educational psychology
R E A D E R

The Art and Science of How People Learn

GREG S. GOODMAN, EDITOR

PETER LANG
New York • Washingt
Frankfurt • Berlin • Bi

Library of Congress Cataloging-in-Publication Data

Educational psychology reader: the art and science of how people learn /
edited by Greg S. Goodman.
p. cm. — (Educational psychology: critical pedagogical perspectives vol. 1)
Includes bibliographical references.
1. Learning, Psychology of. 2. Child psychology.
3. Educational psychology. 4. Critical pedagogy.
I. Goodman, Greg S.
LB1060.E56 370.15—dc22 2009043514
ISBN 978-1-4331-1072-6 (hardcover)
ISBN 978-1-4331-0627-9 (paperback)
ISSN 1943-8109

Bibliographic information published by **Die Deutsche Nationalbibliothek.**
Die Deutsche Nationalbibliothek lists this publication in the "Deutsche
Nationalbibliografie"; detailed bibliographic data is available
on the Internet at http://dnb.d-nb.de/.

The paper in this book meets the guidelines for permanence and durability
of the Committee on Production Guidelines for Book Longevity
of the Council of Library Resources.

This book is dedicated to Shirley Steinberg.

Through her tireless commitment to human justice and her love, dedication, and generosity for her students and colleagues, Shirley is the personification of critical pedagogy. For all that she has given, I offer these words of admiration and my profound gratitude.

Contents

Section Three: Piaget and Vygotsky

Section Four: Paulo Freire's Legacies

Section Five: Motivation

Section Six: Complex Ecologies for Educational Psychology

Section Seven: Enlivened Spaces for Enhanced Learning

Section Eight: Parents and Other Relationships

Section Nine: Educational Psychology Inside the Classroom

Section Ten: Discursive Practice in Educational Psychology: How the Subject Tells the Truth about Itself

Acknowledgments

I would like to express my gratitude to all of the *Reader*'s authors for their contributions to this text. Their scholarship and dedication to the improvement of people's learning reflect a true appreciation of the values of educational psychology and critical pedagogy within the multiple processes of learning.

A work of this size and magnitude requires the effort of many individuals. As the days turned to months, and the months turned to years, the staff at Peter Lang are foremost on my indebtedness list. Bernadette Shade, Sophie Appel, Patty Mulrane, and Chris Myers all deserve my greatest appreciation for their hard work, patience, and perseverance in seeing this project through to completion.

I am eternally indebted to Brenda Stahlman from Clarion University's PAGES for her work in acting as the co-compositor of this tome. Brenda invested long hours in the process of re-composing manuscripts from their original forms to this new arrangement.

Great gratitude is extended to the following permission editors and their respective publication's boards for releasing copyrights and re-print permissions for these chapters and articles:

Peter Lang Publishing for permission to reprint from:

Educational Psychology: An Application of Critical Constructivism (2008) by Greg S. Goodman, ed.

Chapter 1. *Critical Thinking: How Good Questions Affect Classrooms* by Greg S. Goodman.

Chapter 2. *Coming to a Critical Constructivism* by Greg S. Goodman.

Chapter 14. *English Language Learners: Understanding Their Needs* by Binbin Jiang.

Chapter 16. *Affective and Motivational Factors for Learning and Achievement* by Patricia Kolencik.

Chapter 24. *Cultural Collision in Urban Schools: What Pre-service Teachers Should Know* by Floyd Beachum and Carlos McCray.

Chapter 26. *Creating a Classroom Community Culture for Learning* by Suzanne Gallagher and Greg S. Goodman.

Chapter 30. *Teacher and Family Relationships* by Tamar Jacobson.

Chapter 44. *Assessment* by Karen T. Carey.

Chapter 49. *Toward a Psychology of Communication: Effects of Culture and Media in the Classroom* by Joanne Washington.

Educational Psychology: Disrupting the Dominant Discourse (2003) by Suzanne Gallagher:

Chapter 36. *Toward a Poststructural Analysis* by Suzanne Gallagher.

Chapter 37. *Disciplining the Discipline* by Suzanne Gallagher.

The Psycho-social dimensions of Multicultural Education by C.T. Vang.

Chapter 15. The Psycho-social dimensions of Multicultural Education.

No Education Without Relation, C. Bingham and A.M. Sidorkin, Eds.

Chapter 31. *Personal and Social Relations in Education* by Barbara J. Thayer-Bacon.

Chapter 32. *Relations Are Difficult* by Cris Mayo.

Jean Piaget: Primer by D. Jardine.

Chapter 9. On the Origins of Constructivism: The Kantian Ancestry of Jean Piaget's Genetic Epistemology by D. Jardine.

Chapter 10. Jean Piaget and the Origins of Intelligence: A Return to "Life Itself" by D. Jardine.

19 Urban Questions by S. Steinberg, Ed.

Chapter 42. Urban Dropouts: Why Persist? by G.S. Goodman & A.A. Hilton.

Paradigm Publishers for permission to reprint from Sonia Nieto's *Dear Paulo: Letters from Those Who Dare Teach* (Boulder, CO: Paradigm Publishers 2008.

Chapter 12. *To Study Is a Revolutionary Duty* by Jeff Duncan-Andrade (pp. 154-163).

Chapter 13. *Eating, Talking, and Acting: The Magic of Freire* by Herb Kohl (pp. 115-119).

Thank you to Charlie Finn for permission to quote these lines from *Please Hear*. The full poem can be found at http://www.poetrybycharlescfinn.com

Chapter 3. I also wish to thank Shirley Steinberg for the permission to print Joe Kincheloe's *Beyond Reductionism: Difference, Criticality, and Multilogicality in the Bricolage of Postformalism*. This work appears for the first time in *Educational Psychology Reader*.

Chapter 5. Reprinted by permission of the publisher: www.nasponline.org Barkley, R. (2007). School interventions for Attention Deficit Hyperactivity Disorder: Where to from Here? In *School Psychology Review, Vol. 36* (2), 279-286. Copyright 2007 by the National Association of School Psychologists, Bethesda, MD.

Chapter 8. Reprinted by permission of the publisher: *Purdue University Press* (2008) Bryan Shaffer, Editor: Mayer, S.J. (2008). Dewey's Dynamic Integration of Vygotsky and Piaget by Susan J. Mayer. *The Journal of the John Dewey Society of Education and Culture 24* (2), 6-24.

Chapter 17. Reprinted by permission of the publisher Rightslink: Zimmerman, B. (2000). Self-efficacy: An essential motive to learn. *Contemporary Educational Psychology, 25*(1), 82-91.

Chapter 20. Reprinted by permission of publisher Mort Morehouse: *Analytic Teaching: Encouraging the Discouraged* by Julia Ellis, Susan Fitzsimmons, and Jan Small-McGinley

Chapter 21. Reprinted by permission of the editors of *Teaching Educational Psychology*:

Hanich, L. (2009). Using student interviews to understand theories of motivation. *Teaching Educational Psychology, 3*(3), 1-5.

Chapter 22. Reprinted by permission of the publisher, Rightslink: Lee, C. (2008). The centrality of culture to the scientific study of learning and development: How an ecological framework in educational research facilitates civic responsibility. *Educational Researcher, 37*(5), 267-279.

Chapter 23. Reprinted from *Multicultural Learning and Teaching, Volume 3 Issue 2* by permission of the editors: Through the fire: How Pretext Impacts the Context of African American Educational Experiences by Carlos McCray and Floyd Beachum.

Chapter 27. Reprinted by permission of publisher Alan Jones: www.csse.ca/cacs/jcacs

Ellis, J. (2004). Researching Children's Place and Space. *Journal of Curriculum Theorizing, 20*(1), 83-100.

Chapter 29 Reprinted by permission of publisher Alan Jones: www.csse.ca/cacs/jcacs

Ellis, J. K. (2002). The importance of attending to children and place. *International Journal of Educational Policy, Research, and Practice, 3*(3), 69–88.

Chapter 33 . Reprinted with permission from the publisher: National Middle School Association.

Lenski, S. J. & Caskey, M. M. (2008). Using the lesson study approach to plan for student learning. *Middle School Journal, 40*(3), 50-57.

Chapter 34. Reprinted by permission of the authors: Shen, J., Zheng, J., & Poppink, S. (2007). Open lessons: A practice to develop a learning community for teachers. *Educational Horizons, 85*(3), 181-191.

Chapter 35. Reprinted by permission of the authors: Shen, J., Poppink, S., Cui, Y., & Fan, G. (2007). Lesson planning: A practice of professional responsibility and development. *Educational Horizons, 85*(4), 248-258.

Chapter 38. Reprinted by permission of the editors of *Teaching Educational Psychology*:

Deemer, S. (2009). Using action research methodology to unite theory and practice. *Teaching Educational Psychology, 3*(3), 1-3.

Chapter 40. Reprinted by permission of the publisher, Hampton Press: J. Jelmberg & G.S. Goodman (2008). *The Outdoor Classroom: Integrating Learning and Adventure*. Cresskill, NJ: Hampton Press.

Chapter 46. Reprinted by permission of the *Canadian Journal of Educational Administration and Policy*, Issue #32, July 1, 2004. © by *CJEAP* and the author(s): Seifert, K. (2004). Learning to feel like a teacher: Personal identity from within and without. *Canadian Journal of Educational Administration and Policy, 32*.

Chapter 47. Reprinted by permission of the publisher: Teaching Educational Psychology (2005).

Zambo, D., & Hansen, C. (2005). Once upon a theory: Using picture books to help students understand educational psychology. *Teaching Educational Psychology, 1*(1), 1-8.

* And a tremendous, sincere and loving thank-you to my wife, Andy, for her patience during the 18 month hiatus required for this project.

Introduction

Educational Psychology: The Art and Science of How People Learn is an ambitious dream of hope for our school children and their teachers and an amalgam of diverse realities representing the pluralistic community of America's schools. As I glance back over the process of creating this tome, I am awed by the collection of genius assembled within these pages. Carol Lee, Russell Barkley, Julia Ellis, Barry Zimmerman, Suzanne Gallagher, Joe Kincheloe, Herb Kohl, Cathrene Connery, Floyd Beachum. . .all of the individuals included within these pages provide daunting evidence of the range and intellectual rigor of the field of educational psychology at this historic juncture. A diversity of both established and emerging scholars' perspectives is represented within this 50-chapter collection of education's most essential subject: educational psychology, the study of how people learn.

At the same time that we are presented with great opportunities for the expression of pluralistic possibilities, we are struggling with a quest for answers to some very vexing problems. Most of our urban environments are in a dire and prolonged crisis. Cities like Baltimore, the Bronx in New York City, Cleveland, and Los Angeles are plagued with violence and physical decay. Schools share these crises and mirror the decay with atrocities, including violence, inadequate staffing, decaying buildings, chaotic classrooms, and drop-out rates ranging from 50–70 %. One thousand entering freshmen in Bridgeport, CT, yield 400 high school graduates four years later. For those who have paid attention and who are not inured to the pain evoked by the daily repetition of these facts, we've witnessed the killing of over 150,000 Americans since the terrorist attack of September 11, 2001. Much of this violence occurs in and around the schools our children attend each day. Compounding these extreme social problems, we face economic realities resulting from bad policy choices that impair our opportunity to provide essential services to those in the most need. Questions abound concerning America's future, yet, ironically, the schools continue to be the #1 scapegoat for fear-inspired reform movements like No Child Left Behind and the Race to the Top. Simple rhetoric does not resonate in a knowledge economy or within a global competition for greatness. What does educational psychology have to offer in response to these enormous social and political issues?

Within these pages, you will experience a sampling of some of the best of the answers to today's difficult educational issues and challenges. The core of this conversation is that we must confront stultifying, boring, and irrelevant curricula and turn our attentions to the real needs of our students—their environment, their souls, and their futures. The core issues and values of educational psychology presented in these pages reflect the art and science of individual and collective research on improving student learning. But still, there is no silver bullet. What we have is a multicultural and multi-intelligenced quilt of complexity and opportunity. Educators and educational psychologists need to remember that America was never a 'one size fits all' nation. We are, by our constitution and our rebellious heritage, fiercely independent, and this *Reader* is true to that tradition. Yet, what we do have is a common mission: true democracy is the catalyst for the provision of equity and equal opportunity. This means giving those who need specific pedagogy and educational psychology the instruction that best meets their needs and does so in the most caring and loving way. Serving autistic children in California requires totally different praxis than what is required to meet the educational needs of a gifted child in New Hampshire. Solutions for Oakland, CA, are not the same in Jonesport, ME. But the love and interpersonal relationships necessary for quality education to be delivered are universal qualities.

In the world of education, our challenges are great. Scholars of educational psychology represent some of the best minds in education today, but we are confronted with myriad problems. It is not just that there are no simple solutions; the crux issue may be the complex of chaos that surrounds us. While policy makers try to apply business models, seek value added assessments, and attempt to throw technical rationality at the problems, the outcomes only add frustration and confusion for our teachers. Frustration is the direct result of the misrepresentation that 100% of all children could be 'on grade level' by 2014. Confusion comes from the scramble to fix a system that was designed to prepare children for jobs that either no longer exist or will cease to be available within the next ten years. Certainly, American schools are facing serious and vexing problems. But fixing American schools is not simply a matter of increasing math and science test scores. For the past 60 years, we have been among the lowest performers on standardized assessments of achievement when compared to other industrialized nations such as England, Germany, and Switzerland. However, test scores are not the arbiter of success. If American schools are such a failure, and for so long, how can we continue to be the world's leading economy? Is John Gatto correct in saying that we are a success because our schools are doing exactly what they were designed to do: prepare future workers for America's three largest employers: Walmart, McDonalds, and Burger King? Is academic failure on standardized tests inversely correlated with economic success? Are we really focused upon the essential elements of our school's mission: preparing productive citizens for a democracy? Will fear of failure on standardized tests ironically be the driver of the end of our global economic success? Who is really being left behind?

I am, as Freire prompted, a prisoner of hope. I believe that we can demonstrate that our greatest strength is our diversity and our fresh, creative spirit. There is much to consider if we truly desire to help our children learn, and this *Reader* provides the student and practitioner of educational psychology with a sense of the great breadth of the discipline. More importantly, this *Reader* extends an invitation to engage in the dynamic dialogue of how children and adults learn. As we all work to transform the schools into real successes for our communities, not just factories producing future workers for low-paying, low-status dead-ends, the key point is that it is the collective wisdom of our teachers and leaders that makes for successful outcomes for all of the diverse learners to whom we attend. Creative cooks go beyond the recipe's routine, and successful educators are no different. Creativity is the ingredient that has given America its greatest moments, and creative educational psychologists can educate us in ways to reclaim our sense of purpose, soul, and dignity by leading learners into the future. And the best teachers, true practitioners of educational psychology, represent hope and demonstrate to us how to make these dreams of relevant and rewarding learning become a reality.

Constructivist and Postformalist Perspectives on Educational Psychology

ONE

Critical Thinking:
How Good Questions Affect Classrooms

Greg S. Goodman

This chapter presents the notion that critical thinking is one of the keys to your success as a person: be that as a citizen or as a teacher. Developing ways to use your mind to explore concepts, theories, events, or assumptions is a good place to start. To begin this discussion, let us ask ourselves some questions: How is critical thinking different than thinking in general? Is it always necessary to think critically? What values or benefits exist in asking critical questions? How do we begin to create critically meaningful questions?

Many professors of education consider John Dewey (1944) to be one of the foremost philosophers in Americans history. Philosophers are valued for their critical thinking and intellectual contributions to society. As an educational philosopher, Dewey gave us many ideas to ponder. One of the best of Dewey's contributions was the notion that learning is the process of thinking about experience. In Dewey's (1944) words, "No experience having meaning is possible without some element of thought" (p. 143). This contribution is immediately simple to understand, yet it is profound in its implications for us as teachers, and it is worthy of a deeper investigation. To assist in displaying how Dewey's words affected me as a teacher, I will share this example from my favorite teaching lesson: rappelling.

As a young college student, fresh out of 13 very boring years of public and private schooling, I was eager to learn of exciting and new ways to use my mind. Encouraged by my mentor Peter Ordway to attend a school called Outward Bound, I discovered how to rappel (how to descend mountains using a rope). Having had this experience of scaring myself half to death and realizing that I could do very bold things and not be limited in my experience by fear, the thing that I wanted to do most was to share this natural high with others. To teach outdoor education became my goal, and teaching rappelling would become my best lesson.

The days of climbing and rappelling always held excitement, and they were never boring. This is not to say that teaching on the edge of the cliff was sufficient for me as a teacher. I took inspiration from some instruction by Jed Williamson, president of Sterling College. Jed once shared with me that my rappelling lesson had a high "C.T." factor. When I asked what "C.T." meant, Jed smiled and said, "Cheap Thrills." For those unable to get beyond the immediate experience of rappelling, this is true. Jed inspired me to seek something more from the experience. My challenge as a teacher was to help my students see this experience as a metaphor for other challenges in their lives. Rappelling was my best teaching aid for overcoming fear and personal obstacles. The real learning for climbers is not the obvious technique business of knots, slings, and belays, but it is in the internal examination of one's fear, courage, ingenuity, integrity, and identity.

I would instruct my students that for some of them, the courage to attend this class on the cliff required more character than it does for the ones who blithely hop down the rock face, high on adrenaline. In my introductory safety, outdoor "bathroom" rules, etcetera lecture, I would allude to Dewey's words, learning is the process of thinking about experience, to communicate the message that this day and lesson were not about learning to rappel. Today's lesson was about reflecting upon your own courage and ability to overcome personal limitations. To give this meaning to sixth graders, I would add, "There are no chickens on the rock today. For several of you, it took more courage to get up and get on the bus to come out here than it will take for others to descend this cliff."

Rappelling can be a pathway to personal discovery; however, the real learning comes from reflecting on the experience and using that knowledge for your life's benefit. Learning that you can overcome obstacles and that you do have the courage that you will need to endure: these are the big lessons. Teaching something as important as this was the reason I so enjoyed my lesson on rappelling. I was really trying to teach students to think critically about themselves. What does it mean to have courage? What is a moral equivalent for your bravery today? In what ways did you confront your own perceptions of self by doing this rappel? How did today's experience change the way you see someone else in your class?

As a climbing teacher, it is relatively easy to make learning exciting. It is all in the rock. What about math, English, or social studies teachers? How will you make your subject have personal meaning for your students? Some would argue that the subject matter is not relevant. What is important is teaching learning processes: logical thinking, creative and divergent thinking, critical thinking, and using the mind's multiple capacities or intelligences (Gardner, 1983). For all teachers, assisting in the development of the knowledge, dispositions, and skills of critical thinking may be the most valuable of the contributions they can imbue upon their students regardless of the specific subject matter at hand. In fact, educators may argue that some of the most important work ahead in this century is in engaging students through meaningful and relevant discourse to consider their potential role and become critical citizens (Giroux, 1998). Critical citizens are individuals who take seriously their ethical, moral, and philosophic responsibilities to create communities that care about the environment, the culture, and the people they include.

> More than ever, the sheer magnitude of human knowledge renders its coverage by education an impossibility; rather, the goal of education is better conceived as helping students develop the intellectual tools and learning strategies needed to acquire the knowledge that allows people to think productively about history, science and technology, social phenomena, mathematics, and the arts. Fundamental understanding about subjects, including how to frame and ask meaningful questions about various subject areas, contributes to individuals' more basic understanding of principles of learning that can assist them in becoming self-sustaining, lifelong learners.
>
> From "How People Learn: Brain, Mind, Experience and School" (p. 5) http://newton.nap.edu/html/howpeople1/ch1.html

The Bellevue Community College "Critical Thinking and Information Literacy Across the Curriculum" faculty have developed a solid rubric for defining critical thinking.

Critical Thinking recognizes:

- Patterns and provides a way to use those patterns to solve a problem or answer a question
- Errors in logic, reasoning, or the thought process
- What is relevant or extraneous information
- Preconceptions, bias, values and the way that these affect our thinking
- That those preconceptions and values mean that any interferences are within a certain context
- Ambiguity—that there may be more than one solution or more than one way to solve a problem

Critical Thinking implies:

- That there is a reason or purpose to the thinking, some problem to be solved or question to be answered
- Analysis, synthesis and evaluation of information

Critical Thinkers:

- Can approach something new and in a logical manner
- Look at how others have approached the same question or problem but know when they need more information
- Use creative and diverse ways to generate a hypothesis, approach a problem, or answer a question
- Can take their critical thinking skills and apply them to everyday life
- Can clarify assumptions and recognize that they have causes and consequences
- Support their opinions with evidence, data, logical reasoning, and statistical measures
- Can look at a problem from multiple angles
- Can not only fit the problem within a larger context but decide if and where it fits in the larger context
- Are comfortable with ambiguity (www.bcc.ctc.edu/lmc/ilac/critdef.htm)

THE ROLE OF CRITICAL THINKING IN THE PROMOTION OF SOCIAL JUSTICE

One of the most important functions of a relevant educational pedagogy (philosophy of teaching) is to confront social injustice and environmental destruction with some meaningful and relevant questions. Some philosophers have suggested that the notions of what is right or wrong are already within us. We begin as children questioning simple fairness. In adulthood, we look at right and wrong as more complex questions, with answers other than simply yes or no.

As David Jardine (2000) has shared in his book *Ecopedagogy,* the word "educate" derives from the Latin root *educatus:* to bring out or to rear (raise). We take this meaning literally to state that we, as educators, are helping to develop, or to bring forth, the whole collective of body, knowledge, mind, soul, and character within our students. The important questions are within us and stem from the life experiences we have lived with our families, our friends, and our foes. What burns inside our students, future teachers, are the questions of meaning-making and the discovery of truth. When we present real questions to our students, relevance and meaning-making enhance our perspectives and help us to feel worthwhile.

Conversely, our disaffected (at risk or turned-off) students are overloaded with frustrations, and they often display a refusal to learn or even look inward. In the book *I Won't Learn from You,* Herb Kohl (1994) called this phenomenon (refusing to learn) "creative maladjustment." Could a student's refusal to learn also stem from her inability to create questions of real personal and social relevance? That often our students are frustrated by a lack of personal power and disconnected from the real issues of their time may be the logical consequences of an educational system that has been imposed upon them by distant leaders and policy makers. Educational and social change begins with the questioning of the ideas that have maintained a broken system in which many of our students fail. In our culture, we need individuals who dare to come forward to question the big problems such as: "Why do we continue to wage wars outside our borders?"; "How can we judiciously resolve the issue of 12.5 million illegal aliens living in our country?"; "How can we allow such large numbers of our students to fail or drop out of high school?"; and "Why are we failing to correct the achievement gap between minority and poor students and their white and affluent classmates?" These are just some of the critical questions.

From John Lennon "Give Peace a Chance" to Eminem "Feel the Love" to John Mayer "Waiting for the World to Change", the call is for real pedagogical changes: to question the boredom and the alienation brought on by teachers and schools that perpetuate policies of social reproduction. We cannot continue to operate schools that foster failure through poor educational practices. The new psychological and educational knowledge required to facilitate human growth and learning should be a primary focus of today's teacher. How we can enliven a passion for discovery and teach relevant learning processes with critical questioning is one of the keys to creating classrooms that match the requirements of today's youth.

Technology and related information-age advancements have changed our world in many ways (Peters, 2006). Knowledge and new information emerge from academic, business, and private organizations with such speed and volume that the total amount of info-data/knowledge available far exceeds anyone's capacity for comprehension. Even the processes we are using for the creation of this book may become obsolete within a short period.

As you read this book, assuming you are holding a hard copy, the 5,000,000 books in print are being electronically copied to supplant and possibly to replace actual hard-copy manuscripts. This act symbolizes the dynamic growth of information and communication technologies (ICTs). As our world continues to "shrink," a factoid's value will diminish, too. What this implies for educators is that learning as a process of thinking and evaluating new information is much more important than rote memorization. Of course, the need to learn facts will continue to be of value; however, its importance is of diminished significance in comparison to one's ability to assimilate new information and to accommodate that information in relation to this rapidly changing world. This process-driven quest for learning is inspired and enlivened by critical questioning.

HOW TO CREATE CRITICAL QUESTIONS

Changes in technology call for a re-examination of old paradigms of critical thinking and beg the development of new behaviors to execute pathways for understanding our role within these new ICT defined cultures (Peters, 2006). Thinking critically will be key to one's ability to negotiate life's chaotic and confusing constellation of choices. Because of the importance of this skill, thinking, it is important for students to begin to build understanding of the ways one develops critical questioning skills and dispositions. For purposes of applying educational psychology, you, as a student/teacher, can implement the processes of critical thinking for every developmental level from emergent critical thinkers (pre-school) to fully matured critically thinking citizens (college graduates?).

One of the many markers of the educated person is the ability to think critically. This activity, critical thinking, is associated with informed query (questioning) and concomitant intellectual attributes, including linguistic facility and research-based knowledge foundations. When these attributes are linked with an attitude or disposition of inquisitiveness characterized by honest curiosity (versus a haughty snobbishness defined as hubris), the quality of interaction is markedly higher. Critical thinkers are lively discussants at political events, participants in positions of community leadership, or situated within academic communities as professors or students. Supporting traditions of discursive activity has been a primary function of the academy, the name given to all members of institutions of higher learning. Interactions between academy members (for example, dialogues and published papers) are opportunities for publicly displaying and testing research and newly developed ideas. In fact, the tradition of dialogue is older than the academy. As an example, the *Meno,* Plato's dialogue of virtue, pre-dates the inception of academic institutions such as the university.

Historically, the activity of critical thinking is foundational to the Western tradition of intellectual endeavor. Most scholars would concur that Socrates (father to the Socratic method) taught us all to further our investigations into truth and knowledge until we answered the questions fundamental to our being, such as "What is virtue?" "Can virtue be taught?" In the ancient Greek dialogue *Meno,* Socrates seeks to find the answer to how virtue connects to humans (Phillips, 2006). His explorations in search of an answer lead him to question Meno as to the nature of education and knowing. How do we come to know virtue?

SOCRATES: And thus we arrive at the conclusion that virtue is either wholly or partly wisdom?

MENO: I think that what you are saying, Socrates, is very true.

SOCRATES: But if this is true, then the good are not by nature good?

MENO: I think not.

SOCRATES: If they had been, there would assuredly have been discerners of characters among us who would have known our future great men; and on their showing we should have adopted them, and when we had got them, we should have kept them in the citadel out of the way of harm, and set a stamp upon them far rather than upon a piece of gold, in order that no one might tamper with them; and when they grew up they would have been useful to the state?

MENO: Yes, Socrates, that would have been the right way.

SOCRATES: But if the good are not by nature good, are they made good by instruction?

MENO: There appears to be no other alternative, Socrates. On the supposition that virtue is knowledge, there can be no doubt that virtue is taught.

SOCRATES: If virtue was wisdom [or knowledge], then, as we thought, it was taught?

MENO: Yes.

SOCRATES: And if it was taught it was wisdom?

MENO: Certainly.

SOCRATES: And if there were teachers, it might be taught; and if there were no teachers, not?

MENO: True.

SOCRATES: But surely we acknowledged that there were no teachers of virtue?

MENO: Yes.

SOCRATES: Then we acknowledged that it was not taught, and was not wisdom?

MENO: Certainly.

Socrates may well have believed that teaching was truly the way in which virtue was acquired, but his method of teaching was to push others to deeply investigate each question. As we seek to apply this process of developing critical questions in our classes today, we are fortunate to have had a series of mentors following these lines of query and refining the applicability to meet the changing needs of our students and the world they inhabit. Socrates, though important in the tradition of Western thought, is of note historically. Bringing the concepts forward 2,000 years, perhaps Bob Dylan, Mary Oliver, 50Cent, Tupac, or other members of hip-hop or other cultures would frame it better for the youth of today (White, 1997).

As an example, let us critically look at questions of virtue from some of these more current challenges of mainstream thinking: Mary Oliver and Tupac Shakur. Mary Oliver is a widely anthologized American poet who lives in Provincetown, Massachusetts. She grew up in eastern Ohio, and as a young woman, she summered in the woods of western Pennsylvania in a place called Cook Forest. Living in an old army tent, she would imagine herself a poet, and she spent her time as a *flâneur:* an idler. She would roam the forest in search of herself, and she used the time to observe nature's beauty and man's destruction. Years later, she would write *The Wild Geese*, the poem that won national attention and admiration.

> *You do not have to be good.*
> *You do not have to crawl through the desert for a hundred miles repenting.*
> *You just have to let that soft animal in yourself love what it loves.*

This poem frees; it liberates. Reading this brings back our childhood and the time of our freedom from oppression of schedules, responsibilities, and obligations. It relates to our work as educators, but how does it connect? What rules do you need to adhere to and what callings do you answer?

Tupac Shakur grew up in the shadows of America's 1960s. His mother, Afeni Shakur, was a Black Panther, and Tupac's life was just starting as the civil rights movement had achieved national attention. The hope and the frustration of civil rights failed promises left Tupac as a ten-year-old proclaiming: "I want to be a revolutionary!" (White, 1997). Tupac took this calling and transformed himself into an icon of hip-hop. His lyrics were both a rant and raging against a world of racism and discrimination of the black man. The words of his songs were also an appeal to bring the changes necessary to free oneself of the oppression of the hood:

> *We gotta make a change....*
> *It's time for us as a people to start makin' some changes.*
> *2PAC Lyrics "Changes"*

Tupac challenges us to look at the injustices of the inner city and to feel the pain of ghetto traps: pimps, drugs, violence, and alienation. Tupac calls to his brothers and sisters to examine the situation they find themselves in and to adjust their lives before the violence changes them. Unfortunately, Tupac was a victim of his own prophesies. On September 13, 1996, in Las Vegas, Nevada, Tupac Shakur died from gunshots inflicted upon him six days earlier (White, 1997).

However, his lyrics live on as a reminder of the continuing need to "make a change." As future teachers, you are in a unique position to ask questions of your own. What role will you play in the production of social change? As a teacher, what aspects of social change do you want to incorporate within your classroom? Do the women's movement, civil rights, democratic processes, students with disabilities, and care for the environment have a place within your curriculum or classroom culture?

For the authors of this book, the dynamic and pressing issues of social change and the problems associated with our modern civilization's ecological mismanagement are drivers of our motivation to increase the critical thinking capacity of our students. We take inspiration from the mentor to many subscribers of critical thinking: a man named Paulo Freire (1970). Freire's work has ignited a new political revolution in American educational dialogue (Goodman, 1999; Kincheloe & Steinberg, 1997; McLaren, 1997). Informed by Freire's thought and word, educators for social justice are inspired to have hope for the future through Freire's critical pedagogy: the pedagogy of love. Love in Freire's eyes was a love for humanity. This love is not a romantic love, but a mindful compassion and connectedness with all people to create successful communities. Successful communities, in Freire's eyes, were ones in which all citizens could read, develop personal agency, and safely co-exist in an atmosphere of collective harmony and social justice.

Following the loving legacy of Paulo Freire, we feel a responsibility to prepare our students for the world of diversity and the demands of proper earthly stewardship. Helping to prepare future teachers of yet unborn generations of citizens makes the issues of critical thinking and its application into a real and relevant problematic not a solitary, esoteric, or academic exercise. Critical thinking and questioning will make your classroom come alive!

Paulo Freire's critical pedagogy is deeply imbedded into the practice of the teaching. His teaching has given us a sense of personal responsibility that motivates and guides us to help our students to work toward issues of social justice and to confront problems of our environment. These important activities require thinking that is critical and well informed. Freire's goal was to bring literacy to an illiterate and exploited mass of millions of Brazilians. By forming literacy circles, he applied social learning theory to support individual learning. The result was the creation of literacy for thousands of Brazilians (McLaren, 2000).

CONSTRUCTIVIST ACTION LEARNING TEAMS

From Freire, I have taken the notions of critical pedagogy and literacy circles and created a process called Constructivist Action Learning Teams (CALT). Constructivist theory comes from the work of developmentalists Jean Piaget and his contemporary, Lev Vygotsky. These men affirmed our ability to create and construct our own lives through the multifaceted and experientially based existence that we continuously evolve and participate in. We are the agents of our own destiny. This agentic process posits people as the essential creators of their own life experience. Students' experiences contain relationship choices, activity decisions, and learning opportunities. Constructivists believe that individuals re-structure the chaos of life to create meaning and order within their own worlds. In this model, teachers provide stimulation, guidance and extrinsic motivation in order to maximize the intrinsic motivation of our students and to help them to further their understandings and knowledge.

In the CALT process, I begin by teaching my students about framing critical questions. This teaching includes a rationale for using critical query. Critical query reflects the knowledge of the conversationalist, and it furthers the discussion beyond simple reductive yes and no questions. Questions and their quality do reflect upon the individual, and there are, contrary to popular wisdom, "stupid" questions. Questions like, "Is our children learning?" (Begala, 2000) reflect extraordinarily dim light upon the interrogator. I want my students to get beyond the reductive "Yes" and "No" conversant critique and to move the conversation deeper into an intellectual and informed discussion.

How to achieve this higher learning is no mystery. The information and grist for the student's mental mill are located within the research of the topic at hand. Using the common research forms contained within the literature review process, the students will find information and fact to bring meaning to their questioning. Within the books, journal articles, and myriad other sources of information, students will find facts (or untruths) upon which they can build questions and arguments for discussion.

Adolescents are known for their developmentally linked, reductive, either/or thinking. As adolescents mature in their ability to define their world, they begin to eschew perceptions of either/or. As college students, it is incumbent upon you, as emerging adults, to see that over-generalizations are invalid and that the answers to important questions are not "Yes" or "No," but are complexities of response belonging rightfully upon a continuum ranging widely across a spectrum of culturally driven and diverse possibilities. Questions like, "As a nation, what policies should we develop to reverse global warming?" are not answered with simple solutions.

The writers of this book want you to share in the knowledge contained in the readings we have selected for your edification. Some of these readings are deep, and some of them are easy to comprehend. However, all of these readings are made meaningful by your thinking about the reading's content and by developing critical questions to make their investigations more enlivened and experiential.

Related to each chapter assignment in the classes I teach, I ask my students to create a critical question and to bring it to class with them. At the end of my lecture, I ask the students to query their peers with their question and to spend some time in discussion. What I get from this process is an enthusiasm and a participation that is lively. The students enjoy each other's company, and they like having the ability to share their opinions and to challenge their learning. Topics such as racism, discrimination, poverty, No Child Left Behind, hip hop culture, and other relevant issues spark a dialectical discourse that makes the traditional, teacher-directed questioning pale in comparison. In my classroom during CALT, the noise level picks up and the interaction is healthy and enlivened. I believe that higher levels of learning are accomplished through the CALT process and the use of critical pedagogical practices.

College is a time of great intellectual and emotional growth. However, the greatest purpose of college may be in the social learning that can occur within the classroom and throughout the campus community. Learning how to work with diverse student groups and to develop dispositions that foster successful team working skills can be among the most beneficial tools one can acquire during the college years. Using the CALT process helps students stretch themselves and ask the tough questions. Students like to challenge each other's thinking and to investigate multiple pathways for solving problems. Hopefully, by building positive cultures of learning and fostering values of respect for diversity (of opinion, personality, style, etc.) within our classrooms, we can help our larger university community and extend these pro-social behaviors for everyone's benefit.

THE REAL QUESTIONS

Carlos Santana demands, "Give me your heart, make it real, or else forget about it." It is time to "make it real" in the classrooms. Our students have been mesmerized into boredom with the traditional curricula of sterilized textual representations of cultural reproduction. The frontier of education and the point of adventure and excitement are within working through problems of the present moment to meet the challenge of preparing our students for the future. Valid questions for today's students confront inequalities and alienation from hope of ever changing our culture. John Mayer sings, "We're waiting…waiting for the world to change." But if all we are going to do is wait, the world is never going to change in a direction other than the direction corporate and political leaders choose for their profit. Building more fences around our nation's borders and producing gated communities to surround our suburban estates changes nothing of the inequality or alienation most Americans experience. Instead, we need our future citizen/leadership to ask, what can I do to stop the violence in my communities? What are the real reasons for drug use of epidemic proportion in this country? What is wrong in our communities that gangs are viable social units? How can I work to stop the spread of sexually transmitted diseases? When will our schools stop focusing on standardized assessments of the past with no plans to prepare students for a future? When will we experience a real and meaningful connection with our earth instead of viewing it as an object to be trashed and exploited? These are examples of the types of questions students of a critical constructivist educational psychology need to ask themselves in preparation for teaching today's youth.

Questions of social justice and personal relevance are the critical problems to examine if we want to make a difference in the lives of those we teach. Until we engage our students in the types of real questions that need confrontation, the process of education will work to reproduce the same alienated, disconnected, mind-numbed citizens who are unprepared to find solutions to the vexing social and political questions of our time. It will not be their fault that they cannot see the solutions, because they were tacitly taught to deny their complicity and to blame or ignore the victims of social malaise. Just like the miscreants at school, society shoves misfits aside and attempts to coerce them back to work (Goodman, 1999). Meanwhile, in other locations, the shootings continue; the drug cartels have a lucrative market for their goods; and the criminal justice system finds work for the unemployed. These are the real, present issues that need questioning, and the indignation of young people is the fuel for possibility and change.

The leadership in the teaching of educational psychology must ask: what are our social and professional responsibilities as educators? The root of the word psychology…psyc…comes from the Greek word "psyche." Psyche means "soul," and it also, in psychiatry, means "mind." The mind is "an organic system reaching all parts of the body and serving to adjust the total organism to the needs or demands of the environment" (Friend & Guralnik, 1953, p. 1175). If our soul is our essence, then we need to consider questions of essential importance to the education of our future citizens. As the children of Birmingham, Alabama, seized the day and left the schoolhouse for the jailhouse to force the end of segregation, we need to bring the spirit of the civil rights movement back to our classrooms and communities needing equally important transformations. Teaching our youth how to develop critical questioning may allow their minds to develop the congruence and courage to empower greater social changes.

REFERENCES

Begala, Paul. (2000) *"Is our children learning?" The case against George W. Bush.* New York: Simon & Schuster.

Bransford, J.D., Brown, A.L., & Cooking, R.R., Editors. (1999). *How people learn: Brain, mind, experience, and school.* Washington, D.C., National Academy Press. http://newton.nap.edu/html/howpeople1/ch1.html

Dewey, John. (1944). *Democracy and education.* New York: The Macmillan Company.

Freire, Paulo. (1970). *Pedagogy of the oppressed.* New York: Continuum Press.

Friend, J.H. & Guralnik, D.B. (1953). *Webster's new world dictionary.* Cleveland, OH: The World Publishing Company.

Gardner, Howard. (1983). *Frames of mind: The theory of multiple intelligences.* New York: Basic Books.

Giroux, H. (1998). *Channel surfing: Racism, the media, and the destruction of today's youth.* New York: St. Martin's Press.

Goodman, G. S. (1999). *Alternatives in education. Critical pedagogy for disaffected youth.* New York: Peter Lang Publishing.

Jardine, David. (2000). *Under the tough old stars: Ecopedagogical essays.* Brandon, VT: The Foundation for Educational Renewal.

Kincheloe, Joseph & Steinberg, Shirley. (1997). *Changing multiculturalism.* Buckingham, England: Open University Press.

Kohl, Herb. (1994). *"I won't learn from you" and other thoughts on creative maladjustment.* New York: The New Press.

Lennon, J. (1970). "Give peace a chance."

Mayer, J. (2006). "Waiting for the world to change."

McLaren, Peter. (2000). *Che Guevera, Paulo Freire, and the pedagogy of revolution.* Lanham, MD: Rowman & Littlefield.

———. (1997). *Revolutionary multiculturalism: Pedagogies for dissent for the new millennium.* Boulder, CO: Westview.

Peters, Michael. (2006). *Building knowledge cultures: Education and development in the age of knowledge capitalism.* Lanham, MD: Rowman & Littlefield.

Phillips, J. "Memo." (Lecture, Clarion University. Clarion, PA, April 10, 2006).

White, Armond. (1997). *Rebel for the hell of it: The life of Tupac Shakur.* New York: Thunder's Mouth Press.

TWO

Coming to a Critical Constructivism: Roots and Branches

Greg S. Goodman

How do children learn? How can my teaching positively affect the future lives of these young people? What can I do in my classroom to make a contribution to our environmental quality? What are the components of the democratic classroom? As you consider becoming a teacher, you may have already asked yourself some of these questions. If you have, you are not alone. Most pre-service teachers are filled with questions as they consider their future in education.

One of the most important questions to ask concerns the style of teaching you will adopt: what type of pedagogy should I practice? Pedagogy, the philosophic and theoretical foundation for teaching, has been one of the fundamental foci of teachers since Socrates, the ancient Greek philosopher, first questioned Meno about how we obtain knowledge (Sesonske & Fleming, 1965). During the past fifty years, educators have been presented with a wide array of pedagogical possibilities: objectivism, behaviorism, social learning theory, cognitive learning theory, constructivism, and critical constructivism. Today, the pedagogical positions or perspectives recommended by postmodern learning theorists reflect the growth of educators' knowledge of what makes for both better teaching and improvements in student outcomes or learning. The continuing conversation on teaching and learning is supported by thousands of volumes of scientific research (Wheldall, 2006). As you begin your career in education, you will be well informed by reading some of the literature of educational research and considering questions you may like to investigate on your own.

There is much to consider in the development of your own pedagogy for professional practice (praxis). Arguments for pedagogical positions are enlivened by political, humanistic, sociological, philosophic, and artistic appeal. A good example of this can be taken from the recent film *Freedom Writers* (2007). As the film begins, the protagonist, Mrs. Gruwell, is confronted with her own naiveté, or innocence, concerning how to run a classroom within an urban high school. As she considers the students' needs to understand historic events like the Holocaust, she begins to help them understand the implications of their own racist and prejudicial behaviors. In a perfect world, perhaps Mrs. Gruwell would have been better prepared for her first teaching assignment. If she had come to her first teaching assignment prepared for critical constructivist praxis, she would have been ready to present relevant challenges to her students. However, in that scenario there would have been no story, because there would not have been the essential conflict that captivates us as viewers.

Despite its distorted, Hollywood depiction of a middle-class woman saving the hood/ghetto, *Freedom Writers* can give you good insights into the application of the pedagogy identified as critical constructivism. Critical constructivism is an engaging process of enriching students' learning experiences by challenging the known world with intellectually and spiritually invigorating experiences (Kincheloe, 2005). Mrs. Gruwell wanted to attack the racism and sexism in her classroom by using dynamic, experiential processes. She learned, as did her students, that the best way to teach is through authentic engagement with relevant issues.

To assist you, the pre-service teacher, in developing a pedagogical position to inform your future teaching, some of educational psychology's most recent research, philosophic thought, and pedagogical theory will be discussed. I will briefly cover some of the traditional constructivist concepts and theory from the Swiss psychologist Jean Piaget and his Russian counterpart Lev Vygotsky before branching out into an approach more congruent with today's research and the youth you will serve. Although the eclectic, critical constructivist position will be strongly suggested to you, you are encouraged to create your own unique and personal pedagogy. The major purpose of this chapter is to inform you of some of constructivism's foundational thought and then to aid you in the development of your own, unique pedagogical stance. The knowledge of constructivism past and the critical constructivism of the present can be an essential tool for enhancing your teaching practice in the classroom and the larger community.

A secondary purpose of this chapter is to help to prepare you to pass the section of the Praxis Two examination titled "The Principles of Teaching and Learning." In most states, beginning teachers must pass this examination before they can acquire a teaching credential. The authors of this text do not support the use of single, high stakes tests for any selective sorting. However, over 800 occupations in America currently require a competency examination (Drummond, 2006), and education is aligned with mainstream policy considerations in this regard. Since the passing of No Child Left Behind (NCLB, 2001), the Praxis exam has been required of all prospective teachers in an attempt to ensure their basic literacy (Praxis One tests reading, math, and writing skills) and to evaluate subject specific competency (Praxis Two: mathematics, English, sciences, etc.). Although this author takes exception with both the content and predictive validity of Praxis One and Praxis Two, these evaluations must be passed if one desires to teach in most American public schools (Goodman & Carey, 2004). To deny this reality is to do you, the pre-service teacher, a major disservice. However, you can transcend the banality of the Praxis by understanding the foundational theories and moving beyond their limited perspective (Watson-Gegeo & Gegeo, 2004). Through understanding some of the dominant discourse, you will then be able to grow beyond primary comprehension to improve your professional practice and reach the broad audience of today's multicultural classroom.

JEAN PIAGET: THE DEVELOPMENTAL PSYCHOLOGIST

To better understand and appreciate the significance of Piaget's contribution to our understanding of development, it is helpful to briefly review previous conceptualizations of childhood. Before Piaget's systematic observations and scientific evaluation of children, young people were viewed as either small versions of their adult counterparts or insignificant and bothersome burdens on society (for example: the satire *A Modest Proposal*). Although this was not a universal position, children were often considered cognate with adult roles and activities. In the world of art, they were depicted in adult clothing and formally represented. These artistic images of children portrayed them as iconic prizes of the aristocracy. Yet in real life, young people worked beside adults, or substituted for adults, in factories and in fields. Much of the motivation for these activities was economic. Mouths were difficult to feed. In colonial New England, families would send young boys to wealthier neighbors to live and work during the long, difficult winter months (Kennedy, 2006). When Pilgrim children were released from work to attend school, they read and studied the Bible. Prior to the twentieth century there was no conception of developmentally appropriate reading material or children's literature. Children were treated as little adults in almost every aspect except, of course, in rights and freedoms. There were little to no protections for children or their rights.

To understand the significance of Piaget's scientific inquiry into children's development, some historical facts may help you to understand how children were mistreated. In the late 1800s, one third of Britain's boys and one half of the girls between the ages of five and nine were working 12 to 15 hour shifts in shops and factories (Colón & Colón, 2001). During these Victorian times (circa 1830 through 1900), approximately 100,000 children were employed in factories within the immediate vicinity of New York City (Calvert, 1893). This practice of exploiting children was ubiquitous in industrial and in agrarian cultures around the globe, and it continues today throughout much of what is referred to as the third world; i.e., the undeveloped nations of the world, especially in Asia and Africa (historyplace.com/uniterstates/childlabor/about.htm). Exploitation of children as "sex workers" continues in the United States as thousands of children are smuggled into America to be sold as prisoners of this ethically repugnant and criminal enterprise. Campagna and Poffenberger estimate that 1.2 million children are sexually exploited within the United States every year (Campagna & Poffenberger, 1998).

The sad reality of the history of children in both Europe and America is that children were so widely mistreated and abused (Colón & Colón, 2001). Although child labor laws were first enacted in the 1830s, most children of poor families were manipulated as insignificant pawns in a labor market supported by unconscionable greed. A famous poem penned from the period by Sarah Cleghorn (1917) entitled "Golf Links" laconically laments:

> *The golf links lie so near the mill*
> *That almost every day,*

The laboring children can look out,
And see the men at play.
(In Metcalf & Burnhart, 1997, p. 3)

To combat the continuing subjugation of children as wage slaves to cruel corporations, photographer Lewis Hine (1874–1940) used his camera to chronicle the exploitation of children for the National Child Labor Committee. "From 1908 to 1912, Hine took his camera across America to photograph children as young as three years old working for long hours, often under dangerous conditions, in factories, mines, and fields. In 1909, he published the first of many photo essays depicting children at risk. In these photographs, the essence of wasted youth is apparent in the sorrowful and even angry faces of his subjects. Some of his images, such as the young girl in the mill glimpsing out the window, are among the most famous photographs ever taken" (historyplace.com/unitedstates/childlabor/about.htm).

The stories of the abuses of children and the ignorance with which they were mistreated are a large part of the reason Piaget's scientific study of children has been so influential. Piaget helped to change the way in which society viewed children by adding a scientifically based inquiry into their cognitive development. Consequently, Piaget's work is foundational to modern educational psychology, and his observations of children have been important in our understanding of developmental changes throughout childhood and into adolescence (Piaget, 1969). Piaget is still considered the most influential developmental psychologist in the history of the Western world (Diessner & Simmons, 2000). Piaget brought us out of the dark age of thinking that children were either naïve urchins or small people with lives largely undifferentiated from adults.

Although the world of education, and, more specifically, America's classrooms are fundamentally different than the 100% Caucasian Swiss audience of Piaget's study, Piaget's contributions bring two things to our attention: (1) children's developmental processes change over time, and (2) we can improve as teachers if we make careful observations of how young people construct meaning or knowledge within normal developmental sequences (Piaget, 1964). Piaget applied scientific methods to the study of children, and he paid close attention to the cognitive or thinking processes. Piaget's genius is all the more important when we consider that he was one of the first psychologists to reveal these gradations within a developmental sequence (Vidal, 2000).

The foundation of developmental psychology posits that children progress through stages of growth beginning at the most fundamental and progressing toward the most advanced or "adult" stage. David Jardine (2006) has contributed a "commonsense legacy of Jean Piaget's work" to simplify our understanding:

An astonishing number of near commonsensical beliefs in educational theory and practice owe their origins directly or indirectly to Jean Piaget's legacy, including the beliefs that:

- Children go through stages of development, and one must be sensitive to "where the child is at";

- A student should be presented with materials and curricular expectations appropriate to the stage of development he or she is at;

- The development of intelligence occurs not only in stages but in a traceable sequence of stages;

- Developmentally appropriate curriculum materials must therefore also be sequenced to fit the stages of development in the child;

- In any real classroom, individual children will be at different levels of development;

- "Ages" and "stages" and "grade levels" are not equivalent except as very broad generalizations that are, more often than not, overgeneralizations;

- In order to learn, young children especially (but not exclusively) are greatly helped by active manipulation of objects (an early thread of hands-on learning);

- Children sometimes need to use concrete materials (objects, images, examples, visual or auditory aids, etc.) not only to learn, but also to show, demonstrate or articulate what they have learned;

- Experiencing and knowing the world in deeply embodied, sensory, playful and image-filled ways are ways of being intelligent a thread of what has come to be known as "multiple intelligences" (Gardner, 1993);

- Children's play is a central feature of the development of intelligence;

- The healthy establishment of a previous stage is necessary to the healthy achievement of the next stage, and finally,

- In knowing the world, we don't just take in the world passively—rather, we actively construct our experiences and understandings of the world according to our own concepts, categories, levels of development and previous experiences. (pp. 2–3)

Jardine notes that the stages of development are not set or fixed, but these changes do occur in a systematic, observable order in the lives of healthy, fully-functioning children. Piaget (1969) made thousands of observations of children, and he specifically delineates four distinct periods of cognitive growth that occur in a chronological order. The first period is identified as the sensori-motor stage of development. The sensori-motor stage begins at birth and continues until approximately two years of age. As the stage's name suggests, during this period of development, children explore the world through their senses: smelling, seeing, hearing, tasting, and touching. Through sensory exploration, children come to understand their immediate world and eventually learn to coordinate multiple sensory inputs, for example, hearing mother and seeing mother. This awareness of mother extends over time to knowing mother is nearby even though the child can't see her because he or she can hear her. Piaget called this phenomenon "object permanence." Before this is developed, if the mother is out of sight, she does not exist.

The sensori-motor stage of development is a very exciting time for parents. Parents anxiously await the arrival of developmental milestones such as focusing, grasping, standing, walking, and saying the first word. The key concept in all of the activities was the "operation" of the child.

As the child would develop, more and more "operations" were being conducted by the child. Piaget used this term to define all of the later stages of child development to build a case for expanding capacities of the child.

At roughly two years of age, children begin to transition from the sensori-motor stage into the pre-operational period of development. From two years of age until approximately age seven, children use various forms of play to develop language and other life skills. This is another period of tremendous growth in children. The two-year-old enters this period as a dependent infant and begins to develop some basic independence from mother/caregiver. The primary job of the young child is to develop language and communication skills to represent and interpret the world. This is a time of play and of exploration. As meaning is developed, reality is only of marginal importance. Psychologists often call these the magic years. Many children believe in Santa, and talking animals are within the scope of conceivable occurrences. The fanciful, magic years of children play an importance part in their construction of meaning as they travel through worlds of make believe and experience the loss of innocence.

Many child psychologists believe that healthy and positive experiences are of utmost importance during this period for later school and life success (Jacobson, 2002). There is a strong body of research-based evidence claiming a valid link between the quality of play in the preoperational period and readiness for school instruction (Bowman, Donovan, & Burns, 2000). In his facetious essay, *All I Really Need to Know About Life, I Learned in Kindergarten*, Robert Fulgram reviews for adults the life lessons of the pre-schooler/kindergartener. The lessons of "take turns," "the golden rule," "don't hit or hurt" help the young child move from a life of self-focus (narcissism) to a world of successful intrapersonal and interpersonal relations. In the article, "The Importance of Being Playful" (Bodrova and Leong 2006) conclude, "in classrooms where play was on the back burner, teachers struggled with a variety of problems, including classroom management and children's lack of interest in reading and writing. These results confirm that thoughtfully supported play is essential for young children's learning and development" (p. 29).

As children progress through school years, they enter into Piaget's third stage: the concrete operational stage of development (Piaget, 1969). Beginning at approximately seven years of age (roughly first grade) and continuing until about eleven years of age (roughly fifth grade), children begin to learn addition and subtraction, spelling, and other mental tasks. Before this time, children could manipulate objects physically, but in this new stage, their mind begins to comprehend how people and events can be organized or structured. For example, when preoperational thinkers would see a woman, and they might immediately identify her as a mother or 'mommy.' Concrete operational thinkers can see a woman and simultaneously identify her as a mother, wife, and sister. The ability to classify sets or subsets is the key component of this stage of development.

During the concrete operational stage, students like to actively participate in their learning through group work and using manipulative objects. Making books, building dioramas, and acting out roles in simple plays are all good examples of ways in which students between the ages of 7 and 11 can construct knowledge using their logical and imaginative qualities. Making learning fun, social, and meaningful goes a long way toward creating an effective learning environment for these rapidly growing youngsters. Many educational psychologists credit Piaget with the development of the notion that children create meaning (knowledge) on their own. This phenomenon is known as constructivism, and it holds as one of its basic precepts that children create (construct) their own reality. Therefore, the child's own actions and interactions with the environment are a reflection of unique interests and desires (Langer & Killen, 1998).

The last period of a child's development is the formal operational stage. This stage emerges at roughly 12–15 years of age. The logical thinking ability that developed during the concrete operational stage is enhanced by thought processes that can include abstract and hypothetical ideas. For example, a formal operational thinker can be given hypotheses to test or imaginary scenarios to consider. How much water will a boat's hull displace if the boat weighs a ton, or how would our government be structured today if the British had won the Revolutionary War? Piaget called the adolescent's ability to solve problems and devise solutions hypothetical-deductive reasoning. "What if" questions make good formal operational thinking exercises for the curious adolescent learner.

Adolescents have many unique developmental characteristics. One of their most interesting attributes is their self-centeredness or egocentricity. Adolescent egocentrism (Elkind, 1978) is a term to describe the teenager's belief that the rest of the world is as interested in them as they are. Another term for this phenomenon is "imaginary audience." Problems associated with adolescent egocentrism include a sense of being invincible or invulnerable. This sense that "it will never happen to me" can lead to reckless driving, drug taking, and/or unprotected sexual experimentation. "Egocentrism is a constant companion of cognitive development" (Wadsworth, 2003, p. 130). Knowing about this powerful personal motivator can be the teacher's best aid in gaining the attention of this narcissistic population.

Although Piaget has obtained iconic status among traditional educational psychologists, critical constructivists do not take such a positive view of his work. The main critique of Piaget stems from the reductive division of development into four fixed stages. Although this conceptualization may have been valid in the rigid, strict Swiss monoculture, this perspective fails to account for the diversity of children's experiences within the larger, global context. As Watson-Gegeo and Gegeo (2004) state: "Research has seriously challenged the notion that the 'stages' of human development are universal in the Piagetian sense, because what is expected of children from an early age and the kinds of socio-historical processes in which they are undergoing development vary across cross-culturally in substantial ways…" (p. 244). Piaget is important to know, but it is also essential to situate his study within the 100% white, 1950's Swiss culture. How Piaget's theory applies to twenty-first century American inner-city students (who represent Puerto Rico, Cuba, Mexico, Cambodia, Ethiopia, Somalia, etc.) is certainly up for question and requires critical re-examination.

LEV VYGOTSKY AND THE SOCIO-CULTURAL THEORY OF DEVELOPMENT

All children grow up in a context of a family, a community, and a culture. Lev Vygotsky (1896–1934) theorized that the influences upon our lives by these significant others contributed the most to the individual's cognitive development. Vygotsky (1987) took objection to Piaget, and he wrote, "…our research confirms…and allows us to put the question about using psychological research data on children's concepts applicable to teaching and training problems in a completely different way from Piaget" (p. 235).

Vygotsky contributes several very valuable concepts to the process of teaching and learning, and many of these constructivist notions are still valid. One of the first is the concept of scaffolding. Vygotsky believed that children's growth occurred incrementally within a space he called the Zone of Proximal Development. Vygotsky (1987) stated, "It is the distance between the actual developmental level as determined by independent problem-solving and the level of potential development as determined through problem-solving under adult guidance or in collaboration with more capable peers" (p. 86). A learner needs to be in a position from which they can make the next incremental step in learning. For example, a non-swimmer is not in the Zone of Proximal Development for learning to water ski or to skin-dive. Although this concept is easy to grasp in our minds, it can be very difficult to apply in a classroom of 30 or so students, each on a different learning level.

I like to teach the concept of scaffolding through the example of a term paper. At the beginning of each semester, I assign a 2,000–2,500-word term paper on a research topic of the student's choice. To mitigate the effects of resistance to writing and the inevitable sad consequences of late papers, I give the students four different assignments in one: choosing the topic, writing an outline of the paper, completing the first 1,000 words, and the final draft. By having three assignments to turn in before the final draft is due, most students attend to the paper and complete their work on time. This assignment works to demonstrate the process of scaffolding and its benefit to both the student and the teacher. Necessary corrections and other editing can be completed well in advance of paper deadlines and, most importantly, student outcomes improve.

Vygotsky's work on the Zone of Proximal Development spurred the creation of the notion of cognitive apprenticeship (Collins, Brown, & Newman, 1987). Applying the axiom "Two heads are better than one," you can understand the benefit of using social motivation to improve learning. Vygotsky's thinking that social relations, and the culture from which social interaction is defined, helped to shape the child's cognitive functioning is most useful for teachers to consider. "He believed that the development of memory, attention, and reasoning involves learning to use inventions of society, such as language, mathematical systems, and memory strategies. In one culture, this could consist of learning to count with the help of a computer; in another it could consist of counting on one's fingers or using beads" (Santrock, 2006, p. 51).

Using socially motivated techniques to improve learning provides multiple benefits for the student. Once the teacher has trained or mentored the student in a learning process, the students are able to actively engage the curriculum in an effective manner. For example, I use the teaching of methods to create critical questions to help my students direct their thinking to the daily lesson. Each class, students are required to read the assigned text and to create a critical question using an allusion from the reading. When the student comes to class, they are given time to meet with 2–4 other students and to ask their questions of one another. I call this process CALT, Constructivist Action Learning Teams. When I break from my lecture and students begin CALT, the entire class becomes actively engaged. Sometimes called cooperative learning, student's natural peer to peer motivation is enhanced by the discovery process. Because I am trying to train college age students to think and act like teachers, peer-to-peer teaching through cognitive apprenticeship can be an effective scaffolding tool for developing critical questioning skills.

Both Piaget and Vygotsky have made great contributions to the development of the educational theory known as constructivism. Although these men differed in their perspectives, many teachers combine elements of both theorists to create their own, eclectic pedagogical practices.

Whether you choose to use Piaget's more individual discovery-based learning or Vygotsky's socially motivated cognitive apprenticeship techniques, or a combination of the two approaches, students will appreciate the fact that you trust in their ability to learn.

Criticisms of Piaget and Vygotsky have reflected changes in educational psychology during the last 50 years. Specifically, Vygotsky and Piaget began their scientific investigations before the advent of the civil rights movement, preceding the woman's movement, and ahead of the development of critical pedagogy. Although it may not be fair to critique their contribution's lack of attention to such a key component as social justice education, it may be more appropriate to suggest that their work opened the way to a refinement of their constructivist contributions to what is now referred to as critical constructivism.

CRITICAL PEDAGOGY

Critical pedagogy is the contribution of the mentor Paulo Freire (1970). Paulo Freire was a Brazilian schooling and social visionary. Among his most impressive accomplishments, Freire developed a process of using social motivation to improve learning. He called these groups literacy circles. As described by biographer Peter McLaren (2000), "In 1962, the town of Angicos, in Rio grande do Norte, was witness to a remarkable event: Freire's literacy program helped 300 rural farm workers learn to read and write in forty-five days. By living communally with groups of peasants and workers, the literacy worker was able to help *campesinos* identify generative words according to their phonetic value, syllabic length, and social meaning and relevance to the workers" (p. 143). Freire's project was the development of literacy and the liberation of all poor and oppressed people.

Paulo Freire appealed to the world's educators to consider the provision of social justice as the pre-eminent mission for all teachers. Social justice in Freire's eyes meant giving citizens the ability to read and, therefore, the key to learning how to break away from the oppressive domination of poverty and social inequality (McLaren, 2000). Throughout all of his life, Freire championed concern for the poor, illiterate, and under-represented citizens by developing literacy circles and calling for the education of all, not just an elite few. Out of his love of the people and a desire to provide education for the empowerment of all, Freire has inspired educators interested in social justice to adopt critical pedagogy as essential to the development of meaningful educational practice (McLaren, 2000).

For all students, especially for those attending urban schools, critical pedagogy has wide applicability in our educational community. As our national educational system continues to confront crises of relevance and is challenged in all areas for improvements, the need for educational reform is most critical in urban settings where unemployment and under-employment are pervasive and alienation from successful role models predominates. For most urban youth, large-scale efforts to provide equal opportunity appear to be economically and socially unsupported. In response to the need to bring excitement and relevance back to the schools, educators for social justice link to Freire's critical pedagogy to support and teach underrepresented individuals and groups.

In today's confusing culture, it may be fair to add that almost all youth require authentic activities to build connection to real world meaning for the value of one another and the need to protect our environment. Often lost in a make-believe world of video games and a mass-marketed culture of violence and escapism, today's youth need mentoring to guide them to the world of authentic experience and personal connectedness. We believe Freire, were he still alive, would approve of these efforts to create more robust learning environments and curricula, especially ones that represent and reinforce policies of social justice and environmental education.

CRITICAL CONSTRUCTIVISM

Critical constructivism has evolved from a combination of the philosophic foundation provided by constructivist theory (we create our own unique reality and knowledge) and the contribution of myriad critical pedagogy scholars led by the mentor, Paulo Freire. Despite years of scientific inquiry into the nature of the child and how best to teach them, much of the technical rationality of initiatives such as No Child Left Behind have betrayed educators. Chased by standardized test scores and running away from the fear of the discrediting failure to achieve Adequate Yearly Progress (AYP), today's teachers need support for the good work they do in their classrooms not threatening mis-applications of evaluation. In support of the social justice needs our students require, the authors of this book advocate critical constructivism's democratic and emancipatory perspective. Critical constructivism offers a view of the child and his or her multidimensional and wonderfully unique characteristics that defy any technical or scientific explanations (Jardine, 2006).

Critical constructivists believe that their students can acquire the knowledge necessary to lead productive and satisfying lives. This belief is supported by the conviction that individual students can create meaningful experiences and that these students are capable of not only analyzing the world around them, they can affect change in their world.

Many of the authors of this book believe that the acts of learning which are most important are the ones that directly affect the lives of students and both the immediate and international world they inhabit. To demonstrate the relevant interconnection of children and their real identifications, several of these authors have linked urban culture, hip-hop culture, and the multiple cultural possibilities of youth with a critical constructivist approach. Through the reading, you will see how you can integrate socially just practices within your classroom to make the learning relevant, authentic, and exciting. Because the issues you will address are relevant, the topics will enliven discussions and create discomfort. Your classroom will be a process-driven ecosystem as students construct meaningful discussions and provoke democratic action.

Our schools have a long way to go to help our students to fulfill the failed promise of the signers of the Declaration of Independence. All wo/men have not been created equally, and their opportunities to frequently mirror the inequities brought on by a lack of education, health care, and other "savage inequalities" (Kozol, 1992) are what our poorest 25% of children experience. Critical constructivists are sensitive to the needs of all children, especially the needs of marginalized and abandoned youth. Critical constructivists understand that there is a real need to help these youth create a viable and sustaining life, free from the threat of violence, disease, and poverty. But rather than defining what critical constructivism is, many of these authors wish to show you applications of this theory so you can get to work and change the world of your future students. As Joe Kincheloe observes, "To assume a position which refuses to seek the structural sources of human suffering and exploitation is to support oppression and the power relations which support it (Freire, 1970; Perry, 2001)" (p. 13). I hope you will grow to see critical constructivist applications of educational psychology as a dynamic and relevant method of changing the lives of your students in positive ways.

REFERENCES

Bodrova, E. & Leong, D.J. (2006). The importance of being playful. In K. Cauley, J. Mcmillan, & G. Pannozzo (Eds.) *Educational psychology: Annual edition.* Dubuque, IA: McGraw-Hill (pp. 27–30).

Bowman, B., Donovan, M.S., & Burns, M.S. (2000). *Eager to learn: Educating our preschoolers.* Washington, D.C.: National Academies Press.

Calvert, K. (1893). "The little laborers of New York City." In *Harpers New Monthly Magazine,* Vol. xlvii, no. cclxxix, pp. 325–332 (August 1893).

Campagna, D.S. & Poffenberger, D.L. (1988). *The sexual trafficking in children.* Dover, MA: Auburn House Publishing Company.

Collins, A., Brown, J.S., & Newman, S.E. (1987). Cognitive apprenticeship: Teaching the craft of reading, writing, and mathematics (Technical Report No. 403) BBN Laboratories, Cambridge, MA. Centre for the Study of Reading, University of Illinois, January 1987.

Colón, A.R. & Colón, P.A. (2001). *A history of children: A socio-cultural survey across millennia.* Westport, CT: Greenwood Press.

Diessner, R. & Simmons, S. (2000). *Sources: Notable selections in educational psychology.* New York: McGraw-Hill/Dushkin.

Drummond, R. & Jones, K.D. (2006). *Assessment procedures for counselors and helping professionals.* Englewood Cliffs, N.J.: Prentice Hall.

Elkind, D. (1978). Understanding the young adolescent. *Adolescence, 13,* 127–134.

Freire, P. (1970). *Pedagogy of the oppressed.* New York: Herder and Herder.

Fulgram, R. (2004). *All I really need to know, I learned in kindergarten.* New York: Balentine Books.

Gardner, H. (1993). *Multiple intelligences: The theory in practice.* New York: Basic Books.

Goodman, G. & Carey, K. (2004). *Ubiquitous assessment: Evaluation techniques for the new millennium.* New York: Peter Lang Publishing.

The History Place: Child Labor in America 1908–1912. Photographs of Lewis W. Hine. (retrieved 5/13/2007) http: www.historyplace.com/uniterstates/childlabor/about.htm Para 3 & 4.

Jacobson, T. (2002). *Confronting our discomfort: Clearing the way for anti-bias in early childhood.* Portsmouth, NH: Heinemann.

Jardine, D. (2006). *Piaget and education.* New York: Peter Lang Publishing.

Kennedy, D. (2006). *Changing conceptions of the child from the Renaissance to post-modernity: A philosophy of childhood.* Lewiston, NY: Edmin Mellon Press.

Kincheloe, J. (2005). *Critical constructivism.* New York: Peter Lang.

Kozol, J. (1992). *Savage inequalities: Children in America's schools.* New York: Harper Perennial.

Langer, J. & Killen, M. (1998). *Piaget, evolution, and development.* Mahwah, N.J.: Erlbaum.

McLaren, P. (2000). *Che Guevara, Paulo Freire, and the pedagogy of the revolution.* Lanham, MD: Rowman & Littlefield.

Metcalf, A. & Burnhart, D. (1997). *America in so many words: Words that have shaped America.* Boston, MA: Houghton Mifflin.

No Child Left Behind Act (2002). Public Law 107–110, 1st session (January 8).

Perry, P. (2001). *A composition of consciousness: Roads of reflection from Freire to Elbow.* New York: Peter Lang.

Piaget, J. (1969). *The child's conception of the world.* Totowa, New Jersey: Littlefield, Adams, & Company.

————. (1964). *The moral judgment of the child*. New York: Free Press.

Santrock, J. (2006). *Educational psychology: Second edition*. New York: McGraw-Hill.

Sesonske, A. & Fleming, N. (1965). *Plato's* Meno: *Text and criticism*. Belmont, CA: Wadsworth Publishing.

Vidal, F. (2000). Piaget, Jean. In A. Kazdin (Ed.), *Encyclopedia of psychology*. Washington, D.C. & New York: American Psychological Association and Oxford University Press.

Vygotsky, L. S. (1987). Thinking and speech. In R.W. Weber & A. S. Carton (Eds.), *The collective works of L. S. Vygotsky* (translated by N. Minick). New York: Plenum Press.

Wadsworth, B. (2003). *Piaget's, theory of cognitive and affective development: Foundations of constructivism*. New York: Allyn & Bacon.

Watson-Gegeo, K. & Gegeo, D.W. (2004). Pushing the epistemological boundaries of multicultural education. In G. Goodman & K. T. Carey, Eds., *Critical multicultural conversations*. Cresskill, N.J.: Hampton Press.

Wheldall, K. (2006). *Developments in educational psychology: How far have we come in twenty-five years?* New York: Routledge.

THREE

Beyond Reductionism:
Difference, Criticality, and Multilogicality
in the Bricolage and Postformalism

Joe L. Kincheloe

In both my constructions of the research bricolage (Kincheloe, 2001; Kincheloe and Berry, 2004) and a postformal psychology (Kincheloe and Steinberg, 1993; Kincheloe, Steinberg, and Hinchey, 1999), I have drawn on the power of difference and multilogicality. Both of these concepts have relevance for researchers concerned with issues of multiculturalism and diversity—especially in critical forms of multiculturalism (Kincheloe and Steinberg, 1997) that are focused on issues of race, class, gender, and sexual justice vis-à-vis a complex understanding of power. This chapter concentrates on the power of difference and multilogicality in such a critical multiculturalism in the process exploring how such a focus enhances the research process and the quality of the knowledge we produce about culture and selfhood. Before going any further, it is important to first define the research terms "bricolage" and "postformalism."

DEFINING BRICOLAGE

For the last several years with the help of Norm Denzin and Yvonna Lincoln (2000), I have been working on the extension of their concept of bricolage—a multi-method mode of research referenced by a variety of researchers but not developed in detail. On one level bricolage can be described as the process of getting down to the nuts and bolts of multidisciplinary research. Ethnography, textual analysis, semiotics, hermeneutics, psychoanalysis, phenomenology, historiography, discourse analysis combined with philosophical analysis, literary analysis, aesthetic criticism, and theatrical and dramatic ways of observing and making meaning constitute methodological bricolage. In this way bricoleurs move beyond the blinders of particular disciplines and peer through a conceptual window to a new world of research and knowledge production.

In the middle of the first decade of the twenty-first century bricolage is typically understood to involve the process of employing these methodological strategies as they are needed in the unfolding context of the research situation. While this interdisciplinary feature is central to any notion of bricolage, I propose that researchers go beyond this dynamic. Pushing to a new conceptual terrain, such an eclectic process raises numerous issues that researchers must deal with in order to maintain theoretical coherence and epistemological innovation. Such multidisciplinarity demands a new level of research self-consciousness and awareness of the numerous contexts in which any researcher is operating—a focus on difference and multilogicality in numerous domains. As one labors to expose the various structures that covertly shape our own and other scholars' research narratives, the bricolage highlights the relationship between a researcher's ways of seeing and the social location of his or her personal history. In this context the bricolage with its multiple perspectives is well designed for research into cultural diversity and multicultural concerns.

DEFINING POSTFORMALISM

Postformalism operates to develop new ways of cultivating the intellect and defining intelligence, while concurrently working for social justice and a democratic redistribution of power. It takes its name from the effort to move beyond what Jean Piaget labeled formal thinking. In many ways postformalism involves the application of a critical theoretical system of meaning to the cognitive or socio-cognitive domain. This multilogical system of meaning draws upon critical theory, critical hermeneutics, post/anti-colonial modes of historical understanding, feminist notions of passionate knowing, subjugated knowledges, liberation theological ethics, and progressive pragmatist concerns with justice, liberty, and equality. In this theoretical bricolage we begin to lay the foundation for a new mode of cognition.

Piaget's formal cognition involved an uncritical acceptance of a Cartesian-Baconian-Newtonian mechanistic worldview that is caught in a reductionistic cause-effect, hypothetical-deductive system of reasoning. This Eurocentric, monocultural cognitive construct was unconcerned with questions of power relations and the complex ways they structure our consciousness. In this context so-called formal operational thinkers accept an objective, depoliticized mode of knowing that breaks a social, psychological, or pedagogical system down into its component parts in order to understand how it works. Operating in a "culture of positivism," such formalism emphasizes certainty and prediction as it organizes verified facts into certified theories.

The facts that do not fit into the theory are eliminated, and the theory developed is the one best suited to limit contradiction in knowledge. In this way formalism assumes that resolution must be found for all contradictions—one truth exists and the scientific discovery of that truth is the goal of all rigorous research. Accepting this formalist monologicality many schools and standardized test makers assume that formal cognitive operations represent the highest level of human cognition. Thus, they focus their efforts on its cultivation and measurement. Many researchers and educators who work to transcend formalism are often unrewarded and sometimes even punished in a neo-positivist evidence-based era.

As they move to postformalism, psychological and educational researchers politicize cognition. They begin to understand the race, class, gender, and sexual dimensions of all cognitive acts. In this context they attempt to disengage themselves from socio-personal norms and ideological expectations. The postformal concern with questions of meaning, emancipation via ideological disembedding, and attention to the process of self-production rises above formalist thinking and its devotion to prescribed procedure. Postformalism always engages larger questions of purpose in the process focusing on questions of human dignity, freedom, authority, and social responsibility. Many may argue that postformalism with its emphasis on difference, multiple perspectives, and multilogicality will necessitate an ethical relativism that subverts efforts to engage in social action. Those who would offer such a perspective do not understand that postformalism is a critical theory of cognition. In this context it is interested in multiple perspectives for their insight into helping us cultivate the intellect in ways that eventuate in the alleviation of injustice and human suffering. In this context postformalism is an ethically informed theory of cognition.

Postformalism's emphasis on difference expands the boundaries of what can be labeled intelligence or sophisticated thinking—a concern that never has been but should be a central concern of a critical multiculturalism. When we begin to expand these boundaries under the banner of multilogicality, we find that those who are excluded from the community of the intelligent begin to cluster around exclusions based on the notion that the poor and the non-white as opposed to the affluent and the white live in separate and hierarchical cognitive domains. In monological and mechanistic modes of cognitive theory, intelligence and creativity are seen as fixed and innate dynamics found only among the privileged few. Mainstream psychology's grand narrative of intelligence has stressed biological fixities that can be altered only by surgical means. Such an essentialism is a psychology of nihilism that locks people into rigid categories that follow them throughout life. Thus, the ethic of difference that postformalism brings to the cognitive table changes the nature of knowledge production in the psychological domain. Such changes hold profound ethical and action-based consequences for ending oppression based on ill-considered and prejudicial attributions of cognitive inability.

DIFFERENCE AND MUTUALISM—MULTIPLE PERSPECTIVES AND THE BONUS OF INSIGHT

The concept of difference is central to bricolage. Gregory Bateson uses the example of binoculars to illustrate this point. The image of the binocular—a singular and undivided picture—is a complex synthesis between images in both the left and right side of the brain. In this context a synergy is created where the sum of the images is greater than the separate parts. As a result of bringing the two different views together, resolution and contrast are enhanced. Even more important, new insight into depth is created. Thus, the relationship between the different parts constructs new dimensions of seeing (Bateson in Newland, 1997). Employing such examples of synergies, bricoleurs maintain that juxtapositions of difference create a bonus of insight. This concept becomes extremely important in any cognitive, social, pedagogical, or knowledge production activity. Indeed, one of the rationales for constructing bricolage and theorizing postformalism in the first place involves accessing this bonus of insight.

This power of difference, or "ontological mutualism," transcends Cartesianism's emphasis on the thing-in-itself. The tendency in Cartesian-Newtonian thinking is to erase this bonus of insight in the abstraction of the object of inquiry from the processes and contexts of which it is a part. In this activity it subverts difference. The power of these synergies exists not only in the cognitive, social, pedagogical, and epistemological domains but in the physical world as well. Natural phenomena, as Albert Einstein illustrated in physics and Humberto Maturana and Francisco Varela laid out in biology and cognition, operate in states of interdependence. These ways of seeing have produced perspectives on the workings of the planet that profoundly differ from the views produced by Western science. What has been fascinating to many is that these post-Einsteinian perspectives have in so many ways reflected the epistemologies and ontologies of ancient non-Western peoples in India, China, and Africa and indigenous peoples around the world.

In the spirit of valuing difference, therefore, bricoleurs seek not only diverse research methodologies but search for ways of seeing that provide a new vantage point on a particular phenomenon. As opposed to many mainstream Cartesian-Newtonian scholars, bricoleurs value the voices of the subjugated and marginalized. The idea of subjugated knowledge is central to the work of the bricoleur. With such an idea in mind bricoleurs do not assume that experts in the disciplines possess the final word on a domain of study. Sometimes what such experts report needs to be re-analyzed in light of the insights of those operating outside the discipline. As a scholar of education and multiculturalism, I have often observed how some of the most compelling insights I have encountered concerning pedagogy come from those individuals living and operating outside the boundaries of educational scholarship. Sometimes such individuals are not formal scholars at all but individuals who have suffered at the hands of educational institutions. Such experiences provided them a vantage point and set of experiences profoundly different than more privileged scholars. This phenomenon is not unique to the study of education but can be viewed in a variety of disciplines (Pickering, 1999; O'Sullivan, 1999; Malewski, 2001; Thayer-Bacon, 2000, 2003; Kincheloe and Weil, 2004).

Thus, the concept of difference as employed by bricolage provides new insights into the nature of rationality itself. As bricoleurs draw upon different knowledges, they begin to understand the postformal assertion that there are many rationalities. When diverse rationalities are juxtaposed insights into new ways of seeing emerge that may be greater than the separate parts. Thus, we return to the bonus of insight mentioned above. Transgression of traditional boundaries is an affirmation of the power of these different perspectives and the alternate rationalities they produce. Bricoleurs in their omnipresent awareness of the hermeneutic circle cross and re-cross the boundaries between the certified and the subjugated. This spiraling action of transgression disrupts calcified truths, as it views them in the light of new horizons. In this context individuals are empowered to make meanings that hold the power to transform society and self in ways that are more just and ethical (Allen, 2000; May, 1993).

From the perspective of the bricoleur, rigor in research comes from an awareness of difference and the multiple perspectives it promotes. Indeed, what presently passes for rigor in many traditional disciplinary arrangements involves a monological, uni-disciplinary pursuit of final truth. Under this regime of knowledge production, the treasures of a multicultural society and the multiple ways of seeing by groups around the planet are dismissed. Emerging in place of such multiplicity is an effort to standardize truth, to provide monological answers to complex questions, and to mandate a universal set of steps necessary to the production of certified truth. This is the same logic that underwrites the effort to impose curricula on educational institutions under the name of content standards—a process nearly complete in U.S. elementary and secondary schools and in process in higher education. Why do educators need to be scholars who can interpret and produce knowledge when experts already know what constitutes the truth? Such absolutist epistemological orientations threaten the very notion of a democratic education where students are exposed to diverse ideas and scholarly orientations taught in different ways by different teachers (Berlak, 1999; Abel et al., 2001).

Bricoleurs respect diversity and the kinetic power that accompanies it. They know that insights into solutions to the problems that face the planet and its peoples rest within diversity. Amazing things can happen when unconsidered perspectives and versions of the world around us are encountered. Indeed, when we see things differently and develop new connections between previously unconnected phenomena our sense of who we are undergoes a process of metamorphosis. Because of our encounter with difference we emerge from our conceptual cocoons as different entities. Bricoleurs take the knowledge developed in the context of difference and synergy and run it through the filter of a literacy of power. Such an act helps them disclose the interests particular knowledges serve, as well as exposing the interests complicit with their production.

Such insights have numerous benefits, of course, especially in the realm of ideology and social transformation. They also aid individuals in better understanding the ways they have experienced the world. Indeed, bricoleurs define learning itself as a process of reshaping the world in light of understanding the ways other individuals in other times and places have shaped it. Thus, they come to see what they know and what is "known" in a new web of meaning. Operating in this multilogical manner, bricoleurs, for example, might study some women's capacity to understand the feelings of other individuals because in Western patriarchal cultures women often sense a greater need to develop this capacity. Such abilities often emerge in asymmetrical relations of power, as African American slaves understood their need to interpret their master's state of mind in order to escape punishment. Thus, researchers use diverse voices in differing historical situations to thicken the knowledges they produce (Weinstein, 1995; Noone and Cartwright, 1996; Scering, 1997; Hoban and Erickson, 1998; Hytten, 2004).

USING SUBJUGATED KNOWLEDGES IN THE BRICOLAGE

Cartesian rationalism has consistently excluded subjugated knowledges from validated databases in diverse disciplines. These local, unauthorized knowledges are central to the work of critical multiculturalism and bricolage. Too often in Western colonial and neo-colonial history Europeans have viewed the knowledges and ways of seeing of the poor, the marginalized, and the conquered in a condescending and dismissive manner. Many of these perspectives, of course, were brimming with cosmological, epistemological, and ontological insight missing from Western perspectives. Western scholars, as postformalism has consistently asserted, were often simply too ethnocentric and arrogant to recognize the genius of such subjugated information. Bricoleurs unabashedly take a hard look at subjugated perspectives—not in some naïve romantic manner but in a rigorous and critical orientation. They are aware that Western scientific thinking often promotes contempt for individuals who have learned about a topic such as farming from the wisdom of their ancestors and a lifetime of cultivating the land. Many of the subjugated knowledges bricoleurs employ come from postcolonial backgrounds. Such ways of seeing force bricoleurs to account for the ways colonial power has shaped their approaches to research and has inscribed the knowledges they have produced.

Starting research with a valuing of subjugated knowledges, bricoleurs can spiral through a variety of subjugated discourses to weave a multilogical theoretical and empirical tapestry. For example, using a Hindu-influenced ontology that delineates the existence of a non-objective, purposely constructed reality, a critical theory that traces the role of power in producing this construction, a Santiago cognitive theory that maintains we bring forth this constructed world via our action within and upon it, and a poststructuralist feminist theory that alerts us to the ways patriarchal and other structures shape our knowledge about this reality, we gain a more profound understanding of what is happening when human beings encounter the world. The insights we gain and the knowledges we produce with these concepts in mind move us to new levels of epistemological and ontological awareness. Such an awareness may be similar to what the Vajrayana tradition of Buddhism calls "crazy wisdom." Bricoleurs seek the multilogical orientation of crazy wisdom in their efforts to push the envelope of knowledge production and the boundaries of multiculturalism (Thomas, 1998; Parmar, 2004; Progler, 2001; Berry, 2001; Capra, 1996; Varela, 1999).

With these insights in mind bricoleurs can operate in a wide diversity of disciplines and use an infinite number of subjugated and indigenous forms of knowledge. Ethnomathematical knowledges can be used to extend understanding of and knowledge production about math and math pedagogy (Appelbaum, 2004). Organic African American knowledges of grandmothers, beauticians, and preachers can provide profound insight into the nature of higher order cognition (Dumas, 2004). Hip-hop musicians can help educators working to develop thicker and more insightful understandings of youth cultures and their implications for pedagogy (Parmar, 2004). Ancient African epistemologies and ontologies can help shape the theoretical lenses one uses to study contemporary racism and class bias (Brock, 2005).

Feminist understandings are important to both women and men who are researchers, as they open doors to previously excluded knowledges. Such knowledges often point out the problems with the universal pronouncements of Cartesianism. The presence of gender diversity in this context reveals the patriarchal inscriptions on what was presented as universal, always true, validated knowledge about some aspect of the world. Indeed, this psychological pronouncement about the highest form of moral reasoning may apply more to men than it does to women—and even then it may apply more to upper-middle class men than to lower socio-economic class men or more to Anglo men than to Asian and African men. With these feminist insights in mind, bricoleurs find it easier to view the ways the knowledges they produce reflect the cultural, historical, and gendered contexts they occupy. In this context universality is problematized. Indeed, the more we are aware of those different from us on a variety of levels, the harder it is to produce naive universal knowledges. In our heightened awareness, in our crazy wisdom, we produce more sensitive, more aware modes of information (McRorie, 1999; Burbules and Beck, 1999). Once the subjugated door is open the possibilities are infinite.

A TRANSFORMATIVE POLITICS OF DIFFERENCE

Bricoleurs work with difference in a way that transcends liberal notions of simple toleration—a key assertion of a critical multiculturalism. Engaging difference in its lived expression so that social inquiry is connected to action in the world, they engage in knowledge work grounded upon a transformative politics of difference. In this context researchers study the ways difference is constructed by historical and social processes, in particular the ways power works to shape the meaning and lived expression of difference. In this context bricoleurs work to set up what Ray Horn (2000) calls postformal conversations where differences are acknowledged and used to address individual needs and systemic inequities. All cultural groups differ in profound ways. Knowing this, bricoleurs who engage in the postformal conversation assume a radical humility that leads to a spirit of equality. Such a disposition allows bricoleurs the opportunity to begin the daunting task of developing genuine and egalitarian interactions among the various cultures of the planet (Richardson and Woolfolk, 1994; McLaren, 2000; Allen, 2000). Based on this foundation the research in which they engage harbors a vision of what could be in the realms of race, culture, class, gender, and sexuality.

Thus, bricoleurs make organic connections with social, cultural, and historical traditions in a manner informed by understanding the power relations that shape them. In addition, bricoleurs are aware of where they stand in relation to these important power relations. With this insight they are better prepared to use the knowledges they produce to initiate critical action. Informed by local knowledges from multiple social and cultural locations, bricoleurs avoid the grand narratives of Western discourses that are monological in their dismissal of histories and the cultural concerns of non-Western peoples. In this context they are able to make use of multiple generative narratives emerging from diverse locales that are dedicated to the production of new ways of making meaning and being/becoming human. Difference in this context is negotiated in the womb of solidarity. These multiple generative narratives are central to the bricolage. Such narratives might include poststructuralist feminism, postcolonial discourses, various social theoretical analyses of macro-social structures vis-à-vis interactionist understandings of micro-dimensions of everyday life, critical hermeneutical ways of interpreting, Santiago enactivist cognitive theories, etc.…

Bricoleurs who employ this transformative politics of difference, however, understand the difficulty of producing critical knowledges. In a globalized era marred by historical and contemporary power asymmetries researchers interested in using their knowledges for social change face daunting obstacles. Difference in such contexts too often leads directly to tension and violence. In the post-9/11 landscape dominated by U.S. military power tension and violence escalate. From the international level to the national and local domains difference in the twenty-first century is often not viewed as an opportunity for insight and social and personal transformation. Indeed, diversity without conversation, community, or a web of relationships can lead to hatred and misunderstanding. If a sense of the interdependence of all peoples has not been established, difference can lead to conflict and murder. In a situation where particular power groups have dominated specific peoples for centuries—as in European and U.S. colonialism and neo-colonialism—the possibility for conflict increases manyfold. In this context, difference for the colonized signifies the taking of political, social, epistemological, educational, and economic power and the imposition of culture.

European knowledges in these colonial and neo-colonial contexts are often presented to the colonial other as the one correct point of view. The knowledges of the colonized is demonized and viewed as inherently inferior. Difference is viewed as a marker of deficiency. Indeed, in an epistemological context, more voices are not viewed as a benefit but as a cacophony of confusion undermining the scientific effort to get the correct answer. As such rationalism relegates the local knowledge of those low in status to the margins, it guarantees that official knowledge remains monological and unblemished by difference. In such a monological context Europeans could produce universal knowledge about the "true nature" of the world and its people. Using such knowledge to build theories delineating proper human behavior and development, Europeans gained to power to tell others what to do, how to organize their lives. Employing a transformative politics of difference, bricoleurs as critical multiculturalists seek to throw a monkey wrench into such mechanistic operations (Allen, 2000; Degenaar, 1995; Thayer-Bacon, 2000, 2003; Thomas, 1998; Kincheloe and Steinberg, 2004).

Bricoleurs make sure that Western rationalism is removed from its sacred sanctuary as the only legitimate mode of knowledge production. They take rationalism into the epistemological bazaar, where it assumes its place as simply another way of making meaning and producing knowledge about the world. Here it co-exists with traditions coming from different places and times. It encounters modes of perceiving that utilize both rational and emotional dynamics and make use of context and interrelationship in unique ways. Bricoleurs like their postformalist counterparts like to hang out in the epistemological bazaar. In this locale they can engage in unimagined conversations that move them to new levels of insight derived from juxtaposing diverse forms of meaning making.

In addition to different cultural knowledges and modes of meaning making, bricoleurs study the history of European disciplines and the insights to be gained from traditions of dissent within such disciplines. Here they study the relationship of canonical and counter-canonical ways of seeing. In this interactive setting bricoleurs are less interested in asking about the truth of other traditions and more concerned with inquiring about the origins of such perspectives and their implications for the larger act of knowledge production (Pickering, 1999; Degenaar, 1995; Steinberg, 2001; Kincheloe, 2005).

DIFFERENCE AND COGNITION: BRICOLEURS AS POSTFORMAL THINKERS ABOUT RESEARCH

As noted above, postformalism provides an important foundation for any notion of a critical and complex multicultural cognition informed by difference. The way we conceptualize cognition exerts a profound impact on both the goals of our research and the everyday activities of researchers. Do we think of the mind as a computer that files representations of the world to be accessed when needed? Or do we view the mind in a more complex manner as an entity that constructs knowledge as it interacts with the world and other knowledge producers? As a complex model for a form of thinking that takes seriously the critique of Cartesian rationalism and the multicultural call for difference, postformalism can change the direction of epistemological work. In research shaped by scholars who understand postformalism and the type of analysis that can emerge from it, self-reflection leads inquirers to become detectives of both intelligence and forms of knowledge work in diverse contexts both academic and outside of academia.

The alternative cognitive practices that emerge in these diverse contexts are often grounded in cooperative interaction between and among diverse peoples. In this cooperative domain individuals are privy to the various forms of interrelatedness. Attending to the characteristics of such connections, individuals come to see order instead of chaos. The concept of interconnection moves postformalists to bring Humberto Maturana and Francisco Varela's cognitive theory of enactivism into the bricolage. In such interconnections and the patterns and processes enfolded within them we begin to discern one of the most amazing phenomena uncovered in recent times. Francisco Varela (1999) writes that as unlikely as it may seem

> Lots of simple agents having simple properties may be brought together, even in a haphazard way, to give rise to what appears to be a purposeful and integrated whole, without the need for central supervision. (p. 52)

In this simple statement we begin to uncover a whole new dimension of not only cognitive activity but also of the character of "the self." In this domain we blaze new trails into the epistemological and ontological domains. In the epistemological domain we begin to realize that knowledge is stripped of its meaning when it stands alone. This holds profound implications in research because European science has studied the world in a way that isolates the object of study, abstracts it from the contexts and interrelationships that give it meaning. Thus, to be a multicultural researcher in a manner that takes Varela's enactivist notion into account, we have to study the world "in context." Bricoleurs understand that they have to search for the interrelationships and contexts that give knowledge meaning while avoiding reliance upon decontextualized study. The notion of difference directly references the relationship of different entities. Thus, the bricoleur's concern with difference gains its cognitive and epistemological power in these relationships.

Of course, this cognitive and epistemological power of difference is being subverted by the emergence of an American empire (Kincheloe and Steinberg, 2004) that privileges one way of seeing and one vision of both history and the future. Because a central dimension of the empire involves the production and control of information, possibilities for encountering difference continue to decline. In this context we begin to realize that cognition cannot be separated from the political and the epistemological. Such recognitions are central to the employment of the bricolage in multicultural research. Drawing upon the contextual and perspectival dimensions of knowledge production, bricoleurs understand that we are all dependent on our relationships with others—the power of difference—to facilitate our effort to transcend the blinders of our own limited perspectives. Making use of difference in bricolage becomes a prerequisite for rigorous research and knowledge work.

Indeed, bricoleurs refuse to be confined to one cultural way of seeing and making meaning. In contemporary society they organize communities of conceptual difference operating at a macro-level much like the mind operates in the interaction of its various parts. Thus, difference is expanded into concepts such as the web of life and the web of social, cultural and political reality into which all humans fit. Bricoleurs work to make use of the relationships one encounters in these webs—relationships that were torn apart by the Cartesian fragmentation of the world and its effort to tame difference. Bricoleurs view cognition as a reflection of life processes in general. Such life processes used physical diversity to form interrelationships that led to more complex biological processes. An understanding of human cognition based on relationship—an important dimension of postformalism—operates in a similar way, establishing interactions with different entities to produce more complex understandings of self and world.

One's cognitive development as a researcher utilizing the bricolage, therefore, would seek out difference in multiple historical, cultural, psychological, philosophical, political, social, economic, and educational contexts. One of the most important tasks of the bricoleur involves bringing together diverse individuals and traditions for the purpose of producing a synergistic postformal conversation between them (Horn, 2000). Again drawing upon the work of Maturana and Varela (1987), bricoleurs study the way the complexity of an ecosystem's web of relationships is connected to its biodiversity. In this context biologists have come to recognize that a diverse ecological community is more resistant to destruction than a more homogenous ecological community. In human communities, especially in the domains of cognition and epistemology, we may find similar dynamics at work. In these domains difference involves analyzing and understanding a plethora of relationships between numerous concepts. It involves engaging, for example, diverse approaches to the same problem. In this way cognitive activity and knowledge production are strengthened, as new insights and ways of pursuing knowledge emerge in the interaction of different approaches (Inayatullah, 1995; Williams, 1999; Murphie, 1998; Capra, 1996).

Whenever physical systems are used to provide insight into social systems caution is necessary. Nevertheless, the use of Maturana and Varela's biological insights may be helpful in understanding the ways difference operates in social, cognitive, and epistemological systems. I am aware that such interpretations must be offered with the knowledge that they are constructions developed at a particular historical moment in a particular historical setting. In this context it is important to study the role of difference in self-organizing systems. According to Maturana and Varela self-organization is not possible without difference. In autopoietic systems an entity evolves by reaching out into novelty and constructing synergistic interactions, not by chance mutations and natural selection. Life forms unfold in relation to their exposure to multiple levels of diversity in a manner that can be described as a creative cognitive process. Drawing upon the concepts, bricoleurs in their research reach out for novelty in the social, cultural, political, economic, philosophical, and economic domains.

Even the notion of autopoietic biology itself was developed by connecting biology to non-Western philosophical traditions. Connecting with difference is central in all of these situations. In enactivist biology humans are seen as engaging in a continuous and egalitarian dialogue with the physical world rather than in a unidirectional monologue. Drawing on the Taoist notion that the physical world emerges from the cooperation of all living and non-living things in their diversity, Maturana and Varela theorized life processes and cognitive processes as similar in form and function. Knowing what we know about the role of difference in shaping these processes, only a regressive ethnocentrism prevents Western researchers from making use of the unique insights of Islam, Hinduism, Buddhism, African traditions, and numerous indigenous modes of meaning making. As bricoleurs are coming to realize, these traditions provide tremendous insights into the effort to make sense of and change the contemporary world. When such multicultural ways of seeing are brought together with the power literacy of criticality, powerful epistemological and ontological synergies emerge that further empower the work of bricolage (Varela, 1999; Capra, 1996; Pickering, 1999; O'Sullivan, 1999).

Escaping the orbit of a mechanistic view of humanness: The postformal journey into new domains of knowledge. In the spirit of John Dewey and Lev Vygotsky, postformalism is about learning to think, act, and research in ways that hold pragmatic consequence—the promise of new insights and new modes of engaging the world. In this context, postformalists seek out new bodies of knowledge, not for the simple purpose of committing them to memory but to engage, grapple with, and interpret them in light of other data. At the same time such scholars are confronting such knowledges, they are researching and interacting with diverse contexts. Here the multilogicality of the bricolage and postformalism merge as both constructs search for new modes and levels of diversity. Postformalists as bricoleurs are focused on the process of making meaning and then acting on that meaning in practical and ethically just ways.

Thus, postformalists and bricoleurs are students of complexity and processes. Postformalists move beyond encounters with "formal" properties of information. Cartesian logic and the mechanistic research it supported focused attention on the formal dynamics of defining subject matter, subdividing it, and classifying it. As Dewey put it in the 1930s in *How We Think:* in formal thinking and teaching "the mind becomes logical only by learning to conform to an external subject matter" (p. 82). The scholar in this formal context is told to meticulously reproduce material derived from arithmetic, geography, grammar or whatever. The concepts of meaning making or use in context are irrelevant in the formal domain. Thus, as complexity theory would posit decades after Dewey's work on cognition: objects in the rearview mirror are more complex than they may appear.

In the spirit of complexity postformalists understand that since what we call reality is not external to consciousness, cognition operates to construct the world. It is more important than we ever imagined. Like cream in a cup of dark roast Colombian coffee, complexity theory blends well with Dewey's critique of formalism. Cognitive activity, knowledge production, and the construction of reality are simply too complex to be accomplished by following prescribed formulae. The reductionistic, obvious, and safe answers produced by formalist ways of thinking and researching are unacceptable to postformalists. What are the epistemological and ideological processes, postformalists ask, that operate to confirm such knowledge claims while disconfirming others? Understanding the pluralistic nature of epistemology, postformalists see beyond the one-truth reductionism of formalism. Understanding, for example, that there are many ways to define and measure intelligence moves postformalists to engage in a more rigorous—and diverse—analysis of such a phenomenon. Again, awareness of and action in relation to diversity becomes a key dimension to gaining a rigorous understanding of the world in order to engage in informed, intelligent, and transformative action.

The procedure-based, decontextualized, epistemologically naïve formalist way of approaching research is the method of beginners, not of seasoned, rigorous scholars. Just as physics and biology have retreated from formalist efforts to search for sub-atomic particles and genes as the ultimate organizational components of matter and life, psychologists of a postformal stripe, for example, see mind less as a compilation of neurons and more of a complex set of processes operating in diverse contexts. Such reductionistic formalist obsessions emerge when research topics are dehistoricized and socially and culturally decontextualized. This is why postformalists are dedicated to the study of context. Without such contextualization Abraham Maslow's hierarchy of needs is put forth as a universal truth, just as relevant for a nineteenth century woman in an isolated tribe in an Amazon rainforest as it is for a privileged oil magnate from Midland, Texas.

Without postformalism's contextual intervention, Piaget's formal operational thinking becomes the standard for measuring the highest order of intelligence for African tribespeople in rural Namibia as well as for affluent students from the Upper East Side in New York City. Needs and concepts of higher-order thinking, once historicized and culturally contextualized, emerge as social constructions. Since it is hard to discern the footprints of social construction in the formalist haze, scientific researchers in the cognitive domain deem African Americans, Latinos, various indigenous peoples, and poor people of all racial and cultural backgrounds to be "cognitively challenged." Such pronouncements serve to legitimate centuries of power inequity and oppression. Poverty becomes a marker of intellectual inferiority. Postformalists operating as multilogical bricoleurs refuse to let such neo-racism, neo-class bias, and neo-colonialism go unchallenged.

With these understandings in mind postformalists deepen their appreciation of the importance of experience in the intersection of constructivism, situated cognition, and enactivism. Carefully examining the interaction of experiential learning in everyday contexts with particular critical theoretical insights, postformalism traverses a terrain of complexity leading to new insights about cognition and the multiple forces that shape it (Fenwick, 2005). Here postformalists refuse deterministic and elitist orientations that view individuals as "blind dupes" of social structures. Instead postformalists learn from people's lived experiences, always appreciating the need to question anyone's experience—their own included—for the role power plays in refracting it. No experience—no matter the context in which it is embedded, no matter how "theoretically sophisticated" it is deemed to be—is free from the influence of power. Drawing on insight from experience in postformalism is always accompanied by the hermeneutic act of interpreting the meanings of such experience in light of particular contexts and processes.

The postformal effort to deal with the complexity of experience is intimately connected to the multilogicality of the bricolage. One of the central dimensions of this multilogicality involves the effort to overcome the monological limits of formalistic science and its companion, hyper-reason. In this context postformalists point out the ways that mechanistic notions of intelligence and ability have dismissed the insights and contributions of the socially and economically marginalized and alternative ways of developing found in differing cultural contexts. Formalism's lack of respect for those who fall outside its boundaries is unacceptable in the contemporary world; in this context postformalism constantly pushes the boundaries of cognition and knowledge production with its emphasis on subjugated knowledges and indigenous ontologies. In postformalism complexity theory breaks bread with a literacy of power. In the process a powerful synergy is constructed that shines a new light on the act of research, especially as it relates to multicultural concerns.

In postformalism, critical social theory works in the trenches with diverse discourses in the process expanding our understanding of complexity and challenging critical theory itself. In this context critical theory sees itself in terms of an evolving criticality that is perpetually concerned with keeping the critical tradition alive and fresh. Such theoretical moves challenge educational psychology to ask how it is shaped by its own culture. Postformalism is the uninvited guest in the summer house of cognitive studies that keeps pressuring the discipline's elite to understand that mechanistic psychology—a positivist view of psychology that views the mind as a self-contained machine—is an ideology with devastating effects on those not in the country club of modern, upper-middle class whiteness.

Pointing out that mechanism operates in the low-affect social world of naïve realism, post-formalists chart its values of detachment, neutrality, and amoral technicism. If we keep politics out of psychology, psychometricians insist, we just objectively measure human intelligence and that has nothing to do with the cultural realm. Indeed, multiculturalism is an insult to the objectivity of the science of psychology, such reductionistic, monological researchers assert. In a neo-social Darwinist era, where survival-of-the-fittest perspectives find wide acceptance, these formalist educational psychologies once again provide justification for the failure of the socially, economically, culturally, and politically marginalized. Postformalism will not allow such reductionism to stand.

MULTILOGICALITY AND CONSCIOUSNESS: POSTFORMALISM AND THE POWER OF MULTIPLE PERSPECTIVES

In this context postformalists turn their critical lenses on the complexity of the interrelationship between consciousness and culture. Culture makes personhood possible with the pre-existing world it has constructed. Such a cosmos is made up of ideas, various constructions of the physical world, interpretations, linguistic structures, and emotional registers. Such dynamics are embedded in various social institutions, discursive practices, social relationships, aesthetic forms, and technologies. Individuals construct their lives with the assistance of these cultural inheritances—the concept of identity itself is meaningless without them. Thus, again the point needs to be made: the lived world is more complex than it seems in the mechanistic portrayal. Any science, postformalists maintain, that claims predictive ability in the complexity of everyday life does not appreciate the complications of mind, consciousness, culture, and power.

For example, a mechanistic psychology that assumes I.Q. can predict the future academic performance of students and uses it in this way misses numerous important points of great relevance to postformalists. On one simplistic level there is a predictive element to I.Q. and academic performance, as long as particular conditions are held constant. As long as students do not learn about the social, cultural, political, economic structures of both I.Q. testing and schools and schools continue to emphasize I.Q. test type skills, there is a correlation between test scores and academic performance. The assumption here is that students be kept in the dark about the panoply of forces that help shape their relation to the test. Thus, in order for this predictive dimension to work we must keep test takers as ignorant as possible about what exactly the test reflects about the relationship between the student and dominant culture.

When students are informed about these complex dynamics, they can begin to reshape that relationship. Also, the predictive dimension rests on the assumption that no curricular innovation will take place that will focus students' attention more on meta-understandings of curriculum and the construction of knowledge. As long as these dynamics are ignored and the curriculum is viewed as a body of previously produced truths to be committed to memory, then the logic behind both I.Q. and curriculum are similar. Students tend to act and react similarly to situations grounded on this formalist logic. When such formalist logic is challenged and more interpretive, complex, and activity-based cognition is demanded, the predictive dimension of I.Q. testing evaporates into the mechanistic mist.

Thus, questions concerning the predictive capacity of I.Q. and other forms of standardized testing are much more complex than mechanistic educational psychology has claimed. Thus, postformalists call for a far more complex understanding of the cognitive act as well as its measurement and evaluation. In the spirit of complexity postformalists promote the ability to both appreciate and deal with uncertainty and ambiguity. In this context they are aware of the underside of the Eurocentric mechanistic quest for certainty and the social and personal damage such a trek produces. Given the vast array of abilities human beings can possess and the infinite diversity of contexts in which to develop and apply them, the mechanistic tendency to label individuals as simply "intelligent" or "not intelligent" is an insult both to the field of psychology and the individuals affected by such crass labels.

Intelligence in the postformal articulation is *not* a description of the hereditary dimensions of some central processing mechanism (CPM) located somewhere in the brain and the efficiency of its operation. Understanding complexity, postformalists maintain that intelligence is more a local than a universal phenomenon. As such, postformalist intelligence involves diverse individual responses to challenges that face them in light of particular contexts, access to cultural amplifiers, cultural capital and particular tools and artifacts, specific values, social goals and needs, patterns of construction, linguistic dynamics, and traditions of meaning making—the constructed, situated, and enacted dimensions of intelligence. Thus, postformal consciousness is shaped by specific contexts and is constructed by particular interrelationships in certain domains. It is enacted into existence—that is, it emerges as it acts in relation to these contexts and domains. Understanding the functioning of this mind is never certain and easy, and measuring it in some quantitative manner is even harder. But that's okay, postformalists are comfortable with such complications in the zone of complexity.

Central to this postformalist appreciation of complexity is the general task of understanding both the situatedness of mind in general and the self in particular. In this context we embrace our postformal humility because we come to appreciate just how limited by time and space, by history and culture our perspectives are. A scholar of any discipline would always be humbled if she had access to a time machine that allowed her to view scholars from the twenty-fifth century reading and commenting on her work. And hers was work that was deemed of sufficient quality to merit comment in 2477! This is one of many reasons that postformalists and bricoleurs value the effort to seek multiple perspectives on everything they do. The more diverse the experiences and the positionalities of those issuing the multiple perspectives, the better. In the spirit of subjugated knowledges it is important to gain the views of individuals and the construction of their consciousness from groups that have been marginalized and dismissed from the mainstream scholarly process.

Thus, complexity demands that postformalists pursue multiple perspectives and multilogical insights into scholarly production. One dimension of such multilogicality involves tracing the developmental history of ideas. How was it shaped by tacit assumptions and contextual factors such as ideology, discourse, linguistics, and particular cultural values? These dynamics are central tasks in postformal scholarship and pedagogy. Indeed, students' ability to understand the ways that ideas and concepts are constructed by a variety of forces and how power is complicit with which interpretations are certified and which ones are rejected is central to being a rigorous educated person. Of course, a central contention of postformalism is that hegemonic educational structures operate to undermine the presence of multiple perspectives in the school, to negate the power of difference. Indeed, one of the most important goals of many of the educational reforms championed by right-wing groups in Western societies over the last few decades has been the elimination of such "dangerous" perspectives from the school. With the victory of these forces in the U.S. embodied in the appointment of George W. Bush to the presidency in 2000 and the election of 2004, policies based on these exclusionary practices have been institutionalized. Thus, the multilogical goals of postformalism have suffered a setback.

Social science, psychology, and pedagogy must realize the limitations and monologicality of traditional research methods and sources. For disciplines of study to move forward scholars must work to view their studies from outside of a white, Eurocentric, patriarchal, class elitist position. Some of the most important positions may be the ones with which mainstream scholarship is the most unfamiliar. Employing these knowledges postformalism provides a way out, an escape from the ideological blinders of the mechanistic worldview.

POSTFORMALISM, SYNERGIES OF DIFFERENCE, AND NEW MODES OF COGNITION

Postformalism understands that intelligence, justice, emotion, activity, disposition, context, access, power, justice, tools, process, ethics, ad infinitum cannot be separated in the study of cognition and efforts to move to new levels of scholarship and social action. With these connections in mind postformalists warn scholars about the complexity of the scholarly process they're about to jump into when they seek to engage in postformal knowledge work. Much is asked of those who enter into this realm. Postformalists urge educators as scholars and researchers at every level of theory and practice to enter into research groups, to develop lifelong learning relationships with those interested in the multiple dimensions, the multilogicality of postformalism.

As I write about the process of becoming a bricoleur in my work on social, educational, and psychological research, the multidisciplinarity and multiperspectival demands of the bricolage cannot be learned in an undergraduate, master's or Ph.D. program. Becoming a scholar of postformalism—like becoming a scholar of the bricolage—is a lifelong learning process. Every time I enter a new dimension of postformalism, I feel as if I need to put myself through another self-taught doctoral program. Lifelong interactive learning relations with other individuals—especially individuals different with oneself in diverse ways—make the process much easier. My motivation to engage myself and others in this process never wanes, for we are dealing with one of the central processes of humanness—making ourselves smarter, more ethical, more sensitive to the needs of others, more active in helping alleviate those needs, and more aware of the nature of our connections and interrelationships with various dimensions of the world around us. I want to become smarter and more helpful to those around me in my engagement with these multiple and interrelated domains.

In this postformal pedagogical context as we transcend the "rational irrationality" of formalism and mechanism, we help students get in touch with what John Dewey (1933) called their own "vital logical movement." In the history of mechanistic educational psychology it was these forms of analysis and knowledge production that were denigrated and replaced by formalist logical procedures. In the memorization of these cut-and-dried logical steps millions of children and young people lost their passion for learning and growing. Indeed, they dedicated their lives to getting out of learning situations, in the process relinquishing their disposition to explore themselves and the world around them. Do not mistake this rejection of dry formalistic procedure as a call for a "return to nature" and the hereditary natural developmental process of the child. Postformalists do not constitute some latter day cadre of reincarnated G. Stanley Halls promoting some bizarre recapitulation theory.

The vital logical movement of individuals can be facilitated by good teachers and by entry into Vygotsky's ZPD, where students learn by association with skilled others. Thus, as is generally the case with postformalism, we seek to expand cognitive abilities in ways that are informed by multiple insights while avoiding dogmatic blueprints for how to do it. Formal reasoning is profoundly different from everyday thinking. Formal thinking embraces a subject matter that is impersonal as algebraic formulae and consciously operates to remove itself from the subjectivity, the dispositions and intentions of the thinker. Postformalism categorically rejects this type of cognition and seeks to connect with and understand all that formal reasoning seeks to exclude.

In the postformal context we get smarter, we come to produce more compelling knowledge by constructing our own multilogical ZPDs. In these contexts we construct our own community of experts—whether virtually by reading their work or by interacting with them personally. In our self-constructed ZPDs we build new intellectual and action based relationships and structurally couple with multiple minds. Schools, postformalists argue, should be grounded on these types of cognitive principles—not on the psychometric, abstract individual, decontextualized, and personally disconnected models of the no-child-left-behind ilk. We can teach students to be lifelong learners who understand that intelligence is not a fixed, hereditarian concept but a fluid, socially constructed dynamic that can be learned when individuals are exposed to challenging new contexts—e.g., teacher and/or self-constructed ZPDs. Viewed in this context postformalism offers a cognition of hope that transcends the nihilism of mechanism and monologicality. Postformalists refuse to believe that human beings are condemned to academic hell because of the infallibility and intractability of test scores, that they cannot become smarter as their ZPD pushes the boundaries of difference.

Thus, as a critical discourse, postformalism seeks an empowering notion of learning. Directly challenging mechanistic psychology's passive view of the learner, postformalism is dedicated to a respect for human dignity and the diverse range of talents and abilities that individuals operating in diverse social, cultural, geographic, and economic context develop. In this context postformalism makes difference come alive with tangible lived world consequences. Indeed, postformalists look behind I.Q. and other standardized test scores to uncover the infinite talents that people with low-test scores develop in the idiosyncratic contexts of their lives. When mechanistic influenced pedagogies refuse to consider these amazing talents and pronounce individuals with low-test scores incapable of learning, they commit a psychological and educational crime against such students. Such postformal insights tear down the exclusive walls protecting the community of blind monks responsible for producing knowledge about the world around us. The "barbarians" from communities of color, indigenous backgrounds, working class neighborhoods, and, God forbid, hillbilly hollers from the southern mountains of Tennessee take their place as knowledge producers.

Postformalists in this context believe in the ingenuity of human beings, the power of individuals to learn, the ability of even the wretched of the earth to create their own ZPDs. One of the most important impediments to such human agency is the positivist ideology of mechanistic psychology and other elitist disciplines. This regressive ideology works to convince individuals from marginalized backgrounds that they are incapable of learning like "normal" students, of joining the community of knowledge producers. Unfortunately, mechanists do a good job of convincing such boys and girls, men and women of their "lack of ability." Over the last few decades I have interviewed scores of brilliant people who told me that they were not good at "school learning" or "book learning." Often they told me of their lack of intelligence as they were in the middle of performing difficult and complex forms of mental labor. They may not have done well in school, but they had learned the most important mechanistic psychological lesson—they were not academic material.

In my conversations with those students mislabeled and abandoned by mechanistic educational psychology, I observe powerful intellectual abilities in their interactions with the world. They often illustrate a compelling ability to see things previously not discerned in domains dominated by conventional perspectives. They many times break through the tyranny of "the obvious" with insights gained by viewing a phenomenon from an angle different from the "experts." Postformalists are proud to have "friends in low places" who see schools, for example, from the perspective of those who have "failed." As a postformalist and critical multiculturalist, I treasure these perspectives. Indeed, they have played a central role in how I have come to understand educational institutions. Over the last couple of decades I have written extensively about what such brilliant people have taught me as I work to be a better educator, psychologist, sociologist, historian, philosopher, and student of cultural studies—in my struggle to become a bricoleur.

BRICOLAGE, DIFFERENCE, AND SELF-AWARENESS IN RESEARCH

When bricoleurs encounter difference in the nature of the other, they enter into symbiotic relationships where the identity of the researcher is changed. The researchers are no longer merely obtaining information but are entering a space of transformation where previously excluded perspectives operate to change consciousness of both self and the world. Thus, multicultural research in bricolage changes not only what one knows but also who one actually is. Thus, the epistemological and ontological domains enter into a new relationship that produces dramatic changes. Lev Vygotsky was on the right track as he documented the importance of the context in which learning takes place. Difference in the sense we are using it here expands the notion of the ZPD into the domain of research, drawing upon the power of our interactions in helping shape the ways we make meaning. In the new synergized position bricoleurs construct new realities where they take on new and expanded roles.

Aware of the power of difference, bricoleurs develop a new consciousness of the self: (1) the manner in which it has been constructed; (2) its limitations; and (3) a sense of immanence concerning what it can become. Self-awareness is a metacognitive skill that has historically been more valued in Eastern traditions such as Buddhism, Taoism, and Yoga than in the West. Time and again we see the value of pluralism manifest itself in this discussion of difference and the bricolage. A pluralistic epistemology helps us understand the way we are situated in the web of reality and how this situatedness shapes what we see as researchers. Such an awareness reveals the limited nature of our observations of the world. Instead of researchers making final pronouncements on the way things are, they begin to see themselves in a larger interdisciplinary and intercultural conversation. Bricoleurs pick up on this dynamic focusing their attention on better modes of listening and respecting diverse viewpoints. Such higher order listening moves bricoleurs to new levels of self-consciousness (Williams, 1999; Newland, 1997; Lepani, 1998; Steinberg, 2001).

Of course, difference does not work as an invisible hand that magically shapes new insights into self and world. Humans must exercise their hermeneutic abilities to forge these connections and interpret their meanings. In this context bricoleurs and postformalists confront difference and then decide where they stand in relation to it. They must discern what to make of what it has presented them. With this in mind bricoleurs work hard to develop relationships with those different from themselves that operate to create new meanings in the interactions of identity and difference. In this interaction bricoleurs grow smarter as they reject modernist Cartesian notions that cultural conflicts can be solved only by developing monological universal principles of epistemology and universal steps to the process of research. Too often, bricoleurs understand, the "universal" principles simply reflect colonial Western ways of viewing the world hiding in the disguise of universalism. Rigorous examination of the construction of self and society are closed off in such faux-universalism. Indeed, it undermines the development of a critical self-consciousness.

In the face of a wide variety of different knowledges and ways of seeing the cosmos, human beings' confidence in what they think they know collapses. In a counter-colonial move bricoleurs raise questions about any knowledges and ways of knowing that claim universal status. In this context bricoleurs make use of this suspicion of universalism in combination with global knowledges to understand how they have been positioned in the world. Almost all of us from Western backgrounds or non-Western colonized backgrounds have been implicated in some way in the web of universalism. The inevitable conflicts that arise from this implication do not have to be resolved immediately by bricoleurs. At the base of these conflicts rest the future of global culture as well as the future of multicultural research and pedagogy. Recognizing that these are generative issues that engage us in a productive process of analyzing self and world is in itself a powerful recognition. The value of both this recognition and the process of working through the complicated conceptual problems are treasured by bricoleurs. Indeed, bricoleurs avoid any notion of finality in the resolution of such dilemmas. Comfortable with the ambiguity, bricoleurs and postformalists work to alleviate human suffering and injustice even though they possess no final blueprint alerting them as to how oppression takes place.

REFERENCES

Able, C., C. Abel, V. Alexander, S. McCune, and P. Nason (2001). The ExCET Teacher Exams: History, Promies and Concerns. In J. Kincheloe and D. Weil (Eds.), *Standards and Schooling in the United States: An Encyclopedia.* 3 vols. Santa Barbara, CA: ABC-Clio.

Allen, M. (2000). Voice of reason. http://www.curtin.edu.au/learn/unit/10846/arrow/vorall.htm

Appelbaum, P. (2004). Mathematics Education. In J. Kincheloe & D. Weil (Eds.). *Critical Thinking: An Encyclopedia for Parents and Teachers.* Westport, CT: Greenwood.

Berlak, H. (1999). Standards and the Control of Knowledge. *Rethinking Schools,* **13**, 3. http://www.rethinkingscfhools.org/archieves/13_03/control.htm

Berry, K. (2001). Standards of Complexity in a Postmodern Democracy. In J. Kincheloe and D. Weil (Eds.), *Standards and Schooling in the United States: An Encyclopedia.* 3 vols. Santa Barbara, CA: ABC-Clio.

Brock, R. (2005). *Sista Talk: The Personal and the Pedagogical.* New York: Peter Lang.

Bruner, J. (1996). *The Culture of Education.* Cambridge, MA, Harvard University Press.

Burbules, N. & R. Beck (1999). Critical Thinking and Critical Pedagogy: Relations, Differences, and Limits. In T. Popkewitz and L. Fendler (Eds.), *Critical Theories in Education.* New York: Routledge.

Capra, F. (1996). *The Web of Life: A New Scientific Understanding of Living Systems*. New York: Anchor Books.

Degenaar, J. (1995). Myth and the Collision of Cultures. *Myth and Symbol, 2*.

Denzin, N. and Y. Lincoln (2000). Introduction: The Discipline and Practice of Qualitative Research. In N. Denzin and Y. Lincoln (Eds.) *Handbook of Qualitative Research* (2nd edition) Thousand Oaks, CA: Sage.

Dewey, J. (1933). *How We Think*. Lexington, MA: Heath.

Dumas, M. (2004). Critical Thinking as Black Experience. In J. Kincheloe & D. Weil (Eds.), *Critical Thinking: An Encyclopedia for Parents and Teachers*. Westport, CT: Greenwood.

Fenwick, T. (2005). Experiential Learning. In J. Kincheloe & R. Horn (Eds.) *Educational Psychology: An Encyclopedia*. Westport, CT: Greenwood.

Hoban, G. and G. Erickson (1998). Frameworks for Sustaining Professional Learning. Paper Presented at the Australasian Science Education Research Association, Darwin, Australia.

Horn, R. (2000). *Teacher Talk: A Postformal Inquiry into Educational Change*. New York: Peter Lang.

Hytten, K. (2004). John Dewey and Critical Thinking. In J. Kincheloe & D. Weil (Eds.), *Critical Thinking: An Encyclopedia for Parents and Teachers*. Westport, CT: Greenwood.

Inayatullah, S. (1995). Deconstructing and Reconstructing the Future: Predictive, Cultural, and Critical Epistemologies. http://www.scu.edu.au/schools/sawd/futures/secure/module1/1.5-sohail-inayatullah.html

Kincheloe, J. (2001). Describing the Bricolage: Conceptualizing a New Rigor in Qualitative Research. *Qualitative Inquiry, 7*, 6, pp. 679–92.

Kincheloe, J. (2005). *Critical Constructivism*. New York: Peter Lang.

Kincheloe & Berry (2004). *Rigour and Complexity in Qualitative Research: Conceptualizing the Bricolage*. London: Open University Press.

Kincheloe, J. and S. Steinberg (1993). A Tentative Description of Post-formal Thinking: The Critical Confrontation with Cognitive Theory. *Harvard Educational Review, 63*, 3, pp. 296–320.

Kincheloe, J. and S. Steinberg (1997). *Changing Multiculturalism*. London: Open University Press.

Kincheloe, J. and S. Steinberg (2004). *The Miseducation of the West: How Schools and the Media Distort Our Understanding of the Islamic World*. Westport, CT: Praeger.

Kincheloe, J., Steinberg, S., and Hinchey, P. (Eds.) (1999). *The Post-formal Reader: Cognition and Education*. New York: Falmer.

Kincheloe, J. & D. Weil (Eds.) (2004). *Critical Thinking and Learning: An Encyclopedia for Parents and Teachers*. Westport, CT: Greenwood.

Lapani, B. (1998). Information Literacy: The Challenge of the Digital Age. http://www.acal.edu.au/lepani.htm

McLaren, P. (2000). *Che Guevara, Paulo Freire, and the Pedagogy of Revolution*. Lanham, MD: Rowman and Littlefield.

McRorie, S. (1999). Pentimento: Philosophical Inquiry as Research in Art Education. Xerox manuscript.

Malewski, E. (2001). "Queer Sexuality—The Trouble with Knowing: Standards of Complexity and Sexual Orientations," in J. Kincheloe and D. Weil (Eds.), *Standards and Schooling in the United States: An Encyclopedia*. 3 vols. Santa Barbara, CA, ABC-CLIO.

Maturana, H. & Varela, F. (1987). *The Tree of Knowledge*. Boston: Shambhala.

May, T. (1993). *Between Genealogy and Epistemology: Psychology, Politics, and Knowledge in the Thought of Michel Foucault*. University Park, PA: Penn State Press.

Murphie, A. (1998). Cyberfictions and Hypertext: What Is Happening to Text? http://www.mcs.elm.mq.edu.au/staff/Andrew/307/hypeprt.html

Newland, P. (1997). Logical Types of Learning. http://www.envf.port.ac.uk/newmedia/lecturenotes/EMMA/at2n.htm

Noone, L. and Cartwright, P. (1996). Doing a Critical Literacy Pedagogy: Trans/forming Teachers in a Teacher Education Course. http://www.atea.schools.net.au/ATEA/96conf/noone.html

O'Sullivan, E. (1999). *Transformative Learning: Educational Vision for the 21st Century*. London: Zed.

Parmar, P. (2004). Critical Thinking and Rap Music: The Critical Pedagogy of KRS-One. In J. Kincheloe & D. Weil (Eds.), *Critical Thinking: An Encyclopedia for Parents and Teachers*. Westport, CT: Greenwood.

Pickering, J. (1999). The Self Is a Semiotic Process. *Journal of Consciousness Studies,* **6**, 4, pp. 31–47.

Progler, Y. (2001). Social Studies—Social Studies Standards: Diversity, Conformity, Complexity. In J. Kincheloe and D. Weil (Eds.), *Standards and Schooling in the United States: An Encyclopedia*. 3 vols. Santa Barbara, CA: ABC-Clio.

Richardson, F. and R. Woolfolk (1994). Social Theory and Values: A Hermeneutic Perspective. *Theory and Psychology,* **4**, 2, pp. 199–226.

Scering, G. (1997) Themes of a Critical/Feminist Pedagogy: Teacher Education for Democracy. *Journal of Teacher Education,* **48**, 1, pp. 62–69.

Steinberg, S. (Ed.) (2001). *Multi/intercultural Conversations*. New York: Peter Lang.

Thayer-Bacon, B. (2000). *Transforming Critical Thinking: Thinking Constructively*. New York: Teachers College Press.

Thayer-Bacon, B. (2003). *Relational "(E)pistemologies."* New York: Peter Lang.

Thomas, G. (1998). The Myth of Rational Research. *British Educational Research Journal,* **24**, 2.

Varela, F. (1999). *Ethical Know-how: Action, Wisdom, and Cognition*. Stanford, CA: Stanford University Press.

Weinstein, M. (1995). Critical Thinking? Expanding the Paradigm. http://www.chss.montclair.edu/inquiry/fall95/weinste.html

Williams, S. (1999). Truth, Speech, and Ethics: A Feminist Revision of Free Speech Theory. *Genders,* 30. http://www.genders.org

SECTION TWO
Behaviorism

FOUR

Behaviorism and Its Effect upon Learning in the Schools

Dengting Boyanton

Behaviorism has had a profound impact in a number of disciplines including psychology, clinical therapy, educational research, and instructional design (Driscoll, 2005). As the first theory that was applied directly to educational settings to facilitate teaching, behaviorism is an extremely important theory in the education field. It was the most dominant theory in American educational psychology between the 1920s and the 1960s and still has tremendous impact on educational practices today. However, behaviorism has been criticized by many researchers, teachers, administrators, and policy-makers. The purpose of this chapter is threefold: 1) to develop a correct understanding of behaviorism, 2) to objectively and critically evaluate its effect on learning, and 3) to provide practical guidelines on its applications in school settings.

This chapter is divided into two sections. The first provides an overview of behaviorism, e.g., its history and some key concepts. The second broadly evaluates its effects, both positive and negative, on education. The second part also includes practical guidelines on the applications of behaviorism in actual school and classroom environments. It is my sincere hope that this chapter will help the readers not only develop a deep understanding of behaviorism but also walk away with practical strategies and methods.

OVERVIEW OF BEHAVIORISM

CLASSICAL CONDITIONING BY PAVLOV

Behaviorism began with the Russian psychologist Pavlov and his famous dog salivation experiment in the 1890s. In his experiment, Pavlov and his laboratory staff first presented food to the dog and found that the dog actually started the act of salivating *before* eating the food. When an actual stimulus itself (e.g., food) causes some action in animals or humans, the stimulus is called an unconditioned stimulus. Inspired by this discovery, Pavlov and his staff designed another experiment. This time, they presented the food to the dog together with a tuning fork, hoping that the dog would associate the fork with the food. After repeating this paired presentation several times, Pavlov removed the food and just presented the tuning fork alone. As hypothesized, the dog also started saliva every time when it saw the tuning fork. When an irrelevant stimulus (e.g., tuning fork) alone elicits the behavioral response (e.g., salivation) after training, it is called a conditioned stimulus. "Conditioned" simply means "trained." The technique of using a conditioned stimulus (often referred to as a discriminative stimulus) to elicit behavioral response is called classical conditioning, which can be illustrated as follows:

$$S \rightarrow R$$

(DISCRIMINATIVE STIMULUS) (RESPONSE)

Pavlov's classical conditioning theory contributed to our understanding of animal behavior and learning in at least four areas:

1. Animal behavioral responses are caused by the stimuli around them, or to be more exact, by the associations that they infer about different stimuli.
2. The associations that animals make about different stimuli are influenced by their experiences with those stimuli.
3. Animal behavioral responses can be predicted because certain stimuli always elicit certain behavioral responses (e.g., food-saliva).
4. Animal behavioral responses can be manipulated through training the animal to make the desired association between different stimuli. For example, if Pavlov paired a blue ribbon, and not the tuning fork, with the food, then the dog would have associated the blue ribbon, and not the fork, with the food.

CLASSICAL CONDITIONING BY WATSON

John Watson was the first person to introduce behaviorism to American psychology. Watson extended Pavlov's research in two areas: 1) he changed the research subjects from animals to human beings; and 2) he shifted the research focus from behaviors to emotions (Rilling, 2000b). Watson's most famous experiment was conducted with the 11-month-old baby Albert. In his experiment, Watson first presented a white furry rat paired with a sweet soft voice to baby Albert. Albert loved the furry rat and even became upset when it was taken away from him. For the second experiment, Watson paired the rat with a loud scary noise instead. This time, Albert immediately jumped with fear and started to cry. After repeating the second experiment several times, Albert started to cry and crawl away in fear when the rat was presented alone. This fear extended to other white furry objects (white dog, white rabbit, sealskin fur coat) and lasted for more than a month. From this experiment, Watson concluded that behavioral responses can be conditioned, and emotional responses can be conditioned as well, and so can human interests, hobbies, and career choices. Watson believed that he could control anyone's interests and careers through the right kind of training:

> Give me a dozen healthy infants, well formed, and my own specified world to bring them up in, and I'll guarantee to take any one at random and train him to become any type of specialist I might select— doctor, lawyer, artist, merchant chief—regardless of his talents, tendencies, abilities, vocations, and race of his ancestors. (Watson, 1924, p. 82)

Although different from Pavlov's theory, Watson's theory shared one common principle with Pavlov's: Responses, whether behavioral or emotional, are caused by stimuli or associations of the stimuli. Watson's theory can also be explained by the stimulus-response formula and adds another layer to classical conditioning. Watson contributed to behaviorism in the following areas:

1. Emotional responses—such as fear, love, and anger—can be conditioned in the same way as behavioral responses.
2. Contrary to what most people believed at the time, emotional responses are not instinctual or biological. They can be learned and trained.
3. In addition to human emotional responses, human interests, hobbies, or career choices can also be trained.

OPERANT CONDITIONING BY SKINNER

Following Watson's lead, Skinner also emphasized behavior as the basic subject matter of psychology (Skinner, 1938, 1974). Often seen as a major proponent of radical behaviorism, Skinner's work differed fundamentally from Watson's work and that of his contemporaries who followed Watson. Classical conditioning emphasizes the role of stimuli or antecedents on behavioral change. Skinner, however, believed that the consequences following the responses are more critical in determining behavioral changes.

Skinner's well-known experiment involved an ingenious apparatus known as the Skinner box. This box contained a bar (or lever) and a small tray. Outside the box was a hopper holding a supply of food pellets that were dropped into the tray when the bar was pressed under certain conditions. A hungry rat was placed in the box, and when the rat approached and pressed the bar, it was rewarded with a food pellet. Skinner observed that after being rewarded, the rat pressed the bar more frequently than before. From this experiment, Skinner concluded that behavioral responses are caused by the consequences. People are more likely to perform a task if they know that their behavior will be rewarded. Controlling or predicting human behavior (or its frequency) by manipulating the consequences (often referred to as a contingent stimulus) is called operant conditioning. For example, a teacher can operate a student's behavior of submitting the homework on time by providing praise. In this example, the "submitting the homework" behavior "operates" on the environment to produce a consequence like praise and the "submitting the homework" behavior is therefore called operant response (Skinner, 1935). Skinner's operant conditioning can be shown in the formula below:

$$S \to R \to S$$

(DISCRIMINATIVE STIMULUS) (OPERANT RESPONSE) (CONTINGENT STIMULUS)

Skinner's operant conditioning added the second branch to behaviorism, and it expanded our understanding on human behavior and learning in several ways:

1. Our behaviors are determined by the consequences that follow them.
2. Depending on whether we like the consequences or not, the likelihood of repeating a behavior can be either strengthened or weakened.
3. In order to change a behavior, consequences have to be presented.

CLASSIFICATIONS OF CONSEQUENCES

Consequences can be divided into different categories. First, depending on where the reinforcement comes from, they can be divided into primary reinforcers and conditioned reinforcers. A primary reinforcer is a consequence whose reinforcement value is biologically determined such as food. A conditioned reinforcer acquires its reinforcement value through the association with a primary reinforcer such as gold stars, money, and praise (Driscoll, 2005). Second, depending on whether a stimulus is presented or removed, they can be divided into positive reinforcers (presented) and negative reinforcers (removed) (Skinner, 1989b). Third, depending on whether the consequence strengthens or weakens a certain behavior, it can be divided into reinforcement (strengthen) or punishment (weaken) (Skinner, 1989b). Lastly, consequences can be divided into natural reinforcers—consequences brought about by the behavior itself—and contrived reinforcers—consequence caused by someone else's actions in response to the behavior (Skinner, 1954). Examples of natural reinforcers are playing with toys, painting, going to parties, solving a problem, learning something new, or having the opportunity to advance to the next stage of an activity. Examples of contrived reinforcers are rewarding a child with candies after he finishes his homework on time or getting a paycheck after working. These two types of consequences are similar to the other two concepts of intrinsic (natural) and extrinsic (contrived) motivators.

Behaviors may also be categorized by the consequences that produce them. Depending on how the consequence is applied to the individual, the resulting behaviors can be divided into contingency-governed behaviors and rule-governed behaviors. Contingency-governed behaviors refer to behaviors performed because the subject receives consequences directly. Rule-governed behaviors, however, are behaviors performed not because the subject experiences the consequences him/herself but because s/he is expected or instructed to do so by rules, laws, advice, religious teachings, etc. Rule-governed behavior is learned from others' experiences without the subject directly experiencing any consequence him/herself (Skinner, 1989b).

Consequences are often categorized by combining two or more of the above criteria, such as whether the consequence is presented or removed and whether the behavior is strengthened or weakened. When combining some of these criteria together, consequences can be divided into the following several types.

Positive reinforcement: Positive reinforcement is the presentation of a desirable consequence (satisfying stimulus) in response to a given behavior so that the behavior is strengthened (Driscoll, 2005). "Positive," as Skinner used it, refers to the act of presenting or adding a consequence. It also refers to the desirable nature of the consequence itself from the subject's perspective. The procedures of positive reinforcement are: 1) the subject performs certain behavior, 2) the desirable consequence is presented to the subject, and 3) the subject's behavior is strengthened. For example, a boy dresses himself, and his mother rewards him by giving him his favorite ice cream. The boy will be more likely to dress himself in the future.

Negative reinforcement: Negative reinforcement refers to the act of removing an undesirable consequence to strengthen a response. "Negative" includes two layers of meaning: 1) the removal of a consequence, and 2) the aversive nature of the consequence. Procedures of negative reinforcement include: 1) the subject is aware of the undesirable consequences for failing to perform the required behavior, 2) the subject performs the required behavior to avoid the undesirable consequence, 3) the subject's required performance is strengthened. For example, a boy knows that his mother will scold him if he does not dress himself. Therefore, he dresses himself to avoid his mother's nagging, and the mother does not scold him. The child is more likely to dress himself in the future.

Punishment: Punishment is the presentation of an undesirable consequence in response to a behavior in order to weaken that behavior (Driscoll, 2005). The procedures of punishment are: 1) the subject performs a certain behavior, 2) the undesirable consequence is presented, and 3) the subject's behavior is weakened. Punishment itself can be subdivided into different types. Depending on whether a consequence is presented or removed, it can be divided into: 1) presentation punishment (or type I) punishment, where an undesirable consequence is directly applied, e.g., corporal punishment; and 2) removal (or type II) punishment, where a desirable/pleasant consequence is taken away, e.g., not getting to go play during recess (Skinner, 1953, 1968b).

Negative reinforcement and punishment are often confused by many people since they both involve using undesirable consequences. These two concepts differ from each other in two ways: 1) Implementation of the consequence: with negative reinforcement, the undesirable consequence is not carried out but avoided successfully. With punishment, the undesirable consequence is actually carried out. 2) Effect of the consequence: with negative reinforcement, the subject's behavior is strengthened. With punishment, the subject's behavior is weakened.

Extinction: Extinction is the process of withholding reinforcement to weaken a previously reinforced behavior. Procedures of extinction are: 1) the subject performs a certain behavior with the expectation of receiving reinforcement, 2) the expected reinforcement is withheld through planned ignoring, and 3) the subject's behavior is weakened. It is important to note that although no consequence is applied in the case of extinction, we are still manipulating the consequence by intentionally not providing the expected consequences. In order for extinction to be effective, the subject has to be expecting some kind of consequence, e.g., attention or approval. An example of extinction is a boy who jumps on the bed shouting "Look how high I can jump!" to seek attention from his mother. If the mother keeps asking him to stop, the boy's jumping behavior will be strengthened because the mother is providing him the desired attention. If the mother uses extinction, the jumping behavior is likely to stop on its own eventually.

Time-out: Time-out is the removal (or Type II) Punishment, which involves removing the individual from the circumstances reinforcing the undesired behavior for a limited amount of time. The procedures of time-out are: 1) the individual performs a certain behavior, 2) the individual is removed to a different place where s/he can no longer perform the behavior to receive the reinforcement, 3) the individual's behavior is weakened. In order for time-out to be effective, several conditions have to be met. First, the individual must dislike leaving the original place. For example, if a boy interrupts the class because he is bored and he cannot wait to get out of the class, then being removed from the class will be more like "positive reinforcement" than "time-out" to him. Second, the time-out place should be a place where positive reinforcement cannot be received. For example, if the time-out is in a game room where the boy can play games, then the "time-out" will again become "positive reinforcement." Sulzer and Mayer (1972) added several more cautions for using time-out effectively including: 1) it should not be used from an aversive situation; 2) it should be consistently maintained; and 3) the time period should be kept short (a general rule of thumb is one minute for each year of the individual's age).

Response cost: Response cost is also a Type II Punishment, which intends to weaken a behavior through the removal of reinforcement, such as taking back previously earned reinforcers (Driscoll, 2005). Procedures of response cost are: 1) the individual performs a certain behavior, 2) some of the individual's desirable reinforcements (e.g., money) are taken away from him, and 3) the individual's behavior is weakened. For example, a boy often interrupts others in class. The teacher takes away some of his previously earned gold stars to stop his interrupting behavior. The boy's interrupting behavior is finally stopped.

Spontaneous recovery: Spontaneous recovery also weakens certain behavior by not presenting any consequences. Its procedures are: 1) the individual has stopped certain behavior, 2) the individual's stopped behavior occasionally comes back on its own, but its intensity/frequency becomes progressively weaker, 3) extinction is applied by providing no consequences, and 4) the reoccurred behavior is weakened or stopped eventually. Spontaneous recovery often happens with extinction. When using extinction, the behavior occasionally reappears without being reinforced because it is difficult to decrease the frequency of undesired behavior after one attempt. Under normal circumstances, the time period between spontaneous recoveries lengthens and the intensity of the recurring behavior becomes progressively weaker. The behavior will eventually stop on its own if no consequence is provided. For example, a husband has already quit smoking. He starts smoking again after a month but much less frequently than before. Instead of getting upset by this, the wife does nothing but let him be. The husband eventually quits smoking on his own. Spontaneous recovery can be understood as one phase of extinction. The difference is that in extinction the undesired behavior occurs because the individual expects some desirable consequence, while in spontaneous recovery the recurrence of the undesired behavior is part of a natural process in which the behavior is slowly disappearing on its own over a period of time.

Shaping: Shaping refers to the process of using multiple positive reinforcements to reinforce successive approximations to a goal behavior. Shaping differs from positive reinforcement in that its reinforcer is presented contingent upon incremental progress made towards the desired behavior rather than the fully formed terminal behavior (Driscoll, 2005). In shaping, only actions that move progressively closer to the terminal behavior are reinforced and all other actions are ignored (Skinner, 1953, 1968b, 1989b). The procedures of shaping are: 1) clearly specify the terminal behavior that is to be learned, 2) identify the entry skills (or prior knowledge) of the learners, 3) break the terminal behavior into mini steps and program the subject matter in carefully graded steps, 4) sequence all of the mini steps from simple to complex and teach first things first (Skinner, 1987), and 5) schedule reinforcements so that the ratio of reinforcements to responses gradually increases and the natural reinforcers can maintain the behavior (Skinner, 1989b).

Shaping is effective because it is sensitive to the continuous nature of a complex behavior, and it illustrates the utility of constructing complex behaviors by a continual process of differential reinforcement (Skinner, 1953). The significance of shaping is that it can generate complex behaviors that have low probability of occurring naturally in the final form (Skinner, 1963a). For example, shaping has been found particularly effective with training autistic children's speech acquisition by using bits of food to reinforce their making eye contact, producing any sound, producing specific sounds, and finally saying complete words and sentences (Wolf, Risley & Mees, 1964).

Fading: Fading is the process of slowly removing the discriminative stimuli or consequences that were initially used to establish a desired behavior (Sulzer & Mayer, 1972). Contrary to shaping, in which multiple reinforcers are provided to reinforce mini progress, in fading the stimuli or reinforcers are gradually withdrawn or reduced from the individual as more progress is made. Fading is mostly used during the later stages of shaping after the individual has mastered certain skills and is able to perform the task without cues or reinforcers. The purpose of fading is to help the individual develop the sense of self-regulation and self-independence.

Contingency contract: Similar to shaping, a contingency contract is also used for difficult or complex behaviors. Rather than simply telling the individual what to do, contingency contract involves the individual in the decision-making process. The individual together with another party or parties will decide what behavior needs to be addressed, what kind of performance is expected, and what consequences will be applied for fulfillment or non-fulfillment of the contract. The advantages of a contingency contract are that 1) it empowers the individual by having him/her involved in the decision-making process, 2) it motivates the individual to perform because s/he "decides" to do so, 3) it allows the individual to regulate his/her own behavior rather than being watched by others all the time, and 4) it takes individual differences (learning ability, expectations, background) into consideration to better suit each individual's situation (Driscoll, 2005).

Token economy: Rather than using consequences with actual values (e.g., food), a token economy uses things that do not carry real values—tokens—to reinforce a behavior. Although a token has little or no inherent value itself, it can be used to "purchase" things with inherent value such as a pizza or a T-shirt. The advantages of token economy are that 1) it allows for more flexibility than other commonly used reinforcers, 2) it saves teachers trouble of providing the real reinforcers all the time, and 3) it prevents the real reinforcer from losing its value when used too frequently. For example, if provided too frequently, candies will lose their value quickly, and the high cost of purchasing them will make it prohibitive for most teachers. The token economy has been found to be effective in reducing disruptive behaviors such as talking out of term, being out of one's seat, fighting, and being off task. They are also effective in improving students' learning (Naughton & McLaughlin, 1995; Shook, LaBrie, Vallies, McLaughlin & Williams, 1990).

SCHEDULING OF CONSEQUENCES

Consequences can be provided with different schedules as well. If the consequence is applied immediately following the behavior every time it is performed, it is called continuous reinforcement. Otherwise, it is called intermittent reinforcement. Intermittent reinforcement schedules can be further divided into interval reinforcement and ratio reinforcement. Interval reinforcement provides the consequence after certain periods of time while ratio reinforcement provides the consequences when the desired behavior has been improved or increased in frequency (Skinner, 1953). Also, depending on whether the reinforcement schedule is predetermined or not, schedules can be divided into fixed reinforcement (predetermined and predictable) and variable reinforcement (un-predetermined and unpredictable). If combining these two factors (time and behavior) together, there are four types of reinforcement schedules.

In a fixed ratio (FR) schedule consequences are applied based on a predetermined fixed amount of progress. Every time a certain amount of progress is made, consequences will be provided. For example, a teacher rewards a student every time s/he increases his/her grade by 3 points. Quota systems on some factory assembly lines also use fixed ratio schedules by providing bonuses based on the quantity of employee production.

Like a fixed ratio schedule, a variable ratio (VR) schedule provides the consequences on the basis of behavioral progress; however, rather than reinforce fixed amounts of progress, a variable ratio schedule randomly reinforces varied amounts of progress. For example, a teacher may reward a student when his/her grade increases by 2 points in the beginning, but may reward by 3 or 5 points later on. The advantage of variable-ratio schedule is that it maintains the behavior against extinction when reinforcement is infrequent (Skinner, 1989b). In some situations, however, this schedule can lead to long-term detrimental consequences. For instance, pigeons reinforced on a variable-ratio schedule for pecking a disc at a high rate will peck until their beaks become inflamed. Similarly, a compulsive gambler will keep playing till s/he is exhausted and broke.

Fixed interval (FI) schedules reinforce the behavior by providing consequences after predetermined periods of time (e.g., every ten minutes, every month, every semester). Weekly assignments, monthly quizzes, and mid-term/final exams are all examples of the fixed interval schedule.

Variable interval (VI) schedules present consequences not at a fixed period of time but rather in a random schedule. Similar to variable ratio schedule, the benefit of variable interval schedules is that it induces the individual to work consistently and independently without depending on the consequences. Pop quizzes are a good example of the variable interval schedule.

GUIDELINES FOR APPLYING CONSEQUENCES

Lastly, operant conditioning also specifies five important guidelines for implementing the consequences: specific, immediate/prompt, consistent, sincere, and fair.

Specific: When providing consequences, one should explicitly explain to the individual what behavior exactly is being rewarded/punished, and why. For example, when a teacher gives a toy to reward a boy for his good behavior, rather than saying, "You behaved well today," the teacher should explain that "You helped Johnny with his homework today and this toy is a reward for your helping Johnny." In this way, the student will know exactly how to perform in the future rather than feeling confused.

Immediate/prompt: When applying consequences, it is better to apply them immediately after the behavior. Immediate consequences enable an individual to make a direct association between the behavior and the consequence. "To be effective in altering behavior in a particular way, reinforcement must be immediately contingent on the execution of an appropriate response" (Gredler, 2004, p. 120). If the consequences are applied too long after a behavior, the individual will be confused and the result will be less effective. For example, a student interrupts a teacher's class but is not corrected immediately. Naturally, the behavior continues. Then the teacher finally provides consequences out of frustration. The student's behavior may be stopped, but some problems may occur as well: 1) the student will feel surprised and angry by the teacher's intervention since he was not corrected earlier and assumed it was acceptable, and 2) the student is unable to make a direct connection/association between his/her behavior and the consequence, thus unable to prevent similar behavior from recurring in the future.

Consistent: Consequence should be applied consistently every time when the behavior happens. Being consistent is extremely important but often difficult to practice in reality. Sometimes the behavior happens so frequently with so many students that it becomes exhausting and time-consuming to apply the consequences every time. Sometimes the teacher is simply too busy to apply the needed consequences.

Sincere: Consequences should be sincere and authentic enough to make the individual feel that the consequences really apply to him/her. Verbal compliments can be insincere under several conditions: 1) the consequence-provider lacks the enthusiasm in his/her voice; 2) the comment is too general such as the ubiquitous "Good job!"; or 3) the compliment is unrelated to the quality of the person's work. For example, a teacher says "excellent" to all of the student's assignments regardless of the quality, or s/he gives the same compliment to every student in class. This kind of undifferentiated compliment will lose its value quickly. Research indicates that excessive praise can be both intrusive and counterproductive (Brophy, 1981).

Fair: Being fair means that the individual's behavior should justify the consequences. Fairness may be violated under the following conditions: 1) the individual's behavior does not merit the consequences. For example, a teacher punishes a student for talking in class. This student feels that the punishment is unfair because his/her talk is related to the class topic and should not be considered as an interruption; 2) the individual knows that other similar behaviors did not receive the same consequences. For example, a student together with his classmates cursed his soccer coach. The student was punished but his classmates were not; 3) the individual displayed the same behavior earlier but did not receive the same consequences at that time; 4) the individual was not being informed about the rules or expectations ahead of time; 5) the individual's own ability (physical, cognitive, linguistic, cultural) limits his/her capacity to perform the required behavior, but s/he is punished for failing to perform the required behavior. For example, an international student with limited English has to take the SAT test in English and compete with the native speakers.

Although operant conditioning specified these five guidelines for applying consequences, the complexity of each different situation should be considered, and flexibility is strongly encouraged when implementing consequences in real situations.

EFFECTS OF BEHAVIORISM ON EDUCATION

How has behaviorism influenced our understanding of teaching and learning? What kind of impact does it have on our instructional design, behavior management, and student learning in schools? As mentioned earlier, there is a tendency toward two extreme points of view regarding behaviorism in the field of education today. One extreme is to completely reject it as outdated and useless. The other is to obsessively embrace it as a magic wand and use it in all situations.

When we evaluate the effect of a theory and its impact, it is important that we put this theory back to its original context (e.g., historical and cultural background). This way, we will be able to examine it from a developmental, open, and historical perspective rather than a static, closed, and anachronistic one. Taking this developmental perspective means that we need to consider factors like the historical situations, limitations to knowledge, and cultural backgrounds behind the theory. This developmental perspective will help us see more clearly not only its contributions but also its limitations. As with any other theory, there is much to be learned from behaviorism, both in terms of its contributions and its limitations.

POSITIVE EFFECT ON EDUCATION AND LEARNING

First, as the pioneer in the field of educational research, behaviorism is the first theory that was developed through conducting actual scientific and systematic experiments. Most theories preceding it were developed through philosophical reasoning or hypothetical logic without objective rigorous testing (Gredler, 2004). Pavlov's description on how animals (and humans) can be trained to respond in a certain way to a particular stimulus drew tremendous interest in his time. His experiments brought revolutionary light to the field of psychological research and paved the way for a new, more objective method of behavioral research. Skinner (1953, 1968b) further stressed that researchers must manipulate observable events in a controlled setting, which he called the experimental analysis of behavior. It was behaviorism that shifted the research goal from developing "grand theories" in which learning might be but one aspect to integrating all known facts around the principal theme of describing, predicting, and controlling learning (DiVesta, 1987, p. 207). From this point of view, behaviorism established a new model for conducting educational psychology research.

Second, behaviorism contributed to our understanding of learning by increasing our awareness of human and animal behavior patterns. Classical conditioning showed that certain responses always follow certain stimuli and vice versa. Behaviorism was the first theory to observe that 1) animal and human behavior may appear to be random on the surface but in reality operate according to set patterns, and 2) these patterns are observable and predictable if we know the relationships among events in the environment. When we are able to control and predict human behavior, psychology becomes an objective and experimental science (Watson, 1913).

Third, behaviorism brought fundamental changes to the instructional design. It was the first theory applied to the educational setting to facilitate teaching and learning. When Skinner was developing his theory, one of the major problems he saw in the education system was that the teacher-student ratio was so large that a teacher often had to tutor too many students. Most teachers could neither provide individual reinforcement nor design differentiated instructional programs based on individual abilities and skills. Furthermore, teachers could not adjust their teaching pace according to each student's learning level either. Students who lacked the prior knowledge or basic skills in the subject area often suffered from the whole-group instruction.

Skinner (1989a) stressed that effective instructional design should consider two important issues: the selection of the discriminative stimuli and the use of reinforcement. Based on this principle, Skinner developed the concept of programmed instruction (Skinner, 1961, 1968a, 1968b, 1973). Programmed instruction had a revolutionary impact in the instructional design. In programmed instruction, content is arranged in small steps called frames, which progress from simple to complex and require a response from the learner to go on. Since the steps are small and increase gradually in difficulty, the learner is able to respond correctly most of the time, and his responses are reinforced frequently. Skinner's teaching machine was invented based on similar principles. The teaching machine was designed to facilitate student learning by: 1) providing students individual feedback, 2) giving each individual student opportunities to monitor their own progress at their own pace, 3) allowing for complex sequences of learning by breaking them into small steps, 4) automatically recording each student's responses such as correct answers and errors and even recording the particular sequence followed by each student, 5) enabling program designers to include a variety of stimuli such as complex graphics and synthesized speech along with the text, and 6) providing drill and practice on various academic skills, simulations to enhance problem-solving, or tutorials in various subject matters (Driscoll, 2005). Both Skinner's programmed instruction and teaching machine profoundly shook the traditional methods of instructional design in the schools and inspired many other educational programs.

Fourth, behaviorism emphasized the importance of establishing the right kinds of associations to influence students' motivation and behavior. For example, teachers should always ensure that directives such as to line up for lunch are not followed by disruptive behavior. Otherwise students will make an undesirable association between this directive and disruptions and display disruptive behavior every time when lining up for lunch in the future. When this happens, the teacher should send students back to their seats to respond appropriately to the directive many times till they are able to display the appropriate behavior. Similarly, if we want our students to like school, we should help them build positive associations about school such as being comfortable, exciting, and fun. Research shows that greeting the children warmly in the morning as they arrive and starting the day with fun activities like drawing or coloring can help children develop a positive association with school (Emmer, Evertson, & Anderson, 1980). If students make a negative association with school such as being boring and stressful, they will lack motivation to attend school. When this happens, they may play truant, misbehave, and even drop out. Thus, in order to help students develop an interest in school or any subject, it is essential to associate students' early experiences with positive reactions (Estes, 1989).

Fifth, behaviorism introduced several fundamental principles of teaching and learning to the education field. The concept of shaping, for example, indicates that in order to teach effectively, teachers should: 1) have clear learning objectives, 2) state these learning objectives clearly to the students prior to teaching, 3) consider students' readiness (e.g., their entry skills, prior knowledge) when designing learning tasks, 4) make learning achievable by breaking a task into small learnable steps and teaching them from simple to complex, 5) be patient and allow students to take one step at a time so that the whole learning process is gradual, 6) reward students for their progress rather than the final product, and 7) provide assistance and reinforcement when needed to ensure students' success.

Sixth, behaviorism provided teachers with a variety of practical methods, such as positive reinforcement and negative reinforcement, together with specific guidelines for their application. These methods and guidelines are not only useful with students' learning but also with behavior management. For example, behavioral methods have been found effective with the treatment of school-related behavioral problems such as inattention, hyperactivity, temper tantrums, and any behavior that interferes with learning and the normal conduct of classroom activities. Behaviorism approaches have also been found particularly effective in special education classrooms (Driscoll, 2005).

Seventh, behaviorism helped educators realize the importance of environment in learning. Classical conditioning clearly states that 1) certain stimuli always elicit certain behavior, 2) in order to invoke some behavior, a stimulus is required, and 3) human behaviors are caused by the environment or by the associations of the environment. The traditional teaching approach, however, seldom takes the learning environment into consideration when designing lessons. Most traditional teachers only focus on the teaching content and pay little attention to environmental factors such as teacher behavior or the classroom decorations. This plain and boring environment often does not evoke much response from the students. On the other hand, the outside environment provides a variety of stimuli such as the internet, media, celebrities, and sex appeal to the students. Given the contrast between these two environments, it is not hard to understand why students are bored at school but attracted to the world outside. Classical conditioning shows the importance of making the learning environment more evocative and stimulating to the students. As Skinner stated, teaching is more than just telling and it occurs only when a response is evoked. If no response is evoked, no learning will occur.

Making the environment stimulating does not mean that teachers should constantly provide new stimuli to students. Instead, teachers should keep a balance between routine and stimulation. On the one hand, the association principle of classical conditioning shows that teachers should establish a daily routine for learning activities. This means that teachers should 1) have a well-planned agenda for the daily/weekly/monthly activities, 2) make sure the agenda has a clear pattern to the students, and 3) be consistent in following the routines. For example, a teacher can start each class by a routine of free writing. Once this routine is established, students will automatically walk into the class being quiet and reflective. Having this routine will save teachers a lot of effort and stress calming the students down at the beginning of class. On the other hand, since response needs to be evoked from the students in order for learning to occur, teachers should incorporate novelty and variety in their lessons to keep students stimulated. These two principles ("routine" and "stimulation") are not contradictory but supplementary to each other. For example, a teacher can have students do an interactive activity after learning each new topic (routine). S/he can also create different activities for each lesson to ensure it is exciting (stimulating).

Lastly, behaviorism laid the foundation for later learning theories. It contributed to the field of psychology by pointing out that our behaviors are not only influenced by the environment (stimuli) around us, but more importantly, by our perceptions of and associations with the environment. Thus, behaviorism invited educators and researchers to shift their focus from teachers to students. Influenced by behaviorism, some researchers started to analyze human behavior in the social settings to see how children acquire acceptable forms of social behavior. These researchers borrowed a set of ideas about human learning from behaviorism and developed new ideas from it. In this way, behaviorism influenced later learning theories such as social cognitive learning theory.

NEGATIVE EFFECTS AND LIMITATIONS

Although behaviorism made fundamental and revolutionary contributions in a number of disciplines from the historical and developmental perspective as stated above, it also has its own limitations. However, having limitations is inevitable for any theory because of the historical context as mentioned earlier. No theory, regardless how popular or how perfect it claims to be, is able to explain everything. In fact, having shortcomings can be a constructive aspect of any theory because these limitations provide room for later scholars to continue improving it as they gain more knowledge. Therefore, we should not completely reject a theory just because of its limitations but stay open-minded and keep modifying it to better reflect the complex nature of a phenomenon. As Boring (1950) pointed out, each new theory is scientific progress depending on its previous one.

First, behaviorists tend to seek explanations only from external factors and not internal ones. In fact, Skinner (1950, 1966b) did not think that inner states should be used as a basis for behavioral research. Explaining human behavior from only one aspect inevitably fails to reflect the complexity of human behavior. For example, when a student misbehaves (for example, curses), a behaviorist will automatically try to solve the problem by manipulating the consequences. There can, however, be many reasons for the student's cursing which can be resolved through other methods. For example, if a student simply has never been educated about cursing, then this student should not be punished but educated. Behaviorism tends to downplay the importance of understanding students' reasons for their behavior in its efforts to control student behavior and learning. Because behaviorism does not encourage teachers to critically examine each situation and find out the reasons first, many teachers become mechanical in using the behavioral approaches and lose sight of the learning goal. Some teachers become so obsessed with "order and control" in the classroom that it leads to inappropriate or even unethical use of behavioral approaches. A teacher who is overly obsessed with having students behave in class can stifle students' active thinking and participation. A teacher who is overly concerned with "control" can also easily get into a power struggle with the students, which will sabotage the learning goal no matter who wins in the end. Even if the teacher wins, s/he still loses because the learning goal is unachieved.

Second, behaviorism focuses on extrinsic motivators and often neglects students' intrinsic motivators, e.g., self-esteem, interest, personality, sense of achievement, identity, and connection with others. Skinner (1963b) stated that concepts like purpose, intention, and expectancy should not be considered in explaining future behavior. He believed that intrinsic motivation does not come from inside but outside such as from past positive reinforcement. Therefore, these are not really "intrinsic" but the result of exposure to a gradually increasing variable-ratio schedule of external reinforcements (Skinner, 1968b). By assuming that all behaviors are caused by external factors, behaviorism devalues intrinsic motives and limits a student's motivation to learn. For example, a student who is motivated only to receive an A will put in just enough effort to ensure that grade and no more. If a student develops an attitude that learning is something that s/he does to earn an immediate reinforcer, true learning and self-motivated learning will be impeded. A student who simply enjoys reading for its own sake might even lose the joy of reading if s/he comes to see reading as a means of achieving reinforcement. Overusing extrinsic motivation not only limits students' motivation to learn but also kills students' intrinsic motivation (Lepper & Greene, 1973).

Third, overemphasizing the impact of environment fails to recognize the role of other factors such as personal, biological, or genetic factors in influencing our behaviors. Although Skinner (1989b) admitted the role of biological and genetic factors to a certain degree, both Skinner (1953, 1989b) and Watson (1924) asserted that a well-designed program can help develop new skills in spite of the genetic deficit and that any skills can be taught through proper training. Modern research, however, suggests that these other factors do influence our behavioral responses and should be taken into consideration when teaching students. For example, if a student is weak in the area of mathematical intelligence, no program of instruction is likely to make this student a mathematical wizard. Therefore, educators should not assume that all skills are teachable by manipulating the external factors.

Fourth, although behaviorism recognizes the importance of individualized instruction, it tends to require all students to achieve the same performance. The goal of the behavioral approach is not to help each individual achieve his/her maximal potential but to perform the behavior as required. Since the performance is not individually suited, it can limit student learning and development. For example, gifted students can easily fulfill the requirement without working too hard. They may excel at school, but their talents and potentials are not fully expressed. Similarly, poorer students may be unfairly punished because of their limited ability in certain areas (Sussman, 1981).

Fifth, since behaviorism was developed through researching on simple animal and human behaviors in a controlled setting, its principles apply most effectively to simple behaviors rather than complex ones. For example, behaviorism cannot explain the acquisition of complex behaviors like pigeons playing ping-pong or table tennis and humans working with computers (Gredler, 2004). Most human behaviors, however, are very complex by nature and happen in the natural, uncontrolled environment.

Sixth, behavioral approach can also be exhausting and costly for teachers. Because behaviorism assumes that all of the driving forces of human behavior come from the outside, teachers are expected to be responsible for students' behavior and learning in school settings. Teachers constantly have to create, plan, and try all kinds of strategies to motivate the students. This puts a lot of burden and stress on teachers and can be exhausting for them. It may even create a sense of failure in teachers when they are unable to reach the students after trying all kinds of behavioral approaches. Furthermore, such an approach can place the students in a very passive and dependent position where they are not encouraged to be self-motivated learners, exacerbating motivation problems.

Lastly, behaviorism was developed under the influence of the positivist paradigm. This paradigm asserts that 1) objective truths exist in the world, and 2) these truths can be directly passed on from the teachers to the students and completely mastered by the students in the original form. Behavioral approaches have been used to teach mostly simple facts with a goal of helping the students remember those facts. Students are not encouraged to understand or disagree with the "correct" answers, and different answers are often punished as "incorrect." However, constructivism states that: 1) learning is about meaningful understanding, 2) meaning is individually constructed, and 3) even if an individual does not know the correct answer, s/he may still have learned. Vygotsky (1978) also stressed that learning happens only when an individual internalizes the information, which means that the individual understands, accepts, and knows how to apply the information. Therefore, behaviorism fails to see another level of teaching and learning—meaningful teaching and internalized learning.

CONCLUSIONS

To conclude, behaviorism has had tremendous impact on education. It brought about a revolution in the understanding of behavior and learning to the field of education. It introduced programmed instruction and the teaching machine to the classroom setting for the first time. It provided new principles and philosophies on human behavior and learning. It offered teachers a variety of practical strategies and methods to help with student behavior and learning. It also built the foundation for many later learning theories such as social cognitive learning theory. At the same time, behaviorism has its own limitations. It fails to recognize the importance of intrinsic motivation. Its approach can be rigid and does not allow for critical thinking or flexibility in its application. It does not reflect the complex nature of human behavior. It fails to recognize the importance of meaningful teaching and internalized learning. However, it was these limitations that led many later investigators to propose cognitive, neurological, developmental, and other theoretical constructs as alternative ways of understanding learning. In short, behaviorism has had positive impact upon learning in schools, and its contributions should not be denied just because of its limitations. At the same time, critical thinking should be used when applying behaviorism in the actual school settings because of its limitations.

REFERENCES

Azrin, N. H. (1967). Pain and aggression. *Psychology Today, 1,* 27–33.

Azrin, N. H., & Holz, W. C. (1966). Punishment. In W. A. Honig (Ed.), *Operant behavior: Areas of research and application.* New York: Appleton-Century-Crofts.

Becker, W. D. (1998). Application of behavior principles in typical classrooms. In C. E. Thoresen (Ed.). *Behavioral modification in education: The seventy-second yearbook of the National Society for the Study of Education, Part 1* (pp. 77–106). Chicago: University of Chicago Press.

Bijou, S. W. & Ruiz, R. (Eds.). (1981). *Behavior modification: Contributions to education.* Hillsdale, NJ: Erlbaum.

Boring, E. G. (1950). *A history of experimental psychology* (2nd ed.). New York: Appleton-Century-Crofts.

Brophy, J. (1981). Teacher praise: A functional analysis. *Review of Educational Research, 51,* 5–32.

Crowder, N. A. (1960). Automatic tutoring by intrinsic programming. In A.A. Lumsdaine & R Glaser (Eds.), *Teaching machines and programmed learning.* Washington, DC: National Education Association.

DiVesta, F. J. (1987). The cognitive movement and education. In J. A. Glover & R. R. Ronning (Eds.), *Historical foundations of educational psychology* (pp. 203–233). New York: Plenum.

Driscoll, M. P. (2005). *Psychology of learning for instruction.* Boston: Pearson.

Emmer, E., Everston, C., & Anderson, L. (1980). Effective classroom management at the beginning of the school year. *The Elementary School Journal, 80*(5), 219–231.

Estes, W. (1989). Learning theory. In A. Lesgold & R. Glaser (Eds.), *Handbook of research on teaching* (pp. 1–49). Hillsdale, NJ: Erlbaum.

Gredler, M. E. (2004). *Learning & instruction: Theory to practice.* Upper Saddle River, NJ: Prentice Hall.

Kazdin, A. (1989). Behavior modification in applied settings (4th ed.). Pacific Grove, CA: Brooks/Cole.

Keller, F. S. (1968). "Goodbye, teacher…" *Journal of Applied Behavior Analysis, 1,* 79–89.

Lepper, M. R. & Greene, D. (1973). Undermining children's intrinsic interest with extrinsic reward: A test of the "overjustification" hypothesis. *Journal of Personality & Social Psychology, 28*(1), 129–137.

Naughton, C. C., & McLaughlin, T. F. (1995). The use of token economy system for students with behavior disorders. *B. C. Journal of Special Education, 19*(2/3), 29–38.

Reiser, R. A., Driscoll, M. P., & Vergara, A. (1987). The effects of ascending, descending, and fixed criteria on student performance and attitude in a mastery-oriented course. *Educational Communications and Technology Journal, 35,* 195–202.

Rilling, M. (2000a). How the challenge of explaining learning influenced the origins and development of John. B. Watson's behaviorism. *American Journal of Psychology, 113*(2), 275–301.

Rilling, M. (2000b). John Watson's paradoxical struggle to explain Freud. *American Psychologist, 55*(3), 301–312.

Shook, S. C., LaBrie, M., Vallies, J., McLaughlin, T. F., & Williams, R. L. (1990). The effect of a token economy on first grade students' inappropriate social behavior. *Reading Improvement, 27*(2), 96–101.

Skinner, B. F. (1935). Two types of conditioned reflex and a pseudotype. *Journal of General Psychology, 12,* 66–77.

Skinner, B. F. (1938). *The behavior of organisms.* New York: Appleton-Century-Crofts.

Skinner, B. F. (1950). Are theories of learning necessary? *Psychological Review, 57,* 193–216.

Skinner, B. F. (1953). *Science and human behavior.* New York: Macmillan.

Skinner, B. F. (1954). The science of learning and the art of teaching. *Harvard Educational Review, 24*(2), 86–97.

Skinner, B. F. (1961). Why we need teaching machines. *Harvard Educational Review, 31*(4), 377–398.

Skinner, B. F. (1963a). Behaviorism at fifty. *Science, 140,* 951–958.

Skinner, B. F. (1963b). Operant behavior. *American Psychologist, 18,* 503–515.

Skinner, B. F. (1966a). Contingencies of reinforcement in the design of a culture. *Behavioral Science, 11,* 159–166.

Skinner, B. F. (1966b). What is the experimental analysis of behavior? *Journal of Experimental Analysis of Behavior, 9*(3), 213–218.

Skinner, B. F. (1968a). Teaching science in high school—What is wrong? *Science, 159,* 704–710.

Skinner, B. F. (1968b). *The technology of teaching.* New York: Appleton-Century-Crofts.

Skinner, B. F. (1973). The free and happy student. *Phi Delta Kappan, 55,* 13–16.

Skinner, B. F. (1974). *About behaviorism.* New York: Vintage.

Skinner, B. F. (1984). In J. O. Green, Skinner's technology of teaching. *Classroom Computer Learning,* pp. 23–29.

Skinner, B. F. (1987). *Upon further reflection.* Upper Saddle River, NJ: Merrill/Prentice Hall.

Skinner, B. F. (1989a). The origins of cognitive thought. *American Psychologist, 44*(1), 13–18.

Skinner, B. F. (1989b). *Recent issues in the analysis of behavior.* Upper Saddle River, NJ: Merrill/Prentice Hall.

Snowman, J., & Biehler, R. (2003). *Psychology applied to teaching.* Boston: Houghton Mifflin Company.

Sulzer, B., & Mayer, G. R. (1972). *Behavior modification procedures for school personnel.* Hinsdale, IL: Dryden Press.

Sussman, D. M. (1981). PSI: Variations on a theme. In S. W. Bijou & R. Ruiz (Eds.), *Behavior modification: Contributions to education*. Hillsdale, NJ: Erlbaum.

Vygotsky, L. S. (1978). *Mind in Society: The development of higher psychological processes*. (M. Cole. Trans.). Cambridge, MA: Harvard University Press.

Vygotsky, L. S. (1986). *Thought and language* (A. Kozulin, Trans.). Cambridge, MA: MIT Press. (Original work published in 1934)

Walker, J. E., & Shea, T. M. (1999). *Behavior management: A practical approach for educators* (7th ed.). Upper Saddle River, NJ: Merrill.

Walters, G. C., & Grusec, J. E. (1977). *Punishment*. San Francisco: Freeman.

Watson, J. B. (1913). Psychology as the behaviorist views it. *Psychological Bulletin, 20,* 158–177.

Watson, J. B. (1924). *Behaviorism*. New York: Norton.

Wolf, M. M., Risley, T. R., & Mees, H. L. (1964). Application of operant conditioning procedures to the behavior problems of an autistic child. *Behavior Research and Therapy,* 1, 305–312.

FIVE

School Interventions for Attention Deficit Hyperactivity Disorder: Where to from Here?

Russell A. Barkley

THEORETICALLY DRIVEN PSYCHOSOCIAL TREATMENTS FOR ADHD

I have carped about this issue before (Barkley, 1997, 2006) but it is an issue that still remains to be more systematically investigated. Current psychosocial, largely cognitive-behavioral, interventions were based on what are now outdated assumptions about ADHD and its associated disruptive behavior. Most of our treatments grew out of social learning theory (Pelham, 1986; Pelham & Sams, 1992)—a theory holding that deviant or disruptive behavior should be initially considered developed and/or currently maintained as a result of exposure to faulty contingencies of reinforcement or social modeling. This view came to be supplemented with cognitive behavioral theory, which ascribes some importance to the cognitive (largely verbal) deficits associated with ADHD that should respond to direct cognitive training (Meichenbaum, 1988). This amalgamation of social learning and cognitive-behavioral theory is the original basis for recommending functional behavioral assessment as a prelude to classroom interventions.

Appreciating these initial assumptions helps one understand the reason why psychosocial treatments have been routinely withdrawn after a period of implementation. It was assumed that the increased prosocial and decreased deviant behavior would be maintained as a consequence of the improved natural contingencies of reinforcement for those behaviors that would sustain them (Pelham & Sams, 1992; Ross & Ross, 1982, pp. 250–252; Willis & Lovaas, 1977). Added to this was the view that supplemental cognitive training in verbal self-regulation strategies would result in the internalization of such strategies that would further promote generalization and maintenance of treatment gains (see Abikoff, 1992). Likewise, the assumption was that teachers would sustain their use of these procedures for the reinforcement they, too, received from the reductions in child disruptive behavior and increased positive behaviors shown by the children with ADHD in their classrooms.

It is therefore puzzling to hear researchers now criticize the National Institute of Mental Health Multimodal Treatment Study of ADHD (MTA) methodology for withdrawing the cognitive-behavioral component of this treatment study before the end-point assessment while medication treatment was continued to the assessment point (MTA Cooperative Group, 1999). At the time of implementation, the initial assumptions were likely different for these treatments than they are currently if one can remember such perspectives 17 years ago. As recently as the early 1990s, just before the design of the MTA project, behavioral researchers, including some of those in the MTA, were touting this original rationale for cognitive-behavior therapy for ADHD. Medications for ADHD have never been claimed to produce enduring benefits upon their withdrawal, so it made no sense to withdraw them before assessing their effectiveness. Yet now that these learning theory based assumptions of psychosocial treatments have proven partly or largely erroneous, criticisms are leveled for withdrawing behavioral interventions in various study designs that put them at a disadvantage relative to medications that are continued. This is having it both ways, the cake and the eating it, and it is "a dog that won't hunt" for those of us who have been in this field 30 years. This is not to say that local contingencies of reinforcement have no bearing on children's levels of ADHD and disruptive behavior in the classroom—clearly they can in individual cases. But it does say that such contingencies are not the primary origin of those behavioral problems, are likely not the source of individual differences among children in those behavioral problems (population variation in ADHD traits), and will not, once changed, persist in sustaining any behavioral improvements once the formal interventions are withdrawn. We have now come to view psychosocial treatments, especially behavioral ones, as comparable to medication management in this sense, producing solid benefits as long as they are in place. But they yield little evidence of maintenance or generalization once withdrawn and are not considered the origin of the behavioral problems in the first place. Yet we should not forget that our original rationale for instituting behavioral interventions for ADHD was quite different then than it is now.

Sometime over the last 15–20 years it became obvious that ADHD and its related disruptive behavior and academic impairments were not the consequence of faulty contingencies of reinforcement in natural ecologies like classrooms or homes, as some originally claimed in the 1970s (Willis & Lovaas, 1977). Such behavior does not need to function to gain positive reinforcement nor escape from aversive situations to be produced and sustained. We now recognize the etiologies of ADHD and its various levels of phenotypic expression to be largely in the realm of neurology and genetics (Nigg, 2006). This is not to say that social environments are irrelevant or that certain contingencies make no contribution in individual cases because they certainly pertain to forms of impairment, risk for comorbidities, and treatment resources. But it does say that no serious investigator today could make the case that ADHD can arise purely out of social causes such as bad parenting, intolerant teachers, faulty social learning, or inappropriately learned cognition. There is simply too much evidence against such ideas (Nigg, 2006).

Over this same time, it became evident that the cognitive and behavioral manifestations of ADHD were not confined to just overactivity, inattentiveness, or poor inhibition, but were associated with a broader swath of cognitive impairments, many believed to be in the domain of executive functioning and self regulation (Barkley, 1997; Douglas, 1999). It was also obvious that there were striking genetic contributions to variations in the traits comprising ADHD even within the general population and that a significant minority of variance could be attributed to unique events, most likely pre-, peri-, and postnatal biological hazards to the developing brain (Nigg, 2006). To believe that merely altering contingencies of reinforcement would produce sustainable behavioral improvements long after artificial behavioral methods were withdrawn from natural settings was to believe that Phinnaeus Gage, the classic case of a frontal lobe syndrome in neuropsychology textbooks, was just one token short of returning to normality.

We continue to persist with our behavioral technologies long after we have come to realize both their significant value and significant limitations because, frankly, it is about all we have in the psychosocial realm of interventions that has some empirical support for its use. Yet the theories behind the techniques are no longer valid (faulty learning and cognition) because ADHD does not arise from social learning origins. Over the past 15 years, the use of behavioral interventions has come to be based on a different view, which I have called "designing prosthetic environments" (see Barkley, 1989, 1997). Behavioral treatments, like hearing aids, wheelchairs, ramps into public facilities, lower bathroom fixtures, glasses and large-print books, and prosthetic limbs for amputees, are artificial means of altering environments so as to reduce the adverse effect of a biological handicap on the performance of major life activities. No one would rationally claim that physical disabilities arise from the lack of wheelchairs and ramps. Similarly, no one would claim that using a wheelchair or associated ramps for a month or two would result in their either being internalized or so altering the social environment that they would be sustained by changes in naturally occurring contingencies after the chairs and ramps are withdrawn. And so no one should now rationally claim that ADHD arises from faulty learning or that several months of contingency management produces sustained benefits for ADHD once treatment is withdrawn. Behavioral methods are prostheses—means of rearranging environments by artificial means so as to yield improved participation in major life activities.

ADHD is now thought to be as much a disorder of self-regulation and executive functioning as it is in attention. What we most need now is a theory of how normal self-regulation develops, where it goes awry in producing ADHD, and what this may mean for constructing better interventions. This perhaps explains why there have been no new or innovative psychosocial interventions for more than 20 years. This does not mean there have been no innovations in delivery systems or implementation sites, such as the development of community-based training programs (Cunningham & Cunningham, 2006). But what is being delivered is still largely cognitive-behavioral training. What we are largely witnessing is mostly the combining and recombining of earlier methods into ever more complex treatment packages in the hopes that one combination will eventually open the vault to success.

I am reminded of the status of oncology over the past 20 years where treatment methods largely constituted the study of different combinations of cytotoxins at differing doses and differing cycles of intervention in the hopes that we could kill the cancer cells before killing the patient. Only with breakthroughs in the theory of cell replication, such as selfish gene theory, and switch genes that turn on and off a cell's default tendency to replicate itself, and the focus on means of repairing such switch genes, have new and innovative methods of cancer treatment come to the fore (gene repair or replacement).

We need the same sort of theoretical understanding for ADHD if novel treatments are to be developed that offer even greater hope for success than those we currently have. Indeed, we need a theory of ADHD that even explains why the use of artificial consequences scheduled more intensively in natural settings is even needed for management of ADHD when it is not so required for normal children. Theories of ADHD as a motivational deficit, executive function disorder, disorder of self-regulation, and so on have been efforts to fill this theoretical void with only partial success. Environmentally accommodating executive deficits (Barkley, 1997, 2006) offer one such approach. The still relatively nascent field of cognitive training of working memory (Klingberg et al., 2005) is another example of a pilot or experimental treatment based on more theoretical constructs. This is not an endorsement of cognitive training for widespread school adoption but simply acknowledgment of its theoretical rationale. We should be trying to develop even better theories of this disorder that might offer the hope of more effective and innovative therapies. None of what is said here should be taken as nihilism over the promise of new psychosocial treatments or the effectiveness of current ones—just a call to further theoretical work and not just more recombinations of old treatments.

SEE NO EVIL

As one who studies both psychosocial and psychopharmacological interventions for ADHD, I repeatedly notice the routine absence of efforts to study the side effects or adverse events (AEs) associated with the former treatments when such is not only routine but a matter of utmost importance in the latter. This arises, I believe, from an inchoate belief among mental health professionals that their therapies do no harm even if they are not beneficial. But a moment's reflection shows this is absurd. Any intervention that is truly effective must produce AEs if only because of individual differences among people in their psychological and physical makeup and the variance this must create in their reactions to our interventions. AEs are also to be expected given the likely occasional ineptitude in the use of treatments by clinicians, parents, and teachers. There are other reasons, but these serve to make the point. Psychosocial treatments of any power to influence behavior will produce AEs in some subset of the treated population.

This is not hypothetical. Some years ago in a study of various family therapy approaches for addressing parent–teen conflict in teens with ADHD, we noted a significant increase in conflicts in a minority of our families (10–20%) as a consequence of our largely behavioral interventions (Barkley, Edwards, Laneri, Fletcher, & Metevia, 2001; Barkley, Guevremont, Anastopoulos, & Fletcher, 1992). It was not an isolated event. By using individual change statistics rather than just group level analyses of mean differences among groups, we were able to identify families who not only did not improve but worsened in response to our treatment efforts. The probable reasons for this have to do with teaching parents to set limits on highly disruptive teenagers through various contracting, time-out, and other forms of behavioral containment and punishment that could serve to escalate rather than reduce conflict and teen temper outbursts within these families. It was not as if we were looking for AEs either, but simply that this approach to data analyses permitted the detection of cases that deteriorated in addition to those that improved from treatment. Other studies have documented the adverse effect of group social skills training on a significant subset (20–25%) of children with ADHD that may result in increased aggressive behavior (Antshel & Remer, 2003) by a process known as deviancy training (Dishion, McCord, & Poulin, 1999). This time, the investigators were aware of this possibility and formally assessed its potential occurrence; they were not disappointed.

Rest assured these findings are not isolated instances; their rarity in articles, however, can be attributed to the fact that we simply do not routinely evaluate the potential AEs of psychosocial interventions. This is especially so in school-based programs. The status quo is unacceptable. We cannot, on the one hand, use medication treatments for ADHD and their attendant side effects as the typical straw men we routinely set up in the introductions to our articles on psychosocial treatments for ADHD as the justification for studying our alternative treatments. On the other hand, we cannot turn a blind eye toward the "evils" (AEs) we may do. As one who has designed and implemented numerous classroom management interventions for ADHD children, including an entire special kindergarten program for children with ADHD and oppositional defiant disorder (Barkley et al., 2000), I have seen firsthand some of the AEs we can produce in some children via the various accepted empirically based methods we advocate others to use. And I am as guilty as other researchers of not making any efforts to systematically evaluate their occurrence. They were a given to be ignored.

Several rating scales and clinician report forms exist for evaluating the side effects of medications for ADHD (see my Side Effects Rating Scale in Barkley & Murphy, 2006, for instance). It would be an easy matter to construct similar instruments for behavioral, academic, cognitive-behavioral, and other psychosocial interventions we implement for children and teens with ADHD, especially in schools. It is time to do so. First, we could survey the school psychologists or other clinicians instituting these procedures for the most common concerns and complaints that parents and teachers have raised in response to introducing these programs with their students. Second, we could directly survey teachers and parents themselves for similar reports of potential AEs. Third, it would seem wise to interview the children who have been subjected to our procedures for their insights into the reactions they experienced when introduced to our school-based (and home-based) interventions. Through a process of test–refine–retest we could then whittle down this initial list of potential AEs to those reliably likely to arise in response to these sorts of interventions. We could then routinely evaluate them as a matter of course as we now do for ADHD medications. Does anyone doubt that time-outs, response cost, overcorrection, or other coercive forms of punishment do not have some AEs in some subset of these children? Post extinction "bursts" of heightened disruptive behavior are to be expected upon the cessation of positive attention or other reinforcers for their previous occurrences. This common wisdom does not change the fact that this is a form of AE that can potentially occur even when using differential attention, probably perceived as our most benign and well-intentioned psychosocial recommendation. Yet had a medication produced such an effect, even if only temporarily, we would dutifully record it as an AE in that treatment protocol as a matter of course. Increases in perceived social stigma, performance anxiety, depressive cognitive schemas, social humiliation, aggressive behavior as acts of countercontrol to punishment contingencies, temper outbursts, and so forth are but a few of the many potential AEs that our treatments may induce. The potential for reduced "intrinsic" or self-motivation in response to externally rewarded academic performance has been another concern that has haunted reinforcement technologies for academic performance for years with little definitive resolution to my knowledge, especially in the natural ecology of the classroom. It is time we evaluated our psychosocial treatments for their AEs routinely, systematically, and openly as our medical colleagues have done for years with their psychiatric medications. This is a dissertation crying out to be done. Surely one consequence of our doing so would be a newfound respect for our professions and our treatments among our medical and psychiatric colleagues who have studied medication side effects or AEs for years and who have not failed to notice our double standards.

PATHWAYS AND OUTCOMES

In his opening remarks, DuPaul rightly notes that the pathways by which ADHD may be related to various forms of school maladjustment are complex and may not be the same for each form of academic impairment. Attentional and executive deficits may play a larger role in the academic performance problems associated with the disorder, although even then not in any straightforward, uncomplicated, or univariate way. Moderators and mediators seem to exist even in this pathway, as DuPaul rightly notes and as Rapport, Scanlon, and Denney (1999) earlier reported. Inhibition deficits may play a greater role in problems with classroom-disruptive behavior, rule adherence, social behavior and peer relationship problems, and otherwise unruly behavior in school settings. Yet this pathway as well has its circuitous route and array of moderator and mediator variables. Such complexity suggests that a straightforward functional behavioral analysis (FBA) would be woefully incomplete in identifying the variables that initiate and sustain these behaviors and impairments. This is especially so given that FBA focuses on factors in the immediate setting whereas genetic, neurological, and other historic variables as well as intraperson cognitive or neuropsychological ones may also be serving to generate and maintain some of the ADHD-related behavior and associated academic impairments.

Our recent finding on genetics illustrates this point. We found that the herterozygous pairing of the 9-repeat with the 10-repeat polymorphism of the DAT1 gene may account for effect sizes of 0.4–0.7 or higher in the life course expression of ADHD symptoms, mother–teen conflicts, grade-point average in high school, and even employer ratings of work performance in our Milwaukee longitudinal study (Barkley, Smith, Fischer, & Navia, 2006). There is a more complex causal chain to be understood in ADHD and its academic maladjustment than just momentary contingencies. This is certainly *not* genetic determinism—advocating an unmalleable phenotype—but a warning that more simplistic and largely contingency focused views of ADHD and its classroom treatment are no longer tenable.

It can be said, however, that although FBA has some role to play in serving to identify some of the environmental factors that could be contributing to the expression of a given behavioral problem in a given case, it does not provide the total explanation of that problem and is not likely to involve its total management approach either. Response to intervention approaches that largely eschew efforts to identify causes, pathways, mediators, and moderators of various forms of school maladjustment in children with ADHD, although of some use, may themselves be equally limited and short-sighted. Two other approaches are likely to be needed in combination with these others to appreciate and treat the complexity of factors impinging upon a child's academic successes (or failures in the case of ADHD).

One of these is the more traditional psychiatric model that I shall here dub "diagnosis-driven treatment." Such a medical model view seeks to identify ultimate as well as proximal causes in its taxonomy of disorders and to focus on disease states, initial causes, genetic contributions, biohazards, and even family factors that may be contributing to a given disorder, besides the more proximal contributors of social attention, faulty contingencies that are part of FBA. This approach has shown that ADHD has a striking genetic contribution to its range of expression and is leading to the identification of numerous promising candidate genes (5 at this count, another 15 suspected in a recent genomewide scan) for the disorder (Nigg, 2006; Waldman & Gizer, 2006). The relevance of such research to intervention may not only be that different genotypes of ADHD may have different medication responses but also different responses to psychosocial treatments—a possible linkage yet to be explored. It can also be suggested that psychopharmacology for ADHD is a form of genetic therapy in which medications, such as stimulants, appear to be altering, albeit temporarily, genetic mechanisms operative in neurotransmitter pathways. It may be just possible to view behavioral interventions for ADHD from this same perspective given the very real likelihood that they, too, albeit temporarily, alter neuronal functioning. This is a very different point of view of intervention than that offered by traditional behavior therapy.

It is also my sense that FBA, response to intervention, and diagnosis-driven treatment perspectives on maladjustment can be further augmented with impairment-focused treatment, which starts with the specific form of impairment in a specific major life activity in a given setting of concern in a clinical case. It then selects among the various treatments known to have some effectiveness in that setting for addressing that domain of impairment. One example is the effort to train parents to do reading tutoring and math videogames to address reading and math impairments in children with ADHD (Hook & DuPaul, 1999; Ota & DuPaul, 2002). Alone this will prove inadequate for all the impairments seen in ADHD. It will be as shortsighted in its own way as are FBA and response to intervention. What treatment should one select for an impaired domain without knowing the reasons for, processes that lead to, and disorders that can contribute to such impairments? Yet when combined with these other perspectives, impairment-focused treatment serves to focus the treatment team on the very issues that led to the referral of the client for services to begin with—the harms the child or teen are experiencing and a striving to do something to correct them. Just as a hanging in the morning may serve to sharply focus the mind, so too does a focus on impairment (the consequences of symptoms) serve to sharply focus the selection of treatments on what matters the most to the consumer. Each approach will surely have its fad followers, but examining the child's maladjustment from all four perspectives could serve to provide a more comprehensive picture of the sources of maladjustment and more promising recommendations of what needs to be done for them than will any single perspective alone.

CONCLUSION

Space prevents me from giving detailed attention to other issues. The cost–benefit analyses of our psychosocial versus combined versus medication approaches to ADHD surely deserves greater attention despite the boredom that health economics often elicits in clinicians. That three of the four articles here found that less intensive interventions were nearly as good if not equivalent to more intensive ones and the positive implications that flow there from is worthy of notice and follow-up. Recent findings that ADHD in parents can significantly interfere with parent training and probably other interventions for ADHD deserves note among those studying school interventions (Sonuga-Barke, Daley, & Thompson, 2002). We need to further explore the role of parental ADHD in affecting school intervention (daily school report cards, home–school journals, background support of classroom technology, and so on) and that of teacher ADHD and the larger realm of teacher–child temperamental "fit." Although much has been done in the last 30 years to improve our knowledge of how to manage ADHD in the school setting, as the excellent articles here clearly suggest, there is still much work to be done if we are to improve upon the status quo for children and teens with ADHD.

REFERENCES

Abikoff, H. (1992). Cognitive training in ADHD children: Less to it than meets the eye. In S. E. Shaywitz & B. A. Shaywitz (Eds.), *Attention deficit disorder comes of age: toward the twenty-first century* (pp. 261–272). Austin, TX: Pro-Ed.

Antshel, K. M., & Remer, R. (2003). Social skills training in children with attention deficit hyperactivity disorder: A randomized-controlled clinical trial. *Journal of Clinical Child and Adolescent Psychology, 32,* 153–165.

Barkley, R. A. (1989). Attention deficit hyperactivity disorder. In E. J. Mash & R. A. Barkley (Eds.), *Treatment of childhood disorders* (pp. 39–72). New York: Guilford Press.

Barkley, R. A. (1997). *ADHD and the nature of self-control.* New York: Guilford Press.

Barkley, R. A. (2006). *Attention deficit hyperactivity disorder: A handbook for diagnosis and treatment* (3rd ed.). New York: Guilford Press.

Barkley, R. A., Edwards, G., Laneri, M., Fletcher, K., & Metevia, L. (2001). The efficacy of problem-solving communication training alone, behavior management training alone, and their combination for parent-adolescent conflict in teenagers with ADHD and ODD. *Journal of Consulting and Clinical Psychology, 69,* 926–941.

Barkley, R. A., Guevremont, D. C., Anastopoulos, A. D., & Fletcher, K. E. (1992). A comparison of three family therapy programs for treating family conflicts in adolescents with attention-deficit hyperactivity disorder. *Journal of Consulting and Clinical Psychology, 60,* 450–462.

Barkley, R. A., & Murphy, K. R. (2006). *Attention deficit hyperactivity disorder: A clinical workbook* (3rd ed.). New York: Guilford Press.

Barkley, R. A., Shelton, T. L., Crosswait, C., Moorehouse, M., Fletcher, K., Barrett, S., et al., (2000). Early psycho-educational intervention for children with disruptive behavior: Preliminary post-treatment outcome. *Journal of Child Psychology and Psychiatry, 41,* 319–332.

Barkley, R. A., Smith, K., Fischer, M., & Navia, B. (2006). An examination of the behavioral and neuropsychological correlates of three ADHD candidate gene polymorphisms (DRD4 7+, DBH TaqI A2, and DAT1 40bp VNTR) in hyperactive and normal children followed to adulthood. *American Journal of Medical Genetics: Neuropsychiatric Genetics, 141B(5),* 487–498.

Cunningham, C. E. (2006). COPE: Large-group, community-based, family-centered parent training. In R. A. Barkley (Ed.), *Attention deficit hyperactivity disorder: A handbook for diagnosis and treatment* (pp. 480- 498). New York: Guilford Press.

Dishion, T. J., McCord, J., & Poulin, F. (1999). When interventions harm: Peer groups and problem behavior. *American Psychologist, 54,* 755–764.

Douglas, V. I. (1999). Cognitive control processes in attention-deficit/hyperactivity disorder. In H. C. Quay & A. Horgan (Eds.), *Handbook of disruptive behavior disorders* (pp. 105–138). New York: Plenum Press.

Hook, C. L., & DuPaul, G. J. (1999). Parent tutoring for students with attention-deficit/hyperactivity disorder: Effects on reading performance at home and school. School Psychology Review, 28, 60–75.

Klingberg, T., Fernell, E., Olesen, P., Johnson, M.,Gustafsson, P., Dahlström, K., et al. (2005). Computerized training of working memory in children with ADHD—A randomized, controlled trial. *Journal of the American Academy of Child and Adolescent Psychiatry, 44,* 177–186.

Meichenbaum, D. (1988). Cognitive behavioral modification with attention deficit hyperactive children. In L. M. Bloomingdale & J. Sergeant (Eds.), *Attention deficit disorder: Criteria, cognition, intervention* (pp. 127–140). New York: Pergamon.

MTA Cooperative Group (1999). A 14-Month randomized clinical trial of treatment strategies for attention deficit/hyperactivity disorder. Archives of General Psychiatry, 56, 1073–1086.

Nigg, J. T. (2006). *What causes ADHD?* New York: Guilford Press.

Ota, K. R., & DuPaul, G. J. (2002). Task engagement and mathematics performance in children with attention deficit hyperactivity disorder: effects of supplemental computer instruction. *School Psychology Quarterly, 17,* 242–257.

Pelham, W. E. (1988). Behavior therapy. In E. K. Sleator & W. E. Pelham, Jr. (Eds.), *Attention deficit disorder* (pp. 127–162). Norwalk, CT: Appleton-Century-Crofts.

Pelham, W. E., & Sams, S. E. (1992). Behavior modification. In G. Weiss (Ed). *Child and Adolescent Psychiatry Clinics of North America: Attention deficit hyperactivity disorder* (October, Volume 1). Philadelphia: W. B. Saunders.

Rappport, M. D., Scanlan, S. W., & Denney, C. B. (1999). Attention-deficit/hyperactivity disorder and scholastic achievement: A model of dual developmental pathways. *Journal of Child Psychology and Psychiatry, 40,* 1169–1183.

Ross, D. M., & Ross, S. A. (1982). *Hyperactivity: current issues, research, and theory.* New York: Wiley.

Sonuga-Barke, E. J. S., Daley, D., & Thompson, M. (2002). Does maternal ADHD reduce the effectiveness of parent training for preschool children's ADHD? *Journal of the American Academy of Child and Adolescent Psychiatry, 41,* 696–702.

Waldman, I. D., & Gizer, I. R. (2006). The genetics of attention deficit hyperactivity disorder. *Clinical Psychology Review, 26,* 396–432.

Willis, T. J., & Lovaas, I. (1977). A behavioral approach to treating hyperactive children: The parent's role. In J. B. Millichap (Ed.), *Learning disabilities and related disorders* (pp. 119–140). Chicago, IL: Yearbook Medical Publications.

SIX

A Positive Procedure to Increase Compliance in the General Education Classroom for a Student with Serious Emotional Disorders

Paul Beare, Colleen Torgerson
& Kelly Dubois-Gerchak

Students with serious emotional and behavioral disorders (EBD) often display academic deficits that cause them to lag behind nondisabled peers in most or all academic areas (e.g., Mattison, Spitznagel, & Felix, 1998). Improving academic skills represents a difficult task because of the externalizing behaviors that take place concurrent with academic instruction, particularly in structured environments (Nelson, Benner, Lane, & Smith, 2004). These behaviors interfere with students' ability and motivation to follow directions (Walker, Ramsey, & Gresham, 2004). Noncompliant behaviors may sometimes function as a way for students with EBD to escape undesirable academic tasks (negative reinforcement) or obtain attention from others (positive reinforcement) (Maag & Anderson, 2006). A variety of applied behavior analysis (ABA) strategies have been used to address behaviors characteristic of noncompliance (Maag, 2005).

Video modeling consists of having an individual view a video of himself or herself engaging in a behavior targeted for intervention. Video modeling comes from social learning theory and the concept that individuals learn through observation. Albert Bandura, the father of social learning theory, described video modeling as a technique to increase self-efficacy in that it provides clear information on how best to perform certain actions, strengthening belief in one's competency (Bandura, 1997). Video modeling intervention has an advantage over other strategies in that they rely mainly on allowing a student to watch a video, thus not requiring the application of either extrinsic reinforcement or punishment (Baker, Lang, & O'Reilly, 2009). Modeling has the somewhat unique property of increasing desirable behavior and decreasing inappropriate behavior.

Booth and Fairbank (1984) found the use of videotape as a feedback mechanism to be a strong intervention because it is accurate, can be replayed repeatedly, and can be stopped for review and discussion. Osborne, Kiburz, and Miller (1986) maintained that the videotape medium seems to facilitate recognition of responsibility by a subject who had previously denied responsibility for his or her disruptive behavior. The tape allows the subject to see how his or her behavior appears to others. Advantages include: very little preparation time required, rapid behavior change, cost efficiency, and accuracy. Parents like it for the aforementioned reasons and because it gives them a realistic picture of their child's behavior by allowing them to view it (Austin, 1969). Video modeling has demonstrated its effectiveness with a wide variety of behaviors for students with challenging behaviors in school settings (Hitchcock, Dowrick, & Prater, 2003).

Walther and Beare (1991) used video modeling with discussion of the viewed behavior to increase on-task behavior by a ten-year-old child served in an EBD setting. Each day the EBD teacher would ask, as the student watched, recorded, and graphed his own behavior, what behaviors he had seen that were "good," and what he would "like to change." He was also asked what he noticed most about his behavior. The intervention, which required 20 minutes per day, increased task attention from a mean of 28% during baseline to 58% during intervention in math class and from 24% to 49% during written language. Clare, Jenson, Kehle, and Bray (2000) used a very similar technique to obtain much higher on-task rates for three boys, aged nine to eleven, with mild disability labels. A multiple baseline study using two boys, aged seven and nine, who were served in a self-contained special education classroom, demonstrated the effectiveness of video self-modeling combined with behavioral rehearsal in reducing inappropriate behavior and increasing cooperative behavior (Lonnecker, Brady, McPherson, & Hawkins, 1994). The level of cooperative behavior increased to nearly 100%. An added feature of this research was that the behavioral improvements generalized to regular classroom settings where the boys took speech, math, and science classes.

A number of studies have used video modeling to decrease inappropriate behavior (e.g., Davis, 1979; Embregts, 2000; Kehle, Clark, Jenson, & Wampold, 1986). O'Reilly et al. (2005) used a multiple baseline across subjects research design to demonstrate the effectiveness of video feedback and self-management in decreasing the schoolyard aggression of two ten-year-old boys with behavior disorders. During intervention the boys were shown drawings of both aggressive and pro-social behaviors. They were then shown a five-minute video clip, divided into 30-second segments, of themselves playing in the schoolyard. The students were asked if the behavior in the video was "nice" or "not nice." If they answered correctly, they received verbal praise plus a token. If they accurately labeled 20% of the segments during a session they were allowed to exchange their tokens for a back-up reinforcer at the end of the session. The intervention was highly effective.

The literature reveals few criticisms of video modeling research. One possible criticism concerns the social validity of the intervention (i.e., the suitability of doing it in a general education classroom). It may be viewed as possibly disruptive or it may take more time than a general education teacher could afford to allot (Baker, Lang, & O'Reilly, 2009). The same authors point out that it is also difficult to identify if any one part of the intervention package, the viewing, the recording, the extra interaction with the teacher, etc., is the cause of behavior change, if it does occur. One aspect of virtually every video modeling article reviewed was the inclusion of a self-management strategy. The use of self-monitoring and other self-management strategies for students with behavioral challenges is advantageous for a number of reasons. They are largely internal and do not rely on external controls or adult actions. They are proactive interventions that focus on the development of adaptive behaviors, such as compliance with teacher directions, and can be applied across settings and situations (Dunlap et al., 1995). They avoid the use of any activity that could be viewed as aversive and can clearly facilitate generalization by transferring across settings. A number of studies have examined the use of self-monitoring with a variety of special populations, almost all with marked success in increasing appropriate behavior while reducing maladaptive actions.

Self-monitoring has been successful in modifying the behavior of students with a variety of disabilities including autism, cognitive impairments, behavior disorders and learning disabilities (Ganz, 2008). The strategy is effective in addressing both academic and social behaviors and can be used in special or general education classrooms (Maag, 2004; Hughes et al., 2002). It has changed the behavior of both seriously involved and mildly disabled students (Ganz & Sigafoos, 2005). A recent meta-analysis of literature from the past 30 years concluded that self-monitoring produced meaningful improvements in student on-task behavior, academic productivity, and reduction of inappropriate or disruptive behavior (Reid, Trout, & Schartz, 2005).

The present study examined the effectiveness of video modeling in increasing compliance with teacher directions by a highly intelligent ten-year-old boy with behavioral disorders. Self-monitoring had been attempted previously and failed to change his behavior. Video modeling was seen as a stronger first step to cause the student to move toward self-management of his behavior and increasing and maintaining his compliance with teacher directions. Self-monitoring was planned as a method to help fade the video modeling should it prove to be effective in establishing behavior change.

METHOD

PARTICIPANT

Charles was a ten-year-old male who obtained a full-scale score of 142 on the WISC-III (Wechsler, 1991), placing him in the very superior range of aptitude. His special education categorical label was EBD, and his primary placement was a general education fifth grade classroom with resource services for up to 500 minutes per week, either in pullout for social skills training or task completion in a classroom with the categorical EBD teacher. Charles had significant health-related issues, weighing 146 pounds at 4'8" in height and was considered medically to be obese. He was also severely asthmatic and psychiatrically diagnosed with mood disorders as well as Opposition Defiant Disorder. He was heavily medicated for the asthmatic condition, and this was considered to contribute to his obesity. Reports from two different psychiatrists indicated that he perhaps used the asthmatic condition as a manipulation device to aid in frequent non-compliance.

Charles lived in a single-parent family and was raised by his mother, a registered nurse who regularly worked the night shift. While his mother worked, Charles stayed with either his aunt or grandmother. Charles' father lived a few blocks away but had little contact with his son. Charles' mother felt this was a difficult issue for him; however, Charles did not refer to it while at school and said it was not important when in counseling.

Descriptors of Charles' behavior included aggressiveness to parent, teachers, and peers; somatic complaints; characteristics supporting anxiety and depression; social problems; and severe non-compliance. He was described as being stubborn, having sudden changes in moods, underachieving, and having temper tantrums. On occasion, he would physically attack people and exhibit unpredictable behavior. He made frequent statements concerning his unhappiness, lack of friends, and desire to run away or die.

Charles' refusal to do academic work was a serious concern for his teachers. He fluctuated between wanting to finish work to allow himself time to engage in preferred activities and complete refusal to complete any assigned tasks whatsoever or to comply with the simplest request or demand. This latter behavior, lack of compliance with teacher direction, was perhaps the most troubling. Because of his exceptional intelligence and ability to complete work when motivated, his team placed him in the general education classroom whenever possible. Following the teacher's verbal direction was considered the entry-level behavior to allow him to function therein. Prior to the present research, a number of techniques to improve compliance had been tried and had failed. These included the systematic use of verbal praise for compliance, reprimands for non-compliance, extinction, time-outs, self-recording of on-task behavior, and a token economy with back-up reinforcement. Charles had daily assignment sheets, received counseling with the school psychologist, and was in counseling with his mother outside of school. The token economy, daily assignment sheets, and counseling continued throughout the study.

Charles' strengths were his intelligence, large vocabulary and clever wit. He had great potential but was very manipulative, particularly when refusing to comply. An illustration of his extreme non-compliance, and one that was repeated periodically, occurred during fall of the fifth grade. While in the resource room, the teacher directed Charles to replace materials he was using during the free time he had been awarded for completing an assignment. Charles refused. The teacher set a contingency, "Either replace the materials now or you will do it during recess." Charles replied to the contingency, "I poop in my pants if you make me clean up during recess." The teacher affirmed the direction. Charles looked right at her and had a bowel movement, standing in the classroom. He stated, "I warned you."

SETTING

The study was conducted during Charles' daily 45-minute math period in his general education fifth grade setting. The school building held all of the 5000-student district's fifth and sixth graders, approximately 400 in all. During the period, 30 students were in the classroom receiving instructional methods that included lecture, group work, and individual seat-work on math assignments. Charles was experiencing his greatest difficulty with compliance during math period. On most days during the year, the EBD resource room teacher accompanied Charles to the math class. On the occasion of a crisis elsewhere in the school, the teacher would be replaced by a paraprofessional. On all days during the term of the study, the EBD teacher was present and recorded data.

INTERVENTION

Two weeks prior to commencement of the study, a video camera was positioned in the fifth grade room and the students in the class, including Charles, were told that the EBD teacher would be in and out doing some taping of the class for a project as part of her graduate degree. The class and Charles were very accepting of the camera and did not react to the teacher's presence. Before the study began, Charles was told that "nothing on the tape would be used against him" and that he would "soon be able to view the tapes." Math was the first subject of the day in the class.

BEHAVIORAL MEASURES

Two categories of behavior were measured. The first, and primary, target was compliance with teacher directives. The EBD teacher used frequency recording to record each time the classroom teacher gave a command either to Charles specifically or to the classroom as a whole. The command might be as specific as "Charles, return to your desk," or as general as "everyone take out your math book." Following the tally, using a stopwatch, the EBD teacher recorded whether Charles complied with the command within a 30-second period. If he complied, the tally was circled. The data thus yielded the percentage of teacher directions with which Charles complied during each day's math class.

A second category of behavior recorded was "acting out." Acting out was defined as when Charles exhibited a verbal or physical action that was not in compliance with a teacher directive and which had the connotation of either disrupting another individual or the class or hurting another individual or the class. Specifically, verbal acting out was when Charles was hostile, swore, or made a negative verbal statement directed at another student or a teacher. Physical acting out was when Charles made a negative physical act involving contact with another student or a teacher or when he made overt inappropriate use of a physical object (such as throwing a book or slamming a desk). These behaviors were tracked using frequency recording; however, compliance, not acting out, served as the main target and the basis of changing conditions in the experimental design.

EXPERIMENTAL DESIGN

The planned experimental design was an ABABB'C reversal design followed by gradual fading of the intervention (B') before moving to self-recording. No gradual fading was required; the second reversal condition (A3) resulted in no decrease in compliance. Therefore, there was no intermittent taping of Charles, video modeling was simply stopped, causing what would have been a longer process to became an additional baseline condition prior to self-recording, resulting in the final ABABAC design as seen in Figure 1. During baseline (A1) data were collected for two weeks (eight days of school) with no intervention. Throughout this period the video camera was operating and Charles was clearly aware that he was being filmed. To maintain consistency across math lessons that did vary slightly in length, data were collected for the first 30 minutes

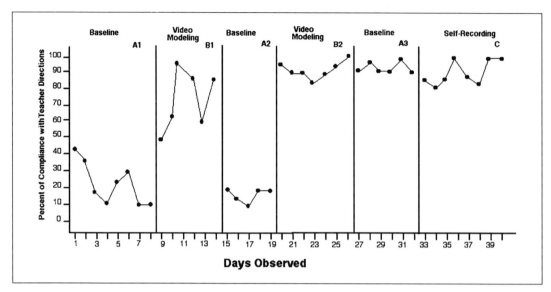

Figure 1. Percent of compliance with teacher commands during math in the fifth grade classroom under baseline, video modeling, and self-recording conditions for a ten-year-old boy with EBD.

of the lesson, commencing when the teacher gave a verbal clue to the class that it was time to start math for that day.

At the end of the math period on day eight, the EBD teacher took Charles to the resource room, and together they viewed a 15-minute sample of that day's math class, beginning the first intervention phase (B1). Note that day nine was thus the first day that Charles knew he would be viewing his behavior with the teacher—thus that was the first day affected by the intervention even though he did the actual viewing on day eight. Each day of intervention Charles was asked what he thought of his behavior. On day eight the teacher explained frequency recording to Charles, and he was directed, as he viewed the tape, to make a tally each time the teacher gave him a direction and to circle it when he followed the direction. While viewing, the teacher spoke with Charles about what he saw in his behavior, what he liked and disliked. Charles understood the behavior he charted, and there was little or no discrepancy between how Charles and the teacher judged behaviors. At the end of the observation, the teacher and Charles marked a graph that showed his percentage of compliance for each day. Acting out was not recorded by Charles but was discussed with him as it occurred on the tape. The teacher's recording from the 30-minute period in the classroom is the data reported in this study, not data from the 10–15 minutes of video review or data that Charles collected during the intervention.

During the first reversal phase (A2), Charles was told the camera was broken and needed repair. No camera was present in the room; however, the EBD teacher was present and continued to record data. After one week of reversal, Charles was told the camera was working again, and re-intervention (B2) was implemented using the same procedure as with B1. After the criterion of six days with over 80% compliance was reached, the decision was made to fade camera and begin self-recording of compliance without the use of the videotape. The plan had been to again remove the camera, this time gradually, using it one day, saying it was needed elsewhere the next. Interpretation of the data, however, showed no deterioration during this second reversal (A3). As a result, after six days without deterioration, the final phase, self-recording of compliance (C) was implemented.

RESULTS

SECOND OBSERVER RELIABILITY

Second observer reliability was collected by having the classroom paraprofessional observe simultaneously during the math period on the first day of each intervention phase a total of six times. Agreement was calculated by dividing the lower observed frequency of compliance, verbal acting out, and physical acting out by the higher observed frequency and multiplying by 100, as recommended by Alberto and Troutman (2005). Observer reliability was thus calculated a total of 18 times for the three behaviors over six days. The reliability for compliance varied from 80% to 96% with a mean of 90%. Reliability for verbal acting out ranged from 100% to 75% with a mean of 95%. Physical acting out reliability was 100% on every occasion.

VISUAL ANALYSIS OF DATA

Data were analyzed using techniques outlined by Tawney and Gast (1984). Level and trend changes were calculated and compared across conditions. The frequency data for compliance were converted to rate by dividing the number of commands delivered during each 30-minute recording session into the number of commands where Charles complied and multiplying by 100, resulting in a percentage score for each day. The acting out data were incidental to the compliance data and thus did not guide the implementation of the various phases. They were recorded and graphed as frequency data.

COMPLIANCE

Compliance data may be seen in Figure 1. During baseline Charles' compliance was variable with a decelerating, worsening trend and a mean level of 24%. There was an abrupt change from 16% compliance on the last day of baseline to 50% compliance on the first day of videotape viewing. The first day was the lowest day of intervention, each subsequent day being higher. During intervention the data were variable, with no clear trend; the mean level was 71%, a 47% improvement over baseline. There was no overlap between the A1 and B1. On day 15 the criterion of a 30% increase over baseline in compliance for 4 out of 5 consecutive days was met and the reversal implemented. On the last day of intervention (B1) compliance was 80%; on the first day of reversal (A2) it decreased to 18%. The mean during A2 was 16%, a marked worsening from the mean of intervention. There was no overlap between the conditions because the reversal was established, on day 20 the intervention (B2) was again applied. On the last day of A2, compliance was 18%; on the first day of B2, it jumped to 94%, an abrupt 76% improvement. The trend during intervention was flat with a mean of 91%, a 75% improvement over reversal. Again, there was no overlap between the adjacent conditions. Every day of B2 was above 80%.

Once the reintervention was judged to be effective, a procedure to fade the intervention while maintaining a high compliance rate was implemented. The plan had been to monitor compliance while removing the camera from the room and have Charles do no viewing of the behavior. If any day dropped below 80%, the camera would be returned until the rate again was over 80%. This was to continue until the criteria of six consecutive days over 80% was reached. Unexpectedly, the first six days were over 80%; thus the fading period became, de facto, A3, a second reversal. The mean remained at 91%, the same as during B2.

To help assure that no abrupt extinction of compliance would occur, at this point the new intervention, considered a less intrusive version of self-monitoring than video modeling, was implemented. In this condition (C), Charles was directed to self-record compliance while in math class, making a tally when a direction was given and circling the tally if he complied. At the end of the math class, he and the EBD teacher would calculate his compliance and graph it, as they had when viewing the videotapes. This condition maintained the high 91% compliance mean of B2 and A3.

ACTING OUT

Figure 2 displays Charles' frequency of verbal and physical acting out. During baseline, verbal acting out was variable with no clear trend and a mean of 6. There was an immediate drop upon the onset of videotape review to a mean of 1. During the first reversal (A2), verbal acting out rose slightly to a mean of 2.2. Upon re-intervention (B2), it dropped to mean of 0.43. It further fell to 0.16 during A3 and was 0.33 during self-recording (C).

Physical aggression had a mean of 3 during A1. Upon application of the videotape viewing it reduced to one occurrence the first day and maintained a mean of 0.33. During A2 the rate rose slightly to a mean of 0.8 incidents per day. Upon re-intervention it obtained a mean level of 0.29 and decreased further to 0 and 0.11 during A3 and C, respectively.

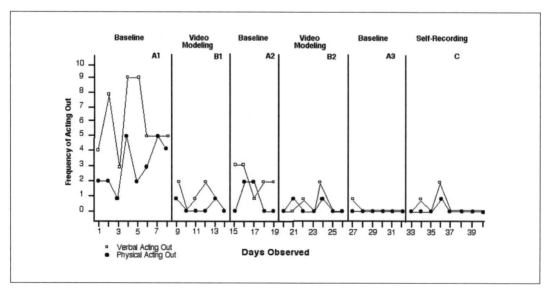

Figure 2. Frequency of verbal and physical acting out behavior during math in the fifth grade classroom baseline, video modeling, and self-recording conditions for a ten-year-old boy with EBD.

SUMMARY

The analysis of this data supports that the use of videotape feedback increased the percentage of Charles' compliance with teacher directives. The abrupt and large level changes and the large mean differences upon application of the intervention support this as does the lack of overlap between adjacent conditions. The sharp and immediate reversal of compliance in A2 verified there was a functional relationship between the video modeling and the change in compliance. The videotape viewing had the effect of reducing the maladaptive verbal and physically aggressive behaviors as an added benefit.

DISCUSSION

The purpose of this study was to determine if a student with EBD could increase his compliance with teacher directives through the use of video modeling feedback. It was implemented to establish whether using a specific behavioral intervention would increase Charles' compliance simultaneously with reducing aggressive behaviors. Accomplishing this, the study would demonstrate that the quality of life and daily school experience, for even an extremely intelligent youth with multiple psychiatric diagnoses as well as serious physical problems, could be improved with a rather simple behavioral intervention that was deemed to be positive in nature. In current special education best practices, reliance on positive procedures is a strong expectation (Alberto & Troutman, 2005).

Charles regularly exhibited both aggressive and noncompliant behaviors; refusing to work, yelling out in class such statements as, "I only do things on my own terms, no one else's!"; "I am in control here!"; and "Math stinks!" He also pushed other students, slammed desks, and punched walls and cabinets. Charles routinely denied his noncompliant and disruptive classroom behavior. The school team determined that he was least compliant during the math period. The intervention of video modeling was selected and a baseline of his inappropriate behaviors taken during math.

When intervention began there was an immediate drop in acting out behaviors and an increase in compliance to teacher directions. While viewing the video of inappropriate behavior, Charles expressed such statements as, "Do I really look like that?"; "Did I really say that?"; "Turn it off!" and "I don't want to see any more!" Initially he would cry as he viewed himself on video. After a few days he seemed to become aware of being polite and he increased his use of "thank you" and "excuse me." He also watched to be sure that the teacher accurately recorded his compliance behavior. After the first intervention Charles' aggressive behaviors diminished and remained down.

During A2 Charles' compliance dropped dramatically to a mean level of 16%. He was angry that the camera was not working, and a typical behavior was to lay his body over his desk and do nothing. Very little work was done in math for those five days. Upon reintervention of video viewing, his compliance increased dramatically to a mean level of 91%. When he charted and recorded his own behavior he was proud of his graph and stated that he wanted to earn 100% compliance. Because of the success of the intervention, the viewing and the camera presence were faded. Charles' compliance remained high. He was taught to self-record and his compliance remained high at 91%.

Charles was an excellent subject for this type of intervention in that he possessed high mental capabilities that enhanced the use of self-control techniques to modify his own behavior. He had a strong desire to be "normal." After video modeling and recording his own behavior, he began to be more responsible, was aware of self-control, and seemed to be a much more pleasant boy to be around. One explanation for the video modeling's effectiveness is that it is accurate, largely inarguable, and is instructive to the student (Baker et al., 2009). Other advantages include the small amount of teacher time it requires, rapid behavior change, cost efficiency due to the ability to record behavior without using trained observers in the room, and the accuracy of the behavior recorded due to the relative permanence of the video (Osborne et al., 1986).

A significant challenge for educators who use the behavioral approach is coaxing the new learned behavior to generalize across settings to situations in which extrinsic intervention or control is not possible (Alberto & Troutman, 2005). The ability to self-manage one's own behaviors without external support has always been a valued goal of education and is considered critical for achieving successful adult adjustment (Sabatos, 1986). Wehmeyer (1996) contended that self-management is essential in the development of self-determination, self-regulation, and self-advocacy skills in numerous settings. Kings-Sears (1999) reported that self-management promotes independence and maintenance of behaviors in various classroom and community settings. Teachers who continually rely on providing extrinsic verbal prompts and reinforcement to individuals encourage the development of dependent behaviors and possibly learned helplessness. The demonstration of self-management is necessary to promote independence and permits an individual with severe challenges, such as Charles, to function more appropriately in all environments, decreasing the need for external support and supervision.

Moon, Inge, Wehman, Brooke, and Barkus (1990) described self-management as a person's act to self-regulate behaviors through the use of techniques that are either external operants (visual prompts, auditory prompts, self-recording, or video modeling) or internal operants (self-instruction, self-evaluation, or self-reinforcement). The use of external operants is more intrusive and requires the application of some type of support. In Charles' case, though minimal, it was the audiovisual support, and review time with the teacher. Internal operants are less intrusive and require individuals to exhibit a greater degree of self-regulated behavior, behavior that can easily cross environments

In a study that rotated three students with cognitive disabilities through three different self-management interventions (self-recording to an auditory cue, the use of an auditory cue but no recording, and recording but not to any cue), Firman, Beare, and Loyd (2002) found all three interventions dramatically improved both on-task and social behaviors over baseline levels. The more extrinsic treatments, recording to a cue and cueing without recording conditions, obtained better results than simply asking a student to record his on-task behavior "whenever he thinks of it"; however, the magnitude of the difference was small. This suggests that teachers must select less intrusive, more normalized self-management training to help students improve and maintain appropriate behaviors.

In Charles' case, the teacher had tried simple self-recording to an auditory cue previously to no avail. The question thus arises as to why the more intrusive video modeling was a necessary step with Charles. Though Baker et al. (2009) concluded that video modeling is not punitive,

Charles' case disputes the notion. Viewing his inappropriate behavior was an aversive stimulus. Though this was intended as a positive procedure, Charles did not perceive it as such, as evidenced by his verbal statements during intervention. The aversive stimulus acted as a negative reinforcer for compliance: Charles increased his compliance to avoid exposure to that aversive stimulus. The same aversive stimulus served as punishment for acting out and reduced it.

The lack of a decrease in compliance during the A3 condition was initially confusing. Compliance had reversed in A2 but stayed exactly level during this second reversal. Did this mean some other factor than the video modeling was controlling Charles' behavior? The explanation probably lay in his very bright nature. He clearly had identified that the EBD teacher was charting compliance during the class; he checked to make sure she did so. Her continued presence and recording may have cued his appropriate behavior. It may be equally likely that he was benefiting from a number of other secondary reinforcers by behaving so appropriately. He earned more points in the token system and more praise from teachers; scores on assignments improved, and other students responded positively to his new way of acting—all possible reinforcers.

The final self-recording condition may have been unnecessary from a scientific point of view to demonstrate a functional relationship between the variables in that positive behavior was being maintained without intervention; however, the self-recording of compliance was an excellent tool to facilitate generalization of the compliance to other settings and to maintain his behavior in the math class. Self-recording was easily transportable and could be used in other classes. The hope in this, like any behavioral intervention, is that the subject will internalize the established behavior and continue it without external control.

CONCLUSION

The use of a behavioral intervention utilizing a single-subject design dramatically changed Charles' success in a school setting. The data provided strong evidence to support the efficacy of the video modeling form of self-management in increasing the compliance of a student with EBD. The intervention was conducted in a manner that limited intrusiveness, and classroom routines were not disrupted. Students not directly involved remained uninformed as to the purpose of taping, reducing possible stigmatization. Actively involving Charles in the self-evaluation process enhanced his ability to accept responsibility. All these features should speak to the external validity of the research, making it easily adaptable to other children in similar settings.

Electronic recording capacity has greatly expanded with the use of video cameras that are widely accessible. Personal computers have become ubiquitous in the American classroom, and most have the capability to record behavior and allow a student to discretley view his own actions. This study was conducted in a general education setting, as opposed to special education classrooms or residential facilities, providing research to support the use of video modeling in a least restrictive environment.

Students with EBD have behavioral characteristics that interfere with both the classroom and student learning such as noncompliance with teacher directives and acting-out behaviors. Teachers often struggle with these characteristics, utilizing extrinsic punishments and feeling ineffective. Effective interventions for teachers must be determined. This study provides an example of how a teacher can use single-subject design to change student behavior and also documents that video modeling is an effective intervention. Video feedback can be used as a strong behavior intervention and clearly demonstrates the effectiveness of applied behavior analysis in promoting positive behavior in a student who is both seriously disturbed and disturbing.

REFERENCES

Alberto, P. A., & Troutman, A. C. (2005). *Applied behavior analysis for teachers* (7th ed.). Columbus, OH: Merrill.

Austin, J. T. (1969). Videotape as a teaching tool. *Exceptional Children, 35,* 557–558.

Baker, S. D., Lang, R., & O'Reilly, M. (2009). Review of video modeling with students with emotional and behavioral disorders. *Education and Treatment of Children, 3,* 403–420.

Bandura, A. (1997). *Self-efficacy: The exercise of control.* New York: W. H. Freeman.

Booth, S. R., & Fairbank, D. W. (1984). Videotape feedback as a behavior management technique. *Behavioral Disorders, 9,* 55–59.

Clare, S. K., Jenson, W.R., Kehle, T. J., & Bray, M. A. (2000). Self-modeling as a treatment for increasing on-task behavior. *Psychology in the Schools, 37,* 517–522.

Davis, R. A. (1979). The impact of self-modeling on problem behaviors in school-age children. *School Psychology Digest, 8,* 128–132.

Dunlap, G., Clarke, S., Jackson, M., Wright, S., Ramos, E., & Brinson, S. (1995). *School Psychology Quarterly, 10,* 165–177.

Embregts, P. (2000). Effectiveness of video feedback and self-management on inappropriate social behavior of youth with mild mental retardation. *Research in Developmental Disabilities, 21,* 409–423.

Firman, K. B., Beare, P., & Loyd, R. (2002). Enhancing self-management in students with mental retardation: Extrinsic versus intrinsic procedures. *Education and Training in Mental Retardation and Developmental Disabilities, 37,* 163–171.

Ganz, J. B. (2008). Self-monitoring across age and ability levels: Teaching students to implement their own positive behavioral interventions. *Preventing School Failure, 53,* 39–48.

Ganz, J. B., & Sigafoos, J. (2005). Self-monitoring: Are young adults with MR and autism able to utilize cognitive strategies independently? *Education and Training in Developmental Disabilities, 40,* 24–33.

Hitchcock, C. H., Dowrick, P. W., & Prater, M. A. (2003). Video self-modeling intervention in school-based settings: A review. *Remedial and Special Education, 24*(1), 36–45.

Hughes, C., Copeland, S., Agran, M., Wehmeyer, M., Rodi, M. S., & Resley, J. A. (2002) Using self-monitoring to improve the performance in general education high school classes. *Education and Training in Mental Retardation and Developmental Disabilities, 37,* 262–272.

Kehle, T. J., Clark, E., Jenson, W. R., & Wampold, B. E. (1986). Effectiveness of self-observation with behavior disordered elementary school children. *School Psychology Review, 15,* 289–295.

King-Sears, M. (1999). Teacher and researcher co-design self-management content for an inclusive setting: Research training, intervention, and generalization effects on student performance. *Education and Training in Mental Retardation and Developmental Disabilities, 34,* 134–56.

Lonnecker, C., Brady, M. P., McPherson, R., & Hawkins, J. (1994). Video self-modeling and cooperative classroom behavior in children with learning and behavior problems: Training and generalization effects. *Behavioral Disorders, 20,* 24–34.

Maag, J. (2004). *Behavior management: From theoretical implications to practical applications* (2nd ed.). Belmont, CA: Wadsworth/Thomson Learning.

Maag, J. (2005). Social skills training for youth with emotional and behavioral disorders and learning disabilities: Problems, conclusions, and suggestions. *Exceptionality, 13,* 155–172.

Maag, J., & Anderson, J. (2006). Effects of sound-field amplification to increase compliance of students with emotional and behavior disorders. *Behavioral Disorders, 31*, 378–393.

Mattison, R., Spitznagel, E., & Felix, B. (1998). Enrollment predictors of the special education outcome for students with SED. *Behavioral Disorders, 23*, 243–56.

Moon, M. S., Inge, K. J., Wehman, P., Brooke, V., & Barkus, J. M. (1990). *Helping persons with severe mental retardation get and keep employment.* Baltimore: Paul H. Brookes.

Nelson, J., Benner, G., Lane, K., & Smith, B. (2004). Academic achievement of K-12 students with emotional and behavioral disorders. *Exceptional Children, 71*, 59–63.

O'Reilly, M. F., O'Halloran, M., Sigafoos, J., Lancioni, G. E., Green, V., Edrisinha, C., Cannella, H., & Olive, M. (2005). Evaluation of video feedack and self-management to decrease schoolyard aggression and increase pro-social behaviour in two students with behavioural disorders. *Educational Psychology, 25*, 199–206.

Osborne, S. S., Kiburz, C. S., & Miller, S. R. (1986) Treatment of self-injurious behavior using self-control techniques with a severe behaviorally disordered adolescent. *Behavioral Disorders, 11*, 60–67.

Reid, R., Trout, A. L., & Schartz, M. (2005). Self-regulation interventions for children with attention deficit/hyperactivity disorder. *Exceptional Children, 71*, 361–377.

Sabatos, M. A. (1986). *Private cues in self-monitoring: Effects on learning disabled students' on-task performance and reading productivity during sustained silent reading.* Unpublished doctoral dissertation, University of Pittsburgh.

Tawney, J. W., & Gast, D. L. (1984). *Single subject research in special education.* Columbus, OH: Merrill.

Walker, H. M., Ramsey, E., & Gresham, F. M. (2004). *Antisocial behavior in school: Evidence-based practices.* Belmont, CA: Wadsworth.

Walther, M., & Beare, P. (1991) The effect of videotape feedback on the on-task behavior of a student with emotional/behavioral disorders. *Education and Treatment of Children, 14*, 53–60.

Wechsler, D. (1991). *Wechsler Intelligence Scale for Children—Third Edition. Manual.* San Antonio: The Psychological Corporation.

Wehmeyer, M. L. (1996). Self-determination as an educational outcome: Why is it important to children, youth, and adults with disabilities? In D. J. Sands & M. L. Wehmeyer (Eds.), *Self-determination across the life-span: Independence and choice for people with disabilities* (pp. 15–34). Baltimore: Paul H. Brookes.

SEVEN

The Limitations of a Behavioral Approach In Most Educational Settings

David Weber

One of the greatest challenges facing those of us who work with young children and adolescents is how to effectively address behavior which interferes with what we're trying to accomplish on their behalf (Freiberg & Lamb, 2009; McIntyre, Gresham, DiGennaro, & Reed, 2007; Reinke, Lewis-Palmer, & Merrell, 2008; Rutherford, Quinn, & Mathur, 2004). Whether it's a parent trying to get a six-year-old to eat fruits and vegetables while trying to get a fifteen-year-old to take shorter showers, or a teacher trying to get a student to stay on task while trying to get another student to stop making rude remarks, the challenge remains the same. We want young children and adolescents to behave differently; therefore, we take action in an effort to change their behavior (Bowen, Jenson, & Clark, 2003).

The behavioral needs of young children and adolescents from early childhood through adolescence are wide-ranging, ongoing, and require an extensive repertoire of proactive plans and response strategies from those of us who work with them (Bowen et al., 2003; Crone, Horner, & Hawken, 2003; Reinke et al., 2008). Parents, teachers, day-care providers, after-school care providers, among many others, are all engaged in the ongoing process of helping young children and adolescents to interact appropriately with others, to make wise behavioral choices, and to increase independence or the ability to manage their own behavior (Crone et al., 2003; Freiberg & Lamb, 2009; Kohn, 2006; Mader, 2009; Walker, 2009). In short, these adults are engaged in the process of teaching new behaviors, reinforcing established desired behaviors, or changing undesired behaviors.

There are many theories and models based upon a plethora of empirical research spanning several decades designed to help adults manage, control, and change the behavior of young children and adolescents (Rutherford et al., 2004). The intent is positive and even admirable—to get young children and adolescents to behave in more appropriate, prosocial ways in order to live more happy, effective, and fulfilling lives. The assumption is that we must behave in certain ways in order to live in, and be accepted by, society. In other words, there are societal norms for acceptable behavior. Although these norms are almost exclusively unwritten, they are commonly understood. Therefore, as schools and families facilitate the assimilation from childhood to adulthood, we look for ways to most effectively help our young children and adolescents to behave as we see fit—in accordance with the societal norms which we have simply grown to understand (Rutherford et al., 2004).

One of the most popular approaches to changing behavior—within both schools and families—is based upon behavioral theory or behaviorism (Austin & Carr, 2000; Freiberg & Lamb, 2009; Kohn, 1999, 2006; Mader, 2009; Rutherford et al., 2004). The foundations of behaviorism are based upon the early work of several early pioneers—Ivan Pavlov, who developed the theory of classical conditioning, Edward Thorndike and John B. Watson, who rejected introspective methods and sought to restrict the study of behavior to experimental methods, and B.F. Skinner, who forwarded the theory of operant conditioning (Austin & Carr, 2000; Rutherford et al., 2004). Watson's classical behaviorism stipulates that there is no mental life, as thought is simply covert speech; that internal states do not exist; and that we can only study that which we see—overt behavior (Buckley, 1989).

Skinner, behaviorism's best known theorist, is widely credited as a seminal pioneer in what has come to be known as behavior analysis (or the experimental analysis of behavior, after variations on the subtitle to his 1938 work, *The Behavior of Organisms: An Experimental Analysis of Behavior* (Austin & Carr, 2000). Today, behavior analysis is a thriving field. "Since 1974, the Association for Behavior Analysis International (ABAI)—the largest organization of its type in the world—has been the primary professional organization for members interested in the philosophy, science, application, and teaching of behavior analysis" (Association for Behavioral Analysis International, n.d.,b). This international organization publishes three separate scholarly, peer-reviewed journals dedicated to the application of behavior analysis and has more than 13,500 members (5,800 in the United States alone) among its 65 affiliated chapters spread over 30 countries (Association for Behavioral Analysis International, n.d.,a). Over the past 10 years, affiliated chapters have enjoyed a 6.5% annual growth rate—a testimony to the viability of an organization focused upon changing human behavior. Consistent with the tenets of behavioral theory, a principal assumption of this organization is that thoughts and feelings do not explain behavior, as evidenced in some of their publicly disseminated literature (Association for Behavioral Analysis International, n.d.,a).

> Behavior analysts make the assumption that all behavior is the product of two kinds of variables: biological and environmental. Biological variables include anatomical structures (birds can fly, people can't), normal physiological processes (digestion, respiration, neurological changes resulting from experience), and anomalies in anatomy and physiology due to injury or disease. Genes influence behavior indirectly through their effects on anatomy and physiology. Environmental variables include any changes in the environment (a rise in temperature, the availability of food, comments by other people, cultural customs). Behavior analysts are primarily interested in the role of environment in behavior change. (Association for Behavioral Analysis International, n.d.,a)

It is important to note that behavior analysts define behavior as "anything a person or animal does that can be observed and measured" (Association for Behavioral Analysis International, n.d., a), thereby not accounting for internal events such as thoughts and feelings unless, of course, they manifest behaviorally in an observable, measurable way.

Another leading organization in the field of behavior analysis is the Behavior Analyst Certification Board (BACB)—the largest organization in the world for the certification of behavior analysts (Behavior Analyst Certification Board, n.d.). A definition of behavior analysis posited by the BACB follows.

> Behavior analysis: Means the design, implementation, and evaluation of instructional and environmental modifications to produce socially significant improvements in human behavior through skill acquisition and the reduction of problematic behavior. A behavior analysis program shall be based upon empirical research, include the direct observation and measurement of behavior, and utilize antecedent stimuli, positive reinforcement, and other consequences to produce behavior change. (Behavior Analyst Certification Board, n.d.)

The BACB has certified thousands of behavior analysts throughout the world in one of two certifications—the Board Certified Behavior Analyst (BCBA) or the Board Certified Associate Behavior Analyst (BCaBA) (Behavior Analyst Certification Board, n.d.). In California alone they have issued 649 certifications, and university training programs in psychology, education, counseling, and school psychology have added coursework which meets the criteria established by BACB for certification purposes (Behavior Analyst Certification Board, n.d.). Information from BACB suggests that the popularity of certification lies in the need for a methodology for improving the behaviors of those with developmental disabilities such as autism spectrum disorders and mental retardation as well as those who have suffered from traumatic brain injury (Behavior Analyst Certification Board, n.d.).

Although it is evident that behaviorism has been clearly established as an approach for changing and improving human behavior, and that its successor, behavior analysis, is currently one of the most popular approaches to changing behavior in young children and adolescents, this approach is not without its limitations.

One common understanding among those engaged in the process of studying human behavior is that behavior is functional and has communicative intent (Association for Behavioral Analysis International, n.d.,a; Austin & Carr, 2000; Buckley, 1989). The principle here—that there is a reason we behave as we do—is vital to fully understanding human behavior in order to facilitate change in behavior. It shows us that behavior is directed towards communicating our needs in such a way as to gain a desired outcome—to meet our needs (Rutherford et al., 2004). More specifically, our behavior is need-driven. Oftentimes an undesired behavior is exhibited as a means of earning some type of seemingly external reinforcement or reward—to satisfy a need. Therefore, our behavior is a direct reflection of, and a means for addressing, our basic human needs (Austin & Carr, 2000; Buckley, 1989; Maslow, 1987; Rutherford et al., 2004). However, often these basic human needs, such as the need for security, the need for acceptance and belonging, the need for friendship and intimacy, or the need to contribute in some way, are complex, profound, and multifaceted (Maslow, 1987; Rutherford et al., 2004). Maslow (1987) posited that when our deficiency needs (at the bottom of his hierarchy of needs—physiological, safety and security, love and belonging, and esteem) are not met, although the body may give no physical indication, individuals will feel anxious and tense and behave in ways to meet those needs.

Although behavior is observable, measurable, and concrete, many of the factors which precede and underlie behavior are not. A limitation of behavior analysis is the failure to acknowledge the multitude of complex factors underlying human behavior and only focus on the ensuing behavior itself and the obvious environmental factors—that which can be observed and measured (Gregory & Ripski, 2008; Kohn, 1999, 2006; Mader, 2009; Wynne, 2004). This would be the conceptual equivalent to a physician treating the symptoms of a condition without addressing the underlying causes. If a physician were to do this, the symptoms would often disappear only to reappear due to inadequate treatment of the real culprit—the underlying causes. Conversely, the physician would be remiss in only treating the underlying causes without also treating the symptoms. The point here is that both the causes of a condition as well as its symptoms must be addressed in order to most effectively treat the patient successfully.

Wynne (2004) has shown that behavior analysis has minimal impact on voluntary adult outpatient services because it is composed of only two of the three theories necessary to effect true behavioral change.

> Behavior analysis continues to have little recognition in the arena of outpatient clinical services to voluntary adults because, while it has a theory of human behavior (radical behaviorism) and a theory of intervention (applied behavior analysis itself), it does not have a theory of deviance to interpose between and connect the two. Consequently, behavior analysts treat unwanted behaviors without considering etiology. (p. 135)

Wynne (2004) vehemently reinforces the importance of this three-pronged theoretical base by emphasizing the current limitation of behavior analysis in neglecting to address etiology.

> The further back in the causal chain of events a psychological problem can be addressed, the more powerful the healing can be. The problem behaviors do need to be addressed, but if they are treated only as mere troublesome behaviors, then the client's improvement is less than it could be, and the problem behaviors are more likely to recur, either in the same form or a different one. (p. 138)

Conceptually, working with the behavior of children in a school setting is similar. The self-imposed limited focus of behavior analysis not only fails to recognize the relationship between the underlying causes of behavior (which may emanate from within us) and the behavior itself but fails to even address the internal underlying causes as a point of focus (Wynne, 2004).

Behavior analysis is focused upon what is known as the behavioral chain which refers to the antecedents of behavior, the behavior itself, then finally the consequences of that behavior—either natural or imposed (Austin & Carr, 2000). This simple, linear, one-dimensional model is commonly referred to as the ABC's of behavior (Antecedent-Behavior-Consequence), and empirical studies support the importance of including these contextual variables in understanding behavior (Austin & Carr, 2000). However, to broaden the contextual scope another level by incorporating the thoughts, perceptions, moods, and emotions offers a more comprehensive, thorough understanding of the factors which underlie behavioral antecedents, thereby maximizing the opportunities to help change behavior (Kohn, 2006; Mader, 2009; McIntyre et al., 2007; Reinke et al., 2008; Rutherford et al., 2004). Again, the more narrow (and shallow) focus of behavior analysis not only fails to examine that which underlies the behavioral antecedent but tragically does not even recognize the existence of any intangible, immeasurable factors involved prior to the antecedent (Doyle, 2009; Gregory & Ripski, 2008; Wynne, 2004).

Many of the most vocal proponents of behavior analysis point to studies which suggest the efficacy of behavior analysis with individuals diagnosed with autism spectrum disorder, a pervasive developmental disorder (Austin & Carr, 2000; Behavior Analyst Certification Board, n.d.; National Association of Cognitive-Behavioral Therapists, 2009; Rutherford et al., 2004). These studies show promise when specific applied behavior analysis is used under controlled conditions for a period of often several weeks. However, it is important to note that those individuals with autism spectrum disorder present with a highly unique constellation of behavioral variables, unlike the vast majority of their school-aged peers (Autism Society of America, n.d.). This is not to say that an applied behavior analysis program which may effectively change undesired behaviors in individuals with autism spectrum disorders should not be employed. However, we must remember that the current prevalence (incidence rates) for autism spectrum disorder is 1:150 (Autism Society of America, n.d.) or less than 1% (0.67%) of the school age population, and that there is not a body of research which indicates that applied behavior analysis alone produces positive, long-term outcomes with the other >99% of students composing the nation's school age population.

Many also question the treatment efficacy of applied behavior analysis on some of these specifically defined populations within the school setting. McIntyre et al. (2007) reviewed all school-based experimental studies conducted with individuals from birth to 18 years of age published between 1991 and 2005 in the *Journal of Applied Behavior Analysis*—the leading journal for applied behavior analysis. The vast majority (95%) of the 152 studies reviewed yielded an operational definition of the treatment variable, yet only 30% yielded treatment integrity data. Additionally, nearly half of the studies (45%) were found "to be at risk for treatment inaccuracies" (McIntyre et al., 2007, p. 659). The authors of this comprehensive recent study conclude with some alarming findings based upon thorough analysis.

> Treatment integrity data were more likely to be included in studies that used teachers, multiple treatment agents, or both. Although there was a substantial increase in reporting operational definitions of independent variables, results suggest that there was only a modest improvement in reported integrity over the past 30 years of *JABA* studies. (McIntyre et al., 2007, p. 659)

A thorough review of six major research databases (Academic Search Premier; PsycARTICLES; PsycINFO; ERIC; Social Sciences Abstract; and Humanities International Index) using the search term "applied behavior analysis" to identify all full-text scholarly (peer reviewed) journals published between June 2004 and June 2009 yielded 411 research studies. Not one of the 411 articles addressed general classroom management of student behavior—they addressed specific disorders (ex. pervasive developmental disorder, autism spectrum disorders, Asperger's disorder), narrowly defined behaviors (ex. sitting at a desk, transitioning from one activity to another, soliciting adult help), or a specific technique (ex. discrete-trials teaching, extinction, fading, shaping, reinforcement) (Austin & Carr, 2000; Rutherford et al., 2004).

Throughout this practitioner's decade of work with adolescents in a group counseling milieu, the limitations of a behavioral approach in helping them to more effectively manage anger were brought to the forefront. As a group facilitator of four to seven adolescents voluntarily participating in a closed, 8–10 week psycho-educational/support group focused on improving self-management of anger (anger management group), students invariably engaged in a process of refocusing their energies from the intended focus on the symptoms of their anger to the source of that anger—resisting attempts to focus on the behavioral manifestations of that anger without first allowing them to share their stories—their experiences and their perceptions regarding the source of that anger. As one group member once shared, "I must know that you care before I care about what you know"—a common retort reflecting the need or requirement for establishing specific, yet indefinable, relational qualities which must precede (and supersede) any interaction taking place between the two (or more) individuals involved in this type of dynamic. Essentially, the establishment of trust, respect and care is often a prerequisite to assuming a position of willingness to become open to change (behavioral or otherwise) being introduced, suggested, proposed, or recommended. In accordance with the principles of applied behavior analysis, this important process would not occur, as trust, respect and care are internal elements which are not amenable to manipulation due to their inherently intangible nature (cannot be observed and measured) (Austin & Carr, 2000; Rutherford et al., 2004).

The significant limitation of behavioral theory and behavior analysis identified here is a manifestation of the fundamental underlying tenet which fervently denies the existence of complex internal forces which cannot be measured, controlled, or even fully explained but are inextricably related to, and have a tremendous impact on, the behaviors humans engage in (Austin & Carr, 2000; Buckley, 1989; Doyle, 2009; Mader, 2009). The limitations imposed through a strictly behavioral analytic approach leave some important questions unanswered in the process of understanding human behavior.

The contention here is that behavior analysis is not wrong but that it is only half right. To incorporate both that which is measurable and observable as well as that which is not is vital in establishing a more complete understanding of human behavior. An expansive, more comprehensive understanding of the full context of human behavior empowers those working on behalf of change in behavior to more successfully effect the desired change (Gregory & Ripski, 2008; Rutherford et al., 2004; Walker, 2009; Wynne, 2004).

Studying the underlying factors of behavior is vitally important in understanding the etiology of behavior and is essential in the process of changing behavior, as to not include this important perspective offers only a superficial and incomplete view of human behavior. Furthermore, a behavioral approach to human behavior change is clearly limited in terms of creating meaningful long-term behavior change (Gregory & Ripski, 2008; Kohn, 2006; Wynne, 2004).

Research into human behavior is currently conducted through two distinctly unique paradigms (Rutherford et al., 2004). The quantitative paradigm—focused on the observable and measureable attributes of human behavior—is consistent with the methodologies employed in applied behavior analysis (Rutherford et al., 2004; Austin & Carr, 2000). The qualitative paradigm—focused on the perceptions, experiences, and meaning behind human behavior—is not a component of applied behavior analysis but is more commonly associated with a human-centered approach to human behavior change (Kohn, 2006; Mader, 2009; Doyle, 2009). The quantitative analysis of behavior helps us to better understand the explicit aspects or characteristics of human behavior, and the qualitative analysis of behavior helps us to better understand the implicit qualities or characteristics of human behavior. Both are important lenses with which to view the full scope of human behavior; however, the system of beliefs underlying behavior analysis does not recognize the role of qualitative analysis and categorically denies its existence, hence its utility (Association for Behavioral Analysis International, n.d., a and b; Austin & Carr, 2000). Quantitative analysis and qualitative analysis should not be viewed as mutually exclusive but as interdependent paradigms to facilitate a more thorough understanding of human behavior (Johnson, 1992). These two distinct paradigms are really two sides of the same coin. Until those who practice behavior analysis begin to acknowledge the qualitative paradigm, their understanding of human behavior is incomplete, and their practice limited.

However, the practice of cognitive-behavioral therapy is but one example of an approach which incorporates both the internal world of cognition as well as the external world of observable, measurable behavior, embracing the interdependent nature of the two constructs (National Association of Cognitive-Behavioral Therapists, n.d.). The National Association of Cognitive-Behavioral Therapists, a leading organization in this field, has chronicled a multitude of studies supporting the evidence-based foundations of this therapeutic approach which marry the theoretical basis of behavior theory with that of cognitive theory (National Association of Cognitive-Behavioral Therapists, n.d.). Limited success in the treatment of depression through the use of a strictly behavioral approach along with the cognitive revolution of the 1960s gave rise to cognitive-behavioral therapy as a distinct field in the 1980s (National Association of Cognitive-Behavioral Therapists, n.d.). The objective of this popular and relatively new psychological treatment approach is to identify and monitor thoughts, assumptions, beliefs, and behaviors that are associated with incapacitating negative emotions in an effort to replace or transcend them with more adaptive, constructive, and functional ones (National Association of Cognitive-Behavioral Therapists, n.d.). A major distinction between behavioral theory (upon which behavior analysis is based) and cognitive-behavioral theory is the acknowledgment, validation, use, and value placed upon thoughts and emotions within cognitive-behavioral theory.

Another approach to human behavior change which acknowledges the intrapersonal dynamics and immeasurable qualitative characteristics which underlie human behavior is the relational approach (also known as a person-centered approach, a human-centered approach, or a student-centered approach) (Doyle, 2009; Freiberg & Lamb, 2009; Gregory & Ripski, 2008; Kohn, 2006; Mader, 2009; Stemler, Elliott, Grigorenko, & Sternberg, 2006; Walker, 2009).

In a recent study on the dimensions of person-centered classroom management (a relational approach), Freiberg and Lamb (2009) found that "after decades of use, the behaviorist model has not caused significant changes in student behavior. Rather, it has limited the ability of the learner to become self-directed and self-disciplined..." (p. 100).

> Public opinion trends over the last five decades show that lack of discipline continues to be one of America's top public educational concerns. This trend suggests that alternatives to the traditional model are urgently needed. In this traditional model of classroom management, based on behaviorism and still common in some areas, discipline is teacher directed. Fifty years of research demonstrates that person-centered, pro-social classroom management may provide that alternative. Person-centered classrooms facilitate higher achievement, and have more positive learning environments with stronger teacher-student relationships than teacher-centered or traditional classrooms. (Freiberg & Lamb, 2009, p. 99)

Another relational approach to classroom management of student behavior—authoritative classroom management—is based upon the following four parenting styles and has been successfully implemented in several states (Walker, 2009):

> Authoritative parents expected mature behavior, used reason to gain compliance, and were warm and supportive. Other parents, labeled authoritarian, were also highly controlling and valued strict obedience but relied on coercion and were less nurturing. A third parenting configuration, permissive, involved few limits or demands, and moderate nurturing or even lack of involvement. Finally, there were neglectful parents, who offered low levels of both control and nurturance. (Walker, 2009)

> Consistent with research on parenting style, the best student outcomes were associated with an authoritative teaching style. Students in this classroom were confident, engaged, and made significant year-end achievement gains. These results likely stemmed from the authoritative teacher's use of positive instructional practices within a highly controlling and nurturing context. This teacher made consistent

demands for compliance and frequent demands for self-management. She also made twice as many nurturing statements as her teacher peers. (Walker, 2009)

It is clear that a non-behavioral approach to the classroom management of student behavior is founded upon a large body of research demonstrating the efficacy of a more student-centered, relational approach to managing behavior (Doyle, 2009; Walker, 2009). Furthermore, "the ability to establish and maintain positive relationships with students, marked by caring, understanding and trust, has consistently been shown to foster student motivation and engagement" (Stemler, et al., 2006, p. 101). When students are motivated and engaged, they are less likely to display inappropriate behavior.

In a recent study, Schussler (2009) discovered that teachers can manage classrooms in such a way that stimulates intellectual engagement in disengaged students. These findings are based on the premise that engaged students are less likely to display inappropriate behavior.

> Teachers create an environment conducive to intellectual engagement when students perceive: a) that there are opportunities for them to succeed, b) that flexible avenues exist through which learning can occur, and c) that they are respected as learners because teachers convey the belief that students are capable of learning. When teachers purposefully manage classrooms so that these elements intersect optimally, students perceive that they are known and valued. Furthermore, opportunities for success, flexibility, and respect generally are present when teachers challenge their students at appropriate levels, provide academic support, use instructional techniques that convey excitement for the content, and make learning relevant. (Schussler, 2009, p. 114)

In a related study investigating a relational approach, it was found "that teachers who consider relationships with students important for their classroom discipline are more likely to have greater trust and cooperation from students who have a history of disciplinary infractions" (Gregory & Ripski, 2008, p. 337). Through a relational approach to classroom management using a meditational model, it was found that the most important factor in minimizing disciplinary issues was student perception of teachers as trustworthy, and that teachers can "earn the trust and cooperation of students if they use relationship building to prevent discipline problems" (Gregory & Ripski, 2008, p. 337).

Even the use of simple strategies such as the Classroom Check-Up—a classwide teacher consultation model—has had a positive impact on disruptive classroom behavior. Results from the use of this interactive/consultative model show an increase in teacher praise directed at students and a decrease in disruptive student behavior. "The results are encouraging because they suggest that consultation at the classroom level can create meaningful teacher and student behavior change" (Reinke et al., 2008, p. 41).

In more than 20 years of experience working across the complete continuum of educational settings, with preschoolers to adults, in programs spanning the full range of human needs, this practitioner has found that the transformative process of significant, long-term behavior change in the vast majority of students cannot be achieved through an exclusively behaviorally based approach. The current trend to view human behavior change from a strictly behavioral perspective and approach appears grounded in an over-simplistic view of human behavior which has evolved from the flawed and seemingly arrogant assumption that even the most complex of human behaviors can be completely understood through observation and measurement. This incomplete perspective does not account for the multitude of complex human variables such as intrinsic motivation, will, and meaning, which are not easily measured or controlled and are oftentimes unpredictable. Furthermore, it does not account for the subtleties, nuances, and idiosyncratic characteristics which contribute to human behavior and therefore are vital to both our understanding of human behavior and our efforts to change or improve human behavior. Consequently, a strictly behavioral approach to an undesired behavior in a typical student rarely results in long-term behavior change unless the intangible, intrinsic, and oftentimes, immeasurable characteristics of the human spirit such as will, values, and meaning are identified and addressed as viable factors in the process of long-term behavior change.

Behaviorism and behavior analysis can collectively be referred to as the science of behavior change; there is also the art of behavior change. The art of behavior change lies in the relationships built between people. Relationships built upon respect and trust in which connections are built—connections which may not always be observable or measurable—upon trust, respect, commitment, and caring.

Exemplary teachers, coaches, parents, and literally anyone working with others to help facilitate their growth and improvement rely not only on behavioral strategies and techniques consistent with the science of teaching/learning but have also mastered the art of their craft through a process of building relationships which significantly (and oftentimes immeasurably) affect motivation, receptivity, focus, and commitment.

Our most talented and effective coaches are not successful simply because of the natural talent of their players, the specific strategies they use, or the training program they have implemented. They are successful because of their ability to touch the spirit of their athletes in a way that inspires change (growth and improvement). Those who adhere strictly to behavior analysis struggle to find something observable and measurable in the dynamic, abstract relationships created between these coaches and their athletes when none exists. The relationship is not concrete; it is art. This dynamic is evidenced routinely in the print and television media, as we see real examples of this consistently. It is evidenced in real-life stories which have been immortalized on the big screen such as *Angels in the Outfield, Remember the Titans, The Rookie, Rudy, Hoosiers, Million Dollar Baby,* and *Believe in Me.*

We also see this dynamic play out in classrooms everywhere, every day, where, although teachers may use behavioral strategies and techniques, their approach is based more upon the care, commitment, respect, and trust—the relationship—they build with their students. This can be seen in classrooms everywhere in which dedicated teachers are committed not to teaching subjects (reading, writing, or math), but to teaching students, and where the emphasis is not on teaching but on learning. Take the time to observe this: it is art. It is also indescribable and generally immeasurable or easily distilled to technical prowess. Many popular movies have brought such true stories to life such as *Stand and Deliver, Mr. Holland's Opus, Lean on Me,* and *The Dead Poets Society.*

Kohn (1999; 2006) speaks to art of pedagogy when he shares his realization of the great divide between teaching the subject matter and students learning the subject matter.

> Once I was out of the classroom, I came to understand that a course is created *for* and *with* a particular group of students. I didn't see it that way before because I wasn't thinking about learning, only about teaching. I was trying to find the most efficient way of giving students the knowledge and skills I already had, which meant that I was treating the students as interchangeable receptacles—rows of wide-open bird beaks waiting for worms, if you will. (Kohn, 1999, p. 13)

Kohn also unveils the true nature of a behavioral approach in his scathing indictment of the behavior control programs popularly implemented in many of our nation's classrooms.

Teachers are often encouraged to rely on rewards rather than punishments, but research suggests that carrots can be just as counterproductive as sticks. Both are forms of manipulation, and neither can produce anything beyond temporary compliance. Students who see themselves as doing an assignment in order to receive a gold star, an A, or an award are actually less likely to develop an interest in the subject matter or to challenge themselves to do their best. By the same token, stickers, popcorn parties, and even praise give students no reason to act responsibly when there is no longer a goody to be gained from doing so. For students to become lifelong learners and good people, we need to work *with* them rather than using techniques like rewards and punishments, which merely do things *to* them. (Kohn, 2006, p. 44)

Mader (2009) found that external incentives have a clearly deleterious effect on internal motivation and overall classroom management in a recent study.

These findings have special relevance to classroom teaching, especially concerning the relationship between contingent rewards and internal motivation: 1) Contingent rewards have the most potential for interfering with internal motivation. (Contingent rewards, as opposed to spontaneous praise or celebration, are those promised in advance if certain conditions are met.); 2) Contingent rewards may create a performance, rather than a process, orientation. (When we are promised rewards for completing a project successfully, we tend to take fewer risks in order to make sure that we succeed—even though we often learn more from our mistakes than our successes.); 3) Contingent rewards may reduce the psychological safety necessary for honest dialogue about personal beliefs and, perhaps, failings. (It is hard enough to share personal doubts at all, let alone with the person who may grant or withhold rewards.); 4) Contingent rewards may diminish the value of a task and thus discourage interest. (If someone has to reward us for doing something, the task must not be very interesting.); 5) Contingent rewards may lose their power when withdrawn. (Rare is the teacher who hasn't heard, "But what's the reward?"); and 6) Contingent rewards may actually serve as de-motivators when individuals are already interested in a topic. (Some people love their work so much they would do it for free, but most probably would not once they began getting paid for it.)(Mader, 2009, p. 148)

The dynamic or construct of personal change outside of the constraints of applied behaviorism is evident in homes, schools, and organizations across the planet. These examples transcend behavioral tenets and occur across political, geographic, cultural, and socioeconomic boundaries. One only needs to observe carefully in one's own little corner of the world to see example after example of the transformative process that takes place between people where oftentimes both the subject of change as well as the catalyst of change experience transcendent change. A plethora of dramatized examples have been chronicled in movies such as *Chariots of Fire, Gandhi, Braveheart,* and *Gladiator.*

American education has always seemed to lean towards pragmatic solutions to issues, and much of today's pragmatic ideas about human behavior and motivation are narrowly rooted in behaviorist theory from the late nineteenth and early twentieth century. To fully meet the needs of American school children, we must move beyond the archaic and obsolete. This does not mean that we should let go of those principles which still work, nor does it mean that we should hold on to them simply out of tradition and fear of change. What this does mean is that we must identify and exemplify those principles, ideas, and methods from the past which remain useful and continue to demonstrate value, while also incorporating new principles, ideas, and methods which also prove useful and demonstrate value. Ironically, it is oftentimes our resistance to change which holds us captive, not allowing us to improve upon current principles, ideas, and methods and ultimately limiting our effectiveness in meeting the needs of our nation's school children.

It is clearly evident that behavior analysis offers efficacious methodologies which benefit our nation's school children. It is also clearly evident that a non-behavioral, relational approach to behavior has also been found to have tremendous value to these children. Unfortunately, it is our collective inability to embrace the value in both—by engaging in dichotomous either/or thinking and rejecting both/and thinking—which constrains our ability to fully intervene on behalf of our nation's school children. Until we change our thinking, thereby our behavior, by acknowledging that both the measurable and observable and that which is not are vitally important in understanding the full scope of human behavior, that both quantitative and qualitative approaches to understanding and changing human behavior have merit, and that both behavioral and relational approaches to human behavior change have treatment efficacy, we will fail to fully meet children's behavioral needs. However, once we embrace the interdependent nature of a relational-behavioral approach in addressing the behaviors of school children, we will transcend the divisive, politicized effects which have polarized the issue of behavior change between two major distinct schools of thought, and empower ourselves—free from an emotional attachment to either approach—to employ the full array of tools and methodologies to most effectively meet the needs of our nation's children.

REFERENCES

Association for Behavioral Analysis International (n.d., a). *Frequently Asked Questions*. Retrieved January 7, 2009, from http://www.abainternational.org/aba.asp.html

Association for Behavioral Analysis International (n.d., b). *Overview of ABA International*. Retrieved January 7, 2009, from http://www.abainternational.org/aba.asp.html

Austin, J., & Carr, J.E. (2000). *Handbook of applied behavior analysis*. Reno, NV: Context Press Autism Society of America (n.d.). *About Autism*. Retrieved February 22, 2009, from http://www.autism-society.org/site

Behavior Analyst Certification Board (n.d.). *About BACB*. Retrieved February 14, 2009, from http://www.bacb.com/cues/frame_about.html

Bowen, J., Jenson, W.R., & Clark, E. (2003). *School-based interventions for students with behavior problems*. New York: Springer Publishing Company.

Buckley, K.W. (1989). *Mechanical man: John B. Watson and the beginnings of behaviorism*. New York: The Guilford Press.

Crone, D.A., Horner, R.H., & Hawken, L.S. (2003). *Responding to problem behavior in schools: The behavior education program*. New York: The Guilford Press.

Doyle, W. (2009). Situated practice: A reflection on person-centered classroom management. *Theory into Practice, 48*(2), 156–159.

Freiberg, H.J., & Lamb, S.M. (2009). Dimensions of person-centered classroom management. *Theory into Practice, 48*(2), 99–105.

Gregory, A., & Ripski, M.B. (2008). Adolescent trust in teachers: Implications for behavior in the high school classroom. *School Psychology Review, 37*(3), 337–353.

Johnson, B. (1992). *Polarity management: Identifying and managing unsolvable problems*. Amherst, MA: HRD Press, Inc.

Kohn, A. (1999). *Punished by rewards: The trouble with gold stars, incentive plans, A's, praise, and other bribes*. Boston: Houghton Mifflin.

Kohn, A. (2006). *Beyond discipline: From compliance to community*. Alexandria, VA: Association for Supervision and Curriculum Development.

Mader, C.E. (2009). "I will never teach the old way again": Classroom management and external incentives. *Theory into Practice, 48*(2), 147–155.

Maslow, A.H. (1987). *Motivation and personality*. New York: HarperCollins Publishers.

McIntyre, L.L., Gresham, F.M., DiGennaro, F.D., & Reed, D.D. (2007). Treatment integrity of school-based interventions with children in the *Journal of Applied Behavior Analysis* 1991–2005. *Journal of Applied Behavior Analysis, 40*(4), 659–672.

National Association of Cognitive-Behavioral Therapists (n.d.). *Evidenced Based Therapy.* Retrieved February 22, 2009, from http://www.nacbt.org/evidenced-based-therapy.htm

Reinke, W.M., Lewis-Palmer, T., & Merrell, K. (2008). The classroom check-up: A classwide teacher consultation model for increasing praise and decreasing disruptive behavior. *School Psychology Review, 37*(3), 315–332.

Rutherford, R.B., Quinn, M.M., & Mathur, S.R. (2004). *Handbook of research in emotional and behavioral disorders.* New York: Guilford Press.

Schussler, D.L. (2009). Beyond content: How teachers manage classrooms to facilitate intellectual engagement for disengaged students. *Theory into Practice, 48*(2), 114–121.

Stemler, S.E., Elliott, J.G., Grigorenko, E.L., & Sternberg, R.J. (2006). There's more to teaching than instruction: Seven strategies for dealing with the practical side of teaching. *Educational Studies, 32*(1), 101–118.

Walker, J.M.T. (2009). Authoritative classroom management: How control and nurturance work together. *Theory into Practice, 48*(2), 122–129.

Wynne, L. (2004). The missing theory: Why behavior analysis has little impact on voluntary adult outpatient services. *Ethical Human Psychology and Psychiatry, 6*(2), 135–146.

SECTION THREE
Piaget and Vygotsky

EIGHT

Dewey's Dynamic Integration of Vygotsky and Piaget

Susan Jean Mayer

Contrary to the assumptions of those who pair Dewey and Piaget based on progressivism's recent history, Dewey shared broader concerns with Vygotsky (whose work he never read). Both Dewey and Vygotsky emphasized the role of cultural forms and meanings in perpetuating higher forms of human thought, whereas Piaget focused on the role played by logical and mathematical reasoning. On the other hand, with Piaget, Dewey emphasized the nurture of independent reasoning central to the liberal Protestant heritage the two men shared. Indeed, Dewey's broad theorizing of democracy's implications for schooling can be seen to integrate the research emphases of the two psychologists.

INTRODUCTION

It has become a fashion among some to oppose progressive educational theory, associated with the scholarship of Dewey and Piaget, with a concern for the pedagogical perpetuation of cultural forms and understandings, currently emphasized by those working within the Vygotskian tradition. Kieran Egan's (2002) recent critique of progressivism may provide the boldest iteration of such reasoning, yet related arguments can be found elsewhere (see, e.g., Kozulin, 1998). In other academic quarters, scholars debate what of Dewey might be claimed as support for a sociocultural tradition that proceeds primarily in Vygotsky's name (See, e.g., Glassman, 2001, 3–14; 2002, 16–20; O'Brien, 2002, 16–20; Prawat, 2002, 16–20).

These contrasting debates are by no means arcane or irrelevant to languishing issues of school reform. Cogent analysis of the intersections between the scholarship of Dewey, Vygotsky, and Piaget promises to inform a set of issues that lies at the very heart of democratic learning and curriculum theory. In particular, Dewey, a philosopher attuned to the contributions of psychology, can help educators in their ongoing struggles to theorize the practical implications of Vygotsky and Piaget for democratic classrooms.

Though often misinterpreted in this regard, Dewey's work deftly negotiates a defining democratic tension between the need to perpetuate established cultural forms and understandings, on the one hand, and the need to foster diverse and novel ideas and perspectives, on the other. As I discuss below, this tension underpins Dewey's central insights about how to build a democratic nation from diverse peoples. For Dewey held that the children of democracies must be apprenticed into collaborative meaning-making processes; they must be allowed to appropriate and reinvent, in terms that they can understand, the practical methods and processes currently in use within their wider society. Rote recapitulation of established material, then, could not even ensure students' adequate mastery of essential cultural content and forms.

Piaget, in seeking to track the development of children's thought, created a dynamic method capable of uncovering the evolving logics of a child's reasoning (Mayer, 2005, pp. 362–382). Naturally, Piagetian findings regarding the distinctive perceptions and assumptions of children were widely seen as supporting established progressive arguments regarding the need for educators to attend to diverse perspectives. Impressed by Piaget's project, Vygotsky responded with investigations into the ways in which existing cultural tools and understandings also necessarily challenge and structure children's nascent thought (Vygotsky, 1986, pp. 12–57). Dewey, intent on explicating democracy's implications for schooling, sought to synthesize most of the underlying philosophical and psychological concerns that shaped both lines of research.

Of the two psychologists, however, it was Vygotsky who grappled with the questions about the perpetuation and advancement of cultural forms that Dewey found central. Dewey and Vygotsky both sought to root a notion of cultural progress within the concrete realities of shared human purposes and social means: human meanings would deepen in a useful and rewarding manner as a function of profound cultural appropriation and renewal. Although the two men emphasized different aspects of this project, their shared attention to the role culture must play in advancing human understanding suggests the deep theoretical intersections that underlay their work.

These intersections are clearly evidenced in the attention that both theorists paid to the nature of learning and of education. Both Dewey and Vygotsky focused on the role of cultural activity in the elevation of human thought and looked to schools to engender an authentic appreciation of the methods and tools that they saw as integral to the work of building their changing nations—an increasingly diverse and industrial America and a postrevolutionary Soviet Union, respectively. Although Piaget did study the role that social interactions play in destabilizing narrow and naive reasoning, his research never focused on the influences of cultural forms per se.[1]

Despite this significant distinction between Piaget's project and the work of Dewey and Vygotsky, one must bear in mind the profound assumptions the three men shared. Although all three worked within different cultural milieus, each scholar questioned how children might be taught to think in new ways and so move beyond lockstep reenactment of the known. Each felt that the necessary quality of intellectual engagement could only be nurtured by giving children developmentally appropriate opportunities to make sense of their worlds in conversation with others.

As I have noted elsewhere, Dewey and Piaget were both raised as liberal Protestants: each emphasized the nurture of independent reasoning central to that heritage (Mayer, 2006; see also Vidal, 1987). As discussed here, Dewey and Vygotsky both pointed toward established cultural forms as the scaffolding upon which human reasoning must climb. Most fundamentally, however, all three theorists looked to the increased vitality and capacity of human intelligence as the only potential source of the social progress they all desired.

SIMILARITIES BETWEEN DEWEY AND VYGOTSKY

Research on the psychological development of individuals has been interwoven with concerns over humanity's prospects since psychology first organized itself into a discipline in Darwin's tumultuous wake (Plotkin, 2004; Richards, 1987). Although this may seem a wide net to cast here, the careers of both Dewey and Vygotsky must be seen in relation to this early disciplinary interest in the links between individual development and social progress. Both scholars' attention to educational method derived from a conviction that the proper nurture of children's intellects would help to build the enlightened social and political orders that each believed his nation promised. Each therefore sought to theorize a new kind of teaching that could elevate the quality of thought of all, elevating the character of all cultural expression in turn.

These shared assumptions and purposes resulted from multiple mingled strains of influence, none more significant than that of Hegel. Well beyond the Darwinian backdrop, Dewey and Vygotsky shared enduring aspects of the Hegelian worldview. Whereas Piaget bound a faith in humanity's forward momentum to the species' evolved capacity for logic and math (Chapman, 1986, pp. 181–194), Dewey and Vygotsky bound their faith in a given society's capacity for historical advancement to the efficacy and sensitivity of that society's cultural resources. For both Dewey and Vygotsky, cultural advancement represented a more diffuse and complex affair and drew upon meanings of every kind.

Kozulin (1990) has identified three key aspects of Hegel's influence on Vygotsky, all of which, I will argue, were shared by Dewey. First, though, it may be useful to remark on the divergent political traditions through which each scholar found his way to Hegel, as these traditions—Marxism and liberal democracy—are opposed in some regards and yet align in the ways that matter here.

Dewey rejected Marxism's faith in historically determined processes and in the revolutionary potential of violent class struggle.[2] As a young scholar, Dewey had shed his own fond attachments to absolutist storylines and had grown averse to their implications for social and political theory.[3] Dewey's radically democratic vision was rooted in the belief that any nation set on greater social equality must enlighten both capitalist and worker.

For Vygotsky, in contrast, the toppling of despotism in the name of humanity's greater equality and fraternity had been ushered in by the political insights of Marx. The banner of Marx provided Vygotsky with a bright (albeit brief) moment of political possibility and with what Vygotsky may well have viewed as historical pretext for his grand overthrow of psychological reductionism.

For the majority of the limited years in which Vygotsky worked as a research psychologist, the revolution had appeared to have arrived (Bruner, 1997, pp. 63–73).

Vygotsky's thinking, however, drew deeply on Western psychological and philosophical traditions: fanatic and antihistoric party lines no more suited Vygotsky's nuanced sensibility than Dewey's. Indeed, Vygotsky was raised within a Jewish tradition of textual interpretation[4] and later studied linguistics and literary theory amidst Russia's cataclysmic transition from royal rule to socialist state. While such an upbringing may have fostered a more tolerant attitude toward Marxist doctrine, Vygotsky's intellectual background did not lend itself to simple social prescription or to radical ideological impositions of any kind. Societies may be reborn, but only in relationship to cultural meanings that derive their value from historically rooted texts and traditions.

From within their disparate cultural contexts, then, both Dewey and Vygotsky studied their Hegel. Along with many others, both scholars found their hopes for a historical progression articulated there; in the company of a considerably fewer number, both then turned to the work of grounding those hopes in the material conditions of humanity. In Vygotsky's case, he naturally traced this effort to Marx. In Dewey's case, this effort was supported through his close personal and professional association with George Herbert Mead.

Unlike Dewey, Mead had spent several postgraduate years in Germany, studying with the famed psychologist Wilhelm Wundt. Germany was not only the intellectual epicenter of experimental psychology at the time, but also of post-Hegelian thought; and Mead became interested in the social theory of one of Marx's contemporaries, Ferdinand Lassalle.[5] Mead was to extend Wundt's attention to the communicative implications of gesture into a social theory of consciousness that served Dewey's purposes beautifully (Scheffler, 1974).

Individual identities, Mead proposed, were entirely shaped by interpersonal interactions and the signs—and sign systems, such as language—that made communication possible. Hegel's notion that social institutions represented an ideal mind could be replaced then by the pragmatic notion that mind itself emerges from the material negotiations that comprise social interaction. Dewey found Mead's work so compelling that he eventually ceded the psychological field to his friend: He felt he would be able to gather all he needed from Mead's social psychology.[6]

Hegel's texts are vast, complex, and arguably indeterminate in even their central meanings (Bencivenga, 2000; Desmond, 1992; Olson, 1992). Yet Dewey and Vygotsky held to several related themes within Hegel, Dewey through the lens of Mead, Vygotsky of Marx. Below, I consider the three Hegelian influences on Vygotsky that Kozulin identified relative first to Dewey and then to Vygotsky (Kozulin, 1990, p. 18):

- The historical nature of the human being;
- The role of work and the notion of "psychological tools";
- The Hegelian dialectic of Becoming.

THE HISTORICAL NATURE OF THE HUMAN BEING

Dewey sought to position all of his philosophical premises and pedagogical claims within the historic sweep of human culture and, more immediately, within the narrative of Western civilization. At the most basic level of consideration, human history provided the grounds from which Dewey wrested the central tenets of his philosophy of knowledge.

> Man who lives in a world of hazards is compelled to seek for security. He has sought to attain it in two ways. One of them began with an attempt to propitiate the powers which environ him and determine his destiny....The other course is to invent arts and by their means turn the powers of nature to account; man constructs a fortress out of the very conditions and forces which threaten him. He builds shelters, weaves garments, makes flame his friend instead of his enemy, and grows into the complicated arts of associated living. (1929/1960, p. 3)

Dewey also identified a specific range of intellectual possibilities that had been constructed by Western civilization and were therefore tied to the material conditions and cultural dynamics of the moment (1916/1944; 1920/1957). Dewey's reasoning at both the more basic and this more proximate level helped to shape his diagnoses of and prescriptions for modern democratic societies and schools.

> Just as theories of knowing that developed prior to the existence of scientific inquiry provide no pattern or model for a theory of knowing based upon the present actual conduct of inquiry, so the earlier systems reflect both pre-scientific views of the natural world and also the pre-technological state of industry and the pre-democratic state of politics of the period when their doctrines took form. (1920/1957, p. ix)

Vygotsky (1986) focused his historical lens on the evolving capacities of language and on the complex relationship between human thought and the sign systems that both enable and express that thought. Drawing upon the work of Köhler and other zoologically minded psychologists of the time, Vygotsky pursued the relationship between thought and speech into both the earliest days of human civilization and into the first conscious phases of an individual's psychological development.

> Verbal thought is not an innate, natural form of behavior, but is determined by a historical-cultural process and has specific properties and laws that cannot be found in the natural forms of thought and speech. Once we acknowledge the historical character of verbal thought, we must consider it subject to all the premises of historical materialism, which are valid for any historical phenomenon in human society. (1986, pp. 94–95)

For both theorists, historic human conditions not only served to determine broad cultural possibilities: they also informed the work of schools in a direct manner. The dilemmas of one's historical moment were a function of the tension between what one's culture had adequately articulated and what now lay in wait just beyond the assurances of such understandings. Only children's active appropriation of those shared understandings could provide the generative framework necessary for their minds to envision relevant new interpretations and possibilities.

One must also remember that, in broad terms, Vygotsky and Dewey did share in a particular historical moment within Western thought. Although Dewey did not read Vygotsky's work (which had not yet been translated into English), he traveled to the Soviet Union in the 1920s, where schools were exploring the implications of Pragmatism in the nation's early years. Dewey's early works were among those being translated and published within Vygotsky's milieu at this time (Cole, 1996). As Popkewitz has pointed out, although the narrative terms and images of their two cultures overlapped in some ways and differed in others, Dewey's and Vygotsky's practical visions for schools more or less aligned (1998).

THE ROLE OF WORK AND THE NOTION OF PSYCHOLOGICAL TOOLS

Dewey, Vygotsky, and their intellectual heirs in the field of education have all concerned themselves with the processes through which children come to appropriate the conceptual and material means of their cultures.[7] Arguments in *The School and Society,* particularly the chapter on "The
Psychology of Occupations," establish the primacy of work as a civilizing force in Dewey's mind.

> It does not follow that all instincts are of equal value, or that we do not inherit many instincts which
> need transformation, rather than satisfaction, in order to be useful in life. But the instincts which find
> their conscious outlet and expression in occupation are bound to be of an exceedingly fundamental
> and permanent type…
>
> However, these interests as [occupations] develop in the child not only recapitulate past important
> activities of the race, but reproduce those of the child's present environment.…He comes in contact
> with facts that have no meaning, except in reference to them. Take these things out of the present social
> life and see how little would remain—and this not only on the material side, but as regards intellectual,
> aesthetic, and moral activities, for these are largely and necessarily bound up with occupations. (1900
> & 1902/1990, pp. 136–137)

Dewey spoke of the individual's "appropriation" of cultural tools and purposes, language
closely associated with the Vygotskian tradition (Wertsch, 1998, p. 138). Though rooted in Dewey's
lifelong preoccupation with democratic political forms, Dewey's insistence that all citizens must
lay claim to the means and purposes of cultural production clearly aligns with Marxist concerns
regarding the dignity of work and the human need to identify with the results of one's labor. As
Dewey put it:

> A society is a number of people held together because they are working along common lines, in a
> common spirit, and with reference to common aims. The common needs and aims demand a growing
> interchange of thought and growing unity of sympathetic feeling. The radical reason that the pres-
> ent school cannot organize itself as a natural social unit is because just this element of common and
> productive activity is absent. (1900 & 1902/1990, p. 14)

Dewey's principal argument here is that the social dynamism needed to nurture a vibrant
society's aims and means must be kindled within schools. Lest I risk the impression, so frequently
gathered from cursory readings of Dewey, that Dewey cared more about spirit than tools, however, I cite at some length below from *The Child and the Curriculum,* Dewey's most explicit rebut-
tal to such mis-readings. For Dewey, common spirit could only live as a function of common
understandings and methods.

> On the face of it, the various studies, arithmetic, geography, language, botany, etc., are themselves
> experience—they are that of the race. They embody the cumulative outcome of the efforts, the striv-
> ings, and the successes of the human race generation after generation. They present this, not as a mere
> accumulation, not as a miscellaneous heap of separate bits of experience, but in some organized and
> systematized way—that is, as reflectively formulated.
>
> Hence, the facts and truths that enter into the child's present experience, and those contained in the
> subject-matter of studies are the initial and final terms of one reality. To oppose one to the other is
> to oppose the infancy and maturity of the same growing life: it is to set the moving tendency and the
> final result of the same process over against each other; it is to hold that the nature and the destiny of
> the child war with each other. (1900 & 1902/1990, p. 190)

Dewey is speaking here—in general terms—about what Vygotsky termed "scientific" and "spontaneous" concepts. The "facts and truths...contained in the subject-matter of studies," which Dewey claims represent the child's "destiny," are, in Vygotsky's language, "scientific concepts."[8] The "truths that enter into the child's present experience" result from a child's spontaneous thought, the course of which Piaget strove to document. Below, Vygotsky speaks of the organizing influences of what Dewey calls "reflectively formulated" knowledge above.

> School instruction induces the generalizing kind of perception and thus plays a decisive role in making the child conscious of his own mental processes. Scientific concepts, with their hierarchical system of interrelation, seem to be the medium within which awareness and mastery first develop, to be trans-ferred later to other concepts and other areas of thought. Reflective consciousness comes to the child through the portals of scientific concepts. (1986, p. 171)

Vygotsky's background in linguistics and in literary analysis set the stage for a lifelong pre-occupation with the role words might play, not only in the psychological development of the young, but also in the liberation of humanity. From Marx's general concern with the material means of labor—leading in Marx's case to an analysis of industrial economic relations—Vygotsky identified language as the defining human tool, the one that supported the inter-subjectivity that made abstract reflection itself possible (Wertsch, 1985). Consequently, and though the influences of Marx and Hegel on Vygotsky are often cited in one breath, Vygotsky can most often be seen moving through Marx to Hegel—and to Hegel's concern with concepts—in his major works (1978; 1986).

For example, Vygotsky ends his final work, *Thought and Language,* with discussion of several excerpts from plays and poetry and with this mention of Hegel:

> The relation between thought and word is a living process; thought is born through words. A word devoid of thought is a dead thing:
>
> > . . . *and like bees in the deserted hive*
> > *The dead words have a rotten smell.*
> > —N. Gumilev
>
> But thought that fails to realize itself in words also remains a "Stygian shadow" [O. Mandelstam]. Hegel considered word as a Being animated by thought. This Being is absolutely essential for our thinking. (1986, p. 255)

Vygotsky's inspired project was to study the development of this Being and the play of its possibilities in the world. Ironically, between Dewey and Vygotsky, the Marxist psychologist arguably proves the more poetic of the two. For although both Vygotsky's focus on semiotics and shared meanings and Dewey's focus on experience and shared purposes were both rooted in the realities of human activity, Dewey's focus can be seen to represent the more elemental and, indeed, the more material set of concerns.[9]

THE HEGELIAN DIALECTIC OF BECOMING

Kozulin also finds Hegelian influence in Vygotsky's commitment to studying learning and development as processes rather than as a series of discrete performances or static states.[10] In considering this claim, one needs to recall that both Dewey and Piaget shared this commitment and that process-oriented models and methods have multiple sources in psychology and in the Western intellectual tradition more generally.[11] Particularly after Darwin, traditional philosophical questions regarding human means and purposes came to be cast in terms of biological and evolutionary processes (Persons, 1950; Richards, 1987).

Certainly, though, Hegel's scholarship continued to play a formative role within these deliberations (Kojève, 1969). Given the care with which both Vygotsky and Dewey read Hegel, Hegel's central notion of Becoming would have likely informed their sensibilities in this regard.[12] Here is a sample of Hegel's language on Becoming:

> The readiest example is Becoming. Every one has a mental idea of Becoming, and will even allow that it is one idea: he will further allow that, when it is analysed, it involves the attribute of Being, and also what is the very reverse of Being, viz. Nothing: and that these two attributes lie undivided in the one idea: so that Becoming is the unity of Being and Nothing. (1873/1975, p. 130)

Although Dewey wrote less on learning science and its methods than did the two psychologists, he called for methods that could study learning as it unfolded (Dewey, 1928/1988; Mayer, 2007). Dewey understood that the static psychometric measures that loom so large within schools today could characterize little of what he sought when he spoke of the rewards of educational experience. He believed that meaningful educational experience, like all experience, is situated and relational; novel juxtapositions generate new qualities of coherence that shift and elevate one's relationship with the world. Below, Dewey speaks of art as experience, but what he says applies in his mind to all true *experiences,* if not to all *experience.*

> Because of continuous merging, there are no holes, mechanical junctions, and dead centers when we have *an* experience. There are pauses, places of rest, but they punctuate and define the quality of movement. They sum up what has been undergone and prevent its dissipation and idle evaporation. Continued acceleration is breathless and prevents parts from gaining distinction. In a work of art, different acts, episodes, occurrences melt and fuse into unity, and yet do not disappear and lose their own character as they do so—(1934/2005, p. 38)

With such language, Dewey strives to evoke a process that subsumes conceptual oppositions—including any absolute distinction between "inner" and "outer" reality—within a greater multidimensional whole. Garrison, in contrasting Dewey's conceptualization of learning with that of Leont'ev (who advanced the Vygotskian research tradition after his mentor's death) argues that Dewey's theory of "trans-action" actually goes further than Leont'ev's in transcending the binary between knower and known (2001). Garrison quotes Vygotsky's work, *Mind in Society,*[13] in order to locate the origins of what he identifies as a continuing Vygotskian tendency to speak of two separate realities that must be mediated, rather than one continuous reality that might be analyzed in various ways in addressing differing purposes.[14] Whether or not such differences of linguistic emphasis result primarily from the analytic demands of psychological research (Miettinen, 2001), Garrison's discussion serves to elucidate Dewey's apprehension of human experience as seamless and dynamic.

Both Dewey (1988) and Vygotsky (1986) also voiced reservations regarding the extent to which psychology could truly be considered a naturalistic science given science's traditional emphases on immutable laws and static formulas. For both scholars, the study of learning and development entailed methods that could move with a child's emerging meanings and that could sensitively mediate between those meanings and an adult's understandings.

While Dewey, as an educator, could call for the study of learning as it unfolded within the context of progressive schools, Vygotsky faced the challenge of inspiring learning within an experimental setting.

> Our method may be called experimental-developmental in the sense that it artificially provokes or creates a process of psychological development. This approach is equally appropriate to the basic aim of dynamic analysis. If we replace object analysis by process analysis, then the basic task of research obviously becomes a reconstruction of each stage in the development of the process: the process must be turned back to its initial stages. (Vygotsky, 1978, pp. 61–62)

For both Dewey and Vygotsky, learning and development were interwoven with each other and the social and material worlds in complicated ways. This complexity did not suggest, however, that methodical studies of learning and development were not possible or necessary, quite to the contrary. The considerable challenges did imply, however, that imaginative methods would be required. Here Vygotsky sums up his introductory section on method in *Mind in Society:*

> *To study something historically means to study it in the process of change:* that is the dialectical method's basic demand. To encompass in research the process of a given thing's development in all its phases and changes—from birth to death—fundamentally means to discover its nature, its essence, for "it is only in movement that a body shows what it is." Thus the historical study of behavior is not an auxiliary aspect of theoretical study, but rather forms its very base. (1978, pp. 64–65)

DEWEY AS MEDIATOR BETWEEN VYGOTSKY AND PIAGET

The disciplinary differences between Dewey's role as a philosopher and Vygotsky's and Piaget's roles as psychologists naturally positions Dewey as a potential synthesizer of the others' scholarship. Although Vygotsky was more the sweeping theorist and less the exacting experimentalist than Piaget, he nonetheless placed his work in conversation with that of Piaget and other developmental researchers, framing the empirical studies that would speak to that world. The time-consuming research that supports scientific theorizing naturally narrows the scope of scientific debate; especially fertile lines of investigation, such as Piaget's, can consume entire careers.

In reflecting on the integrative possibilities of Dewey's vision, it is useful to revisit the organizing purposes of each scholar's project. Again, Piaget sought to explore the ways in which children, in reckoning with material realities, come to construct logical and mathematical reasoning over time.[15] The observation of his close colleague, Bärbel Inhelder, that Piaget was "a zoologist by training, an epistemologist by vocation and a logician by method" well conveys not only the principal dynamics of Piaget's work but also their disciplinary origins.[16]

Of the three theorists, only Piaget drew on Neo-Platonic notions of a transcendent rationality: his oeuvre places great store in the transformative potential of a socially mediated, biologically grounded propensity to discover logical and mathematical forms. In Piaget's view, Western culture was now capable of moving beyond centuries of unconsidered adherence to inherited myths and assumptions and in relation, instead, to a transparent rationality capable of imagining and enacting the greatest good for the greatest number. Although Dewey and Vygotsky shared related hopes, neither of them placed formal logic and mathematical reasoning in so pivotal a role.

In responding to Piaget's project, Vygotsky objected to Piaget's exclusion of the cultural dimension of a child's learning and development, questioning how one could fully appreciate what a child might understand of the world in the absence of a sustained pedagogical interaction. Vygotsky argued that all human thought and speech necessarily implicate language and other cultural tools; a nuanced attention to how children make use of such cultural forms must be involved, then, in any comprehensive attempt to apprehend the nature of their reasoning (1986).

As a Russian scholar who lived to witness Soviet dominion over any number of traditional rural societies, Vygotsky looked to modern Western education to develop more sophisticated forms of thought among these new citizenries. At the same time, Vygotsky certainly expected that Western thought would continue to evolve as a function of ongoing scientific advancements, such as his own and those of his colleagues. Interestingly, it was Vygotsky and Piaget who shared untroubled assumptions regarding the natural links between what they saw as the predictable forward momentum of Western science and the broader forward momentum, therefore, of Western understanding.

Dewey, in contrast, interrogated the relationship between science, art, and morality in modern times, identifying aesthetic and philosophical insight as the ultimate expression of a society's worth.[17] Whereas for Vygotsky, "scientific" thought more or less represented the integrated forward movement of modern rationality, for Dewey, a culture's inherited assumptions and values needed to be continually examined and reborn in relation to a culture's ever more sensitive scientific understandings.[18] If Piaget under-theorized the role cultural resources play in formulating human thought, then, Vygotsky can be charged with under-theorizing the inherent tension between established cultural means and the new and divergent thinking that drives any intellectually open society.

As intellectual inheritors of the Enlightenment rift between free scientific exploration and the dictates of Rome, both Dewey and Piaget were culturally inclined to recognize scientific demonstration and logical reasoning as essential to the struggle against intellectual and political tyrannies of any order. The work of both scholars can usefully be seen, therefore, as moving in opposition to an unreflective appropriation of inherited understandings; at the same time, one must note that Dewey and Piaget took decidedly different tacks in this regard.

Piaget stressed the sensitive nurture of children's developing logical capacity because he believed that by respecting the integrity of children's distinctive thinking one would maximize one's chances of acculturating children to the cultural tradition that mattered most—an interest in and ability to reason logically (see Chapman, 1986). Dewey, on the other hand, had identified lived experience—with its embedded historical, developmental, and cultural contingencies—as the organizing framework for all human understanding. Although he insisted that inherited assumptions must be reexamined in relation to contemporary understandings, Dewey (1934/2005) did not believe that all that mattered could be articulated in propositional, let alone formal logical, terms.

In two central aspects, then, Dewey's scholarship can be seen to integrate the orientations of Vygotsky and Piaget. In insisting on the necessary role of science in the ultimate fashioning of a democratic culture's aesthetic and philosophical vision, Dewey can be seen as placing a Piagetian focus on logical and mathematical reasoning into an active relationship with Vygotsky's emphasis on the necessary (and inescapable) contributions of inherited cultural understandings and methods.[19] In framing lived human experience as the basis for all consideration of human meaning, Dewey engages both the exigencies of individual sensibility *and* the demands of social context.

Again, Dewey found that the people of a democratic nation, in addition to sharing a set of political arrangements, must share a broad array of methods and aims; they must appreciate the rewards and demands of collaborative efforts of many kinds. For Dewey, a particular quality of intellectual involvement with one's world represented both the necessary means and exalted purpose of democracy as a social and political form. It is no accident, then, that Dewey's work provides a synthesizing lens for the work of Vygotsky and Piaget, two psychologists whose research suggests new approaches to fostering children's cultural literacy and analytic clarity, respectively.

IMPLICATIONS FOR CONTEMPORARY EDUCATION PRACTICE

As I have argued, Dewey's insight regarding the organizing social influences of shared means and purposes generated a vision of education that was always at least as much about students' appropriation of cultural methods and understandings as it was about the development of students' critical sensibility. Dewey (1900 & 1902/1990) never imagined that one might replace the other, as much as the balance between them may well shift within various disciplinary and developmental contexts. Students' powers of independent observation, analysis, and theorizing were to be honed within the crucibles of key cultural production and democratic knowledge construction processes.

Current progressive educational practice can generally be seen to embrace this very balance, although the role of cultural forms can remain under-theorized, particularly within work that emerges most directly from the Piagetian tradition.[20] Under-theorized or no, however, essential cultural tools remain reliably in place; Piagetian experiments, and their accompanying paraphernalia, continue to fill investigatory math and science curricula. Piaget's method of engaging children's thinking has now also been adapted to other disciplines. As work inspired by learning theorist Eleanor Duckworth's (1996; 2001) adaptation of Piagetian method to pedagogical purposes has demonstrated, attention to students' meaning-making can uncover not only developmental, but also cultural and individual differences in conceptual framing.

Contemporary interest in Vygotsky's work, set against the more established influences of Piagetian theory, has encouraged educators to consider the tension between an individual and his or her cultural context that Dewey's notion of lived experience subsumes. Sociocultural research and theory has supported educators in articulating the fundamental disciplinary assumptions and methods that democratic citizens must appreciate if they are to take part in the social, intellectual, and political negotiations of the day. In addition, sociocultural scholarship has begun to theorize the pedagogical processes whereby students come to appropriate such assumptions and methods (see, e.g., Lemke, 1990; Kozulin, 1998). All of this work offers a necessary corrective to the field's current preoccupation with thin performance measures and suggests ways of moving beyond the disciplinary uncertainty that has made so extreme an over-reliance on psychometric test scores possible.

Naturally, Dewey's practical curricular interpretations of his work could be spare in places (or, at this point, dated); a scholar interested in outlines that broad will delve only so far into specifics over even a long career (though surely Dewey went further in this direction than most philosophers).[21] Howard Gardner, in a useful discussion of the ways in which later develop-

ments in learning science have informed progressive educational commitments, reminds us that anachronistic criticisms of early progressive theorizing are unfair (1991). I have further argued that the historically insensitive analyses that generate such anachronisms risk derailing needed theoretical syntheses.

CONCLUSION

As we have seen, both Dewey and Vygotsky looked to schools to acculturate the young of their societies into a system of methods and meanings that the children might adapt to their future needs and purposes. Both scholars spoke of their societies as driven by newly emergent material forces and saw the fostering of a critical and informed intelligence within their citizenries as the best assurance that unforeseen challenges might be adequately met by future generations. Both believed that such an education was essential to the development of more just and more enlightened societies.

Although Dewey and Vygotsky both stressed the role of established cultural forms in elevating the condition of their societies, both men also emphasized that children must be taught to claim such means through an active social engagement that provides connections between these forms and the child's worldview. Here, Piaget joins their ranks. Vygotsky and Dewey may have shared more organizing commitments, but Piaget basically agreed with them regarding the implications of developmental learning theory for school practice.[22]

Dewey, Vygotsky, and Piaget all saw reason and culture as informing each other in necessary ways and as advancing together. Piaget's research into developmental constraints helped to frame Vygotsky's subsequent attention to semiotic mediation. Against the dynamic relationship generated by these two sets of contrasting research priorities, Dewey constructed a synthesizing philosophical frame.

Educational theorists detract from this emerging coherence when they emphasize the differences between any two of these theorists to the near exclusion of their shared concerns. Given that Dewey, Vygotsky, and Piaget all sought to transcend the parochialisms of the differing psychological orientations of their day, it seems particularly inappropriate to contrast any two of these scholars based primarily upon their immediate historical circumstances. Although there seems to be no evidence that Dewey, Vygotsky, and Piaget were in direct conversation with each other, they were all in conversation with a particular period of human history and with longstanding philosophical and psychological issues rooted in the Western philosophical and psychological traditions that they shared.

Together, then, the scholarship of these three major theorists underwrites the twentieth century turn toward the study of the ways and means of human intelligence as a basis for pedagogical forms and towards the honing and acculturation of a critical human sensibility as the defining goal of a free and fair educational system. All three have advanced the work of engaging children's creative capacities as a means of initiating them into the complex work of collaboratively making sense of the world. In particular, John Dewey, philosopher of democracy, framed a new form of pedagogical relationship that continues to demand greater elaboration and emphasis within his nation's ostensibly free and fair schools.

ACKNOWLEDGMENTS

I would like to thank David Eddy Spicer for reading and discussing this article with me and also my reviewers for their many useful queries and suggestions.

NOTES

1 An earlier draft of this paper was presented at AERA 2007.

2 Piaget, 1923/1959. This first psychological text of Piaget's explicitly explores social influences on children's thought, an interest to which Piaget returned periodically, particularly toward the end of his career.

3 See Cork, 1950; Farrell, 1950. Both Cork's essay on Dewey and Marx, and Farrell's reflection on his journey with Dewey to Mexico for Trotsky's trial offer nuanced reflections on Dewey's relationships with Marx and with Marxism. See also Ryan, 1995.

4 Dewey, 1939/2003; Shook, 2000. Absolutism not only came to Dewey by way of Hegel, but more personally by way of the Christian intellectual heritage he and Hegel shared. See prologue in Westbrook, 1991, for a brief treatment of Dewey's religious influences as a child. Also, Ryan's 1995 analysis is again pertinent here.

5 In contrast, Marx, though Jewish by ancestry, was raised as a nominal Lutheran by his father, who had converted for political reasons from what appears to have been a similarly nominal Judaism. One can imagine that Marx's appreciation of German idealism owed something to this upbringing. As had Hegel, Marx lived under a socially and politically oppressive Prussian monarchy and would wait in vain for the Prussian state to implode in accordance with his theory. Singer, 2000.

6 See Ryan, 1995 for a treatment of Mead's post-Hegelian influence on Dewey, also Daniels et al., 2007. Cole also traces his efforts to reconcile Soviet cultural-historical psychology with cultural anthropology through Mead by way of Geertz. See Cole, 1996, p. 123.

7 Ryan, 1995. The parallels with Vygotsky's work are striking, raising questions as to the influences of Wundt's work on Vygotsky.

8 Dewey, 1916/1944, 1938/1963; Kliebard, 1987; Kozulin et al., 2003; Vygotsky, 1978; Wertsch et al., 1995.

9 That Vygotsky meant to reference more than the mathematical and scientific understandings Piaget studied with his term "scientific" was evidenced by Vygotsky's investigative accomplishments and ambitions—to study the comprehension of narrative line, for example, or the development of concepts such as "exploitation?" Vygotsky, 1986, p. 162; see also Daniels, 2001. Vygotsky's use of the term "scientific" likely derives from Hegel's and Marx's use of the term to reference systematic conceptual analysis (see Singer, 2000).

10 This is not to suggest that Dewey neglected the organizing role of language. Jim Garrison (2001) quotes Dewey as speaking of mind as "an added property assumed by a feeling creature, when it reaches that organized interaction with other living creature which is language, communication" (pp. 292–293).

11 In speaking of Hegel's dialectic of Becoming, Kozulin does not necessarily reference either dialectical materialism or the Hegelian idealism that helped spur Marxian utopianism. Rather, Kozulin seems to be suggesting that Vygotsky sought to study the movement that results from the play of conceptual oppositions that distinguishes Hegelian dialectical process. In a similar manner, Dewey's attention to transcending dualisms can be traced to a concern with dialectic process, though Dewey renounced transcendent ideals as a dialectical process's ultimate outcome.

12 Chapman, 1988. Though instrumentalist interpretations of Piaget's work emphasize the distinctions between the developmental stages Piaget theorized, Piaget actually saw the evolution of logical reasoning processes as a continuous process.

13 For example, Kozulin may also be evoking Vygotsky's interest in the dialectical process as the source of self-consciousness, a concern that can be traced to Hegel (Kojeve, 1969) and which Dewey shared.

14 Vygotsky's well known formulation was, *"An operation that initially represents an external activity is reconstructed and begins to occur internally,"* Vygotsky, 1978, pp. 55–57.

15 As Garrison (2001) puts it, "Transactional thinking allows us to see things as belonging together functionally, such as lungs and oxygen producing flora that are usually never connected. Transactionalism allows us to recognize them as

subfunctions of a larger function" (p. 286). In other words, the subject and object categories are themselves infinitely malleable and can be constructed in whatever manner might address particular aims.

16 Piaget's hope was that this work would inform the question of how human reason had evolved.

17 Cited in Smith, 1998, pp. 201–219. In reflecting upon this triumvirate of disciplinary influences, contemporary educators are likely to mark the absence of a cultural lens.

18 Dewey saw science as the "handmaiden" of art. See Mayer, 2007, pp. 176–186.

19. On Dewey's vision of the necessary role of science in a democracy, again see Mayer, 2007.

20 Certainly, Piaget's attachment to logico-mathematical thought must be seen as more extreme, and in that sense less balanced, than Vygotsky's broader concern with what he did term, after all, "scientific" language. As we have seen, for Vygotsky, "scientific" language referred to concepts that had been abstracted through established processes of cultural articulation.

21 Kamii, 1994. Kamii, for example, published a series on the practical application of Piaget's work within mathematics classroom that arguably under-theorizes the role established cultural tools play in this approach.

22 This breadth of vision passed out of fashion within Dewey's lifetime. See Westbrook, 1991, pp. 537–552.

23 Although Piaget generally hesitated to speculate on the implications of his work for school practice, he is said to have offered Dewey's work as exemplary.

REFERENCES

Bencivenga, E. (2000). *Hegel's dialectical logic.* Oxford: Oxford University Press.

Bruner, J. (1997). "Celebrating divergence: Piaget and Vygotsky." *Human Development,* 40(1), 63–73.

Chapman, M. (1986). The structure of exchange: Piaget's sociological theory. *Human Development, 29*(2), 181–194.

Chapman, M. (1988*). Constructive evolution: Origins and development of Piaget's thought.* Cambridge, UK: Cambridge University Press.

Cole, M. (1996). *Cultural psychology: A once and future discipline.* Cambridge: Harvard University Press.

Cork, J. (1950). John Dewey and Karl Marx. In S. Hook (Ed.), *John Dewey: Philosopher of science and freedom* (pp. 331–350). Westport, CT: Greenwood Press, Publishers.

Daniels, H. (2001). *Vygotsky and pedagogy.* London: Routledge.

Daniels, H., Cole, M., & Wertsch, J. (Eds.). (2007). *The Cambridge companion to Vygotsky.* Cambridge, UK: Cambridge University Press.

Desmond, W. (1992). *Beyond Hegel and dialectic: Speculation, cult, and comedy.* Albany, NY: SUNY Press.

Dewey, J. (2005). *Art as experience.* New York: Perigee Books. (Original work published 1934).

Dewey, J. (1944). *Democracy and education.* New York: Free Press. (Original work published 1916).

Dewey, J. (1957). *Reconstruction in philosophy.* Boston: Beacon Press. (Original work published 1920).

Dewey, J. (1960). *The Quest for certainty.* New York: G. P. Putnam's Sons. (Original work published 1929).

Dewey, J. (1963). *Education and experience.* New York: Collier Books. (Original work published 1938).

Dewey, J. (1988). Progressive education and the science of education. In S. Brown & M. Finn (Eds.), *Readings from progressive education: A movement and its journal* (pp. 160–167). Lanham, MD: University Press of America. (Original work published 1928).

Dewey, J., (1990). *The school and society* and *The child and the curriculum.* Chicago: The University of Chicago Press. (Original works published 1900 & 1902).

Dewey, J. (2003). Creative democracy: The task before us. In S. Rosenbaum (Ed.), *Pragmatism and religion* (pp. 91–96). Chicago: University of Illinois Press. (Original work published 1939).

Diggins, J. P. (1994). *The promise of pragmatism.* Chicago: University of Chicago Press.

Duckworth, E. (1996). *The having of wonderful ideas.* New York: Teachers College Press.

Duckworth, E. (2001). *"Tell me more": Listening to learners explain.* New York: Teachers College Press.

Egan, K. (2002). *Getting it wrong from the beginning: Our progressivist inheritance from Herbert Spencer, John Dewey, and Jean Piaget.* New Haven: Yale University Press.

Farrell, J. (1950). Dewey in Mexico. In S. Hook (Ed.), *John Dewey: Philosopher of Science and Freedom* (pp. 351–377) Westport, CT: Greenwood Press, Publishers.

Gardner, H. (1991). *The unschooled mind.* New York: Basic Books.

Garrison, J. (2001). An introduction to Dewey's theory of functional trans-action: An alternative paradigm for activity theory. *Mind, Culture, and Activity, 8*(4), 275–296.

Glassman, M. (2001). Dewey and Vygotsky: Society, experience, and inquiry in educational practice. *Educational Researcher, 30*(4), 3–14.

Glassman, M. (2002). Experience and responding. *Educational Researcher, 31*(5), 16–20.

Hegel, G. W. F. (1975). *Hegel's logic.* W. Wallace (Trans.). Oxford: Oxford University Press. (Original work published 1873).

Kamii, C. (1994). *Young children continue to reinvent arithmetic: Implications of Piaget's theory.* New York: Teachers College Press.

Kliebard, H. (1987). *The struggle for the American curriculum.* New York: Routledge.

Kojève, A. (1969). *Introduction to the reading of Hegel.* Ithaca: Cornell University Press.

Kozulin, A. (1986). Vygotsky in context. In L. Vygotsky, *Thought and Language* (pp. xi–lxi). Cambridge, MA: MIT Press.

Kozulin, A. (1990). *Vygotsky's psychology.* Cambridge, MA: Harvard University Press.

Kozulin, A. (1998). *Psychological tools: A socio-cultural approach to education.* Cambridge, MA: Harvard University Press.

Kozulin, A., Gindis, B., Ageyev, V. & Miller, S. (Eds.). (2003). *Vygotsky's educational theory in cultural context.* Cambridge: Cambridge University Press.

Lemke, J. L. (1990). *Talking science: Language, learning, and values.* Norwood, NJ: Ablex.

Mayer, S. (2005). The early evolution of Jean Piaget's clinical method. History of Psychology, 8(4), 362–382.

Mayer, S. (2006). Getting it right: Keeping it complicated. Journal of the American Association for the Advancement of Curriculum Studies, 2. Retrieved Oct. 20, 2008 from http://www.uwstout.edu/soe/jaaacs/vo12/index.htm

Mayer, S. (2007). The ideal as real: John Dewey and the social construction of moral coherence. *Journal of Curriculum 6., Pedagogy,* 4(2), 176–186.

Mead. G. H. (1934). Mind, self and society. Chicago: Chicago University Press.

Miettinen, R. (2001). Artifact mediation in Dewey and in cultural-historical activity theory. *Mind, Culture, and Activity*, 8(4), 297–308.

Olson, A. (1992). *Hegel and the spirit.* Princeton: Princeton University Press.

O'Brien, L. (2002). A response to "Dewey and Vygotsky: society, experience, and inquiry in educational practice." *Educational Researcher*, 31(5), 16–20.

Persons, S. (1950). *Evolutionary thought in America.* New York: George Braziller, Inc.

Piaget, J. (1995). *Sociological studies.* London: Routledge.

Piaget, J. (1959). *The language and thought of the child.* London: Routledge & Kegan Paul. (Original work published 1923)

Plotkin, H. (2004). *Evolutionary thought in psychology.* Oxford: Blackwell Publishing.

Popkewitz, T. (1998). Dewey, Vygotsky, and the social administration of the individual: Constructivist pedagogy as systems of ideas in historical spaces. *American Educational Research Journal*, 35(4), 535–570.

Prawat, R. (2002). Dewey and Vygotsky viewed through the rearview mirror—and dimly at that." *Educational Researcher*, 31(5), 16–20.

Richards, R. (1987). *Darwin and the emergence of evolutionary theories of mind and behavior.* Chicago: Chicago University Press.

Ryan, A. (1995). *John Dewey and the high tide of American liberalism.* New York: W. W. Norton & Co.

Scheffler, I. (1974). *Four pragmatists: A critical introduction to Peirce, James, Mead, and Dewey.* New York: Humanities Press.

Shook, J. (2000). *Dewey's empirical theory of knowledge and reality.* Nashville, TN: Vanderbilt University Press.

Singer, P. (2000). *Marx: A very short introduction.* Oxford: Oxford University Press.

Smith, L. (1998). *Learning and the development of knowledge.* Archives de Psychologie, 66,201–219.

Vidal, F. (1987). *Jean Piaget and the liberal protestant tradition.* In M. G. Ash & W. R. Woodward (Eds.), Psychology in twentieth-century thought and society (pp. 271–294). Cambridge University Press.

Vidal, F. (1994). *Piaget before Piaget.* Cambridge, MA: Harvard University Press.

Vygotsky, L. (1978). *Mind in society: The development of higher psychological processes.* Cambridge, MA: Harvard University Press.

Vygotsky, L. (1986). *Thought and language.* Cambridge, MA: MIT Press.

Wertsch, J. (1985). *Vygotsky and the social formation of mind.* Cambridge, MA: Harvard University Press.

Wertsch, J. (1998). *Mind as action.* Oxford: Oxford University Press.

Wertsch, J., Del Rio, P., & Alvarez, A. (1995). *Sociocultural studies of mind.* Cambridge: Cambridge University Press.

Westbrook, R. (1991). *John Dewey and American democracy.* Ithaca, NY: Cornell University Press.

NINE

On the Origins of Constructivism:
The Kantian Ancestry of Jean Piaget's
Genetic Epistemology

David Jardine

In a recent undergraduate seminar, I held three pieces of white chalk in my hand and asked student teachers to name properties of this object. Their answers came easily: white, dusty, brittle, round, solid, dry and so on. I wrote these on the board.

I then pointed to my open palm and asked, "How many pieces of chalk do I have in my hand?" "Three," someone called out, and I added that to our list.

We used this simple, almost trivial exercise to help us understand and interpret a powerful and puzzling passage from David Elkind (1967, xii), one of Jean Piaget's most articulate interpreters: "Once a concept is constructed, it is immediately experienced so that it appears to the subject as a perceptually given property of the object and independent of the subject's own mental activity."

PROPERTIES OF THE OBJECT

Using Elkind as a guide, we looked back at the white chalk and the easy conversation we'd had, and the equally easy list we had made. In order to "immediately experience" the whiteness of the chalk as a "property of the object," we had used not just our eyes, but also a concept we'd all learned (in English, "white") as a way to communicate our experience to others. We then discussed how this property of chalk—its whiteness—is not a property of chalk alone. It is also a more general concept (a color) that is also the property of many other objects (clouds, this page you are reading, and so on). As one student-teacher put it so brilliantly:

"'White' isn't stuck to the chalk."

Another student-teacher said, with equal metaphorical brilliance:

"It floats above things."

Both of these students were invoking, knowingly or not, all sorts of old mythologies and images about ideas and concepts being "above us," housed not on Earth, but in the heavens.

Our judgment of "brittle" required something more kinesthetic: hitting the chalk against the desk or remembering what happens when you accidentally drop a piece or snap it between your fingers, and so on. We pondered the fact that, as adults, we can simply recall—or imagine—ourselves or someone else having snapped the chalk in the past. This judgment about the "brittleness" of chalk is almost ancient in our individual life-experiences. We've all experienced the brittleness of chalk in a myriad of ways in our lives as well as the analogue of its brittleness in a china cup or a terracotta flowerpot. The lived history of the slow construction, consolidation and reconstruction of this experience—all this "mental activity" as Elkind calls it, and more—of the brittleness of chalk in each of our lives is astoundingly complex and virtually untraceable.

In all of the words from our list, what appeared at first to be simple, obvious properties of the object gave way to a myriad of actual, possible or remembered actions, experiences, sensations, concepts, images, names and fantasies. These actions involved mental activity, but also involved the eyes, the hands, the body and all its housed memories and images of previous experiences. According to Piaget, these seemingly straightforward properties of the object are so familiar to adults that we have lost track of the fact that we had, in each case, to *construct* this familiarity over time. Whiteness, then, is not merely a property of the object, but more difficultly, a property of *the relationship(s)* between the object and the sense-making activities of the person experiencing the object. These sense-making activities are deeply ingrained, almost automatic and numerous in kind: bodily, ideational, imaginative, conceptual, logical, cultural, linguistic, biographical, historical/generational, perceptual, numerical, kinesthetic, playful and so on.

According to Piaget, simply pointing to the object and asserting that it is white is both commonsensical and also, in some sense, naive and unreflective of the nature of knowledge and the profoundly active role that the human being takes in the act of knowing that yes, this chalk is white. Similarly, in speaking with a young child about how many pieces of chalk I have in my hand, it is commonsensical to believe that I *really do* have three pieces; if the child doesn't understand this, the problem is in the child, not in reality. Jean Piaget pushes this commonsense to the point of breaking. On the contrary, he argues, for the young child who cannot understand counting, enumerating, adding up, the world *does not have,* "in reality," a "number" of things, except perhaps "lots" and "none" and "more" and so on. In the presence of a very young child, I do not straightforwardly have three pieces of chalk in my hand because this child does not know how to "do" enumeration. His or her world is not enumerated; it is not constructed, thought of, understood or acted upon in that manner. I know how to enumerate and find numbers commonplace in the world as I experience and understand it, but I know this action so well that I might falsely believe that "three" is a property of the object, rather than a function of my experience and understanding—experience and understanding that the non-numerate child does not share.

Further, since we do not share experience and understanding, it is not just our adult psychological makeups, interior states or conceptual frameworks that differ from children. Since the terms we use to construct the world are different, our *worlds* are different. Hence, from the legacy of constructivism and Piagetian theory, we can sensibly speak these days about "the world of the child" and have it mean something quite disturbing, something quite profound that threatens to interrupt our self-confident ascription of properties to objects. It is the beginning of a self-consciousness regarding just who we mean by "we" and "our."

This is, in part, what Piaget learned from his work with children and with his attempts to standardize Binet's intelligence tests in light of adult standards of knowing: typically, children seemed to put things together differently than adults. As adults, we have learned these standards so well that we tend to "forget" our long and complex agency in the world we experience. We come to think it's all just "the way things really are," forgetting that we have, collectively and individually, *learned* "the way things really are" by collectively and individually *making something* of our experiences.

As can be imagined, my student teachers were not especially happy with this exercise. When we start disrupting seemingly obvious, commonplace things, the first response is often confusion, speechlessness, sometimes frustration and anger. These responses are important: once we have constructed our knowledge of a simple object like white chalk, that construction immediately and automatically appears to be a property of the object. Our constructions, that is, are *objectified*. This process is so deeply ingrained, so deeply buried, that unearthing it can feel humiliating, like a sort of betrayal. In these responses, we see the beginning of an awareness of our ongoing, unintended, often unconscious implication in what we know.

Much more pointed pedagogical consequences also occurred in this incident. One student talked of seeing a teacher hovering over a young child and saying, "Just *look,* would you? Pay attention. There are *six* pictures on the worksheet. *See?*" In this story and others we all got a glimpse of how often we have treated the *outcomes* of our own constructions as if they are absolute properties of the object, becoming frustrated by those who do not understand what is so obvious to any adult.

All of this illustrates a profound idea that underwrites Jean Piaget's work, an idea that has gained great power and, ironically, sometimes even greater obscurity in educational theory and practice: constructivism.

This is not the place to unravel all of the current threads of that phenomenon. Rather, we need to explore another thread in the intellectual atmosphere out of which Jean Piaget's work emerged. In the late 19th and early 20th century in European academic life, an historical figure rose to new prominence, from whom Piaget inherited these images of knowledge as construction: Immanuel Kant (1724–1804).

Immanuel Kant's contribution to the work of Jean Piaget is incredibly important, especially in light of a terrible dilemma that arises if we push this insight regarding constructivism too hard. The dilemma is this: given our differing backgrounds, languages, cultures, constructions, assumptions and experience, it would seem that our knowledge, experience and understanding of the world should be scattershot, too. It would appear that each of us brings only difference and diversity to the act of knowing. Knowledge consequently appears always and only personal; to use the old Greek distinction, knowledge is always and only mere opinion. It would seem, if we push this insight of constructivism too far, that each of us is locked into our own individual "bubble" and that any attempt to escape would only confirm our situation—attempting to understand another person's world would only be an act of *constructing* that other person and their world in light of my own framework. This is a teacher's horror: What if I have imposed my own presumptions, prejudices, constructs and assumptions on a student?

Immanuel Kant brings to this dilemma, and Jean Piaget carries forward, what could be called an Enlightenment ideal: the belief that underlying our myriad backgrounds, languages, cultures, constructions, assumptions, and experiences are commonly held categories, forms or methods of knowledge: commonly held ways of constructing knowledge and objectivity, commonly held ways in which human reason essentially operates. Despite all our accidental differences and idiosyncrasies adult human reason is, in limited and specific ways, always and everywhere the same in its judgments about objects in the world. It is the great task, both in the work of Immanuel Kant and in the world of Jean Piaget, of discovering this universal and necessary—happening in all cases (universal) and happening of necessity and not just by chance (necessary)—character of human reason.

Even though Kant and Piaget share an understanding of knowledge as construction, what each of them claims as universal and necessary to these constructions differs. The rest of this chapter contains a detailed look at how Immanuel Kant took up this task of understanding the universal and necessary character of human reason. This will help us understand both a defining source of Jean Piaget's work (and hence a defining source of educational theory and practice) as well as how Piaget's work departs from that source.

KANT'S "COPERNICAN REVOLUTION"

One can feel very close to the spirit of Kantianism (and I believe I am close to it). (Piaget, 1965a, p. 57)

Immanuel Kant's so-called Copernican Revolution in philosophy reclaimed at the epistemological level what was lost at the cosmological level in the work of Nicolaus Copernicus (1473–1543). In astronomy, Copernicus had overturned the belief that the Earth was the centre of creation, placing the sun at the centre of the physical universe instead. Obviously, this original Copernican Revolution had consequences far beyond astronomy. By unseating Earth from its special cosmological place, humanity itself was de-centered.

Immanuel Kant reclaimed the centrality of humanity by putting human reason and its structures and characteristics at the centre of the knowable universe. Anything "knowable" refers back to the conditions of knowability determined by the essential, constructive character of human reason. But there is an extra step to watch for in this reclaiming of the centre. According to Kant, human reason, by its very nature, puts things together in clearly definable ways. It is an actively organizing, ordering, constructive human faculty, not a passive one. It is, as Kant defined it, a *synthesizing* faculty that, in the act of knowing something in the world, actively constructs orderliness out of the chaos of experience in accordance with human reason's own structures, forms and categories. Over a century later, Jean Piaget (1971c, xii) would call this "imposing cosmos on the chaos of experience."

To be an object in the world, according to Kant, means to have been constructed as an object according to human reason's criteria of "objectivity." To hearken back to the passage from David Elkind and our chalk lesson, we objectify our own constructions; we construct what it means for something to be an object in the world, and we experience the construction not just as mental activity of ourselves as subjects, but also as a property of the object. Human reason, in Kant's work, is thus not merely the centre of the knowable world of objects. It is also the centre of the construction and issuance of the order, structure and reason of that world. To hearken back to our simple example, the world has a number of things only because I am "numerate" and construct the world accordingly, demanding that it answer my questions regarding its number.

Immanuel Kant lays out this theory of knowledge or epistemology in his brilliant and difficult work *Critique of Pure Reason* (originally published in 1787). It is this "spirit of Kantianism" (Piaget, 1965a, p. 57) and its legacies that filled the intellectual atmosphere of Jean Piaget's own thinking. As stated in the preface to Kant's text:

> A light broke upon the students of nature. They learned that reason has insight only into that which it produces after a plan of its own, and that it must not allow itself to be kept, as it were, in nature's leading-strings, but must itself show the way with principles of judgment based on fixed laws, constraining nature to give answer to questions of reason's own determining. Reason...must approach nature in order to be taught by it. It must not, however, do so in the character of a pupil who listens to everything the teacher chooses to say, but of an appointed judge who compels the witnesses to answer questions, which he had himself formulated. While reason must seek in nature, not fictitiously ascribe to it, whatever has to be learnt, if learnt at all, only from nature, it must adopt as its guide, in so seeking, that which it has itself put into nature. (Kant, 1964, p. 20)

Unique here and of especial interest to educators is this new element: conceiving of knowledge as an active, constructive, orderly and ordering, *demand* made upon things. "To know," henceforth, is no longer understood as passively receiving information from an object (think of all those old "filling an empty vessel" images of education, or ones of "writing on a blank tablet," the tabula rasa).

Rather, "to know" is "to impose structure," "to (give) order(s)," "to demand," "to determine," "to make." To know is to *act,* in definable, determinable ways. Kant's work stands at the advent of what has come to be known as constructivism. By examining some of the steps Kant takes in building this image of human reason as an active, ordering, constructive faculty, we'll get a better picture of exactly how Piaget took up this challenge in his own work and transformed it radically in his own genetic epistemology.

TWO TYPES OF KNOWLEDGE: *A POSTERIORI* AND *A PRIORI*

One central argument in Kant's *Critique of Pure Reason* is that **empiricism** does not provide an adequate account of all forms of knowledge. In the theory of knowledge called empiricism, the human mind begins as a blank slate upon which are written the results of empirical, perceptual experience, which forms the basis of all knowledge. All knowledge of objects, therefore, is passively received from objects through the senses. To use the language of David Hume (1711–1776), a central empiricist philosopher, we know what something is because that thing and its characteristics *impress themselves* upon us. Empiricism (from the Greek *empeiria,* "experience," as opposed to *eidos* and *theoria,* ideas and theories) does not deny that humans act upon impressions received through the senses. However, the only sort of human action that can lead to any sort of knowledge, according to empiricism, is an action that occurs *after* this initial "receiving," that is, *posterior* to it. Simply put, all knowledge, for empiricism, is a generalization following from and based upon experience. This is what Kant calls a posteriori knowledge.

According to empiricism, the only warrantable action upon experience is a generalization based upon and limited to the instances of experience. Such generalizations are always subject to the continuing influx of experiences, which may in the next instance prove a generalization incorrect. Hence the conclusions drawn from experience are not universal, necessary or binding, but only general(ized), contingent and dependent upon the next instance. To return to the example of the white chalk: knowing that it is chalk and that it is white can only be understood and judged *after* we have experienced the chalk and seen, over and over, that it is white. Moreover, if we had only ever experienced white chalk and we acted upon that knowledge to suggest that "all chalk is white," we would have generalized those experiences into a false statement. Not all chalk is white. Even with the chalk in our example, empiricism strictly suggests that we cannot say absolutely and necessarily that it is white—or even that it is chalk! We can only say that based upon the past instances we have observed, we judge it to be white chalk, and it is most probable that it will be experienced as white chalk in the future. The more times we experience the chalk, the more probable our judgment becomes (in modern science, it is left to the science of statistics to determine degrees of probability). However, empiricism demands that it is always at least *possible* that future experiences will contradict this judgment, and that it may have to be revised. Empirical judgments are never universal and necessary. They are always only probable and subject to revision. This way of proceeding is, of course, central to the natural sciences. We experience things, we generalize, but those generalizations are always subject to what new experiences might bring. To put a finer point on this, David Hume suggested that the generalizations we make cannot be traced back to a single incident that gave rise to them, since the generalization was not impressed upon the senses by experience, but was, rather, produced by the mind (by what Hume called "association"). Such products of the mind are not, so to speak, "properties of the object" but are only ideas that have no definitive objective reality.

Immanuel Kant's work began elsewhere. He began by affirming the de facto existence of logic, mathematics and Euclidean geometry as forms of knowledge that are precisely *not* empirical generalizations. He argued that there is, in these sciences, another type of knowledge that is not derived from experience *(a posteriori)* but rather is imposed upon experience with a universality and a necessity—with a certainty, we should add—for which empiricism cannot give an adequate account.

Kant maintained that the universality and necessity of logic and mathematics (disciplines that, as we shall see, are central to Jean Piaget's genetic epistemology) were an indication that a type of knowledge exists that is not *a posteriori,* but rather a priori knowledge.

We have *a priori* knowledge of objects *prior to* and independently of empirical experience. Kant maintains (as does Jean Piaget) that when we make the judgment "the chalk is white," not all of this knowledge comes from experiencing the chalk. Some of this knowledge—its general, universal and necessary structure—is known prior to and independently of experiencing the chalk. That is to say, even if I kept my hand closed, and the students in the class had no idea what particular object was in my hand, they would still be able to have some general knowledge of that object.

On the face of it, this sounds very odd. Here are the steps that Immanuel Kant took in making his case, and some of the consequences that follow from it.

Kant began with an age-old philosophical discipline: formal logic. Formal logic delineates the essential, *a priori* (that is, universal and necessary) interrelations between one thought and another. It describes what Jean Piaget (1952, p. 15) called "the organization of thought itself." It is, so to speak, the grammar of thinking, its structure and forms. In formal logic, we have a whole array of formal judgments that can be made. This list of formal judgments extends back in Western thought as far as the work of Aristotle (circa 300 B.C.E.). In the *Critique of Pure Reason,* Kant lists these formal judgments in what he calls the Table of Judgments (see Kant, 1964, p. 107 and following). Formal logic, however, only describes the ways in which one thought might formally, logically relate to another. Here are three simple examples of isolated logical judgments:

A IS A

A IS B

IF A, THEN B.

These statements seem quite abstract and empty until we see what Kant does with his Table of Judgments. The brilliance of Kant's work lies in his suggestion that since these forms of thinking are the universal and necessary forms we always and unavoidably use to think about an object in the world, they thus *prescribe* what we think about that object (at least in general terms). These forms of thinking give shape to our perceptual, empirical experiences and turn our perceptions into objects. They are the forms, therefore, not only of thinking, but of objectivity itself—they are the forms that an object of knowledge must necessarily and universally take, since they are the forms that prescribe how that object is constructed out of perceptions.

In this limited sense, then, we do have knowledge of objects in the world that is not *derived from* our perceptual experience of those objects but rather is a set of demands made by thinking upon perceptual experience; the nature of thinking itself is a demand that forms our perceptual experiences into objects. These formative, constructive demands made upon objects in the world do not therefore constitute a merely formal logic, which simply describes forms of thinking. These formative, constructive demands made upon objects in the world constitute what Immanuel Kant called transcendental logic.

That is, these unavoidable, universal and necessary, formative, constructive demands provide the logic whereby the human subject transcends itself and actively *forms* objects according to its own constructions, its own demands, its own "mental activity" (Elkind, 1967, xii). Transcendental logic thus describes the universal and necessary logic of objectivity itself, the logic of the knowable world that the structure of human reason has itself constructed according to its own demands.

This is a difficult idea. It will become a little less murky if we list some of these formal/logical forms of thought and see how, in each case, they might apply to our knowledge of the white pieces of chalk.

First (and, for many philosophers and mathematicians, most fundamental) is the formal, logical judgment of identity: A = A. Although this seems arcane, it is actually quite simple and very important. When you work with a formula (both in logic and mathematics), each time you run into the term "a," it is always the same "a." Even if "a" is as yet undefined (as, for example, in the equation 2a + b = b-a), we know, we presume, the logic of human thinking *demands* that in both its appearances in this equation, a = a, and likewise, in both its appearances, b = b.

When it functions transcendentally and not just logically, this so-called principle of identity becomes one of the universal and necessary ways that we define and construct what it means to be an object in the world: whatever an object might be, our thinking demands that it is what it is, and it isn't something else. Consider this: even when my hand is closed around those three pieces of white chalk and the students cannot see what the object is, they *already know* that, whatever it is, it is what it is. It is a self-identical thing. Kant borrowed this age-old principle from the work of Aristotle. Consider, from his *Metaphysics:*

> Not to have one meaning is to have no meaning and if words have no meaning, our reasoning with one another, and indeed with ourselves has been annihilated; for it is impossible to think of anything if we do not think of one thing. (Aristotle, Book IV)

We know, independently of our empirical experience of an object (which yields *a posteriori* knowledge), that the object is self-identical, because it is impossible, it is contradictory, it is unreasonable, to think otherwise of things. This is *a priori* knowledge.

Those student-teachers in our example also know a myriad of other things in this *a priori* way: the object in my hand, whatever it is, is a thing which has properties ("A is B," even if we don't know what defines A or B in this particular case); it exists in time and has spatial, geometrical characteristics (to use Kantian terms, space and time are the *a priori* forms of perception, such that even our empirical experience has its own *a priori* forms—this accounts for the *a priori,* universal and necessary character of Euclidean geometry); it is numerable and measurable; it was created or caused by something or other (from the logical judgment "If A, then B," we get the transcendental judgment, "All objects have a cause"); and so on. These things are, in general, and universally and necessarily, what it means to be an object in the world. If we hear a knock at the door, we know that it has a cause, even if we don't yet know *what* the cause is. It is unreasonable to think, for example, that the knock was not caused by anything. It must be someone at the door, or something falling against the door, or some other noise that I mistook for a knock, or an illusion. We cannot reasonably believe that it was caused by nothing at all, that it just happened. That is, so to speak, *unthinkable.* Things in the knowable, objective world don't just happen—they are *caused.*

This bears repeating regarding our example of white chalk. To know that *what* is in my hand is three pieces of white chalk requires empirical experience. To this extent, empiricism is correct, and the knowledge to be had is *a posteriori.* However, to know that it is something self-identical, that it has properties, that it exists in space in measurable ways, that it is a thing that was caused by other things in the world does *not* require empirical experience. To this extent, empiricism is not an adequate account, because this knowledge is had *a priori* and is not a probable generalization but rather universal and necessary.

Here is where Kantian theory (and, following it, Piagetian theory) becomes profound in its consequences and effects. The *a priori* knowledge that my students have of the pieces of chalk in my hand is a knowledge, not just of this chalk, but of *any possible object of knowledge.* It is universal and necessary knowledge about what Kant calls "an object in general." It is now possible to understand what might have originally been a quite contentious assertion: "the *a priori* conditions of a possible experience in general are at the same time conditions of the possibility of objects of experience" (Kant, 1964, p. 138). Or, differently put, "the most the understanding can achieve *a priori* is to anticipate the form of a possible experience in general" (Kant, 1964, p. 264).

A FINAL THREAD OF THE KANTIAN LEGACY

The order and regularity in [what] we call *nature*, we ourselves introduce. We could never find [such orderliness and regularity]…had not we ourselves, or the nature of our mind, originally set them there. (Kant, 1964, p. 147)

This is starting to sound rather bizarre—the orderliness of the world is our construction? Again:

[Human] understanding is itself the lawgiver of nature. Save through it, nature, that is, synthetic unity of the manifold of [perceptual] appearances according to rules [imposed by reason itself], should not exist at all. (Kant, 1964, p. 148)

At this juncture a great distinction arises that has troubled philosophers ever since Kant introduced it into philosophical discourse, a distinction between nature "in itself" and nature "for us." The latter sense of "nature for us" is what David Elkind was hinting at when he spoke about properties of the object which appear to be what the object *itself* is, but are, in fact, what the object is in relation to us and our thinking and acting. For example, when we experience "white" as a property of the object, what we are in fact experiencing is a relation between the object and our mental activity, which has constructed our perceptual experience according to its own categories and concepts. Kant suggests that the question, "What is this object as it exists *independently* of our constructions?" is absurd, because to ask such a question is to think and reason about this object and therefore, to place it back in relation to us and our thinking and reasoning. Thus Kant concludes:

That nature should direct itself [in] conformity to law[s imposed by human reason], sounds very strange and absurd. But consider that this nature is not a thing in itself but is merely an aggregate of appearances, so many representations of the mind. (1964, p. 140)

And:

The question arises how it can be conceivable that nature should have to proceed in accordance with categories which…are not derived from it, and do not mold themselves on its pattern? The solution of this seeming enigma is as follows. Things in themselves would necessarily, apart from any understanding that knows them, conform to laws of their own. But appearances are only representations of things that are unknown as regards what they may be in themselves. As mere representations, they are subject to no law of connection save that which the connecting faculty prescribes. (1964, p. 178)

Here lies the great breakthrough of Kantian theory and the great consequence of constructivism: objectivity in the sciences is not achieved by finding out what things "really" are in themselves but by following the rules of human reason, the very rules that define and determine the essential characteristics of objectivity in the first place. We always and only understand things by striking up a relation to them, a relation in which the human subject is not simply the passive recipient of information from the object but is an active agent in the formation of how the object can be experienced. Things that are in relation to us ("objects of experience and knowledge") are not things-in-themselves. To *know* something is to *put* it into relation with us. Things-as-known are not things-in-themselves. We can never know those things that might "conform to laws of their own." We can only know that which reason produces after a plan of its own. And we can know the universal and necessary characteristics of this plan. We can know the universal and necessary characteristics of the objective world.

To push this one more step, nature-in-itself may, in this epistemology, be preserved from the imposition of human reason, but in such preservation, it is rendered unknowable" *by definition,* since to know nature is to place nature "under the sway" of human imposition. However, as a correlate to such preservation, the knowable world becomes a closed system that has reason as its master. Reason becomes answerable only to itself. It becomes, to use Piagetian terminology, "self-regulating" (Piaget, 1971b, p. 26).

RETURNING TO THE QUESTION OF ORIGINS

> Accordingly, the spontaneity of understanding becomes the formative principle of receptive matter, and in one stroke we have the old mythology of an intellect, which glues and rigs together the world's matter with its own forms. (Heidegger, 1985, p. 70)

In his search for the origins of human reason, Kant draws two conclusions:

1. The origin of human reason is found not in the chance outcomes of and generalizations from empirical experience, but in its universal and necessary *a priori* forms, its categories, its structures, its essential characteristics.

2. Human reason is a demand made upon the world, not unlike a judge compelling his witness to give answer to questions of "Reason's own determining" (Kant, 1964, p. 20). Reason is a giving of order(s), a construction, a making, a forming, a structuring, a categorizing, an organizing.

With Kant's image of the originary character of reason, we have what George Grant called "the wedding of knowing and production" (Grant, 1998, p. 1).

Jean Piaget, as we have noted, feels "close to the spirit of Kantianism," but it is difficult to see yet precisely how this could be. Piaget's work with young children and his work on the Simon-Binet intelligence tests taught him that what Kant takes to be the universal and necessary structures or categories of human reason are precisely *not* universal and necessary: they are not universally and necessarily shared by young children.

This dilemma proves to be the core of Jean Piaget's work: how is it that a squalling, totally dependent infant can, over the course of its life, come to master logic and mathematics in such a way that logic and mathematics appear (as they did to Kant) to be universal and necessary? Or, to put it more colloquially, "How, in reality, is science possible?" (Piaget, 1970a, p. 731). We turn next to Piaget's answer.

REFERENCES

Aristotle. *Metaphysics. Book IV.* http://vms.cc.wmich.edu/~mcgrew/aristotle.htm (assessed January 10, 2004).

Elkind, D. (1967). *Introduction to J. Piaget: Six psychological studies.* New York: Vintage Books.

Grant, G. (1998). *English-speaking justice.* Toronto: House of Anansi Press.

Heidegger, M. (1985). *The history of the concept of time.* Bloomington: Indiana University Press.

Kant, I. (1964). *Critique of pure reason.* London: Macmillan.

Piaget, J. (1952). *The origins of intelligence in children.* New York: International Universities Press.

———— (1965a). *Insights and illusions of philosophy.* New York: Meridian Books.

———— (1970a). Piaget's theory. In P. Mussen (Ed.), *Carmichael's manual of child psychology. Vol. 1* (pp. 703–32). Toronto: Wiley and sons.

———— (1971b). *Biology and knowledge.* Chicago: University of Chicago Press.

———— (1971c) *The construction of reality in the child.* New York: Ballantine Books.

TEN

Jean Piaget and the Origins of Intelligence: A Return to "Life Itself"

David Jardine

AFFINITY AND DISTANCE FROM "THE SPIRIT OF KANTIANISM"

One can feel very close to the spirit of Kantianism (and I believe I am close to it). [However] the necessity characteristic of the syntheses [Kant's *a priori* categories of Reason are the universal and necessary ways that experience is "knit together" by Reason. They are "synthesizing." They are "syntheses"] becomes [in my work] a *terminus ad quem* and ceases to be [as in Immanuel Kant's work] a *terminus a quo*. (Piaget, 1965a, p. 57)

In this passage, Jean Piaget articulates both his affinity to and his distance from the work of Immanuel Kant, which we shall examine briefly to illuminate Piaget's profound originality and contribution to educational theory and practice.

In Piaget's work, the universality and necessity of the categories of human reason articulated by Kant in his *Critique of Pure Reason* are not the starting point *(terminus a quo)* of human reason, but its end point *(terminus ad quem)*. These categories describe, Piaget argues, typical mature adult reasoning and are therefore not the origin of knowledge, but the outcome. They are not present from the beginning and/or present in each case but emergent over time.

In order to unpack the consequences of this insight for educational theory and practice, let's first elaborate on Kant's two conclusions from his search for the origins of human reason discussed in the previous chapter:

  1 The origin (here understood in the sense of most basic, most essential, most "original") of human reason is found not in the chance outcomes of and generalizations from indi-

vidual empirical experience but in its universal and necessary *a priori* forms, categories and structures: those definitive, unavoidable characteristics without which human reason would not be human reason.

2 Additionally, human reason's *a priori* forms, according to Kant, constitute a demand made upon the world. Human understanding is full of agency and determination. It is active, not passive. The ways that humanity *gives* orders are more "original," more fundamental, more basic, than the ways it *takes* orders. The former—the orders we give—*forms* what we take to be the order of the world. Thus, the categories of human reason shape or construct perceptual input into objects. To recall one of our examples: our *a priori* knowledge that the object in my hand is a self-identical thing ("A = A," whatever "A" might be), that it is a thing with properties ("A = B"), and that it has a cause ("If A, then B") is more basic than the particular *a posteriori* knowledge that this piece of chalk is white. The latter is empirical information we learn *from* experience; the former we *impose on* experience. The forms "A = A" and "A is B" and "If A, then B" (there are twelve such categories in the Kantian **Table of Categories**) are basic to any possible object, one particular example of which is the white chalk. To know that I have white chalk in my hand requires empirical experience. To know that I have a self-identical object with properties in my hand does not. Human reasoning is thus an orderly and ordering act of construction, of categorizing, of organizing and synthesizing.

In the passage cited at the beginning of this chapter, Piaget is saying that, although he feels close to the "spirit of Kantianism," the origin of human reason is *not* to be found in its *a priori* forms. In Piaget's work, these structures or categories—those that are characteristics of adult reasoning and that underwrite the disciplines of logic and mathematics—are not "originary." As he discovered in his work with the Simon-Binet intelligence tests and in his detailed conversations with children, those structures or categories:

- sequentially emerged over time, over the history of the species (phylogeny). The "concepts and categories [and methods] of established science"(Inhelder, 1969, p. 23) appear rather late in the history of the human species, and they
- sequentially re-emerge over a lifetime, over the history of the individual (ontogeny). The concepts, categories and methods of established science appear only as the person slowly reaches a certain cognitive maturity.

Since the concepts, categories and methods of established science emerge[d], they cannot be universal and necessary to the character of human intelligence. A newborn infant does not structure the world in these ways, even though, somehow, over the course of that child's development, he or she comes to be able to master logic and mathematics, disciplines fundamental in the Kantian categories. So, here is the rub for Piaget: how is it possible that something like the Kantian categories can be absent in the life of very young children, can develop over time and yet, in the end, can take on the character of universality and necessity in the disciplines of mathematics and logic? How is it possible that established science can emerge out of the embodied, concrete, animistic, image-filled, playful life of a young child chasing and bursting bubbles?

Piaget's work shares this characteristic with Kant's: both argue that the "original" characteristic of human reason is that it is an active, organizing, structuring demand made upon the world. However, typical adult human reasoning (like the type tested for in the Simon-Binet intelligence tests), and its handmaiden disciplines, logic and mathematics, are only a late arriving set of structures and ordering demands. However, they are a reflection of the fact that all of human life—from the frail actions of a newborn infant, to a child bursting bubbles and laughing, to those student teachers counting up pieces of white chalk, to the pristine and abstract intricacies of a mathematician's scrawls—has the character of such a demand:

> *Every relation* between the living being and its environment [not just those in logic and mathematics and the logic of objectivity characteristic of the concepts and categories and methods of established science] has this particular characteristic: the former, instead of submitting passively to the latter, modifies it by imposing on it a certain structure of its own. (Piaget, 1952, p. 118, emphasis added)

Piaget believes that there is a "self-organizing principle *inherent in life itself*" (1952, p. 19, emphasis added). Such order-giving activity is not exclusive, therefore, to logic and mathematics. This self-organizing principle inherent in life itself defines, for Jean Piaget, the origins of human intelligence.

JEAN PIAGET'S BIOLOGICAL VISION OF THE FUNCTIONAL *A PRIORI*

Genetic epistemology is concerned with providing what Piaget maintains is an "indispensable genetic dimension" to our understanding of the concepts, categories and methods of established science, like those articulated by Kant. It is, as we have discussed, interested in the question, "How does knowledge grow?" (Piaget, 1970a, p. 731). How is it that we, beginning, as biological entities apparently possessed of only the simplest of reflexes, are "destined to master science" (Piaget, 1952, p. 372)?

In order to answer these sorts of perplexing questions, it is not enough for Piaget to locate human intelligence and the concepts and categories of established science as simple "relationship[s] among others between the organism and its environment" (Piaget, 1952, p. 19). Logic and mathematics do not just *accompany* the forms of structuring the world displayed by children or the biological functionings and structures of the human organism. The ability to understand logic and mathematics *originates in* and *emerges out of* the life of an organism that begins its days as a helpless infant.

In his *Origins of Intelligence in Children* (1952), Jean Piaget provides us with the clearest and most concise statement of his concerns in these matters, arguing that "from the fact that the living being achieves knowledge and that the child is one day destined to master science, we certainly believe that the conclusion must be drawn that there is a continuum between life and intelligence" (p. 372). Indeed, Piaget and his followers have provided us with a wealth of information that describes the structural differences "characteristic of each [developmental] level" (Piaget, 1952, p. 372) leading to the emergence of logic and mathematics. There are textbooks full of descriptions of the unique characteristics of Piaget's stages of cognitive development, and we will provide our own descriptions in the next chapter.

Piaget's work is also deeply concerned with the issue of "what is permanent in the course of this evolution" (1952, p. 372). In fact, "what is permanent" defines the order, sequence and characteristics of the stages of development. Therefore, the continuum underlying the slow genesis and emergence of the concepts and categories of established science is of great importance in understanding his stages of cognitive development and how they are sequenced and articulated in his work. Piaget believes a continuum defines the slow emergence of knowledge in children, a sense of direction and organization; it is *not* simply the random accruing of empirical experience. Here is Piaget's great challenge to behaviorist theory. Children don't just *change* or modify behavior in response to the whims of experience and stimuli, Piaget argues. Rather, he suggests, they *develop* in ways that have pattern, sequence and continuity.

What is the nature of this continuum? The title of the introductory chapter of *Origins of Intelligence in Children* immediately gives us a clue: "Biological Problem of Intelligence." Piaget writes:

> Intelligence is adaptation. In order to grasp its relation to life in general, it is necessary to state precisely the relations that exist between the organism and environment. Life is a continuous creation of increasingly complex forms and a progressive balancing of these forms with the environment. To say that intelligence is a particular instance of biological adaptation is thus to suppose that it is essentially an organization and that its function is to structure the universe just as the organism structures its environment. (1952, p. 4)

As we have already noted, according to Piaget, *all* interactions between the organism and the environment involve the living being modifying that environment "by imposing on it a certain structure of its own" (Piaget, 1952, p. 118).

Thus, one sense in which there is a universal and necessary continuity across development is that at no level of development can the environment be conceived as a ready-made organization that simply imposes itself on a passive organism-subject. Rather, the underlying organization of the organism, at any and all levels under consideration, actively structures the environment. Thus, once again in line with the "spirit of Kantianism," Piaget speaks against an empiricist conception of the nature of human intelligence that "tends to consider experience as imposing itself without the subject having to organize it" (Piaget, 1952, p. 362).

However, this sense of continuity alone does not yet account for the *emergence* of the concepts and categories of established science in a way that is continuous with "life itself." There must be something about adaptation that leads to this emergence and that provides for this continuity. More fundamental—more "original"—than the varying structures of organism-environment interactions are the ways in which all of those structures *function*. All organism-environment interactions function in precisely the same manner. Piaget variously uses the terms "functional identity" (1952, p. 24), "functional analogy" (p. 237), or **functional invariants.**

These are assimilation, accommodation and equilibration, and they define the a priori character of any relationship between the organism and the environment. Rather than understanding the a priori as a set of structures (following Kant), Piaget believes that the a priori is functional in character and that the structures described by Kant are those that are best adapted to this invariant, universal and necessary functioning (pp. 8–13) and "functional correspondence" (1967, p. 3) to indicate that "the essential fact concerning this functioning is, in effect, absolute continuity" (Piaget, 1967, p. 141, emphasis added) across the wide array of structural or conceptual differences that define human developmental stages. "These functional analogies," Piaget clarifies, "do not at all imply an identity of structure" (1952, p. 240). The particular constructs differ and change over time—even those deemed a priori by Kant. However, despite such difference, "from the simplest of reflexes to the most systematic intelligence, the same method of operation seems to us to continue through all the stages, thus establishing a complete continuity between increasingly complex structures" (Piaget, 1952, p. 153, emphasis added). The newborn infant and the mathematician, it seems, function in exactly the same ways: even though their constructs of the world differ radically, how those constructs function remains continuous.

In Piaget's reworking of Kant, the functioning of life itself becomes what is *a priori,* and constructivism, a currently popular thread of educational theory and practice, is born.

ASSIMILATION, ACCOMMODATION AND EQUILIBRATION AND THE PERVASIVENESS OF "CONSTRUCTION"

The terms that Piaget uses to describe this essentially continuous "method of operation" are assimilation, accommodation and equilibration.

Assimilation is the process whereby features of the environment are incorporated into the structure of the organism. It is a process of "integration into previous structures" (Piaget, 1967, p. 4)—what Immanuel Kant might call a "synthesizing act" (one that involves constructing, ordering, demanding, organizing, bringing together, linking). Thus, when those student teachers named the object I held "white chalk," they were not just passively receiving the input of a perceptual experience but rather were integrating and organizing that input by attempting to assimilate it into "previous structures" (previous organizations of thinking, previous concepts, categories, types, etc.). But note a subtle shift here that once again distances Piaget's work from that of Kant. This "integration into previous structures" is not only an integration into general, abstract structures such as "A = A" (it is a self-identical object), or "A is B" (it is an object with properties), or "If A, then B" (it is an object with a physical, material cause). Even the tentative, empirically general knowledge that "chalk is brittle" is *itself* constructive and ordering in nature. What has occurred here is that the idea of "construction" has become pervasive: *all* interactions between the organism and the environment are "constructive" and "organizing" and "ordering."

This idea has become so commonplace in our contemporary world, especially in the language and thinking of education, that it is difficult to fully experience the profundity of its arrival. To review: even empirically derived concepts—concepts derived from empirically experiencing chalk over the course of time—are ordering and constructive of future experiences. Simply put, because I have experienced chalk dozens of times over the course of my life, when I walk into a new and unfamiliar classroom, that chalk on the board's ledge is experienced by me as brittle because I construct my new experience of this new classroom in light of my previous experiences. Or, to use Piaget's terminology, I assimilate these new experiences to my previous assimilatory schemata or structures. This is how my previous experiences *function*—as ways of ordering my experience of this new classroom into a somewhat familiar place, as ways of "assimilating" this experience. The structuring, assimilating action of my previous experiences thus tends to stabilize my experience of the world. I don't have to constantly experience the immediacy and particularity of every moment. Because my assimilatory schemata provide order to the here-and-now of experience—"the *hic* and *nunc*" (Piaget, 1973 p. 9)—they buffer me from the constant newness of experience. The significance of this point is dual for educators:

- children are functioning in precisely this way—assimilating experience in the classroom in accord with their own "structures" or "schemata"—and, most disturbingly for beginning teachers,
- the previous experiences and order(s) that they bring to the classroom are not identical to those of a typical adult.

Assimilation is not just a cognitive matter or a cognitive function. The same functioning is at work, for example, in my digestion system. Calling something "edible" does not describe, to use David Elkind's phrase, a "property of the object." Rather, it describes the *relation between* my digestive system's "assimilatory structures" and the object. "Edibility," to use the Kantian terminology, is a demand made upon things, a "requirement" of the organism, not just a property of the object. The object is experienced as something edible because it can be integrated into the structures of my digestive system. If it couldn't be thus integrated—assimilated to an already existing structure—it wouldn't be edible. And, as we all know, if I attempt to assimilate it and I do not have the assimilatory structures available to do so, I will, excuse me, "reject" it—in a rather visceral manner.

The brilliance of Piaget's understanding of cognitive development becomes clear as we pursue this line of thought. A young child who does not have the assimilatory schemata or structures that would allow her to "take in" (assimilate into already existing structures) information about, say, place-value in mathematics, will not be able to "understand" (assimilate into already existing structures) certain aspects of a classroom conversation—not because she isn't paying attention, but because her own structures of understanding do not allow for attention to be paid to this idea. So what happens? She'll ignore or reject the conversation altogether, push back against its incomprehensibility (a sort of cognitive "throwing up"), or she will take it in as best she can, given the structures of understanding she has available.

Here is a simple example from a second-grade child: "Twenty plus two is forty because two plus two is four and zero isn't worth anything." This is a perfect example of how the urge to assimilate is indigenous to our nature. Faced with an example like "$20 + 2 = ?$," *all of us*—adults and children alike, even the newborn infant—will bring to bear the structures we have available to assimilate this question and respond to it. Jean Piaget's work provides teachers sensitive to children and their efforts at understanding an opening: "40" is no longer simply incorrect. It is also a wonderful, necessary clue to understanding how this child is thinking, what structures and understandings this child is currently using, and, best of all, what concepts, structures and understandings are necessary for this child to grasp the idea of place-value and how it functions in our mathematics system.

The other essential feature of this method of operation is the process of **accommodation**. Clearly, the function of assimilation doesn't yet account for the fact that we learn and change over time, that the structures to which we assimilate our life-experiences grow and develop. Accommodation refers to the fact that the organism is often incapable of assimilating all elements of the environment into "previous structures." Over the course of development, new elements in the environment "cause the old framework to crack" (Piaget, 1971a, p. 397) and require the previous assimilatory structures to modify themselves to accommodate these new experiences.

The process of accommodation is the "result of pressures exerted by the environment" (Piaget, 1952, p. 6), but it does not function in the ways that behaviorism would suggest. To go back to our place-value example, when the child is confronted—slowly, carefully—with more and more examples of how the idea of place-value functions, her existing assimilatory schemata become systematically perturbed over time. She will begin to experience the fact that her current assimilatory schemata (more simply and commonsensically phrased, her current understandings of these matters) are not adequate to her environment and that something needs to be done. She needs to modify her understanding in order to accommodate new phenomena. If she does not, the pressures of the environment (a school life and a world in which numbers and issues of place-value inevitably exist) will be destabilizing. She needs, in short, to learn.

But "learning," here, is not a matter of simply accumulating more and more input, (as behaviorism would suggest), since the very conditions of her ability to *receive* input are at issue. In the face of these discrepant events, "learning" becomes a matter of modifying the terms of which input is possible—which input is demanded, organized, structured and "constructed." She does not learn the concept of place-value through repeated empirical instances (per the behavioral version of learning). Rather, she must *develop new structures,* new ways of assimilating, constructing and organizing the world. Granted, repeated external stimuli are a necessary condition for learning—they are necessary to the destabilization of previous assimilatory schemata—but they not a sufficient condition. An internal change is also necessary. If the new, discrepant experiences are too severely different, the assimilatory structures will not change—neither will they change if the new, discrepant experiences are too familiar, since the new experiences will not disrupt or disturb the equilibrium of already existing structures.

Understanding this process has a profound effect on how we imagine our tasks as educators. First, development is not especially incremental. As many teachers have witnessed, sometimes children can be presented with repeated opportunities to learn a certain idea or task, but all to no avail—and then suddenly, a shift occurs, and what seemed impossible one day is commonplace the next. Those repeated opportunities have had a hand in this shift, but although the opportunities are incremental, the shift often is not. Sometimes we try to accelerate such shifts by presenting more frequent opportunities, with unreliable results. As the commonsense adage from Piaget's work warns, if children are not "developmentally ready," they cannot learn. All we can do is re-present the experiential opportunities, over and over, and patiently wait. Development takes time. As educators we must each realize this truth: just because I taught something several times, does not mean that students learned.

In the work of Jean Piaget, these functional invariants of assimilation and accommodation do not appear randomly in the life of the developing child. They are deeply rooted in a functioning of "life itself" that guides their appearance and, moreover, that guides the *direction* that development takes. This deeper function, this deeper sense of continuity, is called equilibrium. "Equilibrium" is a term used to describe the relationship between assimilation and accommodation. "Adaptation," of which the concepts, categories and methods of established science are particular instances, "is an equilibrium between assimilation and accommodation" (Piaget, 1952, p. 6).

But here we've reached the same impasse. To say that the functions of assimilation, accommodation and equilibration are universally and necessarily continuous across the different stages of development—all life is adaptation—still doesn't account for the unique *emergence* of the particular adaptations achieved in the concepts, categories and methods of established science. For Piaget, the concepts, categories and methods of established science are not simply one adaptation among others. Science is the end of adaptation, its fulfillment, its goal, its *terminus ad quem.* Human intelligence is, according to Piaget, "an *extension* and *perfection* of all adaptive processes" (Piaget, 1973, p. 7, emphasis original). Here we see traces of Piaget's intellectual ancestry in his profound belief that human reason and human intelligence, as manifest in established science, are the crowning moment of life itself. That adaptation, that way of constructing an understanding of the world, is the goal toward which life is moving, striving, developing. For now, we have to figure out how this absolutely continuous functioning of adaptation (through assimilation, accommodation and equilibration) finds its "perfection" in the workings of established science.

"AN ALL-EMBRACING EQUILIBRIUM" AS THE *TELOS* OF DEVELOPMENT

In Piaget's work, equilibrium is not a mere description of the relation between assimilation and accommodation. Equilibrium is also a **teleological** notion, and as such, it is an expression of "the fundamental reality about living things" (Piaget, 1967, p. 347). Development, in Piaget's understanding, can be characterized as a sequence of increasingly adaptive, increasingly equilibrated and stable plateaus or stages, each characterized by specifiable structures or schemata. In the middle of all these structural changes over time are the continuous and invariant functions of assimilation, accommodation and equilibration. The functional invariant not only appears in every interaction between the organism and environment, it also:

> [Orients] the whole of the successive structures which the mind will then work out in contact with reality. It will thus play the role that [Kant] assigned to the *a priori:* that is to say, [this *functional a priori*] will impose on the structures certain necessary and irreducible conditions. Only the mistake has sometimes been made of regarding the *a priori* as consisting in structures existing ready-made from the beginning of development, whereas if the functional invariant of thought is at work in the most primitive stages, it is only little by little that it impresses itself on consciousness due to the elaboration of structures which are increasingly adapted to the function itself. (Piaget, 1952, p. 3)

In this way, the functioning of "life itself" is formulated as a "progressive equilibrium" (Piaget, 1952, p. 7) worked out through an ordered sequence of stages. But the tendency toward equilibrium is not toward *any* sort of compensation or variation in the organism's structures that will accommodate a new element. Rather, "there is *adaptation*…[only] when this variation results in an increase in the interrelationships between the environment and the organism which are favourable to [the organism's] preservation" (Piaget, 1952, p. 5. Emphasis in original). The modifications that count as adaptive are thus not chaotic or undirected; they are made specifically to create an improved equilibrium in the relation between the organism and the environment.

It is only in light of this teleological sense of equilibrium—equilibrium as an "end" toward which the organism is tending—that the succession of differing structures of organism-environment interactions can be seen as an ordered and comprehensible *sequence*. Moreover, it is only in light of this teleological sense of equilibrium that the succession of structures of organism-environment interactions can be seen to achieve their "perfection" in the concepts and categories and methods of established science. In *The Psychology of Intelligence* (1973, p. 7), Piaget states:

> Every structure is to be thought of as a particular form of equilibrium more or less stable within its restricted field and losing its stability on reaching the limits of the field. But these structures, forming different levels, are to be regarded as succeeding one another according to the law of development, such that each one brings about a more inclusive and stable equilibrium for the processes that emerge from the preceding level.

Development, now understood as a succession of structures oriented toward steadily increasing stability and inclusiveness, "tends towards an all-embracing equilibrium by aiming at the assimilation of the whole of reality" (Piaget, 1973, p. 9).

This tendency toward an all-embracing equilibrium is found in the concepts, categories and methods of established science that, for Piaget, form "an *extension* and *perfection* of all adaptive processes" (Piaget, 1973, p. 7, emphasis original). Again, we see in this Piaget's great participation in an old idea that came to such fruition at the end of the nineteenth and beginning of the twentieth centuries: progress—or better yet, more true to this legacy—that European humanity has developed to the point where it can find its destiny and fulfillment in objective science. We turn now to examine the succession of stages of development that finds its fulfillment in established science.

THE SUCCESSION OF STAGES OF COGNITIVE DEVELOPMENT

The succession of stages of cognitive development in Piaget's genetic epistemology is easy to list, and literally thousands of descriptions of each stage are available: a cursory search on Google gave 9270 hits for "Piaget's stages." Our own brief description of Piaget's **stages of development** follows; we will have a lot more to say about these stages and their characteristics in the next chapter.

SENSORI-MOTOR KNOWLEDGE

Sensori-Motor Knowledge is Piaget's first stage of development (0–2 years old), in which children are centered on their immediate physical environment and learn through bodily activities: grabbing, touching, smelling, eating, etc.

The young infant is possessed, initially, only of reflexes that are themselves organized ways of ordering experience—sucking reflexes, grasping ("palmar") reflexes, the reflex whereby the infant's head turns toward an object that touches its cheek, and so on. These are great instinctual adaptive structures that aid the infant's initial survival. Very young children at this stage also have well-developed, if not yet acute, structures of perception; sensory schemata are extremely prevalent. The world is teeming with sensory input—sounds, smells, touches:

> In its beginnings, assimilation is essentially the utilization of the external environment by the subject to nourish his hereditary or acquired schemata. It goes without saying that schemata such as those of sucking, sight, prehension, etc. constantly need to be accommodated to things, and that the necessities of this accommodation often thwart the assimilatory effort. But this accommodation remains so undifferentiated from the assimilatory processes that it does not give rise to any special active behaviour pattern but merely consists in an adjustment of the pattern to the details of the things assimilated. Hence it is natural that at this developmental level the eternal world does not seem formed by permanent objects. In other words, at first the universe consists in mobile and plastic perceptual images centred about personal activity. (Piaget, 1971a, p. 396)

This "state of chaotic undifferentiation" (Piaget, 1971a, p. 397) is an unstable and exclusive form of equilibrium since, by being restricted to the immediate and momentary aspects of the environment, the infant must constantly adapt to each new element which presents itself. These early assimilatory schemata or structures of the infant—inherited and inborn reflexes—are what Piaget calls "global schema[ta]" (1952, p. 35). Simply put, the newborn child tends, for example, to put anything and everything into its mouth and suck on it, having not yet differentiated these schemata into, say, suckable things that provide nourishment and suckable things that provide comfort to the sucking reflex itself.

Even though these very early sensory inputs are themselves organized by the organism's "assimilatory schemata" (the sense organs), these inputs take time to co-ordinate. **Coordination** is one of the great accommodations that the young child masters to understand, for example, that the object seen and the object grasped are the same object. Grasping, the child realizes, might work in conjunction with seeing. This would be more adaptive and make for a more liveable, more stable world. The young child is thus centred on what is immediate and vivid perceived, through the senses, with all the bodily attachments to those things: touching, smelling, tasting, feeling, grasping, holding, pushing, pulling. This is the sense in which this stage is thus also "motoric"—it is about the slow achievement of motility, movement into the surroundings.

The great Kantian category (for "category," read "form of thinking" or "structure of thinking" or, to use Piaget's term, "schema of thinking") "A = A" has its nebulous beginnings here. Very young children, when presented with objects then covered up or moved, will cease trying to grasp after them, as if the object has ceased to exist. Over the course of the first two years (usually very early on), children slowly develop a sense of what Piaget calls **object permanence**.

This is essentially the belief that "things continue to exist"—A remains A—"even if I don't perceive them immediately." That young girl will go chasing around a tree to find those bubbles that have gone out of sight. This is quite an accomplishment, to realize, "The world is not as unstable or fleeting as my immediate perceptual experience." Young children and their parents are engaged in the developmental establishment of this structure of knowledge when playing peekaboo.

Young children are also very imitative, and they begin to enjoy repetitive games, rhymes, songs and stories. Their imaginations begin to flourish. By far the greatest cognitive accomplishment in this first stage of development is the advent of language. The slow development of language (there are libraries written on the stages in the development of language) provides a near-miraculous change: the child is no longer restricted to thinking about, invoking, naming, objects that are immediately available. Rather than living in a world of presentation (a world of immediate sensory experiences), the child slowly becomes able to *re-present*. By the tail-end of the sensori-motor stage of development, young children can signify, name and ask for objects that are absent by using a representative of the thing, a "stand in" which they have learned through observation and imitation: a word. They no longer have to stretch their arms towards what they want and express delight. That young girl learns to say "Mummy, I want more bubbles." This indicates another structural change in the child's "method of operation." Children slowly become able to be motivated, not by immediacy and reflex reactions, but by setting goals and attempting to carry them out.

PRE-OPERATIONAL KNOWLEDGE

First, we must note that Piaget does not suggest that the characteristics of the previous stage(s) of development simply disappear once a new stage is entered. Many characteristics central to a certain stage persist or are structurally transformed. In the pre-operational knowledge stage of cognitive development, approximately 2–7 years of age, language takes off, so to speak, and becomes a central engine of the child's exploration of the world. One characteristic from the sensori-motor stage that persists through the pre-operational stage is that the child remains egocentric. This does *not* mean that children at this stage are centred on themselves or selfish. Rather, it means that they have not yet developed a sense of themselves and their own point of view and therefore have difficulty seeing another person's point of view—not because they are centred on their own point of view but because they have not yet grasped the whole idea of *having* a point of view. A young child who announces into the telephone, "It's me," for example, has trouble imagining how the other person might not know who it is. A great deal of educational energy is focused on helping children slowly learn that the experiences so immediate to them are not necessarily immediately shared. At this stage, children need to learn to articulate their experience, to share it, speak it, show it and demonstrate it; they are far more able to do so in concrete ways than in abstract or conceptual descriptions.

Coupled with this concrete expression is the dramatic increase in the centrality of play and imagination to development. Young children will spontaneously become involved in what is called "solitary play." A child will move around groups of stuffed animals and talk up a storm, working out elaborate scenarios, rehearsing and repeating things experienced and things imagined—learning all the while about naming, negotiation and narrative structure. Next to coordination, this sort of consolidation of assimilatory schemata through repetition is a major form of accommodation and adaptation. In play and through imagination, accommodations can be tested out, troubles can become objects of speculation or trial-and-error, patterns can be established and remembered. Slightly older children become involved in "parallel play," where two or more children will play alongside but essentially independently of each other. Eventually, and (as any teacher of young children knows) sometimes after many instances of troubles arising when two parallel courses of play collide, "co-operative play" emerges, in which the child begins to be able to actually let go of full control over the course of events and play *with* other children, negotiating, co-constructing, and so on. We get a hint here, too, of what is to come. Children become entranced with concretely exploring how things operate, how things work, how they are put together and come apart. Playing with the workings of things becomes endlessly fascinating and time-consuming. Much of this play is deeply sensory and deeply imaginative, full of alluring, powerful images.

This accounts for young children's often intense interest in stories, especially ones that are full of suspense, adventure, great imaginary figures and monsters, heroes and villains. Children's sense of narrative anticipation and excitement in the face of a rich, imaginative, sensorially laden book full of beautiful pictures and words is uncontainable. In a good children's book, the pictures tell stories at least as compelling as the words. When it comes to learning what the story means, and slowly learning to decode the words themselves, the allure of such images can become an invaluable tool. This makes a case for children coming to understand written language "imaginally," thematically and substantively, rather than simply phonemically. Children learn language narratively, by gathering it into meaningful, belonging-together clusters. A simple example of this is "king, queen, moat, courage, heroes, dragons, castles, battles, horses" and so on. These words are not just stand-ins for lovely, exciting, sensory and bodily things (bold moves, fiery breath, nobility, fear). They are also a cluster of images, ideas and figures that *belong together* in the child's experience of the world. These words form a coherent world. As deeply organizing, assimilatory, constructing beings, children (and adults) crave such coherence and the stability it brings.

By contrast, because young children live imaginatively, a word list that is organized phonemically is rather dull and unalluring: "cat, hat, mat, sat, fat." The phonemic organization "-at words" is very abstract and distant. More bluntly put—and this, I suggest, is a profound and often unnoted consequence of Jean Piaget's insights (Jardine, Clifford & Friesen, 2003a)—understanding and experiencing the phoneme "-at" and the ways in which this phoneme can be prefixed with the letters "c," "h," "m," "s," and "f" is a form of analytic thinking that is a product of a stage of cognitive development to which the young child is not party. As a concept produced by the science of linguistics, "-at" is a logicomathematically produced assimilatory schema in which the young child has very little concrete interest. This is not to say that children are not interested in the sounds of language. At this stage (and before it, and after it), the wonderful sounds of language are linked in the life of the child to the giggly, age-old allure of rhymes, poems and nonsense. Young children love to play with words and their sounds, and the dull, decidedly unplayful spelling or writing list "cat, hat, mat, sat" rarely takes advantage of this developmental tendency. Dr. Seuss, on the other hand, does, as does the first-grade child's discovery that my name rhymes with (giggle) "sardine."

There are two final characteristics that point the pre-operational stage towards future developments. First, children in this stage of cognitive development are certainly capable of what is sometimes too loosely called "abstract thinking," but what we mean by that must be fleshed out. After having read image-rich stories about the perilous journeys of various travellers, even very young children can become engaged in profound conversations and speculations about why people go on journeys, why such things are written about, how perils always seem to appear, how such perils can be lessons, and how learning such lessons might be why authors write such things. But this sort of "abstract" thinking—away from the specific, concrete content of any one story—is still what could be neologistically called "concrete abstract thinking." That is to say, children are capable of gathering the images and themes from these stories in substantive ways full of imagery, examples and "body," full of engaged and engaging questions and concerns. If a teacher moves to a new set of stories—about love, affection, obligation and trust, for example—that teacher must recall that previous example, in all its concreteness and particularity, to use it as a model for the new discussions and explorations. The thematizing that children did on journeys in the first instance is not known, experienced or remembered by them as a general and generalizable way of operating. It is known and remembered only in its concreteness, and the teacher will find that that former way of thinking about the various journey-stories must be re-embodied in this new instance, re-figured. The substance, feel and flow of that former activity must be remembered and re-experienced in order for children to carry it forward into this new territory.

A second characteristic of this pre-operational stage of cognitive development is vital in understanding how it represents a stage on the way to an all-embracing equilibrium. Children near the end of this developmental stage are beginning to be able to explicitly perform very simple operations on objects. Counting, adding, putting things in order, sorting, categorizing, subtracting, are all mathematical "operations" that begin to make sense to children at the end of this stage, thus preparing them for the next.

CONCRETE OPERATIONAL KNOWLEDGE

It is no accident that Piaget named the previous stage "pre-operational." Of growing concern to Piaget over the course of the child's cognitive development is how the concepts, categories and methods of established science emerge, and central—one might say *a priori,* universal and necessary—to this emergence are the functional invariants of assimilation, accommodation and their adaptive balance, equilibration. Piaget calls these functional variants the organism's continuous and invariant "method of operation" in all and every interaction with the environment. What began emerging in the previous stage and now appears dramatically at approximately 7–11 years of age is that the child begins to have a nebulous knowledge not simply of *things in the world* but of his or her own *operations on the world.* In short, their "method of operation" becomes visible to children.

In the stage of concrete operational knowledge children develop the ability to not only have perceptual, empirical knowledge about objects but also to make explicit, very specific operations on such objects—consciously, with knowledge of their own agency. Thus far in development, for the most part, the invariant functions have been operating unconsciously and inexplicitly. Beginning to appear now, albeit in concrete form, is a different type of knowledge. For example, a group of pennies are placed in a circle, and a child counts them. She then starts at a different point on the circle of pennies, counts again and gets the same number. From this sort of example, Piaget extrapolates that what the child is slowly learning is not something about pennies or about some visible, specific starting point on the circle. Rather, the child is slowly learning something about her *actions* and their *organization.* She is learning not about the physical characteristics of the pennies but about the outcomes of the operations she has performed: the operation of counting, enumeration. "Twelve pennies" is neither a physical property of any single penny, nor is it a physical property of the group as a whole. It is, rather, a mathematical "property" that necessarily entails the operation of enumeration, a property tied to the constructive, gathering, synthesizing activity of counting as *an operation* that she *does.*

Take another familiar example: when you place two parallel rows of coins in front of a young child and ask, "Which one has the most?" the child will say that the rows have the same amount. If you then put more space between the pennies to extend one of the rows and ask the same question, very young children will say the longer row has more. This is because, sensorially and motorically, one row is now visibly and undeniably "bigger," and the child is not yet able to detach the knowledge gained from enumeration (in which the number of coins does not change just because you spread them into a longer row) from the perceptually evident fact that one row is now bigger. But in the stage of concrete operational knowledge, children become able to understand that the act of counting the coins and the sensory presentation of the coins are not the same. Moreover—and this is a spectacular breakthrough—the operation of counting is a way of gaining knowledge that is not tethered directly to the objects on which it is performed. Simply put, I can count the chalk, I can count the number of people in the classroom, I can count the pennies in a circle or in a row. A new sort of knowledge emerges, one that entails getting a reflective grasp on my own ways of operating on the world. I can count things and, moreover, this is a general characteristic of things in the world: things can be counted. This general, operational knowledge—that things are countable, enumerable—is, for Piaget, a different *type* of knowledge than the knowledge that I have three pieces of chalk in my hand.

Piaget maintains, however, that at this early stage of the development of concrete operational knowledge, the knowledge gained is still of necessity *concrete,* still rooted in the sensory and motoric actions of the child. That is to say, for the child, counting is still always counting *something,* a number is still always a number of *things,* and a measure is still always the measure of *something.* This insight has had profound effects on educational theory and practice. It suggests that young children, when first becoming engaged in mathematics, need to act upon and actively manipulate concrete objects—pennies, blocks, sticks—in order for them to effectively understand the operations they are performing. They need to see their operations concretely manifest: a pile of five blocks, remove two of them, how many are left? A pizza with twelve slices, divide them up between the three of us, how many do we each get? And, as teachers know, at first the young child faced with a pile of five blocks from which two have been removed will likely look at the remaining pile and count them out anew, because the child needs to concretely "do" the number that are left in order to concretely understand what it means to have five and take away two.

The idea that young children require the use of concrete objects to manipulate in learning mathematics has become commonplace. And this is also true for most adults—we all require, on occasion, a concrete example, an illustration or a demonstration of an abstract idea we can't quite "picture." Graphs can be understood, but it is best, with very young children, to place concrete representations of the objects on the graph. Organizing the children in a classroom by height does not teach them, for example, how to use the abstract concept of height to organize a group of objects. Rather, going through the concrete process of organizing helps children develop, *out* of that activity, a better and clearer understanding of height measurement as a substantial, image filled concept. This can be accomplished best if everyone stands up, moves around and sees this series, so that the concreteness of the differences between, say, 44 and 42 and 39 inches tall can be sensorially and concretely grasped. Other classifications of objects can be understood as well, but it is still necessary to make the new experience of "ordering" or "gathering" similarly concrete and active: for example, to sort things by colour by actively picking them out and re-piling them. Therefore, when a classroom of young children is faced with a new task of, say, putting larger to smaller tomatoes from the garden in order of size, it is not useful to ask "Who can tell me what the rules are for doing this task?" As teachers well know, it is much more useful to ask "Who can tell me what we did last week when we organized the...?" This asks the child to "know" the "rule" of ordering by means of their embodied work and in light of a concrete previous example of an activity wherein that rule concretely appeared.

This is a vital point for educators: when we want children of this age to demonstrate their knowledge about how many different sizes of blocks are in a tub, they may need to do more than think about it. Children need to show us what they know, and in order to do that, they may need to redo the knowing by sorting, naming, enumerating and then answering. Moreover, and equally vital, the next day, when asked the same question, they will probably need to do it all over again, because they don't necessarily "hold" this concrete knowledge in their heads as a concept, but rather as concrete organizations of actions (operations) that they can only know about in performing these actions. Only after repeated experiences like this are children slowly able to abstract from these concrete operational activities and get a glimpse of what forms the core of the next stage of development, formal operational knowledge—knowledge of the abstract organization of the operations themselves, detached fully from any concrete exemplification.

FORMAL OPERATIONAL KNOWLEDGE

At approximately 11–15+ years of age the sort of knowledge requisite of the concepts, categories and methods of established sciences comes into full bloom. Let's go back to the example of knowing that there are three pieces of chalk in my hand. In a commonsense way, in knowing that there are three pieces of chalk in my hand, you do know something about those objects. When we think of what you know according to the previous stage—what you know in a concrete operational way—you know that you counted them and that you could just as well count something else as well; you can detach concretely counting from concretely counting chalk. You can count almost anything. This becomes a charming obsession of some children, who become taken with the numbers of things: How many miles is it to Mars? How many grains of sand are in my hand?

In this new stage of formal operational knowledge, you also are able to gain knowledge simply from a number itself. You can begin to think not just about enumerating physical objects but also about how numbers abstractly work in relation to each other. Numbering, adding, subtracting, multiplying, dividing, measuring, ordering, serializing, graphing—these matters become knowable as orderly, rule-governed, formal, abstract, structured ways of operating. According to Piaget, what a child learns in knowing these ways of operating are the general forms or shapes that knowledge of *any possible object* can take. In coming upon these structured, rule-governed ways of operating on the world, the growing child has come upon a way that knowledge can operate that grows and lives beyond his or her individuality and experience. In knowing concretely that there are three pieces of chalk in my hand, my knowing remains tethered to me and my own experiences; in knowing about numeration in its formal operational sense, I've come upon an instance of "processes common to *all* subjects" (Piaget, 1965a, p. 108, emphasis added). I've come upon a knowledge of the functional or operational character of knowing itself. And, to follow the Kantian logic of knowledge-as-construction, in coming to know the processes or operations common to all subjects, I come to know the general terms in which all subjects can construct the world. To re-cite: "the *a priori* [common to all subjects] conditions of a possible experience in general are at the same time conditions of the possibility of objects of experience" (Kant, 1964, p. 138).

In the stage of formal operations (also called logico-mathematical knowledge) I've discovered, according to Piaget, the logic of objectivity, because I've discovered a knowledge of the invariant functioning or operating of "life itself." This functioning has been going on all along and is common even in the newborn infant, except in that case, the unavoidable processes (the functional invariants of assimilation, accommodation and equilibration) are encumbered by and embodied in structures not yet fully adaptive, not yet fully aware of or in command of those operations. According to Piaget, then, at the logico-mathematical stage of development, I've arrived at a way of knowing that is in command of the functional invariants: the core of the concepts, categories and methods of objective science.

Clearly, "objectivity does not…mean independence in relation to the assimilatory activity of intelligence, but simply dissociation from the self and from egocentric subjectivity" (Piaget, 1952, p. 366). Objectivity is not a static relation between the subject and an object but a form of activity that operates in a de-centred manner, away from the exclusive schemata of the individual and toward schemata common to all individuals (the whole process of **decentration** is itself a fascinating topic in Piaget's work that we won't elaborate on here). Objectivity, far from being an inert state, is a common method of operation, a *methodology*. To know the world in this formal operational way is to "do" science. And, correlatively, established science is most originally and most fundamentally a method of operation.

Even after this long journey, we still haven't directly answered our question: how is it that the concepts, categories and methods of established science form "an extension and perfection of all adaptive processes"? How is it that the concepts, categories and methods of established science provide "an all-embracing equilibrium by aiming at the assimilation of the whole of reality"?

FORMAL LOGIC AND MATHEMATICS AS THE ORIGIN OF INTELLIGENCE

This last twist in Piaget's search for the origins of intelligence is nearly biblical in its import: because of the relationship between logico-mathematical knowledge and the functional invariants that are the origins of intelligence, what comes last is also somehow first. Formal logic and mathematics, which underwrite the methods of operation in established science, are understood by Jean Piaget to embody the functional invariants inherent in "life itself."

Correlative to the developing child slowly decentring away from the individuality and immediacy of concrete experience is a decentring away from the actual situations in which the individual finds him or herself. We become slowly conscious and in explicit command over our invariant and inevitable ways of operating on the world (the functional *a priori*). Thus we also become conscious of and in command over the invariant and inevitable ways that things in the world operate. This, again, is the consequence of constructivism: our ways of operating are a constructing, ordering and organizing demand made upon the world. We are able ahead of time to anticipate "potential" or "virtual" situations (Piaget, 1967, p. 101)—we are able to think about what is possible and what is virtually impossible. Because the assimilatory schemata characteristic of established science are organized around the functional *a priori*, potential or virtual situations can be anticipated, manipulated, controlled and predicted without the organism having to suffer the disequilibrating impact of an actual intrusion of the environment. In other words, we can *think about things*: we can figure them out and, to a degree, affect and control their impact on us by knowing them "objectively," knowing them solely in light of the ways they are constructed vis-à-vis the invariant operations of the organism.

We can therefore deliberately take in hand—but mentally, at a sort of metaphorical arms-length—our immediate well-being and survival, the great functions that define an organism's inevitable and invariant method of operation. We can set forth a hypothesis, an idea or a theory—an assimilatory schema—that we want to check out, and we can explicitly bring to bear upon it events that will attempt to "disequilibrate" it, to "disprove" it. If our original hypothesis becomes shaky, we can accommodate it—differentiate, redefine, consolidate, re-operationalize—and begin again, with the anticipation of either confirming this hypothesis (i.e., reaching some equilibrium) or disconfirming it (i.e., experiencing disequilibrium and the need to accommodate, thus restarting the process). All this can be done formally, logically and objectively. We do not have to physically suffer this process, the way a hungry infant with a functionally similar process of assimilation, accommodation and equilibration suffers. Certainly we can become deeply despondent over a failed experiment. But if we wish to achieve objectivity, we cannot allow this disappointment to enter into the method of operation itself. For a theory to be scientific, then, it has to be kept open to the possibility of being falsified (see Popper, 2002) by future experience. Differently put, for a theory to be scientific, it has to incorporate the possibility of its own disequilibrium and the achievement of a new equilibration, a new theory.

So, to make this final turn, we need to re-cite an extended passage from Piaget's *Origins of Intelligence in Children* (1952, p. 2). The functional *a priori* that defines how life itself operates

> [orients] the whole of the successive structures which the mind will then work out in contact with reality. It will thus play the role that [Kant] assigned to the *a priori:* that is to say, [this functional *a priori*] will impose on the structures certain necessary and irreducible conditions. Only the mistake has sometimes been made of regarding the *a priori* as consisting in structures existing ready-made from the beginning of development, whereas if the functional invariant of thought is at work in the most primitive stages, it is only little by little that it impresses itself on consciousness due to the elaboration of structures which are increasingly adapted to the function itself.

Thus, the sequential development of the structures characteristic of each level of the child's cognitive development is not increasingly better adapted, to the way things somehow "really are" in the world, independently of the functioning of the organism (constructivism has rid us of this naiveté). Rather, over the course of development, we are better and better adapted to *the inevitabilities of adaptation itself*. That is to say, the functions of assimilation, accommodation and equilibration are *a priori,* and the bestadapted structures (most stable and most inclusive) are the ones that are best adapted "to the functioning itself." Development is oriented, therefore, toward continually improving adaptation to the inevitable "organizing activity inherent in life itself" (Piaget, 1952, p. 19).

The peculiarity of the Kantian categories (recall, the Kantian "forms of thinking" that he believed are universal and necessary *[a priori]* to thinking) is that they constitute an extension and perfection of all adaptive processes insofar as they are perfectly adapted to this organizing activity. In this way, the Kantian categories take on the *appearance* of universality and necessity (take on the appearance of being *a priori)* at the end of development because they are perfect expressions of that which *is* universal and necessary: the *functions* of assimilation, accommodation and equilibration (what Piaget calls the functional invariants—the "how" of the functioning—of all interactions between the organism and the environment, *including* logico-mathematical knowledge). Thus "the progress of reason doubtless consists in an increasingly advanced awareness of the organizing activity inherent in life itself" (Piaget, 1952, p. 19). Such an awareness is an "all-embracing assimilatory schema tending to encompassing the whole of reality" since it is an awareness of the organizing activity in terms of which reality itself is constituted.

This helps explain why the sequence of development in Piaget's work moves from sensorimotor knowledge, to pre-operational, to concrete operational, to formal/logical operational knowledge. It has to do with the teleological tendency inherent in adaptation, the sense in which the organism tends toward increasingly stable and inclusive forms of equilibrium. At the highest level of development we have logico-mathematical knowledge, which is in essence a knowledge of the constructive and organizational operations of knowledge itself—knowledge, that is, of the *functioning* that has been going on all along. When we reach the level of formal logic and theoretical mathematics, perfect equilibrium is attained because in these sciences (crystallisations of the methods of established science) we "proceed by the application of perfectly explicit rules, these rules being, of course, the very ones that define the structure under consideration" (Piaget, 1970b, p. 15). That is to say, at the level of logic and mathematics, the rules for doing the operations of logic and mathematics are precisely the rules upon which one operates. Logic and mathematics are thus perfectly equilibrated, for there is no longer any difference between *the operator* (the subject who does logic and mathematics operates only in accord with the rules requisite of logic and mathematics and therefore who operates identically to any subject who does logic and mathematics, in accord only with the general and abstract "processes common to all subjects"), *the operations* performed (logical and mathematical operations), and *that which is being operated upon* (an object in the world constructed according to the ordering demands of logic and mathematics).

These three aspects, so different and mixed in previous stages of cognitive development, are now identical. Logic and mathematics thus emerge as a perfect and pure embodiment of the organizing activity inherent in life itself. The equilibrium embodied in logic and mathematics is thus the *telos,* the "end" of development, and paradoxically, also its origin.

We've reached an unusual spot. By reaching this stage of development, we have also reached the origin that has been present all along, the only difference being that now we have attained an explicit *awareness* of that origin. More strongly put, we are no longer buffeted by the constant striving to adapt. We have reached a command over the origin.

Speaking of origins, it would be very naive to believe that Jean Piaget randomly chose the concepts, categories and methods of established science as his object of study and then just happened to find out that they were an extension and perfection of all adaptive processes. Culturally, historically, philosophically, this belief was already widespread in his time—and still is. Most of us still place great stock in those things that objective science tells us, we still believe (in varying degrees) that science is our best hope at knowing the world, to the extent that knowing the world means being able to control, predict and manipulate objects. And, of course, to a certain extent, this is true. The many ways in which objective science has helped us live longer and healthier lives and to have better control over nature and its vagaries are evident. We still trust—or, in some settings, are *required* to trust—the outcomes of an objective experiment more than the narrative stories a teacher might tell of the life of a child.

However, one didn't pursue the sort of search for origins rampant in the late nineteenth and early twentieth centuries without already believing that one's own culture or age would turn out to be "number one." This provides the transition to our next chapter. We must take into consideration the fact that Jean Piaget's descriptions of, interests in and evaluation of the characteristics of each stage of cognitive development were and are only retrospectively chosen. That is to say, it is only in light of the outcome of logic and mathematics that any particular characteristics of how children think about and understand the world are of interest. The good news is that we, as inheritors of his work, are not under such a restriction. Jean Piaget's explorations have opened up a rich territory that goes far beyond the particular interests of genetic epistemology.

REFERENCES

Inhelder, B. (1969). Some aspects of Piaget's genetic approach to cognition. In H. Furth (Ed.), *Piaget and knowledge: Theoretical foundations* (pp. 9–23). Englewood Cliffs, NJ: Prentice-Hall.

Jardine, D., Clifford, P., & Friesen, S., Eds. (2003a). *Back to the basics of teaching and learning: "Thinking the world together."* Mahwah, NJ: Lawrence Erlbaum and Associates.

Piaget, J. (1952). *The origins of intelligence in children.* New York: International Universities Press.

———— (1965a). *Insights and illusions of philosophy.* New York: Meridian Books.

—— (1967). *Six psychological studies*. New York: Vintage Books.

—— (1970a). Piaget's theory. In P. Mussen (Ed.), *Carmichael's manual of child psychology. Vol. 1* (pp. 703–32). Toronto: Wiley and Sons.

—— (1970b). *Structuralism*. New York: Harper and Row.

—— (1971a). *Genetic epistemology*. New York: WW Norton.

—— (1973). *The psychology of intelligence*. Totowa, NJ: Littlefield, Adams and Co.

Popper, K. (2002). *The logic of scientific discovery*. New York: Routledge.

ELEVEN

A Cultural-Historical Teacher Starts the School Year: A Novel Perspective on Teaching and Learning

Cathrene Connery and Christina Curran

The first day of school has finally arrived. At the shrill of the bell, you survey your classroom one last time. All your hard work and advanced planning has paid off: everything seems to be in order. Brightly colored posters hang on the walls; books peek out from nooks, crannies, and corners. Carefully arranged manipulatives, props, and realia advertise the promise of hands-on and exciting explorations. Name tags stand silently on top of polished desks and tables. As you open the door and call out a greeting, a stream of students enters the room. The final bell signals that the school year has officially started. Closing the door, twenty-five pairs of eyes of diverse shapes and colors examine you nervously from their seats. You smile warmly, moving to the head of the classroom to address your new class for the first time. All at once, your knees buckle and you are moved by the enormity of the responsibility patiently sitting before you.

Each year teachers of all ages and expertise experience the start of the new school calendar in the same manner. The majority of pre-service, in-service, novice and veteran teachers anxiously anticipate the very first moments of the new academic year. Sometimes we worry about our suitability in a new grade level or feel stressed regarding the demands of a new curriculum. Other years, we may have nightmares about potential discipline issues or the uncertainties of teaching with a new colleague. However, underneath these anxieties lies a more profound emotion that cannot be denied. The final days of summer bring us closer to those few minutes in which we simultaneously feel both the weight and the joy, the spotlight and the humility, the power and the privilege of what we do uniquely as educators.

Fortunately, these heart-stopping, breath-skipping moments last only for a few seconds, yet they are an essential part of the reality of *en parentis loci*—a short Latin phrase that means teachers are held legally, ethically, and morally accountable for the lives of the children in their care. Ultimately, this combined sense of awe and responsibility is both positive and necessary because the views and practices we adopt as teachers directly impact children and their families. More important than setting up a classroom or mapping out a curricular plan, the manner in which we define our students, curriculum, and schools holds significant implications for children and society. In the end, our beliefs about the roles of teachers, children and education will determine the success of the academic year for everyone involved.

DEFINITIONS OF EDUCATION: BACKGROUND KNOWLEDGE AND PSYCHOLOGICAL APPROACHES

As educators, we draw on a host of sources to define the student, curriculum, school, and teaching-learning process. Many of us are shocked to hear the exact same tone and words our parents or guardians used tumbling out of our mouths like a script from the past from time to time. We often emulate the example of former teachers, mentors, or religious authorities in our lives. The media also provide us with images that subtly impact our work. These social, historical and political influences, together with our background knowledge, define our stance toward students and schooling. We automatically carry these preconceived definitions into our classrooms without our conscious knowing. In professional teacher education courses, this belief system interfaces with more formal notions about teaching and learning.

In the United States, the field of education has drawn from the science of psychology to define the student, curriculum, school, and teaching-learning process. Educators have traditionally tapped into the philosophical, theoretical, and research approaches of behaviorism and cognitive psychology to describe who we teach, what we teach, where we teach, and how and why we teach. However, these paradigms have come under fire. Educators and other professionals have questioned how well they realistically and humanely characterize our work, students and the families we serve.

In response, teachers and psychologists alike have turned to what has been called cultural-historical, Vygotskian, or sociocultural theory to better describe students, curriculum, schools and the teaching-learning process. This emerging psychological framework is based on the writings of a Russian psychologist named L. S. Vygotsky (1896–1934). This chapter provides a brief history of cultural-historical theory and provides a view of these essential aspects of education for teachers whose success is dependent on a novel definition of the art and science of learning.

VYGOTSKY AND CULTURAL-HISTORICAL THEORY

Who was Vygotsky and what is cultural-historical theory? Lev Semenovich Vygotsky was born on November 5, 1896, in a small town called Gomel in the Byelorussian Republic. The young scholar came of age during a time in which intense discrimination was waged against Russian Jews. Vygotsky wanted to become a teacher, but the czarist government enforced strict laws that forbid non-Christians from becoming government employees (Rosa & Montero, 1990). Undaunted in his career goals, Vygotsky simultaneously attended law school at Moscow University and the Shaniavsky People's Institute to immerse himself in the humanities. After graduating from both institutions in 1917, he returned home (Blanck, 1990). In the wake of the October Revolution of 1917, Vygotsky's professional aspirations were realized. He spent his early career as a teacher in Gomel and worked later as a psychologist in Moscow (Blanck, 1990; Moll, 2000; Rosa & Montero, 1990).

Despite health complications brought on by tuberculosis, Vygotsky sought to articulate a novel approach to psychology that integrated the humanities with the social sciences. His relentless teaching, travels, investigations, and writings were supported and accentuated by fellow collaborators Alexander Luria and Aleksej Leont'ev (Blanck, 1990; Rosa & Montero, 1990). Alexander Zaporozhets, Liya Slavina, Lidia Bozhovich, Natalia Morozova, and Rosa Levina extended "the trio's" work as their first generation of students (John-Steiner, 1999). Together, this collection of *avant-garde* thinkers proposed the basis of an alternative or third approach to psychology (Blanck, 1990).

In 1934, Vygotsky died from complications involving a throat hemorrhage at the age of thirty-seven. By 1936, his writings were blacklisted by the Stalinist regime (Rosa & Montero, 1990). The work of the "trio" and their students remained in relative obscurity until the 1960s, when Luria recruited the assistance of the American developmental psychologist Jerome Bruner to secure the release of Vygotsky's key writings in the United States.

Cultural-historical theory is unique for several reasons. True to its name, it places an emphasis on the social aspects of human psychology. *Culture* is an enduring yet dynamic symbolic system that permits us to establish order in our ever-changing world (Nelson, 1985). Shared cultural patterns, like gender roles, religious rites, and interactional norms allow us to understand, relate, and function in our common quest to survive. However, cultural systems vary from context to context and group to group because people respond and adapt differently in distinct locations or situations. For example, over time, Irish farming communities developed cultural ways of life dissimilar to those of the youth culture found among urban adolescents in New York City. Culture is often perceived as an invisible state of reality until we observe or experience one diverse from our own. This enables us to understand our own culture(s) "as an object of thought" (Cole, 1996, p. 8).

While we often point to food, clothing, and holidays as "culture," it is the imperceptible or obscure aspects like values, principles, and relationships that distinguish a given culture. Moll (2000) describes culture as the lived experience of communities including traditional "means and modes, schemes and patterns of behavior, cognition and communication" (p. 40). Bruner (1990) suggested that these beliefs and practices first originated in the tension that emerged between the individual and family during ancient times. Patterns of behavior, thinking and relating were "converted into human meanings, into language, into narratives and found their way into the minds of men and women. In the end, it was this conversion process that created...the experienced world of culture"(Bruner, 1990, p. 137). Cultures continue to emerge from the ebb and flow of meanings created by solitary individuals and interdependent group members.

In addition to viewing culture as central to the human experience, cultural-historical theory considers how the economy impacts the social, historical, and political aspects of a given culture (Blank, 1990; Rosa & Montero, 1990). It avoids the use of dichotomous, black-and-white, either/or thinking to analyze or explain behavior. Instead of separating the internal/external, individual/social, and psychological/biological aspects of experience, cultural-historical theory uses dialectical or developmental modes of thinking to more holistically test and account for people's thoughts, emotions, and actions. Finally, the cultural-historical framework differs from others because it integrates the humanities with multiple branches of the social and human sciences. A cultural-historical theorist might combine research from anthropology, psychology, sociology, literature, or philosophy to explain how the social and individual aspects of our lives are interdependent (John-Steiner, 1999). Many American scholars have articulated, interpreted, and extended Vygotsky's legacy. Much of their work holds promise and potential for educators, parents, and policymakers concerned with our educational system. A teacher who adopts a cultural-historical perspective would experience the first day of the school year differently than her colleagues. This chapter now relates how she would view her students, curriculum, and school as well as the teaching-learning process.

AN ALTERNATIVE VIEW OF THE STUDENT

Who is the student? Looking out at the fresh faces before her, the cultural-historical teacher considers each child to be a treasure that represents three separate yet interdependent histories. First, whether short or tall, girl or boy, each child is seen to embody all the evolutionary advances humans have ever made as a larger species. Second, and at the same time, each individual student symbolizes the history of their own given family and community. Perhaps a child represents the journey of a Spanish New Mexican family in the Southwest. Another student might characterize the resilience and strength of the African American community in Harlem, New York. Regardless, each child represents a distinct, collective genetic and cultural inheritance that has endured for hundreds of years.

Third, each child embodies their own individual psychological development in that time and space. A student might start the first day of school as a voracious reader while another struggles to sound out words. Another child might be able to write an extended story while her peer has only just learned to draw consonants to label the pictures he has illustrated. The cultural-historical teacher knows that, for each of her students, these separate histories intertwine and braid together, establishing common and unique aspects of their identities, personalities, and competencies. She understands that her students come to her from a constellation of subcultures specific to ethnicity, class, age, gender, religion, language, and region. It will be her job to honor, support and extend these aspects of her students' histories in the days, weeks, and months ahead.

The cultural-historical teacher also recognizes that her students are *meaning makers*. Instead of seeing the children before her as blank slates or empty vessels to be filled with her expert knowledge, she appreciates the fact that her students come to school with common and unique *funds of knowledge* they have acquired from their family's quest to survive and thrive (Moll, 2000). Regardless of age or context, all humans are makers of meaning, as they strive to understand the world and themselves.

As meaning makers, we draw on a rich background to assist us in making sense of new information and experiences. For example, when we get up in the morning and plan our day, we make meanings to guide us in reaching our daily goals. When we interpret the body language of a friend on the bus or a politician on television, we use non-verbal cues to figure out the meaning of the message. When a child reads and understands a social studies chapter on Colonial America, she is making meaning about communities of the past. The cultural-historical teacher harnesses her students' natural propensity to make meaning in all school contexts from the classroom to the cafeteria. The cultural-historical teacher endeavors to capture children's innate curiosity and creativity to nurture lifelong learners.

Cultural-historical teachers additionally know that the meaning makers sitting before them on the first day of school already possess rich, colorful, and powerful understandings about the world and their place in it. In a process called *prolepsis,* adults and more advanced siblings or peers reflect and relate meanings about and to students even before they are born (Cole, 1996). As children gradually experience the larger overlapping social circles that extend from the family into the community, region, state, and beyond, children are exposed to a variety of intellectual, emotional, and experiential sources of knowledge. Because this knowledge is related by people and artifacts from distinct periods in our sociopolitical history, we can say that, individually and collectively, children are shaped by the historical forces surrounding their thought, affect, and experiences. Many students will enrich a classroom discussion about a book using the funds of knowledge they have received from an elderly grandparent or friend. Other children may share their understanding of life as an only child, bilingual speaker, immigrant or political refugee, or member of a particular religious faith. The cultural-historical teacher respects the knowledge and life experiences her students bring to class, helping them to value, elaborate, and extend their understandings.

She also sees her students as vibrant, emotional, and active agents capable of making choices and change. Their personal needs, interests, and emotions play a large role in their meaning making (Vygotsky, 1986). While other psychologists and educators consider thought and affect to be opposites or entirely dismiss the role of emotion in learning, Vygotsky argued that such an approach promotes false notions about cognition as "an autonomous flow of thoughts thinking themselves…separated from all the fullness of real life, from the living motives, interests, and attractions of the thinking human" (cited in Mahn, 1997, p. 284). The cultural-historical teacher knows that her meaning makers' thoughts originate in "the motivating sphere of consciousness, a sphere that includes our inclinations and needs, our interests and impulses, and our affect and emotions" (Vygotsky, 1986, p. 282).

While other psychological approaches might render children as passive participants, a peek into even the most structured classrooms reveals students engaged as intentional *choicemakers*. Children's choices dynamically shape their development by leading to specific actions and inter-actions with other meaning makers (Cole, 1996). For example, in every classroom, there are always a few students who constantly raise their hand to respond to the teacher's questions. For a multitude of reasons, these specific children often become extremely proficient at public speaking. Their peers may be less inclined or even fearful to provide an answer in front of the class.

The cultural-historical teacher would view such hesitancy as a choice that potentially might lead these students down a narrowing educational path. She would therefore use direct and indirect ways to assist such children to feel more comfortable while helping the students to develop skills and strategies that would enable them to answer questions in public. For too long, we have written children's needs, motivations, and choices out of the educational equation. As John-Steiner and

Souberman (1978) describe, children are "active, vigorous participants in their own existence...at each stage of development, children acquire the means by which they can completely affect their world and themselves" (p. 123). The cultural-historical teacher highlights the choices children make, helps them to understand the effects or consequences of their decisions, and cultivates an environment that supports actions and interactions that encourage student growth, development, and informed choice making.

Finally, the cultural-historical teacher identifies children as novice tool users. She understands that her students are in the process of developing expertise in using physical tools like pencils, scissors, calculators, and computers. At the same time, these novices and apprentices are also "mastering certain forms of activity and consciousness which have been perfected by humanity during the process of historical development" (Vygotsky, 1994, p. 352). One of the main goals of socializing children in schools is to help them acquire psychological tools such as language, writing, and number systems. When meaning makers combine these physical and psychological tools, they are liberated from their environment to engage in mental planning and voluntary behavior. For example, when combining the physical tools of paper and pencil with the psychological tools of language and a Venn diagram, a student will be free to compare and contrast the United States and Canada, reptiles and amphibians, or past and present forms of transportation. The cultural-historical teacher realizes that regardless of the age, grade level, or content area in which she works, both student and teacher success depend on how well she assists and supports the refinement of her students' tool use. By appropriating and applying these cultural tools, her students will grow up to become mediums for and makers of history (Vygotsky, 1978; 1986). The first grade reader becomes a fifth grade writer, who eventually chooses a career as a lawyer, politician, or poet. The second grade artist who is fascinated with rulers, learns how to draw with a compass only to one day develop buildings for their community as an architect.

THE CURRICULUM AS SOCIOCULTURAL TEXT

What is knowledge? How is it reflected in the curriculum? In the United States, we tend to view what children learn in school as a physical object or intellectual commodity that can be weighed and measured like a sack of potatoes. Americans additionally define the curriculum as a collection of mandated standards and benchmarks uniformly met and tested at each grade level. People who are unfamiliar with the realities of working with children also have a tendency to divorce the information embodied in or espoused by the curriculum with the manner in which it is delivered. Ironically, most people have experienced that just because a teacher or book states a particular fact, the student may not automatically "learn" it. Many of us consider the curriculum to be a neutral, ahistorical, universal collection of truths easily assessed on an exam.

The cultural-historical teacher defines the curriculum as a collaborative of cultural meanings. She knows that the curriculum she teaches in the first hour, day, week, or months of school is a sociocultural text of richly integrated understandings and practices. What we teach and how we teach it collectively constitute the curriculum. For example, in relating content from an elementary social studies unit on communities, a teacher might directly dictate a list of social behaviors on a chart: "Neighbors live and work by each other."; "Neighbors help each other out"; "Neighbors are not mean to each other"; or "Neighbors use gentle voices to say nice things to each other."

This social studies content is common to early civics lessons that seek to create classroom communities that reflect our democratic values. However, if the same teacher relates the material in a pedagogical or teaching style that degrades or humiliates a restless first grader, the actual curriculum the students learn will be unrecognizable from the curriculum manual or the teacher's lesson objectives. The same is true with regard to reading. Literacy educators have long noted that students who fill out an excessive amount of worksheets during reading time are learning to do just that—fill out worksheets. A cultural-historical teacher interweaves content and pedagogy together, knowing that children learn to read by reading and to write by writing.

CULTURAL MEANINGS AS SOCIOCULTURAL TEXT

A cultural-historical teacher defines the details, information, or meanings represented in the curriculum as cultural knowledge. These understandings—from math facts to scientific explanations—come from the thoughts, behaviors, and actions of people in everyday life (Cole, 1996). As members of a variety of subcultures, we are enmeshed inside a network of social norms, power relations, and cultural understandings. Our life ways directly shape the meanings we make in an unending, generative cycle.

Knowledge or cultural meanings are actually a synthesis of "multiple voices, of unity as well as discord, [including] an imperfect sharing of knowledge; of intergenerational misunderstanding as well as common understandings; of developing both adaptive and maladaptive practices while discarding others" (Moll, 2000, p. 257). Bodies of cultural knowledge undergo quantitative and qualitative changes as they are passed between parents, teachers, and other elders to younger generations. Each new cohort of meaning makers then modifies cultural understandings from their own perspective or stance. In this manner, the curriculum can be seen as potentially evolutionary, transformative, and transforming for each new class of students.

The cultural-historical teacher refutes the idea of knowledge as a personal assemblage of concepts suspended within a child's intellect (Nelson, 1985). Instead, she is confident that her students' knowledge of the world combines thoughts, emotions, and understandings constructed from all of the child's senses. In other words, children acquire cultural knowledge using their heads, hearts, and hands. For example, in certain regions of the United States, the cultural celebration of Halloween is often presented to primary students as a part of the curriculum. Urban children, who may not have immediate access to agricultural produce found in farm fields or suburban gardens, often learn about the symbol of the jack-o'-lantern by listening to stories, talking about pictures, creating decorations, measuring the circumference of pumpkins, and by counting, baking, and eating their seeds. The children "learn" the curriculum in an intellectual, emotional, and experiential manner differently across communities.

Therefore, the cultural-historical teacher considers how to structure and implement the curriculum in a manner that utilizes and supports children's multimodal and holistic meaning making. While it might not be realistic or too expensive for inland teachers to take their students to the beach when studying the ocean, most schools are equipped with facilities and kitchen implements that can be used to demonstrate the effect of the moon on the tides. In this case, the excitement surrounding kinesthetic explorations with water, or other realia, assists children in acquiring important sociocultural text.

One of cultural-historical theory's greatest contributions to our conception of the art and science of learning is the existence of *diverse* sociocultural texts. It is not difficult to understand how cultural meanings or knowledge differ across contexts. For example, the culture of the Cochiti Pueblo emerged from the people's ancient life ways as farmers along the Rio Grande. Their conception of personal property sharply contrasted with that of the Spaniards, who eventually colonized the region. It seems only reasonable that human values, expectations, practices, and beliefs would vary between past and present communities.

However, many of us have difficulty in accepting the presence of varied accounts of cultural knowledge or sociocultural texts based not just on who we are, where we come from, but what we do. John-Steiner's (1999) research found that people develop assorted sociocultural texts as a result of their engagement in diverse roles and practices. A child who learns to sew his own clothes and his sister who is allowed to experiment and disassemble a computer have access to disparate resources, each with their own potential and limitations for developing knowledge or making meaning.

Diverse sociocultural texts account for the wide range of meanings, curiosities, talents, and competencies children bring to school. The curriculum is also a sociocultural text and political document deemed important to the stakeholders who developed it as a psychological tool. The cultural-historical teacher realizes that student and district sociocultural texts do not always match. However, by recognizing the existence of varied cultural knowledge, she does not have to pathologize or privilege specific texts or understandings. The student who cannot successfully cut out a circle using scissors on the first day of school is not necessarily developmentally delayed or culturally impoverished. The same child might be highly skilled at deboning a trout or dressing a deer with a hunting knife, depending on the culture into which they were born.

THE SCHOOL AS A MEANING MAKING SITE

Where and when does learning occur? In what contexts do students engage in meaning making? As children grow up, they come into contact with larger, overlapping social circles. They carry their personal sociocultural texts into these contexts including the cultural institution of the school. Cole (1996) recognized schools as special meaning making sites or developmental niches where "interpersonal planes of parenting, schooling, and apprenticing" socialize the young (p. 190). In the best of circumstances, schools collectively extend the work of children's parents, caregivers, and elders by providing understandings, experiences, and opportunities that facilitate healthy, joyful development and cultural learning while empowering students for a happy and productive adulthood. Indeed, our schools and classrooms are cultures unique unto themselves.

Children make meaning among and across these multiple contexts. Learning occurs through their interactions with the physical features and artifacts of the school, including computer labs, physical education equipment, and art studios. These institutions are also composed of "social, cultural, historical, and political factors as well as the influence of other individuals" (Mahn,

1997, p. 270). Vygotsky (1994) emphasized the importance of schools as meaning making sites denoting the concrete and psychological environment as "the source of development and not its setting" (p. 349). Schools create conditions that nurture, afford, or deny children the opportunity to appropriate cultural tools, practices, and knowledge. Children do not just learn curriculum at school. They co-create their identities, cultures, and sociocultural texts inside our classrooms and on our playgrounds.

The cultural-historical teacher understands that her students will acquire and develop meanings regarding the value of schooling, the fascination of a given topic, their perceived ability to learn, as well as their worth as individuals based on the physical, emotional, and intellectual conditions of the school. It is an American tragedy that many children attend filthy, crowded, and/ or decrepit classrooms and buildings where basic texts and adequate supplies are not provided. The cultural-historical teacher engages in advocacy efforts that ensure safe, clean, well-stocked and appropriately equipped classrooms and schools. She strives to provide positive, comfortable learning environments and relationships where children are physically, mentally, and emotionally valued.

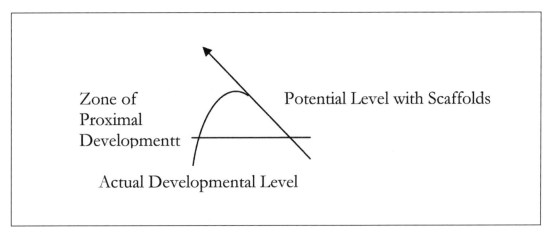

Figure 1: The Zone of Proximal Development (ZPD)

Children also learn or make meanings as the result of interactions and changes in what Vygotsky (1978) called the *zone of proximal development (ZPD)*. These meaning making structures include "the distance between the actual developmental level as determined by independent problem-solving and the level of potential development as determined through problem-solving under adult guidance or in collaboration with more capable peers" (p. 86). In other words, the ZPD represents the dynamic state where learning is bridged from its current individual conception to a more enhanced level of understanding through collaborative support. For example, perhaps a child is able to correctly add two digit by one digit numbers without regrouping by themselves. At their actual developmental level, as represented in Figure 1, they would be able to combine 11 + 8 to produce 19. However, when asked to solve 11 + 9, the same child may come up with 110 for the answer. After a teacher, parent, or more advanced peer explains the concept of regrouping quantities into tens and ones to get twenty, the child's problem solving advances to their potential developmental level with the benefit of assistance. As captured in Figure 1, the

ZPD represents the dynamic interchange that allows for new meanings to be co-created between what the student can achieve independently and with help.

The cultural-historical teacher knows that the ZPD "awakens a variety of internal developmental processes that are able to operate only when the child is interacting with people in his environment and in cooperation with his peers" (Vygotsky, 1978, p. 90). Meaning making or learning occurs because the ZPD scaffolds the thinking of meaning makers with learning resources including people, books, exhibits, displays, media, and other social materials (John-Steiner, 1997). In fact, Mahn and John-Steiner (2002) portray the ZPD as a "complex whole, a system of systems in which the interrelated and interdependent elements include the participants, artifacts, and environment/context, and the participants' experience of their interactions within it" (p. 49). The language an elder or more advanced peer uses with the ZPD, as well as the emotional support that is expressed, directly supports learning and development.

The cultural-historical teacher mindfully creates and modifies multiple ZPDs in the classroom across the school year by implementing a host of grouping patterns and interactional structures. For example, she might begin a lesson on regrouping in addition by having students briefly share with a partner during a whole group discussion. After presenting how to regroup problems like 11 + 9, she might place her students at tables of four children with a white board to collectively solve problems together. After circulating among the groups, she might select students from two groups to become "teachers" for other individual children while working independently with a small handful of students. In this manner, the cultural-historical teacher supports student learning through a variety of two-way interchanges structured by multiple ZPDs.

THE *PEREZHIVANIE* WITHIN THE ZPD

Vygotsky is perhaps best known in educational circles for his concept of the ZPD. However, his writings about *perezhivanie* provide teachers with an additional way of explaining how meaning is made within the ZPD. The Russian term *perezhivanie* roughly translates into "lived experience" in English. *Perezhivanie* can be thought of as a cognitive-affective prism or psychological house through or in which meaning makers perceive, experience, and process the emotional dimensions of their given context (Mahn & John-Steiner, 2002). On one hand, *perezhivanie* refers to the manner in which an individual experiences the ZPD as an internal state including "everything selected from the environment and all the factors related to our personality and are selected from the personality, all the features of its character, its constitutional elements, which are related to the event in question" (Vygotsky, 1994, p. 342). For example, a child's inner experience of conducting a science experiment in middle school might involve excitement at the prospect of collaborating with friends, the need to please their teacher, and/or a strong feeling of being engrossed in a topic of interest. In the exact same situation, a different student might dread the possibility of appearing foolish or incompetent by peers, hold reservations regarding power dynamics between themselves and the teacher, and/or worry about the outcome of the experiment.

At the same time, the *perezhivanie* is "a unit where…in an indivisible state, the environment is represented" (Vygotsky, 1994, p. 342). This meaning making context simultaneously includes elements outside the student including the physical, emotional, and intellectual realities of the immediate classroom. Returning to the previous example, these external factors might include the sensation of manipulating batteries and bulbs, tension among group members to complete the assignment, and the difficulty advanced academic language poses when reading directions. Larger school ethos or teacher ideologies might additionally make up situational factors significant to a child's *perezhivanie*. Because interpersonal relationships between teachers and students, the teacher and the class, and students and students compose ZPDs, issues of power and privilege as well as access and equity shape the nature of the student's *perezhivanie*. The concept of *perezhivanie* explains why students often derive diverse understandings when administered the exact same lesson. The cultural-historical teacher understands the need to create positive, safe, and respectful relationships with her students while providing a challenging and stimulating environment to sustain the *perezhivanie*.

TEACHING AND LEARNING AS AN INTEGRATED MEANING-MAKING PROCESS

What is learning? How do students acquire or create new understandings? What is the connection between teaching and learning? The cultural-historical teacher sees teaching and learning as a complex, integrated meaning making process. Teachers facilitate children's co-creation of knowledge using their hearts, heads, and hands through interactions and activities with other meaning makers. Students internalize the curriculum through their senses, multiple modalities, and physical and psychological tools within the cultural, historical, and political contexts of classrooms and schools (Vygotsky, 1986).

Vygotsky's framework offers teachers a novel definition of the teaching-learning process because it unifies persons and psychological processes usually distinguished as opposites. For example, teachers and students are viewed as collaborative partners instead of opponents, united by their common need and expertise. Instead of isolating thinking into separate skills, meaning making or learning is seen as a complex synthesis of "lower" and "higher" mental forms. Lower psychological functions, such as basic sensation, perception, memory, and attention, are directly associated to the developing physiology of young children. These thought processes are shaped and arranged by specific practices and demands from home and school cultures. Lower mental processes mature and transform into higher forms of thinking over time. For example, emergent readers develop the ability to execute fine motor movements, focus their eyes, and connect specific letters and sounds prior to recognizing words on a page.

Interestingly, higher mental functions such as categorizing, reading, and writing evolve from communication with other people. These complex or advanced forms of thinking are rooted and shaped through shared cultural meanings. For instance, although a child might be able to identify the individual letters c-a-t on a page, it is only through a larger system of cultural agreement that such random marks intentionally refer to a furry mammal with four legs that meows instead of barks. The student's own speech community might use the letters g-a-t-o to express the same concept.

Children's need to feel a sense of control and communicate their lived experience or *perezhivanie* jumpstarts the development of complex forms of thought, language, and literacy. The task of writing one's name on paper means nothing to preschoolers or kindergarteners who first look at letters as random squiggly marks. However, when the same group of students watch their siblings write or must "sign in" to be marked present on an attendance chart, they will come to understand that specific collections of ordered symbols represent themselves or their marks. The cultural-historical teacher sees the development of sophisticated forms of meaning making and semiotic mediation—how we communicate or relay cultural understandings—as the goal of formal education.

Vygotsky's cultural-historical framework also unifies the content teachers and students explore together and the processes we use in such explorations. This is because the curriculum or "knowledge is not internalized directly, but through the use of psychological tools" such as language, number systems, artwork, or other artifacts that mediate meaning (John-Steiner & Mahn, 1996, p. 193). The cultural-historical teacher knows that psychological tools capture, shape, and transform thought. Reading, writing, speaking, and listening acquisition and development are a central focus of the teaching-learning process. Collectively, psychological artifacts make up a cultural tool kit that allows children to "grow into the intellectual life of those around them" (Cole, 1996, p. 88) while uniting the student with the curriculum. Children develop proficient tool use gradually through successive approximations through scaffolding, joint productive activity, and guided practice (Echevarria, Vogt & Short, 2004). Meaning making is the direct result of internalizing psychological tools and cultural knowledge. The acquisition of meaning making tools and practices allows children to communicate with others, make sense of cultural patterns around them, and establish significance in their worlds.

The cultural-historical teacher comprehends that in order to foster meaning making by readers, writers, and thinkers, she must provide her students with multiple opportunities to employ these processes to create new knowledge related through cultural artifacts like poetry, reports, newspapers, and artwork. Vygotsky's (1981a) genetic law of cultural development noted that "Any function in child development appears twice or on two planes. First it appears on the social plane and then it appears on the psychological plane. First it appears between people as an interpsychological category and then within the individual child as an intrapsychological category" (p. 163). In other words, in order to cultivate learning and thinking, a process, proto-type, or example must be evident from the very start. If we are to nurture creative and critical thinkers, children must have the opportunity to observe, engage, and internalize innovative thought structures and processes. When access to a model source of development is absent or impeded, children's development of a particular skill, strategy, disposition, or knowledge will be limited. For instance, many reading programs have eliminated read-alouds with the rationaliza-tion that insufficient time exists during the school day. However, without the opportunity to hear and emulate an expert adult reader, emergent literates will struggle to process, articulate, and comprehend connected text.

The cultural-historical teacher understands the interdependent intricacies of the teaching and learning process. She attunes herself to the unique identities, needs, and strengths of each student. She arranges the curriculum and the multiple ways it might be mediated to bridge col-laborative understandings in the spirit of student advocacy. Within the first week of school, she will implement teaching and learning activities that engage students as apprentices to appropriate the work of scientists, civic leaders, artists, and historians.

Is the teaching-learning process an art or a science? Vygotsky's love for dialectics would prevent him from juxtaposing these two domains. At the end of the day, the cultural-historical teacher would define the teaching-learning process as a collaborative endeavor that looks like both an artful science and a scientific art. Before dismissing the children, she would relish the energetic sense of possibility emerging among her students. Glancing at the children, she would no longer see 25 pairs of eyes but appreciate the unique treasure behind each individual pair. As the bell signals the end of the day, the cultural-historical teacher would joyfully anticipate how to best bridge her students' funds of knowledge with the curriculum in a meaningful manner during tomorrow's lesson. Before closing the door, she would stretch her legs and stand up straight with pride, remembering the weight and the joy, the spotlight and the humility, the power and the privilege of what we do uniquely as educators.

REFERENCES

Blanck, G. (1990). Vygotsky: The man and his cause. In Moll, L. (Ed.), *Vygotsky and education: Instructional implications and applications of sociohistorical psychology* (pp. 31–58). Cambridge, England: Cambridge University Press.

Bruner, J. (1990). *Acts of meaning.* Cambridge, MA: Harvard University Press.

Cole, M. (1996). *Cultural psychology: A once and future discipline.* Cambridge, MA: Harvard University Press.

Echevarria, J., Vogt, M., & Short, D. (2004). (2nd ed.) *Making content comprehensible for English learners: The SIOP model.* Boston: Pearson.

John-Steiner, V. (1997). *Notebooks of the mind: Explorations of thinking.* (Rev ed.). New York: Oxford University Press.

John-Steiner, V. (1999). Sociocultural and feminist theory: Mutuality and relevance. In S. Chaiklin, M. Hedegaard, & U.J. Jensen (eds.), *Activity theory and social practice: Cultural-historical approaches.* Aarhus, Denmark: Aarhus University Press.

John-Steiner, V., & Mahn, H. (1996). Sociohistorical approaches to learning and development: A Vygotskian framework. *Educational Psychologist, 31,* (3/4), 191–206.

John-Steiner, V. & Souberman, E. (1978). Afterword. In Vygotsky, L.S. *Mind in society: The development of higher psychological processes* (pp. 121–133). Cambridge, MA: Harvard University Press.

Kozulin, A. (1986). Vygotsky in context. In Vygotsky, L.S. *Thought and language.* Cambridge, MA: MIT Press.

Mahn, H. (1997). *Dialogue journals: Perspectives of second language learners in a Vygotskian framework.* Unpublished doctoral dissertation, The University of New Mexico: Albuquerque, New Mexico.

Mahn, H., & John-Steiner, V. (2002). The gift of confidence: A Vygotskian view of emotions. In G. Wells & G. Claxon (eds.), *Learning for life in the 21st century* (pp. 46–58). Oxford, England: Blackwell Publishers.

Moll, L.C. (Ed.) (1990). *Vygotsky and education: Instructional implications and applications of sociohistorical psychology.* Cambridge, England: Cambridge University Press.

Moll, L. C. (2000). Inspired by Vygotsky: Ethnographic experiments in education. In Lee, C.D., & Smagorinsky, P. (eds.). *Vygotskian perspectives on literacy research: Constructing meaning through collaborative inquiry* (pp. 256–268). Cambridge, England: Cambridge University Press.

Nelson, K. (1985). *Making sense: The development of meaning in early childhood.* New York: Academic Press.

Rosa, R. & Montero, I. (1990). The historical context of Vygotsky's work: A sociohistorical approach. In Moll, L. (ed.), *Vygotsky and education: Instructional implications and applications of sociohistorical psychology* (pp. 59–88). Cambridge, England: Cambridge University Press.

Vygotsky, L.S. (1978). *Mind in society: The development of higher psychological processes.* London: Harvard University Press.

Vygotsky, L. S. (1981a). The genesis of higher mental functions. In J.V. Wertsch (ed.). *The concept of activity in Soviet psychology* (pp. 144–188). Armonk, NY: Sharpe.

Vygotsky, L. S. (1981b). The problem of the cultural development of the child. In J.V. Wertsch (ed.). *The concept of activity in Soviet psychology.* (pp. 104–180). Armonk, NY: Sharpe.

Vygotsky, L. (1986). *Thought and language.* Cambridge, MA: Massachusetts Institute of Technology Press.

Vygotsky, L. S. (1934; 1987). *Thinking and speaking: the problem and the approach.* Retrieved April 29, 2003 from www. marxists.org/archive/vygotsky/works/words/lev1.htm.

Vygotsky, L. S. (1934; 1987). *Thinking and speech: written, inner, and oral speech.* Retrieved April 29, 2003 from www. marxists.org/archive/vygotsky/works/words/lev1.htm.

Vygotsky, L. S. (1994). In R. Van Der Veer & J. Valsiner. (1994). *The Vygotsky reader.* Cambridge, MA: Blackwell Publishers.

Vygotsky, L.S. (1997). The pre-history of the development of written language. In L.S. Vygotsky; R. W. Rieber (eds). *The collected works of L.S. Vygotsky. Volume IV: The history of the development of higher mental functions.* (pp. 131–148). New York: Plenum Press.

Vygotsky, L.S. (1997). The question of multilingual children. In L.S. Vygotsky; R. W. Rieber (Eds). *The collected works of L.S. Vygotsky. Volume IV: The history of the development of higher mental functions* (pp. 253–259). New York: Plenum Press.

Wertsch, J. (1985). Vygotsky's genetic method. In J. Wertsch (ed.). *Vygotsky and the social formation of mind* (pp. 17–57). Cambridge, MA: Harvard University Press.

Wertsch, J. (Ed.) (1985). *Culture, communication, & cognition: Vygotskian perspectives.* New York: Cambridge University Press.

SECTION FOUR
Paulo Freire's Legacies

TWELVE

To Study Is a Revolutionary Duty

Jeff Duncan-Andrade

> *If we reflect on the fact that our human condition is one of essential unfin-*
> *ishedness, that, as a consequence, we are incomplete in our being and in our*
> *knowing, then it becomes obvious that we are "programmed" to learn, destined*
> *by our very incompleteness to seek completeness, to have a "tomorrow" that*
> *adds to our "today." In other words, wherever there are men and women,*
> *there is always and inevitably something to be done, to be completed, to be*
> *taught, and to be learned.*
> Paulo Freire, *Pedagogy of Freedom (1998)*

June 1, 2007

Dear Paulo,

It seems appropriate that I am writing my first letter to you while on my first trip to the country of your birth. I came to Brazil to give two presentations on how your work has influenced mine. Letter writing is a much more intimate act than presenting, and therefore infinitely more difficult.

This letter presents a particularly difficult challenge because it is asking that I articulate your mentorship of my work. There is simply not enough room in this initial letter to you to capture the depth at which you have impacted my life and my teaching. In fact, I am sure I cannot even fully comprehend it because every time I revisit your work I find something new that challenges me to rethink what I have been doing. So, my hope with this letter is to give you some sense of how I came upon your work, how it has influenced my pedagogy as a high school teacher, how it has influenced my pedagogy as a teacher of teachers, and, finally, how it has led me to formulate my own pedagogical theory, which attempts to connect those two endeavors.

Let me start with some back-story that led me to your work. In 1995, I had been teaching English literature for three years at Westlake Junior High in Oakland, California, and I had never even heard of you. Each of those years I received a March 15 letter of nonrenewal, and in each of those years I also received a "Best Teacher" award from students at the school. When the start of the new school year would near in late August and the school had not found someone to fill my position, they would hire me back with another emergency contract. The reasons for my multiple "nonrenewals" (read firings) were largely the same as the reasons I received accolades from my students. I did things differently from most of my colleagues; I challenged time-honored roles and traditions, and I used a pedagogy and curriculum that encouraged students to do the same.

At the time, I struggled to understand why I was being punished by the leadership of a miserably failing school when my methods were dearly having a positive effect on student engagement and achievement. My students, predominantly of African, Latin American, and Southeast Asian descent, did well in my classes, particularly the students that most of my colleagues complained about as unruly and unmotivated. Parents liked the work I was doing with their children. I believed, wrongly I guess, that the people involved with Westlake Junior High expected me to push and challenge all students.

That belief persisted despite my better wisdom from having attended schools with similarly low expectations of the majority of its students. I recall schooling experiences when students were explicitly discouraged from dreaming beyond their circumstances. In most cases, these forms of discrimination are explained away as minor deterrents that most people encounter in their lives, micro-aggressions against hope. But the frequency with which they happened over time and the lick of challenges to their normality in school culture crushed the spirits of the overwhelming majority of my classmates. As one example, I vividly remember telling my high school math teacher and soccer coach that I wanted to go to the University of California at Berkeley. He laughed out loud in front of the class and told me that Berkeley would never take a student like me.

Years later, after I had graduated from U.C. Berkeley, my father revealed that my math teacher was not the only one who felt that way about me. When I was given a "special admit" to Berkeley, the director of financial aid requested to meet privately with my parents. He told them that they should not be surprised when I returned home before completing my first year at Berkeley. He said I had not attended schools that could properly prepare me for the rigors of such an esteemed institution. Experiences such as these led me to want to become the teacher-coach-counselor that I did not have, one who encouraged critical thinking, hope, and a sense of purpose in all students. The fact that I fall short of that goal every year does not discourage me; it reminds me that I must work harder and be humble enough to critically reflect on my practice as I seek the impossible: perfect pedagogy.

True to this pursuit, discouraging reviews from my administrators in hand, I accepted an appointment to teach an ethnic studies class to a group of thirty East Oakland 9th-grade students in the summer of 1998. I accepted this position because it allowed me to move on to the high school level with many of my Westlake students, but I was struggling to understand the double standard of my calling. On the one hand, the local educational leaders openly admitted that schools like Westlake were failing miserably. On the other, measures that I was taking to effectively confront that failure were punished. It was during that summer, amid my confusion about my calling, that I was introduced to your work. That moment was one of the most significant in my life. It set off a shift in consciousness that has indelibly changed my understanding of myself, my life's purpose, and the nefariousness of deliberate, systematic miseducation.

Another teacher in the summer program handed me a copy of *Literacy: Reading the Word and the World*. He told me he thought I would like what it had to say. It was perfect timing because my treatment inside schools had me believing that there was something wrong with *me*. The more I read, the more I found my critique of the institutions and my pedagogical instincts affirmed. The book gave me clarity about my purpose as an educator. It justified my resistance of the malaise that had embittered and disenchanted most of my teaching colleagues.

The passage that most influenced me comes from the Second Popular Culture Notebook that you used in your adult literacy campaign in São Tome and Príncipe. You quote "The Act of Studying," stating:

> A text to be read is a text to be studied. A text to be studied is a text to be interpreted. We cannot interpret a text if we read it without paying attention, without curiosity; if we stop reading at the first difficulty.…If a text is difficult, you insist on understanding it.…To study demands discipline. To study is not easy, because to study is to create and re-create and not to repeat what others say. To study is a revolutionary duty.

No single passage has more profoundly impacted how I instruct my students about the importance of study. I have posted it in my classroom, and I often reference it when students wonder why I am so demanding. I am so heavily affected by this passage because it transformed the way that I thought about studying for myself. I had never thought of study as a revolutionary act. Before reading your book, study was a means to an end. Studying was a burden, something I had to suffer through to get a degree or to access opportunities and places to which people from my family had never been invited.

To a large degree, this was the promise I gave to my students. My teachers had never told me that there was *any* other use for studying, and I had never read anything that suggested that possibility. Even though I connected to my students, and found ways to inspire and motivate them, before reading your work I was mostly reproducing the same logic systems that I had been taught in public schools. I convinced my students that the system was a game, and that like any game it had rules. Even if they did not come from families that had histories of winning at this game, they could learn the rules and beat the game, just as I had. For the most part, my pre-Freire promise to my students was that studying would allow them to plug into an economic system that had historically exploited their communities. It would allow them the option to go from exploited to exploiter. (As I read more of your work I acquired the language to name this pattern of social reproduction as the suboppressor component of the oppressor-oppressed paradigm.)

I suppose I still agree with this logic to some degree—better them than us. But, reading your work helped me to understand studying as something greater than an individual act, it is a "revolutionary duty." This passage from your work helped me to understand the difference between learning to earn and learning for freedom. Learning to earn is undoubtedly the law of the land in most U.S. classrooms, and it has very little to do with studying. The learn-to-earn paradigm is the pursuit of knowledge for personal gain—it is learning how to become a more effective cog in the economic engine of capitalism. But the studying you were talking about was revolutionary, it was learning for freedom. I *came* to understand the freedom that lies in study when that study is dedicated to an intellectual discipline that challenges the prevailing logic of injustice. As these skills developed, my study progressed toward the creation of a new worldview—freedom. I could actually envision a radically different world, which meant I no longer had to accept the current conditions as inevitable. As I became a student of freedom, I developed the understanding that a major part of my revolutionary duty was to share that path to freedom with others who find themselves trapped in the logic of learning to earn.

The opportunity to share that path presents itself every day that I teach but, as you are aware, there are always moments in teaching when the opportunity to have an impact on an individual student is heightened. For me, this opportunity often presents itself when students ask me why do we have to learn this? Prior to reading your work, I would have given them answers similar to those given to me by my teachers, all of which are both unsatisfactory and unmotivating. That is I would have been dismissive, with something like "Because I said so," or I would have been compliant with the status quo by saying, "Because it's what rich kids learn, *and when* you go up against them in college I want you to be ready to compete." Those answers reflect my own training as a student, but they also reflect my ignorance about the depth and significance of that question. It *is* shameful that so many teachers are unable to give a profound answer to this question. Why should a student learn from me if I cannot answer that question in a compelling way?

Paulo, your work unlocked an answer to this question for me. Now, when students ask me this question, I have two responses for them. First, I turn the question back onto them, and I ask them why they think they should learn. Most claim they don't know or throw back stock responses similar to the ones I used to give. Once I have them thinking about answering their own question, I give them the passage about the importance of studying from your book. I read it to them and I tell them that I did not understand the importance of study until I read that passage. Next, I tell them that somewhere there is a five-year-old child they have never seen, and that child is counting on them to study. In ten years, when that five-year-old is fifteen, their paths will cross. In that moment, they will either change that child's life by sharing knowledge and purpose from what they have studied, or they will miss that opportunity because they have not prepared themselves for it. I tell them that is what you meant when you said that studying is a revolutionary duty, because to be truly revolutionary is to prepare oneself to serve the next generation so that each generation inherits a better world. Finally, I tell my students that every time they get tired or frustrated with what they are studying, I want them to picture that five-year-old because they are not just studying for themselves. They are studying for that child, and that child simply cannot afford for them to give up. We go back to your text and we are both reminded of your challenge—that we insist on understanding that which is difficult, and that this type of study, revolutionary study, is not easy; it demands discipline.

I think most young people understand this, and it helps explain the disconnection between young people and school. We underestimate young people and their desires when we paint them as shallow consumerists. They may be socialized to value consumerism, but the young people I work with end up there mostly as the result of the absence of a viable alternative. They continually ask us why they should learn from us because they have not given up hope that we can offer something more to life than the pursuit of fortune and fame. But, when we fail to offer them a compelling narrative about that alternative possibility, most young people come to see school as an extension of a morally bankrupt society. If studying is a revolutionary duty, then using our studies to inject the promise and the hope of a more just society is a revolutionary imperative.

Your words have taught me this lesson, and I pledge to express my gratitude for this freedom by responding with equal vigor and sincerity each time my students ask me to explain why they have to study.

Eleven years have passed since my first encounter with your work. I remain a high school teacher in my community, but I am now also a teacher of teachers. The responsibility that comes with supporting and mentoring aspiring critical pedagogues has helped me to understand your reasons for describing study as a process of creating and re-creating. I have worked in the last couple of years to study my own practice and the practice of other effective urban educators so that I can help more teachers get access to pedagogical strategies that are effective and give them some explanation about why those approaches work. This process of studying effective pedagogy has led me to be increasingly self-critical as I turn these examinations onto my own teaching. This self-reflexivity is also particularly useful when I work with new teachers because they get to hear about my own struggles as a teacher, and through these struggles I can impart the relationship between effective pedagogy and a lifelong commitment to study and critical self-reflection.

To advance your efforts to stimulate dialogue about critical pedagogy, I have used my study and work with teachers to develop a next iteration of your *Pedagogy of Indignation*. As your wife states in the book, that title was chosen as a counterbalance to your other writings where you articulate so much of your commitment to pursuing and promoting pedagogy that is imbued with hope, love, *conscientização,* and freedom. But in each of those previous books your indignation about the conditions facing the masses has always been obvious to me. You have said many times over that we cannot be pedagogues with any of those aforementioned traits if we are not indignant about the existence of conditions that oppress. Likewise, you have cautioned us to balance our anger with an awareness that the future is not predetermined; anger should be partnered with critical hope that we have the capacity (and responsibility) to act and change oppressive conditions.

Your sagacious advice has been essential because my indignation at miseducation in poor communities is fueled by the fact that it is deliberate. We know how to educate poor children. We have the knowledge and capacity. We lack the courage. We are cowards. Nothing angers me more than cowardice, because cowardice is the confluence of someone knowing what is morally right, having the capacity to act on that moral imperative, and still deciding against that action. Because the educational system in this country has the knowledge and capacity to provide a quality education to all children and chooses to act as though it is tirelessly trying to figure out how to do that, we have systematic cowardice. Systematic cowardice, particularly in regard to services for young people, is the reflection of a morally bankrupt society

As a response to this cowardice, I have begun to write, speak, study and share an adaptation of the pedagogy of indignation that I call THUG LIFE Pedagogy. I borrow the term from Tupac Shakur, someone I am sure you knew both in name and in spirit but perhaps not for his full body of work. Tupac, despite his death in 1996, remains wildly popular among young oppressed peoples around the globe. To be sure, the medium of music and poetry that Tupac used to deliver his message is key to his popularity. But I am convinced that the longevity and extent of his popularity are the result of the portions of his work that speak to the righteous indignation that festers in almost every person who detests injustice. Only twenty-five at his death, Tupac had just begun the development of a theory of humanization for oppressed peoples that drew from their indignation. He argued that oppressed people would need to search within themselves and their communities for freedom, and that this would require adults to pay special attention to children who are born into a society that hates them. For Tupac, hate that is passed to children through the cycle of social inequity destroys communities. He gave his theory an acronym THUG LIFE (The Hate U Gave Little Infants Fucks Everyone), a deliberate turn of phrase against the racist stereotype of urban men of color as street thugs. In an interview, Tupac explained:

> By "thug" I mean, not criminal or someone that beats you over the head. I mean the underdog. The person that had nothing and succeeds, he's a thug because he overcame all obstacles. It doesn't have anything to do with the dictionary's version of "thug." To use "thug" is my pride, not being someone that goes against the law, not being someone that takes, but being someone that has nothing, and even though I have nothing and there's no home for me to go to, my head is up high. My chest is out. I walk tall. I talk loud. I'm being strong.... We gonna start slowly but surely taking our communities back. Regulate our community. Organize. We need to start taking care of our own. We gotta start somewhere, and I don't know about anything else, but this, to me, is a start. (Latin, 2003)

Like Tupac, I believe that the hatred/rage/hostility/indignation that results from any group of people systematically denied their right to food, clothing, shelter, education, and justice will ultimately cause a society to implode. Likewise, properly channeled, those legitimate feelings can be developed into the courage to act and fundamentally change the direction of a society, even in the face of the broader society's cowardice. In fact, the necessary courage to dramatically and justly alter the direction of an empire might only be found among those who suffer under its oppressive weight; this is the type of young person that a THUG LIFE Pedagogy aims to nurture.

Tupac referred to these young people as roses that grow from concrete. They are the ones that prove society's rule wrong. They keep the dream of a better society alive, growing in spite of the cold, uncaring, un-nurturing environment of the concrete. In his poem "The Rose That Grew from Concrete" he wrote: "[L]ong live the rose that grew from concrete when no one else even cared." He expanded this metaphor in his song "Mama's Just a Little Girl," writing "[Y]ou wouldn't ask why the rose that grew from concrete had damaged petals. On the contrary, we would all celebrate its tenacity. We would all love its will to reach the sun. We are the roses. This is the concrete. And these are my damaged petals. Don't ask me why ask me how."

My hope for THUG LIFE Pedagogy is to influence educators (current and future) in urban and poor communities to grow more roses from the concrete. With respect to supporting and developing our current group of teachers, we are challenged by the fact that the majority of the teachers are outsiders (racially and socially) to our communities. I find that a glowing number of teachers have been exposed to your work in their teacher training programs, and a growing number of them find it valuable. Sadly, most people who use your work to train teachers do little to help new teachers interpret its relevance for U.S. urban K-12 classrooms. Many teacher educators do not even mention the fact that your analysis emerged primarily from your experience of working with ads adults. It seems so critically important to me that we understand your pedagogical recommendations, particularly your critique of banking model of education, as an analysis of work you did with adults. You were working with students who chose to come to your classroom. We are working with students who are mandated, by threat of legal repercussions, to come. You were working with students who had the wisdom that comes from surviving and subsisting into adulthood in spite of the hatred given to them as infants. We are working with children who, like any children, have not had the lived experience of adults to guide their decision-making and therefore need a more deliberately structured and disciplined environment.

Sadly, the result of these decontextualized teachings of your work often lead to two more forms of oppressive pedagogy that *we* must battle against. The first of these is a pedagogy guided by fear. Many teachers are so afraid of being labeled as oppressive (read racists) that they shy away from their responsibility as the adult and educational leader *in* the classroom. They shirk their duty to exercise authority for fear of being authoritarian, which results in classrooms that lack structure and discipline under the auspices of being nonoppressive and democratic. As teachers, they are exactly like the parents you describe in the first letter of *Pedagogy of Indignation,* complacent authorities who think of themselves as champions of freedom but find themselves vexed by the "tyranny of freedom." Far too many of these teachers who may consider themselves to be well meaning use democratic sensibilities and social justice leanings to defer to students on decisions that are the teacher's responsibility. In so doing, they fail to establish themselves as a legitimate adult authority with a clear plan for the direction of their students. Inevitably, when the class has spiraled out of control and the teacher decides to hold the young people to some random rule of discipline, the requisite respect of the students is lacking. The two most common results of this situation are equally bad. Either students refuse to recognize the authority of the teacher to the point that the teacher gives up on the class; or the teacher shifts to the role of uncompromising dictator, regains some semblance of control, and then interprets the authoritarian approach to be the most effective one with our children.

Of course, it is usually our students and families who get blamed for this, and the archetype of the unruly ghetto child unable or unwilling to stake a claim to her/his education is reified. Insert culture of poverty "experts" to the rescue who pimp the failing of these teachers with their snake oil solutions that situate the problems with students and the families. Their solution: a "pedagogy of poverty" (a term coined by Martin Haberman): "back to basics" drill and kill scripted literacy social studies, and mathematics lessons; zero-tolerance discipline policies; high-stakes testing; one-size-fits-all standards-based instruction; and phenomenally expensive all-inclusive in-service programs for teachers. The latter of these are particularly disturbing because they are designed by people from outside our communities to help teachers from outside our communities to understand the "culture of poverty" that vexes our communities. The widest-selling of such programs, Ruby Payne's *aha! Process,* claims that teachers should teach their students to examine individuals who have attained prosperity to learn the hidden rules of wealth creation. She argues that teachers should be trained to help individuals who are intent on improving their economic lot. Year after year, these regressive pedagogical methods produce identically low test scores and achievement patterns and questions from teachers wondering how critical pedagogy might help break the pattern. Does critical pedagogy mean that we are not supposed to prepare students to do well on tests anymore? Does it mean that we should throw out state and national standards? Does it mean that college is unimportant? Does it mean that we should not be preparing young people to enter the economy? What does this look like in a classroom? Won't I lose my job if I teach these things?

These questions reflect the second outcome of misinterpretations of your work—pedagogical decisions guided by a false binary. Teachers trained as critical pedagogues sometimes believe they must choose between academically rigorous teaching and teaching for social justice. This false binary is largely the result of the aforementioned pedagogy of poverty whereby teachers are trained to believe that an academically rigorous pedagogy does not have time for critically investigating the material conditions of the society. An academically rigorous pedagogy focuses on skill development to prepare students to score well on state and national achievement tests, most of which are norm-referenced and tend to be more useful (and accurate) as indicative of parental income than of intellect. I find that many teachers believe in the value of a critical and socially just pedagogy at least on a theoretical level. But, under the pressure facing their students to perform on a battery of tests by which their ability as teachers will be judged, they find much more job security in teaching to the test (learn to earn) than teaching students to think critically (learn for freedom). The bitter irony of this decision is that even when they teach to the test, their students don't usually end up doing any better.

To caution teachers against buying into the existence of this binary I return them to your first letter in *Pedagogy of Indignation* where you write:

> The progressive educator does not allow herself any doubt with respect to the right boys and girls from the masses, *the people,* have to know the same mathematics, physics, or biology that boys and girls from the "happier parts" of town learn. At the same time, she never accepts that the teaching of any discipline whatsoever could take place divorced from a critical analysis of how society works. (p. 20)

The disciplined classroom environment, producing the academic rigor and critical social awareness of which you speak, is the foundation on which THUG LIFE Pedagogy is built. Ultimately, THUG LIFE Pedagogy is an effort to ground your theory of critical pedagogy in the U.S. urban context so that teachers understand that all of the standards that students will be tested on are taught when you employ a critical pedagogy. There is no binary; you cannot have critical pedagogy without academic rigor, and you cannot be academically rigorous without drawing from critical pedagogy.

Despite the small number of teachers who struggle to apply critical pedagogy in U.S. urban contexts, I remain hopeful about its potential to improve classroom pedagogy because most teachers I encounter want to be great at what they do. Contrary to prevailing public and governmental opinions, the majority of teachers I come across are more in need of guidance and critical support on how to be effective than they are of mandates and threats. THUG LIFE Pedagogy allows me to encourage, support, develop, and incite educators to grow roses in the concrete. It provides a framework from which to study, and it highlights the work of the best teachers I meet so that people no longer ask why the roses' petals are damaged. Instead, they ask *How can we grow more?*

Working with teachers who are already in the classroom will not be enough to radically alter the quality of education given to most children. I recognize that we must also become more diligent about growing future educators in our communities. This coincides with your insistence that study include the act of creating and Tupac's insistence that we pay attention to nurturing snore roses in the concrete. And, so, I end this letter to you with a promise: I will create and re-create THUG LIFE Pedagogy based on my understanding as a practitioner of it. I will be an educator growing roses in the concrete, nurturing and mentoring those roses so that they can return to the community to grow rose gardens. My promise is to study and practice THUG LIFE Pedagogy so that it too might grow like a rose from the concrete—it is my revolutionary duty.

In solidarity,

Jeff Duncan-Andrade

REFERENCES

Freire, P. (2004). *Pedagogy of indignation.* Boulder, CO: Paradigm Publishers.

——— (1998). *Pedagogy of freedom: Ethics, democracy, and civic courage.* Lanham, MD: Rowman and Littlefield.

Freire, P. and Macedo, D. (1987). *Literacy: Reading the word and the world.* New York: Bergin and Garvey.

Haberman, M. (2006). *Pedagogy of poverty: The pedagogy of poverty versus good teaching.* Retrieved November 14, 2006, from http://ednews.org/articles/610/1/Pedagogy-of-Poverty-the Pedagogy-of-Poverty-Versus-Good -Teaching/Page1.html.

Lazin, L. (2003). *Tupac: Resurrection.* United States: Amaru Entertainment.

Shakur, T. (1999). *The rose that grew from concrete.* New York: Pocket Books.

———— (2002). Better dayz. Los Angeles: Interscope Records.

THIRTEEN

Eating, Talking, and Acting: The Magic of Freire

Herb Kohl

> *I must confess that I am somewhat afraid of people who tell me that they do not like to eat. I become a little suspicious.*
> —Paulo Freire, *The Politics of Education* (1985), p. 196.

Spring 2007

Dear Paulo,

This letter is to your spirit, since your inspiring presence is no longer with us.

I remember the first time we met at Jack London's house in Berkeley in the early 1970s. We had *feijoada* in your and your wife Elsa's honor, a delicious stew full of meats, sausages, and black beans served with fresh tropical fruits and, as Elsa said, the aroma of Brazil. You were still in exile at the time, and the smells of your homeland moved you to eloquence. However, you didn't speak much English at the time, and my first experience your spoken voice was in Portuguese, translated sensitively and thoughtfully by Elsa. I don't remember saying anything at the dinner, but I can visualize even now the pleasure with which you ate and spoke. Without understanding a word, I was struck by the fullness of your love for ideas, food, people, justice. The image of your over-riding passion for life animated your books for me, since I found them overly dense and, though occasionally poetic, abstract beyond necessity.

The first time we actually talked was in 1977. I picked you up at O'Hare Airport in Chicago, and since we were waiting for other people whose planes were late, we had few hours to talk. After we introduced ourselves you asked me about my work. I mentioned my book, *Reading,*

How To which was influenced by your writings. Your response was perhaps the most flattering statement I have ever heard about my work: "I have that book in my small exile's library; it is one I think about."

At that moment exile was much on your mind, and you remarked about how exhausting and depressing it was to be unable to live in Brazil. I'm not sure where you had been before arriving in Chicago, but you were clearly discouraged. You said not once, but a number of times, "I never want to hear the word *conscientização* again." It seems you had just been presented as the guru in residence at a "consciousness raising" seminar, not by your doing, but by the North Americans that orchestrated the session.

In all the times we talked and I observed you with people, I had never heard you talk about individuals in negative ways, and the same was true this time. If I interpret it correctly, you were discouraged and angered by the equation of your revolutionary ideas with the ideas that drove the self-awareness and consciousness-raising movements. You said, "There's no *prache,* no praxis in their work." We talked about how many of the people you encountered in the United States mistook social transformation for personal transformation and applied categories that characterized the lives of the oppressed to their own lives. They individualized what you described as a collective educational process connected with political and social action. This is the dilemma of teaching your words and implementing your ideas in the United States. We are not at a historical juncture where revolutionary practice *is* possible, nor is there a Workers Party that, when you were engaged with it, had strong and explicit socialist ideals.

After speaking to many educators in the United States who said that they were inspired by your work and practiced your ideas, I became very uneasy. All of them were involved in struggling for social justice, were doing the best they could to open up their students to transforming the difficult circumstances of their lives and improving the quality of community life surrounding their schools. They used some of your literacy tactics, built curricula around the lives and the vocabularies of their students. They did everything they could do as individuals and as comrades within small groups of their colleagues. But there was no engagement with a community that was awakening to the possibility that it could liberate itself from the external forms of economic and social repression. There was no radical political movement that connected them. Too often your ideas were turned into formulas for moderate change. I'm guilty of doing it on occasion. I use your pedagogy as much as I can, but I don't see the revolutionary potential of it in the United States. Praxis that emerges from your ideas does serve to help some students become open to their own potential and to engage in social action on a local scale. It also helps community groups clarify their own situation and potential. But very little of this praxis is revolutionary in your sense—it does not explicitly embrace fundamental change in the social and economic structures of U.S. capitalism.

In addition, and perhaps most important, adult non-literacy is not the same issue in the United States as it was in Brazil when you wrote your books. Most people here are either literate or partially and selectively literate. The written word is not alien to them, as it was to many of the poor people you describe in *Education for Critical Consciousness.* That's why it's so important that toward the end of your life you talked about "reading the world" with more passion than you did about reading the printed word. The world is so hard to read and name—that is to describe and encounter without deception. That challenge makes phonics or whole word learning and all the other attempts to provide print literacy seem minor.

Print literacy is one tool for reading the world, but there are multiple sources arising from culture, memory, history, value, and experience that contribute toward revolutionary consciousness. And, as you underline, without love, one cannot read or name the world or understand, through dialogue, the experiences of others. As you said in *Pedagogy*:

> Dialog cannot exist, however, in the absence of a profound love for the world and for women and men. The naming of the world, which is an act of creation and re-creation, is not possible if it is not infused with love. Love is at the same time the foundation of dialog and dialog itself. (Freire, 1970, p. 77)

A number of years ago I decided to teach a graduate teacher education course that had only one text, *Pedagogy of the Oppressed*. The idea was to do a close reading of your text and also read parts of the books you referred to in the footnotes. Each student also had to write a summary of what they read—not of what they thought about the text but what, from their understanding, it actually said. For most of the students this was a new experience. They were accustomed to being asked for their interpretations. I wanted them to look at as you intended.

Most of the students in the class had read excerpts from *Pedagogy* in other classes they had taken and considered themselves enthusiastic Freireans. After they finished reading your book and the texts from Fanon, Sartre, and others that you referred to, and discussing the ideas and structure of your work, the major conclusion was that you were too dangerous a thinker to follow. They agreed that many of your ideas were useful and worth trying out in the classroom, but making a revolution, actually working with oppressed people in ways that assisted them in mobilizing themselves and taking action, was too risky. I hope that the idea of risk was planted firmly in their minds and that some day they might, for moral reasons, be willing to became engaged in confronting systems of oppression in the context of collective struggle. But perhaps the current historical juncture in the United States is not right for revolutionary action. I know these students are decent, progressive people living in the belly of the beast during very difficult times. But the future is not predictable, and the time might soon be ripe for fundamental social and economic change. As my mentor, Myles Horton, once told me, things are always perking during what seem to be quiet times, since the passion for justice never dies and therefore there is no reason to abandon hope.

Paulo, one of the hardest things for U.S. educators who embrace your ideas is to publicly acknowledge an unambiguous rejection of capitalism and advocate some form of socialism. Currently, we have no major Socialist party in the United States, and the language of socialism is not used within the arena of education at all. The language of competition and what you call banking education rules supreme. Yet it is hard to imagine an authentic use of your ideas that is not explicit in its rejection of exploitation of any kind and a passionate identification with those to be educated. This means understanding "the yearning of the oppressed for freedom and justice, and by their struggle to recover their lost humanity" (ibid., p. 28). It also means understanding and respecting the knowledge and intelligence of the people you work with.

I remember an example of learning from poor, oppressed people that you described in *Pedagogy of Hope*. You said that you were at a peasant meeting and one of the members of the audience claimed ignorance and asked you, the expert, how they should go about solving their problems. Your response was to play a game of ten questions with one of the peasant leaders. Each was to ask ten questions of the other based in their own special knowledge. Your first question was 'What is the Socratic method?" Not surprisingly the peasant didn't know the answer but responded with the question 'What's soil liming?' You couldn't answer.

At the end of the questioning the score was ten for you and ten for the peasants. Your response to that was indicative of the profound way you draw people into their own learning:

> As I said good-bye, I made a suggestion. "Let's think about this evening. You had begun to have a fine discussion with me. Then you were silent, and said that only I could talk because I was the only one who knew anything. Then we played a knowledge game and we tied ten to ten. I knew ten things you didn't, and you knew ten things I didn't. Let's think about this." (Freire, 1994, pp. 46–47)

Your ideas about dialogue, the creation of culture, reading the world, and learning from the people have become guiding principles of my life and work. Your work is utopian and full of hope and provocation. Sustaining the battle for authentic democracy and the elimination of oppression is difficult and for many of us one whose fruits we will never experience. The question you raise in *Pedagogy of Hope* is: where shall hope be found when faith in the triumph of revolutionary struggles seems unfounded if not actually confounded by history? This *is* a constant worry for me, not strong enough to make me disengaged but one that tinges all my hopes for a just future with sadness. Your answer to this dilemma pointed to two sources of hope, one involving a reaffirmation and the other a dream. You reaffirmed the role people can play in making history and reminded us that history is process, that it has no end, and that its forms are neither set nor predictable but depend upon the moral actions and dreams of people. The second was to remind us to be utopian and to pay attention to past efforts to build societies based on principles of justice and decency as you said in the book:

> In our making and remaking of ourselves in the process of making history—as subjects and objects, persons becoming beings of insertion in the world and not of pure adaptation to the world—we should end by having the dream, too, a mover of history. There is no change without dream, as there is no dream without hope. Thus, I keep insisting, ever since *Pedagogy of the Oppressed:* there is no authentic utopia apart from the tension between the denunciation of a present becoming more and more intolerable, and the "annunciation," announcement, of a future to be created, built—politically, esthetically, and ethical—by us women and men. Utopia implies this denunciation and proclamation, but it does not permit the tension between the two to die away with the production of the future previously announced. Now the erstwhile future is a new present, and a new dream experience is forged. History does not become immobilized, does not *die*. On the contrary, it goes on. (ibid.)

I find your vision expressed beautifully in this quotation from Pablo Neruda's Nobel Prize acceptance speech, which he called "The Splendid City":

> I wish to say to the people of goodwill, to the workers, to the poets, that the whole future has been expressed by this line by Rimbaud; only with a *burning patience* can we conquer the Splendid City which will give light, justice, and dignity to all mankind. (Neruda, 1974, pp. 33–35)

Our work must be situated in this patience and in our own reading of the world and that of the people we teach. We must also be willing to take risks. Cultural action for freedom is a dangerous enterprise, and your spirit is an inspiration—it is as if you and Miles and other elders (by the way I am seventy now) provide the energy and strength that keeps us going when we feel tired or discouraged or too angry to be effective.

Paulo, I'm honored that you are still with me and with us.

Best,

Herb Kohl

REFERENCES

Freire, P. (2002). *Education for critical consciousness.* New York: Continuum International Publishing Group.

———(1994). *Pedagogy of hope: Reliving pedagogy of the oppressed.* New York: Continuum.

———(1985). *The politics of education: Culture, power, and liberation.* South Hadley, MA: Bergin & Garvey.

——— (1970). *Pedagogy of the oppressed.* New York: Seabury Press.

Kohl, H. (1974). *Reading, how to.* New York: Dutton.

Neruda, P. (1974). *Toward the splendid city.* New York: Noonday.

FOURTEEN

English Language Learners: Understanding Their Needs

Binbin Jiang

English language learners (ELLs) are students whose native languages are not English but are learning English in our schools. ELLs make up over 5 million students, among whom 80% are Spanish speaking, nearly 10.3 percent of public school enrollment. By the year 2025, ELLs under age 18 are projected to be approximately 50% of the American population (American Federation of Teachers, 2006). It will be virtually impossible for a professional educator to serve in any public or private school setting in which the students are not racially, culturally or linguistically diverse. To better prepare each future educator so that she/he can work effectively with this population of students in schools, I will address the linguistic, social, psychological and cultural factors that affect the schooling experience and academic success of these English language learners. Specific attention will be paid to how children and youth acquire a second language in school and how long it takes to acquire conversational and academic language in a second language. It is important to understand the role first language literacy and prior formal schooling have on the student's progress in a second language. Prior social and cultural experiences can have a significant effect on issues of second language learning. The combination of social and psychological factors affect ELLs in their learning of the English language. I will conclude this chapter with a discussion of how cultural differences affect ELLs' academic success and present principles for teachers use in effectively working with these unique learners in schools.

While ELLs may be all ages, come from a wide range of ethnic backgrounds, hail from different economic situations, and may have come to this country for a variety of reasons, they all share the common need to learn English. Throughout the history of American education many different terms have been used to describe or characterize children whose second language is English: students with limited English proficiency (LEPs); students for whom English is a second language (ESLs); or second language learners (SLLs). Currently educators most commonly refer to these children as English language learners (ELLs). This shift in language represents a more accurate reflection of the process of language acquisition.

KRASHEN'S SECOND LANGUAGE LEARNING THEORY & STAGES OF SECOND LANGUAGE ACQUISITION

How do ELLs learn English and become competent in the use of English language? There are many theories about second language learning; however, Stephan Krashen's theory (1981) has been among the most influential in helping educators understand this process. Krashen's theory includes five major components: a language acquisition/learning hypothesis; the natural order hypothesis; the monitor hypothesis; the comprehensible input hypothesis; and the affective filter hypothesis.

The acquisition-learning hypothesis distinguishes between informal learning of a language (acquisition) and formal learning of academic language within the classroom setting. Acquisition is similar in many ways to the process children use in acquiring their first language and is largely subconscious. Learning the academic language is generally the product of formal instruction. The context for first language acquisition is at home and in real-life situations in which children feel free and safe. Conversely, the context for learning academic language is usually in the classroom in which learners are given specific instructions on certain aspects of the target language; for example, vocabulary, pronunciation of words, grammar, listening, speaking, reading and writing. The implication is that teachers who create an atmosphere where students feel free, and safe, to experiment using the target language can successfully promote more active learning.

As a second language learner, I learned English language grammar and how to understand, speak, read and write in English in the formal classroom context where I grew up in China. However, after I came to the United States where English is used in everyday life and professional contexts, I have acquired more native-like English usage. This experience is especially critical in understanding the idiomatic expressions of conversational English.

The natural order hypothesis states that we acquire the rules of a language in a predictable sequence. For example, an understanding of the plural of nouns is acquired more quickly than rules of the third-person singular verb ending of "s."

According to Krashen (1992), "The natural order appears to be immune to deliberate teaching; we cannot change the natural order by explanation, drills and exercises" (p. 2). Another example that Krashen gives is that adults learning a second language acquire the progressive "-ing" marker earlier than the third person singular "-s" even though we do more patterned drills and exercises on the latter. This hypothesis tells us that constant correction of grammatical errors to beginning learners of a second language is not especially helpful.

Krashen's monitor hypothesis suggests that language learned in the classroom serves only to "edit" or "monitor" what the students pick up or acquire. When the student produces language, it may contain errors. A student can "monitor" to make some self-corrections, but his focus will conflict with a focus on fluency and the content of the message. This hypothesis reminds teachers that second language learners are often trying to produce something that is correct using the rules they have learned to plan and monitor the sentence or paragraph before they actually say or write it.

Consequently, teachers need to give students sufficient time to think and not require answers from them before they are ready in the second language. For instance, when I was learning the past tense in English, it took me a very long time to acquire the use of past tense as there are no verb tenses in Chinese (my native language). For a long time, I would actually search for the past tense of the verb in my mind to fit into the sentence before I actually spoke it. The process of searching for the past tense is the monitor or editor function in language learning.

Comprehensible input hypothesis claims that people acquire language when they receive comprehensible input which is slightly beyond their current level of understanding. For example, people learn the rules of language in a natural order, learning rule 1, then rule 2 and so on. When the first rule is learned, they are ready to learn the next.

According to Krashen (1992):

> More generally, if "i" represents the last rule we have acquired, and "i+1" the next rule we have acquired… we move from "i" to "i+1" by understanding input containing "i+1." We are able to do this with the help of our previously acquired linguistic competence, as well as extra-linguistic knowledge, which includes our knowledge of the world and our knowledge of the situation. In other words, we use context. (p. 4)

The point is that the input (i) must be slightly beyond the learners' ability level (i+1) so that acquisition will take place. Krashen (1992) states that "teaching methods containing more comprehensible input have been shown to be more effective than 'traditional' methods…for both beginning and intermediate language teaching" (p. 3). In teaching my beginning adult ELLs, I try to speak slowly, use simple sentence structure, and use visual aids and repetition to make the input comprehensible for the students. I relate to this aspect of second language learning because of a negative experience I had caused by a lack of understanding English.

While I was a college freshman majoring in English in China, I experienced comprehension input difficulty in an American history class taught by an American professor. Because I did not have the background knowledge or the vocabulary necessary to understand the content of the class, his lectures in English were way beyond my comprehension. In addition, the professor used the normal native speaker's speed when lecturing. If he had known about the concept of comprehensible input, I probably would have had a more effective learning experience in that course.

The affective filter hypothesis claims that learners put up a resistance to learning in certain situations. This mental block prevents them "from utilizing input fully for further language acquisition" when they are "in a less than optimal affective state" (Krashen, 1992, p. 9). An optimal state for second language learning is one in which learners have a low level of anxiety, high motivation, self-esteem and confidence. For example, when language learners feel nervous or embarrassed, they can receive comprehensible input but still not acquire the language as their affective filter is high. On the other hand, a student with high motivation can cause the affective filter to be lowered. This hypothesis indicates that students will not acquire a language if their stress level or boredom level is too high. Therefore, we must create a comfortable classroom context and provide materials that will sustain students' curiosity while we teach the necessary content.

Krashen (1985) summarized the five interrelated hypotheses in his book, *Inquiries and Insights*, in one sentence: "We acquire language when we obtain comprehensible input in a low-anxiety situation, when we are presented with interesting messages, and when we understand these messages" (p. 94). In other words, language is acquired in a natural order when students are given comprehensible input in a risk-free environment.

To put Krashen's second language acquisition theory into practice, Krashen and Terrell (1983) developed the Natural Approach teaching method. Based on the Natural Approach method, there are four basic stages or levels that all new learners of English progress through to acquire the target language. It is important to note that the length of time each student spends at a particular stage may vary greatly. In addition, ELLs in the same class may be at different stages/levels of their English proficiency. Knowing the characteristics of each stage/level can be very useful to content area teachers who work with ELLs as they assess which stage/level each ELL is at in order to communicate effectively with each of them and to select appropriate teaching strategies.

The first stage is known as the pre-production/silent period. During this time, students have anywhere from 10 hours to six months of exposure to English, and their vocabulary includes approximately 500 receptive words (words they can understand but don't use yet). They do not usually produce much verbal language at this time, but they communicate using gestures and actions. During this stage, students only understand language that has been made comprehensible. They often rely on modeling, visual stimuli such as pictures and objects, context clues, key words and use listening strategies to understand meaning. These language learners frequently communicate through pointing and physical gestures. For students in this stage of language learning, the teacher should provide activities geared to tap their knowledge but not to force production (speaking). These students benefit from classroom activities that allow them to respond by imitating, drawing, pointing, and matching.

After having spent anywhere from three months to a year immersed in learning English, students begin to acquire a small yet active vocabulary of approximately 100 words. This is referred to as stage two: the early production period. During this time, students grow to have a receptive vocabulary level of approximately 1,000 words, and they begin to feel ready to speak in one- or two-word phrases. At this stage of language learning, students can demonstrate their comprehension of material by giving short responses to easy yes/no questions and either/or questions. They can also respond to simple who, what, when, where questions. They may benefit from classroom activities that employ language they can understand, require them to name and group objects, and call for responses to simple questions.

STAGE THREE: SPEECH EMERGENCE

After somewhere between one and three years of exposure to English, students' development of proficiency increases exponentially. This is known as the speech emergence stage. During this time, they use phrases and sentences, and their active vocabulary grows to about 3,000 words with nearly 7,000 words of receptive vocabulary. There is a noticeable increase in listening comprehension. Students will try to speak in phrases and start to use complete sentences. They often mix basic phrases and sentences in both languages. They will begin to use the social language necessary in the classroom. Ask students at this stage how and why questions that elicit short responses. They will be able to participate in many of the mainstream academic subjects. They may benefit from classroom activities that encourage them to experiment with language and develop and expand their vocabulary.

After about three to four years of exposure to English, students have accumulated approximately 6,000 active words and 12,000 receptive words. This is known as the Nearly Fluent/Intermediate Fluency stage of language acquisition. Students understand most of what is said in the classroom, and they are developing good comprehension skills. They can express their ideas comprehensibly in both oral and written communication. These students expand on their basic sentences and extend their language abilities to employ more complex sentence structures and make fewer errors when speaking. Functionally, they will be able to read most grade-level material. Teachers may ask these students open-ended questions that allow more complicated responses and the use of complex sentences. These sophisticated second language learners may benefit from classroom literacy activities and instruction in vocabulary and grammar.

CUMMINS' VIEW OF SECOND LANGUAGE PROFICIENCY

According to Cummins (1981), there are two important types of language proficiency. Cummins identified these levels of comprehension as Basic Interpersonal Communication Skills (BICS) and Cognitive Academic Language Proficiency (CALP). BICS refers to skills or proficiency in conversational English used in informal interpersonal communications such as at the dinner table or on the school playground. In contrast, CALP is the skill or proficiency in the academic language or formal language used in classrooms and in textbooks. It is the complex syntax of English including forms, rules, and relationships of formal oral and written English. According to Collier's (1989) study, it takes approximately two years for a student to achieve proficiency in BICS, but generally five to seven years to achieve proficiency in CALP. In concert with Krashen and Terrell's four stages of the language development, students begin to develop their BICS at the Pre-Production Stage and reach BICS during the Speech Emergence Stage. At this stage/level, they also begin their initial development of CALP. At the Intermediate Fluency Stage, students continue to develop their CALP and begin to demonstrate their development in CALP through listening, speaking, reading and writing in English. In other words, a student who is fluent in English on the playground is likely to require five to seven years to acquire the level of proficiency needed for successful academic learning. The implication for teachers is not to overlook the fact that academic language can still be challenging and adversely affect the student's academic performance even though she/he is fluent in everyday conversations. Cummins' Common Underlying Proficiency (CUP) Model of Bilingual Proficiency indicates that bilingual students develop proficiency in two languages but with the same underlying proficiency.

The implication of this model is that proficiencies developed in one language are transferable to another. According to Cummins, "Concepts are most readily developed in the first language and, once developed, are accessible through the second language. In other words, what we learn in one language transfers into the new language" (Freeman & Freeman, 1992, p. 176). For instance, in my Chinese literature class in high school, I learned the literary terminology and the related concepts applied to literature, such as flashback, theme characterization, and foreshadowing. When these terms were encountered in English, the concepts were already understood, and, thus, I was able to transfer the knowledge learned in Chinese to English. Evidence for transfer of language skills also comes from research done by Cummins (1979a). He examined the relationship between bilingual children's academic skills in the primary and second language. Correlations between the first language (L1) and the second language (L2) proficiency were statistically significant, which may imply that children who read well in L1 were likely to read well in L2 (Cummins, 1979b).

In my own research (Jiang, 1999; Jiang & Kuehn, 2001), I have also examined the relationship between bilingual students' academic language skills in L1 and L2. Although, my focus was on adult learners, I found similar results regarding the relationship between a bilingual's academic proficiency in L1 and L2 and the issue of transfer (Bossers, 1991; Canale, Frenette, & Belanger, 1988; Carson & Kuehn, 1994; Cummins, 1984; Hoover, 1983; Verhoeven, 1991). As people learn languages, they develop certain skills that may naturally transfer from L1 to L2. The level of proficiency reached in L1 does influence the development of their proficiency in L2 (Odlin, 1986). Empirical studies have indicated that the "transfer of ability to L2 can only occur if individuals have already acquired that ability in their L1" (Carson & Kuehn, 1994, p. 260).

THE ROLE OF FIRST LANGUAGE LITERACY AND FORMAL SCHOOLING

As I have discussed so far, students who have had prior formal schooling and L1 language proficiency in their native country will be more likely to transfer their knowledge and skills to the L2 learning experiences. This experience and prior success can make their transition and learning in the L2 context much smoother. Conversely, the students who have not had formal schooling and L1 literacy will not have the knowledge and skill from their L1 to transfer.

These students can encounter more difficulties and challenges, and it may take them much more time and effort to learn English. These two groups of students are distinguished by Faltis and Coulter (2007) as immigrant students with parallel and nonparallel schooling experiences.

According to Faltis and Coulter, immigrant students with parallel schooling experiences typically enter school at grade level or above and may have had prior exposure to English in school or at home with tutors. These students tend to have smooth transitions into school culture and they often excel academically. Research conducted by Suárez-Orozco & Suárez-Orozco (2001) provides documentation that Salvadoran immigrant children with parallel schooling experiences do succeed academically in school once they gain oral and written proficiency in English.

Zhou (1998) also discusses "parachute kids" in Southern California. These are transnational immigrant children and youth from high-achieving families in China and Taiwan who "drop in" to American schools and live with relatives. These immigrant children and young adults have parallel formal schooling experiences, and they also experience academic success and smoother transition. Conversely, immigrant students with non-parallel schooling experiences and long-term English learners encounter the most difficulty in the schooling experience in the U.S. and present the greatest challenges for schools and classroom teachers.

Non-parallel immigrant students are typically at least two grade levels below where they should be for their age group (Faltis & Coulter, 2007). Gibson (1998) has found that these students also face a number of other obstacles in school. In addition to entering school knowing little or no English, they often have to deal with conflicts between family values and school values. Another challenge many of these students face when they enter school is their minimal knowledge of and experience with computer technology. Computers have become an essential tool for the successful schooling for secondary students (Suárez-Orozco, 2005).

Long-term English learners are immigrant students who have been in English learning programs for at least five years, and they remain English learners. These are students who are below grade level in reading and writing, and they are mostly unable to participate in and benefit from mainstream English-only classrooms unless they can be given individualized instructional practices (Freeman & Freeman, 2002). Specifically, these students need a schooling environment that is inclusive and supportive of their specific language and literacy needs.

SOCIOCULTURAL ISSUES RELATED TO LANGUAGE LEARNING

In both positive and negative ways, elements related to social status and to the students' cultural background contribute considerable influence to the success of ESL students' learning. In their discussion of Labov's (1972) findings, Diaz-Rico & Weed (1995) reached the following conclusion:

> As students learn a second language, their success is dependent on such extra-linguistic factors as the pattern of acculturation for their community; the status of their primary language in relation to English; their own speech community's view of the English language and the English-speaking community; the dialect of English they are hearing and learning and its relationship to standard English; the patterns of social and cultural language usage in the community (Labov, 1972); and the compatibility between the home culture and the cultural patterns and organization of schools (Diaz-Rico and Weed, pp. 40–41). Language is important "in defining the shape of thought." (Hakuta, 1986, p. 79).

Similarly, Ogbu (1986, 1991) discusses the different reasons that immigrants come to the United States and the factors that can lead to social integration or isolation. He describes these groups as immigrant minorities and involuntary minorities who often experience discrimination and autonomous minorities who stay separate from the majority culture (Freeman & Freeman, 1994). New immigrants view the "economic, political, and social barriers against them as more or less temporary problems" which they will "overcome with the passage of time, hard work, or more education" while involuntary minorities view these conditions as "permanent problems" which they "may have little hope of overcoming…" (pp. 222–3). Ogbu is famous for coining the term involuntary immigrants to define those who came to America against their will, for example, slaves.

While Ogbu (1981) looks at minority students in relation to the social and cultural factors that affect their success and failure in general, Schumann examines specific social factors that affect ESL students' acquisition of L2. Schumann uses the term assimilation to describe voluntary immigrants, and the term acculturation to describe immigrants who are in-between since they adapt to the new culture but continue to maintain their own. Schumann defines preservation as the behavior of involuntary immigrants who remain isolated and retain their own culture and reject the new culture. Schumann (1978) posits, "Assimilation fosters minimal social distance and preservation causes it to be maximal. Hence, second language learning is enhanced by assimilation and hampered by preservation. Acculturation falls in the middle" (p. 78).

SOCIAL AND PSYCHOLOGICAL FACTORS

Schumann (1978) developed a model for analysis of the instances in which learners "create both a psychological distance and social distance from speakers of the second language community" (Gass & Selinker, 1994, p. 236). The significance of these differences formed the basis for Schumann's Acculturation Model. Schumann characterized the relationship between the acculturation model and second language acquisition as follows: "Second language acquisition is just one aspect of acculturation and the degree to which a learner acculturates to the target-language group will control the degree to which he acquires the second language…" (McLaughlin, 1987, p. 110). From this point of view, second language acquisition is determined by the degree of social and psychological distance between the learner and the target language culture.

Schumann identified eight influential factors in determining social distance. Social dominance refers to the power relations between speakers of the two languages. The L2 learner may be in a subordinate position that may be related to economic or cultural status. The greater the dominance of the speakers of the target language, the greater difficulty the learners will have in acquiring that language. When there is more equality between the two groups, the second language will be easier to acquire. The integration pattern refers to the full, partial, or limited integration of the L2 learner and depends upon the degree of his or her assimilation and acculturation into the new culture and the degree of the preservation of the L2 learner's native culture. Preservation is linked to an individual's desire to maintain aspects of his or her native culture while living within the new culture. When cultural groups band together this is considered enclosure. Enclosure refers to the confinement of the L2 learner to the native culture and environment. Size of the group has a significant effect, and it refers to the number of a particular cultural group that create or maintain norms.

Cohesiveness is an outgrowth of all of the earlier stages, and it refers to the unity surrounding a specific non-mainstream culture. For example, my Hmong students have enough unity within their group that their need to assimilate with the target language group is alleviated. Cultural congruence is maintained with the cohesiveness, and this refers to the points of correspondence and the harmonious agreement among cultures. Attitude refers to the positive, negative, or neutral attitudes between the groups, more often being negative or neutral. The intended length of stay for the L2 learner also affects the way in which the target language is learned. For example, someone who plans to stay in a country for a short length of time only may have little reason or motivation to become proficient in the target language.

Psychological distance, according to Schumann (1978), results from the affective influence of certain psychological factors: language shock, culture shock, motivation, and ego boundaries (Ellis, 1986). Whereas language shock can lead to doubt and confusion, culture shock can lead to disorientation, stress, fear, and other negative attitudes. A person with high motivation to learn the target language and to learn the culture would probably not suffer from language or culture shock. However, that learner may still have ego boundaries which cause inhibition, defensiveness, and self-consciousness that slow down the process of language acquisition. According to Freeman & Freeman (1994), "In situations where social distance neither strongly promotes nor inhibits language acquisition, psychological distance may play a crucial role" (p. 83).

CULTURAL DIFFERENCES AFFECTING ELL'S ACADEMIC SUCCESS

Because schools are a microcosm of society, many of the same social, cultural, and psychological factors affecting students in society will affect them within the school culture. This can also affect their academic success. For example, students who are not native English speakers must socialize with those who are on campus and in the classroom. More importantly, they must integrate into the school community in order to better understand the school system's organizational structure, policies, and expectations. Second language learners need to integrate within the diverse school population and the classroom in order to better develop the learning and social strategies needed for success.

Teachers also must become sensitive to the second language students' needs and provide support to help them adapt to the new school culture. Part of the responsibility that teachers have is to understand that differences in language and culture are often subtle, but they affect students' classroom participation in several ways. Understanding these will help teachers to respond in ways that will help both ELLs and other students to learn. Cultural differences can mean different rules for classroom behavior. Zehler (1994) recommended the following advice for teachers to be sensitive to the cultural differences among the ELLs in schools. Students from other cultures may behave differently than what is expected in the American classrooms as they may have different views of how to be a student based on their own cultural norms.

For example, in some countries, it is disrespectful to ask questions of a teacher or speak in class. As a result, students from these countries may appear to be reluctant to ask any questions or participate in class discussions. However, as they adjust to the American school culture, they may gradually become acculturated and begin to follow their American peers' behavior.

Cultural differences can also affect students' understanding of content. New knowledge is constructed based on what is already known by an individual learner. Research in reading indicates that reading comprehension involves both understanding the words on the page and one's relevant background knowledge of the topic. However, textbooks used in schools often appear to have been written by authors who assume all students have the same background knowledge. In fact, many ELLs may not fully understand these texts because of a lack of background knowledge or lack of schooling experience in this country. Consequently, they will be less likely to fully comprehend or remember the content material. Students whose experience is not in the mainstream, therefore, will often need additional explanation and examples to help them bridge the gap between the new material and their existing knowledge bases.

Cultural differences can also affect interpersonal relations. Misinterpretation of respect, appreciation and showing interest may occur because of the interaction of multiple cultures in the classroom.

It is common practice in some Asian and Latin American cultures for students not to look the teacher in the eye to show respect when the teacher is talking. Unfortunately, this could be interpreted as the student's lack of attention or as a sign of disrespect if the teacher does not know the culture of the ELL. The way in which praise is given may also be different. For some cultural groups, praise to an individual student is not given in public. In contrast, a quiet word of praise to the student is the norm for them. Teachers need to learn about different cultural practices and be sensitive to student reactions while also helping students to learn about American culture. As a former ELL and as an educator working with ELLs and training teachers for ELLs for over

17 years in the United States and other countries, I have identified developed six principles for integrating instructional practices (Jiang & DeVillar, 2005). As an example, I will use a particular class that I taught with 30 beginning level (Between Pre-production and Early Production in Krashen & Terrell's model) ELLs in an adult school in California (Jiang, 2004).

In my classroom, nine different languages were spoken and many different cultures (Laotion, Hmong, Vietnamese, Miao, Hispanic, Ethiopian, etc.) were present. To illustrate how each principle was implemented for helping these students to succeed in their learning and cultural adjustment in the United States, I will describe each principle in detail.

The first principle involves building the classroom community and culture. As ELLs experience linguistic, psychological, cultural, and other challenges in school while they are striving to learn both English and content knowledge, they need support and understanding from the teacher and their peers. Building a classroom community in which everyone cares about and learns from one another will provide the opportunity for ELLs to feel safe and comfortable to learn and to be willing share their experiences with others. For any teacher with a diverse student population, the American students can also benefit from learning about diverse cultures and be exposed to other languages that will help them to appreciate cultural and linguistic diversity and to broaden their understanding of the world.

One way of building a classroom community is through getting to know one another by sharing everyone's experiences, talents, and families. In my class, I started by sharing about myself, my family and the reasons why I was in the United States. This set the example for my students to tell about their lives, families and the reasons for coming to the U.S. They also brought pictures of their family, cultural artifacts and foods to share with their classmates. Through these sharing experiences, they began to understand and respect one another which marked the beginning of building the classroom community. This cultural sharing helped the class members to have more pride in their own culture and increased their self-esteem and self-confidence. It also motivated students to learn English in order to share with others. These connections resulted in higher attendance rates. Through the code of visual aid, they understood more clearly the content of the discussion and participated in it through verbal and non-verbal communications. Cultural sharing contributed to the development of a positive environment of a community of learners. These students learned to greet each other in one another's native languages as a sign of appreciation of all the cultures represented in the community. This sensitivity helped students to feel more comfortable and to share more deeply personal experiences. It became obvious that they cared about one another.

This cultural sharing activity was also a valuable experience for me. For me to learn about the lives, history and oppression that my students had experienced in their homelands, it helped me to see more relevant themes for future learning units. As a participant and co-learner in the cultural sharing conversations, my respect and understanding for each class member grew as they opened up to our class community by sharing their beautiful culture traditions, their struggles through the wars and hardships, and their talents and knowledge about the parts of the world that I did not know before. These students broadened my perspective on how social, cultural, and historical factors could affect individual learners.

Collaborative group work is another strong tool for promoting student learning. Because of my interest in students' sharing of their cultures, their experiences, and their talents, I took pictures of all the activities we had in class and brought the photos back to class. The students were excited to see themselves in the pictures. In order to celebrate and keep these wonderful memories, we decided to put the pictures on the bulletin board. I further thought it would be even more meaningful if the students could document their own activities. According to the social learning principles of Vygotsky (1962, 1978), students working together can help gain access to new areas of learning beyond those they are able to accomplish alone.

In other words, effective, long-term learning takes place when learners engage in mutually meaningful activities. It is productive for them to work in dyads or small groups, take an active role in the learning process, collaborate with one another, and exercise choice during their activities.

As students collaborate, they learn to externalize their thoughts in order to communicate with each other, to solve problems, and to construct concepts, thus learning (D. E. Freeman & Y. Freeman, 1994). In order to facilitate such learning, teachers become mediators, helping students through their interaction to reach higher levels of proficiency. Vygotsky refers to the distance between the individual level of students and the potential level students can reach in collaborative interaction in the Zone of Proximal Development. According to his theory, learners working together have the potential to reach higher levels of development. Learning to function in groups also helps students to function in society: "In communities of learners, students appear to learn how to coordinate with, support, and lead others, to become responsible and organized in their management of their own learning, and to be able to build on their previous interest to learn in new areas and to sustain motivation to learn" (Rogoff, Matusov, & White, 1996, p. 410). In other words, "Learning must be an active, social, discovery process, guided by the teacher, rather than a transmission process controlled by the teacher…" and "A learner is a thinker and an engaged participant; each role informs and transforms the other" (DeVillar, 1999, p. 45).

Using these principles, I arranged the students into several groups. As members of the class community, they were willing to help each other in their collaborative group work. Each student contributed what he or she could to the writing within their particular group. For example, one person would take the role of scribe and editor; others helped with the vocabulary or assisted with the spelling of a word. Other students would assist with the structures of the sentences. They enjoyed helping with the layout, for example, by determining where to integrate the photographs with the writing. Then, each group shared its text-and-image work with the whole class before placing their individual project on the bulletin board. The level of pride exhibited by students was very high.

The activity of using the pictures (or the codes) from the culture sharing continued to produce results. Most significantly, this activity transformed into more dialogue and action because of the collaborative group work. Students were learning to write about themselves and their activities and learning to read by reading each other's writings. By working together to learn to read and to write in English, they took active steps towards overcoming their language difficulties and towards making positive changes in their own lives.

Freire, the father of critical pedagogy, advocates a dialogical approach in which every member of the community becomes a co-learner in the critical learning process. "The students—no longer docile listeners—are now critical co-investigators in dialogue with the teacher" (Freire, 1998, p. 75). Dialogic approach is applicable to immigrant ELLs, in particular, since most of them come from backgrounds that are similar to the participants in Freire's literacy programs— low socioeconomic status with limited or no access to education in their home countries. After coming to the United States, many of them have experienced emotional and social barriers in learning English, culture shock, lack of self-confidence, homesickness, and a sense of loss and vulnerability in the new environment.

In my teaching with the 30 adult ELLs in my class, I integrated their experiences into our content learning, and they became more active in the learning process. All this engagement made the learning authentic and interesting, thus helping the students learn more effectively. For example, the students enjoyed the weekly cultural sharing time so much that we gradually changed it to the first daily activity. In this activity, students shared experiences of their family and community and their perspectives. However, some students could not understand everything that was being shared because of their lack of vocabulary or their listening proficiency.

They suggested that I write what the class contributed on the board so that they could copy and share them with their family. This started our class journal where we integrated listening, speaking, reading and writing within one activity using the content of students' experiences and reflections.

The daily journals provided authentic reading material for not only the class members but also some of the family members because of the relevant content. This activity was one of the favorite activities—for both the students and me—as it engaged the whole class in a writing project to produce a collective journal and evolved through different students' input over time. This practice adhered to the principle that students needed to be immersed in literature of all kinds to help them progress in writing, to become more proficient writers "through exposure to books and print…" (Weaver, 1994, p. 98).

Cummins contributes the notion of context-embedded instruction as "interpersonal involvement in a shared reality that reduces the need for explicit linguistic elaboration of the message" (Cummins, 1981, p. 11). This is essential to beginning ESL classes, where the instructor can use pictures, realia, activities modeled by the teacher and the language aide, books and prints that have rich illustrations. In the specific adult L2 situation described here, communication was facilitated through the use of appropriate reading materials with pictures, slower and shorter utterances in instruction, and help of a multilingual aide. In order to make learning more meaningful and authentic to the students, my curriculum closely related the students' learning to their daily lives.

When students studied the unit on shopping, they engaged, singly and through group projects, in making up menus, comparing prices for various foods from ads in the local newspaper, and composing related shopping lists. Each group then presented to the rest of the class, telling what they wanted to prepare, what they needed to buy, and where they had decided to purchase the items. Later, when we had potluck lunches, students were able to explain how to make the food they brought, and they provided the name of the dish. In order to make some of these themes more comprehensible to students, we simulated a grocery store with cash registers, canned foods, counters, price tags, and students played various roles.

These context-embedded learning activities provided students with useful tools to become more independent and active in dealing with daily living situations. Daily living problems could be very frustrating to them because they did not know how to communicate. Difficulties could arise with the school about their children's sickness, reporting family emergencies, or even conversing with the clerks at grocery stores. With the improvement of their English literacy, the students gained more confidence in themselves and were willing to take more risks with learning to read and write in English.

A meaningful way in which to introduce and develop students' writing is through immersion in literature of all kinds. The first book we read together in this class was called *What a Wonderful World* (Weiss et al., 1995). It demonstrated the beauty of the world with beautiful pictures and simple verses. The students enjoyed reading along with me. This reading naturally led us into the discussion of their homeland and their writing and drawings about their homeland. Their work amazed me. They used words with codes they knew to define pictures of their homes, rivers, farm animals, trees, flowers. All of these things were personally meaningful and the images represented their lives and their stories. At the same time, I also realized how much help they needed in order to become literate in English (since most of their writings consisted of only words or phrases) so that they could share their stories and have their voices heard. It taught me again that their lives comprised the best themes for learning to read and write.

As the students developed their literacy skills, they were not only able to share their work with a larger community but also demonstrated more critical themes in their writing content and creative format. For instance, during the latter half of the school year, students began to write their own journals. One weekend, a Hmong student witnessed a killing near his apartment. With the help of his children, he wrote about the incident and shared his writing with the class. This journal evoked discussions on gang violence in the local community and resulted in the topic of how to keep children from the gang influence and watch for one another in their own neighborhood. This example also illustrated the unlimited potential motivated learners could have in sharing experiences of their lives (even if negative) which could be transformed into actions that would change the learners' lives. In the month of Lincoln and Washington's birthdays, we read biographical stories about these American presidents. The students learned how these presidents contributed to important events in American history. They also asked many questions about the information contained in the books. The knowledge they gained helped them to pass the citizenship test. We also celebrated President's Day with a group project in which students wrote about the presidents or heroes from their native cultures. They drew pictures of the person and wrote about his or her life and contributions to that particular country.

This project was more challenging to my students than the previous projects since it involved new vocabulary, especially words related to specific historical terms and events. However, with the help of their group members, the aide, and sometimes their family members, we succeeded in completing the project. To showcase the students' efforts, we put these writing projects on display on the classroom bulletin board. This display attracted students' and other teachers' attention from more advanced classes. This achievement, in turn, made my students feel proud about the fact that they could write something that was of so much interest. This was in a sense a community publication and showed the importance recognition plays in building students' self-esteem (Freeman and Freeman, 1994).

FAITH IN THE ELLS

Having faith in your students is the most critical among all of the principles of teaching success. Teachers show faith in their students by organizing teaching and learning in ways that are consistent with all principles for success. Teachers understand that students learn when they are engaged in meaningful activities that relate to their own experiences.

They develop learner-centered lessons, drawing on the interests and needs of their students. Teachers realize that many modes of instruction can be used to provide important resources for learning. Teachers also recognize that during social interaction, students learn a great deal from each other, from teachers, and from the community (Freeman & Freeman, 1998).

In my work with this class, I also used encouragement and first language support to demonstrate my faith in their learning of English. One way I gave encouragement to students was by valuing them as contributing members of the class community in my daily interactions with them and in integrating their experiences into the curriculum. First language support was given in the class for most of my students through the use of bilingual material and with the help of the instructional aide. My positive attitude and high expectations toward my students helped some of them to have the self-confidence to overcome learning difficulties. My encouragement of their use of first language in the classroom not only facilitated their learning of English (Lucas et al, 1990) but also increased their pride and confidence in themselves and their cultures. Most importantly, my encouragement reduced their psychological stress and increased their motivation for learning.

CONCLUSION

All teachers can build a classroom community with culturally diverse learners and provide a safe and risk-free environment so that students are willing to help each other and they are comfortable enough to learn. Using student life experiences as codes in teaching makes learning authentic and interesting. Setting the correct psychological stage, you are helping all the students learn more effectively. Freirean educators also believe that lessons should be learner centered and should have immediate meaning and purpose for learners. One of the best ways to insure this is to promote learning taking place while utilizing social interaction. Learners, themselves, are the ones who actually construct knowledge and thus empower themselves in the collaborative process. Collaborative group work provides scaffolding for the learner (Jiang & DeVillar, 2005), especially for the less advanced student. As students come across difficulties in learning, encouragement is always an important ingredient for turning resistance to success. Using positive psychology and context-embedded instruction makes learning more comprehensible, and it lowers the affective filter of the students.

REFERENCES

American Federation of Teachers, (2006). Where we stand: English language learners. Retrieved August, 20, 2007 from http://aft.org/pubs-reports/downloads/teachers/ellwws.pdf.

Bossers, B. (1991). On thresholds, ceilings and short-circuits. The relation between L1 reading, L2 reading and L2 knowledge. In *ALLA Review*. 45–60.

Canale, M., N. Frenette, & M. Belanger. (1988). Evaluation of minority student writing in first and second language. In Fine, J. (Ed.), *Second language discourse: A textbook of current research,* 147–165. Norwood, NJ: Ablex.

Carson, J. E., & P. A. Kuehn. (1994). Evidence of transfer and loss in developing second language writers. In A. H. Cumming (Ed.), *Bilingual Performance in Reading and Writing.* 257–281. Ontario Institute for Studies in Education.

Collier, V. (1989). How long? A synthesis of research on academic achievement in a second language. In *TESOL Quarterly*, 23 (3), 509–532.

Cummins, J. (1979a, October). Cognitive/Academic language proficiency, linguistic interdependence, the optimum age question, and some other matters. In *Working Papers on Bilingualism*, 19 (1).

Cummins, J. (1979b). Linguistic interdependence and the educational development of bilingual children. *Bilingual Education Paper Service, 3* (2). (ERIC Document Reproduction Service No. ED 257312).

Cummins, J. (1981). The role of primary language development in promoting education success for language minority students. In Office for Bilingual Bicultural Education. (Ed.), *Schooling and language minority students: A theoretical framework*. Los Angeles, CA.:

Cummins, J. (1984). *Bilingualism and special education: Issues in assessment and pedagogy*. San Diego, CA: College-Hill Press, Inc.

DeVillar, R.A. (1999). Developing critical literacy through technology in U.S. schools: Reflections and projections. In Finajero, J.V. & R.A. DeVillar, Eds. *The power of two languages: Effective dual language use across the curriculum. Millennium Edition*. New York: McGraw-Hill School Publishing Company.

Diaz-Rico, L. T., & Weed, K. Z. (1995). *The cross-cultural language, and academic development handbook*. Boston, MA: Allyn and Bacon.

Ellis, R. (1986). *Understanding second language acquisition*. New York, NY: Oxford University Press.

Evaluation, Dissemination and Assessment Center (California State University), pp. 3–49. Cummins, J. (1984). *Bilingualism and special education: Issues in assessment and pedagogy*. San Diego, CA: College-Hill Press Inc.

Faltis, C., & Coulter, C. (2007). *Teaching English learners and immigrant students in secondary school*. Upper Saddle River, NJ: Merrill/Pearson.

Freeman, D. E. & Y.S. Freeman, (1994). *Between worlds: Access to second language acquisition*. Portsmouth, NH: Heinemann.

Freeman, Y.S. & D.E. Freeman, (1998). *ESL/EFL teaching: Principles of success*. Portsmouth, NH: Heinemann.

Freeman, Y., & Freeman, D. (2002). *Closing the achievement gap: How to reach limited-formal-schooling and long-term English learners*. Portsmouth, NH: Heinemann.

Freire, P. (1998). The banking concept of education. In Freire, A.M.A. & D. Macedo, Eds. *The Paulo Freire Reader*. New York: Continuum.

Gass, S. M., & L. Selinker, Eds. (1994). *Language transfer in language learning*. Philadelphia, PA: John Benjamins North America.

Gibson, M. (1998). Promoting academic success among immigrant students: Is acculturation the issue? *Educational Policy, 12*(6),615–633.

Hakuta, K. (1986). *Mirror of language*. New York, NY: Basic Books, A Division of Harper Collins Publishers.

Hoover, W. (1983). Reading: A universal process. In S. Hudelson (Ed.), *Learning to read in different languages*, Washington, DC: Center for Applied Linguistics, 27–31.

Jiang, B. (2004). Problem-posing: Freire's transformational method in adult ESL. In G. Goodman & K. Carey (Eds.), *Critical multicultural conversations*. Cresskill, NJ: Hampton Press, 23–38.

Jiang, B. (1999). Transfer in the academic language development of postsecondary ESL students. Unpublished Dissertation, University of California, Davis and California State University, Fresno.

Jiang, B. & DeVillar, R. (2005). EFL professional development in cross-cultural relief: examining effects of U.S. frameworks on teacher practice in Mexico. In *Journal of Hispanic Higher Education, 4* (2), 134–148.

Jiang, B. & Kuehn, P. (2001). Transfer in the Academic Language Development of Post-secondary ESL Students, In R. DeVillar & J. Tinajero (Eds.) *Bilingual Research Journal, 25* (4), 653–672.

Krashen, S. (1992). *Second language acquisition and second language learning*. New York: Pergamon Press Inc.

Krashen, S & Terrell, T. (1983). The natural approach: Language acquisition in the classroom. Hayward, CA: Alemany Press.

Labov, W. (1972). *Sociolinguistic patterns.* Oxford: Basil Blackwell.

McLaughlin, B. (1987). *Theories of second language learning.* London: Edward Arnold.

Odlin, T. (1986). *Language transfer: Cross-linguistic influence in language learning.* New York: Cambridge University Press.

Ogbu, J. (1991). Immigrant and involuntary minorities in comparative perspective. In M. Gibson & J. Ogbu (Eds.). *Minority status and school: A Comparative study of immigrant and involuntary minorities.* New York: Garland Publishing Co.

Ogbu, J. U. (1981). School ethnography: A multilevel approach. *Anthropology and Education Quarterly, 12* (1).

Ogbu, J. U., & M.U. Matute-Bianchi, (1986). Understanding sociocultural factors: Knowledge, identity, and school adjustment. In Office for Bilingual Bicultural Education (Ed.), *Beyond language: Social and cultural factors in schooling language minority students.* Los Angeles, CA.: Evaluation, Dissemination and Assessment Center, pp. 73–142.

Rogoff, B., & E. Matusov, & C. White, (1996). Models of teaching and learning: Participation in a community of learners. In D.R. Olson & N. Torrance (Eds.), *The handbook of education and human development.* Oxford: Blackwell.

Schumann, J. (1978). The acculturation model for second language acquisition. In Gingras, R. C., Ed., *Second language acquisition & foreign language teaching.* Arlington, Virginia: Center for Applied Linguistics, pp. 27–50.

Schumann, J. (1978). *The pidginization process: A model for second language acquisition.* Rowley, Mass. Newbury House.

Suárez-Orozco, M. (2005). Everything you ever wanted to know about assimilation but were afraid to ask. In M. Suárez-Orozco, C. Suárez-Orozco, & D. Baolian Qin (Eds.), *The new immigration: An interdisciplinary reader* (pp. 67–84). New York: Routledge.

Suárez-Orozco, C. & M. Suárez-Orozco. (2001). *Children of immigration.* Cambridge, MA: Harvard University Press.

Verhoeven, L. (1991). Acquisition of biliteracy. In J. H. Hulstin & J. F. Matter (Eds.). In *Reading in two languages.* Amsterdam: AILA. *AILA Review,* 8, 6–74.

Vygotsky, L. (1978). *Mind in society: The development of higher psychological processes.* Cambridge, MA: Harvard University Press.

———. (1962). *Thought and Language.* Translated by Eugenia and Hanfmann Gertrude Vakar. Cambridge, MA: MIT Press.

Weaver, C. (1994). *Reading process and practice.* Portsmouth, NH: Heinemann.

Zehler, M. (1994). *Working with English language learners: Strategies for elementary and middle school teachers.* NCBE Program Information Guide, 19. Washington, DC: National Clearinghouse for Bilingual Education.

Zhou, M. (1998). "Parachute kids" in Southern California: The educational experience of Chinese children in transnational families. *Educational Policy, 12*(6), 682–704.

FIFTEEN

The Psycho-Social Dimensions of Multicultural Education

Chris Vang

*If civilization is to survive, we must cultivate the science of human relationship,
the ability of all people, of all kinds, to live together, in the same world at peace.*
President Franklin D. Roosevelt

OVERVIEW

The educational climate has changed dramatically, and the change calls for comprehensive multicultural academic programs that reflect pluralistic understanding and acceptance, respect, and tolerance for all children of any group. Because ethnic, racial, cultural, religious, language, political, and sexual diversity is increasing, American schools are now facing tremendous pressure and tough challenges in fulfilling their mandate to teach all students, including students of color. America is an open society that embraces all races, cultures, traditions, religions, and classes. However, the American educational system has been slow to adequately address the socio-cultural issues of diversity. Perhaps the time to engage in academic discourse regarding multicultural and multilingual education is now, and that is the focus of this chapter.

THE GLOBAL PERSPECTIVES ON MULTICULTURAL AND MULTILINGUAL EDUCATION

Historically, multilingual and multicultural education began in the ancient world and has continued into modern times. Societal bilingualism has always played an important role in the civilization of mankind. Merchants, for example, had to speak two or more languages in order to do business or trade goods with tribal villagers. Hmong, for example, are members of a preliterate society, but most older Hmong are bilingual. In the 21st century, very few nations are monolingual or mono-cultural. In the past, religious, political, territorial, and tribal consolidations as well as dominations resulted in the addition of one or more languages to a society's means of communication (Lessow-Hurley, 2000).

Because schooling was limited in the ancient world, bilingualism does not appear to have been an academic matter. Rather, it was a normative societal value necessary for facilitating mutual understanding cross-culturally among diverse linguistic groups. Moreover, in olden days, the scarcity of written materials encouraged people to learn languages other than the language spoken in the home in order to access whatever written information was available (Lessow-Hurley, 2000). Consider, for example, the fact that old religious manuscripts were written only in Hebrew and Greek. Religious scholars compiled the Old and New Testaments from 39 ancient manuscripts written in Hebrew and 27 written in Greek. To translate these manuscripts into other languages, scholars had to be multilingual or at least bilingual.

Many nations around the world still offer courses in foreign languages in their public schools. English, for example, is taught in many countries, and it is perhaps the most popular and widely used language in the 21st century. However, English is ranked the world's fourth most commonly spoken language, with Mandarin the first, followed by Hindi as second, and Spanish as third.

WHAT IS MULTILINGUAL EDUCATION?

Various definitions have been offered for multilingual education. Scholars in the field of bilingual and multicultural education apply the concepts of bilingualism differently, and they would disagree on the acceptance of a single definition. However, for the purpose of this discussion, we will define multilingual education as the use of two or more languages as media in the instructional process for helping students, especially students of color, learn in the classroom setting.

Multilingual education includes the academic ability or speaking ability to function with the use of two or more languages in the process of learning and communicating. Bear in mind that individual levels of fluency and competency in two or more languages could be different, depending on the length of exposure to the languages and the conditions under which the language was acquired or learned. Hmong, for example, have two distinct dialects—White Hmong and Blue Hmong—and Hmong students are generally able to speak one dialect fluently but may not understand the other dialect. Also, having the ability to speak Hmong dialects does not mean that a person is competent in writing those dialects.

Multilingual education should be practical and useful, an integral part of instruction in the multicultural classroom. Teachers with a Bilingual Cross-cultural Language in Academic Development (BCLAD) credential use a primary and a second or third language to provide students of color with primary language support during the instructional process. Monolingual teachers may lack this multilingual approach; however, schools with large numbers of English learners usually hire bilingual instructional aides (BIA) or other paraprofessionals to meet part of the instructional needs in the class, referring to the process as *one teaches and one drifts.*

WHAT IS MULTICULTURAL EDUCATION?

Multicultural education was widely practiced in past centuries and started emerging in America in the mid-1900s. It has continued to be emphasized to the present day. Banks (1988) brilliantly described the historical evolution of multicultural education in the U.S. as occurring in five distinct phases:

1. Phase I, monotonic studies, focused on the black civil rights movement. It advocated for equitable representation related to the needs of African American children and communities.
2. Phase II, multiethnic studies, emphasized the broader need to include other cultural groups in the study of minority experiences.
3. Phase III, multiethnic education, focused on the insufficiency of education to meet the challenges of cultural diversity and demanded educational reform to accommodate societal changes brought about by wars, immigration, the civil rights movement, discrimination, racism, and the presence of diverse languages and religions.
4. Phase IV, multicultural education, focused on a universal approach to understanding cultural diversity through broader perspectives instead of maintaining a limited emphasis on racial and ethnic minorities.
5. Phase V, the institutionalized process, focused on strategies, applications, school curricular efforts, and other reforms that include the teaching of multicultural education in schools.

Ovando, Combs, and Collier (2006) described multicultural education as a concept, idea, reform, movement, process, and affirmation of cultural pluralism that forms the basis of teaching and learning on the foundation of democratic ideals, values, and beliefs.

As with multilingual education, multicultural education has been defined in various ways. At the heart of every definition is a broad emphasis on the academic and social interactions of race, ethnicity, class, culture, religion, gender, language, and socioeconomic diversity of students. Multicultural education stresses educational reform, movement, restructuring, inclusion, and public policy that address multifaceted aspects of cultural diversity in order to provide all students with equal opportunities in the total school environment. Most importantly, multicultural education plays a vital role in advocating for social justice.

ROLES OF MULTICULTURAL EDUCATION

Banks (2008) described the beauty of multicultural education as follows:

> [Multicultural education is] an educational reform movement whose major goals are to restructure curricula and educational institutions so that students from diverse social-class, racial, and ethnic groups—as well as both gender groups—will experience equal educational opportunities. Multicultural education consists of three major components: (1) an educational reform movement whose aim is to create equal educational opportunities for all students; (2) an ideology whose aim is to actualize American democratic ideals, such as equality, justice, and human rights; and (3) a process that never ends because there will always be a discrepancy between democratic ideals and school and societal practices. (p. 135)

Without doubt, discussion of multicultural education produces misconceptions and a great deal of socio-cultural confusion. Proponents view it as a necessity; opponents see it as a handicap. Many feel strongly that the American educational system cannot function well either academically or culturally without including the cultural ingredients of multicultural applications that address inequality, prejudice, and cultural diversity in public schools.

Proponents ask: Who is responsible for educating all American children in Grades K-12 about different cultures? Who can help children understand the differences in race, ethnicities, classes, cultures, religions, and socioeconomic status? Who can differentiate instruction so as to include all students with diverse learning styles, diverse needs, and diverse abilities in the learning process? These questions are not new; they express the daily struggles of every responsible educator.

Pre-service and in-service educators need to think outside the Anglo-centric curriculum when teaching in a pluralistic society. The number of students of color is increasing in nearly every community throughout the United States. Most schools and classrooms have students from at least three different cultural groups: European Americans, Hispanic Americans, and African Americans are the three populations most prominent in many schools. Public policies, such as those embodied in the federal No Child Left Behind Act of 2001 and California Senate Bill 2042, require that new and current teachers devise academic standards, sensible instructional strategies, and purposeful adaptations that will assist English learners learn the English language and mathematical skills. These policies are not requests from parents, children, or community organizations. In fact, these are legal mandates that are required by federal laws, landmark decisions, state legislation, and education codes.

THEORETICAL PRINCIPLES

The definitions of multicultural education describe its principles and purposes; however, they do not capture all its goals. Banks (2008) suggested, "A key goal of multicultural education is to help individuals gain greater self-understanding by viewing themselves from the perspective of other cultures....[This] assumes that with acquaintance and understanding, respect may follow" (p. 2). When respect is present, acceptance of cultural diversity is natural.

Multicultural education has a purpose beyond acquisition of academic knowledge; it is a societal platform as well as an educational philosophy that aims at teaching all people to recognize, accept, respect, promote, and appreciate differences in culture, ethnicity, social class, sexual orientation, religion, special needs, and gender and, at the same time, to advocate on behalf of the marginalized, the powerless, the voiceless, and the oppressed for social justice, fairness, equity, and democracy. It also seeks to instill in educators, during their professional development, a sense of personal responsibility and a civic commitment to work toward democratic ideals.

Despite some opposition to multicultural education, the United States is now a multilingual and multicultural nation with many linguistic groups, and its various cultural groups have enriched the nation in many ways. Multicultural education has as a goal making sure that advocacy for equality is not an option. So far, educators who have embraced multicultural education have made impressive strides in addressing the needs of and advocating for all students, and these advances have benefited both the macro culture and the many micro cultures that exist in America (Banks, 2008). However, to be even more successful, the multicultural education movement requires new understandings, rethinking of old paradigms and practices, and new approaches in the classroom. It also needs the support of parents, teachers, administrators, policy makers, and the community at large in implementing consistent and systematic total-school approaches.

FUNDAMENTAL APPROACHES

An important goal of multicultural education is the elimination of surface level assessments, broken promises, lip service, cosmetic education, and mere talk about cultural diversity. Multicultural education must consist of more than celebrating holidays, giving information, holding cross-cultural trainings, and using on-call interpreters when needed. In fact, intense intentionality is needed to provide quality, effective multicultural education for students and teachers.

As Banks (2008) and Manning and Baruth (2009) suggested, educators can promote appreciation of cultural diversity by doing one or more of the following:

1 Use appropriate multicultural education curricular materials with all students, materials that reflect the cultural backgrounds of the students in the classroom.
2 Have multicultural materials evaluated by experts in the field to make sure they are appropriate for students' age, grade level, development of primary and second language, and gender.
3 Use multicultural materials that enhance and promote self-esteem, positive self-concept, and self-pride to promote learning and understanding among diverse groups of students.
4 Focus multicultural teaching on the development of knowledge, skills, and critical thinking through the process of learning and acquisition of skills.
5 In multicultural education curricular efforts, include authentic and multidimensional approaches to foster understanding of racial, ethnic, class, religion, gender, and language differences as well as cultural diversity.
6 Select curricular materials that meet and align with content-obligatory objectives rather than content-compatibility objectives.
7 Design multicultural lesson plans and instruction according to the length of time the students have been living in the U.S. or have been otherwise exposed to the English language.

8 Base teaching modalities on the results of formal assessments of primary and second-language proficiency.

9 Provide primary language support to accompany instruction in the second language when necessary.

10 Ensure access to equal and high quality instruction for all students.

CONCEPTUAL CONTEXT

Teachers who lack the foundations of multicultural education might have negative feelings about teaching in a pluralistic society and could rely heavily on Western methodologies. However, it is crucial for today's teachers to know and understand the basic concepts of multicultural education. Perhaps the concepts are not completely new; they may simply require relearning to recognize as well as accept the diverse fabric of American culture.

The first concept is that educators in a diverse society must understand the differences in race, ethnicity, culture, religion, class, language, and socioeconomic status that exist among people and the impact of those differences on teaching and learning. This concept is extremely important in a pluralistic society. Socio-cultural discourse must be a part of professional development if teachers are to understand the complexity of cultural diversity. For instance, many university programs require that teachers take multicultural education classes as part of their credential requirements to broaden their views toward culturally diverse student populations. Moreover, some teacher preparation programs require academic experience with a target culture.

The second concept is that social injustice should be eliminated—oppression, marginalization, powerlessness, exploitation, hegemony, prejudice, baggage, bias, inequality, and racial discrimination. Multicultural education targets cultural groups that are subject to blatant unequal treatment. In some cases, multicultural education is portrayed as a concern only for and of minorities. In fact, multicultural education is concerned with quality education for all students, but that goal cannot be attained without special consideration for those students who experience barriers to quality education. For instance, states often require that new teachers learn how to address the special needs of English language learners and students with other specific needs.

The third concept is that every student has constitutional rights—civil rights, human rights, rights to equal opportunities—that require that an equitable system is in place that enables all students to access the total school curriculum so they can acquire meaningful social and academic skills needed for success in life. The American educational system and education policies regarding quotas that address the needs of students of color are inadequate in many areas. However, improvements have been made in some areas. For instance, new elementary teachers are expected to take four methodology courses: math, language arts, social studies, and science. In these courses, teachers learn different techniques for delivering teaching modalities such as ELD, SDAIE, TESOL, and ESL in order to meet the needs of students of color.

The fourth concept is that public policy and education policy should advocate for multicultural curricula that teach students historical events, facts, and cultural characteristics that reflect cultural diversity. For instance, the No Child Left Behind Act requires that schools devise academic standards that measure student learning outcomes regarding cultural diversity and that schools recruit teachers of cultural backgrounds that reflect the cultural diversity of the student body.

The fifth concept is that social empowerment improves human civility and reciprocity in a pluralistic society. Good human behavior, adequate understanding of cultural diversity, racial tolerance, and cross-cultural competency bring a higher level of acceptance and respect among cultural groups. Social empowerment can be achieved by integrating into the social studies curriculum activities related to social events important in various cultures, such as New Year festivals and special holidays. Such activities help students learn about, understand, respect, and accept aspects of other cultures and traditions.

THE MULTICULTURAL CURRICULUM

The goals of multicultural education are achievable and measurable through the use of a multicultural curriculum. Gollnick and Chinn (2009) described a good multicultural curriculum as one that incorporates the histories, experiences, traditions, and cultures of students in the classroom and supports and celebrates diversity in the broadest sense.

At present, not all schools utilize a multicultural curriculum. Some schools are extremely skeptical about offering a multicultural curriculum, and others claim they lack the resources to implement such a curriculum, including materials, teachers, and money. Some schools follow a multicultural curriculum, but they use instructional strategies that are inconsistent with the goals of the curriculum or are capricious. Goals for implementing multicultural education vary, depending on a school's culture, environment, personnel, commitment, and program design. Regardless of the hindrances, comprehensive multicultural curricula are needed in American schools to address differences in race, ethnicity, class, religion, language, gender, and socioeconomic status and the occurrence of prejudice, bias, stereotyping, injustice, inequity, and discrimination.

Setting targeted goals for a multicultural curriculum would help teachers understand its value and how it should be used. Experts and scholars in multicultural education suggest educators consider the following goals for a curriculum that is effective for all students:

1 A multicultural curriculum should be viewed as a positive, a strength, not as a negative or a weakness. It provides opportunities for students to experience, learn, understand, promote, and accommodate other cultures as well as their own.

2 A multicultural curriculum should be used to educate all students regardless of cultural background. All students, rich or poor, bilingual or monolingual, of majority or minority status, need to recognize cultural differences and understand cultural diversity.

3 A multicultural curriculum helps minimize cultural baggage—biases, prejudices, perceptions, values, backgrounds, beliefs, customs, stereotypes, racism, and discrimination. Cross-cultural teaching and learning help educators and students develop attitudes of acceptance and respect of cultural diversity.

4 A multicultural curriculum should be implemented throughout the school as part of the total-school effort to address both majority and minority needs and expectations and to promote understanding, acceptance, and respect among all cultural groups.

5 A multicultural curriculum must provide all students with equal opportunities to succeed academically. Culturally diverse minority students tend to lose their competitiveness when confronted with language barriers, cultural barriers, and odd or different learning styles. They may also lack middle-class characteristics associated with success in academic tasks. These factors often contribute to minority students faring poorly in school and having a high rate of school dropout.

6 A multicultural curriculum should provide a learning climate that reflects the cultural diversity of the students in order to increase awareness of race, ethnic, class, gender, religious, socioeconomic, sexual orientation, lifestyle, and language diversity.

7 A multicultural curriculum should promote cross-cultural understanding and good cross-cultural relationships by downplaying the negative attitudes and mindsets of bias, prejudice, racism, stereotyping, sexism, classism, inferiority, superiority, and discrimination.

8 A multicultural curriculum should help students improve their self-concepts, self-understanding, and self-consciousness by enabling them to view themselves from the cultural perspectives, or through the cultural lenses, of other people.

9 A multicultural curriculum should help students acquire academic knowledge and social skills that empower them to deal with cultural differences and function in the mainstream culture.

10 A multicultural curriculum should help students cope with their internal feelings and thus reduce and heal any pain suffered from the past to the present time.

11 A multicultural curriculum should enable educators to not only teach but also model acceptance and respect for all. Even though the learning process could be dramatic during children's formative years, responsible multicultural education should play a key role in reducing myths, misconceptions, and misperceptions in learners' minds.

12 A multicultural curriculum opens students' eyes to cultural alternatives, helping them gain global perspectives on different cultures.

UNDERSTANDING MYTHS, MISCONCEPTIONS, AND MISPERCEPTIONS

Many people have strong feelings about multicultural education, and the subject has ignited psychological warfare between proponents and opponents. Citizenship education is a tough sell in some parts of today's pluralistic society. Critics feel that use of a multicultural curriculum puts too much emphasis on bilingualism and cultural education. Their objections may stem from xenophobia, the melting pot model, racism, stereotyping, bias, culture shock, or an ethno-centric approach toward cultural diversity.

Of course, anyone looking for examples of inconsistent results of multicultural education can find some. Bilingual education, for example, started more than 30 years ago, but most American schools still have serious problems implementing bilingual education consistently in an academic curriculum that addresses the needs of students of color. Bilingual education is often implemented very differently from the way the program was intended to be operated. Proponents of multicultural education call this difference *espoused policy* versus *policy in use*.

In order to see that education on cultural diversity does not pose a threat to equal treatment and equal education of all students, educators should pay close attention to the students they do *not* serve as the result of cultural and language barriers. Multicultural education benefits all if the design is based on academic content geared to helping students learn, understand, and appreciate differences in race, ethnicity, class, religion, socioeconomic status, language, and gender. Multicultural education faces dire challenges in schools because people have failed to overcome myths, misconceptions, and misperceptions about the practice.

IS MULTICULTURAL EDUCATION ONLY FOR "OTHERS"?

The idea that multicultural education is of benefit only to "others," to minorities, is a single-sided view of the issue from the dominant culture. Some critics view multicultural education as an entitlement program for specific groups of people—people of color, people who are marginalized, the oppressed, minorities, and the underprivileged. The fact is that all people need this education to function civilly and effectively in America. The notion that multicultural education is for "others" must be dispelled. Actually, most cross-cultural training is designed for upper-class and middle-class Americans who may lack cultural sensitivity, awareness, understanding, and appreciation. On the other hand, members of most cultural groups do not receive training on the dominant culture, especially the White culture, or on American culture in general.

Regardless, this author defines multicultural education broadly and does not believe that multicultural education should be only for people who need to understand cultural diversity. The dimensions of multicultural education are framed to educate and empower all people to become sensitive, understanding, knowledgeable, appreciative, loving, caring, altruistic, benevolent, and compassionate citizens in a pluralistic society.

DOES MULTICULTURAL EDUCATION OPPOSE WESTERN VIEWS?

In some sense, multicultural education may appear to be in opposition to Western views on public policy because it advocates for inclusiveness, equality, justice, and democracy. However, according to Banks (2008), most proponents of multicultural education are Western, and multicultural education has been orchestrated by Westerners to address the issues of cultural diversity. Moreover, the conception that multicultural education distorts, minimizes, or attempts to displace Western civilization is false. After all, most school textbooks are written by Westerners. Most importantly, educators should know that the multicultural education movement originated in the West in the mid-1900s, during the civil rights movement. Its framers sought to influence public policy and education policy to deal with issues of equality, freedom, social justice, segregation, and discrimination with the ultimate aim of improving the realization of democratic ideals.

DOES MULTICULTURAL EDUCATION DIVIDE PEOPLE?

The question of whether multicultural education divides people springs from misguided misinformation. Birkel (2000) and Manning and Baruth (2009) explained that multicultural education often has been misunderstood and referred to as a program on race relations, as an affirmative action tool, as a vehicle of the civil rights movement, as an entitlement program, as an anti-assimilation ideology, and as a means to undercut unity. However, none of this is true; multicultural education is not divisive.

On the contrary, it promotes unity, cooperation, empowerment, and cross-cultural competency. People in America are uniquely diverse, and their differences in race, ethnicity, culture, class, religion, socioeconomic status, gender, and language may pose challenges and discomfort for some. However, cultural groups continue to suffer incidents of racism, prejudice, injustice, and discrimination. At one time, Western countries were understandably considered to be racist. Birmingham, Alabama, for example, was called Bombingham during the fight against racial discrimination in the 1960s. In fact, multicultural education has helped reduce racial discrimination and prejudice by actively promoting acceptance and appreciation of diversity.

Banks (2008) asserted that multicultural education is designed to unify rather than divide a nation. Multicultural education supports the notion of "one out of many"—*e pluribus unum*. But Banks cautioned that America is deeply divided along racial, gender, sexual orientation, and class lines, and that social stratification is the most pernicious of the dividing lines.

IS MULTICULTURAL EDUCATION DEBATABLE?

Multicultural education is a social movement as well as an educational philosophy. As with any social movement, the push for multicultural education has sometimes triggered political debate over the restructuring and reformulating of the academic canon. Discussion of implementing multicultural education has also increased racial and ethnic tension in some areas. The struggles are similar to the ways the actions of *Viva La Raza,* a movement to preserve the Latino race, spark heated debate in the educational community as well as in the political arena. However, without a doubt multicultural education has played a vital role in promoting citizenship education that has improved social justice and advocated for equal opportunity for all.

IS MULTICULTURAL EDUCATION DIVIDING INSTRUCTION?

Some critics claim that use of a multicultural curriculum hinders the education of mainstream American students. These critics might feel that all students should learn from the same Anglo-centric curriculum regardless of cultural background. However, if teachers lack an understanding of cultural diversity, do not know how to teach the children in their classrooms, and do not understand how those children learn, the education of all the students in their classrooms is hindered. Moreover, students of color should not be subjected to different instructional modalities; teachers should use one modality for all students. Research shows that the factor that influences student learning the most is the quality of the teacher; in other words, effective teaching is about how to teach, not what to teach. Another important factor is the quality of instruction, not the language of instruction.

IS MULTICULTURAL EDUCATION DESIGNED FOR LEGAL SEGREGATION?

The criticism that multicultural education encourages segregation is not entirely true, but the way the multicultural curriculum is used in some schools appears to be divisive. Instead of grouping diverse students together, teachers sometimes use homogeneous grouping to segregate students of specific cultures. The risk here is that schools put too much emphasis on students' cultures rather than on their education.

IS MULTICULTURAL EDUCATION RESPONSIBLE FOR LOW ACADEMIC ACHIEVEMENT?

Multicultural education does not result in low academic achievement because most standardized testing instruments are either norm-referenced or criterion-referenced. Test results are compared to results from a sample group, which may or may not have the same or similar academic and cultural characteristics as the tested group. In fact, norm-referenced testing is based on a normal curve. Both types of instruments appear to have construct bias when they are used to measure students of color. Test makers are mostly European Americans, and they design tests based on Anglo-centric, or middle-class, values. Moreover, most schools use measurement-driven curricula to drill students on testing strategies. In other words, students of color receive inadequate instructional services to help them perform well on tests. However, schools expect these students to do well on the tests even though they have been subjected to ineffective instruction.

Furthermore, this author supports the argument made by Banks (2008) that schools often use a cultural deprivation paradigm to measure the academic outcomes of students of color. Use of this paradigm blames the students for their academic failure. Instead, schools should use a cultural difference paradigm, which places much of the responsibility for any gap in academic achievement on the school.

Another way to help educators understand student achievement is to examine the distinction between standards and standardization. Sleeter (2005) described standards as measures that provide a quality approach to helping students reach high levels of academic achievement and standardization as an ineffective approach to instruction that focuses on low levels of knowledge and skills easily measured by norm-referenced tests.

IS THE MULTICULTURAL EDUCATION APPROACH EFFECTIVE?

For the most part, if a multicultural curriculum is used appropriately, all students benefit. The instructional methodologies employed in most multicultural education curricula—English

Language Development (ELD), Specially Designed Academic Instruction in English (SDAIE), and Teaching English to Speakers of Other Languages (TESOL), for example—are effective and appropriate for all learners. On the other hand, direct instruction is effective in responding to time constraints and the lack of creative teaching, but it leaves students of color with limited English proficiency out of the engagement process. A multicultural curriculum prefers eclectic methods of teaching that engage all students regardless of cultural and linguistic background or ability.

IS MULTICULTURAL EDUCATION TEACHER-CENTERED?

Direct instruction is teacher-centered instruction. In some senses, the multicultural education approach emphasizes specific teaching techniques for targeting specific group of students. Hmong students, for example, learn English, math, social studies, and science more effectively with a specific teaching scheme designed by Hmong BCLAD teachers because that scheme uses primary language support. In most cases, the multicultural approach is student-centered because teachers prescribe instructional strategies based on the students' levels of comprehension in the English language.

IS MULTICULTURAL EDUCATION APPROPRIATE FOR ALL SUBJECT MATTER?

Multicultural education is absolutely appropriate for any and all subject matter! Methods in multicultural education are appropriate across all subject areas. Manning and Baruth (2009) pointed out that multicultural education is interdisciplinary as an integral part of all curricular areas and should be administered across all subject areas.

For language arts, teachers can use scaffolding and reciprocal techniques to engage English language learners in a variety of ways. For social science, teachers can use prior experiences or embedded skills to engage students of color in activities related to their personal lives and cultural events. Regarding math, most students of color, even those with limited English language skills, can learn because learning math initially does not require a high level of language skills. Also, teachers can use the parts-to-whole approach to help students learn the process. In science, teachers can use hands-on and minds-on activities to introduce science concepts related to personal experiences, such as cooking, cleaning, farming, gardening, grooming, animals, and plants, before going into the more complex science concepts involved in biology, chemistry, physics, and botany.

IS MULTICULTURAL EDUCATION A LEGAL NECESSITY?

The struggle for educational equality for all students has been ongoing for some time. The multicultural education movement started in the mid-1900s and forerunners were present in America even earlier. In 1896, in the case of *Plessy v. Ferguson,* the court ruled that the Civil Rights Act of 1875 was unconstitutional, and the judges approved "separate but equal" facilities. Later laws and court rulings overturned this decision and instead protected human rights, equal opportunity, and justice for all. These legislative and judicial actions eventually led to school desegregation. In 1954, in the case of *Brown v. Topeka Board of Education,* the court ruled in favor of desegregation of Blacks and Whites. A few years later, in 1957, the Commission on Civil Rights was created to investigate complaints of alleged discrimination in violation of human rights.

The Civil Rights Act of 1964 forbade schools that received federal monies from discriminating on the basis of race, color, creed, or national origin. In other words, it mandated that schools protect minority groups. In 1968, Title VII of the Elementary and Secondary Education Act (ESEA), together with the Bilingual Education Act (BEA), assisted American schools in providing services to needy and at-risk students. In 1974, in the case of *Lau v. Nichols,* the court ruled that according to Title VI of the Civil Rights Act of 1964, children must receive equal access to public education regardless of their ability or lack of ability to speak English. In 1975, a national report titled *A Better Chance to Learn: Bilingual, Bicultural Education* issued by the U.S. Commission on Civil Rights recommended that schools provide equal opportunity for language-minority students. In 1994, Public Law 103–382, the Improving America's Schools Act of 1994, reauthorized the ESEA of 1965 along with Title VII, renamed Bilingual Education Language Enhancement and Language Acquisition Programs.

Most recently, the No Child Left Behind Act of 2001 mandated that schools develop sound academic standards to address the academic gap between mainstream American students and students of color and formulate testing strategies to measure reading and mathematics skills of students in Grades 3 through 8 annually.

At the state level, California, for example, passed Senate Bill 2042 that revamped the state's teacher preparation programs to include Teacher Performance Expectations (TPE) and Teacher Performance Assessments (TPA). TPE has thirteen standards. Standard 7 requires that teacher candidates learn how to teach, monitor, and assess English language learners. TPA requires prospective teachers to master four main tasks. Measurement of mastery for each task is conducted with at least four different case scenarios. For Task 1, for example, Case Scenario 3 requires teacher candidates to design lesson plan adaptations for English learners. Furthermore, Task 1, Case Scenario 4 requires teacher candidates to design a lesson plan to respond to the adaptation needs of a student with special needs.

SHOULD TEACHERS BECOME KNOWLEDGEABLE ABOUT MULTICULTURAL EDUCATION?

Absolutely! Today's teachers need a repertoire of psycho-social skills for a variety of applications. Equipping themselves with the knowledge and skills that will enable them to overcome the challenges and complexities from culturally diverse students is critically important. Knowledgeable educators are teachers without borders who can deal with both cultural diversity and different learning styles. Teachers who avail themselves of multicultural education programs at the professional level can remove long-held cultural biases and stereotypes. To be inclusive, competent, and effective teachers in a pluralistic society, educators must possess knowledge (factual information), skills (appropriate applications), and attitudes (ways to respond to the needs of students) that foster learning for all students.

SUMMING UP

This chapter overviews the psycho-social dimensions of multicultural education that have to do with the way people feel, think, learn, know, and understand cultural diversity in today's schools. All issues discussed in this section are designed as a broad base of multicultural education to help perceptive educators as well as students explore the dynamics of diversity in order to understand their school environments and set them free from their own cultural boundaries. Hopefully, it will equip them with democratic perspectives and guide them through the process of acquiring the positive attitudes, the knowledge, and the skills needed to become productive and responsible educators while participating in civic action in the pursuit of social justice, equality, and democracy.

REFERENCES

Banks, A.J. (2008). *An Introduction to multicultural education.* Boston: Pearson Education, Inc.

Banks, J.A. (1988). Ethnicity, class, cognitive and motivational styles: Research and teaching implications. *Journal of Negro Education, 57*(4), 453–462.

Birkel, L.F. (2000). Multicultural education: It is education first of all. *Teacher Education, 36*(1), 23–27.

Gollnick, D.M., & Chinn, P.C. (2009). *Multicultural education in a pluralistic society.* 8th edition. Upper Saddle River, NJ: Pearson Education, Inc.

Lessow-Hurley, J. (2000). *The foundations of dual language instruction.* 3rd edition. New York: Addison-Wesley Longman, Inc.

Manning, L.M, & Baruth, L.G. (2009). *Multicultural education of children and adolescents.* 5th Edition. Upper Saddle River, NJ: Pearson Education.

Ovando, C.J., Combs, M.C., & Collier, V.P. (2006). *Bilingual & ESL classrooms: Teaching in multicultural contexts.* 4th edition. New York: The McGraw-Hill Companies, Inc.

Sleeter, C.E. (2005). *Un-standardizing curriculum: Multicultural teaching in the standards-based classroom.* New York: Teachers College Press.

SECTION FIVE
Motivation

SIXTEEN

Affective and Motivational Factors for Learning and Achievement

Patricia Kolencik

> *"The curriculum is so much necessary raw materials, but warmth is the vital element for the growing plant and the soul."*
> —Carl Jung (1875–1961) Swiss psychiatrist

> *"The extent to which emotional upsets can interfere with mental life is no news to teachers. Students who are anxious, angry, or depressed don't learn; people who are caught in these states do not take in information efficiently or deal with it well."*
> — Daniel Goleman, *Emotional Intelligence*

How are you feeling? Pause for a moment and reflect on your feelings. Are you feeling excited, happy, enthusiastic, energized, elated, content, secure, confident, comfortable, worry free, loved, intelligent, competent, trusting, beautiful, buoyant, creative, honored, respected, revered, sexy, fabulous, gregarious, on top of the world?

Or are you feeling lonely, unsatisfied, hurt, depressed, down-trodden, unintelligent, incomplete, disrespected, unqualified, defeated, unwanted, disconnected, ashamed, unappreciated?

The way that we feel and our perceptions of ourselves in relationship to our feelings have a huge effect upon our functioning within our relationships, our careers, and our education (Bandura, 2001). In this chapter, you will investigate several important aspects of students' **affective** or attitudinal learning. The purpose of this investigation is to help you to make connections between the mind (the combination of thoughts and feelings) and your students' emotional, physical, and cognitive development (Watson-Gegeo & Gegeo, 2004). According to Watson-Gegeo and Gegeo:

> Until now, it has been assumed that the higher cognitive functions are independent of other mental processes, such as feelings, intuition, and so forth—in fact, that they must be kept separate from the latter, less rational mental processes. However, research has shown that emotion for instance) is essential to making logical, rational judgments, including moral decisions (Damasio, 1994), and that emotion "links closely with **cognition** to shape action, thought, and long-term development" (Fischer, Kennedy, & Cheng, 1998, pp. 21–43)

To assist in discovering how these key personal growth components link together as one mind, we will be examining various theories of emotional intelligence and motivation. From this examination, you will be able to understand that if your students come to class with negative emotional **baggage** and troubled minds, they will not function optimally. Through your examination of current research on emotion's role in learning, you will come to comprehend the multitude of factors that influence students' motivation to study, learn, and achieve in the diverse classroom (Damasio, 1994). In addition, you will explore the salient aspects of a supported affective learning environment which works to increase student motivation and promote the understanding of the emotional needs of your students.

The following essential questions guide the foci of this chapter:

1 What roles do emotions (affect) play in learning?
2 What is emotional intelligence?
3 What is motivation?
4 What are the two types of motivation?
5 What are the principal theories of motivation?
6 What psycho-social and familial factors affect motivation?

WHAT ROLES DO EMOTIONS (AFFECT) PLAY IN LEARNING?

Consider these scenarios:

- A twelve-year-old went on a rampage and vandalized a car in the parking lot. The reason: His classmates called him a "sissy" and he wanted to impress them.
- A student reports her classmate is contemplating suicide.
- A fight breaks out between rival gang members
- A student's father dies.
- A student who has just moved to the school is being bullied.
- A student is misbehaving in class and is reprimanded by the teacher. A power struggle ensues.
- A student cheats on an exam.
- A student calls another student "gay."

All of these scenarios: 1) involve examples of relevant emotions such as anger, anxiety, fear, frustration, confusion, bewilderment, disillusionment, uncertainty, and helplessness that students experience on a daily basis; 2) illustrate that learning is not a smooth process but rather a complex emotional process; and 3) are tied to the affective domain in the learning process and contribute to the student's motivation to learn.

Of all the aspects of human growth and cognitive development affecting the learning process, no other is as pervasive and significant as the affective domain (Damasio, 1994). How parents, teachers, and other adults display or deny expression of feelings and react to their own emotional experiences can provide key lessons in their students' developing and regulating personal emotional competence. Because of the critical role of emotions upon learning, it is important for teachers to be aware of the importance of feelings and to be able to discuss interpersonal and intrapersonal issues with their students. Students learn about the nature and expression of emotion from their day-to-day interaction with other individuals. These daily interactions can help students learn to understand and cope with their emotional experiences or they can have inverse, negative consequences.

Even when they are not explicitly stated, affective objectives are pervasive in school work (Smith & Ragan, 1999). Although educators may not always be aware of it, teachers are continuously involved in some form of affective learning. Students look to teachers as models for the development of coping skills, manners, self-discipline, fairness, generosity, courage, compassion, and a host of other interpersonal and intrapersonal qualities. In some cases, affective or attitudinal learning can be one of the main objectives of instruction. Anti-drug campaigns and teaching tolerance for diversity are two examples of this type of emotionally connected instruction.

In the wake of school violence and other risks to student safety, many schools are beginning to take a more active role in students' emotional development (Goodman, 2002). The Collaborative for Academic, Social and Emotional Learning (CASEL, 2005) at the University of Illinois at Chicago has developed five competency areas of social and emotional learning. The five competencies are social-awareness, self-awareness, self-management, relationship skills, and responsible decision making (CASEL, 2005). Schools are developing programs such as PATHS (Promoting Alternative Thinking) (1995) and School Connect (2006) that use these social and emotional learning competencies as the framework to integrate these skills into the curriculum. The book, *The Freedom Writers Diary* (Freedom Writers & Filipovic, 1999), inspired by English teacher Erin Gruwell, is another example of a curricular movement used to help students understand and express their emotions about prejudice, intolerance, racism, and respect for diversity.

Let us now take a deeper look at students' emotions (affect) and its impact on cognitive learning. Affect is the fuel that students bring to the classroom, connecting them to the "why" of learning. As a teacher, you must be cognizant of the fact that students' interest and excitement about the content they are learning are integral factors in the teaching and learning process. How do you feel about learning content knowledge? Are your feelings positive? Are you excited, interested, and curious about learning? Or are your feelings negative? Are you angry or bored? Your attitude about learning is influenced by emotion which researchers call hot cognition (Hoffman, 1991; Miller, 2002; Pintrich, Marx & Boyle, 1993). For example, you may get excited when you read about a new scientific advancement that could lead to a cure for cancer. Or you may feel sad when you read about a tsunami that killed hundreds or people. Your reaction to these scenarios is directed by your emotions; thus, affect is deeply interwoven into cognitive learning. Students are more likely to pay attention, to learn, and to remember events, images, arid readings that provoke a strong emotional response such as excitement, sadness, or anger (Alexander & Murphy, 1998; Cowley & Underwood, 1998). Facts and concepts that are related to the student's personal or situational interests are the most meaningful and create high interest (Renninger, Hidi, & Krapp, 1992; Schraw & Lehman, 2001).

The concept of hot cognition tells us that students are more likely to attend to and remember things that not only stimulate their thinking but also elicit emotional reactions. When the student's emotions are engaged, the brain codes the content by triggering the release of chemicals that single out and mark the experience as important and meaningful (Jensen, 1997). Students will learn more when they become both cognitively and emotionally involved in classroom subject matter. Learning is enhanced when the teachers help their students see the importance of content knowledge by revealing its relevance to them.

One of the most powerful strategies that teachers can use in the classroom to build upon students' interests is to connect new content to students' prior knowledge and experiences (Marzano, 1998). This process is sometimes referred to as scaffolding (Ormrod, 2006). A scaffold is a structure used to support student learning. By both personally and emotionally linking new content to what students already know and understand, teachers provide a scaffold for connecting prior knowledge to the present curriculum (Vygotsky, 1978).

In addition to scaffolding, the following constructivist learning strategies are effective ways to assist the teacher in making these connections and emotionally enhancing learning.

1 Allow students to choose projects or read novels based on their interests.
2 Use primary source materials with interesting content or detail such as personal letters and diaries in history.
3 Predict what will happen in an experiment.
4 Have students design and conduct interviews and surveys to learn about each other's interests.
5 Keep a classroom library stocked with books that connect to students' interests and hobbies.
6 Use graphic organizers and concept maps such as a K-W-L chart as instructional devices.
7 Provide opportunities for students to write their own ideas and feelings about the learning through journaling, learning logs, or discussions.
8 Provide an agenda for the day or the class so that students know what to expect.
9 Jensen (1998) states, "In order for learning to be considered relevant, it must relate to something the learner already knows. It must activate a learner's existing neural networks. The more relevance, the greater the meaning" (p. 84). By making the learning relevant to the students from the beginning of the lesson, the teacher opens the door for better understanding by the students. For example, to begin a unit on estimation, a teacher might bring a jar of marbles to class and ask students to guess the number of marbles in the jar and then discuss ideas about how to estimate the number. By beginning a lesson with a motivational opener like this estimation example, the teacher taps into two very important student emotions—curiosity and fun. Thus, successful, effective teachers capitalize on students' interests and curiosity to create a positive learning climate.

WHAT IS EMOTIONAL INTELLIGENCE?

Because emotions are an integral part of a student's total personality, an understanding of the nature of emotional intelligence and how it affects learning is of vital importance to teachers. Teaching is about the head and the heart: the mind. In other words, the teaching and learning process is not just about imparting didactic knowledge in fundamental content skills. Teaching is also about emotional intelligence (Goleman, 1995), a type of social intelligence that involves the ability to monitor one's own and others' emotions, to discriminate among them, and to use the information to guide one's thinking and actions." (Goleman, 1995, p. 95). The work of Goleman (1995) indicates that motivation is a critical component for school success.

Building on the earlier concepts of "intrapersonal" and "interpersonal" intelligences framed by Howard Gardner's Multiple Intelligences theory (1993), Daniel Goleman (1995) in his book *Emotional Intelligence*, documented that "emotional intelligence (EQ)" is a greater predictor of academic and life success than is IQ (intelligent quotient) as measured by standardized intelligence tests and may be as important as any other type of learning that takes place in school. Goleman introduced the concept of "emotional literacy," a term designating the notion that students' emotional and social skills can be cultivated and developed from infancy throughout an entire lifetime. He calls for a "schooling of emotions" and advocates that teachers play a critical role in developing students' emotional (EQ) as well as intellectual (IQ) talents. Goleman (1995) identifies four areas in emotional competency: 1) identifying, expressing, and understanding emotions; 2) controlling and managing emotions; 3) recognizing emotions toward others; and, 4) managing relationships. Researchers such as Goleman (1995), Gardner (1993), Robert Slavin (1989, 1995, 1996) and Ellen Langer (1989, 1997), have begun to recognize and value this emotional dimension of human intelligence and describe the profound and diverse impact that emotions have on one's lifestyle. These researchers posit that people with emotional literacy skills are more likely to be successful in their professional and personal lives.

How does this theory of emotional intelligence influence teaching and learning? Teachers need to know that their ability to handle students' affective competency skills has a direct impact on instructional delivery, classroom management, and their relationship with students. Effective teachers know that students who have emotional self-control and possess social competency skills are attentive, focused, productive, empathic, and self-motivated. Effective teachers also know that students who lack social competency skills are often distracted from learning, are rejected by peers, and have a history of dropping out of school (Salovey & Mayer 2004).

Emotional intelligence influences teachers' ability to treat students equitably. Teachers should be able to recognize the individual differences that distinguish one student from another. Taking account of these differences makes for sound instructional practice. Teachers need to have the skills to adjust their practice based on observation and knowledge of students' emotional intelligence to foster students' self-esteem, motivation, character, civic responsibility, and their respect for individual cultural, religious, and racial differences.

Successful teachers are adept at dealing with students, both children and adolescents, as they confront personal emotional challenges, sensitive issues, and life-threatening problems as they grow into emotionally mature adults. Many of the challenges and difficulties teachers face concern how to cope with their students' wide variety of needs—some of which are essential for physical survival and others of which are important for psychological well-being—and, how to help young people to grow up as soundly and as trouble free as possible (Eisenberg & Fabes, 1998). For example, if you teach inner-city students whose lives on the street are surrounded by emotions—many of which are negative—you, as a teacher, will want to teach students some self-management skills to help them battle these distressed feelings.

Emotional intelligence is related to discipline problems, dropout rates, low esteem and dozens of other learning and life skill problems. Difficulties in handling emotional experiences may impede students' ability to satisfy their need to feel respected, secure, and socially connected. Thus, teachers need to create a caring, positive and safe learning climate and foster discussion skills that help students actively and respectfully listen to their peers. In the classroom, teachers can function as a role model on how to exhibit and express emotions. Through their own actions, teachers can help students express emotions in socially appropriate ways. Effective teachers model ways of regulating emotions, such as calming down before reacting to a hectic situation or seeking support when stressed or frustrated. Often we teach more by what we do than by what we say.

Teachers can also boost students' social and emotional competency skills by imbedding affective education into the daily academic learning agenda. Suggestions for student involvement include having students create classroom guidelines for dealing with student misbehaviors in the classroom and using class meetings to share feelings about important events or experiences and to build community. Effective teachers also integrate books, stories, plays, poetry, and videos to stimulate discussions of emotional experiences. For example, students could explore the historical effects of racism and learn about institutions, legislation, and movements that sought to right these wrongs.

Simonson and Maushak (2001) have drawn on findings from a number of studies to create a series of guidelines for effective design of affective instruction. These are:

- Make the instruction realistic, relevant, and technically stimulating
- Present new information
- Present persuasive messages in a credible manner
- Elicit purposeful emotional involvement
- Involve the learner in planning, production or delivery of the message
- Provide post-instruction discussion or critique opportunities.

Smith and Ragan (1999) focus on the behavioral aspect of affective learning and emphasize the importance of three key instructional approaches:

- Demonstration of the desired behavior by a respected role model
- Practice of the desired behavior, often through role playing
- Reinforcement of the desired behavior

Teachers need not view academic learning and social and emotional learning at opposite ends but rather bolster support on a daily basis for this affective learning domain. When both academic learning and emotional learning support each other, students are more apt to be engaged and motivated in learning.

Emotion and motivation cannot be considered separately. What and how much is learned is influenced by a student's motivation. And like a revolving door, motivation for learning is influenced by the student's emotional states, beliefs, interests, goals, and habits of thinking.

WHAT IS MOTIVATION?

Why are you reading this chapter? Are you interested in learning more about the topic of motivation to increase your knowledge for future use in the classroom? Are you reading the chapter because there will be a test on this material in the future? Do you need this course to complete your teacher certification requirements? The answers to these questions deal with your "motivation" to study.

Motivation is an elusive concept. Motivation is usually defined as an intrinsic or extrinsic process that arouses, directs, and maintains behavior and relates to the drive to do something. Motivation causes us to get up in the morning and go to school or to work. Motivation drives us to study new things and encourages us to try again when we fail.

Because motivation is an obscure concept, a basic question about motivation always arises, "Where does it come from—within or outside the individual? Consider this example, why do students raise their hand in class? Do they raise their hand because of their interest in the subject matter or because of their interest in earning a good grade? The answer is probably more complicated than either alternative. Nonetheless, motivation is something students must find for themselves, thus, presenting different motivational challenges to classroom teachers.

Teachers, however, can play a powerful role in motivating students through their words and actions. If the teacher is moody or unpleasant or tries to make assignments unnecessarily hard, student motivation and learning will decrease. Effective teachers are caring and provide security—two controlling motivators. If teachers want to motivate students, they must demonstrate sincere concern for student welfare and make them feel as secure as possible.

Effective teachers use a variety of methods so that all students want to learn most of the time. Establishing rapport by showing sincerity and humility, teaching with a sense of humor, maintaining a cheerful, positive attitude, making lessons motivating, increasing student accountability by encouraging and expecting quality work, preparing activities that are authentic, purposeful and connected to real life, and treating students with respect are all effective techniques that can be used to motivate most students to learn. An essential part of teaching is helping students find their own good reasons to learn.

WHAT ARE THE TWO TYPES OF MOTIVATION?

Researchers have identified two types of motivation: intrinsic motivation and extrinsic motivation. Intrinsic motivation is an innate drive, i.e., it is a process nurtured by feelings and needs from within. Students will do something for the sheer joy of doing it or because they want to discover something, answer a question, or experience the feeling of self-accomplishment. For example, you may want to read this chapter because you value learning and want to be knowledgeable about skills you will need as a teacher to understand students' motives for learning. Thus, personal factors such as needs, interests, and curiosity explain the concept of intrinsic motivation, motivation associated with activities nurtured by drives and needs within oneself that are their own reward.

Sometimes students' behavior is directed by outside forces. This type of behavior or process is known as extrinsic motivation. Extrinsic motivation is created by external factors such as rewards and punishments. When students do something in order to earn a grade, avoid punishment, or please the teacher or the parent, they care only about their sole gain and nothing about the task at hand. For example, you detest psychology and read this chapter to earn an A on the test next week. You are motivated to pass the certification requirements and/or to keep your scholarship. Thus, you are motivated by factors external to yourself and possibly unrelated to the task you are performing.

Extrinsic motivators, such as good grades, a teacher's or parent's praise, extra privileges, public recognition, competition, even stickers or candy, are often expected or relied on by students. Often times, these external motivators get in the way of learning because they are sometimes overused or abused. However, many experts believe that extrinsic motivators can be every effective in helping students develop intrinsic motivation to learn or behave.

On the other hand, Kohn (1999) in his book, *Punished by Rewards: The Trouble with Gold Stars, Incentive Plans, A's, Praise and Other Bribes,* argues that extrinsic motivators, including good grades, some types of praise, and stickers, are ineffective and counterproductive to the quality of the learning process. Kohn (1999) contends, "No kid deserves to be manipulated with extrinsics so as to comply with what someone else wants" (p. 34). He states that rewards can have the inverse effect of motivating and take away someone's desire to learn.

Whether or not you agree or disagree with Kohn, the lynchpin to keep in mind is that students are often not as deeply engaged in learning as teachers would like them to be. McCune et al. (1999) found that "students will be more likely to engage in learning activities when they attribute success or failure to things they can control, like their own effort or lack or it, rather than to forces over which they have little or no control, such as their ability, luck, or outside forces" (p. 39). Therefore, an effective teacher recognizes that students vary in their motivation levels. An effective teacher knows how to support intrinsically motivated students and seeks the variety of strategies necessary to provide extrinsic motivation to students who need it. "Students learn when they have a reason and an effective teacher helps students find their own good reasons to learn" (Brandt, 1995, p. 87). Conversely, whether student motivation is intrinsic or extrinsic, teachers must ensure that their students' needs in the context of Maslow's Hierarchy of Needs for physical survival, safety, belongingness, love, and esteem are met.

WHAT ARE THE THEORIES OF MOTIVATION?

Of all the questions teachers have concerning affect, the most commonly evoked query is: "How can I motivate my students to learn?" Good teachers know that students who feel motivated to learn are a joy to teach. But how do our students become motivated, and what can you do to maintain this desire to learn? Theorists, researchers, and psychologists have explored the following principles related to the effect motivation has on students' learning and behavior.

Motivation is defined as a feeling or a force that directs behavior toward specific goals for which people strive (Maehr & Meyer, 1997; Graham & Weiner, 1996; Pintrich, Marx, & Boyle, 1993). This feeling affects the choices that students make—whether to watch a football game or write an assigned research paper; whether to take an active role and try out for the lead in a school play or assume a passive role and sit in the audience and watch.

Motivation can also be self-sustaining. Often this powerful force leads to increased effort and energy. Motivation increases the amount of intensity and the level of involvement that students expend in activities directly related to their needs and goals (Csikszentmihalyi & Nakamura, 1989); therefore, motivation often determines whether students pursue a learning task enthusiastically and wholeheartedly or apathetically and lackadaisically. For example, why do some students start their homework right away while others procrastinate?

Motivation increases initiation of and persistence in activities. Students are more likely to begin a task that they actually want to do. They are more likely to continue that task until they've completed it, even when they are occasionally interrupted or frustrated in their efforts to do so (Larson, 2000). For example, why do some students read the entire chapter in the textbook while others read just a few pages? Some of the answer may be that motivation enhances cognitive processing. Motivation affects what and how information is processed (Pintrich & Schunk, 2002). Motivated students are more likely to pay attention and take pleasure in performing the learning activity. Paying attention and learning for enjoyment results in students' long-term retention and critical understanding of the material in order to construct meaning rather than simply memorizing the facts to pass an upcoming test.

Perhaps most important of all, motivation leads to improved performance. When goal-directed behavior, energy and effort, initiation, persistence, reinforcement, and cognitive processing are all combined, students are totally motivated to learn. These students tend to be the highest achievers (Gottfried, 1990; Schiefele, Krapp & Winteler, 1992; Walbert & Uguroglu, 1980); just the opposite is true of students who are least motivated. The unmotivated, our lowest achievers, are frequently at high risk for dropping out of school before they graduate (Goodman, 2002; Hardre & Reeve, 2001; Hymel, Comfort, Schonert-Reichl & McDougall, 1996; Valerand, Fortier, & Guay, 1997).

FACTORS THAT AFFECT MOTIVATION

To illustrate the practical applications of these principles in a typical classroom setting, I present two student case profiles. These case studies may help you to understand two key emotional and motivational factors: learned helplessness and anxiety. These two psychological phenomena exert significant influence on the teaching and learning process.

Case 1: Michael won't even start the assignment—as usual. He just keeps saying, "I don't understand, or "This is too hard." When he answers the teacher's questions correctly, he "guessed" and he "doesn't really know." Michael spends most of his time staring into space; he is falling farther and farther behind. Michael has trouble starting the assignment right from the beginning. He feels defeated and helpless and maintains that nothing he does matters. "I will always fail because I am stupid," continues Michael.

Case 2: Sarah pretends to be working on her assignment but spends most of her time making fun of the assignment, because she is afraid to try. She fears that she will look foolish in front of her peers and believes that everyone will think she is "dumb." In terms of the principles of motivation, Sarah makes poor choices, procrastinates, avoids engagement, and gives up easily because she is so concerned about how others will judge her. She freezes on tests and "forgets" everything she knows when she has to answer questions in class. Her parents are very high achievers and expect her to become a successful adult, too, but her prospects for this future look dim.

In Case 1, Miguel's actions can be termed learned helplessness, a condition that affects motivation over time. Learned helplessness is based on an experience in which the student feels he or she has no control and is doomed to failure. Students who experience repeated failures might develop a "defensive pessimism" to protect themselves from negative feedback (Martin, Marsh, & Debus, 2001). Learned helplessness can result from a child's upbringing (Hokoda & Fincham, 1995) but also from inconsistent, unpredictable use of rewards and punishments by teachers. Focusing on learning goals (goals of students who are motivated primarily by desire for knowledge acquisition and self-improvement) rather than performance goals (goals of students who are motivated primarily by a desire to gain recognition from others and to earn good grades) can reduce learned helplessness. All students can attain learning goals if they can connect to a personal goal for themselves (Dweck, 1986). Teachers can prevent or reduce learned helplessness by setting consistent, high expectations and accentuating positive outcomes of learning, providing students with opportunities to succeed in small strides, and by giving immediate, encouraging feedback.

In Case 2, Sarah was experiencing debilitating anxiety which was seriously inhibiting her learning and performance. This was particularly problematic during tests. One of the main sources of anxiety in school is the fear of failure and, with it, loss of self-esteem (Hill & Wigfield, 1984). Sarah's feelings of anxiety arose from what she thought and how she felt while she worked. Sarah was experiencing anxiety because she faced situations in which she believed she had little or no chance of succeeding. Her sources of anxiety resulted from concern about what others would think of her and her worry about the future—not meeting her parents' expectations of pursuing a meaningful career. Thus, Sarah's anxiety distracted her attention from the task at hand and blocked her performance.

Teachers can apply many strategies to reduce the negative impact of anxiety on learning and performance by creating a learning environment that is safe and accepting with clear, positive expectations. Teachers should also provide unambiguous instruction and frequent feedback. Another tool for reducing anxiety is to provide students with rubrics for self-evaluation and to give frequent opportunities for self-reflection. In testing situations, teachers can employ a number of strategies to help anxious students perform well. For example, teachers can give students additional time to complete a test and check their work. Tests that begin with easy problems and have standard, simple responses are better for anxious students. Test-anxious students can be trained in test-taking skills and relaxation techniques, both which can have a positive impact on their test performance (Spielberger & Vagg, 1995).

Teachers who have the best success are the ones who deeply care about their students. This caring covers not only the academic competency their students' achieve, but it extends to the whole child. A caring and compassionate teacher knows that the feelings that the child experiences are an integral part of his or her life. These feelings play a dominant role in the interpersonal and intrapersonal world of the student. Without careful and sensitive attention to these feelings, the child may not be able to fully learn and develop. By giving the gifts of love and understanding, teachers can often accomplish educational miracles within their classrooms (Eben, 2006).

REFERENCES

Alexander, P. A., & Murphy, P. K. (1998). The research base for APA's Learner-Centered Psychological Principles. In N. Lambert & B. McCombs (Eds.), *How students learn: Reforming schools through learner-centered education* (pp. 33–60). Washington, D.C: American Psychological Association.

Bandura, A. (2001). Social cognitive theory An agentic perspective. *Annual Review of Psychology, 52,* 1–26.

Brandt, R. (1995). Why People learn. *Educational Leadership.* 53, (1). Available www.ascd.org.

Collaborative for Academic, Social, and Emotional Learning. (2005). *Social emotional learning (SEL) competenies.* Chicago: IL: Author. Available: www.casel.org/about_sel/SELskills.php./

Cowley, G., & Underwood, A. (1998, June 15). Memory. *Newsweek, 131* (24), 48–54.

Csikszentmihalyi, M., & Nakamura, J. (1989). The dynamics of intrinsic motivation: A study of adolescence. In C. Ames & R. Ames (Eds.), *Research on motivation I education: Vols. 3 Goals and cognition.* San Diego, CA: Academic Press.

Damasio, A. (1994). *Descartes' error: Emotion, reason, and the human brain.* New York: Gossett/Putnam.

Dweck, C. S. (1986). Motivational processes affecting learning. *American Psychologist, 41,* 1040–1048.

Eben, J. (2006). *How many wins have you had today?* Clovis, CA: Garden of Eben Publishing

Eisenberger, N., & Fabes, R. A. (1998). Prosocial development. In W. Damon (Series Ed.) & N. Eisenberg (Vol. Ed). *Handbook of child psychology* (5th ed. Vol.3, pp. 701–778. New York: Wiley.

Fischer, K.W., Kennedy, B., & Cheng, C-L. (1998). Culture and biology in emotional development. In D. Sharma & K.W. Fischer (Eds.), Socio-emotional development across cultures. *New Directions for Child Development, 81,* 21–43.

Freedom Writers & Filipovic, Z. (1999). *Freedom writers diary: How a teacher and 150 teens used writing to change themselves and the world around them.* New York: Broadway Books.

Gardner, H. (1993). *Multiple Intelligences: The Theory in Practice.* New York: Basic.

Goleman, D. (1995). *Emotional Intelligence.* New York: Bantam.

Goodman, G. (2002), *Reducing hate crimes and violence among American youth: Creating transformational agency through critical praxis.* New York: Peter Lang Publishing.

Gottfried, A. E. (1990). Academic intrinsic motivation in young elementary school children. *Journal of Educational Psychology, 82,* 525–538.

Graham, S. & Weiner, B. (1996). Theories and principle of motivation. In D. C. Berliner & R. C. Calfee (Eds.), *Handbook of education psychology.* New York: Macmillan.

Hardre, P. L., & Reeve, J. (2001). *A motivational model of rural high students' dropout intentions.* Paper presented at the annual meeting of the American Educational Research Association, Seattle, WA.

Hill, K., & Wigfield, A. (1984). Test anxiety: A major educational problem and what can be done about it. *Elementary School Journal, 85,* 105–126.

Hoffman, M. L. (1991). Empathy, social cognition, and moral action. In W. M. Kurtines & J. L. Gewirtz (Eds.), *Moral behavior and development: Vol. 1 Theory* (pp. 275–301). Hillsdale, NJ: Erlbaum.

Hokoda, A., & Fincham, F. D. (1995). Origins of children's helpless and mastery achievement patterns in the family. *Journal of Education Psychology, 87,* 375–385.

Hymel, S., Comfort, C., Schonert-Reichl, K., & McDougall, P. (1996). Academic failure and school dropout: the influence of peers. In J. Juvonen & K. R. Wentzel (Eds.), *Social motivation: Understanding children's school adjustment* (pp.313–345). Cambridge, England: Cambridge University Press.

Jensen, E. (1997). *Completing the puzzle: The brain-compatible approach to learning* (2nd ed.). Del Mar, CA: Turning Point.

Jensen, E. (1998). *Introduction to brain-compatible learning.* Del Mar, CA: Turning Point.

Kohn, A. (1999). *Punished by rewards: The trouble with gold stars, incentive plans, A's praise and other bribes.* Boston: Houghton Mifflin.

Langer, E. (1997). *The power of mindful leaning.* New York: Addison-Wesley.

————. (1989). *Mindfulness.* New York: Addison-Wesley.

Larson,R. W. (2000). Toward a psychology of positive youth development. *American Psychologist, 55,* pp.170–183.

McCune, S. L., Stephens, D. E., & Lowe, M. E. (1999). *Barron's how to prepare for the ExCET* (2nd ed.).Haupauge: NY: Barron's Educational Series.

Maehr, M. L. & Meyer, H. A. (1997). Understanding motivation and schooling: Where we've been, where we are, where we need to go. *Educational Psychology Review, 9* (4), 371–409.

Martin, A. J., Marsh, H. W., & Debus, R. L. (2001). Self-handicapping and defensive pessimism: Exploring a model of predicators and outcomes from a self-protection perspective. *Journal of Educational Psychology. 93* (1), 87–102.

Marzano. R.J. (1998). *A theory-based meta-analysis of research on instruction.* Aurora, CO: Mid-Continent Regional Educational Laboratory.

Miller, P.H. (2002). *Theories of developmental psychology* (4th ed.). New York: Worth.

Ormrod, J. (2006). *Essentials of educational psychology.* Upper Saddle River, NJ: Prentice Hall.

Pintrich, P. R., Marx, R. W., & Boyle, R. A. (1993). Beyond cold conceptual change: the role of motivational beliefs and classroom contextual factors in the process of conceptual change. *Review of Educational Research, 63,* 167–199.

Pintrich, P.R. & Schunk, D. H. (2002). *Motivation in education: Theory, research, and applications* (2nd ed.). Upper Saddle River, NJ: Merrill/Prentice Hall.

Renninger, K. A., Hidi, S., & Krapp, A. (Eds.) (1992). *The role of interest in learning and development.* Hillsdale, NJ: Erlbaum.

Salovey, P.& Mayer, J. D. (2004). *Emotional intelligence: Key readings on the mayer and Salovey model.* New York: Dude.

Schiefele, U., Krapp, A., & Winteler, A. (1992). Interst as a predictor of academic achievement: a meta-analysis of research. In K. A. Renninger, S. Hidi, & A. Krapp (Eds.), *The role of interest in learning and development.* Hillsdale, NJ: Erlbaum.

Schraw, G. & Lehman, S. (2001). Situational interest: A review of the literature and directions for future research. *Educational Psychology Review, 13,* 23–52.

Simonson, M. and Maushak, N. (2001). Instructional technology and attitude change. In D. Jonassen (Ed.), *Handbook of research for educational communications and technology* (pp. 984–1016). Mahwah, NJ: Lawrence Erlbaum Associates.

Slavin, R. (1995). *Cooperative learning: Theory, research, and practice.* Boston: Allyn & Bacon.

———— (1996). *Every child, every school: Success for all.* Thousand Oaks, CA: Corwin Press.

Slavin, R., Karweit, N., & Madden, N. (1989). *Effective programs for students at risk.* Boston: Allyn & Bacon.

Smith, P. & Ragan, T.J. (1999). *Instructional design.* New York: John Wiley & Sons.

Spielberger, C. & Vagg, P. (Eds.) (1995). *Test anxiety: Theory, assessment, and treatment.* Washington, D.C: Taylor & Francis.

Valerand, R. J., Fortier, M. S., & Guay, F. (1997). Self-determination and persistence in a real-life setting: Toward a motivational model of high school dropout. *Journal of Personality and Social Psychology, 72,* 1161–1176.

Vygotsky, L. (1978). *Mind in society: The development of higher psychological processes.* Cambridge, MA: Harvard University Press.

Walbert, H. J., & Uguroglu, M. (1980). Motivation and educational productivity: Theories, results, and implications. In L. J. Fyans, Jr. (Ed.), *Achievement motivation: Recent trends in theory and research.* New York: Plenum Press.

Watson-Gegeo, K. & Gegeo, D. (2004). Deep culture: Pushing the epistemological boundaries. In G. Goodman & K. Carey (Eds.), *Critical multicultural conversations.* Cresskill, NJ: Hampton Press.

SEVENTEEN

Self-Efficacy: An Essential Motive to Learn

Barry J. Zimmerman

During the past two decades, self-efficacy has emerged as a highly effective predictor of students' motivation and learning. As a performance-based measure of perceived capability, self-efficacy differs conceptually and psychometrically from related motivational constructs, such as outcome expectations, self-concept, or locus of control. Researchers have succeeded in verifying its discriminant validity as well as convergent validity in predicting common motivational outcomes, such as students' activity choices, effort, persistence, and emotional reactions. Self-efficacy beliefs have been found to be sensitive to subtle changes in students' performance context, to interact with self-regulated learning processes, and to mediate students' academic achievement. (2000, Academic Press)

Educators have long recognized that students' beliefs about their academic capabilities play an essential role in their motivation to achieve, but self-conceptions regarding academic performance initially proved difficult to measure in a scientifically valid way. Initial efforts to study students' self-beliefs gave little attention to the role of environmental influences, such as specific features of performance contexts or domains of academic functioning. In the late 1970s, a number of researchers began to assess self-beliefs in a more task-specific way, and one of the most important of these efforts focused on self-efficacy. In 1977(a) Bandura proposed a theory of the origins, mediating mechanisms, and diverse effects of beliefs of personal efficacy, and he provided guidelines for measurement of self-efficacy beliefs for different domains of functioning. In the present article, I define self-efficacy and distinguish it from related conceptions in the literature, describe its role in academic motivation and learning (with special attention to students' capabilities to regulate their own learning activities), and discuss its susceptibility to instruction and other social-cultural influences. Because of space limitations, I cite only key studies and do not consider other issues such as theoretical controversies or gender differences in self-efficacy. For comprehensive reviews of research on academic self-efficacy, I recommend Bandura (1997), Pajares (1996b, 1997), Schunk (1989), and Zimmerman (1995).

SELF-EFFICACY AND ITS DIMENSIONS

Before Bandura (1977a) introduced self-efficacy as a key component in social cognitive theory, he discussed human motivation primarily in terms of outcome expectations. However, during the treatment of phobic individuals with mastery modeling techniques, individual differences in generalization were found regardless of the fact that all subjects could successfully interact with the target of their fear (e.g., touch a snake or dog) without adverse consequences at the end of therapy. Although the subjects developed a strong outcome expectancy that proper techniques (e.g., for handling a snake or dog) would protect them from adverse consequences (such as biting), they still differed in their perceived capabilities to use the techniques outside the therapeutic setting. Bandura labeled this individual difference *self-efficacy* and sought to measure it using task-specific scales. Although self-efficacy and outcome expectations were both hypothesized to affect motivation, he suggested that self-efficacy would play a larger role because "the types of outcomes people anticipate depend largely on their judgments of how well they will be able to perform in given situations" (Bandura, 1986, p. 392).

Bandura (1977a, 1997) formally defined perceived self-efficacy as personal judgments of one's capabilities to organize and execute courses of action to attain designated goals, and he sought to assess its level, generality, and strength across activities and contexts. The *level* of self-efficacy refers to its dependence on the difficulty of a particular task, such as spelling words of increasing difficulty; *generality* pertains to the transferability of self-efficacy beliefs across activities, such as from algebra to statistics; *strength* of perceived efficacy is measured by the amount of one's certainty about performing a given task. These properties of self-efficacy judgments are measured using questionnaire items that are task specific, vary in difficulty, and capture degrees of confidence (e.g., from 0 to 100%).

With regard to their content, self-efficacy measures focus on *performance capabilities* rather than on personal qualities, such as one's physical or psychological characteristics. Respondents judge their capabilities to fulfill given task demands, such as solving fraction problems in arithmetic, not who they are personally or how they feel about themselves in general. Self-efficacy beliefs are not a single disposition but rather are *multidimensional* in form and differ on the basis of the domain of functioning. For example, efficacy beliefs about performing on a history test may differ from beliefs about a biology examination. Self-efficacy measures are also designed to be sensitive to variations in performance *context,* such as learning in a noisy lounge compared to the quietude of the library. In addition, perceptions of efficacy depend on a *mastery criterion* of performance rather than on normative or other criteria. For example, students rate their certainty about solving a crossword puzzle of a particular difficulty level, not how well they expect to do on the puzzle in comparison to other students. Finally, self-efficacy judgments specifically refer to *future* functioning and are assessed before students perform the relevant activities. This antecedent property positions self-efficacy judgments to play a causal role in academic motivation.

SELF-EFFICACY AND RELATED BELIEFS

Self-efficacy beliefs differ conceptually and psychometrically from closely related constructs, such as outcome expectations, self-concept, and perceived control. The conceptual distinction that Bandura (1986) drew between academic self-efficacy and *outcome expectancies* was studied psychometrically in research on reading and writing achievement. Shell, Murphy, and Bruning (1989) measured self-efficacy in terms of perceived capability to perform various reading and writing activities, and they assessed outcome expectancies regarding the value of these activities in attaining various outcomes in employment, social pursuits, family life, education, and citizenship. Efficacy beliefs and outcome expectancies jointly predicted 32% of the variance in reading achievement, with perceived efficacy accounting for virtually all the variance. Only perceived self-efficacy was a significant predictor of writing achievement. These results not only show the discriminant validity of self-efficacy measures, they support Bandura's contention that self-efficacy plays a larger role than outcome expectancies in motivation.

One of closest constructs to self-efficacy is *self-concept*. The latter belief is a more general self-descriptive construct that incorporates many forms of self-knowledge and self-evaluative feelings (Marsh & Shavelson, 1985). Historically, self-concept was defined by phenomenologists (e.g., Rogers, 1951) as a global perception of oneself and one's self-esteem reactions to that self-perception, but this global measure of self-belief was not found to be related consistently to students' academic performance (Hattie, 1992; Wylie, 1968). Perhaps as a result, a number of theorists (e.g., Harter, 1978; Marsh & Shavelson, 1985) reconceptualized self-concept as a hierarchical construct, with a global self-concept at the apex of a self-hierarchy but added subcategories such as academic self-concept in the middle of the hierarchy and academic domain-specific self-concepts at the bottom. The latter self-concept measures emphasize *self-esteem reactions* by posing self-evaluative questions, such as "How good are you in English?" By contrast, self-efficacy items focus exclusively on task-specific *performance expectations,* such as "How certain are you that you can diagram this sentence?" Although prior task reactions and future performance expectations are often correlated, Bandura (1997) notes it is possible conceptually to have high self-efficacy about a capability that one does not particularly esteem as well as the reverse.

There is growing evidence that, although self-efficacy beliefs are correlated with domain-specific self-concepts, self-efficacy measures offer predictive advantages when a task is familiar and can be specified precisely. For example, Pajares and Miller (1994) used path analysis procedures to examine the predictive and mediational roles of these two constructs in mathematical problem solving by college students. Math self-efficacy was more predictive of problem solving than was math self-concept or, for that matter, perceived usefulness of mathematics, prior experience with mathematics, or gender. The effect of prior math experiences on math problem solving was mediated primarily by self-efficacy beliefs, but self-concept played a small but significant role. Thus, when self-concept and self-efficacy beliefs are both included in regression equations, self-efficacy beliefs display discriminant validity by independently predicting future academic achievement. Although self-efficacy questionnaire items should be adapted to specific tasks, the scope of these tasks can vary on the basis of the user's intended purpose, ranging from proficiency in an academic domain (e.g., writing or mathematics) to proficiency in a subskill (e.g., grammar or fractions). This second criterion for developing self-efficacy measures involves their *correspondence* to the performance capability in question. Pajares (1996a) demonstrated that the predictiveness of self-efficacy measures increases as a function of both their specificity and correspondence to a skill. Thus, self-efficacy differs from self-concept in both its specificity and correspondence to varying performance tasks and contexts.

Another closely associated construct to self-efficacy is *perceived control,* which emerged from research on locus of control (Rotter, 1966). Perceived control refers to general expectancies about whether outcomes are controlled by one's behavior or by external forces, and it is theorized that an internal locus of control should support self-directed courses of action, whereas an external locus of control should discourage them. Locus-of-control scales are neither task nor domain specific in their item content but rather refer to general beliefs about the internality or externality of causality. Bandura (1986) has questioned the value of general control beliefs because students may feel anxious about controlling one type of subject matter or performance setting (e.g., solving mathematical problems in a limited time period) but not others. In support of this contention, Smith (1989) found that locus of control measures did not predict improvements in academic performance or reductions in anxiety in highly self-anxious students who underwent an intensive coping skills training program, but self-efficacy scales did predict such improvements.

In summary, measures of self-efficacy are not only conceptually distinctive from closely associated constructs such as outcome expectancies, self-concept, and perceived control, they have discriminant validity in predicting a variety of academic outcomes.

ROLE OF SELF-EFFICACY IN ACADEMIC MOTIVATION

Self-efficacy beliefs have also shown convergent validity in influencing such key indices of academic motivation as choice of activities, level of effort, persistence, and emotional reactions. There is evidence (Bandura, 1997) that self-efficacious students participate more readily, work harder, persist longer, and have fewer adverse emotional reactions when they encounter difficulties than do those who doubt their capabilities.

In terms of *choice of activities,* self-efficacious students undertake difficult and challenging tasks more readily than do inefficacious students. Bandura and Schunk (1981) found that students' mathematical self-efficacy beliefs were predictive of their choice of engaging in subtraction problems rather than in a different type of task: The higher the children's sense of efficacy, the greater their choice of the arithmetic activity. Zimmerman and Kitsantas (1997; 1999) also found self-efficacy to be highly correlated with students' rated intrinsic interest in a motoric learning task as well as in a writing revision task. Furthermore, measures of self-efficacy correlate significantly with students' choice of majors in college, success in course work, and perseverance (Hackett & Betz, 1989; Lent, Brown, & Larkin, 1984).

Self-efficacy beliefs are predictive of two measures of students' *effort:* rate of performance and expenditure of energy. For example, Schunk and colleagues found that perceived self-efficacy for learning correlates positively with students' rate of solution of arithmetic problems (Schunk & Hanson, 1985; Schunk, Hanson, & Cox, 1987). Salomon (1984) has found that self-efficacy is positively related to self-rated mental effort and achievement during students' learning from text material that was perceived as difficult. Regarding the effects of perceived self-efficacy on *persistence,* path analyses have shown that it influences students' skill acquisition both directly and indirectly by increasing their persistence (Schunk, 1981). The direct effect indicates that perceived self-efficacy influences students' methods of learning as well as their motivational processes. These results validate the meditational role that self-efficacy plays in motivating persistence and academic achievement. In a meta-analytic review of nearly 70 studies of persistence and rate measures of motivation, Multon, Brown, and Lent (1991) found a significant positive effect size of students' self-efficacy beliefs.

Student's beliefs about their efficacy to manage academic task demands can also influence them *emotionally* by decreasing their stress, anxiety, and depression (Bandura, 1997). For example, Pajares and Kranzler (1995) have studied the relationship between self-efficacy and students' anxiety reactions regarding mathematics. Although the two measures were negatively correlated, only self-efficacy was predictive of mathematics performance when compared in a joint path analysis. There is also evidence that students' performance in academically threatening situations depends more on efficacy beliefs than on anxiety arousal. Siegel, Galassi, and Ware (1985) found that self-efficacy beliefs are more predictive of math performance than is math anxiety. The strength of efficacy beliefs accounted for more than 13% of the variance in their final math grades, whereas math anxiety did not prove to be a significant predictor. These studies provide clear evidence of the discriminant and predictive validity of self-efficacy measures, and they suggest particular benefit if educators focus on fostering a positive sense of personal efficacy rather than merely diminishing scholastic anxiety.

SELF-EFFICACY AND SELF-REGULATION OF LEARNING

Self-efficacy beliefs also provide students with a sense of agency to motivate their learning through use of such self-regulatory processes as goal setting, self-monitoring, self-evaluation, and strategy use. For example, there is evidence (Zimmerman, Bandura, & Martinez-Pons, 1992) that the more capable students judge themselves to be, the more challenging the *goals* they embrace. When self-efficacy and personal goal setting from the beginning of a school term were used jointly to predict final course grades in high school social studies, they increased prediction by 31% over a measure of prior grades in social studies. Similarly, when self-efficacy and personal goal setting were compared with the verbal subscale of the Scholastic Aptitude Test, there was an increase of 35% in predicting college students' final grades in a writing course (Zimmerman & Bandura, 1994). Although prior course grades and general measures of ability are considered exemplary predictors of achievement, these studies demonstrated that self-efficacy beliefs and goal setting add significantly to the predictiveness of these measures.

The effects of efficacy beliefs on students' *self-monitoring* were studied during concept learning (Bouffard-Bouchard, Parent, & Larivee, 1991). Efficacious students were better at monitoring their working time, more persistent, less likely to reject correct hypotheses prematurely, and better at solving conceptual problems than inefficacious students of equal ability. Self-efficacy beliefs also affect the *self-evaluation* standards students use to judge the outcomes of their self-monitoring. In a path analytic study (Zimmerman & Bandura, 1994), self-efficacy for writing beliefs significantly predicted college students' personal standards for the quality of writing considered self-satisfying as well as their goal setting and writing proficiency. Self-efficacy beliefs also motivate students' use of *learning strategies*. With fifth, eighth, and eleventh grade students, there were developmental increases in perceived verbal and mathematical efficacy as well as strategy use, and there was a substantial relation (16 to 18% shared variance) between efficacy beliefs and strategy use across the three grade levels of schooling (Zimmerman & Martinez-Pons, 1990).

The greater motivation and self-regulation of learning of self-efficacious students produces higher *academic achievement* according to a range of measures. Multon, Brown, and Lent (1991) found an overall effect size of .38, indicating that self-efficacy accounted for approximately 14% of the variance in students' academic performance across a variety of student samples, experimental designs, and criterion measures. This represents further evidence of the convergent validity of self-efficacy beliefs.

INSTRUCTIONAL AND SOCIAL INFLUENCES ON SELF-EFFICACY BELIEFS

In contrast to trait measures of self-perceptions, self-efficacy indices focus on cognitive beliefs that are readily influenced by four types of experience: enactive attainment, vicarious experience, verbal persuasion, and physiological states. *Enactive* experiences are the most influential source of efficacy belief because they are predicated on the outcomes of personal experiences, whereas *vicarious* influences depend on an observer's self-comparison with as well as outcomes attained by a model. If a model is viewed as more able or talented, observers will discount the relevance of the model's performance outcomes for themselves. *Verbal persuasion* has an even more limited impact on students' self-efficacy because outcomes are described, not directly witnessed, and thus depend on the credibility of the persuader. Finally, students base their self-efficacy judgments on their perceived *physiological reactions,* such as fatigue, stress, and other emotions that are often interpreted as indicators of physical incapability. Unlike self-beliefs assumed to have trait-like stability across time and setting, self-efficacy is assumed to be responsive to changes in personal context and outcomes, whether experienced directly, vicariously, verbally, or physiologically. As a result of this sensitivity, self-efficacy beliefs are studied as indicators of change during instructional interventions as well as indicators of initial individual differences.

To facilitate improvements in perceived efficacy, researchers have trained students with learning and motivational deficiencies by modeling specific self-regulatory techniques, describing their form, and providing enactive feedback regarding their impact. For example, youngsters who observed an adult model the use of a cognitive strategy had significantly higher levels of perceived efficacy and academic skills than youngsters who received didactic instruction (Schunk, 1981). Asking students to set proximal goals enhanced self-efficacy and skill development more effectively than asking them to set distal goals because the proximal attainments provide evidence of growing capability (Bandura & Schunk, 1981). Verbally encouraging students to set their own goals improved not only their efficacy beliefs and achievement but also their commitment to attaining the goals (Schunk, 1985). The frequency and immediacy of enactive feedback also created higher perceptions of personal efficacy (Schunk, 1983). When students were taught to attribute their enactive feedback to effort, they perceived greater progress, maintained higher motivation, and reported greater efficacy for further learning (Schunk, 1987). In these investigations, Schunk and his colleagues not only demonstrated the sensitivity of efficacy beliefs to instructional interventions, but also the mediational role of these beliefs in explaining changes in learners' self-regulation and achievement outcomes (Berry, 1987; Schunk, 1981). Self-efficacy beliefs increased prediction of academic outcomes as much as 25% of the variance above instructional influences. Clearly, students' self-efficacy beliefs are responsive to changes in instructional experience and play a causal role in students' development and use of academic competencies.

CONCLUSION

Students' self-perceptions of efficacy are distinctive from related motivational constructs because of their specificity and close correspondence to performance tasks. These cognitive beliefs differ conceptually and psychometrically from trait self-belief measures due to their sensitivity to variations in experience and task and situational context. Two decades of research have clearly established the validity of self-efficacy as a predictor of students' motivation and learning. Although self-efficacy correlates with other related constructs, it has also shown discriminant validity by its unique predictiveness of these outcomes when included in multiple regression analyses. It has shown convergent validity in predicting diverse forms of motivation, such as students' activity choices, effort, persistence, and emotional reactions. Finally, when studied as a mediating variable in training studies, self-efficacy has proven to be responsive to improvements in students' methods of learning (especially those involving greater self-regulation) and predictive of achievement outcomes. This empirical evidence of its role as a potent mediator of students' learning and motivation confirms the historic wisdom of educators that students' self-beliefs about academic capabilities do play an essential role in their motivation to achieve.

ACKNOWLEDGMENTS

I express my gratitude to Frank Pajares and Manuel Martinez-Pons for their helpful comments on an earlier draft of this article.

REFERENCES

Bandura, A. (1977a). Self-efficacy: Toward a unifying theory of behavior change. *Psychological Review*, 84, 191–215.

Bandura, A. (1977b). *Social learning theory*. Englewood Cliffs, NJ: Prentice-Hall.

Bandura, A. (1986). *Social foundations of thought and action: A social cognitive theory*. Englewood Cliffs, NJ: Prentice-Hall.

Bandura, A. (1997). *Self-efficacy: The exercise of control*. New York: Freeman.

Bandura, A., & Schunk, D. H. (1981). Cultivating competence, self-efficacy, and intrinsic interest through proximal self-motivation. *Journal of Personality and Social Psychology*, 41, 586–598.

Berry, J. M. (1987, September). *A self-efficiency model of memory performance*. Paper presented at the meeting of the American Psychological Association, New York.

Bouffard-Bouchard, T., Parent, S., & Larivee, S. (1991). Influence of self-efficacy on self-regulation and performance among junior and senior high-school age students. *International Journal of Behavioral Development*, 14, 153–164.

Hackett, G., & Betz, N. E. (1989). An exploration of the mathematics self-efficacy/mathematics performance correspondence. *Journal for Research in Mathematics Education*, 20, 263–271.

Harter, S. (1978). Effectance motivation reconsidered: Toward a developmental model. *Human Development*, 21, 34–64.

Hattie, J. (1992). *Self-concept*. Hillsdale, NJ: Erlbaum.

Lent, R. W., Brown, S. D., & Larking, K. C. (1984). Relation of self-efficacy expectations to academic achievement and persistence. *Journal of Counseling Psychology*, 31, 356–362.

Marsh, H. W., & Shavelson, R. (1985). Self-concept: Its multifaceted, hierarchical structure. *Educational Psychologist, 20*, 107–123.

Multon, K. D., Brown, S. D., & Lent, R. W. (1991). Relation of self-efficacy beliefs to academic outcomes: A meta-analytic investigation. *Journal of Counseling Psychology, 18*, 30–38.

Pajares, F. (1996a, April). *Assessing self-efficacy beliefs and academic outcomes: The case for specificity and correspondence.* Paper presented at the Annual Meeting of the American Educational Research Association, New York.

Pajares, F. (1996b). Self-efficacy beliefs in academic settings. *Review of Educational Research, 66*, 543–578.

Pajares, F., & Miller, M. D. (1994). Role of self-efficacy and self-concept beliefs in mathematical problem solving: A path analysis. *Journal of Educational Psychology, 86*, 193–203.

Pajares, F., & Kranzler, J. (1995). Self-efficacy beliefs and general mental ability in mathematical problem-solving. *Contemporary Educational Psychology, 20*, 426–443.

Rogers, C. R. (1951). *Client-centered therapy: Its current practice, implications, and theory.* Boston: Houghton Mifflin.

Rotter, J. B. (1966). Generalized expectancies for internal versus external control of reinforcement. *Psychological Monographs, 80*, 148–154.

Salomon, G. (1984). Television is "easy" and print is "tough": The differential investment of mental effort in learning as a function of perceptions and attributions. *Journal of Educational Psychology, 76*, 647–658.

Schunk, D. H. (1981). Modeling and attributional feedback effects on children's achievement: A self-efficacy analysis. *Journal of Educational Psychology, 74*, 93–105.

Schunk, D. H. (1983). Progress self-monitoring: Effects on children's self-efficacy and achievement. *Journal of Experimental Education, 51*, 89–93.

Schunk, D. H. (1985). Self-efficacy and classroom learning. *Psychology in the Schools, 22*, 208–223.

Schunk, D. H. (1987). Peer models and children's behavioral change. *Review of Educational Research, 57*, 149–174.

Schunk, D. H. (1989). Self-efficacy and achievement behaviors. *Educational Psychology Review, 1*, 173–208.

Schunk, D. H., & Hanson, A. R. (1985). Peer models: Influence on children's self-efficacy and achievement behaviors. *Journal of Educational Psychology, 77*, 313–322.

Schunk, D. H., Hanson, A. R., & Cox, P. D. (1987). Peer model attributes and children's achievement behaviors. *Journal of Educational Psychology, 79*, 54–61.

Shell, D. F., Murphy, C. C., & Bruning, R. H. (1989). Self-efficacy and outcome expectancy mechanisms in reading and writing achievement. *Journal of Educational Psychology, 81*, 91–100.

Siegel, R. G., Galassi, J. P., & Ware, W. B. (1985). A comparison of two models for predicting mathematics performance: Social learning versus math aptitude-anxiety. *Journal of Counseling Psychology, 32*, 531–538.

Smith, R. E. (1989). Effects of coping skills training on generalized self-efficacy and locus of control. *Journal of Personality and Social Psychology, 56*, 228–233.

Wylie, R. (1968). The present status of self-theory. In E. Borgotta & W. Lambert (Eds.), *Handbook of personality theory and research* (pp. 728–787). Chicago: Rand-McNally.

Zimmerman, B. J. (1995). Self-efficacy and educational development. In A. Bandura (Ed.), *Self-efficacy in changing societies* (pp. 202–231). New York: Cambridge Univ. Press.

Zimmerman, B. J., & Bandura, A. (1994). Impact of self-regulatory influences on writing course attainment. *American Educational Research Journal, 31*, 845–862.

Zimmerman, B. J., Bandura, A., & Martinez-Pons, M. . (1992). Self-motivation for academic attainment: The role of self-efficacy beliefs and personal goal setting. *American Educational Research Journal, 29*, 663–676.

Zimmerman, B. J., & Kitsantas, A. (1997). Developmental phases in self-regulation: Shifting from process to outcome goals. *Journal of Educational Psychology, 89*, 29–36.

Zimmerman, B. J., & Kitsantas, A. (1999). Acquiring writing revision skill: Shifting from process to outcome self-regulatory goals. *Journal of Educational Psychology, 91*, 1–10.

Zimmerman, B. J., & Martinez-Pons, M. (1990). Student differences in self-regulated learning. *Journal of Educational Psychology, 82*, 51–59.

EIGHTEEN

Teaching Educational Psychology Online: An Examination of Student Motivation and Learning in a Graduate Course

Laurie B. Hanich and Sandra Deemer

Recent research in educational psychology has underscored the importance of incorporating evidence-based psychological principles into practice. For faculty who teach courses in educational psychology, the feat should be possible since the content of the discipline is largely composed of research on "best practices." Yet, an ongoing challenge for many faculty has been how to help pre-service and in-service educators translate such principles into their own instructional practices. In this paper we argue that the most effective way to achieve this goal is by modeling sound instructional strategies and creating classroom environments that reflect best practices.

One of the areas in educational psychology that has warranted much attention in the past decade has been how to effectively utilize instructional technology. This has become particularly important as national and local standards have increasingly required teachers to successfully incorporate technology into their classroom practices. At the teacher preparation level, universities are responsible for showing that pre-service candidates can successfully accomplish this task during their training. Additionally, educators' facility with technology is also important to their own professional development, as many universities and colleges have moved towards offering workshops, courses, and inservices in distance learning formats.

Given the ever-changing needs of society, it is imperative that researchers examine the effects of instructional technology on learning. Current research has found that integrating technology in meaningful ways can motivate students' interest in learning, increase students' higher level learning, and promote significant gains in knowledge related to both educational psychology content and technology-related skills (Drennan, Kennedy, & Pisarski, 2005; Kuo, Parke, & Wells, 2005;

Teng & Allen, 2005). For example, Drennen and her colleagues (2005) found that students in an introductory business course were supported in their learning if the technology utilized within the course did not overwhelm students' competence with using the particular technology. In addition, students with an internal locus of control reported higher levels of satisfaction with an online course when compared to students who had an external locus of control. They suggest that students who assume responsibility for their learning and actions most likely utilized the range of learning materials and learning options available in online courses, becoming more aware of the benefits of online access to materials. Even though students who are self-directed learners appear to enjoy online learning, the need for support and feedback from the course instructor is critical in order to integrate technology in meaningful ways (Kuo, Parke, & Wells, 2005).

Based on the above findings, it is imperative to investigate how students perceive the context of learning within online educational psychology courses and in what ways these environments affect their beliefs about learning. To do such, we utilize self-determination theory, a popular theory in the motivation literature, as a framework for examining students' intrinsic motivation and learning.

Deci and Moller (2005), in a recent review of self-determination theory, identify the environment as a key factor affecting individuals' beliefs about learning. In particular, in order for individuals to be motivated to learn, it is essential that contextual factors support three needs—competence, autonomy, and relatedness. Research by Deci and his colleagues (e.g., Deci, Koestner, & Ryan, 1999; Deci & Ryan, 2000; Deci, Schwartz, Sheinman, & Ryan, 1981) have consistently found that satisfying these three needs relates to enhanced motivation and well-being. Individuals' enhanced motivation and well-being also are associated with increased levels of intrinsic motivation related to learning, which results in higher-quality learning and increased creativity.

According to self-determination theory, students' motivation can range from extrinsic in nature, where students perform simply because it leads to a particular outcome or reward, to intrinsic in nature, where students learn because they find it inherently interesting and enjoyable (Deci & Moller, 2005). The four dimensions along this continuum—external regulation, introjection, identification, and integration—represent differing types of motivation that relate to differing levels of need fulfillment. Although relationships among these dimensions and need fulfillment have been found consistently in students within traditional learning settings, little research has addressed how students perceive the fulfillment of their needs and beliefs about learning within online learning environments.

The purpose of this study is to examine the relationship between intrinsic motivation and participation in an online educational psychology course. Using self-reported survey data and open-ended questions, we extend the literature in this area in the following ways: we target educational psychology courses at the graduate level, we use a strong theoretical framework for examining motivation (i.e., self-determination theory), and we include quantitative and qualitative data analyses about students' perceived motivation and learning in the course. The following research questions were central to our study: 1) Is there a relationship between students' reported relatedness and their participation in group-centered learning activities? 2) Is there a relationship between students' reported autonomy and the frequency in which they accessed the course? and 3) How do students' perceive that their learning was affected by participation in the online course? Research in the arena will contribute to the knowledge base in educational psychology by identifying the effects of technology on students' motivation and learning. Findings from this study will guide responsive instructional decisions based on student feedback as faculty strive to model sound instructional practices and create classroom environments that reflect best practices.

METHODS

PARTICIPANTS

Participants included 33 students (27 females; 6 males) enrolled in a graduate-level educational psychology course at a mid-sized comprehensive university in the Northeast. Twenty-two participants were classroom teachers and 11 were students seeking initial certification. Students' degree programs included elementary education, secondary education, special education, nursing, and sports management. Twelve participants had prior experience in distance learning courses.

The course was offered during summer session in a four-week format. Participants were enrolled in two different sections of the course that were identical in course requirements and format and that were taught by the same instructor. The course was an online course that met once at the beginning of the semester to provide a tutorial on Blackboard (BB), the communication tool in which the course was offered. After the initial meeting, all of the course instruction took place online.

BB is a web-based course management system that is used to support teaching in face-to-face and distance learning classes. It provides tools and management for online communication via group discussion forums, full class discussion boards, and live chat rooms. Course content is posted in templates and is managed by a system administrator, usually a university faculty member. Templates for forums, assignments, quizzes, and a grade book are also available. Students and faculty are able to track a student's progress and participation in a course using the system's course statistics feature. In most cases, data from the course are stored on a university server.

The content for the course in this study was divided into 4 course units: learning, motivation, development, and instructional practices (e.g., management, assessment, etc.). Each unit was divided into several lessons, with each lesson representing a three-hour class period that would occur in a "traditional class meeting." Within each lesson students were required to access three different folders: 1) *instructor's notes,* which were composed of an outline of main concepts and points from the course reading assigned for the lesson, 2) *learning activities,* which required students to communicate on the group discussion board, 3) and *web resources,* which took students to other electronic resources available on the world wide web.

MATERIALS AND PROCEDURE

At the completion of the course, students were mailed a letter that asked for their permission to participate in a research study about online learning and motivation. Students signed informed consent forms and returned their completed paper and pencil measure via the U.S. mail. Sixty-six percent of the students enrolled in the course participated in the study.

To assess students' intrinsic motivation, students completed the Intrinsic Motivation Inventory (IMI) (Deci & Ryan, 2000). The IMI is composed by several scales: interest/enjoyment (7 items);

effort/importance (5 items); perceived autonomy (7 items); perceived competence (6 items), relatedness (8 items); and value/usefulness (7 items). Scores ranged from 1 to 7. The IMI has been used in several empirical studies to assess students' subjective experiences in targeted activities (Ryan, Koestner & Deci, 1991; Deci, Eghrari, Patrick, & Leone, 1994) and has well established reliability and validity (McAuley, Duncan, & Tammen, 1987). The IMI was modified to specifically address students' engagement in an online course (e.g., participation in online discussion, number of times students accessed the instructor notes, etc.) and was administered to students at the completion of the course (see Appendix A). Reliability coefficients, measured by Chronbach's alpha, were 0.91 for interest/enjoyment, 0.83 for effort/importance, 0.83 for perceived autonomy, 0.79 for perceived competence, 0.67 for relatedness, and 0.89 for value/usefulness.

In addition to the IMI, students also responded to several open-ended items on a questionnaire: 1) What did you enjoy about participating in an online course? 2) How do you think your learning was affected by taking Educational Psychology in an online course rather than as a traditional course? 3) Please identify any remarkable features of Blackboard that facilitated your learning and explain how, and 4) Would you enroll in other online education courses? Why or why not? We also collected descriptive data about students' previous experience with distance learning courses and their perceived competence with using technology.

RESULTS

We were interested in the frequency that students accessed the BB course across the 4 weeks that the course met. Although BB has a number of different components that are available for students to access, we were particularly interested in three of the BB features: 1) the announcements page, which was the default starting point for accessing course materials, 2) the group pages, which is where students engaged in small group discussions around learning activities for each lesson, and 3) the content page, which is where the instructor posted course notes that highlighted important concepts from each reading.

The mean number times students logged on to the announcements page, the group pages and the content pages are displayed in Table 1.

Table 1: Descriptive information about participants' logins to announcement page, group pages, and content pages. Note. Scores range from 1–7

	MEAN	STANDARD DEVIATION	MINIMUM	MAXIMUM
Logins to announcement page	91	43	48	257
Logins to group pages	563	152	382	989
Logins to content pages	493	171	259	1087

Students most frequently accessed the group pages. Also notable was the frequency distribution for the number of time students logged on to the announcements page. The number of times students logged on ranged between 48 and 257 across the four weeks of the course.

Table 2 shows the mean scores for the autonomy, relatedness, competence, interest, effort, and value scales of the IMI. Students scored highest on the effort scale and lowest on the relatedness scale.

Table 2: Participants' mean scores and standard deviations on the Intrinsic Motivation Inventory

	AUTONOMY	RELATEDNESS	COMPETENCE	INTEREST	EFFORT	VALUE
Mean	5.11	4.86	5.37	5.18	6.30	5.72
SD	1.04	0.72	0.87	1.21	0.77	1.11

To examine the relationship between students' intrinsic motivation and participation in the course, we conducted correlations between students' scores on the IMI and the number of times students logged on to the announcements page, group pages, and content pages (see Table 3).

Table 3: Correlations between participants' scores on the IMI and logins to announcement page, group pages, and content pages.

	INTEREST	COMPETENCE	EFFORT	AUTONOMY	VALUE	RELATEDNESS	GROUP LOGINS	ANNOUNCEMENT LOGINS	CONTENT LOGINS
Interest	1								
Competence	.70**	1							
Effort	.53**	.58**	1						
Autonomy	.45*	.31	.55**	1					
Value	.76**	.73**	.56**	.47**	1				
Relatedness	.42*	.25	.39*	.31	.39*	1			
group logins	-.32	-.03	-.18	-.32	-.17	-.06	1		
announcements logins	-.05	.02	.18	-.20	.04	.27	.50**	1	
content logins	.11	-.07	.27	.15	.13	.22	.29	.47**	1

Participants' relatedness scores were significantly related to interest ($r = 0.42$), value ($r = 0.39$), and effort ($r = 0.39$) scores but not competence or autonomy scores. Students' autonomy scores were positively correlated with scores on the interest ($r = 0.45$) value ($r = 0.47$), and effort ($r =$

0.55) scales, but not relatedness or competence. Students' competence scores were also positively correlated with interest ($r = 0.45$), effort ($r = 0.58$), and value scores ($r = 0.73$), but not relatedness, autonomy, or participation scores. With regard to the measures of participation, there were no statistical correlations between scores on the IMI and the number of times students logged on to the announcements page, the group pages, or the content pages. The number of times students logged on to the announcement page was related to number of times students logged on to the group pages ($r = 0.50$) and number of times students logged on to the content page ($r = 0.47$). There was not a relationship between number of times student logged on to group pages and content pages.

Did students' perceptions of their competence with technology change as a result of enrolling in an online course? Participants were asked to rate their competence at the beginning of the course and at the end of the course. At the beginning of the course, 1 student rated their competence as *minimal,* 5 rated their competence as *developing,* 20 rated their competence as *competent,* and 7 rated their competence as *advanced.* At the end of the course, 1 student rated their competence as *developing,* 24 students rated their competence as *competent,* and 8 rated their competence as *advanced.*

Using an iterative process involving coding, categorizing, and theme identification (Glesne, 1999), an analysis of the responses to the first open-ended question, *"What did you enjoy about participating in an online course?"* indicated that the majority of students (29/33) enjoyed the flexible work schedule that an online course provided for them. More than one student noted, "I could pace myself and choose when to get online" and "I was able to work at times that were convenient for me." In addition, students (10/33) reported that they liked the nature of interaction within this learning environment. Specifically, they noted that the online learning environment motivated all students to disclose ideas and because of this equity in sharing, many viewpoints and practical ideas were shared. One student noted, "The online course made it easy to hear from everyone, not just a few people on an issue each class period. I also had a lot more time to process the information—I could read things over and over, without asking anyone to repeat anything." Another student communicated, "Usually in a traditional class setting, not everyone has the chance to voice their opinion. In the online setting everyone could voice their opinions and have time to sit, think, and develop better dialogue for class discussion."

In response to the second question, *"How do you think your learning was affected by taking Educational Psychology in an online course rather than as a traditional course?"* several students (9/33) commented on the nature of interaction within the course. In response to this question, they mentioned both the ease of fair, equitable participation by all and the pace of instruction as being beneficial to their learning. One respondent noted, "My learning was more self-directed and I was better able to reflect on concepts and ideas in the participation format." Some students (14/33) reported that learning within an online course was more difficult than in a traditional course due to the lack of immediate feedback from both peers and the instructor when discussing topics. For example, one student noted, "It was more difficult to have your questions answered in a timely manner. You had to wait until it was convenient for your classmates to respond."

Students' responses to the third question, *"Please identify any remarkable features of Blackboard that facilitated your learning and explain how,"* indicated that this technology tool aided their learning. Specifically, it promoted interaction among students about ideas (14/33) and aided them in organizing their learning (18/33) through its calendar, announcements, assignment management, and grading systems. One student noted, "The group discussion board was the highlight and lowlight of the course. The broad range of ideas from classmates truly challenged and helped clarify my thinking at times. But the amount of reading (postings) became overwhelming."

Interestingly, (24/33) of the students responded that they would enroll in another online course when asked in the fourth question *"Would you enroll in another online education course? Why or why not?"* although they reported that their learning benefited from face-to-face interaction. For example, one student noted, "I missed the social interaction. Fact to face meetings/interpersonal relationships formed in person motivate me and spark my interest more than reading a list of comments," and another noted, "I would rather interact with the professor and peers on a face to face basis." In response to this question, students (17/33) again reported that the flexible work schedule was the main reason that they would enroll in another online education course. "I enjoyed the autonomy that an online course offers and the ability to work it into my family time."

DISCUSSION

We examined the relationship between students' intrinsic motivation and participation in an online educational psychology course over a four week summer session. To measure student participation in the course, we analyzed the number of times students logged on to the announcements page, the group pages, and the content pages. Perhaps most notable in the descriptive data was the large range in the number of times that students logged on to the course, via accessing the announcements page. The data in Table 1 suggest that some students logged in 5 times more often than others. There was also a considerably large standard deviation for number of times participants logged on to the announcements page, suggesting large variation in students' participation. At the start of the course, students were told they must log 9 hours of instruction per week and it was suggested they log in every day. Yet, there wasn't a minimum number of log ons that students were required to make. Although this may suggest that there were considerable differences in students' intrinsic motivation for participating in the course, one should be cautious when interpreting this data. The data is a numerical count of how frequently students accessed the announcements page and not how long they spent participating in the course. For example, some students have may logged in one time a day for several hours, thus accessing the announcements page only one time, upon initial log in to the course. Other students may have logged in several times a day, for a matter of minutes, to check the progress of their discussion on the group pages. Therefore, while the number of log ins to the announcements page may provide a general quantitative measure of students' participation in the courses, it doesn't provide a qualitative measure of students' participation.

It wasn't surprising that there was a relationship between the number of times students accessed the announcements and the group and content pages, since the announcement page was set up as the entry to the course. In other words, students couldn't get to the group pages or content pages without first going through the announcements page. However, we were surprised that there wasn't a significant relationship between the content page and the group pages. Students utilized the group pages for each lesson and were asked to engage in a learning activity (e.g., case study analysis, discussion, etc.) for each of the lessons that were posted on the content pages. Thus, we expected students to access the content pages as they were posting comments to the group pages. One reason this may not have happened is because many of the comments on the discussion board built on students' anecdotal experiences in the classroom rather than being steeped in theory discussed in course readings. Students may not have needed to access the content pages to share their experiences on the group pages. Another explanation may be that students' could have printed the material from the content pages and referred to hard copy of the course material as they posted comments on the group pages. Because we didn't ask students to explain the strategies that they used when posting comments in the group forums, we can only hypothesize about the lack of this relationship.

Students' scores on the IMI indicated that students believed that they expended high levels of effort and that they valued the course material. This was pleasing since one of the course objectives was to help students connect theoretical course material to classroom practices, suggesting valuing of course content. We hoped to accomplish this not only with course content but also with pedagogical skills, such as utilizing technology. We were also pleased with students reporting high levels of effort since there was a concern that online courses may be easier than preparing for a traditional class each week. Students have much greater autonomy in the amount of participation for an online course than a traditional course. The online course requires students to self-regulate their learning, whereas a traditional class meeting imposes weekly accountability.

During construction of the course we tried to anticipate ways in which to maximize students' perceptions of relatedness. We attempted to create learning communities by assigning each student to a group they worked with throughout the course. To facilitate working relationships with their group mates, students created homepages and participated in icebreaker activities at the beginning of the course. The instructor provided feedback to each group about their postings at the close of each lesson. Despite these attempts, students reported relatively low levels of relatedness, as measured by both our quantitative and qualitative data.

The amount of student participation (i.e., the number of times students logged on to group and class discussion boards) was unrelated to students' scores on the IMI. We had anticipated that there would be relationships between students' autonomy scores and the number of times they logged on to the course and between their relatedness scores and number of times they logged on to their group discussion page. Neither of these relationships materialized. Students' scores on the effort, value, and interest scales were correlated with all other scales on the IMI. However, students' scores on the autonomy scale, relatedness scale, and competence scale were not related to each other. Although the interest scale is often used as a general measure of intrinsic motivation, the three components (i.e., autonomy, relatedness, and competence) identified by Deci and Moller (2005) as necessary for optimal motivation were not significantly related to each other or any measure of student participation. This suggests that although students reported relatively high levels of interest/enjoyment in the course, it wasn't related to their participation in the course.

The qualitative findings suggest that the majority of graduate students enrolled in this educational psychology course enjoyed the flexibility associated with this learning environment. Many students cited benefits that included the capability to engage in class discussion and review information at any time, to be able to work from home and have no commute time to attend class, and to work at their own pace. Even though these responses are not surprising, it is disconcerting that very few students mentioned responses that related to the content, or the growth, of their learning. In fact, only two students made specific comments about the online environment providing an opportunity for reflecting on course content and allowing them to actively construct their knowledge from other students' comments. This finding is particularly interesting given that these students had completed an online unit on the topic of learning and had engaged in group discussions about the processes of learning and teaching. We hoped they would transfer their knowledge about this content, such as social construction of knowledge and group learning, when asked specific questions about how their learning was affected by participation in the online course. This raises the concern that students may enroll in online courses solely because of the flexibility that they afford with little consideration for how the online course will impact their actual learning of course content.

In regard to students' responses about how their learning was affected by taking this course in an online format rather than a traditional format, responses reveal that feedback may be the key to enhancing students' learning. Many of the students reported that the lack of immediate feedback from both peers and the professor made it difficult to learn in the online environment, although nearly 75 percent reported that they would enroll in another online course. These findings are congruent with Teng and Allen's (2005) suggestion that students need constant feedback from the course instructor in order to maintain their focus on learning within an online course. In fact, Drennan and her colleagues (2005) suggest that a blended course format may be best in promoting student learning because there is an opportunity for both face-to-face and online interaction.

Was students' facility with technology affected by their participation in an online course? At the end of the course, all but one student rated their skill with technology as competent or advanced. This suggests that several students perceived their competence in technology as increasing as a result of engaging in an online course. This is in line with findings from Teng and Allen (2005), which indicated that students' skills and confidence with integrating technology improved following the use of Blackboard in an undergraduate educational psychology course. As K-12 teachers continually face demands about incorporating technology into classroom practices, it becomes increasingly important that they learn to incorporate best practices and demonstrate facility with instructional technology.

In summary, student's motivation, as measured by their scores, on the IMI wasn't related to their participation in the online course. Although students reported high levels of effort in participating in the course and high value of course materials, they reported low levels of relatedness. Students perceived their learning to be affected by the flexibility of the course, feedback from classmates and the instructor, and the organization of the course materials. Few students focused their comments on how their cognitive process of learning was affected by participating in an online course.

There are several limitations of this study. The study is largely exploratory in nature. Thus, the descriptive data only provide us with a snapshot of the perceptions of students in this online course. Additionally, the composition of the sample, both with size and the identity of the participants limits the generalizability of the results. This course is required for students in a graduate program in education, and it was only available in an online format over the summer session. Many students enrolled in the course not by choice, but out of a necessity to complete a degree program in a timely manner. Thus, their autonomy may have been suppressed before the course even began. Finally, the way in which participation was measured was narrowly defined by using counts of student logins. This may have contributed to the lack of relationships between students' scores on the IMI and their course participation.

There are several educational implications from the present study. Instructors who are teaching online courses may use this data to guide course development. In particular, instructors should find ways to increase students' relatedness in online courses. This may include the use of live chats, voice communication tools, feedback to individual students rather than to groups, and the use of blended courses rather than solely online courses. Instructors may also consider how to better measure student participation rather than relying on frequency data of logins. For example, a qualitative analysis of students' postings to the discussion boards may provide fruitful. Finally, instructors may need to explicitly draw students' attention to how the process of learning is affected by participation in online courses and how best practices, such as the social construction of knowledge, are being modeled. The findings from this study are timely given that universities and colleges are increasingly offering more courses via distance learning in order to meet the changing needs of their students and faculty and that K–12 educators are expected to meet state and national standards involving instructional technology.

These data, combined with previous studies on distance learning, add to our knowledge about how students perceive the context of learning within online courses and in what ways these environments affect their beliefs about learning.

REFERENCES

Deci, E. L., Eghrari, H., Patrick, B. C., & Leone, D. (1994). Facilitating internalization: The self-determination theory perspective. *Journal of Personality, 62,* 119–142.

Deci, E.L., Koestner, R., & Ryan, R.M. (1999). A meta-analytic review of experiments examining the effects of extrinsic rewards on intrinsic motivation. *Psychological Bulletin,125,* 627–668.

Deci, E.L., & Moller, A.C. (2005). The concept of competence: A starting place for understanding intrinsic motivation and self-determined extrinsic motivation. In A.J. Eliot & C.S. Dweck (Eds.), *Handbook of competence and motivation* (pp. 579–597). New York: Guilford.

Deci, E.L. & Ryan, R.M. (2000). The "what" and the "why" of goal pursuits: Human needs and the self-determination of behavior. *Psychological Inquiry, 11,* 227–268.

Deci, E.L., Schwartz, A.J., Sheinman, L., & Ryan, R.M. (1981). An instrument to assess adults' orientation toward control versus autonomy with children: Reflection on intrinsic motivation and perceived competence. *Journal of Educational Psychology, 73,* 642–650.

Drennen, J., Kennedy, J., & Pisarski, A. (2005). Factors affecting student attitudes toward flexible online learning in management education. *Journal of Educational Research, 98,* 331–338.

Glesne, C. (1999). *Becoming qualitative researchers: An introduction (2ⁿᵈ ed.).* New York: Longman.

Kuo, Y., Parke, C.S., Wells, J.G. (2005). *Impact of student motivational factors on learning satisfaction in an online environment.* Paper presented at the Annual Meeting of the American Educational Research Association. Montreal, Canada.

McAuley, E., Duncan, T., & Tammen, V. V. (1987). Psychometric properties of the Intrinsic Motivation Inventory in a competitive sport setting: A confirmatory factor analysis. *Research Quarterly for Exercise and Sport, 60,* 48–58.

Ryan, R. M., Koestner, R., & Deci, E. L. (1991). Varied forms of persistence: When free-choice behavior is not intrinsically motivated. *Motivation and Emotion, 15,* 185–205.

Teng, Y., & Allen, J. (2005). Using Blackboard in an educational psychology course to increase preservice teachers' skills and confidence in technology education. *Journal of Interactive Online Learning, 3,* 1–12.

APPENDIX A. INTRINSIC MOTIVATION INVENTORY

All items were scored on a 7 point scale, with anchors at scores of 1 (not true at all), 4 (somewhat true), and 7 (very true). Some items are negatively coded.

1   I enjoyed participating in this course very much.
2   I think I am pretty good at this material.
3   I put a lot of effort into this course.
4   I believe I had some choice about participating in class.
5   I believe this course could be of some value to me.
6   I felt really distant to the people in class.
7   This course was fun to take.
8   I think I did pretty well in this course, compared to other students.
9   I didn't try very hard to do well in this course.
10 I felt like it was not my own choice to participate in class.
11 I think that participating in this course is useful.
12 I really doubt the people in this class and I would ever be friends.
13 I thought this was a boring course.
14 After working with course material for awhile, I felt pretty competent.
15 I tried very hard in this course.
16 I didn't really have a choice about participating in class.
17 I think this course is important.
18 I felt like I could really trust the people in this class.
19 This course did not hold my attention at all.
20 I am satisfied with my performance in this course.
21 It was important to me to do well in this course.
22 I felt like I had to participate in this class.
23 I would be willing to take other online courses because they have some value to me.
24 I'd like a chance to interact with these people more often.
25 I would describe this course as very interesting.
26 I was pretty skilled/knowledge in this course.
27 I didn't put much energy into this course.
28 I participated in class because I had no choice.
29 I think taking this course could help me.
30 I'd really prefer not to interact with these people in the future.
31 I thought this course was quite enjoyable.
32 This was a course in which I couldn't do very well.
33 I participated in class because I wanted to.
34 I believe taking this course could be beneficial to me.
35 I think this is an important course.
36 I don't feel like I could really trust these people.
37 While I was taking this course, I was thinking about how much I enjoyed it.
38 I participated in class because I had to.
39 It is likely that these people and I could become friends if we interacted a lot.
40 I feel close to these people.

NINETEEN

Motivation and Reading: Focus on Content Literacy

Kathleen Murphy

In the summer of 2006, I designed a summer reading day camp at Clarion University comprised of the reading department's literacy assessment and instruction practicum courses, the capstone classes in becoming a reading specialist. During the following two years, Dr. Brian Maguire and I collaborated to create a three-week summer reading camp to promote what is often lacking in our schools—a genuine enjoyment of and interest in reading. Throughout this process, I have been amazed at the fantastic job graduate students have done while working with Pre-K through grade 8 children on phonemic awareness, phonics, fluency, vocabulary, and comprehension on an individual basis as well as collaborating as literacy coaches. Some children arrived at summer reading camp as reluctant readers but left as motivated readers. This phenomenon was particularly evident in our middle grade level students. Much of this success can be attributed to the graduate students' emphasis on selecting instructional materials that related to the children's interests and were highly motivating.

Edmunds and Bauserman (2006) state that when children first enter school, they are excited and motivated to learn. However, over time, motivation begins to decrease in all academic subjects. This waning of motivation is especially vexing in reading. The decline in many children's motivation to read in both the school and home environments reaches a significantly low level in fourth grade. This is further complicated by children's growing awareness of their own performance compared to others. Both standardized testing and instructional practices that place emphasis on competition contribute to this problem. Neither of these activities speaks to children's interests. As Brophy (2005) states, "to the extent that students' motivation and related strategizing includes concerns about peer comparisons and competition, they will be distracted from an exclusive focus on learning the material and doing what they think they need to do to prepare for the test" (p. 172).

Motivation is an inherently complex topic, and we need to consider choices of reading material, readiness to engage in reading, and competence in reading as it relates to fluency and comprehension skills. As educators, we strive to come up with reading strategies as possible solutions to a lack of motivation to read. Unfortunately, the lack of intrinsic motivation to read is the root of many of the problems teachers face in the classroom. To address this issue, several studies have been conducted on the role of motivation in reading (Brophy, 2005; Edmunds & Bauserman, 2006; Smith, 1961). As Smith (1961) states, "reading is one of the few academic areas in which we demand success from all children" (p. 1), yet rarely do we accept the responsibility for successfully addressing this need. As one teacher reported to me, "If students can't read by the time they enter my fourth grade classroom, it is too late to help them learn."

This chapter specifically examines motivation as it relates to reading. Special emphasis will be placed on possible ways for teachers to motivate reluctant readers. In addition to applying techniques for traditional texts, digital media's role will be examined. As teachers face the formidable task of connecting literacy skills to students' expansive technological backgrounds, the application of digital sources will only increase, and the future implications regarding the use of digital media through reading will be explored. In addition, content reading and writing strategies will be discussed.

Motivation is defined by Brophy (2005) as "reference to the qualitative purposes or goal orientations with which students engage in learning activities" (p. 167). It is assumed that a search for understanding or the act of learning through text involves the integration of cognitive and motivational factors (Alexander & Fox, 2004). Since the 1980s, there has been a continued research focus on how motivational and cognitive factors interact and work together to influence student learning and achievement. Linnenbrink and Pintrich (2002) mention that it is recognized that students need both the cognitive skill and motivation to do well in school. Motivation can vary depending on the situation or context in the school. Instructional efforts on the part of classroom teachers and the design of classrooms and schools, according to Linnenbrink and Pintrich (2002), can have an impact in motivating students for academic achievement. Interest in general is defined as the interaction between an individual and his/her environment. Interest "reflects what most laypeople think of when they think of motivation" (Linnenbrink & Pintrich, 2002, p. 318).

The cognitive approach to teaching focuses on a learner-centered approach, taking into consideration the learner's environment, knowledge base, motivation, in addition to improving the learner's ability to process information through both cognitive and metacognitive approaches (Winstead, 2004). The teacher's role is more of a facilitator, using scaffolding strategies that are essential to learning. Teachers need to facilitate learners' strategic processing by helping students to think about thinking. Known as metacognition, reflecting on the knowledge they possess, teachers can better instruct their students in how to apply reading strategies. Metacognition is essential for students to effectively and efficiently process information (Winstead, 2004).

Being aware of the importance of motivating students to become engaged, active learners is one thing. However, finding the right or best ways is quite another matter. Based on a national survey of motivation to read, Brozo and Flynt (2008) state that the large majority of fourth graders in the United States reported that reading was not considered a favorite activity, and the students did not read frequently or for enjoyment. Even motivating students who were provided with the opportunity to select books of their own choosing was a difficult task. Concomitantly, motivating these same students to read content area texts provides an even more daunting challenge.

If content-area textbooks are unappealing or too complex and if the teaching practices fail to engage students, then these students risk an avoidance of reading or of becoming illiterate. This poses two risks according to Brozo and Flynt (2008). First, students who don't read content texts run the risk of never acquiring essential content background knowledge, which is the "most important avenue to effective learning" (Smith, 1961, p. 1). Second, because content area texts require greater effort to process and comprehend information, students need more print experiences with texts, not less. Here is the dilemma for content teachers: How can they provide students with excitement about reading in the various subject areas such as social studies, math, science, and language arts? Another consideration is that middle and high school content teachers have training and advanced knowledge in their respective content fields, yet their reading instructional skills are often insufficient for the task. For example, a social studies teacher is expected to have vast knowledge regarding historical events and a broad range of instructional techniques. Up until recently, the teaching of reading was the responsibility of reading specialists and language arts teachers. Currently, content area teachers are expected to understand reading pedagogy. Some content classroom teachers perceive this arduous responsibility to be part of their already overwhelming curriculum mandates, which come without any additional training.

GUIDELINES FOR MOTIVATING STUDENTS TO READ IN THE CONTENT CLASSROOM

ELEVATING SELF-EFFICACY

Self-efficacy is defined as "the belief and confidence that students have about their capacity to accomplish meaningful tasks and produce a desired result in academic settings" (Brozo & Flynt, 2008, p. 172). Positive self-beliefs have been linked to many benefits, including increased levels of motivation (Putman, 2009). Bandura (1997) noted that negative ability-related beliefs at times incur adverse consequences. Students who have doubts regarding their reading abilities show lower levels of intrinsic motivation, give minimal effort, and believe poor performance is related to the lack of ability. Conversely, research has revealed that students given a feeling of control over an activity display increased motivation (Putman, 2009). Once motivation is achieved, the students demonstrate greater effort and persistence in comprehending reading material that they choose. When children are given access to interesting text and in, particular, multimedia, choice has been demonstrated to be an especially effective motivator (Putman, 2009).

PROVIDING OPPORTUNITIES TO READ BOOKS PERTAINING TO STUDENTS' INTERESTS

Fisher and Ivey (2008) state that it is difficult to find studies of adolescent literacy that do not critically highlight the imperative need for engagement, in particular, the importance of using interesting reading materials. Effective instruction for all adolescents focuses on their personal interests, for example, through the use of trade books and digital texts that students read on their own. Worthy (2002) further states that educational researchers agree that schools must "deliberately and thoughtfully attract children in reading" (p. 568). The difficult question is: How do we motivate these students? As a content classroom teacher, one approach is to take the time to administer reading interest interviews. There are a vast number of animated reading surveys such as the elementary reading attitude (Garfield) survey. Motivation questionnaires can yield valuable insight into a student's literacy environment at home, whether the student enjoys reading in and out of the school setting and what other interests the student has, such as playing video games, sports, and use of computers. I have used reading interest interviews in my classroom, and the results have made significant impacts regarding supplementary materials I've selected as part of my teaching repertoire. Just taking the time and talking to a student about his/her reading interests can be extremely beneficial. If educators listen to students and attend to what they say about classroom instruction and reading materials, this can have profound effects on motivation and engagement in learning. Ultimately, the academic and affective benefits of using materials that students prefer according to their interests can enhance fluency, vocabulary, confidence, and motivation (Worthy, 2002).

SELECTION OF CONTENT TEXTBOOKS

When queried about selecting narrative texts to read, children have often commented on characteristics that affected their motivation to read. For example, Edmunds and Bauserman (2006) relate that exciting book covers, action-packed plots, and the use of humor were frequently mentioned as factors to consider in the selection process. What about content textbooks? Do students look for similar characteristics such as the text cover design? Brozo and Simpson (2003) refer to a learn-ability characteristics checklist that includes criteria such as use of graphs, tables, diagrams, use of appropriate words to signal text structure, use of boldface headings and subheadings, etc. The checklist is provided with columns for each criterion, rated as excellent, good, and poor. I have used these checklists with my secondary, college, and content reading course as part of a content textbook investigation assignment. The learn-ability characteristics checklist is very effective for reviewing content area textbooks.

DIGITAL MEDIA

Today's adolescents bring to school a rich, different set of literacy practices that are underused and often unacknowledged in the classroom (Considine, Horton, & Moorman, 2009). It is the responsibility of educators to establish a connection between the prior knowledge students have and the content they are expected to learn to be successful in and out of the school setting. Much of the different set of literacy practices involves digital media. Technology challenges our understanding as educators as to what it means to be literate. Multiple forms of literacy have emerged such as information literacy, visual literacy, media, and digital literacy. To help students succeed in the content classrooms, teachers must begin to address the complex, high-tech media that adolescents have grown up with, becoming a part of their everyday lives. This is a complicated process as educators we need to grapple with understanding the various forms of digital media and the fascinating issue of what to do with digital media in our content classrooms.

Adolescents now refer to browsing the internet as time spent reading, which can be just as beneficial as printed text. Most students prefer to go online for information as opposed to reading a book (Creel, 2007). Evidence suggests that use of blogs, wikis, instant messaging, and chat rooms appeal much more to students than the traditional schoolwork. Children who have grown up with the World Wide Web are referred to as millennials. Not only are these millennials immersed in the internet content, they are creators as well. Technology-oriented students can easily share creations such as videos, stories, artwork, and photographs in addition to designing web pages, blogs, and online journals.

Public schools have placed restrictions on the use of internet in the schools with sites such as MySpace, YouTube, and Facebook being blocked in computer labs and libraries (Considine, Horton, & Moorman, 2009). The result is a failure to establish a bridge between the classrooms educators expect student to learn in and the ever-expansive technological world these millennials reside in. Educators face an overwhelming undertaking. I was once in this technological predicament as I attempted to develop my first online class. I never envisioned as an associate professor having to teach an entirely web-based course. It has now been three years that I have been teaching web-based courses at the graduate level. I have also set a goal to learn a new way each semester of delivering content online, for example, focusing on incorporating the use of blogs and wikis. Taking small steps to become more technologically savvy is one suggestion for educators so the process does not become too daunting. Even taking time to become immersed in an ebook can offer a reader a first small step and the luxury of enjoying quiet time alone with a great story. "The future for ebooks and digital reading is tantalizingly bright right now" (Harris, 2009, p. 18).

CONTENT READING STRATEGIES

Pressure from high stakes testing currently requires content teachers to teach reading strategies to comprehend the text information. Without this emphasis on reading, students are unable to obtain the necessary content knowledge, and teachers feel ill equipped to address this situation (Boling & Evans, 2008). Content teachers' initial reaction to the idea of incorporating content literacy strategies in the classroom is that they "can't handle one more 'add-on' in my class…and can barely get through the content as it is" (Stephens & Brown, 2005, p. 8). Presently content teachers must understand a multitude of areas ranging from the context of the learning environment, content of their academic discipline, the process that students use to become successful readers, and the imperative role that reading plays in the delivery of the academic content areas (Boling & Evans, 2008). In addition, the content teacher wants to know the factors that direct interest toward reading and that attract the student to specific reading content. Effective reading, as Smith (1961) states, not only creates interest, but it can be a product of interest too.

Many students find the transition from "learning to read" to "reading to learn" problematic. They are not equipped with reading strategies that increase vocabulary acquisition and text comprehension, particularly in the content areas. Students who consciously apply prior knowledge and the use of reading strategies to clearly comprehend a content textbook tend to have a high level of reading motivation.

Content literacy is defined as using reading and writing as tools for learning content subject matter. Content literacy is based upon the constructivist theory, which explains learning in a meaning-making manner (Stephens & Brown, 2005). Reading strategies are defined by Aarnoutse and Schellings (2003) as the cognitive activities, which students can utilize before, during, and after reading a text. Reading strategies are specific procedures, which students apply intentionally and ultimately on an independent basis to understand the content information presented in a textbook.

PRE-READING STRATEGIES

Pre-reading strategies provide many benefits for content learners. One of the main points of emphasis, accomplished through pre-reading strategies, is to organize before starting to read. Pre-reading strategies allow students to activate prior knowledge or "open their minds" so that new knowledge can be shared (Stephens & Brown, 2005). Through the use of some pre-reading strategies, students feel they have a vested interest and motivation in learning various content subjects.

K-W-L CHART

A K-W-L Chart is a form of concept mapping, in which students put work or thoughts into pictures or charts. K-W-L Charts break the topic down in three areas and can expand into a fourth column as described below:

- K—What do you KNOW about the topic?
- W—What do you WANT to know about the topic?
- L—What did you LEARN about the topic?
- +—What did you STILL want to learn about the topic?

QUICK WRITE

This pre-reading strategy helps to activate prior knowledge, connecting previous learning experiences with current ones. Quick Write procedure consists of the following:

- Teacher creates a statement of questions related to the content.
- Students are given 5–7 minutes to respond to the question or statement.
- Students are encouraged to express their thoughts freely without regard to writing mechanics.
- When the time limit has expired, students share their responses with a partner and then the whole class (Stephens & Brown, 2005).

DURING-READING STRATEGIES

Reflective experiences that encourage the development of metacognition are an important component of the during-reading phase. It is essential that students use their metacognitive knowledge to monitor and adapt their learning strategies (Stephens & Brown, 2005).

EXPOSITORY TEXT PYRAMID

Procedures for a story pyramid used for narrative text can be easily modified for use with an expository text. This during-reading strategy requires students to place particular emphasis on the underlying structure of the text. The Expository Text Pyramid can be used with factual information, such as content textbooks, newspapers, and magazines. Researchers have consistently called for engaging instruction that requires the student to understand the organization of content text, ask questions while reading, regulate their learning as well as making connections to prior knowledge (Boling & Evans, 2008). The procedures for an Expository Text Pyramid include the following steps:

- First, identify the topic using one word.
- Describe the topic using two words.
- Describe the setting for this topic using three words.
- Describe a problem related to this topic using four words.
- Describe a fact or an event regarding the topic using five words.
- Describe a fact or an event regarding the topic using six words.
- Describe a fact or an event regarding the topic using seven words.
- Describe the solution to the identified problem in eight words.

X MARKS THE SPOT

With this during-reading strategy, students use a three-part coding system to help them to interact with their content textbooks. This strategy helps students avoid a passive reading of content material by providing students with specific areas of focus such as significant information, newly acquired information, and unclear information.

- The content teacher introduces and models the reading code for students to use as they read their text independently.
- The code includes three parts:
    X means, "I've found a key point."
    ! means, "I've found some interesting, new information."
    ? means, "This is confusing; I have questions about what this means."
- The content teacher specifies what students should look for in their reading (e.g., "Mark 4 key points; 2 interesting, new facts; and 3 questions you have").
- Student use the coding system as they read the text.
- Their responses can be used for class discussion (Stephens & Brown, 2005).

AFTER-READING STRATEGIES

The significance of after-reading strategies is to read, retain, and remember. After-reading strategies provide students with opportunities to act upon or apply the meanings they have constructed through reading text. Some examples are:

RAFT

- R = Role of the writer
- A = Audience to whom the message is directed
- F = Format in which the writing is completed
- T = Topic

The teacher presents RAFT and provides content examples for each of the four steps. Using brainstorming, the class generates and discusses possible responses to the four questions. The students at this point can work individually or in small groups on developing their RAFT.

An example of a RAFT I have used as an example in my classroom for social studies is:

- R = soldier
- A = family
- F = letter
- T = war

THINK-PAIR-SQUARE-SHARE

This after-reading strategy, which also can be used for pre-reading, is a simple discussion technique that can energize and heighten enthusiasm for learning in the content classroom.

- The teacher provides an issue, problem, or question and asks the students to think alone for a short period of time.
- Next, students pair up with someone to share their thoughts.
- Then pairs of students share with other pairs, forming a small group.
- The teacher monitors the brief discussion and elicits responses afterward.
- It is important that the teacher encourages students not to automatically adopt the ideas of their partners.
- These short-term discussion strategies actually work best when a diversity of perspectives is expressed (Brozo & Simpson, 2003), such as in an educational psychology class.

As our culture becomes increasingly more complex, reading plays an essential role (Smith, 1961). Content teachers need to consider the following guidelines: the role self-efficacy plays in reading, using reading surveys to determine students' interests, carefully scrutinizing content area textbooks, utilizing various forms of digital media in their classrooms, and incorporating content reading/writing strategies. Through these efforts, content teachers will play a prominent role in creating environments that make learning interesting and worthwhile, ultimately increasing motivation and engagement in content classrooms.

REFERENCES

Aarnoutse, C., & Schellings, G. (2003). Learning reading strategies by triggering reading motivation. *Educational Studies, 29*(4), 387–409.

Alexander, P. A., & Fox, E. (2004). A historical perspective on reading research and practice. *Theoretical Models and Processes of Reading, 5*, 33–68.

Bandura, A. (1997). *Self-efficacy: The exercise of control.* New York: Freeman.

Boling, C. J., & Evans, W. H. (2008). Reading success in the secondary classroom. *Preventing School Failure, 5*(2), 59–66.

Brophy, J. (2005). Goal theorists should move on from performance goals. *Educational Psychology, 40(3)*, 167–176.

Brozo, W. G., & Flynt, E. S. (2008). Motivating students to read in the content classroom: Six evidence-based principles. *The Reading Teacher, 62(2)*, 172–174.

Brozo, W. G., & Simpson, M. L. (2003). *Readers, teachers, learners: Expanding literacy across the content areas.* Upper Saddle River, NJ: Pearson Education, Inc.

Considine, D., Horton, J., & Moorman, G. (2009). Teaching and reading the millennial generation through media literacy. *Journal of Adolescent & Adult Literacy, 52* (6), 471–481.

Creel, S. L. (2007). Early adolescents' reading habits. *Young Adult Library Services* (Summer 2007), 46–49.

Edmunds, K. M., & Bauserman, K. L. (2006). What teachers can learn about reading motivation through conversations with children. *The Reading Teacher, 59*(5), 414–424.

Fisher, D., & Ivey, G. (2008). Evaluating the interventions for struggling adolescent readers. *Journal of Adolescent & Adult Literacy, 50*(3), 180–189.

Harris, C. (2009). The truth about ebooks. *School Library Journal* (June 2009), 18.

Linnenbrink, E. A., & Pintrich, P. R. (2002). Motivation as an enabler for academic success. *School Psychology Review, 31*(3), 313–327.

Putman, M. (2009). Running the race to improve self-efficacy. *Kappa Delta Pi Record* (Winter 2009), 53–57.

Smith, H. P. (1961). *Psychology in teaching reading.* Englewood Hills, CA: Questia Media America, Inc.

Stephens, E. C., & Brown, J. E. (2005). *A handbook of content literacy strategies: 125 practical reading and writing ideas.* Norwood, MA: Christopher-Gordon Publishers, Inc.

Winstead, L. (2004). Increasing academic motivation and cognition in reading, writing, and mathematics: Meaning-making strategies. *Educational Research Quarterly, 28*(2), 30–49.

Worthy, J. (2002). What makes intermediate-grade students want to read? *The Reading Teacher, 55(6)*, 568–569.

TWENTY

Encouraging the Discouraged: Students' Views for Elementary Classrooms

*Julia Ellis, Susan Fitzsimmons,
and Jan Small-McGinley*

Every teacher is faced with students whose troubled behavior challenges the teacher's sense of pedagogical responsibility. But what would the nature of that pedagogical responsibility be under such conditions, and how could one research this question in a way that retained the living voice of the child? This chapter reports on a project that attempts to address those questions. In the context of a video production project we sought to engage students with a history of behavioral difficulties in sharing their views about how elementary school teachers can transform modes of discouragement into modes of encouragement.

The students discussed many aspects of helpful teacher practices. In this paper we provide a brief overview of the ideas they related and then focus on their specific suggestions and experiences related to encouragement. In examining the encouragement or discouragement stories they shared, we saw that encouragement became linked with experiencing teachers as caring and discouragement became linked with experiencing teachers as punishing. Because punishment interfered with both a student's ability to concentrate on schoolwork and the student's relationship with the teacher, frustration, punishment, alienation and discouragement easily became a self-perpetuating cycle of despair. Students wanted teachers to recognize their limits and provide appropriate help or at least calming, encouraging words. The students prized personal recognition for accomplishment or improvement and treasured any concrete mementos of those instances of recognition. The students listened closely for genuine praise when constructive criticism was given. They needed their teachers to communicate hopefulness for them and trust in their abilities and intentions. Without knowing students well, it can be difficult for teachers to recognize students' limits or correctly discern their intentions or preoccupations. Taken together, the students' stories suggest the value of erring on the side of preserving relationships with students in the same ways one might with any other person. If relationships aren't positive, it is unlikely that they can become genuinely pedagogical.

BACKGROUND

Our work began with a concern for students whose troubled behavior can render them unwelcome in regular classrooms by the time they complete elementary school. These are students who, because of behavioral difficulties in the classroom or school, are often required to attend alternative programs at the junior high level. We wondered how such students experience the classroom in their elementary school years and what we could learn from them about circumstances in classrooms that could have a positive impact on their experiences.

Given the complexity and breadth of social and biological issues that can contribute to students' troubled behavior, teachers and school administrators may sometimes feel at a loss as to what to do or where to begin in order to make any real difference. Further, because school programs are not the apparent "cause" of troubled behavior, it may not seem that changes in school practices are likely to provide any substantial solution. Nevertheless, in this study we endeavoured to learn students' views about how classroom practices could better support students who tend to develop a history of behavioral difficulties in school. We are concerned that educators' awareness of challenging social and cultural conditions can detract attention from what schools can be doing to support students.

We met with the students in a junior high alternative program in a small urban school district and asked for volunteers to work with us to make a video program that would present their views about how elementary school teachers can be helpful to students. Each of the 10 participating students was interviewed 2, 3 or 4 times. The students also expressed their ideas in writing after the second to last interview. All of the last interviews were videotaped, 8 of the first interviews were videotaped, and all interviews were audiotaped.

All of the videotapes, transcripts, and students' writing were coded to identify topics, subtopics and recurring ideas. The professionally produced video program, *Listen Up!: Kids Talk About Good Teaching* (1997) was composed with a view to providing a representative cross-section of all of the students' ideas. Table 1 provides a categorized listing of the students' ideas. The 23-minute video is used in a number of teacher education programs to stimulate discussion about ways that teachers can be proactive regarding classroom management concerns. It is available for purchase very inexpensively. Some teachers show it on the first day of school to stimulate class discussion about how students want their classroom to work. It has been publicly broadcast several times a year on ACCESS Television in Alberta.

When the video was completed, our colleagues expressed surprise that what the students said they wanted wasn't radical at all—what they were asking for was basic. After seeing the video, parents with teenage children typically asked their sons and daughters what they wanted from teachers and were surprised to hear the same ideas our 10 alternative program students had expressed.

Table 1: Students' Views on Helpful Teaching Practices

Practices that are not helpful for misbehavior:
- blaming the wrong student
- believing a student's "enemies"
- blaming the "victim"
- yelling
- using time-out for a young child who already feels isolated and abandoned
- requiring a student to miss recess or physical education
- overusing the principal's office
- becoming angry with the whole class because of one student's behavior
- using time-out for a student who is "goofing off" (as opposed to a student who is angry and needs to calm down)
- failing to respond to misbehavior and then "blowing up" when it persists
- dwelling on or reminding students of past infractions and punishments

Practices that are helpful for misbehavior:
- "coming back after" in order to ask students why they're misbehaving and whether anything is upsetting them
- if a student has "an accident," providing comfort and assistance rather than increasing distress by blaming or accusing about behavior that may have led to the accident
- if a student has done something wrong, explaining it rather than assuming that the student knows what was wrong with the action that is being reprimanded
- if a student persists in talking, *calmly* asking the student to move to another seat
- helping students learn how to get their anger out and giving them opportunities to do so
- being a "friendly father figure" who "shows the way" rather than a stern lecturer
- helping the "class clown" learn when it is or is not appropriate to "entertain" the class (and finding ways to give him/her some attention)
- letting kids know that by succumbing to peer pressure they'll be the only ones getting into trouble and will in fact lose popularity because other kids will then not be allowed to keep company with them
- diffusing tension in the classroom (or the teacher's own negative mood) by interjecting an activity that is fun or relaxing for everybody
- using whole-class incentives such as a movie on Friday afternoon to work towards

"Winning over" is the best way to prevent misbehavior. Winning over entails:
- (a) Respecting students
- (b) Providing encouragement
- (c) Caring
- (d) Making learning enjoyable
- (e) Discerning and supporting students' learning needs
- (f) Being a nice person

(Table continued on next page)

(a) **Respecting students**
- If students feel respected they don't want to be "bad" and risk losing that respect.
- If students feel respected by the teacher, then they respect the teacher in return.
- If students don't respect the teacher, then they don't want to do anything "for" the teacher.
- Students respect a teacher who is "friendly," i.e., asks how they are, participates in games/sports with them in the gym, talks to them at recess or lunch, greets them if they see them at the mall or elsewhere.
- Students respect a teacher who trusts them and is willing to reason and compromise with them.

(b) **Providing encouragement**
- Give recognition for an individual's improvement.
- Respond positively to inept work; e.g., "Close, but good try."
- Say, "You can do it! Leave the hard question, go on and do the others, and then come back to it."
- Make a fuss over creative work; e.g., put story in newspaper, take photograph of art work or construction.
- Be careful with "constructive criticism"; i.e., make it clear that the work is already good and that if the student wants to add things, then provide some ideas.
- Help a child achieve success on a unit or upcoming test by identifying the component pieces of learning and acknowledging success in each part along the way.
- Give compliments, compliments, and more compliments.

(c) **Caring**
- means "being there for" a student.
- means noticing if a student needs help in some way and making sure he/she gets it.
- means making sure that students have a feeling of belongingness and safety in the classroom.
- means letting a student tell you his/her troubles and letting him/her know that you care and that you understand how he/she feels.

(d) **Making learning enjoyable**
- Use humor.
- Use the school grounds for math activities.
- Use games.
- Use group work.
- Focus attention with a riddle before starting class.
- Use decorative or thematic drawings or symbols on the board.
- Give choices.
- Use variety.

(Table continued on next page)

(e) **Discerning and supporting students' learning needs**

- Use a different way to explain something if a student hasn't understood the initial presentation or instruction.
- Notice a student who is struggling and provide an alternative task or set of materials.
- Support the learning needs of students whose strengths are in different modalities; e.g., visual, kinesthetic.
- Provide or obtain extra help for students who have difficulties.
- Allow time for slower students to complete a test rather than collecting it whenever most students seem to be finished.

(f) **Being a nice person**

- "A good teacher is a nice person,…easy to get along with, fun to be around."

The students' ideas about good teaching are not novel. Other researchers (e.g., Loman, 1996; Phelan, Locke Davidson & Cao, 1992) have also found that students want teachers to be friendly, respect them, relate to them as people, be caring, make them feel safe and accepted, encourage them, motivate them, make learning active and enjoyable, use variety, use group work, and have a good instructional repertoire. In undertaking this research, however, we did not expect that students would suggest practices that were previously unheard of. Instead we hoped that students' stories and voices would return the dramatic tension and significance to many good ideas that have become dry, abstract prescriptions. As Crites (1971) has argued, without the human story, abstractions can become hostile to life itself. We also hoped to gain insight into the dynamics of classroom experience from the perspectives of students with histories of behavioral difficulties in that context; that is, to learn how, in their experience, everything was connected to everything else, or how one thing led to another.

We have had some success with both expectations or research purposes. Many teachers who have viewed the video and completed evaluation forms have indicated that the video caused them to reflect and deepened their commitments to supportive practices for students. In terms of the classroom dynamics for students with troubled behavior, we have discerned how easy it can be for students who are most in need of *belonging* or of *encouragement* to get even less than their more advantaged classmates. It is obviously easier to offer approval, affirmation, and encouragement to students whose academic work is strong. It can require more care and imagination to formulate encouraging comments for students who are less adept with assigned tasks. Thus students who come to school with fewer academic skills can become increasingly discouraged where schoolwork is concerned. Similarly, if students do not experience a secure sense of belonging and affiliation in their life outside of the school, they can have particularly high needs for connection, inclusion, and belonging in the classroom itself. Sadly, their lack of emotional nurturance outside of school can lead to troubled behavior in the classroom that may in fact diminish their opportunities for experiencing inclusion there. We realize that teachers can experience disruptive students as taking up more than their fair share of the teacher's time and attention. The nature of the attention they receive, however, is often not experienced as affirming or as enhancing their feeling of belonging in the classroom.

We have revisited the students' stories of events related to belonging or encouragement to attend to the dynamics and meanings of these events for the students. Our work with the theme of belonging has been presented elsewhere (Ellis, Hart, & Small-McGinley, 1998b). A brief overview of key ideas related to belonging and encouragement has also been reported (Ellis, Hart, & Small-McGinley, 1998a). In this paper we wish to offer a more in-depth examination of students' stories of how they experienced encouragement, or in some cases, discouragement, during their elementary school years. The students' perspective can be a rich source for informing reflection on one's own teaching.

METHODOLOGY

RESEARCHING STUDENTS' PERSPECTIVES

While recognized as an expensive and labor intensive undertaking, researching students' perspectives interpretively or ethnographically is understood to be a necessary means for understanding students' behavior. It is the students' own interpretations of classroom dynamics that guide their thoughts and actions in those contexts. Because the child's viewpoint can be distinctively different from the adult's viewpoint, misreadings or misunderstandings of students and their perceptions can impede teachers' best intentions. As Sanders (1996) and others (e.g., Christensen & James, 2000; Graue & Walsh, 1998; Greig & Taylor, 1999; Mergendoller & Packer, 1985; Peevers & Secord, 1973; Shedlin, 1986; Weinstein, 1983; Whitfield, 1976) have contended, children can reliably describe events and experiences in the school setting. In sharing their perceptions, they also reveal their understandings of the events that give structure to their lives. Without access to the meanings of events for students, teachers' best efforts can be hampered by their own broad assumptions about students' perceptions.

The Pilot Study

As a field test for the methodology, an interview was conducted with a grade 7 student who was enrolled in an alternate program because of behavioral difficulties in the classroom and school. As the opening question for the interview, the student was asked what advice he would offer to teachers about how to make the classroom a supportive place. The student talked for 40 minutes with no further prompting. Then he was asked to put his ideas in writing. He was offered an honorarium if he could use his computer word processing equipment to produce 20 double-spaced pages of text on the topics he had discussed. He produced 4 double-spaced pages showing 12 paragraphs on separate coherent topics and then said he couldn't think of anything else. He was paid the whole honorarium. The analysis of the pilot study has been presented elsewhere (Ellis, 1997).

SITE AND PARTICIPANTS

A small urban school district in Alberta agreed to support our research and made it possible for us to meet with 29 students (24 boys and 5 girls) to extend our invitation for participation. All of the students were in the same junior high alternate program. Of these 29 students, 23 were interested, and 10 finally submitted all required signed consent forms. Of the 10 students, 7 were boys and 3 were girls. In age, 1 student was 13, 7 were 14, and 2 were 15.

DATA COLLECTION

Each of the participating students was interviewed 2, 3, or 4 times and completed a piece of writing to express his/her ideas. The four students who were slower to submit signed consent forms had a smaller number of interviews. Students were paid an honorarium for their writing work. All interviews were audiotaped and transcribed. One or two of each student's interviews were also videotaped. Excerpts from videotaped interviews were used in a video program entitled *Listen Up! Kids Talk About Good Teaching* (1997). All interviews and writing took place in October and November 1996.

INTERVIEWS

The interviews with students were unstructured and open-ended. At the beginning of the first interviews students were asked to reflect back on elementary school experiences and to formulate advice they would offer to student teachers or beginning teachers about how to make the classroom a more supportive place for all students. When students ran out of ideas to bring forward, they were prompted to think about memories from specific grade levels or teachers they had particularly admired or appreciated. In follow-up interviews, students were asked to clarify or expand points they made in previous interviews and to offer any further ideas that they could think of. Through this open-ended approach and through following the students' lead in terms of topics, we hoped to avoid introducing language or terminology and ideas that did not come from the students' own perspectives.

Students were asked to write about a number of their ideas after their second to last interview. All students completed four double-spaced typed pages of writing focusing on five or more of the topics that had been of high interest to them in their interviews.

DATA ANALYSIS

Through our analysis of the students' interview transcripts and writing, we sought to understand the significance of various teaching practices to these students. There were a number of teaching practices or teacher characteristics that were commonly mentioned by the large majority of the students interviewed. Examples of these were making learning fun, providing choice, providing help, using humor, using group work, respecting students, encouraging students, caring, talking to students, using incentives and consequences, and using helpful ways to respond to misbehavior. Each of the students also brought forward a unique topic that was particular to his/her own experience. Examples of these topics were: protecting a child who is being bullied or picked on; how to respond helpfully to a class clown; the importance of talking to students about peer pressure; responding to the troubled behavior of a child who is already feeling isolated and alienated; helping a student un-learn the rhythm of frustration and despair with school work; diffusing rather than exacerbating tension or anger in the class; and refraining from asking prying, sensitive questions unless the parents are there.

Although the students' ideas were not necessarily novel, their modes of expressing these ideas often served to remind us of the deep reciprocity in relations between teachers and students. For example, one student talked about the relationship between caring and respect in the following way:

> Like, if a kid thinks a teacher cares about him, it's kind of like how you treat your mother. Some of the ways you treat your mother might start rubbing off on your teacher. Without even thinking, you'd start treating the teacher with more respect. Just because the teacher was nice to you that one time would make the kid feel like there is someone who does care out there and someone who does care where you're going in life.

The majority of the ideas listed in Table 1 have been presented in the students' own voices with their own stories in the video program *Listen Up!* (1997).

For this paper, we have studied all of the students' stories that pertain to encouragement and endeavour to highlight key ideas about how these students have experienced and understood this dimension of elementary school.

Encouragement

Encouragement was a recurring theme in the general advice that students said they would offer to teachers. The following excerpts are from interviews with five of the students.

"Give compliments, compliments, and more compliments!!"

"It [encouragement] makes you want to do more work!"

"Say: 'You can do it! Just try your hardest. And if you can't get that one, go on and do the other ones and then come back and try it again.'"

"And if I didn't get it, she would say 'Close, but good try' and that made me feel like she appreciated my effort."

"Your self-esteem is like a balloon. If someone says to a kid, 'Oh, you're so stupid,' that's just like letting air out of the balloon."

During the interviews, students were asked to share any striking memories they had from earlier grades. They were also asked to recall teachers they had appreciated and any special things these people had done. Students most frequently answered these questions by either describing a "winning over activity" a teacher had used (e.g., letting each child have a turn at being "principal" of the classroom for a day; giving a picnic at the teacher's home), or by relating an event they experienced as extremely encouraging or discouraging.

The Salience of Encouragement Experiences

When students shared memories of events from elementary school years, they became particularly animated when telling stories about encouragement. If the stories were positive ones, their eyes sparkled and their faces lit up as they appeared to re-experience the uplifting quality of the remembered moment. If the stories were negative ones, the heaviness and disappointment of those experiences were palpable in the retelling.

In the following interview excerpt, a student shares a memory of discouragement from the first day of school in grade 1. Notice how at the end of the story he reminds the interviewer of another happier story about a caring teacher who remembered and recognized his August birthday on the last day of school in June. Experiencing encouragement and caring may be closely intertwined for some of these students.

> I had a Grade 1 teacher, and on the first day of Grade 1 she said to everyone, "Write a word on a piece of paper." I didn't really understand the question, so I just started picking letters off the wall and writing this big, long line. She went around to everyone else, saying, "That's really good. Look at this! Look at that!" and I think I was the only one that didn't write a word or something that made sense. I said, "Look how long my word is," and she said, "That isn't a word." It made me feel like I was stupid because I didn't know how to do any of that. That gave me a bad impression for when I got in Grade 2. When I did get that teacher that did give me a pencil and a cupcake because my birthday was in August, that was a good experience, and it prepared me for Grade 3, 4, and so on.

In the following excerpts from interviews with two students, the students share positive memories of experiencing encouragement. Interestingly, both students explicitly connect the encouraging event to feeling cared for.

> STUDENT: I wrote a 19- or 20-page story. I was only in Grade 1. It was a Halloween story, and she liked it so much and I liked it so much that she decided to publish it in the newspaper.
> INTERVIEWER: How did that make you feel?
> STUDENT: It made me feel that people actually cared and made me feel really proud of myself.
>
> ■   ■   ■
>
> INTERVIEWER: Tell me about your Grade 6 teacher.
> STUDENT: She acted like she cared about what you did regardless of the importance of it. This one time I wasn't doing very good in school and I got a 75 on a test, and she said, "That's really good." She let me take a pencil out of this pencil jar, and I thought it was really great. It made me try harder. It picked up my marks too because I thought it was just the best.

Another student told a story about how his teacher took a photograph of a structure he had built out of blocks. Thereafter, he said, he always went to get her whenever he made something out of blocks again, just to see if she'd take another photograph. As we re-visit these encouragement stories, we feel that we see glimpses of the magic of teachers who know how to let students know that they care by seizing any available opportunities to affirm and celebrate students' accomplishments. We hope that these stories will help teachers remember what they always already knew and reassure them of the value of these kinds of encouragement efforts.

PRIZE AS ARTIFACT

The students' stories about recognition that was accompanied by a concrete prize helped us to appreciate the significance of their concrete materiality. Individual recognition for accomplishment or improvement was prized by these students. The concrete materiality of the pencil or the newspaper publication of the Halloween story forever froze these moments of recognition into their memories and into their stories about their own capabilities. The possession of a concrete prize also gave them the opportunity to extend the moment of recognition. One boy spoke insistently and at length about how he preferred it if a teacher wrote a note to his parents about his improved math work during the week rather than simply telling them by telephone. He appreciated being able to present the note to the parent of his choice at the time of his choice. The note was his prize. In concretely presenting it himself, he could count on extending his moment of recognition. Another student treasured a certificate he had received for making the largest improvement in a particular subject area. The certificate remained on the refrigerator at home for three years. We wonder what can explain the potency of these "trophies." Have they been so hard to come by? Have they served as lifelines in a sea of self-doubt? Whatever their meaning, teachers can know that these forms of thoughtfulness on their part are not wasted.

CONSTRUCTIVE CRITICISM THAT ENCOURAGES

The students seemed to be incredibly sensitive detectors of either encouragement or discouragement. They were very ready and able to "teach" us how to "do" encouragement.

One of the students in our study spoke at length about how he experienced constructive criticism as detrimental rather than helpful. He said that if a teacher used constructive criticism all the time a student would feel that there was always one more thing to improve on, that his/her work would never be good enough. He gave the following example in one of his interviews:

STUDENT: A student gets 75% on a language arts assignment, and the teacher comes along and says, "You know, this is not a bad mark, but if you just sound out your words a bit better, you could get 80s on it. You just have to try harder." I took that as a put-down. She thinks I could do better; she's not happy with what I did.

INTERVIEWER: What would you suggest instead?

STUDENT: She could have said, "This 75% is really good!" She may not have thought it was really good, but she could have said that just to keep on good terms with me. She could have said, "Do you want me to give you a secret on how you can do better on tests?" And I'd say, "Yeah," and she'd say, "You know those long words. Sound them out; it might help you a lot. That 75% was really good."

Another student explained the art of constructive criticism metaphorically.

It's like when someone builds a sand castle. Another person might come along and say "You could put a door there." Your response might be "Well, yeah" or you might just knock the whole thing down and say "Build it yourself." Instead the person could say "That's a really great sand castle. Do you want to add something to it?"

The first student above used the phrase "to keep on good terms with me." Perhaps the students are reminding us of the importance of preserving relationships. In our relationships with loved ones, do we not endeavour to exercise tact or discretion when we consider offering constructive criticism? At the very least, the students remind us of the difficult work of teachers who must help students progress while also supporting their sense of accomplishment and capability.

Establishing the Cycle of Discouragement

Students' difficulties with schoolwork, coupled with their behavioral difficulties, sometimes meant that punishment became implicated in discouraging experiences and failed relationships with teachers. Everything became connected to everything else, eventually creating a "knee-jerk" response of high frustration whenever new, difficult tasks were presented.

In the following interview excerpt, a student asks that teachers recognize a child's limits, provide help that may be needed, and if that's not feasible, leave the child with the encouraging words, "That's better. Try a bit more."

STUDENT: I'm a really messy writer because I'm dyslexic, and my handwriting is really messy. My l's didn't look good enough, and she would just go, "Do them right!" and I couldn't do them right. And then she would go, "Go! Go sit down and do it again!"

INTERVIEWER: So that's some advice you'd give student teachers—to encourage students?

STUDENT: Yeah, not hassle the students; encourage them so they will feel better about what they are doing.

INTERVIEWER: Okay, what do you mean by *hassle?*

STUDENT: So instead of "Do this! Make those letters!" I think, Why should I try? That's a hassle right there. That's just like pushing the student too hard to do something that they might take a bit longer to learn how. Instead of that I would try to make the student feel better about what they are doing. You know, say, "That's better. Try a bit more." Encourage them so they feel better about what they are doing, so they will get it done right. Instead of keeping them in for recess or lunch hour because they didn't get it right, sit down with them some other time and let them work, and help them get it right.

Some of the students in this study come to school already upset by their social or biological conditions. They can be easily agitated by negative experiences. As much as other students, and perhaps more than most students, they welcome a calm, patient, encouraging manner. The difficulties they may exhibit with schoolwork or behavior can very likely make teachers feel frustrated and impatient. The students remind us to consider whether our words and our tone can be experienced as encouraging.

The following is a brief excerpt from the above student's lengthy discussion about how he began to experience pressure and frustration in early elementary grades:

INTERVIEWER: Can you give me an example of a teacher hassling a student?

STUDENT: Well, like, the student is sitting in class and does his work, talks to someone, with the teacher being the authority figure, that would be like, "You get down and you do your work, and after, for talking, you can do this and this and this!" Then the student goes back to their work and looks at the question 6 times 7, and instead of getting, like, 42, right off the bat they will be, "Uh, ah, what about the work I have to do after school? What about this? Oh, no! Oh, no!"

The student's discussion of this example and related experiences extended over several pages of transcripts. He talked to the interviewer about how even simple "consequences" for small infractions like talking can be emotionally upsetting and preoccupying for a young child who may already have "problems from home" on his mind. So, for example, if he were told of a pending consequence such as staying in after school and missing play with friends, he would become preoccupied with that and then, in his words, "freeze up" and not be able to figure out his school work. This would be followed by the teacher asking him why he was unable to do his work. This created more frustration because he knew it would be confrontational to tell the teacher the real reason.

Some punishments were also experienced as humiliating and created a feeling of rage. For example, for throwing things into the wastepaper basket from a distance, he was made to not only stay in at recess but also to vacuum the entire classroom floor while the teacher and custodian watched. His stories gave meaning to a simple statement by another one of the students who said that punishment wasn't a good idea and that, yes, "We can learn from it, but it doesn't help us out much." It seems that for students who are already upset about one thing or another, punishment gives them even more to be upset about, distracts them from school work, and distances them from the teacher who is the only present adult who might have been "helpful" in some way. Even the punishment of being yelled at by the teacher in front of the class was a strong one. When asked how that feels, one student replied that "it makes you feel like everyone else in the class is better than you." Just as encouragement was associated with caring on the part of the teacher, discouragement seemed to be connected to a punishing attitude on the part of the teacher.

Hope and Re-establishing Encouragement

The Latin root word for courage is *cor,* meaning heart. If one considers the word *encourage,* what would it mean to *en-hearten* a student? Would it mean to give love? Would it mean to give life force? Would it mean to give hope? In the following interview excerpt, a student offers contrasting stories of ways that teachers can dis-hearten or en-hearten students:

> STUDENT: Well, like at some schools it is harder to be there with teachers that pressure you. Like this one teacher, when you were having problems with your work he'd say, "If you don't get this right you ain't going to pass."
>
> INTERVIEWER: How did that make you feel?
>
> STUDENT: Well, that made me feel that I wasn't going to pass no matter what I did. It made me feel that I wasn't going anywhere. And other teachers encourage students, and they make you feel that you have a really, really good chance to pass, which makes the students feel better. Teachers should have a happy attitude.

Can teachers, being fearful about their students' likelihood of success, communicate that fear, discouragement, or despair to the students? This story suggests that in order to be hopeful themselves, students draw strength, inspiration, courage, and serenity from the teacher's "happy attitude." A teacher who is en-heartening or encouraging is one who communicates hopefulness and a sense of possibility in their interactions with students. If students are to have courage and confidence, they have to see that teachers are at least trying to have confidence in them. As one of our students said, "Encouragement is like a railroad track. It keeps you going."

The student discussed in the section above, "Establishing the Cycle of Discouragement," explained how some teachers were able to support him in breaking out of that cycle.

STUDENT: Teachers like Mr. _____ made me feel like I had the choice to do my work. Like, if I didn't want to do it, I was allowed to take a little time out and go to a little table alone to re-gather my thoughts until I was ready to do it.

INTERVIEWER: So you mean he gave you a break to go re-gather your thoughts. What do you mean?

STUDENT: Like, if I wasn't getting something right and I was getting frustrated about it, he let me go sit in a corner and read a book, put down the book, and then think about what I was just doing, to figure it out when I was not under pressure. When I have all that done I come back to the class. That made it a lot easier because I wouldn't want to sit there for the whole class, getting frustrated. So he gave me five minutes to go figure it out. He didn't pressure me. That makes people feel more mature and more secure about themselves. And they actually feel that they can do it if they set their mind to it. Some students like to do it that way because they know they can get it done. Like, me, I like taking my time and think things out. With the right teachers and the right principals, I can do that.

One of our students said, "You have to trust students; and even if you don't, you have to try." In this story of the student being allowed or invited to take a break to "re-gather his thoughts," we see an example of how teachers can demonstrate trust and communicate confidence in students' abilities.

CLOSING REFLECTIONS

As we searched for a theoretical framework that could most adequately account for or hold together the ideas students had expressed, we found Eric Fromm's (1956) model of positive relationships to be most satisfying and parsimonious. In this model, Fromm identifies *caring, responsibility, respect,* and *knowledge* as four elements that are common to positive relationships. *Caring* entails concern for the life and growth of the person in the relationship. *Responsibility* means being ready to act to meet the needs, expressed or unexpressed, of another human being. *Respect* entails having the ability to see an individual as s/he is and allowing that person to develop without exploitation. *Knowledge* includes not a superficial awareness but genuine understanding of the other's feelings, even if they are not readily apparent.

We expect that elementary school teachers choose their profession because of their *caring,* that is, their willingness to be concerned for the life and growth of students in their classrooms. However, their ability to exercise *respect* and *responsibility,* that is, to recognize a child's limits and to take appropriate action to meet a child's needs, depends on their *knowledge* of the child. *Knowledge,* in Fromm's sense, means being able to read a child's feelings, intentions, and responses. If a child is mis-read, actions which may be intended as helpful can work at cross-purposes.

Getting to know a student can sometimes require more than listening to the stories a student comes forward to share. A number of student teachers and teachers have used a particular interview schedule to invite students to discuss a variety of topics that are most salient for them. This interview schedule and procedures for its use have been reported in previous articles and a book chapter (Ellis, 1992; Ellis 1994; Ellis 1998). Many student teachers using this interview activity often found that simply conducting the interview was enough to transform a previously "difficult" student into a cooperative one. The following is an excerpt from a student teacher's written reflection on the interview experience.

> Finally, the interview served to encourage me to think that I am able to develop the same close, warm rapport with Junior [grades 4, 5, and 6] boys as with girls—and indeed of the value of the interview as a tool for building trust and friendship. Ryan was tremendously supportive following the interview, and volunteered continually for demonstrations, solo musical performances, and generally anything in which I sought input or assistance from the class. He also raised his hand to answer any question I ever posed—all of which reinforced the notion that elementary-aged children typically enjoy only with very few adults a relationship that allows them to talk openly and share concerns.

Although a primary benefit of the interview activity is the relationship it cultivates, the topics the students discuss also alert teachers to their preoccupations, motivations, fears, hopes, and loves. Increased awareness of the student's perspective enables the teacher to support connections between the student's story and the classroom story.

We are also aware that the pressures many teachers may experience to have their "performance" and "achievement" as teachers meet certain standards can discourage them from providing the kinds of support some of their students may need. A number of the students in our study said that they often needed time to calm down or time to just talk to other students, and that a class in which everyone had to be "on-task" at all times was not a good one for them. One of the boys talked about the value of group work as providing a space for "talking about feelings," which he said isn't feasible during the physical activity of recess. Teachers need more space, not less, to accommodate the growth needs of all students in their classrooms.

Teachers in our graduate courses have also reported that the percentage of high needs students in their classes has increased dramatically during the last 10 years. Recognizing that teachers cannot individually provide all the support that so many students need, we turned our research efforts in the direction of school-based mentorship programs, peer support and student leadership programs. These are programs that provide students with opportunities for attachments with adult mentors, contribute to a climate of caring, or empower students to care. In our research with such programs we have endeavored to

- work with schools to collaboratively develop and research mentorship programs for students in the early school years.
- locate and study other existing mentorship programs spanning the years of K-12.
- locate and study peer support programs spanning the years of K-12.
- locate and study student leadership program.

Our intent was not to develop a comprehensive list of existing programs in any specific geographical area, but rather to conduct case studies of a wide range of programs with a view to learning how they work and what their benefits are. We collected data on each of the programs through whatever means were feasible including: audiotaped and videotaped interviews with program coordinators, students, mentors, parents; students' written narrative reports; and program documents. Because most of the programs we found and studied had been in operation for five to seven years, the program coordinators were well informed about program benefits and the practicalities of operating such programs successfully.

In the mentorship programs that we helped to develop, we conducted three intensive studies on the following questions:

- In a short-term mentorship program (8–10 weeks) with minimal training and structure for mentors, do the mentors and children achieve mutually satisfying relationships and are the mentors effective in providing academic support to the children?
- How does the mentor's pedagogy work? What informs or guides the mentor's instructional planning and decision-making? To what extent is the mentor's pedagogy shaped by the child or the child's responses?
- How do the mentors and children develop their relationships? What are the dynamics or key components of non-related adults cultivating relationships with young children in one-hour per week mentorship sessions over an 8- to 10-week period?

These research questions were considered important given that the schedules of schools and available mentors make short-term programs most feasible. Further, there is little research available on mentorship programs for young children and little in-depth qualitative research on mentorship programs for older students. The findings from these three studies were expected to clarify the potential value of such programs and the processes for their successful implementation. An understanding of the dynamics of mentoring young children would be useful to program developers who must make many decisions about the structure, resources, and support for such programs. The results of the completed research have been made available through several publications (Alberta Teachers' Association, 1999; Ellis & Small-McGinley, 1998a; Ellis & Small-McGinley, 1998b; Ellis & Small-McGinley, 1999a; Ellis & Small-McGinley, 1999b; Ellis, Small-McGinley & Hart, 1998; Ellis, Small-McGinley, & De Fabrizio 1999; Ellis, Small-McGinley, & De Fabrizio, in press).

This paper has focused on students' views about how elementary school teachers encourage achievement. Their stories revealed how difficult it was for them to separate discussions about encouragement from discussions about the nature of their relationships with teachers. To support their growth, to give them strength and courage, students need affirmation and encouragement from adults who are oriented to them in a positive way. The students have given many examples of how teachers accomplish this. With so many students needing school to be their primary site for experiencing belonging and encouragement, it makes sense for teachers to be encouraged to give emphasis to their relationships with students. It also makes sense for schools to coordinate programs such as mentorship, peer support, and student leadership to provide further support for the growth of all students in the school.

In closing we wish to express our own tribute to the many teachers who have taken time to listen to the stories of individual students and who have used their art, heart, and imagination to help students find supportive places in their classrooms. We also thank the students who participated in this research for their trust and their efforts to help us understand their experience.

REFERENCES

Alberta Teachers' Association, Edmonton. (1999). *Volunteer Mentorship Programs.* Videotape. Website for ATA's Safe and Caring Schools Project: http://www.teachers.ab.ca/projects/safe.html

Christensen, P. & James, A. (Eds.) (2000). *Research with children: Perspectives and practices.* New York: Falmer Press.

Crites, S. (1971). The narrative quality of experience. *Journal of the American Academy of Religion, 39*(3), 291–311.

Ellis, J. L. (1992). Teachers undertaking narrative inquiry with children. *Analytic Teaching, 12*(2), 9–18.

Ellis, J. L. (1994). Narrative inquiry with children: A generative form of preservice teacher research. *International Journal for Qualitative Studies in Education, 7* (4), 367–380.

Ellis, J. (1997). What a seriously at-risk 12-year-old would really like to say to teachers about classroom management. *Education Canada, 37*(2), 17–21.

Ellis, J. (1998). Narrative Inquiries with Children and Youth. In J. Ellis (ed.) *Teaching from Understanding: Teacher as Interpretive Inquirer* (pp. 33–56). New York: Garland.

Ellis, J., Hart, S., & Small-McGinley, J. (1998a). Classroom management: The views of "difficult" students. *The Canadian Association of Principals' Journal, 8*(1), 39–41.

Ellis, J., Hart, S., & Small-McGinley, J. (1998b). "Difficult" students' perspectives on belonging and inclusion in the classroom. *Reclaiming Children and Youth: Journal of Emotional and Behavioral Problems, 7*(3), 142–146.

Ellis, J. & Small-McGinley, J. (1998a). *Peer Support and Student Leadership Programs.* Edmonton: Alberta Teachers' Association.

Ellis, J., & Small-McGinley, J. (1998b). *Volunteer Mentorship programs K-12.* Edmonton, AB: Alberta Teachers' Association.

Ellis, J., & Small-McGinley, J. (1999a). Students' perspectives on student leadership programs. *Canadian Association of Principals' Journal, 8*(2), 35–37.

Ellis, J. & Small-McGinley, J. (1999b). *Volunteer Mentorship Programs: A Practical Handbook.* Edmonton: Alberta Teachers' Association.

Ellis, J., Small-McGinley, J., & Hart, S. (1998). Mentor-supported Literacy Programs in Elementary Schools. *Alberta Journal of Educational Research, 44*(2), 149–162.

Ellis, J., Small-McGinley, J. & De Fabrizio, L. (1999). "It's So Great to Have an Adult Friend…": A Mentorship Program for At-Risk Youth. *Reaching Today's Youth: The Community Circle of Caring Journal,* August, 46–50.

Ellis, J., Small-McGinley, J. & De Fabrizio, L. (in press). *Caring for Kids in Communities: Using Mentorship, Peer Support, and Student Leadership Programs in Schools.* New York: Peter Lang Publishing.

Fromm, E. (1956). *The art of loving.* Toronto: Bantam Books.

Graue, M.E. & Walsh, D.J. (1998). *Studying children in context: Theories, methods and ethics.* Thousand Oaks, CA: Sage Publications.

Greig, A. & Taylor, J. (1999). *Doing research with children.* Thousand Oaks, CA: Sage Publications.

Listen up! Kids talk about good teaching. (1997). Videotape. Calgary, AB: Mighty Motion Pictures. Telephone: 800–471–5628. Fax: 403–439–4051

Loman, J. (1996). Characteristics of exemplary teachers. *New Directions for Teaching and Learning. No. 65,* Spring, 33–40.

Mergendollar, J.R. & Packer, M.J. (1985). Seventh graders' conceptions of teachers: An interpretive analysis. *The Elementary School Journal, 85,* 581–600.

Peevers, B.H. & Secord, P.F. (1973). Developmental changes in attribution of descriptive concepts to persons. *Journal of Personality and Social Psychology, 27,* 120–128.

Phelan, P., Locke Davidson, A. & Cao, H.T. (1992). Speaking up: Students' perspectives on school. *Phi Delta Kappan, 73*(9), May, 695–704.

Sanders, S. W. (1996). Children's physical education experiences: Their interpretations can help teachers. *JOPERD, 67*(3), 51-56.

Shedlin, A. (1986). 487 sixth graders can't be wrong. *Principal, 6,* 53.

Weinstein, R.S. (1983). Student perceptions of schooling. *The Elementary School Journal, 28,* 286–312.

Whitfield, T. (1976). How students perceive teachers. *Theory into Practice, 15,* 347–351.

TWENTY-ONE

Using Student Interviews to Understand Theories of Motivation

Laurie B. Hanich

This chapter describes the construction and development of a course assignment that uses student interviews as an instructional tool to bridge the gap between theory and practice in a graduate educational psychology course. The first part of the chapter describes the student interview assignment used to examine theories of motivation. The second part of the chapter focuses on evaluation tools used to measure students' motivation for the task and their beliefs about their learning. Participants included 25 graduate students enrolled in an Advanced Educational Psychology course in the spring semester. After completing the student interview assignment, participants completed the interest/enjoyment and value scale of the Intrinsic Motivation Inventory (Deci & Ryan, 2000). Additionally, participants responded to several open-ended questionnaire items on how their learning was affected by completing the student interview assignment. Quantitative and qualitative data reveal that participants reported high levels of both interest and value for completing the assignment and perceived their learning as affected in positive ways.

Too often, students consider course content as either "book knowledge" or "common sense," and have difficulty seeing the application of educational psychology theories to the practices of teaching and learning. To translate evidence-based psychological principles into practice, scholars in this field have called for faculty to use instructional strategies and create classroom environments that model these same psychological principles (Anderson, Blumenfeld, Pintrich, Clark, Marx, & Peterson, 2005; Deemer & Hanich, 2004) The construction and development of course assignments such as student interviews is one instructional practice I have used to bridge the gap between theory and practice in educational psychology for the pre-service and in-service teachers who take my graduate-level educational psychology course at Millersville University of Pennsylvania.

Although interviews could be used to teach such diverse topics as learning and cognition, development, diversity, management, and assessment, in this assignment, they are used to examine principles of motivation. I have found that many pre-service teachers have difficulty integrating and applying motivational principles that are well established in the research literature (Anderman & Leake, 2006), and in-service teachers often resort to quick fixes for motivational problems. Conducting an interview with a K-12 student on their achievement-related behaviors and motivation provides a context to which my graduate students are able to apply classroom principles of motivation that are being learned in our course. In the following sections of this chapter I describe the motivation assignment and assessment measure that I used to evaluate teachers' perceptions of the effectiveness of the assignment.

THE MOTIVATION INTERVIEW ASSIGNMENT

After completing a course unit on motivation, pre-service and in-service teachers are given an assignment that requires them to conduct interviews with K-12 students, in order to give them an up-close look at students' perspectives on achievement motivation. For the assignment, each teacher must select a minimum of two K-12 students to interview. Each interview is conducted individually, and the questions may differ across the protocols. Teachers may interview primary or secondary students, but I encourage them to work with children above third grade since children younger than this often have difficulty providing specific, detailed responses.

In order to maximize teachers' self-determination (see Deci & Moller, 2005, for a review), as much autonomy as possible is provided in the assignment. Teachers are asked to develop their own protocols, or sets of questions, based on readings from the text or class discussions. Prior to conducting their interviews, teachers are provided with instruction on basic principles for conducting interviews, and as a group we discuss how to develop fruitful questions (e.g., ask open-ended questions, avoid yes/no) and ways to probe students' responses for more detail. Issues regarding informed consent, confidentiality, and anonymity are also discussed. Because the assignment is used for instructional rather than research purposes, teachers do not have to submit proposals to Millersville's Institutional Review Board.

In their interview protocols, some teachers choose to focus on specific content, formulating their questions around one or more specific topics (e.g., use of rewards, goal orientation), while others choose to ask broad questions about students' motivational experiences in school. Teachers are asked to tape-record their interviews and to provide a written transcript of each interview as well.

After completing and transcribing their interviews, teachers write a short paper that summarizes what they have learned from their interviews. There is no predetermined page length for this assignment; rather they are expected to discuss thoroughly how the content they have garnered from their student interviews is related to principles of achievement motivation discussed in class and in their assigned readings. In the paper, they are also expected to provide descriptive information about the students selected for the interviews as well as quotes from students to illustrate specific motivational principles they discuss.

Finally, teachers are also responsible for developing a way to evaluate this assignment. Using a combination of small group work and full class discussions, the class develops a rubric that is used to evaluate their papers. Using a group-developed rubric in this way not only allows pre-service and in-service teachers to self-regulate their own learning, but also introduces the class to principles of assessment, the next unit covered in the course.

ASSESSING THE EFFECTIVENESS OF THE ASSIGNMENT

To determine whether teachers' perceive the motivation interview assignment as an effective instructional tool, teachers completed a paper-and-pencil survey regarding their beliefs about the assignment during the last week of the spring semester. All 25 of the students enrolled in the course that term participated in the study (15 females; 10 males). Sixteen participants were classroom teachers (i.e., in-service teachers) and nine were students seeking initial certification (pre-service teachers and students enrolled in the post-baccalaureate program). Students' degree programs included elementary education, secondary education, special education, nursing, and sports management.

To assess their motivation for the interview assignment, participants completed the interest/enjoyment scale and the value/usefulness scale of the Intrinsic Motivation Inventory (IMI) (Deci & Ryan, 2000). Each scale is composed of 7 Likertscale items, and participants' scored each item between 1 (not at all true) to 7 (very true). The IMI has been used in several empirical studies to assess students' subjective experiences in targeted activities (Deci, Eghrari, Patrick, & Leone, 1994; Ryan, Koestner & Deci, 1991) and has well-established reliability and validity (McAuley, Duncan, & Tammen, 1987). For this study, the IMI was modified to specifically address students' motivation for completing the motivation interview assignment.

In addition to the IMI, students also responded to several instructor-designed open-ended items: 1) What did you like most about the motivation interview assignment? 2) What did you like least about the motivation interview assignment? 3) How did the motivation interview assignment help you connect theories of motivation to practice? and 4) How was your own motivation for learning educational psychology affected by this assignment?

RESULTS

Quantitative Data

I was interested to see if there were differences between the scores of pre-service and in-service teachers on these scales. As displayed in Table 1, there appeared to be very little difference between the groups on either scale, and an analysis of variance (ANOVA) found no significant difference between the group means on either scale ($F(1, 23) = 0.09$, $p > 0.05$ and $F(1, 23) = 0.98$, $p > 0.05$). Thus, it seems that both groups reported similar interest/enjoyment and value related to this assignment.

Table 1: Participants' Mean Scores on the Interest and Value Scales of the Intrinsic Motivation Inventory.

	N	INTEREST SCALE	VALUE SCALE
In-service teachers	16	5.90	6.38
		(0.85)	(0.60)
Pre-service teachers	9	6.20	6.44
		(0.047)	(0.45)

Note: Standard deviations shown in parentheses. Possible scores range from 1 (low) to 7 (high).

Participants' means scores, by item, on the IMI are displayed in Table 1. Overall, scores appeared slightly higher on the value scale than on the interest/enjoyment scale of the modified IMI. There also was less variability in participant's scores for the value scale than for the interest/enjoyment scale, with the scores of many items on the value scale approaching ceiling level (i.e., scores of 7).

Table 1 (continued): Participants' Mean Scores, by Item, on the Intrinsic Motivation Inventory

INTEREST SCALE		MEAN ST.	DEV.
1.	I enjoyed the motivation assignment.	6.12	0.78
2.	The assignment was fun to do.	6.04	0.98
3.	I thought the assignment was boring.	1.36	0.57
4.	The assignment did not hold my attention at all.	1.28	0.46
5.	I would describe the assignment as very interesting.	6.00	1.00
6.	I thought the assignment was enjoyable.	6.04	1.02
7.	While I was completing the assignment, I was thinking about how much I enjoyed it.	4.52	1.58
VALUE SCALE			
1.	I believe the assignment was of some value to me.	6.40	0.65
2.	I think that completing the assignment was useful for understanding motivation.	6.48	0.65
3.	I think the assignment was important to do because it helped connect theory to practice.	6.68	0.47
4.	I would be willing to do this type of assignment again because it has some value to me.	6.16	0.94
5.	I think completing the assignment could help me learn to motivate students.	6.24	0.87
6.	I believe completing the assignment was beneficial to me.	6.48	0.59
7.	I think this was an important assignment.	6.36	0.70

Note: Possible scores range from 1 (strongly disagree) to 7 (strongly agree).

Q

a:
e:
(1
n
w
I
th
p
ri
u
n
at
te
m

ti
cc
th
ac

he
nu
th
en
bu

ter
in
the
to
it e
ha
on
ho

to
Sp
the
in
dai

ategorizing, and theme identification, an
estion indicated that the majority of teach-
ng the perspectives of K-12 students. Most
to see what one of my students feels about
"Hearing a child's perspective about what
wards and punishments, was enlightening."
assignment because it helped them connect
ked the analysis part, connecting theory to
said, "I liked being able to relate the theo-
ife scenario; it allowed me to gain a deeper
hers reported that they liked the authentic
ked that it was a real example. We can read
ared to talking to a real student." Another
bout different approaches I could use with
ner for me."

they liked least about the assignment, par-
of transcribing the interview. Examples of
ing behind it, it was tedious to transcribe
tim took forever." However, several also
quirement:

ibing the conversation. Actually, this aspect
o I could then write a finished report." A
estion or indicated that there was nothing
/25) participants indicated that they didn't
, one teacher said, "I enjoyed interviewing,
l-written paper."

ted that this assignment did help them bet-
lied to understanding students' motivation
mented on the "real world application" of
examples of the theories rather than trying
read about sort of 'came to life.' It made
/25) also commented that the assignment
ctices or experiences: "It helped me reflect
bout what I say to my students more and

the assignment on their own motivation
teachers' desire to increase their learning.
cally motivated by the assignment and by
sponses included, "When I saw the value
h as I could and then implement it into my
tivated the student and learn more about

how they felt about practices that teachers use"; and, "I would like to learn more and apply what I have learned." One teacher referred to an increase in her self-efficacy, saying, "It made me feel more confident because my one concern in the beginning of the course was my lack of familiarity with psychology. This assignment helped me to relate to the material and put it in a context which I was able to understand." Another teacher referred to misconceptions that he had about how to motivate his own students, noting, "I saw contradictions in my thinking with the readings and with what the students said." Finally, one participant valued the depth this assignment brought to his learning of the content. Specifically, he noted, "The assignment was very insightful and beneficial. In a perfect world I would have loved to do an assignment like this for each topic we covered. I think I took the most information from this class in motivation, and I believe this is because the assignment forced me to dig deep through the information on motivation."

CONCLUSION

The above findings from survey data and open-ended responses suggest that in-service and pre-service teachers reported high levels of both interest and value for completing the motivation interview assignment. Interestingly, there were no differences between pre-service and in-service teachers' reported value or interest/enjoyment in the assignment. The motivation interview assignment encompasses all of the elements discussed earlier by Anderson and her colleagues (1995). Specifically, the qualitative responses suggest that teachers perceived this assignment to be an effective tool for helping them connect theories of motivation to classroom and life experiences of K-12 students.

REFERENCES

Anderman, L. H., & Leake, V.S. (2006). The ABC's of motivation: An alternative framework for teaching pre-service teachers about motivation. *The Clearing House, 78,* 192–196.

Anderson, L. M., Blumenfeld, P., Pintrich, P. H., Clark, C. M., Marx, R. W., & Peterson, P. (2005). Educational psychology for teachers: Rethinking our courses, rethinking our roles. *Educational Psychologist, 30,* 143–157.

Deci, E. L., Eghrari, H., Patrick, B. C., & Leone, D. (1994). Facilitating internalization: The selfdetermination theory perspective. *Journal of Personality, 62,* 119–142.

Deci, E. L., & Moller, A. C. (2005). The concept of competence: A starting place for understanding intrinsic motivation and self-determined extrinsic motivation. In A. J. Eliot & C. S. Dweck (Eds.), *Handbook of competence and motivation* (pp. 579–597). New York: Guilford.

Deci, E. L., & Ryan, R. M. (2000). The "what" and "why" of goal pursuits: Human needs and the self-determination of behavior. *Psychological Inquiry, 11,* 227–268.

Deemer, S., & Hanich, L.B. (2004). *Hitting the TARGET: Using Achievement Goal Theory to Translate Evidence-Based Principles into Practice.* Paper presented at the annual meeting of the American Education Research Association, San Diego, CA.

McAuley, E., Duncan, T., & Tammen, V. V. (1987). Psychometric properties of the Intrinsic Motivation Inventory in a competitive sport setting: A confirmatory factor analysis. *Research Quarterly for Exercise and Sport, 60,* 48–58.

Ryan, R. M., Koestner, R., & Deci, E. L. (1991).Varied forms of persistence: When free-choice behavior is not intrinsically motivated. *Motivation and Emotion, 15,* 185–205.

Complex Ecologies for Educational Psychology

TWENTY-TWO

The Centrality of Culture to the Scientific Study of Learning and Development: How an Ecological Framework in Educational Research Facilitates Civic Responsibility

Carol D. Lee

The topic of this article is one with which I have been wrestling for many years. The genesis of my attention to the role of culture in learning dates back to the late 1960s and early 1970s at the beginning of the Black Power and Black Arts Movements (Hughes, 1926; Karenga, 1993; Madhubuti, 1991, 1996; Neal, 1989). This was a period when many people of African descent in the United States actively aligned with their African heritage not only as a source of group pride but, equally important, as a catalyst for political organizing and institution building. Across the country young people like me engaged in bold acts of institution building. In Chicago, we developed Third World Press, which is today more than 40 years old and the oldest continuous Black publishing company in the United States; New Concept School, an independent African-centered school that is now nearly 40 years old and has expanded into three African-centered charter schools that we have developed in Chicago over the last decade; and the Institute of Positive Education, an organization that focuses on community-based issues (Lee, 1992). Much to my mother's dismay, in 1974 I quit my job at Kennedy-King College in Chicago to work with the emerging Third World Press, which then shared a storefront with the New Concept School, the forerunner of the Betty Shabazz International Charter Schools. It was during that period that I met the man who would become my husband, writer and publisher Haki R. Madhubuti. My mother said she knew this man had put the hoodoo on me, and she asked her minister to help her find a psychiatrist to help me. After directing and teaching in the New Concept School for 15 years, I decided to enter a doctoral program at the University of Chicago. That transition shifted my focus from a practice-oriented examination of the cultural basis of learning to theorizing the relationship between culture and learning in terms of the underlying mechanisms that help to explain how culture operates both to facilitate and to constrain learning.

As I entered graduate school and eventually the professoriate with this long-standing interest in the role of culture, it became abundantly clear that the academy operated in a kind of intellectual apartheid. From the 1960s forward, there was a growing shift from seeing cultural differences as deficits to a more liberal, multicultural view of such differences, often as distinct phenomena that could serve as positive resources for learning (Ginsburg, 1972). There was also during this period an emerging attention to cross-cultural learning and development in psychology. Now classic studies by Michael Cole (Cole, Gay, Glick, & Sharp, 1971), Sylvia Scribner (1984; Scribner & Cole, 1981), Jean Lave (1977), Barbara Rogoff (Rogoff & Gauvain, 1984), Patricia Greenfield (Greenfield & Childs, 1977), Geoffrey Saxe (1981), and others moved past deficit theories to document the complexity of reasoning embedded in everyday practices. These studies took place outside Europe and middle-class America—in Liberia, Mexico, Brazil, and Guatemala, as well as in blue-collar workplaces in the United States. This is also the period in which Western scholars, particularly in the United States, discovered the writings of Russian psychologist and socialist Lev Vygotsky (1978, 1981, 1987), who made a compelling case about the role of social interactions and culturally organized activity as the cauldron of individual development.

The field of Black psychology was also emerging in the United States. Black psychologists countered the prevailing deficit-oriented psychological theories about Black development (Boykin, 1979; Jones, 1972). The field of Black psychology offered at least two important contributions to our evolving understanding of human learning and development. These contributions can be seen in research conducted by scholars such as Asa Hilliard (1998), A. Wade Boykin (1979), Wade Nobles (1974), Diana Slaughter-Defoe (Slaughter-Defoe, Nakagawa, Takanishi, & Johnson, 1990), and Harriet and John McAdoo (McAdoo & McAdoo, 1985), among others.

The first contribution was a move away from individualistic, purely person-oriented conceptions of identity and motivation to an ecological focus (Boykin, 1986; Murray & Mandara, 2003; Nobles, 1976). Seminal works in the field argue for the need to understand the macrolevel variables that structure roles and opportunities and the broader contexts for which socialization in families and schools must prepare youth; this approach is applicable to all youth and in particular ways to youth of color (Gurin & Epps, 1974; Hilliard, 2001; Spencer, Fegley, & Harpalani, 2003; Spencer, Swanson, & Cunningham, 1991). The macrolevel variables include societal discrimination and stereotypes. As I will illustrate in this article, the research of Claude Steele (1998, 2004) on stereotype threat began in an effort to understand some underlying mechanisms that account for differences in achievement outcomes; and I emphasize here some, certainly not all. But this initial attention to African Americans from an asset-based and ecological orientation has also yielded fundamental propositions about the ways in which macrolevel negative perceptions can negatively influence displays of competence, with examples of women in math and science and White students perceiving themselves as being in competition with Asian students in math and science.

A second contribution from seminal works in the field of Black psychology has been an understanding of how cultural, racial, or ethnic socialization can serve as a protective factor to influence positive development among youth of color (Caughy, O'Campo, Randolph, & Nickerson, 2002; Crocker & Major, 1989; Mandara, 2006; Marshall, 1995). I argue here that this empirical work also demonstrates how historical variables—in this case, intergenerational beliefs and practices that together constitute a group identity—operate to influence individual development.

I point to this intellectual history because these are the bodies of research that have most influenced me and also because the history illustrates the intellectual apartheid to which I have referred. The cognitively oriented studies of how people learn are not in dialogue with those that focus on culture and cognition (Bransford, Brown, & Cocking, 1999); the multiculturalists are not in *dialogue* with the culture and cognition researchers (Banks & Banks, 1995); cognitively oriented research and the world of human development have little to do with each other. I define dialogue as joint studies and referencing across disciplines and points of view in published research, especially handbooks and research syntheses. In volumes from the National Research Council or the National Academy of Education, it is rare to find any serious attempts to synthesize across these paradigms and empirical research bases to examine how culture shapes learning and development (Cole, 1998).

Although there clearly are differences among these paradigms, they share a number of fundamental propositions:

- Context matters: Contexts help to shape people, and people shape contexts.
- Routine practices count.
- The cognitive, social, physical, and biological dimensions of both individuals and contexts interact in important ways.

Yet, despite these broad points of convergence, as Michael Cole (1996) explains, we are not yet in a position to articulate a unified theory of culture and human development. Human development here includes not only the development of cognitive abilities but, equally, the ways in which emotional and social development and cognition jointly shape goals, attention, persistence, and resilience (Dai & Sternberg, 2004; Zajonc & Marcus, 1984). We have abundant evidence, including our own tacit self-reflections, that learning is influenced by intersections among thinking; perceptions of self, others, and tasks; emotional attributions; and self-regulation. We have abundant evidence that what some call this dynamic and complex self-system is influenced by the contexts, the routine activities in which we participate (Bronfenbrenner, 1979; Fischer & Bidell, 1998; Rogoff, 2003). And yet we are still not able to use these fundamental propositions to understand the range of human adaptations in terms of (a) what such adaptations reveal about mechanisms that are local and situated and (b) what such adaptations reveal about broader mechanisms that are universal in scope and essential to the species.

I want to argue here for two underlying causes for the limited state of our knowledge of such complex, dynamic ecological systems (paraphrased from Cole, 2007).

1 The insistence, in practice, on isolating studies of cultural variation in patterns of learning and development from what is presumed to be the "scientific" study of learning and development (Helms, Jernigan, & Mascher, 2005; Lee, Spencer, & Harpalani, 2003), a legacy of the persistent normative assumptions of White supremacy and class-based hegemony that today are largely tacit rather than explicitly public.

2 The intellectual isolation of core disciplines and of paradigms within those disciplines (i.e., the isolation of cognitive psychology from cultural psychology; and the isolation of cognitive psychology from relevant fields of human development—including the study of identity, personality, emotional development, motivation, attribution theory, social

psychology, and social cognition—and from the field of neuroscience, as neuroscientists are now examining the physiology of the brain to understand how people learn; Cole, 2007).

In this chapter I want to explore what disciplinary collaborations and active interrogation of tacit assumptions about normative development may have to offer for the field of education. That is, I want to explore how attention to the centrality of culture may lead to a more robust understanding of human learning and development.

Let me return to a personal story that sheds light on this intellectual journey of mine. About 4 years ago, I discovered that I had developed a macular hole in my left eye. Prior to that I had never heard of macular degeneration. I had been traveling in London and found that I could not read the fine print of the train schedules without a magnifying glass. In keeping with my usual unfortunate habit of attending to my own health after the fact, I finally went to an ophthalmologist. After the initial exam, where my eyes were dilated, I bravely tried to drive myself home and, yielding to my Type A personality proclivities, I stopped at a grocery store. I found that, of course, I could not read signs. But I noticed that I was consciously using cues from the environment and my prior knowledge to piece together inferences about what I was seeing. Several years ago, at a meeting at the National Science Foundation, a scholar from a research center at the University of Wisconsin, Madison, discussed a device under development that would help blind people to "see" by means of electrode stimulation to their tongues (Bach-y-Rita, Kaczmarek, Tyler, & Garcia-Lara, 1998).

As I reflected later, this project and my experience with macular degeneration reinforced an essential proposition about the human species—indeed, about all living organisms that survive evolutionary time. The ability to adapt is the key to survival. The tongue-stimulating system demonstrates human adaptability in the fact that our brains do not depend on any single pathway for navigating in the world. Here, adaptability means that the optic nerve from our eyes is not the only pathway through which to stimulate the parts of the brain that interpret visual stimuli. We understand this kind of redundancy in the physiological system of human beings from everyday experience as well, including my experience at the grocery store with eyes dilated. We know that blind people develop heightened sensations of sound and touch and that people with hearing impairments develop heightened attention to visual cues. Given such built-in redundancy at the physiological level, there is every reason to believe that redundancy at the psychological level supports human adaptation in the social and cognitive domains. Here I define *redundancy* in terms of the potential functionality of multiple pathways for helping human beings to pursue cognitive and social goals and accomplish things in the world, including academic goals in the context of schooling. Yet our prototypical response to the challenges of academic achievement is to articulate singular and normative pathways through which youth are expected to navigate the waters of the academic disciplines—and, by extension, singular and normative pathways through which teachers as adults may learn the complex and situated demands of teaching.

In this chapter, I plan to offer the following:

1 Warrants for why attention to diversity can contribute to the scientific study of human learning and development.
2 Conceptual implications of a cultural lens on learning and development.

3 Examples of research that document multiple pathways for learning and development, along with new general propositions that we can glean from what have traditionally been viewed as localized studies of "the other."

4 Implications for policy and practice.

WARRANTS FROM NATURAL SCIENCE AND THE FIELD OF HUMAN DEVELOPMENT

Here, I want to explore the scientific basis for the view that attention to diversity in the study of human learning and development is a necessary corollary to the articulation of robust and generative theories and, by extension, to the application of such robust and generative theories to problems of practice. I will make this case on the basis of evidence for adaptability over human phylogenetic development and evidence of an integrated and dynamic psychological self in the human species.

ADAPTABILITY AS A CHARACTERISTIC OF THE HUMAN SPECIES

One basic principle we have learned, from our own evolutionary history as a species and from that of other plants and animals, is that the ability to adapt to changing circumstances is important. If we accept that premise, it follows that understanding the underlying mechanisms that support adaptability should be important. Cultural diversity, I argue, is evidence of the adaptive systems that human beings have developed across societies in order to exist, to replicate ourselves, and to adapt to changing circumstances.

I should first note that I take this argument primarily from a wonderful synthesis of brain science in the book *Liars, Lovers, and Heroes: What the New Brain Science Reveals About How We Become Who We Are,* by Steven Quartz and Terrence Sejnowski (2002). I do not pretend to have any level of expertise in this area, but I find that the evidence from neuroscience and human evolutionary history offers a compelling warrant for the crucial need for attention to diversity in the science of learning. Over human evolutionary history, the physical environment of the earth has undergone significant shifts. As the earth's ecology shifted through the Ice Age and back, the species capable of adapting remained, and those that could not adapt died out. It seems that, in the course of evolutionary history, the structure of our brains developed built-in or hardwired capacities to read patterns, impose meanings, and revise the meanings of those patterns by learning from the consequences of our actions. To understand this dynamic relationship between our biology and our human culture and what they make possible in tandem is crucial. As Geertz (1973) adeptly pointed out,

> Man's nervous system does not merely enable him to acquire culture, it positively demands that he do so if it is going to function at all. Rather than culture acting only to supplement, develop, and extend organically based capacities logically and genetically prior to it, it would seem to be an ingredient to those capacities themselves. A cultureless human being would probably turn out to be not an intrinsically talented, though unfulfilled ape, but a wholly mindless and consequently unworkable monstrosity." (pp. 67–68; cited in Cole, 2007)

As a species we are disposed to pay particular attention to trying to read each other's internal states and goals (Flavell & Miller, 1998). Quartz and Sejnowski (2002) note that "the human brain's expansion does not signify the accumulation of more and more instinctual behaviors, but rather a growing mental flexibility that expands our behavioral repertoire, a flexibility that lies at the core of who we are" (p. 80). It is because of our ability to learn from others in socially organized groups that we are able to pass on behaviors across generations. But it is equally important that our biology makes the sense-making process not one of built-in and inflexible behaviors but one of capacity to create meaning and be self-reflective. This process of reflexivity represents "the intertwining of phylogeny and culture in human mental life" (Cole, 2007, p. 237). Language and other symbol systems that we as human beings create become an important medium through which this sense making takes place, a medium that includes routine cultural practices in which the form, significance, and deployment of such symbol- or meaning-making systems occur. Again, to quote from Quartz and Sejnowski,

> Your biology has primed you to acquire a culture. It has endowed you with an internal guidance system that propels you from within and bootstraps you into culture by making the social world highly significant and fueling your desire to participate in it. (pp. 85–86)

One important trigger for brain activity is the release of the chemicals serotonin and dopamine (Diamond, 1998; Fuster, 2001). The serotonin system is found in the brain stem, which is among the oldest parts of our brain system. Again, to quote from Quartz and Sejnowski (2002).

> One popular way to think of the release of serotonin at nerve terminals is as garden hoses that have small holes punched all along their length. These "hoses" sprinkle your brain with serotonin, which doesn't so much give cells their marching orders as change what they are already doing. (p. 87)

Serotonin signals emotional reactions, and dopamine influences our experience of pleasure.

I take away several propositions from this brief, albeit simplified, description of brain chemistry and human evolution. The first is that we are hardwired to be adaptive, but it is the experience of human culture—ultimately in all its variation—that shapes both how such adaptiveness develops and to what we as groups and as individuals learn to adapt. This is not a linear process in which the morphology of the brain is like a sponge to be filled by cultural experience. Rather, even the physiological development of the brain—in both evolutionary and ontogenetic or life-course time—is influenced by culture; and at the same time, our capacities as cultural beings are made possible by human physiology (Donald, 2001; Li, 2006; Plotkin, 2001).

The second proposition that I take from Quartz and Sejnowski's (2002) observations is that emotion and cognition are intimately and dynamically intertwined (Diamond, 1998; Fuster, 2001). I should note here that abundant laboratory-based studies also document the importance of emotion to cognition and motivation (Dalgleish & Powers, 1999; Nadel, Lane, & Ahern, 2000; Ortony, 1979).

The third proposition is that what counts is our perceptions of other people and activities (Spencer, 2006). These perceptions, which result from our efforts to make sense of other people, serve as the central guideposts for how we as human beings adapt to, or navigate in, the world. I take this proposition as rooted in human evolutionary history and in the findings of neuroscience with regard to how our brains operate.

These three propositions support the idea that culture—the medium through which intergenerational resources are passed on and through which novel constructions occur—is essential to human development. Culture and human biology are intricately intertwined.I now move to discuss another warrant for this set of broad propositions. I seek to integrate studies of human cognition with studies of human developmental processes that I think, when taken together, support the same findings I have noted from the brain science and human evolution perspectives. However, the integration of these two bodies of research introduces another important dimension that the first argument does not account for: that is, how power relations within and across cultural communities must also be taken into account if we are to articulate an integrated, robust, and generative theory of human learning and development. In this argument, I am most deeply indebted to Margaret Beale Spencer of the University of Pennsylvania, whose work I will describe, and more recently to a younger scholar, Nailah Nasir of Stanford University.

WARRANTS FROM THE FIELD OF HUMAN DEVELOPMENT

Broadly speaking, we can define cognition as thinking and problem solving. In terms of the work of schools, we typically think of cognition as the knowledge required to solve problems in the academic disciplines. Although, clearly, we as human beings solve problems in virtually every aspect of our daily lives, I want to focus here primarily on learning in the academic domains. People are already fairly good at everyday problem solving, but we in the field of education research have a long way to go in understanding academic learning in the disciplines, especially for youth from racial and ethnic minority communities, youth from low-economic-resource communities, youth whose first language is other than English, and youth with disabilities. Even for learning in schools, cognition includes not only knowledge of tasks—in this case academic tasks—but also knowledge of self, settings, and others.

Knowledge of self involves one's identity—or we might say one's identities—as a member of a family, of peer social networks, and of larger communities, including those defined by ethnicity, race, and nationality (Phinney, 1990; Sellers et al., 1998; Spencer et al., 1991). Knowledge of self also involves one's identity as a learner of particular subjects and a learner in general (Dweck, 1999; Eccles, Wigfield, & Schiefele, 1998) and as a participant who identifies to a greater or lesser extent with the culture of a classroom and a school (Wigfield, Eccles, & Rodriguez, 1998). One's construal of the self serves as an important guidepost for a range of affiliations that one seeks and works to sustain. The self is connected with the ego such that we seek experiences that support ego development, not necessarily in terms of a purely individualistic conception of the self but rather in terms of a psychological state that is affirming and in which basic human needs are met. Maslow (1954) defines a hierarchy of human needs that range from safety through love and belonging, competency, self-esteem, and self-actualization. How these needs are manifested differs across cultural communities. However, I have no doubt that in the broad sense they are basic to human psychological functioning in all communities.

From a human development perspective, the goals we set and our persistence in efforts to accomplish them—especially in the face of challenges—are influenced by our motivation, our attachments to people, our sense of ability as fixed or malleable, our conception of the task (as interesting, as doable, as relevant, and weighed against competing goals), and our r the people with whom we interact to accomplish the goals (Eccles et al., 1998; N Warren, & Lee, 2006; Spencer, 2006; Spencer et al., 2003).

From a cognitive perspective, our ability to learn to accomplish the goals in terms of academic learning, is influenced by the nature of the supports or available to us for learning to perform the tasks in question, including the structure of the prior knowledge we bring to the table (Bransford et al., 2006). A related perspective from the fields of human development and social psychology indicates that our willingness to articulate goals and make use of the available supports—such as the supports in a reform curriculum—are influenced by our perceptions of how the task, the people around us engaged in the activity (peer learners and teachers), and the effort required to accomplish the goal address our basic social and emotional needs as defined by Maslow. Do we feel safe in carrying out this work? How does engagement with this task weigh out in terms of competing needs? Do we develop a sense of competence as we move forward? And are the people with whom we are working (as peers or teachers) aiming to help or hurt us (see Nasir et al., 2006.) Not all of these needs must be met if we are to be successful, but it is clear that some must be met. There must be some forms of support that help us to make sense of the activity that do not meet our perceived and basic needs (Lee, 2007; Spencer et al., 2003). For example, students who have clear long-term objectives to enroll in college may persist in classes in which they are bored and do not feel particularly successful because the long-term need for efficacy represented by college enrollment gives them a reason to persist.

It is also crucial to note that the understanding and pursuit of basic needs in acts of learning, particularly academic learning, are developmental in nature. For example, the needs of young children for competence and social connectedness are qualitatively different from those of adolescents (Eccles & Midgley, 1988; Eccles et al., 1993). Thus any integrated theory must have a developmental focus. It is equally crucial to my argument to assert that these developmental needs are also going to differ by cultural communities. For example, on the basis of Markus and Kitayama's (1991) descriptions of individualist and interdependent cultural communities (Greenfield, Keller, Fuligni, & Maynard, 2003; Markus & Kitayama, 1991), we would expect that adolescents' sense of social relatedness would develop differently in a community where becoming an adult is marked by separation from one's family of origin than in a community where becoming an adult is marked by assumption of greater responsibilities as one further incorporates oneself into one's family of origin. The picture, however, is much more complex than that. I will say more on this subject later.

I have tried so far, in a very condensed way, to capture propositions that are well established in the learning sciences and the fields of human development and social psychology. The problem, however, is that it is rare to find studies, especially studies of any scale, or educational interventions in schools and communities that actually operate theoretically from such an integrated model. Such a model—one that incorporates both a cognitive and a psychosocial perspective—of necessity requires the idea of multiple pathways. This integrated model assumes that neither a purely cognitive approach, focusing on the structure of knowledge to be learned, nor a purely psychosocial approach, focusing on supports for a sense of emotional well-being, is sufficient to develop learning that is robust, especially in the academic context.

SUMMARY OF WARRANTS

I return briefly to my focus on adaptiveness as the key to human survival. I have argued so far that the available resources that enable us to be adaptive are (a) the biology of our brains, (b) the ʳal or social communities that we rely on both to develop from childhood into adulthood and to sustain cultures that continually re-create communities across time, and (c) the primacy of our sense-making efforts. And I have argued from the learning sciences and the fields of human development and social psychology that our sense-making efforts entail cognition, emotion, and perceptions, always working in tandem.

I do not think there is much controversy about these claims, even if we do not see them integrated in either the practice of research or the practice of schooling. However, we lack consensus about another important elephant in the room, which serves as the conceptual filter through which we take any of these propositions as a basis for the design of our research or our practice. This elephant in the room has to do with our conceptions of culture and cultural membership—how our understanding of culture and cultural membership informs how we think about cognition, emotion, and perceptions as they are brought to bear in acts of learning, particularly in terms of schooling.

CONCEPTUAL IMPLICATIONS OF A CULTURAL LENS: TOWARD AN INTEGRATED THEORY OF LEARNING AND DEVELOPMENT

The United States is born out of a mixed history. The articulation in the Bill of Rights and the U.S. Constitution of the fundamental rights of human beings—including the exercise of individual freedoms as long as such exercise does not infringe on the fundamental rights of others—continues to serve as an anchor for democratic debate and without question represents one of the finest social experiments in human history. At the same time, we cannot ignore the gross contradictions that were in play during the formation of these foundational documents. An African in the United States was legally considered to be three fifths of a human being; women could not vote; men who did not own property could not vote; indentured servitude was legal. The issue that we have had the greatest difficulty in handling throughout our history is the fact that this democracy was born on the backs of at least two human holocausts: The African Holocaust of Enslavement and the dismantling of the indigenous nations in the Americas through war, outright murder, broken treaties, and the systematic dismantling of families. Both holocausts were sanctioned by beliefs about White supremacy and longstanding class biases that were the legacy of much of the political and cultural history of Western Europe (Mills, 1997). For the first 400 years of what we might loosely call U.S. history (from the original settling in the 15th century to the historic *Brown vs. Board of Education* Supreme Court decision in 1954 and the Voting Rights Act of 1965), the attribution of Whiteness as normative served to justify all forms of discrimination against those who were classified as non-White (see Ladson-Billings, 2004, for a critical review of educational implications of *Brown* and antiracist legislation). It is interesting to note the changes over the years in the official definitions of racial classifications. Those of African, Hispanic, Asian, and American Indian descent have always been deemed non-White. Whiteness has been the basis for sordid constructions of race (Du Bois, 1940/1992; Gould, 1981; Lee, 2002). The very construct is itself so bizarre that until the late 19th century, Africans in America, for example, were defined on the basis of "blood" percentages, the so-called quadroons and octoroons determined by what percentage of one's lineage was Black. Stranger still, during periods of high immigration in the early 20th century, the Irish, Italians, and Eastern Europeans were considered non-White (Guglielmo, 2003; Ignatiev, 1996; Roediger, 2006). Particularly for people of African descent, the focus on racial classification has thwarted attention to what it means culturally to live as a person of African descent in the United States—that is, attention to the question of ethnicity (Ladson-Billings, 2004; Ladson-Billings & Tate, 1995).

From a sociological perspective, identity questions with regard to race, ethnicity, and nationality (and, by extension, gender and disability) require careful analysis. Although a similar case can be made for discrimination based on gender or disability, I will focus on race because with ascribed racial classification comes exposure to institutional biases, prevalent cultural stereotypes, and outright persistent, intergenerational discrimination that crosses gender, nationality, and disability. Thus to ignore race is to take our vision away from the ways in which our society institutionalizes challenges to particular groups of people. To focus on nationality alone shifts our attention away from the multiethnic nature of U.S. society and increasingly more nation-states around the world. And it should be noted that the United States has always been a multiethnic society. We see the presence of ethnic identification in the wars in Serbia and Kenya, in the plight of the Roma (historically known as gypsies) across Europe, in Somalia, and in the political tensions among the multiple ethnic groups indigenous in China. We see ethnic identification in both the similarities and the differences among Black populations within the United States—Caribbean Africans, immigrants from the continent of Africa, and descendants of the Africans originally enslaved in this country.

Focusing on ethnicity allows us to consider the impact of how people live, their routine practices, and the consequences of such routine practices for their development. Please note: I do not argue that attention to race and nationality are unimportant. Indeed, I have already argued that attention to race *is* crucial but that we must understand for what ends; likewise, attention to nationality is important, particularly for international comparisons. But I would argue that if national trends are to be used to account for inevitable variation—for example in educational outcomes—our attention must also include differences in ethnicity and class within nationalities. For purposes of this discussion, I will explore how we can think about ethnicity as a lens for understanding the range of variation in pathways to learning and the attendant psychosocial development.

Research focusing on ethnicity and learning or ethnicity and psychosocial development typically tries to address some set of negative outcomes for marginalized youth: learning outcomes explained by stereotype threat, family practices posited as non-canonical (e.g., practices of parents who do not read books to their young children at home), lack of mastery of academic English as a constraint on learning, and so forth. Two implicit assumptions underlie much of this research. The first is that the normative problems of developing human beings do not apply to ethnic minorities or the poor.[2] You see this in a review of the standard handbooks on learning and on development. At best, there may be a single chapter devoted specifically to the problems of ethnic minority youth; and in the standard chapters on the big ideas in the field, there is virtually no mention of ethnic or class diversity. The implicit assumption regarding systematic studies of core constructs such as conceptual change or attachment theory is that their application and validity with regard to ethnic minorities need not be examined. The second implicit assumption, especially with regard to the learning side of the equation, is that the domains of everyday knowledge and disciplinary knowledge are worlds apart—or that if there are connections (such as in the cognitive research on the role of prior knowledge, naive concepts, and misconceptions), the everyday side of the equation is typically the deficit calculation.

My fundamental premise is that we cannot articulate a generative and robust science of learning and development without explicit attention to the diversity of the human experience. The National Science Foundation and the Institute of Education Sciences, the two largest sources of federal funding for education research, both explicitly call for attention to diversity in their RFPs. However, there are no common criteria, or for that matter even idiosyncratic criteria, for what constitutes rigor with regard to issues of diversity in the conduct of education research. There are no definitive syntheses of the existing research or comprehensive articulations, of the many unanswered questions that attention to diversity might raise.[3] Thus the most typical responses to the criteria for diversity in programs of research are either outreach activities aimed at underrepresented minorities but not linked in any way to the fundamental research activity, or attention to helping the colored people and the poor without any expectation that the findings from the research might contribute to the expansion of fundamental knowledge about human learning and development.

These tensions between what has been termed an *etic* as opposed to an *emic* perspective have a long history in anthropology and cross-cultural psychology. With greater attention to cultural diversity in research in psychology, human development, and education, this tension is reflected in the following questions to ask when we study culturally distinct communities of practice:

1. What can we understand that is unique to each community and that reflects the inside perspective of its members?
2. What can we understand that can be extrapolated across cultural communities?
    I think both questions are crucial, and we cannot address the second without addressing the first. That is, attention to the meaning of cultural practices within particular communities is crucial so that we are not imposing normative assumptions that have no meaning for the people we are studying. We have a very long history of making this mistake. At the same time, we need some ways of synthesizing across studies of culturally distinct communities to build generative theories about how we as human beings learn and develop over time.

So to move forward, here are some core propositions that I think we must address:

1. Cultural membership is based on shared routine practices and beliefs that are transmitted through generations, across time and space (Gutiérrez & Rogoff, 2003; Rogoff, 2003; Rogoff, Paradise, Mejía-Arauz, Correa-Chávez, & Angelillo, 2003). This is why we see the maintenance of practices and beliefs even when people immigrate to new nations and live in their adopted nations across several generations.
2. People can and do live in multiple cultural communities of practice, but the meanings and functions of these different cultural communities differ. Often (although not always), the sense of identity associated with ethnicity as it is embodied in the practices of the family in which one grows up will serve as an important psychological anchor for the developing person (Cross, 1991; Lee, 2002; Sellers et al., 1998).
3. Cultural communities are communities precisely because of what they share, but at the same time there is always significant variation within communities. Thus we need what my friend Kris Gutiérrez (2004) at the University of California, Los Angeles, calls a

binocular vision, with one lens focused on what makes communities culturally distinct and a second lens focused on the variations within communities. Understanding variation is very important and, I would argue, fundamental to the question I raised at the beginning of this article about the role of adaptation in human survival. I would argue that understanding human adaptation to our social, political, economic, and biological ecologies is central to the scientific study of human learning and development, and thus that diversity among human groups as captured within and across cultural communities—as well as individual variation within such communities—is the science we want and need to understand.

4 The processes through which human beings learn in and from their environments and adapt to them always entail risks. Here, I draw explicitly from Margaret Beale Spencer's research and her Phenomenological Variant of Ecological Systems Theory (PVEST) model (Spencer, 2006). Spencer argues that to be human is to be placed at risk. On the surface this may seem obvious, but if one examines the research literature in education, human development, and the learning sciences, one leaves with the impression that it is the youth of color and the poor youth who have the problems, that middle-class and upper-class White youth are somehow immune from risk. For example, our term *at-risk youth* is intended as a synonym for youth of color and youth from economically poor communities.[4] Thus understanding the nature of risks faced by individuals and communities, how people actually experience those risks, and the nature of the supports that are or are not available to them, as Spencer argues, is necessary for understanding the range of variation in developmental pathways.

Spencer asserts that the nature of the challenges and needed supports changes with age (Spencer et al., 1991). So, for example, the needs of a young child for a sense of competence and attachment are qualitatively different from those of an adolescent. Spencer's final and perhaps most compelling point is that youth who face persistent challenges based on race, ethnicity, poverty, immigrant status, and so forth, must learn to cope with both the normative challenges of growing up and the specialized challenges of stigmatization (Boykin, 1986; Spencer, 1987, 1999, 2000). Learning to cope productively with these dual challenges can provide sources of resilience. This means that ethnic and racial socialization, for example, can serve as important and necessary supports for holistic development (Caughy et al., 2002; Mandara, 2006).

Let me be very clear. I am not arguing that these propositions should inform research on "culturally diverse populations" (which, by the way, has become our synonym for "non-White groups"). Rather, I am arguing that researchers who seek to examine or generate fundamental theories about how and what human beings learn and the psychosocial processes entailed in such learning need to consider these propositions from the very beginning, when deciding how to formulate their research questions, how to sample, what kinds of data to collect, the validity of instruments, the assumptions underlying the variables articulated, and the potential limitations of their findings (Lee et al., 2003).

RESEARCH EXAMPLES OF THEORY DERIVED FROM EXAMINATIONS OF PRACTICE IN COMMUNITIES OF COLOR

To reiterate, I argue that to generate robust and generative theories about how and what people learn, we must attend to issues of diversity based on conceptually complex frameworks that position diversity as essential or fundamental to the human experience and not as some wayward pathology. In illustration, I will describe in this final section several programs of research that have focused on populations of color and have articulated insights about human learning and development that are generative—that have application and meaning across cultural communities, without being normative. Although there are many fine, long-term research programs that I could use, I will limit myself to three: Nailah Nasir's work on nonschool settings, the work of Douglas Medin and Megan Bang among the Menominee, and my own work in Cultural Modeling.

LEARNING IN EVERYDAY SETTINGS IN THE RESEARCH OF NAILAH NASIR

Nailah Nasir situates her research within the African American community and seeks to examine a set of fundamental propositions about what makes a learning community robust. It is precisely because she examines settings and populations where the dual challenges of normative development and racial, ethnic, and class identities are clearly at work that she has been able to contribute to our understanding both of conditions under which transfer may be maximized and of the fundamental features of robust learning communities.

Nailah Nasir (2000, 2002, 2005; Nasir, Hand, & Taylor, 2008; Nasir et al., 2006; Nasir & Saxe, 2003) has examined two routine practices with cohorts of African American youth: playing dominoes and playing basketball. For each of these domains, Nasir, like Margaret Beale Spencer, has taken an explicitly developmental focus by examining youth at different ages with different levels of expertise. She has documented the computational skills and the development of strategic planning processes in child, adolescent, and adult domino players. She has documented the knowledge of simple statistics among adolescent basketball players, many of whom do not transfer their mathematical competencies from the basketball court to mathematics classes in school. She has also examined the structure of scaffolding in an after-school track team. All of these are out-of-school environments where youth learn complex skills. She contrasts a more expansive view of how people learn in these settings with the more restrictive view of learning in schools.

Among the notable findings of Nasir's research are the following: (a) the importance of making problem-solving strategies explicit and public; (b) the importance of timely feedback on performance; (c) the importance of positioning learners as competent; and (d) the importance of social relationships between teachers and learners and among peers. And how these practices play out is not generic. Rather, they are responsive to the cultural histories of the communities in which youth live. These practices are intended to help youngsters understand the challenges they face and to provide them with repertoires for coping with challenge and for excelling in the face of adversity. The strategies are not generic practices that can be simply imported anywhere. Rather, they require that those who design or teach them understand their students as individuals, as members of families, and as members of historical communities. Like Margaret Beale Spencer's

PVEST model, Nasir's research seeks to articulate adaptive principles that are responsive to local conditions and local histories; however, the underlying principles are generative.

STUDIES OF ECOLOGICAL REASONING IN INDIGENOUS COMMUNITIES: MEDIN AND BANG

My second illustrative example is the program of research carried out by Douglas Medin of Northwestern University and Megan Bang of TERC (Atran & Medin, 2008; Bang, Medin, & Atran, 2007; Medin & Atran, 1999; Medin, Unsworth, & Hirschfield, 2007; Ross, Medin, & Cox, 2007). Medin has worked for more than a decade with the Menominee Nation in Wisconsin. Bang is Ojibwe and an outstanding young American Indian scholar. Medin has documented the prevalence of ecological reasoning about the natural environment among the Menominee. The Menominee are known for rich ecological practices with regard to sustainable forestry and maintaining a balance in the wildlife of that area. Medin and Bang argue that the prevalence of ecological reasoning among the Menominee can be traced, in part, to intergenerational practices involving fishing. Although nearby European Americans also routinely fish, the two communities give very different cultural meanings to the practice. And Menominee who live in Chicago, for example, still maintain ecological beliefs about the natural world, largely through social ties and traditional belief systems.

In a recent study, Bang et al. (2007) tested a prevalent theory in cognition that children's conceptions of the natural world are anthropocentric (Carey, 1985), meaning that they project human attributes onto animals rather than vice-versa. Medin and Bang found that "rural children [both Menominee and rural European American] generalized more from wolf to other mammals than from humans to other animals" (Bang et al., 2007, p. 5). This finding suggests that children's reasoning about the natural world is predicated on their experiences with the natural world rather than on a universal pattern. However, the researchers found that Menominee children are much more likely to justify their claims on the basis of ecological relations, for example to "justify generalizing from bees to bears because a bee might sting a bear or a bear might acquire the property of eating the bee's honey" (p. 6). They argue that the genesis of these beliefs may likely be the Menominee creation story, in which human beings evolve from the bear, and the prevalence of an animal-based clan system. This research has implications not only for how to teach ecology in ways that are anchored in the routine practices and belief systems of cultural groups but also—equally important—for how to study the development and genesis of children's knowledge of the biological world.

CULTURAL MODELING

I need to abbreviate the discussion of the third illustration, my own work in Cultural Modeling (Lee, 1993, 1995, 2000, 2001, 2005a). I have documented the genesis of disciplinary reasoning in the everyday practices of Black and Brown youth. Specifically, I have shown the prevalence of literary reasoning embedded in signifying among speakers of African American English and how the structure of that reasoning is related to the demands of reasoning about literary texts. That work has also led me to reexamine some fundamental assumptions about what novices need to know in order to analyze canonical literary texts (Lee, 2004, 2007). The idea that there are classic types of problems, generative relations among types of problems, strategies, heuristics, and dispositions or habits of mind has been central to mathematics and science education but not to the teaching of literature. I discuss these ideas in detail in my most recent book, *Culture, Literacy and Learning: Taking Bloom in the Midst of the Whirlwind* (Lee, 2007).

A third insight that I glean from my work is that robust learning environments provide what I call multiple culturally rich contextualization cues (Gumperz, 1986) that signal to novices what roles are available and sanctioned for us to play, who can talk about what and how, and what tasks we are expected to engage in and how (Lee, 2005a, 2005b). Again we revisit the idea of redundancies, or multiple pathways.

This means that the role transition for students is made easier, especially for students with long histories of underachievement in school. Often, the longer these students remain in school, the more skeptical of the whole enterprise they become. Culturally rich contextualization cues include the following:

1 Everyday knowledge embedded in routine practices in which the youth engage directly, themselves, is invited as an object of inquiry and a scaffold to related disciplinary knowledge. This is what we have done in the domain of literature. It is also what Bob Moses' Algebra Project has done with the teaching of fundamental algebraic constructs based initially on analogies of traveling along an urban transit system (Moses & Cobb, 2001). It is what the researchers at Chèche Konnen at TERC (with Beth Warren, Ann Rosebery, and Josianne Hudicourt-Barnes) have documented with the use of Haitian Creole argument structure in science classrooms (Rosebery, Warren, & Conant, 1992; Warren, Ballenger, Ogonowski, Rosebery, & Hudicourt-Barnes, 2001). It is what Arnetha Ball has documented with regard to preferences in expository writing among African American adolescent speakers of African American English (Ball, 1992, 1995; Ball & Farr, 2003). I could go on, but the point is made.

2 Ways of speaking in classrooms that privilege language resources that students bring from their everyday linguistic practices and repertoires outside school create opportunities for participation and the assumption of meaningful roles in the problem-solving and inquiry work of classrooms. We have documented this with a fascinating range of rhetorical moves as the vehicles for conveying deep thought among the African American English speakers in our studies (Lee, 1993, 1995, 2000). We have similar findings about bilingual language resources in the work of Marjorie Orellana (Orellana, Reynolds, Dorner, & Meza, 2003), Guadalupe Valdes (1996, 2002), Olga Vásquez (2002), and others.

These studies do not represent isolated, self-interested investigations of colored peoples, cute multicultural meanderings from the real questions of learning. Rather, they provide the kinds of rich contextual information about the circumstances under which learning of new concepts and modes of reasoning is maximized; that is, the conditions under which adaptability is maximized.

The underlying assumption behind the anchoring of school-based instruction on what kids already know and value is not an end unto itself. Rather, the goal of teaching students to be adaptive—teaching them what the late Giyoo Hatano (Hatano & Inagaki, 1986) and Rand Spiro (Spiro, Feltovich, Jackson, & Coulson, 1991) have called "adaptive expertise"—means helping them to build transitions to that which they do not yet know. Learning environments where this can happen will inevitably require what Kris Gutiérrez (Gutiérrez, Baquedano-Lopez, & Tejeda, 1999) calls *hybridity*. Such learning environments will involve the intermingling, the interanimation if you will, of multiple languages (e.g., African American English and Academic English, Spanish and the English of mathematics), multiple worldviews (the ecological orientation of the Menominee and the ecological orientation of the sciences), multiple ways of reasoning (reasoning about rap lyrics and reasoning about canonical literary texts), and multiple role playing (students assuming the role of teachers and teachers assuming the roles of learners within their classrooms). Gutiérrez argues that it is specifically this attention to hybridity that is the fulcrum for creativity, the medium that provides opportunities for new constructions that neither teachers nor students could anticipate ahead of time and thus makes for the most exciting and generative kinds of teaching and research. Scott E. Page (2007) makes a similar argument about the generative role that diversity plays with regard to creativity and deep thought.

IMPLICATIONS FOR POLICY AND PRACTICE

We face challenges in the field of education. These challenges are highlighted by the overwhelming evidence of inequity in educational outcomes and opportunity to learn (Moss, Pullin, Gee, Haertel, & Young, 2008; Perle, Moran, Lutkas, & Tirre, 2005). Yet there is an underlying hope that education research can provide our society with the intellectual tools for addressing these pressing problems through the generation of theories that are sufficiently robust to be responsive to the wide variation in the life circumstances of youth and families and in the institutional resources available to them. As education researchers, we cannot be satisfied with overly deterministic pronouncements like the following:

1 If parents don't read books to their children before they come to school, the children are not likely to become competent readers.
2 If parents don't engage in the kind of talk that we imaginatively think goes on in middle-class homes, the children's vocabulary will be so limited that they can never catch up.
3 If children haven't learned the alphabetic principles and how to count to 10 before they reach kindergarten, they will be behind forever.
4 If children don't speak "the King's English," they cannot be taught.
5 If parents don't come to school, they are not interested in their children's education.

At best, such pronouncements are based on studies of White middle-class samples. At worst, they reflect our stereotypes about poor people and their children. Moreover, these "folk beliefs" presume a monolithic approach to teaching that does not create multiple pathways for reaching common goals.

I ask: What are the foundational principles of learning that can help inform practice anywhere, whether in Wisconsin on the reservation of the Menominee Nation; in Los Angeles, where children in one classroom may be recent immigrants from seven countries of origin; in the Appalachian Mountains, where many White families have lived for generations in persistent poverty; in New York City, where Black students may be Puerto Rican, Dominican, Brazilian, Senegalese, Eritrean, or descendents of Africans who were enslaved; or, for that matter, in the rich, predominantly White suburb of Skokie, near Northwestern University where I teach, with students whose high state assessment scores mask the reality (shown by NAEP trends in reading and mathematics) that fewer than 10% of 17-year-olds in the United States are able to engage in the most complex problem solving tasks (Perle et al., 2005)?

I want to see our field generate theories of learning that take into account all this complexity, that help us to understand the cognitive, social, and emotional dimensions of learning; the ways that identity is linked to goal setting and persistence; and the ways that competence is very much context dependent. I want to see education researchers generate theories of learning that help us to understand how the exercise of power and the availability of resources can affect opportunity to learn; how socialization efforts can help youth learn to make sense of and resist those institutional structures and practices that constrain and impede their opportunities to learn. This kind of understanding, I think, is the essence of learning to be adaptive. And learning to be adaptive is indeed the name of the game called Life.

NOTES

I wish to thank the following colleagues for comments on the manuscript: Arnetha Ball, Michael Cole, Kris Gutierrez, Joyce King, and Margaret Beale Spencer.

1 There is some evolving progress in this area, however. For example, a National Science Foundation—funded center for the science of learning —the LIFE Center at the University of Washington—has an advisory board on diversity in the learning sciences, headed by James Banks.

2 This criterion does not apply to the research on stereotype threat, which has documented that stereotype threats can impede displays of competence across multiple populations.

3 The LIFE Center (see note 1) hosted a conference in January 2008 that called for a synthesis document with regard to the role of diversity in a science of learning, including criteria that could be used in the evaluation of proposals.

4 A. Wade Boykin (2000) addressed the implications of the term *at risk youth* by rephrasing to *youth placed at risk*.

REFERENCES

Atran, S., & Medin, D. L. (2008). *The native mind and the cultural construction of nature.* Cambridge, MA: MIT Press.

Bach-y-Rita, P., Kaczmarek, K. A., Tyler, M. E., & Garcia-Lara, M. (1998). Form perception with a 49-point electrotactile stimulus array on the tongue: A technical note. *Journal of Rehabilitation Research and Development, 35(4),* 427–430.

Ball, A. F. (1992). Cultural preferences and the expository writing of African-American adolescents. *Written Communication, 9(4),* 501–532.

Ball, A. F. (1995). Text design patterns in the writing of urban African- American students: Teaching to the strengths of students in multicultural settings. *Urban Education,* 30, 253–289.

Ball, A. F., & Farr, M. (2003). Language varieties, culture and teaching the English Language Arts. In J. Flood, D. Lapp, J. Squire, & J. Jensen (Eds.), *Handbook of research on teaching the English Language Arts* (2nd ed., pp. 435–445). Mahwah, NJ: Lawrence Erlbaum.

Bang, M., Medin, D. L., & Atran, S. (2007). Cultural mosaics and mental models of nature. *Proceedings of the National Academy of Sciences,* 104, 13868–13874.

Banks, J., & Banks, C. (1995). *Handbook of research on multicultural education.* New York: Macmillan.

Boykin, A. W. (1979). Black psychology and the research process: Keeping the baby but throwing out the bathwater. In A. W. Boykin, A. J. Anderson, & J. Yates (Eds.), *Research directions of Black psychologists* (pp. 85–103). New York: Russell Sage Foundation.

Boykin, A. W. (1986). The triple quandary and the schooling of Afro-American children. In U. Neisser (Ed.), *The school achievement of minority children* (pp. 57–92). Hillsdale, NJ: Lawrence Erlbaum.

Boykin, A. W. (2000). The talent development model of schooling: Placing students at promise for academic success. *Journal of Education for Students Placed at Risk, 5*, 3–25.

Bransford, J., Brown, A., & Cocking, R. (1999). *How people learn: Brain, mind experience and school.* Washington, DC: National Academy Press.

Bransford, J., Stevens, R., Schwartz, D., Meltzoff, A., Pea, R. D., Roschelle, J., et al. (2006). Learning theories and education: Toward a decade of synergy. In P. A. Alexander & P. H. Winne (Eds.), *Handbook of educational psychology* (pp. 209–244). Mahwah, NJ: Lawrence Erlbaum.

Bronfenbrenner, U. (1979). *The ecology of human development. Experiment by nature and design.* Cambridge, MA: Harvard University Press.

Brown v. Board of Education, 347 U.S. 483 (1954).

Carey, S. (1985). *Conceptual change in childhood.* Cambridge, MA: Bradford Books.

Caughy, M. O., O'Campo, P. J., Randolph, S. M., & Nickerson, K. (2002). The influence of racial socialization practices on the cognitive and behavioral competence of African American preschoolers. *Child Development, 73*, 1611–1625.

Cole, M. (1996). *Cultural psychology, a once and future discipline.* Cambridge, MA: Belknap Press of Harvard University Press.

Cole, M. (1998). Can cultural psychology help us think about diversity? *Mind, Culture, and Activity, 5(4)*, 291–304.

Cole, M. (2007). Phylogeny and cultural history in ontogeny. *Journal of Physiology-Paris, 101*, 236–246.

Cole, M., Gay, J., Glick, J. A., & Sharp, D. W. (1971). *The cultural context of learning and thinking: An exploration of experimental anthropology.* New York: Basic Books.

Crocker, J., & Major, B. (1989). Social stigma and self esteem: The selfprotective properties of stigma. *Psychological Review, 96*,608–630.

Cross, W. (1991). *Shades of black: Diversity in African American identity.* Philadelphia: Temple University Press.

Dai, D. Y., & Sternberg, R. (2004). *Motivation, emotion, and cognition: Integrative perspectives on intellectual functioning and development.* Mahwah, NJ: Lawrence Erlbaum.

Dalgleish, T., & Powers, M. (Eds.). (1999). *Handbook of cognition and emotion.* Sussex, UK: John Wiley.

Diamond, A. (1998). Evidence for the importance of dopamine for prefrontal cortex functions in early life. In A. C. Roberts, T. W. Robbins, & L. Weiskrantz (Eds.), *The prefrontal cortex: Executive and cognitive functions* (pp. 144–164). New York: Oxford University Press.

Donald, M. (2001). *A mind so rare: The evolution of human consciousness.* New York: W. W. Norton.

Du Bois, W. E. B. (1992). *Dusk of dawn: An essay toward an autobiography of a race concept.* New Brunswick, NJ: Transaction. (Original work published 1940)

Dweck, C. S. (1999). *Self-theories: Their role in motivation, personality and development.* Philadelphia: Psychology Press.

Eccles, J., & Midgley, C. (1988). Stage environment fit: Developmentally appropriate classrooms for early adolescents. In R. E. Ames & C. Ames (Eds.), *Research on motivation in education* (Vol. 3, pp. 139–180). New York: Academic Press.

Eccles, J., Midgley, C., Wigfield, A., Miller Buchanan, C. M., Reuman, D., & Flanagan, C. (1993). Development during adolescence: The impact of stage-environment fit on young adolescents' experiences in schools and families. *American Psychologist, 48(2)*, 90–101.

Eccles, J., Wigfield, A., & Schiefele, U. (1998). Motivation to succeed. In W. Damon & N. Eisenberg (Eds.), *Handbook of child psychology* (5th ed., Vol. 3). New York: John Wiley.

Fischer, K. W., & Bidell, T. R. (1998). Dynamic development of psychological structures in action and thought. In W. Damon & R. M. Lerner (Eds.), *Handbook of child psychology: Theoretical models of human development* (5th ed., Vol. 1, pp. 467–562). New York: John Wiley.

Flavell, J. H., & Miller, P. H. (1998). Social cognition. In W. Damon (Ed. in Chief), D. Kuhn, & R. V. E. Siegler (Vol. Eds.), *Handbook of child psychology* (5th ed., Vol. 2, pp. 851–898). New York: John Wiley.

Fuster, J. M. (2001). The prefrontal cortex-an update: Time is of the essence. *Neuron, 30*, 319–333.

Geertz, C. (1973). *The interpretation of cultures*. New York: Basic Books.

Ginsburg, H. (1972). *The myth of the deprived child: Poor children's intellect*. Englewood Cliffs, NJ: Prentice-Hall.

Gould, S. J. (1981). *The mismeasure of man*. New York: Norton.

Greenfield, P., & Childs, C. P. (1977). Weaving, color terms and pattern representation: Cultural influences and cognitive development among the Zinacantecos of Southern Mexico. *Inter American Journal of Psychology, 11*, 23–48.

Greenfield, P., Keller, H., Fuligni, A., & Maynard, A. (2003). Cultural pathways through universal development. *Annual Review of Psychology, 54*, 461–490.

Guglielmo, T. A. (2003). *White on arrival: Italians, race, color, and power in Chicago, 1890–1945*. New York: Oxford University Press.

Gumperz, J. J. (1986). *Discourse strategies*. New York: Cambridge University Press.

Gurin, P., & Epps, E. (1974). *Black consciousness, identity, and achievement*. New York: John Wiley.

Gutiérrez, K. (2004). *Rethinking education policy for English learners*. Washington, DC: Carnegie Foundation and Aspen Institute.

Gutiérrez, K., Baquedano-Lopez, P., & Tejeda, C. (1999). Rethinking diversity: Hybridity and hybrid language practices in the Third Space. *Mind, Culture, and Activity, 6(4)*, 286–303.

Gutiérrez, K., & Rogoff, B. (2003). Cultural ways of learning: Individual traits or repertoires of practice. *Educational Researcher, 32*(5), 19–25.

Hatano, G., & Inagaki, K. (1986). Two courses of expertise. In H. W. Stevenson, H. Azuma, & K. Hakuta (Eds.), *Child development and education in Japan*. New York: Freeman.

Helms, J. E., Jernigan, M., & Mascher, J. (2005). The meaning of race in psychology and how to change it: A methodological perspective. *American Psychologist, 60(1)*, 27–36.

Hilliard, A. G. (1998). *SBA: The reawakening of the African mind*. Gainesville, FL: Makare.

Hilliard, A. G. (2001). "Race," identity, hegemony, and education: What do we need to know now? In W. H. Watkins, J. H. Lewis, & V. Chou (Eds.), *Race education: The roles of history and society in educating African American students* (pp. 7–33). Boston: Allyn & Bacon.

Hughes, L. (1926, June 23). The Negro artist and the racial mountain. *The Nation*.

Ignatiev, N. (1996). *How the Irish became White*. New York: Roudedge.

Jones, R. (Ed.). (1972). *Black psychology*. New York: Harper and Row.

Karenga, M. (1993). *Introduction to Black studies*. Los Angeles: University of Sankore Press.

Ladson-Billings, G. (2004). Landing on the wrong note: The price we paid for *Brown*. *Educational Researcher, 33*(7), 3–13.

Ladson-Billings, G., & Tate, W. (1995). Toward a critical race theory of education. *Teachers College Record, 97*(1), 47–68.

Lave, J. (1977). Cognitive consequences of traditional apprenticeship training in West Africa. *Anthropology and Education Quarterly, 8(3)*, 177–189.

Lee, C. D. (1992). Profile of an independent Black institution: African-centered education at work. *Journal of Negro Education, 61(2)*, 160–177.

Lee, C. D. (1993). *Signifyng as a scaffold for literary interpretation: The pedagogical implications of an African American discourse genre*. Urbana, IL: National Council of Teachers of English.

Lee, C. D. (1995). A culturally based cognitive apprenticeship: Teaching African American high school students skills in literary interpretation. *Reading Research Quarterly, 30*(4), 608–631.

Lee, C. D. (2000). Signifying in the zone of proximal development. In C. D. Lee & P. Smagorinsky (Eds.), *Vygotskian perspectives on literacy research: Constructing meaning through collaborative inquiry* (pp. 191–225). New York: Cambridge University Press.

Lee, C. D. (2001). Is October Brown Chinese? A cultural modeling activity system for underachieving students. *American Educational Research Journal, 38(1)*, 97–142.

Lee, C. D. (2002). Interrogating race and ethnicity as constructs in the examination of cultural processes in developmental research. *Human Development, 45(4),* 282–290.

Lee, C. D. (2004). Literacy in the academic disciplines and the needs of adolescent struggling readers. *Voices in Urban Education* (3), 14–25.

Lee, C. D. (2005a). Culture and language: Bi-dialectical issues in literacy. In P. L. Anders &J. Flood (Eds.), *Culture and language: Bi-dialectical issues in literacy.* Newark, DE: International Reading Association.

Lee, C. D. (2005b). Double voiced discourse: African American vernacular English as resource in Cultural Modeling classrooms. In A. F. Ball & S. W. Freedman (Eds.), *New literacies for new times: Bakhtinian perspectives on language, literacy, and learning for the 21st century.* New York: Cambridge University Press.

Lee, C. D. (2007). *Culture, literacy and learning. Taking bloom in the midst of the whirlwind.* New York: Teachers College Press.

Lee, C. D., Spencer, M. B., & Harpalani, V. (2003). "Every shut eye ain't sleep": Studying how people live culturally. *Educational Researcher, 32(5),* 6–13.

Li, S. (2006). Biocultural co-construction of life-span development. In P. Baltes, R. A. Reuter-Lorenz, & F. Rosier (Eds.), *Liftspan development and the brain: The perspective of biocultural co-constructivism.* New York: Cambridge University Press.

Madhubuti, H. (1991). *Black men, obsolete, single, dangerous? The African American family in transition.* Chicago: Third World Press.

Madhubuti, H. (1996). *Groundwork: New and selected poems of Don L. Lee/Haki R. Madhubuti.* Chicago: Third World Press.

Mandara, J. (2006). The impact of family functioning on African American males' academic achievement: A review and clarification of the empirical literature. *Teachers College Record, 108(2),* 206–223.

Markus, H., & Kitayama, S. (1991). Culture and the self: Implications for cognition, emotion, and motivation. *Psychological Review, 98,* 224–253.

Marshall, S. (1995). Ethnic socialization of African American children: Implications for parenting, identity development and academic achievement. *Journal of Youth and Adolescence, 24,* 377–396.

Maslow, A. H. (1954). *Motivation and personality.* New York: Harper.

McAdoo, H. P., & McAdoo, J. L. (1985). *Black children: Social, educational and parental environments.* Beverly Hills, CA: Sage.

Medin, D. L., Atran, S. (Eds.). (1999). *Folkbiology.* Cambridge, MA: Bradford.

Medin, D. L., Unsworth, S. J., & Hirschfield, L. (2007). Culture, categorization and reasoning. In S. Kitayama & D. Cohen (Eds.), *Handbook of cultural psychology* (pp. 615–644). New York: Guilford.

Mills, C. W. (1997). *The racial contract.* Ithaca, NY: Cornell University Press.

Moses, R. P., & Cobb, C. E. (2001). *Radical equations: Math literacy and civil rights.* Boston: Beacon.

Moss, P., Pullin, D., Gee, J. P., Haertel, E., & Young, L. J. (Eds.). (2008). *Assessment, equity and opportunity to learn.* New York: Cambridge University Press.

Murray, C. B., & Mandara, J. (2003). An assessment of the relationship between racial socialization, racial identity and self-esteem in African American adolescents. In D. A. Azibo (Ed.), *African-centered psychology* (pp. 293–325). Durham, NC: Carolina Academic Press.

Nadel, L., Lane, R., & Ahern, G. L. (Eds.). (2000). *The cognitive neuroscience of emotion.* New York: Oxford University Press.

Nasir, N. (2000). "Points ain't everything": Emergent goals and average and percent understandings in the play of basketball among African American students. *Anthropology and Education, 31*(1), 283–305.

Nasir, N. (2002). Identity, goals, and learning: Mathematics in cultural practice. *Mathematical Thinking and Learning, 4*(2–3), 211–247.

Nasir, N. (2005). Individual cognitive structuring and the sociocultural context: Strategy shifts in the game of dominoes. *Journal of the Learning Sciences, 14,* 5–34.

Nasir, N., Hand, V., & Taylor, E. (2008). Culture and mathematics in school: Boundaries between "cultural" and "domain" knowledge in the mathematics classroom and beyond. *Review of Research in Education, 32,* 187–240.

Nasir, N., Rosebery, A. S., Warren, B., & Lee, C. D. (2006). Learning as a cultural process: Achieving equity through diversity. In K. Sawyer (Ed.), *Handbook of the learning sciences.* New York: Cambridge University Press.

Nasir, N., & Saxe, G. (2003). Emerging tensions and their management in the lives of minority students. *Educational Researcher, 32*(5), 14–18.

Neal, L. (1989). *Visions of a liberated future: Black arts movement writings.* New York: Thunder's Mouth Press.

Nobles, W. (1974). African roots and American fruit: The Black family. *Journal of Social and Behavioral Sciences, 20*(2), 52–64.

Nobles, W. (1976). Extended self: Rethinking the so-called Negro selfconcept. *Journal of Black Psychology, 2*(2), 14–24.

Orellana, M., Reynolds, J., Dorner, L., & Meza, M. (2003). In other words: Translating or "para-phrasing" as a family literacy practice in immigrant households. *Reading Research Quarterly, 38*(1), 12–34.

Ortony, A. (1979). *The cognitive structure of emotions.* New York: Cambridge University Press.

Page, S. E. (2007). *The difference: How the power of diversity creates better groups, firms, schools and societies.* Princeton, NJ: Princeton University Press.

Perle, M., Moran, R., Lutkas, A., & Tirre, W. (2005). *NAEP 2004 trends in academic progress: Three decades of student performance in reading and mathematics.* Washington, DC: National Center for Education Statistics, U.S. Department of Education, Institute of Education Sciences.

Phinney, J. (1990). Ethnic identity in adolescents and adults: Review of research. *Psychological Bulletin, 108,* 499–514.

Plotkin, H. (2001). Some elements of a science of culture. In E. Whitehouse (Ed.), *The debated mind: Evolutionary psychology versus ethnography* (pp. 91–109). New York: Berg.

Quartz, S. R., & Sejnowski, T. J. (2002). *Liars, lovers, and heroes: What the new brain science reveals about how we become who we are.* New York: William Morrow.

Roediger, D. R. (2006). *Working toward Whiteness: How America's immigrants became White: The strange journey from Ellis Island to the suburbs.* New York: Basic Books.

Rogoff, B. (2003). *The cultural nature of human development.* New York: Oxford University Press.

Rogoff, B., & Gauvain, M. (1984). The cognitive consequences of specific experiences: Weaving vs. schooling among the Navaho. *Journal of Cross-Cultural Psychology, 15,* 453–475.

Rogoff, B., Paradise, R., Mejía-Arauz, R., Correa-Chávez, M., & Angelillo, C. (2003). Firsthand learning through intent participation. *Annual Review of Psychology, 54,* 175–204.

Rosebery, A. S., Warren, B., & Conant, F. R. (1992). Appropriating scientific discourse: Findings from language minority classrooms. *Journal of Learning Sciences, 2*(1), 61–94.

Ross, N. O., Medin, D. L., & Cox, D. (2007). Epistemological models and culture conflict: Menominee and European American hunters in Wisconsin. *Ethos, 35*(4), 478–515.

Saxe, G. (1981). Body parts as numerals: A developmental analysis of numeration among the Oksapmin in Papua New Guinea. *Journal of Educational Psychology, 77*(5), 503–513.

Scribner, S. (1984). Studying working intelligence. In B. Rogoff & J. Lave (Eds.), *Everyday cognition: Its development in social context* (pp. 9–40). Cambridge, MA: Harvard University Press.

Scribner, S., & Cole, M. (1981). *The psychology of literacy.* Cambridge, MA: Harvard University Press.

Sellers, R., Shelton, N., Cooke, D., Chavous, T., Rowley, S. J., & Smith, M. (1998). A multidimensional model of racial identity: Assumptions, findings, and future directions. In R. Jones (Ed.), *African American identity development* (pp. 275–303). Hampton, VA: Cobb & Henry.

Slaughter-Defoe, D., Nakagawa, K., Takanishi, R., & Johnson, D. J. (1990). Toward cultural/ecological perspectives on schooling and achievement in African- and Asian-American children. *Child Development, 61*(2), 363–383.

Spencer, M. B. (1987). Black children's ethnic identity formation: Risk and resilience in castelike minorities. In J. Phinney & M. Rotheram (Eds.), *Children's ethnic socialization: Pluralism and development* (pp. 103–116). Newbury Park, CA: Sage.

Spencer, M. B. (1999). Social and cultural influences on school adjustment: The application of an identity-focused cultural ecological perspective. *Educational Psychologist, 34*(1), 43–57.

Spencer, M. B. (2000). Identity, achievement orientation and race: "Lessons learned" about the normative developmental experiences of African American males. In W. Watkins, J. Lewis, & V. Chou (Eds.), *Race and education*. Needham Heights, MA: Allyn & Bacon.

Spencer, M. B. (2006). Phenomenology and ecological systems theory: Development of diverse groups. In W. Damon & C. R. M. Lerner (Eds.), *Handbook of child psychology* (6th ed., Vol. 1, pp. 829–893). New York: John Wiley.

Spencer, M. B., Fegley, S., & Harpalani, V. (2003). A theoretical and empirical examination of identity as coping: Linking coping resources to the self processes of African American youth. *Journal of Applied Developmental Science, 7(3),* 181–187.

Spencer, M. B., Swanson, D. P., & Cunningham, M. (1991). Ethnicity, ethnic identity, and competence formation: Adolescent transition and cultural transformation. *Journal of Negro Education, 60(3),* 366–387.

Spiro, R., Feltovich, P. L., Jackson, M. J., & Coulson, R. L. (1991). Cognitive flexibility, constructivism, and hypertext: Random access instruction for advanced technology acquisition to ill-structured domains. *Educational Technology, 31*(5), 24–33.

Steele, C. M. (1998): Stereotyping and its threat are real. *American Psychologist, 53,* 680–681.

Steele, C. M. (2004). A threat in the air: How stereotypes shape intellectual identity and performance. In J. Banks & C. Banks (Eds.), *Handbook of research on multicultural education* (2nd ed., pp. 682–698). San Francisco, CA: Jossey-Bass.

Valdes, G. (1996). Con respeto: *Bridging the distances between culturally diverse families and schools*. New York: Teachers College Press.

Valdes, G. (2002). *Expanding the definitions of giftedness: The case of young interpretersfiom immigrant countries*. Mahwah, NJ: Lawrence Erlbaum.

Vásquez, 0. A. (2002). La clase mágica: *Imagining optimal possibilities in a bilingual community of learners*. Mahwah, NJ: Lawrence Erlbaum.

Voting Rights Act of 1965,42 U.S.C. § 1973–1973aa-6.

Vygotsky, L. (1978). *Mind in society: The development of higher psychological processes* (M. Cole, V. John-Steiner, S. Scribner, & E. Souberman, Eds.). Cambridge, MA: Harvard University Press.

Vygotsky, L. (1981). The genesis of higher mental functions. In J. Wertsch (Ed.), *The concept of activity in Soviet psychology*. Armonk, NY: M.E. Sharpe.

Vygotsky, L. (1987). *Thinking and speech*. New York: Plenum.

Warren, B., Ballenger, C., Ogonowski, M., Rosebery, A. S., & Hudicourt-Barnes, J. (2001). Rethinking diversity in learning science: The logic of everyday sense-making. *Journal of Research in Science Teaching, 38,* 529–552.

Wigfield, A., Eccles, J., & Rodriguez, D. (1998). The development of children's motivation in school contexts. *Review of Research in Education, 23,* 135–170.

Zajonc, R B., & Marcus, H. (1984). Affect and cognition. In C. E. Izard, J. Kagan, & R. B. Zajonc (Eds.), *Emotions, cognition and behavior* (pp. 73–102). Cambridge, UK: Cambridge University Press.

TWENTY-THREE

Through the Fire: How Pretext Impacts the Context of African American Educational Experiences

Floyd Beachum and Carlos McCray

> *We have a powerful potential in our youth, and we must have the courage
> to change old ideas and practices so that we may direct their power toward
> good ends.*
> —Mary McLeod Bethune

The above quote is a challenge to all who are concerned about the plight of today's youth. The former portion of the statement affirms the ability of African American youth to take the reins of destiny and chart a course into the future. The latter part of the quote challenges us to reexamine what we have been doing and in many cases change the way we think and act for the betterment of students. Across the United States, from politicians and public officials to students and parents, people are calling for reform, restructure, and change in schools. In response, the federal government, over the years, began to emphasize higher graduation rates, accountability, more standardized testing, more rigor in academic subjects, and educational excellence (Obiakor & Beachum, 2005). The pressure placed on schools for educational excellence can promote a paradigm or paradigms based in technical efficiency, empiricism, scientific rationalism, and modernism (Dantley, 2002; Giroux, 1997). Thus, it is assumed that the best way to improve schools is by raising test scores on standardized tests (quantitative data), the promotion of *cookie-cutter,* recipe-style, linear models, and an ideology that treats all students and communities as equals, when equity is what is needed.

To complicate matters, the 21st century has witnessed the explosion of technology, entertainment, and popular culture. Gause (2005) asked a series of relevant questions regarding popular culture and education:

> How are schools and educational leaders keeping up with this global transformation? What type of impact does this transformation of schools from sites of democracy to "bedfellows" of consumerism have upon the school and much larger global community? How are the "souls" of schools affected? (p. 242)

These poignant questions propose significant challenges for today's educators. While trying to survive day to day providing students with a quality education, they must also deal with outside pressures from the national, state, and local levels. Concurrently, they must also prepare students for a future that is sure to be marked by technological advancement, the necessity of innovation, increased conceptual capacity, and the need to deal with people of different cultures, creeds, and characters (Nesbitt, 2009).

Cultural collision is a clash in beliefs, cultures, or values (see Beachum & McCray, 2008). For the purposes of our discussion, we emphasize the clash in cultures between youth (primarily youth of color in urban contexts) with the culture of educators and systems of education. A different, yet related concept is cultural collusion, which can be described as "the negative cultural/societal implications that emerge when complex cultural cues and messages seem to influence individual and group behavior" (Beachum & McCray, 2008, p. 104). This collusion specifically identifies "highly visible youth cultures, in this case violence, materialism, misogyny, and hip-hop culture" (Beachum & McCray, 2008, p. 104).

This chapter provides a historical and contextual foundation for the following chapters of our latest book: *Cultural Collision and Collusion: Reflections on Hip-Hop Culture, Values, and Schools.* This chapter seeks to also broaden horizons in the field of educational psychology. In support of this notion, Goodman (2008) stated that educational psychology needed to be reconsidered and placed in "real settings, where children and adolescents bring to the classroom a wide range of experiences and background knowledge that earlier pioneers of learning theory could not have imagined" (pp. x–xi). This chapter serves as socio-historical background knowledge for African American education and provides crucial contextual information for understanding cultural collision and collusion. In order to grasp the contemporary impact and outcomes of cultural collision and collusion, one must understand how these concepts originated and evolved. This chapter's organization is informed by the insightful work of French sociologist Loic Wacquant (2000), who proposed "not one but several 'peculiar institutions' have successively operated to define, confine, and control African-Americans in the history of the United States" (p. 378). These peculiar institutions are as follows: 1. Slavery (1619–1865); 2. Jim Crow/Segregation (1865–1965); 3. Ghetto (1915–1968); 4. Hyperghetto and Prison (1968–today). Using this framework, we will discuss historical highlights of the time period (what was happening), African Americans' attitudes toward education and shared cultural values at the time, and contradictions and complexities that caused unification or division, harmony or disagreement, and shifts in how African Americans saw themselves and the world.

NOBODY KNOWS THE TROUBLE I'VE SEEN: THE SCOURGE OF SLAVERY

HISTORICAL CONTEXT

Slavery in the United States of America remains a painful part of the nation's history. Its psychological, economic, and educational impacts are still being felt to this day (Akbar, 1984; Kunjufu, 1995). Thompson (2007) described this institution as follows:

> Although the United States has been described as a melting pot of various cultures, European capitalistic values and traditions have dominated this mix since its inception, long supplanting the theocratic system imported to North America by the early settlers. The opportunity to make huge profits in the New World led colonial entrepreneurs to use any means necessary to exploit the vast untapped resources of their recently claimed land. This included using force to extract labor from unwilling participants. After a trial-and-error period with Native American and indentured European workers, the "perfect" labor force for this harrowing task was identified on the African continent. Subsequently large numbers of Africans were brutally uprooted and shipped like cargo to strange lands hundreds of miles across the sea. (p. 50)

This quote encapsulates some of the purpose and processes regarding American slavery. Therefore, this peculiar institution promised huge profits through a massive system of forced labor. The process of obtaining this labor force meant the inhumane capture of human bodies and transporting them from one continent to another. This process would be rife with physical and psychological terror (Beachum, Dentith, & McCray, 2004; Perry, 2003). Blassingame (1979) gives yet another scathing summary:

> The chains of the American Negro's captivity were forged in Africa. Prince and peasant, merchant and agriculturalist, warrior and priest, Africans were drawn into the vortex of the Atlantic slave trade and funneled into the sugar fields, the swampy rice lands, or the cotton and tobacco plantations of the New World. The process of enslavement was almost unbelievably painful and bewildering for the Africans. Completely cut off from their native land, they were frightened by the artifacts of the White man's civilization and terrified by his cruelty until they learned that they were only expected to work for him as they been accustomed to doing in their native land. Still, some were so remorseful they committed suicide; others refused to learn the customs of whites and held on to the memory of the African cultural determinants of their own status. (pp. 3–4)

It is quite evident and well documented that slavery was an evolutionary industry that employed physical and psychic terror for the purpose of financial gain and the solidification of racial supremacy. It is also important to note that even in the midst of overwhelming and impossible odds, the Africans rebelled, resisted, sought ways to keep cultural traditions, and most of all reaffirmed their own humanity and forged ahead with the hope of a brighter day.

EDUCATIONAL ATTITUDES

The enslaved Africans in the United States were certainly discouraged from learning (except for maybe the most basic information). "Law and custom made it a crime for enslaved men and women to learn or teach others to read and write" (Perry, 2003, p. 13). Once again, against these laws and customs, enslaved Africans still made attempts to become literate. The tactics used to discourage the slaves were horrific; this was countered by ingenious strategies employed by slaves in order to learn. Perry (2003) wrote:

There are the stories of slaves who were hanged when they were discovered reading, and of patrollers who went around breaking up Sunday meetings where slaves were being taught to read, beating all of the adults who were present. Slaves cajoled White children into teaching them, trading marbles, and candy for reading lessons. They paid large sums of money to poor White people for reading lessons and were always on the lookout for time with the blue Black speller (a school dictionary), or for an occasion to learn from their masters and mistresses without their knowing. (p. 13)

Here we see the desire and passion for education among slaves. At some point during slavery, slaves became aware of the importance of becoming literate (Perry, 2003). They realized the great power and potential in being educated and what it meant for changing their status. This struggle by enslaved Africans to become educated occurred against an entrenched social system that constantly reinforced the slaves' subordinate status, hopeless plight, and so-called intellectual incapability or inferiority. Interestingly, many slave owners believed that education would "spoil" a slave by making them discontent instead of docile (Douglass, 1968). Thompson (2007) gives additional insight into the mentality of many Whites who supported slavery when he stated, "An educated slave was commonly viewed as dangerous and a direct contradiction to the slavery philosophy" (p. 57). Ultimately, the educational endeavor was much larger than an individualistic pursuit (even though there were obvious personal benefits); what we see is the building of a foundation to launch future freedom struggles. Education would play a critical role in attaining not only physical freedom; it also had the potential to liberate slaves from their psychological chains. In addition, education was viewed as something to be shared with the community. Again, Perry (2003) asserted:

> While learning to read was an individual achievement, it was fundamentally a communal act. For the slaves, literacy affirmed not only their individual freedom but also the freedom of their people. Becoming literate obliged one to teach others. Learning and teaching were two sides of the same coin, part of the same moment. Literacy was not something you kept for yourself; it was to be passed on to others, to the community. Literacy was something to share. (p. 14)

At the same time, we also see that education was not for education's sake; *education was synonymous with liberation* (Beachum, Dentith, & McCray, 2004). This theme would guide the slaves, who would eventually be called African Americans in their long journey to freedom and beyond.

COMPLEXITIES AND CONTRADICTIONS

Indeed, the Africans faced insurmountable odds and a bleak existence in the United States. Somehow they maintained the high value of education (as previously discussed), family cohesiveness, language patterns, and song. It is rather ironic that the slaves were portrayed to be intellectually inferior to Whites, but Africa was home to renowned educational institutions. "During the early 1500s, Sankore was a renowned intellectual center to which scholars from all over Africa, Asia, and Europe came to study" (Thompson, 2007, p. 57). Thus, the negative stereotyping and false imagery was clearly manufactured to support the institution of slavery (Akbar, 1984) and the de-humanization of all Africans. Africans still placed a high value on family even amid the scourge of slavery. It was commonplace for slaves to be separated and sold to far-off plantations by way of slave auctions (Blassingame, 1979). In many cases, fictive kinship relationships developed where another slave would become a surrogate family member. This was very important because the family proved to be an "important survival mechanism" against slavery (Blassingame, 1979, p. 191). Even though traditional African languages and dialects would slowly change to

English, slaves kept their traditional cultures alive by infusing them into English. "Regardless of his previous culture, upon landing in the New World the African-born slave had to learn the language of his master. Taught by overseers or native-born slaves, the African acquired a few European words in a relatively casual and haphazard fashion" (Blassingame, 1979, p. 24) in order to perform tasks and to engage in minimal communication. The slaves retained a special reverence for spirituality, even as Christianity slowly replaced African religions. Similarly, music and dance also played not only a critical role in the lives of enslaved Africans, but also in the lives of Africans in the American diaspora.

Music is more than an avenue for entertainment only. For the slaves, it was integrated into their lives. In this particular time period, spirituals told the collective story of struggle. Stuckey (1987) wrote:

> Too often the spirituals are studied apart from their natural, ceremonial context. The tendency has been to treat them as a musical form unrelated to dance and certainly unrelated to particular configurations of dance and dance rhythm…That the spirituals were sung in the circle guaranteed the continuing focus of the ancestors and elders as the Christian faith answered to African religious imperatives. (p. 27)

Here we find that spirituals incorporated dance, collaboration (together in a circle), with multiple purposes (emphasis on Christian faith and African traditions). Blassingame (1979) summarized the focus and intent of spirituals when he stated:

> The sentiments of the slave often appear in the spirituals. Songs of sorrow and hope, of agony and joy, of resignation and rebellion, the spirituals were the unique creations of the Black slaves. Since, however, the spirituals were derivations from Biblical lore and served as a means of intra-group expression in hostile environment, they naturally contain a few explicit references to slavery…Even when slaves did model their songs on those of whites, they changed them radically. (p. 137)

From this quote we learn that spirituals were uniquely created by the slaves and even when they adopted the songs of whites, they changed the songs to better reflect their experiences. The really important concept to note here is that through this form of musical expression, slaves told a story, their story and by collectively engaging in this activity, it was shared with succeeding generations. Here we find that music can be more than simply an expression of art; it can be intricately intertwined with one's life. We will return to this theme later.

In sum, slavery was a dark period for African Americans in this country. Although it had an economic intent, it also reinforced notions of Black ignorance, inferiority, and incapability. Thus the initial experiences of far too many African Americans in this nation were tainted by this peculiar institution. At the same time, the slaves still struggled to become literate, support family, maintain their culture (language, dance, and spirituals) and ultimately resign themselves to survive in the hope for a brighter tomorrow. Unfortunately, the next phase was not that bright, as slavery gave way to segregation.

I'VE BEEN IN THE STORM TOO LONG: JIM CROW/SEGREGATION

HISTORICAL CONTEXT

Eventually, slavery was totally abolished in the North, while it somewhat intensified in the South. The American West would become contentious territory, as the question of would slavery expand to newly admitted states. At the same time, the competing economic goals of the industrial North and the agricultural south, slowly guided the two large factions of our country into a bloody Civil War, with the status and future of African Americans at the epicenter. The American Civil War ended with the defeat of the South and the collapse of slavery as a formal institution. A short period of relative progress called Reconstruction (1865–1877) occurred in which many former slaves attained voting rights, began to attain a formal education, and, for the first time in the United States, saw a glimmer of hope in the darkness. This glimmer was quickly squelched as the Northern armies that provided protection and maintained order in the South pulled out. The result was a new era which could be termed Jim Crow or segregation.

Jim Crow laws were largely enforced in the South, while the North did have its forms of racism; segregation became law in Southern U.S. states. These laws were marked by the intentional separation of races (i.e., White and Black). Woodward (1974) asserted that these codes "extended to churches and schools, to housing and jobs, to eating and drinking. Whether by law or by custom, that ostracism extended to virtually all forms of public transportation, to sports and recreations, to hospitals, orphanages, prisons, and asylums, and ultimately to funeral homes, morgues, and cemeteries" (p. 7). The newly freed slaves posed a two-fold threat to the Southern social regime. First, the slaves being freed meant the immediate end to a massive free labor force and now the potential competition with Whites for jobs. Second, the new status of African Americans posed a significant threat to the system of deference, dehumanization, and racial superiority that Southern Whites had depended on for so long (Wacuant, 2001). Part of segregation's function would be to deal with both issues. "Under this regime, backed by custom and elaborate legal statutes, super-exploitative sharecropping arrangements and debt peonage fixed Black labor on the land, perpetuating the hegemony of the region's agrarian upper class" (Wacquant, 2001, p. 101). At the same time, "segregation laws sharply curtailed social contacts between whites and blacks by relegating the latter to separate residential districts and to the reserved 'colored' section of commercial establishments and public facilities, saloons and movie houses, parks and beaches, trolleys and buses, waiting rooms and bathrooms" (Wacquant, 2001, p. 101). Not only were these laws supported by White communities, but also by local police regimes. This allowed for the growth and expansion for *domestic terrorist groups* like the Ku Klux Klan. What this also meant was African Americans could not rely on the police or local/state legal systems for protection; therefore, they were vulnerable (West, 2004). Woodward (1974) observed, "Indeed the more defenseless, disfranchised, and intimidated the Negro became the more prone he was to the ruthless aggression of mobs" (p. 87). Although segregation was a harsh reality, African Americans created nurturing communities and endeavored to educate children and instill in them a sense of pride.

EDUCATIONAL ATTITUDES

An interesting phenomenon occurred amid the ever-imposing environment of segregation. Instead of segregation totally devastating the educational aspirations of African Americans, in many cases, it actually strengthened their spirits and resolve. Segregation not only regulated the physical movement of African Americans, but it also took a psychological toll on them as well (Perry, 2003; Thompson, 2007). Schools were of course segregated, and although they were separate they were certainly not equal (even though separate but equal was the law at this time). In fact, "in many areas Negro schools were disgracefully behind schools for whites" (Woodward,

1974, p. 145). What these schools lacked in facilities and resources, they made up for in attitude and determination. While the dominant Southern social order suggested to African Americans that they were nobody (almost sub-human), schools and communities reinforced the refrain "be somebody." This meant to "be a human, to be a person, to be counted, to be the opposite of a slave, to be free" (Perry, 2003, p. 26). Obtaining an education was the key to being somebody. Similarly, schools during this time period not only provided academic preparation to African American students, but it also prepared them for the world beyond the schoolhouse doors (including the world of segregation and Jim Crow). The academic focus was supplemented or grounded in a pedagogy that purposely cultivated student self-esteem. Another example of this would be the *110 rule*. Many educators would tell their students that 100 percent was not good enough; you had to strive for 110 percent (Kunjufu, 2002). Schools in the segregated South with effective and caring African American educators in many cases promoted academic excellence and personal mastery. In sum, Perry (2003) insightfully asserted:

> There was a systematic denial and limiting of educational opportunity for African Americans precisely because they were African Americans. The philosophy of education that developed was informed by the particular ways in which literacy and education were implicated in the oppression of African Americans. It informed the role that education and schooling would assume in resistance and the struggle for freedom from the time of slavery to the Civil Rights era. (p. 51)

The philosophy here was one that viewed education as a process and product of liberation.

COMPLEXITIES AND CONTRADICTIONS

Although it seems rather easy to totally indict the South in its determined focus on establishing and enforcing a system of segregation, it is easy to overlook the contradictory attitudes in the North. Woodward (1974) insightfully wrote, "One of the strangest things about the career of Jim Crow was that the system was born in the North and reached an advanced age before moving to the South in force" (p. 17). Although African Americans in the North did enjoy certain freedoms, such as more freedom of movement and more freedom to challenge overt forms of racism, these freedoms existed in a context of White superiority and Black inferiority. Again Woodward noted:

> For all that, the Northern Negro was made painfully and constantly aware that he lived in a society dedicated to the doctrine of White supremacy and Negro inferiority. The major political parties, whatever their devotion to slavery, vied with each other in their devotion to this doctrine, and extremely few politicians of importance dared to question them. Their constituencies firmly believed that the Negroes were incapable of being assimilated politically, socially, or physically into White society. They made sure in numerous ways that the Negro understood his "place" and that he was severely confined to it. (p. 18)

Although, this quote is primarily describing the North around the end of slavery, it is evident that such attitudes continued well past slavery's demise (Woodward, 1974). A glaring example of Northern apathy toward the newly freed Blacks is seen in the Compromise of 1877. After the American Civil War, Northern armies in the South played a key role in maintaining order while Southern resentment, outrage, and vengeance boiled beneath the surface. This compromise that on the one hand made Rutherford B. Hayes president of the United States, guaranteed the abandonment of African Americans in the South. Although some Southern politicians pledged to protect the rights of African Americans, they soon became empty rhetoric. "But as these pledges were forgotten or violated and the South veered toward proscription and extremism, Northern opinion shifted to the right, keeping pace with the South, conceding point, after point, so that at no time were the sections very far apart on race policy" (Woodward, 1974, p. 70). As white America's attitudes toward African Americans became more apathetic, Blacks found other ways to cope with the backlash. Music became one of the avenues of freedom by means of self-expression.

Music can provide unique insight into the souls of a people. Perry (2003) wrote, "To know what a people believes, one should of course pay attention to what they say, what they portray in music, poetry, and stories" (p. 27). This particular time period was marked by forms of musical expression such as gospel and blues. What we know now as gospel music grew out of the same cultural crucible as slave spirituals. In this era, African Americans now could meet in their own churches and openly worship in their own unique ways. "African American gospel represents the flip side of the blues. Spirituals are a powerful emotional testimonial to the depths of despair, atonement, and redemption, juxtaposed with an unshakeable faith that God will ultimately prevail" (White & Cones, 1999, p. 55). We discover the deep connection to spirituality here along with the belief that a brighter day was ahead. In addition, Blacks found a way to communicate and pass on a shared history and collection of experiences while acknowledging something greater than oneself. The blues on the other hand was a different form of musical expression.

The blues also told the story of African Americans, but in a different way than gospel. "The bluesman articulates the pain and suffering in a patter of African-American speech and images that the listener who has lived the Black experience can understand" (White & Cones, 1999, p. 55). Here again, musical expression is not divorced from the everyday lived experiences of African Americans. It tells of struggle, strife, pity, problems, reality, and resilience. In this way, the blues was more than an impotent outlet for entertainment only; it became a way to communicate the shared cultural set of experiences complete with musical accompaniment. West (2004) wrote:

> As infectious and embracing as the blues is, we should never forget that the blues was born out of the crucible of slavery and its vicious legacy, that it expresses the determination of a people to assert their human value. The blues professes to the deep psychic and material pains inflicted on Black people within the sphere of a mythological land of opportunity…The patience resilience expressed in the blues flows from the sustained resistance to ugly forms of racist domination, and from the forging of indistinguishable hope in the contexts of American social death and soul murder. The blues produced a mature spiritual and communal strength. (p. 93)

Once again, music reinforced a set of values such as spirituality, community, self-expression, self-reflection, and the undying commitment against forms of oppression in that day and time.

WHAT'S GOING ON? THE URBAN GHETTO

HISTORICAL CONTEXT

The time period from approximately 1915 to 1968 encompasses a large portion of the 20th century. This period would witness events such as two world wars, the Great Depression, and a momentous struggle to end segregation culminating in the American Civil Rights movement. During the first part of the century, segregation was still alive and well. Along with segregation came an era of physical and psychological terror for African Americans, as evidenced by brutal lynching, beatings, harassment, and verbal abuse (Thompson, 2007; Woodward, 1974). Wacquant (2000) summarized the plight of African Americans at the time writing:

> The sheer brutality of caste oppression in the South, the decline of cotton agriculture due to floods and the boll weevil, and the pressing shortage of labor in northern factories caused by the outbreak of the First World War created the impetus for African-Americans to emigrate en masse to the booming industrial centers of the Midwest and Northeast (over 1.5 million left in 1910–30, followed by another 3 million in 1940–60). But as migrants from Mississippi to the Carolinas flocked to the northern metropolis, what they discovered there was not the "promised land" of equality and full citizenship but another system of racial enclosure, the ghetto, which, though it was less rigid and fearsome than the one they had fled, was no less encompassing and constricting. (pp. 4–5)

Thus, the North promised a new beginning devoid of the obvious racial barriers that were prevalent in the South. Ironically, while offering a new life, the North also offered new forms of segregation, as African Americans were ushered into certain segments of Northern cities, which came to be known as ghettoes.

The 20th century witnessed the migration of masses of African Americans to the industrial North from the agricultural South. According to Jackson (1996), "From 1915 to the 1930s, 1.8 million Southern blacks migrated to industrial cities in the North and Midwest" (p. 234). Villegas and Lucas (2002) noted, "In 1940, for instance, almost 80 percent of the African American population lived in the South, and 63 percent lived in rural areas; thirty years later, only 33 percent lived in the South, and 75 percent lived in urban settings" (p. 46). It was the hope of many to find better job opportunities, to escape the segregation and violence in the South, and to possibly gain access to a small slice of the "American dream." Unfortunately, life in the North provided only minimal opportunities and a more nuanced and covert form of racism as compared to the South. Rothstein (1996) agreed, "Wherever they went, however, they found the pernicious segregation system. This affected where they went to school, where they worked, and the type of employment they were able to obtain" (p. 163). This would eventually lead to a phenomenon which would increase the "geographic isolation" of people of color from their White counterparts called *White flight*. White flight would be the next event in a chain that would isolate urban dwellers (mainly of color) and their schools.

EDUCATIONAL ATTITUDES

Whites in many urban areas began to leave as the number of African Americans (and other people of color) increased. They escaped to suburbs away from the cities leaving a void. This process became known as "White flight." Malcolm Gladwell (2000) borrows this term in his book *The Tipping Point: How Little Things Can Make a Big Difference;* he opined:

> The expression [Tipping Point] first came into popular use in the 1970s to describe the flight to the suburbs of whites living in the older cities of the American Northeast. When the number of incoming African Americans in a particular neighborhood reached a certain point—20 percent say sociologists observed that the community would "tip": most of the remaining whites would leave almost immediately. (p. 12)

This quote expresses the core attitude against racial integration. The result would be exceedingly different schools: "The suburbanization of the United States has created two racially segregated and economically unequal systems of education—one urban, mostly for children who are poor and of color; the other suburban, largely White, middle-class children" (Villegas & Lucas, 2002, p. 48). This process would have detrimental effects on communities and schools of color in the inner cities. African Americans who moved to the North found a more nuanced, less overt, yet equally if not more damaging form of oppression. The experience in the industrial North gave the façade of limitless opportunities (which were actually very limited) while also making transparent a harsh reality, which included isolation, neglect, and an inferior infrastructure for schooling.

African Americans would try their best to hold on to their deep belief in education as a means of liberation. This philosophy was now challenged by the harsh reality of urban life. While isolated in segregated parts of major cities, crime rates began to increase, businesses began to leave, and the meaning of community for African Americans began to wane.

COMPLEXITIES AND CONTRADICTIONS

During this time period African Americans faced numerous challenges. In the South, segregation was still the rule of the day, undergirded by the terrorist tactics of groups like the Ku Klux Klan. By the mid-20th century, serious resistance to segregation began to mount. A watershed moment occurred with the *Brown v. Board of Education* (1954) decision.

> The landmark Supreme Court decision in the *Brown v. Board of Education* case has been hailed as the single most important court decision in American educational history. The decision in this case overturned the *Plessy v. Ferguson* separate but equal clause by establishing that segregated schools denied African American students their constitutional rights guaranteed to them in the 14th Amendment. *Brown...* would also serve as the impetus for challenging several inequities as Jim Crow laws in the south and, on many levels, for generally protecting the civil rights of African Americans and later individuals with disabilities. (Blanchett, Mumford, & Beachum, 2005, p. 70)

While this movement impacted the physical manifestations of oppression, in conjunction, the Black Power movement started to deal with how Black people felt about themselves, by instilling self-reliance, self-sufficiency, and in some cases self-protection. Similarly, White and Cones (1999) wrote,

> At a deeper, more personal level, it was about the right of self-determination and self-definition. The Reverend Martin Luther King, Jr. used terms like "somebodyness" to define the psychological meaning of the revolution. Other terms coined to reinforce this concept were "Black pride," "Black is Beautiful," and "Black Power"...self-definition from the perspective of one's own experience is the first step in deconstructing the oppressor's negative definitions. (p. 63)

As African Americans strived to dismantle oppressive laws (i.e., Jim Crow) and deal with the psychological effects of ongoing mistreatment, music remained a means of dealing with reality as well as expressing their innermost feelings.

During this time period jazz became popular as well as the growth of rhythm and blues (R&B). Jazz has been hailed a musical form that characterizes imagination and invention. West (2004) wrote, "These great blues and jazz musicians are eloquent connoisseurs of individuality in their improvisational arts and experimental lives" (p. 91). Dyson (1997) characterized jazz as "its heart pumping with the blood of improvisation, its gut-churning with the blues—embody the edifying quest for romantic self-expression and democratic collaboration that capture Negro music and American democracy at their best" (p. 126). With its emphasis on improvisation, individuality, and expression, jazz represented yet another form of music that transcended the boundaries of mere entertainment-laden titillation. According to West (2004), jazz was much more, "The blues and jazz made it possible to engage race in America on personal and intimate terms—with democratic results" (p. 92). West (2008) provided even more clarity when he wrote,

> What is jazz all about? It's about finding your voice. It's about that long, difficult walk to freedom. It's about mustering the courage to think critically. It's about mustering the courage to care and love, and be empathetic and compassionate…Jazz is the middle road between invisibility and anger. It is where self-confident creativity resides. (p. 118)

Thus, in the early to mid-20th century jazz provided African Americans a unique form of musical expression in the midst of Southern segregation and Northern isolation.

The 1960s and early 1970s clearly represented a unique time period for African Americans. Dyson (2007) agrees, "In the 1960s and 1970s, Black folk were struggling for the sorts of political freedoms and economic opportunities that the most fortunate members of the young Black generation now take for granted" (p. 63). The movement towards Black liberation was supported by music that began to reflect the struggle. At this time you also had the Black Arts Movement (BAM). "For the members of the Black Arts Movement, there was no such thing as a serious artist who was not concerned about the struggles for self-determination and political liberty of their people, struggles which in large part inspired their art" (Dyson, 2007, p. 62). So when one hears Curtis Mayfield's "Keep on Pushin," James Brown's "I'm Black and I'm Proud," or Sam Cooke's, "Change Is Gonna Come," one learns that these works cannot easily be separated from the times in which these artists lived. In sum, music can be utilized strictly for entertainment value, but for African Americans, it has historically served a greater purpose. "Music has been our most powerful creative expression. Of course, the music itself is based on communal links of church, family, and social education. Our music reflects our unique sense of rhythm, harmony, and melody" (West, 2008, p. 114).

GET RICH OR DIE TRYIN': THE HYPERGHETTO/HOOD AND 21ST CENTURY BLACK AMERICA

HISTORICAL CONTEXT

The last 40 years has brought even more changes to the world and to African Americans. The final institution that Wacquant proposed was the hyperghetto. Once again, his framework explains how the four institutions "operated to define, confine, and control African-Americans in the history of the United States" (Wacquant, 2000, p. 377). Our utilization of his framework in this chapter is to provide a historical model to better understand the historical, educational, and socio-cultural experiences of African Americans in the U.S. The hyperghetto evolved in a post–White flight era when the residential barriers that barred African Americans from moving into White suburbs were relaxed (Wilson, 2009). Thus, White flight was followed by *Black trek,* as more African Americans with greater wealth left inner-city communities, leaving a dangerous void in what was the ghetto (Dyson, 2004). In addition to the spatial separation, Wacquant (2001) asserted,

> Its economic basis has shifted from the direct servicing of the Black community to the state, with employment in public bureaucracies accounting for most of the growth of professional, managerial and technical positions held by African Americans over the past thirty years. The genealogical ties of the Black bourgeoisie to the Black poor have also grown more remote and less dense. (p. 104)

From this quote, we note the growing stratification in the African American community, as the Black middle class separates themselves from the Black poor. Many scholars and authors have warned of the increasing separation, segregation, and stratification within the African American community (Dyson, 2005; Kitwana, 2002; Kunjufu, 2002; West, 2008). West (2008) elaborated, "Once we lose any sense of a Black upper or Black middle class or a Black upper working-class connecting with the Black underclass with a 'we' consciousness or sense of community, it becomes much more difficult to focus on the plight of the poor" (p. 57). The evolution of the hyperghetto has become a place of increased violence, elicit drug sale and use, economic depravity, police surveillance and brutality, and struggling schools.

It is apparent that today's African American youth (the current generation) has been impacted by certain sociopolitical forces. Kitwana (2002) identified six major phenomena that make the lives of these youth different from previous generations: (1) a different process of values and identity development; (2) globalization; (3) persisting segregation; (4) public policy regarding the racialization of the criminal justice system; (5) overexposure and negative exposure with regard to media representation; (6) the decline in overall quality of life for the poor and working poor. In reference to values and identity formation, there is evidence that they are influenced in different ways. In the past, church, family, and school heavily influenced African American youth identity development (Kunjufu, 1993). Regarding today's identity development, Kitwana (2002) insightfully wrote,

> Today the influence of these traditional purveyors of Black culture has largely diminished in the face of powerful and pervasive technological advances and corporate growth. Now media and entertainment such as pop music, film, and fashion are among the major forces transmitting culture to this generation of Black Americans...For the most part, we have turned to ourselves, our peers, global images and products, and the new realities we face for guidance. (p. 7)

In terms of globalization, today's African American youth have come of age in a time where we have witnessed the upward mobility of a select number of elites and the expansion of the middle class (including Blacks) (Dyson, 2004). At the same time they have witnessed jobs moving away from urban areas and the increasing distancing of the haves from the have-nots (Kitwana, 2002; West, 2004). Contemporary segregation is not evidenced by signs and customs as in the Jim Crow era. "We certainly live in a more inclusive society than existed in pre–civil rights America. However, continuing segregation and inequality have made it especially illusory for many young blacks. The illusion of integration allows for some access, while countless roadblocks persist in critical areas where blacks continue to be discriminated against in often subtle and sometimes not so subtle ways" (Kitwana, 2002, p. 13). White and Cones (1999) agree that contemporary prejudice exists mainly in the form of institutional racism. They explain:

> Institutional racism exists where whites restrict equal access to jobs and promotions, to business and housing loans, and the like. White bankers and mortgage companies can secretly collaborate to redline a neighborhood so that such loans are nearly impossible to obtain. White senior faculty members in predominately White universities (public and private) determine who gets promoted to tenured faculty positions...Good-old-boys' clubs in the corporate structure determine who will be mentored and guided through the promotional mine fields. (p. 136)

African American youth witness the continuing legacy of segregation and racism and its impact on their lives. Related to the persistence of segregation/racism is the criminal justice system and how it is skewed against people of color (particularly black males). This is not to say that if a black male commits a crime that he does not deserve punishment, but the eyes of justice should be blindfolded, making people equal before the law. For instance, young African Americans have grown up with laws that give more jail time for crimes involving crack cocaine as opposed to crimes that involve powder cocaine (largely the drug of choice for more Whites). They have been impacted by the explosive growth in prison construction, zero tolerance policies, and instances of police harassment and constant surveillance (Kitwana, 2002). Dyson (2005) asserted, "The increase in Black incarceration was driven by political considerations, not a boost in, for instance, drug consumption" (p. 88).

Kitwana (2002) eloquently captured the sentiments of many African American youth when he stated, "The collapse of trust in law enforcement and the vilification of Black youth through crime legislation certainly play a role in the view Black youth share about legislation, law enforcement, and criminal justice" (p. 18).

The images of young African Americans are frequently misrepresented by the mainstream media and today's entertainment titans. Still today, young Blacks are overrepresented on the news as criminals and menaces to society (Kitwana, 2002; White & Cones, 1999). In addition, a wave of so-called reality-based television programs now depicts many young African Americans as combative, aggressive, ignorant, materialistic, and sexually obsessed (West, 2008). According to White and Cones (1999) "Not only do European Americans believe that theses caricatures represent the reality of Black male life, but Black male youths [and female youths] may aspire to live up to these images because they are popularized and romanticized" (p. 72).

Finally, today's African American youth recognize the significant issues around quality of life in America. The wealth gap between the rich and poor continues to grow (Dyson, 2005; Kitwana, 2002; West, 2008). West (2004) chides the more recent over emphasis on money-based values or obsession with wealth attainment. He asserted, "It also redefines the terms of what we should be striving for in life, glamorizing materialistic gain, narcissistic pleasure, and the pursuit of narrow individualistic preoccupations—especially for young people here and abroad" (p. 4). Kitwana (2002) discussed the impact of West's statement on the hip-hop generation when he stated, "For us, achieving wealth, by any means necessary, is more important than most anything else, hence our obsession with the materialistic and consumer trappings of financial success" (p. 6). Thus, African American youth realize the rampant wealth inequality in the United States and have in many cases made a conscious choice to pursue materialistic gain. West (2008) again warned, "The marketplace culture of consumption undermines community, undermines links to history and tradition, and undermines relationships" (p. 31). This quote is particularly powerful in relationship to the historical context provided here.

The phenomena presented here are provided to paint a picture of today's contemporary context, especially for African American youth. We recognize that the other time periods we examined earlier related to Blacks in general. We emphasize Black youth specifically here because of the great curiosity around their contemporary plight. Other things that inevitably impact these youth include: employment, relationships, technological growth, and political engagement (Kitwana, 2002; Dyson, 2004) to name a few. Obviously, the world around these youth would impact their outlook on education.

EDUCATIONAL ATTITUDES

In the 21st century, African Americans find themselves in a place of great promise and peril. Today, there seems to be almost limitless opportunities for students who are dedicated, determined, and disciplined. We have even witnessed what some thought was virtually impossible, the election of a Black president of the United States of America. His success is powerfully symbolic for all children of color, but the structures that one must navigate remain intact. Even as we acknowledge the great progress of Black faces in high places (West, 2008), the data tell a different story. According to McKinsey & Company (2009):

- Avoidable shortfalls in academic achievement impose heavy and often tragic consequences, via lower earnings, poorer health, and higher rates of incarceration.
- For many students (but by no means all), lagging achievement evidenced as early as fourth grade appears to be a powerful predictor of rates of high school and college graduation, as well as lifetime earnings. (p. 6)
- Kunjufu (2002) indicates:
  - African American students comprise 17 percent of the U.S. student population. African American teachers comprise 6 percent of U.S. teachers. African American males comprise one percent of U.S. teachers.
  - There is no staff of color in 44 percent of schools.
  - Of inner-city teachers, 40 percent transfer within five years.
  - One of every three African American males is involved with a penal institution, while only one of ten male high school graduates is enrolled in college.
  - Only 3 percent of African American students are placed in gifted and talented programs.
  - If an African American child is placed in special education, 80 percent of the time the child will be male.
  - Thirty-three percent of African American households live below the poverty line.

In light of *Brown v. Topeka* in 1954, schools have become more segregated since 1971. (pp. vii—viii). These data paint a bleak picture for far too many African American youth. The obvious question for many is what happened from slavery to today? The framework provided here gives some insight. Specifically, regarding educational attitudes, the emphasis on education for liberation seemed to decline with the dismantling of segregated, all-Black schools and increasing integration, the conversion of overt racist practices to covert racist practices in schools, and the change in the attitudes of students regarding the value of education. As previously noted, segregated schools provided Black children at the time academic preparation as well as preparation for life in a world that saw them as inept, inferior, and incapable. Schools reinforced their spirits, as segregated society tried its best to tear them apart. This created a kind or resiliency in these students (Perry, 2003). When segregation ended and integration came, many dedicated African American teachers and administrators lost their jobs (McCray, Wright, & Beachum, 2007). In addition, as the doors of opportunity began to open, African American students opted for other majors besides education (Kunjufu, 2002). Therefore, the educators who provided quality education were lost along with the pipeline that would replace them. In their place, White educators largely took up the task of educating African American students, with mixed results.

Today, the teaching force (along with administrators) is predominately White (McCray, Wright, & Beachum, 2007). As a matter of fact, the teaching core in the U.S. is mostly White and female (Kunjufu, 2002; Mizialko, 2005). This in itself is not inherently problematic. The key issue here is teacher expectations. "There are consequences of a primarily White, female, middle class, monolingual teaching force. The consequences are felt by multicultural, urban learners" (Mizialko, 2005, p. 177). Hancock (2006) agreed, "The reality that White women are on the front lines of urban education is clearly evident. While we continue to recruit and retain minority teachers, it is critical that we also focus our attention on helping to educate White women teachers about the realities of teaching students who may hold a different sociopolitical, sociocultural, and socioeconomic perspective" (p. 97). Additionally, Kunjufu (2002) also made the point that African American teachers could have negative attitudes and low expectations towards students of color. The great problem here is that even though we exist in a society absent the visible manifestations of segregation and alienation (i.e., *Whites only* signs, *Jim Crow* laws, etc.), many students still readily get the message by other covert means that their skin color is inferior. Tatum (1997) discussed the concept of cultural racism, defined as "the cultural images and messages that affirm the assumed superiority of Whites and the assumed inferiority of people of color" (p. 6). Similarly, Delpit (1995) described specific examples where teachers would seldom interact with students of color and called this "invisible racism." It is up to all teachers to strive for equity and excellence for all students.

African American students today are strongly impacted by the world in which they live. Today's youth live in a world of high-speed information sharing, texting, and tweeting as major means of communication, life lived online on the Internet, and are used to having many options. Unfortunately, the way we still structure schools is grounded in a 20th century philosophy. For many African American students, especially those from the inner city, seem to concentrate on immediate gratification as opposed to long-term gratification (as with a good education) (Kitwana, 2002; Kunjufu, 2002). In addition, many youth have witnessed relatives who have graduated high school or attended college and still face discrimination or unemployment (Dyson, 2005). "To be effective teaching African American students, you must convince them that there is a "payoff" in education" (Kunjufu, 2002, p. 101). Educators must provide an accurate and convincing portrait of career choices and reinforce the importance of a good education. In addition, education must be viewed as not only a means for financial gain, but a tool for personal development and self-actualization.

COMPLEXITIES AND CONTRADICTIONS

Today, African Americans seem to be both loved and hated by mainstream society. As it stands, when an African American reaches the pinnacle of their field (sports, acting, journalism, medicine, academics, business, politics, etc.) they are hailed as examples and showered with praise. But for the vast majority of African Americans who are struggling to make a way for themselves, they are many times met with resistance, bitterness, sarcasm, and/or resentment (Bogotch, Beachum, Blount, Brooks, & English, 2008; Dyson, 2004; Perry, 2003; Tatum, 2007; West, 2008). This dichotomized view allows the dominant culture to accept a certain select segment of the African American population while at the same time justify the unfair treatment of the great majority who have not reached such lofty heights as their privileged peers. In this manner, the illusion of true equality in American society is allowed to flourish. This is a serious and ongoing contradiction. This kind of contradiction also affects other areas such as hip-hop culture.

Hip-hop culture has emerged in recent years and clearly dominates the lives of many youth. West (2008) exclaimed, "Hip-hop music is the most important popular musical development in the last thirty years" (p. 122). White and Cones (1999) stated, "Hip-hop is a catch-all term for a contemporary, urban-centered youth lifestyle associated with popular music, break dancing, certain dress and hair styles, graffiti, and street language" (p. 96). Hip-hop culture has gone from primarily rapping, break dancing, dj-ing, and graffiti to including dialects, attitude, expression, mannerisms, and fashion (Au, 2005; Kitwana, 2002). Regarding youth, Kunjufu (1993) asserted, "The ages between 13–17 are when they [teenagers] are particularly vulnerable to outside influence and before their values and ideas are fully developed (Kunjufu, 1993, p. 81). Furthermore, Kitwana (2002) wrote, "Today, more and more Black youth are turning to rap music, music videos, designer clothing, popular Black films, and television programs for values and identity" (p. 9). It is apparent that hip-hop culture has the ability to affect the values of youth in general and Black youth in particular.

Hip-hop (or rap) music is yet another form of musical expression that signifies, symbolizes, and structures the African American experience. The music itself, although born out of post-industrial blight and inspired by those who considered themselves outcasts, has transformed over time (Dyson, 2007; West, 2004). Some may now argue that it has become a reflection of the materialism and corporate structures it railed against during its initial phases. West (2004) elaborated,

> An unprecedented cultural breakthrough created by talented poor Black youths in the hoods of the empire's chocolate cities, hip-hop has now transformed the entertainment industry and culture here and around the world. The fundamental irony of hip-hop is that it has become viewed as a nihilistic, macho, violent, and bling-bling phenomenon when in fact its originating impulse was a fierce disgust with the hypocrisies of adult culture—disgust with the selfishness, capitalist callousness, and xenophobia of the culture of adults, both within the hood and in the society at large. (p. 179)

West is referring to hip-hop's more humble beginnings when the music was a form of expression, a canvas for lyrical creativity, and mechanism for sharing the trials and triumphs of urban existence.

In sum, hip-hop may very well be both overestimated and underestimated. It is overestimated by critics and detractors for blaming the music for a host of social ills that existed long before hip-hop came into being (e.g., rampant materialism, deadly violence, drug proliferation, and malicious levels of misogyny). West (2008) levied a fair critique when he wrote, "Too often, hip-hop still lacks deep vision and analysis. It's just escapism, it's thin. It's too morally underdeveloped and spiritually immature. In the end, it has to be more of a turning-to in order to constructively contribute" (p. 127). At the same time hip-hop is underestimated because of its awesome potential to make money, motivate people, and inspire young minds. It cannot be expected to solve all of the problems in the African American community, but at the same time it does have the potential to at least "do no harm" or at least do not exacerbate the situation. Dyson (2007) eloquently described hip-hop as follows, "Hip hop is fundamentally an art form that traffics in hyperbole, parody, kitsch, dramatic license, double entendres, signification, and other literary and artistic conventions to get its point across" (p. xvii). If the message in hip-hop is disturbing, then its creators are trying to tell us something about the contemporary African American experience.

DISCUSSION

Our discussion here has covered a great majority of the African American experience. The authors acknowledge that this brief analysis cannot begin to address the comprehensive and complex nuances involved in this kind of socio-historical critique. It is our hope to shed a modicum of light for additional insight. What follows is a summation of the information gathered from our rendering of the Wacquant (2000) framework.

CONTEXT MATTERS

In each phase observed we acknowledged historical context. In addition, African Americans are linked to the occurrences, happenings, and experiences of the past. In addition, this is not simply a form of misguided nostalgia when we discuss African Americans and their history. There are pitfalls to extreme forms of this. Dyson (1997) warned, "Nostalgia is colored memory. It is romantic remembering. It recreates as much as it recalls" (p. 117). Our perspective here advocates the recognition of the comprehensive historical experience, even when the memories are painful (i.e., slavery and segregation). The lesson here is to *respect* the history, and also to *protect* the history, so the next generation will not *reject* the history. The acknowledgment of our tragic past, as African Americans begin to experience what some would consider modest success. West (2008) stated,

> It's easy to think that somehow, because there's been relative progress for a significant number of Black people, that there has been some kind of fundamental transformation. Therefore, we lose sight of the degree to which the history of New World Africans, in this hemisphere for 400 years, still affects us all. (p. 50)

Ultimately, our perspectives, attitudes, and views of reality cannot be totally separated from our context.

EDUCATION FOR LIBERATION

Black people have historically struggled for the right to learn, be educated, and be liberated. Education has been valued even at a time when it carried harsh penalties and was against the law (Perry, 2003). As we observe the current statistics regarding African American students regarding dropout rates, achievement gaps, etc., we must question current practices. Earlier, we discussed several problems in the American educational system. Here are some promising ideas:

- All educators should engage in continuous self-improvement/self development. This may include additional readings/reading groups, professional development workshops, and/or attending educational conferences. The goal is to create educational environments that value both equity and excellence (Beachum & Obiakor, 2005).
- Teachers should strive to increase the rigor of their lessons, make their lessons relevant, and continuously build relationships with their students.
- Educational leaders should provide resources to support measurable efforts to create time and space for teachers and administrators to reflect on their practice, engage in

discussion/debate, and imagine as well as develop new and innovative school structures, programs, and activities.

- Parents should monitor and manage your child's educational progress. Attend parent-teacher conferences if possible; if not schedule a specific time to talk to your child's teacher(s). Provide your child with a quiet place to study as well as the proper materials (writing utensils, books, computer, globe, dictionary, calculator, etc.) (Kunjufu, 2002).

- Community members should "hold all leaders and elected officials responsible and demand that they change current policy" (Gordon, 2006, p. 34).

Improving the situation regarding African American education requires individual as well as collective action. Above, we discussed what different constituencies can do individually. The collective urgency is captured in the following quote, "We must demand that local communities provide the resources to educate *all* children, that the state and federal governments provide sufficient resources. The mandate of educating all of America's children rests on all of us" (Gordon, 2006, p. 34).

THE CONTINUITY OF CULTURE

From our read of African American's experiences in the U.S., we identified many complexities and contradictions. As a theme we continuously looked at the role of music in each historical epoch. The role of music is multifaceted. It was a way to communicate and share information during slavery. In segregation, it expressed the pain in the blues and the promise in spirituals. During the American Civil Rights/Black Power era it enhanced the struggle for freedom. Even today, the music still has the potential to do all of the things of the past or reflect the reality of today (as so much of the music seems to do). Music is indeed a form of entertainment and artistic expression. At the same time, it has meant so much more to African Americans. In all of the historical periods, the music is trying to tell us something. Encoded in the music are strife, distress, and powerful emotion. The music also can also contain joy, peace, contentment, jubilation, and hope. This is the magic of music, to be able to take listeners on a journey to places they may have never imagined, or to give the listener an in-depth look into the soul of the person or persons making the music. This is the essence of the African American experience; the highs and lows, the good and the gloom, the realization of the American dream in the midst of the American nightmare.

CONCLUSION

In this chapter, we have taken a socio-historical look at the experiences of African Americans in the U.S. Wacquant (2000) provided a framework of "peculiar institutions" that informed our work: 1. Slavery (1619–1865); 2. Jim Crow/Segregation (1865–1965); 3. Ghetto (1915–1968); 4. Hyperghetto and Prison (1968–). In each era, we delved deeper into historical context, educational attitudes, and complexities and contradictions. From our analysis we gleaned three lessons: context matters, education for liberation, and the continuity of culture. These lessons are illuminating for educational psychology as they challenge the dominant discourse, by advocating the importance of history, culture, and social context. Ultimately, the core of our work may be best expressed by West (2008) when he wrote, "Black people have never had the luxury to believe in the innocence of America. Although we've experienced the worst of America, we still believe that the best of America can emerge" (p. 23).

REFERENCES

Akbar, N. (1984). *Chains and images of psychological slavery.* Jersey City, NJ: New Mind Productions.

Au, W. (2005). Fresh out of school: Rap music's discursive battle with education. *Journal of Negro Education, 74*(3), 210–220.

Beachum, F. D., Dentith, A. M., & McCray, C. R. (2004). Administrators' and teachers' work in a new age of reform: Understanding the factors in African American student success. *E-Journal of Teaching and Learning in Diverse Settings, 2*(1). Available: http://www.subr.edu/coeducation/ejournal/EJTLDS.%20Volume%20 2%20Issue%201.Beachum%20et%20al.pdf

Beachum, F. D., & McCray, C. R. (2008). Dealing with cultural collision: What pre-service educators should know. In G. Goodman (Ed.), *Educational psychology: An application of critical constructivism* (pp. 53–70). New York: Peter Lang.

Beachum, F. D., & Obiakor, F. E. (2005). Educational leadership in urban schools In F. E. Obiakor & F. D. Beachum (Eds.), *Urban education for the 21st century: Research, issues, and perspectives* (pp. 83–99). Springfield, IL: Charles C. Thomas.

Blanchette, W., Mumford, V., & Beachum, F. D. (2005). Urban school failure and disproportionality in a post-*Brown* era: Benign neglect of the constitutional rights of students of color. *Remedial and Special Education, 26*(2), 70–81.

Blassingame, J. W. (1979). *The slave community: Plantation life in the Antebellum South.* New York: Oxford University Press.

Bogotch, I., Beachum, F. D., Blount, J., Brooks, J., & English, F. (2008). *Radicalizing educational leadership: Dimensions of social justice.* Rotterdam, Netherlands: Sense Publishing.

Dantley, M. (2002). Uprooting and replacing positivism, the melting pot, multiculturalism, and other impotent notions in educational leadership through an African American perspective. *Education and Urban Society, 34*(3), 334–352.

Delpit, L. (1995). *Other people's children.* New York: New Press.

Douglass, F. (1968). *The narrative of the life of Fredrick Douglass: An American slave.* New York: Signet.

Dyson, M. E. (1997). *Race rules: Navigating the color line.* New York: Vintage Books.

Dyson, M. E. (2004). *The Michael Eric Dyson reader.* New York: Basic Civitas Books.

Dyson, M. E. (2005). *Is Bill Cosby right? Or has the Black middle class lost its mind?* New York: Basic Civitas Books.

Dyson, M. E. (2007). *Know what I mean?: Reflections on hip hop.* New York: Basic Civitas Books.

Gause, C. P. (2005). Guest editor's introduction: Edu-tainment: Popular culture in the making of schools for the 21st century. *Journal of School Leadership, 15*(3), 240–242.

Giroux, H. (1997). *Pedagogy and the politics of hope: Theory, culture, and schooling.* Boulder, CO: Westview.

Gladwell, M. (2000). *The tipping point: How little things can make a big difference.* New York: Back Bay Books.

Goodman, G. S. (Ed.). (2008) *Educational psychology: An application of critical constructivism.* New York: Peter Lang.

Gordon, E. W. (2006). Establishing a system of public education in which all children achieve at high levels and reach their full potential. In T. Smiley (Ed.), *The covenant with Black America* (pp. 23–45). Chicago: Third World Press.

Hancock, S. D. (2006). White women's work: On the front lines of urban education. In J. Landsman & C. W. Lewis (Eds.), *White teachers/diverse classrooms: A guide to building inclusive schools, promoting high expectations, and eliminating racism* (pp. 93–109). Sterling, VA: Stylus.

Jackson, K. (1996). *America is me: 170 fresh questions and answers on Black American history.* New York: Harper Perennial.

Kitwana, B. (2002). *The hip-hop generation: Young Blacks and the crisis in African American culture.* New York: Basic Civitas Books.

Kunjufu, J. (1993). *Hip-hop vs. MAAT: A psycho/social analysis of values.* Chicago: African American Images.

Kunjufu, J. (1995). *Countering the conspiracy to destroy Black boys* (vol. 4). Chicago: African American Images.

Kunjufu, J. (2002). *Black students—Middle class teachers.* Chicago: African American Images.

McCray, C. R., Wright, J. V., & Beachum, F. D. (2007). Social justice in educational leadership: Using Critical Race Theory to unmask African American principal placement. *Journal of Instructional Psychology, 34*(4), 247–255.

McKinsey & Company (2009, April). *The economic impact of the achievement gap in America's schools.* New York: Author.

Mizialko, A. (2005). Reducing the power of "whiteness" in urban schools. In F. E. Obiakor & F. D. Beachum (Eds.), *Urban education for the 21st century: Research, issues, and perspectives* (pp. 176–186). Springfield, IL: Charles C. Thomas.

Nisbett, R. E. (2009). *Intelligence and how to get it: Why schools and cultures matter.* New York: W. W. Norton & Company, Inc.

Obiakor, F. E., & Beachum, F. D. (2005). Urban education: The quest for democracy, equity, and excellence. In F. E. Obiakor & F. D. Beachum (Eds.), *Urban education for the 21st century: Research, issues, and perspectives* (pp. 3–19). Springfield, IL: Charles C. Thomas.

Perry, T. (2003). Up from the parched earth: Toward a theory of African-American achievement. In T. Perry, C. Steel, & A. G. Hilliard (Eds.), *Young gifted and Black: Promoting high achieving among African-American students* (pp. 1–108). Boston: Beacon.

Rothstein, S. W. (1996). *Schools and society: New perspectives in American education.* Englewood Cliffs, NJ: Prentice Hall.

Starratt, R. (1991). Building an ethical school: A theory for practice in educational leadership. *Education Administration Quarterly, 27*(2), 185–202.

Stuckey, S. (1987). *Slave culture: Nationalist theory & the foundations of Black America.* New York: Oxford University Press.

Tatum, B. D. (1997). *Why are all the Black kids sitting together in the cafeteria? And other conversations about race.* New York: Basic Books.

Tatum, B. D. (2007). Can we talk about race? And other conversations in an era of school resegregation. Boston: Beacon Press.

Thompson T. L. III, (2007). Historical and contemporary dilemmas facing urban Black male students today: Focusing on the past to correct present and future deficits. In M. C. Brown & R. D. Bartee (Eds.). *Still not equal: Expanding educational opportunity in society* (pp. 49–63). New York: Peter Lang.

Villegas, A. M., & Lucas, T. (2002). *Educating culturally responsive teachers: A coherent approach.* Albany, NY: State University of New York Press.

Wacquant, L. (2000). The new "peculiar institution": On the prison as surrogate ghetto. *Theoretical Criminology, 4*(3), 377–389.

Wacquant, L. (2001). Deadly symbiosis: When ghetto and prison meet and mesh. *Punishment and Society, 3*(1), 95–134.

West, C. (2004). *Democracy matters: Winning the fight against imperialism.* New York: Penguin Press.

West, C. (2008). *Hope on a tightrope: Words and wisdom.* Carlsbad, CA: Hay House, Inc.

White, J. L. & Cones J. H. III, (1999). *Black man emerging: Facing the past and seizing a future in America.* New York: W. H. Freeman and Company.

Wilson, W. J. (2009). *More than just race: Being Black and poor in the inner city.* New York: W.W. Norton & Company.

Woodward, C. V. (1974). *The strange career of Jim Crow* (3rd ed.). New York: Oxford University Press.

TWENTY-FOUR

Dealing with Cultural Collision in Urban Schools: What Pre-Service Educators Should Know

Floyd Beachum and Carlos McCray

I think your ears have lied to you
And your eyes have implied to you
That Urban means undeserving and absent of purpose
So give me back!!
Give me back my identity!!
Give me the opportunity
To break free of influential essentials that my community
  seeks
And have been lead to believe
Either from Hip Hop vultures disguised as moguls
Or mass media outlets that televise and overemphasize
What is deemed a destructive culture
Broadcast and typecast misguided black youth
That lives below the reality of broken homes, economic
  oppression, and a multitude of Half-truths
And finding no salvation in my inner city school
Because educators aren't there to educate
But instead baby-sit and dictate
Further reinforcing and filtrating the messages that distort
  who I am

And who I could grow to be
So I ask why haven't you extended your hand
To enhance my ability, expand my ideals and possibilities
Versus leaving me to discover my identity through manipulated
*   mediums*
And an environment that welcomes my bemused condition
I mean more to this society
My articles of clothing, vernacular, or demographic
Do not define me.
Contrary to popular belief I am also aspiring, inspiring,
*   and operating as a prodigy born out of art*
So it is evident that I have the ability to play more than
*   just this part*
But I am also a product of my surrounding…and my
*   underdeveloped mind often has no protection…*
Then difficult to discover my identity and direction
This is a burden that I cannot overcome alone
Give me something additional to relate to before I become
*   prone*
To embracing what is put into the universe to be adopted
*   as my own*
Way of thinking, living, feeling…I am a king on my
*   way to being dethroned*
Understand me rather than abandon me and pierce me
*   with labels*
This is when you find distrust, despair, and anger
I need positive influence to rival the issuance of negative
*   imagery so common in my world*
I am young, Black, impressionable, but imperiled
Look at me!!
—*"Look at Me"* a poem by Krystal Roberts (of Atlanta, GA)

The goal of educational psychology is to effectively solve problems. In many urban schools, many educational problems remain unsolved. As it stands, we can clearly identify the epidemic of failures for ethnic minorities.…Urban practitioners must become problem-solvers and functional decision-makers. As problem-solvers, they must value ethnic, linguistic, and racial differences to effectively teach in urban schools (Smith & Sapp, 2005, p. 109).

The dispositions and beliefs of pre-service educational professionals are of extreme importance. The fate of urban school children largely rests in the hands of educational professionals who may not share the same cultural backgrounds as their students or clients (Kunjufu, 2002; Landsman & Lewis, 2006). Therefore, it is critically important for these individuals to understand social context, appreciate differences, and champion change for a more multicultural organization (Cox, 1994; Cox, 2001; Irvine, 2003). Sometimes the problem is cultural, where the culture of educators' clashes with that of their students, thereby creating a phenomenon called cultural collision (see Beachum & McCray, 2004). By critically examining and understanding youth culture, educators can gain educational insight (i.e., how to tailor teaching strategies and arrange classroom management policies) and make significant connections with their students, which would help reduce many of the problems African Americans face in schools. The above poem gives an acute voice to the legions of voiceless young people who are trapped in neglected neighborhoods, segregated schools, and cultures of chaos.

African American (the term Black will also be used synonymously) youth identity is unique and multi-faceted. It can be affected by a multitude of factors including parents, peers, music, school, television, religious influences, and life experiences (Harro, 2000). For many inner-city youth in particular, self-identity is a combination of various complexities. These youth may face several critical issues such as socioeconomic despair, pressure from gangs, a lack of faith in institutions, and society's concentration on materialism and individualism (Berman & Berreth, 1997). These issues also have an effect on youth identity. Of the numerous influences and factors that shape youth identity, two, sometimes conflicting factors, Black youth popular culture (hip-hop culture and television) and school culture are of particular importance.

This chapter will concentrate on the development of secondary school-aged urban youth (i.e., those in grades 7–12). Urban Black youth popular culture will be examined by means of hip-hop culture and the media. Both of these variables have the awesome potential to shape youth identity. The American phenomenon known as hip-hop can affect youth in both positive and negative ways (Kunjufu, 1993). In a like manner, television too, can exert a powerful influence over youth. The media have the power to alter the habits, feelings, and minds of young people, especially Black youth (Kunjufu, 1990). This chapter is written to assist in the understanding of psychological and cultural/social forces on urban youth, with special emphasis on Black youth culture. For you, the emerging teacher, this information is critically important in your work with these impressionable young people.

NOTIONS OF CONTEMPORARY AMERICA AND SCHOOLS

If you work hard can you really be "successful" in America? How much of your success is due to individual merit (your own efforts)? To what extent do structural barriers inhibit the life chances of certain groups in America? Are schools agents of change or do they perpetuate the inequalities found in American society? These are difficult questions, especially if you have never really considered them. Though difficult, these are important questions for educators and professionals dealing with diverse populations. Why can't we readily identify oppression, inequity, and injustices? The answer might very well be that we are socialized into believing and acting out various roles as related to race, class, gender, ability, status, age, and social class (Harro, 2000). Tatum (1997) states that this socialization process is similar to smog in the air that we all breathe and are inevitably impacted by. This smog is found in notions of meritocracy, individualism, and old-fashion hard work. The cultural ethos of the United States is full of idealistic concepts such as the Protestant work ethic, and the Horatio Alger myth (belief in the idea of going from rags to riches as applied to everyone equally). Such ideas are ingrained into the psyches of nearly all Americans. Writing of pre-service educators, Villegas and Lucas (2002) asserted:

They are insensitive to the fact that power is differentially distributed in society, with those who are affluent, White, and male having an advantage over those who are poor, of racial/ethnic minority groups, and female. They lack an understanding of institutional discrimination, including how routine practices in schools benefit young people from dominant groups while disadvantaging those from oppressed groups; and they have an unshakable faith that American society operates according to meritocratic principles and that existing inequalities in social outcomes are thereby justified. (p. 32).

Thus, you must be willing to question deeply held beliefs and be willing to challenge foundational assumptions. Of course, you might be thinking to yourself, "I made it, why can't anyone else?" Villegas and Lucas responded, "Because the educational system has worked for them (pre-service teachers), they are not apt to question school practices, nor are they likely to doubt the criteria of merit applied in schools" (p. 31). The next factor in understanding how cultural collision operates is to realize how people are affected by the geographic isolation of many urban areas.

THE URBAN CONTEXT AND POPULAR CULTURE

For the purposes of this discussion it is important to also understand the significance of the urban context. Many urban areas across the nation are plagued with all types of social and community problems. Urban schools in these areas face challenges such as inadequate funding and teacher apathy. Resentment from external powers fuels the fire for the marginalizing and criticism of these schools (Ayers, 1994).

As it appears, the urban context creates an environment that affects urban schools and the youth within them. "The situation in far too many schools is one of despair, poverty, isolation, and distress" (Obiakor & Beachum, 2005, p. 13). Noguera (2004) wrote, "In poor communities, the old, persistent problems of overcrowded classrooms, deteriorating facilities, and an insufficient supply of qualified teachers and administrators remain largely unaddressed" (p. 176). These are but some of the many problems that these schools and sometimes districts encounter. The attitudes and behaviors of urban youth of color begin to reflect the structural inequities that create their environments. Kozol (2006) traces the segregation, poverty, and inequity found in such schools in his book, *The Shame of the Nation*. At the same time, this situation has resulted in the increasing pseudo-police state found in many urban areas and schools (Wacquant, 2001) as well as feelings of alienation (Rothstein, 1996; Yeo & Kanpol, 1999).

Black popular culture, many times, tends to originate from this urban context. According to Damen (1987), "Culture is learned and shared human patterns or models for living; day-to-day living patterns; those models and patterns pervade all aspects of human social interaction; and culture is mankind's primary adaptive mechanism" (p. 367). Black popular culture was born amidst "social, cultural, political, and economic segregation—initially as a vibrant expression of Black political and cultural strivings" (Guy, 2004, p. 48).

Gause (2005) stated that "popular culture is the background noise of our very existence" (p. 336). When we consider the origin, expansion, and influence of "Urban America" we realize that its inhabitants are molded and shaped by history, experience, and social context. The global phenomenon known as hip-hop culture can be viewed as an expression of Black popular culture with its roots found in the plight and promise of the urban context.

HIP-HOP CULTURE

Hip-hop culture has a great influence on American youth. White and Cones (1999) write, "Hip hop is a catch-all term for a contemporary, urban-centered youth lifestyle associated with popular music, break dancing, certain dress and hair styles, graffiti, and street language" (p. 96). Hip hop culture has gone from primarily rapping, break dancing, dj-ing, and graffiti to including dialects, attitude, expression, mannerisms, and fashion (Dyson, 2001; Kitwana, 2002). In reference to its wider appeal, Kitwana (2002) asserts, "Rappers access to global media and their use of popular culture to articulate many aspects of this national identity renders rap music central to any discussion of the new Black youth culture" (p.11). This emphasis on media opens up rap artists to audio and visual media. McCall (1997) writes:

> Dr. William Byrd, a Black clinical psychologist, pointed out that for young, impressionable people the mere fact that explicit gangsta lyrics are aired on the radio lends credence to their messages as truth. "When you bombard someone with those messages, it causes conflict, even with those young people who may have been taught other values. With these rap messages, not only are they being bombarded with radio, they also get video." So it's what you hear and what you see. It confirms that these are acceptable values in a subculture (p. 60).

Therefore, this "message bombardment" can be influential to impressionable youth. Kitwana (2002) agrees, "Today, more and more Black youth are turning to rap music, music videos, designer clothing, popular Black films, and television programs for values and identity" (p. 9).

Hip-hop culture has become an integral part of the lives of many urban youth. Through its influence they develop various ideas about sex, relationships, success, and life (Kunjufu, 1993). In addition, these influences can have positive or negative effects on youth identity. "The ages between 13–17 are when they [youth] are particularly vulnerable to outside influence and before their values and ideas have fully developed" (Kunjufu, 1993, p. 81). Hip-hop culture is expressed through songs on the radio, glamorized by video, and reinforced by peers. The result is a particularly powerful form of infiltration and indoctrination. However, this influence can be good or bad. Most of the controversy surrounding hip-hop culture has to do with its emphasis on male chauvinism, open gunplay, and illegal drug usage.

Much of the criticism revolves around a certain mode of hip-hop expression called gangsta rap. Gangsta rap usually refers to a style of rap that references/overemphasizes drug selling, hyper-macho posturing, disrespect for authority, the use of violence to settle disputes and to gain respect, and negative attitudes towards women (Guy, 2004; Kunjufu, 1993; White & Cones, 1999). In reference to this form of rap, Dyson (1997) wrote:

> The gangsta rap genre of hip-hop emerged in the late 1980s on the West Coast as crack and gangs ruled the urban centers of Los Angeles, Long Beach, Compton, and Oakland. Since hip-hop has long turned to the Black ghetto and the Latino barrio for lyrical inspiration, it was inevitable that a form of music that mimicked the violence on the streets would rise (p. 113).

In recent years, the label gangsta rap has seemed to apply less to the contemporary forms of hip-hop displayed in popular culture. Today, much of the music incorporates strands of this theme along with others making it into an eclectic combination of macho-posturing, **misogyny**, violence, and materialism. Thus, gangsta rap is less identified as a societal pariah of previous years but now a common part of "normalized" hip-hop culture. Hip-hop culture has the ability to affect the values of Black youth through various media. Another important medium is television.

TELEVISION MEDIA

The American media are a source of news, entertainment, and information. They include radio, newspapers, the Internet, and television. For our purposes, the authors will concentrate on the media as represented by television. The media have the ability to spread truthful and positive knowledge or misrepresent people, events, and data. Unfortunately, many times the latter is the case. Moreover, television is responsible for imagery that negatively influences youth (Bush, 1999). Consequently, this imagery has the ability to affect youth identity.

Television is an important part of life to many Americans. Black youth, in particular, watch seven to eight hours of television a day, as compared to four and a half hours for White youth (Browder, 1989). Bush (1999) notes, "negative images presented in all of the media conspire with many hours of television viewing to produce a negative effect on Black children's self-image" (p. 36). In reference to Black youth and television, Browder (1989) observes the following:

- Black children tend to use TV as a source of role models. They imitate other people's behavior, dress, appearance, and speech.
- TV provides examples of relationships with members of the opposite sex.
- TV is used as a primary source of learning and perfecting aggressive behavior.
- Black children closely identify with television characters—particularly the Black characters. (p. 47)

Given the amount of television watched by Black youth and its influence on their development, the images portrayed by the television medium become extremely important.

Television many times promotes gender stereotypes and negative images of Blacks. A study conducted by Mamay and Simpson (as cited in Bush, 1999) concluded that "women in commercials were typecast according to three stereotypical roles: mother, housekeeper, and sexual objects" (pp. 35–36). This research indicates that television has the ability to affect the way people view gender roles. Katz (1995) writes:

> Stressing gender differences in this context means defining masculinity in the opposition to femininity. This requires constantly reasserting what is masculine and what is feminine. One of the ways that is accomplished, in the image system, is to equate masculinity with violence (and femininity with passivity) (p. 135).

In addition to gender, the television medium also influences many youth towards violence. For instance, a 14-year-old Black male was sentenced to life in prison for the murder of a six-year-old girl. He was imitating pro wrestling moves he watched on television (Ripley, 2001). Today's Black youth are many times criticized and labeled as violent or rebellious (Dyson, 1997; Kitwana, 2002). Wilson (1990) asserts, "Deeds of violence in our society are performed largely by those trying to establish their self-esteem, to defend their self-image, or to demonstrate that they too are significant" (p. 54). This is not to excuse individuals for violent behavior, but it provides insight into other influences impacting behavior. Moreover, the television medium promotes a value system based on materialism and immediate gratification (Kunjufu, 1990). In accordance with these values, too many youths resort to violence. Thus television exposure to negative imagery could possibly encourage an inner-adversarial conflict of self-identity.

IDENTITY THEORY AND BLACK YOUTH

Black youth who are matriculating through middle and high school deal with a considerable amount of transition. The transitions here are related to grade levels, geographic location of schools, maturation, and identity development (to name a few). Considering the latter, young adults share a certain amount of curiosity, exploration, and discovery with regard to the development of identity (Tatum, 1997). However, Black youth in particular, begin to examine their own ethnic/racial identities even more than their White counterparts (Negy, Shreve, Jensen, & Uddin, 2003). Tatum (1997) posits that "given the impact of dominant and subordinate status, it is not surprising that researchers have found that adolescents of color are more likely to be actively engaged in an exploration of their racial or ethnic identity than are White adolescents" (p. 53). In this state of heightened identity awareness is where salient and unconscious messages and imagery can influence ideas and values. Black youth are more sensitized to society's view of them with regard to race. "Our self-perceptions are shaped by the messages that we receive from those around us, and when young Black men and women enter adolescence, the racial content of those messages intensifies" (Tatum, 1997, p. 54). Hence, identity development for Black youth is complicated by notions of race/ethnicity more than for their White peers, making this a time of complexity and vulnerability. This situation creates the need for direction and guidance from influential individuals and institutions, one of which is the school.

SCHOOL CULTURE

The school itself can have a major impact on the development of students. During school, students are afforded opportunities for academic, emotional, and social growth. Students also interact with teachers and administrators within this educational environment that is founded upon certain values. Academics, opportunities for growth, different types of interaction, and value systems all play a role in a school's culture. The school's culture also has the ability to shape student identity.

A school is commonly defined as a place of teaching and learning. The culture of an organization is the set of values and beliefs of the organization, and these values and beliefs are normally shared with the majority of people in the organization (Cunningham & Cordeiro, 2006; Fullan, 2004; Karpicke & Murphy, 1996). Thus, school culture is the shared value system of a given school. Specifically, school culture involves certain components. According to Pawlas (1997), "The key components of a strong effective school culture include shared values, humor, storytelling, empowerment, a communication system for spreading information, rituals and ceremonies, and collegiality" (p. 119). School culture is important to all who are involved with the school.

The school culture can affect student identity. Banks (2001) notes "the school culture communicates to students the school's attitudes toward a range of issues and problems, including how the school views them as human beings and its attitudes toward males, females, exceptional students, and students from various religious, cultural, racial, and ethnic groups" (p. 24). When the school's culture is characterized by value disagreement, lack of communication, and little collegiality (among teachers and students), many students see themselves as incapable, incompetent, and worthless. However, when an environment promotes a schoolwide value system, good communication, collegiality, and the utilization of ceremonies, students' attitudes are much more positive. Karpicke and Murphy (1996) agree that a healthy (school) culture has a great impact on the success of students.

Taking all of this into account we find that those teachers who are interested in changing a culture must first try to understand the existing culture. In doing this, those teachers would have to begin by understanding the various cultures that come to the schoolhouse on a daily basis, before imposing another culture.

INTERSECTION OF SCHOOL CULTURE AND BLACK POPULAR CULTURE

The values as dictated by negative hip-hop culture and the media many times conflict with the values of the school. Kunjufu (1990) notes that gangs and negative media promote immediate gratification and materialism, while many parents and teachers promote long-term gratification and qualities such as moral integrity and honesty. Kunjufu (1993) also states that there is a concern about some hip-hop artists' misogynistic and violent messages. In effect, students obtain certain values from this segment of hip-hop culture and television and then bring those values to the school. Therefore, there is a conflict of value systems, which sometimes results in discipline problems and lack of communication between students and educators. In addition, peers can have a great influence on each other, even more than the influence of adults (Kunjufu, 1990). Thus, the values are shared and become pervasive because of the influence of peer communication and pressure. Furthermore, Black youth spend much more time with peers, listening to music, and watching television than they do having meaningful conversations with teachers and parents (Bush, 1999; Kitwana, 2002; Kunjufu, 1994). The task for educators is to familiarize themselves with youth culture/value systems and realize the subsequent effect on youth identity.

Hip-hop culture has undergone tremendous growth as an artistic form of expression, fashion, as well a money-making venture. Many have advocated censorship in order to curtail much of the negative influence of rap music. However, censorship may not be an appropriate or realistic response. It sends the message that artistic expression can be stifled by those who simply disagree. But what are we to make of the violent themes readily found in hip-hop culture? In response to this over-emphasis on violence in hip-hop, Dyson (2005) explained:

> …hip-hop has been nailed for casting glamour on thuggish behavior and for heartlessly painting violent portraits of urban life. It's all true, but still, the whole truth of hip-hop as art form and, because of generational lag, as agitator of adults, must not be overlooked.…At its best, hip-hop summons the richest response in the younger generation to questions of identity and suffering (p. 115).

Dyson (1996) wrote, "While these young Black males become whipping boys for sexism and misogyny, the places in our culture where these ancient traditions are nurtured and rationalized—including religious and educational institutions and the nuclear family—remain immune to forceful and just criticism" (p. 186). Therefore, a certain amount of responsibility must be placed on parents, guardians, and school officials. In effect, parents and educators should take a greater role in involving themselves in the lives of these youth. One must remember that hip-hop culture has a business aspect and the supply will meet the demand. What would happen if the consumers demanded more positive conscious images?

The media also have to be held accountable for negative imagery. If not, then youth identity could be at stake. Chideya (1995) writes, "In the final analysis, it's up to the reader and viewers to keep the media honest...pointing out times that the media has misrepresented the African-American community can only make the community better. The media belongs to all of us. If we want it to work, we have to work" (p. 11).

IMPLICATIONS FOR EDUCATORS

In summary, there are many factors that influence the identities of urban Black youth. Hip-hop culture, television media, and school culture do have a serious impact on this particular group. At the heart of this analysis is the creation of a healthy positive value system. Consequently, those students who develop this strong value system have less of a chance to be affected by negative aspects of hip-hop culture and misrepresentation in television media and more of a chance to be influenced by the "positivity" exemplified in a healthy school culture.

Educators have a critical role to play in students' academic and social development. First, you must recognize the inherent inequities within our society and how they impact people, especially in urban areas. Secondly, realize how cultural collision plays out in our schools. By acknowledging the background experiences of urban students, which includes their cultural expressions, educators can gain insight into addressing student behavior, communication, and values. Lastly, Milner (2006) proposed some questions for educators as they begin to self-examine; he referred to it as *relational reflection*. The questions are as follows: 1) Why do I believe what I believe?; 2) How do my thoughts and beliefs influence my curriculum and teaching [managing and disciplining] of students of color?; and 3) What do I need to change in order to better meet the needs of all my students? (p. 84). Educators engage students in a mutual process of liberation for completeness. "Completeness for the oppressed begins with liberation. Until liberation is achieved, individuals are fragmented in search of clarity, understanding, and emancipation. This liberation is not outside of us or created or accomplished through some external force. Rather, it begins with a change in thinking" (p. 85). The essence of this "education for liberation" is a change in thinking for educators, making them realize their own power with students and potential in society.

Due to the increasing amount of cultural and social diversity found in society and in our schools, educators must find the right balance which promotes a healthy school climate while also embracing some degree of cultural pluralism (Villegas & Lucas, 2002). There should be a willingness and effort among educators to structure the school culture to ensure that individuals of diverse backgrounds are well positioned to achieve regardless of their predispositions in life. A school culture structured in a pluralistic manner can lead to the self-efficacy and self-determination of students who may bring conflicting values from their environment (Banks, 1995). Banks (2001) insists "The culture and organization of the school must be examined by all members of the school staff...in order to create a school culture that empowers students from diverse racial and ethnic groups" (p. 22). This is extremely important because it helps to ensure that students are not being labeled incorrectly and are not subjugated because of inadequate cultural capital. Therefore, it is important for educators to help such students develop the kinds of value systems that encourage positive self-identities and give them the legitimate opportunity to become successful in school as well as in life.

REFERENCES

Ayers, W. (1994). Can city schools be saved? *Educational Leadership, 51*(8), 60–63.

Banks, J. A. (2001). Multicultural education: Characteristics and goals. In J. A. Banks & C. A. McGee Banks (Eds.), *Multicultural education: Issues and perspectives* (4th ed.), (pp. 3–30). New York: John Wiley & Sons, Inc.

———. (1995). Multicultural education: development, dimensions, and challenges. In J. Joll, (Ed.), *Taking sides: Clashing views on controversial education issues* (pp. 84–93). New York: The Dushkin Publishing Group, Inc.

Beachum, F. D., & McCray, C. R. (2004). Cultural collision in urban schools. *Current Issues in Education, 7*(5). Available: *http://cie.asu. edu/volume7/number5/*

Berman, S., & Berreth, D. (1997). The moral dimensions of schools. *Educational Leadership, 54*(8), 24–27.

Browder, A. (1989). *From the Browder file: 22 essays of the African American experience.* Washington, DC: The Institute of Karmic Guidance.

Bush, L. V. (1999). *Can black mothers raise our sons?* Chicago: African American Images.

Chideya, F. (1995). *Don't believe the hype: Fighting cultural misinformation about African-Americans.* New York: Penguin Books.

Cox, T., Jr. (2001). *Creating the multicultural organization: A strategy for capturing the power of diversity.* San Francisco: Jossey-Bass.

———. (1994). *Cultural diversity in organizations: Theory, research, and practice.* San Francisco: Berrett-Koehler Publishers.

Cunningham, W. G., & Cordeiro, P. A. (2006). *Educational leadership: A problem-based approach* (3rd ed.). Boston: Allyn and Bacon.

Damen, L. (1987). *Culture learning: The fifth dimension on the language classroom.* Reading, MA: Addison-Wesley.

Dyson, M. E. (2005). *Is Bill Cosby right? Or has the Black middle class lost its mind?* New York: Basic Civitas Books.

———. (2001). *Holler if you hear me: Searching for Tupac Shakur.* New York: Basic Civitas Books.

———. (1997). *Race rules: Navigating the color line.* New York: Vintage Books.

———. (1996). *Between God and gangsta rap.* New York: Oxford University Press.

Fullan, M. (2004). *Leading in a culture of change: Personal action guide and workbook.* San Francisco: Jossey-Bass.

Gause, C. P. (2005). Navigating the stormy seas: Critical perspectives on the intersection of popular culture and educational leadership. *Journal of School Leadership, 15*(3), 333–345.

Guy, T. C. (2004). Gangsta rap and adult education. *New directions for adult and continuing education, 101,* 43–57.

Harro, B. (2000). The cycle of socialization. In M. Adams, W. J. Blumenfield, R. Castaneda, H. W. Hackman, M. L. Peters, X. Zuniga (Eds.), *Reading for diversity and social justice: An anthology on racism, anti-Semitism, sexism, heterosexism, ableism, and classism* (pp. 79–82). New York: Routledge.

Irvine, J. J. (2003*). Educating teachers for diversity: Seeing with a cultural eye.* New York: Teachers College Press.

Karpicke, H. & Murphy, M. E. (1996). Productive school culture: Principals working from the inside. *National Association of Secondary School Principals, 80,* 26–32.

Katz, J. (1995). Advertisement and the construction of violent white masculinity. In G. Dines and J. Humez (Eds.). *Gender, race and class in the media: A text reader.* Thousand Oaks, CA: Sage Publications.

Kitwana, B. (2002). *The Hip Hop generation: Young Blacks and the crisis in African American culture.* New York: Basic Books.

Kozol, J. (2006). *The shame of the nation: The restoration of apartheid schooling in America.* New York: Crown Publishing Group.

Kunjufu, J. (2002). *Black students—Middle class teachers.* Chicago: African American Images.

———. (1994). *Countering the conspiracy to destroy black boys* (vol. IV). Chicago: African American Images.

———. (1993). *Hip-hop vs. MAAT: a psycho/social analysis of values.* Chicago: African American Images.

———. (1990). *Countering the conspiracy to destroy black boys* (vol. III). Chicago: African American Images.

Landsman, J., & Lewis, C. W. (Eds.) (2006). *White teachers/diverse classrooms: A guide to building inclusive schools, promoting high expectations, and eliminating racism.* Sterling, VA: Stylus.

McCall, N. (1997). *What's going on.* New York: Random House.

Milner, H. R. (2006). But good intentions are not enough: Theoretical and philosophical relevance in teaching students of color. In J. Landsman & C. W. Lewis (Eds.), *White teachers/diverse classrooms: A guide to building inclusive schools, promoting high expectations, and eliminating racism* (pp. 79–90). Sterling, VA: Stylus.

Negy, C., Shreve, Jensen, B. J., & Uddin, N. (2003). Ethnic identity, self-esteem, and ethnocentrism: A study of social identity versus multicultural theory of development. *Cultural Diversity and Mental Health, 9*(4), 333–334.

Noguera, P. (2004). Going beyond the slogans and rhetoric. In C. Glickman (Ed.), *Letters to the next president: What we can do about the real crisis in public education* (pp. 174–183). New York: Teachers College Press.

Obiakor, F. E., & Beachum, F. D. (2005). Urban education: The quest for democracy, equity, and excellence. In F. E. Obiakor & F. D. Beachum (Eds.), *Urban education for the 21st century: Research, issues, and perspectives* (pp. 3–19). Springfield, IL: Charles C. Thomas.

Pawlas, G. E. (1997). Vision and school culture. *National Association of Secondary School Principals, 81,* 118–120.

Ripley, A. (2001, March). Throwing the book at kids. *Time, 157* (11), 34.

Rothstein, S. W. (1996). *Schools and society: New perspectives in American education.* Englewood Cliffs, NJ: Prentice Hall.

Smith, R., & Sapp, M. (2005). Insights into educational psychology: What urban school practitioners must know. In F. E. Obiakor & F. D. Beachum (Eds.), *Urban education for the 21st century: Research, issues, and perspectives* (pp. 100–113). Springfield, IL: Charles C. Thomas.

Tatum, B. D. (1997). *Why are all the Black kids sitting together in the cafeteria?: And other conversations about race.* New York: Basic Books.

Villegas, A. M., & Lucas, T. (2002). *Educating culturally responsive teachers: A coherent approach.* Albany, NY: State University of New York Press.

Wacquant, L. (2001). Deadly symbiosis: When ghetto and prison meet and mesh. *Punishment and Society, 3*(1), 95–134.

White, J. L. & Cones III, J. H. (1999). *Black man emerging: Facing the past and seizing a future in America.* New York: W. H. Freeman and Company.

Wilson, A. (1990). *Black on black violence.* New York: African World Info Systems.

Yeo, F., & Kanpol, B. (1999). Introduction: Our own "Peculiar Institution": Urban education in 20th-century America. In F. Yeo & B. Kanpol (Eds.), *From nihilism to possibility: Democratic transformations for the inner city* (pp. 1–14). Cresskill, NJ: Hampton Press, Inc.

TWENTY-FIVE

Understanding Educational Psychology:
A Case Study Approach

Anthony A. Pittman

During a discussion with a teacher's aide who wanted to know more about becoming a certified teacher, I discovered that the route to certification for many applicants can be challenging for a variety of reasons. The individual with whom I spoke had not gone to school in the United States and was not a native English speaker. She had taken the state-mandated examinations for teacher licensure several times. However, each time the results came back, she expressed how disappointed she was to learn that she had not received the minimal passing score on the writing and reading portions of the Praxis I exam. She was not only upset by her failure but noted how expensive her efforts to become a certified teacher had become, and she was on the brink of deferring her dream to be in charge of her own classroom. My conversation with this individual generated an interest in talking with others who might have faced similar situations. Although I did not know of many persons who fit this profile, a colleague of mine who taught at a middle school in a town nearby recommended Alberto, who will serve as the focus of this chapter.

This chapter is a unique departure from traditional approaches to educational psychology in that it discusses psychological theories within a case study framework. If I have been successful, readers will be exposed to various aspects of educational psychology, identity development, in particular. I address these theories through the lens of the experiences of Alberto, a thirty-three-year-old Hispanic male who, at the time the research was conducted, was employed as a teacher's aide at Celebrity High School (pseudonym). I will present some contextual information about the school, data gathered from its website, because it was the site of the interviews with Alberto. In addition, I share some of my impressions of the school and relate them to some of the concepts that are usually addressed in educational psychology courses. Additional impressions of the institution emerged during my interviews with Alberto.

Celebrity High School is located in Connecticut and is considered by most people within the surrounding area to be an inner-city school. It has roughly 1,100 students with a large concentration of Hispanics and African Americans. About 15 percent of the school's students are enrolled in special education programs. With a median household income just slightly above $30,000, at least 59 percent of Celebrity's student population qualifies for free or reduced lunches. Despite these demographics, the number of teachers and administrators of color employed at Celebrity is significantly disproportionate. The school is required by state law to provide written testament regarding how its students interact with persons from diverse backgrounds. In addition to referencing in its statement the success of the school's diversity club, Celebrity High School hails its celebration of diversity week each year.

For my first interview with Alberto, I arrived at the school much earlier than expected but figured I would spend some time in the library while I waited to speak with him. When I entered the school, I was greeted by the security guard who inquired about the purpose of my visit. After signing in, I was directed to the main office, which was filled with a number of students who appeared to have been late arrivals for a class and had been sent to the office for an admission slip. Two administrative assistants were talking on the phone while another individual who must have been in charge of handling the late admits was busy carrying out her duties. I was taken aback by her combative attitude with one of the students who insisted that he be permitted to enter class late so that he would not miss an exam. "You shouldn't have been playing in the hall and should've gone to class on time and you wouldn't be here," she told the young man. Much to his chagrin, he was not permitted to enter the class and was directed to a study hall in another area of the school. When the attendant haughtily addressed me, I explained politely who I was and that Alberto was expecting me. I was given unclear and confusing directions to the classroom and left the main office to begin the odyssey.

While traversing the hallways, I encountered two female passersby who were engaged in a conversation about a teacher at the school. From what I was able to overhear, they were talking about how uncaring and strict the teacher was. I glanced into several of the open-door classrooms while I made my way to my destination. I was surprised by the uni-directionality of instruction and the pervasive teacher-centered pedagogy at the school. With the exception of the voices of teachers, the rooms were quiet. There appeared to be no accommodations for students who might prefer to take more active and participatory roles in their learning process. Not one of the classes I passed by and looked into contained students working collaboratively in groups. Instead, teachers were standing in front of the classrooms disseminating content while some of the students appeared to be taking notes without question or discussion and without interaction with either the teachers or the other students. The arrangement of the desks in the rooms was traditional—five rows across and six rows deep. Just about all of the seats were filled.

I began to wonder what *Bruner* might say about the methods of instruction that seemed to be carried out at Celebrity. His research validates *discovery learning*, suggesting that to the extent teachers permit students to be actively engaged with the content at hand, the more maximized student learning will be. *Guided discovery*, according to Bruner, requires the educator to provide some direction during the instructional process. However, the learning is expected to be problematized by asking students questions that would agitate their minds and coerce them to exercise the higher-order and critical thinking skills required by complex questions. I witnessed none of the above and felt pity for the students who were sitting in the rooms, many of whom exhibited signs of boredom and restlessness.

My initial impressions of Celebrity High School reminded me of Lisa Dietrich's (1998) many criticisms of public educational establishments. In one of her earlier writings she asserted:

> Public education is supposed to be the means by which all individuals, regardless of ethnic or class background, achieve social mobility. However, education is a tool by which powerful interest groups selectively transmit skills in order to reproduce the class, gender, and ethnic inequalities of the wider social structure. (p. 79)

As I peered into these rooms I saw teachers who seemed distant and remote from their students. Several of them had barriers between them and the students. A desk, a podium, or a table represented an imaginary line of demarcation that separated the teachers from the learners. The backs of teachers faced students as some of them transcribed content on dusty chalkboards that appeared not to have been cleaned in quite some time. When I approached the first classroom with a closed door, I decided to take a more sustained look into the room. I watched as a student passed a folded sheet of paper to another student, who passed it on to someone else. The note surreptitiously made its way from the back of the class to a student in the front row of the right-hand side of the classroom. I was amazed that as the paper exchanged hands, it was not read by anyone other than its intended recipient. I chuckled softly as I thought about my own high school days. When nefarious activity like what I was observing happened, it was almost guaranteed that one of the more immature and nosey students would read the note before it reached its destination. I surmised that this was a common occurrence in this particular classroom and that an honor code among the students had somehow been developed. Completely oblivious to what was taking place, the teacher continued writing on the board. Indeed if any social mobility, as referenced by Dietrich, is to emerge for these students, it would have to be because of a paradigm shift in the manner in which instruction is executed at this school.

Alberto had agreed to meet after school in the classroom where he worked as an instructional aide. To ensure that he could speak candidly with me, he scheduled the interviews on the days when the teacher to whom he had been assigned would be occupied with departmental responsibilities. Quite generous with his time, Alberto afforded me the distinct pleasure of vicariously entering his educational world for a span of three hours on three separate occasions. I was pleased to learn that he is a graduate of the same school system in which he now works, as this allowed him to provide honest, firsthand accounts of his experiences as a student there and enabled him, under a guarantee of anonymity, to speak freely about what he had been able to observe as an employee. Based upon themes and patterns from each interview, I will present his case in the following manner: first, I provide details about Alberto's upbringing and how his home environment adversely affected his attitude towards school, academic performance, *self-concept*, and *self-esteem*. Second, I examine his school community and its inherent problematic issues with its *English Language Learners* (ELLs). Finally, I conclude the chapter by discussing some of Alberto's thoughts about what teachers in training should consider if they want to be effective educators. I undergird many of his recommendations with theories advocated by educational psychologists.

When I knocked on the open door and entered the room, Alberto was reading *Their Eyes Were Watching God*. I introduced myself and made a few comments about Hurston's work. He seemed genuinely interested in my perspectives about the novel, and made many comparisons of his experiences to those of the various characters. After a brief conversation on the book, I reiterated the purpose of the project and entertained his questions, many of which were related to anonymity. I obtained his permission to tape-record the interview, and we began. I learned he had once wanted to become a teacher but was unable to fulfill his goal for various reasons. Some of these stemmed from his lack of self-confidence, but others were the result of educational malpractice. He explained how his home environment had negatively affected him:

> One incident in particular stands out in my mind. I remember it being around three in the morning when my dad came home really, really drunk. I thought I was having a bad dream, but then I realized what was happening was real. He turned on the radio and blasted it as loud as it could go. He wanted to dance and wanted somebody to dance with him. I remember my mom trying to convince him to come to bed, but he wouldn't and then began hitting her. I tried to stop him, but he hit me too and told me I would never be anything because I disrespected him. Eventually, he passed out and I went to the bathroom to clean up the blood from my busted lip. It wasn't long before my alarm clock went off and I had to get ready for school.

Alberto recounted several incidents when his father physically, mentally, and emotionally abused him. He recalls being angry with several of his teachers who, according to him, displayed no interest in the physical or *behavioral indicators* (Woolfolk, 2009) of his unhappy home life. Woolfolk notes that contusions or other physical indications of injury or a student's lethargic behavior may be signs of abuse. Although she cautions that these signs are not always evidence of abuse, such situations should be investigated. Unfortunately for Alberto, none of his unsympathetic teachers (many of whom were White) noted his behavioral and physical metamorphosis. Alberto explained his attitude towards school:

> There once was a time that I liked to learn new things. I remember in class one day hearing a White student use the word "accumulate". I never heard my mother use the word. If she did it, wasn't in English; it was in Spanish. I looked it up in the dictionary and learned what it meant and began to use it. Sometimes teachers called on me to help the other students who weren't doing so well in the class. The better at the language I became, the more teachers called on me to tutor students in not only English, but in math as well. I think this situation sparked my fascination with the English language, but all that changed as the school year went on and I got older and the abuse at home got worse.

Alberto explained how he became aware of his social and economic disadvantages. His mother had not attended school beyond the sixth grade, and his father had dropped out in grade seven. He described his father as a drug addict and an alcoholic, and his mother was the sole breadwinner. Her income was insufficient to support them, and the family became dependent upon the state's welfare system. Alberto believes the lack of financial resources precipitated his father's illegal drug activity, which resulted in the home being raided by the police on several occasions. Although he had once exhibited an interest in school and was motivated to excel academically, his grades now declined and he became less sociable.

> I used to think of myself as a nerd. I was enrolled in honors courses, was making good grades, and had plans to go to college, but I sometimes became depressed when I thought about my life. I wasn't even able to go to my senior prom because I couldn't afford the ticket, and I didn't have the money to rent a tux. But to be honest with you, I don't think I would have gone anyway, because I was ashamed of where I lived and wouldn't have liked to have my date to come to my house. I didn't have a car to pick up a friend for the prom, and I lacked the confidence to even bother asking anybody to go with me.

By the time Alberto graduated from high school, his grades had plummeted significantly. He attributes this to his abusive father.

> After dealing with that [alcoholic father] I was like "f___ school." I went from an A and B student and started dropping down to Cs and Ds. I would hear all these happy White kids talking about what a great life they were having…you know…how their fathers were doctors and lawyers, and it's like what do I have… an a-hole…for a father…you know. I was like "f__ that s__." Who wants to hear that? I didn't.

His family's economic situation grew worse. An older sibling had been attending one of the local universities, so rather than place an additional financial burden upon his family, Alberto pretended he did not wish to pursue a college degree and opted to enter the workforce in an effort to improve his family's financial predicament.

> I knew my family couldn't afford to send the both of us [to college], and I always thought about family first, so I let him go. There were times when we had to sacrifice the grocery money so that my brother could purchase the necessary books for school. Sometimes we would just have to wait for my mom's next welfare check, because financial aid wasn't in place at the time.

The concept of *motivation* is evident in Alberto's case study, both *intrinsically* and *extrinsically*. Davis and Buskist (2002) claim, "Extrinsic motivation sometimes enhances intrinsic motivation" (p. 505). However, they warn, "Do not expect instant perfection from your students, but strive for steady improvement…" (p. 505). Woolfolk (2009) notes:

> When we are intrinsically motivated, we do not need incentives or punishments, because the activity itself is rewarding…. In contrast, when we do something in order to earn a grade, avoid punishment, please the teacher, or for some other reason that has very little to do with the task itself, we experience extrinsic motivation. (p. 373)

Proof of Alberto's *intrinsic motivation* was reflected in his discovery of neologisms, the use of which brought about the kind of satisfaction that resulted in his continuation of language exploration simply because it pleased him. Evidence of his *extrinsic motivation* is best represented in his recollection of a childhood event that he described during this interview.

> There was so much abuse in my house that me and my brother learned what not to do when my dad was so-called sober. Anytime he asked us to do something, we did it because we didn't want him to hurt us or our mom. I remember being so hungry one time and sneaking in the refrigerator looking for something to eat. There was one piece of bologna left, and I know my mom probably would have told me to leave it for my dad, but I ate it. It wasn't too long after that that he came to the kitchen and asked me what I was doing in there. I lied and told him I was on my way outside but wanted some water before heading out. He didn't bother me that day luckily, and from that moment on, I pretty much learned that not telling the truth was a way to escape getting my lights punched out…sometimes it worked, sometimes it didn't and he'd just hit me for the hell of it.

According to Ormrod (2008), motivation has significant implications for human behavior and how one's environment affects the learning process, what she refers to as *situated motivation*. Acknowledging that students may lack internal motivation to achieve certain tasks in the classroom context, Ormrod suggests that situated motivation is facilitated by the classroom practitioner. Similar to his experiences of intrinsic motivation, situated motivation was manifested through Alberto's sense of empowerment when a teacher assigned him a tutorial role. However, according to Alberto, teachers did not capitalize upon his fascination with language in such a way that it was sustained. Consequently, his motivation to engage in word discovery and language manipulation became ephemeral at best.

Educational psychologists also highlight the distinction between *self-concept* and *self-esteem*, although some use the terms interchangeably (Woolfolk, 2009; Ormrod, 2008; Harter, 1990a). Generally, self-concept is an assessment of one's strengths, weaknesses, characteristics, and attitudes. Self-esteem constitutes any judgment or value related to one's worth, behaviors, and abilities (Woolfolk, 2009; Ormrod, 2008; Byrnes, 2002; Harter, 1990). Perhaps the best way to apply the terms to Alberto's case and differentiate them accordingly is apparent in the information he had shared earlier. For example, his ideas and feelings about being good with words and a great speller pertain to his self-concept. His self-esteem was increased when his teacher valued his manipulation of the English language and allowed him to tutor other students who struggled with words during a variety of oral and written tasks.

Recent estimates indicate that English Language Learners (ELLs) comprise more than 5 million students in American public schools (Jiang, 2008). A large percentage of the language spoken by this population is Spanish, with Vietnamese and Hmong ranking second and third, respectively (Kindler, 2002). Alberto's native language is Spanish, a growing demographic in United States schools. Unfortunately, the challenges he experienced as a student have not been ameliorated. Alberto spoke about a situation in one of his high school math classes that he recalled vividly:

> For some reason, I got put in a class with a teacher...she couldn't communicate the content to the students and didn't know what she was doing. Sometimes the students were so confused they would ask me or some of the others in Spanish what the teacher was talking about. Anytime that happened she demanded that we speak English. "You're in America now; get used to it" was like her favorite thing to say. I remember being so frustrated, and she must have noticed the expressions on my face because one day she just up and asked me if I thought I could do a better job than what she was doing, I could come up and teach the class. I really didn't mean any harm, but I was just tired of sitting there and waiting for her to make sense. Some teachers think they're all high and mighty...you know? They're sarcastic, and they're not as caring as I think they should be. They have their favorites, and if you're not one of them, you can forget about getting a good education. I can't really honestly tell you who the good teachers are because they're gone already. The best teachers have left [this school] and gone to where the money is...like Fairfield and Greenwich. They leave because they want to make more money, but the reward is not in the money, but in the teaching. They're more concerned about their wallets and not the kids. I've seen teachers treat students like s__! I'm sorry to say that, but they do, which is part of the reason why I don't wanna be a teacher anymore. They killed it for me, man. As it is now, this is just a job for me. Since I'm here, I try to do the best I can, but if I had something else, I would be out. I have two kids of my own. One's a third grader, and I try to protect my son extremely because of what I know. I'm right there and I see it. I see how a lot of kids get pushed through the system, and I'm not gonna let that happen to my son.

He continued talking about some of the teachers with whom he had worked as an instructional aide in the school district. One of his narratives was particularly poignant, especially given how it underscored elements of both racism and discrimination:

> I've seen them humiliate other Black and Hispanic students, sometimes because of the way they talk or the way they dress. I remember an incident where my own professionalism and authority, if you wanna call it that was called into question. One of the White teachers and another Hispanic student got into an argument in class one day. The kid was really having a bad day, and I could tell because he had been crying and went to the back of the room and pulled his cap over his face. He was trying not to be bothered or to bother anybody. Well the teacher just kept f___ with him, you know? She went on and on and just wouldn't leave him alone. She was demanding that he participate in class, and when he wouldn't, she called him a slacker and told him he was lazy and that just because he was quote unquote having a bad day that he needed to suck it up and get over it. She was like everybody has bad days; get over it. I guess it was wrong of me, because I went over to try to get the teacher to calm down, and she ended up going off on me...right there in front of the students. It's not like I made a scene or anything. I mean, I waited to what I thought was a good time to approach her, and when I

did, I was like, I can't believe this sh__. This ended up bringing me before the principal of the school where I had to validate my attempt to resolve what I thought was a hostile situation. I think if I was a white male, then the situation would not have got blown out of proportion. There've been times when me and other aides, are standing in the hallways and administrators just walk by and introduce special guest visitors to the teachers only. I wonder if they ever think how this sh__ is supposed to make me and my coworkers feel.

Many ELLs experience prejudice in present-day public U.S. schools despite the regulations that have been designed to protect them. Current data show that schools continue in their struggles to adequately identify appropriate resources to meet the educational needs of linguistically diverse students. Guided by three primary research questions that examined (1) teacher attitudes, (2) contributing factors towards the development of these attitudes, and (3) how the attitudes varied contextually, Walker, Shafer, and Jiams (2004) found that mainstream educators possessed less than favorable views of their ELL students and did not adequately support their migrant student population. Referring to one of the nation's largest cities ("River City, Great Plains State," an obvious pseudonym) that experienced an influx of Bosnian, Somalian, and Sudanese students, the authors reported that according to interviews with the district's white teachers, they "relied on sink-or-swim immersion practices" (p. 137) and overpopulated special education programs with students of Hispanic origin. They note that:

> In 2000, however, a large school district in the region was cited for violating a migrant student's civil rights to ELL services and new legislation was passed in the state placing stricter requirements on schools serving limited English proficient students. There has also been a dramatic increase in the past few years of migrant parents finding year-round employment opportunities in these communities and permanently settling. Tensions in this region are high as schools find themselves forced to confront an issue that they have historically ignored. (p. 137)

When they examined broader "Great Plains State" contexts, these researchers found that

> For many rural schools, their only experience with linguistic diversity has been with Western European foreign exchange students. While smaller cities are seeing an increase in their language-minority populations, the schools are not overwhelmed as they have been in River City/West River City. (p. 137)

Other salient aspects of the study revealed that an alarming 70 percent (288 of 422) of mainstream teachers interviewed "were not actively interested in having ELLs in their classroom," (p. 140), and 14 percent "directly objected to ELL students being placed in their classrooms" (p. 140). The qualitative component of the study was equally disturbing to the researchers. They admit being awestruck by some of the written comments by participating interviewees. For example, patterns in the narrative comments indicated that teachers felt burdened by the presence of ELLs within their classrooms and that some of the schools' administrative personnel held similar beliefs about ELLs.

The kind of attitude that Alberto witnessed firsthand as a student and that he has seen in several of the teachers with whom he works is commensurate with the perspectives of some of the teachers in Walker, Shafer, and Jiams's study (2004). Data showed that teachers were ambivalent about engaging in professional development related to adapting curricula to the unique needs of their ELLs:

> Teachers who answered negatively to wanting professional development in the area of ELL education echoed similar thoughts, responding with comments such as "At some point, but right now. I feel too busy to fit that training in." Other teachers were more blunt and flatly stated they would be interested in professional development only if it were "on school time." (p. 27)

Alberto confirmed that he felt unwelcome in some classroom contexts, even as an instructional aide. The more we talked, the more apparent it became that little collegiality exists at Celebrity High. He said that some teachers have just recently started speaking to him, although this is his seventh year at the school. "I know I'm not as educated as they are, but I treat them with respect, and I expect the same in return. I just don't always get it," he said. Once he entered the teacher's lounge and noticed that conversation came to an immediate halt as soon as he walked in:

> I overheard them talking about me before I went in, so when I did go in, it was like this awkward silence in the room. I noticed they were talking about a piece of writing that I had helped a student with after school. I guess Ms.___[the teacher Alberto assists] had made copies of it and given it to them. The student got an A on the paper, because she came back to show me her grade a few days later. Why had that piece of writing ended up being the topic of conversation for teachers who I don't even think had this student in their class? I don't know the answer to that. I spoke to everybody in there, but not everybody responded. I just walked out of the lounge in the same quiet way I walked in.

Alberto believes the school's administration has failed to provide its teachers with professional development that could potentially heighten the educators' cultural sensibilities.

Efforts to capitalize upon the cultural and linguistic diversity that ELLs add to any classroom have been advocated by numerous organizations. Chief among these is the National Council of *La Raza* (NCLR). As reflected on its website, NCLR is the largest organization in the United States that advocates civil rights for American Hispanics. Enhanced educational, health, and employment opportunities for American Hispanics are among the goals of the organization as well as the implementation of applied research to ensure the general welfare of its Hispanic constituents. Contrary to popular conjecture, recipients of services rendered by NCLR are not just persons of Hispanic origin. Approximately 32 percent of those who benefitted from the organization were of other ethnicities. The website denotes, "...NCLR's bylaws, personnel policies, and institutional values contain explicit prohibitions against discrimination" (www.nclr. org). While the organization purports to embrace diversity in many respects, many educational institutions have yet to embody a similar philosophy. Consequently, many students from under-represented linguistic backgrounds continue to be dis-serviced.

During our second interview, I asked Alberto to reflect briefly upon our discussion and to share any thoughts that came to mind right away. He began by telling me how our sessions had caused him great anxiety, because he had to remember incidents from his past that he preferred to forget. "But at the same time, I think it helped me too," he said. When asked to clarify, he explained:

> Well, for me, school was pretty much like a sink or swim kind of thing, even though I really did like to learn new things at first. I thought about this last night and had a conversation with my wife about it. I think people who are put in sink or swim positions usually don't succeed unless they have strong family support. I already told you a lot about what my family life was about, so you know I didn't have that kind of support. I've been a teacher's aide here for seven years, but you know what? When it comes to dealing with some of these people around here, I think I lack self-esteem because of my background. Sometimes I don't think I'm good enough, but my son and my family are motivating factors for me. I'll be damned if I let the school system just push them through, kinda like what they did with me...understand?

Alberto also talked about his concern for the students at Celebrity. He believed mainstream teachers' perceptions of the Black students at the school were negative. "Some of the teachers try to judge the book by its cover without reading the content inside," he said. Regarding the Hispanic students, he thought the teachers' views of them were worse:

> I've actually heard them tell kids right to their face that the scores of their classes were gonna drop because of the number of people in the class who struggled with English and writing and reading. I've heard them actually say to kids what's the use…you're gonna be leaving anyway. How do you think those kids feel when they hear sh__ like that? There's some serious racism going on at this school, man…I'm telling you. I went here as a student, and nine times out of ten, I see it as an employee. What makes it really bad is they have no shame in saying this crap in front of people who work with them… people like me. For the most part, I think the school has some really good kids…sure you have a few knuckleheads here and there, but they really don't cause too much trouble. I look at the way they treat the kids and the way they treat the ones who don't look like me and you. I don't see anybody patting them on the back and saying good job, but as soon as one of them does something spectacular, the teachers, the principals, everybody is all over them. It's a real shame, man.

During our final interview, I asked if he could share any suggestions for aspiring educators. Empathy for students, respect for diversity and culture, and awareness that students have lives separate from scholastic activity were central themes that emerged in his response:

> Well, I think first and foremost, you gotta show that you care about the students. I can probably count on one hand the number of teachers who really cared about me, and I can almost guarantee that I wouldn't use all five fingers…and that's sad man, real sad. I also think teachers shouldn't judge their students by what they see on the outside…you know? They gotta be willing to learn about other cultures and step outside of the culture they're familiar with and get involved with other cultures, cause that's the only way they're gonna learn something new. I also think that teachers gotta be human and not forget that students don't eat, sleep, and drink school twenty-four seven. A lot of the kids here have a whole hellava lot going on in their lives, and I think everybody deserves a break sometime, especially if the kid in a class is having not so good of a day. I don't know for sure if any of the teachers who work here live in this community, but I do. I know a lot of the problems some of these kids have because at one time or another I had the same kind of problems. When they see things aren't right, they should at least have enough respect for the kids and say you know what…listen…hey everything's gonna be ok. I'm gonna cut you some slack just for a day. I'm not saying they have to do it all the time, because that's crazy and doesn't make sense, but every now and then, they gotta look out for the kids.

Some of his suggestions were more concrete; one was curricular and multicultural in nature. For example, Alberto believes that schools wait too long before they start teaching young people about embracing racial, socio-economic, and cultural differences. "We have got to start teaching the kids not to grow up to hate. We have to teach them the true history of America. It's ugly, but it needs to be taught. This is the only way they will grow up and become better parents and train their own kids not to hate," he said.

Also among Alberto's recommendations is improvement of the rapport between students, faculty and staff, and parents, at Celebrity High School. He claims he is good friends with his son's teacher because he is involved, something that he feels more parents need to become. While on and off his job, Alberto believes he does a significant amount of preventive work:

> When I see them [students from his school] on the streets, I give them the same respect that I do in the school. The teachers and administration don't know these kids. They don't know where they come from, but I can relate to them. A lot of them come from troubled homes, and I can relate to that… it allows me in…allows me to communicate with them and talk them out of trouble. I'm able to do what the teachers and administration can't do. People like me do all of the work, and the credit goes to the teachers and the principals. They're the ones who get all of the rewards, but it's people like me who do all of the work.

Alberto said that the teachers in Connecticut are mostly White even when they serve a predominately Hispanic population. In order for white teachers to be successful in the classroom, Alberto thinks they need to eradicate their inflated egos. "They can't walk the earth like they're better," he said. He believes also that teachers and administrators have to show a genuine interest in their students by taking them aside and inquiring about how things are going in their home environment. This, in Alberto's view, rarely occurs where he works, and this fact confirms his belief that more needs to be done to demonstrate concern for the students by all parties in the educational process. Moreover, Alberto remains hopeful that an African American, Hispanic, or female principal will replace the three white male administrators at Celebrity High.

SUMMARY AND IMPLICATIONS FOR PRACTICE

The purpose of this chapter is to link educational psychology theories to the case study of an individual who, at one time in his life, wanted to become an educator. Although significant variables in his home life thwarted him, I think it is ironic that the behaviors of teachers and administrators also caused him to rethink his formal career path. Readers may have noticed the applicability of a variety of psychological theories to Alberto's case, but I wish to end the chapter by focusing particularly on Alberto's identity formation and his unique sense of self (Woolfolk, 2009).

Data collected during interview processes suggest that the *parenting styles* (Woolfolk, 2009) of Alberto's mother and father were incompatible. He portrayed his mother as much more *authoritative*. The victim of her husband's abuse on multiple levels, she was characterized as more nurturing and loving. She maintained high expectations for both her sons and though constrained by her fear of her husband, she attempted to promote their independence as best as she could. These factors manifested in Alberto's identity and are observable in his initial sense of curiosity and his motivation (at least early on) to explore further his consuming interest in words and language. He was quite respectful of others' needs, oftentimes sacrificing his own objectives to ensure those of others were fulfilled. For example, he downplayed his wishes to attend college, having recognized that his family's financial status would not permit both sons' simultaneous pursuit of post-secondary education.

In contrast, when talking about his father, who clearly was much more *authoritarian* (Woolfolk, 2009) than the matriarch of the household, Alberto's descriptions were unfavorable. Swift obedience to rules was expected, and less emotional caressing was exhibited by his father. It can be argued that much of Alberto's unhappiness, high levels of anxiety, and diminished self-confidence may be attributed to the mistreatment he received frequently from his father. It is noteworthy that of the four parenting styles (*authoritarian, authoritative, permissive, rejecting/neglecting*) discussed by Woolfolk, Alberto's father seemed to both reject and neglect him. In fact, Alberto, his older brother, and mother were afraid in the majority, if not all, of their interactions with the patriarch.

Authoritative approaches are recommended when dealing with children, as the implications for their behavior in classrooms are usually positive. Ormrod (2008) states:

Children of authoritative parents appear well-adjusted, in part because their behaviors are considered ideal by many people in Western cultures: They listen respectfully to others, can follow rules by the time they reach school age, try to be independent, and strive for academic achievement. (p. 66)

However, she cautions that educators should not make value judgments about the ways parents raise their children. She suggests that a number of variables may influence parenting styles, including challenges that threaten the marital and financial status of a family. Without question, in Alberto's case, financial struggles were evident and often resulted in child maltreatment (Ormrod, 2008).

One of the more widely cited protocols related to the way in which a person views himself was articulated by Erik Erikson (Woolfolk, 2009; Ormrod, 2008). The eight stages, commonly referred to as the stages of *psychosocial development* or the *eight stages of man* are as follows:

1. *Trust versus mistrust*—Usually takes place from birth to 18 months. During this stage the child learns whether his primary needs will be met from a caregiver. When the needs are met, trust is usually developed. If basic needs like love are not provided, the child learns mistrust.

2. *Autonomy versus shame/doubt*—The timeframe identified by Erikson at stage two is from 18 months to 3 years. It is at this stage that toddlers generally increase their physical capabilities and become more self-directed with their actions. When encouraged by caregivers to explore self-directed activities without exertion, autonomy is developed. However, if caregivers are too demanding, shame and doubt manifest.

3. *Initiative versus guilt*—Generally takes place between ages 3 to 6, also known as the preschool years. Individuals at this stage experience increased independence and initiate activities on their own. When discouraged by authority figures, senses of guilt are generally developed.

4. *Industry versus inferiority*—This stage occurs between the ages of 6 to 12 and is where self-confidence may or may not be formulated. It is a crucial stage for risk-taking and may result in a sense of industry when tasks are completed or a feeling of inferiority if the individual's efforts are not supported and are blatantly disregarded or ridiculed.

5. *Identity versus role confusion*—Occurs during adolescence. It is during this stage that peer relationships are formed, gender roles are identified, along with a sense of direction related to where one's life is headed.

6. *Intimacy versus isolation*—Occurs during young adulthood. If no intimate relationships are formed during this stage, sentiments of isolation and loneliness may develop.

7. *Generativity versus stagnation*—This stage takes place between middle adulthood. Concern with posterity emerges, usually resulting in the exploration of related to how one may contribute to the enhancement of society. A person not willing to advance society in some way may experience a feeling of stagnation.

8. *Integrity versus despair*—Occurs during late adulthood or around the age of one's retirement. As one examines the course of his life, a sense of achievement and satisfaction may emerge. Conversely, if the individual's reflection on his life results in the recognition of goals not obtained, despair and disappointment may emerge.

According to Erikson, all human beings progress through the aforementioned stages. Some do so more effectively than others, ultimately determining how successful one may be able to interact not only with himself but with others in the world around him. Alberto mentioned that he had often wondered about how different his life might have been had he been born under a different set of circumstances. He suggested that most of the second-guessing about his identity and self-worth was due primarily to his financial deprivation and sensing that his father did not genuinely care about him or his family. However, since he has begun a family of his own, Alberto believes he understands his place in the world. He has established goals: chief among these are to be a good father to his children, a good husband to his wife, and not to emulate many of the behaviors he witnessed and modeled as a child. His self-esteem is gradually increasing, and he receives constant reinforcement from his wife that he is "a good man" (Alberto's words).

Although he remains dissatisfied with the treatment he sometimes receives at his job, Alberto is not cynical about the future course of his life:

> Because of my wife and kids, I'm happier now than I have ever been. You wanna know why? These are the facts man. I was born prematurely. I had no money. I had an abusive father, and I never thought I would never live past the age of twenty-three. When times were difficult, I thought about suicide, but I never attempted it. I like to think of myself as a very genuine person who's compassionate and relatively calm. I currently own a house. I have a wife, beautiful kids, and a dog, and I worked for that. Although I've gained some success in life, I'll probably always struggle financially, but for the most part, life is good for me.

He believes his current employment is the result of divine intervention, especially for the young adults whose struggles are similar to those of his past:

> There's this song that we sing in church. I won't sing it for you because I don't have a good voice, but I like it because it goes something like if I can help somebody then my living will not be in vain. I think that's part of the reason that I'm here, not just for me, but for somebody else who may need me. And being in the right place at the right time for the right person is all that matters to me.

Alberto's case study underscores the fact that any individual who would enter the teaching profession must be keenly aware of his sense of self and understand that self-confidence is needed to influence positively the students under one's charge. In addition, an educational practitioner must be committed to educational equity and be willing to advocate for the fair treatment of all students. The latter tenet is just as important as the former, and both should serve as guiding principles within any educational establishment, irrespective of the population's race, ethnicity, gender, sexual orientation, and the like. It seems that Celebrity High School has a long way to go before this philosophy is adopted.

Vygotsky informs us that we are all shaped by the immediate environment that surrounds us, what he referred to as *lived experience* (Woolfolk, 2009). Speaking of his work, Woolfolk notes:

> Vygotsky believed that human activities take place in cultural settings and cannot be understood apart from these settings. One of his key ideas was that our specific mental structures and processes can be traced to our interactions with others. These social interactions are more than simple influences on cognitive development—they actually create our cognitive structures and thinking processes. (p. 39)

Although his views about becoming a certified teacher have changed, in his own way, Alberto applies Vygotskian principles when he works with the students who come to him after school for additional help on classroom projects and assignments. He spoke of the method that he used with every student when his assistance is solicited:

I usually began by asking them to write down at least one or two goals that they want to accomplish, depending on how much time we've got to work together. This usually helps the kids get focused and on task which is important, especially when I have more than one who comes to me for help. Once they get their goals down, we take it from there. I think this helps out a lot because some of them come and they're all over the place and have no sense of direction about how to get from point A to point B. I do this with my own kids when I work with them on their homework too. We get a sense of direction and work from that point on. I try to teach these kids here that they gotta stick together if they wanna succeed. So when I see some of them struggling in class, I tell them to come see me after school. I partner them up or I work with them one on one, depending on what's needed. For the most part, though, we tackle problems together as a team, and that usually works best. I think what they're learning from me is really a life skill that they can use not only in this class but in their other classes as well.

It is clear that Alberto knows a great deal about the teaching profession. He endeavors to work with the learners at Celebrity High School to promote their sense of self and to engender a spirit of collective responsibility for the success of all. From him, students appear to gain a sense of what it means to be self-regulated learners, and as he suggests, he teaches them how they can transfer this skill set to a variety of subject matters.

As I reflected on the totality of Alberto's case and read some of my comments in a reflective journal that I had kept throughout our interviews, I remember feeling a tremendous sense of loss with regard to his reconsideration of his role. He seemed to possess many of the character traits that make up a good educator. He was patient, compassionate, and had strong knowledge of English curriculum content. Perhaps more importantly, because of his experiences, Alberto understood many of the students at Celebrity High School. I did not sense that he was as distant as the other teachers he described during our few times together. He was a visible presence in the community and had a good rapport with many of the students' parents at the school.

In comparison to the teacher to whom he was assigned as an instructional aide, Alberto possessed the wherewithal to be in charge, despite his intermittent struggles with self-confidence. Although this is true of his personality, he understood his position in the teaching relationship and did not seek to usurp the teacher's power. My hope is that a case study like Alberto's may be used as a springboard for initiating discussions in educational psychology classes and courses in general about what educators, administrators, parents, and all those involved in the educational enterprise can do to prevent others from experiencing forms of educational malpractice like that I have chronicled in this chapter. It is a disgrace for any individual's dream to be deferred because of the malpractice of another, especially when that individual holds great potential and promise to be a great educator.

REFERENCES

Bridges, R. (1999). *Through my eyes*. New York: Scholastic Press.

Byrnes, B. (2002). Validating the measurement and structure of self-concept: Snapshots of past, present, and future research. *American Psychologist, 57,* 897-909.

Davis, S. & Buskist, W. (Eds.). (2002). *The teaching of psychology: Essays in honor of Wilbert J. McKeachie and Charles L. Brewer.* Mahwah, NJ: Lawrence Erlbaum Associates, Incorporated.

Dietrich, L. (1998). Chicano adolescents: Bitches, ho's and school girls. Westport, CT: Praeger Publishers.

Harter, S. (1990a). Causes, correlates, and the functional role of global self-worth: A life-span perspective. In R. J. Sternberg & J. Kolligian, Jr. (Eds.), *Competence considered.* New Haven, CT: Yale University Press.

Harter, S. (1990a). Issues in the assessment of self-concept of children and adolescents. In A. LaGreca (Ed.), *Through the eyes of a child* (pp. 292-325). Boston: Allyn and Bacon.

Jiang, B. (2008). English language learners: Understanding their needs. In G. S. Goodman (Ed.), *Educational psychology: An application of critical constructivism* (pp. 185-212). New York: Peter Lang.

Kindler, A. (2002). Survey of the states' limited English proficient students and available educational programs and services, 2000-2001 Summary Report.

Kozol, J. (2005). *The shame of the nation: The restoration of apartheid schooling in America.* New York: Crown Publishers.

Morrison, T. (2004). *Remember: The journey to school segregation.* New York: Houghton Mifflin Company.

National Council of La Raza (n.d.). Retrieved from http://www.nclr.org

Ormrod, J. (2008). *Educational psychology.* (6th ed.). Upper Saddle River, NJ: Merrill, Prentice Hall.

Spring, J. (2009). *American education.* (14th ed.). New York: McGraw-Hill.

Tyack, D. & Cuban, L. (1995). Tinkering toward utopia: A century of public school reform. Cambridge, MA: Harvard University Press.

Walker, A., Shafer, J., & Jiams, M. (2004). "Not in my classroom": Teacher attitudes towards English language learners in the mainstream classroom. NABE *Journal of Research and Practice, 2,* 130-160.

Webb, D. (2005). *The history of American education: A great American experiment.* Upper Saddle River, NJ: Merrill, Prentice Hall.

Woolfolk, A. (2009). *Educational psychology.* (11th ed.). Upper Saddle River, NJ: Merrill, Prentice Hall.

TWENTY-SIX

Creating a Classroom Community
Culture for Learning

Suzanne Gallagher and Greg S. Goodman

Only in Hollywood visions of school does classroom chaos and blatant teacher disrespect dissolve and turn to loving relations based upon mutual positive regard. Looking back at a movie such as *To Sir with Love* and continuing up to the more recent film *Freedom Writers,* we view gross mismatches of teacher-cultures of control versus the post-modern youth culture that stereotypically appears unmanageable, oppositional, and disrespectful. As these scripts go, the 30 minutes of agony teachers such as *Freedom Writers'* Erin Gruwell endure are typically followed by 90 minutes of resolution and teaching bliss. Students are transformed, and lessons are learned. Just do as Gruwell does, and you'll have students metaphorically eating out of your hand. What was so hard to understand about that?

The stereotypical script of the teacher movie and its conflict of students versus teacher make for a good plotline, but the reality of today's classroom is missing. Our students are not paid actors, and we, unfortunately, are not pulling in seven digits for our performances. As teacher-viewers, we're always in awe of the quick transformations the movies bring to kids who have been at war with systems more invested in forcing compliance and control than in promoting liberation and individual free expression of thought, life-style or action! The conflict for professional educators is that we are real teachers who have taught in actual schools, not virtual ones! Our problem is real. If we don't control our students properly, we're seen as loose, anti-disciplinarians, and we are jeopardizing the authority of the other teachers in our building. If we let our students "have fun" or appear to have fun, they will expect that in every class. How will other teachers view us when their students say, "Mr/s…doesn't make us raise our hands if we want to comment in class"? Many traditional teachers equate rigid, regimented adherence to rules regarding turn-taking with authority. Their every move seems to communicate, "I'm in control here!" For you, the pre-service teacher, don't be fooled by Hollywood scripts. The reality of the classroom for many teachers and students is that the climax of the story is a tragedy, not a romance.

Embedded in real scenarios of **classroom management** are issues related to authority, power, control, and leadership. Without question, the teacher is vested with authority as the instructional leader in the classroom. However, critical constructivists view the role of the teacher/instructional leader in a different light than is reflected by the traditional control and authority models. For critical constructivists, the emphasis is on building a classroom community culture. To show how these models differ, let us first examine some of the traditional classroom management approaches.

TRADITIONAL MODELS

In our many years of teaching experience, we have seen the promotion of a wide array of techniques touted to promote classroom management. The major focus of these techniques is **teacher centered**; the focus is on what the teacher does to the classroom environment in order to effect the desired behavior in the students. This is a good example of technical rationality (Gallagher, 2003). These techniques may be thought to have some merit in that they can produce the desired behavior in students (Marzano, 2007), and there is clear evidence to reinforce the importance of having clear rules and expectations (Stage & Quiroz, 1997). Teachers reinforce this notion as they witness students learning to conform and to follow directions (Evertson & Neal, 2006). An emphasis on reward for compliant behavior and punishment for infractions is the general mode. As in authoritarian parenting styles, the teacher has complete authority over students. Control and domination is often the cardinal rule in many traditionally structured classrooms.

Most teachers experiment with the practices of classroom management until they find a formula that brings them success. And the winning of control is reinforced in the majority of cases. The goal from this perspective is the same regardless of your stance concerning ethics or social justice: maintaining control of the classroom. However, the moral and ethical issues under-girding the rationale for classroom control play a significant role in the professional's practice. If your reason for control is to mask poor teaching and to quell the rebelliousness spurred by boredom and the concomitant anger your students feel toward you, no classroom management system will work effectively or be justifiable in the eyes of students. Conversely, if you understand that a certain amount of order will provide an environment where you can teach and your curriculum and process are in sync with student interest and ability, that is the best classroom management system and the need to deal with student misbehavior is only rarely needed.

Although it is hard to imagine in our present time, within the real world of the public schools corporal punishment is still legal in 28 states. This antiquated form of punishing students, paddling them on their buttocks with a wooden object, is still permissible under statute of law in the majority of states. Obviously, corporal punishment should never be invoked; however, this form of punishment is mentioned to give you, the student of educational psychology, some foundational knowledge of the crude beginnings of managing student behavior. Using fear and physical domination to control behavior is not only primitive, it is psychologically and physically damaging of students. These laws are criminal, and they need to be stricken from educational statutes, as was done in Pennsylvania during the fall of 2005.

Even in states where corporal punishment is not outlawed, most school districts have sanctions against this form of punishment. However, a behavior that is more apt to be found is psychological belittling or verbal expressions of disrespect of students. The National Educators Association (NEA) has a code of ethics that pre-service teachers need to study and all teachers need to adhere to. One of the principles of ethical behavior is the commitment to students. It reads: Teachers "shall not intentionally expose the student to embarrassment or disparagement" (http://www.nea.org/aboutnea/code.html).

EFFECTIVE LEARNING ENVIRONMENTS

Effective learning environments are ones that are pro-social and positively reflect a respect for both the participants and the process of education. As we have emphasized earlier in the works by Beachum and McCray and by Duncan-Andrade, harmony is achieved when there is an acceptance of the students by the teacher and mutual positive regard for the teacher by the students. Teacher leadership and authority are enhanced by the mutually respectful culture of the classroom (Marzano, 2007). This includes both the positive and negative aspects of culture the students represent and the often gnarly and cacophonous chorus of complaints, criticisms, and commentary that attend their lives. Despite the marketing of *Teen* magazine, the experience of adolescence is not an endless series of glorious encounters with clothing and cosmetics! Adolescence is a time of tremendous growth and personal discovery. Much of this experience is dramatically portrayed within the harsh reality of teenage crisis and conflict.

The concept of positive mutual regard has been a mainstay of humanistic psychology since Carl Rogers coined the term in the early 1950s. Rogers espoused a profound belief in the power of individuals to adapt and become themselves. On valuing the worth and dignity of each person, Rogers said, "The primary point of importance…is the attitude held by the counselor (read: teacher) toward the worth and significance of the individual" (1951, p. 20). These words still resonate with constructivist educators. What has changed is the time and situation students and teachers must confront. Building a safe space for student learning based upon this attitude of mutual positive regard is the art of an excellent teacher.

Traditional classroom management approaches have also focused on the relationship between effective teaching practices and the lack of behavioral infractions by students. In contrast, we present the concept of **learning-centered** environments where students share in the responsibility for learning and building community in the classroom (Evertson & Neal, 2006). The major focus from this perspective, is that students construct meaning in social environments. Students are engaged in meaningful, productive activities with others, and they share authority and responsibility with teachers.

We need to be clear that in a learning-centered classroom the teacher never abdicates authority or responsibility for the class process or content; the teacher "still manages the class in the sense of establishing the environment and creating learning opportunities for students" (Evertson &

Neal, 2006, p. 11). However, in this environment the students have responsibility as well. In the day-to-day life in these classrooms, student voices are respected and taken seriously. Through the modeling of the teachers in this environment students learn respect for others, valuing of others, and a more democratic working out of problems. This is akin to what is termed authoritative style, akin to the parenting style of the same name.

BUILDING A CLASSROOM CULTURE

In a climate of respect and responsibility students are much less likely to be motivated to disrupt or misbehave. Classroom management systems often suggest that an ounce of prevention is worth a pound of cure. Following the advice of author Kolencik, by accepting and effectively dealing with feelings, many behavioral infractions can be avoided.

In the development of the best classroom management system, one of the first foci the teacher will address is the rules and procedures of the classroom. Expert classroom manager, Harry Wong, thinks that training students in the procedures and rules of the classroom is the most important aspect of making an effective learning environment. Wong has made a fortune promoting his system of procedural routines and rules governing classroom behaviors. From greeting the students at the door with a handshake and a "good morning" salutation to the commencement of an immediate task for the student's engagement, every bit of the student's experience is orchestrated. Wong and Wong (1997) leave no room for fooling around! Having sold 3,000,000 copies of their book, *The First Days of School,* we'd say there is a lot of demand for a bomb-proof system.

One critique of Wong's system is that it is too regimented, and there is little room for individual deviation from the procedures or control. Students who grow up experiencing such excessive control tend to lack individual initiative and make good followers. If the leadership is good, this may not be problematic. However, when the leaders are suspect, good followers are just as much a part of the problem.

Rules need to be a part of every classroom, and the developmental needs of each grade will require slightly different interpretations of the same principles. A major theme of critical constructivism is to build respect for the diverse cultural community within each classroom and to encourage the development of social consciousness for living in a democratic society. Leadership is the gift that good teachers model for their students. In a learning-centered classroom students are considered capable and competent to assist the teacher in providing leadership and formulating classroom rules. As they mature, our students have gained experience with classroom living, and we believe they often have a very good understanding of what works and what doesn't. Teachers need to take the time to reflect on their students' beliefs about good classroom practices and to continually re-examine their own beliefs on what rules support effective practice.

Rules need to be part of the life of the classroom from the beginning of the year or semester. Establishing them early is time well spent in helping the students get acclimated to the classroom. Waiting until unhelpful instances occur takes the rules out of the community-building category and makes it appear as a kind of negative disciplinary action. The best policy is to state rules in a positive voice and to avoid negative wording. "Treat others with respect" is more effective than "no put downs." Say what you want, not what you don't want.

Consistency is an important aspect of rules becoming a support in the classroom atmosphere. Implementing rules and the reinforcing procedures require constant attention. Students figure out very quickly if the classroom rules are merely bulletin board decorations or if they really are serious procedures needing their recognition and cooperation.

Enforcement of the rules also requires delicate negotiation. Using the authority as the teacher, consequences for rule violations need to be appropriate and never excessive. Excessive use of punishment can lead to the demise of the teacher's authority. Fairness is the rule, and under-statement of power use is preferable to over-application. The over-application of punishment could be an act of hegemony; the excessive exertion of power and control over a weaker person or subject. Hegemony requires the subjugated to give the power to the person in control or the subjugator. This is not the relationship a teacher wishes to have over students. Hegemony is a misuse of power through subjugation of subordinates, and it debilitates the students' sense of personal agency and control over their own behavior.

Before doling out harsh consequences and/or punishments for misbehavior, the teacher is advised to seek alternative methods for correcting the behavior. Giving the students a chance to self-monitor their behavior is better than relying on the teacher to change the students' actions. Sometimes a cue, "What are we supposed to be doing right now?," is sufficient to redirect a student. Perhaps praising a proximal student for good behavior can stimulate reciprocal positive behavior. Telling the student in a clear voice to stop doing the misdeed and start doing the correct action is very effective. The last action to take is the consequence stage. It should be clear when consequences are meted out that every opportunity to self-correct had been attempted. We work for the successful inclusion of every student.

DREIKURS' LOGICAL CONSEQUENCES

One of our criticisms of many behavior management systems is the absurdity of their logic. Sometimes the consequences for student misbehavior reflect a lack of thoughtfulness. For example, the consequence of smoking in school is often suspension or permanent removal such as expulsion. Smoking is (or can lead to) an addiction, and controlling one's urge to smoke often requires tremendous self-discipline. Self-discipline is not gained when one is sent home for a day or two or more. When students are away from school, they can smoke whenever they want. Behavioral psychologists would call this a positive **reinforcer**, because the suspension has the effect of supporting or continuing the behavior, not extinguishing or ending it. Reinforcers are consequences of behavior that perpetuate or support the continuance of the behavior. Teachers often confuse the meaning of this technical term of behavioral psychology. Just because we assume the act we do is a punishment for the child, for example, sending the child out of our room, the child may like to be removed, and he will continue his misbehavior when he returns to class to be reinforced yet again by being forced to leave. The test of reinforcers is to see if they cause repetition of the behavior. If the behavior is maintained or increases, it has been reinforced.

Simple as this appears on the surface, the actual implementation of a behavior modification plan is complex and challenging.

Because behavioral psychology is highly clinical, training in its application is rigorous. Despite its technical difficulty, it has viable applications within some settings; for example it is often used in special education as teachers work with students who have severe mental and psychological issues such as autism, emotional and mental disabilities. Because of the highly technical nature of behavioral psychology, implementation of these techniques requires extensive training before they can be an effective tool for teachers. As a result, the techniques of behavioral psychology are better used in conjunction with cognitively based psychological principles such as the system Rudolph Dreikurs (1982) developed.

Rudolph Dreikurs (1982) proposed that students misbehave to meet the needs of one of four mistaken goals: attention, power, revenge, or inadequacy. By understanding the reason for the child's misbehavior, the teacher can redirect the child to accomplish his or her real goal of being accepted and or loved by others. According to Dreikurs, if the students cannot meet their goals in a positive manner, they will revert to misbehavior to avenge or correct the denial of that acceptance.

Dreikurs and other cognitive and behavioral psychologists made a major contribution to the processes of classroom management in the discovery of the use of logical consequences. The philosophic foundation of this approach is that children need to learn how to behave appropriately, and that logical consequences can be a better teacher than the use of *aversive punishment*. Logical consequences have to do with what is happening now. Punishment deals with the past. To go back to the example of our smoker, what would be a logical consequence of smoking in school? There does not have to be one answer. The child can help to develop a relationship between what was done and what needs to happen to restore order or harmony. Possible consequences could be counseling with the school nurse on the effects of smoking. Watching a film on the relationship of smoking to disease. Joining a stop smoking group with the school counselor. Coming to a special Saturday school session where students visited the cancer ward at the hospital and visited patients to provide company.

The goal of logical consequences is to teach corrective actions. The tone of the process is collaborative, not harsh and stimulated by anger or rejection. Many students lack understanding of social conventions. They do not know the right thing to do. This is not necessarily their fault. Over the years we have witnessed many forms of student misbehavior, and depending on the developmental level of the student, each misbehavior may have a different communicative intent ranging from no message at all to a very significant act. For example, a first grader may raise a middle finger to another student in "the" gesticulation of disrespect. However, when queried by the principal about the event, the child may not know what that gesticulation means, and the reason they committed the act was imitation of an older sibling's actions. The same behavior in a junior high student may be conducted to make a joke or just to tease another student. The communicative intent was not to express anger or rage but to take a risk and show some bravado. Last, the finger may be used by a high school student as a clear message of contempt. The message is, "I'm angry and this is what you can do!" The logical consequence for the specific behavior needs to address the communicative intent in order to be an effective agent of behavior change. The student needs to cognitively connect behavior to the consequence to learn to adjust and find a more appropriate response.

The system of logical consequences makes tremendous sense for adults, but what about the children it is supposed to affect? Education critic Alfie Kohn (1999) suggests that this process may actually make more sense to the adults than to the children. Children may just see the logical consequence as a thinly disguised punishment. They are not happy to say, "I'm sorry," when in fact they are not sorry at all. Developing compassion is not always an easy or straight-forward process. Often the hurt that killed the compassion is deeper than classroom teachers' capacity or skill to address in a brief intervention.

CRITICAL CONSTRUCTIVIST MODEL: A CULTURE OF MUTUAL ENHANCEMENT

Critical constructivists base their classroom community culture on the egalitarian principles of mutual enhancement (Miller, 2003) and social justice (Kincheloe, 2005). Mutual enhancement is a feminist concept, and within critical constructivists' classrooms it means that both the teacher and the students receive benefit from the interactive processes of teaching and learning. Developed by Jean Miller of the Wellesley Center for Women, mutual enhancement does not imply that the teacher gives up any of their authority or leadership, as we said above. Rather mutual enhancement means that there is an air of equanimity and universal respect that imbues the classroom culture. In an analogy to therapy, both the client and the therapist benefit from the interaction. Growth occurs for both individuals. In the classroom, learning and growth occur for both the students and the teacher. To differentiate between traditional forms of top-down control and domination, it is more accurate to identify critical constructivist educational leadership as creating a classroom community culture.

A classroom community culture is a set of rules and understandings that are specific to the individuals included in the group and reflective of the values and identities of the world these individuals inhabit. A perfect metaphor for understanding this issue is imbedded in the Ebonics debate. Ebonics, derived from the words "ebony" and "phonics," is a specific language of the urban African American community; it reflects members' situated experience. This language is strongly tied to identity and membership pride. The critical constructivist understands and accepts Ebonics as a communicative tool and includes these neologisms along with other attributes of the families or neighborhood within the classroom community culture. In this context, the teacher is embracing the diversity of the students and affirming the values of those individuals in a truly democratic praxis of the classroom.

Mutual enhancement applies to classroom community culture as it extends to the social atmosphere within the classroom. In a classroom based upon the principles of mutual enhancement, a spirit of shared social responsibilities allows for inclusion and equality. These classrooms develop dispositions of openness to diversity and explorations of other identities. Learning activities promote mixing it up and sparking conversations about differences and similarities.

Mutual enhancement allows for the growth of one's self and promotes the acceptance of others. This is especially meaningful when the "other" is comprised of those who have been marginalized because of minority identifications and economic disparities. Mutual enhancement dovetails with critical constructivist philosophy and practice as a further application of *social justice* initiatives. Social justice takes on many meanings in the modern schools, but among the most important is the legitimate recognition of the diversity distributed within the school. Legitimizing diversity is opposed to token, simplistic Cinco de Mayo trivializations. One-day food festivals are not examples of socially just pedagogy (Banks, 2006). Valid programs to promote social justice in the classroom and on the campus provide ubiquitous benefit to the school community. Social justice in school means many important things to groups intimate with experiences of oppression and persecution. For example, Gay/lesbian/bisexual and transgendered (GLBT) youth experience horrific persecution in the public school (Gray, 2004). Although the vast majority of today's students on public school and college campuses have gained the knowledge to radically reduce racist attitudes and behavior, we continue to witness overt forms of anti-gay behaviors in and across campuses. Continuing efforts to build a culture of complete acceptance of all diversity is the goal of social justice educators.

Of utmost concern to critical constructivist educators is the implementation of policies to promote social justice in both the classroom and in the community. Working to promote social justice in your classroom is negated within a school where the conversation of social justice gets no air time. When school administrators ignore disproportionate numbers of suspension or expulsion among specific targeted groups, their actions may reflect institutionalized racism. Against a backdrop of bigotry, the efforts you make in your classroom will work to expose the larger problems, but they may not come close to meeting your needs to achieve a socially just culture for your students.

The entire school must buy in to promoting socially just education and social culture. We are convinced that if proper attention to issues of social justice were in place at Littleton, Colorado's Columbine High School, the persecution of two students (whom we refuse to recognize by name) would not have been allowed nor would it have escalated to their hate-based killing of faculty and students. On dynamic, rapidly changing campuses across this country, critical constructivist educators are continually taking the pulse of their student body and reinventing their responses to revolutionize the process (Kincheloe, 2005).

RULES TO LIVE BY...

Certainly rules and procedures are a natural part of any group experience, and the classroom is no different as a social group. Rules and procedures need to mirror the philosophies of mutual enhancement and social justice. With any system of rules, those responsible for the rule adoption must support the goals of the governing system. There must be buy-in by all the members of the community. These rules are not just window-dressing or pseudo symbols of our beliefs. The rules exemplify our core beliefs, and what could be considered the culture's Tao.

The best rule systems are the simplest to learn; however, they may not be the easiest to implement. In our classroom, we choose just two rules. The first is a "Respect" rule. This means that everyone is treated with respect within the classroom, and no one is devalued for any reason. This is in concert with the concept of mutual enhancement. In a respect-governed classroom, there is no hegemony or subjugation of anyone. The goals of gaining knowledge and learning pro-social behaviors are clearly evident.

Implementing the respect rule requires significant reconceptualizing of social relations for many students. Coming from homes and neighborhoods where "doing the dozens" is the game: yo mama. Leaving this put-down interaction out of the classroom needs to be viewed as positive and additive, not negative or rejecting. Although this may seem to contradict the acceptance of community culture, that is too reductive an explanation. The dozens is a game to build strength and test resolve. Putting someone down with clever word play continues until the loser reveals vulnerability and exposes emotion. The goal is stay strong: don't give in or show hurt.

We agree with the goal of building strength. However, the strength needs to flow from positive, collaborative contributions, not competitive and destructive gaming. The point of the dozens is to stand up to the hegemony of stereotypic representations of poverty, racism, and other put downs. We contribute that the paradox of refuting the process by handing double doses of disrespect to one's classmate or schoolmate may reveal a validation of those derogatory remarks when the loser succumbs to the pain. As Jeff Duncan-Andrade argues about Hip-Hop culture in "Best Friend/Worst Enemy," elements of the anger and alienation youth experience can be used a positive force and deliver energy to transform the rage into something Freire would call love.

Another rule of our classroom is confidentiality; everything that is said in the classroom is potentially sensitive and personal information, and what is said in the classroom needs to stay in the classroom. Therefore, if a personal conversation is going on and a student mentions her parent's divorce (perhaps as it relates to the plot of a novel or theme of a poem), that student does not need to fear that the entire school will be discussing her personal life after school. This rule is hard to monitor, but it pays big dividends for supporting the development of trust within the classroom. Students know when they are being talked about, and they resent gossip just as much as any adult. Protecting confidentiality is a cornerstone of respecting the individual and his or her privileged information.

REDUCING HATE CRIMES AND VIOLENCE IN THE SCHOOL AND COMMUNITY

We live in the most violent society in the industrialized world. Since 9/11, there have been over 130,000 murders committed in America (Herbert, 2007). Sadly, Americans are so inured to the violence that news of such outrageous violence is more often met with resignation and denial than more appropriate emotions like repulsion. Violence is ubiquitously enmeshed in our culture's movies, television, and entertainments (paint ball, smack-downs, and gang initiations). Movies such as *Really Bad Things* and *Pulp Fiction* make parodies of the violence through grotesque over-use, but these "jokes" are more reflective of the malaise in our culture than they are successful strokes of sarcasm. Cornel West (1995) accurately sums this up saying, "Post-modern culture is more and more a market culture dominated by gangster mentalities and self-destructive wantonness" (p. 559).

None of American violence is spared on our children. Schools are often sites of violence, and this is too common news.

> Violence in America is too frequently appearing in schoolyards.…According to a Justice Department report on juvenile justice and delinquency, "American kids are the most violent. Teenagers have 'alarmingly high' rates of violence compared with those of youths in other nations, a comparison that also

holds for adult crime rates. An American teenager is ten times more likely to commit murder than a Canadian teenager." (Hinds, 2000, p. 3) (Goodman, 2004, p. 5)

The first job of the critical constructivist educator is to create a culture where students are safe to learn. Accomplishing this feat is the single most critical aspect of the school community, and we do not want to imply that this is anything shy of huge. Making a safe school is a long-term project, and it requires the buy-in of all of the community's citizens. Everyone must not only see the value in maintaining safety and decorum but the need to commit to the daily maintenance of the values that can support harmony.

One of our favorite slogans from the sixties admonished, "If you want peace, then support justice!" The values of social justice undergird safe schools. Critical constructivist schools are organizations that fairly represent all of the constituents of the community. Staff represent the student body in cultural identity and shared understandings. Realia and other school artifacts demonstrate the contributions of students, staff, and parents. As you walk through these schools, you will see yourself represented in the people and things in evidence.

Safety is also protected by participation. The engagement of all of the members of the community in the preservation of the community values speaks louder than words. Walking the talk of critical constructivism is accomplished by participating in active conversations about racism, class, and sexual identities. From "Teaching Tolerance" to others of the myriad social justice initiatives available through the National Association of Multicultural Educators (N.A.m.E. org), the Southern Poverty Law Center (teachingtolerance.org), or the Tolerance Museum, there are many ways to revive the movement to provide social justice programs in your school.

Creating a classroom community culture with affirming values can diminish the need for safety and discipline concerns. However, teaching will always require vigilance and the need to courageously respond to the demands of challenging situations. Prevention and intervention programs, police and metal detectors, dogs and security cameras will remain in many of our schools, but these things cannot replace the courage it takes to personally confront violent acts and other criminal behaviors. Teachers practice their profession within real communities, and as we work to build a new world, we still confront violent vestiges of our dark side. By applying critical constructivist social justice praxis, we are moving toward a harmonious and idealized reinvention of ourselves. Following Freire (1970), "To teach is to be a prisoner of hope" (p. 91). The teacher in each of us hopes that you are excited to take up this challenge to reinvent our schools and the communities they serve.

REFERENCES

Banks, J. A. (2006). *Diversity and citizenship education: Global perspectives*. San Francisco, CA: Jossey-Bass.

Dreikurs, R. (1982). *Maintaining sanity in the classroom*. New York: Harper Collins.

Evertson, C. M., & Neal, K. W. (2006). http://www.eric.ed.gov/ ERICWebPortal/Home.portal?_nfpb= true&_pageLabel=ERICSearch Result&_urlType=action&newSearch=true&ERICExtSearch_Search Type_0=au&ERICExtSearch_SearchValue_0=%22Neal+Kristen+W.%22 Looking into learning-centered classrooms: Implications for classroom management. [Working Paper]. Washington, DC: NEA [ERIC Document Reproduction Service No. ED495820]

Freire, P. (1970). *Pedagogy of the oppressed*. New York: Contiuum.

Gallagher, S. (2003). *Educational psychology: Disrupting the dominant discourse*. New York: Peter Lang Publishing.

Goodman, G. (2004). *Reducing hate crimes and violence among American youth: Creating transformational agency through critical praxis.* New York: Peter Lang Publishing.

Gray, M. (2004). Finding pride and the struggle for freedom to assemble. In G. Goodman & K. Carey (Eds.) *Critical multicultural conversations.* Cresskill, NJ: Hampton Press.

Herbert, B. (2007). 100,000 gone since 2001. *New York Times.* August 14, p. D 18.

Hinds, Michael deCourcy (2000). *Violent kids: Can we change the trend?* Dubuque, IA: Edward J. Arnone Publisher.

Kincheloe, J. (2005). *Critical constructivism.* New York: Peter Lang Publishing.

Kohn, A. (1999). *The schools our children deserve: Moving beyond traditional classrooms and "tougher standards."* Boston, MA: Houghton Mifflin.

Marzano, R. (2007). *The art and science of teaching: A comprehensive framework for effective instruction.* Alexandria, Virginia: Association for Supervision and Curriculum Development.

Miller, J.B. (2003). Telling the truth about power. In *Research and Action Report 25* (1 Fall/Winter). Wellesley, MA: Wellesley College for Women.

Rogers, C. (1951). *Client-centered therapy.* Boston, MA: Houghton Mifflin Company.

Stage, S.A. & Quiroz, D.R. (1997). A meta-analysis of interventions to decrease disruptive classroom behavior in public education settings. *School Psychology Review,* 26(3), 333–368.

West, C. (1995). Race matters. In *Race, class, and gender: An anthology,* edited by Margaret L. Anderson and Patricia Hill Collins. New York: Wadsworth Publishing.

Wong, H. & Wong, R. (1997). *The first days of school.* Fresno, CA: Harry K. Wong Publications.

Enlivened Spaces
for Enhanced Learning

TWENTY-SEVEN

Researching Children's Place and Space

Julia Ellis

In an autobiographical reflection on how her rural childhood currently shapes her experience of academic work, Jipson (2000) begins with the following recounting.

> It is the third time since July that I have caught myself picking berries, making pie, while my academic projects sit waiting at the computer....My mother and grandmother taught me to harvest every ripe berry, slice and can each carrot and beet....Learning to do the "real work," the sort that is done with your hands not your head, was an essential part of my growing up....It was a way of life that defined time and value as well as survival. But now, in this other-world of academe, I wonder how to frame my identity as a worker. (p. 37)

In the remainder of the article, Jipson's analysis stands as an insightful and articulate testimony to the way in which we always carry as part of ourselves the places where we have lived. Making this point on the basis of an extensive literature review, Chawla (1992) has argued that children's place attachments are important both for what they contribute to the quality of their lives and for the enduring effects they leave after childhood is over. Our experiences are circumscribed by our places and our personalities and perspectives are developed from the experiences we have in the places available to us.

Industrialization, urbanization, and the effects of processes of globalization associated with late capitalism are dramatically altering place and space for people's lives throughout the world. Adults with "good" jobs can make themselves sufficiently "at home" in many localities, can occasionally escape the routine of the home base, or may have action-spaces among many far-flung locales. The poor, the disabled, the elderly, and the young, however, are much more restricted in terms of the environments they can access or enjoy.

At the University of Alberta, I teach a course entitled Children and Place in the hope of drawing attention to the quality of life that places afford for children. Although questions about children and their environments have traditionally been taken up within cultural geography and urban planning, I argue that research on children's "place and space"—both within and outside of the school—should also inform policy and practice in education.

In this chapter I offer a discussion of the significance of *place* and *space* for children, describe examples of place research initiatives that engage children or youth in a participatory way, and discuss research approaches for studying children's place and space for educators' purposes.

THE SIGNIFICANCE OF CHILDREN'S PLACE AND SPACE

In the introduction to his landmark book *Space and Place: The Perspective of Experience,* Yi-Fu Tuan (1977) directed attention to the potential significance of the concepts of *place* and *space.*

> Place is security, space is freedom: we are attached to the one and long for the other....Space and place are basic components of the lived world; we take them for granted. When we think about them, however, they may assume unexpected meanings and raise questions we had not thought to ask. (p.3)

Cultural geographers have studied place and the social organization of space for over three decades (Holloway & Valentine, 2000). Expressing a widespread understanding about the significance of place, Eyles (1989) offered the following comments.

> Place is seen as a centre of felt value, incarnating the experience and aspirations of people. Thus it is not only an arena for everyday life—its geographical or spatial coordinates—it, in itself, provides *meaning* to that life. To be attached to a place is seen as a fundamental human need and, particularly as home, as the foundation of our selves and our identities. Places are thus conceived as profound centres of human existence. (pp. 108–109)

In cultural geography literature, *place* is understood to be a source of security, comfort, stability, nurturance, belonging, meaning, and identity. As Hay (1992) and others have argued, bonds to place facilitate meaningful relationships, which then make the place itself more meaningful. Being an insider in a community gives a person a strong center from which to face the unknowns of the larger world. Good places are seen to also include *space* for growth and creative self-development. When places lack such space, people often have to leave in order to escape drudgery or to change who they can be. Lynch (1981), in the early Growing Up in Cities project work, found that place supports children's and youths' development of self-identity either by affording opportunities for young people to try out predefined roles in conventional settings or by offering unprogrammed space. The notion of "unprogrammed space" will be elaborated in the following discussion of Chawla's (1992) research findings.

To conceptualize childhood place attachments, Chawla (1992) brought together a discussion of four diverse literatures: psychoanalytic theory, which has considered the role of places and things within their social context; environmental autobiography, which has evaluated places saved through the sieve of memory; behavior mapping, which has observed where children and adolescents congregate; and favorite place analyses, which have explored the reasons for their preferences. This review showed patterns of place preference and use by children and youth and clarified the significance of stable, nurturing places and the availability of space.

Chawla noted that place provides three types of satisfaction: security, social affiliation, and creative expression and exploration. She concluded that while security must be a primary feature of place experience in the preschool years for the development of healthy place attachments, and probably remains a taken-for-granted prerequisite, the empirical literature showed the greatest sources of satisfaction to come from opportunities for social or creative self-development. Given reliable care, children and youth are free to turn their attention to environmental exploration. Chawla (1992) emphasized the importance of the availability of space for children and youth at all ages:

> At every age there is a need for undefined space where young people can formulate their own worlds: for free space where preschoolers can manipulate the environment and play "let's pretend" in prepara- tion for middle childhood demands; for hideouts and play-houses indoors and out where school-age children can practise independence; and for public hangouts and private refuges where adolescents can test new social relationships and ideas.…In conventional settings, these rights [of presence, use, appropriation and modification] are conveyed through adult acceptance. In creative settings, they are conferred by the place's malleability and remoteness from adults. (p. 69)

Access to the outdoors, to nature, and to freedom in the environment appeared to be of considerable significance in middle childhood. Both favorite place analyses and environmental autobiography research showed cherished places to be neighborhood woods, fields, undeveloped waste spaces, or waterways. Here, children could physically manipulate and explore the environ- ment with intensity—unbound by adult rules of order, neatness, and propriety—enjoy individual challenge and group play, or find a refuge from the interpersonal tensions of social relations. Similarly, hideouts, forts, and small leftover spaces in the home or outdoors were spaces these children could appropriate in undisturbed privacy and shape to their will.

Public hangouts and private refuges are highly desired by adolescents. Hendry et al. (1993, cited in Matthews & Limb, 1999) observed that these meeting places become "theatres for self- display, observation points for assessing roles of others." Addressing the significance of young people's group membership, and places for groups to congregate, Matthews and Limb (1999, pp. 69–70) reiterated the work of Allison James, a social anthropologist researching the acquisition of language. James argued that

> children develop their own vocabulary and particular patterns of use. Through their own discourse children carve out their own identities and "patterns of belonging are laid down" James (1995: 59)… children are not a subcultural group in their own right, but there is a temporal culture which children move into and out of in the process of their socialization. Each step along this social transition is associated with patterns of language and behavior which define membership.…place, like language acts as an emblem of groupness…important for belonging and identification…setting apart, being different and special. (p. 69)

Thus, James saw young people's use of street corners, indoor shopping centers, and parks as cultural gateways where they could meet and carve out their own identities. In addition to using space as a cultural location, teenagers also have a preference for adventurous environments where they can experience "safe dangers" or be stretched physically without coming to any harm (Burgess et al., 1988, cited in Valentine, Skelton, & Chambers, 1998).

Regrettably, it is more and more the case that children and youth in urban settings may find themselves without desirable "open space" or public space for their social interactions (Valentine,

1996; Valentine, Skelton & Chambers, 1998). This is significant because, as Moore (1986a) has observed, just as friendships prompt environmental exploration at this age, so, too, exploration may intensify relationships. As Tuan (1986, p. 106) has asserted "good personal relationships are at the core of the good life." Many recognize that young people are appropriating digital space as a place for forming relationships, finding communities, and developing identities (Bingham, Valentine & Holloway, n.d.a; Bingham, Valentine & Holloway, n.d.b; Sefton-Green, 1998; Tapscott, 1998; Turkle, 1995). Brey (1998) argues that although people can be understood to "inhabit" virtual space, this does not entirely replace their need and desire for participation in face-to-face relationships. The research discussed in this section has underscored the importance of certain kinds of space that can become places that facilitate social affiliations and the development of identity among children or youth.

In addition to facilitating social affiliation and identity, places that support creative play among children and youth are also contributing to the development of culture that is rooted in place. Drawing on the theoretical work of Winnicott (1971) and others and their own research with children in the UNESCO Growing Up in Cities project, Cosco and Moore (2002) have argued for the significance of children's creative play and free individual expression in the process of culture building or enriching culture. They observed that "through play, children explore and discover places, transforming them as potential spaces to create culture" (p. 53). They noted that "the richer and more diverse the world is socially and physically, the richer this potential space, and the greater the possibilities for developing a rich culture rooted in place" (p. 53). Cosco and Moore (2002) offered the following articulation of the qualities of the world of children that make it a potential space where they can play creatively and build culture.

> Places should be stable and predictable, discovered at an early age through play, and contain features that provide a strong identity that is the essence of the place. At the same time, places should be flexible enough to accommodate creative exploration. They should be highly differentiated into component parts that stimulate many creative relationships for all types of children. They should support children's needs especially in terms of scale and diversity. Places should be sufficiently safe physically, socially, and psychologically. These conditions facilitate the emergence of popular culture and collective transformation as a natural outcome of playful exploration.... (pp. 53–54)

In the Growing Up in Cities project (to be described in more detail in the next section), researchers also learned that a culturally rich neighbourhood supports healthy development and helps children gain positive identification and higher self-esteem.

The Growing Up in Cities project entailed research in eight cities in both developed and developing countries across the globe. One of the key findings from this research was that young people want to feel connected to their locality. The following is an excerpt from Malone's (1997) summary on this point.

> Beyond a basic level of material well-being, the factors that mattered most to young people in terms of their sense of connection to their locality were nonmaterial: a positive identity, integration within a cohesive community culture, accessible and active public spaces and places that they could claim as their own for socializing and play with peers. When communities lacked the above ingredients, young people expressed high levels of alienation, despite relatively higher material standards of living....it was evident that once basic needs were met (food, shelter, health, water) those young people in developing countries experienced a rich and engaging life and they were on the whole "happy." In the developed cities we found that material possessions often meant isolation, loneliness and unhappiness. (p. 8)

This section has related key ideas and research findings with regards to the significance of place and space for children. Places are good places for children when they provide for their material well-being, are culturally rich and provide for positive identity and integration within a cohesive community, and include desirable undefined space and accessible, active public space. Such dimensions of place support belonging and growth for children while also enriching culture.

Currently, cultural geographers are engaged in asking questions about the social and physical conditions in which children live from place to place and how these contribute to the social, cultural and political identities children form (Monaghan, 2000). In North America, key question is: How well served are children by the built environments provided for them, by the erosion of autonomous play in favor of tight schedules of supervised activities, by the privatization of public space, and the corporatization and commercialization of children's play?

EXAMPLES OF PARTICIPATORY PLACE RESEARCH WITH CHILDREN AND YOUTH

This section discusses (1) the UNESCO Growing Up in Cities project, (2) two initiatives in North America and the United Kingdom that have provided leadership in improving school grounds, and (3) teens' use of public places as featured in the Project for Public Spaces. These projects or initiatives vary widely in scale and location. Each offers an informative backdrop for considering the possibilities of research related to children and place.

UNESCO GROWING UP IN CITIES PROJECT

The Growing Up in Cities project builds on ideas about children's rights and has been designed to understand children's own perspectives on the places where they live as a basis for partnerships between children and adults to improve urban conditions (Chawla, 2002). The project, which is still expanding, has entailed fieldwork conducted from 1996 through 1998 in eight cities: Buenos Aires, Argentina; Melbourne, Australia; Northampton, United Kingdom; Bangalore, India; Trondhelm, Norway; Warsaw, Poland; Johannesburg, South Africa, and Oakland, California in the United States of America. It was first conceived by the urban planner Kevin Lynch in the 1970s and was reintroduced by the Norwegian Centre for Child Research and Childwatch International in 1994. Lynch's initial guidelines for the fieldwork have served as the general plan.

> In brief, they [the guidelines] called for interviews with a group of twenty children in early adolescence, all living in one locality. They were to be asked how they used, conceived of, and felt about their surroundings. Investigators were to observe how the children actually used the setting, make a careful physical description of the place, and conduct comparative interviews with parents and with officials concerned with the public planning of the locality.

Thus the research entailed (1) objective descriptions of each location's physical and social features; (2) observations of people's use of public and semi-public places with a particular focus on the presence of children; (3) extended interviews with children supported by drawings, photographs taken by children, child-led tours, and other means; and (4) interviews with parents and urban officials. As Chawla (2002) reports, the 1996–1998 fieldwork used larger numbers of children, typically 10–15 years of age, and invited them to use words, drawings, photographs, neighborhood tours and other means to clarify the nature of their lives in their communities and their own priorities for improvement. There was remarkable consensus among the children from these diverse places and countries regarding the qualities that create places where children can thrive as opposed to conditions that produce alienation and marginalization. Children's ideas for improvements were also seen to be realistic ones. Key findings from this research contributed to the empirical basis for the first section of this paper. The project has endeavored to progress through a research phase, an action phase, and a dissemination phase. As part of dissemination, the project has generated a manual entitled *Creating Better Cities with Children and Youth* (Driskell, 2002), which details the project's principles and methods for others to use.

INITIATIVES TO IMPROVE SCHOOL GROUNDS

The Natural Learning Initiative (NLI), directed by Robin C. Moore, Professor in the Faculty of Landscape Architecture in the School of Design at North Carolina State University, is dedicated to assisting communities to create environments that bring experience of the natural world into the daily lives of children. Moore's related work extends over 30 years. Through research and development projects, he has demonstrated how physical diversification of school grounds and other sites can transform them into significant educational environments that support a wide range of playing and learning activity. By replacing asphalt with natural environments thoughtfully designed for diverse use by children, his projects have supported children's well-being and contributed to their physical, intellectual, and social growth. Children themselves have typically participated in the planning of the redesigned sites. Using naturalistic and ethnographic methods, Moore and his colleagues have studied the impact of these projects on children's growth and behavior (e.g., Moore, 1989; Moore & Wong, 1997).

In the United Kingdom, an independent national organization called Learning through Landscapes (LTL) provides a program of support, based on research, to help schools to develop their grounds. The emphasis is on improving educational opportunities and the educational environment of schools. This organization recognizes that school grounds as an external environment have become even more important to children in contemporary society. Their work is based on the belief that by recognizing how children think and feel about the outdoors, school managers can make improvements that promote the kind of activities and features which are likely to produce positive social interaction and learning opportunities. One of their publications, *LTL Primary School Grounds Toolkit: Managing the Process of Change,* by Liz Russell, provides guidance for the processes of making and evaluating improvements to school grounds. Another package from LTL for Grades K-8, *Special Places; Special People: The Hidden Curriculum of School Grounds* by Wendy Titman reports on research about children's perceptions about their environment, implications of these findings for all schools, and suggestions for changing how school grounds are designed and used.

Projects by NLI and LTL have served to transform schoolyards into places that can evoke place attachment or sense of place for children. The inclusion of child-scale, flexible elements and diverse natural environments support imaginative and dramatic play (Moore, 1986a, 1986b). Children learn about nature, find it endlessly engaging, experience its restorative, healing powers, and appreciate both the social interaction and solitude it supports.

PROJECT FOR PUBLIC SPACES AND TEENS TURNING PLACES AROUND

The Project for Public Spaces (PPS), whose president is Fred Kent, has been helping communities across North America to transform their public spaces into community gathering areas. The project has identified key features of successful places. Some of these are: a mix of uses and users; a mix of ages; a welcoming appearance with lots of places to sit; accessible; social; the likelihood of seeing other people you know; good maintenance; effective security; amenities (e.g., food, washrooms, telephones, waste receptacles); something interesting to do or look at. An important dimension of successful places is management that has the authority to introduce or change temporary elements such as movable furniture, art displays, street vendors, and so forth. The project has found that kids have great ideas and a much more holistic view of spaces.

The PPS website also features case studies of projects in which teens have participated to turn places around and build community. For one example, Phoenix's central downtown library dedicated a 4,000-square-foot space for a teen program called Teen Central. An architect and his staff held five focus groups with teenagers to design the space. It became a large space exclusively for teens, with technology, food, videos, books, comics, CDs, magazines—all free. Each day, 400 teens use the space. Some use it as a quiet room to do homework; others make new friends around the computers; some enjoy watching videos, and so on.

In New York, Riverside Skate Park was developed when Riverside Park was in the midst of restoring underused facilities as sites specifically for a teen project. A volunteer from the community, who was an avid skateboarder, contacted the New York Department of Parks and Recreation with a proposal to build a place for skateboarders and in-line skaters. Twenty-four "at-risk" local high school students were selected to design and build the skate area in Riverside Park. They were taught the basics of construction and participated in a weekend retreat as part of a training program in teamwork and conflict resolution. On a typical weekday afternoon, an average of 50 skateboarders, bikers, and in-line skaters use the skate park. Weekends are much busier, when over 100 enthusiasts of all levels, ranging in age from 9 to 30, come to the skate park from all over the metropolitan area. Skaters say they try to come about three times a week and stay between one and five hours. Parents come to watch and senior citizens come to sit on the benches and also enjoy watching.

As further examples, in Chicago, Illinois, students converted a vacant lot near their high school into a pocket park and community gathering place that has become a center of activity and cultural pride for their largely Puerto Rican neighborhood. In Hampton, Virginia, to help create an all-around more "youth-friendly" city, two teenagers hold part-time jobs in the city planning department, representing their peers and working to improve parks, transportation, and more.

These and the many other teen projects reported on the PPS website attest to how the quality of life for youth and communities can improve when there are opportunities for young people to contribute to the creation of public places that work. Without such initiatives, the constraints of urbanization and rational planning can leave children and youth isolated, alienated, and marginalized.

CHILDREN AND PLACE RESEARCH IN EDUCATION

It would be worthwhile to engage place and space as central ideas in any research on students' experiences in classrooms or schools. If researchers do not take seriously the *place* of students' everyday lives, they risk emphasizing individual agency and control without discerning the societal contexts or structures of everyday life which may significantly shape and constrain experiences (Eyles, 1989). Further, the notions of place and space as discussed in this chapter can invite researchers' ongoing attention to students' opportunities for belongingness and creative self-development in schools. Finally, to make questions about place and space the focus of research in schools is to ask whether classrooms and schools support adequate human development as opposed to contributing to alienation and unhappiness.

Policy and practice in schools can also be usefully informed by research on students' place and space outside of the school. Knowledge about what is present or absent for students in their locales ought to have implications for classroom practice, programs, activities, events and use of facilities and resources at the school. Do the students' locales have positive self-images and do they afford friendly adults, available playmates, accessible and engaging public spaces where interesting activities can be found and places that children can claim as their own for socializing and play? Children and youth in the Growing Up in Cities project expressed satisfaction with their communities when these attributes were present and alienation when they were not (Chawla, 2002). Further, researchers should ask whether students' locales serve as culturally rich educational facilities, as places to explore and learn about the world (Lynch, 1981).

The remainder of this section is divided into two parts. The first discusses the importance of narrative or ethnographic case study research to study children's place and space. When such intensive, holistic work is not feasible, researchers may wish to use favorite place analyses using drawings, maps, interviews, and student-led tours. The second part discusses these methods.

NARRATIVE OR ETHNOGRAPHIC CASE STUDY RESEARCH

As Adams, Hoelscher, and Till (2001) have outlined, the last three generations of humanist geographers have moved from quantitative to phenomenological to qualitative methodologies employing critical or contextual perspectives to study place. They suggest that narrative and ethnographic approaches should remain prominent in research on the experience of place and space. Tuan (1991) has argued for a narrative-descriptive approach in studies of place. In observing Tuan's recommendations, researchers would give great care to crafting an adequate presentation of stories or cases prior to offering their own insights, interpretations, or theoretical analyses of the significance of place narratives. In Polkinghorne's (1995) terms, researchers would choose "narrative analysis" rather than "analysis of narratives." In presenting a well-crafted narrative rather than simply an analysis of narratives, researchers would be recognizing that stories mean more than they can say.

> All narratives and descriptions contain at least interpretive and explanatory strategems, for these are built into language itself. In a narrative-descriptive approach, however, the explicit formulation of a theory is not attempted, if only because such a theory, by its clarity and weight, tends to drive rival and complementary interpretations and explanatory sketches out of mind, with the result that the object of study—a human experience, which is almost always ambiguous and complex—turns into something

schematic and etiolated…in the narrative-descriptive approach, theories hover supportively in the background while the complex phenomena themselves occupy the front stage. (Tuan, 1991, p. 686)

Tuan notes that this approach has been favored by cultural and historical geographers, historians in general, and cultural anthropologists.

Similarly, Eyles (1989) has argued that examinations of everyday life that genuinely grasp the totality of everyday life rely on a small number of cases rather than on representative samples.

> Such ethnographic analyses, emphasizing case-studies and analytic induction, represent a rediscovery of anthropological methods. These methods involve the overt or covert participation in the lives of those investigated to ask questions, to listen to what is said and to watch what happens. Their great strength is that they are the bases of in-depth descriptions set in a theoretical context. They also represent perhaps the most likely route to a profound understanding of the complexity of everyday life… circumstances which not only enable the creation of self and identity but also significantly constrain the range of possible activities, constructions and creations. (pp. 114–115)

Employing the ethnographic case study approach discussed by Eyles would serve to facilitate Chawla's (1992) recommendation that researchers consider the development of place feelings within the holistic context of the family system, social and economic conditions, and available environmental resources. Chawla credits Hart (1979) for pioneering family research of this kind and notes that he has had few imitators.

Although not specifically situating her work as "place" research, Li (2002, 2000) has completed exemplary ethnographic research on the everyday life of a three-year-old girl in a Chinese family in Saskatoon in Canada. The family operated a small restaurant in a lower socio-economic neighborhood. Recognizing that "literacy as a social construction situated in specific contexts emphasizes the *place* [my italics] of oral practice," Li (2000) became a participant-observer in the family restaurant for a nine-month period to study the child's social realities and lived literacy experiences. Li completed this research with the expectation that an understanding of such children's experiences can inform literacy practices in the classroom.

Understandings of the socio-cultural basis of literacy together with contemporary concerns about social justice have given rise to an increasing amount of case study research on the places of children's lives. One example is *Literacy in Its Place: Literacy Practices in Urban and Rural Communities* (Breen et al., 1994). This study generated a descriptive account of literacy practices in six different urban and rural communities across Western Australia. Communities were selected that represented, as far as possible, the linguistic, cultural, and social diversity of Australia. Such studies recognize that everyday life provides the backdrop of meaning for events and a person's actions (Eyles, 1989)—in this case, events such as doing homework, going to school, reading, writing, and so on.

Both children's and adults' perspectives are needed to develop the most adequate interpretations of the significance of children's everyday lives and the places and spaces for these (Holloway & Valentine, 2000). Matthews and Limb (1999) emphasized the importance of understanding children from the perspective of their own multiple lifeworlds. They argued that research should capture the immediacy of young people's lives and "places should be evaluated in terms of their quality to the here and now and not just as training grounds for adulthood" (p. 68). At the same time, adults' perspectives are needed to analyze the macrostructures that determine the material conditions that shape children's everyday lives. Holloway and Valentine (2000) have suggested that "local" cultures—how children organize their day—are bound up with "global" processes; and that "global" processes do not exist in the ether, but are worked out in "local" places. Global and local studies are not irreconcilably split, rather they intimately bind together. (p. 11)

Smith (2000, 2001), Caragata (1998), and Katz (1998) have discussed how the processes of globalization have resulted in unemployment or underemployment and the spatial separation of the rich and the poor with the resulting loss of mediation between the two. In my own city, in a neighborhood of the "rich," there are plans to transform "a large, nearly empty field" into "a multi-use recreation area for residents of all ages" at the cost of $300,000 (Lutter, 2002, p. 501). I am glad to witness a local appreciation for the need for community-building places. I would like to see a greater sense of shared responsibility for the conditions of the lives of the poor.

Intensive, holistic case studies of the everyday lives of children and youth can correct misreadings of their realities, illuminate the social and physical conditions in which they live, and clarify how improvements to the places available to them could better support the quality of their lives. In the lives of both the rich and the poor, questions need to be asked about how well served children are by their places. When planning human environments, adults have traditionally made assumptions about what children need. Narrative-descriptive case studies can offer a window into the immediacy and complexity of children's daily lives and how they experience the places available for these. Such studies should highlight both children's perspectives and adults' analyses of the macrostructures determining the material conditions that shape children's everyday lives.

FAVORITE PLACE ANALYSES

In contexts where it may not be feasible to conduct intensive, holistic case studies as place research, educators or researchers may nevertheless find it informative to engage children and youth in more manageable favorite place analyses. For example, a high school principal presented some of the students with a diagram of the school and asked them to mark all of their favorite places with an "X." One student, who was sent to her office for disciplinary action, marked an X on only one spot, the "Smoking Pit." He enthusiastically participated in an interview with her about his completed diagram and afforded her an emic perspective on all of the routines, dynamics, and rituals in the Smoking Pit. Besides gaining insight into the significance of a number of interactions and language codes in use in the Pit, the principal was made acutely aware that, for many students, the Smoking Pit was the only place in the school where they could experience community or belonging. At the same time, the principal was experiencing pressure from parents to close the smoking area. Given her concern about students' experience of belongingness in the school, she did not close the Pit. This example shows that even learning about the absence or lack of favorite places can be important information for those who care about children and youth's social and physical realities.

There are many ways to learn about students' favorite places or the paucity of these. Depending on the student's age and the context of the relationship—teacher, researcher, youth worker, etc.—one can invite students to keep diaries; draw and discuss pictures; make posters; write stories, poetry, or essays; give guided tours through the neighborhood; label and discuss aerial photographs of the neighborhood; perform a theatre presentation; take photographs and discuss these; participate in focus groups; and so on. Chawla (1992) cautions that the method can shape the results. For example, Hart (1979) found that in child-led walks, children identified a higher proportion of locations valued for exploration and physical action, whereas in interviews at school, they mainly mentioned social centers such as friends' homes. Chawla also noted the tendency of researchers to conduct "favorite place" studies with articulate children who demonstrated extensive, diversified outdoor ranges. She commented that "almost nothing is known about less articulate children or those kept out of sight indoors" (p. 84).

Since children's drawings are likely to have widespread utility in favorite place inquiries by teachers, youth workers, or researchers, it is worthwhile to consider their particular value. The use of drawings or other art forms can enable children to relate their personal life experiences with expression of personality and emotions (Malchiodi, 1998). Through drawing, children are able to express feelings and perceptions that are difficult to verbalize (Chandler & Johnson, 1991; Silver, 2001). Importantly, children's drawings have the potential to evoke narrative accounts both through what is present in the image and the child's response to what is in the image (Cummings, 1986). Malchiodi (1998) notes that such storytelling is usually necessary and helpful for comprehending the meaning of their art expressions. She suggests that researchers refrain from asking children "why" they drew images as they did. Instead, it can be more helpful to simply describe what one sees or to think out loud as a way to prompt children to speak about the contents of their drawings. For example, one can observe a drawing and offer a comment such as: "I see children lining up to play on a slide" or "This drawing uses bright colors but this one only uses black and gray." Children will then often describe what is happening in the picture, especially if the researcher has missed an important or obvious feature. Any comments or questions that reflect "not knowing" are likely to prompt children's explanations. Children at the age of 7–8 typically have well-established language and communication skills, are able to report on their thoughts and emotions, can understand the perspectives of others, and are able to describe "why" others act in a certain way (Stone & Lemanek, 1990). As in any interview, to work well with children and their drawings, time must be taken to build rapport to increase the comfort levels of both the interviewer and the child and to demonstrate the interviewer's genuine interest in what the child has to say (Boggs & Eyberg, 1990).

Driskell (2002) has offered detailed instructions for having young people complete drawings of their local areas. The drawings provide a starting point for interviews and for sharing information about activities, range of movement and favorite/least favorite places. He notes that observations of the drawing process and the drawings themselves can provide insights about what is most and least important to young people. The drawing activity can be conducted with a small group of children/youth as an introduction to a focus group session with participants displaying and sharing their drawings. Follow-up one-on-one interviews are needed to discuss each of the children's drawings with them. The drawing activity, focus group session, and one-on-one interviews support researchers in forming relationships with the participants and thereby increase everyone's comfort level for "guided tours led by young people" and "behaviour mapping activities." Driskell has provided step-by-step instructions for: informal observations and "hanging out"; interviews; drawings; daily activity schedules; family and support networks; role play, drama and puppetry; guided tours; photographs by young people; behavior mapping; questionnaires and surveys; focus groups and small group discussions; and workshops and community events.

There are many approaches that can be used to research students' places with them. Such research can afford insight into their experience of their schools, immediate locales, and cities.

Place research findings can inform consideration of whether social and physical conditions for children and youth support adequate human development. Awareness of the quality of life supported by the places available to children and youth should have implications for practices in schools. Students' participation in place research can also develop their critical awareness about how to make places better for community life.

CLOSING DISCUSSION

To ask questions about the school as a place entails inquiring into how and whether it is a source of belonging for students and how and whether it includes space for creative self-development. In Osterman's (2000) review of studies pertaining to students' experience of belonging in school, she noted that although belongingness is a precondition for academic achievement, schools tend to offer it only as a reward for compliance and academic success. There are many classroom routines, instructional practices, special events, and school programs that can contribute to students' experience of collegiality with peers (Ellis, 1999; Ellis, Hart & Small-McGinley, 1998, 2001; Ellis, Small-McGinley & De Fabrizio, 2001). Activities that provide space for students to draw upon their talents, interests, outside-of-school knowledge, imagination and humor also work well to support the spontaneous development of students' collegiality (Ellis, 1998). Thus, space for creative self-development in classrooms can also increase opportunities for belongingness. Unfortunately, as Stromquist and Monkman (2000) note, globalization, the rise of technology, and economic competitiveness among countries has led to an increased emphasis on competitiveness in schools. Teachers feel compelled to dedicate class time to activities that appear directly linked to the attainment of academic excellence. It is time to ask whether classrooms and schools are in fact good places for young people. Is belonging and growth supported for all students, or is alienation and unhappiness the plight of many? Place and space can be well used as central ideas to both ask questions about the quality of life for students in schools and to imagine needed improvements.

Similarly, knowledge about the places students rely on or lack outside of school should have implications for practices, programs, events, and use of resources within the school. Does the students' locale have a positive self-mage? Do students feel connected to their locale and experience themselves as integrated within a cohesive community? Is their locale a culturally rich place for exploring and learning about the world? Do they have access to friendly adults and playmates? Do they have access to desirable undefined space and active public space? While schools may not be able to effect immediate improvements to students' locales, awareness of the nature of shortcomings of these should guide school programs and the use of available resources.

REFERENCES

Adams, P. C., Hoelscher, S., & Till, K. E. (Eds.) (2001). Place in context: Rethinking humanistic geographies. In P. C. Adams, S. Hoelscher, and K. E. Till (eds.), *Textures of place: Exploring humanistic geographies* (pp. 403–424). Minneapolis: University of Minnesota Press.

Bingham, N., Valentine, G., & Holloway, S. (n.d.a). *Cyberkids: Children's social networks, 'virtual communities,' and on line spaces*. Retrieved May 17, 2001, from http://www.hull.ac.uk/chidlren5to16programme/details/valentine.htm

Bingham, N., Valentine, G., & Holloway, S. (n.d.b). *Introduction to the programme*. Retrieved May 16, 2001, from http://www.hull.ac.uk/children5to16programme/intro.htm

Boggs, S. & Eyberg, S. (1990). Interview techniques and establishing good rapport. In A. M. Lagreca (ed.), *Through the eyes of a child: Obtaining self-reports from children and adolescents* (pp. 85–108). Boston, MA: Allyn & Bacon.

Breen, M. P., Louden, W., Barratt-Pugh, C., Rivalland, J., Rohl, M., Rhydwen, M., Lloyd, S. & Carr, T. (1994). *Literacy in Its Place: Literacy Practices in Urban and Rural Communities*. Printed out from http://www.gu.edu.au/school/cls/clearinghouse/content_1994_place.html 10/05/02

Brey, P. (1998) Space-shaping technologies and the geographical disembedding of place. In A. Light and J. M. Smith (eds.). *Philosophy and geography III: Philosophies of place* (pp. 239–263). Lanham, Maryland: Rowman & Littlefield Publishers, Inc.

Burgess, J., Harrison, C. M., & Limb, M. (1988). People, parks and the urban green: A study of popular meanings and values for open spaces in the city. *Urban Studies* 25, 455–73.

Caragata, L. (1998). The new meanings of place: The place of the poor and the loss of place as a center of mediation. In A. Light and J. M. Smith (eds.). *Philosophy and geography III: Philosophies of place* (pp. 215–237). Lanham, Maryland: Rowman & Littlefield Publishers, Inc.

Chandler, L. A. & Johnson, V. J. (1991). *Using projective techniques with children: A guide to critical assessment*. Springfield, IL: Charles C. Thomas.

Chawla, L. (1992). Childhood place attachments. In I. Altman & S. M. Low (Eds.). *Place attachment* (Human Behavior and Environment: Advances in Research and Theory, Vol. 12) (pp. 63–86). New York: Plenum Press.

Chawla, L. (2002). Cities for human development. In L. Chawla (ed.), *Growing up in an urbanising world* (pp. 15–34). London: Earthscan Publications Ltd.

Cosco, N. & Moore, R. (2002). Our neighbourhood is like that! Cultural richness and childhood identity in Boca-Baracccas, Buenos Airies. In L. Chawla (ed.), *Growing up in an urbanising world* (pp. 35–56). London: Earthscan Publications Ltd.

Cummings, J. A. (1986). Projective drawings. In H. M. Knoff (ed.), *The assessment of child and adolescent personality* (pp. 199–244). New York: The Guilford Press.

Driskell, D. (2002). *Creating better cities with children and youth: A manual for participation*. London: Earthscan Publications Ltd.

Ellis, J. (1998). Creative assignments that promote learning and understanding. In J. Ellis (ed.). *Teaching from understanding: Teacher as interpretive inquirer* (pp. 57–78). New York: Garland.

Ellis, J. (1999). Children and place: Stories we have, stories we need. *Interchange, 30* (2), 171–190.

Ellis, J. (2002). The importance of attending to children and place. *International Journal of Educational Policy, Research and Practice, 3*(3), 69–88.

Ellis, J., Hart, S., & Small-McGinley, J. (1998). "Difficult" students' perspectives on belonging and inclusion in the classroom. *Reclaiming Children and Youth: Journal of Emotional and Behavioral Problems 7*(3), 142–146.

Ellis, J., Hart, S., & Small-McGinley, J. (2001). Encouraging the discouraged: Students' views on elementary school. *Analytic Teaching, 22*(1), 17–28.

Ellis, J., Small-McGinley, J., & De Fabrizio, L. (2001). *Caring for kids in communities: Using mentorship, peer support, and student leadership programs in schools*. New York: Peter Lang Publishing.

Eyles, J. (1989). The geography of everyday life. In D. Gregory and R. Walford (Eds.), *Horizons in human geography* (pp. 102—117). London: Macmillan.

Hart, R. (1979). *Children's experience of place*. New York: Irvington.

Hart, R. (1997). *Children's participation: The theory and practice of involving young citizens in community development and environmental care*. London: Earthscan Publications.

Hay, R. (1992). An appraisal of our meaningful relationships in place. *The Trumpeter 9*(3) Summer 1992, 98–105.

Hendry, L. B., Shucksmith, J., Love, J.G. & Glendenning, A. (1993). *Young people's leisure and lifestyles*. London: Routledge.

Holloway, S. L. & Valentine, G. (2000). Children's geographies and the new social studies of childhood. In S. L. Holloway & G. Valentine (eds.), *Children's geographies: Playing, living, learning* (pp. 1–26). New York: Routledge.

James, A. (1995). Talking of children and youth: Language, socialization and culture. In V. Amit-Talaii & H. Wulff (eds.) *Youth cultures: A cross-cultural perspective* (pp. 19–42). London: Routledge.

Jipson, J. (2000). Better days: The discourse of work in the lives of rural academic women. *Journal of Curriculum Theorizing, 16*(2), 37–48.

Katz, C. (1998). Disentegrating developments: Global economic restructuring and the eroding of the ecologies of youth. In T. Skelton & G. Valentine (Eds.), *Cool places: Geographies of youth cultures* (pp. 130–144). New York: Routledge.

Li, G. (2000). Literacy outside school: Home practices of Chinese immigrant families in Canada. Unpublished doctoral dissertation, Department of Curriculum Studies, University of Saskatchewan, Saskatoon.

Li, G. (2002) *"East is east, west is west"? Home literacy, culture, and schooling.* New York: Peter Lang.

Li, G. (2003). Literacy as situated practices: Implications for early childhood education. *Canadian Journal of Education, 26*(1), 2003.

Lutter, C. (2002). Improvements planned for Ramsey Park: Changes to make park 'space for all ages.' *Edmonton Examiner Zone 5—Riverbend-Southgate-Heritage* (July 31), p. 501.

Lynch, K. (1977). *Growing up in cities: Studies of the spatial environment of adolescence in Cracow, Melbourne, Mexico City, Salta, Toluca and Warsaw.* Cambridge, MA: M.I.T Press.

Lynch, K. (1981). *A theory of good city form.* Cambridge, MA: M.I.T Press.

Malchiodi, C. A. (1998). *Understanding children's drawings.* New York: The Guilford Press.

Malone, K. (1997) *Young people's right to participate in planning for their future: 'Growing Up in Cities' a model of participatory research with young people. Paper presented at* Young People's Creators of their Future conference, Youth Research Centre, University of Melbourne, July. Printed out from http://www2.deakin.edu.au/GUIC/news/yprihts.htm 8/8/00.

Matthews, H. & Limb, M. (1999). Defining an agenda for the geography of children: Review and prospect. *Progress in Human Geography, 23*(1), 61–90.

Monaghan, P. (2000). A child's place in the world. *The Chronicle of Higher Education* (April 7, 2001) A21-A22.

Moore, R. (1986a). *Childhood's domain: Play and place in child development.* London: Croom Helm, 1986; Berkeley, CA: MIT Communications, 1990.

Moore, R. (1986b). Power of nature: Orientations of girls and boys toward biotic and abiotic environments. *Children's Environments Quarterly, 3*(3), 52–69.

Moore, R. (1989). Before and after asphalt: Diversity as an ecological measure of quality in children's outdoor environments. In M. Bloch & T. Pelligrini (Eds). *The ecological context of children's play.* Norwood, NJ: Ablex.

Moore, R. & Wong, H. (1997). *Natural learning: The story of the Washington School environmental yard.* Berkeley, CA: MIG Communications.

Osterman, K. F. (2000). Students' need for belonging in the school community. *Review of Educational Research, 70*(3), 323–367.

Polkinghorne, D. E. (1995). Narrative configuration in qualitative analysis. In J. A. Hatch & R. Wisniewski (eds.), *Life history and narrative* (pp. 5–23). Washington, DC: Falmer Press.

Sefton-Green, J. (Ed.). (1998). *Digital diversions: Youth culture in the age of multimedia.* London, UK: UCL Press.

Silver, R. (2001). *Art as language: Access to thoughts and feelings through stimulus drawings.* Philadelphia, PA: Psychology Press.

Smith, D. G. (2000). The specific challenges of globalization for teaching and vice versa. *The Alberta Journal of Educational Research, XLVI*(1), 7–26.

Smith, D. G. (2001). Engaging the global struggle between knowledge and misrepresentation. *Interchange, 32*(3), 251–260.

Stone, W. & Lemanek, K. (1990). Developmental issues in children's self-reports. In A. M. Lagreca (ed.), *Through the eyes of a child: Obtaining self-reports from children and adolescents* (pp. 18–56) Boston, MA: Allyn & Bacon.

Stromquist, N. P. & Monkman, K. (2000). *Globalization and education: Integration and contestation across cultures.* New York: Rowman & Littlefield Publishers, Inc.

Tapscott, D. (1998). *Growing up digital: The rise of the net generation.* New York: McGraw-Hill.

Tuan, Y-F. (1977). *Space and place: The perspective of experience.* Minneapolis: University of Minnesota Press.

Tuan, Y. (1986) *The good life.* Madison, WI: University of Wisconsin Press.

Tuan, Y. F. (1991). Language and the making of place: A narrative-descriptive approach. *Annals of the Association of American Geographers, 81*(4), 684–696.

Turkle, S. (1995). *Life on the screen: Identity in the age of the internet.* London: Weidenfeld & Nicolson.

Valentine, G. (1996). Children should be seen and not heard: The production and transgression of adults' public space. *Urban Geography, 17*(3), 205-220.

Valentine, G., Skelton, T., & Chambers, D. (1998). Cool places: An introduction to youth cultures. In T. Skelton & G. Valentine (Eds.), *Cool places: Geographies of youth cultures* (pp. 1–32). New York: Routledge.

Winnicott, D. (1971). *Playing and reality.* London: Routledge.

WEBSITES

Natural Learning Initiative http://www.naturalearning.org/

Project for Public Spaces http://www.pps.org/

Learning through Landscapes http://www.ltl.org.uk/home.html

TWENTY-EIGHT

Envisioning the Environment as the Third Teacher: Moving Theory into Practice

Sheryl Smith-Gilman, Teresa Strong-Wilson, and Julia Ellis

> *If we live in a space and respond to it, little by little, fashioning each part of it into more of what we need and what is pleasing to us, then hings continue to grow. We make a change; then the change alters the way we do things and new possibilities emerge. We are inspired to make another change, and so it goes. This is the way of an alive environment. (Cadwell, 2003, p. 107)*

How is it that what Hannah Arendt calls "the thing character of the world" marks the place from which we begin life and potentially where we also see its end coming? We come to understand who we are in the world from the places that we make; the places that we inhabit; the places to which we are denied access; the places that we find in which to wander freely. Places are not abstract entities but are visceral and real. This does not mean that they are only physical. Rather, or more accurately at the same time, they are also imagined, as in the child whose hand twists away from Louise Cadwell's own, gesturing: "I need space. I have to see and feel this place in my own way. Let me go" (Cadwell, 2003, p. 102). Let me go. The mother of one of the authors communicates the same message when she arranges around the bathtub a set of six coasters with the repeated picture of two ducks hovering near the water's edge. As she bathes, she is drawn into a shimmering world between past, present, and future. Time stands still and Alzheimer's forgetting dissolves. The coasters, bought at a bazaar for less than $1, floated free in the envelope. They were given by the daughter for Mother's Day and were intended to support the "real" contents of the package: a card, and several 5 x 7 photographs showing the beloved but (as the older people saw it) elderly woman and elderly man in the company of their daughter and her children. It is the coasters (liberated and restored to their "thingness") that invite Maggie to enter a watery world, where she played, and plays, for hours on end on the West Coast of British Columbia: on the coast, with the coasters.

In this chapter, we (re)turn to childhood spaces. We draw attention to the environment as a rich source for cognitive, social, and cultural development when it is infused with memory and imagination; we also describe ways in which it can be engaged for critical reflection when adult learners revisit their childhood. The chapter uses a narrative approach, beginning with classroom stories of three Canadian teacher educators who have long been interested in the role of childhood places and spaces in lifelong educational formation. Our writing links scholarship and practice in early childhood education with fields such as the geography of childhood, critical cultural geography, literary studies, and memory studies. Specifically, building on an earlier article (Strong-Wilson & Ellis, 2007), we re-visit the Reggio Emilia approach to early education to illuminate how our practices with children and adults foreground in different ways the environment as a (heretofore neglected) "third teacher": in Louise Boyd Cadwell's words, the environment as "alive." We conclude with recommendations for practice.

We begin with the stories from the classroom. We start with adults' memories of childhood places, which largely refer to outside of school contexts. Julia (of the University of Alberta) writes about how graduate students are invited to compose "place stories," and come to a deeper awareness of place as formative; she situates her story within the literature on the study of place. Teresa (of McGill University in Quebec) then looks at neighbourhood maps and secret spaces and, by drawing on literary theory in childhood studies, memory studies, and curriculum theory, shows how such activities can stimulate critical consciousness. Sheryl (a Quebec pre-school teacher as well as teacher-educator at McGill) offers an account of how her theorizing about Reggio Emilia's notion of the environment as a third teacher has influenced her practice with very young children. She invites her young Jewish students to collectively explore the significance of place within their childhood, thus actively shaping and contributing to their memory formation, as documented in their "Museum Project."

WRITING "PLACE STORIES" (JULIA)

I teach a course on "children and place" with the hope of encouraging educators and others to better appreciate the significance of *place* in limiting or enhancing the quality of life for children and youth. As one of the assignments, students are asked to write a 3500-word story about their experience of a particular place. This is intended to be a topoanalysis—an inquiry exploring the creation of one's personal and cultural identity through place. Initially, students in the course wonder how writing about place relates to writing about relationships with people. Is one writing about a place or is one writing about a relationship or set of relationships? It was helpful when I provided students with a model of such writing before they wrote their own place stories. For the model, I used the first chapter of *Seeing through Places: Reflections on Geography and Identity* by Mary Gordon.

Most of the course participants choose to write a story about a childhood place. As the course proceeds with one or two students reading their place stories to the class each week, students express surprise that so many of these stories make us cry. The emotional power of the stories is understandable, given that significant places are frequently bound up with significant others and given that childhood relationships, or their absence, can scar or strengthen us for the rest of our lives. As Brey (1998, p. 201) and others have recognized, "place attachment reflects a history of human interaction." The child's vulnerability—need for a safe place, need for stimulation, and need for others—speaks to us poignantly through the students' place stories.

My first purpose in working with students' place stories is to have them develop a narrative or lived understanding of a number of abstract ideas from cultural geography literature. Some of these understandings are about:

- place as socially constructed: a result of human agency
- place as meaning the whole experience of being there
- meaningful places being as small as a chair or as large as a continent
- place as a source of meaning (what one gives to and receives from the place; stories about what has happened there, i.e., history) and place as a source of security and belonging (feeling cared for and caring for others there)
- place as a source of identity: (a) who one can be; (b) having status through positive identity that comes from recognition and validation of one's talents, abilities, personal qualities; (c) the commonsense values, knowledge, and motivations one develops through the everyday life routine interactions and activities in the place enable the development of relationships which are so instrumental; place being a source of meaning, security, belonging, and positive identity; place as a source of structures (resources, routines, rules, and available relationships with individuals, ideas and institutions) that inhabitants draw from to shape their everyday lives which then result in identity, belonging, and meaning.

Readings in the course also inform students about research on children's favorite places or place attachment. This research emphasizes children's appreciation of the joy and freedom of autonomous activity in nature or malleable waste space (e.g., Chawla, 1992; Porteous, 1990; Hart, 1979). More generally, children's place attachment has been associated with autonomy, social support, and positive feelings (Langhout, 2003).

Once students have developed a storied understanding of place concepts, these abstract ideas are more functional as lenses or as analytic tools in interpretive frameworks for considering places such as classrooms, playgrounds, and sites for special activity programs. For example, Jil Kohler's story "The Kitchen Table" illustrated a number of place concepts. Jil explained that her favourite childhood memories took place around their kitchen table. She described the daily, weekly, and seasonal family rituals that were lived at the table. For example, whenever Jil and her brother and Dad waited for her Mom to get ready before they all went out together, they played board games at the table, and a winner always had to complete a victory run around the table. Jil and her Mom regularly worked on arts and crafts at the table and enjoyed wonderful conversations when doing so. Through the window by the table the family could see the wooden railing on the deck. It was another ritual to never knock the snow off the railing but to see how high it could get each winter. Jil became a teacher who was comfortable and proficient in talking with her classes about their lives and in using arts and crafts for a variety of purposes with students of all ages. Her place story illustrated ideas about how resources, routines and available relationships can enable forms of everyday life that support many aspects of identity.

Experiences of place reflect both human agency and the available physical and social resources or constraints. These are important ideas for teachers given their opportunities to contribute to the social construction of places for students. Guming Zhao wrote about her favorite childhood place—the place where she lived during the last 6 years of her mother's life. Guming's mother died when Guming was 12. The circumstances of their lives were difficult because the Chinese Revolution was in progress. Guming's father, like many school teachers, was identified as an anti-revolutionary and was incarcerated in a hard labor camp. Guming's mother had tuberculosis, and others were afraid to have contact with the family. Although Guming experienced considerable marginalization, the social acceptance she did enjoy was largely facilitated by the diligent care and wisdom in her mother's efforts and practices. When social disappointments were inevitable, Guming's mother was unfailing in giving her children a safe place to pour out their troubles. With the reliable comfort of their mother's listening ear and the modest but adequate network of social support that was cultivated through her care and thoughtfulness, Guming was able to experience her home as a happy childhood place. Hay (1992) has argued that "even the most limited relationships aid in the development of being-in-place, and thus the feeling of belonging and security" (p. 4). Guming said that before she wrote her place story, she experienced her mother as "memory fragments." In writing the place story she concluded that she came to see how her mother had in fact "created a place where her children could live with dignity." One might hope that every student could say that he or she experienced the classroom as a place where he or she could enjoy everyday life with dignity.

Children's appreciation of their access to natural environments is a recurring theme in many of the place stories. From a number of the stories, our classes have heard about nature being prized as a source of sensorial engagement, as flexible material for imaginative play, as a space for autonomy and adventure, and as a source of healing and restoration when social relationships within or outside of the family are disappointing and troubling. These themes are consistent with earlier research on children's place attachment (Chawla, 1992; Porteous, 1990; Hart, 1979). Some of the students wonder whether we romanticize children's access to natural environments and whether children in urban or suburban settings are deprived in any significant way. This question belongs with other questions about the changing nature of childhood as a function of "changing cityscapes, patterns and styles of habitation, and everyday lives" (Monaghan, 2000, p. A21).

Overall, the place stories helped us to appreciate the multifaceted significance of place and to develop the construct of place as an interpretive framework in our daily perceptions and interpretations. During one of the courses a student was touring potential senior care residences for an older relative. Each week she expressed her analysis of each place in terms of concepts from the course. Another student, a school principal, called in "problem students" to ask about their "favorite places" in the school as a way to gain insight about how to be helpful. A more holistic understanding of experience through the lens of place can help educators and researchers avoid emphasizing the individual agency and control of students without discerning or calling into question the constraints upon their experience.[1]

WEDGED BETWEEN A SHIMMERING ROCK AND A HARD PLACE (TERESA)

What do people remember when you ask them about where they grew up in childhood? "Draw your neighborhood map. It could be a composite of various places where you grew up. Draw the places that were significant to you as a child. You can draw inside and/or outside spaces. Distances do not need to be accurate. This is a memory map." For the most part, they draw trees, woods, bushes, pathways, ravines, fields, parks, rivers, pools, streets, houses (their own, friends,' relatives'), convenience stores, schools, schoolyards, and sometimes churches. They typically begin their drawing with streets and houses, so as to situate themselves in time and space: "This was where I lived; this is where others lived." Then they start to travel: "This is where I went." They assemble in small groups and share their maps. As you listen, the stories come out as journeys: "I/we used to go here...." As in many journey stories, they linger over places where they liked best to stop: to play, to rest, to read, to build and construct, to daydream.

They re-trace the pathways in their mind that their feet came to know so well. They reconstruct a self as if from the bottom up. Janice Simcoe (Ojibway) says that there is something about your feet that knows what is felt underneath and can recognize the geography of home (Wilson, 2000, p. 191). Some maps are rudimentary, so basic that it's hard to imagine how the map could give rise to the stories that are told about it, while others are full of exquisite detail, with fond representations of the branches on which to perch, the rock on which to bask or from which to fend off monsters, or the cramped place under the kitchen sink just big enough for one.

I have conducted this activity for different purposes with close to one thousand undergraduate and graduate students over the past four years. In many ways, it has become the hallmark of my teaching. There was one graduate class when I didn't use it, and a student hotly commented in his final journal that he had waited all term for this activity, only to be disappointed. Another graduate student, a no-nonsense principal with a healthy suspicion for "artsy" activities, sent me a letter two years later referring to the course, and the neighborhood map within it, as the most significant learning experience in his program of study. In undergraduate classes, students communicate their delight by saying how much they enjoyed re-visiting their childhood. The activity is a form of memory work, and it is this aspect that provides the common thread in my teaching across contexts and levels. The neighborhood map and (as I shall next describe) the secret place that I have grafted onto it have proved especially versatile: with undergraduate students, to re-ground them in what it means or meant to be a child, to identify their "touchstone" or favorite experiences (Strong-Wilson, 2006), and to locate their childhood within a particular time and place. With graduate students, it has served those purposes and more; one of its goals is to show that identity formation is "storied" (Strong-Wilson, 2008) and that stories are tied to memories that can be spatially mapped and viscerally re-experienced. The map also ties into Grumet's (1991) notion of curriculum as the art of daily living, with the map foregrounding the "background" curriculum that shaped their educational formation.

People are invariably surprised by the vividness with which their memories come back, as sharp as photographs, complete with not only sights, but smells, tastes, and sensations. Sometimes the pictures are hazy, but the feelings associated with them are acute, re-experienced as fresh. What is it about remembering one's childhood environment that elicits such strong feelings? Part of it lies not just in the map but in the secret spaces, places to "incubate," as Goodenough (2003) puts it: "to build a world apart" (p. 2)—places where children can see but not be seen: a cardboard box, the fort in the tree, the small parting in the hedge beyond which lies a magical arbor; guerrilla-style crawling in a ditch, unseen, as a mother guilelessly plies a hoe in the garden; behind the living room couch, under the kitchen sink, which also serves as a store when open for business; under the bed covers, in the closet, in the space under the stairs, under a fort erected from pillows and blankets; wedged into a cupboard shelf. Some spaces are not so much hidden as known only to the child, as in a marble pillar in open view in the middle of a Japanese home, which the child hugged, deeply attached to its deep color and smooth texture. Some spaces open up when others are sleeping, such as the cupboard dolls who would only come out to play during the hottest time of the day in a town in India. Some secret spaces are communal, shared by many, as in the children who built a world with the scraps of nails, metal, and boards left behind by a construction company. Some spaces are incredibly small, like the place under the table in the greenhouse porch or the tiny space between two beds in which a child sequestered herself. Others are wide and expansive, like the network of bike trails that canvassed a kilometer or more of land on the outskirts of a suburb.

The remembrance of a secret space touches something deep inside; the students are asked not just to identify the place but to recount a story associated with it. Sometimes it is the first time that the stories are being told. Some students share their stories with a parent and may be surprised to discover that the parent knew all along but pretended not to. In at least one case, the student found out that the secret passageway between bedrooms that the siblings thought was their discovery also belonged to their mother as a child. Bachelard (1984) attributes great significance to these spaces that we appropriate as ours and that he says begin in or close to home; concretely, to the house: "Our house is our corner of the world" (p. 4). While many have identified the absence of adult supervision as central to the secret space, it is also the case that some secret spaces can be conspiratorial pockets of time and space that come to belong to child and adult. It is certainly true that reminiscing adults often immediately recognize the "secret spaces" of childhood; children may or may not be aware, at the time, of the deep sustaining significance of such places. "The places in which we have experienced daydreaming reconstitute themselves in a new daydream," Bachelard claims (p. 6). If Goodenough is right, adults yearn for and seek out these spaces—the rock where they sat in the sun and did "nothing" or the woods in which they played all day: "When adults read fairy tales, where do they see themselves? In dying or neglectful parents, cruel stepmothers, and feckless fathers? Or in canny orphans bound for the woods and trials that will transform them into glittering selves?" (p. 2). The answer is: in their "glittering selves."

The impact of the map and secret place would remain on the level of private enjoyment if the artifacts were not shared with others. Through the sharing, students discover that the experiences and environments that they thought were unique are part of a larger social and cultural environment that has shaped who and what they are. This reflection process takes a particular turn in one course, which I describe next.

In the Children's Literature course, I ask the students to re-visit their neighborhood maps after they have read the two novels: *My Name Is Seepeetza* (Sterling, 1990) and *No Time to Say Goodbye* (Olson, 2001). Both are fictionalized accounts, but deeply rooted in lived experience, of Indigenous survivors of the residential school system. This government-mandated residential school system operated in Canada for well over a century; it was also used in other countries (e.g., the United States and Australia). Students were required to attend the schools; otherwise their parents would be jailed. They were not allowed to speak their Indigenous language. Their entry was often abrupt and their stays long; they only went home in the summers. Their connections to family and community were severed. Not only that, the children were often physically and sexually abused, which compounded the injury of their experiences, and even more so when we reflect that parents who had themselves undergone residential school were forced to condemn their children to the same fate, thus perpetuating a cycle across generations. The system had devastating, long-term effects on Indigenous communities in Canada, but Indigenous peoples are also highly resilient, protective of their culture and values. Healing is occurring.

My Name Is Seepeetza takes the form of a diary and, in fact, is based on the diary that Sterling kept during the time that she attended residential school. In *No Time to Say Goodbye*, Olson created composite characters based on her interviews with Tsartlip survivors of the Kuper Island Residential School; they called themselves: Wilson, Joey, Monica, and Nelson. Each novel begins with the children's experiences of home before they are so rudely taken away. In Sterling's novel, which takes place over several years, the narrator recursively visits home. Sterling talks about her love of horses and the apple tree in whose branches she used to read, breathing in its sweet smells. In the residential school, she finds a haven in reading books in the library. In *No Time to Say Goodbye*, each of the characters has memories of home that sustain them or that they try to recreate by finding new spaces even, and especially, amidst their nightmarish reality.

I ask the undergraduate students, whose previous understandings of the residential school system are generally quite limited, to draw a neighborhood map and secret space for either Seepeetza or one of the children in *No Time to Say Goodbye*, just as they had done for themselves early in the term. Students readily identify with the characters' secret spaces, or with the feelings associated with those spaces: the smell of clean sheets; sitting under the apple tree; the feel, texture, taste and smell of homemade food. The discontinuity comes in perceiving the impassable and poignant differences. They become quieter and more thoughtful. Whereas their secret space was by and large enveloped in fond remembrances of family, home, neighborhood and community, and is associated with unwarranted (White) privilege, when asked to compare the two spaces, they recognize that in the residential school stories, the secret space became much more. It had to be fought for as well as kept truly secret so as not to be destroyed. It became a space for keeping alive self and culture under highly adverse conditions. As one of the characters, Nelson, who finds refuge in long-distance running, says: "they can't squeeze the Indian out of me." By juxtaposing their own places (neighborhood maps; secret spaces) with those of the "characters" inhabiting the residential school stories, something shatters inside but without necessarily being broken. They retain their memories of favorite spaces, but the memories have acquired a deeper aura, colored by consciousness and an awareness of joy co-existing with sadness. They leave with a greater attentiveness to space as an aspect of being alive in the world and "aliveness" not to be denied or taken for granted.

"POMEGRANATES IN TSFAT" (SHERYL)

One of my teaching goals is to educate young children about Jewish culture. As an advocate of the Reggio Emilia approach to early childhood, I was instinctively drawn to the arts in order to support this community's cultural awareness and identity. One of the fundamentals of the Reggio

Emilia approach is recognizing and establishing the environment as "third teacher," a concept we will develop in this chapter. Briefly, what is fundamental is that the environment speaks a potential for investigation, while being respected and minded by all protagonists, including, most importantly, the children.

This past year, our group of 5-year-old children had just completed a study of Israel's harvest time, which related to the holiday known as *Tu Bishvat*. Included in that study was a presentation of the Seven Species of Israel. Besides relating to biblical tales, the Seven Species (grapes, pomegranates, olives, wheat, barley, figs, and dates) are elements connected to cultural identity that Jewish people all over the world can identify. When the class was presented with several replicas of Israeli art, they were immediately attracted to a print titled "Pomegranates in Tsfat" by the artist Nachum Gutman. Instantly recognizing one of the species (namely, the pomegranate), the group became excited and they unanimously voted to further explore this piece. (See Figure. 1).

To begin, the children insisted on being able to find Israel on the globe and they uncovered the tiny city of Tsfat in the north of Israel. Our language center became a '"geography hub" where materials were presented so that children could investigate the landscape. Globes, magnifying glasses, maps (authentic and enlarged views of Israel) were available. These young students began to understand the whereabouts of the small country of Israel as well as the tiny city of Tsfat in comparison to the world. Clipboards and pencils were available for students to document their findings as they sketched what they realized. The excitement was palpable as each replica was hung on a clothesline for all to view and revisit. Tarr (2004) perceives classroom displays as having a purpose. Her writing has encouraged me to think beyond just decorating the classroom. The goal is for project documentation to become a catalyst for further investigation and discussions. Indeed, this was what transpired.

As part of project work, reflection is essential at each stage in order that the direction of study follows the children's interest. At even this preliminary phase of investigation, I could not help but notice how these young children were connecting themselves to Israel, considered a homeland by all Jews in the Diaspora. How could such young children make such associations?

What was predominant here was that they were actively learning and collaborating in connecting to their Jewish identity. This common experience, supported by their relationships and active involvement, became the foundation for future learning. The community experience along with the materials made available permitted them to follow their interests. It was evident that they were living in an environment that communicated that this was a place of

Figure 1: The children carefully observed the original print by examining shapes, color, lines, and textures. Content was the next topic.

Figure 2: A completed painting of Tsaft where one child decided to substitute a date palm as her tree of choice.

building memories, a home for collective stories that could set the foundations for a sense of self, learning, and culture.

Our next phase of study included re-investigating the Seven Symbols that they knew only by photographs and name. After purchasing the variety of fruits and grains, our experiences transferred into those of scientific inquiry. Observation, examination, and hypothesizing led us into days of activities. Documentation and recording of all our findings were logged by photographs and excerpts of conversation. *How many pomegranates would it take to make one litre of juice? What happens to the seeds if you plant them? What will happen to dry dates once you soak them in hot water?* With the use of microscopes and magnifying glasses, students actively worked to weigh, measure, and investigate the properties of wheat and barley. The documented procedures and student recordings were hung nearby. Students would re-examine and discuss their experiences, often deliberating on what would happen next. This was proof that having the documentation present in the environment invited further exploration or different directions of study (Gandini, 1998). What's more, the presence of the documented experiences made their "learning visible" to all (Rinaldi, 2001).

Soon after, the children were pleased to artistically recreate the city of Tsfat that Gutman depicted. The language of art became central as conversations about color, line, texture and content helped us analyze and re-establish his work. Magnifying glasses were supplied so students could have a close look at techniques and elements of the composition. Notably, the students selected their preferred species to add to their painting and not necessarily the pomegranates presented by the artist (see Figure. 2). Each segment of reformation was precious; first sketching of the scene, adding the details of color and texture and content, and as a finale, selecting and creating one of the Seven Symbols by accessing various mediums such as clay, wire, or paper. Our culminating activity continued for weeks as each piece was born. To conclude, parents, community members, and friends were invited to an evening vernissage where five-year-old children acted as guides as they presented their experience and representations.

The school and class environment should be one that teaches while being a place that builds a sense of genuine belonging. In order for that to occur, principles of flexibility need to allow settings to change so as to respond to the "voices" of children in the process of constructing their own knowledge (Gandini, 1998). In light of my own experiences, it is apparent that the classroom environment can relate important messages to children. By providing a setting where they are offered rich unique experiences, the tools to investigate, as well as the flexibility to research over time, a Reggio Emilia image of the child is supported. In the Reggio Emilia approach to early education, children are seen as protagonists in their learning: "all children have preparedness, potential, curiosity and interest in engaging in social interactions, establishing relationships, constructing their learning and negotiating with everything the environment brings to them" (Hendrick, 1997, p. 17).

Further, when children work in an environment that allows them to follow and decide on areas of interest, the results speak for themselves. In programs where children make choices, and investigate at their own pace, they demonstrate positive social skills, creative ideas and active learning in the experiences (Phyfe-Perkins & Shoemaker, 1986). Equally important is that the class environment provides for inquiry, where care for aesthetic values can unfold. Collaborative community efforts become the focus, and pro-social behavior is likely to transpire. Throughout the Museum Project I witnessed all of these occurrences.

The evening of our vernissage at last arrived. Children had fashioned their own "guide" badges to designate leadership while taking their families through the learning. The setting permitted them to confidently present a small biography of the artist and a description of their piece of art, which they had studied for several weeks. The precise details of how they developed their creations and understandings surprised not only the families but their teacher as well. It was evident that the pace of investigation allowed the children to reflect and consider each and every aspect of learning. Nothing was taken for granted—every phase was important. *"First we examined what Gutman painted. He loved Israel and loved Tsfat. Did you know that pomegranates grew there?"* one child asked her grandfather. *"It was easy to make the rectangle shapes of the buildings but we needed dots for the cobblestone streets. We chose q-tips 'cause they make great dots—like in a pointillist painting,"* another child informed. *"If I go to Israel I will see every kind of species, but I like dates so I made a date palm." "We found Hebrew writing in one of the branches, we think it was newspaper so we made our branches out of Hebrew newspaper too. You can see the words through the paint"* (see Figure 3).

Figure 3: One child proudly stands holding his preliminary sketch. In the background are his classmates' finished paintings ready for viewing.

The guided tours were respected by the visiting adults and siblings. The environment took on even more meaning as this cumulative session transpired. Young students became the teachers as a result of an environment that had communicated the essential tools of: support, open-endedness, active learning, aesthetics, collaboration, flexibility, and, most importantly, a "palette" of collaboration. Transparency, another Reggio environmental principle (Fraser, 2006), was also evident. This component can imply translucency or simply playing with light and mirrors. However,

Figure 4: The vernissage evening where friends and family witnessed the weeks of learning.

transparency is regarded as a "metaphor for communication" (Fraser, 2006, p. 116). The visible recording and sharing of the phases of this project allowed for a distinctive aperture—a value deemed essential for relationships to transpire and develop (see Figure 4).

The environment needs to inform children: *This classroom is here for your exploration and interpretation belongs to you. It is your place.* Loris Malaguzzi, the visionary founder of the Reggio Emilia Schools, entitled this "the hundred languages of children"—an adage associated with the Reggio Emilia Approach. He speaks of children's "surprising and extraordinary strengths and capabilities linked with an inexhaustible need for expression and realization" (Malaguzzi, 1993, p. 72). This reverence for how children learn, and how they demonstrate their learning, is one that supports a belief in the value of the environment as third teacher. The objective is to transform "dismal places into beautiful, inviting, light filled orderly spaces" (Cadwell, 1997, p. 61), spaces that are social spaces: for children but also for their teachers, parents and other adults.

I have noticed in my work with teachers and student teachers that when the key principles of environmental mindfulness are in place, there is a positive outcome with regard to children's level of involvement and social interactions. It has been repeatedly established that when children are presented with meaningful provocation and are well engaged with the materials and ideas, they are more involved in their learning (Beneke, 2003; Fawcett & Garton, 2005; Gauvin & Rogoff, 1989; Helm & Beneke, 2003; Smith, 1997).

What's more, when children are imparted the respect to take some direction for their learning, to liberally communicate their questions and interests, they can do so with support of an environment that welcomes and responds to them, reflecting their voices in turn. Although many schools may have mandated standards, this approach nevertheless can be successfully implemented provided the environmental components are caringly applied.

THE "ENVIRONMENT" AS THIRD TEACHER

In the Preface to Susan Fraser's *Authentic Childhood: Experiencing Reggio Emilia in the Classroom,* Alan Pence (2006) singles out the Reggio Emilia approach to early education as "revolutionary" (p. xii). He explains his reasons. He is among those who sees in Reggio Emilia's programs and curricula a "paradigmatic" shift rather than an "incremental difference" (p. xi) from early childhood education as it has commonly come to be practiced and understood. Reggio Emilia, Pence argues, "challenge[s] the basic assumptions upon which the ECE establishment in North America has been erected" (p. xii). One of those grounds, we would argue, lies in this attentiveness to the environment: the environment as "third teacher" (Gandini, 1998). Environment may be somewhat of an inadequate word to use, as Julia Ellis suggests, who prefers the language of "place" as it carries stronger associations of the socioaffective dimensions of one's surroundings. The word certainly seems inadequate to capture adult recollections of the significance of particular places (viz., "secret spaces") to their educational formation and how re-visiting those places in new contexts can produce different understandings, as both Teresa and Julia have documented in different ways in their practices. The *Webster's Dictionary* defines environment as the "circumstances, objects or conditions by which one is surrounded" and is linked to the physical and biotic conditions for living. Place, on the other hand, is much more diverse; it can be anything from a space, to a geographical region, to a building, to a spot: a particular part of a surface or body. It can also refer to one's position, as within a social hierarchy or, conversely, a niche. It can also take on associations of time, as in: this is the place, or this is not the place, to engage in a particular activity. Place, being a more nuanced term, is much more closely associated with the particular.

Within Reggio's notion of the environment as third teacher, though, is embedded this goal of making the abstract particular and concrete by infusing it with meaning; when the environment is inhabited, it *becomes* a place. Before that, it is simply a space—a space lacking a theory or, we might say, a story. As Vea Vecchi says, an architect can build a beautiful school "but then if the teachers who go to work there neither reflect on nor prepare to deepen their understanding about what is the meaning of living in a space, nothing happens" (in Gandini, 1998, p. 166). In order for space to be meaningful, the people who use that space need to have "a theory about its use" (p. 165). She gives the example of "piazza," an Italian word that refers to a common space. Malaguzzi contrasts it with the open space in which children and play during "recess"; little thought, he says, is often given to the objects or structures around and through which that space is organized. Indeed, it is more often seen as a time (in a schedule) rather than as a space, which is an afterthought (viz., finding a space large enough to accommodate all of the children who will go out to play). The "piazza" within a Reggio school is a space that deliberately encourages "encounters" (p. 165); light may be streaming in, or the walls may be covered in documentation of a "story" of the school, to which the children contributed, or it may contain "provocations"— objects or structures intended to catch the children's attention and provoke conversations. In this way, the piazza is not simply an open space in which to gather; it is also, says Malaguzzi, a "passage" that allows children "to flow through, to walk, or to linger as they wish" (pp. 165–6) such that children respond to their environment and then carry those understandings into their learning. "The environment becomes part of the individual," and the environment inhibits or facilitates and encourages active and engaged response (p. 166): the kind of response that brings the environment to life and invests it with meaning and purpose.

Purpose is key. Any environment that is invested with purpose potentially becomes a place that lives on in memory and that we seek to construct anew, for the same or a different pedagogical purpose. "Without a philosophical basis that gives meaning to the educational experience to be lived in a space, the identity of the space will not emerge; in fact the risk is to try to live an experience disconnected from the space" (p. 166). Goodenough (among others) has suggested that there is certain affinity between children and outdoor spaces; children find creative ways to infuse their surrounding environment with meaning by making things, imagining scenarios, acting out stories through play. Bachelard argues likewise for the significance of spaces within a house; as children, we incline towards corners, niches, hiding spots, particular places within a house that invite daydreaming and play, or that, with some minor modifications, can be construed as such. From this point of view, we already arrive at school with an understanding of the environment as a "third teacher," and, whether the school is conceived to fulfill this role, we find, or at the least, look for ways to shape it in this direction.

If Reggio Emilia is "revolutionary" in drawing attention to the environment as a third teacher, we are engaged in a similar undertaking whenever, in our pedagogy, we foreground children's or adults' understandings of place. We also suggest that this experience can be heightened when we bring a "theory" about the use of space that has as its goal to stimulate and promote further or different human encounters. From our experiences, this theory or, more precisely, theorizing about place and environment in teaching has roots in both theory and practice: in the productive interaction between what we read and think about and live within and outside of teaching and what we come to understand through listening to the stories that our students tell as a result of their participation in activities around place.

CONCLUSIONS AND RECOMMENDATIONS

"To live an environment that has to be endured or ignored rather than enjoyed
is to be diminished as a human being."
Sinclaire Gauldie, *Architecture: The Appreciation of the Arts*

When observing preschools and kindergartens over the years, I (Sheryl) am frequently surprised by the deficiency in mindful care given to the classroom (including hallways). Learning centers packed with games and manipulatives may be in place, but little provocation is being presented so as to invite discovery. Bulletin boards, often above eye level of the children, are packed with educational fabricated materials. What's more, teachers often comment on children's lack of creative thinking, inventiveness, and resourcefulness. I, in return, question, how they are being modeled these values?

Tarr (2004) passionately exposes the fact that classroom walls can "silence" children's abilities to create and invent. She worries about commercial decorations of "happy children," "perfect school materials," and overloaded typical thematic representations. Life is not so rose-colored for all children. Tarr is firm in her belief that these presentations demean the image of the child and represent more of what the teacher considers childhood to be (Tarr, 2004). She calls attention to the fact that overpacked walls do not authentically showcase children's work or ideas. Because of that, little room is offered to "…reflect who they are in terms of gender, culture and ethnicity but rather in stereotyped ways" (p. 90).

Furthermore, there is a recognized conviction that children are creative by nature. However, at early stages, this inherent active quality may be quashed. Goleman et al. (1992) have indicated that the essential ingredient in nurturing creativity is open–ended time. When children are deeply engaged but abruptly interrupted or pushed to "complete," there is no time for them to "relax into their own rhythm" (p. 63). These authors designate disruption, excessive surveillance and control, and competition to be "creativity killers." Ann Lewin, director of the Capital Children's Museums in Washington, D.C., stipulates the importance of children finding occasions to follow their natural tendencies and individual abilities in order to move ahead with them (Goleman et al., 1992). We have seen many examples of this in our own practices around place.

Conversely, when children work in an environment that allows them to collaborate, decide and follow areas of interest, the results are different. Fraser (2006) notes that the environmental principle of "flexibility" is one of the "joys of the Reggio Emilia approach" (p. 117). In programs where children make choices, and actively investigate at their own pace, they demonstrate positive social skills, creative ideas, and active learning in the experiences (Phyfe-Perkins & Shoemaker, 1986). Gone is the notion of the "numbness" of the classroom and welcomed is the presence of an environment that supports creativity and provocation to proceed. Embracing children in environments that kindle their imagination and interests is at the heart of the "third teacher." Children's aspirations to do more and learn more flourish as a result. What is being established not only reflects on school life but bears on the future as well.

The following principles may be used to develop environments that are important, provocative, and inviting:

1. **Include places where children can work individually or in group projects:** These places need to have adequate furniture and available materials and supplies. Furniture should be arranged so as to indicate to children how they are to work together. Private space is additionally important so that children feel respected to explore alone as well. Also children need places to keep their work, or display their documentation (at child eye level), so bulletin boards or wall space should be present. It is important for them to revisit and reflect and collaborate on where to go next with their ideas.

2. **Have places where children can keep their belongings as well as places to communicate with each other:** Children need to have a place for their belongings—a space they can call their own within their classroom; a true sense of ownership. Included should be some kind of message center where children can communicate with each other by mailboxes or slots.

3. **Ensure the children themselves are well represented in their environment:** Photos of children and families should be welcomed as part of the environment. Cubbies, in-class spaces, school hallways can be utilized as pathways to ensuring a sense of belonging.

4. **Provide flexibility:** Following the Reggio ideals, the environment should speak the components of flexibility: time, space, and materials. In other words, areas can change according to the investigations that are occurring. Time needs to be unlocked so that children are not "hurried" to complete work in one sitting. The openness for children to revisit, discuss, and add to their work creates the concept of spiral learning, where genuine practice of building knowledge is active.

5. **Establish walls that speak:** Classroom walls should reflect the learning of the members of that place. Commercial items need to be set aside to make way for the documentation and provocation under scrutiny.

6. **Be creative!** In conjunction with the principles of the Reggio Emilia Approach, challenging materials and inviting artifacts should be present to rouse inquiry and allow children to investigate (high and low spaces, mirrors, magnifying glasses, authentic tools, light tables, natural items such as shells, rocks, and parts of trees).

7. **Families, too, need to be considered:** There should be a place for parents to sit and talk to educators and children. Bulletin boards where information and documentation can be posted will allow parents to be informed in all respects. What's more, the possibility of revisiting the documentation with their children will allow them to share and communicate about how their children have investigated their surroundings.

NOTE

1. I express my thanks to Jil Kohler and Guming Zhao for permission to discuss their place stories in this writing.

REFERENCES

Bachelard, G. (1984). *The poetics of space: The classic look at how we experience intimate places.* Maria Jolas (Trans). Boston: Beacon Press. (Originally published in French as *La poétique de l'espace,* 1958).

Beneke, S. (2003). Practical strategies. In J.H. Helm & S. Beneke (Eds.), *The power of projects: Meeting contemporary challenges in early childhood classrooms—strategies and solutions* (pp. 8–86). New York: Teachers College Press.

Brey, P. (1998). Space—shaping technologies and the geographical disembedding of place. In A. Light and J. M. Smith (Eds.), *Philosophy and geography III: Philosophies of place* (pp. 239–263). Lanham, MD: Rowman & Littlefield.

Cadwell, L.B. (1997). *Bringing Reggio Emilia home: An innovative approach to early childhood education.* New York: Teachers College Press.

Cadwell, L. B. (2003). *Bringing learning to life: The Reggio approach to early education.* New York: Teachers College Press.

Chawla, L. (1992). Childhood place attachments. In I. Altman and S. M. Low (Eds.), *Place attachment* (Human Behavior and Environment: Advances in Research and Theory, Vol. 12) (pp. 63–86). New York: Plenum Press.

Fawcett, L. M., & Garton, A. F. (2005). The effect of peer collaboration on children's problem-solving ability. *British Journal of Educational Psychology, 75*(2), 157–169.

Fraser, S. (2006). *Authentic childhood: Experiencing Reggio Emilia in the classroom (2nd ed.)* Toronto, Ontario: Thomson Nelson.

Gandini, L. (1998). Educational and caring spaces. In C. Edwards, L. Gandini, & G. Foreman (Eds.), *The hundred languages of children: The Reggio Emilia Approach—advanced reflections.* (2nd ed). (pp. 161–178). Greenwich, CT: Ablex.

Gauvin, M., & Rogoff, B. (1989). Collaborative problem solving and children's planning skills. *Developmental Psychology, 25*(1), 139–151.

Goleman, D., Kaufman, P., & Ray, M. (1992). Playful schools that work. In D. Goleman, P. Kaufman & M. Ray. *The creative spirit.* New York: Penguin Books.

Goodenough, E. (2003). Introduction, in: *Secret Spaces of Childhood* (pp. 1–16). Ann Arbor: The University of Michigan Press.

Grumet, M. (1991). Curriculum and the art of daily life. In G. Willis & W. H. Schubert (Eds.), *Reflections from the heart of educational inquiry: Understanding curriculum and teaching through the arts* (pp. 74–89). New York: State University of New York Press.

Hart, R. (1979). *Children's experience of place.* New York: Irvington.

Hay, R. (1992). An appraisal of our meaningful relationships in place. *Trumpeter, 9*(3), 98–105.

Helm, J. H., & Beneke, S. (Eds.). (2002). *The power of projects: Meeting contemporary challenges in early childhood classrooms—strategies and solutions.* New York: Teachers College Press.

Hendrick, J. (1997). *First steps toward teaching the Reggio way.* Upper Saddle River, NJ: Prentice Hall.

Langhout, R. D. (2003). Reconceptualizing quantitative and qualitative methods: A case study dealing with place as an exemplar. *American Journal of Community Psychology, 32*(3/4), 229–244.

Malaguzzi, L. (1993). History, ideas and basic philosophy: An interview with Leila Gandini. In C. Edwards, L. Gandini, & G. Foreman (Eds.), *The hundred languages of children: The Reggio Emilia Approach-advanced reflections.* (2nd ed), (pp. 49–75). Greenwich, CT: Ablex.

Monaghan, P. (2000). A child's place in the world. *The Chronicle of Higher Education* (April 7, 2000) 46(31), A21-A22.

Olsen, S. (2001). *No time to say goodbye: Children's stories of Kuper Island Residential School.* Victoria, B.C., Sono Nis Press.

Pence, A. (2006). Preface. In S. Fraser, *Authentic childhood: Experiencing Reggio Emilia in the classroom.* Toronto, ON: Thomson/Nelson.

Phyfe-Perkins, E. & Shoemaker, J. (1986). Indoor play environments: The young child at play. *Reviews of Research.* (p.184). Washington, DC: NAEYC.

Porteous, J. D. (1990). *Landscapes of the mind: Worlds of sense and metaphor.* Toronto, ON: University of Toronto Press.

Rinaldi, C. (2001). Documentation and assessment: What is the relationship? In *Making learning visible: Children as individual and group learners, eds.* Project Zero & Reggio Children, 78–89. Reggio Emilia, Italy: Reggio Children.

Smith, L. A. H. (1997). Open education revisited: Promise and problems in American educational reform (1967–1976). *Teachers College Record, 99*(2), 371–415.

Sterling, S. (1992). *My name is Seepeetza.* Vancouver: Groundwood Books.

Strong-Wilson, T. (2006). Touchstones as *sprezzatura:* The significance of attachment to teacher literary formation. *Changing English, 13* (1), 69–81.

Strong-Wilson, T. (2008). *Bringing memory forward: Storied remembrance in social justice education with teachers.* New York: Peter Lang.

Strong-Wilson, T., & Ellis, J. (2007). Children and place: Reggio Emilia's environment as third teacher. *Theory into Practice, 46* (1), 40–47.

Tarr, P. (2004). Consider the walls. *Young Children, 59*(3), 88–92.

Wilson, T. (2000). Conversations with First Nations educators: Weaving identity into pedagogical practice. (Unpublished masters' thesis, University of Victoria, Victoria, British Columbia.)

TWENTY-NINE

The Importance of Attending to Children and Place

Julia Ellis

Place is increasingly being used as a central idea in research in a number of disciplines such as philosophy, sociology, architecture, literary criticism, history, and religion. The more recent work by cultural geographers and scholars in neighboring disciplines has modeled a number of promising approaches for using place as a central idea in researching education and studying the lives of children and youth. Children's place and space can be understood as a form of curriculum—the lived experience that shapes and enables their growth and learning. Pedagogically, place can be understood as facilitating nurturance, especially through meaningful relationships, while space can be understood as affording opportunities for growth and creativity.

This chapter proposes that place become a central concept in researchers' and educators' awareness of children's experiences in and out of school and that the perspectives of children and youth become more of a focus in research on the effects of the various phenomena of globalization such as the privatization of public space and the corporate saturation of media. To invite educational researchers into a consideration of such a proposal, this chapter is organized into three sections. The first section highlights a number of contemporary ideas about place and children's needs for place. The second section presents a hermeneutic of a film as a contextualized way to review a number of key ideas or understandings about place. In this section I will weave themes from the film with formal suggestions about place from the research literature. The film illustrates phenomenologically how the dynamics or processes of place arise in experience. The third section discusses needed research on children and place within education.

THE WHAT, WHY, AND HOW OF PLACE

This section briefly outlines a number of contemporary ideas about place. Taken together, the ideas reviewed in the subsections below emphasize that although globalization—the ever-accelerating flow of goods, people, and information in an internationalizing context—has dramatically altered the meaning of place, it has not diminished its significance (Smith, Light & Roberts, 1998). Places continue to be "significant centres of our immediate experiences of the world" (Relph, 1976, p. 141) and are the most promising foci for inquiries related to social justice (Smith et al., 1998).

WHAT IS MEANT BY PLACE

Cultural geographers recognize that "experience of place can range from part of a room to an entire continent" (Relph, 1976, p. 141). Because the placeness of a place is a subjective or intersubjective creation, it is only apparent to the individuals or group members who create it (Smith et al., 1998). Recognizing the importance of human activity and human conception in the many definitions of place, Brey (1998, p. 240) defines place as "an area or space that is a habitual site of human activity and/or is conceived of in this way by communities or individuals." He argues that cyberspace, the site of an increasing amount of human activity, can also be understood as a place, albeit one that is combined with a physical location for the user. As objects of inquiry, places are usually large ones, called "locales," that are sites of social life and the operation of collectives. These can be at the scale of buildings or cities.

CHANGING CONCEPTIONS OF PLACE

Place was associated with stability and community in earlier work by humanistic geographers who endeavored to study the "essence" of place. It is now widely recognized that communities are defined as much by shared interests and experiences as by common location (Relph, 1976; Smith et al., 1998). Place is furthermore understood as fluid and dynamic, as a "contested terrain" (Agnew, 1989, p. 314).

Places are also seen as fused together by electric media into one place, the global village. Brey (1998) describes how the local characteristics of places are thoroughly invaded by, and reorganized in terms of, distanciated social relations such as those between distant head offices and local branch plants, producing a dialectic of the local and the global. As a consequence, location "in a global web created by space-shaping technologies" (Brey, 1998, p. 243) has increasingly more influence on a place and the people in it than does geographical location. Brey argues that the identity of a place is largely determined by the kinds of human activity enabled by the goods it contains and its nearness to other places and spaces that contain other goods. In the global village, places strive to attract desirable goods such as investments and repel undesirable ones such as pollution.

IMPORTANCE OF PLACE

Philosophers recognize that place "fundamentally structures human experience. It is deeply human to make places and to think in terms of places" (Smith et al., 1998, p. 6). Place is a source of comfort, security, belonging, identity and meaning (Tuan, 1977). Place enables people to share experiences with others and to form themselves into communities with continuity over time (Crang, 1998). As Tuan (1992, p. 44) explains, "culture integrates us into the world through shared language and custom, behaviour and habits of thought." Individual and collective identities are bound to place at multiple scales such as hometown and homeland. Place and place identity are seen as "significant media through which people construct an identity" (Adams, Hoelscher & Till, 2001, p. xxi).

Adams et al. emphasize the critical role of the imagination in the social production of place. As separate groups and individuals evoke geographical imaginations in different and competing ways in the construction of place, concepts such as multiculturalism, racism, nation building, and environmental destruction become linked to the making of place. Recognizing the "multiplicity" of place, critical humanist geographers inquire into how place is at work in the formation of identities related to race, ethnicity, class, gender and sexuality. They also concern themselves with how human creativity is constrained by large-scale social, political, and economic structures.

INTEREST IN PLACE

Increasing interest in place has resulted from the cultural turn in the humanities and social sciences of the mid-1980s (Adams et al., 2001), and also concerns about the social justice of places (Smith et al., 1998), popular interest in place related to the destruction of natural places, and the loss of place attributed to modernization and globalization (Casey, 1997; Crang, 1998). As places have become commodified through globalization, awareness of their importance has increased (Adams et al., 2001).

There is also a growing awareness of the need for a more phenomenological attention to place in the study human experience. For example, Eyles (1989, p. 103) underscores the limitations of researching human experience as though it occurred in a vacuum. Such research risks emphasizing individual agency and neglecting the societal contexts of everyday life which provide the "unquestioned background of meaning for the individual." Postmodern theorists argue that the construction of knowledge has to be engaged, perspectival, hermeneutical, and pluralistic rather than absolute, monolithic, and abstract (Denzin & Lincoln, 1994). Using place as a central idea when researching human experience can ensure a more holistic study of its complexity.

Interest in place also arises from concern about the changing nature of childhood as a function of "changing cityscapes, patterns and styles of habitation, and everyday lives" (Monaghan, 2000, p. A21). Many researchers have been studying the effects of industrialization, modernization, the postmodern condition, and globalization on the experiences of children and youth (e.g., Aitken, 1994; Churchman, 2001; du Bois-Reymond, Sunker, & Kruger, 2001; Holloway and Valentine, 2000; Katz, 1998; Lynch, 1977; Malone, 1997; Matthews & Limb, 1999; Tonucci & Rissotto, 1998).

QUESTIONS ABOUT PLACE

Some of the current questions about place include: How are places and meanings within places constituted humanly speaking? How can places be improved? How is the concept of place changing? How can environmental ethics and social justice be addressed? What are the social and physical conditions under which children live?

Tuan (1977), pioneering the perspective of "experience" in human geography, inspired over two decades of scholars to ask: What is the meaning of place? And how is human identity structured through place. Today, drawing on social theories most notably from cultural materialism, feminism, poststructuralism, postmodernism, and postcolonial theory, critical humanist geographers continue to examine how signs, symbols, gestures, utterances, and local knowledge convey cultural meanings and create places (Adams et al., 2001).

Writing in reaction to the "instant environment machine" and the "pseudo-places" resulting from postmodern approaches to creating a sense of place, Relph (1976, 1993) proposes questions about how to make modernist city centers more vital and modernist housing developments more habitable. He suggests a search for environmental design approaches that are responsive to local structures of meaning and experience.

Wasserman, Womersley, and Gottlieb (1998) note the recent and growing interest in the adaptability of place attachment in the context of residential mobility and cultural homogenization. These inquiries seek to clarify how the character of place attachment may be changing in the forms of community that are now flourishing.

Brey (1998) among others is asking how the geographical disembedding of places through space-shaping technologies has impacted the identity of places, and even our very concept of place. These inquiries recognize that the experience of place is not necessarily linked to a single physical location.

Place is seen as a useful way to approach larger questions about both environmental ethics and social justice (Smith et al., 1998). Many questions about social justice pertain to the social and physical conditions under which children live from place to place (Churchman, 2001; Monaghan, 2001). Researchers from geography and other disciplines ask questions about the ways place relates to the social, cultural, and political identities children form. They also ask: How does adult society create space for children and youth? How do societies build environments for children? How can children's needs be addressed in the planning and design of cities? What is happening for children in the new middle-class, gated neighborhoods? How are children's lives changing in poorer neighborhoods? How does economic restructuring from globalization affect the lives and learning of children in developed and developing countries?

CHILDREN'S NEEDS FOR PLACE AND SPACE

A number of studies have identified children's needs for *place* as a source of security, stability, belonging, and identity and, within place, for *space* which provides opportunity for social or creative self-development. These findings can alert researchers to the significance of place and space when studying the lives, learning, and identity formation of children and youth.

Chawla (1992) conceptualized childhood place attachment through a review of diverse literatures. She noted that place provides three types of satisfaction: security, social affiliation, and creative expression and exploration. Her review revealed the significance of both stable, nurturing places and the availability of space for children. She noted that place supports the development of self-identity both by affording opportunities for young people to try out predefined roles in conventional settings and by offering unprogrammed space. At every age, children were found to need undefined space where they could formulate their own worlds. Cherished places tended to be natural, undeveloped, or waste spaces as well as hideouts and playhouses indoors and out.

James (1995), a social anthropologist studying the acquisition of language, observed that both place and language serve as emblems of groupness in young people's development of identity. "Through their own discourse children carve out their own identities and 'patterns of belonging are laid down' (James, 1995, p. 59)" (Matthews & Limb, 1999, p. 69). Thus, James saw young people's use of street corners, indoor shopping centers, and parks as cultural gateways where they could meet and carve out their own identities.

The Growing Up in Cities 1997 project (Malone, 1997) entailed research in 9 cities in both developed and developing countries across the globe. This study found that young people want to feel connected to their locality. What mattered most to young people in terms of their sense of connection to their localities were: a positive identity; integration within a cohesive community culture; and accessible and active public spaces and places that they could claim as their own for socializing and play with peers. Malone (1997, p. 8) observed that once basic needs (food, shelter, health, water) were met for young people in developing countries, they experienced a rich and engaging life and were on the whole "happy." By contrast, in the developed cities, it was found that for many children "material possessions often meant isolation, loneliness and unhappiness."

The findings of these studies and others suggest important questions to be asking about the quality of life for children and youth in locales of interest. Do they have access to others for social affiliation? Do conditions support a positive identity? Do they have access to desirable, unprogrammed space? Do young people have access to active public space they can appropriate? Do they have opportunities to try out pre-defined roles in conventional settings? Do children and youth have opportunities for integration within a cohesive community culture? How are they using or appropriating new technologies in the making of youth cultures in the digital age (Sefton-Green, 1998; Tapscott, 1998; Turkle, 1995)? As Chawla and others have found, children's place attachments not only affect the present quality of their lives but leave enduring effects after childhood is over.

A PARABLE ABOUT PLACE

The film *Chocolat* serves as an artful parable to illustrate many key understandings about place. The story is set in an imaginary, old-fashioned village in the French countryside in 1959. The opening scenes of the village reflect the traditional understanding of place as consisting of three intertwined elements: a specific landscape with both built and natural elements; a pattern of social activities; and a set of personal and shared meanings (Relph, 1976). To introduce this place and this story, the narrator tells us that

> If you lived in this village you understood what was expected of you and you knew your place in the scheme of things. And if you happened to forget, someone would help remind you. In this village, if you

saw something you weren't supposed to see, you learned to look the other way. If by chance your hopes had been disappointed, you learned never to ask for more. So through good times and bad, famine and feast, the villagers held fast to their traditions until one winter day a sly wind blew in from the north.

The lurking ambivalence reflected in this portrayal is reminiscent of geographers' observations that inquiry is needed to clarify whether the stability of a community reflects embraced traditions or disguises oppression by dominant regimes. Hay (1988) among others has noted that sometimes people have to leave strong places to escape drudgery or to have the opportunity to be someone else.

With the north wind came Vianne and her daughter Anouk, intending to make this village their home and establish a chocolaterie. Vianne, like her mother from Central America and her mother's people, was a wanderer, moving with the north wind from village to village, dispensing ancient remedies based on 2000-year-old recipes using unrefined cacao and chili peppers, and never settling down. Two traditions were about to clash.

The scene of Vianne and Anouk approaching the village shows the two figures bent against the wind, carrying heavy suitcases, against a backdrop of harsh, rugged terrain. This stark image may be symbolic of Tuan's (1992, p. 44, p. 36, in Crang, 1998, p. 112) notions that as human beings we are continually searching for a place to help us "forget our separateness and the world's indifference" or to protect us from the "threatening awareness of being alone in a world that is ultimately unresponsive." Tuan (1992) argues that the forces of modernity have created the need for place as an analeptic for individuality and the world's indifference. Geographers suggest that it is because time and space are intangible and dauntingly infinite, that we "cling intellectually and emotionally to our experiences and memories of the material world that is so reassuringly solid" (Adams et al., 2001, p. xiii).

Vianne and Anouk present themselves to a woman who has an old, run-down patisserie and apartment above for rent. After, "Who the hell are you?" (they've let themselves in as she can't hear them knocking in the stormy wind), the landlady's next question is "Where are you from?" Uneasily and evasively, Vianne responds by naming the last three places they've lived. Both Vianne and the landlady seem to appreciate the significance of the question, "where are you from?" As Crang (1998, pp. 102–103) states: "Crucially people do not simply locate themselves, they also define themselves through a sense of place....The place is standing for a set of cultural characteristics; the place says something not only about where you live or come from but who you are." Because Vianne cannot define herself through a particular place, she cannot use the identity of a specific place to answer the implicit questions, "who are you?" or "what patterns of behavior can I expect from you?" The landlady's initial question, "Who the hell are you?," is also significant, symbolizing the indignation outsiders can experience from insiders when they presume to enter their place.

In the next scene we see the child and the mother alone in the newly rented, dusty, dilapidated old patisserie. The first words we hear from the child are: "What a nice town. How long can we stay?" The tension between the mother's willingness to wander—whether to escape oppression, claustrophobia or to fulfill her dreams—and the child's desire for place is one of the organizing themes of this parable.

In Vianne's transformation of the old patisserie into the new chocolaterie, we witness what Smith et al. (1998) have outlined as the interconnected processes of carving place out of ambient space. The processes include marking, intentional reorganization of the physical world, symbolic transformation through naming, and narration that establishes significance and identity. First, Vianne *marked* the place by putting significant artifacts on a counter and hanging up a decoration that appeared to be a good luck charm, even though nothing in the old patisserie had been washed or dusted yet. Marking of the place brings order and intentionality to an otherwise meaningless terrain. Vianne's cleaning, repairs, and renovations to the patisserie constituted her *intentional re-organization of the physical world* as part of making it her place. Then she hung up the sign, "Chocolaterie Maya" thereby *symbolically transforming space into place by naming it*. As Vianne began sharing her magical chocolates with local residents, stories/*narration* about these interactions and the transforming effects of the chocolates gave *significance and identity* to her new place. Topography is humanized with history and, says Glassie (1982, p. 665, in Smith et al., 1998, p. 4), "history is intrinsic to the idea of place."

What is perhaps most striking in the scenes showing Vianne's transformation of the old patisserie is the enthusiasm and energy she brings to her tasks. Some of my colleagues use the phrase, "road energy" to refer to the adrenaline they know they can count on when establishing homes and offices in new sites of employment. Jedrej and Nuttall (1996, p. 142 in Wasserman et al., 1998, p. 204) have commented on the need people have to "impose meaning on new places to nurture a sense of identity and feeling of belonging as an antidote to the possibility of individual estrangement and despair" even when they are separated from place-based communities.

The mayor of the village, the Compte de Reynaud, is the first caller at Vianne's newly rented old patisserie. He invites Vianne to worship with the villagers at mass on Sundays and expresses concern that she may be considering re-opening the patisserie during Lent. Instead, Vianne doesn't go to church, but immediately sets about transforming and healing the lives of the villagers with her chocolates. The Compte becomes obsessed with driving her out of the village. He tells people she is brazen, a bad influence, indecent, an atheist, a radical, the enemy, shameless, and a vehicle for the devil's work. He forbids the villagers to visit her chocolaterie. He promises Vianne that she'll be out of business by Easter. A student of history, he recollects that the first Compte de Reynaud expelled the radical Huguenots many years earlier.

Although established places need and benefit from new blood, they can also be very unwelcoming to outsiders. Relph (1997, p. 223) observes that "the stronger the belonging, the greater the hostility to outsiders." Similarly, Oakes (1997, in Adams, Hoelscher, & Till, 2001, p. xxii) argues that place "can yield a place-based politics which is reactionary, exclusionary, and blatantly supportive of dominant regimes."

The first time we see Anouk outside of the old patisserie, she is in the playground at school fighting physically with boys who have been teasing her. She and the boys share the same time-out, face-against-the-wall punishment, but it is only Anouk who is verbally reprimanded by the teacher, who says: "In this school we are civilized; we do not strike one another." Such a statement serves to re-inscribe Anouk as an outsider who is inferior. This scene represents the experience of many immigrant or mobile students who must struggle for belongingness in new places. It also serves as a reminder of the challenges teachers face in facilitating social acceptance for "outsiders" who are new to the school or classroom (Ellis, 1999).

Later in the film Anouk comes home in tears after being teased yet again. When prompted, she cries out to her mother: "Why can't we go to church? And why can't you wear black shoes like the other women?" Anouk, like many children of immigrant or mobile parents, welcomes assimilation, wants to participate in what others are doing, and wants to fit in and belong in the community (Crang, 1998, p. 103). Vianne, on the other hand, perhaps like many immigrant parents who lack nearby access to the heritage culture, is at a loss to help her child understand the significance and importance of her own worldview and ways of doing things (Ellis, 1999).

It is noteworthy that when Anouk comes home in tears, she does not rush to her mother's arms but instead seeks comfort in her private nook, a large empty fireplace draped over by a curtain. The production of a private place that can serve as a refuge is an accomplishment attesting to the child's growing skill and independence (Chawla, 1992). Cherished places such as this nook become internalized as resources to provide serenity in times of trouble.

The village is then visited by another set of outsiders, a group of young Irish people who live on a houseboat and follow the river. The Compte suggests that the villagers "help them to understand that they are not welcome." He explains that "These people are rootless, godless drifters. Theirs is the way of slovenly pleasure. They would contaminate the spirit of our quiet town and the innocence of our children." This attempt at organized resistance to the anticipated invasion by the houseboat people reminds us that place is inescapably exclusive in that "the placeness of a place is also a legal and social creation, the product of rules and convention that set territory aside and reserve it as the exclusive domain of certain types of human behaviour and certain types of human beings" (Smith et al., 1998, p. 6). Before long, a demented villager sets fire to the houseboat, consistent with the observations that "violence is the existential ground of place" and "nearly all fighting is over places" (Smith et al., 1998, p. 6).

The arrival and words of the houseboat people also introduce the theme of the "experience of mobility as being about a different sense of belonging" (Crang, 1998, p. 115), of people who are at home with themselves or who find the price of belonging (expectations) too high.

The landlady of the old patisserie has health problems and her daughter wants her to move into a nursing home. She resists this idea, says she wants to eat and drink what she pleases, and expresses dread about the prospect of daily interactions with a nurse bearing a clipboard and checklist and asking her about her bowel movements. In addition to fear of the loss of independence in an institutionalized residence, we can also say that the landlady is expressing displeasure about the way "non-places" are different from places. In the "organic sociality" of places, people have long-term relationships and their interactions do not solely serve an immediate functional purpose, whereas in non-places such as airports or supermarkets, interactions are characterized by "contractual solitariness" as individuals or groups only relate to wider society through limited and specific interactions (Crang, 1998, p. 114).

The landlady's daughter has a young son whom she over-protects. Ever since the death of her husband she fears that the son will over-exert himself if he rides his bike, or injure himself in other ways if he roams about the village freely with other children. Nor is the boy allowed to see his grandmother, the landlady of the old patisserie, as the daughter sees her own mother as potentially a bad influence. This mother's over-protection of her son is reminiscent of contemporary parental fears for the physical and moral safety of their children (Valentine 1996, 1997; Valentine & Holloway, 2001). As shown in this boy's circumscribed experience, one consequence of such fear for children's safety is a limiting of their access to social affiliations (belongingness and identity) and to autonomous play in engaging environments (space for growth and creativity).

Rather than be forced into the nursing home, the landlady chooses to break all of her health rules to enjoy her seventieth birthday party as she pleases. She then dies right after the party. The Compte blames Vianne for her death. Despairing at being misunderstood and wrongly judged, an emotional Vianne attempts to leave with the north wind again. It is a dramatic moment as her daughter Anouk physically resists leaving. The child's need for place is strong. It is a need for security, comfort, belonging, connectivity, identity, and at-homeness. Adults can be happy in a variety of locales so long as they have their things with them and enough meaningful relationships. They primarily concern themselves with work and family or even the pursuit of ideas (Hay, 1988; Tuan 1977). The child, however, needs the whole place to serve as her reliable, supportive, expanding world—a place from which she "can face the unknowns of the larger world beyond" (Hay, 1988, p. 163).

Anouk has many good reasons for the place attachment she has developed. With their apartment above the chocolaterie, she is not separated from the adult world of work. She has opportunities to take her mother's role in identifying best choices of chocolate for new customers who are children, thereby trying out a pre-defined social role in a conventional setting. Playing with children in the village she enjoys exploring undefined space as they slide down the dirt banks at the edges of the roadways or visit the wooded area on the edge of the river. Freedom in exploration of the environment intensifies friendships and friendships intensify exploration of the environment (Moore, 1986).

Because Vianne has befriended and helped many of the troubled and unhappy villagers, to express their support for her after the Compte's injustice, they gather in her chocolaterie and begin the day's cooking of chocolate before she comes downstairs. They want her to stay and they want to show her how much she means to them. It is a touching scene. Relph (1993, p. 36) says that "a place is above all a territory of meanings. These meanings are created both by what one receives from and by what one gives to a particular environmental context."

In the end, true to the genre of comedy, all are reconciled and the village is transformed by the new people and traditions it has accommodated. The priest—also a frustrated newcomer—pronounces in his Easter sermon that "we can't measure goodness by what is excluded. We can only measure goodness by what we embrace, create, and include." The priest's words echo the views of Doreen Massey (1994) and others who see place as "a crucial aspect of the politics of inclusion, where people form multiple identities and marginalized groups contest a dominant ideology. [There exists] the possibility of creating a 'progressive sense of place,' one that meets the challenges of feminism and celebrates the politics of difference" (Adams et al., 2001, p. xxi).

The transformation of the village reminds us that places are not only the contexts of human life but "in some manner are themselves alive, for they grow, change, decline with the individuals or groups who maintain or ignore them" (Relph, 1993, p. 38). The chocolaterie has been established and one of the women Vianne has helped has enthusiastically opened a new café.

The scene that dramatically illustrates aspects of the reconciliation and transformation in a place takes the form of a carnival that involves the talents, foods, and entertainments of all villagers, including those from the houseboat and the chocolaterie. This public celebration seems both unusual and at the same time welcome to the residents of the "tranquil village." The village will be a different place with the traditions and worldviews introduced by Vianne and the house boat people from Ireland. This portrayal of the transformation at work in the village reveals place, not as a space that contains culture, but as formed by the crossing routes of people and cultures. The story in this film is exemplary of why Crang (1998) recommends an optimistic view of the possibilities of mobility and the loss of organic communities.

In summary, the film *Chocolat* is an excellent parable for a number of key themes about place. Within *traditional communities,* it has illustrated the following themes: (1) place is traditionally understood as consisting of the three intertwined elements of a specific landscape with both built and natural elements, a pattern of social activities, and a set of personal and shared meanings; (2) traditional communities can entail embraced traditions or drudgery and oppression; (3) established communities can benefit from new blood, but can be very unwelcoming to outsiders; and (4) typically newcomers are socialized into the patterns of behavior in a community.

The following were themes related to the *need for place:* (1) people need place for comfort, belonging, identity, and as a restorative from the world's indifference and the daunting infinity and intangibility of time and space; (2) people define themselves and others through sense of place; (3) people experience an urgency to impose meaning on new places to avoid individual estrangement and despair; (4) mobility is about a different sense of belonging; (5) non-places lack the "organic sociality" of places; and (6) sense of place, being an insider in a community, gives a person a strong center from which to face the unknowns of the larger world.

A number of themes pertained to the dynamics of *how place works:* (1) there are interconnected processes for making place out of space; (2) history is intrinsic to the idea of place; (3) places are legal and social creations that reserve territory for certain types of people and certain types of behaviors; (4) nearly all fighting is over places; (5) place is a territory of meanings created by what one gives to and receives from an environment; and (6) places are not only contexts for human life but are themselves alive as they grow, change, or decline in response to human care or activity.

The film serves to introduce several themes related to *place as a dynamic, fluid ,and contested terrain:* (1) place is a crucial aspect of the politics of inclusion where people form multiple identities and marginalized groups contest a dominant ideology; (2) a "progressive sense of place" is needed to meet the challenges of feminism and celebrate the politics of difference; (3) places are not spaces that contain culture but are formed by the crossing routes of people and cultures; and (4) there should be an optimistic view of the possibilities of mobility and the loss of organic communities.

The film also serves as a parable for the following themes related to *children and place:* (1) children and adults can have different needs of place; (2) parental fears for children's safety limit their access to social affiliation and to space for creativity and growth; (3) children's private hideouts or playspaces are cherished places and become internal resources; (4) exploration of the environment intensifies children's friendships and vice versa; and (5) children benefit from connection to the adult world of work and opportunities to try out pre-defined social roles.

RESEARCH ON CHILDREN AND PLACE

So far, this chapter has endeavored to provide an overview of a number of key ideas about place and children's needs for place. Although children's lives are shaped by processes for which, increasingly, no "one" is responsible (Mugerauer, 1994), it is incumbent upon us as community members at all levels to take responsibility for the quality of children's lives in our localities. North American suburbs largely fail teenagers (Schiavo, 1988), and both gated communities for the middle-class and housing projects for the poor fail younger children in terms of their needs for access to other children and desirable outdoor spaces (Caragata, 1998; James, 1998).

Employing place and space as central ideas in research with and for children and youth can lead to responsive and responsible action. Understanding school as a place that ought to support belonging and afford space for creativity and growth can give valuable direction to research and practice in schools generally. This section briefly highlights five examples of research in education or school settings that explicitly or implicitly study children and place, while considering school as place. Three studies are concerned with students' opportunities for social affiliation (belonging) and positive identity, and two are concerned with space for students' creativity and growth. The section concludes with a discussion of suggested research directions.

Osterman (2000) reviewed studies pertaining to students' experience of belonging in schools. She noted that although belongingness is a precondition for academic achievement, schools tend to offer it only as a reward for compliance and academic success. For the most part, schools adopt organizational practices that neglect and may actually undermine students' experience of membership in a supportive community. The increasing emphasis on competitiveness vs. child-centeredness and/or equity in schools has been directly linked to three factors: globalization; the need for individuals to have technological knowledge; and the desire for countries to move into higher levels of economic competitiveness (Stromquist & Monkman, 2000).

Ellis, Small-McGinley, and De Fabrizio (2001) studied school-based mentorship, peer support, and student leadership programs in schools in kindergarten through grade 12. These programs made schools better places for students by giving them "someone to talk to" in many different ways. All of the programs were found to be valuable ways to facilitate caring relationships for students within schools, thus making schools more meaningful and positive places for students. Feelings of alienation and poor relationships with peers and teachers have been identified as key reasons for dropping out of school (e.g., Alberta Learning, 2001).

Currently, in the Canadian provinces of Saskatchewan and Alberta a study is under way to examine spatial practices and ethnocultural diversity in urban public high schools (Hurren, Hayford, Carson & Johnston, forthcoming). The study reflects increasing concerns for inclusive practices in public high schools and involves teachers, administrators, and support staff as well as students. The study is designed to focus on the experiences of students over three years of their high school education. "Space" in the context of this study refers to both observable space, with measurable and boundable aspects, and to culturally coded space.

Moore and Wong (1997) have reported on their research on children's social, emotional, and cognitive benefits when asphalt school grounds were replaced with natural environments containing appealing structures and objects for children. Children and teachers were involved in the design process. This project and others like it have been intended to support a strong sense of place or place attachment through the availability of desirable, undefined space in the school yard. In the transformed school yards, children's interactions were characterized by imaginative play and social intimacy rather than competition or conflict.

Ellis (1998) studied the use of open-ended, "creative" assignments in classrooms from kindergarten through grade 12. She found that these activities provided engaging and satisfying opportunities for students to make what they could imagine. At the same time, these activities enhanced relationships (belonging) among students and between teachers and students.

If the school is to serve as a good place for children and youth it should be a place that affords positive identity and belonging and includes space for creativity and growth. The challenge of building community at the classroom level and the school level ought to be a priority in education and research. Without safety, social acceptance, and the absence of fear of ridicule or harassment, students cannot fully participate in or benefit from the learning activities they are invited into (Osterman, 2000). They need to know that they will be cared for and supported by others, and they need to value the other members of the group in return. At the level of the classroom, it must be understood that, just as in a sports team, once you're in, you're in. Such unconditional acceptance must be lived and experienced by all in the class. Just as a sports team will not function well without such inclusivity, neither will a classroom work to accomplish its purposes. In order to facilitate unconditional acceptance and personal relatedness in the classroom in the context of high residential mobility, schools that are often too big while being ethnoculturally diverse must be a focus of ongoing inquiry. As Smith (in press) argues, as a relational activity, being in a conversation together "depends on a certain kind of commitment, the commitment to stay together in the work of gaining understanding." In educational research we need to give our attention to the ways in which teachers can inspire or evoke such commitment on the part of students in diverse classroom contexts. Similarly, at the level of the whole school, diverse practices for facilitating group membership require ongoing inquiry. This is not to say there will not be differences among students; identities will always be multiple. There must, however, be a commitment to the possibility of caring relationships and healthy good-spiritedness among students and teachers, both in educational research and practice.

Inquiries into schools or classrooms as *places* can usefully give attention to the ways in which such places include or fail to include space for creativity and growth. Just as natural environments inspire intense constructivity as children form their own worlds in imaginative play, school and classroom activities can offer opportunities for students to imagine what it is like to be someone else and to create objects or events they may dream about. Creative work and the validation it evokes supports growth and positive identity. Many creative activities, like forms of play, also facilitate group spirit and cohesion. Thus space for creativity and growth can also be a catalyst for the development of a sense of community.

Awareness of the quality of children's place, and the space it includes outside of school, can direct attention to children's needs for place within the school. Research on children's lives in their localities can usefully inform policy, programs, and practices in schools. For some students, school may well be their most stable and nurturing place. While appreciating the significance of place as a form of curriculum—the lived experience that shapes growth and learning—there are also other concerns to bear in mind regarding the affordances of children's place outside of school: What access do they have to other children and adults for social affiliation, meaningful relationships, and positive identity? What access do they have to "left-over" spaces or their own rooms to use as private hideouts or play spaces? What access do they have to desirable unprogrammed space and active public space? What connection do they have with the adult world of work? What opportunities do they have to try out pre-defined roles in conventional settings? What access do they have to educational experiences or resources? What recreational time do they have that is not committed to supervised lessons or activities? Research on the places of students' everyday lives can support understanding of what is meaningful to students and inform programs and practices intended to enhance their growth and learning. It may also inspire leadership or advocacy in improving the localities in which students find themselves.

CLOSING DISCUSSION

Tuan (1986) acknowledged the futility of attempting to define a social ideal for a good community and suggested that how the concept of community finds social expression will be "the principal measure of a people's wisdom" (p. 106). Matoré (1966, p. 6, in Relph, 1976, p. 145) proposed that to compensate for the inevitably more dispersed mode of human activity in the contemporary world, we should "let the occupied, lived-in space acquire more cohesion, become as rich as possible, and grow large with the experience of living" (p. 145). How this can be accomplished in already industrialized, modernized cities is unclear. Children and parents, however, can be expected to have ideas about manageable and useful improvements (Matthews & Limb, 1998). The United Nations Convention on the Rights of the Child (CRC) (1989), now ratified by all but the United States and Somalia, presents children's access to place and space as "a legitimate political right, together with their inclusion in those decision-making processes which concern local environments" (Matthews and Limb, 1998, p. 63).

Research that clarifies the current social and physical conditions of children's lives may prompt imaginative and helpful action. Countries or cities in earlier stages of industrialization can benefit by planning early to be watchful in how they make "places." Children and parents should participate in the design of places. School programs and practices can be responsive to research on the social and physical conditions of children's lives in their found localities. Research with children and schools can serve to support schools in being the best places they can be for children.

ACKNOWLEDGMENTS

I am very grateful to David Geoffrey Smith for his detailed criticism of previous drafts of this chapter. I also express my thanks to both Carol Leroy and David Geoffrey Smith for enlightening discussions I had with each of them on the question of community in the classroom.

REFERENCES

Adams P. C., Hoelscher S., & Till, K. E. (2001). Place in context: Rethinking humanistic geographies. In P. C. Adams, S. Hoelscher, and K. E. Till (eds.), *Textures of place: Exploring humanistic geographies* (pp. xiii-xxxiii). Minneapolis: University of Minnesota Press.

Agnew, J. A. (1989). The devaluation of place in social science. In J. A. Agnew & J. S. Duncan (Eds.), *The power of place: Bringing together geographical and sociological imaginations* (pp. 9-29). Boston: Unwin Hyman.

Aitken, S. C. (1994). *Putting children in their place.* Washington, DC: Association of American Geographers.

Alberta Learning (2001). *Removing barriers to high school completion.* Edmonton, AB: Author.

Brey, P. (1998). Space-shaping technologies and the geographical disembedding of place. In A. Light and J. M.(eds.), *Philosophy and geography III: Philosophies of place* (pp. 239–263). Lanham, Maryland: Rowman & Littlefield Publishers, Inc.

Caragata, L. (1998). New meanings of place: The place of the poor and the loss of place as a center of mediation. *Philosophy and geography Vol. III: Philosophies of Place*, pp. 215–237.

Casey, E. S. (1997). *The fate of place: A philosophical history.* Berkeley, CA: University of California Press.

Chawla, L. (1992). Childhood place attachments. In I. Altman & S. M. Low (Eds.), *Place attachment (Human, Behavior and Environment: Advances in Research and Theory Vol. 12)* (pp. 63–86). New York: Plenum Press.

Churchman, A. (2000). Is There a Place for Children in the City? *Proceedings of the World Congress on Environmental Design, 2000, Seoul, Korea* (pp. 81–93). (In English and Korean).

Crang, M. (1998). *Cultural geography.* New York: Routledge.

Denzin, N. K., & Lincoln, Y. S. (1994). Introduction: Entering the field of qualitative research. In N. K. Denzin & Y. S. Lincoln (Eds.), *Handbook of qualitative research* (pp. 1–17). Thousand Oaks, CA: Sage.

Du Bois-Reymond, M., Sunker, H. & Kruger, H. (Eds.). (2001). *Childhood in Europe: Approaches—Trends—Findings.* New York: Peter Lang.

Ellis, J. (1999). Children and place: Stories we have, stories we need. *Interchange, 30* (2). 171–190.

Ellis, J. (1998). Creative Assignments that Promote Learning and Understanding. In J. Ellis (ed.), *Teaching from Understanding: Teacher as interpretive inquirer* (pp. 57–78). New York: Garland.

Ellis, J., Small-McGinley, J., & De Fabrizio, L. (2001). *Caring for Kids in Communities: Using Mentorship, Peer Support, and Student Leadership Programs in Schools.* New York: Peter Lang Publishing.

Eyles, J. (1989). The geography of everyday life. In M. J. Clarke, K. J. Gregory & A M. Gurnell (Eds.), *Horizons in Physical Geography* (pp. 102–117). Houndmills: Macmillan.

Glassie, H. (1982). *Passing the time in Balleymenone.* Philadelphia: University of Pennsylvania Press.

Hay, R. (1988). Toward a theory of sense of place. *Trumpeter, 5*(4), 159–164.

Hay, R. (1992). An appraisal of our meaningful relationships in place. *Trumpeter 9*(3) Summer 1992, 98–105.

Holloway, S. L. & Valentine, G. (2000). Children's geographies and the new social studies of childhood. In S. L. Holloway & G. Valentine (eds.), *Children's geographies: Playing, living, learning* (pp. 1–26). New York: Routledge.

Hurren, W., Hayford, A., Carson, T., & Johnston, I. (forthcoming). Spatial practices and ethnocultural diversity in public high schools: Students negotiating spaces and identities. University of Regina and University of Alberta.

James, A. (1995). Talking of children and youth: language, socialization and culture. In V. Ami-Talai and H. Wulff (eds.), *Youth cultures and cross cultural perspective* (pp. 19–42). London: Routledge.

James, A. (1998) Imaging children 'at home' and 'at school': Movement between the spatial and temporal markers of childhood identity in Britain. In N. Rapport and A. Dawson (Eds.), *Migrants of identity: Perceptions of home in a world of movement* (pp. 139–160). New York: Berg.

Jedrej, C. & Nuttall, M. (1996). *White settlers: the impact of rural re-population in Scotland.* Luxembourg: Harwood Academic Publishers.

Katz, C. (1998). Disintegrating developments: Global economic restructuring and the eroding of ecologies of youth. In T. Skelton and G. Valentine (eds.), *Cool places: Geographies of youth cultures* (pp. 132–144). New York: Routledge.

Lynch, K. (1977). *Growing up in cities: studies of the spatial environment of adolescence in Cracow, Melbourne, Mexico City, Salta, Toluca and Warsaw.* Cambridge, MA: MIT Press.

Malone, K. (1997) Young People's Right to participate in Planning for their Future: 'Growing Up in Cities' a model of participatory research with young people. Paper presented at Young People as Creators of their Future conference, Youth Research Centre, University of Melbourne, July. Printed out from http://www2.deakin.edu.au/GUIC/news/yprihts.htm 8/8/00.

Massey, D. (1994). *Space, place and gender.* Oxford, United Kingdom: Polity Press.

Matoré, G. (1966). *Existential space. Landscape 15*(3), 5–6.

Matthews, H. & Limb, M. (1999). Defining an agenda for the geography of children: Review and prospect. *Progress in Human Geography, 23*(1), 61–90.

Monaghan, P. (2000). A child's place in the world. *The Chronicle of Higher Education,* (April 7, 2001), A21-A22.

Moore, R. C. (1986). *Children's domain: play and play space in child development.* London: Croom Helm.

Moore, R.C. & Wong, H.H. (1997). *The life history of an environmental schoolyard: Natural Learning: Creating environments for rediscovering nature's way of teaching.* Berkley: MIG Communications.

Mugerauer, R. (1994). *Interpretations on behalf of place: Environmental displacements and alternative responses.* New York: SUNY.

Oakes, T. (1997). Place and the politics of modernity. *Annals of the Association of American Geographers 87,* 509–531.

Osterman, K. F. (2000). Students' need for belonging in the school community. *Review of Educational Research,* 70(3), 323–367.

Relph, E.C. (1976). *Place and placelessness.* London: Pion.

Relph, E. (1993). Modernity and the reclamation of place. In D. Seamon (Ed.), *Dwelling, seeing, and designing: Toward a phenomenological ecology* (pp. 25–40). New York: SUNY Press.

Relph, E. (1997). *Sense of place. In S. Hanson* (Ed.). *Ten geographic ideas that changed the world* (pp. 205–226). New Brunswick, NJ: Rutgers University Press.

Schiavo, R.S. (1998). Age differences in assessment and use of a suburban neighbourhood among children and adolescents. *Children's Environments Quarterly 5,* 4–9.

Sefton-Green, J. (Ed.). (1998). *Digital diversions: Youth culture in the age of multimedia.* London, UK: UCL Press.

Smith, D.G. (in press). The mission of the hermeneutic scholar. In M. Wolfe (ed.). *The mission of the scholar: Essays in honor of Nelson Haggerson.* New York: Peter Lang

Smith, J. M., Light, A. & Roberts, D. (1998). Introduction: Philosophies and geographies of place. In A. Light and J. M. Smith (eds.), *Philosophy and geography III: Philosophies of place* (pp. 1–13). Lanham, Maryland: Rowman & Littlefield Publishers, Inc.

Stromquist, N. P. & Monkman, K. (2000). *Globalization and education: Integration and contestation across cultures.* New York: Rowman & Littlefield Publishers, Inc.

Tapscott, D. (1998). *Growing up digital: The rise of the net generation.* New York: McGraw-Hill.

Tonucci, F., & Rissotto, A. (1998). The children's city: A new way of conceiving the city in which the child is considered a parameter. *Bulletin of People-Environment Studies, No. 8/9,* 16–24.

Tuan, Yi-Fi, (1977). *Space and place: The perspective of experience.* Minneapolis: University of Minnesota Press.

Tuan, Y. (1986) *The good life.* Madison, WI: University of Wisconsin Press.

Tuan, Y. (1992). Place and culture: Analeptic for individuality and the world's indifference. In W. Franklin & M. Steiner (eds.), *Mapping American culture* (pp. 27–50). Iowa City: University of Iowa Press.

Turkle, S. (1995). *Life on the screen: Identity in the age of the internet.* London: Weidenfield.

Valentine, G. (1997). "Oh yes I can." "Oh no you can't": Children and parents' understandings of kids' competence to negotiate public space safely. *Antipode, 29*(1), 65-89.

Valentine, G. (1996). Angels and devils: Moral landscapes of childhood. *Environment and Planning D: Society and Space, 14,* 581-599.

Valentine, G., & Holloway, S. (2001). On-line dangers?: Geographies of parents' fears for children's safety in cyberspace. *The Professional Geographer, 53*(1), 71-83.

Wasserman, D., Womersley, M., & Gottlieb, S. (1998). Can a sense of place be preserved? In A. Light and J. M. Smith (eds.), *Philosophy and geography III: Philosophies of place* (pp. 191–213). Lanham, MD: Rowman & Littlefield Publishers.

Parents and Other Relationships

THIRTY

Teacher and Family Relationships

Tamar Jacobson

Unless you have already experienced parenthood, it may be difficult for you to appreciate fully the enormity of the emotions and roles that parents experience and that affect their ability to function as parents. Even if you are a parent, the diverse cultures, communities and circumstances that influence families in modern America make individual lives unique; one parenting experience and one family will be quite unlike another. (Gestwicki, 2007 pg.1)

CHILDREN AND FAMILIES

Children come with families. When they arrive at our classroom doors, children are already in the process of developing the deepest and most influential relationships of their formative years. Earliest emotional memories will affect them forever, and are being learned and developed with and by the most significant adults in their lives: family members. In order to understand children, the ways they communicate, interact, behave and learn we will need to get to know their families. Knowing the family helps us to understand the child better. Parents have primary responsibility for their children. Teachers and families are partners in helping children learn.

Teachers expect children to be alert and attentive the moment they set foot in the school building, and especially when they enter our classrooms. The reality is children were most likely affected by different family scenarios and situations even just one hour before arriving at school.

Their experiences of diverse and complex situations will influence how they feel when they walk through our classroom doors. For example, they may have witnessed a violent argument, experienced harsh scolding or punishment for taking too much time to get dressed, the car not starting, buses too full, trains late, or laundry undone leaving them nothing appropriate to wear. Some children may not have received breakfast and others were yelled at or called names as they were walking out the door. Some children might be feeling ill or did not sleep well the night before. Others woke up with warmth and security, a healthy breakfast and hugs and kisses of support to send them on their way. As we look around at the faces of children in our classrooms, we realize that each and every one has had a unique experience even a very short while before as they set out to meet us in school that morning.

Getting to know families, building those important relationships with parents, and learning how to communicate with family members is perhaps one of the most challenging aspects of the teaching profession and our work with educating children. There are a number of reasons that developing relationships with the families of children in our classrooms is complex. There are numerous and different ways of parenting, and they are affected and influenced by culture, family style, or socioeconomic status. Every unique way of parenting is developed from generations of different life experiences, ways of interacting, solving problems, and, even, expressing feelings. No one way is right or wrong. Just different. As educators we are expected to respect that. This is not easy and causes us discomfort or anxiety.

> Our survival depended upon learning about the cultural mores of our family and community: How to sit and eat at the table, what to say when, how to say it, when to be silent, how to behave with strangers or different family members, what attitudes to have about school, who we could like and dislike, and so on. When we meet people from cultures with different worldviews from us, we immediately feel unsafe. It is as if we have to give up what we learned to survive in order to open ourselves to different cultural mores. We are not sure of how other people will behave or interpret what we say. A lot of the time we do not understand them at all. That makes us uneasy and anxious. (Jacobson, 2003, pages 44 & 45)

Although it is challenging and uncomfortable, it is our responsibility as educators to overcome our discomfort through **reflective practice** where, as professionals, we come to understand why we do what we do, or how we feel the way we do. We learn to make the necessary connections with personal emotions and our own family cultures and understand and monitor how that influences our professional behavior with children and their families.

REFLECTIVE PRACTICE—BEING THOUGHTFUL, PENSIVE PRACTITIONER

Parents care about their children. Children are precious to them. However, at the same time they experience many complex feelings about their children including love, anger, guilt, fear, anxiety about doing the right thing, and many more. As teachers, it is our responsibility to learn to understand and respect the challenge of parenting while we attempt to develop relationships with families of children in our classrooms. For example, parents are often frightened of teachers and school. Parents might have had bad experiences while they were in school themselves and are not fond of the institution. They have their own memories about schools from when they were children. Some of these memories are unpleasant. School was not always a fun place for many parents of the children in our classrooms.

In addition, they might feel inferior to the teacher, who they believe knows more than they do, and so they will find it difficult to approach the school with ease and openness. Even more frightening for parents is the fact that teachers are able to know their family secrets through how their children behave and what they say. For example if a child wets her pants or behaves aggressively, the parents fear that we will think it is their fault and that they look bad. When a child is sent out into the world the family is exposed. Until a child leaves her or his home to interact with the community at large, all the family secrets are intact. Once the child goes to school the truth will come out, and parents fear being judged for what kind of parent they are through the behaviors of their children. Types of secrets include behaviors like bathroom accidents, not paying attention at group time, learning how to share or socialize, or manners at the lunch or snack table. However, they could also include larger, more serious secrets like family fights, alcoholism, sex abuse, beatings or abuse and neglect. These fears or complex emotions will affect ways that parents interact with teachers. At times they might seem defensive or confronting, or perhaps they will withdraw and keep away from the school even when invited. It is our responsibility as teachers to reach out to parents in all these different situations and find a way to help them feel emotionally safe with us.

Being judgmental, having inappropriate expectations, and not understanding our biases with regards to the diversity of families are all obstacles as we work to develop relationships with families of children in our classrooms. In this chapter, we think about how to develop the types of relationships with families that will enhance and support children's well-being and academic success. Children thrive emotionally, socially and academically when teachers and parents or guardians cooperate and collaborate. We will need to develop skills of communication, reflect on our own biases and emotions in order to break down the barriers, and address the obstacles that prevent us from developing healthy and productive relationships with families.

TEACHERS AS PARENTS

As I write this chapter, the day after Mother's Day, I think about how my son forgot to call me until very late that night. I smile to myself because now that I am older, I have decided that Mother's Day is not about my son remembering me or acknowledgment from others about how good a mother I am. It is not even about how much love I put into my time as a mother. It is about how I loved giving birth to my son. It was a privilege and honor to have him enter my life and accompany me on my turbulent and interesting journeys. I learned so much from him about myself, especially regarding unconditional love and commitment. It is I who should be remembering him on Mother's Day, and thanking him for sharing his joys and sorrows, musical talent, truthful opinions, humor and love, and, especially, for being a child of my womb, who changed my life in so many ways, forever.

Nowadays, I see a tall, lean young man standing before me. My son is thirty-four, a talented jazz pianist, and a credentialed family therapist. I hear his deep voice as he speaks. He was not always like this, for even as I see and hear him now, at the same time I can clearly recall many years ago, as if they were today, his chubby toddler cheeks and sweet little voice. He sat straight and tall in his car seat at the back, when we drove around the neighborhood, pointing at trucks or trains and calling out, "Look! Twucks" or "Look! Twains, Mommy." As a young mother I learned very early on that no one would fight for my son but me. As a result, I would always come to his school to talk with his teachers from pre-school right up until he graduated from high school. I would speak to his teachers about his progress, share with them our changing family situations, discuss ways to treat him better, and talk about concerns regarding appropriate education practices. I was also involved with the community life of his various schools whether they were in Israel (where we lived until he was fourteen), or in America after we immigrated to the States when he was fifteen. I would volunteer to cook, bake, make craft-type things for fundraisers, help out in his classrooms, or attend meetings and parent-teacher conferences. I knew that parent involvement was very important for his well-being and academic success.

You see, I am a teacher myself and learned from the beginning of my career that all children come with families. When a child enters my class, she is like an emissary from her family. Not only did I learn this in teacher education classes or staff development trainings; but I knew it because I was a child once. I have memories of my own parents' participation in my educational life. Indeed, I can recount each time my mother celebrated my accomplishments when I was growing up. I also remember the times she did not show up and how much I missed her, or felt excluded when my friends' parents were present and mine were not. It affected my general sense of well-being one way or the other.

What do you remember about your own family's involvement in your education? Did they show up for all your scholarly events to which they were invited? How did they participate in your school life? How did that make you feel? What would you have liked them to do more of, or less? What kind of a parent will you be or are you now? Will you be defensive or confronting, or will you withdraw and keep away from school? How do you think about involvement in your children's education?

TEACHERS ARE NOT PARENTING EXPERTS

We are teachers of children. Our work is not to know the best way to parent. Either we will parent our children the way we were parented because it worked for us, or, we might try something completely different because it was not pleasant for us as children. Ways of parenting are subjective, handed down from generation to generation, and as teachers we can only know the best way to parent our own children based on our life experiences. Even though teachers are not parenting experts, we care deeply about the well-being and education of children in our classes. This influences how we perceive parenting styles and causes us to be judgmental of family systems and dynamics that are different from our own. We are not here to educate parents how to parent. We are here to educate their children. Teachers do not realize that parenting is not a profession. Therefore, we have expectations of families that are inappropriate or not relevant to who they are and what they do with their children. In other words, we expect parents to be objective, or at the very least, knowledgeable about child development, treating them as if they had studied and learned about the right way to be a parent—as if it were a profession.

Subjective—Being affected by personal views, experience or background.
Objective—Being able to distance oneself from the situation and think it through.

PARENTING IS NOT A PROFESSION

It is difficult for teachers to comprehend that parenting is not a profession. When we say parents are children's first teachers, we must be careful not to confuse that with the education profession, which we have chosen as a career. Parenting is part of life, nature's way of perpetuating and nurturing our species. Teaching is a profession with a code of ethics, policies, knowledge base, which includes pedagogy and curriculum, and licensure. Anybody can be a parent. Teachers must be specialized in education and credentialed. Oftentimes we have expectations of parents that are inappropriate. We want them to understand child development or the best educational practices without having to explain that to them. We send home complicated homework assignments for them to work on with their children. In his book, *The Homework Myth: Why Our Kids Get Too Much of a Bad Thing,* Alfie Kohn describes the way homework affects family relationships (Kohn, 2006):

> Beyond its effects on parents and children, homework's negative impact—and specifically the nagging, whining, and yelling that are employed to make sure assignments are completed on time—affects families as a whole. As one writer remarked, "The parent-child relationship...is fraught with enough difficulty without giving the parent a new role as teacher" or enforcer. Ironically, the sorts of relaxed, constructive family activities that could repair the damage are among the casualties of homework's voracious consumption of time. (page 12)

We mistakenly call this *parent involvement.* We invite family members in for parent-teacher conferences and scold them for how their child behaves, demanding that they fix it at home, expecting them to follow through with what we have decided are the best remedies for improving their child's behavior or learning abilities. We are surprised and frustrated when they do not comply. We even judge them as not caring about their children because they do not follow our instructions. We mistakenly call this *empowering families.*

Some more appropriate ways that teachers can support families are by encouraging them to love their children unconditionally, and to be as subjective as possible. It is natural for parents to be attached emotionally, and, hopefully, unconditionally with their children. We can and should encourage parents that their child is their one and only—the very best—and that we understand that no one will fight for their child but them. On the other hand, as an objective and unbiased professional, we have been taught to be engaged with the whole class and be present for all children. In other words, we have learned not to have favorites and to be fair to everyone. As teachers, we are able to do this because we are the professionals. We have learned to be objective, see the bigger picture, and know what is best for the whole group as well as individual children. We understand that parents must be subjective for the good of their one child. We understand that family support and encouragement is the foundation for a child's self-worth, security and confidence. We have learned about it in child development classes, through keeping up with the current research in our professional field, and by reflecting on our own early childhood experiences within our families of origin. We know that children are more precious to families than anything else in their life.

CHILDREN ARE PRECIOUS TO PARENTS

For many years, I was the director of a large university child care center, which included five preschool and eight infant-toddler classrooms. From time to time I would receive letters from student or faculty parents expressing gratitude for the care and education their children received at the campus center. I was always reminded how precious their children were to them. Following, are examples of two letters I received from different parents when they were preparing to leave the Center. While the letters expressed gratitude, they also described how much these parents cared about their children, how sensitive they were to their children's well-being, the importance of their role as parents, and especially how precious their children were to them:

> Our daughter will be leaving your center at the end of this month. We just wanted to take the time to thank you, the teachers and staff for all your hard work and dedication. In May of 1996 we brought our daughter to your center, a scared and shy toddler, who preferred the company of teachers to children. I can remember how I would sneak in at the end of the day hoping to find her playing happily with some of the children. But a lump would grow in my throat when I would instead find her riding safely in the pack on the back of *"friend teacher"* (that's what my daughter called her). Looking back, I am extremely grateful for the patience and understanding afforded her during her first months at the center. Now my daughter leaves the center a young girl full of curiosity and eager to make new friends. We as parents leave equally anxious and excited about her future at "big school." (It is difficult to leave the security of the family-like atmosphere.) Yet we are certain that the strong foundation provided by wonderfully giving and loving teachers has instilled our daughter with the confidence that will support her throughout her elementary years. You are nurturing the future of the world and that is not an easy task. Keep up the good work! Thanks for taking such great care of our precious one. (Parent one)

> As I prepare to celebrate *my* graduation from school, I am very aware of my struggles to get this far and how so many people have helped along the way. Graduating is certainly an accomplishment—but I am most "proud of" and fulfilled by my role as mother to my children. They are more important to me than anything else in this world. In order to go to school, I had to entrust their care to others—something I found very had to do in light of my beliefs about my duties as a mother. So as I prepare to graduate, I realize just how thankful l am and how blessed I have been to have met all of you and to have your help in caring for and teaching my children. If I did not have your help to care for my children, a duty I feel is so very important I can't imagine anything more so, I would not be graduating now. Thank you, all, so much for all your giving to my kids and me, for all you have taught me about child development, and for all the love you have shown my children. (Parent two)

NEGOTIATING THE RELATIONSHIP: TEACHER AND PARENT COOPERATION

Teacher-parent cooperation is beneficial for children's socio-emotional development and academic achievement. In May 2007 a report was published by *PolicyBridge,* a non-partisan public policy think tank founded in 2005 to monitor urban policy issues affecting the quality of life for minorities in Northeast Ohio (McShepard, Goler, & Batson, 2007: www.policy-bridge.org). In a proposed *"Policy of Personal Responsibility,"* the authors base their recommendation for more involvement from parents on recent research published by the *Southwest Educational Department Laboratory* indicating:

...that students with involved parents, no matter their income or background, are more likely to earn higher grades, have better test scores, enroll in higher level programs, pass their classes, attend school regularly, have better social skills, adapt well to school, graduate high school, and go on to postsecondary education. (p. 15)

While we all know that parent involvement is beneficial, at the same time it often seems difficult for teachers and parents to cooperate. A partnership between adults who care for and educate children is complicated. For, while teachers are professional and objective educators, families are the subjective and emotional caregivers for the children. Indeed, parent-teacher cooperation is very much like a negotiation between those two very different perceptions and attitudes: one subjective and emotional and the other objective and professional.

WHAT DOES IT TAKE TO BECOME A PARENT?

Think about the following questions as you consider what your own choices or decisions might be as you contemplate becoming a parent. Does having an education influence what kind of parent you will become? Why? What kind of a relationship would you need to develop with your partner in the raising of your children? Who would you choose as a partner in life to share in the raising of your children? Would that person be a lover or a friend? What do you think about your partner's beliefs and values? What do you think about your partner's religion or culture? Would these things matter to you in raising your children? Why? Would you be willing to give up time, money, career, or whatever it takes, to become a parent? How would you negotiate that with a partner of choice? How would your financial situation play a part in parenting your children? What do you think about your physical and mental health affecting your ability to parent? What type of support systems would you need to be a competent and capable parent? What do you feel about the child's gender? Would this play a part in your parenting styles? After you discovered you were pregnant or had decided to adopt a child, how would you prepare for the future? What are any other questions you might want to explore as you consider becoming a parent? If you are already a parent, what advice could you give to future parents?

Write these answers down and discuss them with friends, peers, teachers, your own parents or counselors. What were some of the surprises (if any) that you experienced as you thought and talked about this subject? Write a summary titled: *Becoming a parent: What does it mean for me?*

CREATING A SAFE EMOTIONAL ENVIRONMENT

Now that we are reading, talking and thinking about creating a family, becoming a parent or guardian, and are beginning to understand how fearful parents are of being judged and how they all want the very best for their child, let us look at ways to negotiate an effective and productive parent-teacher relationship. But first, some reminders about how parents feel and what some of their anxieties are.

Parents are guilty from the day their child is born. They are expected to raise their children in the correct manner (whatever that means) by family members, society and the popular media.

Advice is abundant and diverse, through books, television talk shows, extended family members, religious leaders, neighbors, pediatricians, professors, teachers, and counselors. It is amazing that people feel capable of parenting at all with all the different advice they are given. Teachers must learn that parents have their own life experiences and different ways of dealing with things. Their ways of interacting, expressing feelings or solving problems could almost be considered a different language from our own. In order to understand parents without judgment, we must learn to listen to their stories. If a parent asks my advice, I usually say something like, "Well, I don't know what would work in your family, but for me, and considering the kind of family I came from, this or that works for me." In fact, my advice might not work for someone else. Our parenting styles are just too different. For example, some families physically express love with hugs and kisses, stroking and close eye contact. Others are a little more distant and not as physical.

One of the ways to make parents feel comfortable is by letting them know that we are human. Let parents get to know who you are. It is important to let parents know that you are human, fallible, flexible, and respectful of their way of parenting. Make yourselves available and approachable to parents. When I was a teacher of young children I always gave the parents my home phone number. At the first parent meeting of the year, I would tell them all about me. I shared with them stories about my marriage, my experiences as a mother, and informed them that I did not have all the answers. I have always told parents that no one will fight for their child but them, and I want them to feel safe to come and tell me anything that would help me in understanding their child better.

Practice an open door policy, where parents can feel free to drop by any time they want. Invite their concerns. If you know that parents are subjective and naturally emotionally attached to their children, you will expect them to be indignant or afraid if their child gets hurt. When a parent confronts you or is upset, the best thing is to acknowledge their pain and listen to what they have to say. Usually I say something like, "I am so sorry that happened." And then I write down all their complaints and concerns and listen carefully to what they are feeling. After that I explain what I can do to see that it does not happen again, and I warn them that it might because when children play together things happen. However, I list all the actions I can take to improve the situation and promise to apprise them of my progress. I make sure to follow through with my promise. It is important that parents feel safe and trusting with their child's teacher in order for effective communication and cooperation. As professionals we must learn to see the whole picture, the bigger picture of the classroom and the best practices for all the children. Respect parents' feelings, including anger and hurt for their child. Give them steps on how you will help, be professional, listen to all the wants and needs of parents even if you cannot meet all of them. Always write down conversation points with a parent. Take them seriously. Remember just how precious their children are to them.

INVOLVING FAMILIES AND FACILITATING COOPERATION

Welcome parents and children into your classroom every day. Mostly, children travel to school on buses, but if they are dropped off by parents, there is nothing as powerful as a warm and welcoming greeting each and every day. Families and teachers will need to communicate about many different issues relating to the care and education of children: things to bring to school; children's clothes, needs, naps, food, behaviors; the child's progress; various and sundry concerns; curriculum; fund raising; participation; meetings; holidays; religion; ideology; philosophy; and beliefs, just to name a few. Almost all of those items listed require discussion, listening, negotiation, explanation and understanding. Some will become complex and challenging conversations and others will be easier to resolve or work through together. The difficulties or ease with which problems are solved and each party is understood will depend on the family's mode of communication and the teacher's biases. It is first and foremost the teacher's responsibility to make it work. It is especially difficult for beginning teachers who feel as judged or as insecure as the parents. If you are unsure about how to react in the beginning, try and listen to the parents and get to know their way of communicating. Before you react or become defensive, try and remember: "Ah, they are being *subjective* and emotionally attached to their child. This is good. This is how it should be. I am the professional, the *objective* person and must work out what to do that will be best for *all* of the children in my class as well as each individual child."

It is important to arrange conferences twice a year where parents and teachers can discuss the child's progress and share information back and forth respectfully. If you remember the parents' subjectivity and fear of being judged, you will make an effort so that by the end of the conversation, parents leave proud and feel empowered and loving of their children. Parent-teacher conferences are not a time for scolding or warnings. Concerns should be shared and discussed all year long in a respectful and caring manner.

There are many different ways to organize whole group activities for parents: Open house before school starts; meetings with an expert guest speaker on curriculum, behavior management, children's literature, or some other topic of interest to parents; holiday parties; and general informational meetings. Inviting parents to participate and become involved in their child's education can also take many forms. For example, as a classroom teacher, I always organized a parent advisory committee where once a month parents, who acted as representatives of all the parents in the class, would meet with me to discuss any issue of concern, including curriculum, facility, teacher interactions, food, equipment, fund raising, playground or anything of specific interest to them. We would notify all the parents about participation and they were encouraged to contact the committee members with concerns that their representatives could bring up for discussion at our monthly meetings.

Parents might want to come into their child's class to share a talent, their expertise or to read a story. When I was director of the campus child care center, parents were invited to celebrate a "special day" of their choosing with their child's class. It could be related to a holiday they liked to celebrate, birthday, or anything at all. Field trips are another excellent opportunity to invite parents to participate. Teachers always need many adults, helping hands when organizing a trip with a class full of young children.

If you invite parents into your class to participate with the class in general, be aware that their child might be sensitive to sharing their parent with others. It is natural for a child and parent to want to spend time together. When parents were invited to participate in my classroom, *I* gave them one simple task—*be with your child*. I did not turn them into a helper or a teacher of the other children. If they wanted to do that and their child was willing for that to happen, I was supportive and encouraging. However, I did not expect them to take on that role.

A bulletin board is a good way to let parents know what is going on in the classroom. Articles or suggested parenting books can be posted there too, or other kinds of information that can suggest parenting support of one kind or another. Newsletters or daily news bulletins are a good way for parents to be kept up to date with what their children are learning day by day. In childcare settings, where children spend many long hours away from their parents, a notebook is a good way to communicate with parents with an intense and busy work schedule who are unable to spend time in the center. Teachers write information and parents can reply if they do not find the time to speak in person with the teacher.

Home visits are an excellent way to get to know children in their own natural environment, away from the institutional setting and the teacher's *turf* that everyone is accustomed to. When the teacher comes to the child's home she opens herself up to the parent's domain and levels the playing field.

> Home visiting has been a central part of working with families and their young children in many programs all around the country, all through the century…. Meeting in a comfortable, relaxed environment opens communication between parents, child and teacher, and can set the tone for a positive home-school relationship. (Fox-Barnett & Meyer, 1992, p. 45)

Child-sensitive home visits, where the teacher does not arrive as an educator of parents, but rather spends time specifically with the child in her home, communicates to the family that their child is of primary concern and reinforces the child's feeling of self-worth (page 46). Home visits can make an enormous difference to the quality of the relationship between teacher and parent and teacher and child. However, they take time and it is often difficult to find a way to fit them into an already busy schedule. It is a dedicated teacher, indeed, who sees this activity as worthwhile and finds a way to visit the children at home at some point in the school year.

THE BEGINNING OR NOVICE TEACHER

If you are a beginning or novice teacher, be compassionate with yourself as you learn to negotiate your relationships with families of the children in your class. Especially during your first year, you find yourself overwhelmed with *learning the ropes,* and understanding the school's culture, rules and regulations. Many of you are just happy to survive the first year and are unable to think further than surviving the day-to-day assignments of organizing and managing a classroom and getting paperwork completed for the administration (Katz, 1995). As we have discussed throughout this chapter, working with families is one of the most challenging aspects of teaching. Overcoming our biases and navigating between the subjective, emotional attachments of parents and the objective professional stance as a teacher are not easy tasks. It takes skill and practice, time, and experience and can be painful as we learn the best way to communicate appropriately and productively with families.

As you experiment with some of the suggested activities for parent participation and involvement, take it slowly and carefully. Learn which activities will be supportive and encouraging for you as a beginning teacher and try not to take on too much at once. Some teachers are comfortable sharing themselves with parents right from the beginning. Others will take a bit longer. Remember, you also come with a family. Just as the children in your class do. Your family's cultural norms are bound to be different to many of the children's families in your classroom. If, in the first year, you try one or two activities and they are successful with parents, the following year will be easier and you can add in more. Remember, if you are afraid of parents who seem defensive and passionate about the care and education of their child, they are most likely even more afraid of you! And, their children are more precious to them than anything else in the world.

However long it takes, and whatever obstacles might rise up to greet you as you develop authentic, caring, professional and respectful relationships with families, teacher-parent cooperation is a most valuable contribution to children's emotional wellbeing and academic achievement in the long run.

REFERENCES

Fox-Barnett, H. & Meyer, T. (1992). The teacher's playing at my house this week! *Young Children,* July; Vol. 47. Number 5. 45–50.

Gestwicki, C. (2007). *Home, School, and Community Relations.* Clifton Park, NY: Thomson Delmar Learning.

Jacobson, T (2003). *Confronting Our Discomfort: Clearing the Way for Anti-Bias in Early Childhood.* Portsmouth, NH: Heinemann.

Katz, L. (1995). "The Developmental Stages of Teachers" in *Talks with Teachers of Young Children: A Collection.* Stamford, CT: Ablex.

Kohn, A. (2006). *The Homework Myth: Why Our Kids Get Too Much of a Bad Thing.* Cambridge, MA: Da Capo Press.

McShepard, R., Goler, T., & Batson, M.C. (2007). The rap on culture: How anti-education messages in media, at home, and on the street hold back African American youth. *PolicyBridge, May 2007. www.policy-bridge.org*

THIRTY-ONE

Personal and Social Relations in Education

Barbara Thayer-Bacon

The term *relation* is ambiguous. Relation signifies the existential connections, a dynamic and functional interaction; it also signifies the logical relationships of terms. We speak of the overlapping and interconnecting of concepts and meanings, and we describe how things affect each other ontologically. Relationships can be personal, one-on-one exchanges as between a teacher and a student, a parent and a child, or between two lovers. We also use the term *relational* in a general manner, to describe social relationships between citizens and their country, or the relationship of men and women. We speak of relations in terms of kinship, and we say we can relate to someone else, meaning we feel sympathy toward that person or we can compare our experiences to the other. The plural use of the term *relation*, is even used to mean sexual intercourse. Given all the different ways we use this term, *relations* has a common theme of "connection" to others, which is what I want it to signify. I find it an advantage, not a disadvantage, that relation means connections in so many ways. My hope is that its many uses will remind us of the transactional nature of knowing (in the Deweyan sense of the term).[1]

For my contribution to this book I would like to explore some of the important implications of a relational approach to knowing for education in terms of personal and social relations. The definition of education is much debated, and we can find a contribution to that debate in the work of Gert Biesta within this volume. For my purposes here, I will assume that education is a studenting-teaching process that involves a teacher and a student (whose roles are fluid, flexible, and often interchangeable) and something that is taught (the curriculum, the content) in some kind of setting and in some manner (the form of instruction, the context). I will look at how the roles of teachers and students change within a school setting, given a relational focus, and I want to consider curriculum issues. We will find that a relational theory of knowing has tremendous implications for all areas of schooling as we know them today in much of the world.

This discussion concerning personal and social relations fits within a project of mine, the development of what I call a relational (e)pistemology.[2] A relational (e)pistemology is an approach to knowing that emphasizes that knowledge is something that is socially constructed by embedded and embodied people who are in relations with each other and their greater environment. We are fallible, our criteria are corrigible, and our standards are socially constructed, and thus continually in need of critique and reconstruction. A relational approach argues that knowing is something people develop as they have experiences with each other and the world around them. People improve on ideas that have been socially constructed and passed down to them by others. They do this improving by further developing their understandings and enlarging their connections. With enlarged relationships, people are able to create new meanings for their experiences. An (e)pistemology that rests on an assumption of fallibility entails pluralism, both in terms of there being no one final Answer at the end of inquiring, and also in terms of the need to be open and inclusive of others who help us compensate for our own limitations. A relational (e)pistemology strives for awareness of context and values and seeks to tolerate vagueness and ambiguities.

I will rely on assorted examples available: my own and others, experiences as teachers and students, the various conversations I have shared with others concerning schools and the tools of intuition, emotions imagination, and reason I/we have available to help me/us constructively think of some new possibilities for schools.[3] I will try to remind the reader of my own limitations and fallibility throughout the discussion by revealing my own biases and not neglecting my own contextuality. I do not want to try to ignore and diminish the political power that philosophers wield in their social roles as legitimators. I do not mean to suggest that the examples I offer or the suggestions I make are in any way final or complete, for I have argued elsewhere for the impossibility of attaining knowledge that is certain, as well as for the impossibility of attaining knowledge that is universal.[4] As a fallible social critic I need others to contribute to this discussion and help me in this redescribing effort. I need a clamor of diverse voices so I encourage your contributions to help us in our efforts to recreate anew schools that take relations to be primary.

PERSONAL RELATIONS

As we learn in Bonnie Lyon McDaniel's and Cherlyn Pÿanowski's papers within this volume, psychoanalytic philosophers focus on intimate relationships we share, as infants; with our childcare providers. More spiritually focused philosophers, such as Martin Buber and Simone Weil, focus on a very intimate relationship that we share as spiritual beings with our Thou.[5] By "intimate" I do not mean sexual, I mean relationships that are close associations, relationships between I and Thou, between one-caring and one-cared-for. Feminist scholars such as Jane Flax, Sarah Ruddick, and Nel Noddings emphasize that all of us begin our lives already in relation with our biological mothers, and that this very close relationship extends for us into the early years of our lives, according to object relations theory, as we continue the psychological birthing process with our adoptive mothers.[6] It is through our personal relationships with others that we develop a voice, an "I," a sense of who we are as unique individuals in relation to Thou. In her book *Caring*,

Nel Noddings does not just explore the intimate relationship of a mother and child in her discussion of caring relations, but she also considers the relationship between a teacher and student as another example of a caring relationship. She further explores the personal relationship between teachers and students in her follow-up book, *The Challenge to Care in Schools*.[7]

Noddings's description of teacher-student relationships in terms of one-caring and one-cared-for is considered controversial in the United States for many reasons, one of which is the distinction that Americans make between private and public relations. It is expected that parents and their children, and friends and lovers, have close personal relationships; these are all considered examples of private relationships. Teachers and students, and bosses and their employees are expected to have a public relationship that is therefore not intimate and personal. In the United States, we fear that if teachers establish personal relationships with their students this means that students will be vulnerable to manipulation and indoctrination, including physical and psychological abuse. We recognize that teachers wield great power over students in their roles as dispensers of knowledge and evaluators and judges of what students have learned. Teachers assign grades to students, work, and these grades help to determine whether or not students have the opportunity for the good life, in terms of employment and higher education. We also recognize that teachers are responsible for the safety and well-being of their students and we realize that teachers have great influence on the quality of students' daily lives as a result of teacher interactions with others. Teachers witness and monitor students' behavior.

Yet certainly parents (childcare providers) wield even greater power over their children than schoolteachers. In fact, children's very survival depends on their patents, and still we acknowledge the importance of parents establishing personal relationships with their children We even argue that if parents are unable or unwilling to establish caring relationships with their children, those children could be hindered in their growth and development and will have to find ways to compensate for this lack. If caring is so important in parental relationships despite even greater risk of abuse, why is the establishment of caring relationships with students not important for teachers in school settings? I want to suggest that in fact it is very important for teachers to establish caring relationships with their students. One of the most vital implications of relations as primary is that those of us working in schools need to focus our attention on the relationships teachers have with their students, as well as the relationships students have with each other. A relational approach to knowing describes knowers as social beings-in-relation-with-others, not as isolated individuals. As social beings-in-relation-with-others, we must not only focus on relationships, but also ensure that these relationships are caring rather than harmful, oppressive ones. Focus on relational education recognizes and attempts to address the political powers involved in relationships, both personally and socially.

Schools in America currently focus predominantly on the outcomes and products of schooling. Often these are entirely disconnected from the relational processes of learning. Students become objects who must produce a certain amount and quality of products in order to graduate, and teachers become the managers of this production effort whose job security and salaries depend on how productive their students are. Current emphasis on proficiency exams in the United States, attempts to hold teachers accountable and make sure all students are able to produce the predetermined outcomes, only further enhance a product focus. A relational approach to education insists that we must focus on the process of learning and consider very deeply how we can help students, as social beings-in-relation-with-others, become knowers. While all are born with the possibility of becoming knowers, we can only actualize that possibility if others, such as our family members and friends and schoolteachers, encourage and support our efforts.

I am suggesting that schooling (and the larger process of educating) at its best is a personal, relational process between a student and a teacher. I want to suggest, in agreement with Noddings, that teachers need to establish caring relationships with their students, in which students are active participants able to reject relationships with their teachers if the latter are not perceived as caring While there are many false forms of caring, a genuine caring relationship is one that is good, not harmful to either the one-caring or the one-cared-for.[8] A caring relationship is based on treating the other with respect and dignity, so that a trusting relationship can develop between the two. In a caring relationship, teachers must focus their efforts on valuing and appreciating students' needs and learning what their interests and desires are. Teachers should, as far as possible, suspend their own beliefs, feelings, and values and listen attentively and generously to their students. This is the only way they can be assured of coming close to understanding their students, and can therefore help to meet students' needs to know. This effort of attending to the needs of others helps assure us that the teaching-student relationship will be a caring one, and not one that is manipulative or harmful to the student or teacher

In most middle schools, high schools, and colleges in America, it is next to impossible for teachers to establish caring relationships with their students. The larger the population in the school is and the more students each individual teacher has, the more difficult the establishing of caring teacher-student relationships becomes. It is not humanly possible to establish caring relationships with a large number of people. There is just not enough time in each day to be able to listen attentively to everyone. One teacher can only be available, approachable, and attentive to so many people, and most teachers are asked to teach more students than they can possibly get to know well. Not only are teachers and students not able to establish caring relationships with each other in most upper-level schools, but also students are not able to establish caring relationships with other students either, for there are too many students in each classroom and too little time to get to know each other.

Even though we make it difficult for teachers to establish caring relationships with their students due to the working conditions, it is easy to point to examples that show we do value caring teacher-student relationships. Schools, including colleges, will advertise that one of their advantages is their smaller number of students, and they will boast about their student-teacher ratio as a way to attract students to their school. They will point out that the smaller the student teacher ratio, the more likely that individual students will receive the attention they need from their teachers to help them learn. Schools that offer flexible, alternative forms of scheduling where students can enjoy more time with their teachers and the possibility of having their teachers as mentors throughout their schooling experience will advertise these possibilities as ways to attract students to their campus. Again, the schools will acknowledge the value of students being able to work closely and over extended periods of time with their teachers, for it helps the students learn and succeed in school. And campuses will offer faculty smaller numbers of classes to teach and fewer students as incentives to teach there. They will point out that faculty teaching there have more time to prepare for their classes as well as more time with their students. The gift of more time and fewer students will make it more likely that potential faculty members will be able to do a good job as teachers and enjoy the intrinsic rewards of teaching, such as getting to know their students and watching them grow as a result of working with them. In general, the more prestigious the university, college, elementary, or secondary school is, the smaller the faculty-student ratio is and the lighter the faculty teaching load is.

The closest the majority of students in public schools come to being able to establish caring relationships with their teachers and their classmates is when students are in preschool, kindergarten, and lower elementary grades. Several states in the United States have established public policies limiting the number of students who can be in lower grade levels to no more than twenty, and often each classroom will have two teachers or a teacher and a classroom aide (non-certified teacher). Again, such policies demonstrate that we do recognize the value of teacher-student relationships. With no more than twenty students, two adults, and most of each day to be together, there is much more of a chance for students and teachers to establish caring relationships with each other.

Sometimes students will have the opportunity to establish caring relationships with teachers if they are placed in special education or bilingual education classes, for these teachers may teach the same students for up to three years, depending on their school's resources and policies. Also, some smaller public schools only have one art, music, foreign language, or physical education teacher, and so that teacher will have the same students for extended periods of time, sometimes stretching over the entire time the student is enrolled in the school. However, many of these teachers are severely limited in terms of the amount of time they spend with students and are even more overwhelmed by the sheer number of students enrolled in a school if they are the only gym, art, or music teacher for the entire school enrollment. Even worse, they can be the "specials" teacher for two or three schools.

As a Montessori teacher, I had even more opportunity to establish caring relationships with my students than most elementary teachers.[9] Not only were my classroom sizes smaller (the largest class I had was twenty-three students), I also had classroom co-teachers, and the students were in my classroom for most of the day. I also had the students in my classroom for three years. Three years of time with a student makes a big difference, and that is the typical structure for Montessori classrooms; students ages 3–6, 6–9, and 9–12 years are together in the same room for three years. As some students graduate each year and move on, and other, younger students move into the classroom each year, the child ideally stays in the same room, with the same teacher, and a core of other students around the same age, for three years. I found that as a teacher in such a setting not only was it possible for me to establish caring relationships with my students, it was necessary. Neither the students nor I could look forward to another year of being together unless we were able to relate to each other in a caring manner. And students could not function effectively with the same students in their classroom year after year unless they were able to learn how to get along. My classroom became like an extended family, which in included the students' family members as well, many of whom I still hear from.

I am not suggesting that teachers and students need to establish caring relationships in schools because students are lacking these experiences in their home settings as Jane Roland Martin does in her book *The Schoolhome*, though that is sadly often true.[10] Like Noddings, I want to suggest that even students experiencing significant caring relationships in their home settings will benefit from experiencing caring relationships with their teachers. The establishment of personal, close relationships with teachers and peers will help students become knowers able to participate in and contribute to the knowing process. It will help them develop their own voice and learn how to express it, for they can feel confident that others will listen generously. And they will be able to learn from other students' voices as well. It will help them gain confidence in their own abilities, for they will feel valued and affirmed by the attention they receive. Students will thrive under such conditions. Why should only a few students be allowed the opportunity to experience close, personal relationships with their teachers and other students—those who come from wealthy families, attend Montessori schools, or live in small, isolated locations? There are many things we can do to help make it possible for all students and teachers to experience caring relationships.

One suggestion is to make classroom sizes smaller, following the early childhood/younger elementary policy of no more than twenty students in a classroom. Another suggestion is to assign more than one teacher to a classroom. A third suggestion is to lengthen the time students spend in one classroom with each other and their teachers, as well as increase the number of times students can have the same teacher. Some schools are trying similar ideas, such as changing their scheduling formats to what many are calling "block scheduling, which gives students more time in a classroom each day with a teacher. Other schools are creating "schools within schools" as ways of breaking down large student populations into smaller groups, and having the same teachers work as a team with the same students so students can become better known in a more holistic manner by their teachers and classmates. Some schools are creating advising/mentoring programs where all teachers are assigned a small number of students to meet with regularly and consistently throughout the student's enrollment in school. These and other related practices will help students and teachers have more chances to develop personal relationships with each other.

Now let's come back to the concerns people express about the studenting-teaching relationship being a personal, caring one. In no way am I suggesting that any student, or teacher for that matter, should have to experience a teaching-studenting relationship with someone who is manipulative or abusive. Students should not have to fear their teachers or protect themselves from teachers (or vice versa). Many teachers do not know how to relate to other people in healthy, constructive ways, and they use teaching as an opportunity to dominate and oppress others. These people should not be allowed to harm our children. And unfortunately, today there are many students who are so troubled that they are a danger to other students and teachers as well. These students should not be allowed to harm each other or their teachers. But these are extreme examples that are signs of unhealthy social conditions The extremes do not diminish the importance of establishing caring relationships with each other; they underscore how important caring relationships are. A relational approach to education, and (e)pistemology, describes knowers as social beings-in-relation-with-others, not as isolated individuals. It therefore emphasizes that education is a relational process between beings who are in relation with each other. Wherever people are together in relation with each other there will be political factors. A relational approach to knowing does not seek the impossible task of getting rid of political factors, nor does it try to ignore them. Rather, a relational focus highlights political factors and underscores them so we can address them. I can now address political factors further by turning to a discussion of social relations, and so I move on to consider social relations in terms of schooling.

SOCIAL RELATIONS

A relational approach to knowing argues that the relationships we experience with others are both personal and social; they are what Dewey called transactional relationships. We are first of all social beings who are greatly affected by others, but we also greatly affect others right from the start. We are social beings who exist in relation to others at an intimate level as well as at a generalized level. We are selves-in-relation-with-others. There is a direct link between our individual subjectivity and our general sociality.

The implications of a transactional view of selves-in-relation-to-others are many. For one we cannot focus just on the individual student, or even the student-teacher relationship, at a personal level alone, for we must take into consideration the larger social context in which both student and teacher are embedded. All of us are historical, locally situated beings. As soon as we widen our lens to take into consideration the larger social context placed within a historical timeframe, all sorts of exciting possibilities become available to us. With a larger social and historical context, we now have a variety of perspectives from which to choose. We now can have a greater understanding of our own situatedness, for we can compare ourselves to others. Others draw attention to themselves and us, through their difference; for while they may have much in common with us, they also are irreducibly distinct and different from us. They offer us contrasting image; they cause ruptures in our understanding, and they cause discontinuities. These contrasts others offer allow us the chance to become more conscious of who we are and more self-reflective These contrasts also expose us to other possibilities and differences and help to stimulate our ideas of what is possible Then we can even change something about ourselves that we do not like. We can grow and develop further; we can enlarge our thinking, as Benhabib says.[11]

Paradoxically, at the same time that a relational approach to knowing and education implies that schools need to offer students and teachers ways to develop caring relationships by lowering the student-teacher ratio and increasing the time students and teachers have with each other, it also implies that students need to be exposed to diversity. A relational approach to knowing argues that we learn more about our own situatedness by having ourselves reflected back to us by others not like us. As Cris Mayo argues next, the more variety and differences in the others we are exposed to, the more perspective we will be able to gain on ourselves Since we begin our lives as immature individuals who have not developed a sense of self yet, we are exposed to our culture before we are able to critique the culture we are exposed to. As Jim Garrison says, culture has us before we have it.[12] We become acculturated by the others who care for us. That acculturation process happens unconsciously, automatically, so that we are not even aware that it is taking place. Thus, when we begin to interact with others not like us, we begin with an assumption that others are like us, not even realizing the concept of difference. As Biesta points out, we become aware of our differences through our interactions with others, through our efforts to establish common meanings so that we can communicate and relate to each other, and all the mishaps and miscommunications we experience along the way. It is others not like us who help us become more conscious and aware of our own contextuality. They wake us up and make us notice what before we had taken for granted.[13]

Therefore, while I recommended that students need to experience small classroom sizes in the previous section, I also want to say that students need to experience diverse perspectives. What does it mean "to experience diverse perspectives"? There are many levels and degrees of diversity. Placing any two students together will create diversity, for there will be differences between the two even if they come from the same family, as any siblings and even twins can attest to Two students from two different families already walk into a classroom with a great deal of diversity, as well as commonality, between them. Add in differences in ages or make the classroom coeducational and we now have more differences that will be represented. If the students come from different socioeconomic backgrounds, then even more differences will be represented, and that's without even introducing differences due to religious and ethnic backgrounds. Because the United States is a very diverse country with people who have immigrated here from all over the world, it is not so difficult to find classrooms with a small number of students in them (twenty) who will still represent a lot of diversity. Even in more isolated parts of the country, or in other countries that are more homogenous, it is still the case that there will be differences represented that can teach us a lot. Yet it is possible to import still more differences into a small classroom community by assuring that diversity is represented in the curriculum. Maybe recommending small classroom sizes that are diverse is not quite so difficult after all. What it requires is the embracing of a multicultural curriculum.

What do I mean by "a multicultural curriculum"? Sonia Nieto's *Affirming Diversity*, is an excellent source for considering the concept of multicultural education. Her book is used in many college classrooms across the United States that focus on helping future teachers understand what a multicultural curriculum should entail.[14] While I have disagreements with some of Nieto's theory—in particular her Marxist critical theory, which risks sliding into a God's-eye view of how the world should be transformed—I do think her definition of multicultural education represents a fine example of what a relational approach to knowing and education implies. Nieto does not recommend that students should enroll in a class on various cultures during the time they are matriculated in schools. She does not recommend we only study various cultures, for example during Black History month, or Latino, Native American, or Women's History month. Nieto defines a multicultural curriculum as one that is basic and pervasive and for all students, in that culture becomes a significant way for framing all subject areas taught each day. Students should not just learn about other cultures in their foreign language classes, but in their English, science, history, math, and geography classes as well on a daily basis. In all subject areas culture should not be just a "tag on" that we add at the end of each chapter, as a supplemental text, but rather, culture should be used to frame the way we learn about the subject areas.

Following her advice, students will not just learn about the American Revolutionary War, but they will learn various perspectives of the Revolution: the British, the Founding Fathers, the indigenous tribes that lived in the area, the black slaves of the Founding Fathers, and the Founding Fathers' wives, as well as the non property owners working in America at the time. The more world views introduced into a subject area, the more students will become conscious that there are differences in opinions and a variety of experiences. Teaching subject areas through a cultural lens allows students to gain a greater awareness of their own embeddedness, as well as greater understanding of others. Importantly, a multicultural curriculum offers students ways to learn how to critique the various viewpoints represented, including the majority view that is easily taken for granted and allowed to remain invisible as the established norm against which other worldviews are measured.

Nieto defines a multicultural education as one that teaches students to be critical thinkers able to critique the very curriculum they are taught. By teaching students subject areas through a cultural framing, they become aware of the situatedness of the various subject areas themselves. They learn not only about science, but also that science is influenced by different schools of thought and that there is more than one way to view science. They learn that scientific theories have changed and developed over time as scientists have gone through paradigm shifts, thus not only helping students critique past scientific theories but also making them aware that the current theories of science they are learning will change over time as well. Students learn not only the situatedness of the various subject areas they study, but also the limitations of their various sources of knowledge, their teachers—including their schoolteachers—and their texts. A multicultural curriculum teaches students about situated truths that are qualified by as much evidence as we can offer. A multicultural curriculum teaches students that criteria and standards for judging the evidence we offer change over time and can be corrected and improved on A multicultural curriculum teaches students that the world in which we live is a pluralistic world supported by a variety of truths. It does not represent our struggles to gain knowledge as leading us to one final answer on which in the end we will all agree.[15]

We can therefore anticipate the kinds of worries a recommendation of teaching through a multicultural curriculum might trigger. Many concerns will center on feats of relativism. People worry that teaching students through a multicultural curriculum will lead them to become cynical and critical of all sources once they realize no source has the Truth and all the Answers. They worry that schoolteachers will lose students, respect and their authority, as teachers will be undermined if students are taught that their teachers cannot serve as a final source of knowledge. Some also worry that whole cultures will be undermined, for students will question the very culture their teachers, including their parents, are trying to teach them. Many fear that teaching a multicultural curriculum will incite the youth to civil disobedience, and it will lead to chaos and the undermining of basic social values (of which Socrates was accused by Athenians).

Awareness of diversity highlights our own fallibility. It emphasizes that none of us has a God's-eye view of the world; we are all embedded and embodied within the world. None of us are absolute authorities, including our schoolteachers. A relational (e)pistemology implies that we must change the way we view our teachers. They can no longer be viewed as the experts they have been historically portrayed as (I am pointing here to the topic of authority, which Charles Bingham addresses in his chapter in this volume). Teachers become other inquirers, along with students. Teachers become facilitators, resources, and guides, but not expert authorities. At the same time, teachers are still able to critique existing knowledge, as are students. Teachers and students become social critics, able to deconstruct and reconstruct, and offer new theories and contribute to the constructing of new knowledge with the help of others.

Others worry that in teaching students about diverse perspectives they will lack a commonality and cohesiveness that pulls them, together as citizens. If we emphasize our differences and strangeness, the irreducibility of our alterity, how can we ever hope to learn how to work together with each other and establish grounds of commonality, on which communities depend? And, if we teach students diverse curriculums, how will we give them a common base of knowledge from which to be able to relate and communicate with each other? Still others worry that in teaching a multicultural curriculum, there are only going to be so many perspectives we can include, simply due to lack of time, not to mention lack of resources and knowledge. So which ones will we include and which ones will we leave out? For every worldview we include in our curriculum, there is another one we must leave out. On what grounds will we decide? For decide we must.

A relational education and (e)pistemology, with its emphasis on social relations, highlights our similarities with others as well as our differences. It highlights how each of us is uniquely affected by our cultural surroundings, while at the same time emphasizing that all of us share that commonality of cultural influences. A relational approach to knowing underscores our limitations and contextuality, while at the same time pointing out that all of us are limited, contextual beings, thus showing how much we also share in common. A relational (e)pistemology is a humbling approach to knowing that insists we must always reconsider the criteria we use to make curriculum decisions about what to include and what to leave out. We must always remind our students and ourselves that we are not able to be all-inclusive, and that there are many worldviews worthy of our consideration that are beyond our reach. At the same time, we must help our students learn how to critique various perspectives, once they have attempted to generously understand them, for some ideas are worth rejecting. Our theories of knowledge are qualified by as much evidence as we can socially muster, so that it is not the case that we must accept anything as good, and yet at the same time we cannot accept anything as certain, fixed, and final. A relational approach to knowing helps us critique cultural influences and avoid social determinism, while at the same time our transactional relationships with others remind us that we are not alone: We are social-beings-in-relation-with-others, thus avoiding solipsism as well.

CONCLUSION

I focused this chapter on some specific recommendations for schools that a relational approach to knowing implies in terms of personal and social relations, in order to help us begin to explore how our schools might look if we see them through a relational lens. The specific recommendations I made include:

Teachers need to establish caring relationships with their students.

All students need to be exposed to diversity through a multicultural curriculum.

I agree with psychoanalytic scholars that all of us begin our lives already in relation with our biological mothers and that this time extends into the early years of our lives with our childcare providers. Psychoanalytic scholars help us understand that we develop a "core identity," as Jane Flax calls it, a "voice," even a multi various, or fractured one through our personal relationships with others. These others are like us and not like us in many ways. The ways in which they are the same and different from us help us develop our identities and make us more aware of our own context and differences. With that awareness come chances for us to critique and change ourselves.

In agreement with Nel Noddings, I have argued that the need for caring personal relationships with others extends into school settings with teachers and other students. Experiencing caring personal relationships in schools gives students chances to further develop their voices by enlarging their social contexts beyond the boundaries of their immediate families and childcare providers. Extending the diversity of voices students are exposed to even further through a multicultural curriculum increases the ranges of social contexts and offers students even more chances to become stable in their self-identities as well as better able to critique and change themselves I tried to bring out tensions and concerns people have about teachers establishing caring relations with students as well as with teachers teaching a multicultural curriculum. These concerns center on fears of social determinism and relativism, for example. They point us to the powerful impact relations have on our lives and underscore their dangers. However, I did not point to these dangers so that we could draw the conclusion that relations should be ignored or diminished. Rather, I pointed to dangers in relations so these dangers could serve to help remind us and emphasize for us the importance of considering carefully the kinds of relationships our children experience in schools and the quality of the curriculum to which they are exposed.

If this discussion has helped to connect theory with practice, enhance the reader's understanding of the relational theories presented in other chapters as well as within this chapter, and demonstrate the kinds of impact a relational approach to knowing can have for our daily living, in particular our schools, then I have achieved my goals. How we teach our children has such a profound affect on how they will relate to the world as adults.

NOTES

1. From introduction to Barbara Thayer-Bacon, *Relational "(e)pistemologies"* (New York and London: Peter Lang Publishers, 2003). Parts of this chapter are derived from Chapter 9 of *Relational "(e)pistemologies"* as well. "Transaction" is a term Dewey used late in his career in *Knowing and the Known*, with A. Bentley. Earlier in his career he used the term "interaction." Whereas "interaction" treated individuals as if they were autonomous, like billiard balls that bounce off of each other without changing each other as a result, "transaction" emphasizes that individuals are not autonomous, but are always in relation with others and are always already affecting each other as a result of their contact with each other. "Transaction" is a more fluid, porous description of individuals that emphasizes how leaky the boundaries are between individuals and others, as well as emphasizing that the relationship between individuals and others is one that is in motion (trans-action). John Dewey and Arthur Bentley, *Knowing and the Known* (Boston: Beacon Press, 1949, 1960).

2. The lower case "e" in (e)pistemology is used to symbolize a non transcendent epistemology, instead of a transcendent Epistemology, which I capitalize to distinguish.

3. Barbara Thayer-Bacon, *Transforming Critical Thinking: Thinking Constructively* (New York: Teachers College Press, 2000).

4. Thayer-Bacon, Relational "(e)pistemologies" , Chapters 1 and 2.

5. Martin Buber, *I and Thou* 2nd ed., trans. Ronald G. Smith (New York Charles Scribner's Sons, 1923, 1937, 1958); Simone Weil, *The Simone Weil Reader,* ed. George A. Panichas (New York: David McKay Co., Inc., 1977).

6. Jane Flax, *Thinking Fragments: Psychoanalysis, Feminism, and Postmodern in Contemporary West* (Berkeley: University of California Press, 1990); Nel Noddings, *Caring: A Feminine Approach to Ethics and Moral Education* (Berkeley, CA: University of California Press, 1984); Nel Noddings, *The Challenge to Care in Schools: An Alternative Approach to Education* (New York Teachers College Press, 1992); Sarah Ruddick, *Maternal Thinking: Toward a Politics of Peace* (Boston: Beacon Press,1989).

7. Noddings, *Caring* and *The Challenge to Care in Schools*

8. Barbara Thayer-Bacon, "The Power of Caring," in *Philosophical Studies in Education* (Ohio Valley Philosophy of Education Society, 1997), 1–32.

9. I am an American Montessori Society (AMS) certified elementary Montessori teacher, and I taught in Montessori schools from 1981 to 1987. My own children all attended Montessori schools from around the age of three for as long as they were able to attend, depending on where we lived at the time (twenty-five years total). Sources for information on the Montes—sori method of instruction include Maria Montessori, *The Discovery of the Child*, 2nd ed., trans. M. Josephy Costelloe (New York , Ballantine, 1972); Maria Montessori, *The Secret of Childhood* 2nd ed., trans M. Josephy Costelloe (New York, Ballantine, 1977), and your nearest Montessori teacher training program. Listings of teacher training programs can be found by contacting the American Montessori Society (AMS) and the International Association of Montessori Societies. (IAMS).

10. Jane Roland Martin, *The Schoolhome: Rethinking Schools for Changing Families* (Cambridge, MA; Harvard University Press, 1992).

11. Seyla Benhabib, *Situating the Self: Gender; Community and Postmodernism* (New York: Routledge. 1992).

12. James W. Garrison, "A Deweyan Theory of Democratic Listening," *Educational Theory* 46, no. 4 (1996). 429–451.

13. See Maxine Greene's work for wonderful discussions on the idea of helping students become awake and aware, especially her *Teacher as Stranger: Educational Philosophy for the Modern Age* (Belmont, CA: Wadsworth Publishing Co., 1973) and *Releasing the Imagination: Essays on Education, the Arts, and Social Change* (San Francisco: Jossey-Bass Publishers, 1995).

14. Sonia Nieto, *Affirming Diversity: The Socio political Context of Multicultural Education* (White Plains, NY: Longman, 1992).

15. What I describe here I have labeled elsewhere "qualified relativism." See Thayer -Bacon, "Pragmatism and Feminism as Qualified Relativism," *Studies in Philosophy and Education,* in press.

THIRTY-TWO

Relations Are Difficult

Cris Mayo

There has been much attention recently to the resistance on the part of white or other majority students to anti-bias curriculum characterized as "non engagement" by Rudolfo Chavez Chavez, and James O'Donnell; the difficulties of bringing majority students into a fuller understanding of their privilege and their active ignorance of social divisions is a key obstacle to pulling white students out of their comfort with the world as they see it into the activity of challenging social inequities.[1] At the base of these concerns over dominant students' resistance is a realization that those students are not relating to the topic of bias. Perhaps because of their social status, some dominant students are disinterested in finding out how their passive acceptance of privilege means that their relationships with nondominant people will be difficult and always negotiated through the experience of power imbalance. In order to address the problem of dominant students opting out of forging relationships across the divides of race, gender, class, and sexuality, some multicultural and anti-bias educators have attempted to make the classroom a place apart from the world of social fractures, a place where dialogue across difference can happen outside the context of difficult relations. I will argue that the attempt to make relationships less difficult does a disservice to the abilities of students to thrash out the challenges that they face in a world rife with inequalities.

While the kind of approach to diversity that reassures students that "we're all different from one another" is one way to engage students, it does so by first providing comfort in everyone's equal participation in the issue of diversity. The comforting form of multiculturalism paints the world as diverse, knowable, and potentially pacific in its unproblematic leveling of different subjectivities. This sort of diversity education seeks to address injustice by making all students feel at home in a world of diversity. It is my contention that the figure of "home" and "domestic relations" does much to derail what I take to be necessary components of anti-racist education. In short, these homeward trends in education forestall precisely the sort of alienation toward ourselves and others that would better facilitate an examination of the power relations undergirding racialized subjectivity and race relations. In addition, by positing some sort of home as the goal and space of education, students are discouraged from entering into relations with others out in the world. So I want to argue that education ought not be home. By doing so, I am not suggesting students learn alone, but that they learn together with others with whom they may not find domestic bliss.

In this chapter I trace out the relationship among the themes of aporia, the uncanny, and vertigo, and use these connections to criticize a trend that links knowledge with the desire for home. First, I examine the necessary break with habit that marks the beginning of thinking and acting differently, of having to face and understand an obstacle in order to stop and think. I connect the educational use of aporia with a form of the uncanny, where the operation of ignorance is not blank, but is instead a weighted ignorance, aware of something that lingers in an uncomfortable state that wavers between familiar and unfamiliar. I contend that vertigo is a state of discomfort that is aware of this fearful familiarity that has been repressed. I suggest in conclusion that the initial suspicions attending the uncanny and the vertiginous responsibility of accounting for one's place in the world are useful antidotes to the problems attending educational comfort.

To illustrate the dynamics of comfort, the uncanny, and vertigo, I examine contemporary writings on feminism, race, and education. Jane Roland Martin argues that schools ought to reflect more of the domestic, while Bernice Johnson Reagon and Minnie Bruce Pratt strongly link critical reflection and political action with a move away from the desire to have a comfortable home, a move toward struggles and relations with others. I want to support this latter move away from caring, not because theorists are incorrect when they assert that we ought to care, but because their message too easily traps us into a therapeutic, one-on-one caring relationship with students. This domestic relation impedes our obligation to push students (and ourselves) out into the responsibility of relations with others in ways that are unlikely to lead to domestic and cozy comfort. I do not mean this as a fully heartless response to dynamics of power, subjectivity, and responsibility, but I want to account for the central role the inequalities of the world have in maintaining home as a place apart and a place of studied ignorance.[2]

In a time when the version of home in education all too often collapses into explanations of student attitude based on their "family background," when students become the objects of care through therapeutic forms of education including calls for empathy and connection, home is a problematic concept as yet to be fully taken apart. This is especially problematic as social inequality collapses into discourses of trauma, and when conservative as well as progressive voices call for home schooling. Each of these moves has in common a representation of learning as comfort, an understanding of relations with others as psychologically integrating. Instead education ought to cultivate alienation and an alienated subjectivity.[3] The aporia, the uncanny, and the unsettling are the very reason we engage in education, and we ought to embrace the discomforts of obstacles and understand our engagements with the world and others fraught with difficulty. Rather than shying away from these difficulties, they should find a central place in education that cultivates an appreciation for the discomforts of the world over the purported comforts of home.

DOMESTICATING EDUCATION

In contrast with the notion of education as necessarily discomforting, some recent theorists have argued that education might be made more socially responsible—more worldly—by making it more homelike. As Jane Roland Martin advocates education for domestic tranquility, she pushes us to think "about the kind of home we want our nation to be and the kind of family we want its inhabitants to be."[4] In her book-length work, *The Schoolhome*,[5] and in other versions of what I will refer to as therapeutic multiculturalism, education is linked also with the development of comfort in the world. These works advocate for schools to more closely resemble the home cultures of all students, just as they have always purportedly resembled the home culture of white middle-class students. What all of these versions of education have in common is the notion that learning ought to be comforting, that situations in which students and teachers confront and interrogate one another and new ideas ought not to be so contentious that students prefer to retreat to the place of home. But the solutions suggested in these calls for homelike versions of schools and family like versions of social space neglect an important distinction: Public space is not private space (and I would argue, following Catharine MacKinnon, neither is private space so private for women, or for other groups). To return public school to the space of family comfort, of course, presupposes that families are comfortable places. Martin is well aware that the domestic sphere[6] as currently constituted is not an ideal model, recounting the pervasiveness of domestic violence in what currently serves as the domestic sphere.' She is not advocating, of course, for the continuation of current domestic problems but for the best form of the domestic.... Martin argues that we give little attention to what we take to be our natural relations of home, and too much attention to cultivating the ability of students to enter the public. As such, she argues, the domestic becomes something "we must learn to go beyond."[7] She argues against an education that concentrates on the civic virtues of citizenship and patriotism, contending that education ought to cultivate "a commitment to safety—bodily and psychological integrity."[8] I think the desire for safety maintains social relationships of inequality and want to instead argue that the very contentiousness of public (and private) spaces is eroded and elided when models of education that seek to soothe students overwhelm models of education that seek to disturb them. I strongly disagree, then, with Martin's assertion that "we reclaim the civic or public realm as a domestic domain"[9] even if this task is undertaken to bring tranquility to the domestic. Tranquility is too close to an easy status quo. Further, the challenges facing anti-bias education are not so easily solved, and cultivating our students' capacities to grapple with difficult relations remains our greatest challenge.

STUNNING IGNORANCE

The process of education confronts the rootedness of home with the unmooring of relations of others; the purpose of liberal education is touted as that which removes students from a world "lapped round with locality."[10] While liberal education has been criticized for installing a particular version of the world that too closely resembles the "home" of some students, it is worth considering the importance of educational projects that attempt to move majority students out of the home that may have maintained their complacent ignorance. Minority students already experience this wrench away from comfort, and already know that they must know at least two worlds in order to negotiate schooling. My point is not to magnify their discomfort but to help to show how the experience of reorienting oneself in a variety of contexts can be of educational use. Honing the critical possibilities of this process can help both minority students who already engage in reorientation as a matter of course, and it can help majority students who haven't felt the need to reorient themselves or who don't experience shifts in context that stun them into reconsideration of their knowledge and practices.

Recentering "aporia" in education may be one way to overcome the "non engagement" of majority students and to illuminate the knowledge-making abilities of minority students. Rather than focusing on what majority students know, centralizing aporia would move the educational project to focus on what they don't know. The task becomes to stun them with their own socially acceptable ignorance. This process recapitulates Socrates' account of the difficulties of learning. Socrates describes the ability to be open to learning in physically uncomfortable and unsettling terms: turning one's head toward knowledge—or, as Meno describes his experience of Socrates' questioning, being stung by a stingray and numbed in the pursuit of knowledge.[11] To stimulate these difficulties, rather than avert them, Socrates sorts through these obstacles to knowledge with interlocutors with whom he disagrees. In other words, he does not shy away from people who most doubt and disparage him, nor does he shy away from people whose practices he abhors. This, to a certain extent, might encourage a view of knowledge as that which requires discussion, dispute, and adversity. Socrates views his place in the world as necessarily contentious. Certainly his refusal to leave Athens and the polis, even when it meant his death, indicates his willingness to remain in conflict rather than seek safety. The polis was of course not ideal; certainly its existence depended on the exploitation of others: slaves, women, non-Greeks. Further, it is plausible to interpret Socrates' turn to knowledge from the otherworld as indicating that knowledge is discovered, not created. But for the purposes of this examination of the educational use of aporia, my focus is on the capacity to grapple with the disabling potential of one's purported "knowledge" in order to get around what is actually one's ignorance.

As much as obstacles pull the learner into a realization of ignorance, the aporia is filled, eventually, by what the learner already knew in the other world. Whether one views this as the capacity to learn that preexists the particular use to which it is put or the social (or spiritual) ground on which all knowledge rests, Socrates indicates that the learner, even in the deepest perplexity, still has familiarity with the knowledge he or she does not know. This process requires, most importantly, the recognition of the contours of ignorance that structure the mistaken presumption of knowledge. So the first aid that Socrates provides for antiracist education is the reminder that ignorance is a necessary starting point, but that ignorance is not empty. Ignorance is the workings of a solipsism that is unable to see that the world may be understood differently by others. When that solipsism confronts itself and sees itself as an obstacle, there is potential for getting beyond the stalled misrecognition of the world. Overcoming the aporia of this solipsism is the realization of having forgotten a problem that needs to be solved because of overconfidence in existing knowledge. But confronting the aporia does not mean that one necessarily stays stunned, it means that one begins to recognize that the capacity to be stunned signifies that something more is required. Thus, the aporia that numbs Meno is the occasion for examining how he had forgotten his capacity to learn the knowledge that he already "knows."[12] For students engaged in antiracist education, developing the capacity to interrogate their "stunning ignorance" means, first of all, recognizing when their confidence in their knowledge and place in the world disables them from viewing it from other perspectives.

But it is not always possible to overcome aporia, nor would it always be right to do so. Part of the problem of living in a position of dominance is the confidence in the ability to know, to always be able to sort out differences of opinion or to fully understand everything in the world. Aporia can be a reminder that some things are beyond the reach of knowledge and understanding that can be assimilated. For learners whose solipsism has disabled them, recognition of the boundaries their place in the world puts on the reach of their knowledge may also be a helpful reminder of the limits of knowledge and the intransigence of ignorance. But at the very least, a suspicion that one does not know as much as one thinks one knows allows one to remain more open to the possibility of difficult relations. Further, a suspicion about one's ignorance can be a motivation to form relations that keep one grappling with one's understanding of the world.

UNCANNY RESEMBLANCE

Part of the reason majority students (and instructors) are reluctant to engage with the aporia of their own ignorance is a lurking or repressed full understanding of the moral implications of the unjust place they occupy in the world. While centralizing the process of recognizing, confronting, and maintaining aporia are important to antiracist education, attention to the uncanny is a further requirement. The uncanny can help to illuminate the reluctance to push beyond what seems to be innocent ignorance. In his discussion of the uncanny, Freud examines how the dynamics of repression undergird what is familiar with a discomforting echo of what is strange, and vice versa. While the focus of his essay is on the techniques of literature that produce the feeling of the uncanny, his observations provide a helpful parallel to one of the central difficulties of antiracist education: the discomfort of white students who simultaneously know enough about race relations to know why they should be uncomfortable in such discussions and who also claim ignorance about race relations. In other words, like the examples Freud uses to explain the particular unsettling quality of the uncanny, these students have a familiarity with problems they have in some way either actively repressed or been encouraged by social norms to ignore. Their repression is, in my view, less of a psychological dynamic than a reflection of the general social tendency to ignore difficult topics. Students' frequent participation in such a form of "social repression," shows that they do know "something familiar which has been repressed" about race.[13]

Highlighting the "uncanny" aspects of race relations may be a helpful pedagogical way to avoid the dogmatism of "just don't be racist" because it calls on students to make an unsettling problem of their race related fear and familiarity. Like the uncanny, this active form of anti-racist problem posing might create an uncertainty in students. Borrowing from Freud, the uncanny might be said to create uncertainty "in such a way that [their] attention is not focused directly upon [their] uncertainty, so that [they] may not be led to go into the matter and clear it up immediately."[14]

There is promise in the uncanny destabilizing the familiar and the strange into mutually constitutive categories. It is promising in terms of anti-bias pedagogy, in terms of a pedagogy reliant on riddles and puzzles that require background knowledge, but also one that should simultaneously trouble the very background that enables such knowledge.

MISTAKING CLICHÉ FOR STUDENT VOICE

All too often discussions about student voice devolve into calls for opening spaces for them to speak what they already know. This inevitably leads us into the sterile problem Dewey argued against: raw experience is not necessarily experience that is educational. This raw experience, where students give voice to what they knew prior to engaging with others, is self-centered, less interested in further association than in concretizing its own place. Thus, this centering of discomfort is particularly critical for teaching students antiracism. As students recall what they know from home, they rely on the comforts of dinner table conversations, the very conversations they feel compelled to repeat uncritically and nearly compulsively as they are face with a world unfamiliar to them. When students, for example, recount their first interaction with a black person as a moment where they looked up from their yard or from their place on their mother's lap and screamed at the sight of an unfamiliar hue, they are recounting precisely why education ought not to be home. Home is where the scream is inculcated and expected, because of a lack of the unfamiliar. Education is where the scream ought to be problematized, where what one had previously thought one did not need to know pushes one into a relation with this self-alienating relationship. I contend that these relationships are self-alienating because one's definition of oneself is maintained through the expectation that the world is a familiar place, that one will not encounter startling or ignored difference.

Families and churches remain the most starkly segregated institutions in our society. Whether or not they manage it in practice, families are supposed to provide for affective support and warm encouragement. Meeting others with whom one is unfamiliar, in contrast, is a potentially aporia-generating experience. Facing the responsibility for race relations, particularly for students who have never considered race relations a problem, ought to generate the numbing effect Meno described. The experience ought not to send them into a comfortable exchange of stories, but should push them into a painful, critical reexamination of their active ignorance about difference. This active form of ignorance is what most troubles me about the desire to make antiracist education or any education comfortable. Many of us have taken great feats of subtle strategy to maintain our ability to be comfortable in the world in ways that directly impede the comforts of others. That this form of ignorance directly involves our actively ignoring the very lack of knowledge that would otherwise stun us—preferably into action against that which we guard ourselves against knowing—means that we are fully complicit even when blissfully unaware. While I am not arguing that we send our white or other majority students into paroxysms of liberal guilt, I am certain that they ought not to require carefully nurtured prodding into concerns about justice.

FAMILY AS THE CAUSE OF RACISM, AUTOBIOGRAPHY AS THE CURE

It might reasonably be argued at this point that Roland Martin's call for the "3 Cs of care, concern, and connection" in her plan for domestic education and Noddings's call for caring in schools are useful antidotes to the apparent trauma of racism. I want to steer us far away from the discourse of racism as the result of individual family-based trauma. One particularly pernicious example, popular in antiracist curricula, is the film *The Color of Fear*, in which a male mixed-race encounter group thrashes out race relations over the course of a weekend at what appears to be a California spa or convention center. As they recount stories of race relations, one white man increasingly becomes the center of their attention as they root through his past to find the kernel of truth that mobilized his racism. This therapeutic setting enables the classic domestic explanation: His father abused him. The problem of race is then the problem of his family, and while the family writ large stands in for the wounded white man's race relations, it is a return to family dynamics that uncovers where the therapeutic cure for his racism lies. We find the same sort of call for domestic healing of racism whenever exhausted teachers and professors turn away from curricular ways to address racism and turn back to the family. As one professor recently put it at a conference on hate crimes at the university, "What can we do when these students come from families whose socio-economic status makes their racism possible, even necessary?" That the particular university in question was unable to recruit or retain students of color at a rate of more than 5 percent clearly points to institutional responsibility, not family failings.

We need to recognize the discourse of family-based racism where racism is "bred in the bone," as an avoidance of discussions of social forces and institutions that require racism. The turn toward domestic or psychological causes of racism individualizes broad social problems and installs a subjectivity doggedly unable to leave home and get to school. This, it seems to me, is precisely the problem with therapeutic-domestic education. Students do not need the comforts of home or home remedies, they need to get out and mingle with others beyond their knowing and begin to understand the world as a place in which they are not meant to feel the arrogance of comfort.

To avoid this arrogance of comfort, we need to sidestep what seems to be an all too common feature of diversity education: the telling of the personal story as if the subject of the story were disconnected from relations of identity. We should not encourage the telling of students' selves without adequately interrogating what a self or subject is, and how the very constitution of subjectivity is part of a discourse of authenticity and authority underwriting racism, as well as other forms of bias. In other words, we should not encourage students to concretize their subjectivity without adequately attending to historical contingency and power relations subtending claims to know oneself. Further, stories often neglect the hidden relationships among other subjectivities and thus maintain ignorance of how, for instance, white racial or ethnic identity is constructed and understood in relation to nonwhite identities. Stories that stand side by side to illustrate that we're all different neglect to show that, whether we acknowledge it or not, we're all related in the terms we use. We are related inasmuch as we use each other to form concretized senses of our own identities.

By now I have been to at least half a dozen diversity training sessions where participants were invited to each get up on a stool and tell their family story. One person might come from a working-class Italian background, another from a middle-class African American background, and so on. The impetus behind this exercise is partially to remind all people that their identities are marked because people in the majority categories may too often consider themselves the universal subject. In the end, the objective always seems to be that we all have complicated lives and would do well to realize that of each other. While this is doubtless a start, understanding that some of us complicate the lives of others differently would help to raise the relational stakes of this exercise. Diversity workshop participants are encouraged to take seriously the role of social positioning in the constitution of their subjectivity, but this process tends to reinstall uninterrogated identity categories and neglect the power relations between identity categories. By conflating all identity as difference, then, we open the possibility that students will assert that being German is necessarily equivalent to being Latina. All difference becomes exchangeable without an understanding of social and political forces; all differences are identified as having (false) family resemblances and thus bring students into what they take as closer understandings of themselves and others.[15]

But here are some stories that don't fit well together. A class discussion of women's sexuality was taken over by the two men in class, who spent the greater portion of the discussion both explaining their own difficulties with women and castigating women in the class for not chiming in with their own stories. Despite numerous attempts to steer these men away from talking, including a long discussion on why some people taking up discussion time meant that other people wouldn't be talking nor would be particularly inclined to share intimate details, nothing stopped the incessant storytelling of the men. We broke into small groups, and most groups discussed why they weren't going to participate, given that the men whose talking had taken up all the airspace seemed, much too paradoxically, to want the women to talk. As a few women pointed out later, they were hardly going to help these boorish men understand women's sexuality, given that they couldn't understand how to listen in the first place. Now, clearly part of this story is also my ineptitude as an instructor, but another part is that the women read the context of story sharing as one in which it really didn't matter what they said and so there was no point in saying it. Add that to the detail that the discussion was about the "myth of the vaginal orgasm" and the general cultural ignorance of the clitoris, and one can see that the men were likely talking to cover their discomfort of the topic and shift that discomfort onto the women in class. The moral of this story about stories is not that everyone should have talked and understood their relationality, although that certainly would have been an improvement. Instead, the difficulty of speaking and even entering into a relationship was highlighted for the women, who had long experience with such things but nonetheless made the incident a central part of their experience of the class. That they had so starkly been reminded of how much men control conversations and sexual knowledge meant that they were able to share an experience with one another and rethink the degree to which they wished to establish classroom relations across the gender divide. They clearly recognized the double bind: To insist on a classroom relationship with the men meant continuing to give the men attention; to ignore a classroom relationship with the men meant continuing to allow them to speak unchallenged. And I was left with numerous office hours trying to explain that the class was not jelling because the men were opting out of recognizing their role as obstacle to the formation of a difficult relationship, while the men continued to assert that it was the women who were opting out.

Another difficult series of stories that wouldn't sit comfortably side by side started with the topic of racial segregation but moved to gay rights. White students initially discussed what they hoped would have been their active response against racial segregation, but more than a few were deeply concerned that they would have accepted the dominant norms. We were talking about how the larger issues of racism and other forms of bias structure social interactions and thus actively limit the spaces in which relations across difference can even happen. While mulling the historical example of legalized segregation, a black student suggested that a white person moving to the back of the bus wouldn't help the situation because he or she was then taking up one of the few seats a person of color could legally occupy. A student of color pointed out that even having shared the space, a white person couldn't fully understand what it meant to be the person who had to sit there and who had to understand the full ramifications across the range of social, political, and economic meanings of sitting there. Ultimately the problem the class grappled with was that one can potentially have a relationship across difference and still be faced with a great divide. Many students had been advocating empathy as a way to bridge the divide but were beginning to be moved away from their belief that they could ever feel what another person felt. In short, they were beginning to see that relation does not necessarily imply a similar viewpoint but rather an active decision to cross a divide that is maintained through activity that looks like passivity.

As the class started to try to ferret out where they were actively or passively allowing divides to be maintained, a lesbian student pointed out that straight people passively decide to go about their lives, all the time ignoring the differences between their lives and the lives of sexual minority people all around them. She pointed out that she had been to multiple weddings, given away multiple small kitchen appliances, but no one had ever noticed that she had been with her female partner for many years. There wasn't an equivalence to their relationship and heterosexual relationships; there wasn't an easily socially sanctioned way to celebrate their relationship, nor was there even an indication from heterosexual friends that they realized that marriage was a segregated institution. Classmates who had imagined themselves perhaps attempting to ride in the back of the bus objected that they could hardly be expected to give up having families because the law prevented gay and lesbian couples from marrying. A few confusedly asked if it weren't true that many places allowed gay marriage and were surprised to find that rumors of gay marriage's legality were greatly exaggerated. All students in class said that they had gay friends, lesbian relatives, or at least some firsthand experience with a person who was not heterosexual. None of them had noticed or been particularly troubled that the major life events and rituals they had been to had excluded celebrations of same sex couples.

So they at once knew gay people as friends or relatives, but didn't notice their absence from the center of social ritual or think about the further implications of that absence (in terms of hospital visitation, adoption, property, simple social recognition). But they all knew that there was a similarity between gay and straight relationships, so at once the resemblance was clear, but unmarked by actual practices like ceremonies. Further, the differences between gay and straight relationships were somehow not recognizable because they simply did not see the exclusions visited on gay couples. As one student said, having prided herself on not seeing the difference between gays and straights, it was difficult to consider that there were, in fact, differences. She said it was particularly hard to realize that her heterosexuality insisted on and maintained those differences through social institutions but that her sense of herself as "kind of progressive" depended on her saying that there weren't differences. In other words, her comfort with herself as social progressive wound up being part of what discouraged her from considering difference as something that needed to be maintained at the forefront of discussions of bias.

MOVING OUT OF THE SELF, OUT OF IDENTITY, AND INTO A VERTIGO OF ACTION

Bernice Johnson Reagon has argued that this sense of comfort is not the point of a political agenda that addresses racism through coalition politics. As she puts it:

Coalition work is not work done in your home. Coalition work has to be done in the streets. And it is some of the most dangerous work you can do. And you shouldn't look for comfort. Some people will come to a coalition and rate the success of the coalition on whether or not they feel good when they get there. They're not looking for a coalition, they're looking for a home. They're looking for a bottle with some milk in it and a nipple, which does not happen in a coalition. You don't get a lot of food in a coalition. In a coalition you have to give, and it is different from your home. You can't stay, there all the time.[16]

Reagon clearly shows the problems of turning diversity and antiracist education into a comfortable endeavor, as she argues that the recognition of similarity and the need to be comfortable with similarity keeps people in "little barred rooms."[17] Whether these rooms are made up of people of particular identity group similarities or perceived similarities is unimportant After a time they become exclusionary.

The difficulties of separation and association are clear, as Minnie Bruce Pratt recounts the pull and the impossibility of home and firm boundaries on identity in her essay "Identity: Skin Blood Heart." For Pratt, the voices of black men in her neighborhood recall her home and at the same time remind her that home is based on exclusion:

I think how I just want to feel at home, where people know me; instead I remember, when I meet Mr. Boone, that home was a place of forced subservience, and I know that my wish is that of an adult wanting to stay a child: to be known by others, but to know nothing, to feel no responsibility.[18]

Rather than staying in the place of nostalgia and comfort, Pratt's experience becomes "fraught, for me, with the history of race and sex and class; as I walk I have a constant interior discussion with myself, question how I acknowledge the presence of another, what I know or don't know about them, and what it means how they acknowledge me."[19] Her very actions of reflection and recounting the impossibility of writing a stable autobiography or returning to the nostalgia of home make home and self themselves impossible. That is by engaging in this kind of work, she is unable to go home, as home is a place where these questions would have been unacceptable. She recounts her father's attempt, when she was young, to introduce her to his view of the world by climbing to the top of the courthouse and tells of her failure to make that climb and have that view. But she is also well aware that her place in the world as a white woman makes that view not something given up by conscience but rather one that remains even in her attempts to actively not have it. As she engages in her work, she effaces her own particular viewpoint: "I am struggling now to speak, but not out of any role of ought-to; I ask that you try not to place me in that role."[20] She explains, "I began when I jumped from my edge and outside myself."[21]

She describes the Greensboro massacre, where Klansmen killed Communist activists demonstrating against racism, as a turning point in her thinking: What else had these Klansmen done to protect white womanhood? Pratt's historical examination of the production of white womanhood and the attendant ills visited on black men and women in its name produced in her "a kind of vertigo: a sensation of my body having no fixed place to be."[22] At one level, this is good, second-wave autobiography whose intent is to explain an authentic experience as a political starting point, but at another level, Pratt wants her own experience not to stand for itself but to encourage the uncomfortable process of her audience's tracing their own positioning in vectors of race, class, sexuality, and power. Like the numbing process of the aporia and the unsettling experience of the uncanny, the point is not the series of events leading to vertigo, but what one does with the vertiginous feeling of losing one's place and with the impossibility of reinstalling comfort as an antidote. Engaging in tracing the space of the uncanny requires the unsettling of one's place in the world and one's place in defining what one takes to be uncanny But for Pratt, the experience of vertigo is a constant reminder of the work that needs to be done, the relationships that need to be formed, and the constant trouble that one's social position brings to any relation or project. She offers a clear reminder that one does not transcend one's position by engaging in relations with others, but rather that social position continues to drag on possibilities for relations. Still, the only option is to relate, not to retreat into the comfort of one's troubling home.

HATE CRIMES, FAMILIES, AND CARING

At a recent conference on the role of the university in preventing hate crimes such as those that occurred a few summers ago in the Midwest, by an Indiana University student, Eva Cherniavsky criticized the affective and family-based response from the dean of students at Indiana University.[23] Faced with explaining how his university intended to address the shooting deaths, he pointed to a program where individuals of different races, himself included, get together, barbecue, meet each other's families and, in the end, become like family themselves: the all too classic refrain resounding through slavery and servitude.

Cherniavsky derided this tactic as reinstalling the embattled white masculinity, via the pater familias, behind the hate crime itself.[24] To encourage educators and students to view their relationships as revisiting family relations may also revisit a pesky gender binary that makes education into a helping profession. No doubt many of us, particularly women faculty, have been warned against baking or giving out our home phone numbers, with the caution that students will need to be reminded that "you are not their mother." In reference to the same hate crime, Stephanie Foote contended that we ought to refuse to engage in the kind of care that a comforting role in education typifies. Instead she advocates dealing with the problems of hate crime and bias in general as structural problems; not problems to be dealt with by what she calls "therapeutic teaching."[25] Too often the therapeutic gesture is directed at the dominant persons trying to deal with the difficult ethical problems that attend their social position. To address the feelings of difficulty without dealing with the power inequities that create those feelings misses the point of education: the formation of difficult relations, not to comfort those involved but to grapple with and address the structuring problems.

Rather than work to make education about difficult issues easier, we do better to maintain anti-bias education as unsettling but necessarily relational. These processes, like all engagements with learning what we find difficult, are uncomfortable. Discussions around topics like racism that have so long been the purview of active, constant ignorance, in the clearest sense of ignoring what is palpably present, are uncomfortable precisely because so much effort has gone into ignoring them. To bring anti-bias education into a comforting environment, then, misses the point. If the world is home because it was ensured that it was not someone else's, we must give up home in order to engage in difficult relations.

NOTES

1. Rudolfo Chavez Chavez and James O'Donnell, eds. "Introduction," *Speaking the Unpleasant: The Politics of (Non) Engagement in the Multicultural Education Terrain* (Albany, NY: SUNY Press, 1998), 2.

2. See also Ann Diller's presidential address to the Philosophy of Education Society, "Facing the Torpedo Fish: Becoming a Philosopher of One's Own Education," *Philosophy of Education 1998*, ed. Steve Tozer (Urbana, IL: Philosophy of Education Society, 1999) 1–9.

3. I see this as connected to Natasha Levinson's work on "belatedness." See Levinson's "Teaching in the Midst of Belatedness: The Paradox of Natality in Hannah Arendt's Educational Thought," *Educational Theory* 47, no. 4 (*Fall 1997*): 441.

4. Jane Roland Martin, "Education for Domestic Tranquility," in *Critical Conversations in Philosophy of Education*, ed. Wendy Kohli (New York: Routledge, 1995), 47.

5. Jane Roland Martin, *The Schoolhome: Rethinking Schools for Changing Families* (Cambridge, MA: Harvard University Press, 1992).

6. Martin, "Education for Domestic Tranquility," 48.

7. Martin, "Education for Domestic Tranquility," 52.

8. Martin, "Education for Domestic Tranquility," 53.

9. Martin, "Education for Domestic Tranquility," 49.

10. Michael Oakeshott, *The Voice of Liberal Learning* (New Haven, CT: Yale University Press, 1989).

11. Other philosophers have also discussed the discomfort of learning—Lyotard contending that education is terror, Gadamer contending that we only think when we are confused or confounded—all versions of learning well in keeping with Meno's reaction to Socrates.

12. That this process occurs through Socrates' dialogue with Meno's slave may underscore the inevitable pull of knowledge beyond the consent of the one being pulled, but it also indicates the different experiences of knowledge based on social position. For Meno, the dialogue is philosophically interesting, for the slave, who knows? .

13. Sigmund Freud, Freud, Sigmund, "The 'Uncanny,'" in *The Standard Edition of the Complete Psychological Works of Sigmund Freud*, vol. 17, trans. and ed. James Strachey (London: Hogarth Press, 1955), 247.

14: Freud, "The Uncanny," 227.

15. Indeed, a closer examination of Wittgenstein's version of "family resemblances" might be helpful here in separating and untangling the different meanings and positions of a variety of subjectivities, not all of whom may, in the end, share a family resemblance.

16. Bernice Johnson Reagan, "Coalition Politics: Turning the Century," in *Home Girls: A Black Feminist Anthology*, ed. Barbara Smith (New York: Kitchen Table: Women of Color Press, 1983), 359.

17. Reagan, "Coalition Politics," 358,

18. Minnie Bruce Pratt, "Identity: Skin Blood Heart," in *Yours in Struggle: Three Feminist Perspectives on Anti-Semitism and Racism*, ed. Elly Bulkin, Minnie Bruce Pratt, and Barbara Smith (Brooklyn: Long Haul Press, 1984), 12.

19. Pratt, "Identity: Skin Blood Heart," 12.

20. Pratt, "Identity: Skin Blood Heart," 15.

21. Pratt, "Identity: Skin Blood Heart," 19.

22. Pratt, "Identity: Skin Blood Heart," 35.

23. In the summer of 1999, a white neo-Nazi Indiana University student went on a hate-driven shooting spree, killing two people of color and wounding a number of others before killing himself during a police chase.

24. Eva Cherniavsky, "Ethnic Cleansing at the University," *American Studies Roundtable*, Indiana University at Bloomington, September 30, 1999.

25: Stephanie Foote, "The Working Conditions of Ethical Teaching," *Concerns: A Journal of the MLA Women's Caucus*, 25 no. 1 (Spring 2000): 33–53. Another panelist, in contrast, called for better relations with the police and FBI, as they bring comfort (as an audience member cat called, "to white people").

Educational Psychology
Inside the Classroom

THIRTY-THREE

Using the Lesson Study Approach to Plan for Student Learning

Susan J. Lenski and Micki M. Caskey

The Lesson Study approach is a method of professional development that encourages teachers to reflect on their teaching practice through a cyclical process of collaborative lesson planning, lesson observation, and examination of student learning. This results-oriented professional development model is an ideal vehicle for improving instructional practice in middle schools. Characteristically, middle schools are (a) learning communities where teachers and students engage in active learning, (b) places with high expectations for every member of the community, and (c) organizational structures that support meaningful relationships (National Middle School Association, 2003). Middle school teachers have to know their students well—who they are and how they learn best—and use this information when planning instruction and assessing student performance (Jackson & Davis, 2000). Most teacher planning focuses primarily on teacher actions rather than on student results (Ornstein, 1997). The Lesson Study approach, however, can provide an opportunity for middle school teachers to work together to strengthen the link between instructional planning and student learning.

WHAT IS LESSON STUDY?

Lesson Study is a "comprehensive and well-articulated process for examining practice" (Fernandez, Cannon, & Chokshi, 2003, p. 171). The Lesson Study approach is the way Japanese teachers have studied their practice for decades. Educators from the United States who studied the reasons for Japan's high scores in mathematics concluded that Japan's success could be the result of their professional development model. These educators discovered that Japanese teachers had developed a way to examine student achievement using a method that Makoto Yoshida (1999) translated as "lesson study." Stigler and Hiebert (1999) introduced Lesson Study to teachers in North America in their book about international methods of instruction. Lesson Study is now one of the fastest-growing approaches to professional development in the United States (Lewis, Perry, Hurd, & O'Connell, 2006).

THEORETICAL PERSPECTIVES

Underpinning the Lesson Study approach is Situated Learning Theory (Lave & Wenger, 1991), which advances the premise that learning is situated in the specific activity and is embedded within a particular context and culture. Lave and Wenger posited that learning is a social process in which individuals co-construct knowledge rather than transmit knowledge from one individual to the next. In the case of Lesson Study, the learning occurs as teachers exchange ideas and collaborate on lessons for their actual classrooms. Situated learning is a model of learning that transpires in a community of practice (Lave & Wenger).

As teachers engage in the process of Lesson Study, they are collectively examining practice; they are functioning as communities of practice. "Communities of practice are groups of people who share a concern or a passion for something they do and learn how to do it better as they interact regularly" (Wenger, n.d.). The members of the community develop a shared practice, a repertoire of shared experiences and understandings. The Lesson Study approach helps teachers to form communities of practice around planning and teaching. In these communities, teachers construct, organize, share, and refine their knowledge of the lesson. Notably, the focus of Lesson Study remains the collaborative intellectual process rather than the output of isolated products such as a collection of model lessons (Chokshi & Fernandez, 2004). This intellectual engagement is a hallmark of communities of practice, which "provide an avenue for teachers with common interests to interact with other professionals with similar interests to solve problems and improve practices" (Angelle, 2008, p. 56).

Developing and nurturing communities of practice require a number of conditions including the legitimatization of participation and provision of support (Wenger, 1998). Legitimizing participation entails giving members time to participate in collegial activities and creating an environment that acknowledges the value of communities. Providing support comes in the form of resources such as meeting space and outside experts. Not only are these cultural conditions critical for fostering and sustaining communities of practice, they also are imperative for creating an atmosphere for effective professional development.

Communities of practice as professional development: In recent years, educators and policymakers have expressed growing concerns about the effectiveness of traditional professional development (Penuel, Fishman, Yamaguchi, & Gallagher, 2007). According to research conducted by Bryk and Schneider (2002) and Desimone (2002), professional development that centers on teacher learning communities rather than the more traditional "workshop" is more likely to be accepted by teachers and implemented in the classroom. Therefore, a growing trend in professional development is to move away from a workshop approach to one that implements some sort of community of practice and encourages teachers to solve educational problems together.

The research base on effective professional development indicates that there are predominantly six components that should be featured: (a) whether it actively fosters a *reform style* (i.e., study group, mentoring relationship, teacher research) rather than a traditional workshop; (b) whether it is of sufficient *duration;* (c) the degree to which it emphasizes the *collective participation* of groups of teachers from the same school, department, or grade level; (d) the extent to which it provides opportunities for *active learning;* (e) whether it promotes *coherence* by incorporating experiences that are consistent with teachers' goals and state standards; and (f) the degree to which it has a *content focus* (Desimone, Porter, Garet, Yoon, & Birman, 2002). The Lesson Study approach is a good match for this type of professional development. Teachers using Lesson Study work as a team, either by grade level, subject area, or as an interdisciplinary group, to examine an instructional problem and determine how to apply the solution to current teaching goals. Lesson Study typically spans weeks or months as teachers meet to talk about the issue, plan the lesson, observe each other's teaching, and meet to discuss student learning. As teachers participate in Lesson Study groups, they actively discuss instructional interventions and share knowledge about how students will respond. Culminating from those discussions, teachers produce a lesson plan that is the result of collective wisdom and experience. Teachers then build on that collective wisdom as they watch each other teach and consider how best to engage students in learning.

RESEARCH ABOUT PLANNING

The research on Lesson Study can be contextualized in the larger body of lesson planning research. The current thinking that lesson planning is a linear path that begins with a teaching objective is based on Tyler's work, which was published in 1949 (John, 2006). Tyler (1949) proposed that lesson planning should consist of four essential elements: educational purposes or objectives, classroom experiences to attain these purposes, effective organization of the experiences, and determining whether the purposes are attained. According to Yinger (1980), "Education, for the most part, adopted a rational model of planning based on models from economics and from national and city planning" (p. 108). The rational method of planning requires teachers to set goals, formulate alternatives, predict outcomes, and evaluate the effectiveness of reaching those goals. This linear, rational type of thinking became the basis for the predominant model of planning that is taught in teacher education programs today and is considered to be the prototype for lesson plans (Jalongo, et al., 2007).

During the 1980s, a flurry of research was conducted about teacher planning that challenged the notion that teachers use linear lesson plans that begin with teaching objectives (Jalongo, Rieg, & Helterbran, 2007). The results of this research indicated that teachers do not use a linear thought process when they plan. Instead, planning can be likened to the composing process in writing (Owen, 1991). Teachers use a pattern of "nested" decision making, focusing on activities rather than objectives, and they plan based on prior successful experiences and institutional elements such as the school schedule, availability of materials, and the interests and abilities of their students (Brown, 1988). When teachers plan, they engage in mental dialogues about teaching rather than writing down their plans. They think about their lessons and envision how they could implement those plans (Clark & Peterson, 1986).

Recent research bolsters the argument that practicing teachers do not plan using what we have called the traditional lesson plan. According to Ornstein (1997), experienced teachers are holistic and intuitive when they plan. Strangis, Pringle, and Knopf (2006) found that teachers begin planning by thinking of activities or texts, not objectives. Sanchez and Valcarcel (1999) found that 78% of teachers in their study began lesson planning by thinking of the content knowledge, and only 22% began with objectives. Instead, teachers consider the lesson objectives as they teach, and the formats of plans vary according to the content of the lesson (Kagan & Tippins, 1992). Because teaching is a complex process that is improvisational in nature, planning generally takes the form of a mental activity, which is a cyclical process that is successively recursive (Yinger, 1980).

Planning using lesson study: When teachers participate in a Lesson Study community, they verbalize the mental dialogue that usually occurs during individual planning. Further, the group interactions provide multiple ways to envision the lesson. As the teachers negotiate their final plan, they are able to examine a wider range of possibilities for lesson instructions, possible student responses, and how to evaluate student learning. Ideas are shared, examined, negotiated, and decided upon. All of these interactions provide teachers with richer and more varied ideas than they could have generated by themselves. Research that has been conducted on Lesson Study indicates that it has strong potential for effective collaborative planning.

One example of research conducted in the United States studied 15 middle school teachers who used the Lesson Study approach as their primary method of professional development for six years (Vandeweghe & Varney, 2006). The researchers reported that this approach helped the teachers form a vibrant learning community in which they examined their teaching practices. Fernandez (2002) investigated two groups of teachers, fourteen K–8 teachers and nineteen middle school teachers, who used Lesson Study as their professional development focus. They found that teachers' intellectual engagement and collaborative work were benefits of using Lesson Study, but that there were also a variety of obstacles to this approach including having teachers find time to collaborate with their colleagues, overcoming their fear of having team members observe their teaching demonstrations, and critically analyzing their teaching practices.

In a second study of 16 U.S. teachers who were mentored by Japanese teachers in the Lesson Study approach, Fernandez, Cannon, and Chokshi (2003) concluded that to really benefit from using Lesson Study, teachers need to learn how to apply a critical lens to their examination of lessons the way a teacher researcher would. The same holds true for teacher candidates. Marble (2006) investigated eight teams of three student teachers each who had learned how to use Lesson Study to collaborate on planning. She found that teacher candidates were able to critically analyze their practice when they had the opportunity to look at their planning in this way.

Researchers in countries outside the United States have also conducted studies about the use of Lesson Study. In Indonesia, Marsigit (2007) conducted a pilot study regarding the introduction and use of Lesson Study with secondary mathematics teachers in three cluster sites (i.e., West Java, Central Java, East Java). Though initial findings revealed improvements in teaching practice, including student achievement, Marsigit cautioned that Lesson Study is only a starting point. In Hong Kong, Lee (2008) investigated secondary English teachers' professional development using a Lesson Study approach. He found that teachers developed subject knowledge and pedagogical skills, engaged in critical self-reflection, and were more attuned to students' learning needs; however, teachers also experienced increased levels of pressure from the additional workload and time commitment. In another case study, Law and Tsui (2007) studied how a team of university tutors, mentor teachers, and student teachers used Lesson Study to support student teachers' classroom teaching. Results indicated that this approach was a transformative professional development experience not only for the student teachers but also for the university tutors and mentor teachers.

Unquestionably, the research on Lesson Study is in its infancy. Lewis, Perry, and Murata (2006) discussed the need for further research on the topic. They recommend that there should be a three-pronged approach to developing the research base on Lesson Study. First, there have been several descriptive studies of Lesson Study projects. Lewis and associates(2006) recommended that more of these studies be conducted and published. In addition to descriptive studies, there needs to be an explication of the mechanics of Lesson Study. For example, what happens when teachers debrief a lesson needs to be examined. Finally, longitudinal studies that investigate how teachers using Lesson Study change their practice over time need to be conducted and reported.

In the next two sections, this column shifts from a review of salient research literature to a focus on the authors' own work with Lesson Study. After explaining how teams of middle school teachers participated in a Lesson Study project, we describe teacher candidates' experiences with this approach.

USING LESSON STUDY WITH MIDDLE SCHOOL TEACHERS

Our focus on Lesson Study was to determine whether this type of collaborative professional development could refocus teachers' thinking on student learning and develop sound instructional practices. We wondered whether the collaborative nature of the Lesson Study approach could help groups of teachers visualize how to plan for student learning as they discussed and agreed upon the components of a lesson.

Teachers from three middle schools agreed to participate in the project and formed lesson study teams, ranging in size from two to eleven teachers. The teams consisted of a mix of content area teachers including language arts, math, science, and social studies teachers, as well as learning specialists (i.e., special education and ESOL teachers). Though the schools' geographic locations differed, all three schools served high-needs students. None of the schools had achieved adequate yearly progress (AYP) in language arts in the past year and all served populations that had at least 50% of the students receiving free and reduced-priced lunches. For two years, these lesson study teams met regularly to design, teach, observe, and evaluate "research lessons" that emphasized sound instructional principles and observations of student learning. The topics of their research lessons varied widely and included science lessons on genetics and sound; math lessons on algebraic equations; language arts lessons on a short story, prefixes, and roots; and social studies lessons on the plague and state rivers. After each school year ended, the lesson study teams from the three schools gathered at literacy symposia to share their lessons and experiences.

LESSON STUDY IN ACTION

In the Lesson Study approach, a community of teachers collaborates to plan a single lesson. The teachers talk about how a lesson fits with the overall school goals and what standards or objectives they want to achieve. To plan the details of the lesson, the teachers use a matrix like the one shown in Figure 1.

First, the teams agree on a lesson that furthers the students' progress toward a school or content goal. Then they outline the teachers' actions and brainstorm possible teacher comments. They script some of the comments that the teachers could use during the lesson at critical points. As they discuss teacher actions, they discuss potential student responses. This discussion tends to set in motion a process of reevaluating and revisioning the teacher actions, and the plan is revised until the teachers agree on their best course of action. As the teams discuss teacher actions and student responses, they also reflect on how to evaluate student learning. The teachers in this project were asked to consider four areas related to student learning: student engagement, student behavior, student learning, and student products.

The teachers in each of the three schools focused their plans primarily on student engagement. All of the teachers felt competent in classroom management and did not consider student behavior a major issue in their classrooms. They felt, however, that a lack of engagement prevented students from learning the concepts they were teaching. Each lesson, therefore, had ways (e.g., tests/quizzes, written notes, or worksheet completion) that observing teachers could chart as evidence of student engagement through the lesson. Some teachers also included an informal check for understanding in their lessons. These informal observations of student learning took the form of having students volunteer to answer questions, looking at student work during the lessons, and listening to student small-group discussions.

The Lesson Study approach includes another powerful component: observing the lesson. Some of the teachers in our project were hesitant about having colleagues watch them teach. During Lesson Study, however, the observers do not evaluate teaching; they observe student learning. One teacher in each group taught the lesson, while the others observed students using agreed-upon criteria. For example, if the team agreed that students would be evaluated on the amount of participation in class discussion, the observers would record participation rates. Observers took note of other classroom events during instruction, but their primary task was to observe *students*.

After the lesson, the team reassembled and reflected on the lesson. The teacher shared his or her perceptions of how the lesson was received. The observers shared the data that they had collected. As a group, the teachers discussed what was successful in the lesson and the elements that could be strengthened. The teachers then revised the lesson, which could be taught again or made public by sharing it at a meeting or publishing it on a Web site.

Developing lessons using this collaborative approach to teaching produces exemplar lessons that can be published as models of instruction. (We provided our teachers with the option of having their lessons posted on the Content Area Teacher Network Web site, http://www.teachers. ed.pdx.edu/.) The benefits of the Lesson Study approach, however, are not only the development of a demonstration lesson; teachers who collaborate on the development of the lesson learn from each other how to think about teaching and student learning.

MENTORING TEACHER CANDIDATES

In addition to introducing practicing teachers to the Lesson Study approach, we brought this approach into our teacher preparation program. Based on our knowledge of the program, we decided to incorporate Lesson Study into our middle school teacher candidates' methods courses.

Teacher candidates have trouble relating to the kinds of lesson plans that they are taught in their teacher education programs, because these types of lesson plans tend to be far removed from what actual teachers do in the classroom (Maroney, & Searcy, 1996). Teacher candidates are typically taught a linear, rational, ends-means sequence of lesson planning that begins with the objectives of the lesson (John, 2006). We taught our candidates a variety of ways to plan (e.g., differentiated lesson plan, inquiry-based lesson plan, PowerPoint lesson plan) including Lesson Study.

Our experiences introducing teacher candidates to collaborative planning were met with enthusiasm. Teacher candidates are novice planners and welcome input into their lesson planning. They also are accustomed to identifying their proposed actions, so they found the Lesson Study format easy to navigate. However, teacher candidates had much more difficulty than the practicing teachers did in thinking of ways to evaluate student learning. Consistent with research on the development of novice teachers, our teacher candidates were more focused on their own instruction than they were on how students responded (see John, 2006). As the teacher candidates moved into full-time student teaching, however, they were able to develop lessons and work samples that indicated growth on planning for both instruction and student learning.

ADVICE FOR TEACHERS AND ADMINISTRATORS

Becoming familiar with Lesson Study is an obvious initial step for teachers and administrators alike. To build an understanding of this approach, educators can engage in a book study (see Recommended Resources), read journal articles (see References), view videos or DVDs (available at http://www.globaledresources.com/), and consult with university faculty or regional education laboratories. Information and links to publications can also be found on Lesson Study Web sites including The Lesson Research Web Site hosted by the Education Department at Mills College (http://www.lessonresearch.net/) and The Lesson Study Research Group at Teachers College/ Columbia University (http://www.tc.edu/centers/lessonstudy/).

Once teachers and administrators share a common understanding of Lesson Study, it is necessary to move from discussions to actually engaging in Lesson Study (Chokshi & Fernandez, 2004). As with other innovative approaches, it is best to start Lesson Study with a small, interested group of teachers. These interested teachers, working as a learning community, are more likely to adopt the Lesson Study approach (Bryk & Schneider, 2002; Desimone, 2002). Together the group can set realistic expectations for implementing Lesson Study in their school.

To engage effectively in Lesson Study will require certain conditions. First, teachers need time for genuine collaboration to occur (Vandeweghe & Varney, 2006), which administrators will need to allocate in the school schedule. In middle schools, common planning time within the teachers' instructional day is an ideal venue for Lesson Study, though other regularly scheduled times for teacher collaboration can work. Second, teachers need to make collaboration routine. In Lesson Study, collaboration entails the collaborative planning, observing, and debriefing of lessons. Such collaborative work can encourage teachers to rely on their peers to inject vital feedback regarding the Lesson Study (Chokshi & Fernandez, 2004). Similarly, the collaborative nature of Lesson Study can help teachers emphasize critical self-reflection and de-emphasize external evaluation (Lewis & Tsuchida, 1998). Finally, teachers need to shift their attention to student thinking and learning when using the Lesson Study approach. When planning, teachers need to adopt the student lens (Fernandez, et al., 2003) and identify indicators of student engagement. During the observation of the lesson, teachers should focus on student work, engagement, and behavior, rather than focusing on the teacher's ability. By keeping the focus on the students, teachers can gain important insights into ways to improve their instructional practice.

CONCLUSIONS

"Effective planning is an essential element of good teaching and of promoting student achievement" (Jalongo, Rieg, & Helterbran, 2007, p. 42). The Lesson Study approach is a way for teachers to engage in professional development leading to activities that promote instructional change. When teachers meet in professional learning communities to discuss planning, they become active participants in reform. Lesson Study has additional benefits by drawing teachers' attention to student learning as they think about their own instructional actions. A further advantage of Lesson Study is that it allows teachers to observe students during the teaching of a planned lesson. As teachers observe students, they begin to see teaching from the students' point of view. This new perspective can change deeply entrenched notions of instruction and result in better student learning.

ACKNOWLEDGMENTS

This publication was made possible, in part, by a grant from Carnegie Corporation of New York and the U.S. Department of Education, Title IIA, University/School Partnership (USP) Program. The statements made and views expressed are solely the responsibility of the authors.

REFERENCES

Angelle, P. S. (2008). Communities of practice promote shared learning for organizational success. *Middle School Journal, 39*(5), 52–58.

Brown, D. S. (1988). Twelve middle-school teachers' planning. *Elementary School Journal, 89,* 69–87.

Bryk, A. S., & Schneider, B. (2002). *Trust in schools: A core resource for improvement.* New York: Russell Sage Foundation.

Chokshi, S., & Fernandez, C. (2004). Challenges to importing Japanese Lesson Study: Concerns, misconceptions, and nuances. *Phi Delta Kappan, 85,* 520–525.

Clark, C. M., & Peterson, P. L. (1986). Teachers' thought processes. In M. C. Wittrock (Ed.), *Handbook of research on teaching* (3rd ed.) (pp. 255–314). New York: Macmillan.

Desimone, L. (2002). How can comprehensive school reform models be successfully implemented? *Review of Educational Research, 72,* 433–479.

Desimone, L., Porter, A. C., Garet, M. S., Yoon, K. S., & Birman, B. F. (2002). Effects of professional development on teachers' instruction: Results from a three-year longitudinal study. *Educational Evaluation and Policy Analysis, 24*(2), 81–112.

Fernandez, C. (2002). Learning from Japanese approaches to professional development: The case of lesson study. *Journal of Teacher Education, 53,* 393–405.

Fernandez, C., Cannon, J., & Chokshi, S. (2003). A U.S.-Japan lesson study collaboration reveals critical lenses for examining practice. *Teaching and Teacher Education, 19,* 171–185.

Jackson, A. W., & Davis, G. A. (2000). *Turning points 2000: Educating adolescents in the 21st century.* New York & Westerville, OH: Teachers College Press & National Middle School Association.

Jalongo, M. R., Rieg, S. A., & Helterbran, V. R. (2007). *Planning for learning: Collaborative approaches to lesson design and review*. New York: Teachers College Press.

John, P. D. (2006). Lesson planning and the student teacher: Re-thinking the dominant model. *Journal of Curriculum Studies, 38*, 483–498.

Kagan, D. M., & Tippins, D. J. (1992). The evolution of functional lesson plans among twelve elementary and secondary student teachers. *Elementary School Journal, 92*, 477–489.

Lave, J., & Wenger, E. (1991). *Situated learning: Legitimate peripheral participation*. New York: Cambridge University Press.

Law, Y. K., & Tsui, A. B. M. (2007). Learning as boundary-crossing in school–university partnerships. *Teaching and Teacher Education, 23*, 1289–1301.

Lee, J. F. K. (2008). A Hong Kong case of lesson study—Benefits and concerns. *Teaching and Teacher Education, 24*, 1115–1124.

Lewis, C., Perry, R., Hurd, J., & O'Connell, M. P. (2006). Lesson study comes of age in North America. *Phi Delta Kappan, 88*, 273–281.

Lewis, C., Perry, R., & Murata, A. (2006). How should research contribute to instructional improvement: The case of lesson study. *Educational Researcher, 35*(3), 3–14.

Lewis, C., & Tsuchida, I. (1998). A lesson is like a swiftly flowing river. *American Educator, 22*(4), 12–17, 50–52.

Marble, S. T. (2006). Learning to teach through lesson study. *Action in Teacher Education, 28*(3), 86–96.

Maroney, S. A., & Searcy, S. (1996). Real teachers don't plan that way. *Exceptionality, 6*(3), 197–200.

Marsigit. (2007). Mathematics teachers' professional development through lesson study in Indonesia. *Eurasia Journal of Mathematics, Science & Technology Education, 3*(2), 141–144.

National Middle School Association. (2003). *This we believe: Successful schools for young adolescents*. Westerville, OH: Author.

Ornstein, A. C. (1997). How teachers plan lessons. *High School Journal, 80*, 227–238.

Owen, F. (1991). Teaching as a composing process. *English Journal, 80*(3), 57–62.

Penuel, W. R., Fishman, B. J., Yamaguchi, R., & Gallagher, L. P. (2007). What makes professional development effective? Strategies that foster curriculum implementation. *American Educational Research Journal, 44*(4), 921–958.

Sanchez, G., & Valcarel, M. V. (1999.) Science teachers' views and practices in planning for teaching. *Journal of Research in Science Teaching, 36*, 493–513.

Strangis, D. E., Pringle, R. M., & Knopf, H. T. (2006). Road map or roadblock? Science lesson planning and preservice teachers. *Action in Teacher Education, 28*(1), 73–84.

Stigler, J. W., & Hiebert, J. (1999). *The teaching gap: Best ideas from the world's teachers for improving education in the class-room*. New York: Summit Books.

Tyler, R. (1949). *Basic principles of curriculum and instruction*. Chicago: University of Chicago Press.

Vandeweghe, R., & Varney, K. (2006). The evolution of a school-based study group. *Phi Delta Kappan, 88*, 282–286.

Wenger, E. (n.d.). *Communities of practice: A brief introduction*. Retrieved August 12, 2008, from http://www.ewenger.com/theory/index.htm

Wenger, E. (1998). Communities of practice: Learning as a social system. *The Systems Thinker, 9*(5), 2–3.

Yinger, R. J. (1980). A study of teacher planning. *Elementary School Journal, 80*(3), 107–127.

Yoshida, M. (1999). *Lesson study: A case study of a Japanese approach to improving instruction*. Doctoral dissertation, University of Chicago Department of Human Development.

RECOMMENDED RESOURCES

To learn more about Lesson Study and its use in schools, the following resources are recommended:

Northwest Regional Educational Laboratory. (2003). Lesson study: Crafting lessons together. *Northwest Teacher, 4*(3), 1–21. Portland, OR: Northwest Eisenhower Regional Consortium for Mathematics and Science. Available at http://www.nwrel.org/msec/nwteacher/

Stepanek, J., Appel, G., Leong, M., Turner Mangan., M., & Mitchell, M. (2007). *Leading lesson study: A practical guide for teachers and facilitators.* Thousand Oaks, CA: Corwin Press.

Wiburg, K., & Brown, S. (2007). *Lesson study communities: Increasing achievement with diverse students.* Thousand Oaks, CA: Corwin Press.

THIRTY-FOUR

Open Lessons: A Practice to Develop a Learning Community for Teachers

Jianping Shen, Jinzhou Zheng, and Sue Poppink

Interest in improving the quality of professional development in this age of educational reform has intensified (Little, 1993) as a growing body of research suggests that teaching practices matter in terms of student achievement (Stronge, 2002). Based upon strong empirical evidence, many researchers have argued for embedding professional development in the context of teachers' work in order to transform both teaching practices and the structures and cultures of schools in which teachers practice (Darling-Hammond, 1994; Grossman, Wineburg, and Woolworth, 2001; Holmes Group, 1990). Consequently, fundamental structural changes in conceptualizing professional development are necessary so that teachers can develop these new and innovative teaching practices.

Promoting this type of professional development will not be easy for several reasons. Teaching is tremendously complex work (Cohen, 1989) and classrooms are complex social organizations (Jackson, 1968). In addition, teaching practices are difficult to change (Cohen, 1990; Shen and Ma, 2006): they require both learning and unlearning by practitioners (Cohen and Ball, 1990; Shen 1994, 2002). Beyond that, both the culture and structure of schools mitigate against changes in teaching (Little, 1990; Lortie, 1975; Sarason, 1982).

Grossman, Wineburg, and Woolworth (2001) developed a set of markers to guide the formation of a workplace-based professional community. To identify issues that should be addressed when attempting to change teaching practice within the context of schools, there are some innovative practices that may be helpful in developing helpful professional-development activities in the workplace. One such professional-development activity that may be useful in an environment of trust is what we refer to as "open lessons." Open lessons, as described in this paper, are habitually used in Asian cultures, but not frequently in the United States (Paine, 1990; Paine and Ma, 1993; Stigler and Stevenson, 1991).

THE CHALLENGE IN OVERCOMING THE ISOLATED CULTURE OF TEACHING

In this brief background statement, we describe the theoretical underpinnings of the workplace-based professional community that Grossman, Wineburg, and Woolworth developed, and the markers of professional community that they argued are important (2001). In our chapter we describe how open lessons could help build a professional community. The theoretical underpinnings of Grossman, Wineburg, and Woolworth's professional-development opportunity took into account the structural features of the high school, learning environments, and subject-specific pedagogy. They state,

> After reviewing the educational literature on community, we formulated a model based on the structural features of the urban high school (e.g., time and resources), departmental organization (based on the work by Grossman and Stodolsky 1995), and intellectual features of cooperative learning environments (drawing largely on Brown and Campione's [1994] work on communities of learners; Brown 1992), as well as our own prior work on pedagogical content knowledge and subject specific pedagogy. (p. 105)

Many have written about the structural features of elementary as well as high schools to which Grossman, Wineburg, and Woolworth refer and how those structures isolate teachers from one another. Dan Lortie, in his seminal *Schoolteacher* (1975), wrote that there are three unique hallmarks of teaching. One is a culture of "individualism" that is reinforced by the structure of schools organized in self-contained classrooms. Individualism and organization work against changing teaching into a more community-oriented undertaking. By individualism, Lortie means that public schools are "staffed by people who have little concern with building a shared technical culture" (p. 67).

Shen has pointed out that the isolation teachers feel in public schools is one reason for high teacher attrition rates (Shen, 1997). Those who stay in public school teaching may enjoy the individualistic nature of the work, yet ironically, those who may be most willing to develop a shared technical culture are most likely to leave. Lortie made a similar argument by stating that the second hallmark of public school teachers is their "conservatism." He argues that "teaching...is more likely to appeal to people who approve of prevailing practice than to those who are critical of it" (p. 29); that is, most teachers like the practice of teaching in individual classrooms and the traditional methods of teaching in those classrooms.

A PRACTICE TO DEVELOP A LEARNING COMMUNITY FOR TEACHERS

Lortie argues that a third feature of the teaching labor force is "presentism"—that is, "the dominancy of present versus future orientations among teachers" (p. 86). Grossman and her colleagues addressed all three of these cultural issues in the way they built the professional community, which was composed of participants from two departments, English and history. Members of those two departments created a cross-discipline curriculum and read literature and history together. According to Grossman, Wineburg, and Woolworth, they did so to address these structural and cultural norms. Much has been written about the occupational norms of privacy that impede joint work among teachers (Little, 1990; Lortie, 1975). The norms are maintained in part by the temporal organization of the school day, which limits teachers' interactions to fleeting encounters at lunchtime or to the rushed minutes before and after school.

Another theoretical underpinning of this work was a community of learners, as referred to in their organizing framework, which allowed teachers to cooperate on two specific tasks—writing the curriculum and reading literature and history together. Finally came the third theoretical underpinning of this work: the teachers used ideas concerning (a) pedagogical knowledge, the "how to" of teaching; (b) disciplinary knowledge, the "what" of teaching; and (c) pedagogical content knowledge, or the knowledge of how teachers teach specific disciplines. Grossman, Wineburg, and Woolworth found that the markers of creating professional communities in the workplace included:

a. forming group identity and norms of interaction
b. navigating fault lines, that is, dealing with deeply rooted conflicts within the group
c. negotiating the essential tension, which in this case meant a tension between the two purposes of the group—teacher learning (the readings) and student learning (building curriculum)
d. accepting communal responsibility for individual growth

When we examined those markers of professional community, we began to think about other activities that workplace professional communities could undertake. Such activities may help groups work through these markers, realizing that the process of working together would take some time. We believe that open lessons might be such an opportunity. In open lessons, teachers develop a common lesson plan; then one teacher pilots the lesson with a group of students, who work to improve the plan before it is demonstrated a final time with a different group for colleagues to observe. The lesson may be either a polished one or something new that teachers are trying out. Teachers then discuss the lesson with colleagues to think collectively about how to improve the lesson's content knowledge and pedagogy.

These open lessons are rooted in the markers that Grossman and her colleagues see as professional-workplace communities because over time, as they suggest, groups would need to:

a. form a deep sense of trust, which would include norms of interaction, in order to share their practice with others
b. allow conflicts in understandings about subject matter and pedagogy to surface in order to understand one another's teaching
c. focus on both teacher and student learning
d. take responsibility for one another's learning.

ABCs OF THE OPEN LESSON

The practice of the open lesson has implications for helping overcome the culture of teacher isolation that prevails in American education (Grossman, Wineburg, and Woolworth, 2001; Lortie, 1975). Some researchers discussed the Chinese concept of the open lesson (e.g., Huang and Bao, 2006; Ma, 1999; Paine, 1990; Paine and Ma, 1993; Stigler and Stevenson, 1991). Below, we will systematically introduce this practice and discuss its implications for the U.S. teaching profession. Open-lesson professional development can be important for sharing teaching experiences, demonstrating new teaching methods and techniques, overcoming the isolated culture of teaching, and improving the effectiveness of teaching.

What is an open lesson? An open lesson is a professional-development activity in which (a) someone, usually a teacher, teaches a lesson to his or her regular class; (b) colleagues—and sometimes researchers and parents—observe the lesson; and (c) the teacher and the observers discuss and reflect upon the lesson. The characteristics of the open lesson include the following: the students are usually the teacher's regular students; the content of the lesson is part of the standardized curriculum; the lesson is usually a demonstration or an exploration; and after the open lesson, there is always a session for collective reflection.

Who teaches open lessons? Classroom teachers present most of the open lessons, although university faculty or other researchers will occasionally do so, too. Classroom teachers who offer open lessons range from novice teachers to the exceptionally experienced. Novice teachers' lessons are usually exploratory, while those taught by experienced teachers are often for demonstration.

Who observes open lessons? The "observers" of open lessons could be teachers from the same school; those who teach the same subject matter within the same county- or city-based school system; or occasionally teachers from all over the country. The number of the observers ranges from as few as three to five colleagues to as many as thirty to fifty teachers, and in very few cases, as many as three hundred to five hundred teachers.

Who sponsors open lessons? The organizers of open lessons could be the county- or city-based education bureau, the school, or the professional association. Every year the bureau will organize open lessons. It will designate teachers who will teach open lessons and then provide those lessons as a professional-development opportunity to other teachers—usually teachers of the same subject matter—within the administrative boundary. A school could also be an organizer. School-based open lessons usually involve exchanging between novice and experienced teachers and promoting certain types of school-based renewal. In recent years, some professional associations have also sponsored open lessons that usually transcend administrative boundaries.

A CASE OF AN OPEN LESSON

The open lesson is a collective effort. From designing the lesson to reflecting on the lesson taught, teacher community is a common theme running through the whole process. The following is an example of an open lesson that took place in Jiading District, Shanghai (Zheng, 2003). In 2003, a group of thirteen teachers who taught eighth-grade Chinese language arts and reading formed an action research group. They wanted to explore ways in which to connect students' experience with reading materials, with a particular focus on the affective domain of students' experience. They decided to offer an open lesson among themselves once a month. One of the teachers taught an open lesson in 2003. The content was a passage entitled "In Memory of Space Shuttle *Challenger*," which came from the middle school textbook series in Shanghai.

The first step in offering the open lesson was that the group of thirteen teachers developed the lesson plan together. This kind of collective approach, not atypical for planning an open lesson, reduced the pressure on the teacher who gave the lesson.

The second step was an instructional rehearsal. Essentially, the teacher taught one of his parallel classes as a trial run. It is common at the eighth-grade level that a Chinese language arts and reading teacher has two parallel classes, so it is feasible to have the instructional rehearsal in one.

The third step was to revise the lesson plan. After the rehearsal, the group of thirteen teachers discussed whether the lesson had achieved its instructional objectives—in this case, connecting student experience with the reading materials. After exploring the strengths and weaknesses of the lesson, the group revised the lesson plan for the formal open lesson.

The fourth step was to teach the open lesson formally. Based on the revised lesson plan, the teacher formally taught the open lesson in his other regular class. The observers were the twelve other teachers in the action research group. Because the classroom was able to accommodate the twelve additional teachers, the open lesson was offered in the regular classrooms. (It is common to move to a larger space if more observers are involved.)

The teacher first introduced the lesson:

> The first human flight was by the Wright brothers. Although it lasted only fifty-nine seconds and flew 259.75 meters, it demonstrated the ambition and courage of human kind and laid a foundation for further explorations.
>
> However, the process of exploration was not without dangers. At 11:38 A.M., EST, January 28, 1986, the space shuttle *Challenger* exploded about one minute after liftoff. The crew of seven astronauts, including a teacher, died.
>
> This was one of the most significant tragedies in the history of space exploration. President Ronald Reagan expressed his sadness for the tragedy, but vowed that the space exploration would continue and that more spaceships and astronauts would be sent into space.

The teacher then asked a question for students to connect their experiences with the tragedy: "How do you think of the tragedy of the space shuttle *Challenger?*"

The students then connected with their own experience and offered answers such as:

"Exploration and failure always go hand in hand."

"Exploration needs courage."

"Exploration should be based on science."

"Exploration creates the future for humankind."

The teacher then gave guidance about using students' personal experiences to substantiate the statements they made and drawing meaning from their experience. The teacher formally introduced the passage "In Memory of Space Shuttle *Challenger*," and students began to read the passage. The open lesson continued. After the formal open lesson, the last step was to reflect upon the lesson that just had been taught and observed. During the reflection, the teacher who taught the open lesson raised three issues for discussion:

a. How much time should be allocated to reading and how much to discussion?
b. How could the time spent on addressing students' spontaneous questions and the time allocated be balanced?
c. What kinds of questions could effectively raise students' interest in reading the passage?

There were two camps among the twelve teachers who observed the lesson. One group felt that it was a successful lesson. The positive comments included: much interaction between the teacher and the students; guidance for students about connecting their experience with the reading materials; and balance between understanding the passage and discussing the materials. The other group felt the lesson needed considerable improvement. The critical arguments included the following: (a) the designed instructional process was too complicated; (b) it took too long to begin the actual reading by the students; and (c) the teacher emphasized the importance of exploration, which limited the ways in which students connected their experiences with the reading materials. As we can see from the case above, individual as well as collective reflection can help teachers transcend the isolated culture of teaching and develop a professional community.

IMPLICATIONS OF OPEN LESSONS

Open lessons provide opportunities for developing the markers of community formation formulated by Grossman, Wineburg, and Woolworth:

a. forming group identity and norms of interaction
b. navigating the fault lines, or handling conflict
c. negotiating the essential tension, or negotiating how to address both student learning and teacher learning
d. creating communal responsibility for individual growth

The first marker, forming group identity and creating norms of interaction, is at least partially addressed in the open-lessons professional development opportunities. The teachers and others don't just observe another teacher's lesson plan, but rather participate in its conception and implementation so that all the teachers have some stake in ensuring a solid and correctly implemented lesson plan. How they work together requires adjustment within the context of the group; that is, moving the group from one of multiple individuals with individual perspectives to a true community of those with a respect for multiple perspectives would be an important aspect of implementing professional community.

The second marker, handling conflict, would also be addressed in open lessons because the two-stage process of implementing the lesson plan allows conflicts to surface before the final exploration or demonstration. In our example, the teachers were not of like mind at the end of the demonstration. Whether teachers would "agree to disagree" on the value of the lesson or not, the process of open lessons would enable them to handle conflict.

The third marker requires that the professional-development opportunity concern both student learning and teacher learning. Open lessons focus strongly on students' learning, the way the open lesson introduced here focuses on connecting students' experience with reading materials, and is tried out twice on two different sets of students. However, it also focuses on the teacher's learning to teach. In China, with a largely standardized curriculum, teachers may be familiar with the content of the lessons, and the focus is more upon pedagogy. In the United States, with a less-standardized curriculum, teachers may increase both their content and pedagogic knowledge through an open lesson as teachers work together to create the lesson.

Finally, the fourth marker requires the community to take responsibility for individual growth. This marker is certainly inherent in the model of open lessons: the teacher teaching the lesson receives feedback from the community while the community ensures that the lesson is well executed, due to the collective nature of its formation.

In terms of overcoming the isolated culture of teaching and creating a professional community, open lessons have great potential. However, developing norms that would allow U.S. teachers to utilize open lessons fully may not be easy. As Lortie (1975) first noted and Little (1990) and others have affirmed, teaching has endured largely as an assemblage of entrepreneurial individuals whose autonomy is grounded in norms of privacy and noninterference, and the very organization of teaching work sustains that tendency.

Therefore, ground rules for open-lesson participation may need further development before undertaking such a task, which would work against the grain of teaching culture and organization in the United States. Those invited to participate in such a professional-development opportunity would need to be willing participants. If they are working in subject-matter-specific areas, they also would need to develop at least some rudimentary shared understandings of the purposes of the curriculum within the context of their school and across disciplines. They would also need to think deeply about the content and pedagogy of each lesson: whether the content worked within their own state standards and benchmarks, and how they would assess student knowledge and understanding of the lesson.

CODA: FUNCTIONS OF OPEN LESSONS

In China an open lesson is a major professional-development activity, introduced by educators from the former Soviet Union in the 1950s. The Soviet experts offered open lessons as a major vehicle to reform teaching in China. Ironically, open lessons are seldom taught in Russia today.

Open lessons provide a forum in which the theory and practice of teaching are integrated, the content of the lesson is part of the regular curriculum, and the teacher and the observers may engage in two-way reflection immediately after the lesson's conclusion. It is indeed job-embedded professional development. Even in today's world, where videotaping and podcasting are readily available, the value of building a professional community to overcome the isolation of teachers is something that new technologies will not necessarily accomplish. The functions of open lessons are:

- First, an open lesson is a forum for sharing teaching experience. Through open lessons, novice and experienced teachers can exchange the wisdom they have accumulated. Open lessons provide interaction between the individual and the collective experience. Open lessons create an opportunity for learning across disciplines and administrative units.

- Second, an open lesson provides an opportunity for action research. "Teachers are action researchers" is a notion generally accepted in China since the mid-1990s. Teachers have many questions in their daily professional lives. The principles of teaching and learning, which tend to be general, cannot give specific answers to all the questions teachers have. They must therefore explore on their own. Open lessons provide a mechanism for exploring complex and perplexing issues in their professional lives.

- Third, an open lesson can also be a platform for demonstration. When a new curriculum is being implemented, or when a new teaching method is being promoted, open lessons offer an effective approach to demonstrating how to teach the new curriculum or how to employ the new teaching method. The open lesson is theory in action.

REFERENCES

Brown, A. L. 1992. "Design Experiments: Theoretical and Methodological Challenges in Creating Complex Interventions in Classroom Settings." *Journal of the Learning Sciences* 2 (2): 141–178.

Brown, A. L., and J. C. Campione. 1994. "Guided Discovery in a Community of Learners." In *Classroom Lessons: Integrating Cognitive Theory and Classroom Practice,* ed. K. McGilly. Cambridge, Mass.: MIT Press/Bradford Books.

Cohen, D. K. 1989. "Teaching Practice: Plus Ca Change…" In *Contributing to Educational Change: Perspectives on Research and Practice,* ed. P. W. Jackson, 27–84. Berkeley: McCutchan.

——— 1990. "A Revolution in One Classroom: The Case of Mrs. Oublier." *Educational Evaluation and Policy Analysis* 12 (3): 327–346.

Cohen, D. K., and D. L. Ball. 1990. "Relations between Policy and Practice: A Commentary." *Educational Evaluation and Policy and Analysis* 12 (3): 249–256.

Darling-Hammond, L., ed. 1994. *Professional Development Schools: Schools for Developing a Profession.* New York: Teachers College Press.

Grossman, P. 1990. *The Making of a Teacher: Teacher Knowledge and Teacher Education.* New York: Teachers College Press.

Grossman, P. L., and S. S. Stodolsky. 1995. "Content as Context: The Role of School Subjects in Secondary School Teaching." *Educational Researcher* 24 (8): 5–11.

Grossman, P. L., and S. S. Wineburg. 1998. "Creating a Community of Learners among High School Teachers." *Phi Delta Kappan* 79: 350–353.

Grossman, P., S. Wineburg, and S. Woolworth. 2001. "Toward a Theory of Teacher Community." *Teachers College Record* 103 (6): 942–1012.

Holmes Group. 1990. *Tomorrow's Schools: Principles for the Design of Professional Development Schools.* Lansing, Mich.: Michigan State University.

Huang, R., and J. Bao. 2006. "Towards a Model for Teacher Professional Development in China: Introducing Keli Source." *Journal of Mathematics Teacher Education* 9 (3): 279–298.

Jackson, P. W. 1968. *The Practice of Teaching.* New York: Teachers College Press.

Little, J. W. 1990. "The Persistence of Privacy: Autonomy and Initiative in Teachers' Professional Relations." *Teachers College Record* 4: 509–536.

——— 1993. "Teacher's Professional Development in a Climate of Educational Reform." *Educational Evaluation and Policy Analysis* 15 (2): 129–151.

Lortie, D. C. 1975. *Schoolteacher: A Sociological Study.* Chicago: The University of Chicago Press.

Ma, L. 1999. *Knowing and Teaching Elementary Mathematics: Teachers' Understanding of Fundamental Mathematics in China and the United States.* Mahwah, N.J.: Lawrence Erlbaum.

Paine, L. W. 1990. "The Teacher as Virtuoso: A Chinese Model for Teaching. *Teachers College Record* 92 (1): 49–81.

Paine, L. W., and L. Ma. 1993. "Teachers Working Together: A Dialogue on Organizational and Cultural Perspectives of Chinese Teachers." *International Journal of Educational Research* 19 (8): 675–698.

Sarason, S. B. 1982. *The Culture of the School and the Problem of Change.* Boston: Allyn and Bacon, Inc.

Shen, J. 1994. "Voices from the Field: Emerging Issues from a School-University Partnership." *Metropolitan Universities* 5 (2): 77–85.

———. 1997. "Teacher Retention and Attrition in Public Schools: Evidence from SASS91." *Journal of Educational Research* 91 (2): 81–88.

———. 2002. "Student Teaching in the Context of School-University Partnership: A Case Study of a Student Teacher." *Education* 122 (3): 564–580.

Shen, J., and X. Ma. 2006. "Does Systemic Change Work? Curricular and Instructional Practice in the Context of Systemic Change." *Leadership and Policy in Schools* 5 (3): 231–256.

Stigler, J. W., and H. W. Stevenson. 1991. "How Asian Teachers Polish Each Lesson to Perfection." *American Educator* 15 (1): 12–47.

Stronge, J. H. 2002. *Qualities of Effective Teachers.* Alexandria, Va.: Association for Supervision and Curriculum Development.

Wilson, S. M., and S. Wineburg. 1993. "Wrinkles in Time: Using Performance Assessments to Understand the Knowledge of History Teachers." *American Educational Research Journal* 30 (4): 729–769.

Zheng, J., ed. 2003. *Cases of Open Lessons Based on the New Curriculum.* Fujian, China: Fujian Education Press.

THIRTY-FIVE

Lesson Planning: A Practice of Professional Responsibility and Development

Jianping Shen, Sue Poppink,
Yunhuo Cui, and Guorui Fan

THE IMPORTANCE OF LESSON PLANNING

Much has been made of teachers' professional development, especially in this era of educational reform, in large part because it enables teacher learning (Ball, 1996; Little, 1993). Teachers in the U.S., it is often argued, need to learn more in order to effectively teach their students. They need knowledge of (a) the content, subject matter or discipline, (b) how students learn and what sense they make of various subject matters, and (c) pedagogical alternatives for enabling student learning in a particular subject, or what many have come to refer to as pedagogical content knowledge (Grossman, 1990; Shulman, 1987; Wilson, Shulman & Richart, 1987).

Some have argued that a set of conditions can better enable teachers to develop this knowledge within the context of their teaching practice, referring to this as a collegial professional community in which teachers can reflect, explore, and improve their teaching practice (Grossman, Wineberg, & Woolworth, 2001; Little, 1987; Putman & Borko, 2000; Wang & Paine, 2003). Researchers have discussed multiple tasks that teachers may undertake in these professional communities, particularly examining student work, using videos to examine others' teaching, and studying multiple subject matters as a group.

One tool that is often overlooked in the U.S. as a source of professional growth is the development of lesson plans, which are used in China as both a tool for personal reflection and development as well as collegial reflection. Heaton (2000) has written about the need for teachers to be well prepared for lessons, because each classroom of students will have various levels of prior knowledge of the subject matter and consequently different questions concerning that knowledge. But few have written about the process of lesson planning itself. In the US, planning and preparation are considered important activities, but lesson plans themselves are seldom more than a list of activities. Developing lesson plans are seldom considered a professional development activity for individuals, or set in the context of a professional learning community or in the context of a given school.

Yet, in China the preparation of a lesson is embedded into the organizational structure of school for both individual teachers and the professional community of a school. It is embedded in two activities: the preparation of the lesson plan and the refinement and preparation of a lesson through "open lessons." In an earlier article (Shen, Zheng, & Poppink, 2007), we explained open lessons and how they help teachers to develop their teaching skills. In this article, we explore not only how Chinese teachers develop lesson plans, but also how the organizational structure of Chinese teaching allows them to use lesson plans as a professional development activity.

Lesson planning allows teachers to explore multiple aspects of what may constitute pedagogical content knowledge: content knowledge, teaching methods, and student learning. In developing lesson plans, teachers have opportunities to think deeply about the subject matter, including the way the subject matter is represented in particular textbooks or another aspect of the curriculum such as standards and benchmarks. They also have time to develop pedagogical activities or methods that enable the students to grasp the subject matter. Finally, they have opportunities to ponder their students' knowledge and how they may best understand the content.

AMERICAN AND CHINESE TEACHERS' CONTEXT OF PROFESSIONAL WORK

Su, Qin, and Huang (2005) summarize the differences in the organization of teaching between Chinese and American teachers, by defining a set of activities each undertakes during the day to show that while Chinese teachers work in a social environment with an emphasis on improving the practice of teaching with time to reflect and improve; American teachers work alone, in an isolated environment that requires them to be in front of the classroom for a great majority of their time, with little time to reflect or conduct other activities that may improve their practice. They point out that Chinese culture is one that emphasizes collectivism, while American culture emphasizes individualism, a point that Cohen and Spillane (1993) also made when discussing the governance of American schools and its role in instruction.

In their case study, Su, Qin, and Huang (2005) found American teachers teach in front of a classroom for six or seven hours a day, which means they have very little time, in school, to undertake activities that may improve the practice of their teaching, including lesson planning. They have (a) about 30 minutes for lesson planning, almost no time for correcting student class work in school, or to give feedback on homework to the class as a whole or to individual students; (b) a short, isolated lunch break; and (c) few social or recreational activities with other teachers, few in-school professional development activities, and few opportunities to study with colleagues.

Chinese teachers, on the other hand, teach only one or two hours a day and in one core subject area. This means they spend a fair amount of time on lesson planning: two hours a week with colleagues on one core subject, and informally two hours a day with colleagues on one core subject. It also means they have one or two hours a day to correct student homework and class work, 30 minutes for feedback on homework and classwork with individual students, 40 minutes of lunch time with colleagues plus 40 to 60 minutes of rest time, 30 minutes of recreational time with other teachers, professional development activities every Friday afternoon, and 90 minutes a week studying with colleagues.

LESSON PLANNING BY CHINESE TEACHERS

With these kinds of differences, preparing for each lesson is considered a very important responsibility for Chinese teachers. At the elementary level, a teacher has at least two periods a day to prepare for lessons. At the secondary level, even more time is usually available for planning lessons. It is widely held that lesson planning is a very important factor in determining the quality of the lesson taught.

Textbook, student, and teaching method are the three foci of lesson planning. A teacher is expected to study thoroughly the *textbook* to understand the content of a particular lesson and how the lesson is situated in the larger context of the subject matter. To understand *students' knowledge level* within the textbook contents is also an expectation for the teacher. Based on the knowledge of the textbook and students, the teacher selects the most appropriate and engaging *teaching methods*. Therefore, textbook, student, and teaching method are the three foci for lesson planning.

THE PROCESS OF LESSON PLANNING

Careful lesson planning takes place at both the macro and micro levels. A teacher begins with the preparation for the semester, mapping out the content for the whole semester. The teacher then moves on to planning for the unit, and finally to each lesson in the unit. Therefore, there is a continuum from semester to unit and to each lesson.

An important aspect of lesson planning is emphasizing that the function of each lesson could also be different—some focusing on introducing new content, others on reviewing materials, and still others on applying what has been learned through solving problems. Therefore, not all lesson plans will follow the same pattern.

There are some traditional steps in planning lessons which are emphasized both in textbooks concerning pedagogy, and in practice. First, a teacher prepares for writing the lesson plan, a process that includes understanding how a particular lesson is related to the content of the semester and the unit, learning from professional colleagues' work by studying their lesson plans or seeking input from colleagues, and finding ways to connect the content with students' everyday lives. Second, a teacher engages in writing the lesson plan. As the actual lesson plan that follows shows, this step includes (a) specifying the cognitive and affective objectives, (b) identifying the key points of the content, (c) anticipating the difficult points for students, and (d) designing the flow of the lesson from introducing the topic, presenting the new knowledge, strengthening the understanding of new knowledge by application with increasing complexity, summarizing the learning, and assigning homework. After preparation for and writing of a lesson plan, the lesson planning continues. For example, a teacher finds or makes the most appropriate teaching aids and designs the presentation to show on a projector or blackboard. A teacher is also expected to take notes after the lesson for reflection and improvement. This shows the care with which the teacher must attend to lesson planning.

ADMINISTRATIVE CONTEXT FOR LESSON PLANS

Lesson plans are a critical criterion in the evaluation of teachers. The school provides resources for planning lessons, such as preparing for a lesson in a group setting, sharing lesson plans with different teachers, organizing site visitations to other schools, and holding open lessons to promote learning among teachers. In this way, the lesson plan becomes much more than a simple paper exercise as it may be in the U.S. The lesson plan becomes a larger part of the organization of teaching in China, as teachers develop lessons and share them with one another both on paper and in practice.

ISSUES IN LESSON PLANNING

Generally speaking, lesson planning as a professional activity is successfully carried out by teachers in China. However, based on our experience, the activity of lesson planning in China also has some issues. The first is that a class usually has about 40 students in the developed areas of the country and up to 80 in those still developing. Therefore, class size may make it difficult to individualize instruction. A second issue is that lesson planning occupies much of a teacher's professional day, so much so that some teachers feel they could spend that time productively on other responsibilities. A third issue is that to plan too much might lead to teachers' neglect of the students' learning issues that arise spontaneously in the class. A fourth issue is that in China, each geographic area uses the same set of textbooks; therefore, teachers are usually within a few days of teaching the same lesson. The rigidness in timeline constrains, to a certain extent, teachers' creativity in designing lesson plans.

AN ACTUAL LESSON PLAN ON THE SUM OF MEASURES OF INTERNAL ANGLES OF POLYGONS

The following is an actual lesson plan prepared by Qing Zhang of Weifang Experimental School, Shandong Province, for a lesson using *Mathematics for the Seventh Grade (for the Second Semester)*, a textbook series published by the East China Normal University Press. It illustrates the format and content of a lesson plan that introduces new content. It is common in China to publish compilations of lesson plans and even verbatim transcriptions of lessons that were actually taught. The compilations become an important resource for teachers. This allows other teachers to examine how students reacted to a particular lesson in terms of content and methodology.

INSTRUCTIONAL OBJECTIVES

The cognitive objectives are: (a) to be able to define a quadrangle, polygon, and regular polygon; (b) to be able to interpret, prove, and calculate the sum of internal angles of the quadrangle and polygon.

The ability objectives are: (a) to develop the ability for analogical and divergent thinking through studying the definition of polygon and the sum of internal angles of the polygon; (b) to develop the ability to diagnose and solve problems by dividing polygons into triangles and utilizing the knowledge about triangles.

The affective objective is: to develop students' interest in geometry through studying the similarities and differences between triangles and polygons.

KEY POINTS AND DIFFICULT POINTS

Key points: (a) the ability to interpret, prove, and calculate the sum of internal angles of the quadrangle and polygon; and (b) the ability to actively investigate a new phenomenon.

Difficult point: a student's understanding that the vertices of a polygon must be on the same plane, a necessary condition that is difficult for students to understand.

Ways to emphasize the key points and teach the difficult points include: (a) developing and using teaching aids designed by the teacher (b) facilitating students to think about how to derive geometric theorems; (c) helping students master both individual sets of knowledge, as well as helping them realize the relationship between and among the sets of knowledge; (d) using a table to systematize students' web of knowledge; and (e) designing and implementing exercises with increasing level of difficulty and complexity.

FIRST STAGE OF THE LESSON: CREATING A SITUATION FOR LEARNING

Use multimedia to display a plane view of a weather station. Ask students to find triangles, rectangles, squares, parallelograms, and trapezoids. Ask students to use their knowledge on triangles to define quadrangles and the uses of quadrangles in agriculture, industry, and everyday life.

SECOND STAGE OF THE LESSON: STUDENT-CENTERED EXPLORATIONS ON DEFINITIONS OF QUADRANGLES AND POLYGONS WITH "N" SIDES

(a) Students first recall the definition for triangle. Through analogy students try to define quadrangle. The teacher uses self-made teaching aids to emphasize the necessary condition that all four vertices must be in the same plane. Students then define polygons with "N" sides.

(b) Students then explore the elements in the definitions of quadrangles and polygons. With teachers' Socratic questioning, students complete the following table.

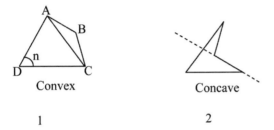

Definition			
How many sides?			
How many internal angles?			
How to notate?			

(c) The teacher emphasizes that when quadrangle is mentioned, we mean (1) rather than (2).

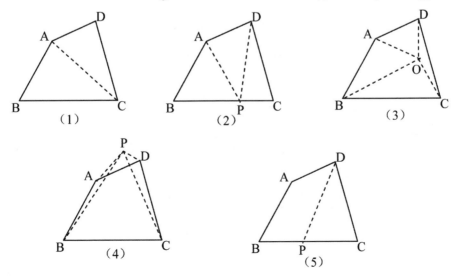

Convex   Concave

1   2

(d) Students solve questions to reinforce their definition of quadrangles and polygons.

THE THIRD STAGE OF THE LESSON: COLLABORATIVE APPROACH TO EXPLORING THE CALCULATION OF INTERNAL ANGLES OF A QUADRANGLE

(a) The teacher raises the questions: The sum of measures of the internal angles of a triangle is 180°, what is the sum of measures of the internal angles of a quadrangle?

(b) Students try various methods of solving the question, and the teacher summarizes their approaches using the following diagrams. Through comparing methods (1) to (5) as illustrated in the following, students will realize that (1) is the optimal approach.

(c) The teacher and students summarize the finding on the sum of the internal angles of a quadrangle.

(d) Students engage in exercises to deepen their understanding of the finding.

THE FOURTH STAGE OF THE LESSON: EXERCISE WITH VARIATIONS

Students work in groups to solve the following problem. Please refer to the diagram below. OB AB. OC AC. What is the relationship between A and BOC? Please explain your answer. In the diagram, are there any angles that are the same as A in measure?

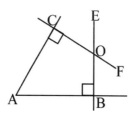

THE FIFTH STAGE OF THE LESSON: EXTRAPOLATING THE FINDINGS FROM QUADRANGLES TO POLYGONS

(a) Based on the knowledge that the sum of internal angles of a quadrangle is 360°, students inquire into the sum of internal angles of polygons with 5 sides, 6 sides, and n sides?

Number of Sides of a Polygon	3	4	5	6	7	...	n
Sum of Internal Angles	180°	360°				...	

(b) Draw the conclusions that the sum of internal angles of polygons with 5 sides, 6 sides, and n sides is $(n-2) \times 180°$.

THE LAST STAGE OF THE LESSON: SUMMARY

(a) Discussing the methods for solving problems: observe, analyze, guess, analogize, explain, and apply.

(b) Discussing the methods for studying geometrical concepts: how to define, and how to specify the elements in the definition such as sides, angles, and sum of internal angles (briefly mention that the sum of external angles is a topic for future study).

(c) Discussing the thinking processes and methods used in drawing the conclusion that the sum of internal angles of a quadrangle is 360°.

(d) Discussing the notation that triangles, quadrangles, and other polygons are related to each other; and that geometric knowledge comes from everyday life and can be used in everyday life.

SUMMARY AND DISCUSSION

Lesson planning, then, is part of professional development of teachers in China, including teachers' individual reflection and study to prepare the lesson, and the collegial activities undertaken to prepare. It is considered an important professional responsibility. In a case study of Ms. Zhen, written to explain the interaction of the organization of curriculum and teaching in China, Wang and Paine (2003) write of Ms. Zhen's personal preparation,

> In planning this lesson, Ms. Zhen first spent considerable time reading and analyzing the textbook and teachers' manual to understand "what the important and difficult points were, which area needed to be stressed in teaching, and where students would likely make mistakes." Then she individually developed a preliminary lesson plan by considering "how to teach it in an active way and by involving students in it." (p. 9)

This quote shows the importance of (a) content knowledge—particularly as it is portrayed in the textbook, (b) understanding what students will make of the content, and (c) how to link the two of them together. It also shows the careful study that teachers undertake individually.

Support for this kind of lesson planning is woven into the structure of the organization of teachers' work in China in at least two ways. First, the organization of teachers' work in China is that they teach one or two hours a day in one subject matter, and they spend the rest of the day in preparing for teaching, or reflecting on students' work and what could have been done better. Second, the lesson planning can be used as a part of the preparation for what Wang and Paine (2003) refer to as a "public lesson" and we refer to it as an "open lesson" (Shen, Zheng, & Poppink, 2007). In the case of Ms. Zhen, the authors continue explaining her lesson preparation by explaining the social aspects of her preparation. They write,

> Next, she shared her lesson plan with several senior mathematics teachers in the teaching research group and revised it based upon their suggestions. Ms. Zhen then taught a trial lesson in one of the two 6th grade classes she taught which was observed and critiqued by her colleagues in the teaching research group. She revised the lesson plan again based upon her experience in teaching the trial lesson and suggestions from her colleagues. In the end, she formally taught this public lesson, which was again observed and critiqued by the teachers in the teaching research group.

American teaching is unlikely to be restructured to resemble teaching in China any time soon. Still there are valuable lessons to be learned from the Chinese practice that lesson planning is an important professional development activity which requires an increase in knowledge on the part of teachers together with collegial support for improving the practice of teaching. Teachers' individual and collegial planning and working time may be a necessary condition to improve the quality of teaching in American schools, and detailed lesson plans provide a way for American teachers to better understand content, student learning, and pedagogical content knowledge.

REFERENCES

Ball, D. L. (1996). Teacher learning and the mathematics reforms: What we think we know and what we need to learn. *Phi Delta Kappan, 77*(7), 500–508.

Cohen, D. K., & Spillane, J. P. (1993). Policy and practice: The relations between governance and instruction. In S. H. Fuhrman (Ed.), *Designing coherent education policy: Improving the system* (pp. 35–95). San Francisco: Jossey-Bass Publishers.

Grossman, P. L. (1990). *The making of a teacher: Teacher knowledge and teacher education.* New York: Teachers College Press.

Grossman, P., Wineburg, S., & Woolworth, S. (2001). Toward a theory of teacher community. *The Teachers College Record, 103*(6), 942–1012.

Heaton, R. M. (2000). *Teaching mathematics to the new standards: Relearning the dance.* New York: Teachers College Press.

Little, J. W. (1987). Teachers as colleagues. In Richardson-Koehler (Ed.), *Educators' handbook: A research perspective.* New York: Longman.

Little, J. W. (1993). Teacher's professional development in a climate of educational reform. *Educational Evaluation and Policy Analysis, 15*(2), 129–151.

Putnam, R. T., & Borko, H. (2000). What do view of knowledge and thinking have to say about research on teacher learning? *Educational Researcher, 29*(1), 4–15.

Shen, J., Zheng, J., & Poppink, S. (2007). Open lessons: A practice to develop a learning community for teachers. *Educational Horizons, 85* (3), 181–191.

Shulman, L. S. (1986). Those who understand: Knowledge growth in teaching. *Educational Researcher, 15*(2), 4–14.

Shulman, L. S. (1987). Knowledge and teaching: Foundations of the new reform. *Harvard Educational Review, 57*(1), 4–14.

Su, Z., Qin, H., & Huang, T. (2005). The isolated teacher: What we can learn from the Chinese. *Wingspread Journal,* 7–13.

Wang, J., & Paine, L. W. (2004). Learning to teach with mandated curriculum and public examination of teaching as contexts. *Teaching and Teacher Education, 19*(1), 75–94.

Wilson, S. M., Shulman, L. S., & Richart, A. E. (1987). "150 different ways" of knowing: Representations of knowledge in teaching. In J. Calderhead (Ed.), *Exploring teacher thinking* (pp. 104–124). Sussex: Holt, Rinehart and Winston.

Discursive Practice in Educational Psychology: How the Subject Tells the Truth about Itself

THIRTY-SIX

Toward a Poststructuralist Analysis

Suzanne Gallagher

As a student of educational psychology I had "learned" the discipline at one level. It was not until I began "teaching" an introductory course to preservice teachers that I began questioning the discipline. The act of questioning took me to another level of understanding. What I had accepted as "real," "stable," "true," and "neutral" within the discipline's knowledge base I gradually began to read as a "reflection of conventions" (Kincheloe, 1993) imbued with political interests. It was an uneasy reading. As I became aware of the way power and knowledge implicate each other, I began to critique educational psychology's mainstream discourse as a "regime of truth" (Foucault, 1980).

The analysis presented in this chapter is meant to be an example of a critical poststructuralist analysis. As reflected in discussions in the preceding chapters, this analysis is facilitated by an oppositional reading, necessarily partial, and coming from a particular social and political location, i.e., it assumes and acknowledges my own situated knowledge (Collins, 1990; Haraway, 1991; Harding, 1991). It is illustrative and by no means exhaustive. It represents a sample not a synopsis of all possible critiques (Murphy, 1993). It is a counterdiscourse, and serves to "talk back" to and denaturalize the dominant discourse of the discipline of educational psychology.

Two aspects of the discipline of educational psychology are examined in the critical discourse analysis that follows. First, the *disciplinary principles* that form the internal features and particular rationality of educational psychology's discourse are highlighted. Then the *nondiscursive* aspects of the discipline, including the political and social networks in which the discourse is embedded, are examined. These aspects are discussed briefly as the chapter begins.

Disciplinary principles are apparent in the particular rationality, i.e., *technical rationality*, of the discipline. A technical rationality provides the meaning-making system, a kind of internal regulation (Foucault, 1972), of the discipline of educational psychology. It is evident in the rules, relations, and regularities that lie just below the surface of the discourse. This internal regulation is generally considered a resource for the discipline as it provides a "grounding" for the discipline's perspective. It is powerful in that it influences thought and by extension the knowledge and practice of the discipline itself.

While the internal system of the discourse is considered a resource from a particular standpoint, it also can be considered a constraint from another perspective. The technical rationality of the discipline presents *problematics* when read critically. In the use of the word problematics I adopt Foucault's notion of developing something that is accepted (i.e., a given) into a question (Caputo & Yount, 1993). Problematics can remain invisible if the technical rationality of the discipline is "taken for granted" and becomes transparent or invisible, or is considered "natural." Usher (1993) aptly describes the possibility that educational psychologists are "*enfolded* in an implicit conception of disciplines as neutral bodies of knowledge" (emphasis added, p. 17). It is possible that educational psychologists are caught in our own unself-reflexive meaning-making system. Educational psychologists will remain prisoners of the discourse unless we gain access to the constitutive forces of the discipline's rationality.

Educational psychologists, through a critical reading and analysis, can make explicit and interrogate the disciplinary principles of the discipline and the problematics they suggest. Viewed from a critical perspective the science of the discipline in general as well as its truth claims do not cease to exist; instead, "they become representations that need to be problematized rather than accepted as received truths" (Aronowitz & Giroux, 1991, p. 75).

This section of the chapter is an appropriation of Foucault's (1972) notion of archeology, i.e., an investigation of the human sciences as systems of knowledge. Archaeology has been described as a "critical investigation of disciplinary systems of knowledge with the goal of understanding the discursive practices that produce those systems of knowledge" (Prado, 1995, p. 25). Dreyfus and Rabinow (1983) emphasize that Foucault's aim was "to rediscover on what basis knowledge and theory became possible" (p. 17). Once this is understood it is possible to begin to think differently and to understand "what what we do does" (Foucault, quoted in Dreyfus and Rabinow, 1983, p. 187).

The *nondiscursive aspects* of the discipline are discussed in the second section of this chapter. Nondiscursive aspects pertain to the "background practices" (Dreyfus & Rabinow, 1983), the human activity, and institutional processes operating within the discipline (Foucault, 1972) as well as those within which the discipline is embedded. These include the social, political, economic, and historical contexts and contingencies of the discipline that are prior to the "truth" of the discipline and are potent in the hegemonic construction of the discourse.

Educational psychologists, for example, persevere in the belief that the discourse is developed and controlled through rigorous scientific activity (Cherryholmes, 1988). This activity yields a body of knowledge able to be put to positive use in education. However, this commonsense assumption can "work behind our backs in powerful and constraining ways" (Gitlin, 1990, p. 444). The discipline is embedded in power relationships (Foucault, 1980). By ignoring these various power relationships, the relationships that enable and facilitate the discipline's discourse and practices (Cherryholmes, 1988), it is possible to take as natural and necessary, as transcendental truth, that which is actually of our own making. As Gergen (1985) insists, "a given understanding that prevails…is not fundamentally dependent on the empirical validity of the perspective in question, but on the viscidities of social processes" (p. 268). All the things that are said through the discipline's dominant discourse, what metaphors and values are endorsed, what remains unsaid, and what knowledge is marginalized are actually the result of social negotiations and power relationships more than rigorous scientific activity. As Thomas (1997) points out, what is considered knowledge is "what is *agreed* to be correct rather than the product of compelling justifications" (emphasis added, p. 92).

DISCIPLINARY PRINCIPLES

WHAT IS A "DISCIPLINE"?

A "discipline," in one sense of the word, is considered a "neutral, scientifically validated body of knowledge whose…effects are enlightening and empowering and which thus enable effective action" (Usher & Edwards, 1994, p. 48). David Berliner, a preeminent educational psychologist and coauthor of a "classic" textbook, expresses confidence in the discourse of the discipline as a body of knowledge marked with an empowering character. He asserts: "I think that in the past few years we have come closer than ever before to providing direct scientific underpinnings for the art of teaching. In some cases, the need for highly inventive, creative minds has been lessened, as research provides ideas and technology that are *almost* directly applicable to classroom life" (emphasis in original, Berliner & Rosenshine, 1987, p. 3). He continues: "We now have something that an ordinary person does not have—a knowledge base consisting of facts, concepts, and technology that can transform our profession.…Knowledge is clearly power, a kind of social power" (p. 31). Berliner's quotes portray the discipline as producing a body of systematized knowledge that is cumulative; this body of knowledge is produced through the scientific practice of a specific group of persons and conveys faith that it is able to be applied in positive ways to the practice of teaching. These tenets are implicated throughout the classic texts of the discipline of educational psychology.

Gage and Berliner (1991) have stated in their preface that the purpose of the textbook is "to give prospective and practicing educators…an introduction to what educational psychology can provide by way of facts, concepts, principles, and research methods that will be both theoretically enlightening and practically useful. We want our students to take what we present as theory and put it into use in their classrooms" (p. xvii).

> Woolfolk (1995) similarly tells readers that "the major goal of this book is to provide you with the best and the most useful theories for teaching—those that have solid evidence behind them…[these theories] are ways of understanding the challenges that teachers face" (pp. 16–17).

DISCOURSES OF DISCIPLINES—SITES OF STRUGGLE

Textbooks typically present the mainstream discourse of disciplines. A discourse is important in poststructuralist research but for reasons other than those traditionally understood. Poststructuralists are skeptical that knowledge can be systematized because knowledge claims are considered local, partial, and always permeated with power and human interests (Usher & Edwards, 1994). Claims of neutrality are always suspect as discourses, even scientific ones, act in the interests of some persons over others. Therefore, the work of discourse analysis is undertaken not because a discourse is understood as delivering "truth"; rather, a discourse is selected for analysis because its "truth" is seen as relational, situated, and partial (Luke & Gore, 1992), and needs to be understood and critiqued as such.

Discourses are sites of encounter and struggle. McNay (1994) explains: "*Discourses and meaning are the site of social struggle.* The process through which hegemonic social relations are achieved and maintained often involves the stabilization of discursive relations and the fixation of meaning.... Similarly, resistance to hegemonic meaning entails the contestation and disruption of naturalized forms of discourse" (emphasis added, p. 75). Once we recognize that the discourse of educational psychology is a site of social struggle we are able to enter the dialogue, to engage in debate, and offer criticism that "provides important opportunities to break with dominant readings and interpretations" (Cherryholmes, 1988, p. 158).

RATIONALITY OF A DISCIPLINE: IDEOLOGY

A hallmark of modernity is entrusting "reason" as the way to know the "truth," ascertaining universal laws through which order may be maintained. Reason was/is understood as "the source of progress in knowledge and society, as well as the privileged locus of truth and the foundation of systematic knowledge" (Best & Kellner, 1991, p. 2). Rationality is the means by which a person or group puts the world in order. In other words, rationality is the sense-making activity of a particular community evidenced in the community's discursive formation. Rationality is evident in the particular views of knowledge, set of interests, beliefs, expectations, meanings, and methodological forms of inquiry that are held by a person or group (Giroux, 1983a). The dominant discourse of educational psychology has a particular rationality, as do other examples of discourse.

The sense-making function of rationality is akin to a meaning of "ideology." Words like "ideology" are seldom part of the discussions regarding disciplines in the social sciences such as educational psychology. The assumed neutrality of the science eschews words like ideology often considered in a pejorative sense; it is something another group subscribes to, while "we" have, or at least search objectively for, the "truth" (Burbules, 1995). The way ideology forms a perspective, or influences work and relationships, is easily overlooked. As mentioned in the beginning of this chapter, another possible reason educational psychologists rarely consider the ideology of the discipline is that we are so embedded in it that we take the sense-making activity of the discipline as "natural."

The ideology to which I am referring permeates social life—we all participate in it (Giroux, 1983a). Ideology is evidenced in "the production and representation of ideas, values, and beliefs and the manner in which they are expressed and lived out by both individuals and groups" (McLaren, 1989, p. 176). Van Dijk (1993b) explains ideologies as "the fundamental social cognitions that reflect the basic aims, interests and values of groups" (p. 258). This "sense-making" characteristic of ideology is important as it is involved in the "production, consumption, and representation of meaning" (Giroux, 1983b, p. 16). This is the sense of "ideology" I am concerned with here, rather than with specific political ideologies, such as socialism, communism, or conservatism (Giroux, 1983b).

Another characteristic of ideology gives it significance. Ideology's potency only "becomes clear when it is linked to the concepts of struggle" (Giroux, 1983b, p. 16). A critique of ideology, therefore, serves to present the interests of some persons in dialectical relationship to the advantage of others. This is why a critique is "useful and necessary…because it helps identify the struggles that are central" (Sarup, 1996, p. 70).

The dynamic of the struggle to be considered along with rationality is expressed through the "problematic" (Giroux, 1981, 1983a). As explained earlier, the problematic represents a questioning of an assumption or belief communicated in the discourse. Problematics have an added dimension in that they also raise questions regarding what is not expressed in the discourse, or what has been silenced by the discourse. In this way problematics reveal "the ideological source that lies beneath the choice of what is considered important and unimportant in a mode of thinking" (Giroux, 1981, p. 9). That is, the way things are understood affects the kind of questions that seem intelligible or important, and, at the same time, pins other questions outside the realm of comprehension or reasonableness. However, questions that seem unfathomable if taken seriously could transform our basic assumptions (Giroux, 1983a); they form a counterdiscourse to the dominant ideology. Therefore, problematics are important considerations.

A particular rationality "grounds" the dominant discourse of educational psychology and is quite evident in the discipline's classic texts. This is explained as a *technical rationality*, which becomes obvious through a close reading of the codes found in the texts of the discourse. Technical rationality is understood as "an epistemology of practice derived from positivist philosophy" (Schon, 1987, p. 3). It has been described as indicative of embeddedness in a "culture of positivism" by Giroux (1981) because it is based "upon the logic of scientific methodology with its interest in explanation, prediction, and technical control" (p. 42). As the natural sciences provide the model for its theoretical development (Giroux, 1983a), it is understandably explained as a "normal science version of social science" (Schon, 1995); it allows for a kind of "scientific management" (Kincheloe, 1993) of education.

Technical rationality is rooted in the modernist need to control and bring order to an objective world. It operates through the following interrelated assumptions expressed by Giroux (1983). *Control* is the goal of technical rationality (and therefore, educational psychology's goal) and is made possible through the application of educational theory, or law-like propositions, derived from empirical research. *Discovery of causation* is possible through this scientific management and makes credible the possibility of prediction and control. The knowledge derived from this inquiry is understood as *value-free* and represents neutral, objective reality. Therefore, educators using its knowledge believe they *act in a value-free manner.*

Technical rationality is evidenced not only in the discourse of the texts; it is built into the structures and practices of modern educational activity and educational institutions themselves (Bloland, 1995; Schon, 1995; Usher & Edwards, 1994). In the following discussion, first, evidence is presented to show how technical rationality pervades the discourse of educational psychology (Giroux, 1981) as expressed in its classic texts; second, the problematics provoked by this perspective are discussed.

CONTROL AND THE POSSIBILITY OF CAUSATION

The purpose of gaining control of the educational experience is central to educational psychology's discourse found in classic textbooks (e.g., Gage & Berliner, 1991; Woolfolk, 1995). Gage and Berliner (1991) explain that the "objectives of educational psychology, like those of any science, are to explain, predict, and control the phenomena with which it is concerned" (p. 16). Hence, educational psychology is intent on controlling the processes of teaching and learning. Scientific research is the means by which control of educational settings is thought possible.

The primary and fundamental position of scientific research and theory building is clear throughout both classic texts. Both texts provide a defense against the position that educational psychology is merely an exercise in "common sense." This defense operates to answer the historical critique that educational psychology is "putting what everybody knows in language which nobody can understand" (quoted in Welton, 1912; Grinder, 1970, p. 4). Gage and Berliner (1991) assert that research in educational psychology, like research in the social sciences in general, is of high quality. "Despite popular belief to the contrary, the consistency of results compares favorably with that of the physical sciences….The relationship between variables often is even stronger than those on which some medical practice is based" (p. 28).

In a similar manner, Woolfolk (1995) highlights the research of educational psychology in contrast to common sense. She comments that "frequently the principles set forth by educational psychologists—after spending much thought, research, and money—sound pathetically obvious. People are tempted to say…'Everyone knows that!'" (p. 11). She alerts readers that there is a "danger" in thinking, "educational psychologists spend a lot of time discovering the obvious. When a principle is stated in simple terms it can sound simplistic" (p. 13). Readers are warned that it is not a case of what "sounds sensible" but "what is demonstrated when the principle is put to the test" (Gage, quoted in Woolfolk, 1995, p. 13).

It is interesting to note that despite the attempt to differentiate and privilege "scientific research" over commonsense theorizing, there appears a contradiction in that commonsense is called upon frequently to witness a shared understanding, e.g., "Everyone knows what intelligence is" (Gage & Berliner, 1991, p. 51). "Everyone knows what motivation is, how it makes a difference between resentful boredom at one extreme and ravenous interest at the other" (p. 326). Even as the scientific basis of the discipline is defended, it is imperative that at some point the knowledge claims of educational psychology appear "so correct that to reject them would be unnatural, a violation of common sense" (McLaren, 1989, p. 175). This is when hegemony takes hold, i.e., when that which appeals to common sense is accepted as universal truth (Giroux & Purpel, 1983).

Woolfolk (1995) notes that "research is the primary tool" (p. 16) for understanding teaching and learning. Toward this end "descriptive studies and experimental research can provide valuable information to teachers. Correlations allow you to predict events that are likely to occur in the classroom; experimental studies can help indicate cause-and-effect relationships and should help you to implement useful changes" (p. 20). There is little indication regarding just how little cause-and-effect relationships are possible in the social sciences, although Gage and Berliner (1991) do state that "Good experiments, those that allow for clear causal interpretations, are less likely than we would like" (Gage & Berliner, 1991, p. 25). The confidence in scientific method prevails and is reiterated in an appendix titled "Research in Educational Psychology" that is provided because students "must know how information in the field is created" (Woolfolk, 1995, p. 588).

There are limitations placed on what may be said and not said through the discipline by privileging scientific research over other forms of knowledge. For example, the legitimacy of a complaint by some "parents in low-income areas, whose children often tend to do poorly on intelligence tests" (Gage & Berliner, 1991, p. 72) is recognized. Gage and Berliner (1991) explain that these parents may "believe that teachers and school systems hold hereditarian views [regarding intelligence]. And they [the parents] believe these views lead educators to stop trying to help their children" (p. 72). The perspective that parents offer as the result of their own personal knowledge is discounted by citing a 1967 survey reporting that only "6% of American adults, and only 1 and 2 percent of students and teachers believed that intelligence tests measure only inborn intelligence" (Gage & Berliner, 1991, p. 72). The evidence of this 1967 research study is used to nullify the possibility of merit in an argument coming from personal knowledge of a group.

"NEUTRAL" KNOWLEDGE

In a discourse based on technical rationality, knowledge arrived at through scientific means is treated as value-free, representing neutral, objective reality. This is an indispensable tenet of the scientific method. It follows that teachers using the discipline's knowledge are judged as acting in neutral and objective ways.

Gage and Berliner (1991) are clear in stating that *the act of teaching*, in general, is not value-free as "teachers must combine insights from educational psychology with ethical thinking about what is good for their students and for society" (p. 7). However, they also emphasize that ethical discussions are not the concern of their educational psychology text: "But educational psychology, and hence this book, is most concerned with the teaching and learning processes in classrooms. More precisely, we deal primarily with the problems that arise in carrying out the tasks of teaching" (p. 7). They explain that the style of writing found in this textbook, "like most textbooks is...neutral and dispassionate" (Gage & Berliner, 1991, p. 7).

Similarly, Woolfolk (1996), reflecting on her purpose in writing textbooks, contends that while other educational psychologists have course goals that include deepening students' "social and ethical understandings [or] capacity to be planful and reflective" (p. 41), she has other goals she considers the "heart" of courses in educational psychology. For Woolfolk the "main goal... is to help perspective teachers understand, value, and use the knowledge and processes of educational psychology" (p. 41).

An assurance is expressed that better teaching can result through learning and applying educational psychology. Woolfolk (1995) states: "If you can become a more expert learner by applying the knowledge from this text...then you will be a better teacher as well" (p. 50). Woolfolk (1995) explains that expert teachers, "like expert dancers or gymnasts, have mastered a number of moves or routines that they can perform easily, *almost without thinking*" (emphasis added, p. 5). Consider the quote from Berliner and Rosenshine (1987) above, "In some cases, the need for highly inventive, creative minds has been lessened" (p. 3).

PROBLEMATICS

The discussion of technical rationality in this section has the purpose of displaying the sense-making activity of the discourse. Because discourses are recognized as sites of social struggle, they need to be interrogated. This interrogation is necessary not just to argue or to interpret on the level of ideas, but because theoretical choices have implications for practice (Luke & Gore, 1992). Problematics are posed regarding the following issues: the relationship of theory and practice; a reductionist focus of the discipline; the teachers' role; the limitation of questions and behaviorism; and the possibility of neutral, value-free knowledge.

RELATIONSHIP OF THEORY AND PRACTICE

There is an implicit understanding that the theory generated in the name of educational research can be applied directly to the practice of education. This is especially clear in each of the classic textbooks as disciplinary knowledge is placed in a foundational position to the practice of teaching. "We have presented a view of educational psychology as a foundation discipline that helps to accomplish the tasks of teaching" (Gage & Berliner, 1991, p. 47); "My goal in writing this book…[is] so you will have the foundation for becoming an expert" (Woolfolk, 1995, p. 18). Thus, both the vital role that disciplinary knowledge plays (Giroux, 1981), and the one-way relationship of theory-to-practice (Carr & Kemmis, 1986) are highlighted in these classic textbooks.

Many of the criticisms of the foundational understanding of the relationship of theory and practice regard the decontextualized learning of theories and concepts and then applying them directly to practice (Anderson et al., 1995). The theoretical knowledge is sometimes judged to be inaccessible or too "scientific" for practitioners. However, the foundational model has proved to be resistant to arguments leveled against it. Despite criticisms, it has been difficult to disconnect from the "formative power" psychology has had on education (Usher & Edwards, 1994). What is it that the foundational model provides that keeps it viable in the midst of so much criticism?

The foundational metaphor is meant to convey a sense of security in that "grounding our thinking about practice on a simplified and scientifically accurate foundation should make it more comprehensible and reliable" (Doyle & Carter, 1996, p. 24). The need for security is heightened as the practice of teaching is recognized as a serious and complex enterprise. This is the optimistic message expressed in both classic textbooks and the dominant discourse of the discipline in general.

Thinking about the knowledge of the discipline as foundational also serves to establish a certain hierarchical order within the discipline. A foundational approach distances those who do research from those who teach it and from those who learn it and eventually apply it to practice. By privileging theoretical knowledge over the practical knowledge of teachers, students, and parents, the conventional power arrangements within the educational process are supported.

Also supported are the inequalities constructed by its knowledge claims in a way "so powerful it is almost invisible" (Cherryholmes, 1988, p. 98).

REDUCTIONIST FOCUS

Technical rationality's aim of gaining control through the development and application of theory is advanced when variables can be manipulated in the interest of bringing about "a certain state of affairs or to prevent its occurrence" (Giroux, 1981, p. 43). In order to complete experimental activities, through which theories and principles can be formulated, variables need to be reduced to simplest terms. Necessarily, this directs attention toward the "trivial—on that which can be easily measured by empirical instruments" (Kincheloe, 1993, p. 129.). The "illusion" of certainty in practice is supported, but as Kincheloe (1993) remarks, "[r]arely do the most significant questions of human affairs lend themselves to empirical quantification and the pseudo-certainty that often accompanies numbers" (p. 129). The underside of reductionism is that it may "simplify a particular phenomenon so as to mask its complexity" (Leistyna et al., 1996, p. 36).

A plain example of reductionist thinking is found in the material regarding writing objectives that are categorized as cognitive, affective, or psychomotor. Both texts recognize the impossibility of separating these areas from each other: "none of these kinds of activities is isolated from the others.…The three types of objectives are intertwined" (Gage & Berliner, 1991, pp. 42–43); "In real life, of course, behaviors from these three domains occur simultaneously" (Woolfolk, 1995, p. 447). However, they are separated in these texts, because "it often is useful to focus on one at a time" (Gage & Berliner, 1991, p. 42–43) . In what way is this useful? For whom is this useful? This distinction, "devised by a group of educational measurement experts" (Gage & Berliner, 1991, p. 43), is a "fiction that we tell to make our lives as educators simpler" (Apple, 1994, p. x). These distinct categories have made their way into the realm of a commonsense understanding of educational psychology. They are examples of simplistic ways of understanding phenomena that mask their complexity.

An important issue in this criticism is the emphasis on the efficiency of action, or the "means," by which the control is produced, not on the value of the goal of the practice itself. This implies a separation of factual information intended to facilitate teaching from questions of values that is indicative of technical rationality's goal of gaining control through mastery of theory. The concern is with how to do things, and how to do them more efficiently, rather than on what it is that should be done. Teachers internalize this logic of efficiency.

TEACHERS AS FUNCTIONAL PROBLEM SOLVERS

Teachers-as-problem-solvers is a favorite role of teachers expressed in classic texts: "Whatever your situation, the tasks you must accomplish raise problems that teachers have always had to face. And these problems arise in some form from the first day and every day you teach.…Educational psychology serves teachers…by helping them deal with these problems" (Gage & Berliner, 1991, p. 7). Woolfolk (1995) highlights this bias regarding the teacher as a problem solver by playing off Schon's (1983) call for a more "reflective practitioner." Because Woolfolk is discussing the "artistry" of teaching and the need for teachers to be reflective, inventive, and creative she suggests that her readers might find this discussion "a bit idealistic and abstract" (p. 9). She then submits that "[r]ight now, you may have other, more down to earth, concerns about becoming a teacher. You are not alone!" (p. 9). For Woolfolk the more pertinent concerns of beginning teachers include: "maintaining classroom discipline, motivating students, accommodating differences among students, evaluating students' work, dealing with parents" (p. 10). These are the issues of educational psychology. Students of the discipline are told that "by applying the knowledge from this text…you will be a better teacher" (p. 10). Anything that keeps teachers from their task of efficiently solving technical problems is apparently considered secondary.

Two important themes can be inferred from Woolfolk's (1995) discussion. First, the "real" concerns of teachers are defined and delimited by those who write the texts. These become the issues in which educational psychology can be useful to teachers; these are the problems and solutions addressed in the text that are to be learned and internalized by readers. Second, focus is directed away from the need of teachers to be reflective about the work that they do and the ends for which teachers teach. The focus becomes the problem-solving activity.

Kincheloe (1993) refers to the "how-to" emphasis as an example of "crude practicality" that characterizes so many technically oriented teacher education programs. Cherryholmes (1988), likewise, alerts us to a "vulgar pragmatism" that is "instrumentally and functionally reproducing accepted meanings and conventional organizations, institutions, and ways of doing things for good or ill" (p. 151). Teachers in this perspective are seen primarily as instrumental problem solvers who "select technical means best suited to a particular purpose" (Schon, 1987, p. 3). This image of teachers constructs a specific view by which a "technical ethos is created which eventuates in….a constricted view of teacher cognition, which reduces the act of teaching to merely a technique" (Kincheloe, 1993, p. 10).

It is ironic that through an enculturation into the discipline, through internalizing the mindset of educational psychology, teachers can become complicitous in their own de-skilling (Apple, 1993; Giroux, 1983a; Kincheloe, 1993; Macedo, 1994). Even so, teachers are not necessarily so "malleable and powerless that they submit to their own victimization" (Giroux & Purpel, 1986). People do have and can be encouraged to be reflective, to develop a sense of the social, political, and historical contexts in considering the mainstream discourse of this discipline. Teachers can be self-reflexive and realize that there are multiple texts that support and facilitate, or contest and interrogate, particular meaning-making systems. However, the discipline itself supports and privileges thinking within the established paradigm.

LIMITING OF QUESTIONS

Technical rationality limits the kind of questions that may be considered legitimate within the discipline. Questions are confined to those that have a specifically technical solution, those that can be addressed through scientific research. Questions about "problems" that teachers face have to be handled within an empiricist tradition and, therefore, need to be reduced to variables that are treated in isolation. This manner of thinking "creates a form of tunnel vision in which only a small segment of social reality is open to examination" (Giroux, 1981, p. 46). Ignoring complexities is in sync with Edward L. Thorndike's (1910) recommendation in an early educational psychology textbook. He stated in a discussion of laws of learning that "the complexities of human learning will in the end be best understood if at first we avoid them" (p. 6).

Besides limiting questions to those that can have technical solutions, questions are also transformed or recast as problems with technical solutions. Thus, issues regarding the social, cultural, and political situations that arise in educational institutions and classroom life are explained through "neutral" scientific means. This allows for a very subtle entrenchment of hegemony as scientific justification provides for the ideal solution to social, political, and ideological problems (Apple, 1990).

Problems dealing with diversity in tracking, for example, are managed as scientific issues. Through the use of scientific technologies of testing of "intelligence" the differential control of access to high status knowledge is not seen as a power play of agents of the dominant culture, but rather rationalized as the commonsense dealing with the varying "abilities" of students.

Behaviorism, for another example, is effective in advancing the empiricist perspective of technical rationality in that it is concerned with efficiently controlling the environment through the manipulation of discrete (and often minute) variables. A commitment to a behavioral perspective is presented as a commitment to efficiency and effectiveness, but it can also express a commitment to control, manipulation, and a vulgar pragmatism (Cherryholmes, 1988).

Classic texts manifest their behavioral proclivities in the perspective they present in several areas. Although theories other than behavioral ones are covered to some extent, the preponderance of space and endorsement is afforded to the behavioral perspective. A small sampling communicates this bias.

Gage and Berliner (1991) provide a good illustration in their definition of "learning," as "a process whereby an organism changes behavior as a result of experience" (p. 225). They go on to state that "it is the overt behaviors of talking, writing, moving and the like that allow us to study the cognitive behaviors that interest us—thinking, feeling, wanting, remembering….The overt behaviors of the organism—pigeon or school-age child, dog or teacher—are always our starting point" (p. 225). Social interactions between teacher and students are described as "two or more people stimulating and responding to one another" (p. 503). The handling of a category of behavior described simply as "too much," "calls for extinction or punishment" (p. 511); behavior of the "too little" variety "calls for reinforcement, which strengthens behavior" (p. 512).

Personality is described as "a concept derived from behavior. We see only behavior. But we create names for that behavior to talk about the different kinds of behavior we notice" (p. 147). Gage and Berliner (1991) go on to explain that "we need to emphasize more that behavior is controlled, to a large degree, by the way rewards and punishments occur in the environment" (p. 148). In the discussion of "motivation" the authors explain that their text explores "the operant-conditioning approach to the understanding and improvement. This approach concentrates on the environment—particularly the reinforcement contingencies in the environment" (Gage & Berliner, 1991, p. 327).

Despite a reliance on behaviorist psychology, Skinner is mentioned only in citations in Gage and Berliner (1991). The knowledge claims and practices of this perspective appear ahistorical or transhistorical with no mention of the social or political context that influenced its popularity in the 1940s and 1950s in the United States. The role of teacher as "social engineer," which characterizes Skinner's theoretical perspective (Sprinthall & Sprinthall, 1990) might be unpalatable to teachers, yet that is the implication of the behavioral approach. Although teachers should be able to evaluate and question theories, this is difficult to do because of the assumption of neutrality and objectivity, the authoritative tenor of the text, the limiting of questions, and the emphasis on technical problem solving.

TEXTS AS NEUTRAL AND VALUE-FREE

Giroux (1981) comments that generally, values are dismissed as inappropriate for discussion from a perspective embedded in technical rationality. Questions of value must be eschewed within a technocratic worldview as values are thought to weaken the scientific process. Giroux (1981) explains: "Information or 'data' taken from the subjective world of intuition, insight, philosophy and nonscientific theoretical frameworks is not acknowledged as being relevant. Values, then, appear as the nemeses of 'facts' and are viewed at best, as interesting, and at worst, as irrational and subjective emotional responses" (p. 44). Although classic texts claim a stance of value-free neutrality, they can be read as expressing very clear values, usually the values of the dominant culture. These values are presented as normative and natural. Value statements appear so frequently that their authors subvert their own claim to neutrality.

Values are revealed in what is included and what is excluded from texts, and the type of rhetoric connected with issues. For example, Gage and Berliner (1991) expound on the effectiveness of small class size and cite studies supporting this assertion. They proceed to add another value factor, cost-effectiveness, to the discussion. They conclude: "Knowing that smaller classes are more effective and creating them are two different things. A major problem is cost" (p. 502). They report that it would cost $34.5 million to reduce class size by one, from 30 to 29. Readers are presented with the conclusion that "reducing class size at all grade levels from 30 to 15, to obtain substantial improvement in education, would increase the cost even more" (p. 502). The unreported message is that this cost is more than "we" would want to pay. This position displays a stark contrast to the critique of the "savage inequalities" in funding educational resources exposed by Kozol (1994). It also assigns cost-effectiveness as a premier value in education, over quality and equity. This value-laden assertion ignores the political and economic issues related to the fact that some school districts can and some cannot "afford" small class size. In accepting as a matter of course that small class size is just not "feasible" inequality becomes "naturalized."

Another example of values being very much an aspect of purportedly neutral texts is obvious in the discourse expressing the differential treatment of students. It is the discourse of scientifically solving problems, so characteristic of technical rationality, that allows discussions like the following to be viewed as acceptable within "neutral" discourses.

Woolfolk (1995), for example, presents a discussion of between-class ability grouping as a way to make teaching "*more appropriate* for students" (emphasis added, p. 118). However, the text states that there are several "problems" with the practice of ability grouping. The following problems are listed:

> Lower ability classes seem to receive lower-quality instruction in general. Teachers tend to focus on lower-level objectives and routine procedures. There are more management problems. Teacher enthusiasm and enjoyment are less in the lower-ability classes....[and] lower expectations are communicated to students. Student self-esteem suffers almost as soon as the assignment to "dummy" English or math is made. Attendance may drop along with self-esteem. The lower-tracks often have a disproportionate number of minority-group and economically disadvantaged students, so ability grouping, in effect, becomes resegregation in school. (pp. 118–119)

The problems connected with ability grouping are attributed to "difference in instruction and/or the teachers' negative attitudes" (p. 119). These problems are attributed to technical difficulties with tracking. Even with the listing of problems of such a profound nature, the practice of ability grouping itself is represented as neutral and remains unproblematic. The real violence done to students seems invisible or trivialized as this method of instruction is conceptualized as "more appropriate."

The importance of this issue is further minimized by the little attention that is given to examine the consequences of this grouping on students' daily lived experience of schooling. A single paragraph is used to report these negative effects. The complexities of the social struggles that produced the current configuration of practices and how these practices fit relations of ruling in the wider society (Rizvi, 1993) remain obscured.

Only if the instructor chooses to present the information in the background section (located in the margins, printed in light blue, and available only in the teacher's edition) is the educational psychology class offered a brief summary of a well-known and important research program. *Keeping Track: How Schools Structure Inequality,* originally published in 1985 by Jeannie Oakes, discusses the deleterious effects of ability grouping and tracking, and, more important, places the issue within its historical and social context. However, this material is not readily available to students who are using this text.

Gage and Berliner (1991) address the issue of ability grouping in a section titled *"Coping with Individual Differences"* (emphasis added, p. 449). The situation of individual differences among students is reported to have "complicated" the teacher's task (Gage & Berliner, 1991). The discourse presents certain individual differences as a "problem" to students of educational psychology, something that will need coping with and an issue that will complicate their life as a teacher.

Again, a technical solution to the "problem" of individual differences is presented, and it is based on the assumption of innate ability: "to set each student to work on tasks appropriate to his or her particular abilities and interests...appropriate to the student's temperament....to move each individual ahead at his or her own rate" (pp. 449–450).

Ability grouping is presented as a step toward individualized instruction. The idea behind this method of instruction is that "teaching is *more effective* with students of similar ability" (emphasis added , p. 450); even so, it is noted that conflicting results have been reported regarding "achievement, self-concept, attitudes toward others, and behavior" (p. 450) in employing this teaching strategy.

Gage and Berliner (1991) also refer to the findings of the Oakes (1985) research (mentioned above). The text states, in reference to this study, that "ability grouping has been suspected, and often found guilty, of fostering social-class discrimination: Lower-income students wind up in one group; higher-income students in another" (p. 450). The assignment to low-track is even characterized as a "life sentence" (Gage & Berliner, 1991). Once again, the practice of ability grouping of students itself remains unproblematic; it is characterized as a "plausible" way of coping "with individual differences in *stable* characteristics...(scholastic abilities, interests)" (emphasis in the original, p. 450). How is it that the discourse can reconcile the admission of such negative effects as *more effective* and *plausible*?

Contrastingly, another group of students, i.e., gifted and talented, receives quite a different presentation: "Gifted and talented students contribute greatly to society and should be considered a precious human resource. Our investment in identifying and developing these students should at least rival—in interest, time, and money—the investment we make in gifted athletes" (Gage & Berliner, 1991, p. 217).

Woolfolk (1995), like Gage and Berliner (1991) asserts the importance of providing for the special educational needs of "gifted" children." The characterization of gifted students by a former secretary of education as "our most neglected students" is repeated. Gifted programs formulate yet another "track" allocated for students who "contribute greatly to society and should be considered a precious human resource" (Gage & Berliner, 1991, p. 217). These "remarkable individuals" (Woolfolk, 1995) are represented as a scarce commodity that must be developed for our national security and well-being (Sapin-Shevin, 1993.

Through the discourse of educational psychology such differential valuing and treatment of children are authorized and perpetuated despite conflicting effects and long-standing accusations that ability grouping does not work (Slavin, 1987), is not fair (Oakes, 1985), and is undemocratic (Giroux & McLaren, 1989). Nevertheless, ability grouping continues to appear reasonable and is accepted as tolerable from within the meaning-making system of the discipline. General acceptance of this practice as a commonsense way to organize schooling experiences is achieved through the work of the discourse.

The discourse constructs the situation in such a way that the semblance of neutrality and meritocracy is upheld. This understanding is promoted by assigning children to ability groups on the basis of the assumption of the biological reality of innate ability, i.e., "intelligence." Since innate ability can be determined through the use of "neutral" standardized tests, the social stratification that results from this differential access to curriculums appears efficient, reasonable, and is taken as common sense. The historical, social, and political contexts in which students' access to curriculums is sorted and selected is cast as scientific and value-free.

An uncritical reading of the dominant discourse contained in classic texts does not engage the complexity of meaning or examine the value-laden aspects of issues that are seen, at first glance, as "neutral" and acceptable. In contrast to the traditional understanding of the discipline's discourse as a neutral body of information, a critical reading presents the discourse of educational psychology as a site of struggle. Meanings in the discourse can be contested and struggled over, and they are. Even so, the dominant discourse prevails. To more fully understand why the discourse exists as it does, it is necessary to look beyond disciplinary principles to the "effects of power [that] shape a discursive practice" (Cherryholmes, 1988, p. 59). The effects of power are infused in the nondiscursive background practices that precede the text and talk of educational psychology. They are the human, social, institutional activities that make the discipline possible in the first place (Dreyfus & Rabinow, 1983). These nondiscursive practices are presented in the remainder of the chapter.

NONDISCURSIVE PRACTICES OF EDUCATIONAL PSYCHOLOGY

In an earlier work, I used Foucault's (1980) idea of discourse of a modern science, such as educational psychology, as a "regime of truth." Foucault's famous quote deserves repeating: "Truth is a thing of this world: it is produced only by virtue of multiple forms of constraint. And it induces regular effects of power. Each society has its regime of truth, its general politics of truth: that is, the types of discourse it accepts and makes function as true" (Foucault, 1980, p. 131).

Understanding the discipline of educational psychology as a "regime of truth" contrasts with the view of the discourse of the discipline as a neutral body of scientifically validated knowledge. In discussing the discourse as a "regime of truth" it is important to foreground and interrogate those social, political, economic, and institutional networks in which the discipline is embedded. Discussions need to be taken up concerning the relationship of power and knowledge; the social construction of knowledge; the impossibility of neutrality of knowledge; the division of labor in knowledge production highlighting a power hierarchy regarding as to who controls knowledge production and whose meanings are legitimated.

POWER–KNOWLEDGE

Understanding that "knowledge is power" within a traditional perspective of educational psychology contrasts with what Foucault means in the quote above. The traditional contention is that the development of the knowledge of the discipline (i.e., the discipline's "truth") has given educational psychologists power. The relationship is understood as *causal*: knowledge causes power. The "direct scientific underpinnings…the knowledge base consisting of facts, concepts, and technology" (Berliner, 1987, p. xvii) give educational psychologists power. In other words, use of the technical knowledge of the discipline gives one knowledge. For Foucault (1995) the relationship of power and knowledge is correlational: "power and knowledge directly imply one another…there is no power relation without the correlative constitution of a field of knowledge, nor any knowledge that does not presuppose and constitute at the same time power relations" (p. 27). Foucault, therefore, always refers to power and knowledge together, i.e., power-knowledge, a "solidus [suggesting] that for his purposes power and knowledge are not to be studied separately" (Sarup, 1996, p. 72). They are "immanent in one another, each a condition for the possibility of the other" (Usher & Edwards, 1994, p. 87).

Power relations pervade the knowledge-making activity, affecting the one who knows, that which is known, and the mode and practice of knowing (Foucault, 1995). The implication of this relationship of power-knowledge for the human sciences is that the "truth" expressed by the discipline is both produced and confined by the power relationships of the discipline. In other words, "truth" is what the discipline says is "truth." As Usher and Edwards (1994) point out, knowledge "does not simply represent the truth of what is, but, rather, *constitutes* what is taken to be true.…It's what counts as true that is important" (p. 87).

Aronowitz (1988) pushes this power-knowledge dynamic a step farther. He insists that "The power of science consists, in the first place, in its conflation of knowledge and truth" (p. vii). The truth that is being produced by the specific scientific manipulations of the discipline is a specialized knowledge that has been conflated with truth.

When the understanding of how power and knowledge implicate each other is recognized, a radically different perception of knowledge follows. What counts as knowledge is considered the "truth" of the discipline. However, this truth is also understood as the product of social activity imbued with power relations. There is always a political struggle over knowledge, and it is not something that resides solely in the realm of ideas. Rather, it is a matter of mechanisms of power that are prior to discourse and often unspoken. These mechanisms decide who may speak, when, and what may he said; this is a "general politics of truth" (Foucault, 19805, p. 131) that pervades the discipline. Thus, the knowledge of any discipline can never be received as neutral; it is always situated, contingent, and partial and the result of social struggle.

THE SOCIAL CONSTRUCTION OF KNOWLEDGE

The way the world is known and explained is the result of "historically situated interchanges among people" (Gergen, 1985, p. 267). This pertains to scientific knowledge. Scarr (1985) insists that we "should not be disturbed that science is constructed knowledge. Rather, the recognition of our own role in scientific knowledge should make more modest our claim to truth" (p. 500). Nevertheless, those who do science have consistently failed to examine the social practice of producing knowledge and the historical, economic, and political context that give it meaning in the first place. It seems as though at times educational psychologists have forgotten that they have "invented the knowledge they apply.…they do not discover, they invent" (Caputo & Yount, 1993, p. 7).

The mainstream educational psychology community may not recognize that the dominant discourse contained in classic texts has been socially constructed. A textual style of *narrative realism* and the appearance of consensus lend to the discourse the ambience of objective knowledge.

Textbooks are usually written through a textual strategy of narrative realism (Usher & Edwards, 1994) that accentuates the "reporting of already existing ready-made reality" (p. 150). Using this genre the text is understood as a "neutral medium for conveying pre-existing facts about the world.…[its] neutrality exempts it from consideration as a species of social/cultural activity" (Woolgar, quoted in Usher & Edwards, 1994, p. 150). This strategy also allows the text to appear as an authoritarian source of what the discursive community considers the truth of the discipline (Kuhn, 1970). Rizvi (1993) describes this as a type of "rhetorical appeal that is by its very nature uncritical" (p. 137).

Narrative realism is affected frequently by statements made in a matter-of-fact style. Gage and Berliner (1991), for example, state: "It became possible during the twentieth century to measure individual differences in intelligence" (p. 50). This simple statement masks the historical and political context and struggle in which the statement is embedded.

An argument could be made that there is some evidence in the mainstream discourse that the knowledge of the discipline is recognized as the result of negotiated understandings within the educational psychology community. This is because the pronoun "we" is used throughout both textbooks. For example, Gage and Berliner (1991) explain that:

> A concept is the organized information *we have* (emphasis added) about an entity.…The meaning, boundaries, and relationships connected with a concept are derived from everything *we know* (emphasis added) about that concept.…What *we mean* (emphasis added) by a concept is partly a matter of definition and partly a matter of the methods of studying the concept.…for example, the meaning of the concept of intelligence depends in part how *we define* (emphasis added) *intelligence* (emphasis in the original). (pp. 12–13)

The "we" of this discussion could be referring to the educational psychology community, Gage and Berliner being "authorized" (Usher & Edwards, 1994) to speak in its name. However, it is more likely that it is the editorial "we" that is reflected here and throughout the text. This makes it difficult to know to whom the text is referring. Contrary to Gage and Berliner's assertion, there is no universal agreement among educational psychologists about a construct as complex and politically charged as "intelligence" let alone with other educationalists or the general public. However, their use of the pronoun "we" builds the impression that there is universal agreement. Apple (1993) remarks "the very use of the pronoun 'we' simplifies matters all too much" (p. 49). The continual use of the editorial "we" serves to create the illusion of consensus around an "objective" discourse of educational psychology. There is an attempt to build what Rizvi (1993) calls a "collective phenomenon." Van Dijk (1993) points out that consensus building is a major function of any dominant discourse. In a climate of consensus, acceptance and legitimacy of knowledge allow a particular discourse to dominate and achieve hegemonic control.

Textbooks and the discourse they support need to be understood as important artifacts of culture (Gergen, 1985) that "signify through their content and form, *particular* constructions of reality, *particular* ways of selecting and organizing the vast universe of *possible* knowledge" (emphasis added, Apple, 1993, p. 49). At any time there are competing discourses, competing paradigms, and their respective proponents can be imagined as "practic[ing] their trades in different worlds....[they] see different things when they look at the same point in the same direction" (Kuhn, 1970, p. 150).

Gage and Berliner (1991), for example, recognize that deliberations related to the construct of intelligence are connected with "different social and political ideologies" (p. 51). They are clear in presenting the definition that they support, characterized as "traditional," i.e., "Intelligence=what tests measure" (p. 51). Readers are told that this definition stems from "the intellectual tradition of the developed nations" (p. 53). Gage and Berliner (1991) explain that this tradition is "only one approach to human learning and instruction—namely, that appropriate to a middle-class segment of an industrialized society in which learning takes place in a certain kind of classroom in an institution called school. If *our* society were different...we would probably have to redefine intelligence" (emphasis added, p. 53). Even while both texts acknowledge that there is no agreement on what intelligence really is (Gage & Berliner, 1991; Woolfolk, 1995), their perspective on intelligence is utilized as the standard perspective. This traditional psychometric perspective is privileged as it is presented as neutral, normative, and unproblematic. There seems to be no recognition of the psychometric perspective's alignment with any social and political ideology through which students are included, excluded, or marginalized in schools and in society on the basis of such measurements.

In summary, although there is a growing acceptance of knowledge as a social construction (e.g., Gergen, 1985; Kincheloe, 1993; Scarr, 1985), it is questionable whether traditionally educational psychologists have recognized the knowledge claims of the discipline as socially constructed. The genre of narrative realism generates the appearance of consensus and neutrality in textbooks. These can be considered a "pre-text" (Usher & Edwards, 1994) that needs to be interrogated and subverted as there is a "hidden politics of neutrality" (Kincheloe, 1993, p. 42). It is the impossibility of neutrality of knowledge that is discussed next.

THE IMPOSSIBILITY OF THE NEUTRALITY OF KNOWLEDGE

The claim of neutrality of knowledge needs to be discussed. As mentioned earlier, neutrality can be used as a "cloak" covering scientific research. As long as knowledge is considered neutral, it can claim a place separate from human interests, biases, and power.

The fact that knowledge can never be neutral is an assertion that crosses disciplinary lines and epistemological stances. Those who offer feminist critique of science (e.g., Blier , 1984; Harding, 1991; Hubbard, 1989; Namenwirth, 1986) join critical educational theorists (e.g., Apple, 1993; Freire, 1992; Giroux, 1981, 1983; Kincheloe, 1993; McLaren, 1989), and feminist poststructural-ists (Luke & Gore, 1992) in this assertion. McLaren (1989), for example, challenges traditional ideas regarding the neutrality of knowledge: "Knowledge acquired in school—or anywhere, for that matter—is never neutral or objective but is ordered and structured in particular ways; its emphasis and exclusions partake of a silent logic. Knowledge is a *social construction* deeply rooted in a nexus of power relations" (emphasis in the original, p. 169). Even so, the claim of "neutral-ity" is a strong and important condition for the human sciences. It is the representation of the knowledge of a discipline as neutral and objective that facilitates an assumption of certainty and universality. In this way the knowledge of educational psychology is able to function as a founda-tion on which to base practice or as a resource that informs practice. However, as Giroux (1981) explains, this view of knowledge "not only undermines reflective thinking, it does this and more. It is also a form of legitimation that obscures the relationship between "valued" knowledge and the constellation of economic, political, and social interests that such knowledge supports" (p. 53). When the acceptance of the neutrality of knowledge is subverted, a whole new discernment is required. If knowledge cannot be accepted as neutral, a demand follows to know more about the political implications that permeate it. New questions surface concerning whose interests does the knowledge serve? Whose experience is legitimated or marginalized? Who profits through this knowledge? Many critical educational theorists have written persuasively on this subject. Banks (1993) has explained that "knowledge that people create is heavily influenced by their interpre-tations of their experiences and their positions within particular social, economic, and political systems and structures of a society" (p. 5). Apple (1993) asserts that "what counts as legitimate knowledge is the result of complex power struggles among class, race, gender, religious groups" (p. 46). It is not a question of what knowledge is of most worth, rather it is *whose* knowledge (Apple, 1993, 1996) is privileged and made to appear "natural," "normal."

Alison Dewar addresses the question of "whose" knowledge is normative. She explains suc-cinctly: "The knowledge we teach in our educational system has a white, middle class, androcentric bias. More importantly, this bias is not presented as one possible version of reality, but more often is taught as the only, legitimate and therefore, representative version of reality" (Dewar, quoted in Lewis, 1992, p. 42). This white, middle-class, andro-centric knowledge is the knowledge that counts (Sleeter & Grant, 1994), and this is the knowledge that "provides formal justification for and legitimation of prevailing institutional arrangements" (Anyon, 1978, p. 40, quoted in Giroux, 1981, p. 531). Generally this is the knowledge found in textbooks (Banks, 1993; van Dijk, 1993).

It is often easy to discern the bias of whose knowledge gets privileged in the dominant discourse of educational psychology. Numerous examples attest to this fact in educational psychology's mainstream discourse. One example is obvious, again using the psychometric understanding of intelligence. Gage and Berliner (1991) admit that "A society will always have a problem testing the intelligence of minority-group members because, by definition, they do not belong in important ways to the majority culture that usually develops the tests" (p. 54). In the very next sentence these authors state simply: "We measure intelligence with tests" (Gage & Berliner, 1991, p. 55). Later in the chapter, Gage and Berliner (1991) state that, "Because minority-group and poor children less often do well on these tests their parents have a right to worry about how the information from the tests is used" (p. 74) . Indeed, assignment to a "slow group early on can be like a *life sentence with no likelihood of parole*" (emphasis added, p. 74). Children who belong to economically disadvantaged groups and especially when they are also part of a minority are essentialized and seem almost alien (Rizvi, 1993). This kind of representation also presents the dominant group as homogenized. There is a clear admission that this normative practice of psychometric testing in the discipline benefits those in the dominant culture.

This situation is naturalized by being represented as "the way things are." Note Gage and Berliner's (1991) assertion: "A society will always have a problem testing certain groups of children." The assumption is that it could not be otherwise (Rizvi, 1993). Thus, this purportedly "neutral" discourse functions to sustain the power relations of the status quo. More important, it trivializes the violence done to children through testing procedures. Mainstream educational psychology has left the concrete reality of many children's lives unchallenged.

THE DIVISION OF LABOR IN KNOWLEDGE PRODUCTION

Implied in the above discussion is the existence of a hierarchy of power (van Dijk, 1993) in the production of the knowledge of the discipline. There are some who speak with authority; they are "author-ized" to speak. Others must listen. Van Dijk (1993) refers to the former group as the "power elites," i.e., those who have "special access to discourse; they are literally the ones who have the most to say" (p. 255). The elites of the discourse have a particular social power.

Social power could be understood as involving control of one group over others regarding acts in limiting freedom, or cognition, i.e., how people think (van Dijk, 1993). The social power referred to here is primarily concerned with the cognitive aspects of power that involve knowledge production, or "managing the minds of others...a function of text and talk" (van Diik, 1993, p. 254). Although the idea of "managing minds" may be startling, it is the latent purpose of the dominant discourse of educational psychology. The dominant discourse is aimed at initiating novices into a particular meaning system, i.e., "facts, concepts, principles, and research methods that will be both theoretically enlightening and practically useful" (Gage & Berliner, 1991, p. xvii).

Those who arc considered authorities purport to clarify meaning. Meanings that are accepted generally are understood as *social cognitions* (van Dijk, 1993). These social cognitions influence "beliefs, understandings, attitudes, ideologies, norms and values" (van Dijk, 1993, p. 257). Clearly, classic textbooks take this as a goal, i.e., reproducing social cognitions by supplying meanings and definitions for various concepts.

Teachers of educational psychology may accept their task as "transmitting" the meaning of the discourse to students. Students are, in a sense, positioned as receivers of knowledge, "consumers" of the dominant discourse presented in textbooks. Of course, the teaching-learning process is more complex than simply determined by the reproductive metaphor. On the one hand, students of educational psychology are active participants in their own learning, and their learning could never be determined by these texts. My student in the opening story is a good example. On the other hand, the rationality of the dominant discourse does steer students in the direction of particular interpretations.

As the discussion on narrative realism pointed out, meanings in textbooks often appear to be fixed; they are presented as objective and static. "Textual" features are used to reinforce these meanings. The Gage and Berliner (1991) text supplies a glossary that provides "brief definitions of key terms" (p. xx) and marginal notes "highlighting important points...quick guides to key ideas and issues" (p. xix). Woolfolk (1995) furnishes readers with a margin glossary that "defines terms of the text to provide *easy access* to the terms and their relevant examples as the student studies" (emphasis added, p. ix).

A poststructuralist analysis problematizes the idea of meanings as fixed. What is necessary is recognizing how power infiltrates language (Cherryholmes, 1988) constructing social cognitions. Cherryholmes insists that: "Culturally sanctioned, positive, and authoritative knowledge is incomplete, interest-bound, tied up with existing power arrangements, and cloaked in certainty. As the illusion of certainty is dispelled, it becomes possible to uncover the origins and commitments of our structures and the effects of power that led to their production" (p. 70). Modern textbooks bear the effects of power and represent a privileged view of the material they present. The school knowledge they contain "reveals which groups have power...[and] which groups are not empowered by the economic and social patterns in the society" (Anyon, 1983, p. 49). These become obvious in omissions, stereotypes, and distortions that are found even in updated versions of textbooks (Anyon, 1983). Consider the following examples of stereotypes regarding Native American cultures: "Some place high value on the skills required in weaving. Some of them depend on spearfishing for much of their food. If industrial society valued these skills in the same way, our educational system would focus on them and our definition of intelligence would give them greater importance" (Gage & Berliner, 1991, pp. 53–54). There are several problematic assumptions in this statement; one is that all members of given groups share the same cultural and behavioral patterns (Sleeter & Grant, 1994). This refers not only to the minority groups, but the assumption pertains to the dominant groups as well. Do all Native American groups weave and fish? What about the economic, social, and cultural contexts in which members of groups weave and fish—or do not? How do the authors use the word "our" to exclude persons considered outside the group in power? Another implication is that the minority group is deficient in comparison to the dominant culture, i.e., industrial society, that determines the type of tests given in the society. These assumptions, though erroneous, serve to reinforce stereotypes, perpetuate social cognitions, and disguise oppression or power relations.

Meanings attributed to "race" are especially noxious and significant. Gage and Berliner (1991) note that "race" "typically should refer solely to such psychologically unimportant characteristics as skin color, eye shape, and facial configurations" (p. 79). Woolfolk (1995) defines "race" as: "A group of people who share common biological traits that are seen as self-defining by the people of the group" (Woolfolk, 1995, p. 165).

The essentializing of race as a stable and biological characteristic persists in both texts, although this representation is generally considered anachronistic within the scientific community (Harding, 1996). It continues to be used in some discourse communities despite the fact that all scientific attempts to show any biological definition of race have been exposed as untenable. This representation persists. The biological representation is useful, however, as it serves to perpetuate the prevalent social cognition of race as fixed. This has a *naturalizing effect* that constitutes social, cultural, and political differences among people *as if* these differences were merely the effect of nature.

There is a professed "disinterest" in "race" evident in the Gage and Berliner text through its representation of race as referring to characteristics that are "psychologically unimportant." Again, this representation is useful as it limits how readers think of race by taking it out of social and cultural contexts. In this way the understanding of meritocracy that is based on individual merit, hard work, and achievement (Haymes, 1996) can be preserved.

How is it that stereotypes and incorrect information continue to be presented in current textbooks? The possibility of the effects of power relations must be considered. Some individuals may dominate a field, not because of their arguments but because of their positional authority (Cherryholmes, 1988). What is important to recognize is that often those considered the "elites" of the discourse may "enact, sustain, legitimate, condone, or ignore social inequality or injustice" (van Dijk, 1993, p. 252) supported by the official knowledge of the discipline. Thus, knowledge in a dominant discourse needs to be interrogated as the "property of an elite establishment working to maintain its power" (Usher & Edwards, 1994, p. 198). When this is understood, it facilitates a critical position in both teachers and students.

The work of this chapter focused on beginning an interrogation of the dominant discourse of the discipline of educational psychology using two classic textbooks. The first part of the chapter discussed disciplinary principles understood in terms of technical rationality. These principles, although supplying a grounding of the discipline, are rarely examined. Although often considered a resource, they also constrain the discourse of the discipline and, therefore, are problematic and need to be interrogated. The remaining portion of the chapter considered the nondiscursive aspects of the discipline that include the social and political contingencies in which the discipline is embedded.

This discussion is important not solely on the level of ideas. The meaning-making system and power relations of the discipline are important because they affect the everyday discursive practices of schooling and the material conditions of children's lives. These practices are the focus of the next chapter: "Disciplining the Discipline."

REFERENCES

Anderson, L. M., Blumenfeld, P., Pintrich, P. R., Clark, C., M., Marx, R. W., & Peterson, P. (1995). *Education psychology for teachers: Reforming our courses, rethinking our roles. Educational Psychology, 30*(3), 143-157.

Anyon, J. (1983). Workers, labor and economic history, and textbook content. In M.W. Apple & L. Weis (Eds.), *Ideology and practice in schooling.* Philadelphia: Temple University Press.

Apple, M.W. (1994). Series editor's introduction. In A. Gitlin (ed.), *Power and method: Political activism and education research* (pp 1-12). New York: Routledge.

———— (1993). *Official knowledge: Democratic education in a conservative age.* New York: Routledge.

———— (1990). *Ideology and curriculum.* New York: Routledge.

Aronowitz, S. (1988). *Science as power: Discourse and ideology in modern society.* Minneapolis: University of Minnesota Press.

Aronowitz, S. & Giroux, H.A. (1991). *Postmodern education: Politics, culture, and social criticism.* Minneapolis: University of Minnesota Press.

Banks, J.A. (1993). The canon debate: knowledge construction, and multicultural education. In *Educational Researcher, 22*(5), 4–14.

Berliner, D. C. & Rosenshine, B.V. (Eds.). (1987). *Talks to teachers.* New York: Random House.

Best, S. & Kellner, D. (1991). *Postmodern theory: Critical interrogations.* New York: The Guilford Press.

Bleier , R. (1984). *Science and gender.* New York: Pergamon Press.

Bloland, H.G. (1995). Postmodern and higher education. *Journal of Higher Education, 66*(5), 521–559.

Burbules, N.C. (1995). Forms of ideology-critique: A pedagogical perspective. In P.L. McLaren & J.M. Giarelli (Eds.), *Critical theory and educational research* (pp. 53–70). Albany: State University of New York Press.

Caputo, J.D. & Yount, M. (1993). Introduction. In J.D. Caputo & M. Yount (Eds.), *Foucault and the critique of institutions* (pp. 3–23). University Park: The Pennsylvania State University Press.

Carr, W. & Kemmis, S. (1986). *Becoming critical.* Philadelphia: The Falmer Press.

Cherryholmes, C.H. (1988). *Power and Criticism: Poststructural investigations in education.* New York: Teachers College Press.

Collins, P.H. (1990). *Black feminist thought: Knowledge, consciousness, and the politics of empowerment.* New York: Routledge.

Doyle, W., & Carter, K. (1996). Educational psychology and the education of the teachers: A reaction. *Educational Psychologist, 31*(1), 23-28.

Dreyfus, H.L. & Rabinow, P. (1983). *Michael Foucault, beyond structuralism and hermeneutics.* Chicago: The University of Chicago Press.

Foucault, M. (1995). *Discipline & punish: The birth of the prison* (2nd ed.). New York: Vintage Books.

Foucault, M. (1980). Truth and power. In C. Gordon (Ed.), *Power/Knowledge: Selected interviews and other writings.* New York: Pantheon Press.

Foucault, M. (1972). *The archeology of knowledge.* New York: Pantheon Books.

Freire, P. (1992). *Pedagogy of the oppressed.* New York: Seabury Press.

Gage, N.L. & Berliner, D.C. (1991). *Educational psychology* (5th ed.). Boston: Houghton Mifflin Co.

Gergen, K.J. (1985). The social constructivist movement in modern psychology. *American Psychologist, 40*(3), 266–275.

Giroux, H.A. (1983a). *Theory and resistance in education: A pedagogy for the opposition.* South Hadley, MA: Bergin & Garvey Publishers, Inc.

——— (1983b, Winter). Ideology and agency in the process of schooling. *Journal of Education,* 165, 12–34.

——— (1981). *Ideology, culture, and the process of schooling.* Philadelphia: Temple University Press.

Giroux, H.A. & McLaren, P.L. (1989). *Critical pedagogy, the state, and cultural struggle.* Albany: State University of New York Press.

Giroux, H.A. & Purpel, D. (1983b). *The hidden curriculum and moral education.* Berkeley: McCutchan Publishing Company.

Gitlin, A.D. (1990). Educational research, voice, and school change. *Harvard Educational Review, 60*(4), 443–466.

Grinder, R.E. (1970). The crisis of content in educational psychology courses. *Educational Psychology, 8*(I), 4.

Haraway, D. (1991). Situated knowledges: The science question in feminism and the priviledge of partial perspective. In D. Haraway (Ed.), *Simians, cyborgs, and women: The reinvention of nature* (pp. 183–202). New York: Routledge.

Harding, S.G. (1991). *Whose science? Whose knowledge? Thinking from women's lives.* Ithaca, NY: Cornell University Press.

Harding, S. G. (Ed.). (1996). The racial economy of science: Toward a democratic future. Bloomington: Indiana University Press.

Haymes, S. N. (1996). Race, repression, and the politics of crime and punishment in the Bell Curve. In J. L. Kincheloe, S. R. Steinberg, & A. D. Gresson III (Eds.), *Measured lies* (pp. 237–251). New York: St. Martin's Press.

Hubbard, R. (1989). Science, facts, and feminism. In N. Tuana (Ed.), *Feminism and science.* Bloomington: Indiana University Press.

Kincheloe, J. L. (1993). *Toward a critical politics of teacher thinking: Mapping the postmodern.* Westport, CT: Bergin & Garvey.

Kohl, H. (1994). *I won't learn from you: And other thoughts on creative maladjustment.* New York: The New Press.

Kozol, J. (1991). *Savage inequalities: Children in America's schools.* New York: Harper Collins.

Kuhn, T. (1970). *The structure of scientific revolutions.* Chicago: The University of Chicago Press.

Leistyna, P., Woodrum, A., & Sherblom, S.A. (1996). *Breaking free: The transformative power of critical pedagogy.* Cambridge, MA: Harvard Educational Review.

Lewis, M. (1992). Power and education: Who decides the forms schools have taken, and who should decide? In J. L. Kincheloe & S. R. Steinberg (Eds.), *Thirteen questions: Reframing education's conversation* (pp. 39–64). New York: Peter Lang.

Luke, C. & Gore, J. (Eds.). (1992). *Feminisms and critical pedagogy*. New York: Routledge.

Macedo, D. (1994). *Literacies of power: What Americans are not allowed to know*. Boulder, CO: Westview Press, Inc.

McLaren, P. (1989). *Life in schools*. White Plains, NY: Longman.

McNay, L. (1994). *Foucault: A critical introduction*. New York: The Continuum Publishing.

Murphy, K. (1993). *Pedagogy for postmodernity: Travels in poststructuralism, feminism, and education*. Unpublished doctoral dissertation, University of Alberta, Edmonton, Alberta.

Namenwirth, M. (1986). Science seen through a feminist prism. In R. Bleier (Ed.), *Feminist approaches to science* (pp. 18–41). New York: Pergamon Press.

Oakes, J. (1985). *Keeping track: How schools structure inequality*. New Haven, CT: Yale University Press.

Prado, C.G. (1995). *Starting with Foucault: An introduction to genealogy*. Boulder, CO: Westview.

Rizvi, F. (19930. Children and the grammar of popular racism. In C. McCarthy & W. Crichlow (Eds.), *Race, identity, and representation in education*. New York: Routledge.

Sapon-Shevin, M. (1993). Gifted education and the protection of privilege: Breaking the silence, opening the discourse. In L. Weis & M. Fine (Eds.), *Class, race, and gender in United States schools* (pp. 25–44). Albany: State University of New York Press.

Sarup, M. (1996). *Identity, culture, and the postmodern world*. Athens: The University of Georgia Press.

Scarr, S. (1985). Constructing psychology: making facts and fables for our time. *American Psychologist, 40,* 499–512.

Schon, D.A. (1987). *Educating the reflective practitioner*. San Francisco: Jossey-Bass.

———— (1995, November–December). The new scholarship requires a new epistemology. *Change 27*(6), 12–25.

Slavin, R.E. (1987). Ability grouping and student achievement in elementary schools: A best evidence synthesis. *Review of Educational research, 57*(3), 293–336.

Sleeter, C.E. 7 Grant, C.E. (1994). *Making choices for multicultural education: Five approaches to race, class, and gender* (2nd ed.). New York: Merrill.

Sprinthall, N.A. & Sprinthall, R.C. (1990). *Educational psychology : A developmental approach* (5th ed.). New York: McGraw-Hill Inc.

Thomas, G. (1997). What's the use of theory? *Harvard Educational Review, 67*(I), 75–104.

Thorndike, E.L. (1910). *Educational psychology*. New York: Teachers College Press.

Usher, R. (1993). Re-examining the place of disciplines in adult education. *Studies in Continuing Education, 15*(I), 15–25.

Usher, R. & Edwards, R. (1994). *Postmodernism and education*. New York: Routledge.

van Dijk, T.A. (1993). Principles of critical discourse analysis. *Discourse and Society, 4*(2), 240–283.

Woolfolk, A. (1995). *Educational psychology* (6th edition). Boston: Allyn and Bacon.

THIRTY-SEVEN

Disciplining the Discipline

Suzanne Gallagher

This chapter takes as its focus an examination of the practices sanctioned by educational psychology's dominant discourse and investigates the effects of these practices. The earlier discussion regarding technical rationality and the nondiscursive power-knowledge relationships of the discipline facilitates the turn to this focus. This turn is imperative as the ideas generated by the meaning-making structure evident in the discursive principles of educational psychology "gain strength and are a form of power [because]…they take concrete shape in the actions of our daily lives" (Freire & Faundez, 1992, p. 26).

Through the process of education students are "socialized" so as to adapt to the world. Students are judged, labeled, sorted, and selected according to how well they fit in. Through its knowledge base and practices the discipline of educational psychology claims to explain characteristics of the student and the teacher; the assertion of the discipline is "to know those objects truthfully.…[by their] 'natural characteristics'" (Usher, 1993, p. 18).

Using the perspective of Foucault, a different view of socialization is proposed. Foucault is skeptical regarding modern disciplines (1980a), especially those connected with education (Ball, 1990). Foucault's position is that knowledge of the modern disciplines is organized around the power to define and name others—especially to define persons as *normal* and as *abnormal*. Human beings are defined and made subjects of the society through the process of *normalization* often understood as *socialization*.

The knowledge and the practices of the human sciences are central to this process. Through their specific knowledge claims and practices, human beings are thought to be simply described and categorized. The language used to convey the reality of the person is considered neutral and unproblematic in itself. However, from a critical perspective language is considered to have a productive characteristic; it is through the language, the discourse, of the discipline that subjects are formed and constituted.

Modern sciences through their specialized knowledges produce a new subject, a subject of a particular kind (J. D. Marshall, 1990), i.e., subjects who are docile and useful. Foucault's contention is that every modern discipline is "a general formula of domination" (1995, p. 137). Thus, the knowledge of modern discipline "ceases to be a liberation and becomes a mode of surveillance, regulation, discipline" (Sarup, 1993, p. 67). The specific disciplinary practices derived from the knowledge claims of educational psychology are implicated and interrelated in the processes whereby societies control and discipline their populations (Philip, 1989), through the educational process.

Foucault's idea of the meaning of the human sciences as "disciplines" is a central theme in this chapter. The contemporary understanding is tied to the former meaning of discipline, i.e., it is concerned with the control of bodies. The understanding of "trope" discussed below helps illuminate this connection. A discussion of the formation of the discipline follows beginning with an appropriation of Foucault's concept of *genealogy*. Foucault uses genealogy to explicate how every historical era has sought control over populations, changing only the strategies through which control is achieved (1980b). The human sciences are the current means through which control is gained. Next, three disciplinary technologies are presented that Foucault suggests form the basis of the disciplinary practice, i.e., *hierarchical observation, normalizing judgment,* and *examination*. These disciplinary practices are utilized by disciplines to normalize students and are located in the everyday activities of school life. Finally, I use these disciplinary technologies to inform my critical reading of the dominant discourse of educational psychology expressed in two classic textbooks.

A thorough examination of these various points is important in order to render visible what has been taken for granted, i.e., to make the familiar strange (Foucault, 1995). The presentation of the everyday practices can and must be looked at differently because "as soon as one can no longer think things as one formerly thought them, transformation becomes both very urgent, very difficult, and quite possible" (Foucault, 1988, quoted in Dales, 1992, p. 83).

DISCIPLINE: CONTROL OF BODIES

"Disciplines" are discussed as they are usually considered "neutral, scientifically validated bodies of knowledge whose only effects are enlightening and empowering and which thus enable effective action" (Usher & Edwards, 1994, p. 48). However, this chapter takes up a different meaning of discipline. The word discipline can be understood more fully through a consideration of "trope." Tropes are words in which new meanings contain residues of former uses of the word; new meanings are understandable in connection to the original sense of the word (Briscoe, 1993). Tropes help us notice what could have been missed without their recognition; they make our thinking swerve (Haraway, 1996) and we are able to "see" things differently.

In thinking about discipline as a trope it is helpful to consider its various lexical meanings:

1 Training expected to produce a specific pattern of behavior.

2 Controlled behavior resulting from disciplinary training.

3 A systematic method to obtain obedience.

4 A state of order based on submission to rules and authority.

5 Punishment intended to train or correct.

6 A set of methods or rules (that regulate) practice.

7 A branch of knowledge or of teaching. (Soukhanov, 1984, p. 383)

It is not until the sixth and seventh meanings that a match is found for our commonsense understanding of the word "discipline" used in the context of a "body of knowledge." Educational psychology, for example, as a discipline and branch of psychology includes laws, principles, theory, and practice aimed at improving teaching and learning. However, recognizing discipline as trope helps one appreciate Foucault's meaning of "disciplinary power"; it is important to see the connection with the other meanings listed for the word "discipline." The discipline, the human science, of educational psychology is connected with managing and controlling the bodies of students, e.g., behavior. The recognition of the dynamic relationship among power, knowledge of the discipline, and the control of bodies is necessary for understanding the practices of educational psychology.

In *Discipline and Punish* Foucault (1995) connects the control of the body and the growth of the scientific knowledge of disciplines since the seventeenth century. Foucault studies the spread of "disciplinary mechanisms…[as] techniques through which modern societies train and regulate individuals" (Sarup, 1996, p. 72). In modernity, as "objective" science developed so did "a radically new regime of power/knowledge" (Fraser, 1989, p. 22) through the discipline's discourse. This shift in regimes of power from the classical age through modern times will be discussed later in the chapter. However, it is important to emphasize here that the aim of the disciplinary technologies remains the same, i.e., the control of the bodies of human persons.

Foucault explains two manifestations of power over the body. One manifestation is *bio-power*, a "modern form of power…characterized by increasing organization of population and welfare for the sake of increased force and productivity" (Dreyfus & Rabinow, 1983, pp. 7–8). Dreyfus and Rabinow explain that bio-power is so ubiquitous that it appears as a "strategy, with no one directing it and everyone increasingly enmeshed in it, whose only end is the increase of power and order itself" (p. xxvi). This modern form of power is a control and regulation of the masses, a kind of macropolitics. However, it did not emerge as a coherent management process. It was preceded by Foucault's other manifestation of power, micropolitics.

Micropolitics developed as administrators in various institutions were faced with the daily government of large numbers of people. The historical process of growing and shifting populations, for example, was connected to the formation of the disciplines (Smart, 1985). In order to manage and control the growing number of those in their charge "a variety of 'microtechniques' were perfected by obscure doctors, wardens, and schoolmasters in obscure hospitals, prisons, and schools.…only later were these techniques and practices taken up and integrated" (Fraser, 1989, p. 22). In other words, specific tactics were "invented and organized from the starting points of local conditions and particular needs…in piecemeal fashion" (Foucault, 1980b, p. 159). Only later were these procedures gathered to form a coherent discourse.

An example of the development of the local conditions generating specific practices can be found in writings about the history of educational psychology. Hilgard (1996), for example, notes that the later part of the nineteenth century before educational theory and teacher education became "centered in the universities, most of the adaptations of education were made by school administrators" (p. 992). Hilgard's recounting of the work of William Torrey Harris (1835–1909) is instructive here. Harris was superintendent of the St. Louis, Missouri, school district as the Civil War was ending, a time of increased industrialization and immigration to the area. Hilgard (1996) explains the need for specific procedures to manage the burgeoning numbers of children in the schools of St. Louis:

> The problems of school buildings, school management, and teacher training loomed large as the heterogeneous population expanded, and Harris took seriously his efforts to provide universal education on an efficient and effective basis. He did this by adopting the graded school so that the curriculum could he planned according to the movement of pupils through school, with careful records of attendance, of ages at leaving school, and of the progress of learning. (Hilgard, 1996, p. 992)

The specific procedures, or micropolitics, utilized by Harris (i.e., graded classes, records of attendance, and progress of students) imposed an order or governmentalism on the schooling of children in a particular time and locale. It was much later that these practices, and others were gathered and generalized into an integrated system of management.

Another notable example of the development of a tactic of micropolitics is the development of the first so-called "intelligence" tests by Alfred Binet (1857–1911) and his student Theodore Simon (1873–1961). Universal education, mandated in France in the nineteenth century, meant that all French children be given several years of public education (Fancher, 1985). It is noted that for the first time "retarded children were included, who in earlier years would have dropped out early or never attended school at all" (Fancher, 1985, p. 69). A diagnostic tool was thought to be needed to identify children who "could not profit from instruction in the regular public schools in Paris" (Lewontin, Rose, & Kamin, 1996).

In 1904, Binet and Simon responded to this local need and formulated an intelligence test and scale. Binet's original intention was to "construct an instrument for classifying unsuccessful school performers" (Mensh & Mensh, 1991, p. 23) into different groups: idiots, imbeciles, and "debiles" or "weak ones," later translated to "moron" in America (Fancher, 1985). Sorting students in this way, bringing a kind of "order" to the educational system of the time, was a function of the tests.

Later, the scales of Binet and Simon were appropriated for a variety of uses in the United States. For example, the army used variations of the test during World War I "not primarily for the exclusion of intellectual defectives…but rather for the classification of men in order that they may be properly placed in the military service" (Yerkes, quoted in Fancher, 1985, pp. 117–118). Postwar analyses of the results helped frame the rationale of the Immigration Act of 1924 defining immigrant groups thought suitable to become U.S. citizens. The testing movement is also linked to the passage of a series of sterilization laws declared constitutional by the Supreme Court in 1927 (Lewontin et al., 1996).

Not long after these applications, educational institutions adopted the tests as a tool for studying individual differences in order to make "formal schooling a successful and rewarding experience for the whole school-age population" (Jensen, 1987, p. 61). According to students' "ranking" in tests they could be sorted into "appropriated instructional programs [that] can make it possible for the vast majority of children to attain at least the basic scholastic skills during their years in school" (Jensen, 1987, p. 86).

The point that needs to be clear is that the discourse of the discipline of educational psychology did not emerge self-contained and coherent. The shift in demographics led to the need to govern growing student populations on local levels, micropolitics. Gradually, the formalization of the practices of management was established. Of particular importance were the practices of sorting students. This was deemed necessary to bring order to local school situations. The demographic shift was precipitated by the shift toward industrialization and growth of capitalism and formed a particular historical conjuncture with an emphasis on increased production and efficiency.

There is another historical process occurring at the same time, referred to as a juridico-political process (Smart, 1985). The juridico-political historical process refers to the formal and legal structures of societies that were established around the existing power relations of the eighteenth and nineteenth centuries simultaneous to the demographic shifts that were occurring. This process of modern lawmaking took over the power of the sovereign of premodern times. The juridico-political process that developed guarded the status of the group wielding political power. An example of this historical process can be found in the contradiction of the framers of the U.S. Constitution. At the same time that freedom was guaranteed to all, provisions recognizing and protecting slavery were also included (Bell, 1997).

This is the milieu in which the growth of scientific knowledge gains importance. The scientific historical process refers to the increasing complex relationship between the formation of knowledge and the exercise of power.

THE FORMATION OF DISCIPLINARY PRACTICES

Foucault is skeptical about the ability of modern human sciences to fulfill the dream of linear progress. He bases his skepticism on the "historical evidence…that what looks like a change for the better may have undesirable consequences" (Sawicki, 1991, p. 27). Foucault offers the *genealogy* as a way to critique totalizing discourses of modern sciences. The genealogist "is a diagnostician who concentrates on the relations of power, knowledge, and the body in modern society" (Dreyfus & Rabinow, 1983, p. 105). The genealogy that Foucault presents is a particular history, clearly not history in the usual sense. Foucault (1980a) asks us to see a genealogy as a "kind of attempt to emancipate historical knowledge from that subjection, to render them, that is, capable of opposition and of struggle against the coercion of a theoretical, unitary, formal and scientific discourse" (p. 85).

Sawicki (1991) explains genealogy as resistance that "involves the use of history to give voice to the marginal and submerged voices that lie 'a little beneath history'—the voices of the mad, the delinquent, the abnormal, the disempowered" (p. 28). The purpose of highlighting these subjugated and disqualified knowledges is both "modest and profound…to disrupt commonly held conceptions about events and social practices rather than to proffer, from on high, proposals for reform" (p. 62).

Foucault (1995) in *Discipline and Punish* presents the genealogy of the prison. Foucault believes that the prison is the "most characteristic of disciplinary institutions, one which schools, factories, and hospitals all come to resemble" (Shumway, 1989, p. 133). It is Foucault's intention that his history of "the birth of the prison" can or "must serve as a historical background to various studies of the power of normalization and the formation of knowledge in modern society" (p. 308). Normalization and a particular knowledge of each student are key aspects around which educational psychology is organized.

Foucault (1995) explains that every society had its means of control of the body. He describes this control within the historical recounting of the birth of the prisons beginning with the classical age, through the reform era, and arriving at the formation of the modern penal system.

In the *classical age* Foucault (1995) recounts the torture of Robert Francois Damiens, accused of trying to assassinate Louis XV, in 1757. The story delineates torture as a means whereby the sovereign is able to reinstate his authority, with public torture being a kind of political ritual (Dreyfus & Rabinow, 1983). The brutality of the torture is fierce. The punishment leaves its marks, literally, on the body of the condemned who is the subject of the sovereign. The retelling of this torment, however, is meant as an exercise in defamiliarization (Shumway, 1989); the cruel torture is obviously of another era. One finds oneself thinking, "We've come a long way from such barbarism!"

Foucault continues with a review of the eighteenth-century reforms for the punishment of crimes and criminals. This is the *era of reform* in which public torture decreases. The body of the wrongdoer continues to be visible to the public. However, the accent in this era is the restoration of the social contract, with penalties meted out according to the crime committed (i.e., the punishment for murder was death; arrogance was punished by humiliation; the lazy person was sentenced to hard labor). The "corrections" notion was put in place as each "punishment would function as a deterrent, a recompense to society, and a lesson, all immediately intelligible to criminal and society" (Foucault, 1995, p. 148). The body in this era is marked, but marked differently than in the classical age. The body bears the representation of the evil of the crime (Shumway, 1989). Hester Prynne's wearing of the "scarlet letter" in Hawthorne's novel is an apt example.

Describing the crime accurately was of utmost importance in this era of reform. Only in knowing the crime exactly could the proper punishment be given, and the correct ordering/reordering of social life made possible. Precise knowledge of the crime and the criminal allowed for "reformers…to construct a comprehensive table of knowledge in which each crime and its appropriate punishment would find its exact place" (Dreyfus & Rabinow, 1983, p. 149).

Foucault reports that the model for this kind of individualization was taking place in natural history of the late eighteenth century. He refers to the prison reforms as a "Linnaeus of crimes and punishments, so that each particular offense and each punishable individual might come, without slightest risk of any arbitrary action, within the provision of a general law" (Foucault, 1995, p. 99). Knowing the crime and the criminal exactly emphasized the importance of the practice of representation. The marks on the body of the classical model are replaced by "signs, coded sets of representation" (Foucault, 1995, p. 130) in the reform period.

The third era of development within the penal system is the *modern model*. Foucault (1995) refers to it as "the gentle way" where "power must act while concealing itself beneath the gentle force of nature" (p. 106). This development is characterized by the appearance of the physical building, the prison, where economy and morality were combined (Dreyfus & Rabinow, 1983) in the methodical use of time (e.g., timetables were enforced) and space (e.g., isolation in cells).

Prisoners were isolated from the rest of society as they were to be feared by society and more easily controlled behind the prison walls. Solitary confinement within the prison was added, so as to facilitate penitence by the prisoners for their transgressions. All activities of the prisoner's day, including required work for economic reasons, were under strict surveillance. The acquiring of exact knowledge of the prisoner was very important and made possible through "dividing practices": separating prisoners from society and often from each other; separating the person of the prisoner into segments, e.g., the crime, intention, or psychological state of the prisoner. In this way, reform was sought to affect the "soul" of the prisoner in the resocializing effort.

Distinct breaks appear with the reforms of the previous era in this third model of punishment. The focus is on the modification of the prisoner's behavior, rather than public representation of a violation and punishment. The primary aim becomes the reform of the soul of the transgressor. The body in this era is like a machine (Shumway, 1989), and the success of the incarceration depended on the training and production of a "docile" and useful body (Dreyfus & Rabinow, 1983). However, it was really the soul that was being formed and reformed. Instead of the commonsense understanding of the soul as the prisoner of the body, what Foucault wants to emphasize is that the body is actually the prisoner of the soul. The control of bodies remains the primary goal of state control. The means of this control is the "gentle way" as the soul internalizes the rules and codes of the society. It is through the conversion of the soul that the body is reformed and conforms, and thereby is rendered docile and useful.

In summary, Foucault (1995) explains in *Discipline and Punish* how, in modern times, the focus has shifted from the overt control of the body, exemplified by monarchial power (Sarup, 1993) to another distinct form of control, although it is still focused on the control of the body. This shift is characterized by an exercise of power over the body that is covert; it is constant, regular, efficient, and unseen. Foucault (1995) characterizes it as the "gentle way" of control, yet it is every bit as potent as the control of former eras.

DISCIPLINARY TECHNOLOGIES

Foucault's major concern is the way modern modes of power form and reform individuals. It is a process of normalization often disguised as socialization. The socializing process is a key effort and effect of institutions and is facilitated by the disciplines of the human sciences.

Foucault (1980c) understands disciplines as "systems of power" with particular "structures and hierarchies...inspections, exercises and methods of training and conditioning" (p. 158) that have been "developed, refined, and used to shape individuals" (J. D. Marshall, 1990, p. 15). Disciplines of educational institutions, not unlike the prisons described by Foucault, exercise a kind of bio-power, a modern form of power. This is accomplished in the "increasing ordering of all realms under the guise of improving the welfare of the individual and the population....a strategy, with no one directing it and everyone increasingly enmeshed in it" (Dreyfus & Rabinow, 1983, p. xxvi).

Foucault's *gentle way* is an apt description of this control through a discipline's normalization of students, as they are rendered docile and useful. The dominant discourse of educational psychology, although using other words, seems to concur with normalization as the goal of the discipline as it is stated: "Because education is aimed at *causing* wanted changes in people—in their knowledge, skills, and attitudes—the discovery of ways to cause these changes has great practical importance" (emphasis in the original, Gage & Berliner, 1991, p. 14). This perspective of causing "wanted" changes echoes what Thorndike (1910) asserted as the discipline was developing in the beginning of the twentieth century: "The aim of education is...changing [the student] for the better—to produce in him the information, habits, powers, interests and ideas which are desirable" (p. 4).

The "way" to cause these "changes" is the stuff of educational psychology, its knowledge claims and practices. The normalizing practices of the discipline are utilized to render bodies docile as the individual is "subjected to habits, rules, orders, an authority that is exercised continually around him and upon him, and which he must allow to function automatically in him" (Foucault, 1995, pp. 128–129). Freire (1992) critiques this goal of modern educational practice: "the educated man is the adapted man, because he is better 'fit' for the world...the purposes of the oppressors, whose tranquility rests on how well men fit the world the oppressors have created, and how little they question it" (p. 63). Foucault (1995) specifies disciplinary practices as the technologies of *hierarchical observation, normalizing judgment,* and the *examination.* These major disciplinary "technologies" are understood as the "methods which made possible the meticulous control of the operations of the body that assured the constant subjection of its forces and imposed upon them a relation of docility-utility" (Foucault, 1995, p. 137). Even so, they are very simple instruments. Perhaps it is their simplicity that makes them so effective.

Each of the three disciplinary technologies will be presented next. A discussion of the way these disciplinary technologies pervade the discipline of educational psychology follows.

HIERARCHICAL OBSERVATION

Hierarchical observation is the disciplinary technology understood as a kind of "optics of power" (Dreyfus & Rabinow, 1983). It signifies the alliance between visibility and power (Smart, 1985). It is both a literal and a figurative observation. The purpose of requiring that individuals be visible is to make it possible to know them; when people, are known they can be changed, thus controlled and rendered docile. First in importance is determining the "nature" of the person or seeing the individual as he or she really is.

Foucault (1995) explains the importance of understanding the significance of architecture to this optics of power. The palace, for example, was built in the classical era to be seen, a symbol of the sovereign ruler; the fortress was built in such a way as to allow those inside to observe the space external to it. However, the school (as well as the prison) was constructed "to render visible those who are inside it...to act on those it shelters...to make it possible to know them, to alter them" (p. 172). The schoolhouse, then, became figuratively and literally an apparatus of observation, a kind of "microscope of conduct" (Foucault, 1995). Through observation, knowing, and training the socialization (read normalization) of students can take place.

The ideal situation is a single eye of authority seeing everything constantly (Smart, 1985). As numbers grew in school situations it became increasingly difficult for a "single eye" to supervise all students. A division of the work of the optics of power or a system of "super-vision," developed as a "disciplinary gaze" that took the form of a hierarchy of continuous and functional surveillance (Smart, 1985). The example discussed earlier of William Torrey Harris initiating the graded schoolhouse is a useful reference for this system of supervision. As students in the one-room schoolhouse could no longer be supervised effectively by one person because of growing numbers, they were separated into the grades, and the graded school appeared. Several teachers watched over their separate grades, and a supervisor watched over them. Foucault (1995) refers to hierarchical observation as the continual play of "calculated gazes."

Surveillance is an important aspect of hierarchical observation. Foucault (1995) introduces the image of the panopticon to demonstrate the efficiency and potency of surveillance used in prisons. The panopticon of Jeremy Bentham (1748–1832), the English philosopher and reformer, was meant to produce the effect of "the state of consciousness (and permanent visibility) that assures the automatic functioning of power" (p. 201). Bentham's model called for a central watchtower surrounded by tiered rows of cells. Light from windows in each cell and an open space facing the center tower allowed for prisoners to be in the constant view of the supervisor.

The economy of this mechanism is a major feature of the panopticon's usefulness. The panopticon allowed for the constant surveillance of each prisoner and, at the same time, did not require constant surveillance of each prisoner. Because prisoners knew that they *could* be watched at any time, they never could be sure *when* they *were* being watched. The economy and effectiveness of this model were exacerbated as the prisoners began to internalize the gaze of the supervisor; they watched themselves.

Foucault (1995) tells us that this mechanism, a form of hierarchical observation sets up a "network of relations from top to bottom, but also to a certain extent from bottom to top and laterally; this network 'holds' the whole together and traverses it in its entirety with effects of power that derive from one another: supervisors, perpetually supervised" (pp. 176–177). The internalization of the gaze of the supervisor is extremely significant in the formation of the subject. This internalization has implications for teachers as well as students. Teachers know that they are under the watchful eye of administrators as well as subjected to public scrutiny. Teachers, too, internalize the gaze of those in authority and of the dominant culture; they learn to watch themselves. To be effective and economical, the cooperation of those who are watched must be enlisted.

NORMALIZING JUDGMENT

Hierarchical observation allows for judgment and evaluation, and the basis of judgment is the norm. The technology of normalizing judgment is said to be at the heart of any system of disciplinary power (Foucault, 1995; Smart, 1985). Disciplinary practices need standards around which their operations can organized so individuals and groups are assessed by "comparisons with a favored paradigm real or imagined" (Prado, 1995, p. 61).

Normalizing judgment has the simultaneous action that marks its power; that is, it assumes and imposes homogeneity and simultaneously introduces individuality:

> The power of normalization imposes homogeneity, but it individualizes by making it possible to measure gaps, to determine levels, fix specialties and to render differences useful by fitting them into one another. It is easy to understand how the power of the norm functions within a system of formal equality, since within a homogeneity that is the rule, the norm introduces, as a useful imperative and as a result of measurement, all the shading of individual differences. (Foucault, 1995, p. 184)

Persons are recognized as individuals when they are described in terms of the norm and with reference to the norm finer and finer differentiation and individualization are possible. Through the normalizing judgment, behavior can be quantified and ranked as it falls on a field between two poles, normal and abnormal, good and bad (e.g., grades on tests, student cooperation, effective and ineffective teachers). A continuum is established and subjects can be placed along it in an objective manner. Foucault (1995) tells us that it has become possible through the modern sciences to "quantify this field and work out an arithmetic economy based on it" (p. 180). More specifically, "an objective hierarchy can be established by which the distribution of individuals is justified, legitimated and made more efficient" (Dreyfus & Rabinow, 1983, p. 158).

A system of penalties and rewards is effective in establishing and supporting normalization. Punishments are exacted for the slightest deviation from the norm, referred to as micropenalties. Micropenalties grew to include more and more areas of life (Dreyfus & Rabinow, 1983). Examples of micropenalties include issues around the following: time (e.g., lateness, absence), activity (e.g., inattention, lack of zeal), behavior (e.g., impoliteness, disobedience), speech (e.g., idle chatter, insolence), body (incorrect gestures, attitudes, cleanliness), sexuality (e.g., impurity, indecency) (Foucault, 1995).

THE "EXAMINATION"

The "examination" is at the "heart of the procedures of discipline" (Foucault, 1995, p. 184). It combines the other two disciplinary instruments, hierarchical observation and normalizing judgment, into what Foucault (1995) calls the "normalizing gaze." This is the disciplinary technique in which can be found "a whole domain of knowledge, a whole type of power" (p. 185) that allows for differentiation, classification, and judgment of its subjects. Foucault (1995) considers this technology as a kind of tiny, slender, widespread "ceremony of objectification" (p. 187). As such the examination marks a definite exemplification of the connection between power and knowledge.

Increased visibility is a key effect of the examination. Foucault reminds us that in feudal times the most visible people were the most important people, e.g., the king, the epic hero. With the rise of modern sciences the common folk are the ones who become visible as they are subjected to the mechanisms of objectification through the examination. This disciplinary technique of examination has the power to bring the individual into view, able to be seen in multiple ways and with finer and finer differentiation from others.

An important issue in this is that the examination is the "gaze" of the one with more power upon the one with less or no power (Shumway, 1989). The visibility of the subject, or student, is heightened as more and more features of the person are tested and gathered into a file. Individuals become "cases" through the gathering of common occurring attributes and differences (Smart, 1985), a case that can be described and analyzed, known, categorized, and eventually reformed.

The way Haraway (1991) highlights the metaphor of vision is helpful here. She insists that the visualizing technologies, exemplified in the examination, "are without apparent limit; the eye of any ordinary primate like us can be endlessly enhanced....Vision in this technological feast becomes unregulated gluttony" (pp. 188–189). Haraway insists that vision is always embodied. The eyes that see belong to/in somebody. This understanding exposes the impossibility of a "gaze from nowhere." The image of the eyes of the knower as always embodied renders problematic the claim of modern scientific methods that profess to "factor-out" or "control-for" the personality and bias of the scientist as the results or findings are understood to speak for themselves. On the contrary, the only possibility is vision from somewhere, from somebody, i.e., situated knowledge.

The effectiveness of the disciplinary technique of the examination is intensified through an inversion of visibility; as the individual becomes more visible the disciplinary power itself becomes invisible. Foucault (1995) explains:

> Disciplinary power…is exercised through its invisibility; at the same time it imposes on those whom it subjects a principle of compulsory visibility. In discipline it is the subjects that have to be seen. Their visibility assures the hold of the power that is exercised over them. It is the fact of being constantly seen that maintains the disciplined individual in his subjection. And the examination is the technique by which power, instead of emitting signs of its potency, instead of imposing its mark on its subjects, holds them in a mechanism of objectification. (p. 187)

Thus, despite its potency, the technology of power that facilitates the rendering of subjects as objects is itself invisible, i.e., the productive character of the examination is itself invisible, even as it renders its subject visible. In its ubiquity the normalizing activity of the examination is not questioned. The necessity of the examination in its multiple forms is a commonsense practice; it is taken for granted, considered natural or normal, as though things could not be otherwise.

Through the technology of the examination classifications and comparisons of persons become possible along increasingly finer gradations. Individual differences become significant. Foucault highlights the point that the modern individual is a historical achievement. Subjects are the products of the disciplinary power by which subjects are objectified, analyzed, and fixed (Dreyfus & Rabinow, 1983). Modern sciences have yielded the individual who is both the effect of power and the effect of knowledge, an example of questionable progress, from a "dubious science" (Foucault, 1995). This is a key example of what Foucault calls the productive aspect of power: "We must cease once and for all to describe the effects of power in negative terms: it 'excludes,' it 'represses,' it 'censors,' it 'abstracts,' it 'masks,' it 'conceals.' In fact, power produces; it produces reality; it produces domains of objects and rituals of truth. The individual and the knowledge gained of him belong to this production" (p. 194). In other words, professionals in the discipline produce the knowledge they apply, "they create the knowledge they require in order to fashion functioning, well-formed individuals" (Caputo & Yount, 1993, p. 7). Through this normalizing technology students become objectified; they become their "scores" as they receive their "marks."

This is an inversion of a modernist understanding that knowledge of the subject emerges through the technologies of the discipline. Subjects are *inscribed* by the technologies of the discipline rather than *described* by them.

DISCIPLINARY TECHNOLOGIES IN EDUCATIONAL PSYCHOLOGY

The disciplinary technologies (i.e., hierarchical observation, normalizing judgment, examination) described by Foucault (1977/1995) are operative in the discipline of educational psychology's discursive practices. The illustration of these technologies provides a way to interrogate how educational psychology uses power and knowledge to normalize students, i.e., to render students docile, neutral, and appropriate subjects. This interrogation highlights practices of the dominant discourse given expression in classic texts with the hope of "making the familiar strange" (Foucault, 1995). When practices seem strange they are more open to critique and more readily able to be changed.

The technologies of the discipline come together in various practices generated and perpetuated by the discipline of educational psychology. The specific areas to be discussed are:

1. The surveillance practices that pervade educational settings.
2. Classroom management practices.
3. The practice of testing, especially standardized resting.

In using these practices, teachers step into the web of power relations through which students are normalized. Through an uncritical use of these practices teachers participate in their own normalization as well, i.e., they become docile and useful.

SURVEILLANCE PRACTICES

In today's educational settings developing the capacity to see students clearly is represented as key to teacher effectiveness. Bentham's panopticon is a metaphor for a characteristic teachers are encouraged to develop, i.e., "withitness." The panopticon was meant to effect "the state of consciousness and permanent visibility that assures the automatic functioning of power" (Foucault, 1995, p. 201). Gage and Berliner (1991) describe a similar effect of "withitness": "the knack of seeming to know what is going on all over the room, of having 'eyes in the back of your head.' A teacher's awareness, and the students' awareness of it, makes a difference. Teachers with high "withitness" make few mistakes in identifying which student is misbehaving, in determining which of two behaviors is the more serious, or in timing an effort to stop a misbehavior" (p. 512).

Woolfolk (1995) also highlights the importance of "withitness" as a characteristic of effective classroom managers whose classes are "relatively free of problems." These are contrasted with ineffective managers whose classrooms are "continually plagued by chaos and disruption" (p. 416). Woolfolk states that withitness "means communicating to students that you are aware of everything that is happening in the classroom, that you aren't missing anything" (p. 416). Woolfolk repeats the optic power image of "eyes in the back of your head" and adds that "withit" teachers

> ...avoid becoming absorbed or interacting with only a few students, since this encourages the rest of the class to wander. [With-it teachers] are always scanning the room, making eye contact with individual students, so the students know they are being monitored... These teachers prevent minor disruptions from becoming major. They also know who instigated the problem, and they make sure the right people are dealt with. In other words, they do not make...timing errors (waiting too long before intervening) or target errors (blaming the wrong student and letting the real perpetrators escape responsibility for their behavior). (pp. 417–419)

"With it" teachers convey to students that they can be seen and are being monitored continuously. Students know they will be punished for a transgression. An important effect of the proper development of this quality in teachers is so they will be able to "catch" and correct misbehaving students.

The economy of this surveillance technique is a key factor in its utility. Since students know that there is always the possibility that they are being watched, they are encouraged to internalize the gaze of their supervisor learning to monitor themselves and each other. The direction is clear, "Teach students to monitor themselves" (Woolfolk, 1995, p. 420). Thus, the power relations in the classroom are diffused as teachers watch students, students watch teachers, themselves, and each other, and so forth. There is a web of relations of surveillance being weaved as Foucault (1995) insists "from top to bottom…bottom to top…and laterally" (pp. 176–177).

CLASSROOM MANAGEMENT

Despite the promised effectiveness of surveillance, or because of teachers' ineffective use of surveillance techniques (Gage & Berliner, 1991), children do "misbehave." Classroom management programs and practices are recommended by the mainstream discourse as explicitly aimed at maintaining an atmosphere conducive to learning, yet there is another side to these practices. Management practices are powerful tools (i.e., technologies) used in the normalization of students as they effect increasingly finer differential categories of what it means to "misbehave." The discursive practices of classroom management attend to the finer and finer differentiation of the specific aspects of everyday behavior.

Classroom management is a topic of special and growing import in educational psychology. There has been a marked increase in discussion of this topic in the past few decades, and it has been characterized as the number one concern of classroom teachers (Randolph & Evertson, 1994). According to a report of content analysis of educational psychology textbooks (Ash & Love-Clark, 1985), classroom management increased in amount of actual text space by 75% from 1954–1964 to 1965–1975. There was reported a 100% increase from 1965–1975 to 1976–1983 in text space. The authors of this analysis speculated that the increased discussion might reflect the movement of textbooks toward the more pragmatic concerns of teachers and away from the 'softer' side of educational psychology (Ash & Love-Clark, 1985). Despite their lack of ability to draw definitive conclusions from this descriptive report, the authors state that there have been changes in textbooks used in educational psychology. These changes are reported to be aimed at the practical aspects of classroom life and away from theoretical considerations.

The Woolfolk (1995) text then is representative of this shift in its attentiveness to the importance of issues related to classroom management. Woolfolk (1995) notes that classroom management is "one of the main concerns of teachers, particularly beginning teachers, as well as administrators and parents (p. 401). Woolfolk (1995) cites a Gallup Poll of the public's attitude toward public schools to substantiate this claim. Sixteen of the first seventeen polls list "lack of discipline" as the "number one problem facing schools" (p. 402). Since the late 1980s only "drug use" and "funding" issues have seized first place.

Gage and Berliner (1991), likewise, relate that all classroom needs fall into a "rough order of priority…the first [being] the establishment of classroom discipline, control, and management" (p. 509). It is claimed that "without it [classroom discipline, control, and management] nothing much of educational value can be done" (p. 509). Gage and Berliner (1991) also state that the issue of classroom management and discipline is considered by many administrators and teachers to be the most important cause of teacher failure…[and the] leading cause for dismissal" (p. 510). If teachers are judged as being ineffective in their management of classrooms, they can be dismissed. This indicates that the web of power relations in classroom management practice affects teachers and students alike.

There are many points that could be made in a critique of the discourse and practices of educational psychology regarding classroom management. Three areas are particularly problematic. The practices of classroom management are based on a preemptory perspective indicative of hierarchical observation. The question of who is "empowered" through management practices needs to be addressed. There is a question of a shift in emphasis from management as a way to access the curriculum to curriculum as a way to ensure good management.

The discursive practices of traditional classroom management come out of a modernist view that the social world is locked into irrationality. Chaos will reign if order is not established and controlled (Ball, 1990). Practices are directed to the "problems" that arise in classrooms. As discussed in the earlier chapter (chapter 36) , these problems are viewed through the perspective of a rationality that looks for technical solutions that can be applied to restore or maintain order. Teachers and educational psychologists define, interpret, and judge both the students who resist the management practices and students' action from a hierarchical position in ways that limit the meanings that the behavior may have.

These judgments are based on an "assumption that there is a proper, correct, standard, or agreed manner of carrying oneself" (Berry, 1995, p. 89). The teacher and educational psychologist know what that proper deportment looks like, and they can easily spot improper behavior. The judgment of proper/improper behavior is based on a "norm" and increasingly fine deviations from the "norm." In such an atmosphere the "non-conformist, even the temporary one, [becomes] the object of disciplinary attention" (Dreyfus & Rabinow, 1983, p. 158). Although the judgments of both students and their actions are always historically, socially, and politically contingent, they are seldom problematized as such.

For example, Woolfolk (1995) recognizes that difference in behavior may have cultural links. The critique that American schools, "typically reflect the white, Anglo-Saxon, middle-class, male-dominated values that have characterized mainstream America" (p. 155) is accepted as a valid appraisal. Readers are told that schooling formerly was thought to be "the fire under the melting pot" (p. 154). The importance of moving away from this assimilationist perspective, which takes this mainstream perspective as normative, is espoused; a new image of "mosaic" (p. 157) that "celebrates" and values diverse cultural behavior is introduced.

However, the mainstream norm and the deficit orientation model that judges nonmainstream behaviors as inferior resists displacement in the meaning-making basis of the text. Readers are instructed to "teach students directly about how to be students. In the early grades this could mean directly teaching the courtesies and conventions of the classroom: how to get a turn to speak, how and when to interrupt the teacher, how to whisper....You can ask students to learn "how we do it in school" without violating [the] principle...respect your students" (Woolfolk, 1995, p. 189). What needs to be highlighted is that while Woolfolk recognizes that "how we do it in school" exhibits the values of the dominant culture and is regarded as problematic, it is never disrupted or displaced. Standards of the Anglo, male, middle-class culture remain the favored paradigm and retain the privileged position. These "standards" become the universal norm that is used to judge behavior as proper or not, and children are judged for their compliance to these norms.

Earlier in the chapter normalizing judgment was discussed as both imposing homogeneity and constructing individuality simultaneously. This dual effect is obvious in classroom management practices as conformity to the homogeneous norm is privileged as the universal standard. Once the norm is established, finer differentiation from the norm can be perceived and measured; eventually individuals can be ranked in relation to each other.

Other examples from Gage and Berliner (1991) explicate the privileged and uninterrogated view of teachers judging the behavior of students from a universalized norm. Activities of students' "misbehavior" are placed in two simple categories: too many unwanted behaviors and too few wanted behaviors. Unwanted behaviors are listed as "physical aggression, moving around the room at inappropriate times, making too much noise, challenging authority at the wrong time or in the wrong way, and making unjust or destructive criticism and complaints" (p. 511). Behaviors that are wanted and need to be increased include "volunteering to recite, standing up for his or her own opinion, paying attention to what is being explained or discussed in class, being involved and active in individual or group projects" (p. 516). What these actions mean to the students themselves is ignored or marginalized as unimportant. Behaviors are simply assigned to one category or another, and the ambiguous nature of students' behavior is eschewed. For instance, a student may view his or her own behavior as "standing up for his or her opinion" (a wanted behavior), while the teacher judges the same action as "challenging authority in the wrong way" or making "unjust criticism." Deeper meanings of student behavior seem unimportant as the focus is on maintaining order and control. More frequently, that which is labeled misbehavior is lack of compliance to the preferred norm. What is ignored is that students are the ones producing the behavior that needs to be managed in the first place (Everhart, 1983). Students give meaning to their behavior.

Everhart (1983) explains that student behavior has social and political contingencies, and these extend beyond the classroom experience. Students, for example, understand their assignment to roles within the classroom and in the broader social context. Their activity forms a subculture as they struggle with the social and political aspects of schooling. As Everhart (1983) explains:

> Classroom management must be understood as a social system, but also as an interface between the state educational system and students. Classroom management mediates social life as students attempt to "make" themselves in a world in which political consciousness, class interests, and cultural regularities enter into the calculus of appropriateness and certitude by which students define themselves. (p. 170)

Students, from a sociopolitical perspective, are viewed as active agents. As such they comply or resign themselves to their assigned roles, or they devise various strategies through which they contest and resist the management practices of teachers and their assignment to low status positions in classrooms and schools. Oppositional behavior of students may well be an appropriate response to an oppressive education (Kohl, 1994). Students have a sense that an oppressive education is preparing and directing them to life in subordinate positions in society. Their minimal involvement in school activities, explicit signs of boredom, or oppositional behavior may signify their own feelings of alienation from the process and product of their work. Through their own oppositional activities students act to reappropriate control of their labor process (Everhart, 1983). In recognizing the sociopolitical aspects of classroom relations, much may be learned by teachers and students alike.

Teachers and students need to learn from students' oppositional activity. Frequently these activities are a mark of student agency; however, they also have a negative impact on students' lives. Perhaps one of the most dramatic forms of oppositional behavior that a student can perform is actually dropping out of school. "Dropping out" is seldom mentioned, questioned, or explored from a sociopolitical perspective in the mainstream discourse of educational psychology. Woolfolk (1993) notes, for example, that in the high school years teachers can focus on academics more than procedures and rules because "[b]y this time, unfortunately, many students with overwhelming behavioral problems have dropped out" (p. 405). The lack of attention supports

Fine's (1991) critique that the exodus of students, especially low-income students of color, from high schools "is represented as if it were all quite natural" (p. 8).

Classroom management is generally represented as a way to promote the empowerment of students. Even so, both texts advance models that focus on the empowerment of the teacher-manager (Ball, 1990). Students are not considered in terms of their own learning, agency, desires, and fears as discussed above. In the models presented in the discourse of the classic texts, the focus is on what teachers do to maintain control and compliance; the technical rationality of the discipline is obvious as the activity of the teacher is central.

Gage and Berliner (1991), for example, present classroom teaching practices in terms of how the teacher gains power in contrast to the students who have none:

> From the teacher's point of view you'll be looking at classroom teaching as an activity in which you have the power to shape the process. You probably had little of that power when you were in the student's role. Then you did pretty much what your teacher wanted you to do. Now, as the teacher, you have the determining role and the responsibility that goes with it....We will introduce you to a diverse set of teaching behaviors that can help you plan and actually be more effective whatever the subject or grade. (p. 494)

In discussing issues of classroom management the perspective of Gage and Berliner (1991) is clearly based in behavioristic psychology. The teacher gains power, and order is maintained through this system set in a discourse of control; management is a case of extinguishing unwanted behavior and increasing wanted behavior. Several strategies are suggested:

> One-way of stopping misbehavior is to extinguish it, to withhold reinforcement. This usually means not paying attention to it....Where it is feasible, simply ignore the [misbehaving] student. Turn your back, pay attention to a student who is behaving properly, walk away....Extinction takes time. It may be a while before a child's misbehavior begins to decrease. But be careful. Even an occasional reinforcement on your part can undo the whole process. (p. 513)

This is an example of a traditional prescriptive approach to classroom management in that the focus is directed toward the activities the teacher needs to perform in order to keep students on task and attentive (Everhart, 1983). Educational psychology's purpose is to equip the teacher with techniques through which he or she is more able to control classroom agendas.

Gage and Berliner (1991) recognize that the perspective presented in this text is *traditional* in that it "centers more on the teacher than the student" (p. 492). This perspective is represented as having an advantage over other perspectives of classroom management and teaching (e.g., student-centered instruction, open and humanistic education). The advantage that is reported is that traditional, teacher-centered educational practices have lasted over so many decades; they are "viable." As Gage and Berliner (1991) explain, "it has one important advantage—viability. It is the kind of teaching toward which teachers gravitate and to which they return" (p. 492).

However, it is noted that this perspective and its practices are not entirely in the best interest of students. Gage and Berliner (1991) report the comment of Cuban that this model "has been extremely viable, *for better or worse*" (emphasis added, p. 492). This method of classroom management is accepted as normative and unproblematic despite the expressed possibility that it may not be in the best interest of students.

The practices encouraged in the text manifest a vulgar pragmatism (Cherryholmes, 1988) as the emphasis is focused on what works, regardless of the underside of the effects. What Gage and Berliner (1991) leave out in reference to Cuban's work, and the discussion of classroom management in general, is the reason teacher-centered styles of classroom management persist. Cuban

(1984) theorizes that "[s]chools are a form of social control and sorting" (p. 9), echoing the social reproduction and correspondence theory of Bowles and Gintis (1976). Cuban (1984) argues:

> The ways schools are organized, the curriculum, and teaching practices mirror the norms of the socio-economic system....teacher practices become functional to achieve those ends . [i.e.,] reinforcing the teacher's authority to control the behavior of the class...the practices encouraged by student-centered instruction ill-fit the character of the society children will enter and classrooms became inhospitable arenas for small group instruction, expression, student decision making, etc. Teacher-centered instruction, however, endured because it produces *student behaviors expected by the larger society*. (emphasis added, p. 9)

Cuban (1984) has connected the micropractices of schooling with the macrovalues of the larger society. These issues are left unquestioned, even obscured, in the classic educational psychology texts. Through the traditional practices of classroom management students can be normalized, made proper citizens of the state, i.e., docile and useful.

The use of behavioristic psychology, so typical of traditional teacher-centered classroom management practices, exemplifies clearly the "shaping" of students to conform to norms that have become naturalized. What also needs to be noted as well is that humanistic psychologies also are useful in the normalization of students, albeit their role in government is subtler. In student-centered classrooms that espouse humanist psychology the emphasis is on the empowerment of the student. Students are understood as active meaning-makers striving to know themselves and to become self-actualized. Gage and Berliner (1991) explain self-actualized students as: "people who come to accept themselves, their feelings, and others more fully. These people are self-directed, confident, mature, realistic about their goals, and flexible. They've gotten rid of maladjustive behaviors. They become like the people they want to be" (p. 479).

This student-centered perspective seems to be an improvement on the teacher-centered, traditional model. However, while students are perceived as central to the meaning-making system, they are considered self-contained, separate, and isolated from the social and the political contingencies that generate the categories into which they place themselves. Getting rid of "maladjustive behaviors" mentioned in the quote above could be indicative of an even subtler interiorization of a dominant and possibly oppressive norm.

Usher and Edwards (1994) state that humanistic discourses can be more powerful than the objectifying discourses generated by behavioristic psychology. In "subjectifying discourses, within which humanistic psychology has been strongly implicated...[d]iscipline is not something externally imposed by teachers since students discipline themselves" (p. 51); it is possible to argue that "regulation works by empowerment" (p. 50). Humanistic psychology, too, provides the "justification and the means for intervention and 'shaping'" (p. 53) students under the illusion of self-governance.

There has been a discernible shift toward the control of students through the use of the curriculum. McNeil (1983) asks readers to picture a one-room schoolhouse of the last century. The students sit on hard benches or at desks in rows facing front; students stand to recite; for much of the day they are silent and still. The teacher or schoolmaster is stern, perhaps wielding a hickory stick. There the purpose for the discipline is *to help the students access the curriculum*. Classroom management and discipline traditionally are viewed as instrumental to the learning of the curriculum.

To a major extent, classroom management procedures of the current day are much different, although they purportedly are intended for the same purpose, i.e., to help students access the curriculum. Woolfolk (1995) lists more time for learning and greater access to learning as reasons for management practices. Gage and Berliner (1991) insist nothing educational happens without good management practices. However, there is an indication of an obvious shift in the idea of management practices of educational psychology. While classroom management practices are instrumental in helping students access the curriculum, there is also evidence that there is an inversion, i.e., the curriculum is a means of classroom management. For example, Gage and Berliner (1991) connect "misbehavior" of students with the way schools are organized. They note: "behavioral problems…[can] stem from the way schools are organized. Sometimes school structure forces students to take courses that are inappropriate for them, that do not allow for their individual needs or level of achievement" (p. 510). They continue to explain that schools that do not allow for students' "individual needs or levels of achievement," as well as a variety of other issues that are outside the teachers' control, contribute to the "crime, delinquency, and problem behavior that exist in [the schools]" (p. 511). The assumption is that the needs of students are met when they are correctly placed in appropriate learning groups and given the appropriate information. When students receive their proper educational experience, they will not misbehave. Thus, there is signaled an inversion of means and ends. Where the practices of classroom management were intended as means toward the end of accessing knowledge, there is a shift. The curriculum may also be used as a means through which schools control students.

TESTING AND THE PRODUCTION OF STUDENTS

Following Foucault's (1995) position that normalization is a major aspect of the role of schooling, the formation of the "norm" is a key consideration. As presented above, there may be a tacit endorsement by educationalists of what is "normal" or normative based in the commonsense acceptance of certain values, beliefs, and behaviors. These norms are reflective of the preference of the dominant groups and adopted as universal norms by social institutions, schools in particular. Norms grow in power through hegemonic control, i.e., they are validated by meaning-making systems and granted consent by members of subordinate as well as dominant groups. They need to be continually exposed and critiqued. However, there is another area that needs to be highlighted regarding the establishment of norms.

Foucault (1995) has noted the increasingly complex nature of the normalization process in that it has become "possible," through the human sciences, to measure or quantify what is judged to be "normal." The technologies of hierarchical observation and normalizing judgment come together in the quantifying of an evaluative judgment. This is so much of the work of educational psychology exemplified by its emphasis on testing.

That "testing of students is ubiquitous" is a truism. Woolfolk (1995) remarks that "if you have seen the cumulative folders that include testing records for individual students over several years, then you know the many ways students are tested in this country" (p. 528). Hanson (1993) asserts that the testing associated with schooling can begin with examinations toddlers take to enter nursery school, and "that is just the beginning of an endless torrent of tests that will probe every corner of their nature and behavior for the rest of their lives" (p. 1). Gage and Berliner (1991) report that a "reasonable estimate" of teacher time devoted to the testing process is 20% to 30%.

Woolfolk (1995) states: "Measurement is evaluation put in quantitative terms—the numeric *description* of an event or characteristic" (emphasis added, p. 514). Educational psychology advances the understanding that through testing practices that produce these measurements the "truth" about an individual can be known. In other words, testing increases the ability to see and describe students. It is necessary to interrogate this familiar notion. It is argued in the following discussion that testing processes, i.e., forms of examination (especially the norm-referenced variety), are *technologies of differentiation and individualization* that *inscribe* rather than describe students, Examinations are also technologies of power that work to establish hierarchies among students, that are a means of control and a method of domination (Foucault, 1995).

An important issue in the understanding of testing practices is the notion of validity, particularly construct validity. Validity is defined by Woolfolk (1995) as the "degree to which a test measures what it is intended to measure" (p. 525). What is generally avoided in mainstream discussions of construct validity is the social construction of these abstract characteristics. Social constructs are considered and treated "as if" they are "real." This exemplifies the problem of *reification*. However, reification of abstract concepts is imperative in testing practices because only "real" things can be measured. Within the ideology of meritocracy, these "real" characteristics need to be understood as innate properties of individuals, stable over time, and varying in measurement in individuals.

Another important issue regarding testing is that it yields "objective" measurements according to a scale that is metric. The "normal distribution" of students along the bell-shaped curve is critical to this understanding. Although the social construction of the normal or bell-shaped curve has been presented and critiqued, the discursive practice continues to be advanced unproblematically in classic texts of educational psychology. It is presented as "natural" as well as "normal."

For example, Woolfolk (1995) states that the "bell-shaped curve, [is] the most famous frequency distribution because it describes many naturally occurring physical and social phenomena" (p. 519). Gage and Berliner (1991) make the connection as well between physical and social characteristics in stating that "both measures of intelligence and height are normally distributed within any specific age, ethnic, and gender group" (p. 57). The argument is that a "naturally occurring" physical phenomenon (e.g., height) and "naturally occurring" social phenomenon (e.g., intelligence) are normally distributed within a specific population.

These authors construct the illusion that there is a metric scale used to measure both phenomena. However, while there is a standard of measure for height (e.g., feet and inches), only an ordinal system can measure "naturally occurring social phenomena." It is more than an illusion that is created though, as Gage and Berliner (1991) state: "One reason for the popularity of tests is that they give us a quantitative estimate of ability or achievement; they tell *us how much*. In education the attributes that interest us emphasize the abilities and achievements of students—such things as intelligence, creativity, spelling ability, science knowledge, and interest in art" (emphasis added, p. 570).

Mensh and Mensh (1991) refer to the bell-shaped curve as a "particularly mystifying aspect of IQ" (p. 75). Although normal distribution may occur regarding the "metric characteristics of animals such as birth weight in cattle....IQ tests do not possess the characteristics for creating a normal curve" (Mensh & Mensh, 1991, p. 172). Nevertheless, educational psychologists continue to insist that the IQ does possess these metric characteristics.

The bell-shaped curve is an arbitrary and social artifact (Lewontin et al., 1996). Testers create tests so that a bell-shaped curve will appear. This approach preserves the illusion that the "tests measure a real characteristic" (Mensh & Mensh, 1991, p. 76). Intelligence and ability tests "have been composed of items selected after trial for observed conformity with the normal distribution. Items that showed little correlation with the overall expectations, or with the previous tests of the kind have been systematically excluded" (Morrison, 1977, quoted in Mensh and Mensh, 1991, p. 76).

Woolfolk (1995) refers to this process in the following explanation of basic concepts in standardized test making: "The test items and instructions have been tried out to make sure *they work* and then rewritten and retested as necessary" (emphasis added, p. 517). What is meant by making sure "they work" is that the tests successfully correlate intelligence or ability scores of students taking the test with the placement of students in the social order (Mensh & Mensh, 1991). That "they work" is an indication of their power to differentiate (Gage & Berliner, 1991).

Gage and Berliner (1991) assert that developers of tests use "the tests' differentiating power as their guide" (p. 51). This differentiating power is further explained:

> Partly because of the way the tests were made, and partly because of the way human intelligence functions, the resulting IQ scores…fell into a *normal distribution* [emphasis original[which has the bell shape… Why do IQ tests tend to be normally distributed? *Is it simply because the test is rigged? Not entirely* [emphasis added]. Remember that the tests consist of many items, each designed to differentiate among individuals. That is, the items are written so that on some items only about half of a given age group responds correctly, while on other items a higher or lower percentage of that group responds correctly. (p. 56)

The standard on which the tests' differentiating power is based is middle-class knowledge. Gage and Berliner (1991) recognize this and give many examples of this bias, and then they excuse it; as bias is renamed "relevance":

> Middle-class bias has proved much more difficult to eliminate than was anticipated. For tests of intellectual abilities useful in modern American society, a "middle-class" and "urban" orientation may constitute not bias but *relevance*….So we may not want to change the tests so much as we might want to change the environments that promote low test performance. (emphasis added, p. 90)

The suggestion of changing environments as a way to ameliorate low-test scores is contradictory and seems disingenuous. It is contradictory in that "intelligence" is repeatedly represented in the same text as an innate, stable, and inherited characteristic (Gage & Berliner, 1991). How can it improve with a change in environment? It seems disingenuous in that standardized tests *are constructed* to rank a certain percentage of students below the normal range. Effective standardized tests are guaranteed, or, to use Gage and Berliner's term, "rigged" to separate and sort children. This is the differentiating power that guides the development of the tests in the first place. This is how *they work*, why they were developed, and why test questions have to be written and rewritten.

The "differentiating power" of tests is central to their use in educational institutions. The particular "norm" around which they are organized is never made problematic. On the contrary, the middle-class "relevance" is accepted as normative. Award or violence is distributed to students according to their scores or their "marks." Lewontin et al. (1996) explain succinctly:

> …the power of the "norm," once established, is that it is used to judge individuals who have been located along its linear scale. Deviations from the norm are regarded with alarm. Parents who are told that their child is two standard deviations from the norm on some behavioral scale are led to believe that he or she is "abnormal" and should be adjusted in some way to psychometry's Procrustean bed. Psychometry, above all, is a tool of a conformist society that, for all its professed concern with individuals, is in reality mainly concerned to match them against others and to attempt to adjust them to conformity. (p. 149)

Norms are established by validating what works in differentiating those considered "normal" from those who are not. The argument is circular. The process of standardized testing establishes what is "normal" based on information gathered on those who are considered normal. The deficit view of those outside this norm is a form of "popular racism" (Rizvi, 1993).

Although the classic texts never say exactly who the norming sample is, it is noted that "social class, race, gender, and ethnicity can be relevant considerations" (Gage & Berliner, 1991, p. 574) if there is a concern with equal opportunity. It is stated that there is a "problem that many African American, Chicanos, and Native Americans face with norm referenced testing when the norms are based on distant but supposedly representative, peer groups" (Gage & Berliner, 1991, p. 574). When this information is added to the "problem" that a hypothetical student named "Lisa" is having with her national percentile rank, then all the clues point to the norm group. The norm group is male, Anglo, and middle class. It is important to note that although Gage and Berliner (1991) regard social class, race, and gender to be "relevant" considerations in discussions of equality, these same characteristics become "irrelevant" when the interest is in selecting "highly competent rather than mediocre" (p. 574) students.

The "objective" evaluation of students according to scores produced through testing needs to be regarded as a process that produces normalcy. This process also describes deviance from the norm. As more tests are taken by students, their cumulative folder expands, and "more knowledge leads to more specification" (Dreyfus & Rabinow, 1983, p. 159). There is developed a new visibility and a more minute describability. The "examination is at the center of the procedures that constitute the individual as both effect and object of power, as effect and object of knowledge" (Foucault, 1995, p. 192).

There is a certain "alchemy" in this process. The properties of a discipline's regime, i.e., its norms, values, procedures, become attributes of persons. Rose (1989) expresses this well:

> The procedures of visualization, individualization and inscription that characterize the mental sciences reverse the direction and domination between human individuals and the scientific and technical imagination. They domesticate and discipline subjectivity, transforming the intangible, changeable, apparently free-willed conduct of people into manipulable, coded, materialized, mathematized, two-dimensional traces which may be utilized in any procedure of calculation. The human individual has become calculable and manageable. (p. 129)

Disciplines are ways of naming and ordering differences. Through their testing procedures, they allow educators to categorize all the complexity students by reducing them to scores that can be illustrated on graphs and tables. The result of testing practices has profound effects on lives of students. Gage and Berliner (1991) remind us: "All your life you've been taking tests. They have brought you success or failure, joy or sorrow, a sense of justice done or outrage suffered" (p. 569). That there is not more outrage attests to the hegemonic control this disciplinary practice of educational psychology exerts.

This chapter is entitled *Disciplining the Discipline* in order to highlight the activity of placing the discursive practices of the discipline under scrutiny. Utilizing the process of critical reading and Foucault's methods of critique, it is possible to look at the modern science of educational psychology differently. The practices of the discipline, its disciplinary technologies, are usually considered progressive. In other words, they are considered a means of enabling students, i.e., practices are used in the liberatory interest of education. However, the limits of these technologies need to be recognized as they are utilized to judge, construct, and normalize students as subjects of a particular kind, docile and useful.

The questioning of the discipline's practices is not aimed at looking for answers or universal solutions. Rather, questioning is regarded as a way to engage the issues of the discipline more deeply and complexly. Questioning indicates a desire to interrogate "what what we do does" in the real-life experiences of children so that we can think about students and our own practice differently. A critique of the discipline needs to become an important part of the disciplinary practice.

REFERENCES

Ash, M.J. & Love-Clark, P. (1985). An historical analysis of the content of educational psychology textbooks. *Educational Psychologist, 20*(I), 47–55.

Ball, S.J. (1990). Introducing Monsieur Foucault. In S. J. Ball (Ed.) *Foucault and education: Disciplines and knowledge* (pp. 1–10). New York: Routledge.

Bell, D. (1997). Protecting diversity programs from political and judicial attack. *The Chronicle of Higher Education, 43*(30), B4–B5.

Berry, K. (1995). Students under suspicion: Do students misbehave more than they used to? In J.L. Kincheloe & Shirley Steinberg (eds.). *Thirteen questions: Reframing education's conversations* (2nd ed.) (pp. 89–96). New York: Peter Lang.

Bowles, S. & Gintis, H. (1976). *Schooling in capitalist America.* New York: Basic Books.

Briscoe, F.M.(1993). *Knowledge/power and practice: A Foucauldian interpretation of nineteenth century classrooms.* Unpublished doctoral dissertation, University of Cincinnati, Cincinnati, Ohio.

Caputo, J.D. & Yount, M. (1993). Introduction. In J.D. Caputo & M. Yount (Eds.), *Foucault and the critique of institutions* (pp. 3–23). University Park: The Pennsylvania State University Press.

Cuban, L. (1984). *How teachers taught: Constancy and change in American classrooms: 1890–1990.* White Plains, NY: Longman.

Dales, B.L. (1992). *Power relations surrounding access to sources of information in public schools.* Unpublished doctoral dissertation, Miami University, Oxford, Ohio.

Dreyfus, H.L. & Rabinow, P. (1983). *Michael Foucault, beyond structuralism and hermeneutics.* Chicago: The University of Chicago Press.

Everhart, R.B. (1983). Classroom management, student opposition, and the labor process. In M.W. Apple & L. Weiss (Eds.), *Ideology and practice in schooling* (pp. 114–142). Philadelphia: Temple University Press.

Fancher, R.E. (1985). *The intelligence men.* New York: W.W. Norton & Co.

Fine, M. (1991). *Framing dropouts: Notes on the politics of an urban public high school.* Albany: State University of New York Press.

Foucault, M. (1980a). Truth and power. In C. Gordon (Ed.), *Power/Knowledge: Selected interviews and other writings.* New York: Pantheon Press.

Foucault, M. (1980b). The will to truth. In A. Sheridan (Ed.), *Michael Foucault: The will to truth.* New York: Tavistock Publications.

Foucault, M. (1980c). The eye of power. In C. Gordon (Ed.), *Power/knowledge: Selected interviews and other writings* (pp. 146–145). New York: Pantheon Books.

Foucault, M. (1995). *Discipline & punish: The birth of the prison* (2nd ed.). New York: Vintage Books.

Fraser, N. (1989). *Unruly practices: Power, gender, and discourse in contemporary social theory.* Minneapolis: University of Minnesota Press.

Freire, P. (1992). *Pedagogy of the oppressed.* New York: Seabury Press.

Freire, P. & Faundez, A. (1992). *Learning to question: A pedagogy of liberation.* New York: The Continuum Publishing company.

Gage, N. L., & Berliner, D. C. (1991). *Educational psychology* (5th ed.). Boston: Houghton Mifflin Company.

Hanson, F.A. (1993). *Testing testing: Social consequences of the examined life.* Berkeley: University of California Press.

Haraway, D. (1996).Modest witness: Feminist diffractions in science studies. In P. Galison & D.J. Stump (Eds.), *The disunity of science boundaries, contexts, and power* (pp. 428–441). Stanford: Stanford University Press.

Haraway, D. (1991). *Simians, cyborgs, and women: The reinvention of nature.* New York: Routledge.

Hilgard, E.R. (1996). History of educational psychology. In D.C. Berliner & R.C. Calfee (Eds.), *Handbook of educational psychology* (pp. 990–1004). New York: Macmillan Library Reference.

Jensen, A.R. (1987). Individual differences in mental ability. In J.S. Glover & R.R. Ronning (Eds.), *Historical foundations of educational psychology* (pp. 61–88). New York: Plenum Press.

Kohl, H. (1994). *I won't learn from you: And other thoughts on creative maladjustment.* New York: The New Press.

Lewontin, R.C., Rose, S. & Kamin, L.J. (1996). IQ: the rank ordering of the world. In S. Harding (Ed.), *The racial economy of science.* Bloomington: Indiana University Press.

Marshall, J.D. (1990). Foucault and educational research. In S.J. Ball (Ed.), *Foucault and education: Disciplines and knowledge* (pp. 11–28). New York: Routledge.

McNeil, L. (1983). Defensive teaching and classroom control. In M. W. Apple & L. Weis (Eds.), *Ideology and practice in schooling* (pp. 114–142). Philadelphia: Temple University Press.

Mensh, E. & Mensh, H. (1991). *The IQ mythology: Class, race, gender, and inequality.* Carbondale: Southern Illinois University Press.

Philp, M. (1985). Michel Foucault. In Q. Skinner (Ed.), *The return of grand theory in the human sciences* (pp. 65–82). New York: Cambridge University Press.

Prado, C.G. (1995). *Starting with Foucault: An introduction to genealogy.* Boulder, CO: Westview.

Randolph, C.h. & Evertson, C.M. (1994). Images of management for learner centered classroom. *Action in Teacher Education,* 55–64.

Rizvi, F. (1993). Children and the grammar of popular racism. In C. McCarthy & W. Crichlow (Eds.), *Race, identity, and representation in education.* New York: Routledge.

Rose, N. (1989). Individualizing psychology. In J. Shotter, & K. Gergen (Eds.), *Texts of identity* (pp. 119–132). London: Sage.

Sarup, M. (1996). *Identity, culture, and the postmodern world.* Athens: The University of Georgia Press.

Sarup, M. (1993). *An introductory guide to post-structuralism and postmodernism* (2nd ed.). Athens: The University of Georgia Press.

Sawicki, J. (1991). *Disciplining Foucault: Feminism, power, and the body.* New York: Routledge.

Shumway, D.R. (1989). *Michael Foucault.* Charlottesville: University Press of Virginia.

Smart, B. (1985). *Michael Foucault.* New York: Routledge.

Soukhanov, A.H. (1984). *Webster's II new Riverside university dictionary.* Boston: Houghton Mifflin Company.

Thorndike, E.L. (1910). *Educational psychology.* New York: Teachers College Press.

Usher, R. (1993). Re-examining the place of disciplines in adult education. *Studies in Continuing Education, 15*(I), 15–25.

Usher, R. & Edwards, R. (1994). *Postmodernism and education.* New York: Routledge.

van Dijk, T.A. (1993). Principles of critical discourse analysis. *Discourse and Society, 4*(2), 240–283.

Woolfolk, A.E. (1995). *Educational psychology* (6th ed). Boston, MA: Allyn & Bacon.

THIRTY-EIGHT

Using Action Research Methodology to Unite Theory and Practice

Sandra A. Deemer

Courses in educational psychology typically contain readings and discussions that are centered on pivotal research studies in the field. Whether studies relate to the foundational work of key theorists in our field (e.g., Piaget) or recent examinations of current issues in education (e.g., studies about achievement motivation and high stakes testing), these studies help us analyze classroom situations. Yet, many preservice teachers fail to understand the importance of learning about, and conducting, educational research. In fact, many fail even to see the link between being a critical consumer of educational research and developing into an outstanding teacher (Sowell, 2001). In order to develop these skills, teacher candidates need to be actively involved in an authentic process in which they can critically analyze and utilize research in educational psychology.

Action research methodology is an authentic research process that is typically viewed as a tool for inservice teachers to understand and respond to situations in their classrooms (Mills, 2000). The action research process differs somewhat from the traditional scientific research process in that it evolves from an educator's struggle with a very particular issue in the classroom and the main focus of the research is on solving a specific, local problem. For example, Capobianco and Lehman (2006) utilized action research to resolve the struggle they were having with involving all students in discussions during science classes. In addition to drawing on previous academic research to understand and respond to this problem, they discussed how they also gained information about solving this problem from conversations with colleagues. Within the action research methodology, this type of local knowledge, often so useful to educators, is considered just as valuable as knowledge derived from large-scale academic research. Instead of a tension between theory and practice, in action research the two are united and provide an impetus for discovering solutions to authentic classroom problems. According to Shuell (1996), relieving this tension is necessary in the field of educational psychology and reflects the reality of how teachers actually practice in the classroom.

Clearly, action research is a process that can aid current teachers in responding to dilemmas in their classroom, but the students in many educational psychology courses are not yet certified nor are they teaching in their own classrooms. At Millersville University, I have found that the same methodology can be adapted to both develop preservice teacher's research-related skills and to aid them in uniting theory and practice. Even though they are not yet teaching, allowing these students to draw on their own previous classroom experiences permits the authenticity of the problem needed to begin the action research process to be maintained. For example, a student may recall being anxious when exposed to timed multiplication tests during her elementary years. As an aspiring elementary teacher, she could use action research methodology to investigate the educational soundness of this approach and possible alternatives to teaching multiplication skills during the elementary years.

DESCRIPTION OF ACTION RESEARCH ASSIGNMENT

The action research methodology described by Mills (2000) represents an approach that is most amenable to current teachers. As mentioned above, this methodology needs to be adapted so that preservice teaching students can benefit from the approach. The first step in this process is having students identify an educational problem they have observed in a classroom or experienced themselves as a student. Students can also identify an educational issue that is being experienced by a child that they know personally; this could include a child of their own. Second, students consult class readings and seek out additional research in educational psychology in order to understand the context and background of their chosen problem. This same research base can serve as a source of potential solutions to the problem. Third, students collect additional information regarding possible solutions to the problem from one or more individuals who have experience with, or expertise related to, the problem. Students can gain this information from a variety of sources (e.g., experienced teachers, parents, other students, administrators) through an interview, a survey, or an observation. Finally, students summarize and analyze the potential ideas for action that they gained from the research in educational psychology and their informant(s). After examining the validity, feasibility, and possible "side effects" of these potential solutions, students recommend the "best" intervention to take and then discuss how the action would be expected to affect the student, teacher, and classroom context if it were taken, based on the knowledge they have gathered.

In addition to completing a written paper, which can be done individually or collaboratively, students also share their action research at the end of the semester in a formal presentation and an informal question and answer session with their classmates. This sharing is invaluable in further validating the usefulness of educational psychology research in understanding educational contexts and in offering solutions for educational problems (Sternberg & Grigorenko, 2004). The presentation provides another forum for students to convey their knowledge about a particular topic and their understanding of the action research process. Students receive confidential written feedback from their classmates following the presentation; this aspect keeps all students involved in this important sharing and learning process.

ASSESSING THE EFFECTIVENESS OF THE ACTION RESEARCH ASSIGNMENT

In order to assess the impact that this action research project had on students, I gave a six-item survey to all students who took Advanced Educational Psychology at Millersville University in the fall of 2006 and spring of 2007. Participants included 30 students who were enrolled in this masters-level Educational Psychology course in the fall of 2006 (n=16) and spring of 2007 (n=14); both males and females, between 21 and 55 years of age were included in the sample. The classes included students receiving post-baccalaureate certification in elementary and secondary education and students obtaining masters' degrees in various areas of elementary, secondary and special education.

This self-designed survey included the following items:

1. What was the topic of your action research project?
2. Did you work individually or in a group on this project? How would you evaluate the experience?
3. Describe what you learned in regard to the process of action research.
4. Describe what you learned in regard to the key ideas, concepts, and theories in educational psychology.
5. How did the action research presentations (yours and your classmates') help you learn in this course?
6. How could this project be improved? Consider both the written and the oral parts of this project.

Although students' responses to the first two questions did not directly address the effectiveness of the action research assignment, they clearly showed the variety in the topics selected for this project and the different ways in which students chose to complete it. This variety (e.g., *Motivating non-dominant students to learn secondary social studies in an urban setting* and *Integration of core subject content into the visual arts curriculum*) exposed the students to topics that I would not necessarily discuss throughout the semester. Thus, by hearing students' presentations about their classmates' action research, students received a much more comprehensive course that if I alone had dictated the topics for all of our weekly class meetings. In addition, 25 out of 30 students reported favorable experiences working within small groups, partner arrangements, or individually. For example, one student who worked in a group claimed it was "*extremely valuable to integrate peers' ideas, experiences, writing/learning styles,*" while another student who worked individually said working alone, "*helped me to understand the process of exploring educational issues.*" It appears that the elements of choice in regard to the topic for the action research and the way in which it is completed (e.g., group, partner, or individual) actually fostered learning about key topics in educational psychology such as learning styles and cooperative learning.

Their responses to the third question indicated that students did gain an understanding about the process of action research. Specifically, the majority (26 of 30) of the students indicated that the action research methodology introduced them to a valuable problem-solving process of which they had not been aware, prior to taking this course. One student stated, *"You choose a specific topic and take time to really think about this topic that will impact your teaching career. Researching for articles is important and necessary for a contemplative practitioner."* Students also indicated that uniting academic research with information from a live informant fostered cooperation among educators that aided them in suggesting meaningful strategies to address their issue of concern.

In regard to the fourth question, which most clearly asked about students' learning related to key ideas, concepts, and theories in educational psychology, all students listed topics that were highlighted in class readings and discussions. These included references to theories of development (Piaget, Vygotsky, Gilligan, Kohlberg, Erikson), theories of motivation (Ames' TARGET framework, goal theory, Maslow's hierarchy of needs) and paradigms of assessment (assessment as inquiry, assessment as measurement). The action research project seemed to help students articulate their understanding of educational psychology in meaningful ways as they applied these key psychological ideas to solving a problem of personal interest to them. For example, one student described how she utilized learning theories in her classroom as she adapted her lessons to reflect multiple intelligence theory.

Students' responses to the fifth question, about the action research presentation, indicated that they learned from both creating and presenting their work, and listening and responding to their classmates' presentations. One student stated, *"I got to hear different ideas, sources, and information used for the action research papers."* Several (15 out of 30) others indicated that the presentations further allowed them to unite theory and practice. For example, a student reported that, *"The presentation gave an opportunity to draw linkages between theories discussed in class and research—these ideas clicked."*

Students' responses to the last question on the survey revealed some aspects of the assignment that could be improved. Ten of 30 students said they would have liked more time to present their work while 10 of 30 students also would have preferred more direction in choosing topics for the project. Ten of 30 students indicated that no changes were necessary and that they appreciated the class time devoted to working on this project and the review of their written draft of the action research paper.

Although the sample of students used to assess the effectiveness of this assignment was quite small, these findings suggest that action research methodology does offer one way to aid students in uniting theory and practice. By situating students' thinking within an authentic situation, as called for by Anderson and her colleagues (1995), this assignment helps students develop a deep and generative understanding of how knowledge in educational psychology can serve as a foundation for solving problems in the classroom. In addition, it gives students an appreciation of, and experience with, a research process that they can use as future practitioners.

REFERENCES

Anderson, L. M., Blumenfeld, P., Pintrich, P. H., Clark, C. M., Marx, R. W., & Peterson, P. (2005). Educational psychology for teachers: Rethinking our courses, rethinking our roles. *Educational Psychologist, 30,* 143–157.

Capobianco, B., & Lehman, J. (2006). Integrating technology to foster inquiry in an elementary science methods course: An action research study of one teacher educator's initiatives in a PT3 project. *Journal of Computers in Mathematics and Science Teaching, 25,* 123–146.

Mills, G. E. (2000). Understanding action research. In *Action research: A guide for the teacher researcher (pp. 36–52).* Upper Saddle River, NJ: Prentice Hall.

Shuell, T. J. (1996). The role of educational psychology in the preparation of teachers. *Educational Psychologist, 3,* 5–14.

Sowell, E. J. (2001). *Educational research: An integrative approach.* Boston, MA :McGraw-Hill.

Sternberg, R. J., & Grigorenko, E. L. (2004). Successful intelligence in the classroom. *Theory into Practice, 43,* 274–280.

Alternative Education, Urban Youth, and Interventions

THIRTY-NINE

Therapeutic Art, Poetry, and Personal Essay: Old and New Prescriptions

Mary Hollowell and Donna Moye

Within the field of educational psychology, issues of how to motivate children to learn often discuss and deconstruct traditional dimensions such as cognitive, social, behavioral, and humanistic perspectives. Edith Kramer's *Art Therapy in a Children's Community* presents us with a fresh explication for motivating children to learn. Published over fifty years ago, her insights into troubled children, based on their artwork, are still applicable today. Post-modern technological inventions such as MP3 players, iPhones, videogames, and online social networking have not changed the universal themes found in the art of wounded children and youth, as they learn about themselves and others while they progress towards healing.

Kramer's art therapy first began in Prague during WWII, as she began to see patterns while working with refugee children. She is described in a wealth of literature as a pioneer in the field of art therapy. In fact, art therapy was not formally recognized in the United States until it was introduced by Kramer in the 1940s, following her immigration. She has been identified as a major theoretician-practitioner by Jean Keller in *Activities with Developmentally Disabled Elderly and Older Adults* (1991). When Melvin Miller and Susanne Cook-Greuter interviewed her in 1997 at the age of 82, they wrote, "Kramer's activities have bridged continents, integrated disciplines, and crossed domains of high expression" (p. 99). In contrast to her predecessors, who heavily psychoanalyzed artists, Edith Kramer focused more on artwork itself. Scholars Aubrey and Nya Fine write, "Edith Kramer, on the other hand, placed emphasis on an alternative direction, more towards a humanistic approach. Her work with children emphasized the healing properties of the creative process" (p. 263). Kramer was a brilliant and talented woman who sculpted, painted, and etched as well as taught art and wrote books.

From 1950 to 1957, Kramer worked as an art therapist at the Wiltwyck School in Esopus, New York, a rehabilitation center for emotionally disturbed boys. Her school was very similar to our own, fifty years later. We, Mary Hollowell and Donna Moye, taught at Peachtree Alternative School in Georgia, in different capacities. One of us was a regular substitute teacher, and the other was an art teacher at this school, for many years. Students at both Wiltwyck and Peachtree Alternative had mental health issues. Most of them were on probation and had been referred by judges. The schools were also similar in that they had racially diverse student populations averaging 100 students. According to Kramer, Wiltwyck had a caring and qualified staff, as did Peachtree Alternative. Wiltwyck School had a staunch supporter in the form of Eleanor Roosevelt, who served on the board of directors for the last twenty years of her life. Mrs. Roosevelt hosted an annual picnic for the whole school, every summer on the grounds of her Hyde Park home, where she regularly grilled hot dogs. Similarly, Peachtree Alternative School had strong community support in the form of a vocal child advocacy group comprised of ministers, foster parents, sheriff's deputies, social workers, and health care providers, who hosted school events. At Wiltwyck School, Edith Kramer used to tell her students Grimm's fairy tales in order to keep them from fighting, and at Peachtree Alternative School, the art teacher used to play soothing classical music.

Wiltwyck School differed from the contemporary alternative school, however, in that it was a treatment facility with beds and was entirely for boys. Peachtree Alternative School was a day school and almost a quarter of the students were girls. Wiltwyck was the setting for the academy award-winning classic film *The Quiet One,* and Peachtree Alternative School is depicted in the book *The Forgotten Room* (Hollowell, 2009).

THEORY

In her four major books published between 1958 and 1979, Edith Kramer subscribes to the Freudian school of psychoanalysis. She writes that creating art can lead to emotional maturation and sublimation, the overcoming of basic instincts by the ego. Art is a means by which children who have been traumatized by war, poverty, crime, abuse, addiction, and other societal ills can express themselves, reach catharsis, and develop well-being. Art therapy is also a way to unearth repressions and overcome denials. Students can take pride in their work, particularly if it is displayed or published. At Wiltwyck School, art was regularly displayed in the dining hall and at Peachtree Alternative School, art, poetry, and personal essays were published in annual anthologies.

Kramer defines sublimation as "any process in which a primitive asocial impulse is transformed into a socially productive act" (1958, p. 11). She gives an example. When a toddler who throws blocks becomes a child who stacks them, sublimation has occurred. Similarly, a baby matures from throwing and smearing food to spooning food; thus, he achieves sublimation.

As educators in a public alternative school filled with chronic disrupters, we saw many students lash out in ways that indicated they had *not* achieved sublimation. We saw tantrums with things that had been smeared (including walls smeared with blood), people shoved, work destroyed, and items thrown. Some psychologists equate smearing by teens with an anal fixation, an arrested stage of development. Punches were also thrown during fist fights. A few tantrums were violent enough to be called rampages, and they involved breaking walls, throwing furniture, self-injury, or injury to others. In response to violent tantrums, we observed that the best teachers, who had the most strength and fortitude, remained calm and stayed around to clean up and continue their efforts to establish relationships with students. They stayed for months and years afterwards.

We also watched preadolescent students regress into toddler-like thumb sucking and hiding inside closets and boxes. We later witnessed some of these students evolve into mature young adults, who managed to conquer their aggressive impulses, obtain educations, and lead productive and peaceful lives. Many pieces of art, poems, or personal essays in the anthologies were tributes to teachers, and it is relationships with caring teachers that usually helped turn alternative students around. Specifically, caring teachers role modeled respect, allowed students to be creative, boosted their self-esteem, and gave them hope. In many cases, there were no other adults in students' lives to help motivate them, certainly not immediate family members, many of whom experienced depression, domestic abuse, addiction, and/or incarceration. Peachtree Alternative students were teenagers who had to survive on their own, beginning at young ages, and they did not have the time or resources to develop hopes and dreams, not when they were struggling to take care of themselves. They did not even have much energy left for academic learning, but their trusted teachers gave them hope for the future and reasons to want to learn. In the absence of caring adults at home, it fell upon teachers to help at-risk adolescents achieve sublimation.

Kramer also identifies the need to possess as a basic instinct, while the desire to preserve is a more mature response. She equates a boy's desire to devour his mother (reflective in some raw student artwork, complete with huge teeth) with primitive headhunting and cannibalism. Interestingly, she cautions that we don't want student artists to be too sublimated or too rigorous, for relying on instinct while painting, sculpting, drawing, or using other mediums is an integral part of creating art. Master artists learn to channel their instincts.

The pioneer art therapist also writes, "Children naturally crave the adults' appreciation of their art, as they need appreciation of all accomplishments. Thus pictures are often given as presents to beloved adults" (1958, p. 20). We experienced much of this at Peachtree Alternative: poems and drawings given as gifts and anthologies with heartfelt dedications to teachers. Kramer also advises, "Success in treatment depends on teamwork, mutual respect, and unity among staff members" (1958, p. 32). With the exception of a couple of ineffective teachers, we definitely saw teamwork at Peachtree Alternative School. In order to help angry, disruptive, or disaffected youth, teachers relied on one another and supported colleagues when their spirits waned. Teamwork for successful alternative schooling cannot be overemphasized. Peachtree Alternative had a number of critical support specialists such as a media specialist, a registered nurse, and a school psychologist, although these positions were eliminated or reduced to part-time in the school's final year.

Kramer is a master of identifying dichotomies, and she asserts that in order to be successful, an art therapist must be both accepting and discriminating, accepting of the aggressive first attempts of alternative students while still maintaining an eye for quality. Her additional advice is that art teachers carefully balance leeway and structure, allowing students to be creative but not so boisterous that they can't hear directions.

In the foreword to Edith Kramer's second book, *Art as Therapy with Children,* public school psychologist Muriel Gardiner states that others "can learn from Edith Kramer's insights and methods, even if working in a quite different field" (1971, p. x). We, too, believe that Kramer's insights are keen, her advice is sound, and her compassion is inspiring to today's generation of educators.

LITERATURE OF LEARNING AND WOUNDED STUDENTS

Essential components of successful learning, which appear in James Banner and Harold Cannon's *The Elements of Learning,* are beyond alternative students without hope in their lives. To expect them to be diligent in their studies while they have so many physical and emotional needs or to persist towards an intellectual goal when they have no goal at all is to ask them to hoist themselves up by their bootstraps. When teenagers are solely and by necessity present oriented, they cannot be studious as an investment in their futures. Intellectual models may be few, and intellectual capital is a foreign concept. To alternative students seeking attachment who have been mired in isolation, the loneliness required in traditional studying in libraries and laboratories is not appealing, especially not without practice. Passion for learning is often something that is ignited by supportive parents, intriguing material, or outstanding teachers; it is not the result of spontaneous combustion. Curiosity is not easily aroused in students who are numbed in self-defense or are oppositional. In addition, aspirations towards endurable creations or discoveries require the assumption that you will survive to a certain age. Several nonfiction books set in urban landscapes such as *There Are No Children Here, Our America: Life and Death on the South Side of Chicago* and *Gang Leader for a Day* demonstrate that many inner-city males in our nation's ghettos do not expect to live very long. Therefore, they seek immediate gratification.

The Elements of Teaching, which preceded *The Elements of Learning,* inspired a multitude of teachers who saw themselves as the compassionate, creative, and authoritative characters described in the pages. The attributes identified as necessary for successful learning, however, only apply to a select group of highly motivated students. Teens who have been excluded from educational opportunities, housed in poor schools with no resources, or labeled failures from an early age simply cannot attain lofty criteria for successful learning without substantial assistance.

Another contemporary book, however, is particularly applicable to our study of alternative students and their art and writing. In *Reaching the Wounded Student,* Joe Hendershott (2009) shares his observation that in response to a question about their futures, wounded students "will just look at you with a strange look or a blank stare. This question is totally foreign to their thought process" (p. 22). He goes on to ask, "If a student has no hopes and dreams, how can an education make sense to them? What would be the point?" (p. 22). When it comes to working with severely traumatized teens, restoring hope takes precedence over academic learning. Hendershott also reminds readers, "true change happens for most people on the emotional level and not on the cognitive level" (p. 61). Wounded students must be guided from despair and into hope before they can focus on traditional school subject matter. One way to ease this transition is through therapeutic art and writing.

We have encountered those blank stares, ourselves, in our work with at-risk teenagers. We have also encountered them in films and in literature. Megan, one of the two main characters in the documentary film *Girlhood: Growing Up on the Inside,* springs to mind. When the filmmaker asks her, on camera, to name three wishes, Megan stares hopelessly around her ghetto neighborhood and then says, "I don't know. It ain't no sense in wishing for anything." In Alex Kotlowitz's book *There Are No Children Here,* a boy living in a blighted urban housing project says, "If I grow up, I'd like to be a bus driver" (p. x). He does not take growing up for granted. Such hopeless children with weary, ancient faces are all too familiar to us.

In some cases, particularly in the absence of parental figures, teachers may be the only ones who can rescue adolescents from boredom, poverty, or despair. We must help wounded students develop hope and aspirations, then channel them further towards academic achievement. This shepherding must be done in a gentle and flexible manner. Trying to sweep alternative students along through a straight and narrow channel doesn't work. Greg Goodman echoes this when he writes "in chaotic spaces, meaningful pedagogy requires nonlinear and complex processes to examine and negotiate the fractal borders that disaffected youth occupy" (2007, p. 16). For example, in art therapy, recovery might involve temporary regression into a monster phase to face fears before progressing to self-portraiture and portraits of family members.

An important caution that Hendershott gives is "understand that we cannot always understand where these students have been" (p. 13). This is very sound advice. He emphasizes that, in some cases, the damage wrought to students may be so severe and so hidden that we may never uncover it. In this event, we must just proceed with our shepherding. Hendershott is advocating an attitude of acceptance. So often, teachers struggle to try to understand the origin of a learning problem. It is a relief to be directed, to just proceed. Some pain and injustice are completely beyond our comprehension. It is all right, sometimes, to not know the full extent of student hardships.

Many school systems cannot afford an adequate number of school psychologists and counselors. Hendershott reassures us that in times of grave shortages of specialists, it is okay for teachers to take the lead. The caring teacher may become the expert. The overall tone of *Reaching the Wounded Student* is soothing, reassuring, and uplifting. It resonates within us.

METHODOLOGY

This chapter is based on qualitative methods: document analysis of four years worth of Peachtree Alternative School anthologies, along with personal observations and interviews with former teachers. The rawest, most aggressive artwork was censored from the anthologies by adult advisors and relegated to a "Do Not Publish" pile. The rejected work included hideous monsters with serpent heads, enormous claws, and sinister smiles.

The patterns in the final, more evolved products, can be assessed and some have been reproduced, here. Young artists and writers at Peachtree Alternative often depict painful scenes. They face fears and express anxieties in order to overcome them. They draw or write about their demons as a step towards conquering them.

There is a scarcity of first-person data from alternative students. Greg Goodman also recognizes the need for "the deeply personal stories that alternative education students have to tell" (2007, p. 7). Alternative students have encased themselves in protective shells for so long that it is usually very difficult for them to open up during interviewing. Interviewing alternative students is often hampered by their communication problems, and it is ethically challenging. Their identities must be carefully safeguarded, and sometimes they reveal crimes that they have committed. Instead of interviewing, we studied alternative student annual anthologies, which proved to be very enlightening. We were also able to track down a handful of drop-outs and graduates in order to obtain permission to reproduce their artwork. Student signatures have been blackened in the reproductions in order to maintain anonymity.

While we are not psychoanalysts who are able to delve deeply into the pasts of young artists and writers, we are both concerned educators who have worked with troubled teens. We can identify patterns, provide a basic overview of student work, and depict regression and progression for readers.

Peachtree Alternative School, in its tenth and final year, was so overcrowded and lacking in resources that an anthology was not produced, but the four previous anthologies brimmed with high quality work, thanks to talented student editors. While she is too modest to admit it, the anthologies are also largely due to the hard work of the English teacher. She conceived the project, sought funding for copying and equipment, inspired and guided student editors, and carefully preserved original materials.

In this chapter, we have chosen to include art and writing that is non-stereotypical. The student work that is reproduced or quoted is not bland or saccharine sweet. The images of monsters and heroes will speak to wide audiences. Edith Kramer argues that stereotypes begin to appear during the teenage years and that "younger children do not seem to be able to produce false sentiment in art" (1971, p. 122). The heroes that we display are not hollow heroes but ones with grace and energy.

RESULTS

In the following paragraphs, we describe the prominent patterns and symbols in the artwork of Peachtree Alternative students (many of whom were on parole for acts of violence such as assault, burglary, vandalism, weapons violations, drug dealing, and terroristic threat). The patterns in Peachtree Alternative student art over a four-year period included monsters, prisoners, and warrior/heroes. They were the very same patterns that Kramer found in Wiltwyck student art, fifty years before. At Peachtree Alternative, these patterns also crossed disciplines from art into writing. In addition, symbols in the artwork such as flaming hearts, bleeding jesters, and thorny roses depicted inner conflicts.

BEGINNING SUBLIMATION

Peachtree Alternative students faced fears and uncovered scars in their art and writing. In one drawing that could not be reproduced due to the ravages of time, a student drew a portrait of himself hanging from a hook. He was hanging from the hook by his collar with his feet dangling high in the air. Facing him was a dark knight in a helmet and full armor, who stood poised to stab him. The art was quite an expression of vulnerability, and to admit his fear on paper was a step in the right direction. Other fearsome monsters in the student artwork, besides the dark knight, were large vampire bats and werewolves with very sharp teeth. They were metaphoric monsters in students' lives. In contrast to alternative students, regular students in mainstream schools do not draw such fearsome monsters or draw them with such regularity.

Students also depicted realistic, as opposed to fantastical monsters, in the forms of drugs and alcohol, weapons, and crime. In Figure 1, there are bloody handprints on a burglarized house on the right side of the picture. They are depicted in red in the original color drawing.

Figure 1: The Monsters in My Life Montage

Blood was common in a number of works of art. Fangs, hearts pierced with swords, and roses with prominent thorns all dripped blood. A closer inspection of Figure 1 shows excellent use of proportions and perspectives. The marijuana leaves are in proportion. The limbs of the punctured and bleeding paper doll are also in proportion with its body. The burglarized home is set at a believable angle, with the doors and windows well spaced. The artist makes good use of shading and maximizes contrasts by boldly outlining a human figure, while leaving the inside white. The cutting seen in the sliced wrists and the realistic razor blades are two of the more vivid elements of the drawing. The artist makes excellent use of space by filling the entire page with bold elements. The weapons that she depicts include nails, drugs, razor blades and, on a smaller scale, junk food. Altogether, it is a powerful, confessional drawing by a talented artist that depicts sorrow and pain.

As audience members viewing this art, we are both disturbed and impressed. It is distressing to see such a preponderance of problems spelled out in black and white. They range from academic failure to crime to drug use to cutting behavior, but we cannot help but admire the honesty, courage, and artistry involved.

Just as Kramer indicated in 1958, Peachtree Alternative students were also quite fearful of jail. It loomed as a prominent specter in their lives. Most of them had been to jail, and quite a few had parents in prison. Students were so fearful of jail, in fact, that they refused to have their picture taken inside a paddywagon (a photographic prop discovered on a field trip). Finally, with much coaxing, we managed to have two students climb on board the paddywagon for a picture.

Peachtree Alternative students chose to use black-and-white striped prisoner graphics in the anthologies. Prisoners in Peachtree County, today, still wear black and white striped jumpsuits while working on the sides of the road. Peachtree Alternative students also began to face their fears by writing about their own experiences in jail. As Kramer says, "To delinquent children who live in a delinquent environment, prison is a serious menace. The subject, therefore, is usually avoided" (1958, p. 73). To address the topic in any form is a breakthrough.

Reflections on youth detention or prison, in the anthologies, include a very frank personal essay in which a former inmate shares her fears of being assaulted while in the shower. She escaped this, she believes, by maintaining a low profile. She avoided inmates who tried to start fights. "I ignored them so I would not get more time," she writes. To share such fears in a school-wide anthology, along with her name, is an act of courage.

Another student, who writes anonymously, shares the heavy impact of regularly visiting her sister in prison. Her sister was a crack addict who was in prison for larceny and forgery. The author concludes, "I've learned a lot of what not to do. She's really destroyed her life."

Troubled students often depersonalize their artwork and avoid painting faces. Facial features are not particularly hard to draw compared to hands and feet, yet at-risk teens avoid them by incorporating devices such as helmets, profiles, hoods, and masks. This represents their fear of emotions and was quite common in Peachtree Alternative student art.

The alternative school principal, who sanctioned the revealing anthologies, sent a strong message to students in poem format. The principal was a former English teacher and a writer herself. She also loved poetry and selected a poem about a mask for the last page of Anthology 3. The poem by Charles C. Finn is titled "Please Hear What I'm Not Saying." In the following stanza, he writes about his insecurity as a new teacher.

> *My surface may seem smooth but my surface is a mask,*
> *ever-varying and ever-concealing.*
> *Beneath lies no complacence.*
> *Beneath lies confusion, and fear, and aloneness.*
> *But I hide this. I don't want anybody to know it.*
> *I panic at the thought of my weakness exposed.*

In the 100-line poem, Finn makes additional references to his shield and his façade. In the end, he encourages kindness, gentleness, and sensitivity in order to scale his walls.

The principal felt strongly enough about the importance of confronting insecurities to relay this message to all of her charges. It is valuable advice for insecure and fearful adolescents, and it encapsulates what they have done in the anthologies.

The English teacher included one of her very own poems in an anthology that revealed her own insecurity. Both women are avid readers and practicing writers, as well as therapeutic educators. They work alongside students and convey their humanity. It is one of Kramer's most important lessons.

On a more somber note, we were able to observe a number of young artists at Peachtree Alternative School working on spontaneous drawings that reflected great hostility. One very angry young man drew an especially violent volcano that spewed wide rivers of lava, thick plumes of black smoke, and giant boulders. While grandmothers are usually idealized in children's book illustrations as gentle and loving characters, this particular boy drew his grandmother as a troll. He also entertained himself in time out by creating monstrous paper claws, swiping the air with them, and making vicious faces. He was an overtly aggressive preadolescent in a less mature stage of emotional development. In fact, he was so disruptive that he was later transferred from the alternative school to a psychoeducational center for more intensive treatment.

Figure 2: Drugs Make You Crazy

Figure 2 shows an adolescent's confusion and despair over drug use. This artwork was created using a computer graphics program. The teen in the piece is isolated, for most alternative students draw single figures as opposed to multiple or interacting ones, and his hair is in wild disarray. He clutches his head in torment. A smoking joint is nearby, and he is surrounded by darkness, representing the absence of light in his life.

Former alternative teachers recall this teenager as being one of the most talented young artists that they ever taught. Sam (a pseudonym) did not make it, though, and is now in prison for murder. His tale is reminiscent of one that occurred at Wiltwyck, as conveyed in the book *All God's Children: The Bosket Family and the American Tradition of Violence.* The author, Fox Butterfield, won both a Pulitzer Prize and a National Book Award. At Wiltwyck, a boy named Walter (Kramer's pseudonym for Butch) was a master painter, but after his release, he killed a store clerk during a robbery. He stabbed the clerk once, the clerk staggered, then he stabbed him five more times. He committed two more murders before killing himself during a police shootout. Butch's son Willie attended Wiltwyck, years later, and is now serving life in prison. Violence was perpetuated from one generation to the next. Robert Coles concludes his 1995 review of *All God's Children* with the following observation. "Butch and Willie were each a living loaded gun, waiting to be triggered by anyone and anything, each with resentments difficult for those of us luckily raised in solid families to imagine, never mind comprehend" (p. 12).

At Wiltwyck, Butch revealed the depths of his despair and rage to Edith Kramer in his self-portrait of a young man holding a knife. Similarly, at Peachtree Alternative, Sam revealed the magnitude of his pain and turmoil in his "Drugs Make You Crazy" portrait. Butch and Sam were two talented artists and disturbed young men, living similar lives but separated by half a century. Their stories are eerily similar and both end tragically.

The details of Sam's last crime are horrendous. In October of this year, he robbed a convenience store, shot the clerk, then shot him twice more. The clerk staggered away but died in the hospital. He had immigrated from India, three years before, and was described by a friend as "one of the most spiritual and courageous people I knew" (Hedge, 2008, p. 3). Sam was apprehended hours later and is now in jail, awaiting trial for murder. It is the culmination of a list of crimes including burglary and drug offenses. The agonizing art that Sam created as a teenager foreshadowed his life as a young man. Had Sam received therapy earlier and for an extended period of time, this tragedy might possibly have been prevented.

For those who subscribe to Freudian psychoanalysis, Sam also wrote a telling monster story that is published in an anthology. The short story is a classic example of the previously identified consumption fantasy (i.e., devouring something in order to possess it). Sam writes about a monster eating his dog. Later, his new dog eats his clothes and dies.

We do not wish to paint a portrait of utter doom for any of our former students, especially those who might one day read this chapter. There is indeed spiritual redemption for those who seek it. We firmly believe this.

ADVANCED SUBLIMATION

Additional patterns in the artwork were warriors, heroes, and superheroes. One student drew a fierce warrior with a mighty shield and a raised spear. The warrior was embellished with a decorative shield and armor that was aesthetic as well as functional. The artist readily identified with the heroes of Greek mythology and also drew a powerful image of Zeus in the sky amid lightning bolts.

He also demonstrated growing confidence in his writing. "Now I do all of my work without any help and I know I can do it," he writes in an essay. In fact, the student repeats this realization twice more in the same essay. He also writes that he is more adept at making friends after having attended the alternative school. The student concludes, "I've learned many things while I've been over here" and goes so far as to say that he may have learned more than any other student. He likes his teachers at the alternative school and indicates that he may become a lifelong learner.

"I just keep learning," he writes. This particular student has experienced advanced sublimation, benefitted from therapeutic art and writing, and had a successful alternative school experience.

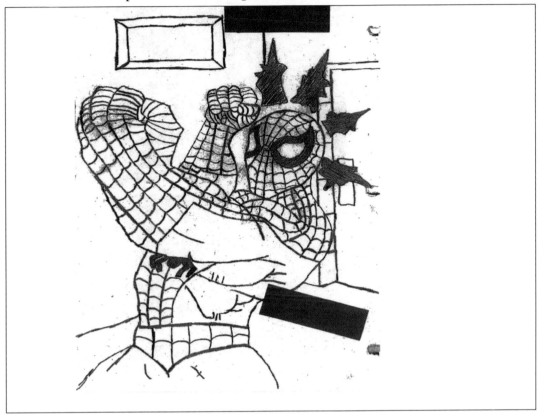

Figure 3: Superhero

Figure 3 shows a superhero, Spiderman, with unusually large fists, making him extra powerful. In his own way, Figure 3 is a glamorous character. The Spiderman looms large on the page, with obvious muscles and bolts of energy emerging from his head. It is safe to assume that, in drawing stand-alone heroes, students were imagining themselves in heroic positions. Aspiring to be a hero is a sign of health.

One interesting assignment at Peachtree Alternative was to create a collage using construction paper, glue, and magazine clippings (Figure 4). The assignment led to the creation of honest and, in some cases, hopeful collages.

Solid values are evident in words cut from magazines. In Figure 4, the words "good" and "brave" are pasted, along with "Black!," which shows pride in one's culture. (On another boy's collage, which is not shown, the words "ready," "brave," "healthy living," and "brains" are stuck to the page.) By pasting the word "ready" to the page, the artist indicates that he is prepared to advance.

The confident artist who created the "Black!" collage also wrote a humorous and clever poem about a hero. He describes a blonde riding a horse with the wind whipping her hair. She starts to fall, her foot is caught in the stirrups, and she's in danger of a concussion. Suddenly, the hero goes over, unplugs the mechanical horse, and rescues the tot. The young poet has succeeded in startling his readers with a surprise ending.

Figure 4: A Boy's Collage

Symbols that are repeated in the anthologies included flaming hearts (Figure 5), bleeding jesters, and thorny roses, which depicted teens' inner conflicts of broken hearts, dual identities, and troubled relationships.

Figure 5: Flaming Heart

Flowers were particularly common. Half of the flower drawings were unhealthy or ominous in that they had brittle leaves or big thorns, while the rest were quite lovely, sprinkled with dewdrops or surrounded by butterflies. Either way, the flowers are commendable for being honest or hopeful.

In addition to symbols, inner conflict is revealed in poetry. Nothing more clearly indicates the conflict between adolescent dual identities than the original line from a poem, "He is a creature with two faces...very few see his second face." The poem is titled "Liar." It is not hard to imagine the writer's conflict. She could be struggling with any number of opposing identities that are common to alternative students: promiscuous young man or monogamous boyfriend, absentee dad or involved adolescent father, someone in the spiral of addiction or a person in recovery, criminal or law-abiding citizen. Alternative students experience more severe internal conflicts than most mainstream students but dual identity is a universal human dilemma.

ON FAMILIES, FRIENDS, AND THEMSELVES

Kramer observed that students at Wiltwyck had such terribly broken homes that they never depicted their families in artwork. Only one Wiltwyck child, as he neared recovery, was able to paint his mother. Similarly, other than one grandmother troll, we never saw family members in artwork by Peachtree Alternative students. It is a heartbreaking observation.

In "A Poem to an Abusive Father," a boy reveals a history of abuse, drug addiction, homelessness, and jail. The climax of this poem is when he is shot in the leg by a police officer. The tragedy is so extreme that it is almost incomprehensible, and the most dramatic line in this ode to his dad reads, "I wanted to grow up not being like you." It is one of the most powerful poems in the entire anthology series, along with a poem about a car wreck and one about a murdered aunt.

On the other hand, another alternative student pens an ode to his mother titled "My Family." He writes, "First there is my mom; she is my world....She is always there to pick me up when I fall." Thank goodness this young man has such a mother. It takes just one caring adult to help make a child resilient, be it a parent, a minister, a teacher, or an extended family member. The opposite of aggressiveness is tenderness, and the alternative student who can convey a tender family scene in art or writing is on his way to recovery.

According to Kramer, flattering portraits and accurate self-portraits indicate very advanced stages of development, and the artists who complete them have achieved a measure of healing. The artist who drew a warrior in decorative armor and developed self-confidence went on to draw a lovely portrait of the alternative school principal wearing a beautiful smile.

Figure 6: Hooded Figure   *Figure 6.1:* Face in Detail

Figure 6 is an interesting self-portrait in which a teen is depicted as scowling, wearing a hood, and having baggy pants and an unlaced shoe—a very common way for teenaged boys at the alternative school to dress. The student also regularly wore a state university baseball cap. He conveyed his own early demeanor quite well and is seen in several early school photographs slouching and unsmiling.

When the face is examined in detail in Figure 6.1, a teardrop is seen under the right eye. It is unclear whether this represents an actual teardrop or a tattoo. Teardrop tattoos have signified losing a loved one or, in gang culture, they have indicated that the wearer has committed murder. This particular student, however, had no facial tattoo.

A collection of this student's artwork is available, and he also drew hearts in flames (Figure 5), flowers, and crosses. He is a young man who has excised his demons and begun to move towards a higher level of maturation in the form of religious thinking. The superego that governs moral decision-making is taking over. Elsewhere in the anthologies, angels and poignant writing about heaven appear, additional signs of advanced sublimation and spiritual evolution. The artist who drew Figures 5 and 6 married his high school sweetheart and has gone on to become a family man and hard-working father.

DISCUSSION OF LEARNING

As indicated in the center of Figure 1, alternative students have a history of academic failure. Many have reading problems, communication problems, and learning disabilities. Consequently, they are resistant to pencil and paper testing and other forms of traditional assessment such as oral reporting. We have witnessed entire classes of students groan in response to testing, violence in response to testing (one dangerous student threatened to stab his teacher, who dropped the testing procedure in self-preservation), and classrooms disintegrate into chaos in order to distract teachers from testing. Alternative students are more open, though, to activities perceived as nonacademic such as art, poetry, and the personal essay.

In the last year of Peachtree Alternative School, before it was replaced by a computer center for at-risk youth, dramatic staff cuts led to the elimination of high school art although poetry writing continued in the English teacher's classroom. Given its valuable therapeutic effects, eliminating art for alternative students was a grave error. Art, poetry, and personal essay all require patience, reflection, and concentration. Practicing these skills and gaining confidence in these fields can pave the way for success in other subject areas.

Edith Kramer elaborates on the value of alternative assessments, such as an art display and a published anthology. "A child who is unable to learn in the classroom needs other learning experiences. As long as learning continues in other areas, a child's development need not be seriously stunted" (1958, p. 126). According to Kramer, art, in addition to serving as a path towards more academic subjects, enables the expression of conflict and fantasies that predominate in alternative students; whereas, traditional math and science have fewer fantasy outlets.

CONCLUSION

Again, the very patterns of monsters, prisoners, and heroes that Edith Kramer found in the artwork of troubled children at Wiltwyck can be found in a similar population in a different region, half a century later. The maintenance of these patterns over time is impressive and well worth investigating in other regions and cultures. They are the same monsters, portraits, collages, and heart-shaped imagery found in Cathy Malchiodi's book *Breaking the Silence: Art Therapy with Children from Violent Homes,* and Malchiodi even includes a checklist to evaluate therapeutic art. Lani Gerity's *Creativity and the Dissociative Patient: Puppets, Narrative and Art in the Treatment of Survivors of Childhood Trauma* is yet another recommendation for the therapeutic arts, based on Kramerian theory, albeit for younger children.

Kramer states why art is so useful to delinquent children and youth. "Art can absorb and contain more raw affect than most other equally complex and civilized endeavors" (1971, pp. 184–185). She also asserts that it has the power "to relieve pressures or to contain what is unbearable" (1971, p. 207). We believe that writing serves the same functions, and we have provided evidence of containment and relief in both areas.

It is important to add that verbal therapy was also available to Peachtree Alternative students in the form of group counseling sessions and visits with a school psychologist, but not all alternative students could successfully discuss their feelings. Art and writing remained important alternative outlets. Finally, Kramer cautions readers that therapeutic arts are not easy, and we have learned this lesson ourselves. Therapists must "be willing to accept defeat time and again" (1971, p. 221).

In preparing this chapter, we interviewed four other former alternative teachers and a former school resource officer. All were transferred to mainstream schools, after the alternative school was closed. During interviews, we sat together, reviewed the anthologies, and discussed student outcomes.

The English teacher said she tried to structure the anthologies as loosely as possible so students could include pieces that had personal significance. If students revealed something painful, she would try to discuss it with them but they wouldn't always open up in person. She had to resolve herself to not knowing, just as Hendershott advises.

She smiled as she reread the story of the hero who saved a tot in a superstore by unplugging a mechanical horse. She remembered the author well. "He was a great kid. He had a great personality," she said. He married another former alternative student, and they had a child. Later, he was arrested for theft. "I hope he had a good reason," the English teacher said, "like he had to feed his family."

The English teacher was in the process of moving out of a portable classroom and into a main building. "About a week before you called, I was thinking of throwing these out," she said, referring to the anthology boxes. "Now, I know why I didn't." Her saving the materials was fortuitous.

"I thought about doing anthologies, here," she said about her mainstream school, "but it just wouldn't be the same. There wouldn't be the same emotion." The publishing of a loosely structured anthology at a regular school wouldn't be as emotionally cleansing and as useful to students therapeutically.

A former school resource officer remembers the final years of Peachtree Alternative School, during which these anthologies were produced, as being especially rough. It is an important observation, coming from a highly qualified Officer of the Year and a Gulf War veteran. The resource officer shakes his head in disbelief, recalling some of the students. He vividly remembers having to drag thrashing teenagers down the hall past four-year-olds, who attended preschool in an adjacent building. He also thought that the Central Office put the principal in water over her head by putting her in charge of four programs under one roof: an alternative high school, a preschool, an alternative special education program, and a state-funded psychoeductional center for severely emotionally disturbed students. He was genuinely touched by the goodbye poster he received when he was transferred. It was signed by many of the students. "That meant a lot to me," he says, "considering it was kids I had to lock up." He remembers that they wrote "Keep your head down," advising him to stay safe.

Prior to our interview with the former alternative school academic counselor (now also a high school English teacher), she was distributing candy in her classroom. She had a big candy box in her lap and was rolling up and down the aisles in an office chair, passing it out, which made for a funny image. "You see what I've resorted to," she said, "bribing them." She was rather sheepish about it but we've done it ourselves.

During our meeting, a student dropped by, asking her advice. "I love you," she told him, afterwards. "I love you, too," the boy said, without hesitation. The exchange was testimony to the strength of her relationships.

We left her classroom with sad stories and fistfuls of chocolate. The author of the poem about an abusive father had a stroke following a drug overdose and is permanently impaired. He had to learn to walk all over again. One artist now resides in a mental health facility, while another joined a gang and is lost to the streets. One student did receive his GED, however.

Our favorite phrase from Kramer's first book *Art Therapy in a Children's Community,* is "every teacher remains something of a witch or wizard to the student" (1958, p. 128). This is a positive metaphor that we haven't heard before. By this, Kramer means that the best and most gifted alternative educators appear to have almost magical powers. They have the power to transform something mundane into something relevant and engaging, and the talent to help bring the empty canvas or page to life. We have been privileged to see many such alternative educators in action, and their work does seem miraculous, at times. The trusted teachers who manage to instill hope in formerly hopeless students are truly miracle workers. Perhaps, "fairy godmothers" or "fairy godfathers" would be a more apt, given the historically negative connotation of witches.

Hendershott's prescription to school administrators struggling with growing numbers of wounded students is to focus on emotional well-being *before* focusing on academics. Starting points include art and reading/writing therapy, yet art and libraries are often cut in times of financial hardship. They (along with music and physical education) are programs which should take precedence for emotionally disturbed children and youth in public schools.

While some aspects of alternative schooling have not changed in over fifty years, the vocabulary of alternative schooling has begun to evolve. New terms are being applied, and there is a great need for these terms. Hendershott describes the overwhelming response to one of his early wounded student presentations. While he anticipated twenty-five people in the audience, the crowd swelled to a thousand. Clearly, a great many educators are concerned about the futures of disruptive and disaffected youth and are seeking answers. The calls for grace, mercy, serenity, and soul in education coming from Joe Hendershott and Greg Goodman are steps beyond the professionalism, forgiveness, peace, and caring traditionally espoused in colleges of education. They are calls for human spirit strong enough to address the dire needs of deeply troubled students. Beyond simply being decent, alternative educators must be noble. We are thankful to have encountered these new terms in the literature of education, and we know educators who embody them. They are powerful words which definitely apply to alternative schooling. They have enriched the language of education and our own aspirations.

REFERENCES

Banner, J. & Cannon, H. (1999). *The Elements of Learning.* New Haven, CT: Yale University Press.

Banner, J. & Cannon, H. (1997). *The Elements of Teaching.* New Haven, CT: Yale University Press.

Butterfield, F. (1995). *All God's Children: The Bosket Family and the American Tradition of Violence.* New York: Vintage Books.

Coles, R. (1995). "Blood Ties: Fox Butterfield's History of Willie Bosket's Family Is also a history of American Violence." New York: *The New York Times Review of Books:* 12.

Fine, A. & Nya. (1997). *Therapeutic Recreation for Exceptional Children: Let Me In, I Want to Play.* Springfield, IL: Charles C. Thomas.

Finn, C. C. (2002). "Please Hear What I Am Not Saying." Available at http://www.poetrybycharlescfinn.com

Garbus, L. (2003). *Girlhood: Growing Up on the Inside.* Santa Monica, CA: Genius Entertainment.

Gerity, L. A. (1999). *Creativity and the Dissociative Patient: Puppets, Narrative and Art in the Treatment of Survivors of Childhood Trauma.* Philadelphia: Jessica Kingsley.

Goodman, G. (2007). *Reducing Hate Crimes and Violence Among American Youth: Creating Transformational Agency Through Critical Praxis.* New York: Peter Lang.

Hedge, J. (November 20, 2008). "Convenience Store Clerk Shot to Death." Atlanta: *NRI Pulse: The South's Premier South Asian Newspaper.*

Hendershott, J. (2009). *Reaching the Wounded Student.* Larchmont, NY: Eye on Education.

Hollowell, M. (2009). *The Forgotten Room: Inside a Public Alternative School for At-Risk Youth.* Lanham, MD: Lexington Books.

Jones, L., Isay, D., & Newman, L. (1998). *Our America: Life and Death on the South Side of Chicago.* New York: Simon and Schuster.

Keller, M. J. (1991). *Activities with Developmentally Disabled Elderly and Older Adults.* New York: Taylor and Francis.

Kotlowitz, A. (1992). *There Are No Children Here.* New York: Knopf.

Kramer, E. (1971). *Art As Therapy with Children.* New York: Schocken Books.

Kramer, E. (1958). *Art Therapy in a Children's Community.* Springfield, IL: Charles C. Thomas.

Malchiodi, C. (1997). *Breaking the Silence: Art Therapy with Children from Violent Homes.* Levittown, PA: Brunner/Mazel.

Meyers, S. (1949). *The Quiet One.* Narbeth, PA: Alpha Home Entertainment.

Miller, M. & Cook-Greuter, S. (Eds.) (1999). *Creativity, Spirituality, and Transcendence: Paths to Integrity and the Wisdom of the Mature Self.* New York: Ablex.

Venkatesh, S. (2008). *Gang Leader for a Day: A Rogue Sociologist Takes to the Streets.* New York: Penguin.

FORTY

Alternative School Adaptations of Experiential Education

Greg S. Goodman

The ignorant man is not the unlearned, but he who does not know himself,
and the learned man is stupid when he relies on books, on knowledge and
on authority to give him understanding. Understanding comes only through
self-knowledge, which is awareness of one's total psychological process. Thus
education, in the true sense, is the understanding of oneself, for it is within
each one of us that the whole of existence is gathered.
—Krishnamurti (1953, p. 17)

Ever since Outward Bound and the National Outdoor Leadership School's (NOLS) beginnings in the late 1960s and early 1970s, individuals trained within these schools have branched out and sought sites to apply the skills and dispositions they acquired. One of the most popular applications of experiential learning has occurred within alternative educational and therapeutic communities. In this chapter, I attempt to articulate a pedagogy and praxis for use with those identified as needing affective, social, or other psychosocial education and/or therapy. Also included in this chapter are some stories that help to experientially connect the pedagogy of outdoor education with the daily praxis of the leadership.

At-risk youth require a psychosocial atmosphere that acknowledges these adolescent's essential and unique needs for safety, trust, and recovery following the many years of educational and other social failure that preceded their placement in an alternative program (Baker, Bridger, Terry, & Winsor, 1997). Because of these needs, the pedagogy for outdoor programming within alternative education must be well founded in psychological theory and supported with sound educational praxis (Goodman, 1999; Pianta & Walsh, 1996; Rogers, 1969). For purposes of enhancing the personal and relational needs of these students, the pedagogy for an outdoor program within the alternative education setting is distinguished from more traditional outdoor education philosophy in several important ways. The primary difference is the emphasis on psychological and psychosocial components such as individual and interpersonal growth. These psychological and psychosocial components are viewed as a precondition for the development of intellect and the enhancement of traditional goals of learning such as reading, writing, or science education. In our descriptions of outdoor educational programs, outdoor education pedagogy and praxis were designed to primarily enhance student academic achievement, and the secondary benefit was increased sensitivity and compassion for one another (i.e., psychological and psychosocial goals). In outdoor educational pedagogy and praxis for alternative education students, this paradigm is inverted to place the psychosocial before the academic. In fact, when the academic is even reached with disaffected youth, it will be cause for significant celebration for the teaching staff. Yet, no matter what the principal goals of one's specific program or school happen to be (recovery, re-education, or therapeutic), the needs of alterative education students match perfectly with outdoor education's experiential approach (Goodman, 1999).

As stated earlier, to understand how the experiential education philosophy is differentiated from the traditional, epistemological approach, it is instructive to examine their specific ideologies. Traditional pedagogy posits the school's mission as an academically driven, subject-centered process. This fact is apparent from the structure of the daily schedule to the reliance on formative and summative assessments such as standardized testing to evaluate outcomes. Traditional schools sometimes support the emotional wellness of the students with psychological components, for example, a guidance counselor. However, the main goals of guidance are to further the academic success of students, not supplant academics with therapeutic or psychologically motivated interventions such as counseling (Goodman & Young, 2005).

Epistemological philosophy fails the needs of at-risk youth and reinforces their exclusion by woefully under-acknowledging their psychological requirements. However, as an outdoor education teacher or instructor with these youth, you won't need a text to instruct you as to their proclivities. If you try to teach them without first establishing a positive connection, these former failures of our public schools will tell you straight up, "F**k you!"

One of my earliest learnings of the extreme difference between regular education and alternative education occurred while I was working as an outdoor education teacher at "The Alt." At the end of a magnificent climbing day at Rockhouse Pond, my instruction started. Up to this point, the day had been "perfect" (that should be the first clue that things are awry!), and the students were anxious to get back to the van and make the drive back to Hampton. Unaware of their true intention, I said. "Go on. I'll coil up the last rope and meet you shortly." Fairly humming with joy along the trail, my high from the success of the day's activity was quickly returned to earth's floor by the hanging scent of marijuana on the trail's corridor.

When I reached the van, I let my rage descend on the students and I pummeled them with questions until one of them admitted to the discipline breach. After the barrage of emotions, the van was silent for the 40-minute trip back to school. When we arrived back at school, I went to the appropriate disciplinarian and then promptly went outside to pace and reflect on the day's events. My frustration was palpable, and I could not let myself get into my truck to drive home.

In my continuing rage and disappointment, I brought myself into the counselor's offices and sat down with friend/colleague Jamie Marston. I began by telling her of the day and my continuing issues with my new students in the alternative program. She knew these students well, and she had heard of the "head banging" that was going on between them and me over who was in charge at the Alt. As I spoke and she listened, all of my tangled-up feelings began to unravel and I broke down in tears. I was so frustrated that these students would not listen to me or obey my rules. I felt as though I was a damn good teacher and that these students were wasting my time and theirs. I wished that I had never come to teach at that school and regretted my decision to leave the comfortable security of my old position as a middle school counselor. My situation was painfully disturbing and I didn't know what move to make. Hitting such a wall of rejection, I couldn't believe that I was fool enough to take that job at the alternative school! The students were rejecting me, and I felt like a failure!

The counselor was a great comfort to me. Knowing the students whom I was teaching, she said that their resistance was normal. She offered, "Perhaps part of the problem is that you are having trouble accepting your new students? Maybe the resistance you are getting is from the students' feelings that they are not acceptable to you?" After dismissing my first response of wanting to swear and reiterate that I was the teacher, I let Jamie's words penetrate. Maybe I was causing the resistance of the students to be exacerbated because of my rejection of them? This was now the time for my education—time to learn that the teacher of alternative education students needs to learn from the class before she or he can teach—period. My job was to accept them as they were and then, hopefully, they would accept me. I needed to stop trying to make them into something they weren't. The expectations that I had were unrealistic.

The adjustment that I made over the ensuing weeks and months improved my ability to win the students' trust and respect. I continued to learn about my students and to try to see the world through their eyes. Through understanding their point of view, I was able to meet the students in the middle between their ability to work and conform to rules and my ability to communicate a warmth and affection for them no matter what they felt about the given tasks. Why I thought the students would accept me unconditionally when I wouldn't do that for them stands out as one of the most naive notions of my career! The students and I both needed to come to the point of accepting each other through a natural process.

BRIDGING MULTIPLE WORLDS

Alternative education students have been fighting the molds of conformity for many years. They are much better at smashing a system than the adults are at maintaining these students within a tightly controlled classroom. Furthermore, it can be instructive to see this mismatch of the school's authoritarian or control pedagogy and the needs of at-risk youth through the lens of cultural reproduction theory (Bourdieu, 1977). Cultural reproduction theory states that groups or social classes tend to develop systems that reinforce the power and position that those groups hold. In the case of schools, success is marked by grades and advanced placement. These successes are the product of having the cultural capital (Bourdieu, 1977) to succeed within that system. Examples of cultural capital are homework, vocabulary, and personal experience. According to

McLaren (1994), "Schools systematically devalue the cultural capital of students who occupy subordinate class positions" (p. 198).

I would suggest that a pervasive lack of hope of future success is also a part of the equation that sums as student failure. A student without the tools for success—for example, a strong and supportive family or habitus—is at a disadvantage because of his or her lack of resiliency (Goodman, 2002). In cultural reproduction theory, these students are already marked to repeat the failing from which they came. Again, according to McLaren (1994), "The end result is that the school's academic credentials remain indissolubly linked to an unjust system of trading in cultural capital which is eventually transformed into economic capital, as working-class students become less likely to get high-paying jobs" (p. 198). The net effect of a traditional, epistemological approach on disaffected youth is, simply, an ever-growing group of school dropouts.

The pedagogy for an outdoor program for at-risk youth must be fundamentally different than the epistemological foundation for regular education. Alternative schools need to work in a holistic fashion incorporating the best practices of mental health, education, and systems thinking (Pianta & Walsh, 1996) to build programs that address the needs of the youth they serve. This methodology is stated well by Altenbaugh, Engle, and Martin (1995) in their study of Pittsburgh's "school leavers." They state:

> Simplistic solutions, therefore, will only change the form of schooling, bur not the substance and structure. Solutions must be comprehensive, acknowledging the complexities of the school leaving process. They must transcend the limits of the existing paradigm of public schooling and seek creative and flexible approaches, overlooking nothing. All of this must begin with an atmosphere of caring and sensitivity. (p. 155)

It is paramount that the alternative school outdoor education pedagogy reflect a deep understanding of the needs of the students and their family as a system of human resources (Pianta & Walsh, 1996). For this reason, alternative education praxis is best structured so that it is primarily psychosocial in nature. This relates to the philosophical paradigms of existentialism and phenomenology. The focus is on the individual and his or her development as authentic self. To this end, all of the processes of the outdoor program need to reflect a positive valuing of the students and their culture. In daily instruction and programming, emphasis needs to remain on the dignity and respect of the student and his or her family.

The experiential process of the outdoor classroom helps to build a positive relationship bridge between the student, the family, and the school personnel. This connection is fundamental in demonstrating the school's desire to include in an educational experience those who have previously known exclusion (Comer, 1988). Inclusion begins with a psychological process to develop a self-esteem that allows growth and learning. Joy Zimmerman (1994), rephrasing the work of Bonnie Benard, said this well. "Essentially . . . all youngsters can thrive despite otherwise risky environments if in some area—home, school or the community—a child feels loved and supported; is the object of high expectations; and is given the opportunity to participate and contribute in meaningful ways to the world" (p. 3).

The foundation for alternative education students' success is clearly rooted in their seeing themselves as lovable and capable individuals (Harris, 1969). It is from a foundation of acceptance of the individual and his or her culture that a successful relationship with school and society can be built.

ADD COMPASSION

For at-risk youth to achieve success of any kind, it is paramount that they have a close and personal relationship with their teacher, and the basis of this relationship is the teacher's compassion for the student. Compassion is defined as an empathy for the individual based on knowledge of the individual's history and a deep understanding of his or her experience. It is from this relationship or connection with the teacher that alternative education students then develop a personal reason to learn. This connection is very similar to the relationship that one develops with a mentor. In order to reach and teach these students, the teacher needs to recognize and remember that the influences that lead to the patterns of failure are deeply imbedded in the habitus of that student (MacLeod, 1995). Only compassionate acceptance will allow the teacher to overlook the resistance these students bring with them so that a connection can be forged.

Jay MacLeod eloquently described the role of habitus and social reproduction theory in his ethnography of disaffected youth in a Massachusetts housing project. MacLeod (1995) stated, "Put simply, the habitus is composed of the attitudes, beliefs, and experiences of those inhabiting one's social world. This conglomeration of deeply internalized values defines an individual's attitudes toward, for example, schooling" (p. 15). From this habitus, there tends to be a reproduction of values over time. Although not all poor and delinquent youth perpetuate habitus characteristics among themselves, the large majority continue the "traditions" set by older siblings, parents, and close friends. Breaking away from those values is the exception to the rules of social reproduction. In order to break the chains of habitus and to develop routines that foster success in school, a major paradigm shift needs to occur within the alternative education student. For teachers to gain the trust of at-risk youth, the students must first abandon their old connections and belief systems (habitus) before they will learn new ones.

Learning follows the development of safety and trust (Maslow, 1968). This is why the implementation of the "full value contract" is so essential (Schoel, Prouty, & Radcliff, 1988). One's locus of safety and trust is where the learning is taking place (Hart, 1983). The need for the development of trust is especially strong within the minority, at-risk learners. According to Ogbu (1995). "Because they do not trust the schools, many minority parents and adults in the community are skeptical that the schools can provide their children with good educations" (p. 98). The cultural capital or set of knowledge and experience that frames one's culture must be respected in order to build a bridge from one's culture to that of the school (MacLeod, 1995). The impact of disregarding the student's cultural capital (Bourdieu, 1977) is the subject of a recent research study by the California School Climate and Safety Survey (Bates, Chung, & Chase, 1996). This work revealed that approximately 40% of the students in the sample disclosed low levels of trust in their school. In the case of at-risk students, the failure to address their pain and alienation leaves the traditional school unable to reach these potential learners. Without compassionate teachers, these students will look for love outside the system in what is very often an antisocial affiliation such as a gang. Teaching at-risk or urban youth requires that outdoor education teachers develop respect and competency in the cultural identifications of their students (Andrade- Duncan, 2005).

MORE ON EXPERIENTIAL LEARNING FOR STUDENTS AND TEACHERS

One of the learnings I have derived from teaching disaffected youth is that they are developmentally delayed as well as educationally deficient. The impact of years of substance abuse, truancy, and nonparticipation in learning has been to keep these students from achieving personal growth in all areas. Ironically, they appear mature; however, their social reasoning, decision making, and self-esteem are often more characteristic of preadolescents. To teach and reach these students, a student-centered curriculum works best. Using a team-teaching approach, the alternative school can focus on the needs of the individual first and the content of the curriculum second. As with the early adolescent, the challenge of teaching outdoor education in the alternative school is to change the self-esteem of the learners and to teach them by utilizing innovative and effective methods. Many educators have found the process of "integrated learning" has much to contribute to middle school-age and alternative education students (Eggebrecht et al., 1996). According to Eggebrecht et al., "integration provides engaging experiences in which students encounter essential content in multiple and meaningful contexts in response to their own inquiry" (p. 5). Integrated learning uses the students' natural curiosity as the motivator for inquiry. As in Bruner's (1966) thematic teaching, students can participate in the learning of seminal skills through the process of exploring projects both grand and motivating. Outdoor education programs provide natural pathways for this application of knowledge.

Experiential learning also reinforces relevancy and enriches the learning process (Rogers, 1969). Experiential process, although everything we do is an experience, implies active learning. Learning by doing helps the kinesthetic learners as well as those who learn best through the auditory and visual modalities. This type of learning has been popularized by Outward Bound and Project Adventure (Gass, 1993; Rohnke, 1981). Many alternative schools in the United States and abroad use techniques based on this philosophy. This methodology is especially effective in the teaching of life skills (Moore & Wodnarski, 1997). Life skills, according to Brown and Mann (cited in Moore & Wodnarski, 1997) are those abilities that include self-efficacy, communication, and problem solving critical to the successful functioning or adaptive behavior of the individual.

Relevance continues to be a fundamental issue within an alternative setting. Students benefit from "reading" about specific content areas and relating their reading to their topic of interest. For example, students interested in whales can read about whales, write about whales, and research whales to achieve their desired knowledge. Additionally, all reading that is individualized and directed toward vocational or recreational interest has purpose and improves reading (Smith, 1978). High interest is achieved and reading is accomplished!

Paralleling reading strategies, math needs to be taught using the most highly motivating methods. Similar to reading, the successful math program needs to be individualized (Coxford & Hirsch, 1996. Coxford and Hirsch stated, "The individual work accommodates differences in ability, interest, and mathematical knowledge and challenges students in heterogeneous classes" (p. 25). The salient point within all instruction is to motivate and inspire interest within the students.

A lot of the fun for alternative education teachers is in developing specific courses to address the psychological and social needs of these students. Courses in life decisions, health science, psychology, communication, outdoor education, community service, understanding cultural diversity, our environment, and conflict resolution can provide impetus for learning the reading, math, writing, and socialization skills these students must have to survive, or better still, to discover purpose and success! To call the classes by the same old names is to reinforce the resistance that an alternative education student loves to express.

In the period before I moved to California, I taught outdoor education in the Winnacunnet Alternative School (the Alt). The undisclosed motto of the Alt School was, "F**k that shit!" That motto was a true reflection of how my students felt about traditional education! Our challenge as educators was to devise curriculum that didn't evoke that expletive as a response. The students' challenge was to extinguish schoolwork that made them miserable and to reinforce us for providing lessons that were enjoyable for them to complete. I appreciate the fact that often the learning was two way. We both held opportunities for growth!

I joined the staff of the Alt in Fall 1985. The staff was comprised of a director, Ken Grossman; an academic teacher, Chris Spiller, an aide, Judy Hallisey; and an outdoor education teacher, me. Occasionally, our staff was supported by a part-time teacher or a counselor in times of large enrollment. Large for us was 55 students. The students chosen for the Alt were selected by counselors at the comprehensive high school, Winnacunnet High School. Winnacunnet was a school with an enrollment of approximately 1,000 students. Ninety-nine percent of the student body was Caucasian. The alternative education students were chosen from the cohort of students who had failed ninth grade. Many of these students were considered to be conduct disordered, and they were well known to the high school administrators. From that freshman cohort, we attempted to select 20 students whom we felt would be successful in our program. They would become our core group.

The core students would spend at least 1 year with us. They would take all of their academic classes with the alternative school staff. Outdoor education supplanted physical education. On Tuesdays and Thursdays, the core would split in half. One half would go on an outdoor education field trip and the other half would stay at the Alt. Their schedule was a bloc type. Several periods were combined together so that our schedule was not dependent upon the bell. We could have the students for as long as 8 hours at a time. In the case of our summer program, we had them for 3 weeks! After successfully completing Grade 9, our students could return to the alternative school to take a two-credit class called Life Decisions. This class was designed as a follow-up to the more intensive alternative core and as a way to maintain contact with our students. The class also included an outdoor education component. Because Life Decisions was a seminar-styled class, the students were free to discuss topics of interest to them. This requirement left the class loosely structured. It could be repeated in both the junior and senior years. One of the goals of the alternative school was to reconnect its students with the high school and to have them graduate from there. To this end, the Life Decisions class acted as a link between the Alt and the comprehensive high school.

The habitat selected for our alternative school was very successful in its ability to connect students with their teachers. The alternative school's building was an old colonial period house. The house was vacant and located behind the campus of Winnacunnet High School, conveniently separated from the high school by a vocational building and a cemetery. For an alternative high school, the housing could not have been better. We had a kitchen to prepare meals and a home-like atmosphere. Most of all, we had large blocks of time to spend in the uniquely structured outdoor settings and within the alternative school itself. Those ingredients contributed greatly to the creation of a sense that the students were truly having an alternative school experience.

An especially effective component of the alternative school was the staffing. We almost always team taught. Therefore, our staffing allowed two adults on all trips and two adults to stay at school. This student-teacher ratio meant that there was always a person free to talk with an individual student, to answer the phone, to provide relief for a bathroom break, or to generally support the person teaching. Given the resistance that was often the companion to the alternative student's repertoire, the support of another adult was not a luxury, it was essential!

Our staff arrangement also recognized the importance of the influence of male and female staff persons working together. This balance was instrumental in developing feelings of familial support within the students. Often, we were in the roles of nurse, counselor, listener, or surrogate parent. Because our success with the students was accomplished by having their trust, having gender balance and respectful relationships among ourselves had a significant carry-over with our students. Trust (Bates et al., 1996) was enhanced by having the time and the sensitivity to address our students' personal needs. Conversely, when we were not exhibiting our most positive and professional behavior, the students used that opportunity to reinforce negative attributes concerning the teacher, the work, or the school as a whole. Fortunately, discord among our staff was rare.

One of our earliest discoveries as teachers was that schoolwork was best accomplished at the moment. Readings that spanned a period of 20 to 40 minutes were more successful than lengthy articles or full books. The average attention span of our students coincided perfectly with that strategy. We also found homework to be essentially non-existent. Homework is an example of the type of cultural capital that our students lacked. Home life for alternative education students often lacks the protective features necessary for any of the requisite factors for work completion: quiet, space, or support. Therefore, assignments due the next day were a sure flop. The best practice was to have an activity that lasted about 20 minutes and then to move on to another. If the activity was a winner, great! If it was the inverse of winner, then no one had to suffer it for long.

Assignments that were tied to themes were more successful than work done in isolation or seemingly unrelated to any larger issue. When the students' "boredom button" was pushed, their internal alarms would rally them to full resistance! However, if entertainment could somehow be tied to the assignment, it was a guaranteed winner. The best example of what grabbed our students' attention had to do with a local blues man, T. J. Wheeler. T. J. would come to the alternative school on a regular basis. His lessons would fuse the topics of rock and the blues with stories about the old blues men of the south who worked their way across the country. The students were fascinated to learn how rockers from Elvis to today got their styles by emulating various obscure blues men. T. J. would mesmerize the students by playing his guitar and demonstrating styles of play to show rock and blues interconnectedness. The music experience led naturally to further discussion of history and related language arts activities.

The film *Crossroads* is a good example of a language arts activity that was a natural follow-up to T. J.'s work with the students. After T. J. would come to the Alt, we would show the film *Crossroads* to reinforce the stories that T. J. shared and give additional credence to the role that the blues men played in the evolution of rock history. Whenever we could include a current film in the construction of a lesson or a unit, student interest was markedly increased.

The timely manner in which the work was introduced was also very closely related to the probability that it would get done or be met with a tsunami of resistance. We learned that if the students came to us with feelings unresolved from any earlier encounters or interactions, that those feelings would continue to hover about until they were resolved. It mattered not how enthralling our lesson was. If two of our students were angry at one another, those issues needed to be addressed before any teaching could take place!

Therefore, to facilitate any business or learning that needed to be attended, we would start our afternoon session with a whole-class meeting. The meeting would begin with a teacher or a student going to the blackboard and listing everyone's agenda for the day. Of course, the teachers would say, math, social studies, and the like. The students would interject break, movie, or whatever was on their minds. We would then divide up our time and vote on what went where in the day. Then we would all try to follow the schedule. This worked well in democratizing the experience and empowering the students in the process of their own education. This experience gave the students voice and feelings of validity in the process of their learning!

One of my former students, Raylene Davis, sums up the importance of being able to deal with her feelings and the benefit that process provided. Raylene said,

> Like most of the kids that were there, I had a hard time coping with my feelings and the life that I had been living. [At the Alt] I was given the freedom to feel any way I needed to at the moment. I was also given the freedom to have space to deal with it. Rather than be carted off for inappropriate behavior, I was shown a better way. I felt like I had the freedom to ask for what I needed. I learned how to express myself in my own unique way, how to have respect for others.

Raylene further concluded, "When you learn [to] trust the small group around you, you will find something of your own trust and self-worth." These learnings demonstrate how the process of listening to our students developed into the substantive social learning that made our program effective.

In addition to our teaching/counseling style, we found that the more divergent and engaging the topic of study, the more our students would get involved. When they had a successful day, it was very apparent in their faces. Conversely, when the students hated a lesson, we would have to teach through the gales of resistance. There is a lot of learning for a teacher in an alternative setting. Much creativity is required as well as a thick skin.

When I started at the alternative school, I was filled with excitement and idealism. I had wanted that outdoor education job since the school first opened in the 1970s. After I was hired, I was on cloud nine! However, after I met the students, I was shocked at the amount of resistance 1encountered! The students basically said that they weren't ready to accept me as their new outdoor education teacher. They liked the old one, and they didn't want to follow me or any of the rules that I had established for them. The students informed me that the old teacher didn't make them do such and such. The old teacher was cool, and the old teacher understood them. In a nutshell, I didn't know what I was doing.

Alternative education students carry considerable frustration. They are angry to have failed in the traditional system, and they are unsure of their ability to succeed. The result is a confusion about where to place their blame—on themselves or on the system that did this to them. This phenomenon I call the "failed" student's dilemma. Letting go of the blame and anger is a hard process. To travel from anger and self-hate to acceptance and self-respect is the quest of all time. Since Plato's "Know thyself," teachers of the humanities have struggled to find the way to help students learn how to better themselves. In alternative education, it is the continual and quintessential question.

One of the best examples of a method to allow the venting of student anger came serendipitously on a gray March day. Lying innocently beneath us on the Alt school's basement floor were a large number of antiquated metal folding chairs. These former student desks were of the bomb-proof, attached writing arm variety. Because they were school property and symbolically significant, the chairs took on one last utility for our students.

Matt appeared in the Life Decisions class with a load of rage on that March day. Failing to mitigate his anger with the usual counseling strategies, we discovered the chair's last utility. I suggested to Matt that he take one of the chairs from the basement, bring it out to the driveway in front of the school, and destroy it. This appealed to Matt. He took the chair outside and spent the better part of 30 minutes pounding the chair into the asphalt. Vented and sweaty, he came back into the class relieved. The process became known as "doing a chair." The point of the process was that it gave recognition to the feeling of anger, and it legitimized the process of venting one's anger against a tangible object and not hurting oneself in the process. So often, our students would be carrying anger only to have the release of that anger come back and hurt them further. A good example of that was when an angry boy would punch a wall or other hard object only to hurt himself more. Other examples of personal abuses abound—drug abuse, fights, body carving. Having an awareness of the true utility of intervention strategies that work for alternative education students is the difference between being able to survive as an observer to the wars they are waging or falling victim to the students' own undermining of their progress and education. At the Alt School, we were constantly experimenting with our methodologies to find pragmatic and psychologically correct techniques to help our students find successful solutions to their real life problems.

MODULATING THE EMOTIONAL TONE

The emotional tone of an alternative school is critical to the school's success. Developing feelings of support and trust between the students and the faculty is the single most significant component in the change process for the alternative education student (Schoel, Prouty, & Radcliff, 1988). Whereas these students were previously looking at education as an adversarial process because they were only experiencing the negative consequences of their inappropriate behavior, they now need to be convinced of the school's sincere wish to be an ally in their success.

The most important element in reversing the student's sense of failure is in demonstrating the school's understanding of the "failed" student's dilemma. Adolescents are notorious either/ or thinkers. Their experience is most often expressed as black or white. Therefore, teenagers will usually be giving either one of two opinions. The response tends toward "It's the bomb!" or "This sucks!" Adults, too, can fall victim to the trap of reductive, either/or thinking. In the case of a "failed" student, often the reason for school failure is placed squarely on the shoulders of the student. Educators have become proficient at placing the responsibility for student failure outside the school. Examples of blaming the victim abound! "The parents don't support the teachers or demand the student complete homework." "The student doesn't attend frequently enough to earn credit to pass." "Despite modification, the student is not completing any of the work." These examples of reductive thinking resound in schools. Denial of the school's complicity protects the school from change.

The "failed" students' dilemma lies in overcoming the irony that they have been to blame for their school failure for the past 8 or 10 years. Why now would the new teachers treat them differently? Countering the blame of the schools, the students' response to the either/or summation has been to conclude that school sucks. In order to overcome the naturally ingrained resistance on the part of the alternative education student, special understanding is required. These students need to let go of their ingrained assumption that they will be to blame if their school experience does not change for the better and that the school is a damned place for its historic condemnation of them. These realities require special expertise of psychological understanding and often personal counseling finesse, to overcome the resistance that often accompanies these formerly failed students.

One of the solutions to restoring self-esteem after school failure is built on demonstrated student successes. Success is first experienced through the development of a positive relationship with the teacher and then through a positive relationship with the work There is the belief within the student that he or she is safe (Hart, 1983), and it is possible for him or her to achieve success.

Key to the development of trust at the Alt was the establishment of a few simple rules. The first and foremost of the rules was the no put-downs rule. Put-downs include the entire range of racial, ethnic, gender, intellect, and other comments meant to place one student above another in a verbal joust. Put-downs are the leading cause of fights, disruption, and chaos in most groups and families. Often, the put-down is an expression of anger that is thinly disguised as a joke. Called "doing the dozens" within the African American community, this experience is contrived to build a shield of defense against verbal abuse. In reality, the game is dangerous and leads to major social problems, not the least of which are fights.

Establishing the no put-down rule takes constant vigilance; however, the reward in terms of school climate is huge! We all can work to remind ourselves that none of us is any better or any less than anyone else (Kopp, 1989). Our lives are experienced within communities defined by varying amounts of diversity. In this context, our individuality requires nurturing and acceptance. We are all human, capable of mistakes, and, conversely, experiencing the rewards of our correctness!

The second rule of the alternative school was that everything that was spoken about at the alternative school stayed at the alternative school (except as required by laws regarding child abuse). This rule reinforced the trust that we wanted to develop among the students. Often, on hikes or other trips, comments of a personal nature would slip out. We didn't want the students to feel that once a personal situation was revealed, that the story would spread throughout the community. The confidentiality rule was hard to monitor, but the students generally respected it.

The significance of these two rules was within the emphasis on mutual respect and the protection of the individual. The value of these rules revealed itself in helping to establish a friendly tone within the Alt. Students certainly had their differences, but they were able to live within a culture based on mutual respect.

Balance of gender, race, ethnicity, and other human qualities is essential to the emotional tone of the school. An alternative school needs to reflect the positive values of the community that it serves and to be balanced accordingly. In this way, the staff can model the benefits of diversity and help the students see the value everyone possesses. This contributes considerably to the development of a positive atmosphere within the school. Although there are many factors that work together to shape the emotional tone of an alternative school, the fact that a person's psychological feelings are pre-eminent cannot be overstated. Staff and students alike are the essential players in the development of the school's tone, spirit, and atmosphere. Without buy-in to enhance the resiliency qualities partner to adolescent growth and development, learning is an uphill battle, and the development of trusting relationships will never occur. The net result will be both student and school failure. Just how those resiliency factors are enhanced is the focus of the remainder of this chapter.

Using outdoor educational methods within an alternative school requires that the teacher view the process of personal change and growth as being dynamic. Although this process encompasses the mistakes and learning of the past and aspires toward goals and benefits of a healthy future, alternative education exists in the here and now (Gaines, 1979)! The focus is immediate and very much present tense. The actions of the moment and the challenges they present provide numerous opportunities for learning and growth. Successful alternative schools incorporate modem psychological and resiliency theories to create an atmosphere that fosters the trust that allows positive development to occur. According to Bonnie Benard (1991), "Just as in the family area, the level of caring and support within the school is a powerful predictor of positive outcome for youth" (p. 10).

Alternative education philosophy and method allow each student opportunities to grow from self-defeat to self-fulfillment (Goodman, 2002). The word *alternative* implies that this process will be uniquely and deeply personal and developed individually (Bomotti, 1996). For the entire community, all individuals need to be successful and productive members. Alternative education recognizes and celebrates cultural pluralism and the need for meaningful inclusion of all. This means equal opportunity for each student with regard to ethnicity (Page, 1996), gender, and ability. Apple (1995) underlined the necessity for including a truly democratic process within the process of the alternative school by suggesting the following:

If the development of clear alternative programs is essential, these alternatives need to be based on the democratic strength that actually exists in the United States. Without clear programs that seem to provide for at least partial solutions to local and national problems, most people will accept the dominant view, which is inherently undemocratic and anti-egalitarian. Thus, these programs need to be sensible not only to hard-core activists but to working people with families and jobs.

SPECIAL METHODOLOGIES FOR ALTERNATIVE EDUCATION

How shall we approach oppositional and defiant students? By surprise and in a way that they have not been solicited for learning before. When I began working at the alternative school, the principal of the high school, James Hawthorne, called me into his office and asked me how it was going at the alternative school. I told him that the students were a real challenge and that I had to think fast in coming up with new techniques to get their attention. James asked for an example and I hesitatingly offered this one. I told James that the students used the word "funk" all the time and that I needed to develop a "funk" lecture. James asked, "What's a f**k lecture?!" I replied that in response to the gross overuse of the word, I called my students together and said, "Hey, listen up! 'Funk' is my favorite word, but you guys are going to ruin it for me. Every day I hear, 'Oh funk. I've got to get my f**kin' lunch out of my f**kin' locker to go on a f**kin' trip in the f**kin' van.... "'I said, "Whoa, you are going to ruin this word for me. If you want to say the word 'funk' that is perfectly OK. But save it for something really good, like if a canoe fell on your foot or something!" The student response was to stare at me with their mouths agape. Then came the comment, "That's cool."

James thought that this story was one of the funniest things he had ever heard in his tenure as principal. For months after our meeting, I would be somewhere and be approached by someone recalling my "F**k" lecture. Showing that you can waltz to the edge of the envelope on occasion builds your credibility with the alternative education student. However, for your own professional security, you may want to check out some of the local linguistic norms first.

Swearing or obscenity is defined, psychologically, as displaced aggression. Displaced aggression is a term from Freudian psychology that defines the concept of displacement (Hunt, 1993). If, for example, students were angry at themselves for their current straits, that anger could more easily be released by swearing at some object or external person. As alternative education students are almost always carrying anger as a form of personal baggage, the attendant strings of obscenity are a natural vent.

The other aspect of obscenity that bears regard relates to the local norm. Coming from New England where the weather could foul the tongue of a saint, the "F" word is often used merely as punctuation. Exclamation becomes "Oh, F**k!" Interrogatives degrade to "What the F**k?" My biggest culture shock came after moving to the central valley of California, an area of predominantly White, middle-American values. Here the use of the "F" word is reserved for gutters and prisons. I made the mistake of using the word during an Individual Educational Plan meeting with some of my new colleagues. The resultant meeting with my supervisor was most instructive! I confess to still being linguistically challenged at times when there just doesn't seem to be a better word, but in deference to my survival needs, I try to be careful and pick my spots for that pleasant indiscretion.

Because language and image are so intertwined, at the Alt School I tried to strike deals with my students to keep the language appropriate to the situation. In the woods, and far removed from civilization, the linguistic standards were different than they were in the classroom or in the local grocery. The rationale was respect; respect for ourselves and the Alt as a whole.

True to the nature of adolescence, risk is one of the teenager's favorite companions. In the domain of risking, alternative education students pride themselves! Alternative education students are very desirous of adventure and challenge, fundamentals in a methodology first proposed by Kurt Hahn, refined by Willie Unsoeld, and utilized by Outward Bound. This methodology of outdoor and experiential learning well suits these heretofore resistant learners. Rock climbing, canoeing, skiing, and other outdoor activities give opportunity for the satisfaction of the need to risk. The outdoor education component was essential in making our school alternative.

The outdoor/experiential approach also connects the students in a holistic way to their learning (Gass, 1993). Lab-like in structure, the school lets the students learn by doing (Leugers, 1997). The focus is on the process of the learning, and participation and cooperation are the only requirements. In the language of adventure-based counseling, this is referred to as a part of the "full value contract" (Schoel et al., 1988). No one is devalued in the learning process!

One of the unique characteristics of the outdoor education approach is the way in which it can feature multiple invitations to rejoin a learning experience. Using a variety of positive methodologies, we break new ground away from memories of past failures. Within a supportive small-group atmosphere, the alternative school teacher can foster a relationship that can achieve positive results. Between 1970 and 1989, I spent approximately 150 days teaching climbing and rappelling at a local ledge called Stone House. One of New Hampshire's most beautiful sites, Stone House afforded excellent climbing; solid rock, gorgeous views, and bomb-proof belays. Over the years, I developed a lesson routine at Stone House that had a 100% success rate for getting students to rappel (Reif, 1984). I accomplished this success by telling all of the students that for some of them, rappelling wasn't scary at all. For the unafraid, because they trusted me, the exercise was just another thrill like riding a roller coaster. However, for a few of the students, showing up at the top of that 200' cliff was the most courageous thing that they had ever done! Having redefined success, everyone was a hero and the term "chicken" was never evoked. This methodology maximized the use of social psychological theory by including everyone in the process of the day. "Doing" became the best demonstrator to overcome a lack of self-esteem that supported nonparticipation. No one was devalued in the exercise.

Another successful tool to turn a "dropout" into a student is to let the student be the teacher. The peer instruction method has been proven to be very effective for both teacher and learners. Especially with peer-centered adolescents, the focus shifts from the adult to their own (ownership) of the learning process. One of the keys to success in this methodology is that we are not perceived as interfering with their learning! With all students, we are most successful when we remember to be the "guide on the side," not the "sage on the stage."

The strategy that I have found to be the most effective for the teacher's personal and professional survival in dealing with at-risk youth is humor. The alternative education students possess a great need to laugh and release frustration. The teachers, also, need to psychologically detach themselves from the immediate stress of their jobs to maintain their role as good-humored participants. To serve these purposes, the constructive use of irony, paradox, and humor in a variety of forms (remember, no put-downs!) can make the difference between a disaster and success. Humor can provide the release necessary to keep an absurdity in its place. Often the alternative education student is facing multiple paradoxes, and, of these, the "stupid" teacher is one they constantly watch for. Having been put down many times by teachers, it is no wonder that the inverse of this hostility has found a home. By overstating our stupidity and showing our foibles, we allow the kids the opportunity to laugh at us in ways that enhance our relationship.

An example of the constructive use of humor relates to an old camp song. Often when we were in the woods, we would come across a beaver dam or lodge. To mark this event I would call the students together, point out the lodge, and sing "The Beaver Song." The words are, "I'm a beaver, you're a beaver, we are beavers all; and when we get together we give the beaver call." For the finale of the song, you put your two index fingers in front of your mouth to simulate beaver's teeth and yell, "Hey!" This rendition's obvious silliness would always generate a flood of appropriate moans and laugh. Of course, the double entendre when I sang, "I'm a beaver" was not lost on many of our libidinous learners! The song became a part of the legend at the Alt (Goodman, 1999).

Although not a methodology per se understanding the power and effect of alcohol can enhance understanding of one of the other dilemmas that alternative education students face. An alternative education parent may verbalize that he or she wants his or her child to be successful in the world; however, the parent's alcoholism is a glaring example of his or her inability to overcome personal obstacles and have a healthy resolution of his or her problems. This irony can be interpreted in many ways, but students often misunderstand their parent's disease as a justifiable alienation from the world. The alcoholic parent blames the world for his or her own shortcomings. The boss fired him or her. The coach cut his or her son from the basketball team. In other words, the result of the alcoholic parent's effort or his or her child's effort is undermined by someone else. Blame is the defense of choice.

In any alternative school, more than a couple of the students will be coming from alcoholic and dysfunctional families. The rule in these families is chaos first! Don't count on anything! Dad could be home, or not. Mom could cook dinner, or be back in the hospital. This is a very insecure world! Because of their insecurity, any deviance from their school schedule hits these students right between the eyes. The message to them is that they are just like their parents; they are not trustworthy!

This "alcoholic" thinking of the parent is visited on the child. "The world is wrong!" This child comes to school looking for the teacher to be the "deceiver." "What time do we do math?" "What time do we get to go to the bathroom?" Endless questions. I used to think that these students were put in my classes just to delay the class from starring! It took me years to see that these children of alcoholics were so insecure char they needed to know what was going to happen minute to minute because in their personal lives, chaos was the clock. Life for them was totally unpredictable!

To be able to reach these students, tremendous understanding and patience are required (Baker, Bridger, Terry, & Winsor, 1997). Again, humor can be the fuel that keeps the engine of education going when the resistance is running at its highest. My favorite example of how the changing of the schedule can cause a predictable fury and how humor can be used to diffuse it has to do with one afternoon at the alternative school. The basic schedule for the alternative school was generally predictable. Although students and staff would negotiate the order of the day's activities, Mondays were an academic day. Tuesdays and Thursdays were trip days. Wednesdays were movie days, and Fridays were, well, TGIF!

One Wednesday, the academic teacher, Charles, usurped control of the daily calendar and declared that there would not be a movie that afternoon because he was behind in his teaching chronology. He dictated that there would be a math test in place of the movie. The students went wild! They declared, "You can't take away our movie!" "You're not fair!" The upshot of all of this is that they stormed out of the classroom and milled around outside the building, smoking cigarettes and complaining. In a word, they went on strike! One girl even made a picket sign that said, "No Movie....No Test.... F**k Math!"

After giving the students time to vent, my response was to get a camera and to go out and join the strikers. One of my favorite mementos from the alternative school is a picture of myself making the worst face I can make and holding the sign of protest. Shortly after I joined the strike it dissolved. It dissolved because adults got involved. The protest wasn't against anything anymore. For an oppositional and defiant teenager, nothing wrecks a parry more than adult permission and consent. To move against something, that is the joy!

This example of the strike is a good one for understanding the two issues of schedule and oppositional and defiant behavior. Alternative education students are with us because they are not compliant. Realizing that, we need to not fuel their defiant nature by changing their schedule. A school works when it enlists the participation of its students. In an alternative setting, this requires finesse! Throwing a change in the schedule does no more than create angst.

Understanding the student's dilemma, alternative school educators can use humor to diffuse real and imagined catastrophes. Having the ability to see things differently has to be a key characteristic of an alternative school educator. This ability to work with conduct disorder is one of the premier skills of a successful alternative education teacher. As the students at the Alt would proudly disclaim, "What the Funk! I go to the Alternative School!" We, the staff, would sometimes echo, "What the Funk? We teach there!"

The ideal environment for alternative education invites discovery and doing. It inspires curiosity and participation as students are actively engaged in their education. Because of the unique needs of alternative education students, they require an environment that is not reminiscent of the one where they previously experienced failure. In my experience, I have found that atmospheres that are close to nature, or natural environments, provide the greatest opportunity for establishing a mental set conducive to learning.

Moreover, the value of differing environments is strongly supported in educational research literature (Kellmayer, 1995). The modern educational system has created many examples of learning environments that diverge from the traditional classroom such as science labs, shop classes, demonstration kitchens, gymnasiums, outdoor learning centers, and technology labs. As noted by Cairns and Cairns (1994), "The lessons are not restricted to the classroom . . ." (p. 259).

Because our desire is to achieve a more responsible and positively engaged citizen, these students need to see applications of their learning outside the classroom and in relationship to a real-world setting. The best subjects include those relevant to the lives of the students and their families. The biggest gripe of at-risk students is that the schoolwork and teachers in a traditional setting are not related to their lives. In MacLeod's (1995) ethnography, *Ain't No Makin' It*, the words of one of the "Hallway Hangers" sum up this sense of alienation well.

> Chris: I hate the f**king teachers. I don't like someone always telling me what to do. Especially the way they do it. They make you feel like shit. I couldn't take their shit. (p. 108)

Whatever the setting, be it outdoors or in a career lab, we recognize that the ideal environment for at-risk students is one that reflects their dynamic and physical nature. The appearance of the traditional classroom reinforces reminders of their experience of the past. Many of these students have attention deficit disorder, are anxiety disordered, learning disabled, and/or impaired in their mental process. Placing them in an environment that produces déjà vu does not convince them that this is any "alternative." It looks like the same old structure in a different location or, as is the case in some districts, the location isn't all that different, either. The alternative education class is often on the same campus.

The first place alternative education should look for constructive change is in its environment. John Kellmayer's (1995) work on alternative schools places great emphasis on the value of setting for students. Kellmayer stated, "The richer the site, the more powerful the effect of the site on modifying the cognitive and affective performance of at risk students" (p. 93). Of all possibilities, the outdoors offers one of the best choices for alternative education. "Climb the mountains and get their good tidings. Nature's peace will flow into you as sunshine flows into trees" (Teale, 1954, p. 311). My first work in an alternative high school was as an outdoor education teacher at the Winnacunnet High School in Hampton, New Hampshire. For 3 to 5 days a week, I would load up to 10 students and another adult into a 12-passenger van, and away we'd go. Being located on the campus of the comprehensive high school, administrators would often breathe a sigh of relief to see the students that I had with me leaving the campus for the day! We would leave the confines of the high school campus and cruise off to mountains, seasides, rock faces, and rivers for a day of adventures and misadventures. Overall, the students loved these trips. The trips provided a challenge and a release from the ordinary. These adolescents loved risk taking, and the outdoor education program provided plenty of opportunity for adventure. Whether the challenge was climbing up an icy mountain or screwing up the process, there was something they could sink their soul into and get a response.

Above all, through the course of our experiences, we learned to respect and understand each other. There was not a single physical fight during my 4 years at the alternative school. Disagreements, arguments, and even a walk-out style strike, but no fights. I feel that the role that outdoor education played in providing an outlet for some of the frustration was a key ingredient in the process of keeping everyone going.

Not all alternative schools are as fortunate as those in New Hampshire in their proximity to natural habitats. However, the experience of getting out of the confines of a classroom is key to expanding the experience of the students. As Freinet used "learning walks" to inspire curiosity and develop literacy, the alternative school can incorporate outside experiences to build links with the community and enhance the inquisitiveness of its students.

In urban communities where fear is rampant, students and their families are even more alienated and fearful about the world around them. In his insightful ethnography of growing up as an African American in Portsmouth, Virginia, Nathan McCall (1994) wrote:

> Shortly after we moved in, a neighbor warned my parents, "Be careful not to drive through Academy Park. Them is some mean crackers over there. They'll stone your car and shoot at you for driving through there." One night, when I was about ten years old, a little girl my age was shot to death while sitting near a picture window in her living room on Freedom Avenue. The killing brought home the fact that, nice neighborhood or not, we still weren't safe in Cavalier Manor. (pp. 9–10)

In communities where safety is a concern, looking for protective factors and working to maintain them are important roles for the alternative school teacher. Without a sense of safety and trust within the immediate environment higher functions such as learning will not be accomplished. To this end the entire community is key to the enhancement and betterment of itself. Within the contexts of our multifarious environments, we must seek affirmations for our students' future as well as our own. We cannot minimize the environment's value within the overall development of outdoor programs within alternative education settings.

REFERENCES

Altenbaugh, R. J., Engel, D. T., & Manin, D. T. (1995). *Caring for students: A critical study of urban school leavers.* Bishop, PA: The Falmer Press.

Andrade-Duncan, J. (2005). Identifying, defining, and supporting culturally competent teaching in urban schools. Paper presented at the annual AERA convention, Montreal.

Apple, M. W. (1995). *Education and power.* New York: Routledge.

Baker, J. A., Bridger, R., Terry., T., & Winsor, A. (1997). Schools as caring communities: A relational approach to school reform. *School Psychology Review, 26,*586–602.

Bates, M., Chung, A., & Chase, M. (1996 Summer). Where has the trust gone? *CASP Today,* pp. 14–15.

Benard, B. (1991). *Fostering resiliency in kids: Protective factors in the family, school and community.* Portland, OR: Northwest Regional Educational Laboratory.

Bomotti, S. (1996, Ocrober). Why do parents choose alternative schools? *Educational Leadership,* pp. 30–32.

Bourdieu, P. (1977). *Outline for a theory of practice.* Cambridge: Cambridge University Press.

Bruner, J. (1966). *Toward a theory of instruction.* New York: Norton.

Cairnes, R B., & Cairnes, B. D. (1994). *Lifelines and risk: Pathways of youth in our time.* Cambridge, England: Cambridge University Press.

Comer, J.P. (1988). Effective schools: Why they rarely exist for at-risk elementary school and adolescent students. In *School success for students at risk: Analysis and recommendations of the council of chief state school officers.* Orlando, FL: Harcourt, Brace, Jovanovich.

Coxford, A. F., & Hirsch, C. R. (1996). A common core of math for all. *Educational Leadership, 13*(8), 22–25.

Eggebrecht, J., Dagenais, R., Dosch, D., Merczak, N., Park, M., Styer S. & Workman, D. (1996). Reconnecting the sciences. *Educational Leadership, 13*(8), 4–8.

Gaines, J. (1979). *Fritz Perls: Here and now.* Tiburon, CA: Integrated Press.

Gass, M. (1993). *Adventure therapy: Applications of adventure programming.* Dubuque, IA: Kendall Hunt.

Goodman, G. (1999). *Alternatives in education: Critical pedagogy for disaffected youth.* New York: Peter Lang.

Goodman, G. (2002). *Reducing hate crimes and violence among American youth: Creating transformational agency through critical praxis.* New York: Peter Lang.

Goodman, G.S., & Young, I.P. (2006). The value of extracurricular support in increased student achievement: An assessment of a pupil personnel model including school counselors and school psychologists concerning student achievement as measured by an academic performance index. *Educational Research Quarterly, 30*(1).

Harris, T.A. (1969). *I'm okay—you're okay.* New York: Harper &Row.

Hart, L. A. (1983). *Human brain and human learning.* Oak Creek, AZ: Books for Educators.

Hunt, M. (1993). *The story of psychology.* New York. Doubleday.

Kellmayer, J. (1995). *How to establish an alternative school.* Thousand Oaks, CA: Corwin Press.

Kopp, S. (1989). *Rock paper scissors.* Minneapolis, MN: CompCare Publishers.

Krishnamurti, J. (1953). *Education and the significance of life.* New York: Harper & Row.

Leugers, S. (1997, Summer). Experiential education: Learning by doing. *Paradigm,* pp. 14–15.

MacLoed, J. (1995). *Ain't no makin' it.* Boulder, CO. Westview Press.

Maslow, A. H. (1968): *Toward a psychology of being.* New York: Van Nostrand Reinhold.

McCall, N. (1994). *Makes me want to holler.* New York: Vintage Press.

McLaren, P. (1994). *Life in schools: An introduction to critical pedagogy in the foundations of education.* New York: Longman Publishing.

Moore, G. T., & Wodnarski, J. S. (1997). The acquisition of life skills through adventure-based activities and programs: A review of the literature. *Adolescence, 32*(125), 143–167.

Ogbu, J. U. (1995). Literacy and black Americans: Comparative perspectives. In V.L. Gadsden & D. A. Wagner (Eds.), *Literacy among African-American youth.* Cresskill, NJ: Hampton Press.

Page, C. (1996). *Showing my color: Impolite essays on race .and identity.* New York: Harper Collins.

Pianta, R. C., & Walsh, D.J. (1996). *High risk children in school.* New York: Routledge.

Reif, L. (1984, September). Writing and rappelling. *Learning Magazine,* pp. 73–76.

Rogers, C. (1969). *Freedom to learn.* Columbus, OH: Charles E. Merrill.

Rohnke, K. (1981). *High profile.* Hamilton, MA: Adventure Press.

Schoel, J., Prouty, D., & Radcliff, P. (1988). *Islands of healing: A guide to adventure based counseling.* Hamilton, MA: Project Adventure.

Smith, F. (1978). *Reading without nonsense.* New York: Teachers College Press.

Teale, E. W. (Ed.). (1954). *The wilderness world of John Muir.* Boston, MA: Houghton Mifflin.

Zimmerman, J. (1994, May). Resiliency versus risk: Helping students help themselves. *Far West Focus,* p. 3.

FORTY-ONE

A Comprehensive Evaluation of Life Space Crisis Intervention (LSCI)

Larry F. Forthun, Jeffrey W. McCombie,
and Caroline Payne

INTRODUCTION

Crisis intervention skills are essential for all educators. However, many teachers enter the profession feeling unprepared to manage a student crisis (Lewis, Parsad, Carey, Bartfai, Farris, & Smerdon, 1999; Merrett & Wheldall, 1993), and as a result, it falls upon the local school district to provide training and support. For most classroom teachers and staff, professional development typically consists of short-term (1 day or less) in-service seminars and workshops (Parsad, Lewis, & Farris, 2001). However, there is concern that short-term training may not be enough to effectively learn crisis intervention skills and generalize the skills to the classroom (Parsad et al., 2001). Life Space Crisis Intervention (LSCI) is different. Life Space Crisis Intervention is a competency-based professional development training for educators. Unlike traditional professional development opportunities, LSCI is a highly intensive, strength-based training that teaches educators a new approach to intervention for students in crisis. It trains educators in crisis intervention skills from verbal de-escalation of a crisis to intervention strategies that help students develop better coping skills. Studies have shown that educators who implement LSCI in the classroom often experience fewer disruptive behaviors among students and are less likely to refer students for disciplinary action (Dawson, 2003; Forthun, McCombie, & Freado, 2006; Grskovic & Goetze, 2005; Naslund, 1987).

Life Space Crisis Intervention (LSCI) is a competency-based approach specifically designed to help classroom teachers, guidance counselors, administrators, and other school staff reduce the negative psychological, social, and emotional consequences of poor decision making and promote positive development among students. No longer just the purview of administrators or school counselors, classroom teachers and other school staff are being called upon to assist in addressing the social and emotional needs of students (Long, Morse, Fecser, & Newman, 2007). Many children and youth with behavioral and emotional difficulties are being integrated (mainstreamed) into the regular classroom, and more students than ever are entering the classroom with difficulties that are not severe enough for enhanced educational services but may be disruptive to the learning process (Farrell & Tsakalidou, 1999; Landrum, Katsiyannis, & Archwamety, 2004). Research suggests that the overall quality of teacher-student interactions and the academic progress of the students both suffer when disruptions are not managed effectively (Shores & Wehby, 1999). LSCI offers educators specific skills to focus their efforts to addressing the *central issue* (e.g., the underlying pattern of self-defeating behavior) rather than getting bogged down in attempts to determine who is at fault and who should be disciplined. The goal is to encourage more adaptive problem-solving behaviors among students that will lead to an improved quality of life and a reduction in disruptive behaviors at school (Long, Fecser, & Wood, 2001).

However, as a promising approach to crisis intervention, the research on LSCI has been limited to only assessing its impact on student behaviors, mostly within alternative or special education classrooms. For example, DeMagistris and Imber (1980) found that the use of LSCI significantly decreased maladaptive behavior (up to 72%) and increased academic performance among those who received the intervention within a special education classroom. A more recent study by Dawson (2003) found similar results among male junior high special education students. Compared to a similar classroom that did not use LSCI, students in the LSCI classroom experienced fewer crises, fewer suspensions, and better attendance by the end of the school year. In other research, Naslund (1987) kept daily records of the classroom use of LSCI among classroom teachers of elementary school children in an emotional support classroom. Over the course of a school year, daily reports showed that although LSCI continued to be used quite frequently, the content of the interviews changed from complaining about rules to discussing with the student new ways (skills) to be more successful in the classroom. For Naslund (1987), the change in the content of the interviews demonstrated that the students were making progress. Similarly, Grskovic and Goetze (2005) recently reported a significant decrease in challenging behaviors among learning-disabled students exposed to LSCI in the classroom.

Although LSCI results in significant changes in student behaviors, little is known about *how* LSCI is implemented within the schools and *how* training and implementation of LSCI might work in changing the attitudes and behaviors of the educators who are trained (Dawson, 2003; Forthun et al., 2006). The purpose of the study that is the subject of this chapter, then, was twofold. First, we sought to evaluate the *implementation* of LSCI by educators (see Forthun, Payne, & McCombie, 2009 for a full description). A successful LSCI requires a commitment from educators to work with the student to address their immediate and long-term needs. Yet most educators do not have the luxury of spending large amounts of time with a student in crisis. Therefore, as a goal of the implementation, or process, evaluation, it was important to understand how teachers learn to adapt the quasi-therapeutic skills of LSCI into the natural flow of the school day.

A second goal for the study was to examine the impact of LSCI on educators' responses to student misbehavior (e.g., the frequency of use of crisis intervention skills in response to crisis, referrals for disciplinary action, quality of teacher-student relationships) and on the causal beliefs, sense of self-efficacy, and emotional reactions of educators to student misbehavior (see Forthun & McCombie (unpublished) for a full description). Past research suggests that changes in the knowledge and beliefs of educators are a necessary precursor to the successful implementation of new skills or educational strategies (Adalbjarnardottir & Selman, 1997; Stein & Wang, 1988; Tillema, 1995). In fact, Hoy and Weinsten (2006) suggest that teacher's beliefs about students are a significant influence on teaching practices, which ultimately leads to improved student learning and behavior. For example, research has shown that causal beliefs that focus on child temperament or parental divorce (e.g., characteristics that are less amenable to change) often result in negative emotional reactions such as anger or resentment (Hastings & Brown, 2002; Poulou & Norwich, 2002). These negative emotional reactions can lead to a lowered sense of self-efficacy in intervening with disruptive students and a greater likelihood of using restrictive or punitive disciplinary strategies or removing students from the classroom (Hughes, Barker, Kemenoff, & Hart, 1993; Poulou & Norwich, 2002). This study was designed to assess the impact of LSCI on an educator's beliefs, emotions, and behaviors regarding student misbehavior and how this may translate into improved teacher-student relationships and reduced referrals outside of the classroom.

BRIEF OVERVIEW OF LSCI

During LSCI training, current conceptions of students with emotional and behavior problems as "disordered" are challenged and replaced with a "reclaiming" philosophy that views students as individuals who may be acting out as a result of developmental or psychosocial anxiety or pain (Brendtro & Shahbazian, 2004). For example, students may experience developmental anxiety as they struggle to develop a sense of identity or psychosocial pain because of a break-up in a close relationship. In addition, LSCI teaches educators that emotional and pychological *pain* can develop from a variety of sources leading to stress, anxiety, conflict, and crisis, even among well-functioning students (Long et al., 2001). As a result, educators are taught specific skills to disrupt the crisis, thereby reducing negative emotional reactions. These skills are taught through an understanding of the six steps of the LSCI process and the six types of LSCI interventions.

As shown in Table 1, the first three steps of the LSCI process are the Diagnostic steps that are designed to reduce the intense feelings of the student and educator (drain off), validate the student's perceptions (timeline), and identify the underlying issue leading to the current crisis (central issue) (Long, et al., 2001). Once complete, the next three steps (the Reclaiming steps) use one of six interventions to promote *insight* and encourage the development of *new skills* that can be generalized to other situations (transfer of training). The six types of interventions reflect specific intervention skills that target common crises among youth. For example, a student who becomes hostile in the classroom may receive a Red Flag intervention, while a student who is unfocused may receive a Reality Rub intervention. Overall, the goal of LSCI intervention is to use the current crisis as a learning opportunity to encourage the student to take responsibility for her/his own behavior by promoting self-awareness and encouraging behavior change (Long et al., 2001).

Table 1: Steps and Interventions for Life Space Crisis Intervention (LSCI)

STEPS	DESCRIPTIONS
DIAGNOSTIC STEPS	
1. Drain Off	Student "cools down" and teacher holds back any counter aggression feelings s/he may be experiencing toward student
2. Timeline	Obtain and validate the student's perception of the crisis by having the student help create a timeline of the incident
3. Central Issue	Determine which one of the six patterns of student self defeating behaviors is being used by the student
RECLAIMING STEPS	
4. Insight	Help the student develop insight and accountability for the specific self-defeating behavior the student used during the crisis
5. New Skills	Teach the student new social/interpersonal skills to overcome their pattern of self-defeating behavior
6. Transfer of Training	Help the student generalize the new social skills and/or behaviors to other situations

INTERVENTIONS	DESCRIPTION
Red Flag	This intervention addresses emotional problems that are "imported" from outside of the immediate context; for example, a student who "explodes" on another student in the classroom because of a personal or home issue. The emotionality of the issue is carried with the student into the classroom where the student is easily set off by another student.
New Tools	This intervention is designed to teach new social and interpersonal skills to students who may be "acting out" or having difficulty with their peers because of inadequate skills. Generally this intervention is with students who want to succeed socially, but lack appropriate social skills.
Reality Rub	This intervention is designed to address misperceptions or misattributions about the nature of the situation that triggered the crisis; for example, when a student focuses exclusively on how she/he had been wronged by another. This intervention is to help students "see" the situation in a more neutral, rational way.
Symptom Estrangement	This intervention is used with students who attempt to avoid blame by avoiding responsibility or shifting responsibility to someone else; for example, when a student caught fighting blames the other student for starting the fight.
Massaging Numb Values	This intervention is designed for students who feel anxious, guilty, or inadequate; for example, a student who was physically or sexually abused at home. The intervention is to help the student develop better self-efficacy regarding her/his ability to cope in social situations.
Manipulation of Body Boundaries	This intervention is used for a student who is being exploited or manipulated by their peers; for example, a student who misbehaves to gain the approval of other peers.

Definitions taken from Long et al. (2001)

RESEARCH QUESTIONS

To evaluate the process of implementing LSCI in the school setting, we designed an assessment tool that allowed us to answer the following questions: How frequently was LSCI used with students in crisis? What was the average length of an LSCI? How many steps of the LSCI process were typically completed? What type of LSCI (e.g., Red Flag, New Skills) was typically used and for what types of problems? What was the average outcome of an LSCI?

The answers to these questions would provide an important foundation for understanding how educators adapt LSCI to meet the needs of students while continuing to fulfill their educational responsibilities. Second, we asked educators to complete a comprehensive survey of their attitudes, emotional reactions, and behaviors toward students. It was expected that causal beliefs about student misbehavior that blame the family or the child would be positively related to negative emotional relations, negatively related to self-efficacy in managing student behaviors, negatively related to the use of crisis intervention skills, and positively related to disciplinary referrals. Furthermore, negative emotional reactions to student misbehavior would be negatively related to self-efficacy, negatively related to the use of crisis intervention skills, and positively related to disciplinary referrals. To measure the impact of LSCI on each of these processes, a post-test comparison was performed between LSCI-trained educators and educators who were untrained. It was expected that LSCI-trained educators would be (a) less likely to adopt child- or family-focused causal attributions of student misbehavior; (b) less likely to react negatively to student misbehavior; (c) more likely to feel obligated to help a student in crisis; (d) have a higher sense of self-efficacy in managing student crises in the classroom; (e) report using crisis intervention skills more frequently in response to student crises; and (f) be less likely to refer students out of the classroom to counselors or principals.

METHOD

SAMPLE

The training and evaluation of LSCI was part of a long-term initiative of a rural school district in the Northeastern United States. The purpose was to change the school environment from "zero-tolerance" to a reclaiming environment in which teachers and staff would promote belonging, generosity, mastery, and independence among all students (see Brendtro, Ness, & Mitchell, 2002; Brendtro & Shahbazian, 2004). However, the school district was unable to train all school personnel in the district during a single academic year. Instead, approximately 25 to 50 school personnel, primarily from the middle school and high school, were invited to participate in annual trainings. This study was conducted among those who participated in the first three annual trainings with approximately 39 school personnel trained during the first year, 51 trained in the second year, and 25 trained in the third year (see Table 2). All but three participants agreed to participate in the study (n = 112).

Table 2: Demographic Characteristics of LSCI and Comparison Participants*

VARIABLE	VALUE	FREQUENCY LSCI	FREQUENCY COMPARISON
Gender	Female	66 (58.4%)	39 (57.4%)
	Male	46 (40.7%)	29 (42.6%)
Ethnic Origin	Am. Ind./AK Native	2 (1.8%)	1 (1.5%)
	Hispanic/Latino	2 (1.8%)	
	White/Non-Hispanic	108 (95.6%)	66 (97.1%)
Grade Level	Elementary School	9 (8.0%)	
	Middle School	39 (34.5%)	8 (11.8%)
	High School	61 (54.0%)	56 (82.4%)
	Across Schools	1 (0.9%)	
Teaching Experience	No Experience		1 (1.5%)
	First year teaching		2 (2.9%)
	1-4 yrs	34 (30.1%)	8 (11.8%)
	5-9 yrs	15 (13.3%)	14 (20.6%)
	10-14 yrs	17 (15.0%)	18 (26.5%)
	15-19 yrs	14 (12.4%)	11 (16.2%)
	20-24 yrs	16 (14.2%)	4 (5.9%)
	25-29 yrs	8 (7.1%)	1 (1.5%)
	30-34 years	5 (4.4%)	8 (11.8%)
	35-39 years		1 (1.5%)
	Over 40 years	1 (0.9%)	0
Academic Position	Principal/Administrator	6 (5.3%)	2 (3%)
	Reg. Ed. Teacher	66 (58.4%)	8 (13%)
	Sp. Ed. Teacher/Aide	18 (15.9%)	2 (3%)
	Alternative Ed./Aide	3 (2.7%)	
	Guidance Counselor/ Psychologist	15 (13.3%)	1 (1%)
	Other	4 (3.5%)	3 (4%)
	Missing		52 (76%)
	Total	112	68

* *not all percentages add up to 100% due to missing data*

A comparison sample of 68 untrained teachers and staff were recruited from two demographically similar schools in the region (see Table 2). Approximately 31 were teachers at a vocational/technical school and 37 were faculty who taught in a middle school or high school. In all, participants in both groups were primarily female (58%), predominately White, non-Hispanic (97%), taught in the middle school or high school (94%), and had, on average, 10 or more years of experience (58%).

PROCEDURES

Process Evaluation

Those trained in LSCI were asked to complete a report following each interaction with students where LSCI skills were used. The report asked them to identify the type of LSCI intervention that was used, the number of steps that were completed, the length of the intervention, the intensity of the situation (on a scale from 1 [low] to 5 [high]), a brief description of the situation, and a brief description of the outcome. Although not all of the participating educators completed a report after each LSCI, approximately 702 reports were submitted over the course of the 3-year study.

Written descriptions of the situation that precipitated the LSCI and the outcome that followed were coded using a content analysis approach. First, descriptions of the LSCI situation were compared to a list of common disciplinary infractions obtained from each school (e.g., disciplin-

Table 3: Definition of Situations Coded from the LSCI Reports

SITUATION CODES	DEFINITIONS
Misbehavior: Non-Physical	The situation involved a behavior that was disruptive to the class, school environment, teacher, or other students but was not physical, i.e.: talking at inappropriate times, inappropriate comments or writings, harassment, or disrespect for others.
Misbehavior: Physical	The situation involved a behavior that was disruptive to the class, school environment, teacher, or other students and was physical, i.e.: fighting, pushing, or hitting.
Academic Issues	The situation took place as a direct result of an academically centered issue, i.e.: failure of a subject, difficulty with homework.
Family Issues	The situation was the direct result of an issue stemming from the student's home environment, i.e.: parental divorce, death of a family member, or sickness in the family.
Relationship Issues	The situation took place between two individuals who were experiencing difficulties in their romantic relationship or as a result of a romantic relationship.
Personal Issues	The situation took place as a result of a personal or emotional issue that the individual student was experiencing, i.e.: depression, eating disorder, or suicidal thoughts.
Peer Issues	The situation involved two or more students having social problems with one another. The problem may have escalated to become verbal or physical, but was still centered around peer difficulties, i.e.: trouble making friends, disagreements between friends, or clique status.
Teacher-Student Issues	The situation took place between a teacher and a student, i.e.: disagreement over grades, or miscommunication.
Follow-up	A meeting was scheduled in which the student-educator met to further discuss a previous situation.

ary codes). When a description mirrored a coded infraction, the situation was coded similarly (e.g., bullying, disrespect, etc).. For those descriptions that were not disciplinary infractions, new codes were developed (e.g., parental divorce, fighting with friend, etc.). Once complete, the new codes were reanalyzed to consolidate codes that reflected similar themes (e.g., misbehavior, personal issues, etc.). This process continued until no more higher-order themes could reasonably be identified. In the end, nine situation codes were used to describe the specific events that precipitated most LSCIs (see Table 3).

Coding for outcomes proceeded similarly. Initially, each outcome description was coded using very specific categories (e.g., insight to emotions, detention, returned to class, etc.). Following the initial coding, specific codes were consolidated into higher-order categories that reflected the general theme of the outcome (e.g., discipline, peer meeting). As a result, twelve outcome codes described most of the outcome descriptions provided by the educators (see Table 4).

Table 4:: Definition of Outcomes Coded from the LSCI Reports

OUTCOME CODES	DEFINITION
Central Issue Identified	The central issue of the problem was established.
Conference Requested	A meeting took place between the parents and teacher/administrator.
Discipline	The result of the intervention was some form of punishment i.e.: suspension, detention, or sent home for the day.
Drain Off Established	The student calmed down, relaxed, and was able to discuss the incident.
Promoted Insight	The educator gathered enough information from the student on the specifics of the situation and was able to encourage the student to look at the situation in different ways.
New Skills Discussed	The educator was able to discuss new skills that could be applied to the specific situation.
Ongoing Discussion	The situation was not resolved and actions were taken to continue the discussion at a later time.
Peer Meetings	The intervention resulted in a peer meeting of some sort either between the individuals involved in the situation, or between other peers.
Plan Developed	A plan was developed to help the student resolve the situation and prevent the situation from reoccurring.
Referred Outside School	The student was referred to an individual, program, or service outside the school.
Referred Inside School	The student was referred to someone else within the school that was trained in LSCI, i.e.: teacher, principal, guidance counselor, or other.
Resolved	The educator felt that the situation had been resolved as a result of LSCI.

OUTCOME EVALUATION

Participants in the LSCI group completed a battery of questionnaires immediately prior to training and again approximately 6 to 8 months following the start of the academic year (e.g., a pre- and post-assessment). Data were collected from trained educators during the first year following training with data from all three cohorts (first year only) combined to form the LSCI-trained group (n = 112). Comparison group participants were evaluated only once at approximately the same time as the post-assessment for the third LSCI group (e.g., 6 to 8 months from the start of the academic year). The comparison group was assessed only once to avoid pre-test sensitization. As a result, only the post-test data from the battery of questionnaires were subjected to statistical analysis.

Participants who were trained in LSCI were also asked to participate in a focus group at the end of the school year in which they were trained. Focus group questions included: What was the most important impact of LSCI on your values as an educator? What traditional beliefs about school discipline or misbehavior have been done away with? Give an example of a significant impact of LSCI on a student.

The focus groups were conducted by the LSCI trainer, and participants were allowed to interact with one another. Focus group members were asked to write their reactions/responses on note cards that were analyzed by the researchers using a similar content analytic approach as described above.

MEASUREMENT

The *Attribution Inventory* was designed by Poulou and Norwich (2000) to evaluate teachers' causal attributions about student misbehavior and their subsequent cognitive, emotional, and behavioral responses. Participants are asked to read a vignette about a problem student and asked to respond to the following scales.

CAUSAL ATTRIBUTIONS

Causal attributions for the student's misbehavior described in the vignette were evaluated in four domains: family environment, child, teacher, and school. Five to seven items were used to assess each domain. Examples of items in the family environment scale included: "poor attachment between parent and child" and "parent's inability to help their child." Reliability estimates for this scale were adequate with Cronbach's alpha estimated at .69 for the LSCI group and .79 for the comparison group. Examples of items in the child scale included: "Child cannot control his behavior" and "child's low intelligence level." Reliability estimates for this scale were also adequate with Cronbach's alpha estimated .65 for the LSCI group and .71 for the comparison group. Examples of items from the teacher scale included: "Teaching style" and "poor classroom environment." Reliability estimates for this scale were excellent with Cronbach's alpha estimated at .87 for the LSCI group and .86 for the comparison group. Finally, examples of items from the school scale included: "Irrelevant curriculum for the child's interest" and "class size too large." Reliability estimates for this scale were good with Cronbach's alpha estimated at .74 for the LSCI group and .83 for the comparison group.

REACTIONS TO MISBEHAVIOR

Three items were used to assess *self-directed emotional reactions* to the student in the vignette. Examples of items in this scale included: "I would feel stressed/anxious" and "I would feel helpless/depressed." Reliability estimates for this scale were adequate with Cronbach's alpha estimated at 0.63 for the LSCI group and 0.79 for the comparison group.

Three items were used to assess *child-directed emotional reactions* to the student in the vignette. Examples of items in this scale included: "I would feel angry/resentful toward the child" and "I would feel sympathy/compassion toward the child" (reverse coded). Although reliability estimates for this scale were adequate for the comparison group with Cronbach's alpha estimated at .74, the reliability estimate for the comparison sample was poor at 0.55. Items were examined to identify their contribution to the overall estimate of reliability; however, given the low number of items, removing a single item did not improve the estimate. Results for this scale for the LSCI group should be interpreted with caution.

Three items were used to assess the *level of felt responsibility* in helping the student in the vignette. Examples of items in this scale include: "I would feel responsible to help" and "I would feel committed to help the child." Reliability estimates for this scale were good with Cronbach's alpha estimated at 0.75 for the LSCI group and 0.86 for the comparison group.

SELF-EFFICACY

Participants complete the Perceived Self-Efficacy in Classroom Management subscale of the Teacher Interpersonal Self-Efficacy Scale (Brouwers & Tomic, 2001; Brouwers, Tomic, & Stijnen, 2002). Examples of the 13 items in this scale include: "I am able to respond adequately to defiant students" and "I am always able to make my expectations clear to students." Reliability estimates for this scale were excellent with Cronbach's alpha estimated at 0.90 for the LSCI group and .88 for the comparison group.*Crisis Intervention Skills and Referrals*

Finally, both the LSCI and comparison group participants were asked to answer several questions on their use of, and comfort with using, skills for managing crises (see Dawson, 2003). LSCI participants were asked about their use of LSCI skills, while the comparison participants were asked about their use of general crisis management skills. Participants were asked to rate on a scale from 1 (very uncomfortable) to 5 (very comfortable) how comfortable they felt working with students in "crisis." Participants were also asked to rate how frequently they used their skills with youth in crisis from 1 (not at all) to 5 (very frequently). In a separate line of questioning, participants were asked to rate on a scale from 0 percent to 100 percent, the percentage of time their interventions with students resulted in positive outcomes and the percentage of time interventions resulted in a referral to the principal or counselor.

DESIGN AND ANALYSIS

Qualitative procedures were outlined previously. To analyze the quantitative data, relationships between variables were first examined using Pearson's correlation. We expected the variables in our analysis to be related to each other in a theoretically consistent manner. Second, mean scores of the scale items were statistically compared between groups by using a 2 (LSCI group; comparison group) X 2 (male; female) ANOVA on the post-test scores only. Gender of the educator was included as an independent variable in the analyses based on previous research that suggested that outcomes may differ based upon the participant's gender (Forthun et al., 2006). Years of experience was included as a covariate. To avoid potential Type I errors (concluding a mean difference between groups is significant when it is not), the probability level was set at 0.01 for all ANOVA analyses.

RESULTS

LSCI PROCESS EVALUATION

Data gathered from the LSCI reports are summarized in Table 5. To ease interpretation, the educators were separated into five groups: classroom teacher/aide, alternative teacher/aide (including special education, alternative education, and emotional support), principal/administrator, guidance counselor/psychologist, or other staff (e.g., school resource officer, student liaison). On average, principals and guidance counselors spent the most time with students (about 30–35 minutes), while classroom teachers spent the least amount of time (about 22–24 minutes). Likewise, on average, most educators only completed four of the six steps of the LSCI process (see Table 5). Most reported the completion of the first three steps in the order in which they occur in the model: Step 1 (Drain Off), Step 2 (Timeline), and Step 3 (Central Issue). However, Step 4 (Insight) and Step 5 (New Skills) were often completed independently when the completion of Step 5 (New Skills) occurred by skipping Step 4 (Insight) in the process. Transfer of Training, the last step in the LSCI process, was least likely to happen (22.7% of the time). The results suggest that all educators completed the first three LSCI steps relatively consistently, although the limited time with students may have led to adaptations of the last three steps.

Table 5 summarizes the three most common student difficulties by educator group. The most common student difficulty reported by principals and classroom teachers was student misbehavior. For mainstream teachers and guidance counselors, personal and peer issues also prompted an LSCI. In fact, alternative education teachers were the only educator group with academic issues as one of the top three issues addressed. This suggests that when students are experiencing personal difficulties, mainstream classroom teachers, along with guidance counselors, are the educators who are most likely to be able and available to intervene. On the other hand, given that many of the student difficulties were either for misbehavior or were personal in nature, it is not surprising that the most common LSCI interventions used were the Red Flag (35% of the time), New Tools (23% of the time), and Reality Rub (15.5% of the time) interventions (see Table 5). The only variation in the frequency of use of the three LSCI interventions was for guidance counselors who were more likely to use the New Tools intervention.

In the analysis of the outcomes of each reported LSCI, the most frequent outcomes were Promoting Insight (e.g., efforts by the educator to gather information from the student to encourage them to think or behave in a different way), Ongoing Discussion (i.e., educator to continue discussion at a later time), New Skills Discussed (i.e., educator noted discussing prosocial skills), and Resolution (i.e., educator felt issue was adequately resolved). As expected, Discipline (e.g., detention, suspension, etc.) was a common outcome only for school principals.

Table 5: Summary of LSCI Implementation by Type of Educator

TYPE OF EDUCATOR	# SUBMITTED	MEAN # OF STAGES	MOST COMMON INCIDENT CODES	MOST FREQUENT LSCI	AVERAGE INTENSITY OF CONTACT	LENGTH OF LSCI (MINUTES)	MOST COMMON OUTCOME CODES
Principal/ Administrator	82	3.96	1 Misbehavior: Non-Physical 2 Misbehavior: Physical 3 Peer Issues	1 Red Flag 2 New Tools 3 Reality Rub			1 Insight 2 Discipline 3 Resolved
Emotional/ Special/ Alternative Ed	247	3.09	1 Misbehavior: Non-Physical 2 Academic Issue 3 Personal Issues	1 Red Flag 2 New Tools 3 Reality Rub			1 Insight 2 Resolved 3 Ongoing
Classroom Teacher/Aide	233	3.95	1 Misbehavior: Non-Physical 2 Personal Issues 3 Peer Issues	1 Red Flag 2 New Tools 3 Reality Rub			1 Insight 2 Ongoing 3 Resolved
Guidance/ Psychologist	42	4.09	1 Personal Issues 2 Peer Issues 3 Family Issues	1 New Tools 2 Red Flag 3 None			1 Resolved 2 Insight 3 New Skills
Other Staff	91	3.95	1 Peer Issues 2 Misbehavior: Non-Physical 3 Personal Issues	1 Red Flag 2 New Tools 3 Reality Rub			1 Insight 2 Referred inside school 3 New Skills

OUTCOME EVALUATION

Using correlation analyses to evaluate the relationships among the quantitative variables (see Table 6), results showed that, consistent with expectations, attributing the cause of the student's misbehavior to the family environment was positively related to both self-directed negative emotions ($r = 0.19$) and child-directed negative emotions ($r = 0.22$) (see Table 6). These negative emotional reactions, in turn, were negatively related to both the comfort of using crisis intervention skills with students ($r = -0.27$ with self-directed emotions; $r = -0.22$ for child-directed

Table 6: Correlations between Variables in the Study for All Participants Combined

	CHILD CAUSES	TEACHER CAUSES	SCHOOL CAUSES	SELF EFFICACY	SELF DIR EMOT	CHILD DIR EMOT	RESPONSIBLE	COMFORT WITH SKILL	FREQ OF SKILL	POSITIVE OUTCOME	REFERRAL
Fam Env Causes	.15*	.03	.18*	.07	.19**	.22**	−.08	−.05	−.04	.01	.20*
Child causes		.52**	.60**	−.03	−.09	−.21**	.12	−.06	−.02	−.06	−.14
Teacher causes			.67**	−.01	−.08	−.18*	.16*	.08	.00	.01	−.11
School causes				−.13	−.05	−.17*	.13	.00	−.07	−.09	−.12
Self-efficacy					−.15*	−.07	.05	.17*	.15	.16*	.03
Self dir emotion						.65**	−.14	−.27**	−.26**	.03	.11
Child dir emotion							−.34**	−.22**	−.21**	−.07	.18*
Responsible								.23**	.16**	.14	−.20*
Comfort with skills									.54**	.39**	−.15
Freq of skills										.29**	.00
Positive outcome											−.10

* $p < .05$
** $p < .01$

emotions) and frequency of the use of crisis management skills with students ($r = -0.26$ with self-directed emotions; $r = -0.21$ with other-directed emotions). Additionally, child-directed emotional reactions were positively related to student referrals ($r = 0.18$). However, when attributions were focused on the child, teacher, or school as the cause of the student's misbehavior, teachers and staff were less likely to report child-directed negative emotional reactions (r = −0.17 to -.21). When causal attributions were directed at themselves, teachers and staff were more likely to report feeling responsible to intervene (r = 0.16); and therefore, were less likely to refer students.

ANOVA ANALYSES

Causal Attributions

In separate analyses comparing the LSCI group with the comparison group, the LSCI group (see Table 7) endorsed three of the four causal factors more strongly. They were more likely to

Table 7: Analysis of Variance for LSCI and Comparison Participants (Main Effects Only)

VARIABLE	LSCI MEAN (*SD*)	COMPARISON MEAN (*SD*)	*F*	ADJUSTED *R*²
Family Environment Causes	3.09 (.525)	3.52 (.793)	14.02**	.136
Child Factor Causes	2.92 (.615)	2.47 (.757)	17.79**	.145
Sex	*Female* *2.60 (.701)*	*Male* *2.94 (.680)*	*11.87***	
Teacher Factor Causes	3.17 (.623)	2.59 (.849)	24.84**	.123
School Factor Causes	3.15 (.527)	2.72 (.817)	17.08**	.08
Negative Emotions Directed at Self	1.91 (.639)	2.59 (1.05)	25.18**	.143
Negative Emotions Directed at Child	1.61 (.523)	2.31 (.969)	33.02**	.178
Felt Responsible To Help	4.31 (.648)	3.70 (.950)	21.15**	.119
Self-Efficacy in Classroom Management	4.99 (.465)	4.95 (.478)	.120	.00
Frequency of Use of Crisis Management Skills	3.38 (1.04)	3.09 (1.18)	2.73	.00
Comfort Working with Students in Crisis	4.05 (.776)	3.53 (.915)	15.86**	.086
% Positive Outcomes in Crisis Interventions	73.69 (22.60)	70.52 (21.54)	1.09	.00
% Intervention Results in Referral	19.46 (22.18)	40.98 (31.71)	20.40**	.137

* $p < .05$
** $p < .01$

identify, teacher ($F (1, 160) = 24.84, p < 0.01$), school ($F (1, 160) = 17.08, p < 0.01$), and child ($F (1, 160 = 17.79, p = 0.01$) factors as influential in explaining the student's disruptive misbehavior. On the other hand, mean scores were lower for LSCI participants on family environment factors ($F (1, 159) = 14.02, p < 0.01$). Additionally, a significant interaction emerged by group and gender for family environment causal beliefs ($F (1, 159) = 8.01, p < 0.01$). Females in the comparison group ($M = 3.72, SD = 0.79$) were much more likely to endorse family environment causes than those in the other groups (comparison group males ($M = 3.24, SD = 0.74$), LSCI group females ($M = 3.05, SD = 0.53$), or LSCI group males ($M = 3.15, SD = 0.52$)). The opposite occurred for child factor causes with males ($M = 2.94, SD = 0.68$), regardless of training, endorsing child factor causes significantly more often than females ($M = 2.60, SD = 0.70$) ($F (1, 160) = 5.11, p < 0.01$). These trends suggest that LSCI training had its greatest impact on reducing the endorsement of family environment causes among female educators.

REACTIONS TO MISBEHAVIOR

Significant main effects were found for negative emotional reactions directed toward the self (F (1, 160) = 25.18, $p < 0.01$) and toward the child (F (1, 160) = 33.02, $p < 0.01$) with mean scores significantly lower for LSCI participants. LSCI participants reported that they were much less likely to respond to the misbehavior of the student with anxiety or stress, and they were much less likely to report child-directed reactions like feeling angry at the child or feeling indifferent. On the other hand, a significant main effect was found for the level of felt responsibility to help the disruptive child (F (1, 159) = 21.15, $p < 0.01$). The LSCI group felt a greater sense of responsibility to respond to the misbehavior of the student.

SELF-EFFICACY

There were no statistically significant differences between groups on the self-efficacy scale. Comparison participants were just as likely as LSCI participants to feel confident in their ability to manage student misbehavior in the classroom.

Crisis Intervention and Referrals

Both groups reported that they use crisis management skills relatively frequently (no statistically significant differences between groups); however, a significant main effect (F (1, 164) = 15.86, $p < 0.01$) showed that LSCI participants felt more comfortable implementing their skills in crisis situations. At the same time, while both groups reported positive outcomes as a result of interventions with students in crisis (~70% of the time), the LSCI group was much less likely, on average, to refer students outside of the classroom (only 20% of the time compared to 40% of the time for the comparison group;) F (1, 150) = 20.40, $p < 0.01$.

FOCUS GROUP RESPONSES

Impact on Beliefs of Those Trained

During focus groups, LSCI-trained personnel were asked to share how implementation of LSCI had affected them, and two themes characterized those responses. First, educators reported that they were more willing to listen and provide encouragement to students: "I believe I can make a difference." They reported that they had become more tolerant, kind, gentle, and compassionate towards students, that they were more understanding and aware of students' needs, and that they were more patient and calm when discussing issues with students, avoiding overreaction and criticism. Second, they also reported that they were more reflective and open-minded toward students. The following participant had this to say about the change in attitudes and beliefs regarding disruptive students:

> It has helped me to reframe my thoughts as I approach student problems. It helps in providing a framework from which to begin instead of blindly asking questions in order to find out who's to "blame." This approach focuses more on getting at the root of a problem in order to help a student solve it.

BELIEFS THAT WERE CHALLENGED

LSCI participants noted that many strongly held beliefs about student problems and effective management strategies were challenged. The strongly held beliefs that were challenged included:

1. Punishment first; lock-step discipline; send the student to the office when they misbehave.
2. Schools *must* use traditional discipline strategies (e.g., suspension, detention, and expulsion) in response to misbehavior.
3. Intimidation of student by teachers to encourage appropriate behavior.

These long-held beliefs were substituted with the following beliefs and practices:

1. Talking to the student rather than sending them to the principal's office.
2. Traditional detention has been replaced with other consequences.
3. Fewer "write-ups" and more flexibility in managing disruptive behavior.

IMPACT ON STUDENTS

LSCI participants related many personal stories about how their different approach to student misbehavior impacted their relationships with students. Several themes characterized these stories. First, many stories emphasized the positive relationships that were created and that previously disruptive students had become their "buddies" or would often stop by the classroom/office "just to talk." This transformation in the teacher-student relationship occurred through a series of steps beginning with the teacher stopping and listening to the student's needs followed by more self-disclosure from the students (i.e., trust). One teacher noted, "I have several students who just "hang out" in my room before and after school. This used to annoy me. Now I know that my room is a comfortable, safe place for them. They need this."

Second, school personnel commented on the transformations they had observed in student behavior both in and out of the classroom. For example, previously disruptive students were more able to control their temper, get along better with peers, be more respectful toward others, and accept responsibility. One teacher stated: "One student who has 'issues' at home and was on the path to failure has developed some level of trust in me and is succeeding academically in my classroom."

DISCUSSION

The purpose of this study was to more fully evaluate the efficacy of Life Space Crisis Intervention (LSCI) as a training tool for classroom teachers and other school personnel. Our goal was to evaluate both the process of implementation and the outcomes among educators. The goal of the process evaluation was to assess how educators implemented LSCI and adapted the skills to best meet the needs of all students. The goal of the outcomes evaluation was to assess the impact of LSCI training on the attitudes, beliefs, and behaviors of educators. More specifically, the goal was to examine causal beliefs about student misbehavior, negative emotional reactions to misbehavior, self-efficacy in classroom management, intent to intervene with student misbehavior, use of crisis intervention skills, and typical outcomes of crisis intervention (i.e., referral and teacher-student relationships). The results of this study suggest that training and participation in LSCI had a significant impact on these processes.

Results from the evaluation of LSCI implementation suggest that educators throughout the school system, not only special education teachers, were able to successfully use and implement LSCI with students. Mainstream classroom teachers not only intervened with student misbehavior, but they also acted as "counselors" and discussed personal and peer issues with students. In fact, educators who used LSCI spent a great deal of time with each student discussing one situation (between 22 and 35 minutes). That is a significant investment, an indication of the educator's commitment to the process. The results also indicate that educators who used LSCI saw little need to refer students outside of the classroom, an indication that they felt confident in their abilities to intervene. On the other hand, educators reported that they rarely completed all 6 steps of the LSCI process, on average completing the first three steps (see Table 5). However, the outcomes of Promoting Insight, Ongoing Discussion, and Resolution may reflect less formal ways of addressing Step 4 (Insight), Step 5 (New Tools), and Step 6 (Transfer of Training).

Results from the outcome evaluation show that those trained in LSCI were more likely to report child, school, and teacher causes for misbehavior and were less likely to adopt family-environment causes. That scores for only family-environment causal attributions were significantly lower, and not child causal attributions as we expected, is curious. It may be that LSCI participants evaluate family-environment causal attributions as less amenable to change than child factors. This is partially supported by the correlation results that showed family-environment attributions were significantly positively related to both self and child-directed negative emotional reactions while the relationship with child attributions was significantly negative. On the other hand, causal attributions directed at teachers and school were beneficial because they were negatively related to negative emotional reactions directed at the child. Although speculative, the results appear to confirm the hypothesis that when adults attribute causes for misbehavior to characteristics that they see as unchangeable (either in the child or in the family), they may be more likely to respond with frustration, resentment, and negative disciplinary actions (Hastings & Brown, 2002).

Additionally, differences between LSCI trained and untrained educators showed that LSCI participants were less likely to report negative emotional reactions, either directed at the self or the child. It may be that this difference in the likelihood to respond with negative emotions plays a pivotal role in shaping the teacher-student relationship (Montague & Rinaldi, 2001). Focus group responses confirm the importance of positive emotional responses on improvements in the teacher-student relationship, beginning with the simple step of stopping and listening to the student's needs. Educators reported that they had become more tolerant, patient, and compassionate towards students and were more willing to listen and less willing to criticize. These responses lead to a more positive teacher-student relationship and improved behavior within the classroom.

The results also showed that LSCI educators were more likely to feel comfortable using their crisis intervention skills with students. However, the higher level of comfort was not generalized to self-efficacy in classroom management. This may be due to differences in the measurement of each construct. Classroom management self-efficacy was measured using a questionnaire that assessed the perceived ability of educators to maintain order in the *classroom* (Brouwers & Tomic, 2001); whereas, the frequency of use of crisis intervention (or LSCI) skills was assessed with a single question that focused on implementation of specific skills with *students* in crisis.

Finally, LSCI educators were less likely to report referring a student out of the classroom (20% of the time compared to 40% of the time for untrained educators). This is important given that referrals may result in students falling behind in their classes. According to the correlation results, educators who endorsed family environment causes for a student's disruptive behavior and who experienced negative emotions directed at the student were more likely to refer the student outside of the classroom. This suggests that decisions to refer a student outside of the classroom are influenced by both the attributions and the emotions of the educator, with LSCI educators much less likely to endorse family environment causal beliefs or report experiencing negative emotions. This was mirrored in focus group responses when LSCI educators reported that their beliefs about "dealing with problem students" shifted from a focus on punishment to a focus on cooperation. Traditional disciplinary beliefs including detention, suspension, and expulsion were substituted with more cooperative beliefs that focused on prevention and natural consequences.

Based on these findings, it appears that LSCI is an effective intervention for students in crisis. However, the process evaluation results suggest a few necessary modifications. A useful model for guiding these modifications is offered by Long, Fecser and Wood (2001) in their description of an LSCI "safe and reclaiming school." Similar to the "pyramid of interventions" that is being adopted in school districts across the U.S., a safe and reclaiming school would distinguish between the needs of all students (base of pyramid), the needs of at-risk or occasionally involved students (middle of pyramid), and the needs of high-risk students (top of pyramid); (Blankstein, 2004). For Long, Fecser and Wood (2001), the three levels of student needs could be addressed by three levels of training. Primary prevention training would begin with training all school employees on the basic concepts and skills of creating a positive and predictable school environment and managing their own emotional reactions towards student misbehavior. The second level of training in early intervention skills would be taught to all classroom teachers and support staff and teach more specific skills for connecting with and supporting students who are experiencing difficulties (e.g., the first 3 steps of the LSCI process). Finally, LSCI (or advanced reclaiming strategies) would be taught to members of the *crisis reclaiming team,* composed of principals, guidance counselors, and special education teachers. The reclaiming team is called upon when initial efforts at crisis intervention are unsuccessful.

LIMITATIONS AND STRENGTHS

Several limitations to this study warrant caution when interpreting the results. First, the primary measurement tool used in the process evaluation, the LSCI report, was developed for use in this study and has not been validated in other studies (however, see Naslund, 1987). Additionally, the educators who completed the LSCI reports may have been a selective group of educators who were more highly motivated to succeed with LSCI. They may have offered more socially desirable responses on the LSCI reports or only selectively submitted reports that showed positive outcomes. However, if social desirability was an issue, one would have expected a greater number of reports submitted with more LSCI steps completed and more outcomes seeking resolution.

For the outcome evaluation, the inability to randomly assign educators to groups could not guarantee that the groups were similar. It may be LSCI participants volunteered to participate in the training and research because the values/beliefs that were taught were consistent with existing beliefs (Tillema, 1995). Likewise, the participants may have differed in other ways that could not be controlled for in this study; although years of experience was included as a covariate and a post-test only design does control for testing effects within the comparision group. Finally, the child-directed emotional reactions scale demonstrated poor reliability. Given the sensitivity of estimates of internal consistency to sample size and the number of scale items, the poor estimate may reflect greater variability in responses among the LSCI group.

Appreciating these limitations, the strengths of this study included the comprehensive evaluation of both the process and outcome of LSCI training on educators including their cognitive, emotional, and behavioral responses to the disruptive behavior of students. It is clear from past research that the relationship between attributions and beliefs about the reasons for student misbehavior and emotional and behavioral responses of educators was a key component to successful implementation of LSCI (Alvarez, 2007; Hastings & Brown, 2002; Hughes et al., 1993; Poulou & Norwich, 2000). An additional strength of this study was that it was conducted on a program that was initiated within the local school district. One of the difficulties in large-scale rigorous experimental studies of intervention programs is that the program often fails to survive once the grant funding is removed (Greenberg, 2004). This study was conducted on a program that was initiated by the local school district and could be realistically sustained over time. This type of research is important because it evaluates whether programs that are implemented in "real world" settings can be effective.

CONCLUSIONS

LSCI is an intensive strengths-based program that not only meets the needs of students in crisis, but it also offers a practical set of skills that can be used with all students (Forthun et al., 2006). Previous research has shown that experienced classroom teachers generally become more punitive in their interactions with students (Woolfolk & Hoy, 1990), and it is more difficult to change beliefs and behaviors once existing beliefs and behaviors have become established (Tillema, 1995). The results of this study are remarkable because training in LSCI appeared to change the educator's style of interacting with students. An additional implication of this study is the importance of evaluating the emotional, cognitive, and behavioral responses of educators because it is critical that professional training change the way educators think and feel about students and their role as educators if behavior change is to be successful. This knowledge could not only lead to a better understanding of how to ultimately change educators' responses to students in crisis but also how to design and implement successful crisis intervention training programs.

ACKNOWLEDGMENTS

The authors would like to gratefully acknowledge the financial assistance of the Pennsylvania Department of Education, Division of Student and Safe Schools Services in supporting the implementation and evaluation of Life Space Crisis Intervention. We would especially like to thank Myrna Delgado, Division Chief, for her continued encouragement in this evaluation project.

REFERENCES

Adalbjarnardottir, S., & Selman, R. L. (1997). "I feel I have received a new vision": An analysis of teachers' professional development as they work with students on interpersonal issues. *Teaching and Teacher Education, 13*(4), 409–428.

Alvarez, H. K. (2007). The impact of teacher preparation on responses to student aggression in the classroom. *Teaching and Teacher Education, 23*(7), 1113–1126.

Blankstein, A. M. (2004). *Failure is not an option: Six principles that guide student achievement in high-performing schools.* Thousand Oaks, CA: Corwin Press.

Brendtro, L. K., Ness, A., & Mitchell, M. (2002). No disposable kids. *Behavioral Disorders, 27*(4), 423–424.

Brendtro, L. K., & Shahbazian, M. (2004). *Troubled children and youth: Turning problems into opportunities* (1st ed.). Champaign, IL: Research Press.

Brouwers, A., & Tomic, W. (2001). The factorial validity of scores on the teacher interpersonal self-efficacy scale. *Educational and Psychological Measurement, 61*(3), 433–445.

Brouwers, A., Tomic, W., & Stijnen, S. (2002). A confirmatory factor analysis of scores on the teacher efficacy scale. *Swiss Journal of Psychology/Schweizerische Zeitschrift für Psychologie/Revue Suisse De Psychologie, 61*(4), 211–219.

Dawson, C. A. (2003). A study on the effectiveness of life space crisis intervention for students identified with emotional disturbances. *Reclaiming Children and Youth, 11*(4), 223–230.

DeMagistris, R. J., & Imber, S. C. (1980). The effects of life space interviewing on academic and social performance of behaviorally disordered children. *Behavioral Disorders, 6,* 12–25.

Farrell, P., & Tsakalidou, K. (1999). Recent trends in the re-integration of pupils with emotional and behavioural difficulties in the United Kingdom. *School Psychology International, 20*(4), 323–337.

Forthun, L.F., & McCombie, J.W. (unpublished). The impact of Life Space Crisis Intervention (LSCI) on educators' cognitive, emotional, and behavioral reactions to students in crisis.

Forthun, L.F., McCombie, J. W., & Freado, M. (2006). A study of LSCI in a school setting. *Reclaiming Children and Youth: The Journal of Strength-Based Interventions, 15,* 95–102.

Forthun, L.F., Payne, C., & McCombie, J.W. (2009). LSCI in a school setting: Final results. *Reclaiming Children and Youth: The Journal of Strength-Based Interventions, 18,* 51–57.

Greenberg, M. T. (2004). Current and future challenges in school-based prevention: The researcher perspective. *Prevention Science, 5*(1), 5–13.

Grskovic, J. A., & Goetze, H. (2005). An evaluation of the effects of life space crisis intervention on the challenging behavior of individual students. *Reclaiming Children and Youth: The Journal of Strength-Based Interventions, 13*(4), 231.

Hastings, R. P., & Brown, T. (2002). Behavioural knowledge, causal beliefs and self-efficacy as predictors of special educators' emotional reactions to challenging behaviours. *Journal of Intellectual Disability Research, 46*(2), 144–150.

Hoy, A.W., & Weinstein, C.S. (2006). Student and teacher perspectives on classroom management. In C.M. Evertson & C.S. Weinstein (Eds.), *Handbook of classroom management: Research, practice, and contemporary issues* (pp. 181–219). Mahwah, NJ: Lawrence Erlbaum Assoc.

Hughes, J. N., Barker, D., Kemenoff, S., & Hart, M. (1993). Problem ownership, causal attributions, and self-efficacy as predictors of teachers' referral decisions. *Journal of Educational & Psychological Consultation, 4*(4), 369–384.

Landrum, T., Katsiyannis, A., & Archwamety, T. (2004). An analysis of placement and exit patterns of students with emotional or behavioral disorders. *Behavioral Disorders, 29*(2), 140–153.

Lewis, L., Parsad, B., Carey, N., Bartfai, N., Farris, E., & Smerdon, B. (1999). *Teacher quality: A report on the preparation and qualifications of public school teachers. statistical analysis report* No. NCES-1999–080. Retrieved: http://nces.ed.gov/pubsearch/index.html

Long, N. J., Fecser, F. A., & Wood, M. M. (2001). *Life space crisis intervention: Talking with students in conflict* (2nd ed.). Austin, TX: Pro-Ed.

Long, N. J., Morse, W.C., Fecser, R.A., & Newman, R.G. (2007). *Conflict in the classroom: Positive staff support for troubled students* (6th ed.). Austin, TX: Pro-Ed.

Merrett, F., & Wheldall, K. (1993). How do teachers learn to manage classroom behaviour? A study of teachers' opinions about their initial training with special reference to classroom behavior management. *Educational Studies, 19*(1), 91–106.

Montague, M., & Rinaldi, C. (2001). Classroom dynamics and children at risk: A followup. *Learning Disability Quarterly, 24*(2), 75–83.

Naslund, S. R. (1987). Life space interviewing: A psychoeducational intervention model for teaching pupil insights and measuring program effectiveness. *Pointer, 31*(2), 12–15.

Parsad, B., Lewis, L., & Farris, E. (2001). *Teacher preparation and professional development: 2000.* E.D. *tabs* No. NCES-2001–088. Retrieved: http://www.nces.ed.gov

Poulou, M., & Norwich, B. (2000). Teachers' causal attributions, cognitive, emotional and behavioural responses to students with emotional and behavioural difficulties. *British Journal of Educational Psychology, 70*(4), 559–581.

Poulou, M., & Norwich, B. (2002). Cognitive, emotional and behavioural responses to students with emotional and behavioural difficulties: A model of decision-making. *British Educational Research Journal, 28*(1), 111–138.

Shores, R. E., & Wehby, J. H. (1999). Analyzing the classroom social behavior of students with EBD. *Journal of Emotional and Behavioral Disorders, 7*(4), 194–199.

Stein, M. K., & Wang, M. C. (1988). Teacher development and school improvement: The process of teacher change. *Teaching and Teacher Education, 4*(2), 171–187.

Tillema, H. H. (1995). Changing the professional knowledge and beliefs of teachers: A training study. *Learning and Instruction, 5*(4), 291–318.

Woolfolk, A. E., & Hoy, W. K. (1990). Prospective teachers' sense of efficacy and beliefs about control. *Journal of Educational Psychology, 82*(1), 81–91.

FORTY-TWO

Urban Dropouts: Why Persist?

Greg S. Goodman and Adriel A. Hilton

As we are all too keenly aware, the national educational statistics tell a very troubling and foreboding story about life for students within America's urban classrooms (Banks & Banks, 1989; National Center for Education Statistics, 2006). African American students embody 17 percent of the total U.S. student population, but African American teachers represent only 6 percent of all teachers in the U.S. (*Leaving Schools*, 2004). For Hmong and other minority groups, the gap can be even more acute. African American male teachers comprise just one percent of America's total teaching force. Underscoring those dismal numbers is the fact that there is no staff of color in 44 percent of the nation's schools (National Center for Education Statistics, 2006). Based upon these demographics and the cultural mismatch they portray, is it any wonder that inner city schools are failing their students and continuing to fall further behind (Beachum & McCray, 2008)? This is failure by design (Duncan-Andrade & Morrell, 2008). Why persist? Indeed!

The Children's Defense Fund reports the alarming fact that one American high school student drops out every nine seconds ("Leaving Schools," 2004). In 2007 that statistic equated to 6.2 million students in the United States between the ages of 16 and 24 dropping out of high school. These data are further substantiated by the Center for Labor Market Studies at Northeastern University and the Alternative Schools Network ("High School," 2009): these demographics represent roughly 16 percent, or one student in eight, of all of the students in the United States who were in that age group. As these data consistently show, most of the students who are dropping out of school are minority youth, specifically African American and Hispanic (National Center for Education Statistics, 2006), and they are living in our nation's largest urban areas. Seventy-one percent of students nationwide graduate from high school but less than half of the students of color graduate (Greene & Forster, 2003). These data spotlight the fact that our young African American and Hispanic men are the most prone to drop out of high school. For most urban youth, the question 'why persist?' is a metaphor of their dilemma in the struggle for survival.

WHY DO URBAN STUDENTS FAIL TO PERSIST IN SCHOOL?

Angela Pascopella (2003) pulls no punches when she states that the schools themselves are to blame for most students dropping out of high school. Why persist when the school is large and alienating, students are confronted with less-experienced teachers in their classrooms, schools are given fewer resources and support, and it is clear that the majority White policy-making community is complicit in undermining the education of its urban youth (Duncan-Andrade & Morrell, 2009)? According to Pascopella (2003), even the teacher's unions work to support a corrupt system of ineptitude. Teacher contracts can result in the more knowledgeable and skilled teachers being rewarded for their performance by moving from low-performing schools to escape the ghetto. These systems support a vicious cycle of cultural reproduction. Students who lack qualified teachers and pupil personnel services in their schools fall further behind (Bourdieu, 1993; White & Cones III, 1999). Why persist when the scene is set for failure? Research also demonstrates that a significant number of students drop out of urban high schools because their schools are not offering real-life opportunities for learning (Duncan-Andrade, 2008). The curriculum is not relevant, and the mismatch between student lives and the experience within the classroom is grossly disconnected. Teachers are presenting materials that are proscribed by central office administrators in a misguided attempt to increase standardized test scores (Goodman & Carey, 2004). When students are exposed to the mandated curriculum within their classrooms, the subject content often has no relevance to the real problems they confront on a daily basis. Schools must be held accountable for what they are teaching and how it translates to the real world of their community, not to the dictates of Educational Testing Service (ETS) or a central office oligarchy fearful of losing cushy, politically parceled jobs (Carnevale & Desrochers, 2003). Researchers tie at least part of the problems facing urban schools to their makeup. Although these schools are populated mainly by students of color, educators within these settings are mostly White and female (National Center for Education Statistics, 2006). Hancock (2006) notes,

> The reality that White women are on the front lines of urban education is clear. While we continue to recruit and retain minority teachers, it is critical that we also focus our attention on helping to educate White women teachers about the realities of teaching students who may hold a different sociopolitical, sociocultural, and socioeconomic perspective (p. 97).

The effect of the cultural mismatch is supported by the work of Malloy and Malloy (1998). These researchers discovered that many urban teachers consider the culture of the student and the classroom to be a hindrance. A solid example of this mismatch is found in the debate concerning the use of Ebonics in schools. To teachers supporting White curriculum, the wealth of opportunity that a mix of experiences brings to the classroom is threatening, unappreciated, and devalued (Goldenberger, Kunz, Hamburger, & Stevenson, 2003). In urban school districts, as many as 95% of the students are minority. Large urban states such as New York report 86% of the teachers are White (National Center for Education Statistics, 2006). In rural states such as New Hampshire and Maine, the population of White teachers climbs to 98 and 99%, respectively!

According to Cross (2003), concerns related to race and culture are of tremendous significance in today's educational environment. Issues of an irrelevant curriculum and the attitudes, color, and disposition of the educators charged with teaching our youth bring additional evidence to support our fundamental question: Why persist? Why persist when you cannot see yourself represented in any of the identifications of your school?

An urban school is so designated, generally, because of its location, rate of poverty, percentage of students of color, and the proportion of students who are limited in English proficiency (i.e.; Hispanic and other English Language Learner (ELL) students). Most teachers going into urban schools for the first time face unexpected challenges as they confront the everyday problems of inner city classrooms (McKinsey & Company, 2009). For inexperienced and untrained White teachers, the adjustment is even more profound. Season four of the critically acclaimed, award-winning HBO series *The Wire,* focuses on the stories and the lived experiences of several young boys in Baltimore City Public School System. The youth featured in this dramatic television series continuously grapple with authentic problems within their homes and the Baltimore ghetto/community. In this fourth season, the writer/producer David Simon focused on an urban middle school in West Baltimore that faced a critical shortage of teachers, especially in the important areas of science and math. *The Wire* provides viewers with a drama accurately representing most urban school districts. The drama exposes the policy of urban school systems that elect to employ teachers who are not certified but are offered alternative methods for certification such as teaching residency programs. The training represented in *The Wire* is positively ludicrous. Teachers are instructed to chant "I am lovable and capable" with their charges. This 1960s pabulum nourished hippies, but in this episode of *The Wire* it effectively demonstrates how out of touch trainers and administrators are with the urban classroom of the twenty-first century.

The series' director, David Simon, is acutely aware of both the research and the lived experience of the people existing within the ghetto of Baltimore. *The Wire* is set in an urban district that is one of the largest in the nation. The City of Baltimore includes a very highly educated and affluent community, yet it also is home to significantly large number of under-educated and poor. In 2006, 33 percent of the 25-and-older population had a college degree, and conversely, Baltimore City had one of the highest rates of people over the age of 25 without a high school diploma (State of the Region Report, 2006).

Season four of *The Wire* features a suspended police detective who seeks a career change with the goal of impacting the lives of youth. Naively, our protagonist decides to teach math in an urban school district. Driving the drama, this White male with little experience in urban schools has no idea what challenges are ahead. As he begins to struggle with gaining command and order within the classroom, the students are more engaged in creating a brutal and hectic culture reflective of their lives on the street. As one could expect, our protagonist was surprised to learn just how little help was available to teachers or students. Director Simon depicts a system characterized by a lack of intervention and support mechanisms; a system designed to perpetuate failure. Why persist as either teacher or student within this mismatch?

The Wire reveals many of the reasons why urban students drop out of high school. A recurring theme in the show identifies the role of the gangstas and their grip on the young and vulnerable wanna-bes. To fulfill the need for quick, if not always easy, money to take care of themselves and their loved ones, the gangstas enlist the children of their block to distribute drugs (mules) to drive-through customers. As the show deftly demonstrates, the lure of quick money in real time makes education for a future and distant reward appear meaningless and disconnected. Within a culture of violence, the lure of gangs is clear. Joining can help young people feel and be more protected within the violent inner city neighborhoods where they live. Gangs are a support network that fills the void manifested by society's abandonment of the ghetto's inhabitants. The gang is the family, the court, the administration, and the authority.

Urban school districts, such as Baltimore City, are facing major problems, made worse by a very nomadic student and teacher population. Of inner city teachers, 40 percent will transfer within five years of placement. Sara Neufeld (2006), a reporter with the Baltimore *Sun,* stated that only 38.5 percent of Baltimore's high-school students graduate four years after entering. Too much of the city's workforce is under-educated and poorly prepared for the economy of today, much less the future. The ripple effect on quality of life issues throughout our nation is apparent—it leads to more crime, a less healthy and less wealthy population. Employment opportunities are few because businesses will not locate in areas where schools are sub-par. Further driving the economic and social downturn, businesses choose to re-locate away from communities with such issues; meaning fewer jobs, a declining population and, of course, higher taxes for those who stay.

When segregation ended to make way for integration, many dedicated African American teachers and administrators lost their jobs. Black schools were closed and their students were bused to White schools (McCray, Wright, & Beachum, 2007). Also exacerbating the lack of Black educators for our urban students, young African American college students opted to major in fields of study other than education (Kunjufu, 2002). These shifts left a void of teachers who had traditionally provided quality education to America's Black students. In their place, White educators largely took on the job of educating African American and other urban students. Despite multiple efforts to recruit minority candidates within urban school districts, the teaching force (along with administrators) continues to be predominately White (McCray, Wright, & Beachum, 2007).

While we live in a more inclusive society than that which existed in pre-civil rights America, continuing segregation and inequality have made the hope of living 'The American Dream' illusory and an irony for many young Blacks. "The illusion of integration allows for some access, while countless roadblocks persist in critical areas where blacks continue to be discriminated against in often subtle and sometimes not so subtle ways" (Kitwana, 2002, p. 13). White and Cones (1999) agree that contemporary prejudice exists mainly in the form of institutional racism. They explain:

> Institutional racism exists where whites restrict equal access to jobs and promotions, to business and housing loans, and the like. White bankers and mortgage companies can secretly collaborate to redline a neighborhood so that such loans are nearly impossible to obtain. White senior faculty members in predominately white universities (public and private) determine who gets promoted to tenured faculty positions....Good-old-boys' clubs in the corporate structure determine who will be mentored and guided through the promotional mine fields. (p. 136)

African American youth witness the continuing legacy of segregation and racism and its impact on their lives. They see their schools continuously underfunded, lacking in modern facilities, supplied with inadequate and inappropriate textbooks, and staffed with teachers who are poorly trained and who have low expectations of the youth. Why persist when those who need to support you are so conspicuously absent?

Wacquant (2000), a noted sociologist, takes the racism theory several steps further, proposing the notion of hyperghetto to describe African Americans who were steered to certain areas of Northern cities, areas that came to be known as ghettoes. Wacquant (2000) created the neologism hyperghetto to identify the environment of urban African Americans from 1968 to present day. He points out the relationship between hyperghetto and prison in the way African Americans are forced to live. According to Wilson (2009), hyperghettos are characterized by increased crime, illegal drug activity including addiction, economic depravity, police surveillance and brutality, and struggling schools, all of which forces businesses to relocate to the suburbs.

The hyperghetto evolved in a post-White flight era when the residential barriers that barred African Americans from moving into White suburbs were relaxed (Wilson, 2009). When Blacks move up and make it to middle or upper class status, they often move out of inner cities and develop amnesia concerning where they come from, and they neglect to reach back and uplift their former community. The lack of involvement in their old community, including the schools, can only be described as abandonment. This alienation between middle and upper class Blacks and the hyperghetto exacerbates the recurring problems of inadequate urban school funding, parental detachment from the schools, and the continuing cycle of conditions detrimental to student success. Many scholars and authors have warned of the increasing separation, segregation, and stratification within the African American community (Dyson, 2005; Kitwana, 2002; Kunjufu, 2002; West, 2008). West (2008) elaborated, "Once we lose any sense of a black upper or black middle class or a black upper working-class connecting with the black underclass with a 'we' consciousness or sense of community, it becomes much more difficult to focus on the plight of the poor" (p. 57).

Urban school districts have their share of problems that are not often experienced by suburban schools. Dropout rates of 70 percent and higher are common in many inner city schools (Alexander, Entwisle & Horsey, 1997). The impact of these students' decision to dropout can be felt throughout their communities and into society as a whole. Communities already plagued by high rates of crime and physical and mental challenges often find those problems are exacerbated by high numbers of citizens experiencing disenfranchisement. Dropouts, for example, have been shown to account for half of the nation's prison population (Coley, 1995; Goodman, 2007). One of every three African American males spends time in a penal institution, but only one of ten male high school graduates is enrolled in college (Coley, 1995).

URBAN DROPOUTS: PEOPLE MAKE THE DIFFERENCE

The recurring question, why persist? gets a resounding round of reinforcement: it's cool, schools sucks, my teachers hate me, I don't fit, 'America ain't right,' everybody else does.....It is the truth that arguments for dropping out too often outweigh the cries for persistence. "The situation in far too many schools is one of despair, poverty, isolation, and distress" (Obiakor & Beachum, 2005, p.13). As we stated in the first half of this chapter, the student dropout problem is reinforced with obsolete and counter-productive pedagogical practices that extend beyond the individual classrooms into the halls, cafeteria, bathrooms, and the entirety of the culture known as school. Often the result of this complex ecology is a "cultural collision" (Beachum & McCray, 2008), "....the culture of educators clashes with that of their students..." (Beachum & McCray, 2008, p. 55), and the mismatch is devastating. Jeff Duncan-Andrade and Ernest Moreno (2008) take this argument one step further and make the claim that urban schools are performing exactly as they were designed to function. "If urban schools have been decried for decades as 'factories for failure' (Rist, 1973), then their production of failures means they are in fact successful at producing the results they are designed to produce. To the degree that we continue to misname this problem by calling schools designed to fail 'failing schools' we will continue to chase our tails" (p. 5).

Consequently, for students facing the paradox of successful "factories of failure" (Rist, 1973), what could be the counter-narrative to the urban question: why persist? What factors contribute to students' resiliency and school persistence? In this second half of our investigations into the questions of urban middle and high school dropouts, we will explore some of the successful initiatives that have been utilized in building healthy learning communities. The complex ecologies of these learning communities will be explored and deconstructed to reveal the ways in which they work to keep students connected and on track toward graduation. These are not presented as simple panaceas to the huge problem of dropouts. All of these initiatives require hard work, courage, tenacity, intelligence, emotional toughness, and, as Barack Obama observed, audacious hope.

James Comer (1980) has been one of the undisputed leaders in the development of successful learning communities for the past thirty years. Comer was one of the first urban educators to identify the holistic nature and the complex ecology of the learning community. "When satisfactory home and school conditions exist the caretaker and the school staff constitute an alliance and are both able to interact with a child in a series of social and teaching experiences in which the child can gain personal control, motivation for learning, a balance between individuality and cooperation, interpersonal and social skills, and a sense of responsibility for his or her own behavior" (Comer, 1980, p. 33–34). Although Comer's work centered on pre-school and elementary school children in New Haven, which is not New York or Los Angeles, his model School Development Program (SDP) was innovative for its attention to all of the ecological factors contributing to student success: the school, the home, and the community.

This early work applied social and behavioral science to the operation of the whole school and community environment. Comer's SDP also has spurred the growth of interest in addressing the myriad elements of each of these complex ecologies. "Our work over the years shows that curriculum and instruction are at the heart of the education enterprise, but that relationships must be such that young people can imitate, identify with, and internalize the attitudes, values, and ways of the meaningful adults around them in order to be motivated to learn academic material and, eventually, to become self-motivated, disciplined, self-directed learners capable of taking advantage of the resources of our society" (Comer, 1980, p. 295). Comer re-defined and revitalized the role of psychology and social science within the school.

Unfortunately, attempts to widely reproduce the Comer School Development Program (SDP) proved limited in their possibilities for replication. The reality is that people, not programs, are the change. Within the culture of each school and the community they represent, there are key individuals who are responsible for the myriad factors that contribute to the success or failure of the school organization's complex ecology. Dropouts are the result of the failure to successfully resolve the issues of 'cultural collision' (Beachum & McCray, 2008), and each community needs a leader who can interpret both the existing research on urban school reform and translate this into a workable program for their unique community.

California's Clovis East High School is an example of an urban high school that has developed a culture effective in reducing school dropouts and creating strong and personally meaningful bonds within its community's shareholders. Drawing its students from a mix of diverse socioeconomic and cultural sub-communities located in California's Central Valley, Clovis East High School's 3,000 students are typically Californian as exemplified by being majority minority in racial identification. In addition to the racial diversity of the student body, the academic abilities of the students are wide-ranging. The majority of the students are well-below grade level in both reading and math scores.

When the school opened in the fall of 1999, there was a new principal, Jeff Eben, greeting the students as they walked onto the campus. Jeff Eben is a quadriplegic, yet his stature in his Quickie wheelchair resembles a professional basketball center. His presence on campus is ubiquitous, and his sensitivity to issues of culture is unparalleled. "On the day we opened, our students brought with them varied experiences in school. When we looked at the test results on the academic records of our first group of students, almost seventy percent couldn't read at grade level. Many of them had never been on teams or part of performing groups. School had not been a friendly place for a large portion of our clientele and our community didn't come in with a great deal of trust in education....We had no credibility, and it felt like we were actually starting at whatever comes before square one" (Eben, 2006, p. 193). The tasks were daunting, but the persistence of this principal and many of the staff caused the culture to form and take hold.

In his autobiographic book, *How Many Wins Have YOU Had Today?*, Eben (2006), recounts his experiences of the early days of Clovis East:

> If we were going to have any academic success, we had to be able to teach our kids how to read, a tough task with teenagers. A struggling reader will have trouble in every discipline, so we had to find instructional practices that were innovative and effective, and we aren't necessarily trained at the secondary level for that type of instruction. Motivation was critical, and I thought our students would try harder if they participated in activities outside of class. We wanted to create opportunities for our young people to participate in sports, the arts, agriculture, and any other programs that would make their school experience more fun. Many of our students had not been part of high profile groups, but they would be here. We even adopted a schedule with eight class periods as opposed to the typical six to force students to take elective classes. Finally, I wanted students to feel safe and was concerned about how well our different cultures would interact with each other. It seemed natural to use our diversity as an on-going tool to teach inclusion, social tolerance and justice, and caring. So we took our Feel the Love motto and defined it with three words 'Competence, Connectedness, and Compassion.' These words combined our goals of helping students achieve academically, provide them with a sense of belonging, and create an environment where we care about each other. We put these words on a poster and hung them in every room and office in the school. It became who we were and caught on quickly. Two of my colleagues even gave us the name of "The Love Shack" and our marching band still plays the song as a way of celebrating our identity. (p. 194)

Eben's work at Clovis East follows a line of thought well-accepted and articulated within current critical constructivist pedagogical perspectives. Constructivists ascribe to the belief that the individual must invest of themselves in order to acquire knowledge. Using a combination of external and internal motivations, the individual learner is engaged in learning and meaning-making. Critical constructivists further the championing of an individual's self-efficacy as a learner with an application of social justice education. Social justice education is focused upon the liberation of all individuals from the destructive forces of racism, sexism, poverty, and the oppression of ignorance and hate. Dropping out of school reflects the victory of these destructive forces by being self-perpetuating and contributing to the cultural reproduction of failure (Bourdieu, 1993). More than any other factors, critical constructivist pedagogy can provide a positive intervention for ecological and educational success. "Understanding the problem of high school dropouts requires looking beyond the limited scope of individual student characteristics to include school (read: ecological) factors in student decisions to stay in or leave school" (Knesting, 2008, p. 3).

Eben's culture of caring has replicability. In her research on dropout prevention in high school students, Knesting (2008) lists a caring culture and three other factors as key to promoting student school persistence and dropout resistance. "Four factors emerged as critical for supporting student persistence: a) listening to students, b) communicating caring, c) the school's role in dropout prevention, and d) the students' role in dropout prevention" (p. 3). The generalizability of caring and compassionate teachers is clear. What is not so obvious is the tremendous effort and persistence that is required of staff. Knesting concludes: "Developing caring, supportive, and mutually respectful relationships with students in a large, comprehensive high school is not an easy task…" (p. 9). This is why people, not programs, are the key to success in creating 'wins' with our students.

Another important and successful school reform for improving students' school persistence is found through the creation of charter schools, school within a school, and other alternative ecologies for learning, for example, smaller learning communities (SLC). Transitions from grade to grade and school to school are disrupting and threatening to adolescents. When these transitions from school to school are not supported with the creation of solid bonds to either the new school's culture, individuals such as teachers or counselors, or another emotional and/or social anchor for the student, the risks of dropout loom large. Conversely, the literature is replete with examples of 'reclaiming youth' through the development of alternative educational programming featuring adventure activities, relevant curriculum, and the development of close bonds between students and staff (Goodman, 2007; Brendtro, Brokenleg, & Van Bockern, 2002). SLCs have been proven to significantly contribute to student school persistence (Darling-Hammond, 2002).

Very often the failure of students to bond with the new school and its culture result in social frustrations and academic failure (Diller, 1999). Across the nation, the dropout rate for freshmen in urban settings hovers around 40% (EPE, 2006). In many schools, students get stuck in ninth grade, and their experience is one of a continuing cycle of repeating because of a failure to win the credit-banking game of high school (Freire, 1970). Patterson, Beltyukova, Berman, and Francis (2009) explain:

> For many urban school districts, the response to the dehumanizing condition of the large urban high school has been the creation of smaller learning communities (SLC). The impressive benefits of SLCs have been well-established in the literature, with increasing examples of success across the country (Cotton, 2001; Darling-Hammond, 2002). Hundreds of SLCs have been created in urban areas, including Chicago, Denver, Los Angeles, New York, Philadelphia, Seattle, and Ohio. Small school researchers are careful to assert, however, that shrinking the size of schools is not a panacea; rather, smaller environments make it easier to give kids the things they really need to succeed: collegiality among teachers, personalized teacher-student relationships, and less differentiation of instruction by ability (Cotton, 2001; Gladden, 1998; Raywid, 1999) (p. 128).

Although this process of creating dropout preventions can sound simple as described in these pages, what is not easy is finding instructional and support staff with the strength, courage, conviction, and love of humanity to pull this off. Jeff Duncan-Andrade is a professor who walks the talk. A member of the faculty at San Francisco State University, Jeff also teaches a 12th grade English literature class at the Oasis Community High School, in Oakland, California. Jeff understands and communicates caring as a primary value, but he demonstrates his love (Freire, 1970) for his students by providing them with a rich, culturally relevant curriculum. This curriculum places students' cultural identification and icons at the center of their educational experience. Duncan-Andrade (2008) says,

> A curriculum that draws from youth culture would embrace...expanding definitions of literacy by viewing students as producers of and participants in various cultural literacies, such as: image, style, and discursive practices. This more inclusive approach to literacy instruction recognizes students as cultural producers with their own spheres of emerging literacy participation. This pedagogy of articulation and risk (Grossberg, 1994) values and learns from the cultural literacies students bring to the classroom and assists them as they expand those literacies and develop new ones. Teachers should aim to develop young people's critical literacy, but they should also recognize students as producers of literacy and support that production (p. 140).

Duncan-Andrade also trusts his students. He believes in their ability to know the truth and their skills in detecting elements of the popular and school's culture that enhance and scaffold their success. This is the ultimate show of respect and caring. Students don't dropout of Duncan-Andrade's class: they are practically breaking down the doors to get in. Within Jeff's classroom, his students have the opportunity to learn how to create an activist agency to transform themselves and their community's ecology by applying an authentic social justice and critical pedagogy. Jeff has dubbed this process "Doc Ur block." "The Doc Ur Block project was a commitment to those principles of humanization by providing young people an education that prepares them to analyze their world critically. It put tools of critical thinking, research, and intellectual production in the hands of young people so that they could counter-narrate pathological stories of their families and communities. Along the way, many students discovered that they too had come to believe the dominant discourse about their community and had lost sight of the countless indicators of hope and strength that are present on their blocks every day" (Duncan-Andrade & Morrell, 2009, p. 147).

CONCLUSIONS

The examples we have provided are evidence of some of the successes that can be achieved in countering successful factories of failure, of promoting school persistence, and reversing the tsunami of student dropouts. All of these examples are the products of individual's efforts; the real results of work by teachers and staff who are leading a revolution in education (Ladson-Billings, 1994). These individuals are bucking social and political forces that act to perpetuate the dropouts; and their work is nothing shy of courageous. As we witnessed in *The Wire,* standing in front of a class of urban youth and chanting "I am lovable and capable" is an exercise in pretending to make the changes that real love can bring (Freire, 1970). Perpetuating absurd, trite, trivial, and outdated practices maintains the hegemony of the dominant culture upon a failed community and its main socializing institution: the school.

Resisting hegemony, schools can produce a counter-narrative to the forces trying to perpetuate student failure (as success). Although the story was typically Hollywood, the portrayal of Erin Gruell's struggle to transform her students through her own metamorphosis is absolutely on point (*Freedom Writers,* 2006). Many urban sites are centered in 'the war,' and winning these battles begins with the courage to transform one's self into a warrior's character much like heroine Erin Gruell: to fail and to come back; to risk defeat and to refuse to accept losing; to persist and not to yield! This is the circle of courage required to answer the question: Urban dropouts: Why persist? This is what the pedagogy of love means.

REFERENCES

Alexander, K., Entwisle, D., & Horsey, C. (1997). From first grade forward: Early foundations of high school dropout. *Sociology of Education, 70,* 87–107.

Banks, J.A., & Banks, C.A.M. (1989). (Eds). *Multicultural education: Issues and perspectives.* Boston: Allyn and Bacon.

Beachum, F. & McCray, C. (2008). Dealing with cultural collision in urban schools. In G. Goodman (Ed.) *Educational psychology: An application of critical constructivism.* New York: Peter Lang Publishing.

Beachum, F. D., & Obiakor, F. E. (2005). Educational leadership in   urban schools. In F. E. Obiakor & F. D. Beachum (Eds.), *Urban education for the 21ˢᵗ century: Research, issues, and perspectives* (pp. 83–99). Springfield, IL: Charles C. Thomas.

Brendtro, L., Brokenleg, M., Van Bockern, S. (2002). *Reclaiming youth at risk: Our hope for the future.* Bloomington, Indiana: National Educational Service.

Bourdieu, P. (1993). *The field of cultural reproduction.* New York: Columbia University Press.

Carnevale, A.P., & Desrochers, D.M. (2003). *Standards for what? The economic of K-16 reform.* Princeton, NJ: Educational Testing Service.

Coley, R. (1995). *Dreams deferred: High school dropouts in the United States.* Princeton, NJ: Educational Testing Services.

Comer, J. P. (1980). *School Power: Implications of an intervention project.* New York: The Free Press.

Cotton, K. (2001). *New small learning communities: Findings from recent literature.* Portland, OR: Northwest Regional Educational Laboratory.

Cross, B.E. (2003). Learning or unlearning racism: How urban teachers transfer teacher education curriculum to classroom practices. *Theory into Practice.* 42(3), p. 203–209

Darling-Hammond, L. (2002). Redesigning schools: What matters and what works. Stanford, CA: School Redesign Network at Stanford University. Retrieved from http://www.schoolredesign.net

Eben, J. (2006). *How many wins have YOU had today?* Clovis, CA: Garden of Eben Press.

Educational Projects in Education. (EPE). (2006). Ohio graduation report. *Education Week.* Retrieved from http://www.edweek.org/ew/toc/2006/06/22/index.html

Diller, D. (1999). Opening the dialogue: Using culture as a tool in teaching young African American children." *Reading Teacher, 52,* p. 820–27.

Duncan-Andrade, J. (2008). Your best friend or worst enemy: Youth popular culture, pedagogy, and curriculum in urban classrooms. In G. Goodman (ed.), *Educational Psychology: An Application of Critical Constructivism* (pp. 113–143). New York: Peter Lang Publishing.

Duncan-Andrade, J. & Morrell, Ernesto (2009). *The art of critical pedagogy: Possibilities for moving from theory to practice in urban schools.* New York: Peter Lang Publishing.

Dyson, M. E. (2005). *Is Bill Cosby right? Or has the Black middle class lost its mind?* New York: Basic Civitas Books.

Freire, P. (1970). *Pedagogy of the oppressed.* New York: Continuum.

Goldenberg, I. I., Kunz, D., Hamburger, M., Stevenson, J. M. (2003). Urban Education: Connections Between Research, Propaganda & Prevailing Views of Education. *Education, 123*(3), 628–634.

Goodman, G.S. (2007). *Reducing hate crimes and violence among American youth: Creating transformational agency through critical praxis.* New York: Peter Lang Publishing.

Goodman, G.S. & Carey, K.T. (2004). *Ubiquitous assessment: Evaluation techniques for the new millennium.* New York: Peter Lang.

Gladden, R. (1998). The small school movement: A review of the literature. In M. Fine & J. Sommerville (Eds.), *Small schools, big imaginations: A creative look at public schools* (pp. 113–133). Chicago: Cross City Campaign for Urban School Reform.

Greater Baltimore State of the Region Report. (2007). Greater Baltimore Committee: Retrieved June 15, 2009, from http://www.gbc.org/reports/GBCSOR2007.pdf

Greene, J., and Forster, G. (2003). *Public High School Graduation and College Readiness Rates in the United States.* Manhattan Institute for Policy Research.

Grossberg, L. (1994). Bringin' it all back home—Pedagogy and cultural studies. In H. Giroux & P. McLaren (eds.), *Between Borders: pedagogy and the politics of cultural studies.* New York: Routledge. Youth Popular Culture and Curriculum, 335.

Gruel, E. (2006). *Freedom writers: How a teacher and 150 teens used writing to change themeselves and the world around them.* New York: Broadway Books.

Hancock, S. D. (2006). White women's work: On the front lines of urban education. In J. Landsman & C. W. Lewis (Eds.), *White teachers/diverse classrooms: A guide to building inclusive schools, promoting high expectations, and eliminating racism* (pp. 93–109). Sterling, VA: Stylus.

High school dropout crisis continues in U.S., study says. (2009). CNN.com: Retrieved June 18, 2009, from http://www.cnn.com/2009/US/05/05/dropout.rate.study/index.html

Kitwana, B. (2002). *The hip-hop generation: Young blacks and the crisis in African American culture.* New York: Basic Civitas Books.

Knesting, K. (2008). Students at risk for school dropout: Supporting their persistence. *Preventing School Failure, 52* (4). Retrieved June 3, 2009 from ERIC EBSCO.

Kunjufu, J. (2002). *Black students—Middle class teachers.* Chicago: African American Images.

Ladson-Billings, G. (1994). *The dreamkeepers: Successful teachers of African American children.* San Francisco, Calif.: Jossey-Bass, 1994.

Leaving schools behind: When students drop out. (2004). University of Minnesota: Retrieved June 16, 2009, from http://education.umn.edu/research/ResearchWorks/checkconnect.html

Malloy, C.E., & Malloy, W.M. (1998). Issues of culture in mathematics teaching and learning. *The Urban Review, 30,* pp. 245–57.

McCray, C. R., Wright, J. V., & Beachum, F. D. (2007). Social justice in educational leadership: Using Critical Race Theory to unmask African American principal placement. *Journal of Instructional Psychology, 34*(4), 247–255.

McKinsey & Company (2009, April). *The economic impact of the achievement gap in America's schools.* New York: Author.

National Center for Education Statistics. (2006). *Status and Trends in the Education of Racial and Ethnic Minorities.* Retrieved: 07/10/2009 http://nces.ed.gov/pubs2007/minoritytrends/

Neufeld, S. (2006, June). Schools challenge report: Journal says city graduates 38.5 percent of students; Only Detroit fared poorer. *The Baltimore Sun.* Retrieved June 12, 2009, from http://www.redorbit.com/news/education/551340/schools_challenge_r eport_journal_says_city_graduates_385_percent_of/index.html

Patterson, N.C., Beltyukova, S.A., Berman, K., & Francis, A. (2007). The making of sophomores: Student, parent, and teacher reactions in the context of systematic urban high school reform. In *Urban Education,* Volume 42 (2). Downloaded from http://uex.sagepub.com. Retrieved on May 24, 2009 at York College of Pennsylvania.

Pascopella, A. (2003, November). Drop Out. *District Administration, 38*(11), 32–36.

Raywid, M. (1999). *Current literature on small schools.* Retrieved from http://www.ael.org/eric/digests/edorc988.htm.

Rist, R. (1973). *The urban school: A factory for failure.* Cambridge, MA: MIT Press.

Wacquant, L. (2000). The new 'peculiar institution': On the prison as surrogate ghetto. *Theoretical Criminology, 4*(3), 377–389.

West, C. (2008). *Hope on a tightrope: Words and wisdom.* Carlsbad, CA: Hay House, Inc. White, J. L. & Cones III, J. H. (1999). *Black man emerging: Facing the past and seizing a future in America.* New York: W. H. Freeman and Company.

Wilson, W. J. (2009). *More than just race: Being Black and poor in the inner city.* New York: W.W. Norton & Company.

SECTION TWELVE
Matters of Assessment

FORTY-THREE

Test Anxiety: Contemporary Theories and Implications for Learning

Jerrell C. Cassady

Few constructs in psychology and education have broader accessibility to students than test anxiety. We all encounter a measured response to evaluative situations that can be characterized as tense, uneasy, disquieted, nervous, fearful, and simply anxious. As a researcher with interest in this field, I frequently ask my undergraduate students if they experience test anxiety. In an average semester, I will receive a response somewhere in the range of 70% self-diagnosed test-anxious learners. Naturally, they are correct—they do have an anxious reaction to tests. These feelings of apprehension and concern over test anxiety are appropriate. Research on test anxiety has demonstrated negative correlations with IQ in math, statistics, reading, foreign language, science, and psychology courses; study skills and abilities; coping procedures in learning events; admittance into advanced programs; problem-solving skills; and basic memory processes (see Hembree, 1988, for meta-analysis).

However, most of these students do not have a conception of the pervasive and detrimental role test anxiety plays in the educational and academic experiences of a sizable portion of the population. More systematic examinations of the prevalence of test anxiety place estimates closer to the 25%–40% of the population, with higher rates of prevalence for racial minorities and females (Carter, Williams, & Silverman; 2008; Ergene, 2003; McDonald, 2001; Putwain, 2007). However, these estimations are difficult to validate given the absence of a clinical diagnosis and the select sampling that often occurs in test anxiety research (e.g., undergraduate student populations). While we are not entirely clear on how many people reliably *have* test anxiety, there is wide consensus that females have a higher degree of test anxiety than males (Hembree, 1988), but the higher rates of test anxiety have been shown to be unrelated to their ability levels (Cassady & Johnson, 2002). Rather, as with other forms of academic anxiety (e.g., Britner, 2009; Jameson, 2009), the heightened test anxiety appears to be a function of greater emotional responsiveness in general, or perhaps stereotype threat (see Osborne, Tillman, & Holland, 2009).

The field of test anxiety has a long history—and has recently seen a resurgence in interest connected to recent trends in high-stakes testing (Ryan & Brown, 2005; Whitaker Sena, Lowe, & Lee, 2007) as well as intentional connections to broader models of emotional control, coping, and self-regulation (Stowell, Tumminaro, & Attarwala, 2008; Zeidner & Matthews, 2005). This chapter attempts to provide both historical and contemporary guidance to address the role of test anxiety in academic settings.

In essence, three primary trends in test anxiety will be explored. First, I will summarize the evidence that confirms there is variance in both the degree and type of test anxiousness that may assault a learner and influence performance. Second, test anxiety is not an isolated event that occurs during an exam period; it permeates all phases of the learning-testing cycle in various ways. Finally, the perpetual absence of consensus on overcoming test anxiety successfully is likely driven by wide variations in these forms of test anxiety that are commonly overlooked in research studies.

TYPES OF TEST ANXIETY

Several conceptualizations for test anxiety have been offered over the past 50 years. However, only a few have stood the test of time and served to guide research and intervention attempts. Historically, the view of representing test anxiety has moved predictably from models of context-specific anxieties and personality traits to more contemporary views that adopt a process framework or systems approach (see Zeidner & Matthews, 2005).

STATE VS. TRAIT ANXIETY

Initially, the challenge for test anxiety researchers was to identify that there was indeed a distinct anxiety relevant for tests alone rather than merely general anxiety that was elevated during evaluations. In a sophisticated and compelling model built upon 20 years of research, Spielberger and Vagg (1995) outlined a transactional process model that relied on trait and state anxiety interacting with the contextually specific occurrence of tests to produce the condition of test anxiety. In this model, the individual's trait anxiety level predicted a predisposition to view evaluative situations as threatening, and when the test situation arose, the state of anxiety would also be activated, leading the child to a negative emotional response.

Zohar (1998) proposed a similar additive model of test anxiety, where the impact of test anxiety was an "additive function" of the person's level of trait anxiety and situational factors relevant to each assessment event (e.g., low self-confidence for the content, high-stakes testing event). Kurosawa and Harackiewicz (1995) demonstrated support for this additive feature, with the evidence that the state and trait components were detrimental to the cognitive processes of the learner in a collective fashion.

Naturally, the student's perception or appraisal of the test in question is a primary determinant in the level of test anxiety that will be encountered in this orientation. My research on perceived test threat has repeatedly confirmed that the students who report high levels of test anxiety across multiple tests also have high ratings of perceived test threat for specific tests and adopt a hopelessness attribution to future testing events (Cassady, 2001; Cassady, 2004b; Cassady & Gridley, 2005). Davis, DiStefano, and Schutz (2008) extended the knowledge base on test perceptions, identifying five common test appraisal patterns in undergraduate students that influence their views of tests, approaches to test preparation, and emotional regulation during testing events.

This parsimonious view of test anxiety has the appeal of connecting test anxiety to potential for anxiousness in other contexts, which explains the common correlations among various forms of individual anxieties. In addition, this view of test anxiety allows greater translation of research to findings relating various types of anxiety to models of motivation, emotional control, and self-regulation. However, most researchers in the field of test anxiety tend to isolate the construct given the consistent variance noted between test anxiety and other forms of anxiety (Zeidner & Matthews, 2005).

EMOTIONALITY VS. WORRY

The earliest work on test anxiety per se came from the pioneer in this field, Irwin Sarason. Sarason's (1961) classic work provided both conceptual and psychometric guidance to the field that persisted for decades. In his initial work on test anxiety, he proposed that test anxiety could be effectively measured with a unidimensional scale of testing anxiety. However, he did acknowledge that the manifestation of test anxiety could arise in two forms: "heightened physiological activity" and "self-deprecating ruminations" (Sarason, 1961, pp. 201–202). This classification scheme took hold in the research, and the two domains were named "emotionality" and "worry" in subsequent work by Liebert and Morris (1967), a guiding distinction that rightly differentiated the two primary manifestations forecast by Sarason.

Emotionality

The emotionality aspect of test anxiety is generally referred to as physiological reactions to stressful or evaluative events. These reactions tend to include (a) galvanic skin response, (b) elevated heart rates, (c) dizziness, (d) nausea, (e) feelings of panic, or (f) disruptions to sleep/rest (Deffenbacher, 1980; Hembree, 1988; Morris, Davis, & Hutchings, 1981). Sarason (1984; Sarason, Pierce, & Sarason, 1996) provided a more fine-grained analysis of the emotionality factor, claiming that there were two distinct forms of emotional responses to tests—tension and bodily symptoms—however that distinction has not been universally maintained and evidence using Sarason's (1984) four-factor Reactions to Tests scale failed to replicate the differentiation of two dimensions of emotionality (Kalechstein, Hocevar, Zimmer, & Kalechstein, 1989).

The emotionality component of test anxiety has traditionally been shown to have a lesser impact on performance as compared to worry (Bandalos, Yates, & Thorndike-Christ, 1995; Williams, 1991). However, it is a pervasive and disconcerting aspect of test anxiety that can drive subsequently higher rates of worry because of drawing the learner's attention away from relevant test preparation and performance matters and focusing upon the manifestations of anxiety (Cassady, 2004b; Deffenbacher, 1980; Hembree, 1988).

Worry

The worry component proposed in the 1960s has been given more attention in most test anxiety studies due to the consistent finding that the worry component is tied to performance deficits while the emotionality construct is not (Hembree, 1988; Zeidner & Matthews, 2005). Classic manifestations of worry include (a) making comparisons to other learners, (b) worrying over the potential of failing, (c) reduced self-confidence and self-efficacy, (d) fixation on the testing event, (e) reporting a feeling of underpreparedness (which tends to be exacerbated during the test session when the first few items are difficult), (f) losing self-worth or esteem within the peer group, and (g) engaging in avoidance thoughts during both the test preparation and test performance periods (Cassady, 2004b; Deffenbacher, 1980; Depreeuw, 1984; Hembree, 1988; Morris et al., 1981).

This broad array of cognitive issues captured within the worry component has led some to adopt more inclusive language. My work has focused primarily on the dimension I call "cognitive test anxiety" (Cassady & Johnson, 2002), which has been similarly applied in other forms of evaluation anxiety (Zeidner & Matthews, 2005). While the term is updated and differs from that proposed by Liebert and Morris, the underlying anxious responses are essentially the same—or at a minimum consistent with their orientation.

ZEIDNER'S TYPOLOGY FOR TEST-ANXIOUS LEARNERS

The most comprehensive exploration of types of test anxiety and the relations with other forms of anxiety has been compiled over the past ten years by Moshe Zeidner (1998; see also Zeidner & Matthews, 2005). Zeidner has demonstrated that the various forms of anxiety tend to correlate—leading some researchers to assume that test anxiety is a mere context-specific form of generalized anxiety—but that the correlations are weak enough to identify that the constructs are distinct in some fashion. This representation of test anxiety is a fundamental advancement in the theory and research in the field because we are able to differentiate between the "types" of test anxiety students encounter—which sets the field ahead such that we can begin to identify why certain types of interventions work with specific individuals and not with others who have "test anxiety" (see Hembree, 1988; Naveh-Benjamin, McKeachie, & Lin, 1987). Zeidner's six types of test anxiety are summarized below, with corroborating research provided to illustrate the widespread support afforded to this conceptualization.

Study or Testing Skill Deficiencies

Moshe Naveh-Benjamin (1991) has provided a strong account of an information-processing perspective for test anxiety that illustrates that the relationship between test anxiety and performance is explained—for many students—by the inability of students with test anxiety to effectively comprehend, organize, and recall the core content in question (Naveh-Benjamin et al., 1987). Research with students in contrived tasks that reduce or eliminate the presence of salient evaluative pressure has consistently demonstrated students with high test anxiety have difficulty with recall or recognition tasks for studied materials (Benjamin, McKeachie, Lin, & Holinger, 1981; Cassady, 2004a; Mueller, 1980; Naveh-Benjamin, 1991; Tobias, 1986). These pervasive failures highlight the reality that test anxiety can influence a learner's experience with content at all phases in the learning-testing cycle (Cassady, 2004b) and that the failure for the testing situation need not be due to an emotional response to the testing content but is merely an indication of underlying cognitive failures to acquire, store, and organize content in an effective way. Alternatively, researchers have proposed that test anxiety is a reactive response once the learner encounters a testing situation and recognizes that s/he is insufficiently prepared for the exam due to subpar study practices (Desiderato & Koskinen, 1969; McKeachie, 1984).

The study skills of test-anxious students have been an area of considerable investigation. It has long been known that test-anxious learners are more prone to procrastination (Cassady & Johnson, 2002; Kalechstein et al., 1989), take less informative notes from course lectures and readings (Cassady, 2004b), engage in more repetition study strategies as opposed to elaborative strategies (Wittmaier, 1972), and are prone to more surface-level representations of content (Naveh-Benjamin et al., 1987). Curiously, the research on test anxiety continues to support work by Culler and Holohan (1980) that demonstrated that high-test anxious students studied more hours per week than those without test anxiety. When examining the relation to performance, among those students with test anxiety alone, study time was positively linked to performance. When compared to the non-anxious peers who studied more efficiently, the test-anxious students were outperformed regardless of time devoted to studying (Culler and Holohan).

Anxiety Blockage and Retrieval Failure

In the classic view of test anxiety held by many, test anxiety is a problem during the testing session itself. Presumably, the learners have mastered the content, but when confronted with the test threat, they have an anxious reaction that interferes with their performance. This anxiety blockage phenomenon is therefore a failure at the retrieval phase of information processing (Covington, 2000; Zeidner & Matthews, 2005). That is, the learner has effectively encoded and stored the target information, but in the face of a threatening evaluative setting, the information is not available to the learner. This is a clear distinction from the study skills deficit model, because content is firmly entrenched in long-term memory, but the learner is incapable of retrieving it during the testing context due to debilitating or interfering contextual anxiety (Benjamin et al., 1981; McKeachie, 1984; Mueller, 1980; Onwuegbuzie & Daley, 1996).

Covington and Omelich (1987) explored this hypothesis, putting to the test the common claim that "I knew it cold before the exam." The results of that study provided support—anxiety blockage was present in a subset of individuals. In particular, anxiety blockage was noted as a factor for high-test anxious learners who possessed genuinely good study skills on test items that were considered "easy" in the manner that they did not require extensive critical thinking or cognitive embellishments to arrive at the correct answer.

Explanations for this phenomenon generally converge on the belief that anxiety arising in the test situation prompts interference, distraction, and inefficient cue utilization strategies (Cassady & Johnson, 2002; Geen, 1980; Sarason, 1986; Schwarzer & Jerusalem, 1992). Regarding cue utilization, the learner is actually hypothesized to have a difficulty in restricting the range of cues necessary to answer the questions on a test. When this occurs, the searching process through long-term memory becomes unduly cumbersome and bound to failure (Cassady & Johnson, 2002; Easterbrook, 1959). Naveh-Benjamin (1991) also proposed that test-takers are likely to show loss for those content topics for which they have less elaborate and complete representations for the information (such as may occur when "cramming" for a test). The condition is exacerbated for learners during tests when they begin to perceive the test as threatening—the students begin to lose confidence in their knowledge base, and continue to question the accuracy of the responses they have offered (Bar-Tal, Raviv, & Spitzer, 1999), a situation that becomes particularly salient in multiple-choice tests with distracters that "look good." This is one reason that a common suggestion for test-anxious learners is to work from their strengths during a testing situation—that is, when encountering a test and finding the first few items are difficult or unknown to the learner, a common strategy is to skip those items so they can build confidence and overcome the cyclical process of self-doubt and anxiety arousal.

Failure-acceptance

Several motivational models exist to explain why some test-takers simply believe they cannot succeed and do not make any effort to change their pattern of failure, ranging from social influences to internal beliefs about ability (e.g., Schunk, 1999). Zeidner and Matthews (2005) liken these attitudes and behaviors to learned helplessness, which Cassady (2004b) identified as a common orientation when examining test performance attributions for the test-anxious learners. Learned helplessness manifests in students who have a history of testing failures and recognize that any collection of strategies employed before have been fruitless, leading to "giving up" on test preparation. Perhaps the most reticent of the test-anxious learners, these individuals may very well be able to overcome their performance deficits with effort but have resigned themselves to failure already.

Failure-avoidance

A dramatically different set of goals are established by learners who are failure-avoidant (Dweck, 1986; Elliot & McGregor, 1999; Schunk, 1990). Students who strive to avoid failure will generally set personal achievement motivation goals that have a lower level of difficulty. Setting goals to be easier to attain helps stave off the specter of failure—even if the achievement in question is not impressive or does not advance the individual. Learners with this orientation will frequently avoid challenging tasks in favor of simplistic activities because failing will lead to a negative self-appraisal and detrimentally impact self-efficacy and self-esteem (Lay, Edwards, Parker, & Endler, 1989).

Self-handicapping

Self-handicapping is a relatively new manifestation for test-anxious learners and is closely aligned with the failure-avoidance construct. The self-handicapper is working to preserve his or her self-concept or self-worth (Covington, 2000), and will identify reasons and explanations for failure for specific evaluative situations that can place "blame" on anything other than personal ability, which is commonly under public scrutiny (Midgley, Arunkumar, & Urdan, 1996; Urdan, 2004). While many self-handicapping test-anxious learners will actively avoid studying through procrastination (Cassady & Johnson, 2002; Wolters, 2003), test-anxious learners also use their test anxiety as the handicap. That is, reporting that their test failure is due to the fact that they have test anxiety provides the learner with a ready explanation for failure that does not lead to an undue negative impact on self-worth (Thomas & Gadbois, 2007; Zeidner & Matthews, 2005).

Perfectionism

In contrast to failure-avoidant learners, perfectionists set excessively high personal achievement goals (Frost, Marten, Lahart, & Rosenblate, 2005). In addition, these students subject themselves to overly harsh and critical self-evaluations of achievement and performance, which contributes to both anxious and depressive tendencies for perfectionists (Kawamura, Hunt,

Frost, & DiBartolo, 2001). The perfectionist test-anxious students also strive to build order and organization to their academic work (Covington, 1992) and tries "to avoid errors and failure through an endless cycle of self-defeating overstriving" (Zeidner & Matthews, 2005, p. 146). Like other categories of test-anxious students, there is no clear exit from the self-deprecating process that influences their perceptions and behaviors across the learning-testing cycle. Curiously, even in the face of performance that many students would be pleased with, the perfectionist learner will maintain a state of anxiety over exams because nothing is ever "good enough" in their own estimation (Covington, 2000; Matthews & Zeidner, 2005).

TEST ANXIETY AND THE LEARNING-TESTING CYCLE

The classic views of test anxiety were dominated by strong research supporting cognitive interference views of testing conditions that demonstrated that interfering thoughts, deficient working memory strategies, and retrieval barriers during the testing situation were driving the performance deficits observed for those with high test anxiety (Ikeda, Iwanaga & Seiwa, 1996; Sarason, 1986; Sarason et al., 1996). However, progressively researchers in the field have adopted more process-oriented views of test anxiety that recognize that there are test-anxious beliefs and behaviors that manifest differentially across three phases of the "Learning-Testing Cycle" (Cassady, 2004b). These three phases are defined in relation to the target-evaluative scenario and include test preparation (also referred to as forethought), test performance, and test reflection (Schutz & Davis, 2000; Zeidner, 1998). Covington (1985) provided an initial process model in this line of inquiry that highlighted that the final phase (test reflection) naturally flows into the next forthcoming evaluative event's test preparation phase—making test anxiety ever-present in the academic arena.

TEST PREPARATION PHASE

As outlined in Zeidner's typology, a sizable portion of test-anxious individuals have primary difficulty in merely accessing, encoding, organizing, and effectively storing material (Naveh-Benjamin, 1991). Similarly, test-anxious learners commonly have deficient study skills that interfere with their abilities to successfully prepare for exams (Culler & Holohan, 1980). To summarize the various characterizations for the impact of test anxiety during the test preparation, the research can be partitioned into test-anxious learners common beliefs, abilities, and behaviors related to test preparation.

Test Preparation Phase Beliefs

The standard orientation toward the test that individuals with high-test anxiety encounter is one of a perceived threat (Cassady, 2004b). This threat appraisal is conjured from the interpretation of the evaluative session as posing potential harm to the student's academic standing, self-esteem, or peer status (Lay, Edwards, Parker, & Endler, 1989; Schwarzer & Jerusalem, 1992). This view of the test as an agent of negative impact is heightened for learners with low self-efficacy (Bandalos, Yates, & Thorndike-Christ, 1995), in academic content areas that are complex in general (Everson, Tobias, Hartman, & Gourgey, 1993), or in situations where the student merely identifies no potential for control over the situation (Davis et al., 2008). The comparative peer group within the evaluative setting has also been shown to influence the perception of threat for students in gifted classes, consistent with the threats to self-concept encountered for students in these situations (Goetz, Preckel, Zeidner, & Schleyer, 2008). However, this comparative analysis with the peer group's likely performance level has been shown to be specific to the cultural context of the learning group. Specifically, although test-anxious students in the U.S. have been shown to devote considerable attention to worrying over their peers' abilities and performances, research with students in Kuwait (Cassady, Mohammed, & Mathieu, 2004) and Argentina (Furlan, Cassady, & Perez, 2009) have demonstrated that these comparisons simply are not universal.

It is this intersection of self-efficacy, motivation, and perceived test threat that sparks the learner on the process of emotional and cognitive preparation for the exam and underlies the attentional focus, goal structures, metacognitive strategies, and eventual behavioral output during the test preparation phase (McGregor & Elliot, 2002; Smith, Sinclair & Chapman, 2002; Vasey, El-hag, & Daleiden, 1996; Wolters, 2003; also see Fletcher & Cassady, 2009). Therefore, interventions targeting the appraisal of testing events are anticipated to have a sizable influence on positively influencing test-anxious learners' preparatory responses to the testing event. Helping students adopt views that are focused more on mastery-oriented goals and recognizing the testing event in the framework of a challenge rather than a threat can help the learner recast the impending evaluative episode as a more manageable undertaking (Davis et al., 2008; McGregor & Elliot, 2002). With this adjusted interpretation of the evaluative event, the learner has a greater chance of developing a goal structure and coping process that actively targets successful test preparation strategies (see Fletcher & Cassady, 2009, for example).

Test Preparation Phase Abilities and Behaviors

The negative outcomes connected to test anxiety during the test preparation phase follow naturally from behaviors students engage in prior to their exams. Failure to study effectively (for whatever reason) will inevitably lead to reduced content knowledge and conceptual understanding and lack of eventual success in test situations. As reviewed before, test-anxious learners in the test preparation phase have been shown to have lower levels of working memory capacity for verbal learning materials (Ikeda et al., 1996), incomplete cognitive representations for target content (Cassady, 2004a; Naveh-Benjamin et al., 1987), inefficient study skills and strategies (Cassady, 2004b; Wittmaier, 1972), and are prone to procrastinate over tests as a task-avoidant coping process (Cassady & Johnson, 2002; Wolters, 2003).

When both the behaviors and abilities of the learner in the preparation phase are challenged, the combined effect is understandably worsened. For instance, this is particularly evident for students in universities during the final exam period. As our research demonstrated, students with procrastination tendencies and test-anxious responses were particularly impacted during the final exam phase—we presume that the significantly greater decline in test performance for that period was a function of the inability to regulate the poor study behaviors for multiple assessments during a short period of time (Cassady & Johnson, 2002). While test-anxious students are bound to procrastinate over tests and assignments in general, they generally encounter only limited performance decrements because they can generally put in a large amount of study or work in a "cramming" session (Milgram, Dangour, & Raviv, 1992; Rothblum, Soloman, & Murakami, 1986). It is during the final examination period, when the average student may have to prepare for 4 exams in a 3–4 day period that these last-minute efforts begin to break down because poor time management interferes with multiple test preparation needs.

As Zeidner (1998; Zeidner & Matthews, 2005) summarized, failure by students in this test preparation phase is not isolated to one form of test-anxious manifestation. That is, there is no single manner by which test anxiety interferes with success of students during this phase of the learning-testing cycle. Some students will engage in avoidance behaviors (based on a fear of failure perspective) while others will actively attempt to prepare for the test—but may employ strategies that are not useful (e.g., surface-level note taking; Cassady, 2004b) or have insufficient cognitive skills to manage the content (Naveh-Benjamin, 1991). Regardless of the form of faulty test preparation behavior, failure to navigate the test preparation phase successfully will result in subsequent failure in the test performance phase, influencing both beliefs and behaviors once again.

TEST PERFORMANCE PHASE

During the test session itself, students with test anxiety encounter differential experiences that typically lead to lower performance or at least a considerably more stressful event. Traditional work in test anxiety has effectively documented the collection of cognitive and emotional responses during this phase that interfere with success.

Test Performance Phase Beliefs

The perception of tests as threatening held during the test preparation phase carries into the test performance phase as well (Cassady, 2004b), particularly at the beginning of an assessment period (Meijer & Oostdam, 2007). This initial rush of test anxiousness has been proposed to prompt skewed early judgments of test difficulty, personal readiness to perform, emotional responses to the testing event, and foster self-doubt (Sarason, 1986; Schutz & Davis, 2000). Another set of beliefs that students can develop is an appraisal that they are insufficiently prepared for the test event, which can arise in response to perceived insufficient poor preparation strategies (Desiderato & Koskinen, 1969; McKeachie, 1984) or unrealistically high expectations as seen in perfectionists (Kawamura et al., 2001).

It is important to recognize that individuals with test anxiety can react differentially to testing events that have varied perceived threats to the learner. That is, our appraisal of the threat in the testing situation *at hand* provides a significant influence to our final level of anxiety (Fletcher and Cassady, 2009). Zohar (1998) demonstrated this effect in support of an additive model for test anxiety, revealing that specific expectations for isolated exam performance levels influenced the overall level of test anxiety experienced for three different subtests on a college entrance exam. Thus, learners do not have a set level of test anxiety that functions in all situations—their appraisals for each testing situation dictates the level of experienced test anxiety. Individuals form differential appraisals for a variety of testing conditions, including item format (e.g., multiple choice *vs.* open ended; Birenbaum & Feldman, 1998), delivery format (e.g., online *vs.* paper; Cassady & Gridley, 2005), or perceived importance to future school or career placement (Putwain, 2009).

Test Performance Phase Abilities and Behaviors

During the test session itself, students are faced with the burden of balancing the interfering stimuli generated by the content of the test, the stress imposed by the test event, and their emotional responses to both. During the session, examinees with test anxiety may face a variety of difficulties impairing performance including: (a) attentional biases toward threatening stimuli in the evaluative session (Vasey et al., 1996), (b) comprehending written content required to answer items (Cassady, 2004a; Ikeda et al., 1996; Naveh-Benjamin, 1991), (c) marshaling cognitive resources with effective self-regulating and coping processes to stay focused on the task at hand (Eysenck & Calvo, 1992; Sarason, 1986), or (d) effectively accessing relevant and established retrieval cues (Cassady & Johnson, 2002; Easterbrook, 1959; Zeidner, 1998). Conversely, students with effective coping mechanisms can stave off the negative influence of test anxiety on academic performance through effective emotional and cognitive regulation (Fletcher & Cassady, 2009; Hembree, 1988; Zeidner, 1998). Onwuegbuzie and Daley (1996) demonstrated that these examination-taking coping strategies were particularly effective in supporting performance on timed tests, which appear to activate the highest levels of perceived threat for examinees.

TEST REFLECTION PHASE

The test reflection phase is often overlooked due to the indirect manner in which it influences actual test performance and function. Although there is no temporal point of transition where the learner has clearly moved from the reflection phase to the next exam's preparation phase, there is a clear distinction in the types of beliefs and behaviors that occur in the phases. The direction of projection seems to shift between the two phases—although they are obviously intimately intertwined. Specifically, during the test reflection phase, the beliefs and behaviors that are enacted tend to be a process of taking information gleaned from a recent evaluative session and developing beliefs about the self (internalizing external cues). Conversely, during the test preparation phase these established beliefs about our abilities are used to dictate our interpretations of the events as threatening or challenging.

Test Reflection Phase Beliefs

Once the test has been completed, the test reflection phase commences and test appraisals are activated. In response to the exam, test takers develop an attribution for their level of performance (positive or negative) with examinees with high-test anxiety prone to develop more externalized attributions for successful test completion (e.g., "I was lucky"; "the test was easy") and attributing failure to internal constructs such as ability or testing skill (Bandalos et al., 1995). This phase sets the stage for continued self-doubt of ability to perform or validation of a student's view that she has test anxiety and that makes her incapable of performing (Covington, 1985). Over time, learners with test anxiety who repeatedly fail to achieve their goals also demonstrate a pervasive presence of perceived helplessness (Cassady, 2004b; Schwarzer & Jerusalem, 1992).

As Zeidner and Matthews (2005) summarized, attributional differences formed in this test reflection phase among test-anxious learners can account for wide variation in the experience of test anxiety and the behaviors and beliefs that are likely to follow. For instance, self-worth-protecting students will offset responsibility for failed evaluative events (Thompson, Davidson, & Barber, 1995), generating a failure-avoidant motivation perspective. For these students, subsequent testing situations are likely to be met with indifference, avoidance, and a perspective that no level of effort could be successful in overcoming failure (because the locus of failure is external; Covington, 2000). Unfortunately, learners tend to overestimate how much time was spent and how effective their study tactics for a given test were—which can easily lead to an inaccurate attribution of test performance related to their test preparation strategies from earlier assessments and subsequent abandonment of strategies that were merely not used enough or properly (Winne & Jamieson-Noel, 2002). Conversely, perfectionists will internalize perceived failings and develop even more self-critical views of self and ability (Kawamura et al., 2001).

Elliot and McGregor (1999) demonstrated the importance of recognizing the interplay among achievement motivation, goal structure, and test-anxious responses and attributions within a broader evaluative situation. It is during the test reflection phase that these attributions are developed, strengthened, or tested explicitly—and can easily lead to the establishment of more firmly entrenched test behaviors and beliefs in subsequent evaluative situations. Interestingly, students with high levels of procrastination (and an appraisal that the procrastination affected their performance) are more likely to "promise themselves" that their actions will be different next time (Lay et al., 1989)—illustrating that the foundation for future motivations and behaviors is reviewed in this phase (even when those promises to self are unlikely to be carried through).

Test Reflection Phase Abilities and Behaviors

In the test reflection phase, students with test anxiety exhibit similar behaviors related to upcoming tests as noted in the preparation phase, each type of test-anxious learner developing a set of behaviors that balances the need to appear personally competent and their actual performance. Behaviors in this phase are directly related to the motivational set and types of learning goals that the learner tends to adopt (i.e., task-approach, task-avoidance, mastery; Eccles & Wigfield, 2002). These established goal orientations will determine the likelihood of instigating processes of ego-preservation, self-handicapping, and academic disengagement (Bandalos, Finney, & Geske, 2003; McGregor & Elliot, 2002; Smith et al., 2002).

MANAGING TEST ANXIETY

The literature on test anxiety repeatedly demonstrates that there are no universally effective strategies to support learners with a meaningful correction to the feelings or influences of test anxiety. Originally, this was a puzzling and frustrating trend leading to erroneous conclusions about the nature of test anxiety interventions (Hembree, 1988). However, as Zeidner and Matthews (2005) highlight, this trend has largely been due to the insensitivity in our identification of types of test anxiety.

Promoting learners' abilities to form more proactive goals and motivation structures centered on meeting the task at hand (successfully completing the test) rather than focused upon the stressful aspects of the evaluative situation ("what happens if I fail?") will help both the learner and her support network to build a personalized intervention strategy to meet the challenge. This process is best addressed within a process that accounts for both the cognitive challenges imposed by drawing resources from the task at hand and emotional management skills that will help the learner diffuse the mounting evaluative stress. In previous writing, Kathryn Flether and I outline models of coping, self-regulation, and emotional information processing that are proposed to assist in identifying the point at which a learner is experiencing a problem with developing these positive goal structures or interpretations of testing events. In those models, helping learners to recognize the limited threats imposed by a testing event—or isolating strategies that can promote the likelihood of success in such testing events—can promote their ability to successfully manage their beliefs about the tests and their behaviors as they prepare for, engage in, or reflect upon testing situations.

Regardless of the form of test anxiety that a learner is challenged with, the success of intervention efforts will be based upon the match of that intervention with the actual barrier to success. Matching study skills training to those individuals with reasonable interpretations of the threat imposed by tests but with poor study skills is an effective application (Naveh-Benjamin, 1991). However, when a student has effective study skills, the focus needs to be on the appraisal of the test challenge and personal efficacy. Furthermore, attending to the threats to cognitive and emotional regulation posed by testing events in all three phases of the learning-testing cycle will further support effective resolution of anxiety. We must help students recognize that their pre-evaluative beliefs and behaviors are as detrimental to their final performance levels as the during-test thoughts and behaviors. In this way, they can apply emotional regulation controls that we have trained to students to employ during tests for decades (Hembree, 1988) during the study phase as well to support successful performance on the upcoming test.

REFERENCES

Bandalos, D.L., Finney, S.J., & Geske, J.A. (2003). A model of statistics performance based on achievement goal theory. *Journal of Educational Psychology, 95,* 604–616.

Bandalos, D. L., Yates, K., & Thorndike-Christ, T. (1995). Effects of math self-concept, perceived self-efficacy, and attributions for failure and success on test anxiety. *Journal of Educational Psychology, 87,* 611–623.

Bar-Tal, Y., Raviv, A., & Spitzer, A. (1999). The need and ability to achieve cognitive structuring: Individual differences that moderate the effect of stress on information processing. *Journal of Personality and Social Psychology, 77,* 33–51.

Benjamin, M., McKeachie, W. J., Lin, Y., & Holinger, D. P. (1981). Test anxiety: Deficits in information processing. *Journal of Educational Psychology, 73,* 816–824.

Birenbaum, M., & Feldman, R.A. (1998). Relationships between learning patterns and attitudes towards two assessment formats. *Educational Research, 40,* 90–98.

Britner, S.L. (2009). Science anxiety: Relationship to achievement, self-efficacy, and pedagogical factors. In J.C. Cassady (Ed.), *Anxiety in schools: The causes, consequences, and solutions for academic anxieties* (pp. 80-95). New York: Peter Lang Publishing.

Carter, R., Williams, S., & Silverman, W.K. (2008). Cognitive and emotional facets of test anxiety in African American school children. *Cognition and Emotion, 22,* 539–551.

Cassady, J. C. (2001). The stability of undergraduate students' cognitive test anxiety levels. *Practical Assessment, Research & Evaluation, 7(20).* Available online: http://PAREonline.net/getvn.asp?v=7&n=20.

Cassady, J. C. (2004a). The impact of cognitive test anxiety on text comprehension and recall in the absence of salient evaluative pressure. *Applied Cognitive Psychology, 18(3),* 311–325.

Cassady, J. C. (2004b). The influence of cognitive test anxiety across the learning-testing cycle. *Learning and Instruction, 14(6),* 569–592.

Cassady, J. C. & Gridley, B. E. (2005). The effects of online formative and summative assessment on test anxiety and performance. *Journal of Technology, Learning, & Assessment 4(1).* Available online: http://www.jtla.org

Cassady, J.C., & Johnson, R.E. (2002). Cognitive test anxiety and academic performance. *Contemporary Educational Psychology, 27,* 270–295.

Cassady, J.C., Mohammed, A., & Mathieu, L. (2004). Cross-cultural differences in test anxiety: Women in Kuwait and the United States. *Journal of Cross-Cultural Psychology, 35(6),* 715–718.

Covington, M. V. (1985). Test anxiety: Causes and effects over time. In H. M. van der Ploeg, R. Schwarzer, & C. D. Spielberger (Eds.), *Advances in test anxiety research* (Vol. 4; pp. 55–68). Lisse, The Netherlands: Swets & Zeitlinger.

Covington, M. (2000). Goal theory, motivation, and school achievement: An integrative review. *Annual Review of Psychology, 70,* 141–156.

Covington, M.V., & Omelich, C.L. (1987). "I knew it cold before the exam": A test of the anxiety-blockage hypothesis. *Journal of Educational Psychology, 79,* 393–400.

Culler, R.E., & Holohan, C.J. (1980). Test anxiety and academic performance: The effects of study-related behaviors. *Journal of Educational Psychology, 72,* 16–26.

Davis, H.A., DiStefano, C., & Schutz, P.A. (2008). Identifying patterns of appraising tests in first-year college students: Implications for anxiety and emotion regulation during test taking. *Journal of Educational Psychology, 100,* 942–960.

Deffenbacher, J. L. (1980). Worry and emotionality in test anxiety. In I. G. Sarason, (Ed.) *Test anxiety: Theory, research, and applications* (pp. 111–124). Hillsdale, NJ: Lawrence Erlbaum.

Depreeuw, E. A. M. (1984). A profile of the test-anxious student. *International Review of Applied Psychology, 33,* 221–232.

Desiderato, O., & Koskinen, P. (1969). Anxiety, study habits, and academic achievement. *Journal of Counseling Psychology, 16,* 162–165.

Dweck, C.S. (1986). Motivational processes affecting learning. *American Psychologist, 41,* 1040–1048.

Easterbrook, J. A. (1959). The effect of emotion and cue utilization and the organization of behavior. *Psychological Reports, 66,* 183–201.

Eccles, J.S., & Wigfield, A. (2002). Motivation beliefs, values, and goals. *Annual Review of Psychology, 53,* 109–132.

Elliot, A. J., & McGregor, H. A. (1999). Test anxiety and the hierarchical model of approach and avoidance achievement motivation. *Journal of Personality and Social Psychology, 76*(4), 628–644.

Ergene, T., (2003). Effective interventions on test anxiety reduction: Meta-analysis. *School Psychology International, 24,* 313–328.

Everson, H.T., Tobias, S., Hartman, H., & Gourgey, A. (1993). Test anxiety and the curriculum: The subject matters. *Anxiety, Stress, and Coping, 6,* 1–8.

Eysenck, M. W., & Calvo, M. G. (1992). Anxiety and performance: The processing efficiency theory. *Cognition and Emotion, 6,* 409–434.

Fletcher, K.L., & Cassady, J.C. (2009). Overcoming academic anxieties: Promoting effective coping and self-regulation strategies. In J.C. Cassady (Ed.), A*nxiety in schools: The causes, consequences, and solutions for academic anxieties* (pp.177-200). New York: Peter Lang Publishing.

Frost, R.O., Marten, P., Lahart, C., & Rosenblate, R. (2005). The dimensions of perfectionism. *Cognitive Therapy and Research, 14(5),* 449–468.

Furlan, L.A., Cassady, J.C., & Perez, E.R. (2009). Adapting the cognitive test anxiety scale for use with Argentinean university students. *International Journal of Testing, 9(1),* 3–19.

Geen, R. G. (1980). Test anxiety and cue utilization. In I. G. Sarason (Ed.), *Test anxiety: Theory, research, and applications* (pp. 43–61). Hillsdale, NJ: Lawrence Erlbaum.

Goetz, T., Preckel, F., Zeidner, M., & Schleyer, E. (2008). Big fish in big ponds: A multilevel analysis of test anxiety and achievement in special gifted classes. *Anxiety, Stress, and Coping, 21(2),* 185–198.

Hembree, R. (1988). Correlates, causes, and treatment of test anxiety. *Review of Educational Research, 58,* 47–77.

Ikeda, M., Iwanaga, M., & Seiwa, H. (1996). Test anxiety and working memory system. *Perceptual and Motor Skills, 82,* 1223–1231.

Jameson, M.M. (2009). Math anxiety: Theoretical perspectives on potential influences and outcomes. In J.C. Cassady (Ed) *Anxiety in schools: The causes, consequences, and solutions for academic anxieties* (pp 50-64). New York: Peter Lang Publishing.

Kalechstein, P., Hocevar, D., Zimmer, J. W., & Kalechstein, M. (1989). Procrastination over test preparation and test anxiety. In R. Schwarzer, H. M. van der Ploeg, & G. D. Spielberger, (Eds.) *Advances in test anxiety research* (Vol. 6; pp. 63–76). Lisse, The Netherlands: Swets & Zeitlinger.

Kawamura, K.Y., Hunt, S.L., Frost, R.O., & DiBartolo, P.M. (2001). Perfectionism, anxiety, and depression: Are the relationships independent? *Cognitive Therapy and Research, 25,* 291–301.

Kurosawa, K., & Harackiewicz, J. M. (1995). Test anxiety, self-awareness, and cognitive interference: A process analysis. *Journal of Personality, 63,* 931–951.

Lay, C. H., Edwards, J. M., Parker, J. D. A., & Endler, N. A. (1989). An assessment of appraisal, anxiety, coping, and procrastination during an examination period. *European Journal of Personality, 3,* 195–208.

Liebert, R. M., & Morris, L. W. (1967). Cognitive and emotional components of test anxiety: A distinction and some initial data. *Psychological Reports, 20,* 975–978.

McDonald, A.S. (2001). The prevalence and effects of test anxiety in school children. *Educational Psychology, 21,* 89–101.

McGregor, H.A., & Elliot, A.J. (2002). Achievement goals as predictors of achievement-relevant processes prior to task engagement. *Journal of Educational Psychology, 94,* 381–395.

McKeachie, W. J. (1984). Does anxiety disrupt information processing or does poor information processing lead to anxiety? *International Review of Applied Psychology, 33,* 187–203.

Meijer, J., & Oostdam, R. (2007). Test anxiety and intelligence testing: A closer examination of the stage-fright hypothesis and the influence of stressful instruction. *Anxiety, Stress, and Coping, 20(1),* 77–91.

Midgley, C., Arunkumar, R., & Urdan, T.C. (1996). "If I don't do well tomorrow, there's a reason": Predictors of adolescents' use of academic self-handicapping strategies. *Journal of Educational Psychology, 88(3),* 423–434.

Milgram, N. A., Dangour, W., & Raviv, A. (1992). Situational and personal determinants of academic procrastination. *The Journal of General Psychology, 119,* 123–133.

Morris, L. W., Davis, M. A., & Hutchings, C. H. (1981). Cognitive and emotional components of anxiety: Literature review and a revised worry-emotionality scale. *Journal of Educational Psychology, 73,* 541–555.

Mueller, J. H. (1980). Test anxiety and the encoding and retrieval of information. In I. G. Sarason, (Ed.) *Test anxiety: Theory, research, and applications* (pp. 63–86). Hillsdale, NJ: Lawrence Erlbaum.

Naveh-Benjamin, M. (1991). A comparison of training programs intended for different types of test-anxious students: Further support for an information-processing model. *Journal of Educational Psychology, 83,* 134–139.

Naveh-Benjamin, M., McKeachie, W. J., & Lin, Y. (1987). Two types of test-anxious students: Support for an information processing model. *Journal of Educational Psychology, 79,* 131–136.

Onwuegbuzie, A.J., & Daley, C.E. (1996). The relative contributions of examination-taking coping strategies and study coping strategies to test anxiety: A concurrent analysis. *Cognitive Therapy and Research, 20(3),* 287–303.

Osborne, J.W., Tillman, D., & Holland, A. (2009). Stereotype threat and anxiety for disadvantaged minorities and women. In J.C. Cassady (Ed.), *Anxiety in schools: The causes, consequences, and solutions for academic anxieties* (pp 119-136).New York: Peter Lang Publishing.

Putwain, D.W. (2007). Test anxiety in UK schoolchildren: Prevalence and demographic patterns. *British Journal of Educational Psychology, 77,* 579–593.

Putwain, D.W. (2009). Situated and contextual features of test anxiety in UK adolescent students. *School Psychology International, 30,* 56–74.

Rothblum, E. D., Solomon, L. J., & Murakami, J. (1986). Affective, cognitive, and behavioral differences between high and low procrastinators. *Journal of Counseling Psychology, 33,* 387–394.

Ryan, R.M., & Brown, K.W. (2005). Legislating competence: High-stakes testing policies and their relations with psychological theories and research. In A.J. Elliot & C.S. Dweck (Eds.) *Handbook of competence and motivation* (pp. 354–372). New York: Guilford Press.

Sarason, I. G. (1961). Test anxiety and the intellectual performance of college students. *Journal of Educational Psychology, 52,* 201–206.

Sarason, I. G. (1984). Stress, anxiety, and cognitive interference: Reactions to tests. *Journal of Personality and Social Psychology, 46,* 929–938.

Sarason, I. G. (1986). Test anxiety, worry, and cognitive interference. In R. Schwarzer (Ed.), *Self-related cognitions in anxiety and motivation* (pp. 19–34). Hillsdale, NJ: Lawrence Erlbaum.

Sarason, I. G., Pierce, G. R., & Sarason, B. R. (1996). Domains of cognitive interference. In I. G. Sarason, G. R. Pierce, & B. R. Sarason (Eds.) *Cognitive interference: Theories, methods, and findings* (pp. 139–152). Mahwah, NJ: Erlbaum.

Schunk, D.H. (1990). Goal setting and self-efficacy during self-regulated learning. *Educational Psychologist, 26,* 207–231.

Schunk, D.H. (1999). Social-self interaction and human behavior. *Educational Psychologist, 34,* 219–227.

Schutz, P.A., & Davis, H.A. (2000). Emotions and self-regulation during test taking. *Educational Psychologist, 35,* 243–256.

Schwarzer, R. & Jerusalem, M. (1992). Advances in anxiety theory: A cognitive process approach. In K. A. Hagtvet & T. B. Johnsen (Eds.) *Advances in test anxiety research* (Vol. 7, pp. 2–31). Lisse, The Netherlands: Swets & Zeitlinger.

Smith, L., Sinclair, K.E., & Chapman, E.S. (2002). Students' goals, self-efficacy, self-handicapping, and negative affective responses: An Australian senior school student study. *Contemporary Educational Psychology, 27,* 471–485.

Solomon, L. J., & Rothblum, E. D. (1984). Academic procrastination: Frequency and cognitive behavioral correlates. *Journal of Counseling Psychology, 31,* 503–509.

Spielberger, C.D., & Vagg, P.R. (1995). Test anxiety: A transactional process model. In C.D. Spielberger & P.R. Vagg (Eds.) *Test anxiety: Theory, assessment, and treatment* (pp. 3–14). Washington, D.C.: Taylor & Francis.

Stowell, J.R., Tumminaro, T., & Attarwala, M. (2008). Moderating effects of coping on the relationships between test anxiety and negative mood. *Stress and Health, 24,* 313–321.

Thomas, C.R., & Gadbois, S.A. (2007). Academic self-handicapping: The role of self-concept clarity and students' learning strategies. *British Journal of Educational Psychology, 77,* 101–119.

Thompson, T., Davidson, J.A., & Barber, J.G. (1995). Self-worth protection in achievement motivation: Performance effects and attributional behavior. *Journal of Educational Psychology, 87,* 598–610.

Tobias, S. (1986). Anxiety and cognitive processing of instruction. In R. Schwarzer (Ed.) *Self-related cognitions in anxiety and motivation* (pp. 35–54). Hillsdale, NJ: Erlbaum.

Urdan, T. (2004). Predictors of academic self-handicapping and achievement: Examining achievement goals, classroom goal structures, and culture. *Journal of Educational Psychology, 96(2),* 251–264.

Vasey, M.W., El-Hag, N., & Daleiden, E.L. (1996). Anxiety and the processing of emotionally threatening stimuli: Distinctive patterns of selective attention among high- and low-test-anxious children. *Child Development, 67,* 1173–1185.

Whitaker Sena, J.D., Lowe, P.A., & Lee, S.W. (2007). Significant predictors of test anxiety among students with and without learning disabilities. *Journal of Learning Disabilities, 40,* 360–376.

Williams, J. E. (1991). Modeling test anxiety, self concept and high school students' academic achievement. *Journal of Research and Development in Education, 25,* 51–57.

Winne, P.H., & Jamieson-Noel, D. (2002). Exploring students' calibration of self reports about study tactics and achievement. *Contemporary Educational Psychology, 27,* 551–572.

Wittmaier, B. C. (1972). Test anxiety and study habits. *The Journal of Educational Research, 65,* 352–354.

Wolters, C.A. (2003). Understanding procrastination from a self-regulated learning perspective. *Journal of Educational Psychology, 95,* 179–187.

Zeidner, M. (1998). *Test anxiety: The state of the art.* New York: Plenum Press.

Zeidner, M., & Matthews, G. (2005). Evaluation anxiety: Current theory and research. In A.J. Elliot & C.S. Dweck (Eds.) *Handbook of competence and motivation* (pp. 141–163). New York: Guilford Press.

Zohar, D. (1998). An additive model of test anxiety: Role of exam-specific expectations. *Journal of Educational Psychology, 90,* 330–340.

FORTY-FOUR

Paying Attention and Assessing Achievement: Assessment and Evaluation: Positive Applications for the Classroom

Karen T. Carey

Are children making academic achievement? Are we competitive with other countries? Does anyone know what we are doing in our schools? Questions continue to arise about how our children are doing despite the Federal Government's No Child Left Behind Act (2002).

How do we know if anyone is progressing in any academic area? How do you know when you have *learned* something? How do I know if you have learned something? Most of us demonstrate what we have learned. Our actions show what we know, our character, and our views about the world. However, we are rarely evaluated academically by our actions and how we function in our day-to-day activities. Progress is generally assessed in schools through standardized, objective multiple choice item testing, and in actuality these tests tell us very little about the student, the classroom, or the learning that has taken place.

HISTORY

During the middle 1800s the state superintendent of instruction in Massachusetts required the assessment of students' skills through written examinations to hold schools accountable (Linn & Gronlund, 2000). Other districts around the country also began to assess students, and following World War I schools began using multiple choice tests to assess students in academic areas. Following World War II the assessment of students in schools became accepted practice in most districts around the country. In 1983, *A Nation at Risk: The Imperative for Educational Reform* was published by the National Commission on Excellence in Education. Several recommendations for the use of tests to enhance students' educational achievement were made by the Commission. *A Nation at Risk* (1983) also advocated further educational overhauls including the certification of a student's credentials, the identification of the need for remedial intervention, and provisions for the opportunity to complete advanced work. The report enticed many to action with concerns about where students in the United States ranked in comparison to other countries and the need for schools districts to demonstrate that all students were learning and progressing. All of this political dialogue resulted in a heightened interest in accountability.

In 2002, the federal government passed the No Child Left Behind (NCLB) Act (2002) requiring each state to develop "world class" standards for children in the third through eighth grades. NCLB was to help all children, especially those from impoverished backgrounds and to close the achievement gap between the highest and lowest academic performers. To meet the letter of the law, each state developed assessment measures aligned with the state's curriculum to meet specific standards. NCLB further mandated that educators assess all students in grades three to eight annually. Because they are conducted on a massive scale, the traditional multiple-choice format was selected as the most cost-efficient way to meet the letter of the law. Should schools and/or districts not meet their annual goals set forth by the state as outlined in NCLB, monies are withheld from those sites, and remediations are put in place for the teachers at those schools (No Child Left Behind, 2002). Today, every school district includes some form of traditional standardized assessment of students, and many also now require their seniors to pass high school exit exams in order to graduate.

Although many good arguments are offered defending school improvement through assessments, there are many critics of this approach to school reform and improvement (Goodman & Carey, 2004). Assessment is a necessary and critical ingredient for student success, but is standardized assessment and punishment for underperformance the answer? According to Apple (2006) the characteristics of NCLB "include a massive centralization of control, a loss of local autonomy, and a redefinition of what counts as good or bad education that is simply reduced to scores on problematic tests of achievement" (p. 25). Perhaps there are better ways to find out how your students are learning and what you need to know to teach them better.

As mentioned above, states are required to develop specific standards, and many have gone as far as to identify the specific curriculum to be used at every grade level. Unfortunately, only in rare instances do the assessment tools selected by the states to be used at the end of year match the curriculum used by classroom teachers. This results in deleterious consequences for students when there is no match between what is taught and what is tested. The only way students' can actually do well on such standardized assessments is if teachers prepare students for these specific tests or if the students possessed the cultural capital to do well on these measures of reading and generally accepted knowledge. Cultural capital is defined as family background, vocabulary, opportunity, and experience (Bourdieu, 1993). But no matter what we think may be assessed, only if the tests and the curriculum are well aligned can teachers be sure that students will be tested on what they have been taught.

Another problem with standardized group tests is that such tests do not allow for any kind of changes in instruction or informed decision-making by teachers. They are "one-shot" evaluations that result in students potentially being stigmatized and teachers made to suffer whatever consequences the politicians and state agencies deem to be necessary. Such assessments tell us little about how students learn, what they need to learn, and the best way to teach students the skills they will need for the future. In order to understand the problem more fully, a brief review of some of the most common group standardized tests follows below.

STANDARDIZED GROUP TESTS

The most common standardized group tests currently in use are the California Achievement Tests (CAT), the Iowa Tests of Basic Skills (ITBS), the Metropolitan Achievement Tests (MAT), and the Stanford Achievement Tests (SAT). Despite millions of dollars spent and thousands of hours invested to create unbiased and fair assessments, there are significant problems and deficiencies with all of these tests. Because your students will be taking these tests, it is important to note that many of the negative consequences of these assessments are related to the test instruments themselves, not the teaching that goes on within your school.

The California Achievement Test, Form 6 (CAT6), also known as the Terra-Nova Second Edition (CTB/McGraw-Hill, 2002), includes subtests in reading/language arts, mathematics, science, social studies, word analysis, vocabulary, language mechanics, spelling, and mathematics computation. There are 13 levels of the test, one for each grade kindergarten through twelve. The test was normed on over 264,000 children during fall and spring standardizations and includes students identified as eligible for special education. The problem with the CAT6 is that there is minimal evidence of any type of validity and no evidence of test-retest or alternate form reliability. A further criticism of this assessment tool is that it does not align with California's state standards for instruction even though it bears California's name and by implication implies it relates to instruction in that state (Bell, 2002; CVERC, 2002). For many reasons the use of this test in schools to assess the overall achievement of students must be viewed with extreme caution.

The Iowa Tests of Basic Skills (ITBS) (Hoover, Dunbar, & Frisbie, 2001) consist of ten levels for students in grades kindergarten through eight and were normed in 2000. Subtests include vocabulary, word analysis, reading comprehension, listening, language, mathematics, social studies, science and sources of information for students in grades kindergarten through third, and vocabulary, reading comprehension, spelling, capitalization, punctuation, usage and expression, math concepts and estimation, math problem solving and data interpretation, math computation, social studies, science, maps and diagrams, and reference questions for students from grades three to eight.

Additional standardized achievement tests such as the Tests of Achievement and Proficiency (TAP) (Scannell, 1996) and the Iowa Tests of Educational Development (ITED) (Forsyth, Ansley, Feldt, & Alnot, 2001) are available for students in grades 9–12. Subtests for the TAP include vocabulary, reading comprehension, written expression, math concepts and problem solving, math computation, social studies, science, information processing. The ITED tests vocabulary, reading comprehension, spelling, language: revising written materials, math concepts and problem solving, math computation, analysis of social studies materials, analysis of science materials and sources of information. The TAP was constructed in 1992 and is primarily a norm-referenced test, while the ITED was standardized in 2000 and is a norm-referenced and curriculum referenced test. The ITBS and ITED were normed on approximately 180,000 students. The construct and criterion validity of these tests are lacking and there is no test-retest reliability reported. In sum, the use of these tests must be questioned when technical adequacy is so poor.

The Metropolitan Achievement Tests, Eighth Edition (MAT8) (Harcourt Educational Measurement, 2002) consists of 13 levels from kindergarten through twelfth grades. Subtests include sounds and print, reading vocabulary, reading comprehension, open-ended reading, mathematics, mathematics concepts and problem solving, mathematics computation, open-ended mathematics, language, spelling, open-ended writing, science and social studies. The test was normed on a total of 140,000 students during fall and spring standardizations in the 1999–2000 academic year. Again, as with the other tests discussed, content and construct validity are insufficient for evaluating student progress. Further reducing the test's value, reliabilities reported for internal consistency and test-retest are too low to be used to make individual decisions about students.

The Stanford Achievement Test, Ninth Edition (Harcourt Brace Educational Measurement, 1996) consists of 13 levels and includes five to 13 subtests at each level. Subtests include sounds and letters, word study skills, word reading, sentence reading, reading vocabulary, reading comprehension, mathematics, mathematics problem solving, mathematics: procedures, language, spelling, study skills, listening to words and stories, listening, environment, science, and social science. The test was normed on approximately 250,000 students. Validity is addressed in the manual, and the authors did go to some lengths to insure the test had strong content and construct validity by having the items reviewed by subject matter experts, people of differing cultures and ethnicities, and teachers involved in the standardization. Reliability is reported for internal consistency and alternate form. However, conclusions concerning individuals based upon results of this assessment need to be viewed with caution.

Of the four tests reviewed, only one appears to have adequate technical adequacy for screening students on academic achievement. However, all of these tests are used by state departments to meet the No Child Left Behind requirements of yearly testing. Without technical adequacy, they tell us virtually nothing. Of gravest concern are the high stakes consequences of such tests upon students and their families, teachers, and schools. Stigmatizing students and penalizing schools based on technically inadequate tests is unethical and unprofessional.

Professional psychometrist's knowledge about good assessment practices has been virtually ignored by the states' school administrators and the federal government's legislative and administrative branches. Large-scale assessments, such as the California Achievement Test, were developed and implemented despite other assessment initiatives that were recommended which, if actually attempted, could benefit students on an individual level. This desire to provide improved outcomes for individual students has led to the more recent developments of performance-based assessments.

APPROPRIATE ASSESSMENT

Performance-based assessments allow us to "observe students while they are performing or we examine the products they create and evaluate the level of proficiency demonstrated" (Stiggins, 2001, p. 184). Students are required to perform some activity rather than simply answering or knowing an answer (Linn & Gronlund, 2000). Other types of assessment have grown from this movement as well, including outcomes-based assessment, authentic assessment, and alternative assessment. Outcomes-based assessments refer to the "products" schools produce in terms of the knowledge and experiences students take with them (Ysseldyke & Thurlow, 1993). Authentic assessment identifies the "knowledge, thinking, problem-solving skills, social skills and attitudes exhibited by those in the community, on the job, or in advanced courses as part of their normal work" (Tombari & Borich, 1999, p. 4). Those skills that are necessary outside of the school setting and are needed in the real world are the abilities and knowledge that are stressed. Alternative assessment may be defined as anything other than the traditional model of multiple-choice and other standardized tests.

The assessment of a student's classroom may be the most important part of any evaluation conducted. Teachers are generally concerned about children in their classrooms because these children are having difficulty in the classroom, not in contrived settings. School professionals hired to assist teachers often fail to take the time to observe students in the classroom, interview teachers, or assess the learning environment. Paying attention and assessing academic achievement require more than multiple choice tests. The best and most appropriate ways to assess achievement are the goal of every successful teacher, and we will now examine a few of these tools.

TEACHER-MADE ASSESSMENTS

Teacher-made evaluations, sometimes referred to as formative assessments, are the most common form of academic measurement and provide the teacher with student outcomes concerning what they have been exposed to in the classroom. To know how students can perform teacher-made assessments should be experiential and use the material actually taught in the classroom. Unfortunately, many teacher-made assessments have no relevance to learning outcomes and often are only given in order for the teacher to issue the students grades. True-false and multiple choice tests still tend to be the methods of choice for classroom assessments and often only one test is given on a particular area of content. Such assessments do not provide teachers with information needed to modify instruction in order that students can succeed, and no information related to a student's daily or weekly progress is obtained. Most importantly, teacher-made assessments have generally not been used with any other group of students, or if they have, the data collected are not analyzed in any way to determine if the scores obtained are meaningful, that is, valid or reliable.

Teacher-made assessments can be improved by insuring (a) the assessments match the content covered in class, (b) the assessment provides an adequate representation of the material covered, and (c) each question measures one or more learning objectives (Braus, Wood, & LeFranc, 1993). In addition, teacher-made assessments should evaluate students' abilities to think critically. Critical thinking is best assessed by using some type of performance-based or experiential assessment. Often, classroom assessments tell how students perform (i.e., based on the grades obtained), but information relative to how students arrive at answers can be lacking. Taking the time to analyze students' responses requires extra time on the part of teachers; however, it may in the long run be far more beneficial in terms of the students' actual attainment of knowledge.

CLASSROOM ASSESSMENT

The review of common standardized group assessments and teacher-made tests, demonstrates over and over again the problems evidenced with such tools. The question then arises, "How can I appropriately assess the students in the classroom?"

In contrast to the great number of standardized tests in use at this time, a number of far more useful methods can be implemented to provide teachers with the information needed to truly make a difference for their students. While alternative assessments take additional effort, when one considers the wasted time and energy that go into evaluating students in the classroom through the use of standardized tests, these techniques more efficiently provide information that can help teachers make informed educational decisions for all of their students.

CONSULTATION WITH OTHER TEACHERS AND PARENTS

One of the first steps in assessing a student's functioning often involves engaging in consultation and assessment with the child's previous teacher, a teacher's aide, their parent, or some other individual. Consultation is a systematic way to guide problem-solving which involves identifying the problem and then developing interventions approaches to rectify the situation. As discussed in the chapter on parents, the role of the child's care-giver is critical in the development and success of each individual. Often we cannot understand the difficulties the child experiences until we hear the story of the child's life from the parent's perspective. This understanding can build compassion for the child's struggles with learning and socialization (Goodman & Carey, 2004).

CLASSROOM OBSERVATIONS

Classrooms should be viewed as ecosystems that provide support for student learning. The interactions between teacher and student and student to students can provide a wealth of information about how the classroom is functioning and whether successful learning can take place. Evidence supporting the value of psycho-social and pro-social conditions within the classroom is voluminous. For example, Hobbs (1966) wrote, "The group is important to the child. When a group is functioning well, it is extremely difficult for an individual child to behave in a disturbed way" (p. 112).

Classroom observations can result in useful information for developing change strategies concerning students. Well-functioning classrooms have teachers who utilize an age-appropriate curriculum and who teach adaptive behavior skills that can help to prevent behavior problems and increase pro-social interactions (Dunlap & Kern, 1996; Nordquist & Twardosz, 1990). Highly functioning and experienced classroom teachers can assess students as they engage curriculum in a natural environment. In this sensitive setting, any change for individual students may affect other childrens' and teachers' behaviors. Thus, teachers and others need ways to evaluate what is happening in the classroom setting, and the most effective technique is the use of structured observations.

The best method of evaluation for developing effective interventions is to carefully assess your students to obtain usable data by planning, conducting, and using classroom observations. Using structured observations based on carefully developed problem-solving, the teacher can assist in the identification of selected specific behaviors to observe and help create appropriate interventions. The emotional distancing of the teacher as observer enhances the teacher's objectivity and improves the validity of the intervention.

Teachers need to develop good observation skills. They need to be objective, collect data, and be able to analyze observation data to determine exactly what is occurring in the classroom. When conducting classroom observations, the teacher must decide what to evaluate in the natural environment of the classroom. The best practice is to attempt sampling of behaviors across several classes or units and different days. For many students, time of day is also an important aspect to explore. Some behaviors only occur at certain times of the day, for example, right before lunch. This information can only be obtained through an individualized problem-solving strategy, making sure observations are conducted at specific times. Observing throughout a class period or unit at selected times addresses the teacher's decision related to when to observe. Selecting time checks as observation units require that the 1) sessions must be equivalent in opportunities for the occurrence or nonoccurrence of behavior; and 2) conditions must be the same for all observation periods (Cooper, Heron, & Heward, 1987). From the consultation session, teachers can get an idea of the usual time periods for activities, making it possible to have comparable sessions. Finally, it is important to select an adequate observation length. Behaviors that do not occur often may require longer time periods; behaviors that occur more often may require shorter time periods. Sample behaviors from the observations must be representative and accurate.

Many teachers have developed simple ways of observing without taking away from instructional time. In some cases, students can monitor their own behavior by keeping track of how many problems they complete, how many words they can read, or how often they engage in disruptive behavior. Teachers can "count" behaviors by transferring tokens or pegs or some other small item from one pocket to another or use small note cards in their pockets to record occurrences of events.

METHODS FOR OBSERVING AND RECORDING BEHAVIOR

Observation includes "recording the stream of behavior, dividing it into units, and analyzing the units" (Wright, 1967, p. 10). The observation should be a "detailed, sequential, narrative account of behavior and its immediate environmental context as seen by skilled observers" (Wright, 1967, p. 32). Observations need to be guided by specific questions related to the environment, instruction, behaviors, skills, and tasks (Wolery, 1989). There are several useful ways to observe behavior in the classroom. Oftentimes observers conduct so-called observations by simply writing down everything they see (or think they see) and developing impressions about a student's behavior. Conducting observations in this manner is haphazard and subject to bias and incomplete information (Linn & Gronlund, 2000). In order to get an accurate picture of a student's behavior in the classroom, whether it be academic or social-emotional, we must collect objective data on the problem behavior identified during our consultation.

REAL-TIME OBSERVATIONS

The natural environment allows for on-going observations to be conducted as the behavior actually occurs. If the teacher is unable to record these events, a teacher aide or other adult may be able to make the recordings. Barnett and Carey (1992) recommended that preliminary observations be done using real-time observations to select those behavior and environmental features that are important to note and may add to our understanding of the behavior identified during consultation.

Real-time observations focus on the child's situation (including actions of peers and teachers toward the child) as well as specific child behavior. The procedure shown in Figure 1 requires the teacher or other observer to record the exact times of the beginning and ending of behavior. Activity changes are recorded by time notations, and arrows are used for the observer to note the the appropriateness (↑) and / or inappropriateness (↓)of the child's behavior. Each line of the observation protocol should include only one unit of behavior, and each behavior should be mutually exclusive (one activity is recorded) and exhaustive (all time is accounted for) (Sackett, 1978; Suen & Ary, 1989). Time notations can be made at prespecified intervals such as one minute (Wright, 1967), two minutes (Bijou and colleagues, 1969), or a variation (Barnett & Carey, 1992).

Data derived from real-time observations include:

1. Frequency or Event recording. Frequency equals the number of times behavior occurs in an observation session. Frequency can be useful for describing aggressive behaviors, time on task, or transition times.
2. Rate of Occurrence. Rate of occurrence is the frequency of behavior divided by the length of the observation session. Using the rate of occurrence allows for comparisons of frequency across sessions of different lengths, providing us with measures of reliability and validity. This is useful when our time is limited but we need to make comparisons across different days, again to insure reliability.

Figure 1: An Example Of Real-Time Recording

Setting: Special Day Class for Emotionally Disturbed Students
Time: 8:15–8:35 Child: D

8:15   D. enters classroom and tosses book bag on table. Walks to get chair from stack for his desk. Takes chair back to his desk.

8:16   D. sits down and then runs to the classroom door, shouting for S. Teacher intervenes and attempts to get D. back to his seat

8:17   D. agrees to go back to his seat and as soon as he is seated he runs to the door again and starts shouting for S. Teacher intervenes and asks D. to come with him to the office space in the classroom.

8:19   D. and Teacher go to the office space in the classroom and the Teacher asks, "What is going on, D.?" D. states that he "saw S. earlier but that S. said he wasn't coming to class today."

8:21   Teacher says for "D. not to worry about S., that he would find out what is going on, but that D. needs to get back to his desk and get to work." D agrees and leaves the office area.

8:22 D. returns to his desk, opens his backpack and removes a notebook and a pencil. Other students in the class are working on writing in journals. D. takes out his journal and begins completing the assignment.

8:24 S. enters the room and D. jumps up to greet him. D. states "I thought you weren't coming today." "I thought I would have a good day but now you're here. How am I supposed to get any work done with you here?"

8:25 D. begins to scream at S., telling him he hates him and that he is ruining everything for D. D. hits S.

8:26 Teacher and aide tell D. to not hit S. but D. continues.

8:27 Teacher and aide tell D. again to calm down and D. begins to move away from S. toward the Teacher. Teacher tells D. three times to stay calm which D. does.

8:29 D. moves closer to the Teacher and when he is about three feet away says to the teacher, "I am really sorry, I don't know what happened." Teacher tells D. he must apologize to S.

8:30 D. tells S. that he is sorry and hopes they can still be friends. S. says he is sorry too about telling D. he wouldn't be in class. Teacher encourages them to shake hands and they do.

8:32 Teacher directs D. back to his desk to continue working on his journal. D. follows the Teacher's directions, returns to his seat and begins working.

8:34 D. continues working quietly.

Frequency: D. engaged in inappropriate behavior five times and appropriate behavior nine times.

Two episodes of shouting.

Two episodes of hitting.

Rate of Occurrence: 2 D. engaged in yelling behavior.

Bout duration: For hitting—lasted for two minutes

Prevalence: Four bouts of behavior.

3. Bout duration. Bout (one occurrence of behavior) duration is the length of time the behavior occurs. Bout duration can be useful for recording states of behavior (tantrum), on-task behavior (paying attention during instruction), or activity engagement (such as art instruction).

4. Prevalence. Prevalence is the proportion of time a bout is found within an observation session. Bout durations are totaled and divided by the session length (expressed in the same time units) and the result is multiplied by 100. Using prevalence allows us to compare states of behavior, such as paying attention in class, across observation sessions of different lengths.

5. Inter-response time (IRT). IRT is the time between bouts and is calculated by recording the time period from the end of a behavior to the beginning of the next behavior. The mean IRT is calculated by dividing the sum of all IRT durations by the number of non-occurrences of behavior. IRT is useful for setting observation intervals, particularly when only limited time is available for several observations.

ANTECEDENT-BEHAVIOR-CONSEQUENCE ANALYSIS

Antecedent-Behavior-Consequence Analysis or ABC Analysis is a basic strategy for the functional analysis of behavior (Bijou, Peterson, & Ault, 1968). All behavior that we engage in is thought to have a function.

Functional analysis of behavior refers to what function a behavior serves for a student. Antecedents are events that precede a behavior and may increase or decrease the behavior. Consequences can be either reinforcing, punishing, or neutral depending which type is administered. In general, the setting is first described and then observations are recorded on a three-column form (see Figure 2). Similar to Real-Time Observations, a time column is also included.

Figure 2: Antecedent-Behavior-Consequence Analysis

Date: _____

Behavior of Concern: _____

Time: _____

What activities / behaviors / processes were going on before the behavior of concern?_____

What was the behavior of concern? _____

What happened after the behavior was exhibited? _____

FREQUENCY OR EVENT RECORDING

Frequency recording involves simply tallying the number of times a behavior occurs in an observation session. Only behaviors or events that are predefined are recorded. To use this technique successfully, only behaviors of brief and stable durations, such as activity changes, calling out, or aggressive acts can be recorded. There are many ways to record frequencies and events including simply making tally marks on a piece of paper or using counters of some kind.

Duration recording is the recording of the elapsed time for each occurrence of a behavior, and the total duration or the behavior. This method is used when the concern is the length of time a student engages in a specific behavior. For example, when a student is not paying attention during seatwork, duration recording is the method to use to record how long the student does not pay attention. In addition, the latency of the response can be recorded. Latency is the amount of time before beginning a behavior, such as the length of time it takes a student to begin to pay attention (Barnett & Carey, 1992).

OTHER METHODS

Many other methods exist for observing and recording behaviors. These include discrete skill sequences or task analysis where every component required to complete an activity is first recorded and then the student is observed to determine where she/he has difficulty. Another example is category sampling. This technique is used for behaviors that can be categorized, such as on-task behavior. All evidence of on-task behavior is recorded even if it takes different forms. Artifacts of student work are good examples of productivity. Permanent products, which may include work and homework completion, give the teacher and parent a specific point of reference for evaluation of student performance. All teachers should take the time to review actual student work products as they can tell us much about teacher's own expectations and how the student performs relative to her/his peers.

Direct observation of the student's attempts at work completion are also effective means of measurement. Trials to criterion define how many times a "response opportunity" is presented before the student performs the task to a specified criterion (Cooper, Heron, & Heward, 1987, p. 74). In other words how long does it take a student to meet some teacher expectation given the opportunity to do so? Levels of assistance include recording the amount of support a student needs to complete a task or participate with peers. Some students need additional support from teachers and/or peers, and knowing how much support is necessary can provide us with information in terms of how to insure the student gets such support. Probes include structuring tasks in such a way that data can be collected. Oftentimes it is not possible to actually observe the behavior in the real world, and we need to "set up" situations for the behavior to occur in order that we can observe it.

OBSERVING MORE THAN ONE CHILD

Micro-norms refer to the norms accepted in a classroom. This is also referred to as classroom culture. What is acceptable behavior for this classroom? Each teacher sets behavioral expectations and rules differently. Intra-group or whole group observation can be especially useful for teachers observing students coming to their own classrooms the next academic year. Appropriate comparison students (3–4) must be selected, and generally observations are conducted using momentary time sampling, where each student is observed for one interval, before moving on to the next. Each student is observed engaged in a task for preset time period (e.g., 10 seconds). Such data can help us see whether or not the student identified is actually behaving in ways significantly different from her/his peers.

SELF-OBSERVATION

Self-observation is used when we are interested in the emotions and thoughts of a student. Although self-observation can be used to assess overt behaviors, it is best utilized when we want to know if the student is cognizant of her/his behaviors. In order for self-observation to be effective, the student must be able to discriminate the occurrence from the nonoccurrence of a behavior. The results of self-observations must be recorded by the student. Based on the data recorded, the student needs to evaluate him/herself. Generally the student needs to be trained in order to self-observe.

Although several strategies can be used to improve accuracy, students are often not accurate at self-observation. Aids to success include combining self-observation with other strategies used by adults to monitor the student's behavior. Agreement checks can be conducted to improve performance through the surveillance of the teacher. It is important to recognize that complete accuracy is not necessary for the student to derive benefit from self-observation (Kanfer & Gaelick, 1986).

CURRICULUM-BASED ASSESSMENT

Although many of the standardized tools currently used to assess students in the classroom are neither reliable nor valid, a useful tool for developing academic interventions is found in the process of assessing the student with her/his actual curriculum. Assessing the student on what s/he has actually learned provides us with information we can use to change the instruction and see the student make real gains. Curriculum-based assessment allows for continuous, ongoing observations of the student's performance in the classroom setting. By analyzing the student's level of skill development, we can determine the appropriate level of instruction for that particular student in a specified area (Barnett & Carey, 1992).

According to Barnett et al. (1999) "the information gained from curriculum based assessment includes: (1) current level of performance or functioning; (2) rate of learning new skills; (3) strategies necessary to learn new skills; (4) length of time the new skill is retained; (5) generalization of previously taught skills to a new task; (6) observed behaviors that deter learning; (7) environmental conditions needed to learn new skills (individual, group, peer instruction); (8) motivational techniques used to acquire skills; and (9) skills acquisition in relationship to peers" (p. 66). Curriculum-based assessment has been relegated in the past to students in elementary school. However, this assessment tool can be used with any curriculum that is based on developmentally sequenced tasks and ongoing assessment (weekly or more often). For example, at the high school level where computer literacy classes are now required, the curriculum for these classes is based on an appropriate developmental progression. A student's knowledge of computer literacy can be assessed in such classes by conducting brief probes of his/her knowledge. One example would be asking students to find a particular file on the computer (a task that should take no longer than one minute). By gathering information on this task the teacher would know whether or not the student is able to turn on the computer, find the correct program, use the mouse or keyboard in the appropriate way, go to the correct tool bar icon, and locate the file. Should the student break down at any step along the way, the teacher would know exactly when to begin instruction for that student in order to insure the student continues to make progress. By engaging in such activities once, twice or three times a week, students are less likely to fall behind their peers.

In many school districts such assessments are relegated to the use of local norms developed to determine student eligibility for special education. However, that is not what we are referring to here. Curriculum-based assessment should be viewed as a part of the seamless process from assessment to intervention. By continually assessing a student's areas of weakness and changing instruction, we can be assured that we are doing everything possible for the student to make academic, behavioral, and social gains.

SUMMARY

This chapter provides teachers with the basic, necessary tools to begin to engage in ubiquitous assessment: continuous assessment of the functioning of themselves and their students within the classroom (Goodman & Carey, 2004). Daily and continuous assessment means going far beyond the one-test requirement of NCLB. Truly understanding the complexities of the classroom and the methods for assessing what happens in the educational setting can provide the teacher with meaningful assessment data to ensure change and growth for all students.

The primary goal of all teachers is the outcome of learning: both academic and social. It is critical to remember that the student is a whole person. The whole person is one that embodies a mind, body and a spirit. This view allows us to see the student beyond his or her test scores and to see them as personal agents with other people with whom the student interacts within their environment.

Furthermore, every teacher has his or her own, unique way of presenting material, structuring the classroom, and using academic time. Some students benefit from a classroom with lots of activity, group work, and noise; others simply do not. Knowing the students with whom we work through our interactions with them, observations of them in the natural environment, interviewing important persons in their lives, and assessing them regularly in the instructional material to which they have been exposed can provide us with the knowledge we need to make instructional and psycho-social decisions in students' best interests. Paying attention and assessing achievement are two important tools for professional mastery. The ubiquitously aware and "with it" teachers are the one's who achieve the best in student outcomes.

REFERENCES

Achenbach, T. M. (1991). *Manual for the Child Behavior Checklist/4–18*. Burlington, VT: University of Vermont, Department of Psychiatry.

Alessi, G. J., & Kaye, J. H. (1983). *Behavioral assessment for school psychologists*. Washington, DC: National Association of School Psychologists.

Apple, M. W. (2006). *Educating the "right" way: Markets, standards, God, and inequality*. New York: Taylor & Francis Group.

Barnett, D. W., & Carey, K. T. (1992). *Designing interventions for preschool learning and behavior problems*. San Francisco: Jossey-Bass.

Barnett, D. W., Bell, S. H., & Carey, K. T. (1999). *Designing preschool interventions*. New York: Guilford.

Bell, T. (2002). State adopts new school tests. *San Francisco Chronicle*, 26 April, p. A. 1.

Bijou, S. W., Peterson, R. F., & Ault, M. H. (1968). A method to integrate descriptive and experimental field studies at the level of data and empirical concepts. *Journal of Applied Behavior Analysis, 1,* 175–191.

Bijou, S. W., Peterson, R. F., Harris, F. R., Allen, K. E., & Johnson, M. S. (1969). Methodology for experimental studies of young children in natural settings. *Psychological Record, 19,* 177–210.

Bourdieu, P. (1993). *The field of cultural reproduction.* New York: Columbia University Press.

Braus, J. A., Wood, D., & LeFranc, L.E., (1993). *Environmental education in the schools: Creating a program that works.* Peace Corps.

Brown, L, & Hammill, D. (1990). *Behavior Rating Profile* (2nd ed.). Austin, TX: Pro-Ed.

Carey, K. T. (1989*). The treatment utility potential of two methods of assessing stressful relationships in families: A study of practitioner utility.* Unpublished doctoral dissertation, University of Cincinnati.

Central Valley Educational Research Consortium (CVERC) (2002). *What works: Characteristics of high-performing schools in the Central Valley.* Fresno, CA: California State University, Fresno.

Cooper, J. O., Heron, T. E., & Heward, W. L. (1987). *Applied behavior analysis.* Columbus, OH: Merrill. CTB/ McGraw-Hill (2002). *Terra Nova,* Second Edition. Monterey, CA: Author.

Dunlap, G., & Kern, L. (1996). Modifying instruction activities to promote desirable behavior: A conceptual and practical framework. *School Psychology Quarterly, 11,* 297–312.

Forsyth, R. L., Ansley, T., Feldt, L., & Alnot, S. (2001). *Iowa Tests of Educational Achievement.* Chicago: Riverside Publishing Company.

Goodman, G. & Carey, K.T. (2004). *Ubiquitous assessment: Evaluation techniques for the new millennium.* New York: Peter Lang Publishing.

Gutkin, T. B., & Curtis, M. J. (1990). School-based consultation: Theory and techniques. In C. R. Reynolds & T. B. Gutkin (Eds.). *Handbook of school psychology* (pp. 796–828). New York: Wiley.

Harcourt Brace Educational Measurement. (1996). *Stanford Achievement Test, Ninth Edition.* San Antonio, TX: Psychological Corporation.

Harcourt Educational Measurement, Inc. (2002). Metropolitan Achievement Tests, Eighth Edition. San Antonio, TX: Author.

Hartmann, D. P. (1984). Assessment strategies. In D. H. Barlow & M. Hersen (Eds.). *Single case experimental designs: Strategies for studying behavior change* (2nd ed, pp. 107–139). New York: Pergamon.

Hobbs, N. (1966). Helping disturbed children: Psychological and ecological strategies. *American Psychologist, 21,* 1105–1115.

Hoover, H. D., Dunbar, S. B., & Frisbie, D. A. (2001). *Iowa Tests of Basic Skills.* Chicago: Riverside Publishing Company.

Kanfer, F. H. & Gaelick, L. (1986). Self-management methods. In F. H. Kanfer & A. P. Goldstein (Eds.), *Helping people change: A textbook of methods* (3rd ed., pp. 283–245). New York:Pergamon.

Kaufman, A., & Kaufman, N. (1998). *Kaufman Tests of Educational Achievement-Normative Update-Comprehensive form manual.* Circle Pines, MN: American Guidance Service.

Linn, R. L. & Gronlund, N. E. (2000). *Measurement and assessment in teaching* (Eighth edition). Upper Saddle River, New Jersey: Merrill.

Markwardt, F. (1998). *Peabody Individual Achievement Test-Revised- Normative Update.* Circle Pines, MN: American Guidance Service.

National Commission on Excellence in Education (1983). *A nation at risk: The imperative for educational reform.* Washington, DC: U.S. Government Printing Office.

No Child Left Behind (2002). Public Law 107–110, 1st session (January 8).

Nordquist, V. M., & Twardosz, S. (1990). Preventing behavior problemsin early childhood special education classroom through environmental organization. *Education and Treatment of Children, 13,* 274–287.

Peterson, D. R. (1968). *The clinical study of social behavior.* New York: Appleton-Century-Crofts.

Psychological Corporation (2001). *Wechsler Individual Achievement Test,* Second Edition. San Antonio, TX: Author.

Reynolds, C. R., & Kamphaus, R. W. (1992*). Behavior Assessment System for Children.* Circle Pines, MN: American Guidance Service.

Sackett, G. P. (1978). Measurement in observational research. In G. P.

Sackett (Ed.). *Observing behavior: Vol. 2. Data collection and analysis methods* (pp. 25–43). Baltimore: University Park Press.

Salvia, J. & Ysseldyke, J. E. (2004). *Assessment in special and inclusive education* (9th Ed.). Boston: Houghton Mifflin.

Scannell, D. P. (1996). *Tests of Achievement and Proficiency.* Chicago: Riverside Publishing Company.

Shinn, M. R. (1989). *Curriculum-based measurement: Assessing special children.* New York: Guilford.

Stiggins, R. J. (2001). *Student-involved classroom assessment* (3rd Ed.). New Jersey: Merrill Prentice Hall.

Suen, H. K. & Ary, D. (1989). *Analyzing quantitative behavioral observation data.* Hillsdale, NJ: Erlbaum.

Tindall, G. A. & Marston, D. B. (1990). *Classroom-based assessment: Evaluating instructional outcomes.* Columbus, OH: Merrill.

Tombari, M., & Borich, G. (1999). *Authentic assessment in the classroom: Applications and practice.* New Jersey: Merrill Prentice Hall

Vedder-Dobocq, S. (1990). *An investigation of the utility of the Parenting Stress Index for intervention decisions.* Unpublished doctoral dissertation, University of Cincinnati.

Wolery, M. (1989). Using direct observation in assessment. In D. B. Bailey, Jr. & M. Wolery (Eds.). *Assessing infants and preschoolers with handicaps* (pp. 64–96). Columbus, OH: Merrill.

Wright, H. F. (1967). *Recording and analyzing child behavior.* New York: Harper & Row.

Ysseldyke, J. E., & Christenson, S. L. (2002). *Functional assessment of academic behavior: Creating effective learning environments.* Longmont, CO: Sopris West.

Ysseldyke, J. E., & Thurlow, M. L. (1993). *Self-study guide to the development of educational outcomes and indicators.* Minneapolis, MN: National Center on Educational Outcomes, University of Minnesota.

Teaching Educational Psychology & Teaching Teachers

FORTY-FIVE

Learning to Feel Like a Teacher

Kelvin Seifert

PERSONAL IDENTITY FROM WITHIN AND WITHOUT

In this postmodern age, searching for identity has become a risky business. Who am "I," and how do "I" compare to the various "me's" which others (hopefully) notice? Erik Erikson described how individuals gradually become able to answer this question, at least when all goes well (1950/1967)—though as optimistic as he was, even Erikson admitted that developing a *felt* identity was fraught with risk. In Erikson's world, shadowy clouds of "identity diffusion" lingered in the blue skies of self-knowledge, even for the best of us. Others of a psychological bent have echoed his description, often with more detail about the cloudy weather: descriptions are plentiful about factors that frustrate identity development, about how the self as experienced can go wrong even when it *looks* healthy enough (see, for example, Marcia, 1993; Waterman & Archer, 1990). Identity goes right, it seems, in more singular, predictable ways than it goes wrong. So personality psychologists often end up echoing Leo Tolstoy: "Happy families are all alike; every unhappy family is unhappy in its own way" (Tolstoy, 1912). As with families, so with individuals when viewed as examples of identity development: individuals tend to *look* more similar when happy, positive, and successful, than when doubtful, anxious, or unsure. At least that is how they are portrayed.

While we might therefore complain that psychology has not tried hard enough to describe the diversity in positive identity, we could just as easily decide that "identity development" is simply an ambiguous and partial concept. There may be no such thing, or at least nothing very stable, when experienced from within. It may be one thing to look like "I" have my life together, and something else to *feel* that I do. In slightly roundabout ways, psychologists with a postmodern bent may simply be making this distinction and claiming it as a "fact" of life. Kenneth Gergen, for example, has suggested this possibility in describing a "saturated self" (1991). There is no singular, stable "me," he asserts; there are only various "me's" activated in diverse contexts and witnessed by diverse others. I am saturated with identities that I and others call my own. It is not that I am "full of myself," so to speak, but that I am burdened by the confusion of experiencing so many selves. For all practical purposes, when seen by others, I am Person #1 at school, Person #2 at home, Person #3 alone with my spouse or partner, Person #4 with my parents, and so on. Each persona is too complex to be considered a mere role in the conventional sociological sense. We could call the selves "mega-roles," I suppose, except that the name would be awkward and perhaps less accurate than calling them "multiple identities."

Generally, the complexity of my identity is not a problem for others, since each persona is activated in a distinct social context inhabited by a distinct community or group. But the complexity can deeply challenge the one person who not only sees but also experiences *all* of the selves: the individual him/herself, the experiencing "I." How can "I" reconcile the differences and contradictions I witness myself enacting from one situation to the next? Where is the stable autobiography in all of these transformations? "I" would like to believe that the fluidity of my behaviors and roles is mere surface appearance and that a deeper, steadier core lies within if I can just find it—just "identify" with it. As psychoanalysts and even neurologists keep pointing out, finding a transcendent, existentially based identity feels crucial, in spite of my difficulty in naming or describing it (Damasio, 1999). Otherwise "I" feel out of control, empty on the inside, a victim of the changing circumstances that trigger performances of the various "me's."

RECONCILING STABILITY AND FLUX: THE FUTURE TEACHER'S DILEMMA

Imagine, therefore, how teachers-in-training might experience this state of affairs. More than usual, they seek control and stability in their work: classroom management is, without a doubt, their most serious concern about their professional future (MacDonald, 1999; Rosenblum-Lowden, 2000). Will "I" be in charge and keep control well enough in spite of the flux of classroom events? The sheer diversity of children, activities, and daily surprises makes "me" unsure. As a teacher, it looks as if I will have to tailor my actions, behaviors, and roles constantly. I worry about striving to be all things to all people, as they say, and expect to be at least many things to many students. The behavior that I enact prominently with one student may not be what I display prominently with another, even if I value consistency in teaching. Because of the inevitable diversity of students' experiences of me as a teacher, there can easily get to be one student who sees (or "identifies") me as a somewhat angry or stern person, for example, but another student who sees me as a supportive and nurturing person. Still another may come to see me as changeable, or even moody.

The diversity of others' perceptions, responses, and experiences will defy easy to characterization of the teacher who performs them all. But it will most especially challenge the teacher himself or herself, at least if the teacher takes an honest look. Who am "I," I ask myself after seeing me behave so differently with different students and situations? How can the same "I" criticize or even punish one student's behavior, but praise and enjoy another's? How can "I" nearly fail one student's academic effort, but reward another's effort handsomely? At times "I" seem to contradict myself in class; and even when I do not, "I" often seem like an eclectic conglomeration of behaviors, as if I have been guided incoherently by an eclectic internal committee.

On the surface, inconsistencies in the performance of teaching can be interpreted easily: seemingly diverse behaviors are simply expressions of the single role of teaching, not expressions of conflicted personal identity. Distinguishing between the personal and professional allows for radical reinterpretation of anomalous behaviors and a consequent rescue of the image of "my" self—meaning both the impressions that I make on others and, more importantly my felt, lived experience of who "I" am. Just as a soldier who shoots at an enemy need not consider himself a murderer, so a teacher who (for example) scolds a student need not think of herself as a cruel person. That, at least, is what we are told by social convention, and that is what is often assumed in third-person descriptions of professional identity(ies). As long as I distinguish the personal from the professional, "I" am not an uncaring person even if I sometimes reprimand a student, nor am I inconsistent or conflicted if I reprimand one student but praise another, nor uncommitted if I take less time with one student than with another. I am simply performing my duties—enacting my "professional identity" as externally defined.

That much seems easy to accept. The problem is that distinguishing the personal from the professional may not be appropriate when being professional tends to mean "caring personally" about others (Hansen, 2001). Good teaching, it seems, is heartfelt by definition: it is partly about caring for others sincerely and not just about looking like you care. Yet heartfelt feelings, to be heartfelt, cannot be commanded into existence. They must appear of their own accord. For the newcomer to teaching, this requirement can be especially worrisome. Whatever my performance as a teacher may suggest, how do I actually *feel* about my work? And what, if anything, does my performance—my externally visible identity—show about how I actually feel and what my professional motives actually are? How can "I" describe myself as a teacher, not just to others, but to myself? Watching myself in action over many days and weeks, across many students and situations, I can easily fret about my identity. "Don't just do something; stand there!" goes the aphorism, and privately I may sense the wisdom in it.

To be effective, those of us involved in teacher education need to understand the troubling vividness of these questions, even though they are by nature experienced inwardly. Future teachers are worried about *more* than outward "professional identity," about how they look in the classroom. They worry as well about whether they *feel* committed to teaching as a calling. This is not merely a practical concern about employability, but a more intimate anxiety. In private moments it is expressed in terms of whether they feel "sincere" about teaching, whether they "actually like students," or whether they can "be themselves with students." In the short term, such doubts can be banished, covered, and quelled by performing outward signs of professionalism: I can distract myself by saying and doing what others "identify" as good teaching. But in the long term, merely looking professional is not good enough. The problem is that satisfying others with good teaching performances does not, by definition, encourage mindful attention to *self*-identification.

It is here that we teacher educators can make important contributions to preservice students' identity development, if we can just be sensitive to the complexity of students' lives and to our own limits in being helpful. Our challenge is not to coach or entice future teachers to perform particular acts of teaching; like budding artists in other fields, most will pick up performance skills to a respectable degree. The true challenge is to help novices *feel* like teachers and to love as many moments of teaching as possible, even while they unfold. Giving this sort of help calls for a more counseling-like approach: we must invite students to talk and reflect on how they feel about themselves as teachers, while at the same time providing a stable and safe environment for doing so. As in any successful counseling experience, the "client" (student) does much of the real work of discovering her true passions (teaching or whatever). The "therapist" (teacher educator) primarily provides mindful attention—attention that focuses, reflects back, and interprets the client-student's efforts. At its best, this approach promises deep satisfaction and value for both the student and teacher educator: the student feels cared for, and the teacher educator feels valued (Noddings, 2002). But as with other counseling-like relationships, there are also real limits to what it can accomplish.

SORTING THROUGH THE CONFUSION OF DISCOURSES

The limits come from the sheer variety and magnitude of influences on preservice students, and from the fact that teacher educators may be prone to underestimating the variety and magnitude. In particular, in sorting through their experiences, both the student and the teacher educator encounter a variety of *discourses* relevant to teaching and learning in general and to professional identity formation in particular. A discourse is a pattern of thinking and is speaking that socially constructed over time and that is used by a particular community or group of people, such as a family, an occupation (like teachers), or a national society (Bahktin, 1981). Discourses contain and express beliefs, values, and perspectives, and they are used by individuals to communicate with each other. To participate in a group, in fact, individuals need to adopt one or more of the discourses used by that group. Using the local discourse(s) successfully makes mutual understanding possible and also allows the individual both to self-identify with the group and to be identified as such by other members.

In teacher education programs for the younger grade levels, for example, two of the most prominent discourses used by instructors might be called the discourses of *progressive education* or *developmentally appropriate practice*. These are beliefs about good teaching based on assumptions about the nature of "normal" and/or preferred individual development and relationships with families, coupled with beliefs about the importance of basing teaching on real, lived experiences of both teacher and students (Egan, 2001; Bredekamp & Cottle, 1997). These discourses are promoted heavily to preservice students by faculty members in early childhood or early years education and in a sense become major "languages" for communicating with and among individual faculty members. Preservice teachers in these programs must therefore learn the discourses of progressive education and of developmentally appropriate practice if they also wish to be part of the teaching profession, or at least of the early childhood/early years branch of the profession. Those few teachers who happen to move from early childhood teaching to secondary teaching experience an interesting change of "languages." The discourses of progressive education and developmentally appropriate practice that circulate so prominently in early childhood education become somewhat less prominent in secondary education. In their place, a *curriculum* discourse—beliefs about the importance of "knowing the subject matter"–takes on added importance.

As teacher educators, it is tempting to believe that the above description tells most of the story about discourses in teacher education, and perhaps therefore about the professional identity development of novices. After all, talk about developmentally appropriate practice, progressive education, and curriculum occupy most of *our* working time, and a good deal of our encounters with preservice students. Our job, it would seem, is to help individual students to acquire these discourses—to help them learn to "talk like us educators," so to speak. Unfortunately, this view of our mandate overlooks a multiplicity of additional discourses that impinge on students' lives in a variety of ways and frequently are at odds with the officially privileged discourses of teacher education. The competing discourses are largely beyond our control as teacher educators, and perhaps as a result, they frequently go unnoticed.

Consider a relatively pointed example in order to understand this point clearly. In addition to working amidst beliefs and assumptions about "developmentally appropriate practice," teacher educators and preservice teachers also live among particular beliefs and assumptions about sexuality and sexual orientation—beliefs and assumptions that might collectively be called a heterosexuality discourse. In this discourse, personal relationships that are intimate, long-lasting, and mutually supportive are also assumed both to be heterosexual and to be appropriate topics of everyday conversation. Homosexual relationships that have these same qualities are generally excluded from this discourse, or more precisely are included by being dismissed as inappropriate or worse. Unfortunately, the widely assumed and/or spoken heterosexual discourse directly clash with elements of progressive education promoted by the discourses of developmentally appropriate practice. It clashes, for example, over whether teachers should be "authentic" with students and should therefore share their personalities and personal lives with students. The contradictions thus created create serious, chronic challenges for teachers with same-sex orientations, both during their teacher education programs and later when working in schools (Evans, 2002). From the point of view of a teacher education student, the contradictions are a problem not just because common discourses about sexual orientation create social prejudices. The contradictions are also a problem because they are rendered invisible to everyone except one person—the individual who prefers an intimate partner of the same sex.

Discourses about sexuality may be especially marked in their impact because teacher education programs tend to deal with them so little. But similar conflicts occur even with topics that do have a nominal role with preservice programs. One of these, for example, is *multicultural education*. Although this term is grammatically singular, it really contains (and sometimes conceals) several competing and partially contradictory discourses about the nature of and relationships among people of diverse race, ethnicity, and language (Marsh, 2003). In a version that is reminiscent of anthropology, for example, the discourse of multicultural education refers to a relatively innocent celebration of selected differences among peoples—comparisons of their holidays, their clothing, their living arrangements, and the like (Britzman, 1991). In a version more reminiscent of politics and social criticism, however, the discourse calls attention to fundamental, institutionalized injustices of one people against another. This version is about the privileging of one race over another, the existence of real or *de facto* slavery, the "necessity" of poverty for certain groups within society, and the like (Grieshaber, 2001). In a third version of multicultural education, the discourse circumvents the anger implicit in social injustice by emphasizing the importance of positive individual human relationships; in this view, racial prejudice has not been institutional-ized by society, but exists merely within (quite a few) persons individually (Levine-Rasky, 2002).

These three versions are supported and contradicted in various degrees both within and without teacher education programs. The resulting position—and self-identity—of students will therefore vary depending on individuals' exposure to the different discourses. Within teacher education programs, for example, the human relations version of multicultural education might indeed be supported within foundations courses—some version of it may be expressed in courses on educational psychology and foundations of education and may be implied in curriculum classes as well. The "celebration of selected differences" version, on the other hand, might find a compatible home in certain curriculum courses. But the political/social critique might be more problematic. While a foundations course might call attention to it, it is unlikely to sit comfort-ably with the usual emphasis on individuality found in educational psychology, nor with the commitment to positive human relations necessary for the smooth functioning of a classroom curriculum (Kincheloe, 1999). Psychology, furthermore, is especially likely also to promote what might be called a discourse of normalization: the idea that children and youth "normally" develop through a series of predictable steps that lead to a particular identifiable outcome in maturity. An exemplar of this viewpoint that is widely studied in educational psychology courses is Jean Piaget, but there are numerous others as well (Seifert, 2001). Although the discourse of normalization seems innocent enough on the surface, it can be inconsistent with multiculturalism when taken seriously. Normalization has two problematic implications: first, that cultural differences are psychologically unimportant (mere window-dressing for more fundamental uniformity among individuals), and second, that differences are really deficits of some sort (more or less adequate versions of being human). Ironically, therefore, preservice education students are "normally" exposed to contradictory discourses in their professional education. Understandably, therefore, the effects on novices' identity development are both variable and challenging for individuals.

The variability and challenge are compounded when individuals' experiences outside their programs are taken into account. No matter how hard preservice students work at their assign-ments and classroom teaching responsibilities, they experience a variety of important discourses *outside* their programs—beliefs and attitudes that circulate in family and society, or that students carry forward from their pasts. While some of these fit comfortably with beliefs and attitudes promoted publically within teacher education, it is likely that others do not, and teacher educa-tors' knowledge of them is correspondingly obscured. In addition to discourses about queerness, about developmentally appropriate practice, and about multiculturalism, for example, preservice education students are likely to experience discourses about gender roles, about family rights and responsibilities, and about the significance of economic disparities. All of these are double-edged "preparation" for teaching, sometimes supporting beliefs and assumptions promoted by teacher educators and sometimes contradicting or undermining them. What all the discourses share is a tendency to cause some experiences or feelings to remain hidden, from both peers and instructors. Table 1 lists some of these experiences and feelings, in no particular order. To some degree, every item poses a challenge to its possessor about how, when, and whether to "come out" (to borrow a term from the queerness discourse) about the information, precisely because every item in the table contradicts some part of more officially sanctioned discourses about teaching and personal development.

Table 1: Personal Information Which Students Might Not Share in Reflective Writing

(not in order of frequency or importance)

Queerness: "I'm gay/lesbian/bisexual/etc."

Health conditions: "I have colitis, lupus, fibromyalgia, eating disorder, etc."

Weight problems: "I'm overweight."

Visible disabilities

Unwanted pregnancy, recent or current

Self-assessment of "wrong" personal qualities:

"Privately, I think I'm too shy to teach."

"Privately, I think I'm too intellectual to teach."

"Privately, I think I am the 'wrong' gender (e.g., male teaching kindergarten, female teaching physics)

"Privately, it seems like I believe in the 'wrong' [i.e., minority] religion" (e.g., Judaism, Islam, or some versions of Christianity)

Shameful stories of relatives (e.g., a parent or sibling in jail or on drugs)

Immigrant family background: "I'm self-conscious about their manners or lack of money."

Serious money problems: "I'm on welfare," "My family has just gone bankrupt."

Personal divorce, recent or current

Divorce of parents, recent or current

Physical or sexual abuse: in family or origin or in current marriage/partnership

Victim of recent rape or personal assault

Perpetrator of undetected crime (e.g., shoplifting or minor theft)

While the items in Table 1 vary in severity and frequency, they suggest that preservice teachers, as a group, have much more to think about than getting a grasp of the discourses sanctioned officially by teacher education programs. Developing professional identity, it seems, amounts to more than understanding developmentally appropriate practice, multicultural education, or Piagetian stages. It also includes reconciling these public discourses with private and personal experiences and discourses. If teacher educators can recognize the need for these reconciliations, as well as their extent, then they might have more success at encouraging students to adopt the official discourses. Yet how can teacher educators do so if the alternate discourses are by definition personal, private, and sometimes mutually contradictory?

THE POSSIBILITIES AND LIMITS OF BEING TRULY HELPFUL

Teacher educators have two general strategies available for influencing education students: they can select and modify academic assignments, and they can arrange for students to have particular social experiences. Although both strategies can be helpful under the right conditions, they also have limitations and unintended consequences. The limitations and consequences, at bottom, come from the impossibility of establishing a vantage point about teaching that is truly outside of all prior social discourse or influence. There is no such thing, in other words, as a haven for reflection that is reliably and fully authentic, real, or "objective."

ASSIGNMENTS MEANT TO FOSTER PROFESSIONAL IDENTITY DEVELOPMENT

Can we encourage preservice students to develop professional identities—especially to "feel like a teacher"—by giving assignments that encourage thoughtful reflection? It would seem, at first glance, that the widespread practices of journal writing and of autobiographical writing might do so. On the face of it, these activities would seem to require new and future teachers to confront their personal histories and assumptions about teaching, learning, and students, and thereby develop awareness and self-identity. A closer look, though, suggests that reflection and reflective writing usually serves too many purposes to guarantee these results (Rodgers, 2002; Feldler, 2003). In teacher education, reflective and autobiographical writing is variously used to demonstrate students' self-consciousness, to plan teaching systematically, to explain a general perspective about the value of education, to recommend ways of remedying social inequities, and to express an "authentic inner voice" that is somehow independent of its social context. While it is possible that these activities can stimulate thinking that is genuinely new and there-fore a basis for personal development, the tautological quality of reflection makes this outcome problematic. The difficulty is that the mental furniture and "space" available for reflection has itself been molded and constituted by the very practices and discourse which it is supposed to critique (Foucault, 1997). Without even realizing it, students (and their instructors) may write about what they already know and believe.

When this logical problem is coupled with the differential privileging of discourses described earlier in this chapter, it is easy to imagine reflective writing to have effects that are at best unpre-dictable and diverse. Imagine, for example, the ways that individual students might perceive an assignment to write reflectively or autobiographically. At one extreme, for example, will be stu-dents whose life experiences or private beliefs are seriously at variance with his or her peers and instructors, and who therefore consider reflective writing to be unsafe as a forum for personal expression. These students' reaction will not depend on whether the instructor actually gives a formal mark for journal writing, but simply on the accurate expectation that the students' ideas and activities will be evaluated informally. Such students are at risk of dropping out of the program, either psychologically or literally, without their feeling safe enough to explain why. But even if such students complete the reflective writing assignment, they are likely to withhold their most important concerns. Either way, they must deal with alienation from teaching.

At another extreme will be students whose experiences and beliefs, by good fortune, coincide almost fully with peers and instructors and who find their voices magnified, so to speak, by reflective writing. For these individuals, such writing will not be a burden, but an opportunity simultaneously to be recognized and to see themselves: the perfect combination, in other words, for developing identity that is both personally felt and socially conferred. Like others in privi-leged, dominant circumstances, however, these relatively fortunate students may not develop empathy with classmates who struggle more—and sometimes much more—to reconcile personal and social identities. The privileging of certain discourses over others, and silencing of certain non-dominant discourses, may escape their notice. Classmates who do experience discourse conflicts may seem deficient, rather than embodiments of useful insights about the limitations of teacher education.

In between these extremes will be many others who experience varying mixtures of partial success (and failure) at reflective writing. Some of these students, for example, may decide to share their thinking through reflective writing, but only selectively. In following this path, they help to create the impression held by many preservice students that education assignments include a lot of "busy work," or thoughtless, ritualized tasks. Others in this group may accept the requirement to write reflectively, but approach the task too literally, only to find themselves later regretting certain private information they have disclosed. For them, the eventual result is private anger, anxiety, and/or apprehension. If the instructor-reader of their reflections does not respond to such "overdisclosures" appropriately and respectfully, these students may end up feeling *less* confident of their ability to teach, and even of their worthiness as human beings.

Note that these speculations assume that reflective writing will lean toward an introspective style, with perhaps a measure of social criticism thrown in for spice. As other commentators have pointed out, however, there are no logical or empirical grounds for assuming that introspection is especially effective for promoting the identity development of preservice students (Feldner, 2003; Zeichner, 1996). Teachers who reflect primarily on technical questions (e.g. "How can I prepare my students for a multiple-choice test more efficiently?") may be guided by educational philosophies just as humane as those guided by psychological or philosophical questions (e.g. "What is the best way to assess my students?"). Both may be motivated by deep concern for students' welfare. Yet the technically oriented thinking would not be considered reflective by some educators, perhaps including the majority of teacher educators. As Kenneth Zeichner has summarized this problem, "there is no such thing as an unreflective teacher"—only teachers whose reflections may not be recognized as such (Zeichner, 1996, p. 207). If teacher educators can understand this possibility more fully, they may teach students a bit more effectively.

ADMINISTRATIVE ARRANGEMENTS MEANT TO FACILITATE IDENTITY DEVELOPMENT

The considerations just discussed suggest a need for additional ways to support the development of students' personal and professional identity. Other than by giving academic assignments, however, there really is only one other strategy at the disposal of teacher educators: they can organize how students spend class-related time, and with whom they spend that time. Program leaders can arrange, in particular, for preservice teachers to spend more or less time in classrooms, or they can arrange for preservice teachers to spend more or less time with each other. To a limited extent, they can also try to guide or constrain what happens when these contacts are arranged. As discussed below, though, instructors' guidance and constraint decrease markedly once students' interactions focus on persons *other* than the instructors themselves.

Much has already been written and studied about how practice teaching affects preservice teachers (see, for example, Cecilia, Buttery, & Gatton, 1996; or Bullrush & Griffin, 2001), and about how initial teaching experiences affect novice teachers (see Bullrush & Bagman, 1997). For purposes of understanding students' professional identity development, the research can be summarized by saying that (1) time in classrooms easily overwhelms the emotional impact of other aspects of teacher education, and (2) practice teaching has highly individual or idiosyncratic effects on new teachers' confidence and self-image. In a general way, the reasons stem from the same considerations discussed earlier in this chapter: student teachers face conflicting discourses and expectations about teaching and about what it means to be a "good teacher." Although nearly all preservice education students do in fact complete their certification programs and most do complete practice teaching in particular, job statistics following completion are typically mixed (Bureau of Labor Statistics, 2003). This chronic statistical fact suggests that many preservice teachers either do not become or do not remain committed to teaching. They learn to *perform* as teachers, it seems, but necessarily to *feel* like teachers. Because this topic has already been researched so well elsewhere, however, it will not be discussed further here; interested readers should refer to the reviews cited above.

Instead, consider one other administrative arrangement that might influence students' identities: teacher educators might arrange for students to spend more time with each other. A cohort model is the idea here: a group of peers who take many or even most of their courses together (Dika & Singh, 2002). Fellow students therefore share both the stress and the excitement of learning to teach. Because of their class schedules, furthermore, they even share much of their *non*-class time. Hopefully, these arrangements might make individuals feel less alone and more able to give and receive support from each other. In addition, students would not have to deal with the usual powers of instructors individually. Instructors could still require assignments and other teaching-related "performances," and they would still have the power to evaluate the performances. By belonging to a cohort, however, individual students would have others to consult for advice and support about these matters. In this way a cohort would resemble a professional association or (more debatably) a labor union.

When it comes to developing professional and personal identity, in particular, cohorts could (theoretically) offer an arena safely away from instructors. Peers could assist individuals to sort through personal reactions to and beliefs about teaching—assist individuals to ask themselves what kind of teacher they really want to be, or even *whether* they wish to teach. The cohort might even offer a safe place to lose one's composure (literally) when courses, practice teaching, or instructors become especially stressful or confusing. These features, it would seem, might help students to clarify their personal commitments, and perhaps eventually to perfect their classroom performances as a byproduct.

Presumably peers *would* still exercise influence on individuals, of course, because of individual students' desire to belong to and be accepted by the community. Whether such influence would create its own problems is an empirical question, but it seems reasonable to expect that peer-generated problems would at least have the advantage of *differing* from professor-generated problems (Dika & Singh, 2002; Bennington, 2002). It seems reasonable to expect, therefore, that teacher education organized around student cohorts might offer a more balanced social diet to its members, even if the diet amounted only to mutual limitations on the influences of instructors and peers. With a cohort organization, the stage should be set—or at least a stage should be set *better*—for individuals to "identify themselves" as teachers, as well as to be identified as such by others. That, at least, is the theory.

But do cohorts really work this way? Does personal and professional identity really develop more effectively if students have greater contact with each other? Much the literature of the social sciences argues for the wisdom of cohorts of various forms, although it does not always justify the experience by its benefits for identity development. In sociology, the benefits are often described as gains in *social capital* (Coleman, 1988; Putnam, 2000; or Mandzuk, Hasinoff, & Seifert, in press): improved information because of contacts with others, and greater access to services because of exchanges of favors. In psychology, the benefits are seen as increases in emotional and intellectual support and as reductions in isolation and alienation (e.g., Slavin, 1995; Salomon & Perkins, 1998). In education, group work—whether temporary or long-term—has been tried experimentally and often found to be successful, though there are also examples where it has *not* worked well (Dika & Singh, 2002; Melnychuk, 2001). But most of these benefits, including even the psychological ones, are not about identity in the sense discussed in this chapter. They do not, that is, concern whether an individual develops a stable *feeling* of self from spending a lot of time with a group, nor do they concern whether cohorts might lead *others* to identify an individual member as a stable self.

There are other cautions about the impact of cohort groups as well. Much of the theory and research, for example, assumes groups much smaller than typical in teacher education cohorts. The reviews by Slavin and by Salomon and Perkins, cited above, really refer only to handfuls of students (4–6 individuals) working together. The "communities" assumed in social capital theory are usually larger—in fact similar to classroom-size groups—and therefore more appropriate for comparison to experiences in teacher education. But the "capital"—the ties and favors—exchanged in such groups tends to be immediate and specific, and rarely permanent or institutionalized. These qualities make it easier for classroom-sized groups to be "democratic," in the Deweyan sense of allowing and encouraging appropriate responses by individuals to the needs of the group (Porter, 1995; Schutz, 2001). But this sort of democracy also has limitations, both as a test for the benefits of community and as an avenue for individual identity development. In particular, and perhaps paradoxically, the "democracy" of moderate-sized groups also promotes shallow homegrown or group self-stereotyping (Prentice & Miller, 2002). Individuals, that is, talk themselves and fellow group members into simplified individual and group identities—a sort of "school spirit" effect. The identities thus assigned are definitely not the kind that are the focus of this chapter, because they obviously overlook the internal complexity of individuals, the diversity among group members, and the diversity within and between other comparable groups. As research reviewed by Prentice and Miller suggests, the constraints and alienation on individuals from homegrown stereotyping are very real, but usually poorly acknowledged by the group itself.

When cohort program experiments are tried in teacher education, therefore, the evaluations of the programs need to take these cautions into account. Given the cohort and cohort-like experiences in other domains of human activity, it seems likely that cohort organization of preservice education may often be successful, but not for the reasons often thought. Cohorts may work, in particular, in *spite* of their interpersonal cost, and not only *because* of their interpersonal benefits. In an earlier review of cooperative learning, for example, Slavin (1983) noted that successful cooperative learning has generally been embedded in *non*-cohort, individualistic contexts, a circumstance that gives individuals respite from peer pressures between group-oriented "opportunities." Similarly, cohort models in teacher education may work best when they are not overdone.

What about identity development in and by cohorts? How would the promises and constraints of groups affect how future teachers make peace with the complexity of their own classroom and personal behaviors? The research on cooperative learning and on non-education cohorts, described above, does not really answer these questions directly, even though it implies that cohorts at least tend to be positive experiences and do not *interfere* with identity development. Research specifically about cohorts in preservice education has not focused directly either on students' sense of self development or on their felt sense of professionalism. In a combined survey and interview study of one cohort program, for example, Mandzuk, Hasinoff, and Seifert (in press) found that students reported *liking* assignment to class-sized groups, because, as expected, they felt supported by peers and therefore better connected to the teacher education program. These are obviously positive outcomes, but they are not precisely equivalent to students' reporting that they feel more like *teachers* as a result of support from cohort members. A number of students in the Mandzuk study also reported that cohorts constrained their individual behavior; but in the data reported so far, they did not indicate whether the constraints limited their eventual professional self-identification. Individuals commented, for example, that peer influence in cohorts sometimes became *too* strong, but they did not clearly indicate whether the excesses were about social, academic, or personal matters. They also spontaneously mentioned factors that inhibited participation in the cohort to some extent, such as being a "mature" or older student, being a parent, and living out of town, among others.

In any case, students' opinions in single interviews and on written surveys cannot be taken as reliable indicators of their thinking about a matter as central as personal and professional identity. The reasons are reminiscent of the problems surrounding reflective writing, discussed earlier. In essence there are competing discourses affecting individual students, many of them are mutually contradictory, and a few are—strangely—expected to remain "unseen" (or more accurately, unheard though known). In various combinations, individuals must confront and sort out beliefs and expectations about queerness, about gender roles, about multiculturalism, about socioeconomic class, and the like. In this case, however, they must do so orally and in the intellectual and social company of peers more than of instructors. Given the likelihood that individuals will bring rather different backgrounds and starting points to these dialogues, it seems more likely that the results will be unpredictable and diverse. As Table 1 suggests, many students will have *something* to hide, and some may feel they have much to hide. Individuals will also have various ideas and experiences they wish to share with peers, but their meanings and motives for sharing will be diverse and often unconscious. Under the circumstances, it seems likely that much of the learning will simply reproduce existing preconceptions of the preservice university students. This unfortunate result has already been found, it might be noted, among cooperative work groups of elementary-age children (Cohen, 1994). The children within such groups express and enact prejudices—about race, gender, and the nature of schooling and of intelligence—toward each other that parallel those found in society at large.

ASSISTING IDENTITY DEVELOPMENT IN SPITE OF IT ALL

If identity development really is so fraught with risk, unpredictability, and diversity, what then is a teacher educator to do? The simplest answer may simply be to cultivate a taste for ambiguity and to proceed with humility and respect for students when trying to influence them. Although the idea of diversity is easy to accept with regard to children and youth, it seems harder for us to accept when applied to ourselves, including when applied to the next generation of ourselves, the students enrolled in teacher education programs. But we need to move away, it seems, from unified conceptions of our identities as a profession and as individuals—away from difference models of teachers and toward the diversity models we urge our preservice students to use.

Will this shift limit our role as teacher educators? In spite of any impression possibly given earlier in this chapter, teacher educators *can* sometimes be helpful when preservice students struggle with whether they feel like teachers yet. But for the diversity-related reasons already indicated, teacher educators may not be able to influence students' identity development in major or sweeping ways, even if we can point to success stories with selected individuals (Danielewicz, 2001). Efforts to exert influence too strongly or comprehensively, in fact, may sometimes hurt or interfere with students' real struggles to decide for themselves how, why, and whether they wish to teach. As the medical doctors often remind us and each other, our guiding professional ethic must be this: first of all, to do no harm.

REFERENCES

Bredekamp, S. & Cottle, C. (1997). *Developmentally appropriate practice for children from birth to age eight.* Washington, D.C.: National Association for the Education of Young Children.

Britzman, 1991. *Practice makes practice: A critical study of learning to teach.* Albany, NY: State University of New York Press.

Bullough, R. & Griffin, A. (Eds.). (2001). *Becoming a student of teaching, 2nd edition.* New York: Routledge Falmer.

Bullough, R. & Baughman, K. (1997). *First-year teacher eight years later: An inquiry into teacher development.* New York: Teachers College Press.

Bureau of Labor Statistics. (2003). *Occupational outlook handbook, 2002–2003.* Washington, D.C.: United States Government Printing Office. Also available online at <http://www.bls.gov/oco/ocos069.htm>

Cohen, E. (1994). *Designing groupwork, 2nd edition.* New York: Teachers College Press.

Coleman, J. (1988). Social capital in the creation of human capital. *American Journal of Sociology, 94,* Supplement S95-S120.

Damasio, A. (1999). *The feeling of what happens: Body and emotion in the making of consciousness.* New York: Harcourt Brace.

Danielewicz, J. (2001). *Teaching selves: Identity, pedgogy, and teacher education.* Albany, NY: State University of New York.

Dika, S. & Singh, K. (2002). Applications of social capital in educational literature: A critical synthesis. *Review of Educational Research, 72*(1), 31–60.

Egan, K. (2001). Why education is so difficult and contentious. *Teachers College Record, 103*(6), 923–941.

Erickson, E. (1950). *Childhood and society.* New York: Norton.

Erickson, E. (1968). *Identity: Youth and crisis.* New York: Norton.

Feldner, L. (2003). Teacher reflection in a hall of mirrors: Historical influences and political reverberations. *Educational Researcher, 32*(3), 16–25.

Foucault, M. (1997). Subjectivity and truth. In P. Rabinow (Ed.), *The essential works of Michel Foucault 1954–1984: Volume 1, Ethics: Subjectivity and truth* (pp. 87–92). New York: The New Press.

Gergen, K. (1991). *The saturated self: Dilemmas of identity in contemporary life.* New York: Basic Books.

Grieshaber, S. (2001). Advocacy and early childhood educators: Identity and cultural conflicts. In S. Grieshaber & G. Cannella (Eds.), *Embracing identities in early childhood education: Diversity and possibilities,* 60–72.

Hansen, D. (2001). Teaching as a moral activity. In V. Richardson (Ed.), *Handbook of research on teaching, 4th edition,* pp. 826–857. Washington, D.C.: American Educational Research Association.

Kincheloe, J. (Ed.). (1999). *Rethinking intelligence: Confronting psychological assumptions about teaching and learning.* New York: Routledge.

Levine-Rasky, C. (Ed.). (2002). *Working through whiteness: International perspectives.* Albany, NY: State University of New York.

Lightfoot, S. (1983). *The good high school: Portraits of character and culture.* New York: Basic Books.

Lyons, N. & LaBoskey, V. (Eds.). (2002). *Narrative inquiry in practice.* New York: Teachers College Press.

MacDonald, R. (1999). *Handbook for beginning teachers, 2nd edition.* New York: Longman.

Mandzuk, D., Hasinoff, S., & Seifert, K. (in press). Learning to teach in student cohorts: A social capital perspective. *Canadian Journal of Education.*

Marcia, J. (1993). *Ego identity: A handbook for psychosocial research.* New York: Springer-Verlag.

Marsh, M. (2003). *The social fashioning of teacher identities.* New York: Peter Lang.

Melnychuk, N. (2001). A cohort practicum model: Physical education student teachers' experiences. *Alberta Journal of Educational Research, 47*(3), 259–275.

Mishler, E. (1986). *The research interview: Context and narrative.* Cambridge, MA: Harvard University Press.

Neuman, Y. & Bekerman, Z. (2001). Cultural resources and the gap between educational theory and practice. *Teachers College Record, 103*(3), 471–484.

Noddings, D. (2002). *Educating moral people: A caring alternative to character education.* New York: Teachers College Press.

Pennington, D. (2002). *The social psychology of behavior in small groups.* New York: Taylor & Francis.

Porter, T. (1995). *Trust in numbers.* Princeton, NJ: Princeton University Press.

Prentice, D. & Miller, D. (2002). The emergence of homegrown stereotypes. *American Psychologist, 57*(5), 352–359.

Putnam, R. (2000). *Bowling alone: The collapse and revival of the American community.* New York: Simon and Schuster.

Rodgers, C. (2002). Defining reflection: Another look at John Dewey and reflective thinking. *Teachers College Record, 104*(4), 842–866.

Rosenblum-Lowden, R. (2000). *You have to go to school: 250 classroom management strategies for beginning teachers, 2nd edition.* Thousand Oaks, CA: Corwin.

Salomon, G. & Perkins, D. (1998). Individual and social aspects of learning. In D. Pearson & A. Iran-Nejad (Eds.), *Review of research in education, vol. 23,* pp. 1–24.

Schon, D. (1987). *Educating the reflective practitioner.* San Francisco: Jossey-Bass.

Schutz, A. (2001). John Dewey and "a paradox of size": Democratic faith at the limits of experience. *American Journal of Education, 109* (3), 287–319.

Seifert, K. (2001). Sociable thinking: Cognitive development in early childhood. In O. Saracho & B. Spodek, (Eds.), *Contemporary perspectives on early childhood curriculum, Volume 1,* 15–40. Also available at <home. cc.umanitoba.ca/~seifert>

Seifert, K. & Mandzuk, D. (2004). Student cohorts: Learning communities or dysfunctional families? Unpublished manuscript available at <home.cc.umanitoba.ca/~seifert>.

Sikula, T., Buttery, T., & Guyton, E. (Eds.). (1996). *Handbook of teacher education, 2nd edition.* New York: Macmillan.

Slavin, R. (1983). When does cooperative learning increase student achievement? *Psychological Bulletin, 94,* 429–445.

Slavin, R. (1995). *Cooperative learning: Theory, research, and practice, 2nd edition.* Boston: Allyn & Bacon.

Tolstoy, L. (1912). *Anna Karenina.* New York: E. P. Dutton.

Waterman, S. & Archer, S. (1990). A lifespan perspective on identity formation: Developments in form, function, and process. In P. Baltes, D. Featterman, & R. Lerner (Eds.), *Lifespan development and behavior (Vol. 10).* Hillsdale, NJ: Erlbaum.

Zeichner, K. (1996). Teachers as reflective practitioners and the democratization of school reform. In K. Zeichner, S. Melnick, & M. L. Gomez (Eds.), *Currents of reform in preservice teacher education* (pp. 1–8). New York: Teachers College Press.

FORTY-SIX

Once upon a Theory: Using Picture Books to Help Students Understand Educational Psychology

Debby Zambo and Cory Cooper Hansen

Imagine a college instructor reading the picture book *Lilly's Purple Plastic Purse* by Kevin Henkes (1996) to her class of 38 preservice teachers enrolled in an educational psychology course. As she reads, the students listen to the story and focus their attention on the story's illustrations being projected on a screen at the front of the room. After reading each page and examining each illustration, the instructor poses questions to spark discussion about the main character, Lilly, and how her actions are typical of children in the preoperational stage of cognitive development (Piaget & Inhelder, 2000). The students' replies indicate that they are connecting the story to experiences in their intern classrooms and their assigned textbook readings. For example, after reading the page where Lilly disrupts story time because she wants to share her purple plastic purse and movie star sunglasses, one student tells the class about a child in his mentor's classroom who is just like Lilly. He talks about the thinking of preoperational children and the strategies his mentor uses with children this age. Another student connects Lilly's behavior to the word egocentric, a term she read in the course text. She notes that preoperational children, like Lilly, can be egocentric in their thinking: they do not see the perspectives of others and believe that their view is the only one. When the story ends, one student says she understands why Lilly's teacher punished her for disrupting story time but she empathizes with Lilly because she was reasoning the best she could, given her stage of cognitive development. The responses of these preservice teachers demonstrate that they are relating the story to their experience working with children and to the theories they are learning in the college classroom. The fact that they are thinking about Lilly's behavior and cognitive development shows that they are beginning to look at children through a theoretical lens.

This type of interactive learning demonstrates the power children's picture books can afford when they are used to make psychological theories come alive. As instructors within a teacher preparation program, we have consistently found this practice to be motivating and cognitively stimulating for our students over our collective thirteen years of college teaching. Initially, some students are taken aback when we read out loud to them and wonder why we use children's picture books at the college level. However, once we begin to link theory to the behavior and thinking of various characters, our students begin to develop an appreciation for interpreting theory through the medium of children's picture books.

Students at our institution are required to take an introductory educational psychology course in their initial semester (junior year) of our teacher preparation program. The institution itself is a satellite campus within a large, southwestern, research-one university. Our location and commuter status bring us a unique group of students: many come from working-class families, have families themselves, and while work full time they pursue their degrees. The majority of our students are Anglo, 95 percent of them are female, and they average between the ages of 22 and 26. Our classes tend to be relatively small (between 20 and 28) and students are cohorted by majors: early childhood, elementary, and bilingual education.

Courses in educational psychology are the backbone of college preparation programs for students seeking degrees and/or certification for jobs that that lead to careers with children (Alexander, 2006; Woolfolk, 2004). While students are usually enthusiastic about taking practicum courses because they provide hands-on activities for immediate and direct use, they are often less enthusiastic about studying theories explaining cognition, moral and social development, and motivation. Enthusiasm may wane because students do not see the practicality of theory or understand how it applies to their immediate needs. Typically, educational psychology courses are taught in a lecture format, and this also can make theory seem dry and removed from real life. To appreciate the practical nature of educational psychology theory, students must bridge the gap between what they learn in their courses and their interactions with children in the field. One way to do this, as the opening scenario shows, is to enrich lectures and course work with well-chosen picture books.

Researchers and instructors have discovered the motivating appeal and cognitive benefits of children's literature for students of all ages and abilities (Evans, 1998; Hansen & Zambo, in press; Ho, 2000; Routman, 1994; Zambo, 2005). We are partial to children's picture books (32 pages that convey a message through both story and picture) because they are entertaining, can be read and discussed in a short period of time, and, when carefully selected, present theory accurately both in words and pictures. Sipe (2001) calls this text-picture relationship "synergy" because it is neither the text nor the illustration that creates understanding but a combination of the two. Images contribute to a deeper understanding of text, and text helps one see and learn from the images. Along these same lines, Mitchell (1994) uses the term "imagerytext" to convey the cognitive advantages of an image juxtaposed with the text. Text and image converge to become multi-modal input, and this is a powerful way to learn. When learning is energized, motivation is enhanced.

MOTIVATIONAL ASPECTS OF CHILDREN'S LITERATURE

Many people think of picture books as simple texts for beginning readers. Parents read picture books to children at bedtime, and primary teachers use picture books within early childhood education. This may have been true in the past (Demers & Moyles, 1982), but contemporary picture books have emerged as a key literary form within children's literature as a source of enjoyment and inspiration for people of all ages. For example, many of our students report receiving *Oh, the Places You'll Go!* (Seuss, 1990) as a high school graduation gift and share positive emotions towards a work typically considered to be written for younger readers.

Few articles were found in a review of the literature for using picture books in educational psychology courses, but other disciplines have reported increased motivation when this genre is used. For example, Juchartz (2004) uses the work of Dr. Seuss to get his community college students, who struggle with reading, engaged with text. Juchartz uses the books of Seuss to scaffold learning and bridge the gap between his students' levels of literacy proficiency, their personal experience, and the meaning found in complex text. An example of this is his use of *The Sneeches* (Seuss, 1989). Reading about the prejudice faced by the Plain Belly Sneeches helps his students understand social injustice and challenges that minorities face in the world today. Once students relate this story to their lives, Juchartz is able to lead them to more complicated texts with similar issues and themes. Juchartz (2004) finds his students are "consistently delighted to engage in such nontraditional material" (p. 337).

Smallwood (1992) is another instructor who advocates the use of picture books in the college classroom. Smallwood uses the "synergy" of picture books to teach literacy skills to her adult English as second language learners. She uses the stories to provide insight into the customs and concepts of a new culture, and she uses illustrations to visually depict new vocabulary terms and ideas. One example is her use of the dramatic illustrations in *Brother Eagle, Sister Sky* (Jeffers, 1991) that in her words, "convey the deeper meaning of the story, that is, respect for our environment" (p. 2).

College textbook writers recognize that picture books are powerful ways to illustrate concepts and ideas. The teacher's edition of *Child Development* (Santrock, 2004) suggests using *Miss Rumphius* (Cooney, 1982) to spark discussion about adolescent thinking and idealistic views. *Fish Is Fish* (Lionni, 1970) is recommended in a book called *How People Learn* (National Research Council, 2000) to help readers understand Piaget's concept of assimilation. The audience for picture books has broadened, and the use of picture books has expanded well beyond childhood.

THE COGNITIVE ASPECTS OF PICTURE BOOKS: STORIES AND ILLUSTRATIONS

Bruner (1966) notes that when learners see something happen, as well as read or hear about it, they encode this information both visually and verbally in their long-term memory store. We agree with Bruner and document the cognitive benefit of picture books with evidence from the work of Paivio (1971; 1991). According to Paivio's dual coding theory, two cognitive systems are used to process and store information: a verbal system for linguistic information and an imagery system for non-verbal input. Both language and images are stored independently and k together through associative cross-code links. This means, and has since been confirmed with neuroscience (Miyake & Shah, 1999), that a word in the verbal system can spark an image and an image in the non-verbal system can prompt recall of a verbal fact. Experiencing a picture book in a readaloud encourages dual coding because the narrative provides verbal input and the illustrations show the concept in non-verbal form. Picture books are unique learning tools because they not only provide input in tandem but also do it contiguously in time. Mayer and Anderson (1991) call this the contiguity principle, and it supports our claim that picture books help students learn and understand theory at a deeper level. Contiguity of input helps students form a coherent mental model of theory in both images and words.

STORIES AND NATURAL COGNITION

Historically, humans have enjoyed listening to and have learned about themselves and their world through story. Stories have been created to explain natural forces, social contexts, and cultural mores (McCauley, 2000). Thinking about story, in this broader sense of the word, emphasizes how learning from narratives is an innately human, natural way of thinking, learning, and understanding what is important in one's world. Hearing the stories of others (as through a readaloud) can provide individuals with vicarious experience and may lead to insight beyond what is personally known. This is especially important when students lack background knowledge or practical experience to understand theory and how it connects to the children with whom they are working. The stories we use with our students helps them understand what that theory looks, sounds, and feels like in the context of a character's experiences.

Effective teachers often use story intuitively when they teach. They use anecdotes, analogies, and metaphors to simplify and clarify concepts, make them more concrete, and build vocabulary. Instructors share personal experiences to enrich ideas presented in the classroom and students relate to that insider perspective. Deeper understanding occurs when a more knowledgeable other assists with vocabulary understanding and points out connections that bridge initial knowledge to life experiences (Cazden, 1988; Vygotsky, 1978). Picture books and focused discussions can be used to supplement presentation of theory and concepts, allow teachers to make their point without lecture, challenge current ideas, and advance the reasoning skills of their students (Koc & Buzzelli, 2004).

ILLUSTRATIONS: A PICTURE IS WORTH A THOUSAND WORDS

Proficient readers often ignore the illustrations in a picture book, focusing on the words rather than noticing how the message of the text is reinforced through the pictures (Anderson, Kauffman & Short, 1998). In doing so, they neglect three cognitive benefits: development of visual literacy, awareness of abstract concepts, and the use of imagery.

- Visual literacy, or the learning from pictures as well as from print (Evans, 1998), is dependent on analysis of illustrations within the context of the story. Promoting visual literacy teaches students to look at pictures for the details and information they contain. Students who develop this ability move beyond concrete, literal interpretations of what they see to deeper and more complex understanding of characters, contexts, and thoughts.

Encouraging the use of visual literacy helps students look beyond the surface to the deep complexity and subtleties that exist in the world (Falk, 2005).

- Abstract concepts can come to life through illustrations in tandem with text. Drawings allow students to see theory in the context of a character's experiences and interpret the reactions, responses, and decisions that a character may make. For example, how it feels to have dyslexia is poignantly portrayed on the 24th page of *Thank you, Mr. Falker* (Polacco, 1998). Without words, the message comes through loud and clear.

- The use of imagery allows learners to form mental representations in their mind and helps make theory more concrete. Neisser (1987) notes that imagery is constructive in nature and promotes active learning, deep processing, and superior recall. A picture is worth a thousand words, and supplementing course readings and lecture with the richness of illustration can be of cognitive benefit.

Theory learned with story and illustrations is better understood, remembered, and transferred. This is a powerful way to round out learning about theory but finding and using picture books with adult learners takes know-how, time, and skill.

PICTURE BOOK SELECTION AND USE

Key points to successfully using picture books with adult learners are a thorough knowledge of theory, access to picture books, and an ability to make connections between theory and appropriate books. Stories and illustrations should match the theory presented in a clear and well-defined way. Books should contain literary elements that encourage lively discussion, problem solving, and critical thinking. We like stories with human characters, or animal characters with decidedly human characteristics that display a wide range of cognitive, and social, and emotional features.

When using picture books in our classrooms, we take steps to ensure that students can both hear the story and see the illustrations at the same time. Technology has helped us achieve this goal. We have scanned pictures into our PowerPoint presentations, and now that document cameras are available, we project the corresponding page onto the screen while we read. If technology is not available, we achieve the same goal by obtaining multiple copies of the book and small groups of students examine the illustrations as we read aloud to the whole group.

Carefully selected books are used in five ways: to introduce theory, to build background knowledge, to make theory understandable, to create an image of theory and vocabulary terms, and to help students make connections between theory and their work with children.

To introduce theory: The opening scenario is an example of how we would use a picture book to introduce a theory. Students read an assigned section from the course textbook before presentation of the theory in class. To start the session, the book is read aloud and the illustrations are projected. During the readaloud, students discuss the story and pictures as we facilitate connections between theory, the story, and the children in their classrooms. This introductory session usually entails a book that provides a broad overview of the theory because our purpose is to engage students' thinking, discussion, and wondering about the finer points and nuances of the theory.

To build background knowledge: Sometimes introductory sessions reveal that students have read the course text but lack background knowledge or practical experience to understand what the theory is truly about and how it connects to the children they see. For example, students who teach young children may not understand ethological attachment theory, or how important toys and blankets are to their young students and how they are used as a secure base (Bowlby, 1989). *Owen* by Kevin Henkes (1993) presents this theory in appealing story with delightful illustrations. A toddler named Owen attaches himself to a fuzzy yellow blanket to help self-regulate and manage stress as he experiences life's little stressors like "nail clippings and haircuts." Unfortunately, for Owen, his attachment to Fuzzy becomes a source of concern for his parents, and they try to wean him from his beloved blanket. The more they try, the more tensions arise and the more Owen needs Fuzzy. Eventually, a solution that respects both Owen's needs and those of his parents is discovered. The blanket is cut up into smaller pieces, like handkerchiefs, that Owen keeps as a secure base when he enters school. Attachment—the strong emotional bond between young children and their caregivers—is a key concept in understanding socio-emotional development (Ainsworth, 1973; Bowlby, 1989), but students may not have experience with this concept in the context of a classroom.

To make theory more understandable: Besides using picture books to help students build background, we also use them make theory understandable by placing it in the context of a story and providing a visual of what to expect when working with children. For example, when we study memory, we provide small groups of students with a copy of *Wilfred Gordon McDonald Partridge* by Mem Fox (1985). As a pre-reading activity we ask students to discuss what memory means to them. Then we have them read the book and look closely at the illustrations. This story is about a young boy named Wilfred Gordon who sets out to help ninety-six-year-old Miss Nancy find her fading memory. Because memory was a new concept, and an abstract one for a little boy, Wilfred Gordon solves the problem by talking to other people, like Mrs. Jordan, who tells him a memory is something warm. To make sense of this information, Wilfred Gordon takes a fresh, warm egg from under a hen and brings it to Miss Nancy. As she holds the warm egg, a smile crosses her face and she begins to recall her lost memories.

After finishing the story, we ask students to construct a definition of memory in the context of information processing and ways to enhance it with retrieval cues. We then explore memory strategies found in the college text like mnemonics, keywords, and acronyms.

To create an image of theory and vocabulary terms: The fourth way we use picture books is to help students form an image of theory and vocabulary terms. To help students understand the words modeling and imitation contained in Bandura's (1977) social learning theory, we read Robert Munsch's (1996) *Stephanie's Ponytail* and vary our presentation style by *not* showing the pictures. We ask students to imagine how Stephanie styled her hair and how the other children imitated her. Then our students look at copies of the book in small groups and talk about what they had imagined and what the illustrations really looked like. We then go on to introduce the pros and cons of imitation, the role models children follow today, and introduce factors that influence observational learning like a model's age, prestige, competence, or enthusiasm (Bandura, 1977). Our students inevitably begin looking at illustrations with a new view: looking for evidence of accurate interpretation of theories of educational psychology in the pages of a children's picture book.

Piaget's notion of assimilation is often a difficult concept to explain and a difficult one for students to grasp and recall. *Fish Is Fish* by Leo Lionni (1970) has become instrumental to help our students understand this abstract concept. The story creates a visual of assimilation because it illustrates a fish's mental images as he assimilates new information, heard about the world, into his existing fishy scheme. When Fish hears about cows, he envisions them as large fish with horns and udders. When Fish hears about birds, he imagines them as flying fish with wings. Each of the Fish's mental representations is a slightly altered fish-like form that builds on his existing view of his world. The illustrations in this book provide a memorable visual of how the mind assimilates new information into an existing scheme.

To help students make connections between theory and their work with children: Learning theory removed from real life or not using it to improve teaching is pointless. So is reading picture books aloud merely for the sake of a good story. Effective use of picture books happens when they help students make connections between what they learn in their educational psychology courses and the children in their lives. One way we encourage connections is to read humorous portrayals of life in the classroom like *David Goes to School* (Shannon, 1999). After listening to and examining the pictures in this short story, students get into small groups to discuss David's behavior in the context of behaviorism. Students discuss rewards and punishments that could be used with David, the Premack principle, and behavior contracts. Our students enjoy talking about their internship

Table 1: Theory and Its Connection to Picture Books

THEORY/CONCEPT/VOCABULARY	TITLE, AUTHOR, YEAR OF PUBLICATION
Piaget's theory of cognitive development preoperational thinking, imagination, pretend play, and constructing knowledge	*Lilly's Purple Plastic Purse* (1996) and *A Weekend with Wendell* (1986) both by Kevin Henkes
Piaget—assimilation—prior knowledge	*Fish Is Fish* by Leo Lionni (1970)
Vygotsky's—sociocultural perspective of cognitive development	*Once There Were Giants* by Waddell (1989)
Vygotsky's zone of proximal development	*The Three Bears* by Paul Galdone (1972)
Erikson's psychosocial development—identity	*The Big Box* by Toni Morrison and Slade Morrison (1990); *The Sissy Duckling* by Harvey Fierstein (2002); *Whomever You Are* by Mem Fox (1997)
Self-esteem, self-concept, resiliency	*Stand Tall, Molly Lou Melon* by Pati Lovell (2002)
Kohlberg and Gilligan—moral development	*Rose Blanche* by Christopher Gallaz and Roberto Innocenti (1985); *The Butterfly* by Patricia Polacco (2000); *Pink and Say* by Patricia Polacco (1994)
Information processing, long term memory	*Wilfred Gordon McDonald Partridge* by Mem Fox (1985) and *Something to Remember Me By* by Susan V. Bosak & Laurie McGraw (1999)
Attention difficulties	*Waiting for Mr. Goose* by Laurie Lears (1999)
Behaviorism—rewards and punishment	*David Goes to School* by David Shannon (1999)
Motivation—Attribution Theory	*Ronald Morgan Goes to Bat* by Giff (1990); *Willie the Wizard* by A. Browne (1995)
Reading disabilities, differentiated instruction, emotions, stress, resiliency	*Thank You, Mr. Falker* by Patricia Polacco (1998)

ιassrooms and the behavior plans being used. This connection bridges the gap between picture book character, theory, and classroom. Virtually every theory or principle, with a little creativity and a good selection of picture books, can be interpreted from within a character's perspective. Table 1 provides a list of theories commonly taught in beginning educational psychology courses and titles we have used successfully to scaffold connections.

CONCLUSION

Supplementing educational psychology instruction with picture books is not without its disadvantages. There is only so much time in a seventy-five minute class period, and we have had to forego case study discussions in lieu of responding to a picture book. Generally, we save case studies from our textbook for areas that we have not yet found a suitable picture book. Another disadvantage is problems with documenting student achievement with empirical evidence. Measuring differences in retention of theory is difficult because we cannot ethically withhold what we feel to be a highly effective teaching method from a control group. However, our teaching evaluations are consistently high, and many students mention our use of picture books in the written portion of our course evaluation forms. Comments include:

> "You gave me a new understanding to a picture book I already loved."
> "The more information I have, presented in different formats, helps reinforce my learning of concepts."
> "I am very open to the idea of picture books in the classroom."
> "I think using picture books is a creative and fresh way to teach themes."
> "I enjoyed your psychological interpretations of the picture books."

Our background in teaching reading with children's literature has, undoubtedly, contributed to our success. It may be difficult for instructors to adopt this approach without that prior experience. Nonetheless, our best lessons have been the ones that our students created by responding to the picture books from their unique perspectives and surprising us with their interpretations.

Picture books are one way that educational psychology instructors can transition theory gained from textbooks and lecture to its application in authentic interactions with children. Skilled authors and illustrators help us place theory in context and provide a visual image of it in action. Thinking about practical applications of theory and concepts, coupled with a solid foundation in educational psychology, increases the likelihood that our students will apply theory in their classrooms. The possibilities are limitless, and with a little creativity and ingenuity, theory can come alive through the pages of a picture book.

CHILDREN'S BOOKS CITED

Cooney, B. (1982). *Miss Rumphius*. New York: Puffin Books.

Fox, M. (1985). *Wilfred Gordon McDonald Partridge*. Brooklyn, NY: Kane/Miller Books.

Henkes, K. (1993). *Owen*. New York: Greenwillow Books.

Henkes, K. (1996). *Lilly's purple plastic purse*. New York: Greenwillow Books.

Jeffers, S. (1991). *Brother Eagle, Sister Sky*. New York: Dial.

Lionni, L. (1970). *Fish is fish*. New York: Scholastic.

Munsch, R. (1996). *Stephanie's ponytail*. New York: Annick.

Polacco, P. (1998). *Thank you, Mr. Falker.* New York: Scholastic.

Seuss, Dr. (1989). *The Sneeches and other stories.* New York: Random House.

Seuss, Dr. (1990). *Oh, the places you'll go!* New York: Random House.

Shannon, D. (1999). *David goes to school.* New York: Blue Sky.

REFERENCES

Ainsworth, M. (1973). The development of infant-mother attachment. In B. M. Caldwell & H. N. Ricciuti (Eds.), *Review of child development research* (pp. 1–94). Chicago, IL: University of Chicago Press.

Alexander, P. A. (2006). *Psychology in learning and instruction.* Upper Saddle River, NJ: Merrill Prentice Hall.

Anderson, C., Kauffman, G., & Short, K. G. (1998). Now I think like an artist: Responding to picture books. In J. Evans (Ed.), *What's in the picture? Responding to illustrations in picture books* (pp. 146–165). London, UK: Paul Chapman Publishing Ltd.

Bandura, A. (1977). *Social learning theory.* Upper Saddle River, NJ: Prentice Hall.

Bowlby, J. (1989). *Secure attachment.* New York: Basic Books.

Bruner, J. S. (1966). *Toward a theory of instruction.* New York: Norton.

Cazden, C.B. (1988). *Classroom discourse: The language of teaching and learning.* Portsmouth, NH: Heinemann.

Demers, P., & Moyles, G. (1982). From instruction to delight: An anthology of children's literature to 1850. Toronto: Oxford University Press.

Evans, J. (1998). *What's in the picture: Responding to illustrations in picture books.* London: Paul Chapman Publishing Ltd.

Falk, L. (2005). Paintings and stories: Making connections. *Arizona Reading Journal, 31*(2), 19–21.

Hansen, C. C., & Zambo, D. (in press). Piaget, meet Lilly: Understanding child development through picture book characters. *Early Childhood Education Journal.*

Ho, L. (2000). Children's literature in adult education. *Children's Literature in Education, 31*(4), 259–271.

Juchartz, L. R. (2004). Team teaching with Dr. Seuss and Shel Silverstein in the college basic reading classroom. *Journal of Adolescent and Adult Literacy, 47*(4), 336–341.

Koc, K. & Buzzelli, C. A. (2004). The moral of the story is…Using children's literature in moral education. *Young Children,* 92–96.

Mayer, R. E., & Anderson R.B. (1991). Animations need narrations: An experimental test of dual coding hypothesis. *Journal of Educational Psychology, 83,* 484–490.

McCauley, R. N. (2000). The naturalness of religion and the unnaturalness of science. In F. C. Keil & R. W. Wilson (Eds.), *Explanation and cognition* (pp. 61–86). Cambridge, MA: MIT Press.

Mitchell, W. J. T. (1994). *Picture theory: Essays on verbal and visual representations.* Chicago: University of Chicago Press.

Miyake, A., & Shah, P. (1999). *Models of working memory: Mechanisms of active maintenance and executive control.* New York: Cambridge University Press.

National Research Council. (2000). *How people learn: Brain, mind, experience, and school.* Washington, DC: National Academic Press.

Neisser, U. (1987). *Concepts and conceptual development.* New York: Cambridge University Press.

Paivio, A. (1971). *Imagery and verbal processes.* New York: Holt, Rinehart and Winston.

Paivio, A. (1991). Dual coding theory: Retrospect and current status. *Canadian Journal of Psychology, 45,* 255–287.

Piaget, J., & Inhelder, B. (2000). *The psychology of the child.* New York: Basic Books.

Routman, R. (1994). *Invitations: Changing as teachers and learners K-12.* Portsmouth, NH: Heinemann.

Santrock, J. W. (2004). *Child development teacher's edition.* (10th ed.). Boston, MA: McGraw-Hill.

Sipe, L. (2001). Picturebooks as aesthetic objects. *Literacy Teaching and Learning, 6*(1), 23-42.

Smallwood, B. A. (1992). *Children's literature for adult ESL literacy.* Washington, DC: National Clearinghouse on Literacy Education. (ERIC Document Reproduction Service No. ED353864).

Vygotsky, L. S. (1978). *Mind in society: The development of higher psychological processes.* Cambridge, MA: Harvard University Press.

Woolfolk, A. (2004). *Educational psychology* (9th ed.). New York: Pearson Education, Inc.

Zambo, D. (2005). Using the picture book *Thank You, Mr. Falker* to understand struggling readers. *Journal of Adolescent and Adult Literacy, 48*(6), 502–512.

FORTY-SEVEN

An Educational Psychology of Development for Preservice Teachers

James R. Jelmberg

The mission of the Five Year Teacher Education Program at the University of New Hampshire is "to prepare beginning teacher leaders who demonstrate excellence in classroom practice and who will become educational leaders" (Department of Education, 2008, p. 3) and who will eventually play a major role in staff development with their peers, in continued in-service education, and in initiating curriculum changes. This program begins the preservice teacher's development with a field-based seminar entitled Exploring Teaching. This Phase I course for sophomores is followed by professional education courses and a liberal arts major in the junior and senior years: Phase II. Phase III features a nine-month capstone, post-baccalaureate internship, and seminar leading toward a master's degree.

The principal goal of Exploring Teaching is to help prospective teachers make realistic career decisions by experientially learning what teachers do while they also critically analyze their personal and professional goals. To accomplish this goal, students spend five to seven hours per week assisting an experienced and successful classroom teacher. University instructors conduct weekly seminars to integrate the classroom experience through focused discussions in a supportive atmosphere. A range of issues is discussed related to curriculum and instruction with classroom teachers as seminar participants. A student description of their experience in the course includes this comment:

> Not only did I learn about teaching through an interaction with the students, but I learned about myself as a person and as an individual. I've learned about my strengths and weaknesses, and I've realized my potential in various capacities. I firmly believe that students allow teachers to grow, develop, and learn,

just as teachers foster the development and growth of their students. I now view teaching as a dynamic process of living and learning about one's self as well as others. I wouldn't change the experiences I've shared with the students for anything!

I believe the reason that the teaching profession has become so very appealing to me is that teaching will allow me to fulfill many of my life-long personal values and goals. Simply put, one of my greatest desires is to work with people. In this capacity I will be able to give something back to society. To me nothing could be more rewarding than helping young people develop by exposing them to many and varied ideas. This is exactly what teaching revolves around. Through exposure to knowledge, people are able to develop their own personalities, values, goals, moral ideas and life styles.

The purpose of this investigation is to attempt to answer the question: what is the effect of Exploring Teaching on the preservice development of undergraduates? This qualitative investigation examined student journals, self-assessment papers, and final interviews for evidence of preservice teacher growth that may have occurred in two distinct seminar sections over the course of one year. The population of this study was comprised of thirty-six University of New Hampshire students enrolled in two sections of the Exploring Teaching seminar. These prospective teachers were mostly (but not limited to) sophomores and ranged in age from 19 to 40 years.

A common objective of the Exploring Teaching seminar students is to decide whether or not to enter the next phase of the Five Year Teacher Education Program. To accomplish this objective, the students were strongly encouraged to participate in as many of the roles of the teacher and to do as much actual teaching as the cooperating teachers considered feasible. This process aligns with the Kohlberg and Turiel developmental growth theory. "The stimulus for helping people move into higher stages of abstract reasoning comes primarily from the interaction with others who are functioning at more advanced stages. The assumption is at more advanced stages, people can promote the conditions, set the environment, offer the support, and provide the probing questions or ideas to stimulate and challenge the thinking of those at lower stages" (Oja, 1991, p. 42).

Accompanied by support and encouragement from the cooperating teachers, the university students performed challenging teacher roles. This experiential aspect was accompanied by reflective journal writing and a focused, supportive discussion in seminar. It has been the premise of this program's process that through the tandem experiences of exploring teaching and reflecting on the experience there exists both the challenge and support necessary for preservice teacher development. Preservice teacher development is defined as a change in outlook or practice that would represent the higher abstract thinking that a teacher often uses to solve complex instructional problems.

Prompting my interest in the question of the effectiveness of the Exploring Teaching program was a discovery that followed several months of involvement with the Collaborative Approach to Leadership in Supervision Project (1987), a three-year study of teachers' stages of development at the UNH Education Department. While co-leading my second Exploring Teaching seminar section, I found an engaging entry in the journal of one of my music education students that caused me to think of Exploring Teaching as a possible strong force for preservice teacher development. Dana had just seen a middle school performance of *The Mikado* during which several groups that he had observed came together to create an impressive overall performance. Prior to this performance, he was skeptical of his cooperating teacher's methods. "Each part was so imperfect in rehearsal I never thought the whole could come together." After seeing the final performance, Dana began to develop a more holistic view:

I was knocked out at how well it was done. I saw a great deal of things pull together from the classroom that I did not expect to see. I am sure that this production taught the kids more than they will know. It certainly opened my eyes to an alternative way of teaching. It has shown me better classroom values, and it is an experience I won't forget.

Dana had prior experience giving instrumental lessons to high school students and assisting his former band director. However, despite entering Exploring Teaching with preset ideas, he was able to change his outlook by working in the middle school program. His cooperating teacher challenged him to develop some of his weaker skills, such as piano and choral activities, and Dana began to see himself as a motivator. "I'm much less dictatorial, I see my job as getting the students excited. I think it's a much better approach. I want to make them come to me." Later, in the exit interview, he reflected on the seminar. "I've learned a lot. I can't think of one session that didn't make me see things differently. The special ed. kids…I'm always thinking what am I going to do to get them involved?"

Dana's reflections show a willingness to adopt alternative teaching methods, in this case a new style of teaching that emphasized motivation. His change in outlook is one indicator of a preservice teacher's developmental growth and is an example of the type of evidence I began to find in the self-assessment papers of the students who took the course. These self-assessment papers, written at the end of the course, included students' feelings about the development of teaching within the context of their goals and values. Personal insights and plans to improve weaknesses were also included. Student experiences are included to demonstrate this educational psychology of development process more clearly.

TEACHER DEVELOPMENT

One of the authors we read who has done significant research in ego development in the context of teacher development in the CALS Project was Jane Loevinger (Hy & Loevinger, 1996). While Loevinger has identified eight stages of ego development, for the purpose of this investigation the five middle stages are most appropriate to the discussion of students in this course and their development toward understanding and solving complex instructional problems.

SELF-PROTECTIVE STAGE (STAGE 3)

The Self-Protective stage is egocentric and "the first step toward control of impulses and character development and occurs when the child becomes capable of delay for immediate advantage." People at this stage "appreciate rules and know it is to their advantage to play by them." They are opportunistic and "lack long term goals and ideals." "They want immediate gratification and will exploit others" to get their way. They are defensive and self-protective and see "interpersonal relationships as exploitative." They do not take responsibility when they get into trouble, as they "assign blame to others" or to circumstances. Most adults move beyond this stage, but those who do not "see life as a zero-sum game."

CONFORMIST STAGE (STAGE 4)

Normally there is a transition from the self-protective stage to the "group centered Conformist stage where a person identifies with the group or its authority such as peers or authority figures." Rules are accepted with little question. There is a "right way and a wrong way, and it is the same for everyone all of the time." What is right is what is "conventional and socially approved." One is overly concerned with "appearance, material things, and social acceptance and belonging." People are not seen in terms of individual differences.

SELF-AWARENESS STAGE (STAGE 5)

Self-aware stage people realize that many do not always conform and are "open to begin examination of self." Interpersonal relations are described "not merely as actions but also in terms of feelings." Many self-aware people "distinguish between self and group." They see "alternative possibilities in many situations" and exceptions to the rule are sanctioned. These exceptions are not stated in terms of individual differences but in "broad demographic terms." For example, some activities are sanctioned because of being part of a group, not because of individual merit.

CONSCIENTIOUS STAGE (STAGE 6)

The most prominent characteristic of the Conscientious stage is "self-evaluated standards." Conduct is sanctioned not just because others approve, but "because it is what I personally feel." "Motives and consequences are more important than rules per se." What ought to be becomes more important. The "recognition of multiple possibilities in situations leads to a sense of choice; decisions are made for reasons." Goals are important, and "one tries to live up to ideals, and to improve the self." Moral issues are seen as distinct from "conventional rules and from esthetic standards…involving greater conceptual complexity." Achievement is very important, not just for social approval, but "in terms of one's own standards." People think "beyond their own personal concerns to those of society." People are seen as "having and being different in different roles."

INDIVIDUALISTIC STAGE (STAGE 7)

While the Conscientious stage person has "a vivid sense of individual differences, the person at the next stage (Individualistic) has a sense of individuality, of the personality as a whole or the style of life." There is a "greater tolerance for individual differences, and relationships with other people have become deeper and more intensive." In this later developmental stage, people are seen as "having and being different in different roles." These developmental stages reveal themselves as students move through the Exploring Teaching process. The following examples demonstrate how our sophomores develop through the stages to achieve appropriate maturity to become preservice educators.

GINA'S STORY

Gina began her Exploring Teaching experience not as a prospective teacher but as a sophomore strongly influenced by peers who had negative opinions about teaching.

As I entered into my first seminar, rather than a prospective teacher, I was quite skeptical about teaching, and rather confused about the particular pathway I should follow when choosing a viable career. As a person guided by outside pressure and the strong opinions of the people closest to me, I looked at the teaching profession "half-heartedly," often with a glib smile, saying to myself, "Yes, but…"

The doubt that I experienced had surfaced through discussion with those around me, people who view teaching as a "lowly profession." These people feel that teaching is for those "frustrated intellectuals who can't make it in the real world." Some of the many questions and comments that have been posed to me include:

"Why waste your time teaching?"

"You'll starve if you become a teacher."

"You're too smart to be a teacher."

"Use your brains and talent in the pursuit of a real profession."

"You'll be bored after one year of teaching."

"Teaching isn't challenging enough for you."

In essence, these people have been trying to determine what is right for me. In their eyes, teaching isn't worth the time or the effort. If nothing else, the University's Exploring Teaching program has opened many closed doors for me, and I have now come to the realization that only I can determine what is right for me! Furthermore, I can now answer all of the questions posed, and comment on all of the skepticism in a confident manner, for I now know that I want to be a teacher. Despite all of the negative feedback I've received, having experienced teaching first hand, I feel that I have made a well informed career decision. Not only am I elated, but I am personally satisfied and completely fulfilled when I stop to ponder the decision I've made.

Despite anxiety approaching panic, Gina decided to "dispel" all of her preconceived notions about teaching and "learn first hand just what teaching really entails." She worked with two very different cooperating teachers. Demonstrating flexibility, Gina saw this as a challenging opportunity that could offer a better support system.

Working with two individuals who differ greatly in teaching styles, attitudes, approaches, and other areas, I had the ideal situation for forming an understanding of teaching through comparison and contrast. I found it very enlightening to hear both viewpoints concerning the profession. I felt that this specific situation was perfect for completing the task at hand. Through discussions with my cooperating teachers, I would gain invaluable insight into the teaching profession which could be used in my final decision making process. The nervousness was beginning to dissipate, and that strong sense of confidence in myself and what I was trying to accomplish came rushing back. The motivation and excitement had become very evident.

Gina began to grow and to see herself in a new role. At that point she began to adopt certain behaviors appropriate for developing a unique and mature relationship with each student.

There wasn't a time I left school without thinking about the students and the events of the day. I began looking forward to Mondays when I could go back to school, learn more about teaching, and learn more through teaching. I truly began to feel a sense of belonging, a sense of worth, a sense of pride. I had become enthralled with teaching and awed by it.

I find it difficult to express in words just how fulfilling it was for me to work with the students. Being able to answer their questions, clear up any misconceptions they had, and help them to achieve and grow, truly gave me a high. I think that my success in this area was one of the deciding factors in my choice to pursue teaching. I came to know all of the students in the Chemistry lab class, and I developed a different relationship with each and every student. I can truly say that I love them all and I greatly respect them as individuals. Each relationship has opened my eyes, and each relationship has been special.

The idea of the right amount of challenge combined with support as being all important ingredients for adult development (Kohlberg, 1976) can be seen in Gina's reflection after she taught her first large group class.

> Although nervous, I took a long, deep breath, cleared my throat, and proceeded to the front of the classroom. Once behind the podium, I slowly lifted my head, fearing that once my eyes met theirs, I would not be able to speak. No such luck! It wasn't as bad as I had imagined; in fact, I actually felt rather comfortable in the position. I presented the entire lesson, answered all of their questions, and successfully got the necessary material across. I was thrilled! I had proven to myself that I could function effectively in many of the necessary roles of a teacher. I had become confident that through my experiences within the school, not only had I tapped many of my hidden resources, but I had successfully unlocked one of my most hidden desires, the desire to teach.

> As is extremely evident, my experience as an Exploring Teaching student was nothing but positive and reinforcing. Both of the teachers I had the privilege and honor to work with were extremely cooperative and helpful, and above all friends. They understood the purpose and goals of the program and worked very hard and with a great deal of patience, while guiding me through the acclimating process. The students I had the privilege to work with were exceptional, and I just can't say enough about them.

Gina began to set her goals and express her thoughts in terms that reveal a new self-awareness and possibly the beginnings of self-definition as a teacher. Expressing a strong sense of her own values, Gina saw these values as integrated with her newly chosen career.

> Something else that I greatly value is my individuality. It is very important for me to be able to express myself through words, actions, and emotions. I feel that honesty and trust are essential in any relationship whether it be with those individuals one comes in contact within his or her career or with a friend. I feel that teaching will enable me to express myself in many and varied ways. I will be able to use my imagination as well as express my individuality through the workings of my classroom.

> Through teaching, a sense of confidence and accomplishment can also be obtained. Through teaching I hope to enable people to strive and reach new heights through academics. A sound education is the basis for so very many things throughout an individual's life. I want to have an opportunity to make a difference. I want to be of significance to others.

Gina also saw teaching as being compatible with her lifelong goals of marriage, having a family, and having a challenging career.

> I feel that growth, development, and learning should never stop. As stated before, I see teaching as a dynamic career which presents possibilities for growth in all areas constantly.

Gina then briefly defined her action plan to attain these goals.

> My goal as a student at the university is to further myself through education, while growing and developing personally. I feel that success within the university system is gained through learning about one's self and challenging one's self in all capacities.

This plan also includes a yearlong internship and a master's degree. Revealing further self-awareness in response to the question "What problems do you see confronting you with a teaching career?" Gina expressed a realistic view about meeting the needs of her students.

> As a teacher I would have to realize that I will not be able to reach every single student all of the time. It will become necessary to focus on the very little and sometimes not so obvious accomplishments on a day to day basis. It will become very important for me to realize that I will be able to succeed with some of the students some of the time, but I won't be able to reach all of the students all of the

time. I further believe that I will have to draw a line between school and my students, and my own personal life. I know that my first tendency will be to get more and more involved with the students both academically and with extracurricular activities. I will have to take the time out to reach some sort of equilibrium between the two very early in my career.

Realizing the significant self-direction and identity changes that she has made, Gina finished her self-assessment paper with:

In conclusion, Exploring Teaching has been the most rewarding class I've taken thus far at the university. Not only have I been able to clear up all of my misconceptions about teaching as well as come to the realization that a teaching career is definitely for me, but I have learned more about myself than I thought possible.

By the end of the semester Gina had clearly emerged from a period of peer conformity to a point where she was not only thinking independently, but she was aware that teaching was a way to achieve both her personal and professional goals. Confirming our original premise, Gina's Exploring Teaching experiences appear to have provided an optimum amount of support and challenge to bring about this development of self-direction.

Gina's example of preservice development is dramatic. To further demonstrate the wide range of growth among these students, I will compare and contrast two other student experiences with Gina's. Tricia demonstrates much potential as a future teacher but shows few insights about her personal development.

TRICIA'S EXPERIENCE

Like Gina, Tricia expressed her independent point of view in the self-assessment paper. She, too, was keenly aware of peer opinion.

I had heard from other Music Education majors that the Exploring Teaching class was really boring because they could not relate to the other future educators. I totally disagree with this statement. I believe that if you cannot interact with your colleagues in other subject areas, you will not be a successful teacher. It is important that it combines all aspects of education. In order to sing you need to read; you need to count and divide in order to accurately read rhythms. Exploring Teaching taught me this as well as many other important aspects of teaching.

Also like Gina, her goals were altruistic.

As young children we all have dreams and often that dream changes because of different people or because of our parents. I have always wanted to make a difference in people's lives. I want to educate, counsel, and help young people with the difficult decisions of life.

I still do have dreams and aspirations but they are now more directed. These dreams and aspirations involve education and more directly, music education. As a music educator, my first and foremost responsibility to the educational community is to be able to effectively diffuse my musical knowledge to the students. To do this I must be the best musician that I can be. However, I feel that it is very important to also teach the aesthetic appreciation of music, art, and society to the students.

I believe that socialization is an important part of education. All too often I think that academics are stressed too much. I am not saying that academics are not important, because they are. We could not get anywhere in this world without our academic system. But what I am saying is that people have to get along with each other so that academics will work effectively. As educators, I believe that it is our responsibility to pick up where the parents leave off and teach self-respect, pride, and communication skills at the school. If there is an apparent problem with a student, this student should be pointed in the right direction to receive help.

Recognizing that the child's point of view is important, Tricia endorses an approach to classroom discipline that stresses flexibility and compromise.

While I was observing gym at ORMS, I learned a lot about kids. I learned how to be an effective disciplinarian, through the art of compromising. I learned that if I took a stand and was not wishy-washy about my decision, then I would be respected. When I took a stand and stuck to it then my decision was met. Through Mr. Smith, one of the teachers that I was working with, I learned the idea of positive communication. I like the way that he sends notes to let the kids know that he cares. If they do something nice for someone else or if they do well on something academically, he reinforces this positive behavior with a positive reaction. This process diffuses from the student to their peers and to their teachers. He lets the kids know that someone cares about than. At the same time he still has control in his classroom. When he says no, the kids know that he means no; however, he is willing to debate the issue if the student feels the need. The student is his main concern, as it should be.

Receiving support from her cooperating teachers, she changed her attitude from: "I'm not looking forward to this…" to "This might not be a bad semester after all."

After that first class, both Mrs. Green and Mr. Smith came up to me and said that even though I had forgotten my sneakers, they were impressed because I was on time and I had jumped right in and participated. I told them that I had decided to treat this just like a job, and essentially it was. Their compliment made me feel great and made me think, hey, this might not be such a bad semester after all. The kids were great, energetic, and did not seem to mind taking gym for the most part. I think that this is because inside the gym they were treated fairly.

Tricia began to reflect on her philosophy of education which shows a well rounded approach with an emphasis on citizenship.

They were taught respect for themselves and their peers, not just how to play different sports. This concept is part of my philosophy on education. This philosophy is that students should receive a well-rounded education. Rounded is the key word here, meaning that students should be educated in all areas of our society: English, math, science, foreign languages, art, music, and socialization. Citizenship should be accentuated so that our communities may be a little more pleasant. Maybe the socioeconomic situation would be better and the crime rate would be lower if people were more positive about themselves, if their dreams, goals, and aspirations were helped along by educators, and made more attainable.

Tricia then outlined her action plan to accomplish her goals.

One of my dreams is to be comfortable economically. The lifestyle that I plan to lead is going to be tough if I am to survive only on the salary of a teacher, period. However, I plan to teach private lessons, play in shows, at weddings, direct extra functions at the school that I am employed by. These functions would include jazz band, marching band, pep band, and musicals. During the school year my life will be very student oriented and during the summer I will continue as I have for the last three summers. I will work.

Further plans included continuing education and providing extracurricular activities to students.

I think it is very important for the teacher to always be learning. Education never ends even when you are a teacher of education. Our society is always changing, and new philosophies and techniques are always being developed. As educators we have to be on top of that change. We have to be one step ahead because it is our responsibility to educate the kids, not for them to educate us. We cannot close our eyes to chemical problems, such as drugs and alcohol, emotional problems, such as deaths, suicides, and divorces, and personal problems, such as pregnancy, sexuality, and relationships. Kids are our main concern, not just their education but their well-being.

In order to be an exceptional teacher, I think graduate studies are very important. I believe that I will wait for a few years before I attend graduate school for Music Education. The reason that I have decided to wait is not so much financial as it is professional. I want to make sure that my philosophy of education is rounded, valid, and reasonable.

In addition to making educational experiences available to myself, I plan to always make educational experiences available to my students. As a music educator, I will make all musical opportunities available to my students. I will make them aware of and help them prepare for musical events such as regional and district competitions, solo and ensemble festivals, all-state, and scholarship opportunities. I will inform them of all musical functions that I know about and help them prepare. I will always be willing to recommend teachers for interested students if they are beyond my abilities of teaching on that particular instrument.

Showing a good approach to a problem, Tricia already has a plan to solve her greatest fear.

Although I want to be the best teacher that I can be, I do have fears. One of my greatest fears about becoming a teacher is that I will get so wrapped up in teaching that I will overlook some things. These things include my own musicianship. I am afraid that by the time I get done teaching for the day and going to rehearsals that I will not practice as much as I should. I am also afraid that I will have so much energy that I might want more for the kids than they want for themselves. How do you make someone want to be interested, or how do you help that kid that is interested in music but afraid of the typical failures? Is there any other way besides having sell-out musicals or touring groups with state-wide or nation-wide recognition to participate in musical events such as band concerts or vocal concerts? This is one problem that I plan to address head on. Hopefully my colleagues will have the same concerns and we can all brainstorm together and tackle the problem.

Other indicators of development include creativity with children.

When I began babysitting in the sixth grade, I was always the babysitter that the kids wanted back because I always played the games that they wanted to play. I always had so much fun adding different twists to their pre-adolescent fun. Everyone always told me how good I was with children and suggested that I should consider teaching as a profession.

Like Gina, Tricia has overcome her peers' attitudes toward teaching and has clearly established her own direction. She has outlined her goals and plans to meet these goals and the beginnings of an educational philosophy. Tricia also shows creativity and a strong desire for self-improvement.

Both Gina and Tricia seem to have begun Exploring Teaching at what Loevinger would describe as the Conformist stage (Hy & Loevinger, 1996), strongly influenced by the opinions of others and very skeptical about entering teaching as a career. Although they both appear to have moved quickly to Self-Aware stage (Hy & Loevinger, 1996), with their "sense of distinction between self and group" (p. 5), the development curve throughout the rest of the course seemed quite different. Unlike Gina who "came to know all of the students" in chemistry lab class and "developed a different relationship with each student," Tricia shows no evidence of having a well-developed child orientation. Nowhere in Tricia's journal or paper is it clear that she recognized individual differences among students or that she had thought about individual students very much. In contrast, Gina wrote, "There wasn't a time I left school without thinking about the students...."

Tricia, following the Music Department's guideline, explored her teaching in another subject. While she was enthusiastic, she clearly took fewer risks than Gina and challenged herself less. Also unlike Gina, Tricia's journal entries were more mechanical than reflective. Tricia's lack of introspection and her few references to specific inner feelings would place her at a less-developed level than Gina.

Gina's conscious concerns and interpersonal style advanced quickly through reflection and expression of self, feelings, and ideals. Loevinger characterizes this as the Conscientious stage. Gina then moved on to recognizing individual differences and increasing tolerance for herself, her students and her significant other, developing "a sense of individuality, of the personality as a whole." She seemed to show "greater tolerance for individual differences" (p. 6), and her "relationships with other people have become deeper and more intensive" (p. 6). These traits and her understanding of what she was feeling and perceiving at the moment would seem to place her concerns and interpersonal style in the Individualistic stage (Hy & Loevinger, 1996), two stages above where she started and Tricia ended.

While Tricia had begun to develop a philosophy about the importance of fostering citizenship and a well rounded education, she showed fewer changes in her outlook as a result of Exploring Teaching. In contrast, Gina wrote about her experience in terms of how it had changed the meaning of her life. Gina had developed her stronger sense of self by challenging herself more and by deeper reflection. She taught in her subject and energetically volunteered for many teaching opportunities including substitute teaching.

> Not only did I learn about teaching through interaction with students, but I learned about myself as a person…my strengths and weaknesses, and realized my potential in various capacities. I firmly believe that students allow teachers to grow, develop, and learn, just as teachers foster the development and growth of their students.

Because Gina sought more challenges and reflected more intensely about them, she achieved more dramatic changes in self-definition. Gina's and Tricia's examples illustrate Kohlberg's (1976) position that the right amount of support and challenge leads to development. Since students appear to begin Exploring Teaching at different stages, these supports and challenges need to be individualized. Seminar leaders and cooperating teachers need to recognize this entry level and challenge their exploring teachers accordingly. Requiring Tricia to explore in her own subject, music, could have provided much more challenge and in turn more opportunities for meaningful reflection. Finally, some students may begin at such a low stage that it may be too difficult for them to be an acceptable candidate despite significant levels of support and sufficient challenges.

ANNE

In contrast to all of the other students in her section, Anne showed few changes and almost no growth throughout the semester. Despite feedback from her cooperating teacher, seminar instructors, and peers, she remained resistant to ideas both in the classroom and in seminar. Anne appeared to have difficulty developing sensitivity to her environment. During a visit to the seminar by the administrator of a local alternative school, Anne's inflexibility surfaced. Anne's query to the guest speaker from the local alternative high school for potential dropouts was "How are they going to be prepared for later life if you don't have higher academic expectations at your school?" Despite suggestions from her classmates that she had missed the point and that academic growth could come only after improved self-image, she remained critical of the relational approach being presented.

When her cooperating teacher used a student-planned medieval festival as an approach to a topic in seventh grade social studies, Anne felt that the approach took too much time. When I pointed out the enthusiasm, planning, teamwork, and ideas that the students would remember for a long time, she remained unconvinced. Rather than examining her own approach, she was shocked when the same students were not attentive to a fifty-minute lecture she had presented.

Why this lack of growth? Perhaps there is a correlation between the lack of challenge and lack of development? Anne remained completely resistant to alternative methods. Her lack of risk-taking is exemplified by her conclusion in the self-assessment paper. "I intend to seek certification...but do not intend to teach until my daughters are finished with school." Anne was very quick to criticize her children's teachers but apparently was not willing to take a teaching position in the near future. Rather than reflect on the advantages and disadvantages of new instructional methods, she rejected them outright and remained defensive, inflexible, and seemingly fixed in the Self-Protective stage (Hy & Loevinger, 1996). Gina, Tricia, and Anne leave us with at least two questions. Is there an identifiable and consistent pattern of preservice teacher growth and development among a whole section of students? What are the specific aspects of the course that might further stimulate and foster the development of the preservice teacher?

A CONFIRMATION AND MORE QUESTIONS: FOUR STEPS

A preliminary review of the self-assessment papers of the other students reveals a general and consistent tone of naiveté and idealism blended with a certain amount of assignment-induced direction setting. Once past these predictable attitudes and barriers, there are indications of personal and pre-professional growth that could be considered more permanent. These indicators appeared in the form of changes in outlook and/or practice that seem to fall into several categories.

The first was a change in their perspectives. Students often saw teaching in a much different, usually more positive way than they had imagined it to be. This new outlook often resulted from the confidence they gained from their new role as preservice teacher. Sometimes this was described as a kind of revelation about some unexpected personal achievement, and other times it showed a clear endorsement of alternative teaching methods. Gina exemplifies developmental transformation when she writes:

> I presented the entire lesson, answered all their questions, and successfully got the necessary material across. I was thrilled! I had proven to myself that I could function effectively in many of the necessary roles of a teacher.

This new outlook appeared in many of the Exploring Teaching students' journals based upon their first experiences in the classroom. These conclusions were often confirmed and developed during the third seminar session when students shared their initial reactions. This 'Ah-ha!' moment was experienced again half-way through the semester when the students shared their emerging career decisions.

The next category became clear when, in response to the second self-assessment paper guideline, almost all students set their academic and career goals. Not nearly as many chose to respond to the part of this guideline which asked them to discuss their values. Most students then outlined their action plan to accomplish their goals in response to guideline No. 4 which queries, "What steps can you begin to take now to capitalize on your strengths and weaknesses in working toward a satisfying career choice?"

Last, several students described what might be called a new sense of self-direction often related to either career direction, or a statement of values, probably in response to either guideline No. 5, "What have you learned about yourself...?" or guideline No. 1, "What are your lifelong, personal values...?"

RESULTS: THE SECOND SECTION

The following results for the second section do confirm a pattern of developmental changes in our students. Although three of the four steps are assignment induced, once the students respond to the questions, it would appear that they actually begin to change their outlook, set new goals, plan action steps, and become more aware of their self-direction.

NEW OUTLOOK

After several weeks, 17 of the 18 students adopted a new outlook (Step 1) on either the profession of teaching, themselves, or both. Examples of this new outlook range from learning "how demanding and challenging the profession is" to "how the students are open, friendly, and want to learn." Other examples include: "I've learned to appreciate them and treat them like people, not like children." and "It's not the end of the world if you flop in front of the class."

GOALS

All students began to set goals (Step 2, assignment induced) for their teaching or, in one case non-teaching, career choice. Many of these goals show independent thinking, and in at least three cases, these are clearly altruistic. One exploring teacher decided to go beyond her extremely successful cooperating teacher and have more discussion groups, arrange furniture differently, and "help students verbalize thoughts among themselves rather than with a higher figure." The student elaborated:

> Teaching fits into my goals in life. I want to be in the company of kids. I want to teach with creativity, enthusiasm, and care...using student interests...and diverse projects....I want to coach a swim team. I've taken so much from the sport, I want to give it back.

ACTION PLAN

Thirteen students (72%) responded to assessment guideline No. 4 and formed an action plan to capitalize on their strengths and minimize weaknesses in working toward their career choice. These planned activities are in addition to courses and range from immediate investigations to correct weaknesses to longer range courses of action, such as the master's degree option. Immediate activities include tutoring, talking to students over lunch, becoming an assistant yearbook advisor, assisting a former band director, coaching a hockey team, substitute teaching, and counseling in Upward Bound. These activities represent such opportunities for improving communication skills, decision making, and knowledge of students, that it is not difficult to see the potential for later teacher development.

SELF-DEFINITION

Eight students (44%) expressed a strong sense of self-definition, probably in response to guideline No. 5, "What have you learned about yourself…?" One student wrote a philosophical statement about teaching that expressed a clearly developed child-centered orientation, showing an awareness of individual differences in her students:

> The trick is to locate their strength and apply it to other areas. To be fair in the classroom and treat all the students in the same fashion is important in building a durable student-teacher relationship….Even if they aren't the best student in the class but have some accomplishments they can look back upon with pride that can spur them into continuing learning….My philosophy of teaching caters to the student. The student comes first. I want the classroom to be a place that they desire to come to….I want to know each of than individually before starting the school year so I have a background to work with.

Another student's philosophical statement expressed that the Exploring Teaching experience reinforced her altruistic and egalitarian beliefs: "There is little value in education without the simultaneous growth of the individual in terms of a positive perception of his or her own value as a human being." She does not want to "exclude those less able to compete. I believe every child is already complete and is there to be discovered."

Another student expressed a clear sense of always being herself. She wrote:

> I think they could sense that I cared, that I was patient, and that I am just as fallible as they are. When I made mistakes, it brought us closer in some strange ways. I am also the type of person who never puts on an act, be someone that I'm not. I was always myself with each student, and they were open and honest with me.

Other expressions of self-direction include strong feelings of self-direction and satisfaction about teaching as a career choice and formation of independent thinking regardless of parental or peer opinion. One student, despite parental pressure, has changed her goals from making money to wanting to "make a difference in the lives of individuals, a school and a community." Another sees teaching as compatible with her lifelong desire to communicate and clarify ideas and her preference for happiness over material gain.

This recurring theme of making career decisions despite peer or parental pressure is contrary to the stereotype of the teacher candidate as a person who conforms to the status quo. This theme, often voiced in both seminars, would argue that many of these people are at a point in their development where they are self-directed enough to withstand pressures to conform. This independent thinking is also consistent with the Five Year Program goal of teacher leadership.

Another independent thinker said,

> Maybe we should have…peer evaluations within Exploring Teaching class. I would be eager to hear what my peers feel about me, because I feel we can learn a lot from our peers….Also, I feel it would be beneficial to have to spend a week or two at one of the worst districts. Where we teach (eventually) may not be so nice with such great kids.

Showing confidence, he writes,

> In evaluating the qualities that should help in my teaching, I feel first and foremost is my ability to think on my feet. The ability to come up with ideas off the top of my head should help in keeping classes interesting or…in getting out of a situation that is going nowhere. I also feel that I am a clear speaker, relatively easy to understand. Thirdly and fourthly come patience and creativity….A teacher must be patient to those who are having difficulty yet at the same time creative enough to keep everyone interested. Lastly I feel I'm young enough to still understand where the students are coming from

and combine that with the fact that I've lived, worked with and experienced all kinds of kids from the problem streets, to jocks, to upper crust exceptional students.

Many of these exploring teachers show much independence and self-confidence in their thinking. Asking students to state and explain their values and goals, plan activities to reach these goals, and describe what they have learned about themselves, as the self-assessment guidelines do, is an effective way to help exploring teachers begin to think for themselves and develop toward a sense of self-awareness.

SUMMARY

Rooke and Torbert (2005) were greatly influenced by Loevinger and describe three general levels in adult development. The pre-conventional behavior is described as impulsive and self-protective, while the conventional stages are characterized by the integration of social convention and efficacy within a framework of established norms. Post-conventional stages are marked by a reappraisal of accepted conventions, a better understanding of the complexity and interdependence of problems, and an interest in both individual and societal transformation. While the steps described in this preliminary study of Exploring Teaching for sophomores do not exactly replicate the adult development stages in either Hy and Loevinger's (1996) or Rooke and Torbert's (2005) findings, they seem to represent important beginnings from which later development could be enhanced, especially with the supports and challenges of the later professional courses and internship.

IMPLICATIONS

What have been the elements of the Exploring Teaching course which seem to provide the stimulus for such growth? I offer the following as a list of possible answers for future seminar leaders to consider as they contemplate the continued psychological and professional growth of their students:

(1) Support from cooperating teachers combined with the challenge of continually adopting increasingly responsible teacher roles.

(2) Reflection in journals focused on self and preservice teacher growth following each classroom experience.

(3) Supportive and focused seminar discussions with a high degree of student participation through specific and stimulating questions, assignments, and ideas.

(4) Assignment-induced decision making on goals and action steps to correct weaknesses and capitalize on strengths.

(5) Assignment-induced reflection on values and self-learning.

REFERENCES

Department of Education. (Revised 2008). *The Schoolhouse Book: Programs in Teacher Education.* Durham, NH: University of New Hampshire.

Hy, L.X. & Loevinger, J. (1996). *Measuring Ego Development* (2nd ed). Mahwah, NJ: Lawrence Erlbaum Associates.

Kohlberg, L. (1976). Moral stages and moralization: The cognitive-developmental approach. In T. Lickona (Ed.), *Moral Development and Behavior.* New York: Holt, Rinehart, & Winston.

Oja, S.N. (1991). Adult development: Insights on staff development. In A. Lieberman & L. Miller (Eds.), *Staff Development for Education in the Nineties.* (pp. 37–60). New York: Columbia Teachers College.

Oja, S. N., & Ham, M. C. (1987). A collaborative approach to leadership in supervision: A three year study of teachers' stages of development in relation to collaborative action research in schools. Project funded by: U. S. Department of Education (OERI), October 1985 to September 1988.

Rooke, D. & Torbert, W. R. (2005). Seven transformations of leadership. *Harvard Business Review.* 83: 1–11.

FORTY-EIGHT

Toward a Psychology of Communication: Effects of Culture and Media in the Classroom

Joanne Washington

Advances during the past twenty years have sparked a revolution in technology and communication systems. Today, communication is instantaneous as it travels in digital form via a wide variety of media. Communication has shifted from passive to active. No longer does the student sit passively in the classroom, eyes fixed on the teacher—center stage—the focus of attention.

Think about the changes in communication that have occurred: Twenty years ago telephones were only used for spoken communication and television and film were our primary entertainment outlets. Advances in communication technology have changed the way we use technology and how we depend on it for most of our communication. We expect instant connections and expect that our interactions will garner immediate responses (think instant messaging). What this means for teachers is that we enter the classroom with the expectation that when we communicate with our students, we will be understood and they will give us the responses that we desire. To that end, most schools of education require prospective teachers to take courses on how to use communication technology in the classroom. The most recent trend is the use of cell phones to teach (Mickey, 2005). Yet, will the ability to download textbook readings to students' cell phones, use a blazing PowerPoint presentation, design an interactive wiki or post a blog comparing the writings of Emily Dickinson and Willa Cather actually improve the way you, as a teacher, effectively interact and communicate with your students? Perhaps it will. I believe media technology, when used effectively in the classroom, can enhance instruction. Several years of research conducted on the usefulness of media technology as a tool for instruction concludes that media, while useful for storing and delivering instruction, have little effect on learning outcome. Noted educational technology researcher Richard Clark, summarized the findings of this research writing:

> The best current evidence is that media are mere vehicles that deliver instruction but do not influence student achievement any more than the truck that delivers our groceries causes changes in nutrition (Clark, 1983, p 445).

Some believe that Clark's findings are outdated. This is understandable given that his **meta-analysis** was conducted more than twenty years ago. Yet, recent work in this area has not yielded any differ ent results. Although students enthusiastically use media technology at home, little technology is used in the classroom experience (Clark, 1998; Molenda and Sullivan, 2001; Peck et al., 2002a).

In interviews with high school students in San Francisco (close to Silicon Valley and the world headquarters of high-tech industries), it was found that these students used computers but not in the way educational experts expected.

> …most students surveyed at each school reported home access and serious rates of usage…Some used computers mostly for schoolwork; others used their home access mostly for social pursuits. Students also expressed much enthusiasm about computers and other technologies. Yet despite experience with home computers, enthusiasm for technology, and abundant access to technology in school, technology had but little impact on students' school experiences (Peck et al., 2002b, 477).

Hopefully, no one believes that the use of media technology alone has the power to effectively connect the student and teacher in meaningful ways that communicate interest and care about the relationship between the two. Nor, can technology alone create a classroom environment that impacts the students' learning experience. The teacher creates the culture of learning and effectively communicates the instructional message using the various channels at his or her disposal. This can only be accomplished through the establishment of a communication relationship between the student and teacher. The next section will examine exactly how this communication link is formed.

WHAT IS COMMUNICATION?

There's a famous old comedy routine from the radio days of the 1940s by Bud Abbott and Lou Costello called "Who's on First." A simple synopsis of the routine follows:

ABBOTT: Costello, I'm going to be the new manager of the New York Yankees.

COSTELLO: Good deal. Since you're the manager, will you introduce me to all of the players?

ABBOTT: I certainly will, my friend.

COSTELLO: Do you know all the players' names?

ABBOTT: Why, yes I do.

COSTELLO: Well, who are the main players?

ABBOTT: Let's see…we have Who's on first…

COSTELLO: (interrupting) Wait a minute. You're the manager and you don't know who's on first?

ABBOTT: Why aren't you listening? I just told you Who's on first.

COSTELLO: I'm gonna give you one more chance. Who's on first?

ABBOTT: Yes, that's what I just said![1]

Most people find the exchange humorous because of the obvious wordplay and confusion about the baseball player's name. The player on first base is actually named "Who." The second is named "What" and the third base player is named, "I don't know." Abbott believes he is providing Costello with the baseball player's name, and Costello is trying to communicate his frustration with Abbott's explanation.

The routine was originally heard on radio and had quite an effect on the listening audience as Abbott and Costello delivered their lines using a rapid fire technique. More than 60 years later, this routine may seem somewhat outdated to us, yet the lesson of distinguishing the difference between simply providing information and engaging in effective communication is worth learning. Information is the giving of facts and data about a particular subject while communication requires a much deeper level of understanding.

Communication is defined as *a shared experience between a sender and receiver that contains a message that is understood by both the sender and receiver.* The message may hold thoughts, feelings, information, ideas, and a range of activities that can be intended for communication. For example: How many examples of communication can you find in the following passage?

Thandie, a first-year middle school teacher, checks her reflection in the mirror a few minutes before the bell rings. "Wow," she exclaims out loud, "I shouldn't have stayed up watching that movie last night. My eyes are blood red!" "Oh well," she reflects, "they'll all be here in a few minutes—nothing I can do about it now." (Thandie moves to the front door of her classroom to greet her students). Thandie pats a few students on the shoulder, says good morning to most and returns a hug from an enthusiastic girl who always seems to smile even on the grayish days. Last, but not least, comes Tish. (Tish is big for her age and stands at Thandie's height). "Hey Tish," Thandie begins, giving Tish her most engaging smile. However, before Thandie can ask Tish about her weekend, Tish exclaims in a loud voice "Ms. Mills, what was you doin' last night? *You gotta lay off the bottle—you just gotta.*" Tish breaks into raucous laughter and the whole class joins in. Thandie feels her face tighten and her body tense as she thinks about what to say next....

First, let's look at how Thandie used intrapersonal communication. Thandie begins her day by speaking audibly about her bloodshot eyes although no one is present to answer her. Sometimes when we *self-talk*, we speak out loud even though there is no one present to answer. The most common type of intrapersonal communication is the self-talk that occurs in our thoughts. We reflect on past events and ponder our future. We think about what we're going to say and do when a situation arrives. Sometimes we rehearse scenes and play out the potential consequences of our actions. Intrapersonal communication is the most basic level of communication. It functions by allowing us to examine our innermost feelings, process events in our lives as they are happening, and prepare us for future potential communication situations. Intrapersonal communication takes on an important function in the communication process by helping prepare a person to communicate. Our self-talk can make us very relaxed in communication situations or create anxiety which, in turn, can negatively impact our communication. Many times, the receiver of our communication attempts can sense our comfort or anxiousness in a situation based on the verbal and non-verbal signals that we send out. Let's look at a basic communication model.

The *sender* is the person who initiates the communication. The *receiver* is the intended target of the communication. The arrows go both ways because a communicated message must be

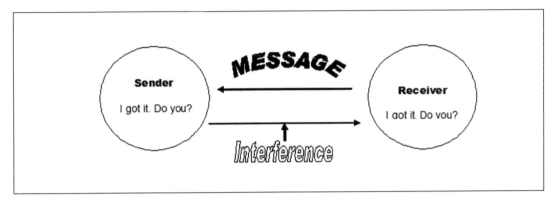

recognized as such. A message that goes out without a means to determine if it has been received as intended is no longer a message but is simply an *informational give and take*.

There are occasions in which our communication efforts fall short of the desired effect. The communication attempt fails and both the sender and receiver are left pondering why they were misunderstood. Because our verbal and non-verbal communication is prone to message interference, our messages become distorted or are misinterpreted. To better understand the dynamics of both of these modes of communication; the following section examines the characteristics of verbal and non-verbal communication.

VERBAL AND NON-VERBAL COMMUNICATION

Verbal communication is the messages we send audibly through language. Our words can be abstract or concrete. Abstract words are open to many interpretations while concrete words have fewer interpretations. Abstract words need not be complex. They simply must have several meanings. Concrete words, on the other hand, have limited meanings and are therefore less likely to be misinterpreted. Here are a few examples of *abstract* and *concrete* words we commonly use in communication.

In communication, our tendency is to use several abstract words to explain concepts that are already very complex. For example, most textbooks on the high school and college level use abstract words to explain complex ideas and principles. I have many students who open their

ABSTRACT WORD	MANY WAYS TO INTERPRET MEANING
Dog	What is the dog's color, type or size?; She was dog tired; or The sawyer placed a dog on the oak log to keep it from moving on the sawmill's carriage.
Home	What is the home's color, type or size? Is the home (meaning home life) happy or sad?
Music	What is the music style or genre? What can be considered music? Is rap or metalcore considered music?

CONCRETE WORD	LIMITED WAYS TO INTERPRET MEANING
Tricycle	A small peddled cycle with three wheels
Sun	A star that is the source of light and heat for a planet
Doctor	Distinguished by area of specialty.

communication theory books and are literally horrified by the thought that their whole school term will be spent reading a 300-page book that contains no illustrations or pictures. Conversely, books on the elementary and middle school levels use many illustrations, charts, graphs, maps, pictures and cartoons. Edgar Dale, noted educationist, was the first to promote the importance of auditory and visual communication in education through the *Cone of Learning Experience Model*. This model advanced the theoretical notion that the most effective way to communicate concepts is through direct experiences. The least effective way is through abstract symbols—or words (Dale, 1969). Overall, Dale suggested that learning will be enhanced if the relationship between direct experiences and abstract symbols is effectively communicated (Seels, 2004). In general, we only tend to remember twenty percent of what we hear (abstract symbols). Yet, that percentage is more than tripled if we also use communication as an active process of both reception and participation to obtain our learning goals (Catt et al., 2007; Dale, 1969). *Communication is an active process that engages both the sender and receiver in direct meaningful experiences that will ultimately translate into a richer and more rewarding learning environment.*

Non-verbal communication involves the messages we send without the use of language. Sometimes non-verbal communication is used alone, and other times its purpose is to emphasize key points given in a verbal message. Even silence is a form of non-verbal communication in a specific communication context. How much then, can you really communicate without the use of words? Probably more than you think.

Look back at Thandie's story. When Thandie is standing at the door of the classroom greeting her students, does she talk to everyone? Some students are greeted with hugs, others with a pat on the shoulder. One student even greets Thandie with a smile. A pat on the shoulder is a type of non-verbal communication called a haptic. Oftentimes, non-verbal communication is used to accompany verbal communication and is used to emphasize the verbal symbols (words). There are several types of nonverbal signals in communication. Following are a few that are more widely used.

If Thandie greets 30 students in the morning, she has potentially 30 different communication situations—all within the same relative context. Things appear to go smoothly until Thandie greets Tish. One way to analyze the exchange between Thandie and Tish is through the cultural influences that affect their communication.

CULTURAL COMMUNICATION INFLUENCES

One of the most difficult tasks for communication mediators is to diffuse a verbal conflict before it accelerates into a non-verbal confrontation or altercation. As you can imagine, non-verbal conflicts are more difficult to assess because the parties are not talking. You can only get a barometric reading through sensing the changes in the communication participants. Some people when reassessing a volatile conflict will make comments such as "You could feel the chill in the air" or "I could sense something wasn't going right." Actually, those individuals don't have a sixth sense nor are they clairvoyant. They are simply highly skilled at reading non-verbal signals and the cultural influences that are impacting the communication context.

Recently, a student told me of a late night incident in which several African American college-aged girls were walking past a dormitory that housed elementary girls who were on campus for a summer sports camp. Some of the elementary girls leaned out the window and called out to the college students, "Hey b-————, you think you're d——cute don't you?" Well, needless to say, the college girls yelled back for them to stop and a verbal confrontation occurred between the two groups. The African American girls went to the dorm to look for the camp girls' counselor but found no one. They then returned to their dorms and a few minutes later, the campus police arrived with the girls' counselor. The counselor told the college-aged girls that she had been around Black girls before and knew that the only reason they came up to the camp floor was to fight the elementary girls. Unfortunately, this communication situation accelerated so rapidly that both the counselor and the college girls filed harassment complaints against each other.

So, what can we learn from this situation? And, how would understanding Tish's cultural communication help Thandie respond appropriately to Tish's comments? First, let's look at the definition of culture as defined by Samovar and Porter:

TYPE OF NON-VERBAL	COMMON USE IN COMMUNICATION
Haptics	The use of touch to communicate. A soft touch generally communicates gentleness while a hard or rough touch (for example, a hit, slap or punch) can communicate anger depending on the communication context.
Proxemics	The use of space to communicate. The closer a person is to us when communicating, the closer the intimacy. Therefore, we generally only allow close relationship within our personal space while communicating.
Kinesics	The use of body movements to convey messages. It could be facial movements like a smile, raised eyebrow, frown, or the lowering or raising of our eyes. Shrugging your shoulders or kicking at something also conveys a message without words.
Appearance	A person's visual aspect that is not altered cosmetically. This may include a person's body type and size, ethnic and racial characteristics that communicate an image, idea or belief about an individual.
Vocalics	The use of voice inflection, tone, or accent to add a particular emphasis to the verbal communication.
Affects	Personal mannerisms that give insights about an individual's comfort level in communication situations. Also serves as a calming mechanism. Examples are twisting hair, nail biting, lip biting, finger tapping, wringing hands, clinched fists, thumb sucking, folding arms, hands in pocket, etc.

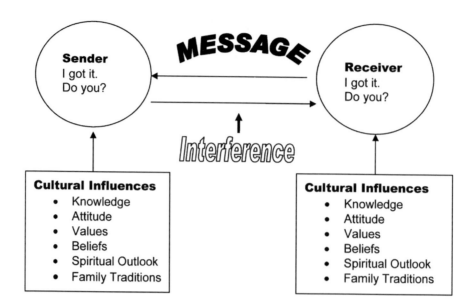

Culture—the deposit of knowledge, experience, beliefs, values, attitudes, meanings, hierarchies, religion, notions of time, roles, spatial relations, concepts of the universe, and material objects and possessions acquired by a group of people in the course of generations through individual and group striving (Samovar and Porter, 1994, pg. 11).

I use this definition to illustrate the importance and impact of an individual's culture on the communication process. If we look at our original model of communication and add the cultural influences, we do indeed see a greater sphere of factors that impact the flow of effective communication.

Having specific knowledge of the subject matter is a key influencer in the communication process. If, for example, the sender has more knowledge of a topic than the receiver, how might that person communicate that fact nonverbally? Will he or she show it in their facial expression or tone of voice? How then will the receiver interpret the message? Will he or she resent the sender if the message is sent with a hint of sarcasm or frustration? What if the message is sent with an open expression communicating respect and willingness to accept any response? The same holds true for our attitudes, values, and beliefs.

ATTITUDES, BELIEFS AND VALUES

I know individuals who, after having a bad night's sleep, wake up in a bad mood. If I speak to them (especially in a cheerful voice) before they have time to adjust to their day, I will inevitably receive a wince and a growl in response to my greeting. Yet, their attitude or mood is temporary and does not reflect their attitude or belief about me. We all have biases and hold stereotypes of individuals and groups that can influence our communication. While these biases and stereo-typical attitudes don't generally affect our choice of words, the manner in which we deliver the words can be greatly affected. As we communicate, the non-verbal signals that accompany our verbal messages are delivered as part of the normal reactions to a communication context. If we are not aware of the personal values we bring into a situation, we can unduly influence the outcome of our communication attempts.

Much of what we hold as personal values is learned early in life and is a direct result of our religious and spiritual upbringing as well as our family values and traditions. Think about conversations you may have had with your family members and what might be discussed if the topic were about an individual in any of the following circumstances:

- Someone living in a trailer park
- A person living in a high-rise apartment in Manhattan
- A person living (insert your hometown)
- A person of color living in a (rich, poor) section of town

Our biases are very much a part of life experiences as are the positive events that have occurred during our lifetimes. In Thandie's encounter with Tish, we witness a whole range of communicative reactions, mostly non-verbal which may give us clues to our hidden biases:

- Tish's size can be perceived non-verbally as being on the same level as her teacher. While not directly communicated, Tish may feel free to communicate with her teacher as if she were her peer or equal.
- Thandie makes a friendly gesture by smiling at Tish. While this gesture has been met with a positive response from the other students, Tish does not respond to Thandie as expected, thereby creating a bit of dissonance in Thandie's mind resulting in her self-talk: "Have I somehow offended Tish? Why is Tish trying to embarrass me?"
- Tish uses a non-verbal method—vocalics—to question Thandie's previous night's behavior. Tish also makes a stereotypical and biased remark suggesting that Thandie's red eyes are a result of a night of drinking. Tish then ends her communication with laughter—another vocalic.
- The class joins in the laughter—generally a cultural non-verbal shared by many groups of people who see it as a sign of happiness. However, laughter can also be interpreted as offensive in certain contexts and can sometimes reveal our biases towards certain groups of people.
- Thandie's face tightens and her body tenses. Her body is non-verbally communicating her discomfort.

How much of the communication that is occurring between Tish, Thandie and her class is culturally influenced? We have little information regarding the cultural, social, economic or racial backgrounds of the parties involved. Yet, we do know that the cultural backgrounds of both Thandie and Tish are going to influence the next communicative event that will occur. What can Thandie do to lessen her tenseness in the communication exchange? How can she improve the interpersonal communication *first* between Tish and herself?

IMPERSONAL AND PERSONAL INTERPERSONAL COMMUNICATION

Interpersonal communication is the most frequent used level of communication. Most of our everyday exchanges occur on the interpersonal level. Interpersonal communication can be face-to-face but is also commonly transacted through media technology (cell phones, Internet, etc.). Interpersonal communication allows both parties in the communication exchange to respond immediately to the communication situation. Therefore, if there is miscommunication, it can be handled right there on the spot. Each individual in the communication exchange can adjust his or her message to better reach the intended outcome.

Interpersonal communication can be either impersonal or personal. Most of our everyday exchanges are conducted using impersonal communication. We use this type of interpersonal communication when exchanging messages with individuals we interact with based on the person's role. We see no further than that person's function within our need to accomplish a short-term goal. If you're purchasing an item at a local convenience store where you, let's say, purchase gas frequently—chances are that you've seen the clerk many times. Yet, the communication most likely never goes beyond exchanging a few pleasantries. Your goal is to make a purchase. Sometimes we ask questions of individuals and never go beyond receiving the answer we desire. The information exchanged is superficial and we primarily regard the person in his or her role. We are more apt to interact with that person from our perspectives of their cultural or stereotypical role. Even though you may communicate with that person a number of times and over a long period of time, the nature of the communication never goes deeper. It remains on the superficial level.

In contrast, while personal communication may begin similarly to impersonal communication, reasons for developing a deeper communication evolve. You find that you have commonalities that grow into both parties sharing more *personal* information. You communicate with the person as a distinct individual. And, as you continue the relationship over time, a deeper understanding of the person's communicative needs develop.

Both impersonal and personal interpersonal communications are needed to navigate through daily interactions. It would be impractical to engage in personal interpersonal communication with each person you greet. As well, our lives would not be enriched without the personal communications we have with significant individuals within our social spheres. Look at a comparison between impersonal and personal interpersonal communication.

So then, how can Thandie manage her communication interaction with Tish? What are Thandie's communication goals? Here are a few short-term goals with action steps and anticipated effects. What other goals can you think of?

All of these goals are understandable if Thandie primarily uses impersonal communication with Tish and does not want to develop a communication relationship based on respect and individual character. However, for unknown reasons, Tish felt that she could make a personal comment about Thandie's personal appearance—her red eyes. This comment presumes that Tish is in a personal relationship with Thandie or that she assumed she could be.

There are several levels of personal relationships from our most intimate (family, spouse, close friends, etc.) to personal relationships that evolve from daily and lengthy interaction. If Thandie has been teaching over a period of time and is still treating the communication with her

IMPERSONAL INTERPERSONAL	PERSONAL INTERPERSONAL
Persons interact by role and/or stereotype	Persons interact as distinct individuals with distinguishing characteristics
Accomplishes short-term communication goals without sharing personal information	Accomplishes long-term communication goals over time through the sharing of personal information
Relationships remain superficial even though there may be several contacts over time. Individuals are rarely perceived as anything more than an assigned role or stereotype.	Relationships grow deeper over time and develop into an understanding of each individual's personhood as a result of shared communication.

students as impersonal (i.e., seeing each student in their cultural and stereotypical roles), then a smooth resolution of this communication situation is doubtful.

Let's examine a few options with the assumption that Thandie does use personal communication with Tish on a level appropriate between teacher and student.

It is important to determine a person's motivation before crafting a response in order to resolve a potential communication conflict. If Thandie can understand Tish's motive for making the comment that she…"*gotta lay off the bottle*" she will be in a better position to improve the genuine personal communication that is desirable between a teacher and student. Most miscommunication occurs because individuals interact superficially based on stereotypical perceptions. Regarding the personhood of an individual with the goal of improved communication will gain rewards that will continuously pay off. Knowing the "why" of a person's actions and remarks helps to reach the individual's mind, desires, and heart of expression. In this way, the teacher becomes more than a giver of information and a repository of facts and data. The teacher becomes a medium of grand expression on several levels as she or he peels back layers of meaning to reveal the true essence of the individual within each student. Reaching this overarching goal will ultimately make the teacher an effective communicator in and out of the classroom.

MEDIA INFLUENCES IN THE CLASSROOM

A study by the Kaiser Family Foundation reports that children ages 2–18 spend approximately 5.3 hours using media each day. While sixty-five percent of kids aged 8–18 have a television in their room, the average child spends about 20 hours a week at a minimum in front of the television (Roberts et al., 1997). The point of these statistics is not to point to an overuse of media but to underscore the fact that a teacher's communication is only one of many media messages and influences that impact student lives on a daily basis.

In the beginning of this chapter, I wrote about communication technology in the classroom—specifically the prevalence and use of cell phones (not to mention Ipods and other communication devices) in the classroom. This propagation of media influence presents a significant challenge to the teacher who wishes to encourage thoughtful and provocative communication between students and between student and teacher. How much of what your students see and hear is based on stereotypical and market-driven images? What are the commercial messages that are sent along with text messages, instant messages, ringtones and the like meant to communicate?

THANDIE'S SHORT TERM COMMUNICATION GOALS	ACTIONS	ANTICIPATED EFFECT
Immediately stop students from laughing	Tell students to stop laughing or "else"	Depends on Thandie's relationship and/or her authoritative position. Will not improve personal or impersonal communication
Stop Tish from laughing	Tell her to stop or "else"	Thandie continues to regard Tish stereotypically and accelerates the potential for conflict by adding a veiled threat.
Take control by letting Tish know that Thandie, as the teacher is in control and that Tish, as student is being disrespectful.	Immediately confront Tish in a voice and tone loud enough for the other students to hear	Accelerates potential for conflict and sets up more communication hurdles
Let Tish know that Thandie has been embarrassed by her.	Immediately confront Tish in a low, stern tone but maintain non-verbal signs (affects) of embarrassment	Tish may be confused by Thandie's mixed communication. Thandie's sternness is an attempt to control the communication situation but her non-verbal communicates uncomfortability. The situation maintains its awkwardness.

How much of these messages seep into our everyday communications? As a teacher, how much have *you* been influenced by the same messages and images that influence your students?

The fact of the matter is that you, as teacher, are the primary medium in the classroom. For six hours a day, you are in control of the communication flow. Your continual presence, method for managing the classroom environment and respect shown for each student as an individual will set the communicative tone from the first class meeting until the last day of school.

FIRST CLASS MEETING PREPARATION

One of the most unnerving tasks for a beginning teacher is to walk into a new school building and stand in front of a classroom of 30 sets of eyes. This is not student teaching but the real thing. You can't leave your class after eight weeks; you have these same people for a whole year—for better or worse. It is like a marriage of sorts. And like any long-term relationship, you don't walk into it unprepared.

Literature related to factors that contribute to effective classroom instruction generally list the following as critical teacher attributes: credibility, delivery, fairness, knowledge, organization and rapport (Catt et al., 2007; McCroskey et al., 2006). Credibility, delivery and rapport are all communicative elements. While delivery and rapport are elements that are implemented while in the classroom, credibility is developed before you teach your first class.

THANDIE'S COMMUNICATION GOALS	ACTIONS	ANTICIPATED EFFECT
Deepen the understanding of Tish's communication motives: Is Tish attempting to divert everyone's attention away from her and onto Thandie? Does Tish really want to know something about Thandie's personal life? Does Tish understand what appropriate comments between children and adults are?	Use light tone that acknowledges Tish's remark. or Redirect Tish's attention: "Never mind what I did last night. What about …" or Tell Tish and the class that you stayed up late watching television. Talk to Tish privately about her comments.	Furthers personal communication by recognizing the individual and by sharing the appropriate level of personal communication. Helps Tish improve her personal communication skills.
To refocus class attention	Quiet class and give them a task	This accomplishes an appropriate short-term goal and is communicated on an *impersonal* level. Thandie communicates using her role as 'teacher.' A communication context (such as a classroom) in which you engage the same people over a long period of time appropriately uses both impersonal and personal communication.
To learn not to tense up when in uncomfortable situations.	Immediately engage in calming non-verbal communication. Relax face muscles and engage in self-talk using soothing phrases learned beforehand to cope with stressful situations.	

Credibility asks the question whether or not a speaker is believable and confident. While credibility is related to knowledge of the subject matter, it also gets at whether or not you, as teacher, are able to project an air of confidence, responsiveness and assertiveness.

> Responsiveness indicates the teachers' positive reactions to students' needs and a willingness to listen to their students. Assertiveness suggests that the teacher approach students as a leader and maintain appropriate control in the classroom (McCroskey et al., 2006, 404).

Responsiveness is also not learned in a classroom but is practiced each day in the interactions you have—especially with people who are close to you. How well do you listen? How perceptive are you about others' needs? Effective communicators do not focus on themselves; they are attuned to the communicative needs of their receivers and adjust their communication styles accordingly.

Assertiveness deals with your personal comfort levels. How at ease are you in new situations? What methods do you use when resolving conflicts with friends and loved ones? When you walk into a room and others are present, do you speak first or do you wait until someone acknowledges your presence? Hopefully, in asking yourself these questions, you will begin a plan of developing those areas in which you do not assert yourself. Remember, assertiveness is not being "pushy" or belligerent. Someone who is assertive knows when and how to make her point

SCENARIO	CONFIDENCE-BUILDING PRACTICE EXERCISES
Meeting your new supervisor	First look in a mirror and practice your greeting saying the supervisor's name. Use direct eye contact and a smile. Then, practice with a friend, adding a firm handshake while you make your greeting. Do this as many times as necessary until it becomes natural. Also, try to get a friend to introduce you to an adult that you don't know. Then practice your greeting.
Going to a club or organization meeting alone where you don't know anyone	Use the same exercise as above. However, many people do not shake hands when they first meet in casual situations. Instead, practice saying your name and then following up with a question such as, "I didn't know there would be —— many people here." Eye contact is important and remember, being natural is the key.
Making a presentation or a speech in front of a class.	The best preparation is to take a public speaking course sometime during college. Also, learn to speak up and express your opinions in group and classroom situations whenever you have the opportunity. Of course, preparation is the key. Knowing what you're talking about is paramount. Again, practicing in front of a mirror is useful. Also, having someone videotape you (even using a cell phone is helpful) will provide you with the best assessment of your communication style. Finally, when the big day comes and you're standing in front of your class, just relax. Find a friendly face and look directly at him or her. Smile and move your eyes across the group as you speak. Move around and you will gain confidence with every step. Use your hands as gestures and if you need to hold on to something, place something (pen, pencil, eyeglasses) in one hand. Remember, at this point, you're the pro—not perfect—but willing to try and to make it work.

and how to inform individuals (without becoming overly anxious or angry) when a boundary has been crossed.

Confidence is learned through experiencing missteps and mistakes but not allowing those life situations to hinder personal growth. "If at first you don't succeed—try, try again" may seem to be a trite cliché; however, not giving up can be a big confidence enhancer. Confidence is gained through practice and experience. If you want to gain confidence in a particular area, you must be able to first visualize your success and then put yourself in situations where you can put your skills to the test. Here are some scenarios that may test your confidence and practice exercises to boost your confidence quotient.

HANDLING THE UNEXPECTED

Loss of control, fear, and dealing with personal prejudices and biases are probably some of the most challenging barriers to overcome in teaching. Even the most seasoned teacher experiences a temporary loss for words or must deal with unexpected conflicts and confrontations. One important indicator of how a teacher will respond to the unexpected is to determine the type of rapport or communication relationship between the teacher and his or her students. Earlier in the chapter we discussed Thandie and Tish's conflict and determined that the outcome would be predicated on Thandie's communication goals and her relationship (personal or impersonal) with Tish. While education books abound on the topic of handling discipline or managing student behavior in the classroom, it is the communication education literature that focuses on the impact of teacher–student rapport and the importance of teacher non-verbal behavior that we now address.

Face-to-face communication is considered to be the most powerful and effective means of insuring a message is delivered correctly (Witt and Schrodt, 2006). Like the difference between a movie and live theatre, the teacher performing his or her craft in a classroom setting is an authentic, vibrant, and convincing medium. Therefore, the things the teacher says or does will be watched very closely—similar to the way people focus on a television screen. The gestures and words spoken cannot be erased and taped over. So, every word and gesture must be weighed and evaluated before delivery, especially because of the closeness of the teacher as medium to his or her audience (students).

A teacher's immediacy behavior is "conceptualized as both the message of closeness and the behaviors that enhance that sense of closeness…. The immediacy principle [is described as] "one's tendency to be drawn towards persons and things they like" (Rester and Edwards, 2007, p. 35). One mistake some new teachers make is to attempt to become their students' friend. As discussed earlier, teaching requires both impersonal and personal communication. The teacher will always occupy the role of "teacher" but it does not have to be a stereotypical role. Your communication style, non-verbal mannerisms that convey trust and respect will draw you to your students and them to you. Cautions must however be given against inappropriate touching and the sharing of comments about your personal life and those of your students that are too intimate. Too often boundaries are crossed that prove difficult to rebuild. Many times the teacher then only has the use of fear and other threatening consequences as a means of exacting student compliance. While the use of fear alone has been shown to have some effect on student behavior, it does not positively influence student outcome nor the student-teacher relationship for long-term instructional impact (Sprinkle et al., 2006).

In conclusion, each person seeks to be known by his or her individual make-up—as created by a distinctive pattern. There will never be another person as uniquely formed as you–or the students that you will teach over the coming years. Communicate your confidence as you believe in who you are and the importance of what you express to others. That is the best we have to offer and the ultimate hope of all communicators.

NOTES

1   If you would like to read the radio script of hear the original broadcast, go to http://www.abbotttandcostello. net or one of the several hundred websites on Abbott and Costello.

REFERENCES

Abbott and Costello (retrieved August 1, 2007). The official abbott and costello website. http://www.abbottandcostello.net/.

Catt, S., Miller, D. & Schallenkamp, K. (2007). You are the key: Communication for learning effectiveness. *Education, 127*(3), 369–377.

Clark, R. (1983). Reconsidering research on learning from media. *Review of Educational Research, 53,* 445–59.

Clark, R. (1998). Motivating performance: Part I—diagnosing and solving motivational problems. *Performance Improvement,* 37(8), 39–46.

Dale, E. (1969). *Audio-visual methods in teaching,* 3rd Edition. New York: Holt, Rinehart and Winston.

Heinich, R., Molenda, M. & Russell, J. (1998). *Instructional media and the new technologies of instruction.* New York: Macmillan Publishing Company.

Knapp, M. (1980). *Essentials of non-verbal communication.* New York: Holt, Rinehart and Winston.

McCroskey, J., Richmond, V., & Bennett, V. (2006). The relationships of student end-of-class motivation with teacher communication behaviors and instructional outcomes. *Communication Education,* 55(4), 403–414.

Mickey, K. (2005). Companies look at educational potential of cell phones, but questions linger. *Electronic Education Report,* 12(6), 1–4.

Molenda, M. & Sullivan, M. (2001). A watershed year for technology in education. *Techno, 10,* 14–19.

Peck, C., Cuban, L., & Kirkpatrick, H. (2002a). High-tech's high hopes meet student realities. *Education Digest,* 67(8), 47–54.

―――. (2002b). Techno-promoters dreams, student realities. *Phi Delta Kappan, 83*(6), 472–480.

Rester, C. & Edwards, R. (2007). Effects of sex and setting on students' interpretation of teachers' excessive use of immediacy. *Communication Education, 56*(1), 34–53.

Roberts, D., Foehr, U., Rideout, V., & Brodie, M. (1997). *Kids and media @ the new millennium.* Menlo Park: Kaiser Family Foundation Report.

Samovar, L. & Porter, R. (1994). *Intercultural communication: A reader,* 7th Edition. Belmont: Wadsworth Publishing Company.

Seels, B. (1997). *The relationship of media and ISD theory: The unrealized promise of Dale's Cone of Experience.* Albuquerque, NM: Proceedings of Selected Research and Development Presentations at the 1997 National Convention of the Association for Educational Communications and Technology. (ERIC Document Reproduction Service No. ED 409869).

Sprinkle, R., Hunt, S., Simonds, C. & Comadena, M. (2006). Fear in the classroom: An examination of teachers' use of fear appeals and students' learning outcomes. *Communication Education, 55*(4), 389–402.

Witt, P. & Schrodt, P. (2006). The influence of instructional technology use and teacher immediacy on student affect for teacher and course. *Communication Reports, 19*(1), 1–15.

FORTY-NINE

The Self in Teaching and Learning

Henry Brzycki

> *"Instruction is about connecting content with human beings,*
> *sharing ideas that matter with people who matter.*
> *When we connect with a student, we know that student*
> *in enough depth to see his or her vulnerabilities and*
> *to see how our teaching can contribute to that student's well-being."*
> —Carol Ann Tomlinson, 2007

To make teaching and learning possible, the *self* of the student needs to be engaged. As teachers, we may refer to our "self" and the "self" of each of our students frequently, but we do not always know what we mean or have an effective set of teaching tools to nurture the "self" in the classroom. The educational approach of engaging the "self" of the student as a prerequisite for learning is described directly and concretely through a research-based theory known as the Self Theory in Schooling: Pathways to Adolescent Well-Being (Brzycki, 2009). The thesis of the theory and this chapter is that if teachers focus upon empowering the "self" of students, this will result in enhanced academic and well-being outcomes.

The Self Theory in Schooling: Pathways to Adolescent Well-Being has applicability to: classroom practices; teaching and learning; psychology as it is applied in education; and educational policy at the national, state, and local levels. If college students in pre-professional teacher education programs learn the Self Theory in Schooling, they will be more effective as professionals, and apable of manifesting their innate, higher purpose in service to children. When teachers upon a number of distinctions about the self in the classroom, children will emerge from their schooling experiences more able to be well, with a greater understanding of what it means to be healthy—emotionally, physically, spiritually, intellectually, and psychologically. Academic learning *and* success will stem from student well-being rather than be the sole purpose of schooling or occur without regard to larger humanistic concerns.

These changes become imperative when we consider we are currently in the midst of an education revolution in which children are learning about life through their schooling. People are spending much more of their lives in school, yet little is known about the complex development that occurs through schooling. School has become the dominant paradigm in a child's life for learning about himself and others. The purpose of this chapter is to provide future teachers and current educators with a framework and a set of tools to draw upon when manifesting their innate calling in life to impact the whole child in their care.

DEFINITION OF SELF SYSTEM AND POSITIVE PSYCHOLOGY ATTRIBUTES

The self may be defined as the essential or particular qualities that distinguish one person from another, such as personality traits or talents. However, it can be even more useful in teaching and learning to think of the self as a holistic system with three major components: the body, the mind, and the spirit. All of these aspects of the person unite as one's self.

The study of the self in cognitive developmental psychology has taken on heightened importance because of the increasing awareness of the central, functional role that the self plays in human development across the life span. Current research shows that through teaching and learning at all grade levels, the totality of a student's self needs to be engaged whenever content is introduced in the classroom. Therefore, the teacher plays a critical role in imparting the student's awareness of self in everyday interactions and lessons. This critical role is enhanced when teachers learn two key distinctions about the self: the "self system" and "positive psychology attributes." If new and master teachers alike learn these distinctions through their teacher training or through professional development course work, they will dramatically increase their teaching and learning effectiveness.

Self system: Developmental psychologist Susan Harter offers an integrated construct of the self she calls the "self system" (Harter, 1999). By "system" she does not mean to refer to a systematic or predictable view of how the self operates. She does mean, however, to offer a holistic view that is consistent with that of influential American educational theorists John Dewey (1900; 1902; 1916) and William James (1900; 1992). The self is the sum of numerous component parts, and, perhaps more importantly, it is continuously in the process of developing and evolving. Building upon Harter's components to include some additional ones of my own, the "self system" consists of self concept, self-esteem, self-efficacy, self-understanding, identity, locus of control, self-affects, and self-schemas.

Positive psychology attributes: Positive psychology is a result of the evolution of cognitive developmental and humanistic views of the self. Positive psychology is not "positive thinking," but rather, put simply, a study of individual strengths. Some "positive psychology attributes" (Csikszentmihalyi, 1993; Seligman & Csikszentmihalyi, 2000; Lopez & Snyder, 2009) are life purpose, life satisfaction, life meaning, happiness, intrinsic motivation, inspiration, and possible selves—all components of the self that contribute to psychological and subjective well-being outcomes (Ryan & Deci, 2001; Lent, Singley, Sheu, & Gainor, 2005). These essential components are important protective factors for educators to incorporate in their classroom practices. The self system and positive psychology attributes reinforce one another through development across the life span and mostly through early formal schooling experiences. An analogy would be a mobile, where one element when moved, impacts all other component parts to varying degrees. By way of example, if a student is clear about her unique purpose in life, this may impact her motivation to succeed by making larger contributions to the greater good envisioned.

Each of the self system components and positive psychology attributes is worthy of an investigation unto themselves; therefore the reader may want to research and reflect on their role in the classroom. For example, how often do we ask our students what inspires them, or help them think about lifelong dreams and potential and how learning could help in their manifestation? In another example, a student with self-understanding of his/her unique talents may not be able to express these talents with self-efficacy, a connection that the classroom teacher could encourage. Previous research conducted on self system and positive psychology attributes typically isolates one of the many attributes or at most looks at the relationship between only one attribute and school achievement. That view minimizes the holistic nature and dynamic interaction that exists among all component parts of the self.

SELF THEORY—FOUNDATIONS

The Self Theory in Schooling: Pathways to Adolescent Well-Being draws its foundation primarily from philosophers, psychologists, and educational researchers from the 20th and 21st centuries and from the Western tradition, although educators find it is relevant in a wide variety of cultural settings. Philosopher and psychologist William James (1900) offered a view of the self in the early 1890s by observing, "a man's self is the sum of all that he can call his" (p. 291). According to James (1900) this included the inner and outer dimensions of self. Examples of the inner dimensions include feelings, thoughts, and spiritual understandings, while the outer dimensions were represented as physical and social. James represented this inward life as the central nucleus of the self. James' views had a tremendous influence on 20th-century educators.

John Dewey (1900; 1902; 1916) extended key distinctions about the self in psychology and their application to education to include moral development, interests, conscious purpose, desire, and reflection. He placed these distinctions at the center of teaching and learning. The phenomenon known to educators as child-centered pedagogy characterized the progressive movement throughout the 1920s and up through the early 1950s (Cremin, 1964). Dewey (1916) encouraged educators to never see the self as complete. The self is always becoming; it is always changing, growing, and developing.

The founder of the school of humanistic psychology, Carl Rogers (1961; 1980), placed our experiences in life at the center of the process of constructing or coming to know ourselves. He ᴄᴀᴌᴌed this process client-centered therapy. Client-centered therapy continues to be widely used today in the discovery of the self. The client is at the heart of well-being and success pathways. Humanistic psychology scholars consider self-actualization, discovery of self concept, and self-understanding critically important to learn through life's experiences. Rogers (1961; 1980) theorized that education should have a "whole person" focus, which he defined as the bringing together of the affective (emotions) with the cognitive and the mind and the body. He asserted that the whole person goes to school, not just the intellect.

At approximately the same time that Rogers developed client-centered therapy, Harvard University psychologist Jerome Bruner (1960; 1996) initiated the cognitive revolution. According to Bruner, the study of mind, with its various levels of consciousness, was central to the cognitive sciences. The mind includes cultural influences and is shaped by both internal and external forces. Cognition and emotions are equally important to the process of meaning making in the construction of ourselves and of our realities. For Bruner, "the role of schools in 'self' construction is very much a part of education" (Bruner, 1996, p. 13). Education is perhaps the most influential cultural institution that operates at the crossroads of individual development and societal values and, therefore, is an essential pathway for developing the self. It is through Bruner's (1960; 1990; 1996) work that we have an understanding that the self of a person combines the mind, which is a dynamic system of internal cognitive and affective processes, with the external cultural and social influences. This intersection of internal process and social influences brings greater importance to the role that schooling has on the development of children and heightens the influence of a teacher in a child's life.

The interplay between the individual, the self, and society is a complex one. The self is a social construction, while at the same time, it is the mediator of the social construction of reality (Berger & Luckmann, 1967). The self mediates the cognitive with the environment. In essence the self of the learner is the context of all personal meaning and the place where reality gets created in one's life. For children and adolescents, the chance to negotiate this interplay between self and society occurs most readily in their schooling environment.

With the publication of *Self-efficacy: Toward a Unifying Theory of Behavioral Change,* Stanford University psychologist and researcher Albert Bandura (1997) facilitated a breakthrough in our understanding of the importance of self-efficacy as one component part of the self. Bandura's social cognitive theory has become a critical model for teachers to know and apply in that schooling can encourage or repress a child's belief that he can achieve a goal.

In an important study that linked learning about the self to schooling (Lent, Singley, Sheu, & Gainor, 2005), the researchers proposed an integrative model—a unifying theory of well-being and psychosocial adjustment. Their model includes personality traits and affective dispositions, life satisfaction, self-efficacy expectations and environmental supports and resources. They found that the most direct path to life satisfaction was through "domain satisfaction"—a specific and memorable experience of success in at least one area of life, such as succeeding at an assignment at school that is deemed important to the individual. If a child comes from a vulnerable population with few chances for after-school or family activities, the importance of achieving domain satisfaction within the school setting intensifies. "Domain satisfaction was found to be the single most consistent predictor of overall life satisfaction" (Lent et al., 2005, p. 439). These research findings demonstrate the importance of helping an adolescent develop a self system through the domain of schooling as a protective factor and the start of a positive life course (Patrick et al., 2007; Shanahan , 2000).

Educational psychologist Frank Pajares (1992; 1996) underscores the need for educ....us to consider their own (as well as their students') beliefs about students' capabilities and how much they can accomplish. "Self efficacy is considered an important component of an individual's self concept. The literature on self-schemas and possible selves provides a concept of self with four dimensions, one of which, the efficacy dimension, is characterized by individuals' beliefs about their potentialities" (Pajares, 1996, p. 557). It is important for teachers to impart "beliefs" about their students' "potentialities" frequently through the teaching and learning process. When a teacher helps a student develop the self-efficacy attribute, the teacher is making a difference in the life of a student who may not believe that he can manifest his own unique potential in life.

A study of elementary school aged children conducted by University of Missouri researchers (Herman et al., 2008) found that there are direct links between students' academic performance in elementary school (first through fifth grades) and their self-perceptions and well-being (such as depression symptoms) when they reach middle school (sixth grade). The key factor is the experience of success, so the researchers found that "along with reading and math, teachers and parents should honor skills in other areas, such as interpersonal skills, non-core academic areas, athletics and music" (p. 406). As teachers, we need to give students as many opportunities for success in order to establish a positive learning and life course trajectory.

THE SELF THEORY IN SCHOOLING: PATHWAYS TO ADOLESCENT WELL-BEING

The Self Theory in Schooling aligns teacher beliefs with classroom practices that focus upon an integrated self that leads to developmental outcomes. The Self Theory in Schooling situates the integrated self at the heart of teaching and learning. This alignment will lead to both adolescent developmental outcomes and academic outcomes and at new levels of each. Academic success, well-being, and positive life course trajectories result when adolescents learn that they have control over their own destinies in life. Having the self-understanding that they have control over their futures is a basic motivation or self-determination (Deci & Ryan, 1995) of all human beings that can be learned in everyday classroom lessons. The development of this sense of control over one's destiny begins in childhood during the elementary school years and is particularly important during the social awakening of the middle school grade levels and continues throughout the self-defining years of high school and college.

In a study conducted with middle school teachers, I found teachers believed that students who do poorly in academic outcomes often do not feel good about their abilities to control their own destinies or future success, showing the reciprocal causal connections between self-esteem and academic performance, and academic performance and self-esteem (Brzycki, 2009). The study also investigated teacher beliefs and practices for imparting self system and positive psychology attributes to discover if there was a critical link between the construction of the self in schooling and happier, healthier, and more successful children. The study considered the interactions between the *beliefs* that teachers hold about the importance of their role in the development of the selves of their students and the classroom *practices* they use to impart self system and positive psychology attributes. Although many studies that are conducted within a school context consider academic achievement as the dependent variable or outcome of a child's schooling, this study was designed to measure the impact that teachers could have upon the human development of their students.

Teachers are important in the life of a child not merely for imparting academic content knowledge, but additionally, and more directly than is generally known, in aiding cognitive and human development in terms of an integrated, whole view of children. There is a dynamic and integrated network between academic outcomes and the self system and positive psychology attributes. If teachers better understand and focus upon these attributes as outcomes through curricula, then their students will be more successful in academic schooling outcomes *and* well-being outcomes. In this process, a teacher is teaching a whole person, not merely the intellect. Therefore, academic outcomes are equal in importance to well-being outcomes when empowering the full potential of children.

Teachers and teacher educators can mistakenly view these two outcomes—academic and well-being—as separate, neither integrated with, nor deeply connected to, the components of a larger self. The available pedagogical tools and methods teachers are required to utilize focus upon more narrow learning results and may be contributing to a decrease in the well-being of school-aged adolescents (Brzycki, 2009; Herman et al., 2008). In an educational environment dictated by No Child Left Behind 2001 (NCLB), school systems may be decreasing the overall quality of life of young people. Teachers see these negative consequences and attach blame to the increased administrative responsibilities, lesson planning, and governmental requirements that focus upon narrow academic learning outcomes and away from the human development outcomes for their students.

Of major concern is the current out-of-balance focus upon just two intelligences—mathematical and linguistic (Baker, 2009; Baker et al., in press; Gardner, 1983; Robinson, 2001). Cognitive functions of critical thinking and creativity are two capabilities required for 21st century learning and skills development. Professor Ken Robinson finds creativity as essential in the 21st century as literacy was in the 19th and 20th centuries (Robinson, 2001). Because NCLB does not encourage creativity, the gains in intelligence and cognition through schooling over the past 100 years could level off or be reduced if this out-of-balance pedagogy continues. Teachers communicate their frustrations with this overemphasis on only two measures of what it means to succeed in the value system of schooling, at the expense of other cognitive and human development attributes.

The Brzycki study (2009) found that in spite of the negative influences of NCLB, teachers believe in trying to develop the self of their students, even though they do not always work with a refined set of distinctions about the self. In one interesting finding, teachers revealed that they strove to develop a close relationship with students as their key strategy to empower their students. As one teacher described one of her students: "He was always drawing these amazing graphics. So I would ask him about that. He would show me. It got to be kind of like…every time he would draw something, he would come back and show me later and tell me where he got the idea from, the video game or something. And later on, at the end of the year, we were talking about 'What are your goals for the future?' 'What do you think you might like to be?' even after high school—it was only sixth grade—but I told him if you could think ahead that far, 'what do you think you might like to do later on?'" (Brzycki, 2009, August, Interview, 2).

Through her personal connection with this particular student, the teacher was encouraging the student's awareness of his potential life dream and even a higher life purpose. However, while she felt she was providing encouragement, she was unaware that she was actually actively helping to impart the student's sense of his dream and purpose, and further, she was unaware that these were important positive psychology attributes. If she had this awareness of the distinctions of life dreams and life purpose, she could have been more consistent and effective at teaching both personal well-being attributes and academic outcomes as well as imparting them more often to her students.

At the same time that teachers believe in relationship-building, they are finding it increasingly difficult to accomplish it in the current schooling environment of technical rationality, with its emphasis upon assessing young people based upon numbers (standardized tests) in place of human qualities (such as personal purpose in life). Indeed, teachers and administrators state that there have been "climate killers" over the recent past, including the increased administrative responsibilities that take time and energy away from building personal relationships with children. Also, widespread policies that don't allow appropriate student touching, such as pats on the back or "high fives" as ways to acknowledge good work, has also contributed to a cold classroom climate. Taken altogether—the focus upon testing, the more extensive and rigid lesson planning, and no touching—core teacher beliefs that they can impact the well-being of students through empowerment of the self have been impeded dramatically.

INTEGRATING THE SELF IN TEACHING AND LEARNING

The dynamic and integrated network of self system and positive psychology attributes is important because "beliefs, attitudes, and values form an individual's belief system" (Pajares, 1992, p. 314), and teachers want or intend to produce these self outcomes in their students, not merely as a strategy to enhance learning outcomes but to empower a positive life course trajectory (Bandura et al., 2001; Hawkins et al., 2008; Herman et al., 2008). The integrated self is at the heart of the Self Theory in Schooling. The integration of the self system and positive psychology attributes melds into a whole view, where each component impacts the other in a dynamic, active relationship. The theory holds that the nexus of teaching and learning is the self—the place where the individual's reality is constructed and where constructive, reflective processing both shapes and is shaped by interactions with the environment.

Figure 1 depicts the dynamic among the self system and positive psychology attributes, as well as some additional concepts from educational psychology.

Teachers can integrate the self of their students in teaching and learning through everyday lessons. Connecting academic learning to the total development of students is indeed possible. Consider this one example: "I was a language arts teacher, and we did poetry in there, and they jumped on the poetry thing just to kind of release, just to kind of get in touch with themselves at the beginning of the year. I don't think I would have seen that, so it was kind of like that was like an outlet for a lot of them, and they started entering poetry contests, and they wanted to share with the class, and I thought that was kind of neat" (Brzycki, 2009, October, interview, 8). What is being demonstrated in this example is that the teacher saw a number of integrated

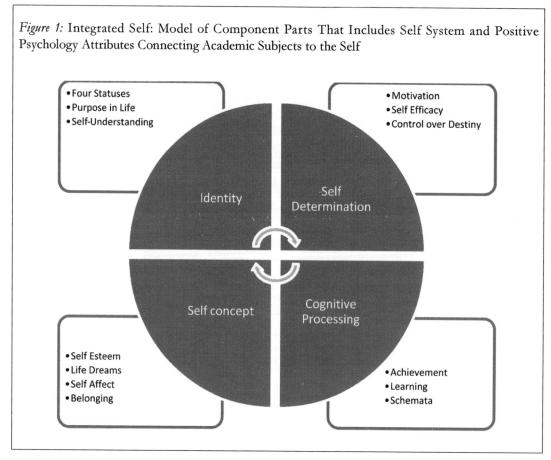

Figure 1: Integrated Self: Model of Component Parts That Includes Self System and Positive Psychology Attributes Connecting Academic Subjects to the Self

self attributes emerge as the students constructed their selves. The students exhibited increased motivation ("jumped on the poetry thing"), self-understanding ("get in touch with themselves"), achievement ("started entering poetry contests"), and self-efficacy ("they wanted to share [more expressively] with the class").

An integrated self even works in a math classroom. Of all academic content areas that are typically taught in school, math is seen perhaps as the most challenging for imparting self system and positive psychology attributes, because the components of the self are explained with language rather than numbers. One of the high school students I taught was not motivated to learn algebra and was more interested in maintaining his popular status among his classmates. He was very bright, emotionally aware (of his own and others' emotions), socially talented, gifted physically, and in touch with the modern culture. When asked why he did not do well in school, up to his potential, including in math, he said that he did not know why he should—a response heard and an associated attitude felt often by teachers in all subject areas. I told him a story about Buckminster Fuller's life that would engage his self, including such components as his sense of higher purpose for his life, his own dreams; his self concept and identity; his mathematical, interpersonal; and intrapersonal intelligences; his feelings for helping others; and his desire to make a positive difference in the world.

Buckminster Fuller was an M.I.T.-trained mechanical engineer who invented the geodesic dome. This design is often used in large athletic arenas such as the Superdome in New Orleans or in freestanding camping tents. The math and physics concept of the dome is that each piece of the structure reinforces the other, which is the source of structural strength. If any one piece is weak or structurally unsound, the entire structure is weakened or could collapse. At one level, the intellectual level, this concept is wonderfully creative, inventive and very useful. Yet, at a deeper level, Buckminster Fuller's intention or guiding purpose of his conception was critical to this math student's transformation from a weak student with no direction in life to one who was motivated to learn about math, physics, and his self through schooling. The geodesic dome represents a model for the way human beings could live that would make the world a better place. Metaphorically, if each person understands his purpose in life and is actively manifesting that unique purpose, thus reinforcing each other's purposes, then the structure of humankind would work better, or even optimally. If any one of us is not in touch with this component of self understanding, or actively manifesting it in the world, then the structure of humanity is weakened and could collapse.

This story helped this student realize that he too had a higher and unique purpose for his own life, and maybe he could study architecture as a way to utilize his math skills and make a difference in the world using these skills. From this point on he had a stronger sense of self efficacy in school and the motivation to excel was no longer an issue for him. His life course trajectory soared.

THE SELF-SCHEMA COMPONENT

The self-schema is one important component of the self system that bears further discussion. The self-schema is a rather complex concept, yet critical to the teaching and learning process, because it represents how people become aware of, structure, and create their own realities. Psychologist and Tufts University professor Robert Sternberg (2007) wrote: "The children have the abilities, but they are not brought out by the ways in which they are taught, which divorce academic content from the children's realities" (p. 152).

Cognitive sociologist and Princeton professor Paul DiMaggio (1997) focuses upon "schema theory as especially relevant to the representation of social phenomena" (DiMaggio, 1997, p. 283) and "the ways in which social identities enter into the constitution of individual selves" (DiMaggio, 1997, p. 275). Cultural beliefs are integrated into the self as schemata, which are acquired "by individuals during development" (DiMaggio, 1997, p. 280). The "development of self-knowledge grows out of the social process" (Scheffler, 1985, p. 25). DiMaggio's (1997) view is that "individuals experience culture as disparate bits of information and as schematic structures that organize information" (DiMaggio, 1997, p. 263). Schemata are beliefs learned from life experiences, and they shape our views of reality. Therefore, schemata are important to include in our broader construct of self in education. According to DiMaggio, "culture is stored in memory" and the individual "organizes the information in the form of schemata" (DiMaggio, 1997, p. 268), where "schemata are both representations of knowledge and information processing mechanisms" (DiMaggio, 1997, p. 269). This view marries the cognitive with the philosophical understandings of knowledge; "in schematic cognition we find the mechanisms by which culture shapes and biases thought" (DiMaggio, 1997, p. 269).

Individuals in everyday classroom lessons bring "mental structures that influence perception, interpretation, planning and action" (DiMaggio, 1997, p. 270). Hence reality gets constructed through the self in everyday teaching and learning processes that occur in the classroom. As teachers, when we present a new piece of information, it requires our students to either assimilate that information into their existing paradigm of reality or create a new paradigm of reality in order to accommodate it. We need to teach our students the mental processes at work when constructing a self with schematic representations of one's identity (Markus, 1977). "Work on identity suggests the possibility that 'the self' may be an emotionally supersaturated cluster of schemata tending toward consistency and stability over time. Schemata that are embedded in the self-schemata, then, are more closely articulated with other schemata than those that are not incorporated into the self" (DiMaggio, 1997, p. 279). This means that teaching and learning effectiveness is dependent upon "schemata embedded in the self-schemata" in that they will be more deeply learned.

Educational psychologist, philosopher, and theorist Pajares (1992) discusses the important role of schemata in the teaching and learning of the self: "knowledge is fluid and evolves as new experiences are interpreted and integrated into existing schemata" (Pajares, 1992, p. 312). Further, "Sigel defined beliefs as 'mental constructions of experience—often condensed and integrated into schemata or concepts, whereas Harvey defined belief as an individual's representation of reality" (Pajares, 1992, p. 313). For our purposes as classroom teachers, the shaping of a student's self is the process of constructing reality out of experiences in the form of beliefs and knowledge. I would suggest that this learning how to construct a self is paramount in our system of education, especially a construct of the self with positive psychology attributes. If our students know that they are in charge of creating their own destinies in life through their construction of reality and of their selves, they will more readily want to learn academic content. There is a natural self-interest.

THE BROKEN PSYCHOLOGICAL CONTRACT

The discipline of educational psychology (Thorndike, 1914) emerged out of the need to measure people's intelligence in the early 1930s in order to justify categorizing students during a time of dramatic growth and the industrialization of America. At this same period in American education history, John Dewey (1900; 1902), the father of progressive education, provided a vision of child-centered pedagogy where he "formulated the aim of education in social terms. He was convinced that education would read its successes in the changed behaviors, perceptions, and insights of individual human beings" (Cremin, 1964, p. 122). When taking a look at who won this struggle for the hearts, minds, and souls of American educators from today's No Child Left Behind (NCLB) era, former Harvard University School of Education dean and historian Ellen Condliffe Lagemann declared, "Thorndike won and Dewey lost" (Lagemann in Gibboney, 2006). The findings in the Brzycki study (2009) support this declaration. When viewed from both schooling and the well-being of our children perspectives, and our schools are cold inhuman places, and trends in child well-being statistics are tragic.

There is a psychological contract between teacher and school and between teacher and student. This contract represents mutual beliefs, perceptions, and informal obligations. It sets the dynamics for the relationship and defines the detailed practicality of the work to be done. Teachers often indicate that the psychological contract has been broken in three places, between the (1) the school and teachers; (2) the teachers and their students; and (3) students and responsible adults (administrators and testers) who make decisions about what to teach the next generation. This broken contract is an underlying reason why students lose their motivation to learn as they go through our PK-12 system of education. Students know that the system of education is not about them, their futures, or their well-being, and they have disengaged in schooling processes. McCombs (2003) underscores this point.

> When the educational paradigm or reform agenda puts something other than the learner or learning at the center of instructional decision making, all learners suffer. Students know that the system is not about them and is not responsive to their needs. In such a system, learners recognize they are not important, because who they are and what they need are not at the heart of the learning process. At worst, they feel left out, ignored or alienated; at best, they feel the system is impersonal and irrelevant. (p. 96)

Teachers are frustrated with NCLB and associated programs such as the Focused Schools lesson planning program, because although they want to make a big difference in the lives, well-being, and self-esteem of their students, they do not have all of the available tools, notably self system and positive psychology distinctions. Teachers are feeling the tensions that are emerging at the crossroads of our society's needs. There are two emerging and conflicting needs: the need to take care of our children's emotional well-being, help them develop a strong sense of self, and experience happiness, and the need to produce academic outcomes that are measurable. Teachers are feeling the frustrations that accompany working for an institution that fails to represent the hopes and dreams of each student, and the future of our society. Schools and schooling hold at once those values held special by previous generations with those newer ones required for future success, in this case the 21st century emphasis on science, technology, and math with measurable outcomes. Their views are clearly articulated by one teacher:

> It is extremely difficult [teaching in the current climate]. I feel extremely overwhelmed and if I am feeling this way whether I can express it to the kids or not they pick up on that....For teachers the time and the caring that you can put into helping the [students' human] development along is [getting] smaller and smaller [due to the] push for standards and [state standardized tests] and certain lesson plans and development of certain things that way. I think we are losing more time to focus on areas like that with the kids. (Brzycki, 2009, November, Interview, 7)

We can conclude from teacher statements and the growing chorus of dissatisfaction with NCLB policies that a new model is needed with a broadened focus upon teaching and learning. This new broader focus includes imparting positive psychology attributes through schooling processes so that our system of education produces happier children with a strong sense of self foundational to well-being and success.

ASSESSING WELL-BEING OUTCOMES

Well-being outcomes can actually be assessed just as readily as academic outcomes if educators were to employ a number of instruments already in use by counselors. These instruments include scales and questionnaires for measuring: Psychological Well-Being (Ryff & Singer 1998), Subjective Happiness (Lyubomirsky & Lepper, 1999), Meaning in Life (Steger et al., in press); Satisfaction with Life (Diener et al., 1998). Using the proposed theory—where teacher beliefs are aligned with teaching and learning practices that place the integrated self at the center of schooling—we will have the possibility of reversing downward trends in child well-being.

Figure 2 is a chart (adapted from Stiggins, 2007) of how the proposed Self Theory in Schooling could provide for a new outcome from both a child's and a teacher's perspective. The chart represents the academic/self-understanding relationship dynamic with two possible pathways and well-being outcomes that can be assessed.

Figure 2: The Self Theory in Schooling: Pathways to Adolescent Well-Being

POSITIVE WELL-BEING OUTCOMES	UNDESIRABLE OUTCOMES
Teacher beliefs, practices, and assessment results provide	
Continual evidence of success	Continual evidence of failure
The student feels	
Hopeful and optimistic.	Hopeless.
Empowered to take productive action.	Initially panicked, giving way to resignation.
The student thinks	
It's all good. I'm doing fine.	This hurts. I'm not safe here.
See the trend? I succeed as usual.	I just can't do this…again.
I want more success.	I'm confused. I don't like this—help!
School focuses on what I do well.	Why is it always about what I can't do?
I know what to do next.	Nothing I try seems to work.
Feedback helps me.	Feedback is criticism. It hurts.
Public success feels good.	Public failure is embarrassing.
The student becomes more likely to	
Seek challenges.	Seek what's easy.
Seek exciting new ideas.	Avoid new concepts and approaches.
Practice with gusto.	Become confused about what to practice.
Take initiative.	Avoid initiative.
Persist in the face of setbacks.	Give up when things become challenging.
Take risks and stretch—go for it!	Retreat and escape—trying is too dangerous!
These actions lead to	
Self-enhancement.	Self-defeat, self-destruction.
Positive self-fulfilling prophecy.	Negative self-fulfilling prophecy.
Acceptance of responsibility.	Denial of responsibility.
Manageable stress.	High stress.

Feeling that success is its own reward.	No feelings of success; no reward.
Curiosity, enthusiasm.	Boredom, frustration, fear.
Continuous adaptation.	Inability to adapt.
Resilience.	Yielding quickly to defeat.
Strong foundations for future success.	Failure to master prerequisites for future success.

Adapted from: Stiggins, 2007, p. 24.

Rick Stiggins, president of the Educational Testing Services (ETS), has called for educators to broaden their perspective when assessing schoolchildren and to more fully understand that throughout the entire assessment process the young person is experiencing either success or failure, and this yields results in terms of positive or undesirable well-being outcomes:

> When we use assessment for learning, assessment becomes far more than merely a one-time event stuck onto the end of an instruction unit. It becomes a series of interlaced experiences that enhance the learning process by keeping students confident and focused on their progress, even in the face of occasional setbacks…even the most valid and reliable assessment cannot be regarded as high quality if it causes a student to give up. (Stiggins, 2007, p. 22)

If a school-aged child is reminded constantly that she is an academic failure, then this produces a self-schema of thinking and feeling that includes hopelessness, anxiety, and defeat. If a student thinks "nothing I try seems to work" or "public failure is embarrassing," she is likely to avoid initiative or attempting to learn new concepts and approaches. She may retreat and escape through emotional withdrawal, excessive computer gaming, or substance abuse. These actions lead to "self defeat, self destruction," "negative self-fulfilling prophecy," and "failure to master prerequisites for future success" (p. 24). Considering the well-being of our children, teachers confirm the dynamic between self, curricula, and outcomes. Making meaning is a constructive process through the interaction of the self and classroom practices where teachers can teach children to construct personal meaning of self-worth and high potential.

If, on the other hand, teachers teach students to focus upon winning through schooling experiences by generating and collecting evidence of success, this leads the student to feel "hopeful and optimistic" and "empowered to take productive action" (p. 24). Cognitively the student thinks "I'm doing fine," "I want more success," and "school is a place that focuses upon what I do best and really cares that I grow and develop as a person." This leads the student to "seek challenges; seek exciting new ideas, take initiative, and persist in the face of setbacks." Possible new ways of being in the world consist of: self-enhancement, positive self-fulfilling prophecy, acceptance of responsibility, manageable stress, resilience, and a strong foundation for future success." It is clear that the second pathway in our two examples would produce two very different types of people, well-being profiles, and attributes.

MENDING THE PSYCHOLOGICAL CONTRACT: USING THE SELF THEORY IN SCHOOLING

Teachers and administrators could work together to develop a renewed understanding of the importance of teaching to the self of each student and an interest in learning about new approaches that will impact the health and well-being of their students as well as their academic achievements. This renewed understanding may inform teacher best practices now being collected by many state departments of education. University teacher education programs and professional development programs could use the new conceptual framework and proven practices to manifest deeply held beliefs about the mission of a teacher, thus assisting in training teachers in how to be more effective when reaching the hearts, minds, and souls of children.

The Self Theory in Schooling can help to inform educational psychology and teacher education, thereby further bringing together psychology and education through a teaching and learning paradigm that includes the self. With the Self Theory in Schooling we can envision the following results:

1. Teachers will have a pathway to expressing and manifesting their deeply held beliefs and mission to impart a significant protective factor in a child's life course: a healthy and positive self system.

2. Students' well-being and their academic achievement will improve as they learn that a positive self system is where meaning is made, and it engages their natural interests to learn and excel (Hunter & Csikszentmihalyi, 2003).

3. Policy makers may want to adopt the researched teaching best practices and put them into their own best practices toolkits for teachers to draw upon. Additionally, they may take action to shift the balance toward a whole child focus.

4. It is my hope that the self theory in teaching and learning becomes a guiding framework for future K-12 reform. All teachers want children to learn how to be well for the entirety of their life spans—psychologically, emotionally, physically, and spiritually.

POLICY IMPLICATIONS

Noted educational theorist Nel Noddings (2003) asserts: "educational aims always reflect the aims—explicit or implicit—of the political society in which they are developed" (Noddings, 2003, p. 88). Education policy must be based upon an understanding of where we want to go and with a clearer vision of future possibilities for our society and for equipping our children to thrive in the 21st century. Therefore, policy makers at the federal and state levels would do well to listen with respect to teacher beliefs as well as take note of the child well-being statistics.

One possible vision of how to inform the policy debate is to design and implement a school-based program that includes outcome measurements that demonstrate that the health and well-being of our youth are important and that we can positively impact the growing health and well-being crisis in America. We can shift our view to a more balanced one between academics and well-being and measure both to the satisfaction of parents, students, and teachers. What if policy makers called for a "well-being center" in every middle school if not all schools? This would be a preventative strategy to the health and well-being crisis and improve academic readiness even in the midst of our present model of education characterized by NCLB.

A "well-being center" would be in a central location where resources are available to distribute to students, teachers, and parents. Resources would not be therapy or counseling services directly administered. They would be educational services where teachers are introduced to a workbook of distinctions about the self that could be incorporated into daily lesson plans by subject. Teachers are accustomed to this model when drawing upon new methods for teaching writing across the curriculum, such as when an earth science teacher draws upon a teaching and learning center's resources to better understand how to help her students write better while learning science concepts. Another example of a widely used center in public schools today is that of a peer mediation center. In this type of center students with the help of trained student facilitators address disrespectful and harmful behaviors most often based in anger and frustration. Thus, students help prevent escalation of fighting and bullying, which contribute to an unsafe school environment.

If teachers were measured on the well-being of students, perhaps using Psychological Well Being scales (Ryff & Singer, 1998), and not just on the academic performance of students, then they would be happier, especially seasoned teachers who have been in the system for a while. There appears to be a growing gap between a teacher's belief that it is important to empower students and the increased requirements to adhere to administrative requirements imposed by NCLB. As a society, we are trying to meet the new demands for healthier people, so that they will not be a financial drain on the health care system, and for new skilled workers in the 21st century workplace, but we are using the old and out-of-date assumptions associated with the NCLB educational model (Robinson, (2001). I am suggesting that placing the self of the learner at the center of a new school reform framework would empower teachers and students alike to higher levels of achievement and outcomes aligned with the needs of our society.

TEACHER PREPARATION

In the state of Pennsylvania new education legislation known as Chapter 49 and 49–2 calls for teacher certification levels and increased training in child and adolescent development. This is a positive direction, but the legislation does not simultaneously call for more course work in educational psychology or human development and learning. How will new teachers understand self distinctions within the new levels? The answer lies in integrating educational psychology concepts into teaching methods courses, which typically have aimed to increase academic outcomes solely using standards and standardized tests and *not* through the motivation, self-understanding, or well-being of young people.

However, expecting more out of current teaching methods courses will be a challenge. Consider two informative research studies. In the first study, Harvard education professor Kane looked at the effectiveness of teachers trained at a number of teacher education programs and concluded that there is no difference in the quality of teachers measured by student achievement. In the second study, Arthur Levine (2006) is largely critical of the way teachers are educated today because they are becoming technicians responsible for merely two learning outcomes—language arts and math. Levine found that teacher education programs do not make a difference in the lives of either those going though them or in the ability to produce results in students. Levine (2006) characterizes what teacher education programs need to focus upon in order to prepare teachers effectively in the NCLB era:

They should educate teachers for a world in which the only measure of success is student achievement. They should educate teachers for subject matter mastery, pedagogical competence, and understanding of the learning and development of the children they teach. The challenge facing education schools is not to do a better job at what they are already doing, but to do a fundamentally different job. They are now in the business of preparing teachers for a new world: an outcome-based, accountability driven system of education in which all children are expected to learn. (p. 104)

Levine's (2006) study reveals a "new world" reality in which schools of education are in the business of producing teachers for an outcomes based system, yet they are not succeeding at their task. This study's stunning conclusions suggest that teacher education programs are not producing the results intended. Teachers believe that schools are in the business of child or adolescent development, empowering young people in their care. This is a direct contradiction working at cross purposes with the current NCLB model. The teachers at the middle school in the Brzycki (2009) study were all trained at various teacher education programs yet were collectively consistent in their beliefs about empowering children's human development. If teacher education programs built upon the sustaining beliefs of teachers, we would have better outcomes both in academics and well-being. Educational theorist Greg Goodman (2008) calls for "teachers to consider their role as fundamental to the development of their students' leadership, and awareness of social justice and equality in education as critical for a healthier and saner world" (Goodman, 2008). Additionally, he challenges educators in our time to take responsibility for developing the professional perspective and skills to empower all children's learning so as to develop their full and unique potentials in life, not merely to be measured in state-administered standardized tests which continue the cold technical rationality begun by Thorndike and maintained through NCLB. There is a growing chorus among experienced educators that education is the pathway to empowering total health and well-being and that NCLB policies and procedures are outdated and ineffective.

As children grow into a more mature and formal operational thinking, I believe they want to dedicate themselves to a higher purpose in life, to making a difference beyond their own self-interest and help make life better for all human beings in our global community. The teaching and learning processes that incorporate the Self Theory in Schooling are meant to release the full and unique human potentials of all people through learning and schooling processes.

TEACHER AND ADOLESCENT WELL-BEING

Schools are where children learn how to be well, how to succeed in life, and where they construct a paradigm of self that empowers their understanding of their full and unique potential. Yet many school systems are designed for children to fail. They focus upon children's weaknesses, and teachers remind them constantly that they are not achieving. Students are driven further and further into the mindset of survival, fearing that they are not measuring up. Will they survive? This is also true for teachers; they are being asked to teach contrary to their own beliefs and homegrown practices that make an impact with children. Positive psychology attributes applied to education can help build academic skills and life skills based upon strengths. We can give teachers more resources and training on self system and positive psychology attributes and new ways of imparting and measuring these attributes.

Children are often frozen in fear, fear of being judged before they feel ready to be evaluated, and how children see themselves is learned from the system of education/schooling. Children are experiencing a myriad of undesirable well-being symptoms largely due to being unaware of who they are and not merely as a student with an intellect. Children are frozen in fear because their worth is measured by test scores, and they are not understood for the whole being that they are.

Schooling reinforces a disconnection between thinking and feeling, between the intellect and emotions. Today's students are products of the NCLB era of cold technocratic rationality. They want to connect in important and emotional ways to the why of learning, and affect is the fuel that brings this to life. How important it is, especially in this era of disassociated education (a clinical psychologist's term to describe the separation of our feelings from our experiences in life), to teach future educators that the "teachers who have the best success are the ones who deeply care about their students. This caring covers not only the academic competency their students' achieve, but it extends to the whole child. A caring and compassionate teacher knows that the feelings that the child experiences are an integral part of his or her life" (Kolencik, 2008, p. 180).

The schooling model characterized by a cold technocratic rationality and the era of disassociated education is one possible reason why psychological theorist Daniel Goleman (1995) asserts that we need to consider all dimensions of what it means to be human, including the emotional dimension:

> These are times when the fabric of society seems to unravel at ever greater speed, when selfishness, violence and a meanness of spirit seem to be rotting the goodness of our communal lives. There is growing evidence that the fundamental ethical stances in life stem from underlying emotional capacities. For one, impulse is the medium of emotion; the seed of all impulse is a feeling bursting to express itself in action. Those who are at the mercy of impulse—who lack self-control—suffer a moral deficiency. The ability to control impulse is the base of will and character. By the same token, the root of altruism lies in empathy, the ability to read emotions in others; lacking a sense of another's need or despair, there is not caring. And if there are any two moral stances that our times call for, they are precisely these, self-restraint and compassion....The very name, Homo sapiens, the thinking species, is misleading in the light of the new appreciation and vision of the place of emotions in our lives that science now offers. When it comes to shaping our decisions and our actions, [and I would suggest our selves] feeling counts every bit as much, and often more, than thought; we have gone too far in emphasizing the value of the purely rational, of what IQ measures, in human life. (Goleman, in Robinson, 2001, p. 164)

Harvard psychologist Howard Gardner (2007) asks: "what kinds of mind do we need if we are to create a world in which we would like to live?" (p. 88), and answers: (1) a disciplinary mind where students are able to master a major school of thought and at least one professional craft; (2) a synthesizing mind; (3) a creating mind; (4) an ethical mind (one willing to take on responsibilities as a world citizen); (5) a respectful mind. I would add another theory of mind where the self changes and grows toward higher and higher levels of conscious awareness, so as to manifest wellness. By placing the self of the student at the center of learning, the symptoms of not knowing the self will reduce as children come to know themselves more thoroughly and deeply. Knowing one's self is the pathway to healing and well-being and to ameliorating tragic mental and physical health issues and concerns, including obesity, depression, cutting, alcohol and drug abuse, heart disease, among others.

This chapter demonstrates the importance of self in teaching and learning and supports the conclusion that when teachers align their own beliefs toward empowering the mind, body, and spirit of their students, their children's well-being and academic outcomes excel. I choose to conclude this chapter by underscoring the work of a transitional theorist in psychology: social cognitive theorist Albert Bandura. Bandura wrote, "The self-efficacy component of social cognitive theory does more than identify a contributory factor to career development. The theory provides the means for enhancing the personal source of control over the course of one's self-development" (Bandura, 1997, p. 34). If teachers learn to foster these essential attributes concerning students' own destiny in their lives: their self-control and self-efficacy, then those same students will develop a healthy set of behaviors and attitudes for charting their life course trajectories. Then, too, will teachers feel like they have succeeded.

REFERENCES

Baker. D.P. (2009). *The Quiet Revolution: The Educational Transform of Modern Society.* Draft copy available at dpb4@psu.edu

Baker, D.P., Thorne, S.L., Eslinger, P., Blair, C., Gamson, D. (in press). *Cognition, Culture, and Institutions: Affinities within the Social Construction of Reality.* Draft copy available at: dpb4@psu.edu

Bandura, A. (1997). *Self-efficacy: The Exercise of Control.* New York: Freeman.

Bandura, A., Barbaranelli, C., Caprara, G. V., Pastorelli, C. (2001). Self-Efficacy beliefs as shapers of children's aspirations and career trajectories. *Child Development,* Jan/Feb, *72,* 1, pp. 187–206.

Berger, P., & Luckmann, T. (1967). *The Social Construction of Reality.* Garden City, NY: Doubleday.

Bruner, J. (1960). *The Process of Education.* Cambridge, MA: Harvard University Press.

Bruner, J. (1990). *Acts of Meaning.* Cambridge, MA: Harvard University Press.

Bruner, J. (1996). *The Culture of Education.* Cambridge, MA: Harvard University Press.

Brzycki, H.G. (2009). *Teacher Beliefs and Practices that Impart Self System and Positive Psychology Attributes.* (Doctoral Dissertation, Pennsylvania State University, 2009) ETD-3819.

Cremin, L.A. (1964). *The Transformation of the School: Progressivism in American Education 1876–1957.* New York: Vintage/Random House.

Csikszentmihalyi, M. (1993). *The Evolving Self.* New York: HarperCollins.

Deci, E.L., Nezlek, J., & Sheinman, L. (1981). Characteristics of the rewarder and intrinsic motivation of the rewardee. *Journal of Personality and Social Psychology,* 40, 1–10.

Deci, E.L., & Ryan, R.M. (1985). *Intrinsic Motivation and Self Determination in Human Behavior.* New York: Plenum.

Deci, E.L., & Ryan, R.M. (1995). Human autonomy: The basis for true self-esteem. In M. Kernis (Ed.), *Efficacy, Agency, and Self-esteem* (pp. 31–49). New York: Plenum.

Dewey, J. (1900). *The School and Society.* Chicago: University of Chicago Press.

Dewey, J. (1902). *The Child and the Curriculum.* Chicago: University of Chicago Press.

Dewey, J. (1916). *Democracy and Education.* New York: Macmillan.

Diener, E., Lucas R.E., Oishi, S. (2002). Subjective well-being: the science of happiness and life satisfaction. See Snyder & Lopez, 2002, pp. 463–73.

Diener, E., Sapyta, J.J., Suh, E. (1998). Subjective well-being is essential to well-being. *Psychological Inquiry,* Vol. 9, No. 1 (1998), pp. 33–37.

DiMaggio, P. (1997). Culture and cognition. *Annual Review of Sociology, 23,* 263–287.

Gardner, H. (1983). *Frames of Mind: The Theory of Multiple Intelligences.* New York: Basic Books.

Gardner, H. (2007). *Five Minds for the Future.* Cambridge, MA: HBS Press.

Gibboney, R.A. (Oct. 2006). Intelligence by Design: Thorndike versus Dewey. *Phi Delta Kappan.*

Goleman, D. (1995). *Emotional Intelligence.* New York: Bantam.

Goodman, G. S. (Ed.). (2008). *Educational Psychology: An Application of Critical Constructivism.* New York: Peter Lang.

Harter, S. (1999). *The Construction of the self: A Developmental Perspective.* New York: The Guilford Press.

Hawkins, D.J., Kosterman, R., Catalano, R.F., Hill, K.G., Abbott, R.D. (2008). Effects of social development intervention in childhood 15 years later. *Arch Pediatr Adolesc Med. 162* (12), Dec.

Herman, K. C., Lambert, S. F., Reinke, W. M., Ialongo, N. S. (July, 2008). Low academic competence in first grade as a risk factor for depressive cognitions and symptoms in middle school. *Journal of Counseling Psychology. 55*(3), 400–410.

Hunter, J.P. & Csikszentmihalyi, M. (2003, February). The positive psychology of interested adolescents. *Journal of Youth and Adolescence, 32,* 1, pp. 27–35.

James, W. (1900) *Principles of Psychology, Vol. I.* New York: Henry Holt and Company.

James, W. (1992). The psychology of belief. In *Psychology: Briefer Course* (pp. 1021–1056). New York: The Library of America.

Kane, T.J., Rockoff, J.E., Staiger, D.O. (2007). Photo finish: Teacher certification doesn't guarantee a winner. *Education Next,* Winter 2007, *7,* 1.

Kolencik, P. (2008) Affective and motivational factors for learning and achievement. In Goodman (Ed.). *Educational Psychology: An Application of Critical Constructivism.* New York: Peter Lang.

Kvale, S. (1996). The quality of the interview. In *Interviews: An Introduction to Qualitative Research Interviewing.* Thousand Oaks, CA: Sage Publications.

Laggeman, C. (2006) in Gibboney, R.A. (Oct. 2006). Intelligence by design: Thorndike versus Dewey. *Phi Delta Kappan.*

Lent, R.W., Singley, D., Sheu, H. & Gainor, K. (2005). Social cognitive predictors of domain and life satisfaction: Exploring the theoretical precursors of subjective well-being. *Journal of Counseling Psychology, 52,* 3, 429–442.

Levine, A. (2006). *Educating School Teachers.* Washington, DC: The Woodrow Wilson Foundation. www.edschools.org.

Lopez S.J. & Snyder C.R., eds. (2009). *Handbook of Positive Psychology.* London: Oxford Univ. Press.

Lyubomirsky, S., & Lepper, H. S. (1999). A measure of subjective happiness: Preliminary reliability and construct validation. *Social Indicators Research, 46,* 137–155.

Markus, H. (1977). Self-schemata and processing information about the self. *Journal of Personality and Social Psychology, 35,* 63–78.

McCombs, B.L. (2003, Spring). A framework for the redesign of K-12 education in the context of current educational reform. *Theory into Practice, 42,* 2.

Noddings, N. (2003). *Happiness and Education.* Cambridge, UK: Cambridge University Press.

Parjares, M.F. (1992). Teachers' beliefs and educational research: Cleaning up a messy construct. *Review of Educational Research, 62,* 307–332.

Parjares, M.F. (Winter 1996). Self-efficacy beliefs in academic settings. *Review of Educational Research, 66,* 4, pp. 543–578.

Patrick, H., Ryan, A.M., & Kaplan, A. (2007). Early adolescent perceptions of the classroom social environment, motivational beliefs, and engagement. *Journal of Educational Psychology, 99,* 1, 83–98.

Penn Resiliency Program (Cutuli, J.J., Chaplin, T.M., Gillham, J.E., Reivich, K.J., & Seligman, M.E.P. (2006). Preventing co-occurring depression symptoms in adolescents with conduct problems: The Penn Resiliency Program. *New York Academy of Sciences, 1094,* 282–286.

Pennsylvania Department of Education. (2005, June). *Pennsylvania Department of Education Press Release.* (www.pdenewsroom.state.pa.us).

Pennsylvania Department of Education. (2008). Chapter 49 Guidelines for Teacher Preparation Programs.

Prakash, M.S., & Esteva, G. (2005). *Escaping Education: Living as Learning within Grassroots Cultures.* New York: Peter Lang.

Robinson, K. (2001). *Out of Our Minds: Learning to Be Creative.* West Sussex, England: John Wiley & Sons Publishing.

Rogers, C. (1961). *On Becoming a Person.* Boston: Houghton Mifflin.

Rogers, C. (1980). *A Way of Being.* Boston: Houghton Mifflin.

Ryan, R.M., & Deci, E.L. (2000). Self-Determination Theory and the Facilitation of Intrinsic Motivation, Social Development, and Well Being. *American Psychologist, 55,* pp. 68–78.

Ryan, R.M. & Deci, E.L. (2001). On happiness and human potentials: A review of research on hedonic and eudaimonic well-being. *Annual Review of Psychology, 52,* 141–166.

Ryan, R.M., Deci, E.L., & Grolnick, W.S. (1995). Autonomy, relatedness, and the self: Their relation to development and psychopathology. In D. Cicchetti & D.J. Cohen (Eds.), *Developmental Psychopathology: Theory and Methods* (pp. 618–655). New York: Wiley.

Ryan, R.M., & Grolnick, W.S. (1986). Origins and pawns in the classroom: Self report and projective assessments of individual differences in children's perceptions. *Journal of Personality and Social Psychology, 50,* 550–565.

Ryff, C.D., & Singer, B. (1998). The contours of positive human health. *Psychological Inquiry,* 9, 1–28.

Scheffler, I. (1995). *Of Human Potential.* Boston, MA: Routledge & Kegan Paul.

Seligman, M.E.P. (2005). The New Science of Happiness. Quoted in *Time Magazine,* January 17.

Seligman, M.E.P. & Csikszentmihalyi, M. (2000). Positive psychology: An introduction. *American Psychologist, 55,* 5–14.

Shanahan, M.J. (2000). Pathways to adulthood in changing societies: Variability and mechanisms in life course perspective. *Annual Review of Sociology, 26:* 667–692.

Steger, M. F., Frazier, P., Oishi, S., & Kaler, M. (in press). The meaning in life questionnaire: Assessing the presence of and search for meaning in life. *Journal of Counseling Psychology.*

Sternberg, R.J. (2007). Who are the bright children? The cultural context of being and acting intelligent. *Educational Researcher, 36,* 3, pp. 148–155.

Stiggins, R. (May, 2007). Assessment through the student's eyes. *Educational Leadership, 64,* 8. Alexandria, VA: ASCD.

Thorndike, E.L. (1914). *Educational Psychology.* New York: Teachers College.

Tomlinson, C.A. (1999). The differentiated classroom: Responding to the needs of all learners. Alexandria, VA: ASCD.

Tomlinson, C.A. (2000, September). Reconcilable differences: Standards-based teaching and differentiation. *Educational Leadership, 58*(1), 6–11.

Tomlinson, C.A. (2001). *How to Differentiate Instruction in Mixed-ability Classrooms,* 2nd ed. Alexandria, VA: ASCD.

Tomlinson, C.A., & Eidson, C.C. (2003). *Differentiation in Practice: A Resource Guide for Differentiating Curriculum for Grades 5–9.* Alexandria, VA: ASCD.

Tomlinson, C.A., & Germundson, A. (May 2007). Teaching as jazz. *Educational Leadership.* Alexandria, VA: ASCD.

U.S. Department of Education, Office of Elementary and Secondary Education, *No Child Left Behind: A Desktop Reference.* Washington, DC.

Annotated Educational Psychology Bibliography

FIFTY

Annotated Educational Psychology Bibliography

Cathleen Ruble

This annotated bibliography includes most of the published works in the field of educational psychology 2004–2009. These results were collected through an ERIC search conducted at Clarion University of Pennsylvania as a part of a course requirement for the Master's in Library Science. The bibliography is presented here to aid in the quest for information literacy within this burgeoning field.

Al Otaiba, S., Petscher, Y., Pappamihiel, N. E., Williams, R. S., Dyrlund, A. K., & Connor, C. (2009). Modeling oral reading fluency development in latino students: A longitudinal study across second and third grade. *Journal of Educational Psychology, 101*(2), 315–329. doi:10.1037/a0014698

Abstract: This study examines growth in oral reading fluency across 2nd and 3rd grade for Latino students grouped in 3 English proficiency levels: students receiving English as a second language (ESL) services (n = 2,182), students exited from ESL services (n = 965), and students never designated as needing services (n = 1,857). An important focus was to learn whether, within these 3 groups, proficiency levels and growth were reliably related to special education status. Using hierarchical linear modeling, the authors compared proficiency levels and growth in oral reading fluency in English between and within groups and then to state reading benchmarks. Findings indicate that oral reading fluency scores reliably distinguished between students with learning disabilities and typically developing students within each group (effect sizes ranging from 0.96 to 1.51). The growth trajectory included a significant quadratic trend (generally slowing over time). These findings support the effectiveness of using oral reading fluency in English to screen and monitor reading progress under Response to Intervention models but also suggest caution in interpreting oral reading fluency data as part of the process in identifying students with learning disabilities.

Amer, A. (2006). Reflections on Bloom's revised taxonomy. *Electronic Journal of Research in Educational Psychology, 4*(1), 213–230. Retrieved April 15, 2009, from ERIC.gov database.

Abstract: In the application of the "Original" Bloom's taxonomy since its publication in 1956, several weaknesses and practical limitations have been revealed. Besides, psychological and educational research has witnessed the introduction of several theories and approaches to learning which make students more knowledgeable of and responsible for their own learning, cognition, and thinking. Hence, a group of researchers revised the "Original" taxonomy in order to overcome its weaknesses and to incorporate the recent developments. The purpose of the present article is to present a concise and critical review of both the "Original" and "Revised" taxonomy with reference to their underlying philosophy, rationale, structure and potential pedagogic uses. (Contains 6 tables.)

Bidjerano, T. (2005). Gender differences in self-regulated learning. *Online Submission.* (Paper Presented at the Annual Meeting of the Northeastern Educational Research Association). Retrieved April 15, 2009, from ERIC.gov database.

Abstract: Self-regulated learning is a relatively new construct in the domain of educational psychology, but its theoretical relevance and important practical implications have already been well established. The study explored the extent to which the self-regulated learning strategies of metacognition, elaboration, critical thinking, organization, rehearsal, time and effort management, help seeking and peer learning vary with gender. The Motivated Strategies for Learning Questionnaire (MSLQ) was administered to 198 undergraduate students at a large university in the northeastern U.S. The obtained data were analyzed through multivariate analysis of variance. The study uncovered several statistically significant differences. Female students tended to over-report the use of rehearsal, organization, metacognition, time management skills, elaboration, and effort. No statistically significant gender differences were found with respect to studying with peers, help seeking, and critical thinking skills. (Contains 1 figure.)

Blewitt, P., Rump, K. M., Shealy, S. E., & Cook, S. A. (2009). Shared book reading: When and how questions affect young children's word learning. *Journal of Educational Psychology, 101*(2), 294–304. doi:10.1037/a0013844

Abstract: Shared book reading, and the conversation that accompanies it, can facilitate young children's vocabulary growth. To identify the features of extratextual questions that help 3-year-olds learn unfamiliar words during shared book reading, two experiments explored the impact of cognitive demand level, placement, and an approximation to scaffolding. Asking questions about target words improved children's comprehension and production of word–referent associations, and children with larger vocabularies learned more than children with smaller vocabularies. Neither the demand level nor placement of questions differentially affected word learning. However, an approximation of scaffolding, in which adults asked low-demand questions when words first appeared and high-demand questions later, did facilitate children's deeper understanding of word meanings as assessed with a definition task. These results are unique in experimentally demonstrating the value for word learning of shifting from less to more challenging input over time. Discussion focuses on why a scaffolding-like procedure improves children's acquisition of elaborated word meanings.

Byrd, D., Arentoft, A., Scheiner, D., Westerveld, M., & Baron, I. S. (2008). State of multicultural neuropsychological assessment in children: Current research issues. *Neuropsychology Review, 18*(3), 214. Retrieved from http://proquest.umi.com/pqdweb?did=1575650011&Fmt=7&clientId=3405&RQT=309&VName=PQD

Abstract: Research and Clinical Implications: Scientific attention to cultural considerations in child neuropsychological assessment has not developed parallel to the focus these issues have received in adult and elderly neuropsychological assessment. There are limited data on the presence, magnitude, etiology, and implications of culture-related differences in cognitive test performance among children. This preliminary report reviews the available empirical literature on the current state of multicultural neuropsychological assessment in children. The review identified articles by searching PubMed and PsycINFO databases, and the tables of contents of *Developmental Neuropsychology* and *Child Neuropsychology* from 2003 to 2008. Of the 1,834 abstracts reviewed, ten papers met inclusion criteria for the review. Five studies were completed in America; four of these compared performance between ethnic groups while the fifth examined neighborhood-level poverty indicators exclusively in African American children. Of the five international studies, all established local normative data and/or were exploratory investigations of neuropsychological functions in specific cultural groups, including Taiwanese infants, South African youth, and bilingual British children. Taken together, the results yield important clinical and research data that begin to inform many of the complex and fascinating mechanisms by which ethnic identity and culture impact cognitive development and the neuropsychological assessment of children. A critique of the existing literature and directions for future research are provided.

Byrnes, J. P., & Wasik, B. A. (2009). Factors predictive of mathematics achievement in kindergarten, first and third grades: An opportunity–propensity analysis. *Contemporary Educational Psychology, 34*(2), 167–183. doi:10.1016/j.cedpsych.2009.01.002

Abstract: A secondary analysis of the Early Childhood Longitudinal Study—Kindergarten Sample (N = 17,401) was conducted to determine the factors that are most strongly associated with math achievement during kindergarten, first grade, and third grade. Factors from the following three categories were considered: antecedent factors (e.g., family socio-economic status), opportunity factors (e.g., frequency of being exposed to mathematical content), and propensity factors (e.g., pre-existing mathematics skills). Structural equation modeling showed that math achievement was strongly predicted by a combination of specific propensity, opportunity, and antecedent factors. However, propensity factors were the most important determinants of achievement. The amount of variance accounted for by gender and ethnicity was substantially reduced when other factors in the antecedent, opportunity, and propensity categories were controlled. The implications of the findings for intervention are discussed.

Callender, A. A., & McDaniel, M. A. (2009). The limited benefits of rereading educational texts. *Contemporary Educational Psychology, 34*(1), 30–41. doi:10.1016/j.cedpsych.2008.07.001

Abstract: Though rereading is a study method commonly used by students, theoretical disagreement exists regarding whether rereading a text significantly enhances the representation and retention of the text's contents. In four experiments, we evaluated the effectiveness of rereading relative to a single reading in a context paralleling that faced by students in the classroom. Participants read educational texts (textbook chapters or a *Scientific American* article) under intentional learning instructions. Learning and memory were tested with educationally relevant summative assessments (multiple choice, short-answer questions, and text summaries). With only several exceptions, rereading did not significantly increase performance on the assessments. We also found that reading comprehension ability did not alter this pattern. It appears that when using ecologically valid materials such as a textbook chapter, immediate rereading may have little or no benefit for improving performance on educationally relevant summative assessments.

Carlson, L. E., & Rescorla, L. (2008). The use of psychological state words by late talkers at ages 3, 4, and 5 years. *Applied Psycholinguistics, 29*(1), 21–39. Retrieved April 16, 2009, from British Education Index database.

Abstract: The use of four types of psychological state words (physiological, emotional, desire, and cognitive) during mother-child play sessions at ages 3, 4, and 5 years was examined in 30 children diagnosed with delayed expressive language.

Chang, M., Park, B., Singh, K., & Sung, Y. Y. (2009). Parental involvement, parenting behaviors, and children's cognitive development in low-income and minority families. *Journal of Research in Childhood Education, 23*(3), 309. Retrieved from http://proquest.umi.com/pqdweb?did=1685505091&Fmt=7&clientId=3405&RQT=309&VName=PQD

Abstract: The study examined the longitudinal association of parental involvement in Head Start parent-focused programs, parenting behaviors, and the cognitive development of children by specifying two longitudinal growth models. Model 1 examined the longitudinal effects of the parental involvement in three Head Start parenting programs (parenting classes, group socialization, and support groups) on parenting behaviors (home observation of parental linguistic and cognitive stimulation, video recordings of parental cognitive stimulation, parental supportiveness, detachment, and intrusiveness). Model 2 analyzed the longitudinal effects of those parental behaviors on children's Bayley MDI scores. Using Early Head Start Research and Evaluation (EHSRE) study data and longitudinal multilevel analysis, the study also took various ethnic and language differences among families into account. The results revealed that mothers who participated in parenting classes or socialization meetings provided more linguistic and cognitive stimulation at home. Participants of parental support groups were found to have high levels of parental supportiveness and low levels of parental intrusiveness over time. Higher Bayley MDI scores were found for children whose mothers had high levels of parental involvement in Head Start parent programs and provided more at-home linguistic and cognitive stimulation. The African American families, in particular, benefited from attending socialization meetings: attendees displayed fewer parental detachment behaviors and provided more linguistic and cognitive stimulation, resulting in higher Bayley MDI scores of children. The study's findings are theoretically significant and policy relevant.

Clark, M. (2008). Review of *Spectacular Things Happen along the Way: Lessons from an Urban Classroom. Education and Urban Society, 41*(1), 158–165. doi:10.1177/0013124508320548

Abstract: Reviews the book *Spectacular Things Happen along the Way: Lessons from an Urban Classroom* by B. Schultz (2008). Schultz begins his book by explaining how he had come to teach from the corporate world, and in his desire to work for social justice, got a job teaching 5th grade in room 405 at Carr Community Academy, a school adjacent to the project housing of Cabrini Green in Chicago. Frustrated and depleted after more than a year of traditional teaching, he finally decided to use the problem-based strategies he was learning in graduate school and apply them to his classroom. The results, based on a democratic curriculum program called Project Citizen, led to great success and publicity for himself and his students, as he describes throughout the book. Describing his curriculum ideas both at the end and throughout the book, Schultz focuses on two key ideas that have permeated much of the theoretical and practical work on classrooms: democratic schooling and progressive education. The first of these, education as democracy, is explicitly mentioned by Schultz as key to his classroom. The concept of democratic schools, long thought of as vital to education in a democratic society, has existed for many years, yet as many teachers lament, it has recently fallen to the wayside in the era of testing and accountability. In addition to the concept of democratic schooling, the second key theme in Schultz's book, and his classroom, is that of progressive education. Recalling his own elite education, he tells about his experiences with a progressive curriculum, something that he did not initially observe at Carr. He argues vehemently against the attitude that "certain children need to be taught in certain ways dependent on their class" (Schultz, 2008, p. 144) and instead instills the idea that all children, particularly those in poor and urban environments, should learn more than math equations and sentence structure. He writes, "One of the primary purposes of American public schools is to prepare children to be good and productive citizens. Unfortunately, most students do not have any opportunity to develop or practice these skills as part of a typical school experience" (pp. 140–141). In his writing, Schultz remains focused on his students, liberally utilizing their words and actions to illustrate the transformation within his classroom walls. Although he does describe the conflicting emotions he felt during the year, he also provides a hopeful picture for teachers in a variety of environments who would wish to create a similar curriculum. The gap between theory and practice remains, yet Schultz is able to show how these two parts of education do not necessarily need to be adversaries and how inclusion of student voices can work to connect broad ideas and concrete action.

Conrad, N. J. (2008). From reading to spelling and spelling to reading: Transfer goes both ways. *Journal of Educational Psychology, 100*(4), 869–878. doi:10.1037/a0012544

Abstract: This study compares the effects of practice spelling and reading specific words on the orthographic representations in memory involved in reading both practiced words and new, unfamiliar words. Typically developing readers in Grade 2 (mean age = 7 years, 7 months) participated in a training study examining whether transfer can occur between reading and spelling following a series of reading and spelling practice sessions. Practice consisted of either repeated reading or repeated spelling of words with shared orthographic rhyme patterns. A series of mixed analyses of variance was used to examine generalization within skill and transfer across skill. Following practice, word-specific transfer across skill was found. Specifically, children were better able to spell words they had practiced reading and to read words they had practiced spelling. In addition, generalization to new words with practiced rime units was found both within a skill and across skills. However, transfer from spelling to reading was greater than transfer from reading to spelling. Results indicate that the orthographic representations established through practice can be used for both reading and spelling. Subsequently, reading and spelling curricula should be coordinated to benefit children maximally.

Corkum, P., Humphries, K., Mullane, J. C., & Theriault, F. (2008). Private speech in children with ADHD and their typically developing peers during problem-solving and inhibition tasks. *Contemporary Educational Psychology, 33*(1), 97–115. doi:10.1016/j.cedpsych.2006.12.003

Abstract: This study compared private speech of children with ADHD and normal controls during problem-solving and inhibition tasks. Thirty-two children (16 children with ADHD and 16 matched controls) aged 6–11 years participated. Consistent with previous studies, children with ADHD produced more task-irrelevant and task-relevant external private speech than control children during problem-solving tasks but did not differ in their use of task-relevant internal private speech. During the inhibition/attention task (Continuous Performance Test-II), children with ADHD produced more task-relevant external and more task-relevant internal private speech, suggesting that they may have employed a less mature strategy to aid in self-regulation. The educational implications of the current study are that there should be an increased awareness of the developmental nature and functional significance of private speech and how private speech usage may differ in children with ADHD.

Geary, D. C. (2008). An evolutionary informed education science. *Educational Psychologist, 43*(4), 179–195. Retrieved April 16, 2009, from Education Abstracts database.

Abstract: Schools are a central interface between evolution and culture. They are the contexts in which children learn the evolutionarily novel abilities and knowledge needed to function as adults in modern societies. Evolutionary educational psychology is the study of how an evolved bias in children's learning and motivational systems influences their ability and motivation to learn evolutionarily novel academic abilities and information in school. I provide an overview of evolved domains of mind, corresponding learning and motivational biases, and the evolved systems that allow humans to learn about and cope with variation and change within lifetimes. The latter enable the creation of cultural and academic innovations and support the learning of evolutionarily novel information in school. These mechanisms and the premises and principles of evolutionary educational psychology are described. Their utility is illustrated by discussion of the relation between evolved motivational dispositions and children's academic motivation and by the relation between evolved social-cognitive systems and mechanisms that support children's learning to read. Reprinted by permission of the publisher.

Gilmore, C. K. & Bryant, P. E. (2008). Can children construct inverse relations in arithmetic? Evidence for individual differences in the development of conceptual understanding and computational skill. *British Journal of Developmental Psychology, 26*(3), 301–316. Retrieved April 16, 2009, from British Education Index database.

Abstract: The study compared 8- to 9-year-old children's use of a computational shortcut based on the inverse relationship between addition and subtraction, in problems where it was transparently applicable and where it was not. Sixty-eight children (33 boys and 35 girls) participated in the study.

Goswami, U. (2008). Reading complexity and the brain. *Literacy, 42*(2), 67–74. Retrieved April 16, 2009, from British Education Index database.

Abstract: The purpose of the special issue was to encourage researchers and practitioners to share work on reading in order to provide more insight into how educators might support the complexities of the reading process in the arena of teaching.

Gredler, M. E., & Shields, C. C. (2007). *Vygotsky's legacy: A foundation for research and practice.* New York: Guilford Press.

Abstract: Most educators are familiar with Lev Vygotsky's concept of the "zone of proximal development," yet the bulk of Vygotsky's pioneering theory of cognitive development largely remains unknown. This volume provides a systematic, authoritative overview of Vygotsky's work and its implications for educational research and practice. Major topics include how children develop higher-order thinking; the influences on cognitive development of teacher-student interactions, the family, and culture; and critical and stable periods in development from infancy through adolescence. Key concepts and research methods are explained in detail, and classroom examples and instructional suggestions are provided. This book may serve as a supplemental text in such courses as Principles of Educational Psychology, Cognition and Learning, and Learning Theories. Its intended audiences are researchers and students in educational psychology, education, and cognitive psychology; and teacher educators. Following an (1) Introduction, this book divides into four parts and nine chapters. Part I, General Principles, contains: (2) Research Methods; (3) Cultural Signs and Symbols; and (4) Development of the Higher Psychological Functions. Part II, Major Cultural Signs, contains: (5) Speech and Cognitive Development; and (6) Development of Thinking in Concepts. Part III, The Cycle of Development, contains: (7) Structure and Dynamics of Age-Related Development; and (8) Development of World View and Personality. Part IV, Some Implications of Vygotsky's Theory, contains: (9) A New Way of Thinking. Appended are: (1) The Cross-Cultural Study; and (2) Shif's Research. The book also has a glossary.

Gulli, C. (2006). How young is too young? *Maclean's, 119*(36), 52–54. Retrieved April 15, 2009, from Readers Guide database.

Abstract: There is increasing evidence that indicates early childhood education actually harms children. Early learning centers such as daycares and preschools are almost always touted as the most promising arena for early education. Some studies have shown gains among children in high-quality child care, yet cognitive benefits are inconsistent at best. According to one surprising study, a child's social development is more likely to slow down the more time it spends in early learning facilities. The study from Berkeley and Stanford University analyzed the influence of preschool centers on children's development in the United States. It suggests that early learning best serves the poorest children in society and found that children from middle and upper-class homes see only modest gains compared with their peers who do not go to preschool. The most surprising finding, however, was that child care centers suppressed children's social development, self-control, interpersonal skills, and motivation once they entered kindergarten.

Howard, A. A., Mayeux, L., & Naigles, L. R. (2008). Conversation correlates of children's acquisition of mental verbs and a theory of mind. *First Language, 28*(87), 375–402. Retrieved April 16, 2009, from British Education Index database.

Abstract: Sixty 3- and 4-year-olds were given tasks assessing mental verb distinctions and false belief.

Japundza-Milisavljevic, M., & Macesic-Petrovic, D. (2008). Executive functions in children with intellectual disabilities. *British Journal of Developmental Disabilities, 54*(2), 113–121. Retrieved April 16, 2009, from British Education Index.

Abstract: The main objective of this study relates to when the establishment of the quality of executive functions development is set. The eligibility criteria for selection of the 24 participants from a primary school in Belgrade was as follows: an IQ of between 50 and 69 as evaluated on the Wechsler Intelligence Scale for Children; a chronological age of between 8 and 12 years; a school age covering the educational level from 2nd to 8th grade; and absence of neurological, psychiatric, sensory or combined disturbances. The instrument used to evaluate executive functions was the Twenty Questions Test proposed by G.V. Klouda and W.E. Cooper (1990).

Jiménez, J. E., Siegel, L., O'Shanahan, I., & Ford, L. (2009). The relative roles of IQ and cognitive processes in reading disability. *Educational Psychology, 29*(1), 27–43. doi:10.1080/01443410802459226

Abstract: The purpose of the present study was to explore the relative roles of IQ and cognitive processes in reading performance. A sample of 443 Spanish children (264 male, 179 female) ranging in age from 7 to 13 years was classified into four groups according to IQ scores (110) and reading disabled (RD) and normally achieving readers (NR) were compared. The findings indicate that IQ scores were not related to the differences between children with RD and NR. We found that reading-related cognitive deficits do differentiate between RD and NR children. Therefore, IQ scores do not make a significant contribution to our understanding of reading disability.

Kozol, J. (2005). Confections of apartheid: A stick-and-carrot pedagogy for the children of our inner-city poor. *Phi Delta Kappan, 87*(4), 264–275. Retrieved April 15, 2009, from Readers Guide database.

Abstract: An article adapted from the book *The Shame of the Nation: The Restoration of Apartheid Schooling in America*. Practices increasingly considered appropriate for black and Hispanic students are intellectually sterile and indoctrinational in nature and can only intensify segregation. The consolidation of racial isolation and the persistence of inequalities in education funding mean that the principals of many inner-city schools are making decisions virtually unknown to the principals of suburban schools. Skeptical about the possibility of black and Hispanic students attending nonsegregated public schools in large numbers in the near future and about the potential for such schools to ever have the infrastructure and resources of successful white suburban schools, many have been investing huge amounts of time and effort in producing a framework of adaptive strategies that promise incremental progress within the limits inequality permits. Most of these strategies are aimed chiefly at poor children of color, and it is understood that these agendas are maintained primarily as responses to perceived disaster in deeply segregated and unequal schools.

Kuchment, A., & Gillham, C. (2008). Kids: To TV or not TV. *Newsweek, 151*(7), 60. Retrieved April 15, 2009, from Readers Guide database.

Abstract: New evidence suggests that certain kinds of television programming can help children with language development. If a child appears interested in watching television, allowing her to watch brief episodes of shows such as Nickelodeon's *Blue's Clues* and PBS's *Arthur* can help her to learn new words. Preliminary research by Rebekah Richert, an assistant professor of psychology at the University of California, revealed that children as young as 18 months are capable of learning new words from DVDs such as Baby Einstein's *Baby Wordsworth* as long as "parents direct their children's attention to the screen and label particular words."

Lambert, E. B. (2005). Children's drawing and painting from a cognitive perspective: A longitudinal study. *Early Years, 25*(3), 249–269. Retrieved April 16, 2009, from British Education Index database.

Abstract: The article describes a study undertaken with 40 pre-school children in rural, south-east Australia during their last six months in an early childhood center and their first six months at school.

Lany, J., & Gomez, R. L. (2008). Twelve-month-old infants benefit from prior experience in statistical learning. *Psychological Science, 19*(12), 1247. Retrieved from http://proquest.umi.com/pqdweb?did=1613379541&Fmt= 7&clientId=3405&RQT=309&VName=PQD

Abstract: A decade of research suggests that infants readily detect patterns in their environment, but it is unclear how such learning changes with experience. We tested how prior experience influences sensitivity to statistical regularities in an artificial language. Although 12-month-old infants learn adjacent relationships between word categories, they do not track nonadjacent relationships until 15 months. We asked whether 12-month-old infants could generalize experience with adjacent dependencies to nonadjacent ones. Infants were familiarized to an artificial language either containing or lacking adjacent dependencies between word categories and were subsequently habituated to novel nonadjacent dependencies. Prior experience with adjacent dependencies resulted in enhanced learning of the nonadjacent dependencies. Female infants showed better discrimination than males did, which is consistent with earlier reported sex differences in verbal memory capacity. The findings suggest that prior experience can bootstrap infants' learning of difficult language structure and that learning mechanisms are powerfully affected by experience.

Lavigne, N. C., & Lajoie, S. P. (2007). Statistical reasoning of middle school children engaged in survey inquiry. *Contemporary Educational Psychology, 32*(4), 630–666. doi:10.1016/j.cedpsych.2006.09.001

Abstract: The case study examined two groups of grade 7 students as they engaged in four inquiry phases: posing a question and collecting, analyzing, and representing data. Previous studies reported analyses of statistical reasoning on a single inquiry phase. Our goal was to identify the modes of statistical reasoning displayed during group discussions in all phases as children designed and conducted their own inquiry. A content analysis of audio- and video-recorded discussions yielded 10 statistical reasoning modes: six relate to Garfield and Gal's [Garfield, J., Gal, I. (1999). Teaching and assessing statistical reasoning. In L. V. Stiff, & F. R. Curcio (Eds.), *Developing mathematical reasoning in grades K-12. 1999 Yearbook* (pp. 207–219). Reston, VA: National Council of Teachers of Mathematics]. Statistical reasoning types involved in the collection, analysis, and representation of data and four modes deal with an aspect of inquiry not exclusively focused upon in the literature on statistical reasoning—i.e., the problem-posing phase. Although students' reasoning reflected an incomplete understanding of statistics, they serve as building blocks for instruction.

Lonigan, C. J., Anthony, J. L., Phillips, B. M., Purpura, D. J., Wilson, S. B., & McQueen, J. D. (2009). The nature of preschool phonological processing abilities and their relations to vocabulary, general cognitive abilities, and print knowledge. *Journal of Educational Psychology, 101*(2), 345–358. doi:10.1037/a0013837

Abstract: The development of reading-related phonological processing abilities represents an important developmental milestone in the process of learning to read. In this cross-sectional study, confirmatory factor analysis was used to examine the structure of phonological processing abilities in 129 younger preschoolers (M = 40.88 months, SD = 4.65) and 304 older preschoolers (M = 56.49 months, SD = 5.31). A 2-factor model, in which Phonological Awareness and Phonological Memory were represented by 1 factor and Lexical Access was represented by a 2nd factor, provided the best fit for both samples and was largely invariant across samples. Measures of vocabulary, cognitive abilities, and print knowledge were significantly correlated with both factors, but Phonological Awareness/Memory had unique relations with word reading. Despite significant development of phonological processing abilities across the preschool years and into kindergarten, these results show that the structure of these skills remains invariant.

Loyens, S. M., Rikers, R. M., & Schmidt, H. G. (2008). Relationships between students' conceptions of constructivist learning and their regulation and processing strategies. *Instructional Science: An International Journal of the Learning Sciences, 36*(5), 445–462. Retrieved April 15, 2009, from ERIC.gov database.

Abstract: The present study investigated relationships between students' conceptions of constructivist learning on the one hand, and their regulation and processing strategies on the other hand. Students in a constructivist, problem-based learning curriculum were questioned about their conceptions of knowledge construction and self-regulated learning, as well as their beliefs regarding their own (in)ability to learn and motivation to learn. Two hypothesized models were tested within 98 psychology students, using a structural equation modeling approach: The first model implemented regulation and processing variables of the Inventory of Learning Styles [ILS, Vermont ("Learning Styles and Regulation of Learning in Higher Education—Towards Process-oriented Instruction in Autonomous Thinking, 1992")], the second model of the Motivated Strategies for Learning Questionnaire [MSLQ, Pintrich and de Groot (*Journal of Educational Psychology, 82,* 33–40, 1990)]. Results showed that structural relations exist between conceptions of constructivist learning and regulation and processing strategies. Furthermore, students who express doubt with regard to their own learning capacities are at risk for adopting an inadequate regulation strategy. A three-tiered structure of conceptual, controlling, and operational level appeared valid for the MSLQ variables but not entirely for those of the ILS.

Malone, H. J. (2008). Educating the whole child: Could community schools hold an answer? *The Education Digest, 74*(2), 6–8. Retrieved April 15, 2009, from Readers Guide database.

Abstract: An article condensed from the winter–spring 2008 issue of *Phi Kappa Phi Forum.* Community schools could be the solution to educating the whole child. To offer a holistic education for students, many reports have called for the reconnection of schools with families and communities and utilizing existing assets in community groups and agencies to create wider educational opportunities. Found in both rural and urban areas, they serve as community centers, community service, service-learning, mentorships, and internships. Community—or full-service—schools provide important lessons on how a school can help students to succeed and bring about positive changes in its community.

Marsh, H. W., Seaton, M., Trautwein, U., Ludtke, O., Hau, K. T., O'Mara, A. J., & Craven, R.G. (2008). The big-fish-little-pond-effect stands up to critical scrutiny: Implications for theory, methodology, and future research. *Educational Psychology Review, 20*(3), 319–350. Retrieved April 15, 2009, from ERIC.gov database.

Abstract: The big-fish-little-pond effect (BFLPE) predicts that equally able students have lower academic self-concepts (ASCs) when attending schools where the average ability levels of classmates is high and higher ASCs when attending schools where the school-average ability is low. BFLPE findings are remarkably robust, generalizing over a wide variety of different individual student and contextual level characteristics, settings, countries, long-term follow-ups, and research designs. Because of the importance of ASC in predicting future achievement, course work selection, and educational attainment, the results have important implications for the way in which schools are organized (e.g., tracking, ability grouping, academically selective schools, and gifted education programs). In response to Dai and Rinn (*Educ. Psychol. Rev.,* 2008), we summarize the theoretical model underlying the BFLPE, minimal conditions for testing the BFLPE, support for its robust generalizability, its relation to social comparison theory, and recent research extending previous implications, demonstrating that the BFLPE stands up to scrutiny.

Martin, J., & McLellan, A. (2008). The educational psychology of self-regulation: A conceptual and critical analysis. *Studies in Philosophy and Education, 27*(6), 433–448. Retrieved April 15, 2009, from ERIC.gov database.

Abstract: The multiplicity of definitions and conceptions of self-regulation that typifies contemporary research on self-regulation in psychology and educational psychology is examined. This examination is followed by critical analyses of theory and research in educational psychology that reveal not only conceptual confusions but misunderstandings of conceptual versus empirical issues, individualistic biases to the detriment of an adequate consideration of social and cultural contexts, and a tendency to reify psychological states and processes as ontologically foundational to self-regulation. The essay concludes with a consideration of educational research and intervention in the area of students' self-regulated learning in terms of the scientific and professional interests of psychologists and educators and the disguised manipulation of student self-surveillance in the service of the institutional mandates of schools.

Merrell, C. H., & Tymms, P. B. (2007). What children know and can do when they start school and how this varies between countries. *Journal of Early Childhood Research, 5*(2), 115–134. Retrieved April 16, 2009, from British Education Index database.

Abstract: The study was restricted to children who had completed the PIPS On-entry Baseline Assessment in the 2002–3 academic year and whose first language was English. Figures for Scotland were then compared to results for England, New Zealand, and Western Australia.

Messiou, K. (2006). Understanding marginalization in education: The voice of children. *European Journal of Psychology of Education, 21*(3), 305–318. Retrieved April 15, 2009, from ERIC.gov database.

Abstract: This paper illustrates how conversations with children can enhance thinking and practice in relation to the development of inclusive education. In particular, evidence from research carried out in a primary school in Cyprus is used to throw light on notions of marginalization. The study suggests that marginalization can be conceptualized in four ways: when a child is experiencing some kind of marginalization that is recognized almost by everybody, including himself/herself; when a child is feeling that he/she is experiencing marginalization, whereas others do not recognize this; when a child is found in what appears to be marginalized situations but does not view this as marginalization; and, finally, when a child appears to experience marginalization but does not recognize this. The paper concludes that children's voices should not only be used as a strategy for understanding and developing more inclusive practices but, more importantly, that listening to children is itself a manifestation of being inclusive.

Miyahara, J., & Meyers, C. (2008). Early learning and development standards in East Asia and the Pacific: Experiences from eight countries. *International Journal of Early Childhood, 40*(2), 17. Retrieved from http://proquest.umi.com/pqdweb?did=1677879731&Fmt=7&clientId=3405&RQT=309&VName=PQD

Abstract: This paper analyzes how countries in UNICEF's East Asia and Pacific Region (EAPR) have engaged in the Early Learning and Development Standards (ELDS) process. ELDS has been developed by the governments of Cambodia, China, Fiji, Lao PDR, Mongolia, the Philippines, Thailand, and Vietnam over the last 3 years with technical and financial support from UNICEF. The ELDS process allowed each country to define its own domain framework, using terminology and defining dimensions and domains in ways that reflected national perspectives and culture while ensuring holistic child development. No two national frameworks are exactly the same, yet they all include aspects of physical development, socio-emotional development, cognitive development, and language development. Moral-spiritual and cultural development, creativity and approaches towards learning were also included by some countries. Regarding the purpose and objectives for undertaking the ELDS process, there were also commonalities and differences between countries. ELDS is being applied as the basis for curriculum revision, for instructional improvement and teacher training, for program evaluation, for parenting education, for public advocacy, and for national alignment of standards. Lessons learned in terms of factors for success include the need for conceptual clarity on holistic child development and ELDS processes amongst key stakeholders and decision makers from the outset, the necessity of national leadership and shared stakeholder responsibility, and the importance of technical assistance, follow-up, and exchange between countries. Looking to the future, recommendations are made to use advanced countries to support countries just starting the process, to hold a follow-up regional workshop on application and use of ELDS, to develop publications, studies, and reports on using ELDS in Asian countries, and to develop a more standardized Asian ELDS model based on validated indicators from the region, to allow countries to use Asian validated standards for specific purposes or research.

Nasir, N. S., & Hand, V. M. (2006). Exploring sociocultural perspectives on race, culture, and learning. *Review of Educational Research, 76*(4), 449. Retrieved from http://proquest.umi.com/pqdweb?did=1289070001&Fmt=7&clientId=3405&RQT=309&VName=PQD

Abstract: This article explores the potential uses and extensions of sociocultural theoretical perspectives for integrating and further developing research on race, culture, and learning. Two bodies of literature are discussed and synthesized: (1) sociocultural theory and (2) studies on race, culture, and learning. The article proposes how a sociocultural lens might provide insight and suggests new lines of research on issues of race, culture, and learning. The authors argue for the extension of each of four lines of research in the sociocultural tradition: a concern with multiple levels of analysis, cultural practices as a unit of analysis, tools and artifacts as mediating action, and learning as shifts in social relations. In doing so, the authors raise critical questions for the field of education to consider.

Nicoladis, E., Cornell, E. H., & Gates, M. (2008). Developing spatial localization abilities and children's interpretation of where. *Journal of Child Language, 35*(2), 269–289. Retrieved April 16, 2009, from British Education Index database.

Abstract: A total of 48 children between two and five years of age were interviewed for the study.

Paquette, K., Fello, S. E., & Jalongo, M. (2007). The talking drawings strategy: Using primary children's illustrations and oral language to improve comprehension of expository text. *Early Childhood Education Journal, 35*(1), 65–73. doi:10.1007/s10643–007–0184–5

Abstract: Listening and reading comprehension can be assessed by analyzing children's visual, verbal, and written representations of their understandings. "Talking Drawings" (McConnell, S. [1993]. Talking drawings: A strategy for assisting learners. *Journal of Reading, 36*(4), 260–269) is one strategy that enables children to combine their prior knowledge with the new information derived from an expository text and "translate" those newly acquired understandings into other symbol systems, including an oral discussion with a partner, a more detailed drawing, and written labels for the drawing. The Talking Drawings strategy begins by inviting children to create pre-learning drawings. These initial drawings are a way of taking inventory of a child's current content knowledge about a particular topic. After pre-learning drawings are created and shared, children listen to or read an expository text (e.g., information book, passage from a textbook) on the same topic as their drawing. Pairs of students discuss the information and either modify their pre-learning drawings to be more detailed or create completely new drawings that reflect the recently acquired information. Students are encouraged to label their drawings with words in a diagram or schematic fashion. By evaluating the "before" and "after" artwork, educators can identify advances in students' reading and listening comprehension of the terminology, facts, and principles on a particular topic.

Phalet, K., Andriessen, I., & Lens, W. (2004). How future goals enhance motivation and learning in multicultural classrooms. *Educational Psychology Review, 16*(1), 59–89. Retrieved April 15, 2009, from ERIC.gov database.

Abstract: This review examines the impact of future goals on motivation and learning in multicultural classrooms. Across cultures, schooling is a future-oriented investment. Studies of minority students' school achievement have advanced future goals as a crucial protective factor in the face of frequent school failure. At the same time, cultural discontinuities and limited opportunities in minority students' school careers may weaken the motivational force of the future. Our review of the seemingly contradictory evidence on the role of the future in minority students' school achievement calls for a more fine-grained motivational theory of the future. Specifically, converging findings support conceptual distinctions (a) between positive and negative perceptions of the instrumentality of school tasks for future goals and (b) between internal and external regulation of classroom behavior by future goals. Thus, "positive" instrumentality and "internal" regulation enhance intrinsic motivation and adaptive learning in multicultural classrooms. We conclude that the motivational force of future goals can be generalized to minority students and that it depends crucially on perceived instrumentality and internal regulation. Results from Academic Search Complete.

Rodale, A. (2008). Creative learning. *Prevention, 60*(8), 168. Retrieved April 15, 2009, from Readers Guide database.

Abstract: The writer discusses how each child learns and is inspired in different ways and urges readers never to neglect to lift up and encourage children.

Schroeder, K. (2006). Teaching diversity. *The Education Digest, 71*(9), 50–51. Retrieved April 15, 2009, from Readers Guide database.

Abstract: LuAnn Hoover, instructor of family studies and human services at Kansas State University, maintains that even children as young as preschool age can start to learn the value of diversity. According to Hoover, the best thing that parents can do when teaching their children about diversity is to check their own attitudes and beliefs because children pick up on adults' nonverbal actions. Hoover explains that learning about diversity is important because children need to learn to respect all people and understand that everyone is alike but also different.

Schroeder, K. (2004). De-stress to learn. *Educational Digest, 70,* 73–74. Retrieved April 15, 2009, from Education Abstracts database.

Abstract: The Institute of HeartMath says that people should keep in mind that stress and anxiety not only affect the way in which children think and feel but also directly affect their ability to learn in school. HeartMath is a California research and education organization that has spent more than ten years researching the physiology of learning and performance. The organization has found that stress can hamper a child's performance in school.

Spencer, P. (2008). Who's harder to raise? *Parenting, 22*(5), 102–105. Retrieved April 15, 2009, from Readers Guide database.

Abstract: The brains of boys and girls develop at different rates, which influences behavior in a variety of ways. Differences in boys' and girls' hearing mean that girls tend to respond better to verbal warnings, whereas boys are less verbal and more impulsive, requiring a more tactile approach to discipline. Boys are generally more rowdy and aggressive, according to experts, because risk-taking stimulates their brain's pleasure centers. Most boys are less communicative than girls, because girls are geared towards a more people-oriented outlook, whereas boys are more action oriented. Girls are therefore more adept at communication early on, but their communication skills can complicate things after the age of 8. Similarly, the greater level of people-orientation in girls can affect self-image and cause insecurity that boys are less afflicted with. Education is harder on boys at younger ages because they are slower to mature in terms of attentiveness, self-control, and fine motor skills. Conversely, girls may have difficulty with spatial learning.

Stafford, E. (2004). What the pendulum can tell educators about children's scientific reasoning. *Science and Education, 13*(7), 757–790. Retrieved April 16, 2009, from British Education Index database.

Abstract: The Pendulum: scientific, historical, philosophical, and educational perspectives.

Stokes, S. F., & Klee, T. (2009). Factors that influence vocabulary development in two-year-old children. *Journal of Child Psychology and Psychiatry, 50*(4), 498. Retrieved from http://proquest.umi.com/pqdweb?did=1668074 381&Fmt=7&clientId=3405&RQT=309&VName=PQD

Abstract: This research explored the relative impact of demographic, cognitive, behavioral, and psycholinguistic factors on vocabulary development in two-year-old children. Two hundred and thirty-two children (24–30 months) were tested on expressive and receptive vocabulary, cognitive development, word learning, and working memory skills. Parents completed a British adaptation (Klee & Harrison, 2001) of the MacArthur-Bates Communicative Development Inventory (CDI; Fenson et al., 1993), a demographic questionnaire and a questionnaire regarding the child's social-emotional behavior. Several demographic, child and processing variables were significantly correlated with CDI (vocabulary) scores, but the only significant unique predictors of CDI scores were nonword repetition (NWR; R 2 change = 0.36), sex (R 2 change = 0.05) and age (R 2 change = 0.04). Scores were only included when a child completed the entire NWR test (77% of toddlers). The NWR task used in this experiment maximized participation in this group of toddlers and was a strong predictor of vocabulary ability. Longitudinal research is warranted to explore the independent and reciprocal growth in working memory and language skills in children.

Takanishi, R., & Kauerz, K. (2008). PK inclusion: Getting serious about a P-16 education system. *Phi Delta Kappan, 89*(7), 480–487. Retrieved April 15, 2009, from Readers Guide database.

Abstract: A P-16 system must pay particular attention to the P-3 years, from early childhood through third grade, because learning during these years lays the foundation for everything that follows.

Thurston, A. (2004). Promoting multicultural education in the primary classroom: Broadband videoconferencing facilities and digital video; Scotland and Missouri. *Computers & Education, 43*(1), 165–177. Retrieved April 16, 2009, from Education Abstracts database.

Abstract: The aim of this study was to explore the impact of interaction (through gathering local field data and engaging in remote reciprocal presentations) on aspects of multicultural awareness. Sixty-six 11–12-year-old Scottish primary school pupils collected data in the field from their local community through questionnaires, interviews, direct observation, digital images, and video. From this they distilled a multimedia presentation, delivered by videoconference to a partner school in the USA, which reciprocated. There was some evidence of pre-post project gains in the complexity of the children's perceptions of their community environment, the ethnicity of their community, their own ethnicity, and news images. The children's use of language to define ethnicity also became more complex and their attitudes toward ethnic minorities became more inclusive. The implications for practice, policy and future research were explored.

Van, D. S., Bakker Arkema, A. H., Horsley, T. M., & van Lieshout, E. C. D. M. (2009). The consistency effect depends on markedness in less successful but not successful problem solvers: An eye movement study in primary school children. *Contemporary Educational Psychology, 34*(1), 58–66. doi:10.1016/j.cedpsych.2008.07.002

Abstract: This study examined the effects of consistency (relational term consistent vs. inconsistent with required arithmetic operation) and markedness (relational term unmarked ['more than'] vs. marked ['less than']) on word problem solving in 10–12-year-old children differing in problem-solving skill. The results showed that for unmarked word problems, less successful problem solvers showed an effect of consistency on regressive eye movements (longer and more regressions to solution-relevant problem information for inconsistent than consistent word problems) but not on error rate. For marked word problems, they showed the opposite pattern (effects of consistency on error rate, not on regressive eye movements). The conclusion was drawn that, like more successful problem solvers, less successful problem solvers can appeal to a problem-model strategy but that they do so only when the relational term is unmarked. The results were discussed mainly with respect to the linguistic–semantic aspects of word problem solving.

Wills, A. J. (2009). Prediction errors and attention in the presence and absence of feedback. *Current Directions in Psychological Science, 18*(2), 95. Retrieved from http://proquest.umi.com/pqdweb?did=1680523791&Fmt=7& clientId=3405&RQT=309&VName=PQD

Abstract: Contemporary theories of learning typically assume that learning is driven by prediction errors—in other words, that we learn more when our predictions turn out to be incorrect than we do when our predictions are correct. Results from the recording of electrical brain activity suggest one mechanism by which this might happen; we seem to direct visual attention toward the likely causes of previous prediction errors. This can happen very rapidly—within less than 200 milliseconds of the error-causing object being presented. It is tempting to infer that if learning is driven by prediction errors, then little can be learned in the absence of feedback. Such a conclusion is unwarranted. In fact, the substantial learning that is sometimes the result of simple exposure to objects can also be explained by processes of directing attention toward the likely causes of previous prediction errors.

Wouters, P., Paas, F., & van Merriënboer, J. J. G. (2009). Observational learning from animated models: Effects of modality and reflection on transfer. *Contemporary Educational Psychology, 34*(1), 1–8. doi:10.1016/j. cedpsych.2008.03.001

Abstract: Animated models use animations and explanations to teach how a problem is solved and why particular problem-solving methods are chosen. Often spoken explanations are proposed to accompany animations in order to prevent overloading the visual channel (i.e., the modality effect). In this study we adopt the hypothesis that the inferior performance of written text compared to spoken text is due to the fact that written text receives less attention and, consequently, less effortful processing. In a 2×2 factorial experiment (N = 96) with the factors modality (written, spoken) and reflection (reflection prompts, no reflection prompts) the hypothesis is tested that prompted reflection requires learners to explicitly attend to written explanations and carefully process them, thus yielding higher transfer performance, whereas for spoken explanations prompted reflection would have no effect on transfer performance. The results indeed showed the hypothesized interaction between modality and reflection prompts. They suggest that the modality effect can be compensated for when learners explicitly attend to the information and effortfully process it. This has implications for learning situations in which spoken explanations are no option, such as education for the hearing impaired.

Zhou, X., Huang, J., Wang, Z., Wang, B., Zhao, Z., Yang, L., & Yang, Z. (2006). Parent-child interaction and children's number learning. *Early Child Development and Care, 176*(7), 763–775. Retrieved April 16, 2009, from British Education Index database.

Abstract: Participants in the study were 85 parent-child dyads from 14 classes in three childcare centers in Shanghai, China, who had been in the early childhood education program for about six months.

Ziv, M., Solomon, A., & Frye, D. (2008). Young children's recognition of the intentionality of teaching. *Child Development, 79*(5), 1237–1256. doi:10.1111/j.1467–8624.2008.01186.x

Abstract: Two studies examined the role of intention in preschoolers' understanding of teaching. Three- to 5-year-olds judged stories in which there was an intention to teach or not (teaching vs. imitation) for 4 different learning outcomes (successful, partial, failed, and unknown). They also judged 2 stories with embedded instructional intent (e.g., guided discovery learning) and several standard theories of mind tasks. There was an age-related change in the understanding of teaching. Five-year-olds distinguished teaching from imitation and recognized guided discovery learning. Understanding of imitation and false belief was related. The findings indicate that theory of mind is relevant to other means of knowledge acquisition besides perceptual access and that understanding intention could help young children to recognize instruction and identify its different forms.

LIST OF FIVE MOST HIGHLY CITED PUBLICATIONS
(HIGHEST TO LOWEST)

Lonigan, C. J., Anthony, J. L., Phillips, B. M., Purpura, D. J., Wilson, S. B., & McQueen, J. D. (2009). The nature of preschool phonological processing abilities and their relations to vocabulary, general cognitive abilities, and print knowledge. *Journal of Educational Psychology, 101*(2), 345–358. doi:10.1037/a0013837

Blewitt, P., Rump, K. M., Shealy, S. E., & Cook, S. A. (2009). Shared book reading: When and how questions affect young children's word learning. *Journal of Educational Psychology, 101*(2), 294–304. doi:10.1037/a0013844

Al Otaiba, S., Petscher, Y., Pappamihiel, N. E., Williams, R. S., Dyrlund, A. K., & Connor, C. (2009). Modeling oral reading fluency development in Latino students: A longitudinal study across second and third grade. *Journal of Educational Psychology, 101*(2), 315–329. doi:10.1037/a0014698

Jiménez, J. E., Siegel, L., O'Shanahan, I., & Ford, L. (2009). The relative roles of IQ and cognitive processes in reading disability. *Educational Psychology, 29*(1), 27–43. doi:10.1080/01443410802459226

Ziv, M., Solomon, A., & Frye, D. (2008). Young children's recognition of the intentionality of teaching. *Child Development, 79*(5), 1237–1256. doi:10.1111/j.1467-8624.2008.01186.x

Contributors

Russell Barkley has been awarded a Diplomate (board certification) in three specialties, including Clinical Psychology (ABPP), Clinical Child and Adolescent Psychology, and Clinical Neuropsychology (ABCN, ABPP). He is a clinical scientist, educator, and practitioner who has authored, co-authored, or co-edited 20 books and clinical manuals. He has published more than 200 scientific articles and book chapters related to the nature, assessment, and treatment of ADHD and related disorders.

Floyd D. Beachum is the Peter E. Bennett Chair in the Urban Principalship and Associate Professor in the College of Education at Lehigh University. His research interests include: leadership in urban education, moral and ethical leadership, and social justice issues in K-12 schools. He is co-editor of the book, *Urban Education for the 21ˢᵗ Century: Research, Issues, and Perspectives.*

Paul Beare earned his BA in Sociology and his M.Ed. and Ph.D. in Special Education, all from the University of Missouri. After four years in public schools he was a Professor for 21 years it Minnesota State University, Moorhead where he also consulted widely, helping school districts plan educational interventions for students with challenging behaviors. He served as a Special Education Due Process Hearing Officer in Minnesota for five years. For the past ten years he has been a university administrator, the last seven of these as Dean of the Kremen School of Education and Human Development at California State University, Fresno.

Dengting Boyanton is an Assistant Professor of Educational Psychology at Long Island University, C. W. Post. She received her Ph.D. in Educational Psychology from the University of Virginia in 2007. Her research interests lie in classroom learning focusing on interpersonal communication, interpersonal relationship, and motivation. For her dissertation, Dr. Boyanton developed the Mutual Value Theory (MVT), a model which aims to improve classroom learning quality especially in the areas of community building, critical thinking, and deep learning. Dr. Boyanton gives many presentations and workshops on student classroom learning both nationally and internationally.

Henry Brzycki earned his Ph.D. from The Pennsylvania State University. He has over 20 years of experiences as a thought leader in psychology and education. Dr. Brzycki has been both a classroom teacher and counselor and he currently teaches at Pennsylvania State University. The focus of his work is teaching and learning at the intersection of psychology and education; providing a critical bridge between theory and practice in teacher education.

Karen T. Carey is Dean of the Graduate School at California State University, Fresno. Dr. Carey received her Ph. D. in school psychology from the University of Cincinnati and has served as a school psychologist for over 25 years. Her most recent books include *Critical Multicultural Conversations* (Hampton Press) and *Ubiquitous Assessment* (Peter Lang Publishing).

Micki M. Caskey is a professor in the Graduate School of Education at Portland State University, Oregon. She is chair of NMSA's Research Advisory Board and editor of Research in Middle Level Education Online. E-mail: caskeym@pdx.edu

Jerrell Cassady is Professor of Psychology in the Department of Educational Psychology at Ball State University. He serves as the Director of the Academic Anxiety Research Consortium, a collaborative group of researchers and educators working to highlight attention to and prevention of academic anxieties across the lifespan. His research in academic anxiety has been primarily on the construct of cognitive test anxiety as well as the use of emotional information processing skills in regulating the effects of academic anxiety. He is the co-editor of *The Teacher Educator,* and recently co-edited the book *Emotional Intelligence: Perspectives on Educational and Positive Psychology* (Peter Lang Publishing). Email: jccassady@bsu.edu (Test Anxiety & Overcoming Academic Anxieties)

Cathrene M. Connery is Assistant Professor of Literacy at Ithaca College. A bilingual educator, professor and advocate, she has drawn on cultural-historical theory to inform her research and professional activities in language, literacy, and sociocultural studies. Dr. Connery has presented on theoretical, pedagogic, and programmatic concerns surrounding the education of culturally and linguistically diverse children in the United States for the past 25 years. Her expertise in emergent bi-literacy, dual language immersion programs, and multi-modal meaning-making has been recognized by professional associations and international audiences alike. In 2006, she received a national award for her work in promoting diversity by the National Association of Extension 4 – H Agents. Dr. Connery has worked as a grant writer, researcher and consultant for several school districts in the west. Her current research interests include multicultural teacher education, bi-literacy & the development of first & second languages, semiotics in Vygotskian theory, sociopolitical issues in development, learning, and education as well as the social construction of feminist identities by female artists and teachers.

Yunhuo Cui is a professor of education at East China Normal University, where he directs the Institute of Curriculum and Instruction. He is also the vice president of Chinese Association of Research on Curriculum and Instruction.

Christina Curran is an Assistant Professor in the Department of Special Education at the University of Northern Iowa. She has been an education professional for over twenty years, with experience as a classroom teacher in a variety of schools and classroom settings as well as previous experience as a faculty member at Central Washington University for eleven years. Christina has authored book chapters, articles, and is co-author of the book: *The middle school experience: Successful teaching and transition planning for diverse learners.* She has provided numerous national presentations, most recently in the area of literacy access and mathematics instruction for diverse learners and tiered instructional delivery.

Sandra Deemer is an associate professor at Millersville University of Pennsylvania where she teaches courses in educational psychology and educational research. Her scholarships interests include the application of achievement goal theory to both secondary and higher education settings.

Kelly DuBois-Gerchak has worked in education for the past 27 years. After graduating from Concordia College in Moorhead, Minnesota, Kelly taught Physical Education, Health, and Speech Communications. In 1992 she received her M.S. degree in Special Education from Minnesota State University Moorhead and taught children with emotional and behavioral disorders for 15 years. Currently Kelly is teaching theater arts at Horizon Middle School in Moorhead and is the director of the middle school theater program. A particular area of interest is in developing a theatre program for students with moderate to severe disabilities.

Jeffrey M. R. Duncan-Andrade holds a joint appointment as the Assistant Professor of Raza Studies and Education and Co-director of the Educational Equity Initiative, Cesar Chavez Institute, San Francisco State University (415-522-5020; jandrade©sfsu.edu) and he teaches Sociology of Education at East Oakland Community High School.

Julia Ellis is a professor in the Department of Elementary Education at the University of Alberta and the anglophone editor for the Canadian Journal of Education. Her books include: *Caring for kids in communities: Using mentorship, peer support, and student leadership programs in schools,* and *Teaching from understanding: Teacher as interpretive inquirer.* She has a web site for mentorship programs for children and youth:http://www.mentorship.ualberta.ca/. She has a number of recent publications on qualitative research and researching with children, mentorship programs for children, creative problem solving in the classroom, and children and place. Her e-mail is julia.ellis@ualberta.ca.

Guorui Fan is a professor of education in the Department of Education and an associate dean of the Graduate College, East China Normal University. He specializes and publishes widely in educational leadership and policy studies.

Susan Fitzsimmons is an assistant professor in the Education Department at the University of Winnipeg, in Manitoba, Canada. Her most recent research was an interpretive inquiry focused on understanding the nature of aesthetic experience through exploring the perspectives of three adolescent girls who wrote poetry. Current research interests include continued study of aesthetic learning spaces, engaging in teacher research as it relates to pre-service teacher education, and exploring arts-based approaches to research.

Kathryn Fletcher is an Associate Professor in the Department of Educational Psychology at Ball State University in Muncie, Indiana. She is director of the masters and doctoral degree programs in Educational Psychology and teaches undergraduate and graduate courses in child and adolescent development. Her general program of research involves how parents impact children's learning and academic achievement. More specifically, Dr. Fletcher is interested in the role of parenting behavior on how children and adolescents cope with academic stress. She has also investigated the effects of caregiver's reading style and home literacy environment on toddler's language development. Her research has resulted in collaborative relationships with community agencies interested in school readiness. She can be contacted at klfletcher@bsu.edu.

Larry F. Forthun is an Assistant Professor of Human Development in the Department of Family, Youth, and Community Sciences at the University of Florida in Gainesville, FL. His teaching and research interests include the examination of parent-adolescent relationships and its impact on healthy psychosocial development and adolescent risky/delinquent behavior. He is also a Certified Family Life Educator (CFLE) and frequently works with community organizations to design, implement, and evaluate prevention and intervention programming that promotes strong families and positive youth development, and reduces risky and health compromising behaviors among adolescents.

Suzanne Gallagher is an associate professor in the School of Education at Gwynedd-Mercy College in Gwynedd Valley, Pennsylvania. Prior to coming to post-secondary education she worked in elementary education as a classroom teacher and administrator. Lang published her first book *Educational Psychology: Disrupting the Dominant Discourse* (2003).

Greg S. Goodman is an assistant professor in the College of Education and Human Services at Clarion University of Pennsylvania. His career has included working as a school psychologist, school counselor, alternative education teacher, and outdoor education instructor. His most recent books include *The Outdoor Classroom* (2008) and *Educational Psychology* (2008).

Laurie Hanich is an associate professor in the Department of Educational Foundations at Millersville University of Pennsylvania. She teaches graduate and undergraduate courses in educational psychology and research methods. Her research interests focus on the development of mathematical thinking in young children with learning disabilities and on children's achievement-related beliefs. She has also published on the scholarship of learning related to educational psychology. She is currently serving as co-editor of Teaching Educational Psychology, an online journal.

Cory Cooper Hansen is an associate professor in the College of Teacher Education and Leadership at Arizona State University. As an early childhood reading specialist, an offshoot of her research is exploring picture books that present children and developmental theory in accurate ways to provide an alternative perspective on understanding the young child. She taught in the early childhood field for ten years before instructing language and literacy courses for prospective elementary school teachers. Her current research includes the effective integration of technology in developmentally appropriate ways as well as best practice at all levels of teaching.

Adriel A. Hilton serves as the executive assistant to the president and assistant secretary of the Board of Directors at Upper Iowa University. He has also been a public policy fellow at the Greater Baltimore Committee where he worked closely with the CEO and policy advisors to research, develop, and advocate a public policy agenda related to the business organizations work. Dr. Hilton is a graduate of the Higher Education (Ph. D.) program at Morgan State University.

Mary Hollowell is associate professor of education at Clayton State University. She is a former science teacher and museum director of education. She has also worked in a zoo for endangered species, for the National Park Service, and in a marine biology lab.

Tamar Jacobson is Associate Professor and Department Chair in the Teacher Education Department at Rider University, New Jersey. Currently, Jacobson serves on the Advocacy Committee of the National Association of Early Childhood Teacher Educators (NAECTE), was selected to participate on the Consulting Editors Panel for the NAEYC, and is a Fellow in the Child Trauma Academy. Her first book: *Confronting Our Discomfort: Clearing the Way For Anti-Bias*, was published by Heinemann in 2003.

David Jardine is Professor of Education in the Faculty of Education, University of Calgary. He received his Ph. D. in education, and he is the co-author of *Back to the Basics of Teaching and Learning* (2003) and *Curriculum in Abundance* (2008).

James Jelmberg serves on the faculty in the Education Department at the University of New Hampshire. In his role as a student teacher supervisor, he is able to use his 40 years of successful classroom teaching experience to mentor and instruct pre-service teachers in the UNH MAT Program. When not teaching or writing, Jim is skiing, sailing, and exploring the mountains of New Hampshire.

Binbin Jiang is an Associate Professor in the Department of Educational Leadership of the Bagwell college of Education at Kenensaw State University. She has over 20 years of experience in teaching and educational administration in China and United States. Her research and publications are in the areas of Teaching English as a second and foreign language, multicultural education, international education, and professional development in cross-cultural contexts.

Joe Kincheloe's piece, *Beyond Reductionism*, appears for the first time in this volume. Joe died in December, 2008, but his memory lives on in the hundreds of publications he crafted and in the thousands of lives that he touched. Joe's profoundly sincere and committed belief in the rights and dignity of all people will continue to serve as an example of what a pedagogy of love can achieve. Joe's simple words, "Life is good", were his motto. He was the author of numerous books and articles about pedagogy, education and social justice, racism, class bias, and sexism, issues of cognition and cultural context, research, and educational reform. His books include: "Teachers as Researchers", "Getting Beyond the Facts: Teaching Social Studies/Social Sciences in the Twenty-first Century", "The Sign of the Burger: McDonald's and the Culture of Power", "Critical Constructivism", and "Changing Multiculturalism" (with Shirley Steinberg). His edited works include "Multiple Intelligences Reconsidered" and "Classroom Teaching: An Introduction." His co-edited works include "White Reign: Deploying Whiteness in America", "The Miseducation of the West: How Schools and the Media Distort Our Understanding of the Islamic World", and the Gustavus Myers Human Rights award winner: "Measured Lies: The Bell Curve Examined."

Herbert Kohl is an educator best known for his advocacy of progressive alternative education and as the acclaimed author of more than thirty books on education. In addition, he has co-edited *A Call to Character: A Family Treasury*, published in response to William Bennett's book, *The Children's Book of Virtues*. Mr. Kohl received a Bachelor's degree in philosophy from Harvard University; a Master's degree in special education from Teacher's College, Columbia University; and was a Henry Fellow at Oxford in philosophy. He began his teaching career in Harlem in

1962. In his teaching career, he has taught every grade from kindergarten through college. Kohl served as the Eugene Lang Visiting Professor for Social Change at Swarthmore College during the 2005-06 academic year. Prior to that, Kohl was the director of the Institute for Social Justice and Education in the University of San Francisco's School of Education. He has also worked as a Senior Fellow at the Open Society Institute.

Patricia Liotta Kolencik is an associate professor in the Education Department at Clarion University of Pennsylvania, Clarion, Pa. She received her Doctorate in Education from the University of Pittsburgh, Pittsburgh, Pa. Prior to coming to Clarion University, Kolencik taught at the high school level for 27 years. In addition to the publication of her dissertation, *"Building Collaborative Partnerships in the Learning Community."* she has authored a professional handbook for elementary teachers entitled, *Teaching with Books that Heal.*

Carol E. Lee has been on the faculty at Northwestern University's School of Education and Social Policy since 1991. Her research interests center on urban education, cultural supports for literacy, classroom discourse, and instructional design. An AERA member for over 20 years, Professor Lee is currently serving as President. Professor Lee is the author of two books—*Culture, Literacy and Learning: Taking Bloom in the Midst of the Whirlwind* and *Signifying as a Scaffold for Literacy Interpretation: The Pedagogical Implications of an African American Discourse Genre.* Her scholarship on literacy, urban education and other subjects has been published in many journals, including the *Reading Research Quarterly, American Educational Research Journal Research in the Teaching of English, The Journal of Black Psychology,* and the *Journal of Negro Education.*

Susan J. Lenski *is a professor who teaches graduate courses in literacy and leadership at Portland State University, Oregon.*

Susan Jean Mayer is a learning and curriculum theorist whose work focuses on the pedagogical implications of human diversity within democratic societies and on urban middle school reform. Susan is currently vice-president of Critical Explorers, Inc., a non-profit curricular development project, and lectures in the Masters in Teaching Program at Brandeis University. Her published articles treat a range of issues related to democratic authority relations, knowledge construction processes, and classroom research methods. sjmayer@brandeis.edu

Chris Mayo is an associate professor in the Department of Educational Policy Studies and the Gender and Women's Studies Program at the University of Illinois at Urbana-Champaign, Champaign, Illinois 61820. Her research interests include gender and sexuality studies and educational philosophy.

Jeff McCombie is a certified school psychologist with extensive experience in education including gifted education, special education and alternative education. McCombie is active on Pennsylvania state committees in shaping policies and best practice procedures for at-risk youth. McCombie serves as a senior trainer of Response Ability Pathways (RAP) and Life Space Crisis Intervention (LSCI). McCombie presently supervises student teachers at Clarion University of Pennsylvania as well as consults with school districts and social service agencies throughout North America.

Carlos R. McCray is an Assistant Professor at Georgia State University in the Department of Educational Policy Studies. His research interests deal with building level leadership, multicultural-ism, and urban education. He has published in journals such as the Journal of School Leadership and The International Journal of Urban Educational Leadership. He has also presented research at international, national, and regional conferences and consulted with school districts in the states of Ohio, Alabama, Connecticut, and Wisconsin. He is a member of numerous professional organizations including the American Educational Research Association and University Council for Education Administration.

Donna Moye is an art teacher with thirty years of experience, who has taught in both mainstream and alternative public schools. In retirement, she plans to weave, make pots, and design jewelry. She also plans to travel throughout Egypt and Europe.

Kathy Murphy is associate professor in the Department of Education at Clarion University of Pennsylvania, Clarion, PA. She received her doctorate in education from Indiana University of Pennsylvania in 2001 in elementary education with concentration in reading and language arts. Prior to coming to Clarion University, she taught reading and English in the public schools for 13 years.

Caroline Payne is currently writing her thesis on the impact of sex education programs on contraceptive use among sexually active emerging adults. Other research interest focuses on youth policy as well as eating disorders. Caroline plans to begin her doctorate in the fall of 2010 and continue to study youth policy and risky behaviors among adolescents and emerging adults.

Anthony A. Pittman is a former educator for the South Carolina Public Schools and is presently Assistant Professor of Instruction and Curriculum in the College of Education at Kean University in Union, N.J. Pittman earned advanced degrees in education and administration from the University of Massachusetts, Lowell and Sacred Heart University, where he served as the director of undergraduate education. He earned his Ph.D. from the University of Connecticut, Storrs. His research agenda focuses on the achievement gap and the disproportionate percentages of students of color enrolled in gifted and talented, collegiate honors education, and similarly structured programs.

Sue Poppink is an associate professor in the Educational Leadership unit at Western Michigan University. She is interested in the relationship between policy and practice, particularly how teachers, principals, districts and states respond to federal policy concerning teaching and learning such as the Elementary and Secondary Schools Act of 1965 and its reauthorizations including the No Child Left Behind Act of 2002. Dr. Poppink works with many doctoral students in both the K-12 and higher education program, and master's students in the K-12 program.

Cathleen Ruble *lives in Pittsburgh, Pennsylvania with her daughter, Alexis. She received her bachelor's degree in psychology from Seton Hill University in 2008 graduating Suma Cum Laude. Currently, Cathleen is currently completing her masters in library science at Clarion University. She is employed as a software technician and volunteers her time at Parentwise and her local public library.*

Kelvin Seifert is a professor of educational psychology at the University of Manitoba, Winnipeg, Canada. His publications focus on the personal development of teachers, the impact of peers in preservice teacher education, and the development of strategies for blended learning. He is also author of several university textbooks about educational psychology and developmental psychology, and editor of the *Canadian Journal of Educational Administration and Policy*. Recently he served as chair of the Department of Educational Administration, Foundations and Psychology at the University of Manitoba, and as president of the AERA Special Interest Group on Teaching Educational Psychology.

Jianping Shen is the John E. Sandberg Professor of Education in the Department of Educational Leadership, Research, and Technology at Western Michigan University. With about 80 journal articles and several books, he has published widely in the area of educational leadership and policy.

Jan Small-McGinley Jan Small-McGinley is a consultant with Edmonton Public Schools in the area of Special Education. Her work involves assessment, consultation and providing educational and behavioral programming for students with severe developmental disabilities. Jan presents at conferences, and provides in-services and workshops to educators and parents on inclusion, curricular modification, transition planning, proactive behavior programming, social interaction skills and advocacy. Jan has numerous years of teaching experience across various age and grade levels. Jan is actively involved in supporting all people with disabilities and is on the City of Edmonton Advisory Board for People with Disabilities.

Sheryl Smith-Gilman has been involved early childhood education for the past 30 years. Besides continuing as a classroom teacher she is the Director of Montreal's Solomon Schechter Academy preschool programs. She holds a B.Ed. and M.A. in Integrated Studies from McGill University and is presently pursuing her PHD studies. Additionally, Sheryl teaches and supervises at Vanier College in Montreal in the Early Childhood Continuing Education Department as well as at McGill University in the Faculty of Education. Sheryl is the Reggio Emilia consultant for the Kahnawake Mohawk Step by Step Child and Family Center and presents frequently at Concordia University and for McGill University's Center for Educational Leadership.

Colleen Torgerson's degrees include a B.A. in Communicative Disorders at California State University, Fresno, an M.A. in Deaf Education from California State University, Northridge and an Ed.D. in Educational Leadership from the University of California, Davis/Fresno State. She taught in special classes and resources settings in Southern California and Fresno. For 13 years she worked as an administrator in Special Education for Fresno Unified School District. In 1999 she joined the faculty at California State University, Fresno as a professor and for the past five years she has served as the Associate Dean of the Kremen School of Education and Human Development.

Teresa Strong-Wilson is Assistant Professor in the Department of Integrated Studies in Education in the Faculty of Education at McGill University, Montreal, Quebec. Her research interests lie in: story, memory, changing literacies, social justice education, and teacher education. She has published in such journals as: Educational Theory, Journal of Curriculum Theorizing, Changing English, Reflective Practice, and Children's Literature in Education, and is author of *Bringing Memory Forward: Storied Remembrance in Social Justice Education* (Peter Lang, 2008).

Barbara J. Thayer-Bacon is a professor in the Program of Cultural Studies in Education, University of Tennessee, Knoxville, TN 37996. Her primary areas of scholarship as a professor of education are feminist theory and pedagogy, pragmatism, and cultural studies in education. Her publications include: *Philosophy applied to education*, (with Chris Bacon) Prentice Hall, 1998; *Transforming critical thinking*, Teachers College Press, 2000; and *Relational "(e)pistemologies,"* Peter Lang, 2003.

Christopher T. Vang is associate professor of teacher education in the Multiple Subject Credential Program at California State University, Stanislaus. He is the advisor for Southeast Asian Bilingual Cross-cultural Concentration. Dr. Vang has authored several children's books, a handbook in

Hmong for Hmong parents, articles in the Multilingual Magazine and the Language Magazine of CABE, several articles in the Hmong University Journal, one article in the Hmong Study Journal, one article in a book, several newspaper editorial articles, and more than 85 online articles. Dr. Vang has recently completed *An Educational Psychology of Methods in Multicultural Education*.

David M. Weber, currently practices the art and craft of school psychology in the Clovis Unified School District in Central California. He is a Nationally Certified School Psychologist and a Licensed Educational Psychologist in California. Dr. Weber is currently professor and Program Director for School Psychology & School Counseling at the Visalia Center of Fresno Pacific University.

Joanne A. Washington, Ph.D., is an associate professor in the Department of Mass Media Arts, Journalism and Communication Studies at Clarion University of Pennsylvania (jwashington@ clarion.edu). She has traversed a varied career path including stops as a jazz musician, television producer, account executive and college residence advisor. Her research focus is on the impact of media and popular culture on the learning achievements of black and brown youth.

Debby Zambo teaches courses in educational psychology at Arizona State University in the College of Teacher Education and Leadership. She has also taught Master's reading courses in best practices, essential elements, and differentiated instruction. Before coming to the university Debby taught in public and private schools in for 9 ½ years. Most of Debby's public school experience has been working with primary children (grades K-3) with learning and emotional challenges. Her years working with children taught her the importance of helping teachers learn theory and transfer theory into classroom life.

Jinzhou Zheng is a professor of education in the Department of Education, East China Normal University. A well-known scholar in China, he publishes extensively on current educational issues in China.

Barry Zimmerman has had a distinguished history of leadership in educational and school psychology. He was president of APA's Division 15 (educational psychology) from 1996-1997. Notable publications include dozens of research articles and the esteemed textbook *Educational Psychology: A Century of Contributions*. Dr. Zimmerman has also been the APA Division 16 (school psychology) Senior Scientist Award recipient.

Critical Pedagogical Perspectives

Greg S. Goodman, *General Editor*

Educational Psychology: Critical Pedagogical Perspectives is a series of relevant and dynamic works by scholars and practitioners of critical pedagogy, critical constructivism, and educational psychology. Reflecting a multitude of social, political, and intellectual developments prompted by the mentor Paulo Freire, books in the series enliven the educator's process with theory and practice that promote personal agency, social justice, and academic achievement. Often countering the dominant discourse with provocative and yet practical alternatives, *Educational Psychology: Critical Pedagogical Perspectives* speaks to educators on the forefront of social change and those who champion social justice.

For further information about the series and submitting manuscripts, please contact:

> Dr. Greg S. Goodman
> Department of Education
> Clarion University
> Clarion, Pennsylvania
> *ggoodman@clarion.edu*

To order other books in this series, please contact our Customer Service Department at:

> (800) 770-LANG (within the U.S.)
> (212) 647-7706 (outside the U.S.)
> (212) 647-7707 FAX

Or browse online by series at:

> www.peterlang.com